杨良宜 | 著

合约的解释 规则与应用

Construction of Contract Rules and Application

法律出版社
LAW PRESS · CHINA
——北京——

序　言

该本新书是在《合约的解释》(法律出版社 2007 年版)的基础上完成的再版,我在此先说明关于再版的感想:第一,这七年来,普通法在合约的解释方面有了无数的先例,很多法律地位也发生了改变,如果不再版,我担心原版不仅跟不上时代,更可能误导读者;第二,再版对原版进行了大量修改,很多章节都是完全重写或者新写并添加,如果没有原版作为基础,我相信再版不会写得令自己满意;第三,再版也让我有机会改正原版的疏漏与不满意之处,如原版介绍太多我自己擅长的国际货物买卖与航运领域的内容,但中国现在各行各业都在国际层面有了蓬勃发展,我在此次再版中就尽量使内容更加全面,力争令各行业的人士都能够看得明白以及感受到与自身行业的关联。毕竟,英国只有一套适用在所有合约关系的合约法,而所有的商贸活动都是合约关系。又如原版对解释合约大原则的新发展趋势,即从相对强调合约"字面"(text)的解释变为相对强调在解释时要考虑订约时"语境"(context),我也觉得写得不够透彻,希望在再版中有所改善。全书完成之后,我发觉整本书的改动很大,增加了很多新内容,反而保留原版的内容并不是很多。法律出版社的吴昉女士也建议,由于本书与原版的差别太大,如果仅用再版命名,不足以反映这些变化,所以应该给本书重新命名,将它当作一本新书。我完全认同这一建议,事实上这也的确是一本新书,所以最后命名为《合约的解释:规则与应用》。

任何与国际商贸活动有关联的人士都知道英国合约法与商法的重要性。英国、美国(美国的商法基本上依从英国的游戏规则)也普遍认同学习这方面的法律可以培养出适合商贸活动的有组织的常识与思维。这一点也是我所感受与认同的,特别是在有关合约法的书籍,包括早在 1998 年出版的《国际商务游戏规则——英国合约法》中,我就已经提及此点,而我也已经听到不少看过该书的朋友说对思维水平的提高很有帮助。多年来,我看到法律的快速变化,考虑到中国日益增长的实际业务量以及各行业相关从业人员的需要,最后决定写三本书来针对中国人最薄弱的合约法的内容。第一本是 2007 年版的《合约的解释》,但出版后我感觉写得不尽如人意,如今再版,我深信能够改善原版的不足之处;第二本是《损失赔偿与救济》(法律出版社 2013 年版);第三本是希望能够在近两年完成的《合约的履行、弃权与禁止翻供》(暂定名)。我希望所有参与国际业务的朋友都会觉得这三本书有用,并且传播给年轻一代去钻研。

如果大家看本书所介绍的英国合约法的默示地位原则,特别是本书的第七章,可以说英国建立起来这一套法律默示地位原则(虽然可以在个别合约中以明示条文作出改变以彰显订约自由)正是国际商贸活动中被大家所认同的全面、合理、合乎逻辑、配合实际与有可行性、肯定性以及可预测性的游戏规则。中国年轻一代有必要学习,不能只是局限在与国际规则尚未完全接轨的中国自己的游戏规则中,毕竟目前国际商贸活动中大部分的争议最后还是由外国(特别是英国)的法官或仲裁员来决定。这些外国法官与仲裁员考虑问题(包括事实认定与解释合约明示与默示条文)也是与英国合约法和商法理念一致。即使他们非常想要公正,但由于理念上的差异(也可称为文化差异),也往往会对不能理解与不符合国际商贸活动游戏规则的事实和做法作出不利推断,进而导致很多中国当事方容易在判决或裁定中败诉。

本书的大量重要内容还是留待读者自己去阅读。在这里,我要感谢一些帮助本书出版的朋友:法律出版社的吴昉女士,提供第二章之2.4段相关伦敦仲裁案件与部分章节资料的杨大明律师,提供第十一章关键路径图的梁永强教授,在部分章节提供专业意见的何志强律师、陈晓山律师,以及我的助手们,包括帮助我写过大量书籍的司嘉女士、新加入团队的贡航先生以及为本书录入整理与搜集资料作出最大帮助的王可心女士。

杨良宜

2014年12月20日于香港

目　录

第一章 概 述

§1 合约承诺是绝对与严格责任

首先对解释文书合约要明白的重要之处是分析双方各自在一个合约中向对方做出的承诺与合约责任是“绝对与严格”(absolute and strict)。这表示即使不是承诺方的错误导致履行不了,这也难逃是违约与要作出金钱损失的赔偿。在Raineri v. Miles (1981) AC 1050先例,Edmund - Davies勋爵就说明合约的承诺是绝对责任,承诺方没有过错是不足以构成抗辩的。所以,解释合约后作出的判决声称败诉方违约与犯错,这“错”很可能是与道德上的错没有关系。这样就很容易明白许多商业合约为什么这样解释。例如在国际货物买卖合约,买方在明示或者默示的条文下必须准时开出信用证,如果办不到,即使这不是在买方的过错下(如市场下跌而想扯皮),而是由于政府的外汇管制,买方还是难逃要对卖方作出赔偿,因为他违反了对卖方作出的承诺。对这种情况,英国法律是不会作出任何的救济。这是要买方自己在订约的时候预见会发生的这些问题而作出有条件的承诺(如说明开出信用证是以政府的允许作为前提),或者加上一条有“政府干预”(government interference)的免责条文。在一个国际货物买卖的合约中还有许多其他承诺,如准时派船,双方之间作出各种通知,卖方负责申请出口证并提供足够数量与良好质量的货物,卖方及时结汇并交出付运单证,买方准时支付货价与接受货物,安排小工卸货,在约定的卸货时间内卸下货物否则要支付船舶滞期费等,都是一连串的绝对与严格的责任。

合约责任为什么要是绝对与严格也不无争议,因为民事诉讼的另一种类“诉因”(cause of action)就是侵权,这是要根据疏忽或者侵权方没有做到“合理谨慎”(reasonable care)才会产生责任。固然,有越来越多的侵权也走向绝对与严格责任。但这往往是有特定的理由与通过立法才会产生这样的效果。如海上的油污,一直以来只是一个小问题,所以造成侵权的一方(通常是船东/船长)往往是被证明了疏忽或者没有做到合理谨慎才会要负责。但随着油轮体积增大与油污会造成的严重后果并影响太多无辜人士,就有了不同的政策上的考虑。在现实中,对油污作出保险的充分安排也是通过船东的互保协会组织起来比较容易,而要求沿岸居住与靠海吃饭的千万人士各自为油污风险投保并不现实。这一连串的政策考虑导致了国际公约与多个国家的法律(如著名的美国1990年《油污法》)把油污责任从合理谨慎改为是绝对与严格责任强而加于船东。至于另一种法律,就是刑法,更加不用说是犯罪人士必须要有犯罪的意图才会承担犯罪的后果/责任。这样看来,在侵权与刑法,都是与"道德犯错"(morally wrong)有关系,但偏偏合约法就是没有关系。

这里的原因或者解释有好几个。第一个是合约本身就是与承诺有关系。而大家对承诺的解释绝对与严格,除非在承诺中说明例外的情况。说实在,如果一个承诺有太多的例外情况,被承诺方也就会针对这些例外作出其他的安排或者为自己留后路,而不会全盘依赖这种有很多条件的承诺。

第二个解释与上一个十分接近,就是既然它是一个合约,双方都会有机会把这个承诺说清楚,如在怎么样的情况下无法履行。这是侵权与刑法不会有的机会,如承诺方对被承诺方说:"我将在本周星期五送货。"这样,如果在星期五不送货,被承诺方就会不满,认为是承诺方违反承诺。客观看来也应该是如此,虽然承诺方会有解释,如星期五下大雨,所以不送货。但这样,如果同意承诺方的解释,原先的承诺就变为"我将在本周星期五送货,除非下大雨"。但事实上,原先的承诺并没有这样说,岂非是"除非下大雨"这几个字要法律默示才说得通?再说,承诺方也会有许多其他的原因导致在星期五不送货,如交通十分堵塞,送货工人不肯超时工作,没有空的车辆,等等。这种问题通常也是承诺方自己比较了解或可以预见到,所以与其让他作出一个看来是毫无保留的承诺之余,而办不到又可依赖法律作出许多不同默示以作出救济,倒不如把责任放在承诺方,在例外情况作出承诺的同时说明与作出条件或限制,好让被承诺方决定是否接受或有了心理准备。

第三个解释是合约承诺可被解释为两个层次的承诺,一是承诺做一件事或者达至一个后果,二是承诺在办不到时作出足够的金钱损失赔偿。[1] 这样,违约方败诉要作出损失赔偿也就不必与道德犯错扯上关系了。

§2 道德与法律

已经解释过就是合约法与商法并没有道德上的对错,但两者之间也并非是完全没有关系。当道德上普遍被认为是错的事情,时间一长,显然是会影响法律的改变(也就是默示地位[2]的改变)或者对明示条文故意地作出解释。举例说,以前法院是不认为在一个公开招标中由投标者之间私底下达成协议不去抬价有什么问题,但

---

〔1〕 有关合约首要义务与次要义务的说法在笔者的《损失赔偿与救济》一书第十一章之1.1段有简单介绍,首要义务就是其中一方承诺做一些事情。而次要义务就是指做出承诺的合约方违反了他做出的首要义务承诺要作出金钱上的赔偿让受害方可以回复到合约被履行的地位。详见 Diplock 勋爵在 Photo Production v Securicor (1980) 1 Lloyd's Rep 545 先例的著名说法。

〔2〕 这在本书之第七章有详述。

这一以前被视为是合法的事情在今天讲起来就被认为是不道德与错误了:Rawlings v. General Trading Co. (1921) 1 K. B. 635 先例。但法律与道德扯上太密切的关系,特别是在个别的案件,就会带来至少两个大问题:一是违反人性,特别当事人是商人;二是导致法律的不肯定。

首先是探讨人性以区分出什么是道德与不道德,这种问题在两千多年前已经在欧洲被探讨过,例如在《On Duties, III, Cicero, Selected Works》(Penguin Classic, trans. Michael Grant, 1971 revision)一书之177页所提到的一个问题或者假设,如下:"Suppose that there is a food - shortage and famine at Rhodes and the price of corn is extremely high. An honest man has brought to the Rhodians a large stock of corn from Alexandria and he has seen their ships making for Rhodians with substantial cargoes of grain. Ought he to tell the Rhodians this? Or is he to say nothing and sell his stock at the best price he can get?"

显然在上述的假设下,一般的人性(不管是中国人还是西方人),更不用说是唯利是图的商人,都不会在这种情况下向买方宣告另有其他船舶装有大量谷物即将抵达,会把高昂的谷物价格很快的压下去。同一个情况出现在近期的 Walford v. Miles (1992) 2 AC 128 先例,它将在本书第二章之6.4段有详细介绍,不在此重复。

2.1 英国普通法对合约没有善意的要求

所以如果法律(特别是商法)把道德的标准定得太高,违反一般人性,这只会造成法律的不现实与商人尽量有法不依。也是这个原因,英国的合约法,特别是商法,没有一个规定是订约双方必须是"善意"(good faith)。[3] 而对合约的解释,也从来不会以善意与否作出任何扭曲。这可节录 Falconer 勋爵在 The Commercial Bar Association Lecture (2005年10月18日)这一个讲座中提到英国法律会这么受全球的欢迎,并且变成英国的一个"生金蛋"的产业,就是由于可循性、肯定与公平。合约的严格履行也不会受到任何善意不善意的干预。他是这样说:"English law is respected by the commercial community - our common law of contract is now a world - wide commodity. It has become so because it is a system that people like. In ever more complex, sophisticated and inter - related markets, English commercial law provides predictability of outcome, legal certainty, and fairness. It is clear and built upon well - founded principles, such as the ability to require exact performance and the absence of any general duty of good faith."

只有在个别的商业活动环节中,因为有特别的原因,才会通过立法提升这一道德的标准。这里最出名的例子就是保险合约,在英国1906年的《海上保险法》,第17条文就说明海上保险合约是要有"最大程度的善意"(utmost good faith),如下:"A contract of marine insurance is a contract based upon the utmost good faith, and, if the ut-

〔3〕 有关善意的课题,在本书第九章有更详细的介绍。

most good faith be not observed by either party, the contract may be avoided by the other party."另在第18条文规定了被保险人在投保时的严格披露责任,如下:"18. Disclosure by assured (1) Subject to the provisions of this section, the assured must disclose to the insurer, before the contract is concluded, every material circumstance which is known to the assured, and the assured is deemed to know every circumstance which, in the ordinary course of business, ought to be known by him. If the assured fails to make such disclosure, the insurer may avoid the contract. (2) Every circumstance is material which would influence the judgement of a prudent insurer in fixing the premium, or determining whether he will take the risk. ..."

注意是《海上保险法》在这些方面的要求也适用在所有岸上的保险合约,这是主要考虑到保险合约的产生是保险人对投保的风险一无所知或所知不多,完全是要靠被保险人诚实与全面的披露才能决定是否接受这一份投保与保费规定是多少。所以如果被保险人不诚实或者漏掉一些披露,就有可能对保险人造成极大的不公平。但合约关系往往就会是这个后果,即对一方公平就可能会对另一方不公平。然而在出现不少案件由于被保险人无辜漏了披露而导致保险合约被保险人拒赔后,英国法院看来在解释这一个最大程度的善意也在放宽对被保险人的要求,不是动辄让保险人以这个理由拒赔。例如在 Pan Atlantic Insurance Co. Ltd and Another v. Pine Top Insurance Co. Ltd (1994) 2 Lloyd's Rep. 427 先例中,贵族院就改变了过去二百年的一些看法,判《海上保险法》第18条文是要求保险人证明被保险人所漏掉的披露是的确会导致损害才能逃避这个保险合约的赔偿。Templeman 勋爵就指出了他的看法与感受,如下:"The law is already sufficiently tender to insurers who seek to avoid contracts for innocent non - disclosure and it is not unfair to require insurers to show that they have suffered as result of non - disclosure."

在现实中太强调善意还有一个困难就是举证。笔者已经见过不少这种指控,说对方"恶意"(bad faith)。这是一个严厉的指控,照常理说要成功,这举证责任也会相应加重。往往指控方不能做到这一点,甚至是毫无证据可言。

另一个大问题是太强调善意就会带来法律上的不肯定。例如在德国《民法典》第22条有规定了善意的要求,如下:"The debtor is obliged to perform in accordance with the requirements of good faith, regard being had to ordinary usage."同样对善意的要求,也出现在第157条文针对合约方面。这看来是非常通情达理的条文却带来了大量的诉讼,在《Staudinger's Kommentar zum Burgerlichen Gesetzbuch》(第13版,1995年)一书就有500页以上的篇幅针对这一方面。

2.2 英国普通法只针对合约条文或合约本身违反公共政策

但要说明,合约法与商法也不是绝对与道德毫无关系。如果这是严重到违反一般人"最基本的道德理念"(basic notion of morality),这就构成违反"公共政策"(public policy)。在订约自由下,合约如果有个别条文或者整个合约本身是违反公共政策,这就不被法律承认。法院或仲裁庭也不会给予执行,不论合约明示条文/文字是如何明确肯定。这种情况最明显就是双方订一个合约犯罪或者侵权,外贸与航运最明确与常见的例子就是以一份保函作为交换,欺诈性地签发提单。显然,这个保函作为合约的一种,不论怎样写与用字明确肯定,也因为本质上属欺诈性而导致法院不予执行,变为废纸一张:Brown Jenkinson & Co Ltd v. Percy Dalton (London) Ltd (1957) 2 Q. B. 621 先例。

再举一个情况,是类同违反公共政策,就是一些合约条文局限一方作为个人的自由。显然,如果一个合约约束其中一方的人士要其奴隶性地为另一方工作,必须宣誓效忠与从令,这就会令该合约无法执行:加拿大的 Archer v. Sacred Heart (1905) 9 OLR 474 先例。又如男女之间的一个婚姻协议/合约是被视为有效,但如果有一个合约限制对方结婚就无法执行了,因为这是限制了对方婚姻的自由。这种例子还很多,如在仲裁就曾经有 Czarnikow Ltd v. Roth, Schmidt & Co (1922) 12 Lloyd's Rep. 195 先例,案情涉及一条仲裁条文约定了仲裁就是终局,不能上诉法院,被英国上诉庭判是无效,因为其中主要的理由是限制了希望上诉方寻求法院救济的自由。这一个普通法的地位是直到 1979 年英国《仲裁法》通过立法作出改变以支持仲裁的终局。

这一方面最多的诉讼就是一种叫做"限制商贸/就业"(restraint of trade/employment)条文,[4]这方面在笔者与杨大明律师的《禁令》一书中第二章 3.1.6 段有详细介绍。这种合约或者规定是为了阻止/干预个人将来自由进行一些有关的贸易/生意或专业。如在一个二手船买卖合约中,有一条文约定买方不准在某些班轮航线经营出售的船舶,以免与卖方形成竞争。另一个例子是可口可乐(为例)雇佣一位高级职员,在雇佣合约内与他约定,如果离职,今后 50 年不准涉及有关饮料的业务或者雇佣。这种千变万化的情况很多,但它们都涉及局限另一方的自由而有可能变为无效。当然法律是要顾及现实与合理的一面,就是坚持有这种约定的一方,如可口可乐,会怕高级雇员离职后投靠百事可乐并带走商业机密,就会造成很大危害。所以法律的地位是找出一条分水线,即一条合理公平的限制商贸/就业条文就可以取得法律的承认并予以执行。这样,只要在时间上订得合理并且限制范围不要太广,就会有效。例如上述的可口可乐限制的期限长达 50 年就不可能是公平合理了。这表示拟定一条限制商贸/就业条文需要很高的技巧且了解有关的判例。既要订得肯定,也必须不能过火,而且也要能够证明是有一个合法权益需要保护而要加上一些限制。

再一大类的合约或者条文被视为是无效,也会是与违反公共政策有点关系,就是有国际公约或立法规定了不准豁免的责任。这里对外贸与航运人士最出名的是美国的《哈特法》与《海牙规则》中的第 8 条:"Any clause, covenant, or agreement in a contract of carriage relieving the carrier or the ship from liability for loss or damage to or in

---

〔4〕 这个课题在本书第七章之 3.3.1 段有更详尽的解释。

connection with the goods, arising from negligence, fault, or failure in the duties and obligations provided in this section, or lessening such liability otherwise than as provided in this Act, shall be null and void and of no effect. A benefit of insurance in favour of carrier or similar clause, shall be deemed to be a clause relieving the carrier from liability."

这种规定在其他较近期的很多立法中也有出现,主要还是为了保护消费者或者弱者。例如1964年的《Hire - Purchase Act》,1977年的《Unfair Contract Terms Act》,1999年的《Unfair Terms in Consumer Contracts Regulations》(英国参加了欧共体后)。即使是笔者熟悉的1996年英国《仲裁法》,内中也包括了许多的地方是禁止订约自由,而即使这样约定也不会有效。例如,不能以订约自由排除英国法院对仲裁员违反自然公正的救济。这首先是二十多条所谓的"强制性条文"(mandatory provisions),在Schedule 1有说明。另外可举的例子是第60条文,说明如下:"An agreement which has the effect that a party is to pay the whole or part of the costs of the arbitration in any event is only valid if made after the dispute in question has arisen."

在这个条文下就表示双方在没有产生争议,也就是一开始订约时,加上一条条文说明将来如果有诉讼,各自承担自己的律师费用或者所有诉讼费用大家对半开等内容,实属无效。至于为什么有这样的立法规定,是否在这种事情上违反公共政策这么严重,也不必深究了。

总结而言,除了上述的罕见情况,双方同意了的合约都会被法院解释与执行。英国合约法在订约自由的原则下基本上是完全尊重一个合约的实质内容,这是完全由双方自由约定。正如Bingham大法官在Pagnan SpA v. Feed Products Ltd (1987) 2 Lloyd's Rep. 601先例所说的:"The parties are to be regarded as masters of their own contractual fate."

法院与仲裁庭并非是订约方,他们无权插手与指手画脚。英国合约法关注的反而是有否一个公平的程序达成一份有效的合约。所以,如果是通过"非法胁迫"(duress)、"误述"(misrepresentation)(普通法下即使是无辜的误述也有一样的救济)等所达成的合约,就不会被法院接受是有效并且作出救济让受害方有权终止合约。

§3 法律的肯定性、可循性与公平之间的冲突

法律的"肯定性"(certainty)是不断被英国法院所强调,在现实中,笔者也非常同意肯定性的重要性。因为不论好坏,事先知道了就可以趋吉避凶了。做法上可以以行动回避(如明知道对自己十分不利的合约条文/文字,就拒绝确立,或订约后小心处理或投保等)或更普遍的就是利用订约自由加上对自己保障的条文/文字。笔者还记得Denning勋爵的一句话,就是不肯定的法律是文明社会中最大的不公平。

对上述所讲,可节录有同样说法的Bridge勋爵在The "Chikuma" (1981) 1

Lloyd's Rep. 371 先例中所讲的:"It has often been pointed out that shipowners and charterers bargain at arm's length. Neither class has such a preponderance of bargaining power as to be in a position to oppress the other. They should be in a position to look after themselves by contracting only on terms which are acceptable to them. Where, as here, they embody in their contracts common form clauses, it is, to my mind, of overriding importance that their meaning and legal effect should be certain and well understood. The ideal at which the courts should aim, in construing such clauses, is to produce a result, such that in any given situation both parties seeking legal advice as to their rights and obligations can expect the same clear and confident answer from their advisers and neither will be tempted to embark on long and expensive litigation in the belief that victory depends on winning the sympathy of the court. This ideal may never be fully attainable, but we shall certainly never even approximate to it unless we strive to follow clear and consistent principles and steadfastly refuse to be blown off course by the supposed merits of individual cases."

上诉庭的 Robert Goff 大法官在 The "Scaptrade" (1983) 2 Lloyd's Rep 253 先例中说(这在贵族院被 Diplock 勋爵所认同):"The English courts have time and again asserted the need for certainty in commercial transactions – for the simple reason that the parties to such transactions are entitled to know where they stand, and to act accordingly."

另 Steyn 大法官在 The "Ulyanovsk" (1990) 1 Lloyd's Rep. 425 先例也认为肯定性是至关重要,说:"Certainty of rights and duties, and predictability of dispute resolution, is the first imperative of a system of commercial law. It is of fundamental importance, not so as to ease the task of Judges, but because it enables businessmen and their advisers in the drafting and negotiating stage to consider properly the risks attendant upon an adventure, and to make suitable arrangements by way of contractual stipulations and the procuring of insurance cover. Moreover, certainty and predictability is also of vital importance when a dispute arises, so that in so far as it is possible, the way in which it will probably be resolved will not usually be a complete mystery to businessmen and their advisers."(在一个商业法律的制度下,对权利、责任与有了争议的可循性是有基本重要性。这不仅减轻了法院的工作,也让商业人士与他们的法律顾问知道怎样在草拟与谈判时可以考虑这一交易有什么风险,以及可作出应对的办法,如在条文方面或投保风险。此外,肯定性与可循性也至关重要,当有争议产生,大家可预测争议会是怎样的结果,而不会是对商业人士或其法律顾问来说是一个完全无法预测的迷局。)

此外在 The "Starsin" (2003) 1 Lloyd's Rep. 571 先例,Bingham 勋爵也说:"In all mercantile transactions the great object should be certainty: and therefore, it is of more consequence that a rule should be certain, than whether the rule is established one way or the other. Because speculators in trade then know what ground to go upon：*Vallejo Wheller*（1774） 1 Cowp. 143"

最后可以 Steyn 勋爵的另一句名言作为介绍（虽然还有其他许多著名大法官有同样的说法），这就是在 Society of Lloyd's v Robinson（1999） 1 All ER（Comm） 545 先例中，Steyn 勋爵说："Loyalty to the text of a commercial contract, instrument or document read in its contextual setting is the paramount principle of interpretation."（这是指英国法院解释合约是完全效忠或依从商业合约与其他文件中所讲的内容，这也是最基本解释合约的大原则，其基本的原因也是为了商业合约的肯定性。）

这也反映在常年以来西方国家的公司与精明的商业人士一贯的理念与做法，就是对合约的内容十分重视，愿意花费大量金钱（特别是律师费）、时间与精力在合约的谈判。因为他们最后达成的合约就给了他们肯定性与可循性，知道他们自己在有关的合约中必须履行/负责什么承诺以及对方也必须履行/负责什么承诺，以利于作出计划、安排与预算。如果不幸（在商业合约也经常难以避免）有了争议，只要合约按照英国法就会知道英国法院会怎样解释有关的合约，因为传统的做法上法院或仲裁庭会严格地效忠或依从合约内的写法，并根据双方通过合约的条文/文字所显示出来的订约意图客观解释。这与中国的部分商人（甚至是亚洲的部分商人）理念与做法有很大偏差。

上述 Steyn 大法官的说法中，把法律的肯定性与对争议的可循性当作同一回事。讲到英国商法是一套具有可循性的游戏规则，即使是有了一套在英国主要是由法院在很多案件中建立起来完整的游戏规则，也只能做到"可循性"（predictability），而无法做到百分百的"肯定性"（certainty）。这也是好事，如果商法是有百分百的肯定性也就太无趣了。美国有一句名言："人生只有两样事情是有肯定性，一个是缴税，另一个就是死亡"，所以在美国逃税可不简单。但在其他很多国家，恐怕缴税也不是肯定吧。至于死亡虽然是或迟或早可以肯定，但到底是迟是早也只能做到可循性，这可循性是根据一些因素如个人的健康卫生、做不做运动、居住的环境条件等。在商法而言，对合约的解释能够做到可循性就是来自长时间通过无数先例累积而成的"合约解释规则"（principles/rules of construction of contract）。而这解释规则正是本书要着重介绍给大家的，以期望大家能够在完全掌握并融汇贯通后，能够对任何性质与措辞的合约或者文书文件作出合乎逻辑的解释，更能进一步在订立合约时知道怎样维护自己的合约权利与作出自己肯定办得到的承诺（不论有条件与否）。要谨记在国际商业活动中，是通过有关的合约争取对自己的保护与公平，在英国法律而言，是没有对这一方面有任何的救济或者同情。普通法也没有一个公平的理念，完全是任由订约方自己为自己争取公平与合约命运。正如本章之 2.2 段节录 Bingham 勋爵所说："The parties are to be regarded as masters of their own contractual fate."（当事人是他们合约命运的主人）

探讨可循性，首先是要理解在每一个案件做到公平是与整个法律体系的可循性之间相互有冲突的。这是因为每一个案件都会有不同的事实与环境。本来,最好的可循性就是严格依照合约的条文与用字作出客观与一般性的解释,这毕竟是双方所选择用的文字与措辞。其他的事实与环境则一概不理会。但这样做在一个案件看来公平合理,但在另一个案件就完全相反。例如,合约条文说明在某些情况下合约的其中一方可以有权选择终止合约,这是明确不过的字面上的规定。在该种情况出现时,双方都会心里有数,一方知道他可以选择终止合约,另一方知道面临可能被终止合约。这就带来了一定程度的可循性,大家可以不必通过打官司就知道各自的地位,并作出安排,如面临被终止合约的一方尽早另寻找替代合约以减少损失等。但如果失去了可循性,双方都不知道该做什么,直到打一场昂贵与漫长的官司,甚至还要上诉,才知道能否合法终止合约,这就会带来严重的不肯定与失去了可循性。这种情况就会出现在法院或者仲裁庭追求个别案件的公道,导致在两个不同案件有同样的合约条文下,却有了不同的判决结果。例如市场情况有差异,导致在一个案件中选择终止合约看来公平合理,因为没有给被终止的合约方带来太大损失,而终止的一方也不像是为了市场变化而取巧。但在另一个案件中选择终止合约就看来不公平合理,有明显的取巧味道,因为当时市场对被终止的合约方会带来极大的损失。又或者合约明示了必须准时付钱,否则收款人可以终止合约。但在一个案件这不准时只是晚了1个小时甚至1分钟,且这不是支付方的疏忽或过错所致。但在另一个案件就是晚了一两个月之久,且支付方有明显的疏忽。这样两个不同案件的事实明确看来有公平合理与否之别。如果对有同样写法与措辞的合约条文/文字在不同的案件中做出相反的解释,法律就再也谈不上有可循性了。所以,英国的法官与法律学者不断强调法律可循性,特别是对商业人士的重要性。

§4 如何解释合约

解释合约的英文有两种说法,一种是"construction of contract",另一种是"interpretation of contract"。针对合约的"construction"是法院或者仲裁庭全面作出的解释,其中包括订约时的背景/语境、口头部分的协议、合约变更与默示条文等对该合约明示条文/文字的增加、否定或者调整。"construction"也包括了"interpretation"。

但"interpretation of contract"只针对一份看来是完整的文书合约,并根据订约方所用的条文/文字与合约内的条文作出"上下文"(context)的解释,反正只是局限在合约的"四个角"(four corners)内,所以面窄得多。这在《Chitty on Contracts》(第31版,2012年)第12-041段有介绍,如下:"Construction. The word 'construction' refers to the process by which a court determines the meaning and legal effect of a contract. As such, it will embrace oral contracts as well as those in writing and implied terms as well as those that are expressed. In this chapter, however, the principles of construction discussed in the following paragraphs have mainly been developed in relation to written documents, and in this context 'construction' denotes the process (some – times referred to as interpretation) by which a court arrives at the meaning to be given to the language used by the parties in the express terms of a written agreement."

在《Implied Terms in English Contract Law》(2011 年)一书,提到 Gerard McMeel 教授的《The Construction of Contracts — Interpretation, Implication and Rectification》(2007 年)一书,说:"'interpretation' must mean the process of gleaning the actual meaning of the wording of a contract; 'construction' can be taken to refer to the process of ascertaining the effect of the contract as a whole. Interpretation does not apply to implied terms, but to express terms."

4.1 找出双方的订约意图

简单而言,解释合约是客观找出双方以文字所表达的订约意图、所能享有的权利以及作出过的承诺与所接受要承担的责任。如果法院或者仲裁庭进行这一工作,他们必须谨记自己不是合约方,所以不能以任何理由(包括公平合理或者不公平)"重写"(rewrite)双方已经达成的协议或者合约。即使这个合约要作出"改变"(variation),这也是订约双方才能做的事情,外人(包括法院或仲裁庭)不能指手画脚。

从合约的条文/文字中找出订约双方的意图,大原则的说法可以节录权威的《Chitty on Contracts》(第 31 版,2012 年)之 12–043 段与 12–044 段如下:"The task of construing a written agreement has often been said to be that of ascertaining the 'common intention of the parties' to the agreement. But this may to some extent be misleading since it is clear that the agreement must be interpreted objectively: the question is not what one or other of the parties meant or understood by the words used but rather what a reasonable person in the position of the parties would have understood the words to mean....

The cardinal presumption is that the words of the agreement mean what the parties have in fact said, so that their words must be construed as they stand. That is to say the meaning of the document or of a particular part of it is to be sought **in the document itself**: 'one must consider the meaning of the words used, not what one may guess to be the intention of the parties'. However, this is not to say that the meaning of the words in a written document must be ascertained by reference to the words of the document alone. The courts will, in principle, look at all the circumstances surrounding the making of the contract and available to the parties (usually referred to as the 'factual matrix' or 'available background') which would assist in determining how the language of the document would have been understood by a reasonable person in their position.

Further it has long been accepted that the courts will not approach the task of construction with too nice a concentration upon individual word. 'The common and universal principle ought to be applied: namely, that an agreement ought to receive that construction which its language will admit, and which will best effectuate the intention of the parties, to be collected from the whole of the agreement, and that great regard is to be had to the clear intention of the parties than to any particular words which they may have used in the expression of their intent.'"(加黑部分是笔者的强调)

根据上述的权威说法,可对一些主要的原则逐一分析如下。

4.2　何谓订约意图

经常见到的说法是解释一个完整的文书合约就是找出订约意图(contractual intention),但这里要说清楚,一直以来,英国法律找出订约意图是指双方所选择用的条文与文字所"表达出来的意图"(intention as expressed),而不是其他单方面在谈判过程中与订约后显示的主观意图。如果有一份文件是双方接受,特别是签署了的合约,可被假设是双方接受的他们所达成的全部合约内容。这份文件也成为解释双方合约的"主要资料"(primary material)。这种做法特别是在一些复杂、国际性与金额庞大的交易中出现,双方就是在谈判的过程中为了避免过早产生合约关系也往往会说明是"以签约为准"(subject to contract),通常表达一天不签署合约,双方就没有合约关系。这样,这一份签署的合约就是找出双方的订约意图的主要资料与依据。

解释的第一步也是最重要的工作,就是客观解释双方在该主要资料中所使用的文字,因为从中才可以看得出订约双方的订约意图。如果追求的是订约方主观的订约意图,这解释也不需要法院/仲裁庭代劳了,可以把双方当事人请来,然后让他们讲出是什么订约意图,随后猜测性地选择一种说法。这显然不妥当。

这里有数不清的权威说法,只节录小部分。如 George Jessel MR 大法官在 Smith v. Lucas (1881) 18 Ch D 531 先例说:"one must consider the meaning of the words used, not what one may guess to be the intention of the parties."(只能考虑所用文字的意思,而不是猜测订约方是什么意图。)

另在 Re Jodell (1890) 44 Ch. D. 590 先例中,Halsbury 勋爵说:"I do not know what the testator meant except by the words he has used. ... For myself, I am prepared to look at the whole of the document and not to part of it; and having looked at the whole of the document to see, if I can, through the document what was in the mind of the testator. Those are general principles for the construction of all instruments, and to that extent it may be said that they are canons of construction."(我不知道订约方到底在想什么,除了看他们所用的文字。我要看整份文件而不仅是其部分内容,并在看了之后,从文件中的文字了解订约方的心里是什么意图。这是解释所有文书文件的一般性大原则,这可以说是解释合约的规则。)

另有 Shaw 勋爵在 Great Western Railway v. Bristol Corp (1918) 87 L. J. Ch. 414 先例中说的:"... one hears much use made of the word 'intention', but courts of law when on the work of interpretation are not engaged upon the task or study of what parties intended to do, but of what the language which they employed showed that they did; in other words, they are not constructing a contract on the lines of what may be thought to have been what the parties intended, but they are construing the words and expressions used by the parties themselves. What do these mean? That when ascertained is the meaning to be given effect to, the meaning of the contract by which the parties are bound. The suggestion of an intention of parties different from the meaning conveyed by the words employed is no part of interpretation, but is mere confusion."(经常听说"意图"这一个词,但法院的工作并非是找出订约方到底想什么,而是从他们所用的文字找出他们应该是想什么。接受订约方的意图与合约文字表现出来不一样的意思只会带来混乱,这并非是解释合约。)

这尤其是针对一些层次比较高的订约方,如在国际商贸或航运,因为可以假设这些人士有足够的知识与水平以清楚与准确的文字表达他们的订约意图。这在新西兰的案例 Board of Trustees of the National Provident Fund v. Shortland Securities Ltd (1996) 1 N. Z. L. R. 45, CA 中,上诉庭说到:"The parties, particularly knowledgeable and experienced parties, legally advised, are to be taken as having intended what they have said."(特别是水平高与有经验的订约方,他们应该被视为是懂得怎样准确表达他们的意图。)

英国这种以文字表达为准的所谓"expression theory"也在大陆法国家有探讨,如在 K Zwigert 与 H Kotz 所著的《An Introduction to Comparative Law》(第 3 版,1998 年)之 402 – 3 段所说的:"The intention theory may have been sound enough in times gone by when contracts were made between neighbourly farmers and amicable merchants who knew each other's personal circumstances, but in the present day of impersonal mass transactions only the expression theory can provide the right solution."(找出订约方主观的意图在过往的比较简单的日子会是好的做法,就是两位作为邻居的农夫或两位大家知根知底的友好商人之间的合约。但到了今天,已经是有大量非个人化的交易在进行,根据文字所表达为准的理论应该才是正确的解决办法。)

4.3 解释合约不接受订约方主观意图

这是指解释合约必须是"客观"(objective)而不是"主观"(subjective),这对法院/仲裁庭来说也应该不困难,因为他们本来就不是订约方。但这里还涉及了其他方面,主要就是法院/仲裁庭不能也不应该接受争议中的订约方所提供的关于他们单方面订约意图的证据,说是协助解释合约,实际上是错误的做法。这也是以前很长一段时间不接受所谓"口头证据"(parol evidence)与"订约后的行为证据"(subsequent conduct)的原因。现在口头证据有一定程度的放松(Investors Compensation Scheme v. West Bromwich Building Society [1998] 1 W. L. R. 896),但口头证据中的有关谈判与订约方主观订约意图的证据还是不被接受。这可节录权威的《Chitty on Contracts》(第 31 版,2012 年)一书之 12 – 126 段,如下:"**Subsequent acts.** The admissibility of evidence to show that the parties have acted upon an instrument in a particular sense is probably confined to ancient documents. Evidence of user, and of acts done in pursuance of an instrument, has been admitted to explain old, or obsolete, or even imperfect expressions to be found in ancient documents. Attempts were, however made to extend admissibility to cases where the document was modern and the ambiguity patent. The acts and conduct of the parties under the agreement were admitted to show the sense in which the parties to it used the language they employed, and their intention in executing the instrument as revealed by their language interpreted in this sense. The House of Lords has decisively rejected this extension and has held that: '... it is not legitimate to use as an aid in the construction of the contract anything which the parties said or did after it was made."

不看订约方主观的意图有几个重要的原因,这将在接下来的段节详谈。

同样道理,法院不会接受一些争辩说是签署合约时没有好好阅读或了解其内容。这是因为法院不会接受订约一方主观与单方面的证据(没有好好阅读),对方很难反驳,法院/仲裁庭也无法确认他订约时的脑海里到底是什么想法。另一个原因是法律不接受以无知作为抗辩。这里可节录 Devlin 勋爵在 McCutcheon v. Macbrayne (David) Ltd (1964) 1 W. L. R. 125 先例中所说的:"It seems to me that when a party assents to a document forming the whole or part of his contract, he is bound by the terms of the document, read or unread, signed or unsigned, simply because they are in the contract; and it is unnecessary and possibly misleading to say that he is bound by them because he represents to the other party that he has made himself acquired with them."

以下对上述所讲逐一分析。

4.3.1 不接受原因之一:主观意图难以证明

这是常识,如果接受"主观"(subjective)意图来解释合约的条文/文字,就存在一有争议,双方就拿出不同的主观解释,法院或者仲裁庭就无所适从了。再说双方在争辩时强调的订约时主观意图往往只能靠空口说,而不会有证据证明在订约时脑中的想法到底是怎么样。事实上很有可能反而是双方在订约时根本没有想到这一方面,谈不上有什么主观意图,只是出了争议后才想自圆其说。而且出争议时可能与订约时时间相隔很久,对双方订约时脑袋里有什么主观意图根本无法取证。所以,针对这一方面既不科学,也不可靠。这也是有许多法官说过,只节录 Wright 大法官在 I. R. C. v. Raphael (1935) A. C. 96 先例所说的:"The words actually used must no doubt be construed with reference to the facts known to the parties and in contemplation of which the parties must be deemed to have used them; such facts may be proved by extrinsic evidence or appear in recitals; again the meaning of the words used must be ascertained by considering the whole document. Terms may be implied by custom and on similar grounds. But allowing for these and other rules of the same kind, the principle of the common law has been to adopt an objective standard of construction and to exclude general evidence of the intention of the parties; the reason for this has been that otherwise all certainty would be taken from the words in which the parties have recorded their agreement or their dispositions of property. If in some cases hardship or injustice may be effected by this rule of law, such hardship or injustice can generally be obviated by the power in equity to reform the contract..."

Goff 勋爵在 President of India v. Jebsens (UK) Ltd (1991) 1 Lloyd's Rep. 1 先例也说他解释合约根本不愿意臆猜订约方一方的意图:"I must confess I am reluctant to speculate on the motives of a party for adopting a clause in any particular form."

另可见 Hoffmann 勋爵在《The Intolerable Wrestle with Words and Meaning》一文中也说道:"... for the purpose of interpreting what other people say, **we have no direct access to their subjective mental states, no window into their minds.** The best we do is to use the background against which the utterance was made, including our knowledge of the speaker, to the maximum extent that we can lay our hands on it. In the end, however, out interpretation is bound to be objective in the sense that it will be our best effort to construe what such person, using those words against that background, would have meant. We may hope that our interpretation corresponds with his or her subjective intentions, but we cannot be sure."(加黑部分是笔者的强调)

4.3.2 不接受原因之二:对另一订约方不公平

另一个原因是对另一个订约方不公平,因为他只能看到的是对方所愿意接受的合约条文/文字,他无法看得见用字不准确或者表达上含糊不清的对方的内心主观意图。这应该也是"禁止翻供"(estoppel)的一种。所以早在 1899 年,《The Theory of Legal Interpretation》一文的作者 Oliver Wendell Holmes 就说:"For each party to a contract has notice that the other will understand his words according to the usage of the normal speaker of English under the circumstances, and therefore cannot complain if his words are taken in that sense."

在 Benjamin Developments Ltd v. Robt Jones (Pacific) Ltd (1994) 3 N. Z. L. R. 189, CA 这一新西兰案例,Gallen 大法官说:"It should not be forgotten that other persons not parties to the contract are also entitled and may need to order their affairs in line with what they understand the agreement to be."(不要忘记订约对方是有权知道与明白同意了什么才能安排他的工作。)

4.3.3 不接受原因之三:对第三人不公平

除了对另一个订约方不公平外,更严重的是一个文书合约如果任由订约方在订约时的主观意图去扭曲文字的意思,就会对依赖该合约的第三人不公平。在今天的商业环境下这种第三人非常多,包括银行会依赖文书合约融资,提单会被转让/转卖,合约权益会被转让等。对这些无辜第三人而言,他们唯一能看到的证据就是一份文书合约。这一点 Devlin 勋爵在 1965 年的一次名为"Morals and the Law of Contract"的讲座中就是这样讲的:"If a man minded only about keeping faith, the spirit of the contract would be more important than the letter. But in the service of commerce the letter is in many ways the more significant. This is because in most commercial contracts many more than the original parties are concerned. The contract is embodied in a document which may pass from hand to hand when the goods it represents are sold over and over again to a string of buyers, or when money is borrowed on it, or insurances arranged. The spirit of the contract gets lost on these travels and the outward form is all that matters. For the common law the sanctity of the contract means the sanctity of the written word in the form in which it is ultimately enshrined. Normally, evidence is not admissible of conversations or correspondence leading up to the contract; they cannot be used to amplify or modify the final document. That document must speak for itself. For the common law has its eye fixed as closely on the third man as on the original parties; and **the final document is the only thing that can speak to the third man.**"(加黑部分是笔者的强调)

4.3.4 不接受原因之四:无法准确提供法律意见

另一个原因也涉及或影响第三人,就是若强调主观意图解释合约,就会令出了争议后双方与其律师也会无所适从。因为寻求法律意见,律师也只能是根据看得见的文书合约条文/文字作出,不会知道对方甚至自己客户在订约时的内心主观意图。对于自己客户还可以查问,但对方的主观意图就根本不会在现阶段能够知道。

4.3.5 不接受原因之五:影响合约本身的有效性

再说一个重大原因,但先要解释在英国法律下看待一个合约是否有效,其中一个要求是双方订约方有"一致想法"(meeting of minds)或拉丁文的 *ad idem*。如果没有一致想法,如针对合约的标的,有效合约就不存在或因"错误"(mistake)而无效。换言之,合约是否有效是要看订约方的真正意图。但一有了合约的约束,有争议要解释合约条文/文字,就不理会订约方的真正意图了。

有关成立有效合约必须是有一致想法,可见 Diplock 勋爵在 The "Hannah Blumenthal" (1983) 1 Lloyd's Rep. 103 先例所说的:"To create a contract by exchange of promises between two parties where the promise of each party constitutes the consideration for the promise of the other what is necessary is that the intention of each as it has been communicated to and understood by the other (even though that which has been communicated does not represent the actual state of mind of the communicator) should coincide. That is what English lawyers mean when they resort to the Latin phrase *consensus ad idem* and the words that I have italicized are essential to the concept of *consensus ad idem*, the lack of which prevents the formation of a binding contract in English law."

这样,如果接受单方面主观意图解释文书合约条文/文字,而最后得出的结论是双方对同一文字的理解是南辕北辙的说法,就会得出一个危险的结论——双方根本没有达成订约的最基本要求,即一致想法。进一步来说,也就会导致该合约根本无效。这个危险实际上一些著名的大法官也提出过,正如 Donaldson 大法官在 Summit Investment Inc. v. British Steel Corp (1987) 1 Lloyd's Rep. 230 先例所说的:"... their actual intentions are happily irrelevant, since, were it otherwise, many, and perhaps most, disputes upon points of construction would be resolved by holding that the parties were not *ad idem*."

4.3.6 不接受原因之六:失去肯定性/可循性

如果接受订约方的主观意图,而不理会文书合约的条文/文字,或加以扭曲,就会失去法律的肯定性/可循性。文字本身会随着每一个不同案件中订约方的主观意图而得出各种奇怪的结论。毕竟在谈判的过程中会有混乱或信口开河,只会带来合约的不肯定。这是早在 Inglis v John Buttery & Co (1878) 3 App Cas 552 先例,Blackburn 勋爵就说:"The formal contract shall supersede all loose and preliminary negotiations ... there shall be no room for misunderstandings which may often arise, and which do constantly arise, in the course of long, and it may be desultory conversations, or in the course of correspondence or negotiations during which the parties are often widely at issue as to what they will insist on and what they will concede."

而商业法律的肯定性/可循性的重要是在本书不断有强调,这也只有对文字本身(不论是在文书合约,立法或其他通用文件如标准格式合约)都给其一个稳定的解释才能做得到。如果在个别的案件中这样解释被当事人认为其订约意图被漠视或曲解,较好的说法就是他们在合约中用错了文字导致被误解,下次再订约时就应该选择另一种更明确的写法。肯定性这方面可节录 Hutton 勋爵在 A. I. B. Group v. Martin (2002) 1 W. L. R. 94 先例所说的:"It is a general rule in the construction of deeds that the intention of the parties is to be ascertained from the words used in the deed and that, with certain limited exceptions, extrinsic evidence cannot be given to show the real intention of the parties. On occasions this rule may lead to the actual intention of the parties being defeated but the rule is applied to ensure certainty in legal affairs."

§5 文字的解释

文字是人与人之间表达与沟通的工具,其重要性不言而喻。在商业关系中,文字就记录下双方约定的权利与责任。但文字并不是一个精密准确的工具,经常会发生这样一种情况,即一方说的话或写的文字被另一方理解为不同的意思。不论是中文或是英文,绝少的文字会是在任何的语境或情况下都只能有一种解释。这可节录 Diplock 大法官在 Slim v. Daily Telegraph Ltd (1968) 2 Q. B. 157, CA 先例中所说的:"Everyone outside a court of law recognises that words are imprecise instruments for communicating the thoughts of one man to another. The same words may be understood by one man in a different meaning from that in which they are understood by another and both meaning may be different from that which the author of the words intended to convey; but the notion that the same words should bear different meanings to different men, and that more than one meaning should be 'right' conflicts with the whole training of a lawyer."

因为文字有这样的缺点,再加上不正确的使用,所以就经常会产生争议,需要法院/仲裁庭根据文书合约条文/文字作出客观的解释。

对文书合约所用的文字给什么解释可先节录一条"黄金规则"(the golden rule),即字典上与"一般性"(ordinary)的解释。这是在 Grey v Pearson (1857) 6 H. L. Cas. 61 先例中,Wensleydale 勋爵所说的:"In construing all written instruments, the grammatical and ordinary sense of the words is to be adhered to, unless that would lead to some absurdity, or some repugnance or inconsistence with the rest of the instrument, in which case the grammatical and ordinary sense of the words may be modified, so as to avoid that absurdity and inconsistency, but no further."

也有其他的说法这些文字应该给其"一般性"(ordinary)、"自然"(natural)、"平易"(plain)、"通用"(popular)、"主要"(primary)、"字义上"(literal)等的解释,因为这也是一般人士(包括订约的商业人士)通常所能合理理解的,毕竟他们不是语言专家或者法律专家。而唯一能够偏离的情况是这一个解释会带来可笑的结果或与合约其他条文/文字有无法协调的矛盾。

5.1 根据字典的一般性解释的做法

找出文字的一般性解释,字典是一个重要的途径。虽然字典并不是什么权威刊物,但这是一般人理解文字的一般性解释。这是 Coleridge 勋爵在 R. v. Peters (1886) 16 Q. B. D. 636 先例中所说的:"I am quite aware that dictionaries are not to be taken as authoritative exponents of the meanings of words used in Acts of Parliament, but it is a well – known rule of courts of law that words are to be taken to be used in their ordinary sense, and we are sent for instruction to those books."

显然,法院经常会参照一些权威性的字典,正如 Cozens – Hardy M. R. 大法官在 Marquis Camden v. I. R. C. (1914) 1 K. B. 641 先例所说的:"It is for the Court to interpret the statute as best they can. In so doing the Court may no doubt assist themselves in the discharge of their duty by any literary help which they can find, including of course the consultation of standard authors and reference to well – known and authoritative dictionaries, which refer to the sources in which the interpretation which they give to the words of the English language is to be found."

同样的说法可见 P. O. Lawrence 大法官在 Mills v. Cannon Brewery Co (1920) 2

Ch. 38 先例所说的:“One of the main objects of every dictionary of the English language is to give an adequate and comprehensive definition of every word contained in it, which involves setting forth all the different meanings which can properly be given to the particular word. The Court, on the other hand, in determining what is the true meaning of a particular word used in an instrument which it has to construe, has to ascertain in what sense the parties to that instrument have used the word: all the help the Court can derive from dictionaries in such a case is, in case of doubt, to ascertain that the meaning which it comes to the conclusion ought to be attributed to the words is one which may properly be given to it.”(字典主要的目标是给一个英文字充分与全面的定义,也包括了一个待定文字所能够拥有的不同意思。但法院解释文件/合约是找出一个特定文字在该文件/合约中当事人给它的意思,所以法院能够从字典得到的协助只是在有怀疑时,对有关特定文字在文件/合约的意思作出结论前,根据字典给该文字的意思看是否恰当。)

根据字典解释合约文字的一般性意思,经常有这样做法的判例。可以举一些例子,第一个是 Yangtsze Insurance Association v. Indemnity Mutual Marine Assurance Co (1908) 2 K. B. 504 先例,一艘船舶的再保险合约内有一条保证条文,即船东保证不装除煤油外的其他货物,并且保证不装战争时的禁运品(warrant no contraband of war)。众所周知,在保险合约中的保证条文在 1906 年英国《海上保险法》有其独特的解释,一有违反,保险公司就不必赔付。当时在日俄战争期间,船舶从上海去海参崴,但被日本巡洋舰扣押。船上发现两名冒充德国人的俄国海军人员,而船东及船长对此事并不知情,结果仍是船舶被日本军方充公而变为全损。船东向保险公司索赔,而保险公司向再保险公司要求补偿,后者拒赔并声称该两名俄国海军人员是“禁运品”,所以船东违反了保证条文,即使船东本身是无辜。法院判是“禁运品”(contraband)一词要给与字典的一般性解释,即只针对货物/物品,不包括自然人,所以再保险公司要作出补偿。

另一个例子是 The “Ante Topic” (1966) 1 Lloyd’s Rep. 566 先例,涉及的是有关船舶装卸时间的停算。这固定装卸时间是算在承租人头上,一旦用完而装卸作业还没有完毕,承租人就要支付滞期费作为损失赔偿。这笔钱在航运市场高涨时十分昂贵,所以承租人自然希望能够停算,且停算越长越好,但船东的心态就刚好相反。在该先例,所争议的条文是规定了船舶从锚地移船去卸货泊位不算卸货时间(time used in shifting from such anchorage to discharging berth not to count as laytime)。双方的争议就是在该条文内中的“移船”(shifting)一词该怎样解释,是宽或是紧。该先例的事实涉及船舶为了等待高潮而无法即时移船,等待的时间长达 4 天之久。问题就是这 4 天是否算是移船的一部分,又或是到了高潮起锚后开航去挂靠卸货泊位的几个小时才能算是移船?结果在高院与上诉庭船东都是胜诉,而整个解释其实十分简单,就是看字典里“移船”一词是怎样解释。这就发现“移船”是指一种动态,所以在等待移船的时间处于静态,不应该包括在这一词的解释内。在上诉庭,Diplock 大法官强调应该给这一词一般性的解释,说:"Why should the words be given their ordinary meaning? ... To give the words their ordinary meaning seems to me in this case to make business sense."

另 Viscount Simonds 大法官这样说:"The word 'shift' is a verb transitive or (less commonly) intransitive, meaning to move or transfer from one place to another. It donates at least an activity. There could not well be a less appropriate word to describe a period during which a vessel, having anchored, lies at anchor (in this case for several days) with no intention of raising anchor until the depth of water in the river permits passage."

有了先例作出这样的解释,就可以在商业社会中有了肯定性与可循性。对先例不满意而且有议价能力的承租人完全可以在惯用的租约条文中作出明示的改变,毕竟有时候因为各种原因等待移船靠泊的时间会比较漫长。所以在英国石油公司的标准航次租约 BPvoy 2 的有关条文就说明船舶从锚地移船与等待移船去装卸泊位的时间不算装卸时间,如下:"... on an inward passage, including awaiting tide, pilot or tugs and moving from anchorage ..."

5.2 根据字典的一般性解释的局限

5.2.1 局限之一:只能解释个别文字,无法解释整体的合约

这方面也有许多严重的局限,无法对解释合约做出太大帮助。毕竟法院/仲裁庭的责任是解释一份合约,而不是把合约切割开来逐字或至多是逐句独立解释。所以,仅靠字典无法解释一份合约。字典只是对单字作出一些通常与字面上的理解,完全"不涉及上下文"(uncontextual)。但单字用在一句话或合约的一条条文,看上下文就往往表示这一个单字可能与字典有不同的解释,因为必须与条文(包括合约中其它条文)的其他文字一并解释。例如,"鸽子"(pigeon)多加一个字为"赛鸽"(racing pigeon),就会涉及在立法或是合约内的解释是否还是与字典一致:Hong Kong Racing Pigeon Association Ltd v Attorney General (1995) 2 HKC 201 先例。

但即使是根据合约整体考虑并作出上下文的解释,这还是局限在合约的四个角内。毕竟合约内的每一个单字、一句话或所有的条文都是订约双方所选择的记录他们的谈判结果与订约意图。这表示即使合约的文字根据上下文作出解释,也不一定双方选用的文字是能够最好准确[5]反映订约双方真正的订约意图。但英国法律传统只是严格解释合约的四个角内的条文/文字,通过不允许"外来证据"(extrinsic evidence)与"口头证据"(parol evidence)的引进帮助解释合约。换言之,不理会合约条文/文字的不同本质(如一份租约或是一份保险合约)以及双方用语的本意或背景的

---

〔5〕 但并不至于错误记录了双方订约意图,否则会涉及另一种衡平救济的"合约变更"(rectification),在本书第三章之13.1段有详论。

问题。这可见 Steyn 大法官在 Arbuthnott Fagan (1995) C. L. C. 1396 先例所说的:"Dictionaries never solve concrete problems of construction. The meaning of words cannot be ascertained divorced from their context. And part of the contextual scene is the purpose of the provision."

Hoffmann 勋爵也在 Investors Compensation Scheme v. West Bromwich Building Society (1998) 1 W. L. R. 896, HL 先例中说:"The meaning of words is a matter of dictionaries and grammars; the meaning of the document is what the parties using those words against the relevant background would reasonably have been understood to mean. The background may not merely enable the reasonable man to choose between the possible meanings of words which are ambiguous but even (as occasionally happens in ordinary life) to conclude that the parties must, for whatever reason, have used the wrong words or syntax."

5.2.2 局限之二:文字有多个解释而要看合约语境

有一些文字是只有一个主要的解释,查字典应该就可以找到正确答案。正如 Slade 大法官在 Earl of Lonsdale v. Att – Gen (1982) 1 W. L. R. 887 先例中所说的:"Of many, perhaps the majority, of the words used by English speaking people there can be little doubt as to the ordinary meaning, or 'literal' or 'primary' meaning, as it is often called. To take an example at random, the court would not, I conceive find much difficulty in attaching a literal or primary meaning to the word 'elephant', if it found it in a written instrument."

但同样有不少文字一般性的解释有多个,则在一个合约内准确的解释就必须看该合约的"语境"(context〔6〕或 factual matrix)与"背景"(background/circumstances),而仅查字典是没有帮助的。这在 Manufactures Mutual Insurance Ltd v. Withers (1988) 5 A. N. Z. Insurances Cases 60 – 853 先例中,McHugh 大法官是说:"... few, if any, English words are unambiguous or not susceptible of more than one meaning or have a plain meaning. Until a word, phrase or sentence is understood in the light of the surrounding circumstances, it is rarely possible to know what it means."

举例说,"warrant"在字典里可以找出好几个不同解释,如授权批准、担保、发票等。如果这一个字出现在保单,如"warrant class",就变成担保船舶是有船级。而如果在保期内船级被撤销,即使是看来无害的短暂时间,也可能有严重的后果。这是因

---

〔6〕 注意是"context"一字在较早前去在四个角内解释一份合约被翻译为"上下文",但"context"在这里与本书其它很多地方,包括近期先例判词中是广泛的包括了合约的本质、双方谈判过程中的订约意图、订约时的环境与背景等等意思。换言之,"context"一字的解释也有不同的语境。而近期在 Investors Compensation Scheme v. West Bromwich Building Society (1998) 1 W. L. R. 896 先例中提到要去广泛根据背景/语境去解释合约条文/文字的做法也普遍被称为是"contextual approach to construction"。

为1906年英国《海上保险法》对保单里面的这种保证必须完全依照，有非常严格的立法解释。这与1979年英国《货物销售法》对“保证”的定义截然不同。这方面会稍后在本书第五章之6.5段另有详论。

再举一个比较常见的字“court”，它可以指法院，也可以是球场、院子，皇室人员的住所或奉承、求爱与殷勤。如果加上一些字典以外的解释，就可能更加多了，如对国际仲裁熟悉的人士就知道有一个著名的ICC Court。要给这一个字准确与贴切的解释，又是要看整句话与整份文件的上下文了。

这种有多个不同解释的例子多不胜数，在本书接下来的章节会不断有其他例子。在此只多举一个例子是“accordingly”（可暂时解释为“所以”），甚至它在一个句子中所处的位子也是关键。这是在上诉庭的The “Pera” (1985) 2 Lloyd's Rep. 103先例，涉及一个油轮租约下的滞期费索赔是否过了12个月时效的争议。有关的条文名为“Petroship Time Bar Clause”，而其中争议的部分是如下：“Demurrage, if any, shall be payable by Charterers against owners invoice supported by notices and statements of fact(s) from loading and discharging port(s) duly signed by shippers. Any claim for demurrage to be accordingly presented within 12 months from completion of final discharge.”（加黑部分是笔者的强调）

本来船东是在12个月时效内向承租人提出了滞期费的索赔，但上述条文第一句说明要求的装港“通知书”(notice)却欠缺了，另“事实记录”(statements of fact)也是一份看不清楚的复印本。船东后来也追加提供了，但时间上过了12个月的时限。这样，双方的争议就在上述条文的第二句，船东的立场是只要滞期费的索赔在12个月内提出就已经符合要求，而句子中的“accordingly”一词只是连接词，可解释为“所以”(therefore)。但拒赔的承租人立场是滞期费的索赔必须是在12个月内呈交第一句中所阐明的所有文件才能避免时效已过，而第二句的“accordingly”一词是一个副词，应该解释为“根据上一句的前提”(in accordance with the premises)。

根据字典的解释，“accordingly”有好几个意思。根据牛津大字典，它被解释为“in accordance with the premises; correspondingly; in natural sequence”。这些解释看来是比较支持承租人的说法。但另一本著名的字典《Chambers》，这一个字被解释为“agreeably; suitably; in agreement (with what precedes); therefore”。这看来是有解释支持承租人，也有解释支持船东。所以仅看字典找出该词的一般性解释不能解决问题。

看来，这一词在整个句子中所放的位置也是很关键。如果一句话是说“My car broke down; accordingly I came by bus”（我的车坏了，所以我坐公共汽车来），这应该是一个连接词。但如果一句话是“Pupils will read the school rules, and conduct themselves accordingly”（学生要熟读学校的规定，并依照行事），这就是一个副词。除了是这句话本身表达这个意思外，“accordingly”也是在动词之后。

但注意在本案例的“accordingly”并不是放在动词的“presented”后面。结果，三位上诉庭的大法官都觉得作出解释十分困难,而最后判承租人败诉,还是只能靠最后的武器,就是针对承租人解释(*contra proferentem*),[7]因为这有关条文是由承租人拟定,它也不是一个标准格式租约条文,所以可以按照个别不同案件去判决,而且本质上是对承租人的免责条文(针对船东索赔的时效,得利的是承租人)。

另在 Investors Compensation Scheme v. West Bromwich Building Society (1998) 1 W. L. R. 896 先例中,也是文字在一个句子里面所处的位置带来了完全不同的解释,要到贵族院才有定案。由于这个重要先例的案情在本章 8.3 段与本书第六章 12.3 段有详细介绍,不在此重复。

5.2.3 局限之三:技术性文字或专业术语

现在许多商业合约中技术性文字或专业术语越来越多,这往往也是无法在一般的字典中找到。这样,不少合约订约双方增加一条明示条文作出"定义"(definition),定义条文或"解释条文"(interpretation clause)将在本书第五章之第 9 段有详论。但如果是漏了或因为定义条文写得含糊而引起争议,就有可能需要订约双方举证(外来证据/口头证据)并协助解释了。例如在 Cooper (Max) and Sons Pty v. Sydney City Council (1980) 54 A. L. J. 234 先例,有关合约中"pay loading"一词,Diplock 勋爵是这样说:"it is not an expression that is used in ordinary speech; without extrinsic evidence from a witness experienced in the building industry and familiar with the technical terms used in it, a judge could only speculate as to the meaning."

这种情况也会在双方的谈判中曾经同意过某一个定义,这种所谓的"私人字典"(private dictionary)在本书第三章之第 14 段有详论。

5.2.4 总结

有关上述所讲可以节录《Chitty on Contracts》(第 31 版,2012 年)之 12 - 051 段与 12 - 052 段部分如下:

"**Adoption of the ordinary meaning of words.** The starting point in constructing a contract is that words are to be given their ordinary and natural meaning. This is not necessarily the dictionary meaning of the word, but that in which it is generally understood. The courts assume that the parties have used language in the way that reasonable persons ordinarily do. So terms are 'to be understood in their plain, ordinary, and popular sense, unless they have generally in respect to the subject - matter, as by the known usage of trade, or the like, acquired a peculiar sense distinct from the popular sense of the same words; or unless the context evidently points out that they must in the particular instance, and in order to effectuate the immediate intention of the parties to that contract, be understood in some other special and peculiar sense.'

Technical words. Prima facie the rule is that technical words must have their techni-

---

[7] 这一课题在本书第四章之第 5 段有详细介绍。

cal meaning given to them unless something can be found in the context to exclude it, for if a word is of a technical or scientific character, then its primary meaning is its technical and scientific meaning. ..."

§6　合理与否的关系

一般而言,明示条文/文字不理会合理与否,这是因为订约自由的大道理,他们完全可以订一些不合理的交易,只要这不违反公共政策。如果其中一方接受对其十分不利的合约条文,这是他自己的选择,可能背后有各种原因(如谈判力量与知识不足,要与对方建立关系等)。普通法在这种情况是没有办法作出救济"重写"(re-write)合约。这种救济往往要依靠立法(如政策要求立法针对垄断或保障消费者)以针对不公平竞争或对社会的弱者作出保护。但默示条文/文字就必须合理,因为这是法律增加合约的内容,必须假设双方同意是合情合理的事情,这方面在本书第七章会详谈。

合理与否也不是与解释合约明示条文/文字毫无关系。以下谈谈涉及合理的情况。

6.1　什么是不合理的约定

这里介绍一些客观看属于不合理的约定,当然它的范围很广,无法逐一介绍。其中一种最常见的类型就是以明示条文改变立法或普通法以及商业习惯做法/惯例所规定的"默示地位"(implied position)。例如,普通法默示有疏忽的一方通常要承担责任,这样,如果订约一方想在他疏忽时也不必承担责任,就要以清楚无误的文字豁免对疏忽的责任。因为豁免疏忽的责任属于一种不合理的约定,必须写得清楚无误,只有唯一的一种解释才会被承认。这也可以让对方订约方在接受这种极不合理的约定时先考虑清楚。有关这方面的解释在本书第十二章之第1段有关免责条文有详论。在这里只节录其中一个重要的先例,就是 Gillespie Brothers Ltd v Roy. Bowles Transport Ltd (1973) 1 Lloyd's Rep. 10,上诉庭的 Buckley 大法官说:"It is, however, a fundamental consideration in the construction of contracts of this kind that it is inherently improbable that one party to the contract should intend to absolve the other party from the consequences of the latter's own negligence. The intention to do so must therefore be made perfectly clear, for otherwise the court will conclude that the exempted party was only intended to be free from liability in respect of damage occasioned by causes other than negligence for which he is answerable."

类似的,要排除普通法给予订约双方的抵销权利或其他违约救济,也需要非常清楚无误的文字。[8] 普通法或立法有很多默示条文，通常可以清楚无误的明示条文排除任何的默示。有关今天十分普遍见到的“完整合约条文”（entire agreement clause）能否排除默示条文，这在本书第十三章之第2段会有详论。

在海事方面，船东的适航责任也是明显的例子。普通法下，船东确保船舶适航是严格/绝对责任。确保船舶适航本身也是十分复杂与琐碎的责任，不容易面面俱到，如船舶船底有一个大窟窿是船舶不适航，一艘大型船舶少了一件看来无关紧要的救生衣亦可构成不适航。所以经常见到租约内有明示条文减轻甚至免除船东的严格/绝对与很容易就会有违反的适航责任，国际船东协会 BIMCO 也有这一方面的标准合约，如著名的金康租约（Gencon Charter - party）。总而言之，只除了在立法中明确禁止以明示条文改变的情况（如根据1924年《海牙规则》立法的1924年英国《海上运输法》），其他情况下只要双方用字清楚无误，明示条文还是可以超越法律的默示。

此外，如果双方约定的合约条文/文字与其所从事的行业习惯做法不同，也可能被视为不合理的约定，因为商业习惯做法有合理性的要求。这种情况下，双方亦只有以清楚无误的明示条文来排除习惯做法/惯例的默示。举一个例子，提单作为“物权凭证”（document of title）是根据当时地中海贸易的习惯做法而在贵族院的 Lickbarrow v Mason (1787) 2 T. R. 63 先例被确认/承认，所以在租约约定船东/船长必须在卸港无单放货就是如此，这明示条文必须清楚无误而且不能涉及非法/侵占。

6.2 以一个合理人士的角度来解释文字

法院或仲裁庭在解释合约时，所关心的不是合约订约方单方面的订约意图，而是客观与合理来看他们通过合约的条文/文字所表达出来的订约意图，而法院或仲裁庭就是以一个合理第三人的身份来理解与判断双方到底约定了什么内容与它们的解释。

6.3 越不合理的约定就越要写得清楚

越是不合理的约定，就越要以清楚无误的明示条文来写明。这个著名的合约解释的大原则是 Reid 勋爵在 L Schuler AG v Wickman Machine Tool Sales Ltd (1973) 2 Lloyd's Rep 53 先例（这一重要先例在本书第五章之6.4段有详细介绍）中确立的，他说：“The fact that a particular construction leads to a very unreasonable result must be a relevant consideration. The more unreasonable the result the more unlikely it is that the parties can have intended it, and if they do intend it the more necessary it is that they shall make that intention abundantly clear.”

这个原则也被 Hoffmann 勋爵在 B. C. C. I. v. Ali (2001) 1 UKHL 8 先例以另一种方式表达出来：“When judges say that ‘in the absence of clear words’ they would be unwilling to construe a document to mean something, they generally mean (as they did in the case of exemption clauses) that the effect of the document is unfair.”

---

[8] 这可看本书第四章之第11段。

在同样的原则下，如果双方约定一些荒谬的东西，也应该以清楚明确的文字表达，尤其是在商业活动。这可以节录在 Tillmanns & Co v. S. S. Lnutsford Ltd（1908）2 K. B. 385 先例，Farewell 勋爵提到在解释商业合约时，有假设是商人不会意图同意一些“荒谬或可笑”（absurd）的事情：“In a mercantile document or a statute there is a presumption that business men do not intend to do anything absurd, which is some slight guide; but in all cases it is a matter of construction.”

另在 L Schuler AG v Wickman Machine Tool Sales Ltd 先例，Morris 勋爵也有类似说法，他说除非用字清楚无误，否则很难接受商人会同意一些绝对“异想天开”（utterly fantastic）的事情，他说：“Subject to any legal requirements, businessmen are free to make what contracts they chooses but unless the terms of their agreement are clear a court will not be disposed to accept that they have agreed something utterly fantastic.”

这个说法也十分公道，因为合约中的内容对订约一方很不合理或荒谬，也就表示用字上必须清楚无误且只能有一种解释，这样才能够在对他不利时，法院或仲裁庭可理直气壮地说他是在订约时接受的。

6.4　法院或仲裁庭选择最合理的解释

这一说法与上一段是同一个理念，如果文书合约的条文/文字只能有一个解释，法院或仲裁庭也就只能这样解释了，不管合理与否。但如果该条文/文字可以有多过一个解释，法院或仲裁庭就要挑一个客观看来比较合理或最合理的解释。

这方面可先介绍 Australian Broadcasting Commission v. Australian Performing Right Association Limited（1973）129 C. L. R. 99 先例，Gibbs 大法官对这方面的原则有详尽的论述，他说：“... If the words used are unambiguous the court must give effect to them, notwithstanding that the result may appear capricious or unreasonable, and notwithstanding that it may be guessed or suspected that the parties intended something different. The court has no power to remake or amend a contract for the purpose of avoiding a result which is considered to be inconvenient or unjust. On the other hand, if the language is open to two constructions, that will be preferred which will avoid consequences which appear to be capricious, unreasonable, inconvenient or unjust, ‘even though the construction adopted is not the most obvious, or the most grammatically accurate’, to use the words from earlier authority cited in *Locke v. Dunlop*（1888）39 Ch. D. 387...”

6.5　商业合约尽量以商业合理性的角度解释

很大部分的争议涉及商业合约，近年来经常有重要的案例判是对待这些合约，应该尽量以一个合理商业人士的角度解释有关条文/文字。这里又存在一个字义上与商业上解释的矛盾，但首先可以节录一些比较著名的说法，这可见 Steyn 勋爵在 Mannai Investment Co Ltd v. Eagle Star Life Assurance Co Ltd（1997）A. C. 749 先例中所说的：“In determining the meaning of the language of a commercial contract, and unilateral contractual notices, the law therefore generally favours a commercially sensible construction. The reason for this approach is that a commercial construction is more likely to give effect to the intention of the parties. Words are therefore interpreted in the way in which a reasonable commercial person would construe them. And the standard of the reasonable commercial person is hostile to technical interpretations and undue emphasis on niceties of language."

在该先例,Steyn 勋爵也说到在过去几十年法院的态度上的改变,并指出现在有转变以商业角度解释的趋势。这一种新的趋势在本章第8段会有详论。

同样的说法也在 The "Antaios" (No. 2) (1984) 2 Lloyd's Rep. 235 先例,Diplock 勋爵说如果在一个商业合约中文字上的分析会带来商业上的不合理,前者就应该服从后者:"While deprecating the extension of the use of the expression 'purposive construction' from the interpretation of statues to the interpretation of private contracts, I agree with the passage I have cited from the arbitrator's award and I take this opportunity of restating that, if a detailed semantic and syntactical analysis of words in a commercial contract is going to lead to a conclusion that flouts business common sense, it must be made to yield to business common sense."

上述说法,就可以 The "Antaios" (No. 2)先例作为典型例子进一步解释。案情是有关著名的期租标准格式合约 NYPE 46,有第5条文说明承租人如果没有准时支付租金,船东就可以撤船。但问题是除了针对准时支付租金外,也同时多了一句说明是"或有任何在本租约下的违约"(or on any breach of the charter - party),船东也可撤船。这就带来很大的问题,因为在一个长期的合约内,违约(特别是一些无伤大雅或技术性的)经常在发生。它们在普通法下都不会有什么救济,因为往往没有带来实际损失。所以,如果根据字义上严格解释,无伤大雅的违约也包括在"任何违约"一词,岂非可以根据这明示条文让船东很容易撤船?毕竟,明示条文可以约定一些完全不合理的内容,只要写得清楚。但这样解释"任何违约"一词,以后很难有长期的期租合约了,就算是约定了较长的租约期,也很容易在中途被船东终止,因为履行的过程中很容易发生轻微违约的情况。再考虑到双方在订立中长期租约时,稍有头脑的承租人与船东绝对不会接受不论大小违约,一出现就可以让船东撤船的条款。这太不符合商业合理性,也几乎肯定不是他们之间的订约意图,否则何必花时间谈判3年5年的期租。这当然也不是默示的问题,因为已经有一条明示条文针对。当然,可以说 NYPE 46 订得不好,应该改变,而不是解释合约的法律要改变。但这也是一个矛盾,因为一份著名的标准格式合约也不是轻易修改,而且即使修改了,市场普遍接受也需要很长时间,正如 NYPE 93 到近期的使用率还是大大比不上 NYPE 46。这个问题在 The "Antaios" (No. 2)先例也有提到,Kerr 大法官说:"Whatever may be the right answer, clause 5 is unsatisfactory and requires consideration from the point of view of what owners and charterers really wish to be their respective rights and obligations in the context of the owners' right to withdraw the ship, thereby effectively endangering any New York Produce charter on a rising freight market. However, it all too frequently happens that admonitions of this kind from the Courts in relation to printed forms of charter - parties in common use have not borne fruit, because of the practical difficulty of securing amendments to the printed forms, and the reluctance of brokers to hazard the successful negotiation of any individual charter by some express amendment or clarification. However, in the context of the right to withdraw, an unsatisfactory clause is clearly a matter of the utmost seriousness."

所以,怎样解释这一句早在 The "Athos" (1983) 1 Lloyd's Rep. 127 先例中已经涉及,案情有关船东指承租人违约,没有尽快支付战争险加保费。当时上诉庭就是面对这一选择,即这一句是否要无节制地解释,或者法院要重写让这一句可被商业人士接受。Purchas 大法官这样说:"Should the clause be allowed to stand unmitigated in its effect or should the Court rewrite the clause so that its effect would be reasonably acceptable in the Court's view to commercial men?"

在第一审,高院的 Neill 大法官判是第 5 条文的这一句"清楚明确"(did not contain any ambiguity),并认为应该被解释为适用在"任何违约",不论轻微或严重。上诉庭的 Kerr 大法官这样评论:"Mr. Justice Neill concluded that these words should be construed without restriction so as to apply to any breach whatever..."

但上诉庭的多数觉得应该给这一句话一点限制,认为只适用在一些涉及承租人不合理拒绝支付的情况,如已经判了承租人要承担战争险加保费,但承租人继续拒绝支付的情况。另一个限制是觉得第 5 条文主要针对准时支付租金,所以假设的订约意图是对待支付租金的违约与租约其他的违约(如承租人的小工装卸时对船舶造成轻微损坏或承租人装运了一批禁止的货物)有所区别。Kerr 大法官这样说:"... since clause 5 appeared to give the owner the right to withdraw the vessel 'on any breach of this charter - party', a restriction had sensibly to be imposed on clause 5 to give effect to the presumed intention of the parties; and the intention of clause 5 was to single out the payment of hire by the due date as a crucial obligation in relation to payments and to draw a distinction between payments other than hire on the one hand and breaches of a different nature on the other hand; The words 'or on any breach' in clause 5 might possibly apply to some unjustified refusal by the charterers to make some payment other than hire but the situation in the present case could not be regard as one of refusal; it was a bona fide dispute as to the amount payable and on the construction of the charter as a whole such a situation fell within the arbitration clause and did not give to the owners the immediate right of withdrawal if the charterers contentions subsequently failed in the arbitration."

这混乱的说法在不久后在贵族院的 The "Antaios" (No. 2)先例才定了调。在这个案例的案情中,可更加明显看到这一句不符合商业合理性之处。它是一个 3 年的期租,承租人是把船舶分租,而分承租人再分租,是"分分承租人"在营运时签发了一些错误的提单。原承租人是完全无辜,但他对分分承租人有"代理责任"(vicarious liability)。船东在运费市场高涨时就以这一技术性的违约撤了船。在仲裁庭,判是承租人的违约并非是"毁约性违约"(repudiatory breach),并针对 NYPE 46 第 5 条文这一句的解释说:"We always return to the point that the Owners' construction is wholly unreasonable, totally uncommercial and in total contradiction to the whole purpose of the N. Y. P. E. time charter form. The Owners relied on what they said was the 'the literal meaning of the word in the clause'. We would say that if necessary, in a situation such as this, a purposive construction should be given to the clause so as not to defeat the commercial purpose of the contract."(我们不断要回到这一点说船东的解释完全不合理,完全不合商业性与违反了整个 NYPE 期租合约的目标。船东倚赖的是该条文的文字上的字义解释。我们可以这样回应,就是如果有需要,在本案件的情况下,一个目的性的解释才不会否定合约的商业目标。)(这"目的"就是指 NYPE 期租合约是用在可能很长的租约期,所以不应该有条文轻易让其中一方随意脱身。)

贵族院认同仲裁庭的判法,其中 Diplock 勋爵就讲了一段上述节录的名言。换言之,NYPE 46 第 5 条文的"any breach of this charter – party"变为或重写为"any repudiatory breach of this charter – party"。

最后节录一个更近期的上诉庭先例,BMA Special Opportunity Hub Fund Ltd & Ors v African Minerals Finance Ltd. (2013) EWCA Civ 416 指出在商业合约的条文有了争议,如果有两个解释,法院应选择与商业常识更一致的解释。这一说法与本章 6.4 段的道理一样,但还是经常会有争议就是双方各执一词,并认为自己的说法与商业常识更一致。在该先例是说明法院(当然也包括仲裁庭)不要根据其中一方的商业常识的解释,更加不要以法院或者仲裁庭的主观看法作出解释。虽然在现实中,后者的情况很难避免,但法院或者仲裁庭还是需要警惕这一原则或游戏规则,尽量客观看待双方的争辩与证据作出什么才是与商业常识更一致的解释。Aikens 大法官是这样说:"There was no dispute between the parties on the principles of construction that the court must use in interpreting this commercial document. There has been considerable judicial exposition of these principles by the House of Lords and the Supreme Court in recent years. There is no point in my going over the same ground again at any length. The court's job is to discern the intention of the parties, objectively speaking, from the words used in the commercial document, in the relevant context and against the factual background in which the document was created. The starting point is the wording of the document itself and the principle that the commercial parties who agreed the wording intended the words used to mean what they say in setting out the parties' respective rights and obligations. **If there are two possible constructions of the document a court is entitled to prefer the construction which is more consistent with 'business common sense', if**

that can be ascertained. However, I would agree with the statements of Briggs J, in Jackson v Dear, first, that 'commercial common sense' is not to be elevated to an over-riding criterion of construction and, secondly, that the parties should not be subjected to '. . . the individual judge's own notions of what might have been the sensible solution to the parties' conundrum'. I would add, still less should the issue of construction be determined by what seems like 'commercial common sense' from the point of view of one of the parties to the contract."（加黑部分是笔者的强调）

商业合约尽量以商业合理性的角度解释的说法也带来另一个疑问，就是法院的法官并非是最适合的以商业合理性解释商业合约的人选。所以，不断见到一些著名法官强调法院不要通过上诉（因为这是一个法律问题）轻易改变由商业人士作为仲裁员对商业合约作出的解释或裁决，因为这些人士会是更适合的人选。在20世纪80年代，上诉庭的Denning勋爵就经常在他的判例中作出这一强调。另也介绍一个名为Andre et Cie v. Cook Industries Inc (1986) 2 Lloyd's Rep. 200的先例，案情涉及一票豆饼的国际货物买卖，有关订约双方对有否以传真往来达成一个合约"更改"（variation）有争议，并开始了GAFTA仲裁。Bingham大法官判是解释任何文书文件是法律问题，但由一些商人写的传真往来，让商人作出解释应是恰当，法院应该尽量避免插手由贸易商作为仲裁员所作出的裁决（这是因为GAFTA的仲裁员名单是贸易商而不是法律人士）。他这样说："I should be very slow to differ from a trade tribunal on the meaning reasonably to be given to telex exchanges of the sort in issue here. Ultimately, of course, the construction of any written instrument is a question of law on which the court is entitled and bound to rule, but the significance of a meaning attributed by the reasonable non－lawyer varies widely from instrument to instrument and according to the circumstances of the case. Here one is dealing with communications by trader to trader in the context of an unexpected and fast－moving situation. A trade tribunal brings to the task of interpretation certain insights denied (to a greater or less extent) to the court: an informed appreciation of the commercial situation as it unfolded, seen through the eyes of a trader; an understanding of the hopes and fears and pressures which moved traders at the time; an awareness of the extent to which, at the time, the future course of events appeared obscure and unpredictable; a knowledge of the language which one trader habitually uses to another. So, in a case such as this the court's task is not one of pure construction and I should be reluctant to differ from the board unless it appeared that the board's construction was fairly plainly untenable."

6.6 假设订约方不会不合理约定一些不可能做到的事情

会有比较少见的情况是双方约定一些不可能做到的事情，当然这不是指一些沉重的责任，需要其中一方花很大的费用与精力，这不是不履行合约承诺的理由。解释合约，也要避免解释双方约定了一些不可能做到的事情，因为这并不合理。但现实中这种情况确有发生，其中很大的原因就是乱订合约，导致作出承诺后履行不了。这在本书第四章之第 14 段有介绍，不重复。

§7 传统解释合约的做法

传统解释合约的做法是比较严格解释一份文书合约，这可被称为“字义”（literalist）解释，也有称为“严格解释”（strict interpretation）。固然，也会根据合约不同的“语境”（context）加以考虑，但这往往是在合约的条文/文字上有“含糊”（ambiguity），即有多过一个解释时才可能这样做。否则，传统的解释就会严格依照合约文字的“一般性”（ordinary）、“自然”（natural）、“平易”（plain）、“通用”（popular）、“主要”（primary）、“字义上”（literal）等解释。如果不只是一个单词而涉及一份文书合约/文件内不同的条文/文字，传统法院的做法就是根据本书介绍的多条“解释合约的规则”（rules of construction）给其一个综合的解释。反正只局限在有关文书合约的“四个角内”（within the four corners），不涉及证据认定事实，如在双方谈判中的一些事实。这里一些权威说法与先例可小部分节录如下。

首先是在权威的《Chitty on Contracts》（第 31 版，2012 年）一书第 12 – 118 段，说：“But under the older restrictive view expressed in this statement, and endorsed in a number of subsequent cases, extrinsic evidence is admissible only where the sense and meaning of the words of the written instrument is doubtful or difficulty arises when it is sought to apply the language of the instrument to the circumstances under consideration. If the words have a clear and fixed meaning, not capable of explanation, extrinsic evidence would not be admissible to show that the parties meant something different from what they have written.”

另在《Norton on Deeds》（1928 年）一书中说明文字上没有含糊的情况下，必须根据字义解释：“When the words used in a deed are in their literal meaning unambiguous, and when such meaning is not excluded by the context, and is sensible with respect to the circumstances of the parties at the time of executing the deed, such literal meaning must be taken to be that in which the parties used the words.”

早在 Robertson v. French（1803）4 East 130 先例，Ellenborough 大法官说：“The same rule of construction which applies to all other instruments applies equally to this instrument of policy of insurance, viz, that it is to be construed according to its sense and meaning, as collected [in the first place] from the terms used in it, which terms are themselves to be understood in their plain, ordinary and popular sense, unless they have generally in respect of the subject – matter, as by the known usage of trade, or the like, acquired a peculiar sense distinct from the popular sense of the same words; or unless the context evidently points out that they must ... be understood in some other special and peculiar sense."

这种英国法律下传统解释合约的做法也可以节录美国历史上一位十分出名的 Learned Hand 大法官曾经在美国的上诉庭先例 Hotchkiss v National City Bank of New York 201 F664 (CA, 2nd cir, 1912) 中生动的说法(但他在 1940 年左右改变了想法: Zell v American Seating Co. 138 F 2d 641 [CA, 2nd Cir, 1943] 先例):"A contract has, strictly speaking, nothing to do with the personal, or individual, intent of the parties. A contract is an obligation attached by the mere force of law to certain acts of the parties, usually words, which ordinarily accompany and represent a known intent. If, however, it were proved by twenty bishops that either party, when he used the words, intended something else than the usual meaning which the law imposes upon them, he would still be held, unless there were some mutual mistake, or something else of the sort."(一个合约的解释,严格地说其实不管订约方个人的意图。合约的承诺只是法律强制双方通过文字表达一个共同意图。如果订约方能够找到 20 个主教证明他订约时所使用的文字有其他的意图或解释,而不是法律想强制的解释,他还是不会成功,除非有一些共同的错误或类似的问题。)

这一传统解释合约 Hoffmann 勋爵在 BCCI v. Ali (2001) UKHL 8 先例中也说:"It is not easy to recover the intellectual background against which the 18th and even 19th century judges decided historical inquiry. What is, I think, beyond dispute is that their approach was for more literal and less sensitive to context than ours today."

7.1 总结传统解释合约的做法

总结传统解释合约的做法可有以下几条大原则:

1. 解释合约是客观找出双方的订约意图,指在文书合约的条文/文字对一个客观的法院或仲裁庭所显示或表达的意图。

2. 这订约的意图是根据条文/文字的一般性、自然、平易、通用、主要、字义上等的解释,而且倾向于"严格"(strict)与"形式化"(formal)对待。

3. 虽然传统解释合约在一些情况[如在文字上有"潜在含糊"(latent ambiguity)时],法院也会考虑合约的语境而不是仅凭字义解释,但总的说是以合约文字字义的解释为主。

4. 这就带来了对证据的排斥,因为要考虑合约的语境就是要靠证据。传统做法是法院不接受文书合约的四个角外的证据显示双方在谈判时的真正订约意图,企图增加、改变或驳斥可能是没有完整或准确记录双方订约意图的合约条文/文字。这些不被接受的文件可称为"外来证据"(extrinsic evidence),其中包括"口头证据"(parol evidence)。这方面包括些什么在本书第六章之第 2 段有介绍。不接受外来证据的原因有几方面,如早期的民事案件的事实由陪审团审理,接受证据是他们的工作,法官只认定法律问题。而在那个年代,经常会有陪审团成员是文盲,但法官就不可能是。

另一个原因是以前文件证据不多,主要依赖口头证据。但证人因为素质以及经常有自己的利益(特别是针对某些文件如遗嘱),所以向其取证十分困难与很不可靠。在以前,法院所见得到的文件也通常由律所拟定,理论上总会比较全面与明确。所以为了肯定性,就索性排除外来证据改变文书合约。Hoffmann 勋爵也在 BCCI v. Ali (2001) UKHL 8 先例中有说到这一点如下:"Courts were reluctant to admit what was called 'extrinsic evidence', that is to say, evidence of background which would put the language into context. This reluctance has to do with a number of factors which are now of purely historical interest, such as trial by jury, under which the construction of documents was treated as a matter of law for the judge, the incompetence of the parties and persons interested to give evidence, the fact that most documents which came before the courts were deeds prepared by lawyers and a general feeling that the less the court took account of extrinsic evidence, the more predictable would be the construction which it gave to the document. As Popham CJ said in the Countess of Rutlan's Case (1604) 5 Co Rep. 25b, 26a: 'it would be inconvenient that matters in writing made by advice and on consideration and which finally import the certain truth of the agreement of the parties should be controlled by averment of the parties to be proved by the uncertain testimony of slippery memory.'"

7.2 传统解释合约做法的弊病

传统解释文书合约做法的弊病主要是会对订约双方真正的订约意图作出错误或片面的解释,因为绝少有一个文书合约能够把双方订约的意图全面与准确地节录下来。这也经常造成"断章取义"(reading out of context),特别是文书合约本身就言辞不详或用错字时。在这种情况下,如果能看双方订约的意图,尤其是近几十年来有了更可靠的文书谈判记录,就,会可能很容易与准确地找出这一真正意图。但传统做法没有这个环境,因为禁止口头证据就等于不能通过这个途径找出真正的订约意图。当然,万事都有例外,有一个说法即如果文书合约的文字显示了有"潜在的含糊"(latent ambiguity),这才允许参照外来证据/口头证据。举例而言,两个朋友相约一起去大剧院听朗朗先生的钢琴演奏音乐会。当其中一位朋友买了该音乐会的票,就告诉他的朋友:"我 3 月 2 日晚上 7 点在大剧院门口等你。"如果这一句话是一个有法律效果的文件,就可以看到在日期上有笔误,因为朗朗先生是在 3 月 1 日有演出。他的朋友明知道朗朗先生只表演一天,就会回来问清楚。但如果这是一个双方签署了的合约,这笔误或错写就会改不了。在一些情况当然可以可以"变更"(rectification),[9] 但如果双方事前没有明确同意过或没有证据来证明,就不能以这个途径解决问题。这样,能否看这两位朋友在订约之前的理解是什么,就很容易找出这一笔误或错写与双方真正的意图是指 3 月 1 日。但问题是解释书面合约/文件不能看口头证据,除非

[9] 这个课题可看本书第三章之 13.1 段。

有潜在的含糊。在这一情况下,如果3月2日根本没有任何表演,这会是一种潜在的含糊。但如果3月2日晚上有表演,但不是朗朗先生,这就表示在文字上没有潜在的含糊而必需依照文字解释,而3月2日不可以被扭曲为3月1日的朗朗先生的演出。

7.3　以前有关先例的介绍

笔者以下介绍这一方面的先例。第一个是是 Doe d. Cox v. Roe (1802) 4 Esp. 185 先例,案情是有关房东给房客一个通知,要收回房屋。该文书通知说要收回:"the premises which you hold of me ... commonly called ... The Waterman's Arms"

但证据显示房客并非"占有"(hold)这一地方,而是占有同一房东的另一个地方名为"The Bricklayer's Arms"。事实上,该地区也没有一个地方名为"The Waterman's Arms"。这被判是构成一种潜在含糊,可以根据外来证据找出该通知的真正意图。看来,如果该地区的确有另一个名为"The Waterman's Arms"的地方,就不能看外来的证据来协助解释该文书通知了。

第二个是 In the Goods of Peel (1870) L. R. 2 P. &D. 46 先例,涉及一份遗嘱委任了"Francis Courtenay Thorpe, of Hampton ... Middlesex"为遗产执行人。但这是不可思议与违反常理,因为他只是一个12岁的小孩。他的父亲名为"Francis Corbet Thorpe, of Hampton Middlesex"是遗嘱订立人的好朋友,明显遗嘱中的遗产执行人应该是委任父亲。但贵族院判小孩是遗产执行人,说:"The testator makes use of a description which applies in fact to one person, and not to any other."

贵族院也知道这样的判法不正确,但不认为有解决办法,Penzance 勋爵说:"If I am at liberty to look at the facts stated in the affidavits, I may possibly have no difficulty in deciding that the person meant is the father, but the question is, whether I am at liberty to do so."

第三个先例也是有关遗嘱,名为 In re Fish; Ingham v. Rayner (1894) 2 Ch. 83。该先例的遗嘱是把住所给遗嘱订立人的侄女名为"Eliza"。但遗产订立人没有一个合法的侄女叫 Eliza,但有一个曾侄女名为 Eliza。证据显示他还有一个非法的曾侄女名为 Eliza,看来大家感情非常好,并且住在一起。根据这些"外来证据"(extrinsic evidence)作出正常的推理,应该明确是想把住所给她。但上诉庭判是住所应该给合法的 Eliza,Lindley 大法官是这样说:"where the person most nearly answering the description is the legitimate grandniece of the testator's wife ... no evidence can be admitted to prove that her illegitimate grandniece was intended."

上述的例子虽然是更严格排除外来证据协助解释一份文书通知或遗嘱,而不是文书合约的例子,但道理一样,反正是被批评为太严格与太"形式化"(formal)。这也带来其中一种例外情况开放外来证据/口头证据,也就是针对文件或合约中的标的与订约方身份,这在本书第六章之2.3.5段有详论。这种情况到了现在解释文书合约或文件的新趋势全面开放外来证据/口头证据,就更加不会发生了,这会在接下来的段节介绍。

§8 近年来解释合约的做法

在最近的三四十年,传统解释合约的做法有了很大改变。这倒不是解释合约要考虑什么有了改变,也不表示传统解释文件/合约的四个角内的做法被摒弃,而主要是在侧重点方面有所转移。现在的侧重点是在订约时的背景/语境与合约的本质等方面,比文书合约中的条文/文字更加重要。这就带来了许多的做法,如大幅度放宽外来证据/口头证据,虽然还是有一点难以划清界限,就是有关谈判与订约方主观意图的证据还是不接受。[10] 另是传统做法必须条文/文字有了含糊(甚至是潜在的含糊)才接受外来证据,[11] 但现在即使是条文/文字毫不含糊,也要考虑背景/语境与合约的本质。[12] 如果两者之间起严重冲突,导致条文/文字从背景/语境看来不可能是订约方的意图,即使程度上不达致"荒谬或可笑"(absurd),法院/仲裁员甚至要扭曲/漠视合约的条文/文字。

这重大的改变可节录 Hoffmann 勋爵在 Investors Compensation Scheme v. West Bromwich Building Society (1998) 1 W. L. R. 896 先例中所提出的重要指引:"The 'rule' that words should be given their 'natural and ordinary meaning' reflects the commonsense proposition that people have made linguistic mistakes, particularly in formal documents. On the other hand, if one would nevertheless conclude from the background that something must have gone wrong with the language, the law does not require judges to attribute to the parties an intention which they plainly could not have had. Lord Diplock made this point more vigorously when he said in *Antaios Cia Naviera SA v. Salen Rederierna AB*, *The 'Antaios'* (1985) A. C. 191: '... if detailed semantic and syntactical analysis of words in a commercial contract is going to lead to a conclusion that flouts business common sense, it must be made to yield to business common sense.'"

这种近期解释合约的做法有几种名称,一是"目的解释"(purposive construction),也有称为"语境解释"(contextual construction),或"商业解释"(commercial construction),或"自由解释"(liberal construction)。举例说,Steyn 勋爵在 Mannai Investments Co Ltd v. Eagle Star Life Assurance Co Ltd (1997) A. C. 749 先例中评论道:"There has been a shift from strict construction of commercial instruments to what is sometimes called purposive construction of such documents. Lord Diplock deprecated the use of that phrase in regard to the construction of private contracts as opposed to the con-

---

〔10〕 这在本书第六章之 2.5.1 段有详论。

〔11〕 这在本书第六章之 2.3.4 段有详论。

〔12〕 这在本书第六章之 1.3.4 段有详论。

struction of statutes... That is understandable. There are obvious differences between the process of interpretation in regard to private contracts and public statutes ... It is better to speak of a shift towards commercial interpretation."(加黑部分是笔者的强调)

这趋势早在一些早期的先例,如 Prenn v Simmonds (1971) 1 WLR 1381 先例就已经有作出呼吁或先兆。著名的 Wilberforce 勋爵说:"The time has long passed when agreements, even those under seal, were isolated from the matrix of facts in which they were set and interpreted purely on internal linguistic considerations. There is no need to appeal here to any modern, anti – literal, tendencies, for Lord Blackburn's well – known judgment in River Wear Commissioners v Adamson (1877) 2 App Cas 743 at 763 provides ample warrant for a liberal approach. We must, as he said, enquire beyond the language and see what the circumstances were with reference to which the words were used, and the object, appearing from those circumstances, which the person using them had in view. Moreover, at any rate since 1859 (Macdonald v Longbottom [1859] 1 E & E 977; 120 ER 1177 [affirmed (1860) 1 E & E 987; 120 ER 1181]) it has been clear enough that evidence of mutually known facts may be admitted to identify the meaning of a descriptive term."

这一新趋势看来有好几个原因,其中重要的是一个现实情况,即很少情况下有一个文书合约能够包罗万有,把双方在谈判中理解(或应该理解)的事情与当时的环境全部与准确记录在一份文书合约中,显示了他们作出的表达的条文/文字所代表的真正订约意图。另有一个可能是更重要的原因是为了与国际接轨。这些原因与其他原因都会在本书第六章详论。

面对这一趋势,也有支持或不支持的说法。例如,不支持的说法马上就可以想到大量引进外来证据的后果会令诉讼变得更昂贵与漫长,而且这种做法会带来不肯定,特别对无辜第三人造成不良影响。这些方面都会在本书第六章详谈,笔者只在这里说这看来是不可逆转的法律趋势,虽然这一趋势还是有一点摇摆不定,如 Rainy Sky SA and others v Kookmin Bank (2012) 1 Lloyd's Rep 34 先例的判法又带来了微妙变化。[13] 此外,英国法律相比其他国家(如欧洲国家与美国)仍被视为太严格与形式化。但只要一天有订约自由,就可以想出对策。例如,商业合约中经常出现的"完整合约条文"(entire agreement clause),虽然凭这一条文目前的一般写法能否做到排除外来证据/口头证据还有疑问。有关这一条重要的条文,在本书第十三章之第 2 段有详论。

接下去在本章介绍这一现代趋势的 6 个主要贵族院先例:Charter Reinsurance Co Ltd v. Fagan (1997) AC 313, HL;Mannai Investments Co Ltd v. Eagle Star Life Assurance Co Ltd;Investors Compensation Scheme v. West Bromwich Building Society;

[13] 这先例稍后会在本章之 8.6 段有介绍。

BCCI v. Ali (2001) 1 UKHL 8;The "Starsin" (2003) 1 Lloyd's Rep. 571 与 Rainy Sky SA and others v Kookmin Bank。

8.1 Charter Reinsurance Co Ltd v. Fagan

在 Charter Reinsurance Co Ltd v. Fagan (1997) AC 313, HL 先例,相关的伦敦保险市场的再保险保单中有名为"责任条文"说明,在每一次事故中如果"最后净损失"(Ultimate Net Loss)超过某一个金额,再保险人要负责赔偿。接下去就有一条文针对最后净损失的定义说:"The term 'Net loss' shall mean the sum **actually paid** by the Reinsured in settlement of losses or liability after making deductions for all recoveries, all salvages and all claims upon other Reinsurances whether collected or not and shall include all adjustment expenses arising from the settlement of claims other than the salaries of employees and office expenses of the Reinsured. . . . "

以上加黑的两个字,可翻译为"真正支付",就是起争议的文字。在该先例,投保的原保单"保险人"(reinsured)名为"Charter"发生经济困难与清盘。有关的事故已经发生,但 Charter 还没有赔付给受保人,估计这些受保人都变为债权人。Charter 的清盘人就转向"再保险人"(reinsurer)名为"Fagan"(一个劳合社保险小组)索赔,但再保险人抗拒支付。理由是根据他们之间的再保保单,是要求 Charter 先真正支付原保单的"被保险人"或在本段可称为"受保人"(assured),完成原保单的赔付责任,才能向 Fagan 要求赔付。换言之,Fagan 的立场是,Charter 必须真正支付了受保人是向他要求赔付的先决条件。但这样的立场就等于 Fagan 不必赔付,因为 Charter 在清盘中根本没有钱先赔给受保人。只有能够向 Fagan 取得赔付,在清盘中的 Charter 才能够有钱分摊给债权人。所以,Fagan 的争辩其实是不符合商业合理性的。但表面看来,这"真正支付"在字义上的确也有 Fagan 所主张的味道。这一判决也非常影响整个伦敦再保险市场,因为再保保单都是这样的措辞。

这里也涉及了再保险市场的本质,因为受保人的原保单与再保单并不完全一样,大家各有不同限制与例外情况。例如,发生了受保的事故,是原保单与再保单都包括的,但原保单的保险人赔付给受保人的金额会有各种变化,如损失是通过和解而打了折,损失可能因为代位求偿部分成功而减少等。这样,在再保险人而言,就需要在再保保单有一条条文规定再保险人的赔付责任与限额。其中最重要的是不能赔付高过原保险人赔付给受保人的金额。最早期的再保保单是这样一条条文:"Being a reinsurance, subject to all clauses and conditions of the original policy or policies, and to pay as may be paid thereon. . . "

但在 Uzielli & Co v. Boston Marine Insurance Co. 15 Q. B. D. 11 先例,法院作出的判法并非是再保险人所希望的。这之后就出现了一种叫"依从原赔付"(follow settlement)的条文,最后就演变成为"最后净损失"(Ultimate Net Loss)条文。

从上述简单介绍的历史与商业背景,可知道"真正支付"所关心的是再保险人自己面对的净损失,而并不理会原保险人到底是否已经在原保单下作出了支付与卸下了责任。Hoffmann 勋爵这样说:"Considerations of history, language and commercial background therefore lead me to the conclusion that the word ' actually ' in the UNL clause is used to emphasise that the loss for which the reinsurer is to be liable is to be net and that the clause does not restrict liability to the amount by which the liability of the re-insured for the loss has been discharged. I think that this is the natural meaning of the clause."

Hoffmannn 勋爵也提到"支付"这一词有不同解释,在很多情况下是指金钱上的易手,为了卸下某一些支付责任,但它完全可以用在另一种语境,即针对有什么责任,但并非指是否卸下该责任。例如,一位妻子回家并给她的丈夫看其买的新时装,丈夫回问:"你支付了多少钱?"这显然是丈夫只想知道有关的支付责任,而不管是否有卸下该责任。也可以再把问答稍微改动下,就是妻子告诉丈夫:"百货商店有大减价,本来这件时装是要 300 英镑。"丈夫就会接下问:"你真正支付了多少?"(So what did you actually paid?)丈夫的问题显然又是关心减了多少,而不是关心有否作出现金的支付,特别在当时的环境下有可能是丈夫知道在该百货商店买东西可以赊账。

Mustill 勋爵也认为在再保险的本质上,"真正"是指"如果最后被确定",而"支付"是指"面对要赔付的责任":"I am now satisfied that the purpose of ' sum actually paid ' is not to impose an additional condition precedent in relation to the disbursement of funds, but to emphasise that it is the ultimate outcome of the net loss calculation which determines the final liability of the syndicates(再保险人的劳合社保险小组)under the policy. In this context, ' actually ' means ' in the event when finally ascertained ', and ' paid ' means ' exposed to liability as a result of the loss insured '."

所以,最后贵族院判是 Charter 不必先赔付受保人就可以先获得 Fagan 的赔付,因为 Charter 要赔付给受保人的责任已经被确定,只是因为 Charter 发生清盘才没能卸下该支付的责任。

这里顺便一提是"船东互保协会"(P&I Club)也有看来类似的条文,这在 The "Fanti" (1987) 2 Lloyd's Rep. 299 先例被判是会员(船东)先要赔付后才能向互保协会要求补偿。互保协会的相关文字是:"shall become liable to pay and shall in fact have paid."

文字从字义上看来是差不多,但在 Charter Reinsurance Co Ltd v. Fagan 先例的上诉庭认为两种写法并不相同,而互保协会的条文是更清楚要会员(船东)先赔付,说:"But if it be asked how such a meaning could have been made any clearer, a simple answer is to be found in the House of Lords decision in *The Fanti* [1991] 2 A. C. 1—namely by adopting the words used in the club rules there under consideration, whereby the members were indemnifies against claims which they ' shall have become liable to pay and shall in fact have paid. ' I recognise, of course, the close similarity between the ' sum actually paid ' and ' claims ... which he ... shall in fact have paid '. But the inclusion in *The Fanti* of the additional words ‘shall have become liable to pay’ made it impossible to argue there..."

同样重要或更重要的是,两个案例涉及两种不同的保险合约在本质上有所不同。The "Fanti" 先例针对的是互保协会的条文,与再保险无关。互保协会是船东组织起来的,互相承保船舶在国际经营中会带来各种责任风险,而且在很长一段时间是无限度地承保责任风险。这表示发生一个数以十亿或百亿美元计的损失,不论是船舶在港内爆炸或是客船乘客集体中毒,有关的互保协会的船东会员都要赔。尤其是,英国有一个法律名为 1930 年《The Third Parties (Rights against Insurers) Act》,它允许受害方直接起诉责任保险人。例如,在一个车祸中受伤的行人不会因为疏忽驾驶的司机在意外中死亡或是穷光蛋而变为没有救济,他可以根据该立法直接向承保汽车第三人责任险的保险公司索赔。所以,互保协会为了怕被受害方直接起诉,特别是出事的船东有违反互保协会章程的行为,如没有按时交保费,就设计这一条文希望绕过此 1930 年的立法,就是要出事的船东先直接支付受害方,互保协会才会有赔付责任,而赔偿与否还要看董事局的裁量权。所以,本质上与再保险十分不同,更不说两者之间的文字也不完全一样。

8.2 Mannai Investments Co Ltd v. Eagle Star Life Assurance Co Ltd

Mannai Investments Co Ltd v. Eagle Star Life Assurance Co Ltd (1997) A. C. 749 先例是有关房屋租赁合约的终止通知,而发生争议的是有关该通知的文字,解释有关文件的大道理与解释文书合约也接近。案情涉及办公楼与停车场所订的为期 10 年的租约,从 1992 年 1 月 13 日起算。该租约内有一条文是在这 10 年的第 3 周年的第一天,租客有权提早终止租约,但要先给 6 个月的文书通知。该 7(13)条文是这样说:"The tenant may by serving not less than six months' notice in writing on the landlord or its solicitors such notice to expire on the third anniversary of the term commencement date determine this lease and upon expiry of such notice this lease shall cease and determine and have no further effect. . . ."

在订了租约之后,伦敦的租金市场大幅下跌,租客就很自然地想根据上述条文合法取巧了。当然在租约终止后,租客可以搬一个更便宜的办公楼。即使不想搬迁,找原房东谈另一个新租约,租金比当时的市场稍高,恐怕原房东也会同意。该租客所发出的终止通知如下:"pursuant to clause 7(13) of the lease we as tenant hereby give notice to you to determine the lease on 12 January 1995..."

请注意上述通知在日期上犯了错误,应该是 1995 年 1 月 13 日而不是 12 日。这就带来了一个问题是该通知是否有效。

这看来是一个很小的笔误或错写，但法律并不简单。[14] 首先节录在 Hankey v. Clavering (1942) 2 K. B. 326 先例中，Greene 勋爵讲到了一个大原则，说："In an option clause the requirement is that a party must strictly comply with the condition for its exercise. If the condition includes the giving of a particular notice, it seems to me that the logical first approach is to interpret the notice, looking at the words and applying legal principles to their construction, and then ask whether it complying with the strict requirements as to exercise of the option."（在合约中有选择权的一方，他在行使时必须严格依照所规定的行使条件。如果这条件包括要给一个通知，逻辑的做法就是解释该通知，看看在文字上可否被解释为完全依照了行使选择权的严格要求。）

这表示如果该条文说明通知必须用蓝纸，以粉红色的纸给出的通知是无效的，正如 Hoffmann 勋爵在本先例 Mannai Investments Co Ltd v. Eagle Star Life Assurance Co Ltd 中所说的："If the clause had said that the notice had to be on blue paper, it would have been no good serving a notice on pink paper, however clear it might have been that the tenant wanted to terminate the lease."

在本先例合约中的第 7(13) 条文，它的要求只有如下条件：一是至少要 6 个月的通知；二是通知必须是文书形式；三是通知必须给房东或他的代表律师。它并没有要求在通知中说明哪一天终止租约，所以租客的通知在这方面看来是有一点多余。有关在这种情况下不必加上终止日期，Goff 勋爵这样说："It is however well settled that, under a clause such as the present which does not require that the date of expiry should be specified as such in the notice but merely that the notice should be expressed to expire on the relevant date, it is enough that the notice should be so expressed to expire in accordance with the terms of the clause. This was made clear by Lord Coleridge C. J. in *Cargner v. Ingram*, 61 L. T. 729..."

另是，如果担心加上终止日期会有错误，另一个办法就是通知所针对的终止期限也一并写进，在本案例就是第 3 周年的第一天。这样，就可以作出补救，估计是因为接到通知的房东或租客就不会有猜疑了，或令 1995 年 1 月 12 日的终止日期变为一个"明显错误"(obvious mistake)。这也是 Goff 勋爵在本先例所说的如下："Furthermore it is also well settled that, if the person giving the notice specifies the actual date but out of caution also specifies, in the alternative, the end of the period at which the notice is required under the clause to take effect, the alternative so given will be effective to save the notice if the actual date so given should prove to have been mistaken. For obvious reasons, therefore, it is a commonplace for notices to quit to take this form, which

---

〔14〕 法律对行使选择权这种"单方面合约"(unilateral contract)有很严格的要求，这在本书第十章之 4.3 段有详论。也可一提就是，方面合约如果有错误不存在合约"变更"(rectification)的救济，因为不存在有双方在谈判中曾经达成协议或有一个共同/分享的订约意图的情况。

avoids the trap into which the tenant fell in the present case."

在通知的日期犯错是有一个重要的上诉庭先例也就是前面提到的 Hankey v. Clavering 先例，该房东给房客代表律师的通知如下："As I may have to be away for some time in the near future, I will be obliged if you would accept the six months' notice to terminate your client's lease which I am allowed to give on 21 June 1941. This would mean that he would have to give up the cottage on 21 December 1941."

但这一个通知在事实上是日期错误，它应是 12 月 25 日而非 21 日。注意是这错误并非是潜在的含糊或明显的错误，变为根据传统的解释方法就只能严格看这份通知文件四个角之内的文字，而这明确是写为 21 日，法官不能将该笔误改为 25 日。所以，上诉庭判是案例非常明确，该通知无效。Greene 勋爵这样说："This appeal raises a short point in connection with a break clause in a lease wherein the plaintiff was the lessor and the defendant was the lessee. By this letter of 15 January 1940, the plaintiff, on the face of it, was purporting to determine the lease by notice on 21 December 1941. The whole thing was obviously a slip on his part, and there is a natural temptation which must be resisted, because documents are not to be strained and principles of construction are not to be outraged in order to do what may appear to be fair in an individual case."

Greene 勋爵也提到这样判的原因如下："Notice of this kind are documents of a technical nature, technical because they are not consensual documents, but, if they are in proper form, they have of their own force without any assent by the recipient the effect of bringing the demise to an end. They must on their face and on a fair and reasonable construction do what the lease provides that they are to do. It is perfectly true that in construing such a document, as in construing all documents, the court in a case of ambiguity will lean in favour of reading the document in such a way as to give it validity, but I dissent entirely from the proposition that, where a document clear and specific, but inaccurate on some matter, such as that of date, it is possible to ignore the inaccuracy and substitute the correct date or other particular because it appears that the error was inserted by a slip. By the clear wording of this notice the plaintiff purported to bring the lease to an end on 21 December 1941. In so doing he was attempting to do something which he had no power to do, and, however much the recipient might guess, or however certain he might be, that it was a mere slip, that would not cure the defect because the document was never capable on its face producing the necessary legal consequence."

现在回来本先例 Mannai Investments Co Ltd v. Eagle Star Life Assurance Co Ltd，它也是犯同一错误的通知，把 1 月 13 日写为 12 日，在贵族院，少数的 Goff 勋爵与 Jauncey 勋爵认为单方面作出行使裁量权的通知必须准确，也不应该偏离 Hankey v. Clavering 等先例而导致这方面的法律不再肯定，所以判该通知因为这看来轻微的笔误而变为无效。Goff 勋爵这样说："I have no doubt that this may indeed be the meaning properly to be attributed to many contractual provisions conferring a right exercisable upon notice. But the difficulty in the way of so holding in the case of clauses in leases, such as the break clause in the present case, is that for well over a century a different construction has been placed upon them. Innumerable leases, many of them still in force, must have been drafted on the understanding that they bear the well known meaning established in the authorities. It follows that, quite apart from the element of uncertainty to which I have referred, the step which your Lordships are being invited to take would have a retrospective effect. In these circumstances I am most reluctant to depart from the established meaning unless I am persuaded that there is very good reason to do so."

但 Steyn、Hoffmann 与 Clyde 勋爵的多数意见是判该通知有效。Hoffmann 勋爵更是说了一句名言,即 Hankey v. Clavering 先例与同样判法的以往先例再也不代表英国法律,是等于 Hoffmann 勋爵在 Investors Compensation Scheme v. West Bromwich Building Society (1998) 1 W. L. R. 896, HL 先例中所指应该抛下的"旧包袱"(old baggages)。他也说到,解释文书合约已经有了不少先例确认可根据案件的背景/语境而肯定所用的条文/文字是错误而作出正确的"扭曲"。但文书合约虽然先走一步,在解释其他的文件如一份通知或遗嘱还没有跟上。Hoffmann 勋爵看不出它们之间的解释做法上为什么要有不同,为什么不能找出书写一方真正意图传达的信息,而一个合理的接收人也知道这一个意图。Hoffmann 勋爵这样说:"In the case of commercial contracts, the restriction on the use of background has been quietly dropped. There are certain special kinds of evidence, such as previous negotiations and express declarations of intent, which for practical reasons which it is unnecessary to analyse, are inadmissible in aid of construction. They can be used only in an action for rectification. But apart from these exceptions, commercial contracts are construed in the light of all the background which could reasonably have been expected to have been available to the parties in order to ascertain what would objectively have been understood to be their intention: *Prenn v. Simmonds* [1971] 1 W. L. R. 1381, 1383. The fact that the words are capable of a literal application is no obstacle to evidence which demonstrates what a reasonable person with knowledge of the background would have understood the parties to mean, even if this compels one to say that they used the wrong words. In this area, we no longer confuse the meaning of words with the question of what meaning the use of the words was intended to convey. Why, therefore, should the rules for the construction of notice be different from those for the construction of contracts? There seems to me no answer to this question. All that can be said is that the rules for the construction of notices, like those for the construction of wills, have not yet caught up with the move to common sense interpretation of contracts which is marked by the speeches of Lord Wilberforce in

Prenn v. Simmonds [1971] 1 W. L. R. 1381 and *Reardon Smith Line Ltd. v. Yngvar Hansen – Tangen* [1976] 1 W. L. R. 989.（即 The "Diana Prosperity" [1976] 2 Lloyd's Rep. 621）The question is therefore whether there is any reason not to bring the rules for notice up to date by overruling the old cases."

另 Clyde 勋爵也强调了在本案例，这个通知是有明确说明根据租约的 7(13) 条文，房东作为接收人对租约的内容完全了解，并在当时的环境下知道房租市场下跌，应该很清楚知道这通知代表什么，并可马上理解到 1 月 12 日实是 1 月 13 日的笔误。他是这样说："In my opinion a like view should be taken in the circumstances of the present case. The notices were expressed to be 'pursuant to clause 7(13)'. It is plain from that that the tenant intended to invoke that clause. It is also plain that the tenant wished to determine the tenancy and that clause is the only clause under which the tenant could achieve that result. The landlord would be expected to know the terms of the lease and the date on which the lease fell to be determined under that clause. He would also be expected to know that there was no formal requirement for the tenant to specify in the notice the date of termination of the lease. There was no evident reason why the tenant should specify 12 January rather than 13 January. The close proximity of the 13th makes it the more evident that it was erroneous and that the date intended was the date which the parties had agreed for a determination of the tenancy under clause 7(13). While there is a discrepancy evident in the notices between the reference to the clause and the statement of the date it seems to me that the notices were sufficiently clear and unambiguous. No reasonable landlord would in my view be misled by a statement of a date which in the context of a clear intention to invoke clause 7(13) was inaccurate. The landlord would in my view recognise that in each case the reference to 12 January was to be read as a reference to 13 January and I would so construe the notices."

笔者总结上述重要先例，可举航运中的例子有关期租合约因承租人迟延支付租金让船东在高涨的运费市场有机会撤船，但在撤船前通常根据租约必须先给出一个"反技术取巧通知"(anti – technicality notice)。法律一直对船东这一通知的内容吹毛求疵，这方面请看杨大明律师《期租合同》一书第十八篇所介绍的 The "Li Hai" (2005) 2 Lloyd's Rep 389、The "Pamela" (1995) 2 Lloyd's Rep 249 与 The "Afovos" (1983) 1 Lloyd's Rep 335 (H. L.) 等先例。

这种"反技术取巧通知"被严格针对解释在以前的先例 Hankey v. Clavering 下可以说是能够理解与判法一致。但现在有了贵族院的 Mannai Investments Co Ltd v. Eagle Star Life Assurance Co Ltd 先例就可能有了冲击，虽然笔者还没有见到这种先例，因为这是要到贵族院（或现在的最高院）才可以作出法律地位的更改，而这种机会可遇不可求。但这一方面可能有变的警告并不是没有人提过，其中可节录 Nicholas Hamblen 御用大律师（目前已经是高院大法官）在 2004 年伦敦召开的国际海事仲裁员大会(International Congress of Maritime Arbitrators)上所讲如下:"The importance of looking at how the notice would be reasonably understood rather than the precise wording of the notice is borne out by the House of Lords decision in *Mannai Investments Co Ltd v. Eagle Star Life Assurance Co Ltd* [1997] AC 749. In that case the Court managed to construe a tenant's notice to determine a lease on 12 January as being a notice to determine it on 13 January (which was the first date upon which it could be determined) as the landlord can have been left in no doubt that that was what the tenant meant. The question is now a reasonable and reasonably informed recipient would have understood the notice, bearing in mind its context and its purpose. The purpose of giving an anti - technicality notice is self - evident. For all these reasons *The Pamela* is a dubious decision on this issue as well. It is therefore an authority of doubtful correctness on two important issues: (1) when a notice is effective and (2) the form of notice required."

看来,作为 The "Li Hai"先例一方的当事人中散公司,如果把该先例一路上诉到贵族院,就可能从败诉方变为胜诉方了。但据悉中散公司在高院败诉后就已经作出庭外和解,所以无法知道该案例上诉贵族院,在 Mannai Investments Co Ltd v. Eagle Star Life Assurance Co Ltd 先例的影响下会是什么结果。

8.3　Investors Compensation Scheme v. West Bromwich Building Society

Investors Compensation Scheme v. West Bromwich Building Society (1998) 1 W. L. R. 896 先例著名是因为 Hoffmann 勋爵在其中总结了解释文书合约与文件的五条大原则,这五条几乎在之后每一个解释合约的先例都有提到。本先例的案情将会在本书第六章 12.3 段有较详尽的介绍。只在此简单说该先例涉及一份索赔表格的一句"Any claim (whether sounding in rescission for undue influence or otherwise)"被贵族院解释为"Any claim sounding in rescission (whether for undue influence or otherwise)"。这样一来,整句话的意思完全不同。这可举一个通俗的例子说明,在离婚时,男方对女方说"我给你任何财产(不论是我目前住的房屋或其他)"如果变成"我给你任何房屋的财产(不论是我目前住的或其他)",两者之间就会有很大区别,特别在该男方十分富有但并非是拥有很多房屋的地产商的情况。

但这样解释文书合约的办法,把这一双方约定的句子作出结构上的改变(将括号内的文字移前出括号),是从来没有先例允许这样做的。但贵族院还是以新思维解释合约,并确定说这才是根据该文件本质与背景/语境的正确意思。Hoffmann 勋爵还说要把以前严格解释合约的一些著名先例就如"旧包袱"(old baggages)一般抛下。看来,今后如果有合约解释的争议,如果对方抖出一些以前的先例支持他的字义上解释,就可以以 Hoffmann 勋爵的这句话作出反击。

总结本著名先例大致上有以下几点可以肯定根据传统解释合约的做法不会这样判的,如下:一是把这一双方约定的句子作出结构上的改变(将括号内的文字移前出括号),这是贵族院的一致意见,包括 Hoffmann 勋爵自己,是严重"扭曲文书合约的语言"(doing violence to the language)。二是贵族院多数的意见这样做只是为了防止"荒谬/可笑"(absurdity)的结果。注意是少数不同意见的 Lloyd 勋爵认为结果并不可笑,可以解释得过。如果不是这个看法,Lloyd 勋爵也会跟从大多数意见这样判。三是贵族院的多数非常重视索赔表格中的"解释注脚"(explanatory note),认为没有受过法律训练的人会看这些注脚,而索赔表格的有关条文却是给律师看的。但该有争议的条文并非与解释注脚一致,所以要把索赔表格的有关条文作出结构上的改变让一般人士看得懂。但根据传统的解释,注脚是没有什么分量的,这可看本书第二章之 12 段。

8.4 BCCI v. Ali

BCCI v. Ali (2001) 1 UKHL 8 先例涉及在 1991 年英伦银行下令把巴基斯坦老板的著名国际银行 BCCI(Bank of Credit and Commerce International SA)接管与清盘,指称该银行涉及欺诈与贪污,这导致该银行在全球出问题,包括香港的 BCCI。在本案例涉及一位在伦敦 BCCI 雇用的巴基斯坦裔雇员 Mr. Naeem。他在 1985 年被雇用,但在 1990 年由于银行重整而被裁员。在被裁时,他被 BCCI 清付了所有的遣散费与工资(完全符合雇佣合约与英国立法的要求),而且还多给了一个月的工资作为"优惠赔偿"(*ex gratia* payment)。但 Mr. Naeem 也签了一份所谓的"解除责任协议"(release agreement),确认这是"全面与最终的和解"(full and final settlement)。这等于是签了一份和解协议。该协议的有关文字非常广泛,可节录如下:"The applicant [Mr. Naeem] agrees to accept the terms set out in the documents attached in full and final settlement of **all or any claims whether under statute, common law or in equity of whatsoever nature that exist or may exist** and, in particular, all or any claims rights or applications of whatsoever nature that the applicant has or may have or has made or could make in or to the industrial tribunal, except the applicant's rights under [the bank's] pension scheme."(加黑部分是笔者的强调)

在清盘的过程中,有雇员向 BCCI 的清盘人提出索赔,说是因为该银行声名狼藉导致目前失业的雇员名誉受损而找不到工作并面临损失。这在另一个贵族院的先例 Mahmud v. Bank of Credit and Commerce International SA (1998) AC 20 被判决是在雇佣合约,应该法律默示一条条文就是雇主不应做一些不诚实与腐败的事情,而这些事情会导致雇员的前途受损。[15] 这样,表示在失业中的 Mr. Naeem 可根据 BCCI 破坏雇佣合约中的默示条文而提出索赔,但 BCCI 清盘人提出的抗辩就是上述全面与最终的和解,文字的内容包罗万有,而且写明包括了普通法下所有的索赔权利,这正是针对这一先例的所谓违反雇佣合约的默示条文。

但即使是这种包罗万有的文字,也应该考虑订约时的语境,这些文字显然有它的默示局限。例如,Mr. Naeem 当时有存款在 BCCI,如果双方对这笔存款有争议,总不

---

〔15〕 这可看本书第七章之 3.3.1 段。

能与上述的和解协议扯在一起，指 Mr. Naeem 再也不能索赔这一笔存款，因为已经有了全面与最终的和解。这种情况根本不会是双方在订立和解协议时有所针对或有意图的。

BCCI 的代表大律师也同意即使有了这么广泛的文字，也仍有一定的默示局限，但这局限应该是在雇佣合约之间的关系以外才不包括在和解协议中。但就是这样解释，也有难以分清之处。如员工因公受伤（这是指一些潜伏性疾病，多年后才会浮现），如吸入石棉而致癌。这是在达成全面与最终和解很久之后才冒出来，这种潜在的立法或普通法下的索赔权利难道也被包括在和解协议内而令员工失了索赔的权利？毕竟，这种索赔也是在雇佣之间的关系范围内。所以，双方的代表律师也同意这个分水线很难界定，但反正就是所谓的全面与最终和解不能以文字广泛的字义作出解释。

有关双方达成全面与最终和解与卸下责任的局限，是有过不少先例说明只局限在订约方所知道或合理应该知道的事情，而不包括不知道的。举例在 Turner v. Turner (1880) 14 Ch D 829 先例，Malins 大法官说："But it has always been the rule of this court to construe releases and documents of that kind with regard to the intention of the parties, and to refer in such cases to the state of the property which was known at the time."

另在一本比较老的合约法书籍《Principles of Contract》（第 13 版，1929 年）一书，Fredrick Pollock 也说："... in equity 'a release shall not be construed as applying to something of which the party executing it was ignorant'..."

比较近期的是 Arrale v. Costain Civil Engineering Ltd (1976) 1 Lloyd's Rep. 98 先例，案情涉及一个工人在迪拜因工伤而失了左臂，但他因为不知道自己的权利而接受了公司一笔赔偿，以为是根据迪拜当地的立法，并签了让公司卸下责任的协议，说是："in full satisfactory and discharge of all claims in respect of personal injury whether now or hereafter to become manifest arising directly or indirectly from an accident which occurred on 3 July 1998."

该受伤工人后来在英国法院起诉，上诉庭的多数意见认为他可以这样做，因为卸下责任协议并没有包括他在普通法下索赔的权利。Denning 勋爵这样说："I would say that, if there was a true accord and satisfaction, that is to say, if Mr. Dohale（受伤工人）, with full knowledge of his rights, freely and voluntarily agreed to accept the one sum in discharge of all his claims, then he would not be permitted to pursue a claim at common law. But in this case there is no evidence of a true accord at all. No one explained to Mr. Dohale that he might have a claim at common law. No one gave a thought to it. So there can have been no agreement to release it. There being no true accord, he is not barred from pursuing his claim at common law."

最后一提是 Torrens Aloha Pty Ltd v. Citibank NA (1997) 144 ALR 89 这个澳大

利亚先例,该先例是判一个在1987年签署的卸下责任协议不能被解释为包括在订约当时双方根本不会考虑的索赔权利,而且当时的法律也站不住脚,直到5年后澳大利亚最高院改变了法律才变为有一个新的诉权。

现在可回来探讨BCCI v. Ali这一先例,贵族院的大多数判是Mr. Naeem在1990年达致的全面与最终的和解/卸下责任协议中并不包括在Mahmud v. Bank of Credit and Commerce International SA先例后新出现的可向BCCI索赔损失权利,因为BCCI违反了雇主对员工的法律默示责任。贵族院认为在订约时,双方根本不可能预见这种索赔与后来普通法作出这样的先例,所以不会在和解协议的文字上被包括在内。

但可能读者会觉得有点奇怪的是Hoffmann勋爵在这一先例中是少数的反对意见,主要的理由是认为在这一先例中的和解/卸下责任协议不存在有上述所介绍的"语境"(context),这不像许多的和解/卸下责任协议是针对当时某一种的索赔,如人身伤亡、合伙人拆伙等,都可找出可能是同样文字的一句"full and final settlement"应该局限在哪一种的索赔类别。但在本先例,Mr. Naeem与BCCI根本没有发生过任何争议,只是涉及裁员。BCCI根据雇佣合约与立法作出补偿,而且多给了1个月的工资。Hoffmann勋爵认为如果BCCI还是将来要面对一些订约时不知情的索赔,这1个月工资就交换不了任何的实质利益了。所以,这笔钱显然就为了针对这一种索赔。如果是BCCI在订约时单方面知道Mr. Naeem有这种索赔权利,但他自己不知道,这样法律是不会允许这种"占便宜的做法"(sharp practice),但现在不是这种情况。

Hoffmann勋爵也看订约时的其他背景,特别是在工业中经常有一些长期的工伤索赔,所以在卸下责任协议中有特别条文针对,排除这种索赔。这表示在本先例,双方(包括Mr. Naeem)在订约时应该知道将来不知情的索赔权利会被排除。Hoffmann勋爵所以认为BCCI付出了一笔合理的金钱但求卸下将来的责任,只要是订约时双方均不知情的,这并没有什么不公平之处。他说:"I do not propose any wider principle: there is obviously room in the dealings of the market for legitimately taking advantage of the known ignorance of the other party. But, both on principle and authority, I think that a release of right is a situation in which the court should not allow a party to do so. On the other hand, if the context shows that the parties intended a general release for good consideration of rights unknown to both of them, I can see nothing unfair in such a transaction."

8.5 The "Starsin"

The "Starsin" (2003) 1 Lloyd's Rep. 571这一个贵族院先例涉及航运人士面对的一个问题,就是提单到底是"承租人提单"(charterers' bill)还是"船东提单"(owners' bill)。这一问题在笔者的《提单与其他付运单证》一书第三章有详尽解释。这个问题非常关键,因为涉及经常发生的货损货差索赔,收货人或代位的保险人应该向谁追偿。一旦出错,1924 年《海牙规则》的 1 年时效转眼即逝,货损货差的索赔也就没有了。这一问题在极端的情况下非常明确,如散货经常使用的 Congenbill。由于它根本没有承租人的名字出现而只有船舶名字与船长的签字,可以说几乎属于船东提单。但只要涉及一些班轮或半班轮所签发的提单,特别是船舶并非该班轮公司自己拥有而是期租进来,这就会变得混乱,特别是班轮公司签发的标准提单经常有一些互相矛盾的条文,如著名的"光船条文"(Demise Clause)与"承运人定义条文"(Identity of Carrier Clause)。

在 The "Starsin"先例,正是这种情况,它被船东期租给了一家走半班轮航线的公司,名为 Continental Pacific Shipping Ltd(CPS)。船舶是用在马来西亚装三夹板与木材去比利时、安特卫普与英国的 Avonmouth 的航线。争议(声称三夹板受到水损)涉及 11 套提单,提单格式都是以 CPS 作为抬头的标准格式,内中有不少印本条文。第一条是对承运人的定义,就是提单签发方。而这些提单是由马来西亚装港的代理人签发,并在提单中写上"As Agent for Continental Pacific Shipping Ltd (The Carrier)",之后该代理人签了自己名字("United Pansar Sdn Bhd")与盖章。

另在提单的背面有一些标准条文,第一条是第 33 条承运人定义条文,第二条是第 35 条光船条文,两条条文如下:

"33. IDENTITY OF CARRIER The contract evidence by this Bill of lading is between the merchant and owner of the vessel ... and ... the ... **ship owner** only shall be liable for any damage ... arising out of the contract of carriage.

35. If the ocean vessel is not owned or chartered by demise to the company or line by whom this Bill of Lading is issued (as may be the case notwithstanding anything that appears to the contrary) this Bill of Lading shall take effect only as a contract of carriage with the**owner ... as principal** made through the agency of the said company or line who act solely as agent and shall be under no personal liability whatsoever ..."(加黑部分是笔者的强调)

从上述的简单节录,可见提单正面的签字部分与背面的条文有直接矛盾。正面看来,特别是签字很明确 CPS 是承运人,但背面说是船东才是承运人与这份提单的订约方。在第一审,Colman 大法官判是承租人提单。但了上诉庭,判决改过来说是船东提单。最后到了贵族院,明确是承租人提单。贵族院认为正面的签字至关重要,而且 5 位贵族院大法官都举信用证的结汇根据 UCP 500 只看提单正面,而不会理会提单背面密密麻麻的标准条文。这里涉及的原因其中一个当然是银行的一般职员看不懂提单背面的标准条文,如他们不会知道什么是第 35 条就是著名的光船条文。Hoffmann 勋爵也说得有道理,就是同样一份提单,总不应该同样的文字在银行结汇时的解释与收货人要提出索赔时的解释有所不同,毕竟商业法律肯定性是至关重要。

虽然这一先例不像 Investors Compensation Scheme v. West Bromwich Building Society (1998) 1 W. L. R. 896, HL 非常明确的针对现代解释合约的方法,所谓的

“目的解释”(purposive construction)、“语境解释”(contextual construction)、“商业解释”(commercial construction)或“自由解释”(liberal construction),但 The “Starsin”仍是一个近期针对合约解释的重要先例。其中 Bingham 勋爵总结了 4 条十分历史悠久与重要的解释合约规则如下:“When construing a commercial document in the ordinary way the task of the court is to ascertain and give effect to the intentions of the contracting parties. Here, the task is to ascertain who, on one side, the contracting party was. But a similar approach is appropriate. Mr. Milligan [船东代表大律师] urged that the House should not seize on a single cannon of construction and give it effect to the exclusion of all others. I am sure that warning is salutary. But there are a number of rules, some of very long standing, which give valuable guidance.

First is the rule to which Lord Halsbury LC alluded in*Glynn v. Margetson & Co* [1893] AC 351, ‘that a business sense will be given to business documents.’ The business sense is that which businessmen, in the course of their ordinary dealings, would give the document. It is likely to be a reasonably straightforward sense since, as Lord Mansfield famously observed (*Hamilton v. Mendes* [1761] 2 Burr 1198):

‘The daily negotiations and property of merchants ought not to depend upon subtleties and niceties; but upon rules, easily learned and easily retained, because they are the dictates of common sense, drawn from the truth of the case.’(第一条重要的解释合约规则是商业文件必须给其商业的意思或合理性。)...

Secondly, it is common sense that greater weight should attach to terms which the particular contracting parties have chosen to include in the contract than to pre – printed terms probably devised to convey very many situations to which the particular contracting parties have never addressed their minds. It is unnecessary to quote the classical statement of this rule by Lord Ellenborough in*Robertson v. French* [1803] 4 East 130...(第二条重要的解释合约规则是必须给订约双方一致同意加在合约中的条文/文字更重的分量,而不是一些预先印好的条文。)

Thirdly, it has long been recognised by very distinguished commercial judges that to seek perfect consistency and economy of draftsmanship in a complex form of contract which has evolved over many years is to pursue a chimera... The court must of course construe the whole instrument before it in its factual context, and cannot ignore the terms of the contract. But it must seek to give effect to the contract as intended, so as not to frustrate the reasonable expectations of businessmen. If an obvious inappropriate form is used, its language must be adapted to apply to the particular case ...(第三条重要的解释合约规则是很多有经验的商业法官接受解释一份经过很长时间不断发展与复杂的合约,想给其完美的协调是妄想。法院当然必须整体解释合约与不应该漠视合约所有有关的条文/文字。但法院最终必须找出该合约的订约意图并给其效力,令商业人

士的合理期望不会受挫。如果明显是订约使用了一份不适用的格式,就必须把文字改编为适用于该有关案件的语境。)

Fourthly, ' In all mercantile transactions the great object should be certainty: and therefore, it is of more consequence that a rule should be certain, than whether the rule is established one way or the other. Because speculators in trade then know what ground to go upon' : *Vallejo v. Wheeler* [1774] 1 Cowp 143. (第四条重要的解释合约规则是所有商业的交易,主要目的是肯定性,让商业人士有所适从。)

This observation is, I suggest, particularly pertinent where the issue is one which, like that now under consideration, has been the subject of repeated litigation over the years. "

该先例还有第二个问题就是有关提单印本条文的第5条名为"喜玛拉雅条文"(Himalaya Clause),该条文在贵族院判是承租人提单就变为有关,因为船东是要根据这一条文的保障才能避免被货方以侵权起诉索赔。但该条文漏了一句,共有17个字,这是双方都接受。估计可能是在印刷这批提单前,打漏了这17个字。贵族院毫不怀疑把这17个字加上来一并解释,Bingham勋爵说:"I take it to be clear in principle that the Court should not interpolate words into a written instrument, of whatever nature, unless it is clear both that words have been omitted and what those omitted words were: ..."

Millett勋爵也说这是最起码的做法令该喜玛拉雅条文可在文法上说得通(minimum necessary for the clause to make grammatical sense)与这是解释合约并非是合约的变更(process was one of construction, not rectification)。

8.6 Rainy Sky SA and others v. Kookmin Bank

在上面介绍的Investors Compensation Scheme v. West Bromwich Building Society (1998) 1 W. L. R. 896先例中,Hoffmann勋爵看来是非常强调在解释时要根据"语境"(factual matrix)或者"订约时的情况"(surrounding circumstances),即使在合约条文表述清楚的时候也一样。但Clarke勋爵在Oceanbulk Shipping & Trading SA v TMT Asia Ltd (2011) 1 Lloyd' s Rep 96先例提到Steyn勋爵曾经评价Investors Compensation Scheme v. West Bromwich Building Society先例时说:"Lord Hoffmann made crystal clear than an ambiguity need not be established before the surrounding circumstances may be taken into account."

问题是解释合约的新趋势如果变为不再是看文书合约的条文/文字或看也没有什么分量,而是要看双方对他们所用文字/句法所希望代表的意思,就很难说只要合约写得清楚,作出解释就不必考虑订约时的背景/语境,因为不能仅看合约条文/文字就得出结论是写得清楚。但这新趋势会对金钱与时间造成很大浪费,令诉讼更加昂贵。而可能造成的结果是,两条完全一样的意思清楚的条文/文字,因为语境与订约时的情况不同,有不一样的解释。这显然带来另一个大问题,也就是不肯定与不可预测。而一直以来在商业社会的做法就是把一份昂贵的合约拟定得全面与明确，也变为不太必要。

但看来贵族院在 Investors Compensation Scheme v. West Bromwich Building Society 先例之后对这方面又有所收紧。在 Rainy Sky SA and others v Kookmin Bank (2012) 1 Lloyd's Rep 34 先例，收紧的是如果在考虑了订约时背景/语境后认为合约的条文/文字清楚无误，法院就必须根据合约的条文/文字作出判决，只有在有两种或以上解释时，才可以选择一种更符合商业常识的解释。贵族院的判决可节录如下："The construction of a contract was one unitary exercise in which the court had to consider the language used and ascertain what a reasonable person, who had all the background knowledge which would reasonably have been available to the parties in the situation in which they were at the time of the contract, would have understood the parties to have meant. In doing so, the court had to have regard to all the relevant surrounding circumstances. Where the parties had used unambiguous language, the court had to apply it. But if there were two possible constructions the court was entitled to prefer the construction which was consistent with business common sense and to reject the other."

案情涉及原告的买方与一家名为 Jinse 的韩国船厂订立了造船合约。被告韩国 Kookmin 银行向原告作出了"还款担保"(refund guarantee)。之后 Jinse 发生经济困难并根据韩国法律需要进行重组，原告的买方根据造船合约的明示条文终止造船合约。该合约中的第 12.3 条文是说："3. If the builder shall apply for or consent to the appointment of a receiver, trustee or liquidator, shall be adjudicated insolvent, shall apply to the courts for protection from its creditors, file a voluntary petition in bankruptcy or take advantage of any insolvency law, or any action shall be taken by the Builder having an effect similar to any of the foregoing or equivalent thereof in any jurisdiction, the Buyer may by notice in writing to the Builder require the Builder to refund immediately to the Buyer the full amount of all sums paid by the Buyer to the Builder on account of the Vessel and interest thereon at seven percent (7%) per annum on the amount to be refunded to the Builder, computed from the respective date such sums were paid by the Buyer to the date of remittance of the refundable amount to the Buyer and immediately upon receipt of such notice the Builder shall refund such amount to the Buyer. Following such refund the Builder may, but shall not be obliged to, by notice in writing to the Buyer give within ten (10) business days terminate this contract..."(这种条文在商业合约经常会有，针对是合约其中一方发生经济困难，需要重整甚至破产的情况。这样，合约还是有效，因为法院委任的管理人或清盘人还是可以代表公司履行可以盈利的合约。合约的另一方也就是没有发生经济困难的一方也就不能从合约脱身。但他的地位十分不利与被动，因为对方的管理人或清盘人可以代表公司要求履行合约承诺或向他索赔。但他向对方要求履行合约承诺否则将会以违约索赔损失就会是空话一

句,因为他充其量只是成了一个债权人,对方显然受到有关破产法的保护。为了避免这种合约履行,不少商业合约会加上一条如本先例的条文,给经济没有发生困难的一方可根据合约条文终止合约的选择权。)

在本案例,Jinse 发生经济困难与被接管是在金融海啸后的 2009 年 1 月底,而买方也很快在 2009 年 2 月选择终止造船合约。估计这里也有取巧(合法的取巧),就是当时航运市场崩溃,买方愿意借这个机会终止造船合约。而终止时,估计离交船日期还有一段时间。在买方选择终止造船合约的同时,也根据该条文要求 Jinse 退还已经支付了的两期付款并加上 7% 的利息。显然当时 Jinse 发生经济困难并且在进行重组中是不会作出这种支付。这导致买方转而向 Kookmin 要求在还款担保下退还支付了的分期付款并加上利息。

Kookmin 拒绝在还款担保下作出支付,而双方的争议只是针对还款担保下明示条文的解释。大致上 Kookmin 是抗辩说还款担保的条文并没有针对以造船合约 12.3 条文为由的经济困难终止合约下的还款。该还款担保部分条款可节录如下:

"[2] Pursuant to the terms of the Contract, you are entitled, upon your **rejection** of the Vessel in accordance with the terms of the Contract, your termination, cancellation or rescission of the Contract... to repayment of the pre – delivery instalments of the Contract Price paid by you prior to such termination...

[3] In consideration of your agreement to make the pre – delivery instalments under the Contract... we hereby, as primary obligor, irrevocably and unconditionally undertake to pay to you, your successors and assigns, on your first written demand, **all such sums** due to you under the Contract..."(加黑部分是笔者的强调)

双方争议的焦点是对"all such sums"的解释,这几个字有不明朗之处,因为它没有明确针对到底怎样的一笔钱。买方认为"all such sums"指的就是交船前支付了的分期付款,没有其他任何限制,买方只要在造船合约下有权取回支付了的分期付款,就包括在内。而银行认为,要把"all such sums"与第 2 条放在一起解释,即条文/文字只针对买方"拒船"(rejection)的情况。毕竟第 3 条里的"all such sums"并没有特别提到经济困难或破产问题。而 Jinse 破产并不属于买方拒船的情况,毕竟离交船日期还远,因此不在还款担保的范围内。

在一审法院,Simon 大法官是判 Kookmin 败诉,认为 Kookmin 所提供的解释"太令人惊奇与商业上无法接受"(surprising and uncommercial),就是还款担保竟然只是局限在交船时被买方合法拒船。但到了上诉庭,以多数意见改判 Kookmin 胜诉,认为 Simon 大法官的解释是否定了第 2 条的文字有任何解释,而第 2 条明确说明只是在买方根据造船合约下合法拒船与终止造船合约下,才涉及该还款担保的退还已支付的分期付款。

最后是上诉到了最高院(也就是以前的贵族院),判是"all such sums"的确含糊不清,因为有两种可能的解释。但最高院最后支持了买方的解释,认为这种解释更符合“商业常识”(commercial common sense)。这就是要求银行作出还款担保只是对一些情况(拒船)有担保,但另一些情况(破产)就没有,这看来说不通。Clarke 勋爵认为(其他所有勋爵也同意)还款担保的有关条文是有含糊之处,必须作出一个最具商业合理性的解释(本章之6.4 - 6.5 段与本书第四章之第3段与第4段)。Clarke 勋爵说:“In these circumstances I would, if necessary, go so far as to say that the omission of the obligation to make such re - payments from the bonds would flout common sense but it is not necessary to go so far. I agree with the judge and Sir Simon Tuckey that, of the two arguable constructions of para [3] of the bonds, the buyers' construction is to be preferred because it is consistent with the commercial purpose of the bonds in a way in which the bank's construction is not.”

Rainy Sky SA and others v Kookmin Bank 先例本身只是一个一般性的合约解释争议,这在商业合约每天都在发生。如果它不是涉及庞大的金额(约5千万美元),也不一定会上诉去了最高院。但这一最高院先例的重要性是对 Hoffmann 勋爵在 Investors Compensation Scheme v. West Bromwich Building Society 先例中的立场作出了一点改变,明确这种考虑语境/订约时环境的解释方法如果在合约条文/文字不含糊的情况下,不能作出扭曲。Clarke 勋爵说:“Where the parties have used unambiguous language, the court must apply it.”

这一点 Hope 勋爵在另一个最高院先例 Multi - Link Leisure Developments Ltd v North Lanarkshire Council (2010) UKSC 47 中的判决说得更加清楚。他说:“Words... should not be changed, taken out or moved ... until it has become clear that the language the parties actually used creates an ambiguity which cannot be solved otherwise.”

9 结论

目前的新趋势明显就是追求订约时双方的意图与共同目的,而找出共同目的就涉及接受有关谈判时的事实背景的外来证据。而不再是像传统做法只在一个文书合约中的条文/文字咬文嚼字地作出解释,以避免一个解释客观看来与双方订约的共同目的不相符,甚至是离题或是“断章取义”(out of context)。这一新趋势解释合约,有英文说法是“from text to context”。

笔者在这里介绍一个案例,就是针对“共识性禁止翻供”(estoppel by convention)发展的主要先例,Amalgamated v. Texas Bank (1982) 1 Lloyd's Rep. 27。在该先例同样是著名与高水平的大法官,第一审的 Goff 大法官与上诉庭的 Denning 勋爵等,他们解释一份“见索即付保函”(demand guarantee)得出了完全相反的结论。Goff 大法官被批评只看该份文件,但 Denning 勋爵是看整个合约的背景以找出该份文件的语境。

首先简单介绍该先例的案情,Amalgamated 是一家英国的地产公司,想要借钱让它的子公司 ANPP 在巴哈马建一栋大厦。英国的一家商业银行 Texas Bank 同意借钱,作为担保,除了之后将建成的大厦抵押,Amalgamated 向 Texas Bank 签发了一份对全部325万美元贷款的见索即付保函。

之后,因为外汇管理的原因,Texas Bank 通过一家名为 Portsoken 的巴哈马子公司将这笔钱借给 ANPP。具体做法如下:(1)Portsoken 从 Texas Bank 得到美元的款项,然后将美元直接借给 ANPP,而无需将钱转为巴哈马元。(2)Portsoken 将取得 ANPP 对该大厦的美元抵押。(3)Portsoken 保留一个美元账户用来收取与支持这个背靠背贷款的本金与利息。

但由于 Texas Bank 的疏忽,Amalgamated 的见索即付保函的受益人没有更改或加上 Portsoken。

这栋在巴哈马的大厦建成后只卖了250万美元,也就是说还欠了75万美元。Amalgamated 的见索即付保函就成了 Texas Bank 剩下的唯一担保。Amalgamated 在伦敦有地产/房子被卖掉,以偿还另外 Texas Bank 作出的贷款,并在偿还后剩下的钱超过了75万美元。Texas Bank 可以也确实从中拿了75万美元来抵销这一笔欠款。但 Amalgamated 申请破产,清盘人质疑了这份见索即付保函,认为这份保函的受益人只是 Texas Bank,但没有包括真正对 ANPP 作出贷款的 Portsoken。换言之,这一份文件只是废纸一张。

在解释这份见索即付保函时,Goff 大法官做出了不利于 Texas Bank 的判决说:"There was a crucial defect in these arrangements; the guarantee furnished by the plaintiffs (Amalgamated) to the bank was not amended. It remains a guarantee in respect of money due or owing or payable to the bank, not to Portsoken."(这一安排有一个严重的缺陷,Amalgamated 提供的担保没有被更改,该份文件仍是只针对银行,但根本没有针对 Portsoken。)

这种解释在上诉庭被推翻,Denning 勋爵批评 Goff 大法官只根据见索即付保函的文字严格解释,而不看订约时的背景/语境,说:

"I take a different view from the Judge. He has construed the guarantee in its strict literal sense - all by itself - without regard to the letters which accompanied it - and without regard to the surrounding circumstances - or the 'factual matrix' to use the modern equivalent.

The guarantee of Sept. 28, 1970 was of no effect by itself. It only took effect on Dec. 31, 1970, when the sum of $3,250,000 was advanced. That sum of $3,250,000 is the connecting link which joins everything together. It was the 'facility' which the bank promised on Sept. 23, 1970, to make available to ANPP and which was to be supported by a mortgage on the Harrison Building(在巴哈马的大厦); and by a guarantee from Amalgamated to the bank. It was the 'banking facilities' contained in the guarantee itself. It was the 'facility' which was in fact granted on Dec. 31, 1970, and supported by a mortgage. The words of the printed form must, in my opinion, be subordinated to the express provisions of the correspondence which brought it into being. That correspondence shows, beyond doubt, that the guarantee was intended to cover the \$3,250,000 let by the bank to ANPP, even though it was done through the channel of its wholly owned subsidiary, Portsoken."

近期的新趋势不仅是在解释文书合约与文件,甚至在解释立法。例如笔者在《Arbitration》的期刊2007年第3号73册第263页看到这样的内容,说这样解释立法是25年前不可置信的:"That can be seen in another European dimension. Art. 10 of the EC Treaty requires domestic courts to interpret domestic law as far as possible in accordance with EC law. Thus, in *Litster v. Forth Dry Dock Engineering & Co Ltd* [1989] 1 All E. R. 1134, the HL, in order to ensure that the Transfer of Undertakings (Protection of Employment) Regulations 1981 properly gave effect to an EC Council Directive〔16〕, construed the words 'a person so employed immediately before the transfer' as including the additional words 'or would have been so employed if he had not been unfairly dismissed before the transfer for a reason connected with the transfer'. Such linguistic gymnastics, unthinkable 25 years ago, will be become increasingly utilized."

在一个角度看来,笔者觉得这个新趋势对亚洲人士(包括中国人)有一些好处。因为在笔者的经验里,在一个复杂的国际交易中,很大部分的亚洲商业人士是没有能力把所有应该放进合约内的内容,特别是对自己有保障性的,完整与明确地记录在一份合约内。就是有作出记录,也经常会词不达意。而且,亚洲的文化是不大愿意花钱雇佣昂贵但称职的律师来代自己谈判与草拟合约。这种文化与做法跟西方商人的做法完全不同。但在解释合约的新趋势下,在一份文书合约没有明确显示出来的事情,或是条文/文字在表达上有含糊,会可以通过外来证据/口头证据向仲裁庭显示有利的背景/语境。但这也不代表可乱订合约,如在本书第六章之12.7段所介绍的Canterbury Golf International Ltd v. Yoshimoto (2002) UKPC 40先例,日本的当事人接受了一条被法院认为不可思议的不利条文,但最终还是无法以案件的背景/语境作出挽救。此外,许多商业合约不像一些针对性的文件有比较明确的目的,如要转让一个权利或做某一件特定的事情。这样,也就不存在可以根据"合约目的解释"(purposive construction)了。正如Lloyd勋爵在Investors Compensation Scheme v. West Bromwich Building Society (1998) 1 W. L. R. 896先例所说的:"Purposive interpretation of a contract is a useful tool where the purpose can be identified with reasonable certainty."

但解释合约可根据外来证据/口头证据考虑背景/语境的新趋势,也经常会对亚洲的商业人士不利。除了亚洲部分商业人士通常会有的弊病如经验不足、不花钱调查或咨询而导致相比西方商业人士往往在一个复杂的交易考虑与理解不全面等外,也通常见到在事前的谈判,西方商业人士很懂得把对他有利的订约背景记录在案。简单的例子就是中方商人在谈判中口头承诺或表示理解的事情,西方商人会随即跟

---

〔16〕 这份文件可以算是外来证据去解释立法的条文/文字。

进一份电文加以确认。所以,即使现在的解释合约方法侧重在外来证据/口头证据而再也不是局限在文书合约的四个角内的条文/文字,恐怕对亚洲商业人士在这一方面的劣势也是帮助不多,因为可以抖出来有利的外来证据/口头证据会很有限。

最后作出警告的就是,由于订约自由,经常有这种有不明确、含糊或与其他条文有冲突的条文/文字发生争议需要仲裁庭作出解释。而仲裁庭在这方面的大量工作现在由于不能再自动上诉到法院,变为有极大权力作出解释。对仲裁员来说,只需要平衡许多甚至越来越多与相互矛盾的解释合约原则(这本身也不是好事,原则应该尽量少与明确),就可以自动发挥。所以现在仲裁员的裁量权很大,不论是对事实的认定,或是对合约条文的解释。这也无可避免带来对合约解释不肯定,特别是一些律师是有法律背景的商业人士。这是因为太"自由"(liberal)、太"根据合约语境"(contextual)与太大裁量权解释一份比较严格拟定的商业合约,有很大危险带来与律师/商业人士在仔细推敲后拟定的合约条文/文字有不一样解释的裁决,会对这些人士有更大影响。正如英国 Richard Calnan 律师收录在 A. Burrows 与 E. Peel 先生编纂的《Contract Terms》(2007 年)一书中的《Construction of commercial contracts: A practitioner's perspective》一文中说:"... the liberalizing effect of Lord Hoffmann's speech leads courts to ignore what the contract said and to impose [their] own view of what it thought was meant."〔17〕

除了不肯定外,笔者还感受在仲裁庭有太自由与太大裁量权解释合约,也带来了相比以前传统文书合约的四个角作出严格与形式化的解释有了另一个大问题。这就是"文化差异"(cultural difference)的冲击,因为以前的解释不大会涉及文化背景。但近期的新趋势需要大量接受与考虑订约时的外来证据/口头证据认定事实背景,就无可避免会受到文化差异的冲击。考虑到今天著名的国际仲裁员大部分都来自西方国家,这一冲击显然也不会对亚洲特别是中国的当事人有利。

---

〔17〕 有关近期新趋势解释合约带来的不肯定在本书第六章之 4.5 段与第 11 段有详细解释。

第二章 合约的达成与内容

§1 概 述

在解释文书合约方面,会要针对双方是否已经达成一个有约束性的合约或是在一个已经达成的合约中的条文/文字找出什么是订约意图。

§2 解释双方是否已经达成有约束性的合约

笔者在这里不多介绍达成一个有约束性合约的各种先决条件,如“要约”(offer)/“反要约”(counter - offer)、“接受”(acceptance)、“约因/对价”(consideration)、“双方想法一致”(meeting of minds 或拉丁文的 *consensus ad idem*)等。这些方面已经在笔者的《国际商务游戏规则—英国合约法》第二章有介绍。这种双方有否已经达成一个有约束性合约的争议经常发生,特别是在涉及中国公司的交易中。法院或仲裁庭认定双方是否达成有约束性的合约的主要依据是双方提供的证据(主要包括一些在谈判中的文件与口头证据)。要注意是这种争议并不排除谈判证据,[1]而且也只有从谈判证据中才能找出双方是否已经达成约束性合约的正确答案。由于需要达成一个约束性合约的要求并不是太多,所以很容易就会让不小心或不熟悉合约法的商业人士掉进一个他以为还没有合约但实际上已经受到约束的陷阱。至于双方根本还没有谈很多看来也是重要的条文,更谈不上已经达成协议的事实,是往往不足以影响一个约束性合约的产生。这是因为这些条文即使是双方没有明示同意过,法律也可以作出默示,[2]不会让该合约无法履行。

还有一个重要原因是英国法院或仲裁庭普遍倾向于支持存在一个合约而不是否定它。所以,商业人士在谈判过程中如果不想产生合约关系,他们有更大的责任说明此意图并将明确的证据显示给法院或仲裁庭看。否则,即使在不明确双方有否达成约束性合约的情况下,也可以断言法院或仲裁庭会倾向说有。至于怎样说明,这可参

---

〔1〕 关于谈判除外规则可看本书第六章之 2.5.1 段。

〔2〕 可看本书第七章,特别是第 4 段。

阅本书第八章有关变数条件条文。显然,还不想产生合约关系的中国公司(原因可能是还有手续要办才能确定,如向领导请示、董事局批准等)就必须清楚明确告知对方这一想法并留下文书证据的"先决条件"(condition precedent)[3]或允许将来自己脱身的"后续条件"(condition subsequent)。[4] 如果还是担心不清楚,不妨以清楚的文字(用中文也没有关系)在与对方谈判的通讯往来中说明,如"直到我取得领导的同意,我们之间是没有合约关系"。

这种争议会导致严重的后果,也经常会涉及庞大的金钱损失赔偿。这是因为双方对有否达成约束性的合约有争议,也就是一个说有合约但另一个说没有合约,其结果往往是存在没有履行的情况。这表示如果后来法院或仲裁庭认定双方已经达成约束性合约,则认为没有合约的一方也就是"违约/毁约"(repudiation),因为他拒绝履行,这如果涉及一个长期与昂贵的商业合约,那损失会是很大的一笔。

这种陷阱特别危险,中国公司中招的频率也很高。经常出现一种情况是在第一线谈判的业务人员还没有向领导请示,就已经被指是与对方达成了一个约束性的合约,从而无法脱身。原因之一显然是负责谈判的业务人员不懂法律,也不知道英国合约法下怎样会构成一个有约束性的合约。部分业务人员更是错误认为双方如果没有签署一份正式合约,就没有合约关系。但在英国法下,对方如果作出了一个要约,即使要约的内容看来简单或不全面,只要中国公司回应说"谢谢"(thanks)或"好消息"(good news)[5]或"同意"(confirmed),[6]就会有危险被指是接受了要约而有了合约关系。也会有其他的情况,如与西方人谈判,他们如果想把中国公司套进一个有约束性的合约,就往往会在文书通讯往来中加上一些显示大家已经谈拢的文字,如"谢谢你的这一票生意"(many thanks for this business transacted),或是"希望将来合作把合约履行好"(looking for to future cooperation in performance)等。这种证据对英国法院或伦敦仲裁庭有很大影响,因为这些词句在西方人眼中不像是双方还在谈判时会说的话。法院或仲裁庭一般也不会更相信中国公司,而质疑西方公司的文书证据只是"自我保护"(self – serving)。但可惜的是,部分中国公司的业务人员对于这些有一定暗示性的词句没有警惕,不会马上回复强调说我们还在谈判之类。

2.1 案例之一:Pagnan SpA v. Feed Products Ltd

针对这类问题,笔者觉得最好介绍一个有明确指引的重要先例,名为 Pagnan SpA v. Feed Products Ltd (1987) 2 Lloyd's Rep. 601。案情是有关一个玉米麸饲料

---

〔3〕 写法可以是千变万化,如"These Heads of Agreement are subject to contract and are not intended to be legally binding . ."。

〔4〕 写法也可以是千变万化,如"Notwithstanding signature by the parties hereto, this Contract shall not come into force until all of the conditions have been fulfilled and confirmed in writing: (1) 领导批准; (2)..."

〔5〕 如在 Glencore Energy UK Ltd v Cirrus Oil Services Ltd (2014) 2 Lloyd's Rep 1 先例。

〔6〕 如在 Proton Energy Group SA v Orlen Lietuva (2014) 1 Lloyd's Rep 100 先例。

的 FOB 买卖,买卖双方都是很有经验的贸易商并通过经纪人进行交易。1982 年 2 月 1 日,经过多次谈判往来谈妥了货物的数量、质量、价格、付运的日期与条件与支付办法等重要条文后,经纪人发了一份电传对双方说:“下述交易在今天谈妥(the following business today concluded)。”但其实在那时还没有谈妥其他也同样十分重要的条文,如装货时间、速遣费与滞期费、“仓储费”(carrying charges)等。后来双方谈不拢,这就带来了争议,即 1982 年 2 月 1 日双方是否已经达成协议。卖方认为已经达成协议,但买方不同意,而令他们各持不同立场的原因很大可能是在相关时间内货物市场价格有了波动。在高院与上诉庭,法官判是卖方胜诉。至于在 2 月 1 日后谈不拢的其他条文,法律都可以作出默示(如装货作业必须是在合理时间内完成,否则卖方要承担船舶的滞期损失),不会令 2 月 1 日达成的买卖合约无法履行。英国法律承认一个以文字表达出来的有约束性的“初步协议”(preliminary agreement),即使订约双方还准备继续谈判其他条文。高院与上诉庭都给了很明确的指引,可详细节录如下:

首先是在高院,Bingham 大法官说:

“The Court's task is to review what the parties said and did and from that material infer whether the parties' objective intentions as expressed to each other were to enter into a mutually binding contract. The Court is not of course concerned with what the parties may subjectively have intended ...

It is furthermore clear that where exchanges between the parties have continued over a period the Court must consider all these exchanges in context and not seize upon one episode in isolation in order to conclude that a contract has been made. There will be some cases where continued negotiations after a contract has allegedly been made will lead to the inference that the parties never in truth intended to bind themselves ... This will the more obviously be so where a term raised by one or other party early in the negotiations had not been the subject of agreement at the time of the alleged contract ...

Where the parties have not reached agreement on terms which they regard as essential to a binding agreement, it naturally follows that there can be no binding agreement until they do agree on those terms ... But just as it is open to the parties by their words and contract to make clear that they do not intend to be bound until certain terms are agreed, even if those terms (objectively viewed) are of relatively minor significance, the converse is also true. The parties may by their words and conduct make it clear that they do intend to be bound, even though there are other terms yet to be agreed, even terms which may often or usually be agreed before a binding contract is made ...

The parties are to be regarded as masters of their own contractual fate. It is their intentions which matter and to which the Court must strive to give effect ... I think, furthermore, that the Court must bear constantly in mind the subject matter with which it is dealing. The relevant principles of the law of contract are, no doubt, of universal application, but the proper inference to draw may vary widely according to the facts of the particular case. One case may concern a protracted negotiation, perhaps conducted in writing through lawyers, between parties who have had no dealings of any kind before. Another may concern a series of quick - fire exchanges between professionals, both of them in the same trade, both having had many previous dealings, and with a wide measure of common experience, knowledge, language and understanding between them. One could not sensibly approach these cases in the same way. Inferences which it would be appropriate to draw in one case might be quite inappropriate in the other. **But the Court's task remains essentially the same: to discern and give effect to the objective intentions of the parties.**"(加黑部分是笔者的强调)

Bingham 大法官在上述所说的主旨是,参考双方在谈判中的通讯往来的主要目的是从中找出这些往来中所客观表达出来的双方当事人的意图,至于双方主观的意图不必理会。法院在作出判断时应该全盘考虑所有的通讯往来,不应该只把其中的一部分单独挑出来说可以证明双方已经达成合约。[7] 现实中会有很多不同的情况,如双方一直在谈判,并没有真正的意图约束双方,特别是其中一方在谈判期间提出过一条条文,而该条文也没有在声称有了合约的一天明确已经被同意过;又或是双方仍没有同意一些重要(如标的)的条文,很自然就要同意后才能说他们有约束性的合约;又有可能的是即使针对的是不重要的条文或只是细节,双方只要以他们的文字[8]或行动显示其只会在所有细节都谈拢后才受到合约的约束,这也是完全可以。订约方在合约中的命运完全掌握在自己手中,只要他们表达清楚意图,法院就会尽量支持。

该先例去了上诉庭,高院的判决除了被支持以外,Lloyd 大法官还给了一些是否达成约束性协议的重要指引,所谓的六个大原则如下:

"(1) In order to determine whether a contract has been concluded in the course of correspondence, one must look first to the correspondence as a whole ...(决定双方在一连串的通讯往来中到底有否订立了合约,是必须整体来看所有的通讯往来。)

---

〔7〕 这特别是在部分口头部分文书达成的合约中会带来风险,因为对文书部分合约的解释被视为法律问题而可以上诉至法院,但口头部分的合约涉及的事实证据就由仲裁庭作出最后裁决。这就会带来仲裁庭考虑了全部证据后作出的裁决被法院断章取义解释部分谈判中的文件后作出的不同判决推翻的风险。这种危险在本章 13. 3 段的 Covington Marine Corp v. Xiamen Shipbuilding Industry Co (2006) 1 Lloyd's Rep. 745 先例有介绍。

〔8〕 这种做法最常见就是在租约的谈判中,在谈妥了一些重要条文并以文书确认时(称为重述要点[recapitulation])加注"subject details"以显示双方的意图是要谈拢细节才会有约束性的合约。这种做法在非航运的合约,如房屋买卖合约也会有,如加注"subject contract"。这些方面在杨大明律师所著的《期租合同》与笔者所著的《船舶买卖法律与实务》一书都有详谈。有关这些变数条件条文,可看本书第八章。

(2) Even if the parties have reached agreement on all the terms of the proposed contract, nevertheless they may intend that the contract shall not become binding until some further condition has been fulfilled. That is the ordinary 'subject to contract' case. (即使双方已经是对所有的合约条文达成协议,但他们的意图是直到一些其他变数条件被满足,合约才有约束性。这是如一些经常见到的"以签署合约为准"的案件。[9])

(3) Alternatively, they may intend that the contract shall not become binding until some other term or terms have been agreed ... (另一种情况,双方的意图是在一些其他的条文或个别条文也达致协议之前合约不会有约束性。这是在航运和国际货物买卖中见到的"以谈拢细节为准"。[10])

(4) Conversely, the parties may intend to be bound forthwith even though there are further terms still to be agreed or some further formality to be fulfilled ... (相反的,双方的意图也可以是立即受到约束,即使还有其他的条文要达成协议或还有其他一些手续/事情需要满足。)

(5) If the parties fail to reach agreement on such further terms, the existing contract is not invalidated unless the failure to reach agreement on such further terms renders the contract as a whole unworkable or void for uncertainty. (如果在上一段的情况下,双方无法在将来对其他条文达成协议,并不会令已经存在的合约无效,除非该达不成协议的其他条文会使已经存在的合约根本无法被履行或变得太不肯定而变为无效。显然这种情况很少,绝大部分的其他条文都可通过法律的默示令合约可以履行。)

(6) It is sometimes said that the parties must agree on the essential terms and that it is only matters of detail which can be left over. This may be misleading, since the word 'essential' in that context is ambiguous. If by 'essential' one means a term without which the contract cannot be enforced then the statement is true: **the law cannot enforce an incomplete contract.** If by 'essential' one means a term which the parties have agreed to be essential for the formation of a binding contract, then the statement is tautologous. If by 'essential' one means only a term which the Court regards as less important or a matter of detail, the statement is untrue. It is for the parties to decide whether they wish to be bound and, if so, by what terms, whether important or unimportant. It is the parties who are, in the memorable phrase coined by the Judge, 'the masters of their contractual fate'. Of course the more important the term the less likely it is that the parties will have left it for future decision. But there is no legal obstacle which stands in the way of the parties agreeing to be bound now while deferring important matters to be agreed later. It happens every day when parties enter into so-called 'heads of agreement'."

---

[9] 可看本书第八章之第4段。

[10] 可看本书第八章之第5段。

(有说法是双方必须同意所有的重要条文才会有合约,这一句话有一点误导成分,因为"重要"一词本身就含糊。如果"重要"是指假如双方没有对这一条文达成协议的话,合约就无法履行/执行[如合约的标的或谁是订约双方还没有同意],该说法是正确,因为法律不会执行一个不完整的合约。如果"重要"是指双方已经同意某一条文对达成约束性合约是重要,这样,有了双方的明确意图,该说法就显得重复了。又如果"重要"仅仅是指法院认为某一条文相比另一条文更重要,这种情况下该说法是不正确的。因为认为某一条文重要与否与双方是否有意图受约束,纯粹是订约双方自己的事情,与法院无关。至多能说的是某一条文越是重要,双方留待将来才谈判的可能性就越低。但如果订约双方明确同意受到合约的约束并把一些十分重要的但还没有谈妥的事情留待将来再试图谈判并希望能够同意,这完全没有法律会否定这一双方的订约意图。这种情况每天都在一些初步协议中发生。)

2.2 案例之二:RTS Flexible Systems Ltd v. Molkerei Alois Miller GmbH & Co KG

Pagnan SpA v. Feed Products Ltd (1987) 2 Lloyd's Rep. 601 先例的判决直到今天也完全有效且具有权威性。在此只多介绍一个近期的关于双方怎样才会被视为达成约束性协议或有合约关系的贵族院先例,名为 RTS Flexible Systems Ltd v Molkerei Alois Miller GmbH & Co KG (2010) 1 WLR 753,Clarke 勋爵说:"The general principles are not in doubt. Whether there is a binding contract between the parties and, if so, upon what terms depends upon what they have agreed. It depends not upon their subjective state of mind, but upon a consideration of what was communicated between them by words or conduct, and whether that leads objectively to a conclusion that they intended to create legal relations and had agreed upon all the terms which they regarded or the law requires as essential for the formation of legally binding relations. Even if certain terms of economic or other significance to the parties have not been finalised, an objective appraisal of their words and conduct may lead to the conclusion that they did not intend agreement of such terms to be a pre-condition to a concluded and legally binding agreement."(双方有否达成约束性协议不是根据他们的主观想法,而是客观看他们之间通过文书、口头与行动的往来是否可以得出他们有意图产生法律关系与双方同意了他们之间认为重要的条文的结论。就算还有一些对双方经济上或其他方面是重要的条文还没有达成协议,但客观分析他们所用的文字与行为[如一种行动是双方或其中一方开始履行]会得出一个结论,即他们并没有想把这些重要但还没有谈妥的条文作为一个达成有约束性合约的先决条件。)

2.3 案例之三:Proton Energy Group SA v. Orlen Lietuva

在 Proton Energy Group SA v Orlen Lietuva (2014) 1 Lloyd's Rep 100 先例,案情涉及石油买卖。合约双方从6月11日开始已经交换过几次邮件,对一些合约条文进行了谈判。在6月14日,卖方在邮件中说:"4. Contractual price is fixed as per the confirmed offer. **All other contractual terms not indicated into the offer shall be dis-**

cussed and mutually agreed between parties upon contract negotiations."(加黑部分是笔者的强调)

之后买方回复"confirmed",双方的争议之一是,此时双方是否已经达成一个有约束力的合约。卖方认为双方交换的最后两封邮件显示双方已经同意有一个有约束力的合约,尽管还有一些合约条文需要进一步同意。但买方认为卖方邮件中的"contract negotiations"显示了双方还没有达成有约束力的合约,还要进一步谈判。法院最后支持了卖方的争辩,说:"This was a classic spot deal where the speed of the market requires that the parties agree the main terms and leave the details, some of which may be important, to be discussed and agreed later. Lay business people from different jurisdictions will not always conduct all aspects of their dealings to fit the conventions of English contract law and Orlen, with whose reasons for cancelling I sympathise, have some points in their favour. But overall the picture is clear. **The language is that of commitment. One side, Proton, committed to Trafigura contractually as soon as this deal had been confirmed.** This shows that it regarded itself as committed to Orlen but does not mean that it was – particularly where the trader was inexperienced. But the fact that Orlen also saw itself as committed means that both sides did. There may well have been internal politics within Orlen but that is no reason to doubt the truth of the firm terms in which the deal was described and progressed within the company."(加黑部分是笔者的强调)

从报道的案件看来,买方回复的同意完全可以被解释为同意在要约没有包括的条文继续谈判。但法院却认为同意是同意有一个有约束力的合约关系,而其他要约没有包括的条文继续谈判并不影响这一份合约。但笔者认为这样判会轻视了双方如果有了合约关系再谈任何条文的难度,因为再也不会有为了达成合约而各让一步的谈判。这样,法院当然可以说如果谈不拢就由法律作出默示,但显然这样做并不理想。反正这一先例又显示了本段稍早所说的英国法院或仲裁庭在解释时会普遍倾向支持存在一个合约而不是否定它。所以,不想被扭曲为有了订约意图去同意一个合约的关系,就必须以文书写得清清楚楚,如本先例的一句"All other contractual terms not indicated into the offer shall be discussed and mutually agreed between parties upon contract negotiations"写为"subject to details"。[11]

2.4 杨大明律师的相关伦敦仲裁案件

最后笔者可以介绍杨大明律师与其团队最近(2014 年 12 月作出的裁决书)帮助一家中国大型公司成功作出抗辩的伦敦仲裁案件。这类案情对于中国公司是非常典型的,就是外国公司指它与中国公司已经有了约束性合约,但中国公司否认有合约关系,导致被外国公司指称违约/毁约,并索赔一笔庞大的损失。该仲裁案件涉及中国

---

〔11〕 详见本书第八章之第 5 段。

一家大型能源公司(因为仲裁的机密性不提供名字),有关事实背景可介绍如下:

1. 案件涉及的10艘船舶(包含一些化学品运输船以及油轮),全部都是一家欧洲船东拥有。这些船舶原本长期出租给一家东南亚的承租人。但因为经济问题,承租人没法继续承租。

2. 为了解决问题,这家东南亚的承租人与中国的能源公司讨论购买这10艘船舶的可能性。初步想法是东南亚的承租人先从欧洲船东手中买下这些船,然后马上转卖给中国能源公司。经过一些书面来往,东南亚的承租人带欧洲船东到中国与能源公司会面,大家签订了一份三方"备忘录"(Memorandum of Understanding)。

3. 这份备忘录是一份简短的文件,提到中国能源公司会以某大概金额向东南亚的承租人购买这些船舶,东南亚的承租人会以另一金额从欧洲船东手中购买这些船舶。备忘录没有提到任何关于船舶的事情,包括船舶质量、交船状态、交船地点与日期,而显然每艘船舶都会涉及不同细节。但备忘录有条文明示中国能源公司需要支付订金,也另有仲裁条文。这份备忘录也有明示规定整个交易需要经过中国能源公司的董事局与股东批准,并以此作为该交易继续进行的先决条件。〔12〕

4. 最终,这份备忘录没有得到股东的同意,因为股东对于有关船舶的质量与价格有保留。但因为在签订备忘录后的书面来往中,中国能源公司处理的不小心,所以转达了给东南亚与欧洲公司已通过全部批准的错误消息,说:"We are pleased to confirm that we have already obtained approvals from our board and shareholder."这一错误的消息莫名其妙,但中国公司不能抵赖备忘录已"生效"。

5. 所以案件的关键问题变为,虽然备忘录具备了生效的条件,但是否是一份足够肯定与完整的合约?

在这方面,仲裁庭认为需要考虑两个不同的问题。第一,必须考虑合约的当事人是否有意图订立一份合约。在这个问题上,仲裁庭认为备忘录的当事人是有意图订立合约。其中一个关键因素是备忘录中有仲裁条文,因为如果没有合约就没有纠纷,也就不需要仲裁。但就算有订约意图也不足够,合约的当事人需要达到第二个条件,即他们所订的合约必须足够肯定与完整。否则就算他们有意图订立一份合约都会失败,达不到这个目的。对于第二个条件,仲裁庭认为这份备忘录不够肯定与完整,因为没有任何关于10艘船舶的条文,也就是较早时提到的船舶质量、交船状态、交船地点与日期等,什么都是需要留到日后再进一步谈判。而这些条文会很多且复杂,无法作出事实的默示。〔13〕 所以,伦敦仲裁庭裁定备忘录是一份"协议将来达成协议"(agreement to agree),因此太不肯定而无效。另是该备忘录也太不完整,正如Lloyd大法官在Pagnan SpA v. Feed Products Ltd (1987) 2 Lloyd's Rep. 601先例中所说,法律不会执行一个不完整的合约。

---

〔12〕 关于变数先决条件,可看本书第八章。

〔13〕 关于事实默示,请看本书第七章之第4段。

除了法律方面，这案件对于中国公司在实际处理伦敦（或其他）国际仲裁或大型诉讼方面也有很多教训。这案件本来是一家中国大陆的律师事务所处理，这家律所对国际仲裁毫无经验，错误与遗漏的地方非常多，完全不理解伦敦仲裁中"文件披露"（disclosure）的关键性，所以没有做好这方面的准备，只抖出几份文件并声称所有有关文件已经披露。原告也就是欧洲船东严厉攻击，指中国能源公司对事实真相有所隐瞒。而仲裁庭也已经明确说明会在事实的认定对中国能源公司作出"不利推断"（adverse inference），这等于还没有审理，中国能源公司就败局已定。中国能源公司转而委托杨大明律师接手，当时距原定开庭时间只有一个半月，时间非常紧张。杨大明律师接手后在中国能源公司查找文件，并最后披露了超过600页的文件证据，从而扭转了伦敦仲裁庭对中国能源公司的敌意。此外，杨大明律师在欧洲船东所披露的文件中挑出蛛丝马迹，发觉欧洲船东已经与东南亚船东达成一些协议，于是要求进一步披露。这被对方抗拒，最后导致伦敦仲裁庭作出命令，强制要求披露，而最后披露出的协议发现是与案件非常有关，并且对欧洲船东不利。这也被仲裁庭接受并在裁决书中引用了英国的说法"the pot calling the kettle black"与中国的说法"五十步笑百步"来形容欧洲船东。

而针对中国能源公司在最后关头替换律师扭转劣势的关键性，裁决书作了以下说明："Concerning disclosure,（仲裁庭）stressed that, on the basis of the（中国能源公司）'s own submissions, it appeared to me to be clear that the topics in relation to which（欧洲船东）had sought further disclosure were topics relevant to issues that I would have to decide, and I informed（中国能源公司）of the importance attached to compliance with obligations as to disclosure in proceedings governed by English law. And I made this further point, namely, that I would not hesitate to draw inferences adverse to（中国能源公司）were I to conclude that they had failed fully and frankly to comply with their disclosure obligations. Two days later ... I, and those representing the other parties, were advised of a change in representation on behalf of（中国能源公司）. From（过了几天）onwards（中国能源公司）were represented by a well known international firm of lawyers clearly familiar with arbitration (and, no doubt, other proceedings) governed by English law."（仲裁庭认为之前中国能源公司所提供的披露文件非常欠缺，也基本上准备好对中国能源公司作不利推断，但幸亏中国能源公司及时更换了律师，委托被仲裁庭认同是明显熟悉仲裁与其他英国法程序的杨大明律师与他的团队处理。）

本章接下去是针对在现实中双方的合约关系会以各种形式出现，而法律要求它们要被整体解释，所以有必要探讨其中一些经常会出现的合约形式与其所包括的部分。

§3 正式与非正式合约

合约是记录双方谈判后所达成的协议,这个协议主要分两种形式出现。第一种形式是“正式合约”(formal contract),这就是一些“盖章的契约”(contract in a deed)。它本质上与其他合约没有区别,只不过是盖了章,显示了订约双方更加小心。另是历史的原因令这种合约有一些不同之处,如它的有效性并不要求约因/对价,索赔时效不是6年而是长达12年。

第二种形式是“非正式合约”(informal contract),或是通常被称为“简式合约”(simple contract)。这种合约在商业活动中最常出现,它可以是口头或文书的形式,甚至是通过行动的形式。但会有个别合约是在有关立法的要求下必须符合一些形式,如要求书面或签署等。这可举例如1677年英国《欺诈法》(《Statute of Frauds》)、1906年的英国《海上保险法》(《Marine Insurance Act》)或1925年的英国《财产法》(《Law of Property Act》)。这些立法对合约形式的要求通常有以下主要原因:(1)希望有关交易中的条文有清楚无误的文书证据;(2)给订约方警告,希望他们不要匆忙、不成熟与不深思熟虑就乱订这种合约;(3)通过对形式的要求可令某一种交易慢慢变得标准化;(4)对某一些形式的要求可以保护合约中较弱的订约方。至于一个合约如果没有依照立法的形式会有什么后果,这主要是看个别立法怎样说。如在1925年《财产法》,Section 40就说明不依照形式要求的合约不能强制执行,是“空的”(nullity)。

至于解释合约内的条文/文字,不论是在正式合约或在非正式合约,实是没有区别。

§4 文件表面看来是双方同意了的全部合约

这是一种比较清楚明确的文书合约,如双方自己或通过代理人已经签署的合约,更不用说是已经盖了章的正式合约。一些比较长期与复杂的合约(如国际性或涉及金额比较大)通常会以这种形式,订约方不会希望以“口头”(oral)形式或“部分口头部分文书”(part oral,part written)的形式达成合约。他们会希望把所有的约定与应该包括在内的条文/文字以文书形式在一个草拟好的合约中显示出来,然后把每一条都看一遍与考虑清楚后才最后以签字确认达成合约。昂贵的商业合约的草拟与谈判工作会有称职律师从旁协助,这会是一个花钱的步骤。不论最后合约能否达成,反正这一笔“交易费用”(transaction cost)省不了。为了避免过早被认定双方已经达成合约,如口头的合约,谨慎的订约方通常会在谈判中写明/说明“以签署合约为准”(subject to contract)这一个先决条件。当然即使没有这一明确的先决条件,也可在谈判的往来中说明不走这一步,双方就还没有达成约束性合约的意图。但毕竟偏离一些已经有无数先例明确了的先决条件的措辞而用其他文字,会是不肯定且有危险将来不被法院或仲裁庭接受。上诉庭的 Jessel 大法官在 Winn v. Bull (1877) 7 Ch. D. 29 先例中说:"When it is not expressly stated to be subject to a formal contract it becomes a question of construction, whether the parties intended that the terms agreed on should merely be put into form, or whether they should be subject to a new agreement the terms of which are not expressed in detail."

这种争议另也可以参阅 The "Polarsol" (1952) 1 Lloyd's Rep. 407 先例与 Concorde Enterprises Ltd v. Anthony Motors (Hutt) Ltd (1981) 2 NZLR 385 先例。

"签署"(signature)本身就是显示签署方受该文书合约/文件约束的意图,以及确认该文件的正确性。以前的说法是解释该合约,就应该局限在该"文件的四个角内"(four corners of the document)。[14] 双方已经签署的文书合约,一般的说法就是除非有欺诈与误述,否则对签署方就有约束力,不论他是否看过合约内容:L'Estrange v. Graucob (1934) 2 K. B. 395 先例。

但即使没有在一份文件内签署,只要双方同意了该文件就是双方达成的合约,效果也是一样。这里可节录 Devlin 勋爵在 McCutcheon v. Macbrayne (David) Ltd (1964) 1 W. L. R. 125 先例中所说的:"It seems to me that when a party assents to a document forming the whole or part of his contract, **he is bound by the terms of the document, read or unread, signed or unsigned**, simply because they are in the contract; and it is unnecessary and possibly misleading to say that he is bound by them because he represents to the other party that he has made himself acquainted with them."(加黑部分是笔者的强调)

在上述的情况下,可以假设双方的意图是该份文件包括了他们之间的全部交易。当然这一假设可以推翻,其中最重要的就是"附带保证/协议"(collateral warranty/contract),这一课题在本书第六章之 2.3.2 段有介绍。

这里也可以顺便谈谈何谓签署一份文件。签署一份文件可以用很多不同的方式,法律上都承认。如可以"草签"(initials):Phillimore v Barry (1818) 1 Camp 513, 170 ER 1040 等先例;"盖章"(stamp):Goodman v J Eban Ltd (1954) 1 Q. B. 550 等先例;另影印与打字的签署也被承认:Brydges v Dis (1891) 7 TLR 215 与 Newborne v. Sensolid (Great Britain) Ltd (1954) 1 Q. B. 45 等先例;一份签署的文件以传真的方法给对方,这也是被认为业已签署:Re a Debtor (No. 2021 of 1995) (1996) 2 All ER 345 先例。

随着电子通讯的发展,法律也加以配合,如在 2000 年英国《Electronic Communi-

〔14〕 可见本书第一章之第 7 段。

cations Act》立法之 Section 7 规定法律诉讼中接受电子通讯中的电子签署的效力，虽然相关证据的分量轻重问题是由法院决定。另是英国法律委员会在《Electronic Commerce：Formal Requirements in Commercial Transactions—Advice from the Law Commission》（December 2001）中除了建议英国政府接受以一个"加密的数码签署"（digital signature using a public key encryption system）就可以满足法律对签署的要求（如 1677 年的《欺诈法》对签字的要求），另是扫描的签署文件也足够。最重要的是该报告还建议在一份电邮中只要在后面加上名字或简写（如 Philip Yang 写作 PY），这也已经足够满足签署的要求。在近期的 J Pereira Fenandes SA v Mehta（2006）EWHC 813 Civ 先例，高院的 Pelling 大法官看来也有接近的说法，如下："I have no doubt that if a party creates and sends an electronically created document then he will be treated as having signed it to the same extent that he would in law be treated as having signed a hard copy of the same document. The fact that the document is created electronically as opposed to a hard copy can make no difference... Thus, as I have already said, if a party or party's agent sending an e－mail types his or her or his or her principal's name to the extent required or permitted by existing case law in the body of an e－mail, then in my view that would be a sufficient signature for the purposes of section 4（《Statue of Fraud》）."

最后一提的是，欧共体发给所有的会员国一个名为《Electronic Commerce Directive》的指引，在第 9 条要求大家排除所有对以电子达成商业合约的障碍。

§5　工作合约（working contract）

在租船业务中，还经常会有一份"工作租约"（working charter－party），是由经纪人根据双方的谈判档案中所达成的各方面协议整理出来的。这样，工作租约很可能有错误，包括经纪人看错或看漏，或用他认为适合的文字草拟但订约方不一定接受。所以，如果签署工作租约，订约方应该十分小心地审阅并肯定自己所同意的内容后才签署。如果仅是一份工作租约，是不被当作双方已经同意的合约，充其量也只能是证明双方到底同意了什么内容的证据之一。

这里可以举一个先例是 The "Pina"（1992）2 Lloyd's Rep. 103，涉及一个"租约链"（Charter－party chain），最后的分承租人是 Coscol。之后，船东在还没有还船前直接找 Coscol，想在租约链中的其他承租人还船后马上把船舶直接租给 Coscol，跳过中间两个承租人 Mitsui 与 OST。在谈判过程中的 1979 年 9 月 5 日，双方以电传确认接受了以"Shelltime 3 subject minor details"为准，并在后来谈判过一些 Shelltime 3 这一份广泛被使用的油轮期租标准格式合约的条文。但双方的谈判是以 Coscol 与 OST 之间现有的租约为准，该租约（对船东而言是一份分租约）也是以 Shelltime 3 的标准格式为基础,但 Coscol 与 OST 在订约时做了大量修改。其中最关键的修改是第 24 条文被大部分删除掉,包括船舶在履行中超越了航速与耗油量的保证对船东有奖励。这种约定在油轮租约非常常见,就是针对船东对航速与耗油量的保证有罚(承租人提出索赔损失)也有奖(提高租金),不像干货轮租约只针对船舶达不到这些保证就要被罚(更准确的说法是船东要赔偿违约的损失)。

船东与 Coscol 在谈判时提到 Shelltime 3 的大部分被删除的第 24 条文,船东曾经说到"稍候告诉你我的意见"(reverting with comments)。但之后没有进一步的谈判,也表示双方对这一点没有达成过协议。后来双方在 1979 年 12 月 27 日对整个租约达成协议。之后经纪人整理出一份工作租约给大家签署,该工作租约保留了 Shelltime 3 标准格式的全部第 24 条印刷条文,这显然是与 Coscol 与 OST 之间原来的租约有很大不同。双方不知道是什么原因也并没有签署这份工作租约,但在后来另约定了五个附件(包括了延长租约期),反而双方每一份附件都有签署,并在附件中说明所有其他条文以原租约为准(All other terms, conditions and exceptions to the Time Charter Party dated September 25, 1979, shall remain unaltered and in full force and effect)。

到了 1983 年,双方已经履行了一段长时间后,船东向 Coscol(在这一个直接的租约,它就是承租人)提出索赔达 200 万美元的奖励,理由是船舶履行超越了航速与耗油量保证。这时候 Coscol 才跳起来,因为它与 OST 之间的租约是删除了这部分的条文。这里就涉及双方到底同意了什么,而船东在谈判的往来中没有办法证明双方曾经同意了第 24 条文的全文。但工作租约倒是有完整的第 24 条文,所以船东争辩说工作租约虽然没有签署但记录了双方的协议并超越了以前所有的口头证据/谈判证据。另外,即使工作租约没有签署,但后来的五个附件都有签署就足够补救。船东是这样说:"For the owners Mr. Rokison (船东代表大律师) first argues that the unsigned charter – party constituted the agreement in writing between the parties. They contemplated that a written record of the fixture reached between the brokers would be drawn up by charterers' brokers and signed by both parties, and that it would provide a working document. According to the owners, when the charter – party was drafted by Mr. de Santis (承租人经纪人) and submitted to the owners for signature, it superseded the oral agreement between the parties and became the agreement in writing which they had contemplated."

但在一审与上诉庭,船东都是败诉,并被判是没有签署的工作租约不能代表双方的合约。上诉庭的 Leggatt 大法官说:"... It therefore was not itself an agreement, though it might have afforded evidence of the terms of the agreement. It is not suggested that the written document was explicitly accepted by the charterers as correctly setting out the terms of the agreement between them, or that the charterers are estopped from denying that it did. If and to the extent that the charterers had accepted the document as correct, its terms would have provided cogent evidence of what had been agreed.... We regard as unsustainable the argument that, when parties agree that an agreement shall be reduced to writing and signed by both of them as the agreement, the document so produced *prima facie* constitutes the agreement notwithstanding that it is unsigned. ..."

而针对五个附件都有签署,上诉庭不同意是补救了本来就没有合约地位的工作租约,而认为它们只是对双方谈判时的口头证据所达成的协议作出了附件所针对的部分"文书更改"(written variation)。Leggatt 大法官是这样说:"In our judgment, that means no more than that the existing charter – party is not to be regarded as having been altered except to the extent of the variation effected by the addendum. It gives no efficacy to the charter – party that the charter – party does not already possess. It does not afford the charter – party incidentally a contractual force that it would not otherwise enjoy. The addenda therefore constituted no more than written variations of the contract made orally. They did not have the effect of rendering the unsigned, non – contractual, written version enforceable subject to rectification. ..."

§6 初步合约(preliminary contract)

英国法律承认初步合约,这在上述介绍的 Pagnan SpA v. Feed Products Ltd (1987) 2 Lloyd's Rep. 601 先例已经提到过。在这里笔者想介绍一些在双方订约时其他会出现的初步合约,如"意向书"(Letter of Intent)、"安抚函"(Letter of Comfort)、"过渡合约"(Bridging Contract)、"互锁合约"(Lock – out Contract)等。

6.1 意向书(letter of intent)

意向书是在一些漫长与昂贵的谈判之前双方达成并签署的协议,如在一些大型的合资、技术转让、工程、造船等合约的签署。内容是明示双方对这一交易计划的理解与一些重要的商业考虑。例如在造船合约,它就会明示出双方意向的船价、买方支付的方法、交船日期、适用法或/与买方可能会有的选择权(如船厂原则上不反对,只要造船合约谈拢就可以让买方照原船价或其他不同船价选择多造一两艘不等的船舶)。在这个时间内,买方可能还没有财务上的安排,如银行融资。所以意向书也会明示即使谈判完毕达成了合约,也是"以财务安排为准"(subject to finance)。而船厂可能也没有备妥订立一个有约束性的合约,如还需要政府的批准。所以,意向书也会明示即使谈判完毕,也"以政府批准为准"(subject to government approval)。意向书的主要目的是让双方按照意向书的理解与列出的重要商业考虑继续谈判直到达成最后的全面协议。显然,如果他们连意向书也无法达成,就根本不值得花时间进行漫长与昂贵的谈判了。

意向书是否有法律效力并约束双方这一问题的答案并不稳定,因为它属于"协议将来达成协议”(agreement to agree)。英国法律认为这太不肯定且无法执行,这方面在本书第三章之12.1.3段会有详论。所以,意向书被不少人视为双方只表达其订约意向,没有法律的约束而只有道德的约束。此外,仅看文件的名称就显示了双方没有建立法律关系的意图。正如在 Associated British Ports v. Ferryways NV, MSC Belgium NV (2009) 1 Lloyd's Rep 595 先例,上诉庭的 Maurice Kay 大法官说:“I regard a letter of comfort[15], properly so called, as one that does not give rise to contractual liability. The label used by the parties is not necessarily determinative. It is a matter of construction of the document as a whole.”

固然,如果意向书涉及了其中一方的恶意,如船厂根本没有建造有关船舶的干坞,但却向船东/买方作出虚假陈述,买方可以根据“欺诈侵权”(tort of deceit)向船厂索赔在谈判中浪费的费用。

但意向书是否有法律效力并约束双方并不在于其名称。在本章之第12段会谈到名称/抬头并不重要,重要的是内容,也就是意向书的条文/文字与其背景/语境。这在 Wilson Smithett & Cape (Sugar) Ltd. v. Bangladesh Sugar and Food Industries Corporation (1986) 1 Lloyd's Rep. 378 先例中,Leggatt 大法官说:“... look at the document itself, at the surrounding circumstances, and at what happened when [the letter of intent] was brought into existence. The fact that it has the particular label that it has does not brand it at the outset as contractual document or as a non - contractual document.”

最明确是一份意向书在内容中说明该文件不约束双方直到谈判完毕。但在另一个极端是意向书有多条条文针对各种不同的双方承诺,特别是加上适用法与管辖权/仲裁条文(因为这代表了文件有法律效力,否则为什么约定一种解决争议的法律救济),这就有可能令意向书被判有法律效力并约束双方。另外,如果在大部分条文都已经谈论并且又是在谈判后期时所订立的意向书,也会有较大可能被视为有法律效力。至于谁有责任举证意向书是否有法律效力可参阅 Edwards v. Skyways (1964) 1 W.L.R. 349 先例与新加坡的 Hong Kong and Shanghai Building Corporation Ltd. v. Jurong Engineering Ltd (2000) 2 S.L.R. 54 先例。

6.2 安抚函(letter of comfort)

这种文件与意向书一样,是否有法律效力或只是在道德上有约束力不能仅看文件的名称/抬头,而主要看其内容,即有关条文/文字以及语境。安抚函通常是由政府或者集团母公司签发给第三人,希望第三人肯与属下的机构或子公司进行交易,针对购买货物或融资等。

有关这种文件有一个著名的先例 Kleinwort Benson v. Malaysia Mining Corporation (1989) 1 Lloyd's Rep. 556,可在此介绍。案情有关 Kleinwort Benson(KB),是

[15] 该先例是针对安抚函,这份文件会稍后在本章之6.2段谈及,但道理是一样,文件名称只是“意向”或“安抚”都显示了双方不想受到法律的约束。

一家著名的英国“商人银行”(merchant bank)。KB 在 1983 年贷款给一家属于 Malaysia Mining Corporation(MMC)的子公司名为 MMC Metals Limited。该子公司是有 150 万英镑注册资本的有限公司,而 MMC 是由马来西亚政府控制的国有企业。由于贷款金额颇大,起初是 500 万英镑,后来增加到 1000 万英镑,所以 KB 向 MMC 要了一份安抚函后才肯融资。MMC Metals Limited 公司唯一的业务是在伦敦金属交易进行期货交易,到了 1985 年 10 月,“锡”(tin)市场暴跌,令“国际锡金属委员会”(International Tin Council)宣布破产,很多相关人士与政府(包括马来西亚)遭受到严重损失。这一个著名的事件在 Maclaine Watson & Co. Ltd. v. Department of Trade and Industry (1988) 3 W. L. R. 1033 先例有报道。MMC Metals Limited 公司也宣布破产,这导致 KB 在当时发出的巨额贷款共 1226 万英镑只能试图转向 MMC 追讨。至于能否成功就要看 MMC 的安抚函是否有法律效力了。在此,先把该文件的全文节录出来,如下:

“We refer to your recent discussion with MMC Metals Limited as a result of which you propose granting MMC Metals Limited: (a) banking facilities of up to £ 5 million; and (b) spot and forward foreign exchange facilities with a limitation that total delivery in cash will not on any one day exceed £ 5 million.

We hereby confirm that we know and approve of these facilities and are aware of the fact that they have been granted to MMC Metals Limited because we control directly or indirectly MMC Metals Limited.

We confirm that we will not reduce our current financial interest in MMC Metals Limited until the above facilities have been repaid or until you have confirmed that you are prepared to continue the facilities with new shareholders.

It is our policy to ensure that the business of MMC Metals Limited is at all times in a position to meet its liabilities to you under the above arrangements.

Yours faithfully, MALAYSIA MINING CORPORATION BERHAD. ”(加黑部分是双方的主要争议)

高院 Hirst 大法官判是安抚函有法律效力,主要理由如下。例如,KB 是依赖了这一份文件才会给出巨额贷款,这表示有约因/对价。另法律上有一个假设是商业人士有意图订立法律合约关系(presumption that commercial parties intend to create legal relationships),而如果没有这一意图就应该明确明示。再一个关键的理由是 Hirst 大法官认为加黑一句是清楚无误的表明 MMC 有法律责任,说:“... the paragraph was crystal clear; it was an understanding that now and at all times in the future so long as Metals was in a position to meet those liabilities; the plaintiffs were entitled to recover damages for breach of contract; there would be judgment for the plaintiffs. ”

但这在上诉庭被推翻,其中最重要的是上诉庭在解释安抚函的内容时得出了与高院大不相同的结论。这也可能是多考虑了背景/语境,就是 MMC 曾经拒绝向 KB

签发保函而改为作出安抚函。而针对该文件的条文/文字,上诉庭认为在主要争议的一句(也即加黑一句)只对在作出安抚函时"所存在的事实作出陈述"(statement of present facts),没有对将来作出任何承诺。MMC 只是说作出安抚函时是"他的政策"(it is our policy)确定子公司能够还债,文法上是"现在时"(present tense)。但如果是对将来作出承诺,文字上就应该要加上如"and will be",令争议的一句变为"It is our policy to ensure that the business of MMC Metals Limited is at all times and will be in a position to meet its liabilities to you under the above arrangements"。注意上一句"we will not reduce our current financial interest in MMC Metals Limited"是对将来作出承诺,即将来不减少对子公司目前的经济利益,如减少股份。但双方起争议的与上一句并没有关系,MMC 也没有违反这一句的承诺。

上诉庭的 Ralph Gibson 大法官判词的部分内容可节录如下:

"... The court would not, merely because the parties had referred to the document as a comfort letter, refuse to give effect to the meaning of the words used. But in this case it is clear, in my judgment, that the concept of a comfort letter, to which the parties had resort when the defendants refused to assume joint and several liability or to give a guarantee, was known by both sides at least to extend to or to include a document under which the defendants would give comfort to the plaintiffs by assuming, not a legal liability to ensure repayment of the liabilities of its subsidiary, but a moral responsibility only. ...

The comfort letter was drafted in terms which in paragraph 3(指主要争议的一句) do not express any contractual promise and which are consistent with being no more than a representation of fact. If they are treated as no more than a representation of fact, they are in that meaning consistent with the comfort letter containing no more than the assumption of moral responsibility by the defendants in respect of the debts of Metals. ..."

在上述案例可以感受到细节的重要,就是西方人的说法"魔鬼是在细节"(devil is with the detail)。在英国法理念中,关键是看条文/文字的内容。如果其中有作出对将来的一些承诺,或是加上了一条适用法与管辖权/仲裁条文,判法就完全不一样了,几个字就可以是涉及上千万或上亿美元的损失。

6.3 过渡合约(bridging or interim contract)

由于一些合约的谈判会涉及很大的一笔费用,但在谈判过程中通常是任何一方都可以自由去中止与撤出谈判,只要有约束性的合约还没有达成。所以这通常会令浪费的费用要双方自己承担,除了在一些非常特殊的情况下会根据"复原的原则"(restitutionary remedy)向对方要回部分费用,如在造船合约,买方在与船厂的谈判中从后者所做的工作与研究中取得了利益:William Lacey (Hounslow) Ltd. v. Davis (1957) 1 W. L. R. 932 先例与 Regalian Properties plc v. London Docklands Development Corporation (1995) 1 W. L. R. 212 先例。

这样,需要承担主要谈判费用的船厂(特别是在建造一些专门船舶,需要个别的设计、检测与向船级社取得批准等工作),如果船厂的谈判力量较强,就会坚持要买方针对谈判费用先签署一份过渡合约,否则就不谈判。在过渡合约中,要求买方即使谈判破裂达不成最后的造船合约,也要根据过渡合约支付给船厂浪费的费用。

通常在最后的造船合约谈妥,会明示或默示合并过渡合约内的一些船厂对设计的保证等内容:British Steel v. Cleveland Bridge (1984) 1 All E. R. 504 先例。

6.4 互锁合约(lock – out contract)

互锁合约的作用是约束双方在谈判期间不能再与其他人同时进行谈判,否则有危险被对方利用、抬价与作出比较,最后突然来一个价高者得。这种情况在租约谈判中经常发生,就是辛辛苦苦谈到差不多时对方突然撤出谈判,因为刚与另一个第三人订了约。这种情况在租船业务经常发生,但租约谈判毕竟浪费的财力与物力还有限,所以双方不会先来一个互锁合约的签署。但换作其他交易需要漫长与昂贵的谈判过程,或者消息泄露出去会招来第三人的兴趣去插手,典型的例子是一些公司收购合约,就很有必要先订一个互锁合约,不准对方在谈判期间与任何其他人进行谈判。如果对方违约,无辜方就可以申请“禁令”(injunction)阻止对方与第三人的订约谈判,或/与索赔损失。

这种很常见与重要的协议应该是有法律效力与约束力,但由于其本质上有“协议将来达成协议”之虞,所以也要在条文/文字上小心拟定。如在贵族院的 Walford v. Miles (1992) 2 AC 128 先例,就是判有关的互锁合约没有一个期限,所以变得太不肯定而无效,总不能把对方永远锁死。该案例涉及收购公司及其办公地点的交易,买方在谈判时出价 200 万英镑,但卖方以一样的价格卖给了第三人。买方跳起来是因为他私下知道该标的价值 300 万英镑,但卖方自己却不知道。所以买方向卖方索赔 100 万英镑的损失,因为卖方违反了互锁合约。可以想象到的是,如果互锁合约没有限期就会造成很大的不公道,特别是在该先例贵族院拒绝默示任何期限。因为买方可以慢慢的谈判,甚至拖延,而如果卖方心急出售套现,这没有限期的互锁合约会置卖方于死地。

但该贵族院的判决还是受到许多批评,如在 Pitt v. PHH Asset Management Ltd. (1994) 1 WLR 327, CA 先例,法院就作出了区分,因为在该互锁合约有一个固定的两个星期的谈判期限。另在 Petromech Inc v. Petroleo Brasilerio SA Petrobras (2006) 1 Lloyd’s Rep 121 先例,上诉庭的 Longmore 大法官也提出了批评并希望贵族院改变这一先例,因为互锁合约在现实中太常见与重要。有关这一方面,在本书第三章之 12.1.3 段探讨“协议将来达成协议”(agreement to agree)与本书第九章之第 2 段与 5.1 段会有详论。

§7 补充协议或多个合约

在一些复杂与长期的交易中,同一个交易就会产生多个合约。如果出了争议怎样协调解释这多个合约,包括区分其分量的轻重是一个复杂的问题。首先在多个合约的情况,解释起来会有三种可能性:一是后来与时间上较晚的补充协议或第二份合约是想超越前一份或第一份合约(可称为原合约);二是补充协议或第二份合约是想与原合约有相同的地位,要一并与协调地作出解释;三是补充协议或第二份合约是想被合并在原合约,如果有矛盾应以原合约为准。这可举 HIH v. New Hampshire (2001) 2 Lloyd's Rep. 161 先例中 Rix 大法官的判词为例:"In essence there are, it seems to me, three possibilities. Either the later contract is intended to supersede the earlier, in which case the above principles apply. Or, the later contract is intended to live together with the earlier contract, to the extent that that is possible, but where that is not possible it may well be proper to regard the later contract as superseding the earlier. Or the later contract is intended to be incorporated into the earlier contract, in which case it is prima facie the second contract which may have to give way to the first in the event of inconsistency."

在多个合约的情况下,它们之间的解释与分量轻重在很多时候会以明示条文规定(特别在补充协议或第二份合约),但如果没有这样做,就会在产生矛盾/争议时需要面对怎样解释的问题。以下会在这一方面探讨。

7.1 情况一:补充协议或第二份合约是想超越原合约

这种情况会是因为各种原因,在租船与保险的商业活动中就会出现。租船会是双方先以传真或电邮的"重述要点"(fixture recap)达成原合约。但由于重述要点写得简单与没有双方的签署,所以针对一些长期的租约,都会有一份完整的租约被整理出来然后双方安排签署。这样做显然是想替代重述要点的原合约,表示有了争议也应该看双方签署的租约。在保险也存在这样的情况,就是先有了一份"承保单"(slip),之后会再出一份"保单"(policy)。它们之间的关系与做法 Diplock 勋爵在 American Airlines Inc. v. Hope (1974) 2 Lloyd's Rep. 301 先例中有说道:

"The slip contemplates its eventual replacement by a policy of insurance in the standard form in use at Lloyd's for aviation risk, but subject to such deletions and as are indicated in the slip. Such additions are generally clauses which themselves follow a standard form and are sufficiently identified in the slip by a reference to a description or a number but some may be specially tailored to the particular requirements of the assured. In the latter case if the slip is for an original insurance the actual clause is set out in the slip itself, although it may be in only abbreviated form..."

Almost invariably the slip provides that the wording of the policy is to be agreed by leading underwriter. Where this is the case the leading underwriter may occasionally consent to someclause going into the policy which was not provided for by the slip, if in his judgment it would not affect the premium. So there is the possibility of minor variations being made in the contract of insurance when terms of the policy are agreed."

在有多个合约的情况,如果发生了争议,在解释最后的一份合约会出现一个问题,就是能否把已经被替代的原合约(如上述介绍的重述要点或承保单)一并考虑,如原合约是怎样的写法与不同之处代表些什么。需要注意的是,英国法律不允许在解释合约考虑谈判时的"草拟合约"(draft agreement):Canterbury Golf International Ltd v. Yoshimoto (2002) UKPC 40 先例。毕竟草拟合约正是本书第三章之 14.3 段与第六章之 2.5.1 段所讲的谈判除外规则的一种文件。Youell v Bland Welch (1992) 2 Lloyd's Rep. 127 先例,一份再保的承保单就不被接受为协助解释再保单的证据。这争议也出现在 HIH v. New Hampshire (2001) 2 Lloyd's Rep. 161 先例,Rix 大法官认为原合约没有理由不可以拿出来协助解释第二份合约,即使是作为背景/语境的证据来看待,但怀疑第一个与被超越的原合约到底能否起什么作用,说:"In principle, it would seem to me that it is always admissible to look at prior contracts as part of the matrix or surrounding circumstances of a later contract. I do not see how the parol negotiation rule can exclude prior contracts, as distinct from mere negotiations. The difficulty of course is that, where the later contract is intended to supersede the prior contract, it may in the generality of cases simply be useless to try to construe the later contract by reference to the earlier one. *Ex hypothesi*, the later contract replaces the earlier one and it is likely to be impossible to say that the parties have not wished to alter the terms of their earlier bargain. The earlier contract is unlikely therefore to be of much, if any, assistance. Where the later contract is identical, its construction can stand on its own feet, and in any event its construction should be undertaken primarily by reference to its own overall terms. Where the alter contract differs from the earlier contract, *prima facie* the difference is a deliberate decision to depart from the earlier wording, which again provides no assistance. Therefore a cautious and sceptical approach to finding any assistance in the earlier contract seems to me to be a sound principle. What I doubt, however, is that such a principle can be elevated into a conclusive rule of law."

另一种情况主要的原因是双方对原合约有"补充"(supplement)或"更改"(vary)的地方,所以约定一个补充协议。该补充协议也是与其他的合约一样,需要满足达成一个有约束性合约的法律要求,如要有约因/对价与双方想法一致等。对有经验与水平的订约方来说,会清楚写明这两份或以上的原合约与补充协议是要一并解释。做法上可以是将后一份文件命名为"附件一或二"(addendum No. 1/2),并在内容中带出较早的原合约与说明除了补充协议所针对的更改内容,原合约的其他内容不变

(all other terms and conditions of the original contract remain unchanged)。这样,补充协议或第二份合约只是增加条文/内容或更改原合约中已经有的条文,而且因为订约时间上较晚,通常增加或更改的内容在分量上比原合约重。正如本章之第5段介绍的 The "Pina" (1992) 2 Lloyd's Rep. 103 先例,Leggatt 大法官说:"The addenda therefore constituted no more than written variations of the contract made orally. They did not have the effect of rendering the unsigned, non-contractual, written version enforceable subject to rectification."

7.2 情况二:补充协议或第二份合约与原合约有相同的地位

在这种情况,往往在第二个合约中有明示条文写明是与原合约有相同的地位或需要一并解释。也会是如果有两个或以上的合约,相隔时间非常接近甚至是在同一时间订立,并针对同一件事或同一个交易,这也会是很强烈的信号显示其应该被一并考虑与作出解释。这可节录 Jessel MR 大法官在 Smith v. Chadwick (1882) 20 Ch. D. 27 先例中所说的:"... when documents are actually contemporaneous, what is two deeds executed at the same moment, ... or within so short an interval that having regard to the nature of the transaction the Court comes to the conclusion that the series of deeds represents a single transaction between the same parties, it is then that they are treated as one deed; and of course one deed between the same parties may be read to show the meaning of a sentence and may be equally read, although not contained in one deed but in several parchments, if all the parchments together in the view of the Court make up one document for this purpose."

对这一方面更清楚的诠释可见 Fletcher Moulton 大法官在 Manks v. Whiteley (1912) 1 Ch. 735 先例中所说的:"... where several deeds form part of one transaction and are contemporaneously executed they have the same effect for all purposes such as are relevant to this case as if they were one deed. Each is executed on the faith of all the others being executed also and is intended to speak only as part of the one transaction, and if one is seeking to make equities apply to the parties they must be equities arising out of the transaction as a whole. It is not open to third parties to treat each one of them as a deed representing a separate and independent transaction for the purpose of claiming rights which would only accrue to them if the transaction represented by the selected deed was operative separately. In other words, the principles of equity deal with the substance of things, which in such a case is the whole transaction, and not with unrealities such as the hypothetical operation of one of the deeds by itself without the others."

在这种多过一个并且解释起来有相同地位的合约的交易,最重要就是在草拟时不要在不同的合约之间产生矛盾或重复。这也是中方当事人在交易中经常出现的问题,其中一种就是在原合约已经有了的条文,在补充协议或第二份合约中又以不同的写法出现。有时甚至不是一两条而是很多条都是这样的情况,这会在产生争议时法院/仲裁庭不确定应该以哪一份为准,又或是在时间相隔不远的第二份合约中双方到底是想作出“更改”(vary)还是有其他意图。

这种问题多不胜数,可以一个笔者处理的仲裁案件为例进行说明。该案涉及一个金额庞大的股权转让合约,其中在2005年6月10日的文书合约中,卖方承诺了“在买方支付款项及履行其他义务后5个工作日内将履行完毕股权转让”。但在该6月10日的合约中,买方其实除了支付外没有什么“其他义务”可言。倒是在7月16日他们之间又追加签署了一个合约,内中有许多新的“其他义务”加于买方。在7月16日的文书合约中,虽然有提到了较早时的几个合约(已经签订了4个合约之多),但只是说几个合约都具有同等法律效力。双方的争议是在卖方收到了股权买卖合约的款项后,一直没有把股权转让给买方,理由就是买方还没有完成“其他义务”,其他义务中还包括一个需要颇长时间来履行的义务。这在对几份合约作出协调的解释时产生了几种不同的争议。对买方有利的解释是在6月10日的合约确立时,双方根本还没有想到将来会有另一份7月16日的合约,所以解释有关条文/文字不应该把后来的合约新增加的义务也包括在内。而只有6月10日的合约才有条文/文字说明在尽了“其他义务”(其实是没有)后5个工作日内卖方就要转让股权,而这句话没有在7月16日的合约中出现。

出现这种矛盾与难以协调的情况,怎样解释也有点拿不准。如果认为7月16日的合约超越6月10日的合约,就表示买方必须要完成所有其他义务(包括需要较长时间来完成的一项义务),卖方才需要转让股权。这带来的后果是买方在支付了一笔昂贵的股权买卖合约的款项后也无法取得股份,这是否符合商业合理性与双方的订约意图?或者也可以协调地作出解释,认为两个合约之间没有这一方面的矛盾,所以不需要把7月16日的合约在有关条文/文字上超越6月10日的合约。这协调解释就是在6月10日的合约中“其他义务”(再强调是实际上没有)完成后,买方支付了有关的款项,卖方就必须在5日内转让股权。至于7月16日合约中新增加的其他义务,如果买方没有按时完成,这就构成违约并让卖方有索赔有关损失或其他的救济权利,但不影响股权按照6月10日的约定进行转让。可见,对一些复杂但有漏洞的合约进行协调解释并不是一件简单的事,毕竟仲裁庭之间也是有不同看法。

7.3　情况三:补充协议或第二份合约是想被合并在原合约

这种情况可举国际货物买卖合约如CIF或FOB在有关装货或卸货时间与滞期费问题经常会合并将来租船时才订立的租船合约(通常是程租合约但也会是“航次期租租约”[Time - Charter - Trip或简写为TCT])的规定。这是因为买卖合约在时间上是第一份合约,而有了买卖才会需要租船进行海上运输。所以租船合约是整个交易中的第二份合约,虽然两份合约涉及不同的订约方:买卖合约是卖方与买方,租船合约是CIF/CFR卖方或FOB买方作为承租人与船东。虽然两份合约肯定有部分内容不相关与不必协调/配合,但还是有不少内容是两份合约要配合与一致。如特定的装港与卸港或地区范围、销约期或Laycan、抵达装港或/与卸港的预先通知、有关货物与数量等。显然买卖合约中负责租船的一方(CIF/CFR 卖方或 FOB 买方)如果不想在装卸货时间与滞期费问题上被夹在中间,就会把将来订立的程租合约中约定的固定装卸货时间与滞期费合并在买卖合约内,以保证在这一方面是“背靠背”(back to back)。这对 CIF/CFR 卖方尤其重要,因为他不想要承担往往是较严重的卸港滞期费而令其在这一宗交易中减少货物出售赚取的利润。但他在订立买卖合约时,不会知道几个月后租船会在与船东的谈判中争取到怎样的固定装卸时间与滞期费条文。所以,最安全的做法就是在买卖合约合并将来程租合约的有关条文。在文字上,可举 OK Petroleum v. Vitol (1995) 2 Lloyd's Rep. 160 先例为例,该 CIF 买卖的有关条文是:“Demurrage: As per Charter Party rate, terms and conditions pro rata for part cargo.”

如果是这样的写法,那么有了争议应该也是清楚明了,应是以原合约为准,后来被合并的第二份合约如果与原合约产生矛盾的话就要靠边站或给予分量较低的考虑了。这与情况一(本章之 7.1 段)刚好是相反。

再多举一个更贴切的例子是保险与再保险合约,虽然通常是先有了保险合约才有再保险合约,但也会有特殊情况。在 HIH v. New Hampshire (2001) 2 Lloyd's Rep. 161 先例中,案情涉及一种很特殊的投资电影/电视拍摄的保险。由于再保险的安排非常重要,所以再保险合约是第一个合约,并以一条文说明合并将来承保投资者的保险合约:“this reinsurance is subject to all terms, clauses and conditions as original.”

正如 Rix 大法官所说的:“A word about chronology is apposite. The first of the three insurance documents in existence as a binding contract (or potentially binding contract) was not the original slip policy, but the reinsurance slip policy.... It is not unknown for reinsurance to precede insurance, especially where the former is vital to the latter.”

§8 合并其他文件

在一份合约中合并其他文件的做法很常见,如只是一份“重述要点”(fixture recap)也经常会出现大量的合并。这些合并会是一些“标准格式”(standard form)与“标准条文”(standard clause)、其他的合约(特别会是双方已经履行过的合约)、一些国际公约或有关的立法或特定规则等。合并主要的目的是节省时间,否则一份复杂的合约如一份期租合约往往会有超过 100 条以上的不同条文,如果不是通过合并而是要整篇内容在租约内重述出来,该份租约就不会只是一份文件而是一本书了。这可节录 Oliver 大法官在 Skips A/S Nordheim v. Syrian Petroleum Co Ltd (1984) Q.B. 599 先例中所说的:“The purpose of referential incorporation is not, or at least is not generally, to incorporate the intention of the parties to the contract whose clauses are incorporated but to incorporate the clauses themselves in order to avoid the necessity of writing them out verbatim. The meaning and effect of the incorporated clause is to be determined as a matter of construction of the contract into which is incorporated having regard to the terms of that contract."

例如"信用证"(letter of credit)普遍合并国际商会的UCP规则,但是不必把UCP的所有条文在信用证中重述。只要是有效与成功被合并的文件都会被视为全面引入有关的主合约,有了争议是需要把合并文件内的每一条文/文字都给予解释,不管订约方是否看过或是理解。

到底怎样才能有效与成功的合并另一份文件,这可介绍Rix大法官在The"Spiros C"(2000)2 Lloyd's Rep. 319先例中所说的:"The first rule relating to the incorporation of one document's terms into another is to construe the incorporating clause in order to decide on the width of the incorporation ... A second rule, however, is to read the incorporated wording into the host document *in extenso* in order to see if, in that setting, some parts of the wording nevertheless have to be rejected as inconsistent or insensible when read in their new context."(合并另一份文件第一条规则是解释主合约的合并条文看到底合并了什么。第二条规则是把合并进来的文字作为主合约的延伸,并看被合并的文字是否有部分因为与主合约不一致或说不通而需要排除。)

在Lewison大法官所著的《The Interpretation of Contracts》(第5版,2011年)一书第105页说:"The first question to be determined is what terms the parties have incorporated into their contract. The second question is what the incorporated terms mean in the context of the contract into which they have been incorporated. These two questions are to some extent interlinked."

8.1 合约成功合并其他文件的先决条件

一份合约要成功合并其他文件(不论是标准合约、双方履行过的合约还是特定规则等),是要求满足一个先决条件,就是所谓的"合理足够通知原则"(contractual doctrine of notice)。这原则是要肯定被通知的一方是合理与足够被告知有一些什么条文将被合并在双方的合约内:Parker v. South Eastern Railway Co (1876 - 77) LR2 CPD 416先例。这显然是公道,否则等于合并一些对方根本无法知道的条文,却令对方受到约束。这完全违反了达成合约的一些基本原则,如双方必须有订约意图与"想法一致"(meeting of minds)。当然,如果给了对方合理与足够的通知但对方不理会合并了什么条文,这是对方的问题。这不仅是合并,就算是明示条文对方也可以不看、不理会、不试图理解,闭着眼睛签字。这种情况在中国公司或企业中经常发生,但显然这不是一个可以不受到明示或被成功合并的条文的约束的抗辩理由。

这一合理足够通知的原则特别适用在订约双方谈判力量悬殊的情况,如一方是提供公共服务的企业(如地铁公司或公交公司)而另一方是普通市民。有关的案例有:Parker v. South Eastern Railway Co; Thompson v. London Midland and Scottish Rly Co (1930) 1 KB 41; Thornton v. Shoe Lame Parking Ltd (1971) 2 QB 163 等。经常发生的情况就是提供公共服务的企业会发出各种形式的票证,如泊车票、车票等,而票面上会合并企业的标准条文,如对服务的时间不准确造成的损失免责,赔偿不超过某一个金额等。同样的原则也适用在双方谈判力量势均力敌的商业案件:Circle Freight International Ltd v. Medeast Gulf Exports Ltd (1988) 2 Lloyd's Rep. 427(涉及在运输时货物在卡车上因司机疏忽失窃,负责安排运输的货代能否依赖被合并的货代协会标准条文中的免责条文); Interfoto v. Stilettp Visual Programmes (1989) QB 433(涉及幻灯片租借公司能否依赖被合并的逾期每张幻灯片每日缴 5 英镑的条文); Poseidon Freight Forwarding Co Ltd v. Davies Turner Southern Ltd (1996) 2 Lloyd's Rep. 388(涉及货代交错了货物,货代能否依赖合并的标准条文中的免责条文)等先例。

在许多包括上述提到的先例,有关合并其他文件的先决条件可简单介绍如下:

1. 有关合并的通知不需要把所有合并的条文写明,只需要清楚提到被合并的是什么就已经足够:Thompson v. London Midland and Scottish Rly Co 先例。这显然符合实际的要求,否则要求把所有合并条文写明或重复,也就否定了合并这一做法简单与快捷的目的。

(2)给对方的通知必须合理足够,而且必须是在合约订立之前。显然如果在合约订立后才通知对方,也就失去了意义。除非双方曾经有过交易,也就是可以"推断"(infer)双方从以前的交往中就应该知道对方有什么条件或条文:Olley v. Marlborough Court Ltd (1949) 1 KB 532;Circle Freight International Ltd v. Medeast Gulf Exports Ltd 等先例。在后一个先例,上诉庭推翻了第一审高院的判决,认为合并"货代协会"(Institute of Freight Forwarders 或简称 IFF)标准条文成功或有效,原因是双方曾经有过交易。此外双方都是有经验的商业人士,货方也知道货代的运输合约通常会合并标准条文。在该先例即使是货方自己不看这些标准条文才订立合约,也不受到影响。Taylor 大法官是这样说:

"Here, the parties were commercial companies. There had been a course of dealing in which at least 11 invoices had been sent giving notice that business was conducted on the IFF terms at a place on the document where it was plain to be seen. Mr. Zacaria(货方证人)knew that some terms applied. He knew that forwarding agents might impose terms which would frequently be standard terms and would sometimes or frequently deal with risk. He never sought to ask for or about the terms of business. The IFF conditions are not particularly onerous or unusual and, indeed, are in common use. In these circumstances, ... I consider that reasonable notice of the terms was given by the plaintiffs(货代). Putting it another way, I consider that the defendants'(货方)conduct in continuing the course of business after at least 11 notices of the terms and omitting to request a sight of them would have led and did lead the plaintiffs reasonably to believe the defendants accepted their terms. In those circumstances it is irrelevant that in fact Mr. Zacaria did not read the notices.

Accordingly, I consider that the learned judge erred in his conclusion on the first issue and Iwould hold that the IFF conditions were incorporated in his contract."

(3)如果合并的条文是"苛刻"(onerous)或"不正常"(unusual),要成功合并条件就会更加严格,通常适用"红手规则"(red hand rule),即要特意提醒对方注意。这一规则来自 Denning 勋爵在 Spurling v. Bradshaw (1956) 1 WLR 461 先例中所说:"... the more unreasonable a clause is, the greater the notice which must be given of it. Some clauses which I have seen would need to be printed in red ink on the face of the document with a red hand pointing to [them] before notice could be held to be sufficient."

(4)什么是足够的通知是根据每一个不同案件的事实来判定。其中 Bingham 大法官在 Interfoto v. Stilettp Visual Programmes 先例给出了一些重要的指引,即要在两个层面分析,一是合约的层面,二是事实的层面。合约层面的分析是指"有关合约的本质与双方当事人的特点"(nature of the transaction in question and the character of the parties to it)。这在 Circle Freight International Ltd v. Medeast Gulf Exports Ltd 先例就可以看出,如果双方都是有经验与水平的货方或货代,货方也已经多次要货代去托运他的货物并对货代的行业做法有一定的认识,这就满足了有关能否成功合并这一问题在合约层面的分析。至于事实层面的分析就要看个别案件的不同事实背景。也是在该先例可以看出一些事实背景,如双方已经进行了 11 次交易,合并的 IFF 标准条文订得十分合理并且在货代行业普遍被使用等。如果另一个看起来差不多的例子但事实背景有不同,如双方也进行了 11 次交易,但这些交易是好几年前并在那个年代 IFF 还没有作出这些标准条文,这事实背景就会带来可能不同的判决。总而言之,这方面的判断还是根据事实,而事实就根据双方提供的证据,至于法院或仲裁庭对事实的认定也会有一定程度的个人看法或裁量权,而且会是片面或"个别"(piecemeal)。

在这里一提的是"提单"(bills of lading)合并租约的做法,在合并后提单作为一份全面的海上运输货物合约,以利其作为物权凭证转让给第三人,也就是收货人。而收货人可以根据 1855 年英国《提单法》或 1992 年英国《海上运输法》以及中国《海商法》与承运人/船东产生合约关系,并在双方发生争议(如货损货差、卸货延误产生滞期费等)时根据有关的提单合约中的条文(包括印在提单上的条文、合并进来的租约条文与有关的立法如根据 1924/1969 年的《海牙规则》/《海牙－维斯比规则》)解决双方的争议。但由于现实中的做法,稍后在本章也会详论,可以看到作出合理足够的通知才能约束对方这一能够成功合并其他文件的先决条件在提单合并租约时无法做到。在绝大部分的情况下,第三人也是收货人受让了提单并与承运人/船东有了合约关系时,是不会见到合并了的租约。这份程租租约或 TCT 也经常没有一份完整与签署了的文件,只是好几份船东与承租人之间的往来谈判传真或电邮,最后有一份他们双方之间的重述要点。这样,根本做不到就有关合并了什么条文作出一个合理足够的通知。更加不会是根据"红手规则"(red hand rule)作出的通知,即使租约中有一些苛刻与不寻常的条文,并且这些条文是与这一个海上运输有直接关系。在承运人/船东没有作出特意提醒的通知下,可否成功合并租约? 在 The "Garbis" (1982) 2 Lloyd's Rep 283 先例,就出现这种情况。仲裁庭认定租约中有一条不寻常的条文,也就是承租人接受石脑油的货物有一定程度的污染。在高院,Goff 大法官认为一般的合并就已经足够,不存在需要特意提醒甚至是在提单内明示该不正常条文,说:"If a receiver of goods accepts a bill of lading in this form without ascertaining the terms of the charter – party, he must accept that his contract with the shipowner for the carriage of the goods, contained in or evidenced by the bill of lading, is subject to the charter – party terms relevant to the loading, carriage and discharge of the goods, **even though they may be unusual terms and may limit the shipowners' liability.**"(加黑部分是笔者的强调)

另一个贵族院的先例 The "Miramar" (1984) 2 Lloyd's Rep 129 涉及收货人是否要支付一笔十分庞大但与其没有太大关系的滞期费(这笔滞期费主要是承租人在较早修改卸港与有严重延误等所造成)。这显然要看提单有否成功合并了租约的滞期费条文,因为这条文显然与海上运输有关。租约的滞期费条文是说承租人要承担,没有说提单持有人要承担。而这种写法比比皆是,在提单成功合并了租约的情况下被接受的做法往往就是简单地把承租人"篡改"(manipulate)为提单持有人或收货人。但在 The "Miramar"先例,判是承运人/船东败诉,也就是租约没有被成功合并进提单,船东索赔滞期费是要找承租人而不是收货人。Diplock 勋爵所给的理由与"红手"规则背后的理由看来十分一致,说:"My Lords, I venture to assert that no business man who had not taken leave of his senses would intentionally enter into a contract which exposed him to a potential liability of this kind; and this, in itself, I find to be an overwhelming reason for not indulging in verbal manipulation of the actual contractual words used in the charter – party so as to give to them this effect when they are treated as incorporated in the bill of lading."

另一提的是,众所周知,提单通常是不会合并租约内的仲裁条文。但这倒不是因为"红手"规则背后没有特意提醒收货人的理由,而是因为仲裁条文不属于与海上货物运输或有关航次直接有关系的条文。这方面的先例有不少,如 The "Merak" (1964) 2 Lloyd's Rep 527; The "Annefield" (1971) 1 Lloyd's Rep 1(CA); The "Rena K" (1978) 1 Lloyd's Rep 545; The "Delos" (2001) 1 Lloyd's Rep 703 等。但这也难不倒精明的船东,因为在最常见的散货提单标准格式 Congenbill 1994,已经明示加进了条文说明租约的仲裁条文被合并在内:The "Ivan Zagubanski" (2002) 1 Lloyd's 106 先例与美国的 The "Sky Reefer" (1997) 63 USLW 4617; AMC 1817 先例等。这样,可怜的收货人(或他背后的代位保险人)就不能说是没有收到特意提醒的通知。但现实的问题是收货人在一个 CIF 或 CFR 买卖往往是想查也不容易查得到到底是怎样的租约条文与仲裁条文,因为船舶不是他租的,而是原卖方所租进的,而经过可能多次买卖后,最后的收货人往往不认识。

有关提单合并租约条文(包括仲裁条文)的问题会在稍后更详尽介绍,内容与上述所讲的有密切关系,但尽量希望不重复。英国商法多年来的发展已是十分现实与灵活,不存在一些僵化与不能变通的大原则。总之主要的目的就是发展一套与不断在改变的实务做法相配合的游戏规则,即使这样发展出来的一套商法或海商法是与一般能成功合并其他文件的普通法做法并不一致。

8.2　被合并文件与主合约起矛盾的情况

一种情况是被合并的标准格式合约或条文与主合约/重述要点起直接矛盾,这就存在要去协调解释或在它们之间作出取舍。显然,在主合约或重述要点明确提到的内容是双方看过,想过与谈判过才自己选用文字去约定,分量应比被合并的文件重。这样,如果在一份租船合约的重述要点中已经约定了香港仲裁,经常被合并的标准格式合约的金康 1994 中的第 19 条文印上的伦敦仲裁或 NYPE 46 中第 17 条文印上的纽约仲裁就要被漠视了。这一方面可去节录《Chitty on Contracts》(第 31 版,2012 年)一书 12 - 079 段如下:

"**Clauses incorporated by reference.** If clauses are incorporated by reference into a written agreement, and those clauses conflict with the clauses of the agreement, then, in the ordinary way, the clauses of the written agreement will prevail. Moreover, the incorporating provision may be so general or wide as to have the effect of incorporating more than can make any sense in the context of the agreement, in which case the surplus may be rejected as insensible or inconsistent, or disregarded as 'mere surplusage'. A term in a proposal for insurance which conflict with a term of the policy will be overridden by the term of the policy."

另可去节录 Parker 大法官在 Sabah Flour v. Comfez (1988) 2 Lloyd's Rep. 18 先例中所说的:

"... if an incorporated document contains provisions which conflict with provisions of the written document, then the terms of the written document would, in the ordinary way, prevail."

8.3　合并标准格式合约或条文

这种情况是经常在商业活动中出现,因为不少行业都有商会去制作一些标准格式合约以协助订约方的谈判,让大家不必从零开始。所以,在租船合约的"重述要点"(fixture recap),最后一句经常就会是"依照金康租约 1994"(as per Gencon Charterparty 1994)或"依照 NYPE 1946"(as per NYPE 1946)。这样,以一个程租合约为例,除了是在重述要点已经规定的内容(往往是一些"重要条文"[main terms]),例如是装港/卸港、销约期、装运的货物、运费、装卸时间与滞期费、适用法、仲裁等,其他没有去规定的内容就一概要去看金康租约 1994 的格式合约是如何规定的了。如果将来出了事故,在责任方面是否可去免责,重述要点经常没有针对,这样金康租约 1994 的第 2 条文就有一条非常保障船东的免责条文,它必须被给予解释。但如果重述要点中有针对双方责任的条文例如是在重要条文中包括了一条标准格式的"首要条文"(paramount clause)去把 1924 年《海牙规则》中承运人/船东责任例如是针对船舶在开航前的适航责任合并进来,这就会在货损货差的责任方面超越了金康租约 1994 的第 2 条文。

8.3.1 标准格式合约的两大类别

有关标准格式合约在本书多个段节有针对,特别是在第四章之第 2 段,这里不再重复。一般能见到的标准格式合约可分为两大类,第一类是如较早时介绍的金康租约 1994 或 NYPE 46,另有提单的 Congenbill、买卖合约 GAFTA/FOSFA 合约等;第二类是比较近期的一些带有垄断性的大公司或企业(如地铁、电力公司、供水公司、通讯公司等,但也可以包括早期班轮公司/公会的标准提单格式)单方面拟定一些标准格式合约,迫使对方(一般是相对比较弱小的消费者/市民)非得接受不可,否则就不交易。这两大类标准格式合约在 Schroeder Music Publishing Co Ltd v. Macaulay (1974) 1 W. L. R. 1308, HL 先例中 Diplock 勋爵说:

"Standard forms of contracts are of two kinds. The first, of very ancient origin, are those which set out the terms upon which mercantile transactions of common occurrence are to be carried out. Examples are bills of lading, charterparties, policies of insurance, contracts of sale in the commodity markets. The standard clauses in these contracts have been settled over the years by negotiation by representatives of the commercial interests involved and have been widely adopted because experience has shown that they facilitate the conduct of trade. Contracts of these kinds affect not only the actual parties to them but also others who may have a commercial interest in the transactions to which they relate, as buyers or sellers, charterers or shipowners, insurers or bankers. If fairness or reasonableness were relevant to their enforceability the fact that they are widely used by parties whose bargaining power is fairly matched would raise a strong presumption that their terms are fair and reasonable.

The same presumption, however, does not apply to the other kind of standard form of contract. This is of comparatively modern origin. It is the result of the concentration of particular kinds of business in relatively few hands. The ticket cases in the 19th century provide what are probably the first examples the terms of this kind of standard form of contract have not been the subject of negotiation between the parties to it, or approved by any organisation representing the interests of the weaker party. They have been dictated by that party whose bargaining power, either exercised alone or in conjunction with others providing similar goods or services, enables him to say: ‘If you want these goods or services at all, these are the only terms on which they are obtainable. Take it or leave it.’”

在上述第一类的标准格式合约,多年来几乎在航运与国际货物买卖的各式各样活动中都有一个或多个可供选择。选择哪一份标准格式或选择后将其修改至面目全非都是订约方自己的事,因为大原则是“订约自由”(freedom of contract)。在这些商业活动,法院通常认为订约双方有同等的水平与谈判力量保护自己,所以订约自由在这个领域充分受到尊重。双方有了争议,法院只是解释有关的合约条文/文字是什么意思,通常对有明示规定的内容是不考虑其合理与否。〔16〕 也有说法是针对这种标准格式合约,肯定性是非常重要,所以一有先例作出解释,就不应该轻易改动,即使是个别案件的背景/语境不一样。〔17〕 当然,标准格式合约也不代表订得公平合理,这还是要看拟定的商会是什么背景。例如,由承租人或货方组成的商会所拟定的租约标准格式难免偏向承租人去考虑问题。毕竟,就算将来在使用的时候有所修改,承租人也已经占了优势,更不必说船东还有各种原因而不要求修改(如看漏了、水平不够、订约时间仓促、谈判力量不够等)。如果法院对一些标准格式合约作出过一些不受欢迎的判决,唯一能作出的救济就是个别的订约方修改该标准格式合约,或有关的商会另作出一个新版本(但这需要时间拟定与推广)。

在一些种类的合约,如期租合约,因在现实中操作变得复杂而令较早前拟定的标准格式合约中的条文/文字变得远远不够。这种情况令标准格式合约被大量修改,订约双方“增加的条文”(rider clauses)在数量上甚至大大超出了标准格式合约中的条文。以 NYPE 46 为例,标准格式只有 28 条条文,而新一版的 NYPE 93 增加至 45 条条文。但即使是 NYPE 93 也远远不能满足现实中的要求,不少在今天见到的期租合约的增加条文动辄上百条,分别针对越来越复杂的国际航运大环境与个别贸易/航线。这导致一些经常租船的承租人在他们的谈判与重述要点中,除了一开始双方就谈妥的一些重要条文,其他的细节条文(有不少条文其实很重要)就合并一份他们熟悉与惯用的期租合约,所谓“租约范本”(proforma charter - party)。这一租约范本可能是以 NYPE 46 作为基础但作出了大量修改并增加了条文,其实再也不是一份标准格式合约,而是一份“一次过”(one - off)合约。即使承租人完全理解有新版的 NYPE 93(甚至将会有另一版的 NYPE 2015),他们也无意摒弃熟悉与惯用的租约范本。而新版的 NYPE 93 即使多了一些好的标准格式条文,但这些条文也很有可能已经以增加条文的形式包括在租约范本之内了。所以在某些比较自由的行业,即使有有关的商会/组织(如船东组织的 BIMCO)拟定一份更加完善的标准格式合约,推广并不容易且需要很长的时间。合并一份租约范本的做法也会出现在船东与承租人同

〔16〕 参见本书第一章之第 6 段。

〔17〕 参见本书第四章之第 2 段与第五章之第 3 段。

意以其不久前交易中用过的一份租约作为范本,毕竟这是双方曾经愿意接受与熟悉的文件。

上述提到的第二类垄断性标准格式合约,在今天已经受立法管制,如英国的1977年《不公平合约法》(《Unfair Contract Terms Act》)与1999年《消费者合约不公平条文条例》(《Unfair Terms in Consumer Contracts Regulations》),而在香港相对应的法律就是1984年的《Control of Exemption Clause Ordinance》。这些主要针对消费者的合约如果出了争议,法院通常不是咬文嚼字地解释合约条文/文字,而是看其合理与否,如果不合理就会"重写"(rewrite)合约。

8.3.2 有不同版本的标准格式合约是合并哪一份

由于世界变化越来越快,有关的商会/组织经常会根据实践中做法的改变而对标准格式合约做出修改与更新版本。这改变一方面是法律上的改变(如近期的恐怖主义、洗钱、贪污受贿、环境保护等重要议题都给租约或国际货物买卖合约带来了很多需要增加或修改的),另一方面是技术上的改变。这样,如果一份普遍被使用的标准格式合约为了追得上时代就需要经常更新。以买卖二手船舶普遍使用的挪威标准格式合约为例,现在就有1966年、1973年、1987年与1993年4份。现实中它们都有被使用,但它们的内容很不同。由于大原则是订约自由,所以订约双方合并时明确约定是1966年格式,解释起来就只能依照该格式。但还会有一个颇多见到的问题,就是如果订约方只约定合并挪威格式而没有提到是哪一个版本,如果仅是看双方已经在重述要点约定的主要条文/文字而不理会明示的挪威格式(说是因为没有规定哪一个版本而变得太不肯定从而不予理会),这就会违反解释合约的主要目的,即客观找出双方订约时的订约意图。双方既然有约定合并挪威格式,就已经显示出其意图是想合并。这样说是没有规定哪一个版本而变得不肯定与无效就不会是双方的订约意图。这方面还可能有一个变数,就是在订约后出了新版本并有许多重大修改。这样,在争议发生时到底是以订约时的版本为准或是也包括了新版本的一些修改就说不清了。

8.3.2.1 合并订约时生效的版本的大原则与例外

表面看来应该合并的文件为订约一天生效的版本,但社会科学总会有例外。这在Lewison大法官所著的《The Interpretation of Contracts》(第5版,2011年)一书第109页有说到这方面的问题:"In some cases the parties intend to incorporate standard terms which are subject to alteration from time to time (for example the Standard Conditions of Sale or a standard freight scale). If the contract is silent as to the possibility of amendment the question may arise as to which version of the terms should be taken to have been incorporated. . . . "

如果合约没有明示规定合并的版本是哪一个,那应该判定是订约时生效的版本。但现实中已经有很多合并条文会明示规定合并也包括将来会对此文件作出的修改,这特别是针对一些经常会被修改的标准格式合约或条文,如一些仲裁机构的仲裁规则。但也会有一些情况没有明示规定,却可以推断合并的条文包括将来适用时可能修改的版本,如针对一套标准运费计算表,即油轮的"世界标准"(Worldscale)。在 The "Bungamwar" (1978) 1 Lloyd's Rep. 263 先例,该案情涉及租约中双方约定的是世界标准的 92.5%,这到底相等于多少美元要根据该世界标准计算出来(有关世界标准的详尽介绍,请参阅笔者的《程租合约》一书第 273 ~ 277 页)。在订约时,世界标准的版本是 1973 年。但到了履行有关航次时,刚刚有了 1975 年 1 月份的新版本。由于通货膨胀,燃油价格上涨等各种原因,1973 年版本的 92.5% 转为美元显然是在金额上大大比不上 1975 年的新版本,在相关的 4 个航次中,共相差 250 万美元。有关的租约合并条文是第 1 条的:"in accordance with the rate provided for by the Worldscale as amended at 92.5%"。另第 33 条的:"All terms and conditions of World-scale Tanker nominal freight scale to apply to this Charterparty."

Goff 大法官判是租约中显示出来的双方的订约意图是以最新版本为准,因为第 1 条文有"as amended"两个字。笔者只说这是一个可能的例外,但也可能不是例外,因为如果第 1 条文少了这两个字就有危险被法院解释是以订约时的版本(1973 年)为准。

有同样说法是在澳大利亚联邦法院的 Ford Motor Company of Australia Ltd v Arrowcrest Group Pty Ltd (2002) FCA 156 先例,Finkelstein 大法官说:"...*prima facie* a reference to standard terms and conditions is a reference to the terms or conditions current at the date of the contract... There will be occasions when the incorporation includes amendments made from time to time ... usually this will only occur when the amendments are of a procedural, and not a substantive, type."

8.3.2.2 合并订约后的程序或实体上的修改

上述 Ford Motor Company of Australia Ltd v. Arrowcrest Group Pty Ltd (2002) FCA 156 先例的第二句话是说法院或仲裁庭会有情况判是合并条文包括了被合并文件在订约后将来可能做出的修改,但这只能针对"程序上"(procedural)的修改而不能是"实体上"(substantive)的修改。这里将程序与实体做出不同对待的原因是,如果包括实体上的修改就会造成很大的不公道。这正如立法作出实体上的修改并追溯适用在立法前发生的行为,就会令正在进行的本来是合法或法律上正确的行为,变为不合法或不正确的。这显然在法治社会是不能被接受,立法如果作出实体上的修改只能适用在其生效以后的行为,可以说立法的追溯权不能针对实质性的权利与义务。相反,如果立法是针对程序上的问题,就可去追溯:The "Boucraa" (1994) 1 Lloyd's Rep. 251。例如,法院在程序上有了一个重大的司法改革,就很难只是新的案件才适用新的规则,而针对还没有审理完毕的案件还是以旧的一套司法程序来处理。

这可节录在 Bunge v Kruse (1979) 1 Lloyd's Rep 279 先例中,Brandon 大法官说到有关程序与实体的修改有不同的看待:"There is, as it seems to me, a difference between a clause incorporating a code containing mainly substantive provisions, i. e. provisions defining or affecting the substantive rights of the parties, on the one hand, and a clause incorporating a code containing mainly procedural provisions, i. e. provisions laying down the procedure to be followed in the arbitration of disputes, on the other hand. In the case of the first kind of clause, of which the provision in the present contract incorporating GAFTA form 100 is an example, it is clear that the code incorporated is that contained in form 100 as existing and in force at the date of the contract. In the case of the second kind of clause, of which cl. 30(a) of GAFTA 100 incorporating the arbitration rules in GAFTA 125 is an example, the prima facie inference, I think, is that the code incorporated is that in force when the time for invoking and acting on the procedural provisions concerned arises."

如果订约方合并一个非强制性的立法或政府的命令,针对订约后有立法或政府命令的改变也是适用同样的道理。但这也并不是绝对,要在个别案件根据有关合约的条文/文字与合约的本质与订约时的环境作出解释。在 Brewers' Company v. Viewplan plc (1989) 2 E. G. L. R. 133 先例,有关的房屋租赁合约合并了 Class III of the Town and Country Planning (Use Classes) Order 1972,之后该政府命令被 Class III of the Town and Country Planning (Use Classes) Order 1987 取代。法院判是合约合并的是 1972 年的立法,不受后来修改的影响。

注意 1979 年 1 月 1 日生效的英国《Interpretation Act 1978》在这一方面有了规定:"Section 17 (2) Where an Act repeals and re – enacts, with or without modification, a previous enactment then, unless the contrary intention appears, —(a) any reference in any other enactment to the enactments so repealed shall be construed as a reference to the provision re – enacted; Section 23 (3) . . . the reference to any other enactment includes any deed or other instrument or document."

8.3.2.3 合并条文没有明示规定但被裁定订约后仲裁规则的修改也被合并的先例

经常会有一些案件涉及仲裁条文合并了过时的仲裁机构规则(这只是针对程序,与实体无关),但经常被解释为新的或修改过的仲裁规则适用在合并条文,而不是否定仲裁条文。这背后原因可节录在 Bunge v Kruse (1979) 1 Lloyd's Rep 279 先例,Brandon 大法官的解释说:"In support of this view it can be said that the other view could lead to considerable difficulties. Procedural provisions can easily become out of date and so become incapable of implementation. For instance, procedural rules might provide for documents to be sent to, or hearings to take place at, an address which later ceased to be appropriate or even to exist; or for members of a tribunal to possess a qualification, or to be appointed by a person holding an office, which is subsequently abolished. In either case amendment of the procedural rules concerned would be necessary to make them workable, and, if a clause incorporating such rules were not construed as incorporating them in their subsequently amended form, the operation of the clause might well be frustrated."这种先例在笔者的《仲裁法——从1996年英国仲裁法到国际商务仲裁》一书第一章之2.12段也有介绍。

另在 Offshore International S. A. v. Banco Central S. A. (1976) 2 Lloyd's Rep. 402先例,涉及仲裁条文合并了"国际商会"(ICC International Court of Arbitration)仲裁规则,这规则后来被不断修改,法院判是以适用时的最新版本为准。

这方面的先例还有 Smith v. South Wales Switchgear Ltd (1978) 1 W. L. R. 165 与 Brett v. Brett Essex Golf Club Ltd (1986) 1 E. G. L. R. 154, CA 等。

8.3.3 合并一份不存在的标准格式合约或条文

在这一种情况下,有两种做法。第一种是有接近的标准格式合约就可以把订约双方视为实际上就是想合并该接近的标准格式合约,只是文字上表达错了,需要在文书上作出改变。这等于本书第三章之13.2段所讲的"明显错误"(obvious mistake)。第二种是根本没有任何接近的标准格式合约,这就只能漠视这一合并了。有关的先例可看 Modern Building Wales Ltd v. Limmer and Trinidad Ltd (1975) 1 W. L. R. 1281。

这一方面的说法,也在《仲裁法—从1996年英国仲裁法到国际商务仲裁》一书第一章2.11段有详论。它是针对仲裁条文明示了一个不存在的仲裁机构,但大道理相同。

8.4 合并其他合约

这与本章之8.3段所针对内容不同的地方就是它合并的并非一个订约双方都熟悉的标准格式合约/条文、仲裁机构的仲裁规则与立法/政府命令,而是合并另一份可能双方完全不熟悉的其他合约。这种合并的危险之处是如果双方同意合并,被合并的其他合约是对双方有同样的法律约束效力,不论双方或其中一方是否了解或者熟悉该被合并的其他合约。

8.4.1 合并不熟悉的其他合约的危险

可以租船合约经常会出现的情况为例阐述合并一份无关合约的危险之处。在租船合约,双方在"重述要点"(fixture recap)中合并双方在很久以前曾经订立过的租约,甚至会有情况是合并其中一方订约方与第三人订立过的租约。这里的危险是,双方或其中一方如果不熟悉该被合并的其他合约,就很容易看漏眼。现实中很少人会小心地把合并的其他合约(已经在较早提到过一份期租合约可能有上百条条文)从头到尾看一遍,即使他并不熟悉该份合约。另一个现实是,即使不熟悉其他合约的一方很努力与小心的从头看到尾,也往往看不懂,看了也白看。这种危险可举一个真实例子,在杨大明先生所著的《期租合同》一书第十一篇之11.2.13.2段有提到,[18]节录如下:

---

〔18〕 该仲裁也涉及合约变更的争议,可看本书第三章之13.1.12段有进一步的解释。

"还有一个伦敦仲裁,[19]也是关于前往美湾的新奥尔良装货的期租案件。这个期租是个循环航次(round voyage),在中国港口交船与还船。交船后装了一票货物从中国到南美。货物卸清之后承租人命令船舶开往新奥尔良港装散粮回中国,船长接受了指示。但船舶到了新奥尔良港外,这个希腊船东开始为难承租人。他依据的理由是双方已签订的租约里有一个承租人没有留意到的漏洞说不准船舶前往美国。估计这一个漏洞是船东埋下的'地雷',所以时机一到,船东马上就跳出来'引爆'。原来本租约谈判所使用的是以前另一艘船舶的租约范本(proforma),上面的一条附加条款未被删除掉或作出逻辑性地修改,而这一附加条款仅仅针对另一艘船舶,而条款题目与内容是针对油污责任,后面有短短一行文字说'不允许前往美国',估计是美国在1990年的《油污法》下的责任严格,但以前的租约估计没有计划去美国,所以加上这一行文字就省了要在该条款针对美国的油污责任。但是在这个循环航次租约里,去美国是非常重要的,在租约重述要点(fixture recap)的文件中根本没有在贸易区除外条款将美国排除。而且在谈判时,也曾提过去美国装货回中国,所以是一个循环航次的租约。希腊船东盯着这个小小的'失误'在一条针对油污责任的条款,拒绝驶入新奥尔良,要求承租人多付15万美元才允许'修改'租约而驶入。尽管后来承租人答应让步付一点钱以息事宁人,但这个"好意"换来更大的剥削与压力,这15万美元被船东随即再提高至25万美元。这案件在后来伦敦仲裁中判承租人胜诉。但仲裁员认为双方签定了租约,就不能漠视'不允许前往美国'的一句,即使它不在贸易区除外条款而是在油污责任条款出现。虽然租约签错之处仍可变更(rectify),但要证明双方到底同意了什么与证明记录在签署的租约中的内容在文书上记录错了却并非易事。这在本案件中更是无法证明双方同意过去美国,顶多只能证明承租人意图从美湾装货回中国,但合同一方的意图并非是双方的约定。但承租人最终能够胜诉,只是依赖了弃权与禁止翻供。这是针对船东在南美卸完货被命令开航去新奥尔良港装散粮,船东照办,然后到了新奥尔兰港外才刁难承租人。如果船东一收到承租人的命令时就提出来,承租人至少还有时间另作安排调动,例如以分租把该船舶改在南美装粮回日本,另去美湾租入其他船舶装运原来备妥的一批散粮去中国等。"

8.4.2 租约提单合并租约条文

有关这一问题已经简单在本章8.1段有提到,以下作出更详尽的介绍。在航运业中最常见的合并其他合约的情况就是"租约提单"(charter - party bill,这种提单普遍被适用在商品/大宗货的运输)合并有关的租约,笔者虽未做过统计,但相信有关合并的案例中以这种案件数量最多。买卖双方订立买卖合约后就需要找船舶在付运期内进行海上运输,第一步先是订一个租约(程租合约或TCT),承租人会是FOB买方或是CIF卖方。有了一个租约,船东才会把船舶开去装港装货。在装完货物后,往往根据当地的有关法律(如中国的《海商法》或英国的《海上货物运输法》),发货人

---

[19] 伦敦仲裁 *The Aka* 10.2.1995(没有报道)。

有权要求船东签发一套提单。这样,如果这一套提单被转让与交出给收货人,就不纯粹只是一份船上货物的收据,而是根据立法提升成为一份船东/承运人与收货人之间的海上运输合约。既然是一份合约,就需要在提单内有一套在海上运输中约定双方权利与责任/义务的条文/内容。现实中极少情况是提单只是作为一份收据,而绝大部分的情况下,提单都会被转让/转卖。提单一去到第三人的手中,就会根据各国的《提单法》或中国的《海商法》被提升为一份运输合约,对船东/承运人与作为提单持有人的收货人有法律约束力。所以出于现实的必要,提单中必需要有一份完整的海上运输合约所需的条文/内容针对有关航次履行中双方的权利与责任/义务。

但由于在签发提单时经常已经有一份程租租约的存在,该租约应该是针对有关航次特别是去卸港卸货会发生的各种事情,如航次中发生共同海损或救助、卸港/卸货泊位、运费的支付、固定卸货时间与滞期费、谁负责卸货、留置货物的权利、船东对货物的责任与免责等。考虑到提单与租约都是针对同一个航次,所以船东与货方不会想在两份运输合约中出现不同的规定而令船东无所适从或影响船东事后向承租人要求补偿的行动。所以一个简单与现实的做法就是在签发提单时干脆把较早时的程租租约的有关条文合并进提单。正如稍早在本章之第8段所说有效与成功的合并是不必把合并的条文逐条重述,做法上就是在提单的表面加上一句,如:"... all the terms, conditions, clauses and exceptions of the Charter Party are incorporated herewith."

8.4.2.1 对提单合并租约相对严格的原因

进一步介绍提单合并租约所带来的困难与其独特的法律地位之前,需要再简单阐述带来这种合并的特殊之处的商业合理性与背景/语境。其中提单合并租约与其他合约的合并情况大不相同体现在:

1. 提单作为物权凭证可令许多无辜第三人作出庞大金额的支付,如银行会以提单作为质押借出一大笔钱或在信用证下作出支付给受益人,无辜买方会以提单进行国际货物买卖等。

2. 提单被转让后在提单持有人或收货人的手中,根据立法(《提单法》)而被提升为一份运输合约,约束船东/承运人与作为提单持有人的收货人。这本就是一个独特的做法,根本不需要有其他合约成立必须有的一些先决条件与过程,如"要约"(offer)、"接受"(acceptance)、"想法一致"(meeting of minds)与或长或短的谈判过程等。也可以说提单作为合约是法律强制的"合约更替"(novation of contract)的结果。这样作为合约方的收货人在现实中经常不知道提单到底合并了什么条文/文字也就不足为奇了。除非是提单对租约的合并也必须满足本章之8.1段提到的有效合并的先决条件,即"合理足够通知原则"(contractual doctrine of notice)。也就是要肯定被通知的一方(提单持有人/收货人)是合理与足够被船东/承运人告知有一些什么条文/文字被合并在提单内。

3. 但看来合理足够通知原则在提单的操作中是完全做不到的,原因有一点复杂,有关的做法与背景部分已经在本章之8.1段提到。其中涉及程租租约或TCT,尤其是短航次的海上运输,经常不会有一份完整与签署了的文件。即使准备一份完整与签署的租约,在国际层面往往就需要在订约后几个星期才能做到,时间上是来不及在签发提单时一并附上。所以,所谓的租约至多是一份电文/电邮中船东与承租人之间的"重述要点"(fixture recap)。另一个大问题是即使有一份签署的租约,但同一航次甚至是同一票货往往会出多份提单,这样只有一份签署的租约应附在哪一份提单?毕竟信用证的结汇必须有正本文件,所以如果只有签署一份甚至两份租约还是不够用。

4. 即使在一个短航次,也会涉及"租约链"(charter – party chain),也就是原船东把船舶出租给"二船东"(disponent owner),二船东再转租给三船东,之后经过多次的转租后才轮到装运有关货物的程租或TCT。这表示有好几份租约(部分签署但部分只是重述要点的一份电文)涉及在内,其中有一两份会是比较配合有关的航次,但也会有其他的租约完全不配合,如光租租约或长期的期租合约。而船舶在订立了有关航次的程租租约或TCT后,往往很快就会去装港装货,也往往很快就会装完货并需要签发提单。而签发的提单不像是"班轮提单"(liner bills of lading),租约提单合并的往往就是根据标准格式提单中的一条印本合并条文,这印本条文中也通常有一个空格填上合并租约的日期。但很少会有准备提单让船长签字的发货人会填上合并租约的日期,因为他往往也不知道,除非他就是承租人,这方面稍后会进一步介绍。

5. 商品买卖也是好像租约链一样,经常涉及"买卖链"(chain sales)。这就会带来十分复杂与千变万化的情况。首先针对准备一份提单让船长签字的"发货人"(shippers)就没有一个明确的定义。在英国的普通法或英国的立法(不论是1855年英国《提单法》或后来的替代立法1992年英国《海上运输法》)都没有对发货人有任何定义。而发货人的定义只能在其他的一些立法或国际公约中找到一些指引,如在英国的1997年《Merchant Shipping (Carriage of Cargoes) Regulation》,对于发货人的定义说:"a 'shipper' is any person who whether as principal or agent for another, consigns goods for carriage by sea."在《汉堡规则》之Article 1.3给的定义是:"shipper means any person by whom or in whose name or on whose behalf the goods are actually delivered to the carrier in relation to the contract of carriage by sea."另在《鹿特丹规则》之Article 1.8给的定义是:"'Shipper' means a person that enters into a contract of carriage with a carrier."

6. 在国际货物买卖中签发提单的做法十分复杂与千变万化,经常会出现提单作为海上运输合约的双方当事人是谁也不清楚与肯定的情况。"承运人"(carrier)固然不肯定,可能是原船东,也可能是承租人。"发货人"(shipper)也同样不肯定,举一个例子,虽然可以说,在大部分的情况下交付货物给船舶付运与托管,并取得一份"大副收据"(mate's receipt)的"委托人"(bailor)就会是提单中印就的发货人,但这也不绝对,因为现实中会有五花八门的做法如将发货人一栏写上FOB买卖中买方的名字，而令提单中印就的发货人并不是“真正发货人”（true shipper）。这样一来，由于提单既是一份收据，也是一份海上运输合约，所以在装港船东交出提单有两方面要兼顾：（1）交出给大副收据的持有人，也就是委托人；（2）根据立法，交出给提单列明的发货人。虽然大部分情况都是同一位，但如果不是，在 Aikens 大法官所著的《Bills of Lading》（2006 年）一书之 3.116 段是说：“Where they are not it will be necessary to examine the facts to ascertain who is entitled to possession of the goods at the time the bill of lading is issued, which is itself likely to turn on whether the shipper has retained a right of disposal of the goods. The carrier will be entitled to issue the bill to the party named as a shipper in the absence of any indication to the contrary.”

7. 在现实中，发货人（不论他是否是委托人）准备一份租约提单让船长签发，通常不知道也不关心合并的是租约链中的哪一份租约。他们往往不涉及租船而不会知道详情，即使是 CIF/CFR 买卖的发货人，他有可能是承租人，但更多的情况是租进船舶由其他人（如一家航运公司或“经营人”[operator]）代劳。反正不是发货人自己干的活，他就不会马上知道几天前租进船舶的租约或重述要点是哪一天。他作为 CIF/CFR 卖方要查也查得到，但他不会关心。因为一份租约提单的合并条文即使没有在空格填上合并租约的日子，也被视为有效与可以在信用证结汇。而签发一份租约提单的船长或他的代理人，往往唯一熟悉的租约就是船东在第一份订立的“原合约”（head charter－party），这会是一份光租租约或长期期租合约。他会理解船舶肯定被转租，但他不会知道转租了多少次与其他细节，更加不会知道有关这一航次的程租合约或 TCT，也是最适合被合并进提单。

8. 这里也可以一提的是，法律对这一多年来国际商品买卖中不需要将提单合并的租约递交给提单持有人/收货人的做法没有肯定的说法，这可看《Benjamin's Sale of Goods》（第 8 版，2010 年）一书之 19－041 段。在 Finska Cellulosaforeningen v Westfield Paper Co Ltd（1940）1 All ER 473 先例，法院判是 CIF/CFR 卖方没有责任把提单合并的租约交给买方检查。虽然《Benjamin's Sale of Goods》一书提到这一先例时，指出它的案情是因为双方以前有过交易所以买方知道合并的租约条文是什么。该权威书籍接下去说：“The case leaves open the possibility that, but for such circumstances, the seller would have been obliged to tender the charterparty. Accordingly, a tender of bills of lading showing the destination to be 'as per charterparty' was held to be bad as it did not enable the buyer to tell from the face of the bills whether they contained or evidence a contract of carriage to the c. i. f. destination.[20] The principle appears to be that the charterparty must be tendered where this is necessary to enable the buyer to tell whether the tendered documents are in accordance with the requirements of the contract of sale. Where this is not necessary, the charterparty need not be tendered e-

[20] SIAT di dal Ferro v Tradax Overseas SA（1980）1 Lloyd's Rep 53 先例。

ven though it is referred to in the bill of lading. However, a requirement to tender the charterparty would cause considerable inconvenience where several bills of lading which had been issued under a single charterparty were transferred to different buyers."

9. 可以对以上的介绍总结,在大部分情况下提单持有人/收货人想要知道提单中合并的租约的条文/文字并不容易。提单持有人唯一得到的通知就是一条印本的合并条文,但该印本条文往往连合并的租约的签订日期也不知道,更不用说是租约的内容。可以说在其他合约,很难接受这是一个有效的合并且已经满足了本章8.1段所介绍的先决条件,也就是合理与足够向对方作出通知。但由于提单的特殊性,包括这是一个立法强制的合约关系,就有了一套通过无数海事先例所建立起来的合并的说法。而其中一个说法就是对提单合并租约条文/内容特别严格。这里的原因可节录Bingham大法官在The "Federal Bulker" (1989) 1 Lloyd's Rep 103, CA先例所说的,如下:"Generally speaking, the English law of contract has taken a benevolent view of the use of general words to incorporate by reference standard terms to be found elsewhere. But in the present field a different, and stricter, rule has developed, especially where the incorporation of arbitration clause is concerned. The reason no doubt is that a bill of lading is a negotiable commercial instrument and may come into the hands of a foreign party with no knowledge and no ready means of knowledge of the terms of the charter-party. The cases show that a strict test of incorporation having, for better or worse, been laid down, the Courts have in general defended this rule with some tenacity in the interests of commercial certainty."

8.4.2.2 提单合并的只能是与货物运输有直接关系的内容

已经有许多案例在解释提单中这一条合并条文时都是将其局限为只能有效地合并有关航次与货物运输有直接关系的条文/文字。早在Gullischen v Stewart (1884) 13 QBD 317先例,Bowen大法官说:"The bill of lading is a document regulating the rights and liabilities of the consignee; only those clause of the charterparty which are consistent with its character as a bill of lading are incorporated in it."

另在Thomas v Portsea (1912) AC 1先例,Atkinson勋爵说:"I think it would be a sound rule of construction to adopt that when it is sought to introduce into a document like a bill of lading—a negotiable instrument—a clause such as this arbitration clause, not germane to the receipt, carriage, or delivery of the cargo or the payment of freight,—the proper subject-matters with which the bill of lading is conversant,—this should be done by distinct and specific words, and not by such general words as those written in the margin of the bill of lading in this case."

比较近期可介绍The "Merak" (1964) 2 Lloyd's Rep. 527先例,上诉庭的Russell大法官说:

"I think a true view of (Thomas v Portsea先例) is that it shows that **clauses which**

are directly germane to shipment, carriage and delivery may be incorporated by general words though the fact that they are found in a charter – party may involve a degree of verbal manipulation to fit exactly a bill of lading; but that where there is a clause whose subject – matter is not thus directly germane, such as an arbitration clause, it is not permissible to construe general words of incorporation as extending to a clause which does not in terms relate to a bill of lading."(加黑部分是笔者的强调)

另在 The "Annefield" (1971) 1 Lloyd's Rep. 1 先例,提单的合并条文是:"... all the terms, conditions and exceptions of [the] Charter Party, including the negligence clause, are incorporated herewith."上诉庭仍是判能被合并的只是租约中与货物运输有直接关系的条文/内容,而租约中的仲裁条文就不包括在内。Denning 勋爵在该案例中判:"that only a clause directly germane to the subject – matter of the bill of lading can be incorporated into the bill of lading contract..."

所以,无论提单中合并条文的文字怎样广泛,如好像 The "Annefield"先例的"所有"(all)一词,或甚至是 The "Delos" (2001) 1 Lloyd's Rep 703 先例的"all terms whatsoever",都不能够把租约的条文/文字全部合并进来。如果租约的仲裁或管辖权条文明确规定所有签发的提单必须包括这一条文也不起作用,在 The "Siboti" (2003) 2 Lloyd's Rep 364 先例就有租约条文说明:"All bills of lading under this Charter Party shall incorporate this exclusive dispute resolution clause..."

不能根据提单中一般合并条文作出有效的合并就是一些所谓的"附带"(collateral)或"附属"(ancillary)租约条文,这包括仲裁条文或管辖权条文。这一方面的英国先例多不胜数,如 Hamilton & Co. v. Mackie & Sons (1889) 5 T. L. R. 677;T. W. Thomas v. Portsea; The "Njegos" (1935) 53 Lloyd's Rep 286; The "Merak"; The "Phonizien" (1966) 1 Lloyd's Rep. 150; The "Annefield"; The "Rena K" (1978) 1 Lloyd's Rep. 545; The "SLS Everest" (1981) 2 Lloyd's Rep. 389; The "Varenna" (1983) 2 Lloyd's Rep. 592; The "Nai Matteini" (1988) 1 Lloyd's Rep. 452; The "Heidberg" (1994) 2 Lloyd's Rep. 287; The "Nerano" (1996) 1 Lloyd's Rep 1; The "Delos"; The "Siboti"(针对一条排外的管辖权条文); The "Epsilon Rosa" (2003) 2 Lloyd's Rep 509; The "Channel Ranger" (2014) 1 Lloyd's Rep 337 等。这方面的问题会后详。

8.4.2.3 提单合并的只能是文书租约条文

在本章之8.1 段与8.4.2.1 段提到,短航次的程租合约往往没有一份签署了的租约而只是一份重述要点甚至更可能只是双方的几封电文往来。如果提单有效合并了相关的程租合约,但双方事后对到底合并了什么条文/文字(如卸货时间的计算或滞期费的金额)有争议,就会需要看租约关于这一特定的航次到底有什么内容。如果没有一份正式签署的租约(也极有可能),就会有可能程租合约属于是部分文书部分口头[21]的情况。针对这方面已经有先例判是提单合并的条文只能是文书租约条文,不能是口头租约条文:The "Heidberg" (1994) 2 Lloyd's Rep. 287 先例。在之后的 The "Epsilon Rosa" (2003) 2 Lloyd's Rep 509 先例,上诉庭也同意 The "Heidberg"先例的判法,Tuckey 大法官同时针对这两个先例作出了以下解释说:"In The 'Heidberg' brokers had agreed the terms of a charter orally. The recap telex erroneously referred to standard terms which provided for arbitration in Paris, whereas the standard terms orally agreed provided for London arbitration. The bill of lading which was in much the same form as the Congenbill incorporated the terms of 'the charter – party dated (blank)'. Judge Diamond held that these words did not incorporate a charter agreed orally. They referred to a charter – party which had been reduced to writing. His reasons for this conclusion include the need for terms incorporated by reference to be readily ascertainable. Extensive investigation as to the undocumented contractual arrangements of third parties would introduce considerable uncertainty. I agree, but do not accept Mr. Dunning's submission that reference to a recap telex would produce similar uncertainty. Take the instant case: a quick look at the telex and the accompanying terms would have left the reader in no doubt that the charter required London arbitration. The same applies to the other important terms of the contract. Although there was an inconsistency between the two forms of cl. 47 the parties clearly expressed their choice of London arbitration from which it would follow that the expanded form with its reference to the LMAA rules was to apply. Arbitration in London subject to GMAA rules would make no sense."

在笔者看来,虽然反正租约条文/文字不论是文书或口头协议,提单持有人或收货人在争议前都不会清楚,但排除口头协议也有道理。因为考虑到将来提单有争议时,如果要看口头协议取证就会很困难,毕竟订立租约与涉及口头协议的当事人根本会是与提单毫无关系,向他取证也会很困难。

8.4.2.4 提单合并的租约条文的其他局限

提单合并租约条文还有其他局限,首先是被合并的租约条文/文字不能与提单内容有冲突/矛盾。这一点倒是与任何其他合约的合并道理一样,而针对提单这种情况也不会是太多,因为提单本身没有太多条文。但这种情况还是有可能发生,如租约的卸港与提单的规定并不一样:SIAT di dal Ferro v. Tradax Overseas SA (1980) 1 Lloyd's Rep 53 先例。有关这一点的权威性说法,可节录上诉庭的 Brett M. R. 大法官在 Gardner v. Trechmann (1884) 15 QBD 154 先例中说:"... those clauses of the charterparty cannot be brought in which would alter the express stipulation in the bill of lading."

另是相比其他合约的合并,提单合并租约条文/文字经常需要作出大量的(verbal

---

〔21〕 本章之第 13 段。

manipulation)。这包括租约条文的"承租人"、"船东"、"租约"等,都需要为"提单持有人"、"承运人"、"提单"等。这可对合并文件作出说法的先例有不少,包括 The "Saxon Star" (1958) 1 Lloyd's Rep. 73; The "Merak" (1964) 2 Lloyd's Rep. 527; The "Annefield" (1971) 1 Lloyd's Rep. 1 等先例。

在 The "Annefield"先例,Denning 勋爵说:"I would follow the test laid down by Lord Justice Russell in The Merak, [1965] P., at p. 260; [1964] 2 Lloyd's Rep., at p. 537, but I would adapt it slightly. I would say that a clause which is directly germane to the subject - matter of the bill of lading (that is, to the shipment, carriage and delivery of goods) can and should be incorporated into the bill of lading contract, even though it may involve a degree of manipulation of the words in order to fit exactly the bill of lading."

提单合并可以对租约条文作出的理由是这是双方的订约意图,假设承运人与发货人/收货人的订约意图。但在一些比较罕见的情况下,如果法院/仲裁庭认为作出后会带来客观看来十分不合理的结果,提单双方(特别是提单持有人/收货人)不可能会有这种订约意图(毕竟解释任何涉及合约关系的文件都需要假设双方订约意图),那么即使提单合并条文与一般租约提单的印本条文一致,用字也十分广泛,法院/仲裁庭也会拒绝作出篡改导致有关的租约条文不能有效合并。这种十分不合理的情况不能成功合并也可以从另外一个角度看,就是如果解释被合并租约条文的提单会导致对提单持有人/收货人带来"商业上荒谬的结果"(commercial absurdity),是可以漠视。[22] 这也属于提单合并租约条文/文字的一个特殊之处,可举两个先例,如下:

1. The "Miramar" (1984) 2 Lloyd's Rep. 129 是一个重要贵族院先例,已经在本章之 8.1 段有提到,有关船舶是装了一船柴油从新加坡去斯里兰卡,收货人只有一个。由于承租人在较早改卸港且有严重延误,产生了 25 万美元的滞期费。有关的提单是以以下的合并条文合并租约条文:"This ship is carried under and pursuant to the terms of the Charterparty dated May 19, 1980, between [the plaintiff] and S. E. A Petrochem Ltd ... Charterer and all the terms whatsoever of the said charter ... apply to and govern the rights of the parties concerned in this shipment."结果是船东以留置货物逼收货人给一个担保,但最高金额只是 15 万美元。之后双方去法院诉讼,其中最关键的一个争议是收货人是否要对提单负上个人合约责任。如果是,收货人就不只是支付 15 万美元,而是全部的滞期费了,只要他还没有个人破产。在高院,上诉庭与贵族院都判是收货人并没有在提单下的个人合约责任,虽然表面看来卸港的滞期费条文明显是与该票货物付运有直接关系。Diplock 勋爵认为租约下的滞期费责任如果可以合并在提单内会带来很多问题,如收货人在接受提单合约的同时接受了不可预

〔22〕 这可看本书第三章之第 4 段。

见的滞期费责任;在部分货物的情况下,不同提单的收货人之间怎样分摊? 如果在卸货时间内先卸下的一票货是否还需要对后来产生的滞期费负责,等等。Diplock 勋爵是这样说:“... I find to be an overwhelming reason for not indulging in verbal manipulation of the actual contractual words used in the charter – party so as to give to them this effect when they are treated as incorporated in the bill of lading. I may add that to do so would raise a whole host of questions as to how the liability is to operate as between different consignees of different parts of the cargo, to which questions no attempt has been made to vouchsafe any answer, let alone a plausible one. To give some examples: is any personal liability for demurrage incurred by consignee of cargo which has been discharged before the expiry of laytime? If the discharge of a consignee's cargo takes place after the vessel is on demurrage is his liability to pay demurrage limited to the amount of demurrage accrued after the expiry of laytime and up to the time when the discharge of his part of the cargo is complete? Is each consignee liable for all demurrage accrued while his cargo remains on board? Is the liability of each consignee to pay demurrage several? If the shipowner choose to sue one consignee of part of the cargo for the full amount of demurrage has that consignee any right of contribution against consignees of other parts of the cargo and, if so, against which of them and upon what basis?”

所以 Diplock 勋爵最后判在租约内即使是与有关航次有直接关系的条文也不能被假设都被合并在提单内,而是要看整体的商业合理性。而租约说明是承租人要负责(如滞期费的支付),也不会被任意“篡改”(manipulate),“承租人”改为“收货人”或者“提单持有人”要负个人合约责任。Diplock 勋爵是这样说:“... this House should take this opportunity of stating unequivocally that, where in a bill of lading there is included a clause which purports to incorporate the terms of a specified charter – party, there is not any rule of construction that clause in that charter – party which are directly germane to the shipment, carriage or delivery of goods and impose obligations upon the ‘charterer’ under that designation, are presumed to be incorporated in the bill of lading with the substitution of (where there is a cesser clause), or inclusion in (where there is no cesser clause), the designation ‘charterer’, the designation ‘consignee of the cargo’ or ‘bill of lading holder’.”

2. 下一个同样结论的先例是 The “Spiros C” (1999) 2 Lloyd's Rep. 91,有关船舶是期租给一家公司名为 Mercator。Mercator 分租给 Tradigrain 跑一个航次装小麦从 Constanza 去摩洛哥。船东也签发了提单,并有合并条文说:“All terms and conditions liberties and exceptions of the charterparty ... are herewith incorporated.”之后 Mercator 经济发生问题而没有支付给船东租金,这导致船东马上向发货人(也是分承租人)留置“分租运费”(sub – freight)。其中由于装港发生了延误,所以一个争议就是提单有否合并航次分租约(提单合并的租约不应该是船东与 Mercator 的期租租约)的卸货时间条文。有关的分租约有第8条文说明滞期费是由承租人负责。另有第49条文规定了卸货时间与通知书的递交如下:“Discharging terms:a) Vessel to be discharged at the average rate of 2,000 metric tons per weather working day of 24 consecutive hours, Saturday noon, Sunday and Holidays excepted, even if used. . . . ”船东同意是分租约第8条文根据The “Miramar”先例是无法篡改“承租人”为“收货人”,换言之,第8条文并没有被合并。Colman大法官是这样说:“In the present case clause 49 is not so expressed as to make reference to ‘the charterer’ and so it could be incorporated without verbal manipulation. However, clause 8 of the sub – charter expressly provides that demurrage is to be paid by ‘the charterer’. Accordingly, as Mr. Meeson (船东代表大律师) concedes on behalf of the shipowners, the reasoning of Lord Diplock makes it impossible to argue that this provision was incorporated into the bills of lading contract. . . . ”接下去Colman大法官就认为第49条文也不能被合并在提单内,因为矛盾重重。如没有道理只合并卸货时间条文,但不合并第8条滞期费条文,这两条条文一般是走在一起等。Colman大法官是这样说:“Could it therefore be that clause 49 alone was incorporated, but not clause 8. There are strong grounds for concluding that this could not have been the mutual intention. Firstly, it is extremely unlikely that a shipper of any of the cargo would agree to a specific laytime clause without also agreeing a demurrage clause. The former is normally devised to fit the latter. They are normally interlocking provisions. Secondly, a shipper of a part cargo would be highly unlikely to agree to a specific laytime provision such as clause 49 because the difficulties of working out the extent of the available time for discharge could be very considerable as between separate consignees particularly because there might be simultaneous discharge of cargo covered by different bills of lading. It is the whole vessel that is to be discharged at the specific average rate and not merely any one parcel of cargo. . . . ”(这一段有关第二个原因双方[发货人与承运人/船东]对租约第49条文没有订约意图合并在提单是部分货物的发货人不可能计算到根据第49条文的固定卸货时间,会将来在卸港给他的一票货有多少时间。毕竟也会有可能是不同提单的不同收货人同时进行卸货。反正第49条文所针对的固定卸货时间只是针对整船的作业,并非是针对同一个航次多票货物的其中一票。)

8.4.2.5 提单合并哪一份租约的疑问

提单合并租约条文的问题并没有告一段落,而且随着60年代后转租越来越频密与期租合约越来越普遍,越来越难以解释租约提单中简单与没有明确哪一份被合并的租约的合并条文。英国法律政策在这方面是明确,就是会想办法找出一个适合的租约,说这就是合并进提单的那一份租约。否则,轻率的说提单合并条文因为太不肯定而导致无效就难以解释承运人与收货人之间的合约关系了。[23] 正如在 The "San Nicholas" (1976) 1 Lloyd's Rep 8 先例，上诉庭的 Roskill 大法官说："I would hesitate long before holding that the mere omission to include the date of a charter – party in a bill of lading negatives an intention to incorporate the terms of that charter – party in to the bill of lading. . . "

在该先例，也明确了合并的应该就是第一份的"原租约"(head charter – party)，因为这往往是签发提单的船长唯一了解与对其有约束性的租约。Denning 勋爵是这样说："It seems to me plain that the shipment was carried under and pursuant to terms of the head charter. The blanks were left because the master and the other people in Recife (装港) did not know its date and the parties to it so as to be able to fill them in. The head charter was the only charter to which the shipowners were parties; and they must, in the bill of lading, be taken to be referring to that head charter. "

同样的判法有 The "Sevonia Team" (1983) 2 Lloyd's Rep 640; The "Nai Matteini" (1988) 1 Lloyd's Rep 452; The "Ikariada" (1999) 2 Lloyd's Rep 365; The "Epsilon Rosa" (2003) 2 Lloyd's Rep 509; The "Kallang" (No. 2) (2009) 1 Lloyd's Rep 124 等先例。

但在 The "SLS Everest" (1981) 2 Lloyd's Rep. 389 先例，上诉庭判是合并的不是第一份的期租合约而是第二份分程租合约。理由很简单也可以理解，因为程租的条文才能够配合提单的运输，如有针对同一个航次的卸港/泊位、卸货时间、卸货费用、滞期费与速遣费、运费等。

在比较罕见的情况下，提单有在空格填上想合并的租约的日期，但有可能还是不解决问题，因为在转租频密的情况下，租约链会有两份同样日期的租约。这种情况在 The "Kallang" (No. 2) 先例中出现，Jonathan Hirst QC 大法官判是："The bills of lading expressly provided that all terms and conditions, liberties and exceptions of the charterparty dated 1 February 2005 "including the Law and Arbitration Clauses" were incorporated. On general principle, as a result of the express identification of the arbitration clause, that would be sufficient to incorporate a charterparty arbitration clause, even if it required a degree of manipulation: The Rena K [1978] 1 Lloyd's Rep. 545. The complication is that here there are two charterparties dated 1 February 2005. Each has an English arbitration clause but slightly different terms. At first, it was thought by Jackson Parton (船东代表律师) that the relevant charterparty was the time charter. That was understandable because it is probably quite unusual to have a time charter and a voyage charter concluded on the same date. It soon became apparent that there was also a voyage

〔23〕 这种判例很早以前曾经有过，在 Smidt v Tiden (1874) L. R 9 QB 466 先例，但早已被后来的说法与判例否定。

charter dated 1 February 2005. The bills of lading also provide that freight is payable as per the charterparty. That is naturally a reference to the voyage charter under which freight (as opposed to hire) is payable. Further the terms of the voyage charter are more naturally germane to a bill of lading. In my judgment, it is clear that the intention was to incorporate the terms of the voyage charter, including its arbitration clause, into the bill of lading contracts."

但如果第一份直到第五份的分租约都是期租,这又怎样解释呢?会否在这种情况下被视为是太不肯定与含糊导致法院或仲裁庭判租约提单的合并条文无效?这一个可能性不大可能存在。这一问题在一个较近期的案例 The "Vinson" (2005) LMLN No. 677 中有针对。案情涉及一份租约提单,以 Congenbill 的标准格式为准。在该航次的背后,先是有一个期租,可称为 Ecotime charter,为期 2 年,仲裁地点是纽约。之后,承租人转租,但以 Baltime 标准格式为准,仲裁地点是伦敦。该 Baltime charter 的分承租人与发货人另又订一个运输合约,但该合约是针对分承租人替发货人作出的服务并不是针对该有关的航次,所以完全不适合合并进提单。

反正是在该航次中发生了货损(香蕉),收货人(提单持有人)向船东索赔并开始了伦敦仲裁,这是因为 Congenbill 94 的格式是印上了合并租约的仲裁条文。收货人这样做,就表示接受该提单合并的是 Baltime charter。但船东提出争议说是提单合并的应该是 Ecotime charter 或其他有关的运输合约,问题是这样一来就再也不是伦敦仲裁了。时间上也不能让收货人去纽约重新提出仲裁,因为《海牙规则》的 1 年时效早已过去。最后 Andrew Smith 大法官判是三份有关的租约中,还是 Baltime charter 的条文比较适合合并进提单,说:"Only the Baltime charter contained provisions relating to liens which could sensibly be incorporated into the bills of lading. Also clause 13 of the Baltime charter (which made provision about the responsibility for delay) contributed something to the bills of lading contracts. Although the provisions of none of the three candidate contracts were particularly appropriate for incorporation into the bills of lading, the terms of the Baltime charter were the most appropriate in view of the lien provision and, in small measure, clause 13."

在更近期的 The "Duden" (2009) 1 Lloyd's Rep 145 先例,Jonathan Hirst QC 大法官认为虽然是合并程租合约会比期租合约更适合,但不是不可能合并期租合约,只是这样做会需要更加多的篡改。

在 Aikens 大法官所著的《Bills of Lading》(2006 年)一书之 7.102 段也讲到另一个在租约链会发生的疑问,说:"The problem is compounded where there are two or more relevant charters of a vessel, typically a head time charter to which the owner is party and a sub – voyage charter to which the shipper is or may be a party. Of the two parties to the bill of lading contract the shipper may well be ignorant of the existence or terms of head charter and the shipowner equally ignorant of the sub – charter. Which, if either, of the two is incorporated? In such circumstances the courts are very reluctant to hold that the contract is void for uncertainty, as this does not give effect to the obvious intention that the terms of a charter are to be incorporated."

从上述所介绍的先例可以看到再也不能假设提单合并的租约条文应该是船东熟悉的第一份租约，也不能假设提单合并的租约必须是程租合约。可以说，假设双方订约意图（现实中会是发货人与承运人签发提单时根本没有想过）来认定租约提单合并了租约链中哪一份租约，看来并不容易也不稳定。这又回到本章8.1段所讲的，凭一条完全不明确与不肯定的提单合并条文，在其他的合约类别，是怎样都不可能被法院或仲裁庭接受是向对方就有关合并些什么作出了合理足够的通知。

8.4.3 租约提单合并租约仲裁条文

从上述所讲，也可以带出这一十分富争议性的课题，就是租约提单通过一般的合并租约条文是否也合并了租约的仲裁条文。在这一方面，针对提单的法律也是与其他合约类别有不同的对待。首先可针对提单的独特之处，在本章之8.4.2.1段要求更严格解释提单的合并条文。另是从上述所介绍的有关提单合约的特殊环境与背景，导致在现实中收货人（或代位的保险人）这些受影响的第三人通常需要时间才能够明确合并的是哪些租约条文与内容。所以如果合并的内容也可以包括租约的仲裁条文，就很容易发生在收货人肯定了仲裁条文后再向承运人/船东提出索赔货损货差时《海牙规则》或适用的相关国家法律的1年时效已经错过。这显然不公道，所以在本章之8.4.2.2段所针对的提单合并条文只能有效地合并与有关航次与货物运输有直接关系的条文/文字，不能合并一些所谓的"附带"（collateral）或"附属"（ancillary）租约条文，包括仲裁条文或管辖权条文。

严格解释提单合并条文（不论在用字上怎样广泛）可节录 The "Federal Bulker" (1989) 1 Lloyd's Rep 103 先例，上诉庭的 Bingham 大法官说：

"**Generally speaking, the English law of contract has taken a benevolent view of the use of general words to incorporate by reference standard terms to be found elsewhere. But in the present field a different, and stricter, rule has developed, especially where the incorporation of arbitration clauses is concerned.** The reason no doubt is that a bill of lading is a negotiable commercial instrument and may come into the hands of a foreign party with no knowledge and no ready means of knowledge of the terms of the charter-party. The cases show that a strict test of incorporation having, for better or worse, been laid down, the Courts have in general defended this rule with some tenacity in the interests of commercial certainty. If commercial parties do not like the English rule, they can meet the difficulty by spelling out the arbitration provision in the bill of lading and not relying on general words to achieve incorporation.

The importance of certainty in this field was emphasized by Lord Denning, M.R. in The Annefield, [1971] 1 Lloyd's Rep. 1 at p. 3, col. 2; [1971] P. 168 at p. 183G, by Sir John Donaldson, M. R. in The Varenna at p. 594, col. 2, and by Lord Justice Oliver in the same case at p. 597 col. 2. This is indeed a field in which it is perhaps preferable that the law should be clear, certain and well understood than that it should be perfect. Like others, I doubt whether the line drawn by the authorities is drawn where a modern commercial lawyer would be inclined to draw it. But it would, I think, be a source of mischief if we were to do anything other than try to give effect to settled authority as best we can."(加黑部分是笔者的强调)

另也可以节录 The "Athena"(No. 2)(2007) 1 Lloyd's Rep 280 先例,Langley 大法官也有解释:"In principle, English law accepts incorporation of standard terms by the use of general words and, I would add, particularly so when the terms are readily available and the question arises in the context of dealings between established players in a well-known market. The principle, as the dictum makes clear, does not distinguish between a term which is an arbitration clause and one which addresses other issues. In contrast, and for the very reason that it concerns other parties, a 'stricter rule' is applied in charterparty/bills of lading cases. The reason given is that the other party may have no knowledge nor ready means of knowledge of the relevant terms. Further, as the authorities illustrate, the terms of an arbitration clause may require adjustment if they are to be made to apply to the parties to a different contract."(原则上英国法律接受以一般合并条文合并一些标准条文,特别是在这些标准条文可以很容易让双方取到并了解合并的内容的情况,而这种情况在一些成熟的行业是司空见惯。这样法律并不将仲裁条文与其他条文作出区分。但如果会影响第三人如租约合并进提单的案件,就有了一个更严格的规则。原因是第三人如提单持有人或代位的保险人不会知道合并了一些什么条文/内容。所以有许多先例显示一条仲裁条文是不会通过一般的合并条文可以有效的合并。)

Langley 大法官接下去也讲到怎样才是有效的合并租约仲裁条文进提单,说:"General words of incorporation may serve to incorporate an arbitration clause save in the exceptional two-contract cases ... in which some express reference to arbitration or perhaps provision of the relevant clause is also required."(Langley 大法官是把租约条文合并进提单视为"两个合约"的案件,也就是两个不同的合约并涉及不同订约方就不这么容易让大家都知道合并的另一份合约会是什么内容。这与一般的"一个合约"合并一些标准条文完全不一样,双方很容易知道合并的内容,如信用证合并 UCP 600。在两个合约想合并仲裁条文,Langley 大法官认为需要有明示适用仲裁或更需要把有关的仲裁条文明示出来。)

Langley 大法官的说法也在 Habas Sinai Ve Tibbi Gazlar Istihsal Endustrisi AS v Sometal Sal (2010) EWHC 29 (Comm)先例被 Christopher Clark 大法官接受。这些先例在 Lewison 大法官所著的《The Interpretation of Contracts》(第 5 版,2011 年)一书

第108~109页被总结说:

"The more restrictive approach requires express reference to the arbitration or jurisdiction clause before it will be taken to be incorporated into the contract. This more restrictive approach will apply to cases in which:[这是指严格解释合并条文是适用在以下(1)与(2)的情况]

(1) A and B make a contract incorporating terms agreed between A (or B) and C.

Common examples are a bill of lading incorporating the term of a charter to which A is a party; reinsurance contracts incorporating the terms of an underlying insurance; excess insurance contracts incorporating the terms of the primary layer of insurance; and building or engineering sub – contracts incorporating the terms of a main contract or sub – sub – contracts incorporating the terms of a sub – contract.(这种会扯上第三人的C就是典型的提单合并租约条文,再保合约合并原保单条文,超额保险合约合并原保险限额的条文,建造或工程分合约合并主合约或分分合约的条文。)

(2) A and B make a contract incorporating terms agreed between C and D.

Bills of lading, reinsurance and insurance contract and building contracts may fall into this category.(这种情况与[1]雷同或接近。)

However, it will not apply where:[但严格解释合并条文是不适用在以下(3)与(4)的情况,换言之仲裁条文不必明示适用也可以通过一般合并条文合并。]

(3) A and B make a contract in which they incorporate standard terms.

These may be the standard terms of one party set out on the back of an offer letter or an order, or contained in another document to which reference is made; or contained in another document to which reference is made; or terms embodied in the rules of anorganization of which A or B or both are members; or they may be terms standard in a particular trade or industry.(订约双方之间只有"一个合约",该合约合并了一些其他文件,或订约双方都属于某一个组织的会员的规则,或一些特定行业中的标准条文。)

(4) A and B make a contract incorporating terms previously agreed between A and B in another contract or contracts to which they were both parties."(订约双方合并了他们以前订立的合约,如在本章之8.3.1段讲的租约范本。)

对Langley大法官的指引,船东(或严格说是他们背后的互保协会)也不敢怠慢,他们普遍喜欢货损货差的争议去伦敦仲裁而不是在卸港被收货人(或代位保险人)在当地法院向他们的船舶提起诉讼,令他们处在不利地位。由于绝大部分的租约都会约定去伦敦仲裁,所以如果能够成功把租约仲裁条文合并在提单,就可以避免要面对在全球不同卸港的法院诉讼的危险,因为根据1958年的《纽约公约》,大部分这样的诉讼都会被中止。这使得船东组织的BIMCO在1994年对商品买卖最普遍适用的标准提单格式Congenbill作出修改,有关的印本合并条文从原来的一般性合并条文加上了以下加黑的一句:"All the terms, conditions, liberties and exceptions of the

Charter Party ... **including the Law and Arbitration Clause** are herewith incorporated."

这一修改已经符合了 Langley 大法官认为需要有明示条文合并租约的仲裁条文的要求，但还没有进一步做到把有关的租约仲裁条文明示出来。但进一步明示有关与特定的租约仲裁条文是印本格式提单合约无法做得到，因为每一个租约的仲裁条文都可能有不同的规定。即使大部分条文都规定去伦敦仲裁，但不同条文会在仲裁员的人数、仲裁员资格、仲裁程序等方面有不同规定。所以对第三人的提单持有人或代位的保险人而言，仅是简单的一句适用租约仲裁条文还难以满足本章 8.1 段所要求的合理与足够的通知。作为提单持有人的收货人，即使根据 Congenbill 1994 知道了租约仲裁条文被明示合并了，还是无法在《海牙规则》或相关国家法律的 1 年时效内采取什么正确的行动保护时效，除非进一步知道有关的仲裁条文的所有内容。但看来英国法律已经明确承认 Congenbill 1994 的合并条文是有效合并了有关租约的仲裁条文，如在 The "Epsilon Rosa" (2003) 2 Lloyd's Rep 509 先例。

笔者听闻这一问题在中国内地的法院还没有定论，这也使得近年来在航运强势的英国法院与伦敦仲裁庭频频涉及 Congenbill 1994 的案件中向中国收货人（或代位的保险人）作出"止诉禁令"（anti - suit injunction），阻止他们在中国海事法院的诉讼。如在 The "Joanna V" (2003) 2 Lloyd's Rep 617 先例的止诉禁令是针对人保，在 The "Alexandros T" (2008) 1 Lloyd's Rep 230 的先例是针对中国太平保险。怎样有效保护中国作为全球最大的商品贸易国的货方利益是另一个大课题，笔者无法在这一小段详论。只是这种困境也可以很容易超越，如中国的收货人如果能够普遍知道 Congenbill 1994 为他们带来的困境，就可以在以后的商品买卖合约与信用证规定不接受 Congenbill 1994 或提单合并租约仲裁条文。正如 Bingham 大法官在 Pagnan SpA v. Feed Products Ltd (1987) 2 Lloyd's Rep. 601 先例所说的："The parties are to be regarded as masters of their own contractual fate."

§9　根据行动合并的合约条文

合约可以是用行动达成，当然也可以从行动中找出合约的条文。在商业活动中经常有这样的情况，这以行动达成的合约的条文可以根据双方以前订立过的合约或他们之间共同的理解来确定。找出什么是被合并的合约条文显然像口头合约或部分文书部分口头的合约一样，是需要证据来支持。

要这样做实在也是没有办法的事情，因为出争议时双方可能已经履行了该合约。这样一来，除了必须要承认合约的存在之外，也需要找出双方约定的是什么条文才能判断谁是谁非。这也不是仅靠默示条文就能够解决的，因为默示条文是在"必要"（necessary）的情况下才会作出，所以不能从零开始就默示一个合约内所有的条文。

上述情况在航运与货物买卖中都会出现,如第一次交易时双方小心地订好一份合约,但如果之后双方还有相同交易,在有了之前的合作经验的基础上,双方在订约方面就会草草了事。例如,买方只给卖方一个传真说"我再订购10箱上一次的商品",而卖方也随即交付。将来如果出了事情,如对货物质量的争议,双方才会要面对在这一买卖的交易中大家到底同意了些什么条文的问题。

显然,如果双方以前有过交易,并且有合约条文的存在,甚至不止是一次,就会可以假设说双方是以以前交易的合约条文为准,事实上也的确很有可能这个就是双方的订约意图。Pearce 勋爵在 McCutcheon v Macbrayne (David) Ltd (1964) 1 W. L. R. 125 先例中说:"It is the consistency of a course of conduct which gives rise to the implication that in similar circumstances a similar contractual result will follow. When the conduct is not consistent, there is no reason why it should still produce an invariable contractual result."

如果以前交易是通过代理人或者是联营公司,也会是足够以以前的合约条文为准:Eastman Chemical International A. G. v. N. M. T. Trading Ltd (1972) 2 Lloyd's Rep. 25;S. I. A. T. di dal Ferro v. Tradax Overseas S. A. (1980) 1 Lloyd's Rep. 53 等先例。

曾有说法是要进行过多次交易才能把以前的合约条文合并进来,大概这里部分原因是为了保护消费者。在一些案例中被认为是足够可以合并以前双方交易的合约条文的情况是:(1)在 Hardwick Game Farm v Suffolk Agricultural Producers (1969) 2 A.C. 31 先例中,连续3年的时间内,每个月有3~4次的交易;(2)在 S. I. A. T. di del Ferro v. Tradax Overseas S. A. 先例中,5年半的时间内,双方共订立了81个买卖合约。

但在 Hollier v Rambler Motors (AMC) Ltd (1972) 2 Q. B. 71 先例中,法院认为5年的时间内双方只订立了3~4个合约是不足够能将之前的合约条文合并进来。

在1977年的英国《不公平合约法》生效后,为了保护消费者,法院可能会在这一方面放宽标准。因为如果是把以前合约中不合理的条文合并进来,也过不了该立法的关卡。一般来说,订约双方如果是势均力敌的商业机构,法院也会在这一方面放宽,不会要求以前有太多的交易次数才可以有效地合并。

这可举 Circle Frei0ght International Ltd v. Medeast Gulf Exports Ltd (1988) 2 Lloyd's Rep. 427 先例为例,其中的一个争议就是货代的标准合约条文(内中有免责条文)是否被合并去合约内,而该合约是出口商与货代通过电话中达成。事实也认定了双方至少有过11次的交易,而其中货代作出的发票中印有一句:

"All business is transacted by the company under the current trading conditions of the Institute of Freight Forwarders, a copy of which is available on request."

在上诉庭,判是以前合约的条文可以被合并进出了争议的合约内,Taylor 大法官的说法在本章之8.1段有节录,这里不再重复。

但毕竟还是有情况是以前进行交易的次数极有限，又或者是每次进行交易都有不同的合约条文，又或者是进行交易是在好几年前。在这些情况下仍然把以前的合约条文合并进来会有点说不通，也很难假设这就是他们的订约意图。这样，会是要通过其他的说法，例如是订约双方的共同理解。这在 British Crane Hire Corp Ltd v Ipswich Plant Hire Ltd（1975）Q. B. 303 先例有针对，案情涉及租用吊车的交易，订约双方之前并没有进行过交易。在订约前供应吊车一方也没有把供应吊车的标准条件去告诉或显示给租用人。但最后还是判在该租用吊车合约，是以供应吊车一方的条件为准。Denning 勋爵是这样说：

"I would not put it so much on the course of dealing, but rather on the common understanding which is to be derived from the conduct of the parties, namely that the hiring was to be on the terms of the plaintiff's usual conditions."

§10　合约格式之争

商业活动中也经常会出现合约格式之争（battle of the forms），特别是在货物买卖。例如，卖方向买方报价，买方随即向卖方下了订单，然后卖方作出交付。期间双方都没有对货价（或至多是一些十分重要的条文如交付时间）以外的其他合约条文（如免责条文、时效条文、仲裁条文等）有过任何谈判，但在他们的交往中也各自附上了自己的标准合约条文。显然，卖方的标准合约条文与买方的标准合约条文不一样甚至很不一样。这如果有了争议，就存在到底其他合约条文以谁的标准合约条文为准。一般说法就是以谁放"最后一枪"（last shot）为准。也就是在双方履行合约之前，谁向对方附上了自己的标准合约条文。这也可以说是根据一般合约的"要约"（offer）/"反要约"（counter - offer）与"接受"（acceptance）分析。也就是 A 附上自己标准合约条文可视为作出了要约，B 回应并附上了其标准合约条文可视为反要约，A 随即履行合约可视为接受了反要约。

这些权威的说法可先节录 Denning 勋爵在 Butler Machine Tool Co Ltd v Ex - Cell - O Corporation（England）Ltd（1979）1 WLR 401 先例所说如下："... it will be found that in most cases when there is a 'battle of forms' there is a contract as soon as the last of the forms is sent and received without objection being taken to it."

在 Tekdata Interconnections Ltd v Amphenol Ltd（2010）1 Lloyd's Rep 357 先例，Longmore 大法官说："The way in which I would put it is to say that the traditional offer and acceptance analysis must be adopted unless the documents passing between the parties and their conduct show that their common intention was that some other terms were intended to prevail."（Longmore 大法官说是要适用传统要约与接受的分析，除非双方交换的文件或他们的行动显示了共同的订约意图是以那份标准合约条文为准。）

Dyson 大法官也说:"The paradigm battle of the forms occurs where A offers to buy goods from B on its (A's) conditions and B accepts the offer but only on its own conditions. As is pointed out in Cheshire, Fifoot & Furmston's Law of Contract, 15th Edition, at page 210, it may be possible to analyse the legal situation that results as being that there is: (i) a contract on A's conditions; (ii) a contract on B's conditions; (iii) a contract on the terms that would be implied by law, but incorporating neither A's nor B's conditions; (iv) a contract incorporating some blend of both parties' conditions; or (v) no contract at all. [这里是指有五种可能性:(1) 以 A 的标准合约条文为准;(2) 以 B 的标准合约条文为准;(3) 合约以法律默示为准,不合并 A 或 B 的标准合约条文;(4) 合约合并了部分 A 与 B 的标准合约条文;(5) 双方根本没有达成合约关系。]

In my judgment, it is not possible to lay down a general rule that will apply in all cases where there is a battle of the forms. It always depends on an assessment of what the parties must objectively be taken to have intended. But where the facts are no more complicated than that A makes an offer on its conditions and B accepts that offer on its conditions and, without more, performance follows, it seems to me that the correct analysis is what Longmore LJ has described as the 'traditional offer and acceptance analysis', ie that there is a contract on B's conditions. I accept that this analysis is not without its difficulties in circumstances of the kind to which Professor Treitel refers in the passage quoted at para 20 above. But in the next sentence of that passage, Professor Treitel adds: 'For this reason the cases described above are best regarded as exceptions to a general requirement of offer and acceptance'. ... But the rules which govern the formation of contracts have been long established and they are grounded in the concepts of offer and acceptance. So long as that continues to be the case, it seems to me that the general rule should be that the traditional offer and acceptance analysis is to be applied in battle of the forms cases. That has the great merit of providing a degree of certainty which is both desirable and necessary in order to promote effective commercial relationships."(不会有一条可以适用在所有不同事实的合约格式之争的规则,到底在多过一份标准合约条文应该适用哪一份取决于客观看双方的订约意图。但当案件的简单事实只是 A 根据其标准合约条文提出要约,B 根据其标准合约条文接受,之后双方就开始履行。在这种情况下,Dyson 大法官认为 Longmore 大法官的传统要约与接受的分析的说法正确,也就是应该适用 B 的标准合约条文。Dyson 大法官同意在其他较复杂事实的案件,这种分析会带来一定的困难。但正如 Treitel 教授所说,这些应该只是属于传统要约与接受的分析的例外情况。传统要约与接受的分析作为适用在合约格式之争的一般性规则是符合商业要求的肯定性与有助于维持商业关系的有效性。)

上述所提到的较复杂事实的案件会是千变万化,但反正就是客观看,双方的订约意图是十分明显不接受对方的标准合约条文。例如,双方在谈判的时候坚持不下,明确表明绝对不会接受对方的标准合约条文。但最后同意把这一问题暂时搁置,希望将来不会出问题,目前先履行如买方支付定金或卖方交付货物。这种相似的情况出现在 Lidl (UK) GmbH v Hertford Foods Ltd (2001) EWCA Civ 938 先例,案情有关咸牛肉的买卖,双方在电话的谈判中各自坚持以自己的标准合约条文为准。之后双方的履行也是各顾各以自己的标准条文为准。后来双方有了争议,法院判是客观看不能以传统要约与接受分析。这样,双方的争议也就只能以法律的默示条文为准〔24〕。Chadwick 大法官说:

"... In my view it is impossible to hold that they were agreed that either set of standard conditions was applicable. As the judge found, they said nothing to each other which indicated agreement on that point; and, for the reasons which I have sought to set out, there is no basis upon which agreement on that point can be inferred.

... On that basis, knowing that they had not — and, in the circumstances, probably could not — reach agreement as to the applicability of either set of standard terms, the only inference that can be drawn is that their agreement was made on the basis that neither set of standard terms would be applicable. That conclusion seems to me at least as likely to accord with reality as a conclusion either that they reached no binding agreement at all or that either agreed to contract on the standard terms of the other."

最后一提的是现在越来越多的网上买卖,双方交易也需要设计程序避免格式之争。这种买卖往往可以通过传统的合约法解释,如卖方在网上对商品的展示与价格是一个"要约邀请"(invitation to treat),买方(可能是来自全球各地)购买就是一个要约,之后就是卖方的接受并在获得支付(或通过信用卡支付)后交付货物。买卖的整个操作都是通过他们的程序,所以卖方如果要坚持适用他的标准合约条文,就首先需要让买方知道与能够"取到"(access)这些条文并可以保存与打印。在程序的设计方面,就要求先取得买方对卖方的标准合约条文的同意之后才可以走下一步作出购买。而如果买方不接受这些标准合约条文,也就不会购买。这一做法大致的陈述会在网站显示出来,如"Precedent 13.14 The terms and conditions of sale set out below shall apply to any contract between us for the supply of items purchased from us via this website (either on this occasion or on any future occasion when you log in using the password you will select as part of your registration process). Please read all of them carefully. They contain exclusions and limitations of our liability under any such contract. If you wish to proceed on the basis that these terms and conditions apply to any such contract, please click on 'ACCEPT' below. If not, please click on 'REJECT' to end this session. If you wish to retain a hard copy of these conditions or save them on your com-

---

〔24〕 有关默示条文请看本书第七章。

puter please click on the 'Print' or 'Save' button below."

§11 序 言

在一些拟定的比较小心的合约中,会出现序言(Preamble / Recitals)。在合约中,序言通常是在订约双方的名称后,但在合约的"履行内容"(operative part)之前。序言会以"WHEREAS"一字开始,然后写下有关合约的一般事实背景,包括双方以前约定的合约,要订立该合约的原因等。但要小心不要把合约的履行、责任或义务加在序言,因为在解释合约时,序言的内容会与履行内容的分量轻重有所不同。

不像下一段会介绍的抬头,序言是在解释合约时应该加以考虑的。其中一个原因是它提供了重要的订约背景/语境。早在 Moore v. Magrath (1774) 1 Cowp 9 先例中,Mansfield 勋爵就说道:"The deed begins with the preamble usual in all settlements; that is, by reciting what it is the grantor intends to do; and that, like the preamble to an Act of Parliament, is the key to what comes afterwards."

但要考虑之余,有新加坡上诉庭的先例说是序言只能作为帮助,不能超越合约的履行内容。这在 The Management Corporation Strata Title Plan No. 1933 v. Liang Huat Aluminium Ltd (2001) BLR 351 先例中有说:"a recital in an instrument can only assist in the construction of the substantive terms thereof, it cannot override or control the operation of the substantive terms, where such terms are clear and unambiguous."

有类似的说法很早就出现在英国的先例,在 Walsh v. Trevanion (1850) 15 QB 733 先例中,Patteson 大法官说:"... when the words in the operative part of a deed of conveyance are clear and unambiguous, they cannot be controlled by the recitals or other parts of the deed. On the other hand, when those words are of doubtful meaning, the recitals and other parts of the deed may be used as a test to discover the true intention of the parties, and to fix the true meaning of those words."

在 Re Moon *ex parte* Dawes (1886) 17 QBD 275, CA 先例中,Esher 勋爵是说:"Now there are three rules to the construction of such an instrument. If the recitals are clear and the operative part is ambiguous, the recitals govern the construction. If the recitals are ambiguous, and the operative part is clear, the operative part will prevail. If both the recitals and operative part are clear, but they are inconsistent with each other, the operative part is to be preferred."

最后可节录《Chitty on Contracts》(第31版,2012年)一书之12-066段,这应该是英国法律当今的地位,如下:"Control by recitals. When the words in the operative part of an instrument are ambiguous, the recitals and other parts of the instrument may be used to fix the appropriate meaning of those words. But clear words in the operative part of an instrument cannot be controlled by recitals."

§12　文件/条文的抬头与条文外的注脚

一份合约中，经常会给个别条文一个抬头（heading），或把几条条文合在一起给一个抬头或名称，主要的作用是为了方便寻找与在合约其他地方可以更容易被提及。甚至合约本身也会有一个抬头，如名为“转让协议”（Assignment Agreement）或“意向书”（Letter of Intend）。抬头通常在解释合约中没有分量，而被认为是一个达到正确的合约解释的不安全的指引。抬头也不能给条文的内容带来不肯定，如抬头是“法院管辖条文”（Jurisdiction Clause），但内容则是针对仲裁。在现实中，抬头与条文内容矛盾或文不对题的情况经常出现。

同样道理也适用在合约条文外的一些注脚（marginal notes）。这里可先举 National Farmers' Union Mutual Insurances Society Ltd. v. Dawson（1941）2 K. B. 424 先例，Caldecote C. J. 子爵认为解释合约考虑注脚是“不安全指引”（unsafe guide）。另在 Cott UK Ltd v. R. E. Barber Ltd.（1997）3 All E. R. 540 先例，Hegarty 大法官针对条文的抬头说：

“[Counsel's] analysis commenced, and indeed concluded, by emphasizing the word 'arbitration', which appears at the head of the clause. He pointed out, correctly, that there is not in this particular contract any provision such as is commonly found, whereby it is expressly stated that the interpretation of the clause.

Accordingly, he says that the word 'arbitration' appearing at the heading, must be taken into account fully in construing the clause, and that in those circumstances one cannot determine, as I have said, whether it is truly a clause requiring arbitration, or a clause requiring expert determination. It does seem to me that the word 'arbitration' at the outset, in the absence of any such common form provisions as I have referred to, must be given due weight. What is due weight, however, must not disregard the fact that it is a catchword, or form of identification, inserted for convenience of reference.

In my judgment, such a catchword or form of identification cannot prevail over the express wording of the clause, or create ambiguity where no ambiguity is present in construing the words of the clause."

但这里也有例外，尤其是在解释文书合约的新趋势下。例如，在本书第六章之 12.3 段介绍的 Investors Compensation Scheme c. West Bromwich Building Society（1998）1 W. L. R. 896 先例，贵族院就认为没有受过法律训练的人士是看这些注脚，而索赔表格的有关条文却是给律师看的，所以如果两者在文字上不一致，令没有受过法律训练的当事人受到注脚的误导，就可改变条文。Hoffmann 勋爵说：“I shall, however, make four points supplemental to those of the judge. First, the claim form was obviously intended to be read by lawyers and the explanatory note by laymen. It is the forms of the claim form which govern the legal relationship between the parties. But in construing the form, I think that one should start with the assumption that a layman who read the explanatory note and did not venture into the claim form itself was being given an accurate account of the effect of the transaction. It is therefore significant that paragraph 4 of the note says categorically and without qualification that the investor gives up all his rights against anyone else and transfers them to ICS. If the effect of the claim form was that the investor retained his claim against the building society, paragraph 4 of the note was very misleading."

可以说,解释合约会被重视的还是条文本身的实质内容,而不是一个简短的抬头或名称。

§13 口头合约与部分文书部分口头合约

没有一份双方签署并看来是完整记录双方所约定内容的文书合约的情况在现实中也不少,这也可以包括了在本章之第5段所讲的有一份尚未签署的"工作合约"(working contract)。这样,有了争议就会要从一份往往是双方之间的文书往来中确定他们之间达成的协议。很多时候,要确定的还不仅是文书文件,也包括了订约方的口头协议,这就变成是一个部分口头部分书面的合约。这样,往往允许双方提供"外来证据"(extrinsic evidence)/"口头证据"(parol evidence)把这些文件联结起来并确定口头协议的内容、范围与解释。而法院或仲裁庭也是要看了所有的证据才能决定什么是双方达成的协议:Carmichael v. National Power plc (1999) 1 WLR 2042, HL先例。这种合约相比一份正式签署的有完整记录的合约缺点就是有争议时会要花费十分昂贵的诉讼费用找出双方同意过些什么或有否同意过,而且通过事后证明与经法院或仲裁庭的解释从而确定双方合约的内容的做法在肯定性方面比较低。毕竟涉及部分口头的合约,提供的口头证据就在肯定性方面比文书证据差得多了,经常会见到水平高的证人讲假话或半真半假也有人相信,但水平低的证人讲真话也没人相信。所以比较严肃一点的合约谈判,经常会在谈判过程的早期就约定"以签署合约为准"(subject to contract)。固然,即使有一份签署的合约,也不代表在发生争议时不会有一方声称它并不能代表全部的合约内容,并以口头证据试图证明双方在谈判时对方曾经作出过一些陈述但没有被加在合约内,或另有一个"附带保证/合约"(collateral warranty/contract)。所以,在现代的商业合约中,为了使文书合约在双方签署后就会被视为完整的记录了他们所有的协议,并带来肯定性,已经有越来越多的合约会加入一条"完整合约条文"(entire agreement clause),并会有同样作用的条文要求只有以文书记录的内容才能有效,从而预防将来履行中如果有争议一方会说双方曾经以口头对合约部分内容作出"更改"(variation)或"弃权"(waiver)的情况。

13.1　部分文书部分口头合约与文书合约的区分

这种需要判断是仅有一份完整记录了双方约定的文书合约还是部分文书部分口头合约的情况在贵族院先例 Carmichael v. National Power plc (1999) 1 WLR 2042, HL 有涉及。案情有关雇佣导游的合约,招聘广告讲明雇佣的导游只是临时工,需要时才按小时付工资。后来的争议是受雇的人士认为他们是公司员工,应该受立法保障,因为这应该算是一个正式的雇佣合约。这样,就涉及要解释他们之间的雇佣合约了。劳工裁判庭根据双方的文书往来中的文字、订约的过程与双方当事人各自对情况理解的证据判是他们不是公司员工。该案去了上诉庭,上诉庭改判,认为这是一份文书合约,所以只需要解释他们之间的文件往来,而解释合约是一个法律问题。但这被贵族院推翻,认为裁判庭判得正确。Hoffmann 勋爵谈到双方往来的信函非常简单,也不是由律师草拟,所以只是看这些文件作出解释是不现实。至少劳工裁判庭有权根据证据找出到底双方的订约意图是否把这些来往信函当作是唯一的文书记录,或这只是部分的合约记录,说:

"The majority of the Court of Appeal thought that the industrial tribunal should have decided as a matter of law that the exchange of letters was an offer and acceptance which gave rise to a contract of employment exclusively in writing. It followed that the construction of the letters would then also be a matter of law. For my part, I do not think that was a very realistic conclusion. The letters were not drafted by a lawyer and their language was extremely concise. To construe them as a complete written contract left the Court of Appeal having to interpret the cryptic phrase 'on a casual as required basis' in what they, as judges, took to be its natural and ordinary meaning, without the assistance of the evidence of what the parties had understood or how the contract had been operated. By this method they arrived at an interpretation different from that given to the words by the unanimous industrial tribunal, to say nothing of the Employment Appeal Tribunal.

Putting the matter at its lowest, I think that it was open to the industrial tribunal to find, as a fact, that **the parties did not intend the letters to be the sole record of their agreement but intended that it should be contained partly in the letters, partly in oral exchanges at the interviews or elsewhere and partly left to evolve by conduct as time went on.**"(加黑部分是笔者的强调)

13.2　解释部分文书部分口头合约是一个事实与法律问题的混合

如果订约双方接受或签署了一份看来是完整记录了双方约定内容的文书合约,特别是该文书合约中又有一条"完整合约条文"(entire agreement clause),之后双方对其中的一些内容有争议,这样解释有关条文/文字的意思是一个法律问题,通常不涉及证据,除非有例外的情况如涉及一个专业性的文字:这方面请看本书第五章之第1段。

如果是部分文书部分口头的合约,解释文书的部分仍是法律问题或是一个"事实与法律问题的混合"(mixed fact and law)。至于是口头部分,这当然全是事实的问题了。

概括的说,事实问题指的是双方对某些事实有争议(如针对其中一方曾经说过一些什么话)而法院或仲裁庭要根据证据找出已经发生过的事实。至于事实与法律问题的混合,可介绍 The "Chrysalis" (1983) 1 Lloyd's Rep. 503 先例,这是关于合约受阻的案例,而受阻的问题也是一个事实与法律问题的混合。Mustill 大法官讲到仲裁庭应该如何考虑问题与步骤是说:"In a case such as the present, the answer is to be found by dividing the arbitrator's process of reasoning into three stages: (1) The arbitrator ascertains the facts. This process includes the making of findings on any facts which are in dispute. (2) The arbitrator ascertains the law. This process comprises not only the identification of all material rules of statute and common law, but also the identification and interpretation of the relevant parts of the contract, and the identification of those facts which must be taken into account when the decision is reached. (3) In the light of the facts of the law so ascertained, the arbitrator reaches his decision."

这是说仲裁庭第一步应该认定事实,主要认定双方在口头的谈判中针对争议之处有否作出了什么承诺与约定。第二步是确定有关法律,这在本段针对的情况是与一些立法或普通法无关,法律问题是根据认定的事实解释双方的部分口头合约中的意思。第三步就是仲裁庭作出决定。

13.3 把部分文书部分口头合约的解释当作是事实与法律问题的混合的弊病

今天绝大部分的商业合约都是以仲裁解决争议。英国是极少数允许将仲裁裁决中关于法律问题的部分上诉至法院的国家,虽然这上诉权利受到一定的节制。这样,如果仲裁庭针对文书合约作出解释,这是法律问题,显然是有机会根据 1996 年英国《仲裁法》Section 68 上诉。但笔者对目前解释文书合约的新趋势,就是要根据订约时的背景/语境解释有关合约的条文/文字,是否仍适合上诉去法院不无疑问。原因是法院不会再重新处理证据(特别是口头证据),这样即使诉讼双方的代表大律师陈述有关仲裁审理所认定的订约背景/语境,但这订约背景/语境会被陈述扭曲与法院难以掌握重点恐怕也在所难免。

而将部分文书部分口头合约中的文书部分(通常是订约双方的文书往来)的解释作为法律问题上诉就会带来更大疑问。笔者可介绍一个自己参与的伦敦仲裁案件,但被上诉法院而成为先例的 Covington Marine Corp v. Xiamen Shipbuilding Industry Co (2006) 1 Lloyd's Rep. 745。由于该先例的案情已经成为"公开资料"(public domain),所以笔者不妨在此介绍。在该先例,笔者与两位著名的英国退休大法官组成了一个仲裁庭,审理的争议是有关双方是否达成了一个造船合约。简单的说,案情涉及中国厦门船厂 4 艘散装船的造船合约。双方先在希腊雅典签了合约,但其中有一条十分奇怪的条文是说明如果双方在 20 天内不能就一个仍未解决的事项达成协议,该签署了的造船合约就自动终止。该仍未解决的事项是该 4 艘船舶的主机到底是韩国或者是中国制造。主机的型号大家已经在造船合约中约定了是 MAN B & W。由于造船历史较久,韩国早已有许可证去建造这种主机并有丰富经验。而中国是刚花了高价取得了 MAN B & W 的许可证,可以建造这种主机。这样,厦门船厂与希腊船东就一直没有办法就这一方面达成协议,包括厦门船厂在雅典与船东的谈判。希腊船东是希望从韩国进口主机,因为虽然大家都是有许可证,但觉得韩国方面因为历史久,主机质量可信度较高。但厦门船厂当然希望用中国有许可证的厂家的供应,一方面是价钱比较低,另一方面是比较容易协调。还有一个重要的方面是有证据显示厦门船厂是先要通过一些手续取得中国有许可证厂家的同意(如中国厂家在时间上来不及或没有能力建造所要求马力的 MAN B & W 主机)才会被允许进口韩国主机。

在经过约 9 天的开庭与仲裁庭的慎重考虑后,包括笔者在内的仲裁庭判是双方并没有达成协议。但希腊船东根据这个协议是否有达成是部分文书、部分口头,而文书部分是法律问题,向英国法院上诉。上诉的所谓法律问题是两封传真,传真是希腊船东与经纪人(ASI)之间的,而 ASI 与厦门船厂之间就只有口头往来(而且厦门船厂否认有这种口头上的承诺)。第一封传真是 ASI 给希腊船东的,时间为 2003 年 3 月 18 日,内容是:

"... after very frank discussion with the yard at length, we think it is necessary to mention the following points:...

B. Main Engine

The Shipyard will agree to import the main Engine Subject to

1. The Buyer shall assist the yard to squeeze the price to the same level as domestic License Supplier or

2. The Buyer bears the costs of price difference after the shipyard present the Buyer clear evidence."

第二封传真是希腊船东给 ASI 的,时间为 3 月 19 日,内容是:

"We refer to our pleasant conversation of earlier today with Mr Edward Jiang(厦门船厂雇员) with respect to the effectiveness of the Shipbuilding Contract. The position under article 21 can be summarized as follows:

1. In accordance with its terms, the Shipbuilding Contract is today fully effective and has been since the date of its execution...

b. Article 21(b)(I) - Main Engine. The Buyer will bear the additional costs, if any, arising from the importation of the main engine from Korea..."

仲裁庭不接受该两封传真已经显示了双方对主机问题达成协议,理由有几方面,部分也没有写在裁决书。如一个原因是在聆听了约 9 天的证据之后,对这两封传真有一定保留,这是在该裁决书的 166 段所显示出来:"We begin by pointing out that

ASI's letter of 18 March 2003 was not the kind of letter, which judging from previous exchanges, Xiamen would have been likely to send if it had intended to make a firm offer as to the supplier of the main engine. ASI's letter is stated to have been the result of an oral discussion with the yard, whereas all previous proposals had been contained in letters or emails sent directly by Xiamen itself. This is not all. When Xiamen had previously made an offer relating to this very topic, it had embodied the offer in a formal document requiring the signature of the buyers; see the draft agreement of 7 March 2003 proposing that the supplier should be a 'Chinese manufacturer under the license of MAN B & W'. The letter from ASI lacks any formality."

另一个原因是仲裁庭认为在3月18日的电传,ASI所用的文字并不肯定是厦门船厂作出了一个要约,接受韩国进口主机。仅是从字面上来看,充其量也就是厦门船厂作出的一个"建议"(proposal)。例如,该电传中的第二点说是要买方(希腊船东)承担主机价格的差额,就不明确这差额包括些什么,是否包括南韩主机运输到厦门的费用与保险费,是否包括厦门船厂可能要赔偿给中国有许可证的工厂的金额?这是在裁决书的167段有针对,如下:"Next, the language used by ASI is not entirely consistent with the making of an offer on behalf of Xiamen. As was pointed out, there is no doubt some uncertainty as to what sums are included in the phrase 'The Buyer bears the (costs) of price difference after the shipyard present the Buyer clear evidence'. Does price difference include any sums that might have to be paid to compensate the Chinese licensees for loss of business? The point however goes somewhat further. If it was open to the buyers to 'accept' the second alternative set out in ASI's letter, then logically one would expect that the first alternative solution proposed in the letter would also constitute an offer open for acceptance. But the first alternative ('The Buyer shall assist the yard to squeeze the price to the same level as domestic License Supplier") is so uncertain in language and effect that it can hardly constitute more than a proposal open for further discussion and more detailed elaboration."

还有其他是仲裁庭感受到或从证据中明显看到的,如船价急升,希腊船东与ASI都很希望造船合约能够确立。但当时希腊船东与厦门船厂关系已经弄僵,厦门船厂根本不回应。所以仲裁庭有点难以接受在这样的气氛下,厦门船厂怎么会像ASI在3月18日的传真中所讲的,无端给了一个要约说只要希腊船东接受价格的差额就答应从韩国进口主机?这是很突然的转变,而希腊船东要承担这价格的差额在谈判一开始就已经不是问题,厦门船厂根本不必争取也是这个结果。仲裁庭也看到一些其他证据是厦门船厂要进口韩国主机在手续上也不容易,而这些在披露出来的文件可以看到有许多问题仍需要解决,厦门船厂不大可能随口做出这样的承诺。

包括笔者所作出的仲裁裁决书被上诉去了法院,法院却改变了仲裁庭的判法,认为该两封传真是可以解释为双方达成一个对韩国进口主机的协议,进一步也等于双方达成了造船合约。Langley 大法官是这样说:"The question whether or not the letters of 18 and 19 March 2003 did constitute a binding agreement was one of law or mixed fact and law... The 18 March letter did constitute the making of alternative offers open to acceptance in relation to the source and cost of the main engine. The 19 March letter was phrased in terms of acceptance and not further negotiation as regards the main engine. An objective reader would readily conclude that there was agreement on the main engine ... **arbitrators were wrong in law to conclude that there was no agreement on the main engine.**"(加黑是笔者的强调)

笔者作为仲裁庭成员之一,评论这一法院的判决也恐怕会有主观。所以在这里只邀请想进一步研究的读者阅读该判例及有关资料并想想怎样能够在做法与制度上改善。笔者感觉三个有经验的仲裁员(包括笔者是有实际造船业务的经验)花了9天时间聆讯大量口头证据后得出的结论,被高院一位法官花了1天至1天半的时间,而且大量口头证据都没有碰过,就根据部分文书证据推翻仲裁庭的裁决,这好像不科学且片面。如果是一份完整记录双方所约定内容的文书合约,不看口头证据解释还有一定的道理,至少这是传统上英国法律的做法。但一涉及了部分口头部分书面的合约,仅看文书部分就作出结论恐怕有断章取义的感觉,尤其是在今天解释合约/文件强调要了解背景/语境。笔者也可依据 Bingham 大法官在 Pagnan SpA v. Feed Products Ltd (1987) 2 Lloyd's Rep. 601 先例中所提的警告说:"The Court must consider all these exchanges in context and not seize upon one episode in isolation in order to conclude that a contract has been made."

经过这一案件,笔者感觉到英国法律认为部分书面的合约是属于法律或事实与法律混合的问题,而法律问题是可以批准上诉去法院的做法存在一定的问题。

第三章　内部解释合约

针对一份看来是完整的文书合约或文件,传统的解释就是看四个角内的内容。在近三十年来的做法上虽然有了改变,导致解释合约从根据“字面”(text)变为“语境”(context),但不表示这种内部解释合约不再重要。毕竟让法院/仲裁庭根据背景/语境认定文书合约条文/文字必须扭曲解释才能体现双方真正的订约意图的案件也不是太多。而且仍有例外情况,如在解释标准合约条文时“肯定性”(certainty)更加重要,导致个别案件的背景/语境就变为不重要。所以,在本章以下段节与第四、第五章都会针对内部解释文书合约/文件的各种规则。

但首先简单一提就是这些众多的解释规则,只能对订约双方的意图作出一般性解读或指引。而且在这种争议,通常双方有水平的代表大律师都会依赖对自己一方有利的部分解释规则,也显示了许多这些一般性的解释规则使用在个别案件往往会引起矛盾。这代表了最终法院或仲裁庭要作出的决定还是主要针对有关案件的双方真正订约意图,而不必受到这些一般性解释规则的束缚。这方面会在本书第四章之第1段有更详尽介绍。

§1　需要整体解释合约且给每一条文/文字有一定解释

文书合约不会只有几个单词或一两条条文,所以解释一份合约是要求全面解释,给每一条有关条文甚至每一个有关单词都有一定的综合解释。毕竟,合约中每一条条文或一个单词都是双方约定了表达他们订约意图的内容,法院/仲裁庭在解释合约时不能漠视/删除,或只断章取义。一份合约必须整体作出解释这个原则,几乎每一位著名大法官都有提到,笔者只挑部分节录如下。

第一个是 Elenborough 勋爵在 Barton v. Fitzgerald (1812) 15 East 530 先例中所说的:“The sense and meaning of the parties in any particular part of an instrument may be collected *ex antecedentibus et consequentibus*; every part of it may be brought into action in order to collect from the whole one uniform and constant sense, if that may be done.”

第二个是 Romilly M. R. 勋爵在 Re Strand Music Hall Co Ltd (1865) 35 Beav. 153 先例中所说的:“The proper mode of construing any written instrument is, to give effect to every part of it, if this be possible, and not to strike out or nullify one clause in a deed, unless it be impossible to reconcile it with another and more express clause in the same deed."

第三个是 Watson 勋爵在 Chamber Colliery Ltd v. Twyerould (1893) (1915) 1 Ch. 268 (Note) 先例中所说的:"I find nothing in this case to oust the application of the well known rule that a deed ought to be read as a whole, in order to ascertain the true meaning of its several clauses; and what the words of each clause should be so interpreted as to bring them into harmony with the other provisions of the deed, if that interpretation does no violence to the meaning of which they are naturally susceptible."

这种同样的说法实际上是近期其他很多出名的法官也有提到,Clarke 大法官在 The "Nerano" (1994) 2 Lloyd's Rep. 50 中说:"However he (原告大律师) submits that the correct approach is to construe the bill of lading as a whole and that the Court should not object any of the terms of the document on the ground of inconsistency unless driven to do so. I accept the submission that the correct course is to try to give effect to all the provisions of the bill of lading. ..."

§2　整体解释合约之一:两条不同条文之间的协调

这是一个经常发生的情况,就是一份合约内有一条以上的条文针对同一件事,但说法不一样且它们之间有一定的矛盾。这样,如果能够协调他们之间的矛盾并且给两条或以上的不同条文都有一定的解释与存在价值,就应该这样解释,即使在协调的过程中会把一些看来清楚无误的个别文字的意思作出一定的扭曲或局限。至于怎样是无法协调的矛盾,这在 The "Lowlands Orchid" (2010) 1 Lloyd's 317 先例,Beatson 大法官说:"... there was inconsistency where the application of one clause would 'almost entirely' deprive the other clause of any effect. ... to one of the clauses being 'emasculated' in a manner which is contrary to its express terms ... In Pagnan SpA v Tradax ... Bingham LJ said that to be inconsistent the contradiction or conflict must be 'such that effect cannot fairly be given to both clauses'."(矛盾必须导致其中一条条文几乎完全剥夺了另一条文的任何解释,或是一条条文"阉割"了另一条文。Bingham 大法官曾经说这一矛盾或冲突必须是无法合理给两条条文一定的解释。)

可以说在这种无法协调的矛盾就只能漠视/删除其中一条被视为是次要的条文,这在本章稍后的第 4 段有针对。

有关把两条或以上起矛盾的合约条文作出协调的解释的权威说法,可部分节录如下:

1. 早在 Joyce v. Realm Marine Insurance (1872) L. R. 7 Q. B. 580 先例,Black-

burn 勋爵针对一份保单就说:"The ordinary and general rule in the case of a policy of insurance, of course, is that we must construe the policy as we find it; it is a printed form, with written parts in introduced into it, and we are to take the whole together, both the written and the printed parts. Although it has sometimes been endeavoured to be argued that we ought to bestow no more attention on the written parts than on the printed parts which are uniform in most policies of insurance, there is no doubt that we do, and ought to, make a difference between them. The part that is specially put into a particular instrument is naturally more in harmony with that the parties are intending than the other, although it must be used to reject the other, or to make it have no effect."

2. 在 Fuller's Theatre and Vaudeville Co Ltd v. Rofe (1923) A. C. 435 先例,是有关悉尼大剧院的一个合约。在枢密院,Atkinson 勋爵这样说:"It is well established, ... that if one finds in a lease a covenant by the lessee not to assign or sublet the demised premises without the consent, in writing, of the lessor first had and obtained, and also a covenant by the lessor that he will not unreasonably withhold his consent to a subletting or such like, the two covenants must be construed together with the result that the covenant of the lessee will be held to be qualified by that of the lessor."(这是针对两条不同条文,一是租客不转租,除非能预先得到房东的文书同意。另一条是房东不会不合理拒绝给予同意去转租。这两条要一并解释,就是租客的承诺受到房东承诺的限制。即是,如果房东的拒绝同意转租被证明不合理,房东就会是违约并要赔偿租客的损失。)

3. 在 The "Caspiana" (1956) 2 Lloyd's Rep. 379 先例,Jenkins 大法官针对提单说:"... a recognised principle, which is not confined to bills of lading, but in its relation to bills of lading may be stated as being that where a bill of lading is concluded by means of a printed form containing general conditions, into which the parties write, type or otherwise incorporated the terms agreed upon in respect of the particular transaction in view (for example the termini of the voyage contracted for), and any of the printed conditions is found to be inconsistent with or repugnant to the main object and intention of the bill of lading as disclosed by the terms specially agreed, the court will limit or modify the conflicting printed condition to the extent necessary to enable effect to be given to such main object and intention, or in a case of complete repugnancy wholly reject it."(提单使用一份印本的标准格式,内有一般性的条件,然后双方当事人写上、打字或合并其他条文,如程租租约,而这与印本条件有矛盾或违背了提单的目的/目标与意图,法院就会限制或更改起矛盾的印本条件,或如果是一个全面的矛盾导致无法协调,会漠视或删除。)

4. 较近期的权威说法是 Goff 勋爵在 Yien Yieh Commercial Bank Ltd v. Kwai Chung Cold Storage Co Ltd (1989) 2 H. K. L. R. 639, PC 先例中说的:"Their Lord-

ships wish to stress that to reject one clause in a contract as inconsistent with another involves a rewriting of the contract which can only be justified in circumstances where the two clauses are in truth inconsistent. In point of fact, this is likely to occur only where there has been some defect of draftsmanship. The usual case is where a standard form is taken and then adapted for a special need, as is frequently done in, for example, the case of standard forms of charterparty adapted by brokers for particular contracts. From time to time, it is discovered that the typed additions cannot live with the printed form, in which event the typed additions will be held to prevail as more likely to represent the intentions of the parties. But where the document has been drafted as a coherent whole, repugnancy is extremely unlikely to occur. The contract has, after all, to be read as a whole; and the overwhelming probability is that, on examination, an apparent inconsistency will be resolved by the ordinary processes of construction."

Goff 勋爵在上述先例中警告说在两条不同条文之间有矛盾时,应该尽量避免漠视或删除其中一条,因为这是"重写"(rewrite)双方订立的合约,这样做只是没有其他办法时"最后的办法"(last resort)。比较普遍发生的情况是双方使用一份被普遍使用的标准格式合约(如租约),然后加上一些有特殊需要的附加条文。这就经常出现附加条文无法全面配合标准格式合约中的印本条文,这样,接受附加条文应该是有更大的可能代表订约双方的意图。但出现这种情况,还是要尽量协调,而不是简单的漠示或删除标准格式内的条文。

5. 在 The "Lowlands Orchid"先例,Beatson 大法官说:"... I have concluded that there is no clear direct and irreconcilable conflict between clause 63 of the pro forma charterparty and the fixture recap. The two clauses can be read together sensibly and in a commercially satisfactory way with the former qualifying the latter."

总结而言,这种在两条或以上不同条文之间的协调,是笔者几乎每天在做的工作。有无数的例子/先例可作介绍。只列举几个如下。

2.1　例子一:协调租约中的保费与加保费的矛盾

在著名的 NYPE 46 期租合约,其第 1 条文是说明"船东必须支付船舶的保险"(The owners shall pay for the insurance of the vessel),没有其他限制的文字。所以从字义上可理解为只要涉及船舶的保险(而不是货物的保险),船东就要承担。但现实中,期租合约经常有附加条文说明如果船舶被承租人命令去战区,战区的船舶保险加保费(有时候去风险高的地区如部分中东国家,加保费会十分昂贵)就要承租人承担,毕竟船舶的营运是承租人的事。本来,一份好的租约就会在第 1 条文中在说明船东必须支付船舶的保险的一句后,马上补充说"附加条文第几条的战区保险加保费除外"。又或是,在附加条文有关战争保险加保费要承租人承担的前面加上一句说"不论本合约其他条文有怎样的不同说法"(notwithstanding any clause in this contract stating to the contrary),以显示附加条文的分量。这样,就可把它们之间的矛盾以明示加以协调与明确。但即使没有这样做,仲裁庭解释时也应该很容易在这一情况下作出协调并且让每一条文都有一定的意思或存在价值。这协调就是船东必须支付船舶的保险,但战争保险加保费是唯一的例外或作为是"限制"(qualify)。毕竟,根据其他解释合约的规则,也很容易得出这一结论。一是附加条文解释起来分量比印本条文重;二是面窄的条文应该比广泛性的条文解释起来分量重,而针对战区保险加保费明显是面比较窄。这在稍后第 5.1.3 段会有详论。

2.2 例子二:协调油轮程租合约中的承租人承诺指定马上可挂靠泊位与免算装卸时间条文的矛盾

The"Laura Prima" (1982) 1 Lloyd's Rep. 1 这个重要的贵族院先例涉及很多船东与承租人的利益,因为它是针对一个经常被使用的油轮程租租约,名为 Exxonvoy 1969 标准格式。起争议的是两条条文,分别为第 6 与第 9 条文,如下:

"6. Notice of readiness: Upon arrival at... port of loading... the Master... shall give the Charterer... notice... that the vessel is ready to load... cargo, berth or no berth, and laytime... shall commence upon the expiration of six... hours after receipt of such notice... **However where delay is caused to Vessel getting into berth after giving notice of readiness for any reason over which Charterer has no control, such delay shall not count as used laytime.**

9. Safe berthing—shifting. The vessel shall load... at any safe place or wharf, or alongside vessel... **reachable on her arrival**, which shall be designated and procured by the Charterer..."(加黑部分是笔者的强调)

另也节录第 7 条文中的相关的一句,如下:"7. ... Time consumed by the vessel on moving from loading or discharge port anchorage to her loading or discharge berth, discharging ballast water or slops, will not count as used laytime."

"Laura Prima"这一艘油轮是在 1978 年 11 月 27 日凌晨抵达利比亚装港,但由于港口拥挤,船舶在锚地等了 9 天后才有空的泊位挂靠。这 9 天的滞期费对一艘大油轮来说可不是一笔小钱,损失应该是船东还是承租人承担就产生了争议,而且马上显示了第 6 与第 9 条文之间的矛盾。承租人说根据第 6 条文的最后一句,即以上节录的加黑部分,清楚说明了如果船舶延误挂靠泊位是因为承租人无法控制的原因所导致,这延误不算装货时间,时间损失也是船东自己要承担。而在该先例的情况下,明确是港口拥挤,泊位被占用与调度属于港口当局的权力,承租人无法控制该 9 天的延误。但船东争辩说根据第 9 条文,承租人违约,因为该条文清楚说明他必须在船舶一抵达装港就要指定一个"马上可以挂靠"(reachable on arrival)的安全泊位。在该先例的情况下,承租人没有履行这一严格的合约承诺。如果港口当局是代承租人指定一个可以挂靠的泊位,这是在抵达装港后 9 天才发生的事情。这样看来,如果支持船东的说法,就会导致第 6 条文没有任何意义了。

在伦敦仲裁,先是由两位当事人委任的仲裁员无法达成一致意见,结果委任了

Bruce Harris 先生为公断人,他认为第 6 条文十分明确,足以保护承租人要支付这 9 天的延误。至于承租人在第 9 条的违约,由于有第 6 条文的保护,承租人还是不必承担这一延误。所以仲裁庭是判承租人胜诉。

但这裁决书上诉去了高院被推翻,原因是解释合约应该协调第 6 与第 9 条文之间的矛盾,而不是像 Bruce Harris 先生否定第 9 条文。协调的做法就是先要求承租人在船舶抵达利比亚装港时,马上根据第 9 条文指定一个可抵达的泊位。此后,如果发生了一些事故导致船舶不能抵达该泊位,如航道突然因另一艘船舶的事故而受阻,逼使有关船舶需要折回锚地等候,这才可适用第 6 条文。固然,这样解释下第 6 条文的适用面就变得很局限,因为指定可抵达的泊位后会在很短时间发生事故导致该泊位变成不可抵达不太可能发生,但毕竟这样解释第 6 条文仍有一定(但是十分局限)的意思与作用。此外,高院也考虑了案件的背景/语境,就是在一个"港口租约"(port charter)下通常是承租人要承担港口拥挤的风险,而船东只承担与航行及船舶有关的风险。Mocatta 大法官这样说:

"Clause 6 and 9 had to be read together in the context of the charterparty as a whole and it was clear that this was a port charter and there was no express provision in the charter that the risk of congestion in the port was to be placed on the owners...

That last sentence in clause 6 only applied and prevented laytime from running if the charterers, pursuant to clause 9, had designated and the procured a safe place or wharf or alongside vessel reachableupon the vessel's arrival, and if an intervening event occurred causing delay over which the charterers had no control; unless clause 6 was construed in this way, it would appear that the last sentence would in many cases, and certainly those of congestion, deprive the words '**reachable upon her arrival**' of the contractual effect given them."

承租人再上诉去贵族院,贵族院完全支持 Mocatta 大法官的判法,就是要整体解释合约。在笔者看来,如果承租人违约不指定一个船舶一抵达即可马上挂靠的泊位,也可解释他的违约令他无法依赖第 6 条文的免责/免算装货时间,并得出同样的结果。因为有另一个合约的解释规则是"假设有过错的一方不能得利"(The presumption that a contracting party cannot take advantage of its own wrong),这在本书第四章之第 10 段与第七章之 10.3 段有介绍。

2.3 例子三:协调法院管辖与仲裁条文之间的矛盾

仲裁条文拟定得有缺陷或不明确的情况经常会遇到,如笔者曾经遇过一条粗糙的仲裁条文说是"香港仲裁,在法院面前"(Arbitration in Hong Kong before the court)。这样,给它一个合理解释就是要给双方约定的每一个文字都有一定的意思。如果双方有了争议可让原告去香港法院,这就是漠视/排除了"香港仲裁"这几个字。但如果要求双方在香港仲裁,原告即使已经在法院开始了诉讼也会被中止,这就漠视/删除了"在法院面前"这几个字。最后笔者参与的决定是给这一仲裁条文全面与协调的解释,就是根据当年的《香港仲裁条例》第13(A)条可委任一位法官作为独任仲裁员。这样,就应该给了每一个文字都有一定解释,因为法官作为仲裁员的话就会在法院内庭审理该仲裁案件了。这一个案子据说后来不了了之,但笔者一直都觉得代表了怎样解释与协调一条条文之间的内部矛盾。

这种协调的工作也出现在合约中有两条条文,一条是仲裁条文,另一条是法院管辖条文。这样就有一个很大的疑问,就是这一严重的不一致会否导致不肯定而判是无效?笔者估计在二三十年前还没有太支持仲裁的年代,认为仲裁条文无效的可能性很大。毕竟,有争议时受法院管辖是当事人基本的权利,也是默示的地位。所以要以仲裁代取或排除法院的管辖,是有必要写得明确无误,这一条解释规则在本书第四章之第11段有针对。

但在近年来,由于各国在政策上大力支持仲裁,特别是在商业合约已经不认为仲裁相比法院是更不合理或次要的争议解决办法,必须明示才能有效替代法院诉讼。这带来一种协调的说法解释这种两条起冲突的仲裁条文与法院管辖条文。其中的两个先例 Smith Ltd v. H & S International (1991) 2 Lloyd's Rep. 127 与 The "Nerano" (1994) 2 Lloyd's Rep. 50 也在《仲裁法——从1996年英国仲裁法到国际商务仲裁》一书第一章之2.5与2.6段有提到,为了方便阅读,笔者把这两个案例节录如下:

"2.5　有缺陷仲裁条文例子之四:协调法院与仲裁的矛盾之一

在 Smith Ltd. v. H & S International [1991] 2 Lloyd's Rep. 127 先例中涉及的是一个名牌运动服专卖合约,其解决争议条文有两条,其中第13条是去ICC仲裁,但第14条说是英国法院有管辖权。它们的文字与措辞如下:

'13. SETTLEMENT OF DISPUTE If any dispute or difference shall arise between the parties hereto concerning the construction of this Agreement or the rights or liabilities of either party hereunder the parties shall strive to settle the same amicably but if they are unable to do so the dispute or difference shall be adjudicated upon under the Rules of Conciliation and Arbitration of the International Chamber of Commerce by one or more Arbitrators appointed in accordance with those Rules.

14. LANGUAGE AND LAW This Agreement is written in the English language and shall be interpreted according to English Law. The Court of England shall have exclusive jurisdictions over it to which jurisdiction the parties hereby submit.'

双方有关支付专利费有了争议,原告企图终止合约。被告向ICC申请与提出仲裁,但原告抗拒说仲裁条文无效。ICC作出了裁决指称该仲裁条文有效,于是原告去了英国法院要求法院对仲裁条文的有效性作出一个'宣告'(Declaration)并同时作出禁令阻止ICC仲裁程序的推进。这种做法是在1996年《仲裁法》生效前的一贯做法。

原告指ICC仲裁条文无效的主要原因是第13条文与第14条文有直接与正面的矛盾与冲突,所以在考虑到法院是正常的程序解决争议,而如果要去仲裁是要清楚说明才能排除法院的管辖,在本案例中就应该否定 ICC 仲裁条文。这是合约'解释规则'(rules of construction)第一条。

Steyn 大法官认为第 13 条文与第 14 条文并非有真正的矛盾与冲突,而是可以协调并给一个综合的合理解释。首先,他认为第 13 条文是一条十分广泛与措辞严谨的 ICC 仲裁条文,所以不能排除。而第 14 条文大可以解释为第一部分约定的是合约的适用实体法,也就是英国法。而第二部分是说明英国法院有管辖权,这管辖权只是局限在对该 ICC 仲裁的监督,而不是取代 ICC。而在英国进行的 ICC 仲裁,程序法是英国仲裁法,但同时照顾到双方明示的 ICC 仲裁规则。这样,第 13 条文与 14 条文综合针对了实体法、程序法与仲裁规则。

2.6　有缺陷仲裁条文例子之四:协调法院与仲裁的矛盾之二

另一个同一判法的案例涉及租约仲裁条文是否有合并提单的热门话题,案例是 The "Nerano"(1994)2 Lloyd's Rep 50。在该货损货差的争议,相关提单有两条条文。在提单前面是有一条写明说:'The conditions as per relevant charterparty dated 02.07.1990 are incorporated in this bill of lading and have precedence if there is a conflict, English law and jurisdiction applies.'可见这条文罕见的把合并的租约日期也写明,并且谈到英国法院的管辖。这样,它就与提单背面的一条合并租约仲裁的条文起了表面冲突。这一条条文是印在最普遍使用的 Congenbill 1994 格式的散货提单,说:'All terms and conditions liberties exceptions and arbitration clause of the Charterparty, dated as overleaf, are herewith incorporated.'

既然提单是收货人与船东之间的运输合约,解释表面看来有冲突的条文就应该看看是否有真正无法协调的冲突与矛盾。结果 Clarke 大法官判是可以作出协调,英国法院起的作用就是监督一个伦敦仲裁。他说:'the correct course was to give effect to all the provisions of the bill; if that attempt was made it led to the conclusion that effect could be given to both the clause on the front and the clause on the back of the bill of lading; there was some overlap but there was no conflict; the notion of English jurisdiction was not inconsistent with a submission to arbitration if only because the English Court retained a supervisory jurisdiction over the arbitration which according to cl. 36 was to take place in England; there was no reason to disregard the specific reference in cl. 1 to the incorporation of the arbitration clause;'

这判法与 Smith Ltd. v. H & S International [1991] 2 Lloyd's Rep. 127 先例的判法一致。"

在上述的两个先例,比较可以理解 Smith Ltd. v. H & S International 先例,因为它的仲裁条文写得很清楚,包括双方先要和解,如果不成功才去国际商会根据有关的国际商会规则进行仲裁。这比简略的一句"英国法院有管辖权"应有更大分量。但到了 The "Nerano"先例,就已经觉得是法院给仲裁条文的明示合并有很重分量,与一贯对提单合并租约仲裁条文的相对严格性有一定程度的不一致。但毕竟还是可以理解,因为提单前面如上所节录的一句只是说"英国法与管辖权适用"。但再举一个更近期的先例 Shell v. Coral Oil (1999) 1 Lloyd's Rep. 72,这种支持仲裁的趋势就更加明显了。

该先例涉及了英国壳牌石油公司与另一家英国公司 Coral Oil Co Ltd 约定了一个技术服务的合约,就是前者协助 Coral 混合与生产润滑油,销售去黎巴嫩与其他中东地区。在该合约中,有第 13 与第 14 条文起矛盾,如下:

"13. Applicable Law This Agreement, its interpretation and the relationship of the parties hereto shall be governed and construed in accordance with English Law and any dispute under this provision shall be referred to the jurisdiction of the English Courts.

14. Arbitration Any dispute which may arise either in contract or at law of or in connection with this Agreement shall be finally and exclusively settled by arbitration by three arbitrators in London, England in accordance with the Rules of the London Court of International Arbitration at the date hereof."

需注意的是,上述两个条文都写得比较全面,特别是英国法院的管辖有说明是针对该合约下的争议,而不是泛泛的一句英国法院管辖,这在较早的两个先例可被一定程度下扭曲成是英国法院在程序上管辖伦敦仲裁。

该先例的案情是壳牌石油公司根据该合约给了 Coral 6 个月的通知来终止双方的合约关系。这虽然是明示规定,但 Coral 作为多年来壳牌石油公司在黎巴嫩的代理商,就面临很大损失,据说高达 500 万美元。而根据黎巴嫩的法律,在这种情况下如果代理人没有过错,委任人就要作出损失赔偿。这样,Coral 就在黎巴嫩法院起诉壳牌石油公司。而壳牌石油公司的反击就是去英国法院申请一个禁令,意图阻止 Coral 在黎巴嫩法院继续起诉,并要去伦敦仲裁。

Coral 的争辩是上述的第 13 与 14 条文直接起矛盾而变得两条条文都无效,所以 Coral 可以在黎巴嫩法院起诉。但 Moore - Bick 大法官不同意并认为这两条条文仍然可以协调,虽然在说法上好像有一点牵强,如下:"The article continues to state: 'Any dispute under this provision shall be referred to the jurisdiction of the English courts'. In my judgment, that can be read as requiring any dispute about the proper law to be referred to the English Courts and all other substantive disputes to be referred to arbitration under article 14. I would accept that provisions of that kind ascribing jurisdiction partly to the Court and partly to arbitrators give rise to an untidy arrangement, but it is quite clear, in my judgment, that the parties did intend substantive disputes between them to be referred to arbitration, even if the Court was intended to have a residual jurisdiction over some kinds of disputes about the proper law. I should prefer not to decide in vacuo whether any particular dispute would fall within the ambit of article 13 or article 14. In my judgment, a question of that sort is better left for decision until a particular issue arises for consideration. Nonetheless I am quite satisfied that these two articles can be reconciled and that the Court should not reject them out of hand as being insensible."

由于订约自由下每一份合约的写法都不一样，笔者希望有一天看到是一个案件针对法院管辖条文是细致的且内容十分有针对性，如说明合约所有有关争议、索赔、救济与解释都要去英国法院解决，被告一定要委任伦敦的代理人/律师接受告票的传达等。而另外一条起矛盾的仲裁条文只简单说"伦敦仲裁"，这样就很有趣，要看看法官如何判法与自圆其说才能支持仲裁了。因为这表示要对许多关系到英国法院管辖条文的内容作出一定的解释，而无法这样做就等于否定这些文字了。

即使在已经介绍过的三个先例中，还是觉得这个协调实际上是有一定的"矫揉造作"(artificial)。因为在现实中就是实质地否定法院管辖的条文了，把法院只说成是管辖仲裁的"程序法"(curial law)。这样的解释与协调显然也不是铁板一块，首先香港的高院就有过不同判法，解释为原告有选择权可去仲裁或可去约定的法院起诉：William Co v. Chu Kong Agency Co Ltd and Guangzhou Ocean Shipping Co (1993, unreported)先例。而即使在英国也有不同的解释与判法：MH Alshaya Co WLL v. Retek Information System Inc (2000, unreported)先例。

先介绍在英国的先例，科威特公司的原告(MHA)与美国公司的被告(RISI)订立了一个向后者"收购软件系统合约"(software agreement)，并加上一个"维修保养合约"(maintenance agreement)，共两个合约。前一个合约有一条英国法院的"排他管辖权条文"(exclusive jurisdiction clause)，但另有一条仲裁条文说明是去美国仲裁协会(AAA)仲裁。而后一个合约只有一条英国法院的排他管辖权条文。之后，双方有了争议，MHA 就去英国法院起诉，但 RISI 去美国开始仲裁。有关的先例就是涉及 MHA 向英国法院申请禁令以阻止 RISI 去进行仲裁。

结果是 Garland 大法官作出了止诉禁令，说是收购软件系统合约下的仲裁条文无效。至于出现一些争议并且同时涉及两份合约，是无法在维修保养合约也作出默示有一条美国仲裁协会的仲裁条文让这些争议都可以去美国仲裁。毕竟在维修保养合约已经有一条英国法院的管辖权条文解决争议，所以不会有"必须性"作出默示。另外，该合约也有一条"完整合约条文"(entire agreement clause)。[1] 所以，在整体上看这一交易的合约结构，仲裁条文是与其"相悖"(repugnant)而无效。

但这一判决还是受到一定质疑，如在 Merkin 教授的《Arbitration Law》一书第 5.14 段就说："While Garland J's conclusion produced a neat solution to the complexities of what had been agreed, there must be several doubts concerning this decision. It is far from obvious that the courts should seek to rescue the parties from deficiencies in their arrangements. Garland J might easily have held that: (1) the proper construction of the software agreement was that the parties were to go to arbitration, while the exclusive jurisdiction clause related to curial matters arising in the arbitration; and (2) disputes ari-

[1] 可见本书第十三章之第 2 段。

sing under the maintenance agreement were to be resolved by the courts, and disputes arising under the software agreement were to be resolved by arbitration—insofar as the issues overlapped, the court could stay its proceedings in relation to the maintenance agreement, and accept the conclusion of the arbitrators on those issues by way of issue estoppel."。(Merkin 教授认为 Garland 大法官大可以判得与其他先例一致,就是有实质争议就去美国仲裁协会仲裁,而英国法院只针对仲裁程序上的问题[笔者看来,英国法院能够在程序上管辖一个美国仲裁恐怕是非常有限]。至于有争议是同时涉及另一个维修保养合约,只能去英国法院解决争议,英国法院完全可以先中止,然后让美国仲裁协会先处理软件系统合约的同一争议。在仲裁裁决了之后,这一结果就可以被法院接受为"一事不再审",而不再对实质争议审理一次。)

2.4 例子四:香港对合约内香港法院、美国法院与纽约仲裁的矛盾条文作出的协调或漠视/删除

再介绍另一个香港上诉庭最近判的 PCCW Global Ltd v. Interactive Communications Service Ltd (2006) Civil Appcal No. 18,涉及一个国际电话服务的合约,合约内所有的管辖权/仲裁条文十分复杂与混乱,如下:

"Clause 4: Differences over billing charges were to be resolved amicably between the parties. Failure to reach an amicable resolution within a reasonable period of time (not to exceed 14 days) meant that the parties would submit their differences to the Hong Kong courts for resolution. (有关支付的争议如果不能在 14 天内友好解决,就去香港法院解决争议。)

Clause 5: The agreement would be subject to the laws of Hong Kong and the parties submitted to the exclusive jurisdiction of the courts ofHong Kong. (本合约根据香港法律与香港法院有专属管辖权。)

Clause 11.2: The agreement would be interpreted in accordance with the laws of the State ofNew York, and any disputes '*shall be submitted to the courts in the State of New York*'. (本合约根据纽约州的法律与任何争议交给纽约州法院审理。)

Clause 11.3: Either partymay require any dispute arising under the agreement to be '*settled by binding arbitration in accordance with the commercial arbitration rules of the American Arbitration Association.... The arbitration shall take place in New York, NY, USA*'. (本合约的争议可以美国仲裁协会的仲裁规则为准。仲裁地点在纽约。)"

双方有了支付的争议,这导致 PCCW 在香港法院根据上述第 3 条文起诉 Interactive,但后者申请中止,要求香港法院强制 PCCW 根据第 11.3 条文去纽约仲裁。

在高院,Interactive 的一个争议是上述的香港与纽约州法院管辖权条文带来了无法协调的情况而只能全部漠视/删除,这就剩下了第 11.3 条的纽约仲裁条文才是唯一有效。这个说法有一点像 Lovelock (EJR) Ltd v. Exportels (1968) 1 Lloyd's Rep. 163 先例,就是仲裁条文第一部分说所有争议去伦敦仲裁而第二部分说所有争议去莫斯科仲裁，结果判是直接起矛盾而全部无效一样。但高院拒绝这样做，并作出了以下的合约解释：主要的原因是第 11.3 条文的纽约仲裁在用字上并非是约束性，而只是“允许性”（permissive）的，因为说是“可以”（may）而不是说“必须”（shall）。高院看来是想协调这两条起矛盾的条文，说是根据第 4 条文双方在 14 天内试图友好解决争议期间，Interactive 从来没有说他要提出纽约仲裁，而是过了 5 个月之后才提出，这对本来允许可以选择去纽约仲裁构成了弃权。

高院也被要求一并解释第 5 与第 11.2 条文之间的直接矛盾，而后者针对纽约州法院用的文字是“必须”（shall）。高院认为第 11.2 条文中也只是允许性的，变成这“必须”被视为“可以”，但这里的原因是因为有第 5 条的“专属管辖权”（exclusive jurisdiction）条文，说：“To read ‘shall’ in clause 11.2 in some other way, as (say) incorporating some mandatory flavor, would be inconsistent with the plain and obvious meaning of the expression ‘exclusive jurisdiction’ in clause 5.”

去了上诉庭，上诉庭认为第 11.3 条仲裁条文可以有约束力与强制性，只要有一方当事人选择去仲裁，而法院也就必须中止法院程序。在本案例，问题就是有关支付的争议到底是属于该第 11.3 仲裁条文管辖或第 4 条文管辖。上诉庭试图根据谈判的“背景/语境”（background/factual matrix）找出双方的订约意图，发觉第 4 条文是依据 PCCW 的标准格式合约，明如果对付款有争议是去仲裁解决。但在谈判时，双方同意把它删除掉而改去香港法院。这样，上诉庭判是针对有关支付的争议，第 4 条文去香港法院是超越了第 11.3 条的纽约仲裁条文。有关以背景/语境找出双方的订约意图在本书第六章有详论，另有关看双方谈判证据的例外在本章之 14.3 段与本书第六章之 2.5.1 段。

总而言之，由于不同的合约条文/文字，与每一个案件有不同的背景/语境，再加上作出解释的法院或仲裁庭会对许多会适用的解释规则各有侧重，导致解释合约并非是完全一致的结果。

2.5　例子五：协调雇佣合约对解雇员工条文的矛盾

近期的 Societe Generale, London Branch v Geys (2011) EWCA Civ 307 先例是一个很简单的协调例子，相关的雇佣合约的第 13 条文规定雇佣关系可以通过雇主或雇员向对方作出 3 个月通知解除。但该雇佣合约又合并了雇员手册，其中 8.3 段说，雇主只要支付一笔钱，就可以立即解除与雇员的雇佣关系。法院判是这两条条文没有矛盾，雇主有两种解除雇佣关系的方式：一是通过作出 3 个月的通知；二是不作出通知，但支付给解雇的员工一笔钱替代通知。

§3　整体解释合约之二：相同文字应该有统一解释

照理说，同一份书面文件中所使用的相同文字或句子应该给予统一解释。这里的判法可举的例子是 The "Laura Prima" (1982) 1 Lloyd's Rep. 1 先例,该著名的贵族院先例在本章 2.2 段已经有介绍,不再重复。贵族院判租约第 6 条文的"泊位"(berth)与第 7 条文及第 9 条文的"泊位"一词是同样解释,即都是指第 9 条文下承租人在船舶一抵达港口就必须指定一个"马上可以挂靠的泊位"(berth reachable on her arrival)。这样,贵族院就可以协调第 6 与第 9 条文之间的矛盾。

可节录 Diplock 勋爵在 Prestcold (Central) Ltd v. Minister of Labour (1969) 1 W. L. R. 89 先例所说:"the habit of a legal draftsman is to eschew synonyms. He uses the same words throughout the document to express the same thing or concept and consequently if he uses different words the presumption is that he means a different thing or concept; ... a legal draftsman aims at uniformity in the structure of his draft."

但有罕见的例子做不到这一点。这可见 Watson v. Haggitt (1928) A. C. 127 先例,案情是有关一个合伙人之间的协议,其第 3 条文有关报酬是说明先支付给每一个合伙人工资,之后在他们之间分摊"净利润"(nett profit)。但另有第 21 条文规定如果有一位合伙人死亡,在世的合伙人就要在之后的 5 年支付给其继承人"每年净利润"(nett annual profit)的 1/3。虽然文字上看来都是一样,说是"净利润",但在枢密院给这两条不同条文的计算方法有不同解释。第 3 条文的计算净利润是在扣除工资之后,但第 21 条文就是在在世的合伙人工资被扣减之前。

§4 整体解释合约之三:两条不同条文起直接矛盾

这与本章第 2 段不同之处是两条直接矛盾的条文没有办法作出协调,而被迫要作出取舍,漠视或删除其中一条。在 Forbes v. Git (1922) 1 A. C. 256 先例,Wrenbury 勋爵说:"The principle of law to be applied may be stated in few words. If in a deed an earlier clause is followed by a later clause which destroys altogether the obligation created by the earlier clause, the later clause is to be rejected as repugnant and the earlier clause prevails. In this case the two clauses cannot be reconciled and the earlier provision in the deed prevails over the later. Thus if A covenants to pay ... and the deed subsequently provides that he shall not be liable under his covenant, that later provision is to be rejected as repugnant and void, for it altogether destroys the covenant. But if the later clause does not destroy but only qualifies the earlier, then the two are to be read together and effect is to be given to the intention of the parties as disclosed by the deed as a whole. Thus if A covenants to pay ... and the deed subsequently provides that he shall be liable to pay only at a future named date or in a future defined event or if at the due date of payment he holds a definite office, then the absolute covenant to pay is controlled by the words qualifying the obligation in manner described."

上述是 Wrenbury 勋爵所举的有关不能协调与能够协调的例子。第一种情况是 A 承诺支付一笔钱，但合约后来另有一条文说明 A 没有任何支付责任，这就是起直接矛盾而必须要漠视其中一条，解决办法如看哪一条条文的分量更重。第二种情况是 A 承诺支付一笔钱，但合约后来另有一条文说明 A 只需要在将来某一天支付，或将来发生某一件事情才需要支付。这样，A 本来是绝对/严格的承诺支付这笔钱就受到了后来所讲情况的限制（或将来某一天才支付或将来必须先发生某一件事情等的限制）。

但上述 Wrenbury 勋爵所讲的前部分的条文分量超越了后面的条文，所谓的"first clause prevails"，已经不再是今天的英国法律地位，这可见《Odgers' Construction of Deeds and Statutes》一书。也可简单介绍 Peabody Trust Governors v Reeve (2009) L & T. R. 9 先例，该先例涉及一份房屋租赁合约。该房屋租赁合约的第 15(a)条文说必须要合约双方书面同意才可以更改除了租金以外的合约条文，但之后的第 15(b)条文又说房东可以通过给租客通知单方面修改合约条文。Gabriel Moss QC 大法官不接受这一条解释规则，说这两条直接起冲突的条文完全有可能倒过来排列，说："I have to add that this solution seems to me to be one of last resort only. It is not clear why the two sub – clauses in the present case come in the order in which they do. It may be that they could just as easily have appeared in the reverse order. That would have led to the opposite solution if this were the only applicable test. It is hardly satisfactory for the true agreement of the parties to be ascertained on grounds which may be arbitrary and I suspect it is only in rare cases that this approach will be applied."

结果判决是以第 15(a)条文为准，而第 15(b)条文就被漠视/删除。原因大致为：一第 15(b)条文如果有效或有一定的解释，该条文会受到保护消费者的《不公平合约法》(《Unfair Terms in Consumer Contracts Regulations 1999》)的管制；二是也有可能是两个直接起矛盾与无法作出协调的条文之间选择一个比较合理的条文，而第 15(b)条文可以单方面修改合约显然比较不合理。

另是在 RSPCA v Sharp (2011) 1 WLR 980 先例，案情涉及一份遗嘱，Neuberger 勋爵说："... as a free – standing point, the mere fact that one clause precedes another seems to me to be of minor potential relevance on the issue of how they interrelate with each other."

对上述的说法，也可以节录《Chitty on Contracts》(第 31 版，2012 年)一书之 12 – 078 段的说法如下："**Inconsistent or repugnant clauses.** Where the different parts of an instrument are inconsistent, effect must be given to that part which is calculated to carry into effect the purpose of the contract as gathered from the instrument as a whole and the available background, and that part which would defeat it must be rejected. The old rule was, in such a case, that the earlier clause was to be received and the later rejected, but this rule was a mere rule of thumb, totally unscientific, and out of keeping with the modern construction of documents. . . ”

今天的地位应该是条文在同一个合约的前后次序,如第 20 条与 23 条,如果它们之间有矛盾是不存在前后次序有分量上的区别。有关条文/文字之间的分量轻重,在接下去的段节详论。

§5 起矛盾条文之间给予分量的轻重

在解释文书合约时经常会对有关的条文作出不同的对待,因为它们之间分量的轻重会有不同。这种做法如在需要协调两条有矛盾的条文,或是在无法协调下被迫要漠视直接起矛盾的两条条文之一。此时会给哪一条较重的分量还有其他耳熟能详的说法,如:(1)“手写”(written)、打印或戳盖的条文/文字超越(或优先于)印本条文/文字,而手写条文/文字超越打印的条文/文字;(2)合约中由订约方自己选用的文字如“修改、附加的部分”(amendments and additions)超越“印本条文”(printed clause);(3)“附件”(addendum)又超越附加条文,时间晚的附件优先于早的附件;(4)面窄与特别针对一件事的条文超越广泛与一般性的条文。

5.1 分量轻重要看订约方刻意显示的重点与选择的文字

上述的说法其实都是出自一个原因,就是找出订约双方所用的文字中表达出来的真正订约意图。而更好能够体现双方真正意图与谈判时有更大可能看过与想过,不论是以任何形式出现在一份合约中,都应该给予更重的分量。这种形式包括上述所讲或其他的,是手写、附件、红字出现在一份黑字的合约、粗体字、针对面比较窄与特别针对该合约特殊的某件事、明示为“首要条文”(paramount clause)、文字说明是“不管其他条文怎样说”(notwithstanding anything to the contrary)等。这里的精神是 Bingham 勋爵在 The “Starsin” (2003) 1 Lloyd' s Rep. 571 先例中认为只是一般的常识,说:“Secondly, it is common sense that greater weight should attach to terms which the particular contracting parties have chosen to include in the contract than to pre – printed terms probably devised to cover very many situations to which the particular contracting parties have never addressed their minds. It is unnecessary to quote the classical statement of this rule by Lord Ellenborough in *Robertson v. French* . . . ”

5.2 手写/打字条文超越印本条文

这方面较出名的案例是在 Addis v. Burrows (1948) 1 K. B. 444,Greene M. R. 勋爵说:“. . . apart from striking any words out, the fact that the parties have deliberately typed into this document words creating a tenancy for eighteen months made it clear that it must be so construed, and that, if necessary, the subsequent words in print must yield to that construction. ”

另是 The “Athinoula” (1980) 2 Lloyd' s Rep. 481 先例,在该案例中 Mocatta 大

法官说:“当一条打字条文与一条印本条文起矛盾时,普遍确立的原则就是打字条文优先。(Clause 18 . . . is a typed clause, whereas clause 8 is a printed clause; and where there is a conflict between two such clauses it is well established that the typed clause should prevail.)”

另 Rix 大法官在 The “Starsin” (2001) 1 Lloyd's Rep. 437 先例说:“the well known maxim of construction that written, stamped or typed words which are inconsistent with printed terms usually take effect by superseding the latter.”

另在《Chitty on Contracts》(第 31 版,2012 年)一书之 12 – 070 段也有说如下:“**Printed and written clauses.** Where the contract is contained in a printed form with writing superadded, the written words, if there should be any reasonable doubt about the sense and meaning of the whole, are to have greater effect attributed to them than the printed words, inasmuch as the written words are the immediate language and terms selected by the parties themselves for the expression of their meaning, and the printed words are a general formula adapted equally to their case and that of all other contracting parties upon similar occasions and subjects. Nevertheless, it is open to the parties to stipulate in their printed conditions of contract that written provisions appended to the printed form are not to override, modify or affect in any way the application or interpretation of that which is contained in the printed conditions, and effect must then be given to such a stipulation even though this is contrary to the ordinary rule.”

但这一条解释的规则正如其他的规则一样,它不是一成不变的教条,必须灵活使用。例如,在使用标准格式合约如一份租约,就经常会有情况是印本条文的空间不够而要以附加条文才能针对。这样,在印本条文部分,针对相应的部分会写上“请参看第××附加条文”。这样,订约意图明显不是给该条文更大的解释分量,而纯粹是现实需要。在 The “TFL Prosperity” (1984) 1 Lloyd's Rep. 123 先例,就涉及一条这样的条文针对船舶的细节,贵族院不接受该条文从印本条文变为第 26 条的附加条文就相比第 13 条的印本免责条文有了更重的解释份量。Roskill 勋爵是这样说:“. . . I will only make this observation. In the charter as executed the whole of the printed preamble was struck out and clause 26 with all its details was clearly intended to replace the printed preamble. If physically clause 26 had appeared as a substitute preamble to the charter, that substitute preamble, whether in type or in print, together with all the other clauses of the charter including clause 13, would have fallen to be construed as a whole and if contrary to either of the charterers' two principal submissions, clause 13 does protect the owners, I am afraid I do not follow why a contrary conclusion should be reached merely because the substitute preamble would appear as a typed clause on the first page of the charter and clause 13 would appear as a printed exceptions clause on the second page.”

5.3 面窄与特别针对一件事的条文超越广泛与一般性的条文

这是一条“面窄”(narrow)与“特别针对”(specific)一件事的条文超越广泛与一般性的条文重要的与经常适用的解释合约规则,这种案例也不少。

5.3.1 案例之一:The “Brabant”

可先举 The “Brabant” (1965) 2 Lloyd's Rep. 546 先例为例。案情是一份期租合约,标准格式是用的是 Baltime,印本条文的第 13 条文,文字上与金康租约的第 2 条文一致,对船东非常有利,豁免了船东对货损货差的责任,即使是由于船员的疏忽与过错所引起。该条文可部分节录如下:“13. The Owner only to be responsible ... for loss or damage to goods on board, if such ... loss has been caused by want of due diligence on the part of the Owners or their Manager in making the Vessel seaworthy and fitted for the voyage or any other personal act or omission or default of the Owners or their Manager. The Owners not to be responsible in any other case nor for damage ... whatsoever and howsoever caused even if caused by the neglect or default of their servants...”但双方在同一个租约也约定了另一条第 28 条附加条文,说明清洁船舱是船东的责任,如下:“28. The decks and holds and other cargo spaces to be properly cleaned at Owners' risk and expense before loading.”

船舶在一个装运木质纸浆的航次中,因船舱肮脏而导致货损,船东在提单下赔款。船东之后向承租人要求补偿,因为有第 9 条文说明承租人要补偿船东所有因签发提单而导致的责任。但要成功,船东必须证明这一货损是在租约下他不必负责的,而是因为签发了提单带来的比租约更重的责任。这就导致了第 13 条文与第 28 条文之间的矛盾。如果根据第 13 条文,船东不必对船员疏忽(这包括在装货前没有认真清洁船舱)的后果负责。但这与第 28 条文有矛盾,因为它说明清洁船舱是船东的责任。而第 28 条文的文字十分清楚,船舱不清洁的后果与损失由船东来承担。McNair 大法官是加上订约背景(如租约为了装木质纸浆这种清洁货物)后,这样解释该条文:“By the clause the owners are at risk that the holds shall be properly cleaned. The owners bear that risk and, if the holds are not properly cleaned, the risk eventuates and they are liable for any damage resulting therefrom. This seems to be the plain meaning of the clause according to its grammatical meaning and accords with what was presumably the intention of the parties to be deduced from the words and the surrounding circumstances, especially bearing in mind that it is an additional clause apparently designed in relation to the known intention that the vessel had been chartered for carrying wood-pulp.”

McNair 大法官也考虑到清洁船舱肯定是船员的工作,船东不会自己干这个活。所以,第 13 条文针对船员疏忽,但没有对船东自己疏忽免责这一点区别在本案背景是没有意思,也无法消除与第 28 条文的矛盾。固然,在本案例中可以以第 28 条文是附加条文,所以比印本格式的第 13 条文分量更重而解释得过去。但这不是每一个案件都说得通,因为有情况是第13与第28条文都出现在印本格式内或附加条文内。在该案例,承租人大律师所争的主要是第28条文有一个特定的目的针对要装运一种十分清洁货物,加上是面窄,应该有更重的分量。他说:"The construction of Clause 28 expressly provided for a specific result to be achieved, namely for the holds to be properly cleaned before leaving. Secondly, it expressly placed the obligation in the clause upon the owners.... Clause 28 made no commercial sense if that plain breach could be offset by reliance on Clause 13."

McNair大法官判是船东的补偿要求败诉,租约的第28条文超越了第13条文。这样,可见是第28条文在整体解释起来分量是比第13条文重,但没有否定第13条文的意义与作用。可想到是第13条文仍然适用在船员疏忽与过错的情况,只要不涉及第28条文的清洁船舱,船东仍然可受到保护。这一判法在The "Mariasmi" (1970) 1 Lloyd's Rep. 247先例也有提到:"Mr. Justice McNair held that the special provisions of clause 28 prevailed over the more general provisions by way of exception in clause 13, and accordingly the owners failed."

5.3.2 案例之二:The "Mariasmi"

接下来介绍这一同样判法的先例,就是The "Mariasmi" (1970) 1 Lloyd's Rep. 247。该先例中所涉及的两条起矛盾的条文均为附加条文,在这种情况下,就不能好像The "Brabant" (1965) 2 Lloyd's Rep. 546先例的说法,可以附加条文超越印本条文解释。这两条起矛盾的条文是:

"Clause 21: Should the vessel not be ready to load in accordance with the definite notice, the Owners to be responsible at loading port(s) for any expenses incurred thereby, such as demurrage on canal barges and or railway wagons, warehousing and extra transport charges in this connection, *force majeure* always excepted. Such expenses to be paid by the Owners or to be covered by deposit to Brokers' Agents at the loading port(s) until the final accounts are available.

Clause 29: Voyage Charter Party Clause Paramount ..."

案情是"Mariasmi"轮在一个程租合约中去欧洲港口装货至斯里兰卡,但不幸在第一装港鹿特丹开航去第二装港安特卫普时,半途因船员航行疏忽而发生船舶碰撞。这导致船舶抵达安特卫普后要检查与修理,又延误了13天才能开始起装货物。承租人损失了额外的仓库费用、驳船的滞期费等。但由于租约的第29条文(所谓著名的租约首要条文)是合并1924年的《海牙规则》,而《海牙规则》是船东对船员的航行疏忽免责。所以,表面看来承租人如果要向船东索赔因船舶碰撞带来的损失将会没有成功希望。在该先例,涉及船东作为原告向承租人索赔滞期费及运费。这样,承租人在同一诉讼中要求在索赔中对冲或反索赔这一笔安特卫普的费用。

但重要的还是看租约条文本身是否有依据可让承租人索赔这一笔安特卫普的费用。承租人说是有,这是根据第21条文,它明确针对如果船舶根据抵达通知未能备妥装货就要对这种额外的仓库费用与驳船滞期费等负责，除非是不可抗力（*force majeure*）的原因导致船舶未能备妥。在这次碰撞事故，涉及的是船员航行疏忽，当然不是不可抗力的免责。船东反驳说第29条文合并《海牙规则》有船东对船员航行疏忽的免责，而且第29条文是说明"首要"（paramount），就应该超越其他与之起矛盾的条文，如第21条文。

Mocatta大法官判是第29条文中的"首要"一词不应该给太多的分量，这种条文也经常在租约或提单见到，它有广泛的针对面，只是被订约双方随手拿来使用。另外，根据船东的解释，就会令第21条文中的一句免责（对不可抗力的免责）失去了任何意义。所以，还是要找一个协调让每一条文都有一定的解释。在Mocatta大法官看来判第21条文超越第29条文最重要的依据就是后者面广且在航运市场上普遍被使用，但前者面窄而且是明显特别被订约方设计的条文，市场上很少见到，更好显示双方订约意图，说："... Here clause 21 is a clause specifically designed - I say this by reason of its language, if by reason of nothing else - to deal with a limited range of circumstances, and to deal with that range only, whereas clause 29 has a vastly wider range of application.... that clause 29 is a clause taken off the peg, while clause 21 is tailor - made for a particular purpose."

5.3.3 案例之三：Sabah Flour v. Comfez

在Sabah Flour v Comfez (1988) 2 Lloyd's Rep 18先例，有关的程租合约有两条关于时效但直接起冲突的条文。其中第23条文是合并了1924年的澳大利亚《海上运输法》（也就是1924年《海牙规则》）的部分条文，如下：The provisions of section 5 and 8 of the Australian Sea Carriage of Goods Act 1924 and of Article III except clause 8 thereof ... of the Schedule thereto shall apply to the Charterparty and be deemed to be inserted in extensor herein."

上述合并的条文表示把《海牙规则》的Article III clause 6的交货后向承运人索赔的12个月时效包括在内。Article III被排除合并的只是clause 8，这一条文是不允许承运人以明示条文减轻或排除《海牙规则》强加的责任。

起冲突的另一条文是第34条文，它规定了船舶抵达最后卸港的6个月内的索赔时效，如下："... any claim must be in writing and claimant's arbitrator appointed within six months of the vessel's arrival at final port of discharge, otherwise all claims shall be deemed to be waived."

案情涉及承租人向船东提出货损的索赔，但委任仲裁员是在6个月时效外，但在12个月内。这表示根据第34条文就已经错过了时效，但根据第23条文就没有错过。船东的争辩主要是根据另一条解释规则，也就是主合约中的文字与目的超越合并文件中的文字，这在本章之5.5段有针对。但一审法院与上诉庭都判船东败诉，原因是其他分量更重的解释规则。就是第23条文十分小心与选择性合并《海牙规则》，它只针对货损货差与向承运人提出的索赔时效。显然，这比第34条文的6个月时效是面窄得多与有针对性。虽然在一个程租合约,很大部分的争议会是货损货差,但也不表示没有其他争议,如经常会有的装卸时间与滞期费争议。所以,第 34 条文的 6 个月不会没有任何意思。

5.3.4 案例之四:The "Eternity"

在 The "Eternity" (2009) 1 Lloyd's Rep 107 先例,也有这方面的争议。但看来是有关的两条条文经过法院的解释并没有起直接冲突,所以 Steel 大法官只是说:"Whilst it is correct that in the face of a conflict between provisions the more specific and tailored provision should prevail, such only arises if the conflict is clear and direct. In Marifortuna Naviera SA v Government of Ceylon (The "Mariasmi") [1970] 1 Lloyd's Rep. 247, the relevant clause imposed a specific obligation to meet certain expenses, with an exception for *force majeure*. It followed that there was a direct conflict since the clause would have been largely redundant if the paramount clause was treated as applicable."

5.4 文字超越数字

从常理看,人们在数字上较为容易犯错,如少打一个零。但相对比较长的文字,出错的机会就比较低。这也是为什么在一些比较严肃的法律文件中,经常会在数字后加上文字,如在 10000 美元后加上一个括号以文字补充(ten thousand dollars)。如果它们之间出现矛盾,如阿拉伯字的 10000 美元多了或少了一个零,应以文字的补充为准。这里的一些说法有 Tindal 大法官在 Saunderson v. Piper (1839) 5 Bing. N. C. 425 先例中说的:"... we can shake the rule of commercial writers, that where a difference appears between the figures and the words of a bill, it is safer to attend to the words."

另可见 Simond 大法官在 Re Hammond (1938) 3 All E. R. 308 先例中也有说到在商业合约中,有这个表面的规则:"No doubt there is a *prima facie* rule that, where words and figures conflict, the words ought to prevail, but no case has been brought to my notice where the rule has been applied otherwise than in the case of commercial documents."

在相对近期的 Durham City Estates v Felicetti (1990) 1 EGLR 143, CA 先例,涉及房屋租赁合约租金调整的通知,通知也必须说明新的租金。该先例的通知中的新租金是"£ 8,850 (Eight thousand seven hundred and fifty pounds)",法院判是以文字为准。

5.5 主合约中的文字与目的超越合并文件中的文字

合并文件虽然被视为主合约的"延续部分"(*in extenso*),要一并考虑与作出协调解释。但显然,分量是主合约为重,毕竟其所用的条文/文字都会经过双方的谈判与考虑后才约定,但合并文件就有机会贪图方便与因为通常的做法将其包括在内。举例说,涉及信用证操作有无数人士,这些有关文件都会合并国际商会的《跟单信用证统一惯例》(UCP 600),但笔者敢说这些人士中不会有超过5%的人曾经把UCP 600从头到尾看过一遍,更不用说充分了解了。这里的一些说法可节录Buckley大法官在Modern Building Wales Ltd v. Limmer and Trinidad Co Ltd (1975) 1 W. L. R. 1281, CA先例中所说的:"Where parties by an agreement import the terms of some other document as part of their agreement those terms must be imported in their entirety, in my judgment, but subject to this: that if any of the imported terms in any way conflicts with the expressly agreed terms, the latter must prevail over what would otherwise be imported."

另可见Parker大法官在Sabah Flout and Feed Mills Sdn Bhd v. Comfez Ltd (1988) 2 Lloyd's Rep. 18, CA先例中所说的:"Those passages lend support to the proposition that if an incorporated document contains provisions which conflict with the provisions of the written document, then the terms of the written document would, in the ordinary way, prevail. For my part I am prepared to accept that is one rule of construction which may be applied in circumstances such as these."

至于在另一种情况,就是主合约中的"目的"(purpose)十分明确,但被合并文件中的文字却有严重矛盾。这样,应该是以主合约的目的为准。在海事著名的The "Saxon Star" (1958) 1 Lloyd's Rep 73. 先例,该先例的租约像大部分的租约一样,以明示条文合并1924年的《海牙规则》或美国1936年的《海上货物运输法》。这种条文被称为"首要条文"(paramount clause),文字上是如下:

"It is agreed that the ... Paramount Clause ... as attached, [is] to be incorporated in this charter – party.

Paramount Clause

This bill of lading shall have effects subject to the provisions of the Carriage of Goods by SeaAct of the United States, approved April 16th, 1936, which shall be deemed to be incorporated herein ..."

很明显,这条文是想把美国的有关法律(《海上货物运输法》, 即美国版的《海牙规则》)合并到租约内。这做法估计是承租人或船东都想在责任与免责方面与提单能配合, 因为提单往往是被装卸港的国家法律强制适用《海牙规则》或类似的立法。这样,双方都比较肯定,知道不论在租约下还是提单下,什么该做什么不该做, 如有适航责任但只是到"恪尽职责"(due diligence)的程度。这也同时可减少事后"补偿"(indemnity)的争议与仲裁。例如,船东或承租人在面对提单下的索赔后,因租约条文责任的不同而事后要求租约另一方作出补偿。

但这做法所带来的困难不少,比如,租约内所有活动远远不止货物的装卸运载,所以,《海牙规则》的适用应到什么程度? 更大的困难是,《海牙规则》,特别是美国《海上货物运输法》,充满了与租约格格不相入的条文,《海牙规则》在Article 5说明其只适用在提单而不适用在租约。所以,要将一套本身有说明不适用在租约的规则合并进租约可能不好解释或协调。

这在 The "Saxon Star"先例可见到这方面的困难与矛盾,即是:(1) 要把《海牙规则》的一些文字,如"提单"变为或篡改为"租约",而"承运人"(carrier)变为"船东"(shipowner),"发货人"(shipper)变为"承租人"(charterer);(2)《海牙规则》只是针对货物装载在船上的航次,所以,租约下的空放航次又如何? 如果装载货物的航次是船东要"恪尽职责"的令船舶适航,但空放航次却不必(因《海牙规则》不适用),这会否令整个租约履行起来矛盾重重,经常出现双重或多重不同标准? (3) 美国《海上货物运输法》第 13 条文说明:"This Act shall apply to all contracts for carriage of goods by sea to or from ports of the United States in foreign trade. . . "这样,是否只有在期租内去美国的航次才适用这条首要条文,其他航次则不受制于美国的《海上货物运输法》?

该案例一直上诉到贵族院,多位著名大法官意见明显相异。在高院,Devlin 大法官的判决被上诉庭推翻,但结果贵族院再次推翻上诉庭的判决。贵族院判是租约合并美国《海上货物运输法》或《海牙规则》有效,也是订约方在主合约的目的,因此要尽量给合并文件中的文字一个宽松与支持目的的解释。这是其中一条解释合同条文规则,就是尽量把双方所同意的合约条文解释为有效,而不轻易否定为无效,该规则的拉丁文写法是"*verba ita sunt intelligenda ut res magis valeat quam pereat*"(这在本书第四章之第 6 段有介绍)或英文中所说的"the contract should be interpreted so that it is valid rather than ineffective"。在该重要案例中,所有 5 位勋爵认为:(1)"提单"与"租约"可被视为相通。(2)按照这样,"承运人"也应被视为"船东",而"发货人"被视为"承租人"。(3)美国《海上货物运输法》/《海牙规则》Article 5 表明不适用于租约就可漠视。

但对于以下争议,贵族院只是 3:2 作出判决如下:(1)有关法律(《海牙规则》)的适用,包括免责条文,不受地理的局限。即船舶不去美国的航次也适用。(2)有关法律(《海牙规则》)也适用于空放航次。(3)船东所拥有的保障不止包括货物实质失去或受损,而且包括承租人在租约下会受到的其他损失(在这案例包括因船东违约带来承租人在租约期内无法完成更多航次)。

所以在 The "Saxon Star"先例之后,可以说著名期租标准格式合约 NYPE 46 的第 24 条文(或附加"首要条文")的法律地位是如下:(1)租约内所有的履行都适用《海牙规则》(或相关的美国法)的规定。(2)所以,不只在"装运航次"(laden voyage),就是在空放航次(ballast voyage),船东也有《海牙规则》要求的开航前恪尽职责令船舶适航的责任。(3)《海牙规则》或相关法律的适用不受地理局限,如要行走美国。事实上,在之后的 The "Satya Kailash" (1984) 1 Lloyd's Rep 588 先例,更是再度确认即使该租约只涉及在印度港外轻载,也完全适用美国《海上货物运输法》(NYPE 46 的第 24 条文)。

但这结果也并非绝对。在一伦敦仲裁 LMLN No. 661,双方删除了 NYPE 46 的

第24 条文,用另一条附加的首要条文代替,这条文提到合并美国或加拿大的《海上运输法》。表明美国首要条文适用于来往美国港口的贸易,也另约定了一份加拿大首要条文适用于来往加拿大港口的贸易。仲裁员认为双方订约意图合并首要条文只针对来往美国/加拿大的航次,不适用于英国去东南亚的航次(该船舶在新加坡港外搁浅,租约如果不合并《海牙规则》或相关的海上运输法,船东就不能依赖《海牙规则》内的航行疏忽免责抗辩承租人的索赔)。所以,在订约自由下最终还是看双方约定的条文/文字为准,如有一句清楚写明租约下《海牙规则》只适用在中国港口之间的运输,就不会被解释广泛适用在全球的运输。

5.6 说明不管其他条文怎样说

如果两条条文起矛盾,而其中一条在开头说说明不管其他条文怎样说(notwithstanding anything to the contrary),这表示订约方明知道会与合约中其他条文起矛盾,并以此说明该条文比另一条更重要。这是 Donaldson 大法官在 The "World Symphony" (1992) 2 Lloyd's Rep. 115 先例中所说的有关第 18 条文开头:"Notwithstanding the provisions of clause 3 hereof... introductory words acknowledging the inconsistency and specifying which is paramount."

该先例的案情有关期租合约中的最后航次,租约期是 6 个月,但在接近还船期时,承租人要求船舶多走一个航次。但船东抗拒,认为这是不合法的最后航次,因为明显超越最后的还船时间。在租约期满的还船期如果碰上运费市场高涨,就经常会有这种争议。显然原来租约约定的租金相对廉宜,承租人如果能多走一个航次会轻易地能赚到 100 万美元以上。

在 The "World Symphony"先例,租约是使用 Shelltime 3 格式,其中起矛盾的两条条文是第 3 与第 18 条。注意这两条条文都是在标准格式内,是印本条文,所以不能以附加条文超越印本条文去解释。第 3 条文说明租约期是 6 个月加/减 15 天,如下:"3. Owners agree to let and Charterers agree to hire the vessel for a period of six months fifteen days more or less in Charterers' option..."

至于第 18 条文是在第二句说明承租人有权以租约的条件与租金完成一个往返航次,如下:"18. **Notwithstanding the provisions of clause 3 hereof**, should the vessel be upon a voyage at the expiry of the period of this charter, Charterers shall have the use of the vessel at the same rate and condition for such extended time as may be necessary for the completion of the round voyage on which she is engaged and her return to a port of redelivery as provided by this charter."(加黑部分是笔者的强调)

这样,这两条条文起的矛盾又要涉及分量轻重问题了。按道理而言,第 18 条文一开头的几个字显示了第 18 条文的分量较重。但这里还有两个区别,如果第 18 条文是对第 3 条文加以局限或补充,针对同一件事的有关租约期,就还是说不通一个普通法下的问题,即承租人不能违约下令船舶走一个最后的不合法航次。即使有一条明示条文允许承租人根据租约的租金完成最后一个航次,也不代表承租人可下令走一个不合法航次,因为“完成”与“下令”是两码事:The “Peonia” (1991) 1 Lloyd's Rep. 100 先例与 The “Black Falcon” (1991) 1 Lloyd's Rep. 77 先例。但如果第 18 条文是独立对待与解释并且超越了第 3 条文,这就只需要看第 18 条文怎样说,它在第二句是允许承租人完成一个往返航次。Donaldson 大法官认为第 18 条文开头的几个字明确承认了两条条文之间有矛盾,所以这不是局限或补充第 3 条文,而是说明以第 18 条文为准。结果判承租人有权下命令走这个最后的往返航次,即使明知道会大大超越租约期。

Donaldson 大法官这样说:“... There is a fundamental difference between a clause which qualifies another clause and one which is inconsistent with and overrides that other clause. A clause which makes provision for what is to happen if, through the fault of no one, the period of hire is exceed is no more than an exceptions clause. By contrast a clause which overrides the terms of another clause - in this case by ‘bolting on’ a round trip charter on to one for a fixed term - plainly involves an inconsistency. It is only the latter type of clause which calls for introductory words acknowledging the inconsistency and specifying which is paramount.”

在同一个先例中,Butler - Sloss 大法官这样说:“In my view, the words in clause 18 ‘notwithstanding the provisions of clause 3 hereof’ are crucial. In construing two clauses in the time charter which, read together, display not only a tension but also an inconsistency, it is clear to me that clause 18 must override clause 3, and consequently the charterer was entitled to give the order for the final voyage in the knowledge that the voyage would overrun the time otherwise stipulated for redelivery under clause 3.”

另一个要介绍的案例是 The “Golden Leader” (1980) 2 Lloyd's Rep. 573,案情是该船舶从朝鲜装杂货去罗马尼亚,船舶在日本海域附近搁浅与沉没,导致货物全损。承租人,也是货主,向船东索赔货物的全损。这样,船东的责任就是要看租约条文/文字的解释。该租约是金康租约,又涉及对船东十分优待的第 2 条文,即船东不必对船长或船员的疏忽或过错所引起的任何损失或延误负责,船东要负责的只是他个人的过错令船舶不适航。在这一先例的案情,看来只会涉及船员航行的疏忽或过错而导致船舶搁浅,与船东本身无关。所以如果船东可以依赖第 2 条文,就不必对承租人负责货物的全损。

但该租约有第 38 条的附加条文,内容是:“**Notwithstanding Clause 2** Owners and Master are responsible for correct and safe stowage, for ventilation of cargo if necessary which to be mentioned in vessel's official logbooks and for delivery of cargo in good order and condition (including responsibility for the delivery of the same number of parcels as mentioned in Bills of lading), Bills of Lading to be drawn up in accordance with Mate's receipt and to incorporate The Hague Rules.”(加黑部分是笔者的强调)

看来,这又是订约双方自己理解到第 38 条文与第 2 条文内容起矛盾,并显示了

第38条文的分量较重。这表示只要看第38条文的内容下,船东是否要对这批货物全损负上责任。承租人认为答案应该是肯定的,因为该条文清楚说明船东有责任让货物在良好状况下交货(Owners and Master are responsible for . . . delivery of cargo in good order and condition),这是一个绝对/严格的承诺,船东要承担对交货的绝对责任。

在笔者看来,解释这一条文也会涉及其他的解释规则,但在案例的报告中没有提到。例如,该条文提到了船东/船长要负责准确与安全的堆货与通风,如果他们有在货物良好状况下交货的绝对责任,就不必再提什么堆货或通风的问题了,因为由于这种原因所造成的货损也应该被前一句包括在内。但在本章第6段会介绍,对双方不约定多余内容的假设并不是一个有力的说法。所以,估计因此双方大律师没有在这一方面多争论。

Lloyd大法官不接受船东在第38条文中有在良好状况下交货的绝对/严格责任。他主要是认为这样解释并不符合商业上的合理性,因为在现实中船东绝少会接受对货物的绝对/严格责任。船东真是这样做,也是超出了互保协会给他的保障,而互保协会的承保范围只是根据《海牙规则》,并没有要求船东绝对适航的责任,而只有恪尽职责的责任。《海牙规则》也豁免了船东对船员航行中的疏忽与过错,表示在这次船舶的搁浅,船东免责。所以,Lloyd大法官为了商业上的合理作出解释,就必须要十分清楚明确且别无其他解释的条文/文字,才会作出这种不合理的解释。而在该条文,Lloyd大法官认为在争议的一句话之后,马上有一句说"包括交出提单上说明的货物件数的责任"(including responsibility for the delivery of the same number of parcels as mentioned in Bills of lading),就说明了这整句话的本质就是要船东/船长负责提单上说明的货物件数与货物状况良好,也就是指清洁提单。换言之,这整句话就造成一个"合约禁止反供"(contractual estoppel),再不准船东推翻提单上的内容。这本来在提单的情况下,被转让去无辜第三人手中,也在法律与国际公约的《海牙—维斯比规则》构成禁止反供,在Article 3的第4段是说:"However, proof to the contrary shall not be admissible when the Bill of Lading has been transferred to a third party acting in good faith."

但这在租约下不适用,而第38条文可被解释起这个作用,而不是承租人所讲的十分广泛但也是商业上不合理的解释,要船东负上交货的绝对/严格责任。Lloyd大法官这样分析:

"What then does the clause mean? The clue lies in the words in brackets 'including responsibility for the delivery of the same number of parcels as mentioned in bills of lading'. The meaning of those words is not, I think, that the owners are absolutely liable to deliver the same number of parcels as mentioned in the bill of lading, but rather that that is the number for which owners are responsible, subject to the terms and exceptions of the charter-party. In other words the owners cannot dispute the number of parcels stated in the bills of lading. The effect of the words is thus to create as between owners and charterers a contractual ‘estoppel’ similar to that which binds the owners when the bills of lading get into the hands of a third party. The provision thus serves the useful function of obviating any dispute as to the numbers shipped.

What then of the reference to good order and condition? The word ‘including’ shows, I think, that that provision is of the same kind as that which follows. The function of the provision is to prevent any dispute as to the order and condition of the goods when shipped. If the owner state that the cargo is in good order and condition in the bills of lading then that is the order and condition in which they are bound to deliver them, subject to the terms and exceptions of the charter – party. What they cannot do is to assert that the goods never were in good order and condition when shipped. Just as the owners are estopped from making such an assertion vis – à – vis the holders of bills of lading, so the clause creates a contractual ‘estoppel’ vis – à – vis the charterers.”

另在 Commissioner for Railways v Avrom Investments Pty Ltd (1959) 1 WLR 389 的枢密院先例,案情涉及土地所有人将土地租给开发商建筑房屋,其中一条条文说:“... the new building ... shall at all times be in accordance with such building design plan and specification as the ... lessor may in his absolute discretion approve ... and **notwithstanding anything hereinbefore contained** the building design plan and specification of the said building shall be subject to the reasonable requirements of the lessor ...”

Somervell 勋爵认为“notwithstanding”一词显示了该条文的后半段超越了前半段:“... clearly indicate the cutting down of a right ‘hereinbefore contained’.”

除了上述介绍的“notwithstanding”一词,也可以有其他文字显示双方对合约内起冲突的条文作出协调,并显示了孰重孰轻。在 Scottish Power Plc v Britoil (Exploration) Ltd, November 18, 1997 先例,相关合约中一条条文写明是“取决于”(subject to)另一条条文,上诉庭的 Staughton 大法官说:“Correctly used, the words ‘subject to’ mean that two provisions in the contract are in conflict, and that the first – mentioned is to be subject to, yield to, the second when the conflict occurs.”

§6 整体解释合约之四:假定双方不会约定多余的内容

这方面先可节录 S. A. Maritime et Commerciale of Greneva v. Anglo – Iranian Oil Co Ltd (1954) 1 W. L. R. 492 先例中 Somervell 大法官所说的:“Although one finds surplusage in contracts, deeds and Acts of Parliament, one learns towards treating words as adding something, rather than as mere surplusage.”(虽然会在一份合约中找到多余的内容,但应该是倾向看待这些文字是为了增加内容,而不是多余。)

这一说法与本章的大精神相配合,即尽量不要漠视/忽视订约双方写在一个合约内的条文/文字。在本书第四章之第8段会介绍"同类规则"(*ejusdem generis*),在此可一提是现在介绍的这个假设也是"同类规则"存在的原因之一。简单说来,所谓"同类规则",就是双方在特别列明了一连串(如免责)个别事项后,在其后加上一句看来很广泛的条文说明"包括一切其他情况"(any other causes)。但如果对此广泛的用字以其字面意思来解释,前面的特别列明的事项就会成为多余,因为它们没有理由不被最后一句包括在内。所以有这个双方不会约定多余内容的假设,就要给此广泛的条文加以局限,变得在前面列明的事项并非多余,就假设后面的"包括一切其他情况"只包括与列明事项同类型的其他事项。

6.1 不同意这一假设的说法

但有不少说法是这一假设对解释合约其实没有什么帮助,如在Tea Trade Properties Ltd v. CIN Properties Ltd (1990) 1 E. G. L. R. 155先例,Hoffmann大法官说:"I have never found the presumption against superfluous language particularly useful in the construction of leases. The draftsmen traditionally employ linguistic overkill and try to obliterate the conceptual target by using a number of phrases expressing more or less the same idea."

另可见在Total Transport Corp v. Arcadia Petroleum Ltd (1998) 1 Lloyd's Rep. 351先例,Staughton大法官这样说:"It is well – established that the presumption against surplusage is of little value in the interpretation of commercial contracts."

还有在Beaufort Development (N. I) Ltd v. Gilbert – Ash (N. I.) Ltd (1999) 1 A. C. 266先例,Hoffmann勋爵又说:

"This is the argument from redundancy; the parties are presumed not to say anything unnecessarily and unless the decisions of the architect were binding, there would be no need to confer upon the arbitrator an express power to open up, review and revise them.

I think, my Lords, that the argument from redundancy is seldom an entirely secure one. The fact is that even in legal documents (or, some might say, especially in legal documents) people often use superfluous words. Sometimes the draftsmanship is clumsy; more often the cause is a lawyer's desire to be certain that every conceivable point has been covered. One has only to read the covenants in a traditional lease to realise that draftsmen lack inhibition about using too many words. I have no wish to add to the anthology of adverse comments on the drafting of the J. C. T. Standard Form Contract. In the case of a contract which has been periodically renegotiated, amended and added to over many years, it is unreasonable to expect that there will be no redundancies or loose ends."

6.2 什么是多余内容

在不少有法律效果的合约,都出现有多余内容,甚至大量存在。即使是由律师或专业人士拟定,也会出现这种情况。多余内容可以是多方面的,如在同一份合约内针对某一件事重复。另一种经常出现的是法律已经有了明确默示,但再以明示条文重复这一默示地位(不是否定)。简单的例子可以是以明示条文说明订约双方要为其疏忽负责,这就是多此一举了。笔者也见过不少涉及庞大金额的合约,由高水平律师协助草拟,其中约定去香港仲裁,就把香港仲裁条例一大半的内容以明示形式搬进此仲裁条文,导致该条文长达好几页。这看来又是多此一举。至于合约内如此多多余内容的原因,除了订约方不懂这一相当重要的原因与上一段节录先例中所说的订约方(包括律师)总是喜欢多讲而非少讲外,另可节录 Staughton 大法官在 The "Eurus" (1998) 1 Lloyd's Rep. 351 先例所说如下:"There is, as it seems to me, a long history of charterparty clauses dealing with the liability of one party or the other for what would without the clause in question still be a breach of contract. To the lawyer this is surplusage; **but to commercial men it is a way of making sure that there has been no mistake or misunderstanding, and to emphasize their rights and liabilities.**"(加黑部分是笔者的强调)

6.2.1 例子之一

这里可先举一条多余内容的著名程租合约条文。在 1876 年版本金康租约中已经出现的一条条文如下:"Indemnity for non - performance of this charterparty, proved damages, not exceeding estimate amount of freight."但这一条文一直不被英国法律承认,当作是多余,所以不会给予解释,不会让船东或承租人在违约/毁约时损失计算只限制在估计的运费。这在《Scrutton on Charterparty》(第 20 版,1996 年)一书有解释如下:"In many charters there appears a clause in some such terms as 'Penalty for non - performance of this agreement estimated amount of freight.' Such a clause is inoperative, and is neglected by the court. ... In past editions of this work, it had been said to be 'a mystery why this clause survives, except upon the supposition that chartering brokers regard it as a piece of sacred ritual'."

另在《Cooke & Others on Voyage Charters》一书也有提到该条文为什么多余,这是因为在违约时,受害方可以在普通法下索赔损失,而金钱损失也往往是唯一的救济,而赔偿的基本原则就是复原,说法如下:"The remedy to which the innocent party most commonly resorts in the event of a breach of the charter is a claim for damages, and this is frequently the only remedy available. The basic principle which lies behind an award of damages is indemnity or *restitutio in integrum* ..."

笔者认为另一个理由是它不像一条清楚明确与有针对性的限制赔偿责任的免责条文,谈不上有明确超越了这些普通法赔偿大原则默示地位。

6.2.2 例子之二

在 BIMCO 一份早期很受欢迎的期租合约标准格式,名为 Baltime,它与金康租约的免责条文中也有多余的内容,在 Royal Greek Government v. Minister of Transport

(1949) 83 Lloyd's Rep. 228 先例有提到。多余的部分如下:"The charterer to be responsible for loss or damage caused to the vessel or to the owners by goods being loaded contrary to the terms of the charter or by improper or careless bunkering or loading, stowing or discharging of goods or any other improper or negligent act on their part or that of their servants."

针对这一部分(第13条文的第二部分),Devlin大法官说是多余,如下:"... the second part of Clause 13 is, from a lawyer's point of view, superfluous. All that it is saying legally is that the charterer is responsible for breach of the charter - party or for negligence."

Devlin大法官也说到是"怀疑商业人士订约会关心重复"(I doubt that the commercial draftsmen pay much attention to overlapping or that they are afraid of repetition)。

6.2.3 例子之三

在 The "Eurus" (1998) 1 Lloyd's Rep. 351 先例,提到了一条在航运特别是油轮租约著名的条文,Scanport clause,其中只有第一句是有用的,剩下的第二与第三句是多余的内容。该条文是用在油轮租约允许承租人在航次半途更改卸港,即使在已经签发的提单中已经明确注明卸港。该条文如下:"Discharge port shown in Bill of Lading not to constitute a declaration of discharge port and Charterers to have right to order vessel to any port within terms of the Charter Party. Charterers hereby indemnify Owners against claims brought by holders of Bill of Lading against Owners by reason of destination."

6.2.4 例子之四

也是在 The "Eurus" (1998) 1 Lloyd's Rep. 351 这同一个先例,涉及一个油轮航次租约,案情是该油轮去尼日利亚装原油,承租人要求船长不要在1992年1月31日11时之前递交准备就绪通知书,因为承租人在1月23日已经知道2月份的原油价格比1月份低,而石油买卖价格的结算是根据提单日期。承租人希望稍后递交通知书,船舶就会在2月1日才装完原油,能够签发2月份的提单。但船舶在1月31日0时30分抵达就马上靠泊,并在6时36分开始装货。之后承租人想办法通过船长减慢装货速度,总算到了2月1日1时30分才装完货。但船东与船长都不知道的是尼日利亚有一个习惯做法是要到了8时之后装完货才能出该天的提单。所以,承租人还是出不了2月份的提单,导致差价损失约70万美元。承租人向船东索赔这笔损失,而其中双方的一个争议是这一习惯做法所带来的损失是否遥远的问题。

这里出现了两个很不同的索赔方法或理念:一是通常的违约下索赔损失,普通法要求损失类别在订约时不能是"遥远"(remoteness),如能够合理预见,加上无辜方有合理减少损失,才能向违约方取回:Hadley v. Baxendale (1854) 9 Ex. 341; Victoria Laundry (Windsor) Ltd. v. Newman Industries Ltd., (C. A.) (1949) 2 K. B. 528 等先例。二是如果根据合约内的“补偿条文”(indemnity clause),则是不必关心损失类别是否遥远,只需关注补偿条文所针对的事情与该事情发生所导致的损失类别是否存在“因果关系”(causition)。可以说,两种不同索赔方法所针对的完全不一样。这一点在本书第五章之6.6段介绍“补偿”一词的解释时另会详论,在此只节录Gerard McMeel教授的《The Construction of Contracts—Interpretation, Implication and Rectification》(2007年)一书之20.57段所说,如下:“It is a surprisingly difficult question whether a claim under an indemnity gives rise to a right to claim in debt or to claim damages. This exercise in categorization is often thought to be the solution to the issues of whether or not the doctrines of mitigation and remoteness of damage are applicable to claims for an indemnity. It is suggested that there is no necessary link between this conceptual question and the practical question concerning whether those limitations on recovery are applicable. The characterization of an indemnity is the subject of a serious conflict of appellate authority.”

可以想到是抗辩索赔的船东希望以第一种方法来计算损失,因为尼日利亚的习惯做法应该是订约时不能合理预见。而承租人希望是以第二种方法,因为有机会(虽然没有明确的先例支持这一点)争议从指示船长稍后才递交通知书的一刻直到后来的提早装完货导致令承租人蒙受损失的一刻,它们之间的因果关系从没有被任何其他事情打断。所以违约的船东就要补偿有关的损失,不存在遥远与否之争。

这里就涉及有关的租约第36条文如下:“36. Owners shall be responsible for any time, costs, delays, or loss suffered by Charterers due to failure to comply fully with Charterers' voyage instructions provided such instructions are in accordance with the Charter Party and custom of trade.”(船东如果没有全部依从承租人的航次指示[只要该指示是与本租约与贸易习惯相符],就要对承租人的损失负责。)

船东指这一条文为“责任与赔偿条文”,而并非补偿条文。毕竟,它不像其他的补偿条文通常会有“补偿”(indemnify)一字。所以,船东需要按照普通法的损失计算作出赔偿。但承租人认为这是一条补偿条文,而“补偿”一字并不重要。这里还涉及本段针对的争议,如果第36条文只针对一般的违约损失赔偿就是多余,因为普通法的默示地位已经明确是这样。所以要给该条文一定的解释,就不能漠视/删除,而这个解释就是将其当作一条补偿条文。

在仲裁,多数的裁决是判船长没有依从承租人的命令,但根据违约索赔,是损失类别不可预见与遥远,所以承租人在这一方面败诉。但承租人根据补偿条文索赔却是成功,原因已经分析过。这导致败诉的船东上诉,并在高院与上诉庭胜诉。

简单地说,上诉庭认为第36条文如果被解释为补偿条文,有一点重要之处说不通。因为整体解释程租合约,就难以理解双方为什么在各种各样的船东违约中只特别针对依从承租人航次指示这一方面的违约才要求补偿,进而让承租人可避开损失类别在本案例下是不可预见的困难。这可见Staughton大法官所说的:“... as to the purpose of the clause there was no reason, why the parties should have wished to provide that, for some breaches of contract by the owners the charterers' loss would be recoverable whether or not it was within the reasonable contemplation of the parties, while for all other breaches the ordinary rule, as to the intention so to provide."

这里笔者也可以进一步解释补偿条文经常在期租合约出现,但在程租合约内就少见。在期租合约有必要是因为船东允许承租人有营运的自由(如去世界各地不同的港口与装运不同的货物、签发各式各样的提单等),而交换的是承租人要明示或默示补偿这些营运自由所带来的船东损失。在许多情况下,补偿所针对的事情不一定与违约有关。由于程租合约没有这种营运的自由,所以不需要补偿(除了一些特殊情况如承租人要求船东同意无单放货并承诺对这样做的后果作出补偿)。但程租合约下船东与承租人各自有作出不同的承诺(如船东承诺准时列名装港、船舶适货与适航、不得延误等,承租人承诺安全泊位、提供货物装船、负责装卸货、在固定装卸时间完成作业等),如果有违反,就要向对方的无辜方根据普通法的损失计算作出赔偿。上述第36条文针对的是船东没有依照承租人的航次指示,而条文也说明了这些指示必须依照租约规定与商业习惯。这表示了船东没有依照航次指示也相当于没有依照租约规定,这正是一个普通法下的违约,本来就不必以明示条文说明。

所以,针对本段所讲的假设订约双方不会约定多余内容,Staughton大法官不同意承租人的说法,说:"... there was an implied term in the charter requiring the owners to comply with the charterers' voyage instructions without clause 36; an implied term derived from clause 36 would therefore be surplusage and the presumption against surplusage was of little value in the interpretation of commercial contracts; and without that presumption there was no basis on which to construe clause 36 as giving the charterers the right to an indemnity for loss resulting from one particular breach of contract..."(法律本来就有默示条文,根本不需要第36条文,第36条文是多余。但假定双方不会订立多余的条文/文字在商业合约的解释没有太大价值,如果承租人只能依赖这一假设,说第36条文给他一个补偿的权利不可以接受。)

§7 合约删除部分

删除合约部分(deletion)会出现在各种情况,一种是双方在谈判时删除对方的草拟本,这代表了什么?可以想得到这种争议会出现在申请"合约变更"(rectification),这在本章稍后的13.1段有详论。这种删除往往属于谈判中的过程,双方的订约意图会变来变去很不稳定,对合约的解释通常不会有任何帮助,也这是本书第六章之2.5.1段谈判除外规则的原因。在近期一个涉及土地买卖先例 Berkeley Community Villages Ltd v. Pullen (2007) EWHC 1330 中,Morgan大法官接受并考虑了有关

合约较早的草拟件被最后删除掉的内容,最后认为没有帮助,说:

"In any event, if I had admitted evidence of the draft consultancy agreements and had compared the terms of the draft agreements with the concluded agreement and had considered whether I derived assistance from that exercise, I do not believe that the exercise would in the end have assisted me...

Even in the cases where the fact of deletion is admissible as an aid to interpretation, there is a great difference between a case where a self contained provision is simply deleted and another case where the draft is amended and effectively re – cast. It is one thing to say that the deletion of a term which provides for 'X' is suggestive that the parties were agreeing on 'not X'; it is altogether a different thing where the structure of the draft is changed so that one provision is replaced by another provision. Further, where the first provision contains anumber of ingredients, some assisting one party and some assisting the other, and that provision is removed, it by no means follows that the parties intended to agree the converse of each of the ingredients in the earlier provision."

另一个极端的情况是双方有了一个有效的合约,事后通过约定删除部分内容。这会是对合约的解释有重大分量。

而最普遍的删除合约部分并带来争议是在使用标准格式合约时,经常有订约双方约定删除部分印本内容,原因有很多。其中一个原因是有了特定的附加条文不同地对待同一个问题,所以删除掉的印本条文再也没有存在价值了。另一个情况是订约双方不接受印本条文而删除,但却没有其他附加条文针对有关的问题而导致合约有漏洞。再另一个情况是双方认为删除的部分印本内容在该合约中没有什么作用,但这样可能会带来"牵一发而动全身"的后果。也经常会有情况是订约方没有太多地考虑就将其删除,这就带来问题是要否在一并解释整份合约时加以考虑。例如,删掉的部分是要其中一方承担某些责任,这样删掉,可否解释为双方约定不要这一方承担这些责任,变为以印本内容的相反意思为准?这种争议不是没有,但很难被接受。显然,如果除了删除其中一方承担某些责任外,另加上一条新条文说明他是否需要承担某些责任,这就清楚无误地显示双方的约定了。这表示删除的分量远远比不上一条清楚无误的条文。

这一方面曾经有不少权威说法,而且大法官的意见也不尽相同。但希望这一方面问题会减少,因为许多标准格式合约已经放到网上,如 BIMCO 的 IDEA 就有大部分的涉及航运标准格式合约,包括经常被使用的金康租约或 NYPE 46,可供订约方下载然后根据谈判后达成的协议直接在电脑的版本上重整。这样,如果标准格式合约中的印本条文被删除,就不会在合约中明显出现,不像以前那样一使用一份已经在纸面印出来的标准格式合约,就肯定要用尺与笔把部分订约方认为不适用的内容删除,并且十分明显。

7.1 印本条文被删除是否可解释为订约双方的订约意图是相反的地位之争

在 The "Golden Leader" (1980) 2 Lloyd's Rep. 573 先例,已经提到案情涉及著

名的航次合约标准格式的金康合约。其标准格式内第2条文的第2段被订约双方删除，而该条文本来对船东非常有保障，说明船东不必对船长或船员的疏忽或过错所引起的任何损失或延误负责："And the Owners are responsible for no loss or damage or delay arising from any other cause whatsoever, even from the neglect or default of the Captain or crew or some other person employed by the Owners on board or ashore for whose acts they would, but for this clause, be responsible, or from unseaworthiness of the vessel on loading or commencement of the voyage or at any time whatsoever."

承租人代表大律师认为这一段被删除就代表了订约双方的意图是希望在船长或船员疏忽或过错的情况，船东要负责。这不被Lloyd大法官接受，说：

"... relies on the deletion of the second and the third paragraphs of the printed clause, particularly the second which provides expressly that the owners should not be liable for the neglect or default of the captain or crew or some other person employed by the owners on board or ashore for whose acts they would, but for this clause, be responsible. The parties must ... have had some purpose in deleting that part of the clause. By deleting the express exclusion of negligence they must have intended to re-instate negligence as a ground of liability, at all events if the undeleted first paragraph is ambiguous.

I do not belong to the school of thought which regards it as inadmissible to look at deletions in a printed clause. Thus the use of a word or phrase in the deleted part of clause may throw light on the meaning of the same word or phrase in what remains of the clause: see The Dominator, [1959] 1 Lloyd's Rep. 125; but it seems to me quite another thing to say that the deletion itself has contractual significance; or that by deleting a provision in a contract the parties must be deemed to have agreed the converse."

7.2 解释合约不应该考虑删除部分的原因与说法

看来，认为不应该考虑删除部分的原因有：(1)解释合约是看双方同意的内容，而不是看没有同意的内容；(2)考虑删除部分与什么原因所造成就会涉及口头证据，以前传统的做法十分抗拒接受这些证据，到现在依然有接受这方面证据的例外，这可看本书第六章之2.5.1段；(3)要删除部分合约内容一定会涉及标准格式合约，但在今天电脑普遍使用，订约方可以很容易将标准格式合约重新整理后"重打一遍"(re-engross)。这样，就不容易分出什么是删除部分。虽然，要刻意与一份标准格式合约比较并挑出到底有否删除部分可以做得到。但笔者的感觉是，比起以前在一份纸面标准格式合约，双方在谈判时刻意作出删除，会是更加没有分量。

这里可先介绍一些著名大法官的说法。例如早在Inglis v. Buttery (1878) 3 App. Cas. 552先例，Hatherlwy勋爵说："When I turn to the deleted words and find that in spite of a line being drawn through them I can read the words ... it appears to me that, those words being deleted, and a material note affixed showing that they were deleted before the contract was finally concluded, it is not in the power of any Court to look at the words, which have been so dealt with and absolutely taken out of the contract, for any purpose whatever connected with the construction of that contract of which they form no part whatsoever.... It is to my mind perfectly immaterial whether the instrument was torn up and rewritten, written out again with those words no longer contained in it, or whether the course was taken of running through those words as they stood in writing ..."

在同一个先例,O' Hagan 勋爵也说:"When those words were removed from the paper which had presented the full contract between the parties, they ceased to exist to all intents and purposes; and whether it was possible, as in point of fact it was, still to read them, in consequence of their simply having a line drawn through them, or whether they had been absolutely obliterated appears to me not to make the smallest difference."

另在 Ambatielos v. Anton Jurgens Margrine Works (1923) A. C. 175 先例,Finlay 子爵说:"... This charter was in a form which was in print. It was a great deal altered, words in print were struck out and words in writing were inserted; and it was said, in tracing the history of these alterations, that it made it improbable that the construction for which the respondents contended should be the true one. I think that all we have to do with is the charter as it finally stands; we must construe the clause with which we have to deal according to the form which the charter ultimately assumed ..."

最后是在 Sassoon (MA) & Sons Ltd v. International Banking Corp (1927) A. C. 711 先例,Sumner 子爵说:"There is a good deal of authority, now old, about the effect of deleting word in a printed form of mercantile contract, which it is not now necessary to cite; but they [i. e. their Lordships] take it to be settled in such a case as this, that the effect is the same as if the deleted words had never formed part of the print at all."(删除部分从来不是合约的一部分。)

7.3 解释合约应该考虑删除部分的原因与说法

但也有不少说法是可一并考虑被删除的部分内容,特别是在剩下的明示部分内容有不明确的情况。这里也可举一些先例的说法,如 Esher M. R. 勋爵在 Baumvoll Manufactur von Scheibler v. Gilchrest & Co (1892) 1 Q. B. 253 先例中所说的:"We have a right to look at what is written in to the printed form and at what is struck out."

还有同样是 Esher M. R. 勋爵在 Caffin v. Aldridge (1895) 2 Q. B. 648 先例中说的:"In order to see what it meant one must look at the rest of the document. We find that the words 'full and complete' which were in the printed form, had been struck out. The plaintiff's counsel contends that, these words having been deliberately struck out, by necessary implication the Court must put them in again. I cannot agree with him."

该很早期的先例涉及一份程租合约,在标准格式合约中要求船舶"装一船满载的货物"(a full and complete cargo),但其中"满载"(full and complete)这几个字被删除,剩下只有"一船货物"。船东认为剩下的"一船货物"几个字还是表示要装满该船舶,但承租人说这样解释等于把双方订约时刻意删除的几个字重新加入合约。上诉庭的多数同意根据删除掉的几个字确定双方在订约时没有约定要满载。

另 Scrutton 大法官也曾在 "Anastiassia" (Owners) v. Ugle - Export Charkow (1933) 46 Lloyd's Rep. 1 先例这样说:"... I am, of course, aware of the conflicting authorities as to whether you may look at clauses struck out of a printed form. I myself always do so, and I think the comparison between the original and the altered form frequently throws great light on what the parties intended by the words they used ..."

但 Scrutton 大法官的说法看来是不被上诉庭的其他两位大法官认同,Greer 大法官在同一案例中说:"... I am not quite sure that I am of the same opinion as Lord Justice Scrutton with reference to the grounds upon which the judgments should be put ..."

接下去介绍在 Louis Dreyfus & Cie v. Parnaso Cia Naviera S. A. (1959) 1 Q. B. 498 先例中,Diplock 大法官持相同观点说:"Where there is a standard form of words familiar to commercial men and contained in a printed form in general use ... it seems unreal to suppose that then the contracting parties strike out a provision dealing with a specific matter, but retain other provisions, they intend to effect any alteration other than the exclusion of the words struck out. I cannot *prima facie*, at any rate, ascribe to them any intention of altering the meaning of the words in the provisions which they have chosen to retain. I say '*prima facie*' because there may be added or substituted words which drive one to the conclusion that they did intend to ascribe to the words retained a meaning modified by the added or substituted provisions; **but while I think that I must first look at the clause in its actual form, without the deleted word, if I find the clause ambiguous, I think that I am entitled to look at the deleted words to see if any assistance can be derived from them in solving the ambiguity, bearing in mind the *prima facie* rule I have indicated.**"(加黑部分是笔者的强调)

Cross 勋爵在 Mottram Consultants Ltd v. Sunley (Bernard) & Sons Ltd (1975) 2 Lloyd's Rep. 197 先例中也说可以将删除部分当作订约时的背景一并加以考虑:"When the parties use a printed form and delete parts of it one can, in my opinion may regard to what has been deleted as part of the surrounding circumstances in the light of which one must construe that they have chose to leave in."

类似的说法也可见 Reid 勋爵在 Timber Shipping Co S. A. v. London & Overseas Freighters Ltd (1972) A. C. 1 先例中所说的:"There is controversy as to whether one can ever look at deleted words in an agreement. If the words were first inserted by the draftsman of the agreement and then deleted before signature then I have no doubt that they must not be considered in construing the agreement. They are in the same position as any other preliminary suggestion put forward and rejected before the final agreement was made. **But it appears to me that striking out words in a printed form is quite a dif-**

ferent matter. The process of adapting a printed form to make it express the parties' intentions requires two things to be done. Those parts which are not to be part of the agreement are struck out and the words are inserted to complete the rest of the form so as to express the agreement. There is no inference that in striking out words the parties had second thoughts; the words struck out were never put there by the parties or any of them or by their draftsman."(加黑部分是笔者的强调)

7.4　目前英国法律在这一方面的地位

英国法律目前最权威的还是节录《Chitty on Contracts》(第31版,2012年)一书,它怀疑法院能否一并考虑删除部分,除非是为了帮助找出余下没有删除文字带来的含糊。它也说到如果一个已经订立的合约事后订约方同意删除部分内容,不论删除的是否是印本条文,这种删除就不一样了。这种删除更准确地应被称为"合约更改"(alteration)。该书之12－069段是这样说:"**Alterations and deletions.** Evidence of prior negotiations is normally not admissible to construe a written contract and drafts will not be admitted either to alter the language of the contract or to help in its interpretation. So, where an instrument appears to have been altered while the parties were negotiating, the court cannot look at it as it originally stood compared with the alterations which were made in it, to see whether those alterations will throw any light upon the question of interpretation. **However, when the parties use a printed form, and delete parts of it, there is some authority for the view that regard may be paid to what has been deleted as part of the surrounding circumstances** in the light of which the meaning of the words which they chose to leave in is to be ascertained. But there is weighty authority to the contrary. **In any event, it is doubtful whether the court can look at the words deleted except to resolve an ambiguity in the words retained.** The position may nevertheless be different where alterations are made to an already concluded agreement. In *Punjab National Bank v. De Boinville* (1992) 1 W. L. R. 1138 Staughton L. J. said: '... if the parties to a concluded agreement subsequently agree in express terms that some words in it are to be replaced by others, one can have regard to all aspects of the subsequent agreement in construing the contract, including the deletions, even in case which is not, or not wholly, concerned with a printed form.' Also **where a one－off contract has been drafted by reference to a standard form contract which formed the basis for its drafting, the court can taken into account the omission from the one－off contract of words that appear in the standard form contract in order to resolve an ambiguity in the former document.**"(加黑部分是笔者的强调)

7.5　有关删除内容应否考虑的实例介绍之一

有关合约删除部分应否在解释时被一并考虑的重要性,可举一个笔者所知悉的在现实中发生的案件,有关一个合约被西方公司索赔将近一亿美元,中国企业坚持在订约时,西方公司口头承诺肯定不会在拿不到担保与批准时向中国企业索赔金钱的损失。结果中国企业就在这个承诺下签署了该合约,其中有条文保证会在1个月内拿到担保与批准。结果是中国企业无法做到而被西方公司提出巨额索赔。首先想到的救济是西方公司"误述"(misrepresentation)而导致中国企业同意签署该份合约,但在笔者所著的《国际商务游戏规则—英国合约法》一书第五章之5.2段有谈到针对将来的意图或是愿望(指西方公司将来不会向中国企业索赔)并非是对事实的陈述,而通常是需要事实的陈述才会构成误述。[2] 下一个救济就是"附带保证"(collateral warranty),指西方公司给了中国企业一个不会向其索赔的附带保证。但该合约有一条十分广泛的"完整合约条文"(entire agreement clause)[3]:Walford v. Miles (1992) 2 AC 128先例。这样只有看该合约本身的条文/文字是怎样写。依照常理,中国企业应该把西方公司这么重要的承诺以明示条文加进该合约,但中国企业根本没有理会该合约的条文/文字,而且对合约解释看来有很大误解。看来唯一根据该合约还有可能争的就是有关条文针对合约半途终止时,格式条文本来是写中国企业要马上退还给西方公司在签署合约时支付的定金,另有后一句话的"无损西方公司可提出索赔损失"(immediately return the deposit and without prejudice to the right to claim damages resulting therefrom)。但格式条文的后一句话被删除,中国企业说删除的原因就是针对西方公司的承诺就不会向中国企业索赔。笔者也相信这的确有很大可能,但看了本章,就可以知道很难依赖被删除的合约部分并说服法院或仲裁庭这就是双方明确的订约意图。如果中国企业不仅是删除这一句话,甚至不删除(因为将会被附加条文超越),而是加上另一句明示了西方公司不能向他索赔损失,就可以安枕无忧了。

7.6 有关删除内容应否考虑的案例介绍之二

以下另介绍一个有关租船合约的案例,它不只涉及是否考虑合约删除内容,也涉及默示条文与整个合约及背景的考虑。该案例是The "Ardgroom" (1966) 1 Lloyd's Rep. 511,是一个以1962年版本的金康租约为准的程租合约。该标准格式的第5条文针对装卸作业与费用,在1962年版本,文字上是反映了普通法的地位:Harris v. Best (1892) 68 LT 76先例,这就是承租人要把待装的货物拉到船旁可让船东把货物以船上吊杆吊上船舶并把它堆装好。这也是在18、19世纪甚至在20世纪前段的做法,而船舶上即使有装卸设备也是由船员来操作。1962年版本的金康租约是这样说:"5. Cargo to be brought alongside to such a manner as **to enable vessel to take the goods with her own tackle** and to load the full cargo in ... running working days. Charterers to procure and pay the necessary men on shore or onboard the lighters to do the work there, vessel only heaving the cargo onboard."(加黑部分是笔者的强调)

---

〔2〕 Edgington v Fitzmaurice (1885) 29 Ch D. 459 先例。

〔3〕 在本书第十三章之第2段有详述。

但到了第二次世界大战后,以前的装卸作业方法已经是过时。一个主要原因是码头工人工会的强大加上各国的立法,往往不容许船员进行装卸作业。当然,船员不干还是可以要船东安排岸上码头工人负责船舶的装卸并支付有关费用,让以前一贯的装卸做法与船东及承租人之间的风险/费用分摊延续下去。但由于船舶要去世界上不同的港口,对某一个装卸港的了解程度安排码头工人的方便性远远比不上承租人。更不用说在不少情况下,装卸是在承租人自己的泊位进行。所以,越来越多从以前由船东负责船舶的装卸并支付有关费用的普通法地位(或简称 Gross Terms)变为全部由承租人负责装卸/堆货并支付有关费用的 Free In and Out, Stow and Trim(或简称 FIOST)。到了 1976 年版本的金康租约,第 5 条文已经印上了两个选择的 Gross Terms 或 FIOST,任由订约方删除其中一个选择。而到了 1994 年版本的金康租约,就只剩下 FIOST 了。

在介绍了金康租约第 5 条文的"背景"(background)后,再回去介绍 The "Ardgroom" 先例的案情。该租约虽然使用 1962 年版本,而当时也只有这个版本的金康租约,但双方约定的是 FIOST,所以在订约时就把上述节录的第 5 条印本条文删除,只剩下了一句针对超过 2 吨的货物必须由承租人负责装卸。这是因为即使根据普通法地位,以前船舶的船上吊杆也通常不能吊超过 2 吨的货物,所以超重货物是要承租人自己负责。这一句没有在印本格式被删除的第 5 条文只剩下是:"Any pieces and/or packages of cargo over two tons weights, shall be loaded stowed and discharged by Charterers at their risk and expense."

另外订约方加了第 19 条的附加条文显示 FIOST 的约定如下:"The cargo is to be loaded, stowed, trimmed and discharged by the Charterers, free of expense to the vessel..."

在上述的有关租约条文介绍后,要介绍的是双方争议。该船舶是去澳大利亚装"废铁"(scrap)去日本,在澳大利亚的装港是墨尔本与悉尼。在第一个装港的墨尔本,船舶的吊杆不被装货工人的工会(Waterside Workers' Federation)与政府当局(Commonwealth Navigation Department)的检验所批准,产生了检验、修理吊杆与装货工人等待的费用与速遣费/滞期费的时间损失。承租人说这是由于船上吊杆缺陷问题,所以船东要负责这些费用与时间损失。但船东抗辩是有关租约针对装卸作业已经明确都是承租人的责任,租约并没有任何其他明示条文要求船东作出承诺提供船上吊杆,所以即使吊杆有缺陷也不构成违约。租约中唯一有针对的地方是在第 5 条印本条文也已经被删除,表示双方的约定根本不要求船舶提供吊杆。虽然在订约后船东曾经回应发货人允许使用船上吊杆,但信函中说明这是"无损害"(without prejudice),而且这是订约后发生的事情,不应该解释订约时的意图。[4]

McNair 大法官接受不应该看删除的部分以协助解释,所以根本不接受船东说把

〔4〕 这方面可看本书第六章之 2.5.2 段。

第 5 条文删除掉就是代表不需要船东提供吊杆的说法。在剩下的明示条文中,包括整体解释合约与得出商业合理的结果,McNair 大法官判是有默示条文即使在 FIOST 条件下船东也有责任提供船上吊杆,也就是不受删除部分的影响。

McNair 大法官首先是从租约的本质与商业合理看待,即这一航次去澳大利亚多个装港与日本多个卸港装卸废铁。这样,如果不能使用船上吊杆,因为没有明示也不能作出默示,就必须要用岸上吊车进行装卸了。但有这么多装卸港,不是每一个港口都有足够的设施与岸上吊车装卸废铁,所以商业上不大可能双方订约的意图是不用船上吊杆。他是这样说:"Accordingly, I apply my mind first to that task, considering whether on this charter – party as it now stands such an implication could be made. The first observation which I would make on that is this: that if the owners are right in their contention, it would mean in effect that this charter – party can only operate in ports where there are provisions for discharging a scrap cargo otherwise than by ship's gear, namely, by shore cranes. Having regard to the fact that the charter – party as originally framed provided for a range of ports – two safe ports between Osaka – Yokohama range – it would seem to me unlikely that it could be postulated as a fact that in all the safe ports within that range shore discharging cranes would be available."

接下去 McNair 大法官看租约内的其他条文,以肯定默示条文不会与其他明示条文不一致。McNair 大法官注意到第 5 条文的印本条文所剩下的一句针对超过 2 吨的货物必须由承租人负责装卸,在本租约是 FIOST 的条件下,这一句话是"多余的"(surplusage)。唯一能够给其解释就是这一句是船东告诉承租人船上吊杆无法吊超过 2 吨重的货物。这样,就显示了在本租约下承租人可以用船上吊杆,除非货物超过 2 吨。McNair 大法官这样说:"I think, too, that that construction is assisted and helped by the provision, to which I have already made reference, in Clause 5 for dealing with heavy cargo. There it is provided that...(在较早时已经有节录,不重复)That surely means, and can only mean that the charterers have not only got to do the work of loading, stowing and discharging, but the ship is saying in clear terms: 'We do not guarantee that our tackle is able to lift over two – ton loads.'"

7.7 有关删除内容应否考虑的案例介绍之三

这是一个近期先例,涉及对国际货物买卖进出口商与船东有十分密切关系的安全港口/泊位争议。这先例 The "Reborn" (2009) 2 Lloyd's Rep 639 的案情涉及船舶去黎巴嫩的 Chekka 港装水泥,但在挂靠泊位时船底被水底隐藏的物体弄破了一个洞。程租租约对装港的泊位是规定"1 BERTH CHEKKA – 27 FT SW PERMISSIBLE DRAFT",显示了 Chekka 是列名港口,但泊位由承租人指定。这在英国法律针对安全的默示地位是港口安全由船东自己负责,因为他接受列名港口,应该有充分甚至更好的能力了解该港口对船舶是否安全。但后者由于泊位是承租人指定,他可以指定列名港口的许多泊位,显然默示地位是承租人要保证对船舶的安全,否则承租人乱指定就会后果严重。要注意本租约的约定没有明示规定泊位必须安全,也就是租约经常的写法"一个安全泊位"(1 safe berth),表示只能看看法律能否作出安全的默示了。

船东认为英国法律的默示地位十分明确,在指定某一个没有列名的泊位装货,安全的风险应由指定泊位的承租人负责。而这一个把船底弄破的风险是承租人指定的泊位所特有的,并非是 Chekka 港所有其他可以使用的泊位都有同样的风险。所以这不安全与 Chekka 港无关,不应该是船东负责。

在这里先一提是有关港口或泊位安全与否的默示属于"事实的默示"(implied by facts)。这一课题在本书第七章之 4 段有详细介绍,并提到这种默示必须符合的先决条件,如有关合约必须默示这一条文,否则不可行。另是必须通过"好事第三人"(officious bystander)的考验,表示双方订约时如果有第三人提出这方面的质疑,双方会异口同声同意并加进一条明示条文。该段也提到了默示必须是肯定双方即使没有明示规定,但明显有这一订约意图。毕竟,大原则是法院或仲裁庭不能自说自话为双方改写他们之间的合约。这也表示如果在双方合约中已经有的明示条文(包括如果使用标准格式合同,但删去了部分)显示没有这一订约意图,法院或仲裁庭就绝对不能默示。

但在该先例,船东败诉,主要原因是在两方面显示了在订约时,承租人不愿意承担港口与泊位的安全,而船东愿意自己承担。第一方面是该程租租约使用著名的"金康格式"(Gencon Charterparty),该标准格式唯一提到对船舶"安全"(safely)是在第 1 条文,这一字被双方删去,如下:"Clause 1: The said Vessel shall ... proceed to the loading port(s) or place(s) stated in Box 10 or so near thereto as she may safely get and lie always afloat ... and being so loaded the Vessel shall proceed to the discharging port(s) or place(s) stated in Box 11 ... or so near thereto as she may safely get and lie always afloat, and there deliver the cargo."(加黑部分是笔者的强调)

第二方面是有一条第 20 条文明示规定船东保证船舶在抵达 Chekka 时,船舶将会符合所有港口的"限制"(restriction),包括泊位与航道,如下:"Owners guarantee and warrant that upon arrival of the vessel to and/or prior its departure from, loading or discharging ports (either in ballast condition prior to loading or laden prior discharging) the vessel including, inter alia the vessel's draft, shall fully comply with all restrictions whatsoever of the said ports (as applicable at relevant time) including their anchorages, berths and approaches and that they have satisfied themselves to their full satisfaction with and about the ports specifications and restrictions prior to entering into this Charter Party."

在这先例,看来是显示了明示条文有含糊之处,上诉庭将删除部分加以考虑,Clarke 勋爵说:"As to clause 1,(船东代表大律师)accepted (in my opinion correctly) that the fact that the word 'safely' in the printed Gencon terms was struck out by agreement was relevant to the true construction of the charterparty. It is the only place in the printed terms that there is any reference to safety. The fact that it was struck out seems to me to be a pointer to the fact that the parties did not intend there to be any express term requiring the port or berth to be safe. It is, however, no more than a pointer. More important is that Mr Bailey(船东代表大律师)correctly accepted that the fact that there is no warranty that the port be safe, when read with clause 1, leads to the conclusion that the charterers were not warranting that the channel to the berth was safe. He submitted however, that a warranty should be implied that the berth itself was safe."

§8 拟订得差劲的合约

拟订得差劲比拟订得好的合约最直接的后果就是带来双方在履约时的争议,甚至会最终导致双方关系破裂与昂贵的诉讼。

在解释方面,对差劲或者好的合约都是适用同一套合约解释规则与大原则。如法院或仲裁庭不能同情身处不利的一方而改写合约。

只简单介绍一个涉及国际性事件与金额庞大的 Kuwait Airways v Kuwait Insce (1999) 1 Lloyd's Rep. 803 先例,案情涉及伊拉克发动战争并占领了科威特后,把科威特航空公司停在机场的飞机与储存的零件占为己有,总额高达 10 亿美元, 其中 3 亿美元是零件的价值。之后科威特航空公司向战争保险商索赔,保险商赔了 3 亿美元后就不肯再赔。针对该战争险保单,Hobhouse 勋爵嘲弄该保单说:"... all points which could easily have been avoided by the exercise of care in the preparation and drafting of the insurance contract. Very large sums of money are involved ... Such disputes are unnecessary. They can be avoided, as has been repeatedly pointed out by those before whom such disputes come for determination, by the exercise of proper care in the drafting of the documents which create and define the relevant contractual obligations."

Hobhouse 大法官认为如果保险合约拟订得好,就根本不会产生争议。在很多争议中,高院与上诉庭对保单的解释不一样,而上诉庭与贵族院的解释也不一样,可见是拟订得差劲的合约所会带来的不肯定与昂贵的诉讼。由于该案情内容很多,而且与海上/航空保险有关,不在本书详细介绍。笔者只挑其中一个争议略为一提。这就是对保险标的的价值约定为每一架飞机不超过 8000 万美元,每一次意外赔偿最高的地面风险限额是 3 亿美元。这表示在任何的事故中,在某一地点的机场,科威特航空公司不能因为战争风险损失多过 4 架价值不超过 8000 万美元的飞机, 否则 3 亿美元就赔偿不足了。但该保单没有特别针对飞机零件是否计算在内,这就成问题了,因为当时被伊拉克占为己有的飞机零件价值就已经高达 3 亿美元。如果包括在内,损失的飞机连一毛钱都赔不到,可见这是订约方考虑不够完整而带来的合约漏洞。

这种拟订得差劲的合约也不仅是上述先例的保单(或是商业人士私下拟定的一

次过合约),甚至会发生在一些著名的标准格式合约,虽然理论上标准格式合约是应该拟定得更完整与更准确。在本书第四章之2.3段介绍过的英国保险市场长达200年在使用的S.G.保单就是差劲的标准格式合约例子。Beaufort Developments (NI) Ltd v. Gilbert - Ash NI Ltd (1999) AC 266先例又是另一个拟定得差劲而被法院批评的例子,在该先例Lloyd勋爵就批评了岸上建造合约的JCT标准格式,说:“Standard forms of building contract have often been criticized by the courts for being unnecessarily obscure and verbose.”

另Hoffmann勋爵也说:“I have no wish to add to the anthology of adverse comments on the drafting of the JCT Standard Form Contract.”

最后节录Denning大法官在British Movietonews Ltd v. London and District Cinemas Ltd (1951) 1 KB 190 CA.先例中曾经度说:“The day is done when we can excuse an unforeseen injustice by saying to the sufferer ‘It is your own folly. You ought not to have passed that form of words. You ought to have put in a clause to protect yourself.’ We no longer credit a party with the foresight of a prophet or his lawyer with the draftsmanship of a Chalmers.”〔5〕但这说法早被贵族院推翻:British Movietonews Ltd v. London and District Cinemas Ltd (1952) AC 166先例。在今天,英国已经有立法保护其想保护的群体,如消费者,针对国际商业合约,在完全的订约自由下有订约方接受一些对其致命的合约条文,肯定就是自己承担后果。

§9 “为什么不说清楚?”

这一个课题与上一个没有直接关系,只能说拟定得差劲的合约有更大机会被对方甚至是仲裁庭质疑为什么不说清楚(why not say it?)。

这是在解释合约中经常会遇到的争议,有不少诉讼律师经常挂在口中,质疑对方为什么不说清楚,正如Dunedin勋爵在Charrington & Co v. Wooder (1914) A. C. 71先例中所提到的,如下:“I do not think it rests with either party to say to the other ‘If the meaning is as you contend, why did you not express it otherwise?’ Both contentions as to the true meaning can be expressed by a gloss ... If either of these glossed had been expressed there would be no possibility of dispute. It therefore comes back to the question, what is the true interpretation of the expression in the contract?”(如果合约说清楚,双方就不会有争议。但既然有争议,法院还是需要给合约条文/文字一个解释。)

不应该这样质疑的原因之一是这个说法是“事后诸葛亮”,也不会对争议解决有什么帮助。正如Gross大法官在GE Frankona Reinsurance Ltd v. CMM Trust No 1400

---

〔5〕 他是英国1906年《海上保险法》与其他重要立法的草拟者。

The Newfoundland Explorer (2006) EWHC 429 先例就将其称为“construction of hindsight”。另是 Mance 大法官在 Dodson v. Peter H Dodson Insurance Services (a firm) (2001) 1 All ER (Comm) 300 先例中说：“It is almost always possible to say after the event that the point could have been put beyond doubt, either way, by express words.”

上诉庭的 Lawrence Collins 大法官也在 Conister Trust Ltd v. John Hardman & Co. (2008) EWCA Vic 841 先例说：“... Nor do I derive any assistance from the point made by Hardmans that Conister could have made the point clear beyond doubt by appropriate wording. That can always be said when parties differ on the meaning of a contract.”

在 Transfield Shipping Inc v. Mercator Shipping Inc (2009) AC 61 先例，Hoffmann 勋爵说：“I suppose it can be said of many disputes over interpretation, especially over implied terms, that the parties could have used express words or at any way expressed themselves more clearly than they have done. But, as I have indicated, the implication of a term as a matter of construction of the contract as a whole in its commercial context .... the court is engaged in constructing the agreement to reflect the liabilities which the parties may reasonably be expected to have assumed and paid for. It cannot decline this task on the ground that the parties could have spared it the trouble by using clearer language.”

最后节录 Neuberger 勋爵在 Re Sigma Finance Corp. (2009) BCC 393 先例中说：“I do not think it is normally convincing to argue that, if the parties had meant a phrase to have a particular effect, they would have made the point in different or clearer terms. That is a game which all parties can normally play on issues of interpretation.... It does not take matters further.”

上述所节录的权威说法只是部分介绍，反正这种争议还是很多。可能一个现实的重要性就是法院/仲裁庭不要被这一种争议所混淆，把原来清楚无误与应该只有一个合理解释的合约条文/文字，却因为有其中一方争辩说可以写得更加清楚无误而认为是属于“含糊”(ambiguous)。如果多过一种解释的含糊就会导致某一些规则的适用，如针对“免责条文”(exception clause)就是“针对规则”(*contra proferentem*)。甚至以前只有在有含糊的情况下才可引入外来证据/口头证据，虽然到了今天已经没有这个局限了。

§10 明显不完整的条文

合约中有不完整的条文也经常遇到，不完整的原因往往是双方订约时没有想到。如果这不完整是在一份合约，而漏掉的内容十分重要，会导致合约被视为还没有成立，因为“无法履行或因为太不肯定而无效”(unworkable or void for uncertainty)。这种不完整的合约在《Chitty on Contracts》(第31版,2012年)一书之2-113段有说:"Agreement in principle only. Parties may reach agreement on essential matters of principle, but leave important points unsettled so that their agreement is incomplete. It has, for example, been held that there was no contract where an agreement for a lease failed to specify the date on which the term was to commence; and that an agreement 'in principle' for the redevelopment and disposal of residential property, which specified core terms but left important matters, such as the timing of the project, for future discussion was an 'incomplete agreement' and so did not amount to a binding contract; that an agreement for sale of land by installments was not a binding contract where it provided for conveyance of 'a proportionate part' as each installment of the price was paid, but failed to specify which part is to be conveyed on each payment; that a convenant in a contract of employment restricting competition in two named counties and in others 'to the south' of them was too uncertain to be enforced; and that where, though agreement had been reached 'covering some significant matters', there was no contract because 'many fundamental matters remained to be resolved.' An agreement is also incomplete if it expressly provides that it is 'subject to' the resolution of specified points; there is no contract in such a case until either those points are resolved or the parties agree that their resolution is no longer necessary for the agreement to enter into contractual force."

但笔者在这里是针对另一种情况,就是合约内的个别条文是明显的不完整,而双方都承认有一个有效的合约或是已经在履行该合约,也等于该不完整合约从"尚未履行"(executory)变为"已履行"(executed),令法院或仲裁庭无法在后者的情况下还坚持该合约无效。这样,最常见的救济办法就是把不完整的地方以"默示条文"(imply terms)来填补。由于这种事实的默示需要该合约必须这样做以填补这个漏洞并让合约有"商业效力"(business efficacy),所以不一定在每个情况都可以这样做(这方面在本书第七章之第4段有详论)。

另一种救济办法就会根据合约的本质与目的,加上其他条文的整体考虑假设这样才是他们一定会有的订约意图,虽然他们没有想到。虽然,这种做法会有一点"矫揉造作"(artificial)。在Bromarin v. IMD Investment (1999) STC 301, CA.先例中,Chadwick大法官这样说:"It is not, to my mind, an appropriate approach to construction to hold that, where the parties contemplated event 'A', and they did not contemplate events 'B', their agreement must be taken as applying only in event 'A' and cannot applying in event 'B'. The task of the court is to decide in the light of the agreement that the parties made, what they must have been taken to have intended to the event, event 'B', which they did not contemplate. That is, of course, an artificial exercise, because it requires there to be attributed to the parties an intention which they did not have (as a matter of fact) because they did not appreciate the problem which needed to be addressed. But it is an exercise which the courts have been willing to undertake for as long as commercial contracts have come before them for construction."

§11 含 糊

含糊(ambiguity)在本章接下去课题的不肯定是十分接近的说法,但两者之间还是有一点区别,所以分段处理。

合约条文/文字如果可以有两个或以上说得通的解释,这就表示有含糊的地方。即使一条条文本身清楚无误也并不一定足够,因为它可能与合约的其他条文冲突一并带来含糊。

如果含糊没有办法通过各种合约解释规则的指引作出一个更加合理与说得通的解释,这就会有危险令合约无效或有关条文变得太不肯定而无效。相反是如果法院/仲裁庭能够找到一个合理与说得通的解释,这一含糊也就不再存在。

很多时候,文件/合约是否含糊很大程度上取决于法院/仲裁庭的主观印象,会有情况是一位仲裁员认为含糊,但另一位并不觉得。在 Ambatielos v. Anton Jurgen Margarine Works (1922) 2 KB 185 先例,Sterndale 勋爵说:"... it is very difficult indeed to say what is ambiguous and what is not, and I do not think any test can be applied except that of the person who is dealing with it. If it does not seem ambiguous to him I am afraid he can only say 'It may seem ambiguous to others, but it does not to me'."

注意是法院/仲裁庭解释商业合约不要刻意挑毛病或含糊之处,这在上一小段为什么不说清楚也有同样的说法。Hope 勋爵在 The Melanesian Mission Trust Board v. Australian Mutual Provident Society (1997) 2 EGLR 128 先例说:"Various rules may be invoked to assist interpretation in the event that there is an ambiguity. But it is not the function of the court, when construing a document, to search for an ambiguity. Nor should the rules which exist to resolve ambiguities be invoked in order to create an ambiguity which, according to the ordinary meaning of the words, is not there. So the starting point is to examine the words used to see whether they are clear and unambiguous."

通常,含糊的合约条文/文字不代表很难找出正确的解释,正如 Wilberforce 勋爵在 L Schuler AG v. Wickman Machine Tool Sales Ltd (1974) A. C. 235, HL 先例中所说的:"ambiguity in this context is not to be equated with difficulty of construction, even difficulty to a point where judicial opinion as to meaning had differed."

而有了法院权威性的解释后,就会令含糊消失,这也是 Wilberforce 勋爵在 Ailsa Craig Fishing Co Ltd v. Malvern Fishing Ltd (1983) 1 WLR 964 (HL)先例中所说:"The possibility of construction of a clause does not amount to ambiguity: that disappears after the court has pronounced the meaning."

英国法律很早以前就已经将含糊区分为两种，一是“表面含糊”（patent ambiguity）；二是“潜在含糊”（latent ambiguity）。这在 Great Western Railway v. Bristol Corp.（1918）87 L. J. Ch. 414 先例有提到，Wrenbury 勋爵说：“It there by ambiguity in the language of a contract itself it may be a patent ambiguity? That is, one apparent on the face of the document itself; or a latent ambiguity? That is, one which arises only when you seek to apply the contract.”

针对第一种含糊，在 Saunderson v. Piper（1839）5 Bing. N. C. 425 先例中有说到：“This is a case of *ambiguitas patens*, and according to the rules of law, evidence is not admissible. Where there is doubt on the face of the instrument the law admits no extrinsic evidence to explain it.”（针对这一种含糊是不接受外来证据，协助解释。）

针对第二种含糊，在 Great Western Railway v. Bristol Corp 先例，Wrenbury 勋爵说：“The words of the instrument may be perfectly plain and unambiguous for example ‘my nephew, Joseph Grant’ or ‘fair market price’. But if, from the surrounding circumstances, when you come to apply the instrument, you find that there are two persons who will satisfy the words ‘my nephew Joseph Grant’ or two markets to which the parties may have been referring, there is a latent ambiguity, and evidence is admissible to resolve it. Extrinsic evidence has created the ambiguity, and extrinsic evidence is admissible to resolve it.”（针对这一种含糊，是有关的文件内的条文/文字是清楚与不含糊，如在一份遗嘱，说“受益人是我的侄女 A 女士”或在一份合约说“公平市场价格”。但订约时的背景是有两位侄女都名为 A，或有关货物有两个市场并且有不同的价格。这样就带来一个潜在含糊，即不知道遗嘱是针对哪一位侄女或合约是针对哪一个市场。这样解释有关文件/合约，就必须引进外来证据/口头证据。例如，外来证据证明其中一位侄女 A 女士是与遗嘱拟定人同住 20 年，但另一位侄女 A 女士却是移居外国，已经有 30 年没有见过面。）

通过上述做法，就可以令一个潜在含糊消失。这也避免有关文件或合约因为不肯定而被判无效。

针对表面含糊，仅是看文件/合约的表面或“四个角”（four corners）内的内容，就已经可以作出解释，根本不需要引入外来证据/口头证据。只有潜在含糊才需要看其他的外来证据/口头证据。所以这种传统区分含糊的类别，就是为了外来证据/口头证据可否被法院接受的问题。这里的原因不必再细究，现在的英国法律已经有了改变，即使文件/合约没有含糊的情况下也已经放开并接受外来证据/口头证据，更加不理会是哪一类的含糊。正如 Steyn 勋爵在《Pepper v. Hart; A Re – examination》（2001）21 OJLS 59 一文所说：“Language is a labyrinth. As in ordinary life, words in a legal text cannot be understood except in relation to the circumstances in which they are used. It is sometimes assumed by judges that the existence of an ambiguity is a precondition to admitting evidence of the context of a legal text. That is wrong. Language can never be understood divorced from its context."

也已经有权威说法是不必再理会表面或潜在的含糊。还是有不少书提到这些说法,所以要涉及。这可节录 Simon 勋爵在 L Schuler AG v. Wickman Machine Tool Sales Ltd 先例中所说:"the distinctions between patent ambiguities, latent ambiguities and equivocations as regards admissibility of extrinsic evidence are based on outmoded and highly technical and artificial rules and introduce absurd refinements."

另在 Lewison 大法官所著的《The Interpretation of Contracts》(第5版,2011年)一书第412页说:"The traditional distinction between these two types of ambiguity does not appear to have survived into the modern law. But then the footnote mentioned Thomas LJ appears to have assued that the distinction remained valid in Wandsworth London Borough Council v. The Co – Operative Bank Plc (2003) EWHC 418 (Comm.)."

另也有说法是都可以翻译为"含糊"一词的"ambiguity"与"vagueness"这两个英文字也有一定区别,但在现实中不必理会。

§12 不肯定

不肯定(uncertainty)会导致整个合约或个别条文变为无效,已经在上一段提到。但由于漠视或删除双方订约所选用的文字会有法院/仲裁庭"重写"(rewrite)其合约与违反如本书第四章之第6段介绍的尽量令合约条文/文字有效的解释规则的危险,所以应该尽量找出一个可以合约整体协调的解释。法院这种想法有很多先例提到过,可部分节录如下:

1. 在 Greater London Council v. Connolly (1970) 2 Q. B. 100 先例中 Denning 勋爵说道:"The courts are always loath to hold a condition bad for uncertainty. They will give it a reasonable meaning wherever possible."

Pearson 勋爵也说:"... the courts are always loath to hold a clause bad for uncertainty if reasonable meaning can be given to it, and it seems to me easy to give a reasonable meaning to this clause."

2. 在 Re Lloyd's Trust Instruments (Unreported, June 24, 1970)先例中,Megarry 大法官说:"I think the starting point on any question of uncertainty must be that of the court's reluctance to hold an instrument void for uncertainty. Lord Hardwicke L. C. once said: 'A court never construes a devise void, unless it is so absolutely dark that they cannot find out the testator's meaning': *Minshull v. Minshull* (1737) 1 Atk. 411. Lord Brougham said: 'The difficulty must be so great that it amounts to an impossibility, the doubt so grave that there is not even an inclination of the scales one way': *Doe d. Winter v. Perratt*. In a well – known statement, Sir George Jessel M. R. said that the

court would not hold a will void for uncertainty ' unless it is impossible to put a fair meaning on it. The duty of the court is to put a fair meaning on the terms used, and not, as was said in one case, to repose upon the easy pillow of uncertainty': *In re Roberts* (1881) 19 Ch. D. 520. That this is not a doctrine confined to wills but is one which applies to other instruments, such as planning permissions is shown by cases such as *Fawcett Properties Ltd v. Buckingham County Council* (1961) A. C. 636, where by a majority, the Delphic language of a condition in a planning permission escaped from being held void for uncertainty largely because of its resemblance to a section in a modern Act of Parliament."

3. 在 Philip Nicholas Shaw v Lighthousexpress Ltd (2010) 1 EWCA Civ 161 先例，上诉庭的 Jacob 大法官说："... void for uncertainty is the last resort conclusion."(以不肯定为由判无效并不予执行是最后没有办法中的办法)

在这种想法下,会以不肯定判无效的例子不太多。特别在近年来宽松的合约解释下,法院或仲裁庭往往在一些十分含糊与不肯定的合约条文中选择一个认为比较合理与符合订约时的"事实背景"(background facts)与双方订约"目的"(purpose)的解释。这在本书第六章有详述。

12.1 不肯定的情况

不肯定在以下情况会发生:一是根本"无法给有关明示条文/文字任何解释"(devoid of any meaning);二是所用的条文/文字有多种解释或/与有关合约其他条文/文字会出现矛盾的解释,所以法院/仲裁庭根本无法确定它的意思或订约双方的想法;三是一个"协议将来达成协议"(agreement to agree)。

这里可先节录 Brown v. Gould (1972) 1 Ch 53 先例,Megarry 大法官所说有关前两种的不肯定情况:"A provision may be void for uncertainty because it is devoid of any meaning. As some critics of certain modern writings might testify, there may be an unintelligible collocation of ordinary English words, or there be mere gibberish ... The other main head is where there is a variety of meanings which can fairly be put on the provision, and it is impossible to say which of them was intended. Mere ambiguities may sometimes be resolved by the application of legal presumptions, and so on; but where the language used is equally consistent with a wide range of different meanings, it may be impossible to discern the concept which the provision was intended to enshrine. If a case is to be brought under this head, the attack will usually start with the demonstration of a diversity of meanings which are consistent with the language used; and if this is not done, the attack will usually fail."

至于第三种不肯定情况,可节录 Denning 勋爵在 Courtney & Fairburn Ltd v. Tolaini Bros (Hotels) Ltd (1975) 1 W. L. R. 297 先例所说如下:"If the law does not recognize a contract to enter into a contract (when there is a fundamental term yet to be agreed) it seems to me that it cannot recognize a contract to negotiate, the reason is because it is too uncertain to have any binding force, no court could estimate the damages because no one can tell whether the negotiations would be successful or would fell through; or if successful what the result would be. It seems to me that a contract to negotiate, like a contract to enter into a contract, is not a contract known to the law."

12.1.1 不肯定情况之一:无法给条文/文字任何解释

这方面一个著名的先例是 Nicolene v. Simmonds (1953) 1 Lloyd's Rep. 189,案情是一宗3000吨钢材的货物买卖。双方通过信件往来达成所谓的合约,其中的一封信函有以下的一段说:"As you have made the order direct to me I am unable to confirm on my usual printed form which would have the usual *force majeure* and war clauses, but I assume that we are in agreement that the usual conditions of acceptance apply."

这一段话带来争议,买方认为双方已经达成买卖合约,但卖方没有交货。卖方认为双方并没有达成买卖合约,因为上述的一段文字太不肯定。结果上诉庭判这一句话的最后几个加黑的字无法给任何解释,因为根本没有这回事。Denning 大法官是这样说:"This case raises a short, but important, point which can be stated quite simply. There was a contract for the sale of 3000 tons of steel reinforcing bars, and the seller broke his contract. When the buyer claimed damages the seller set up the defence that, owing to one of the sentences in the letters which constituted the contract, there was no contract at all. The material words are: 'We are in agreement that the usual conditions of acceptance apply.' There were no usual conditions of acceptance at all, so the words are meaningless. There is nothing to which they can apply. On that account it is said that there was never a contract at all between the parties."

另一个可举的先例是 The "Iran Vojdan" (1984) 2 Lloyd's Rep. 380。该先例所涉及的一份提单中对于适用的法律有如下条款:"2 (a) ... all disputes arising hereunder or in connection therewith shall in the option of the carrier to be declared by him on the merchant's request be governed either by Iranian law with the exclusive jurisdiction of the courts in Teheran, by German law with the exclusive jurisdiction of the courts of Hamburg or by English law with the exclusive jurisdiction of the courts of London."

这种浮动的适用法律条文被视为太不肯定,因为合约在一开始履行就应该稳定受某一个适用法管辖。如果合约履行的半途可以任由一方改变为另一种适用法,就会导致本来正确的做法变为不正确,本来时效没有过变为时效已过等。这进一步令订约双方无所适从,所以被 Bingham 大法官判是上述的条文没有意思与无法理解而无效,说:"I find this, as I feel bound to say, an extremely unattractive clause, introducing maximum complexity and difficulty into what could and should be a simple matter. It is nonetheless the duty of the Court to give a sensible meaning so far as possible to what the parties have agreed and not readily to reject the text of an agreement between the parties as unintelligible. . . . ”

12.1.2　不肯定情况之二：有太多可能的解释

这种情况通常是双方同意的条文/文字有太多可能的解释，而每一种解释都与合约其他条文没有矛盾与说得通，变成法院/仲裁庭无法作出一个比较合理的选择。[6] 这样，就会以不肯定为由判是无效，不论这无效的后果是双方还没有达成协议或是不肯定的条文/文字本身无效。这种案例有不少，如：

1. 这可举贵族院的先例：Scammell & Nephew Ltd v. Ouston (1941) A. C. 251 HL，涉及一个小货车的买卖，但双方说明“以市场有的租购条文为准”（subject to hire - purchase terms being available）的形式买卖。但事后发觉市场上有好几种不同版本的租购条文，每一份都可以适用，难以确定以哪一个版本为准。结果贵族院判合约无效。类似的情况笔者也在仲裁遇到，如在一个造船合约的谈判，船东与船厂除了对一些特定的重要条文达成协议，另加一句“其他条文根据标准造船合约”（other terms per standard shipbuilding contract），就会有争议在这种情况下双方是否已经达成一个合约。因为标准造船合约目前世界上有几个不同版本，如 SAJ，AWES，Norwegian Standard Form Shipbuilding Contract 与 NEWBUILDCON 等。双方到底同意哪个版本适用在其他条文，也会有严重的不同后果，例如，在一些条文，如船舶的“修改”（modification），SAJ 就明显倾向保护船厂的利益，而 NEWBUILDCON 就明显倾向保护船东的利益。如果有关的船东与船厂曾经有过交易，这就可以从以前交易所用的合约格式协助找出答案。但如果没有，就增加了难度。也有可能涉及的船厂在日本，船厂几乎肯定是使用 SAJ 标准格式，就可以说是以 SAJ 为准。毕竟，除了船厂有这样的订约意图外，船东去日本造船也应该有这个准备与订约意图。这些都是根据订约时的“事实背景”（background facts）或“目的”（purpose）协助解释合约条文的例子。但如果是在中国造船，就会涉及许多不同的造船合约，虽然说通常以 SAJ 为基础，但笔者见过一些合约改得面目全非。更不用说现在在中国，有船厂开始接受使用 NEWBUILDCON。这样，就会有危险是法院/仲裁庭可能被迫在非常不情愿的情况下判双方还没有达成一个有法律效力的合约关系，因为“其他条文根据标准造船合约”太不肯定，其中包括一些合约履行必须有的重要条文。也有可能判双方已经达成一个有法律效力的合约关系，因为有关的中国船厂通常是以 SAJ 为基础订约，也是外国买方/船东应该在谈判时知悉，所以标准造船合约指的就是 SAJ。

2. 在 British Electrical and Associated Industries (Cardiff), Ltd v. Patley Pressings, Ltd. (1953) 1 W. L. R. 280 先例，有关不肯定的条文/文字也被 McNair 大法官判是在行业中有很多不同版本的“不可抗力条文”（*force majeure* clause），无从确定是哪一份说：“The terms of a contract note in relation to a sale of steel contained the following clause: ‘Subject to *force majeure* conditions that the government restricts the ex-

〔6〕 这可看本书第四章之第 3 段，在合约条文/文字有两个或以上解释，就选择一个比较合理的解释。

port of the material at the time of delivery.' There was a variety of *force majeure* conditions in the trade, and no evidence that any particular ones had been agreed on. The buyers relied on that note as evidencing a contract."

3. 另一个有相似判法的先例是 The "Agios Lazaros" (1976) 2 Lloyd's Rep. 47，高院的 Donaldson 大法官也是以有太多"首要条文"（paramount clause）版本可选择，难以确定并判该条文无效，虽然这一判决最后被上诉庭推翻。稍后对这一先例有详论，在此不作重复。

4. 在 Lovelock, Ltd. v. Exportles (1968) 1 Lloyd's Rep. 163 先例，该案例中的 CIF 买卖合约是英国买方从俄罗斯卖方进口木材。双方有了争议，一是交货数量不足，二是所交的货物质量有问题。英国买方在英国高院出了告票，但俄罗斯卖方就去高院申请中止诉讼并强制该争议去俄罗斯仲裁。该买卖合约有两条仲裁条文，一是英国仲裁，二是俄罗斯仲裁。这样就存在一个问题，即可否对这两条具有同样效力但文字上稍有不同的条文进行协调，令两条仲裁条文都能够有一定解释。其中俄罗斯卖方提出了五个建议去解释：(1)先去英国仲裁，失败后去俄罗斯仲裁；(2)英国仲裁针对的是金钱上的索赔，俄罗斯仲裁针对的是非金钱上的争议；(3)英国仲裁针对货物在英国交货所产生的争议，俄罗斯仲裁针对交货之前的争议，如买卖合约的履行与否；(4)英国仲裁针对议定金额的索赔，俄罗斯仲裁针对非议定金额的索赔；(5)英国仲裁针对货物运送去英国的争议，俄罗斯仲裁针对货物运送去其他国家的争议。

但这些解释都不被上诉庭接受，认为太牵强与不合理。结果这两条条文被判无法协调，造成不肯定的情况而被判无效。Denning 勋爵是这样说：

"So all five suggestions seem to me to be untenable. **I am forced to the conclusion that the clause is so uncertain that the Court cannot give effect to it.** The clause is divided into two parts which are inconsistent with one another: and it is impossible to reconcile them. The first part of this arbitration clause would send 'Any dispute and/or claim' to arbitration in England. The second part of the clause would send 'Any other dispute' to arbitration in Russia. It is beyond the wit of man - or at any rate beyond my wit - to say which dispute comes within which part of the clause. I think I can see how it has come about. The parties have taken separate clauses from two separate forms and bundled them both together into one clause without stopping to think how they could be applied.

In my opinion the whole clause is meaningless. It must be rejected. The Court cannot give effect to it. The dispute cannot be sent to arbitration. It must be decided by the Court. ..."（加黑部分是笔者的强调）

12.1.3 不肯定种类之三：协议将来达成协议（agreement to agree）

12.1.3.1 协议将来达成协议无效的原因

英国法律认为这种协议等于是协议将来进行谈判一样，因为太不肯定而无效。

主要的原因已经在较早时节录 Denning 勋爵在 Courtney & Fairburn Ltd v. Tolaini Bros (Hotels) Ltd (1975) 1 W. L. R. 297 先例所说的,就是如果在这种协议下违约,如其中一方拒绝谈判,这种违约会带来什么损失没有办法确定与证明。因为难以知道双方谈判出什么结果才是大家可以接受。拒绝谈判一方大可以说“谈下去我也是坚持一分钱也不支付”,这样,希望谈判的一方能够索赔什么损失?

另在近期的 Petromec Inc. v. Petrleo Brasileiro (2005) EWCA Civ. 891 先例,Longmore 大法官多给了几个为什么法律不承认协议将来达成协议的原因,除了不肯定之外,也没有办法知道双方是否是善意/诚意地谈判。他说:“The traditional objections to enforcing an obligation to negotiate in good faith are (1) that the obligation is an agreement to agree and thus too uncertain to enforce, (2) that it is difficult, if not impossible, to say whether, if negotiations are brought to an end, the termination is brought about in good faith or bad faith, and (3) that, since it can never be known whether good faith negotiations would have produced an agreement at all or what the terms of any agreement would have been if it would have been reached, it is impossible to assess any loss caused by breach of the obligation.”

就算是加了一些如要求双方订约方都“尽最大努力”(best endeavours)谈判与同意,结果也是一样。这是 Millett 大法官在 Little v. Courage Ltd (1994) 70 P. & C. R. 469 先例说:“An undertaking to use one's best endeavours to try to agree, however, is not different from an undertaking to agree, to try to agree, or to negotiate with a view to reaching agreement; all are equally uncertain and incapable of giving rise to an enforceable legal obligation.”

12.1.3.2 协议将来达成协议有效的情况

虽然有这个大原则,但也不代表所有的协议将来达成协议都是无效,特别是针对个别履行的条文,这尤其是在有关的合约已经被部分或全部履行了。在商业合约,这种留待将来才达成协议的情况经常有,这样,法院如果能够默示一个双方还没有约定的价格是“公平价格”(fair price),有关协议就可以有效与被继续履行:Corson v. Rhuddlan Borough Council (1990) 1 E. GLR. 255; Money v. Ven - Lu - Ree Ltd (1989) 3 N. Z. L. R. 129, PC 等先例。如果合约有一条仲裁条文,更有一个可以在将来双方无法达成协议时让仲裁庭作决定的机制:The Queensland Electricity Generating Board v. New Hope Collieries Ltd (1989) 1 Lloyd's Rep. 205; The “Didymi” (1988) 2 Lloyd's Rep. 108 与 Mamidoil - Jetoil Greek Petroleum Co v. Okta Crude Oil Refinery (2001) 2 Lloyd's Rep. 76 等先例。

在租船合约,尤其是长期的期租,也经常有条文针对一些留待将来达成的协议,如针对将来还船燃油的价格。在 The “Tropwind” (1982) 1 Lloyd's Rep. 232 CA 先例,有关的条文是要求双方同意最后航次的时间以确定最后一期租金应支付的金额。往往到这个时候,由于租约已经大部分被履行,不可能再说因为不肯定,所以双方没有合约关系。也不能说因为不肯定,所以有关条文无效,毕竟对还船燃油的价格与最后一期要付的租金总要有一个说法。所以双方不能同意,法院/仲裁庭也只能作出默示,如还船燃油的合理价格或最后一期租金的合理金额。Denning 勋爵说:"We often have contracts which contain clauses as to price, time, or other things 'to be agreed'. **Such a provision does not render the clause null or void. We always seek to make it work by making an implication of some kind or other.** As the House of Lords did in W. N. Hillas & Co. v. Arcos, (1932) 43 Ll. L. Rep. 359; (1932) 38 Com. Cas. 23. Clauses such as this are often found in charter – parties. According to the usual practice, the charterers estimate the time and make payment accordingly, deducting the estimated bunkers and disbursements. I cannot believe that the owners can frustrate all the estimates by saying, 'We do not agree'. Nor by making an arbitrary or capricious refusal. It is necessarily implied that each party should act reasonably in endeavouring to reach an agreed time. As a corollary, I think it is to be implied that the owners cannot refuse a bona fide and reasonable estimate of the time necessary to complete the voyage. At any rate, they cannot refuse unless they put forward a bona fide and reasonable counter – proposal which the charterers cannot reasonably refuse. It is only by such implication that the clause can be made to work."(加黑部分是笔者的强调)

关于协议将来达成协议的进一步介绍,在本书第九章多个段节都有详尽针对,这里不再重复。

12.2 不肯定导致的后果

12.2.1 合约不肯定是否有效或只是不肯定条文/文字不被执行

合约不肯定会带来两个后果:一是合约无效;二是将合约视为有效,但漠视/删除不肯定的条文/文字。这可节录 Saville 大法官在 Vitol B. V. v. Compagnie Europeene des Petroles (1988) 1 Lloyd's Rep. 574 先例说:"... If the words are not so clear and admit of more than one sensible meaning, then the ambiguity may be resolved by looking at the aim and genesis of the agreement, choosing the meaning which seems to make the most sense in the context of the contract and its surrounding circumstances as a whole. In some cases, of course, having attempted this exercise, it may simply remain impossible to give the words any sensible meaning at all in which case they (or some of them) are either ignored, that is to say, treated as not forming part of the contract at all, or (if of apparent central importance) treated as demonstrating that the parties never made an agreement at all, that is to say, had never truly agreed upon the vital terms of their bargain."

这两个不肯定导致的后果,Denning 大法官在 Nicolene v. Simmonds (1953) 1 Lloyd's Rep. 189 先例中也说:

"In my opinion, a distinction must be drawn between a clause which is meaningless and a clause which has yet to be agreed. A clause which is meaningless can often be ignored, while still leaving the contract good; whereas a clause which has yet to be agreed may mean that there is no contract at all, because the parties have not agreed on all the essential terms. ...(无法作出解释与没有意思的条文与还需要双方达成协议的条文,是有区别。在前者的情况,可以漠视/删除一条没有意思的条文但不影响其余合约有效。但后者的情况,如果有关的条文是一条很重要的条文,双方还没有达成协议就会表示他们还没有合约关系。)

I would just say a word about the recent decision of Mr. Justice McNair in *British Electrical and Associated Industries* (*Cardiff*), *Ltd v. Patley Pressings*, Ltd. (1953) 1 W. L. R. 280, where the contract note contained the clause 'subject to *force majeure* conditions.' If the true construction of the documents in that case was that an essential term had yet to be agreed, it would fall within the cases to which I have referred; but if the true view was that the excepting clause was agreed but was 'so vague and uncertain as to be incapable of any precise meaning' (which is how Mr. Justice McNair described it, sup., at p. 283) I should have thought that it could be ignored without impairing the validity of the contract. It was clearly severable from the rest of the contract..."

这两个不肯定的后果有时候很难预计到底适用哪一个,这会带来很大影响,因为涉及是否有一个有效合约的问题。可能影响法院/仲裁庭如何判决的因素如下:(1)一般而言,不肯定的条文/文字越是重要,就越有可能带来第一种合约无效的后果。(2)如果是第二种后果,即只漠视/删除不肯定的条文/文字,但合约本身有效,就必须肯定能这样做,即不肯定之处与合约其他条文/文字"能分开来"(severable)。这可以 King's Motors (Oxford) Ltd v. Lax (1970) 1 W. L. R. 426 先例为例,案情涉及一个房屋租赁合约,另有一个长达 7 年续租的选择权,但租金由双方将来达成协议。而合约中没有任何显示这租金是怎样同意,以什么为依据,或是如果双方不能达成协议怎样办。法院判是租约本身有效,但租约的选择权无效。不肯定之处可分开来判无效。(3)如果有不肯定的合约已经开始履行,就有极大可能带来第二种后果。有关这方面在下一段会进一步详谈。

12.2.2　尚未履行与已经部分履行的不同对待

针对不肯定的合约条文,法律对待"尚未履行"(executory)与"已经部分履行"(executed)有很大不同。对尚未履行的合约,特别是不肯定的条文十分重要,可以指双方实际上可能还在谈判阶段或双方还没有"想法一致"(meeting of minds)而否定合约的存在。但如果已经部分履行的合约,就非得找出一个说法,这会被法院/仲裁庭千方百计判一条协议将来达成协议的合约条文是有效与可以解释(即使是牵强的解释)或作出默示。这些说法可列举如下:

1. 在 British Bank for Foreign Trade Ltd v. Novinex Ltd (1949) 1 K. B. 623 先例中,上诉庭同意了以下的说法:"The principle to be deducted from the cases is that if

there is an essential term which has yet to be agreed and there is no express or implied provision for its solution, the result in point of law is that there is no binding contract. In seeing whether there is an implied provision for its solution, however, there is a difference between an arrangement which is wholly executory on both sides and one which has been executed on one side or the other. In the ordinary way, if there is an arrangement to supply goods at a price ' to be agreed' or to perform service on terms ' to be agreed', then although, while the matter is still executory, there may be no binding contract, nevertheless, if it is executed on one side, that is, if the one does his part without having come to an agreement as to the price or the terms, then the law will say that there is necessarily implied, from the conduct of the parties, a contract that, in default of agreement, a reasonable sum is to be paid."

2. 在 Sudbrook Trading Estate Ltd v. Eggleton (1983) 1 A. C. 444 先例中,上诉庭同意了以下的说法:"Where an agreement which would otherwise be unenforceable for want of certainty or finality in an essential stipulation has been partly performed so that the intervention of the court is necessary in aid of a grant that has already taken effect, the court will train to the utmost to supply the want of certainty even to the extent of providing a substitute machinery."

3. 在 Mamidoil - Jetoil Greek Petroleum Co v. Okta Crude Oil Refinery (2001) 2 Lloyd's Rep. 76 先例中,Rix 大法官也有同样的说法,这可看本书第九章之第 9 段。

12.2.3 不肯定不是无效的案例之一:The "Agios Lazaros"

在这一个先例 The "Agios Lazaros" (1976) 2 Lloyd's Rep. 47,有关的租约第 31 条文是说:"... and also Paramount clause are deemed to be incorporated in this Charter Party."

众所周知,"首要条文"(paramount clause)用在租约中是合并《海牙规则》。但问题是航运市场中有许多版本的首要条文,有针对期租,有针对程租,有不同商会的标准条文或个别订约方自己随意约定的条文(如本案例一样)等。有一些首要条文将整个《海牙规则》合并进来,即使许多内容与租约毫无关系。也有只约定将《海牙规则》的第 3 与第 4 条文有关船东的义务与责任合并进来,反正有多个版本可供选择。在本案例,由于没有说明是哪一版本,就带来不肯定的争议。这争议十分关键,因为承租人延迟向船东开始仲裁,如果《海牙规则》的 1 年时效适用,承租人的索赔就无法实现。但如果因为不肯定导致《海牙规则》的合并被视为无效,承租人就有 6 年时效了。在高院,Donaldson 大法官判是该条文由于太不肯定而无效。但去了上诉庭,判决被推翻并认为条文将《海牙规则》全部内容合并进来有效。针对不肯定的争议,Denning 勋爵这样说:

"What does ' paramount clause' or ' clause paramount' mean to shipping men? Primarily it applies to bills of lading. In that context its meaning is, I think, clear beyond question. It means a clause by which the Hague Rules are incorporated into the contract evidenced by the bill of lading and which overrides any express exemption or condition that is inconsistent with it. ...

The Judge (Donaldson 大法官), however, took a different view. He said that there are many different paramount clauses and he could not say which one of them was applicable. So none of them was...

I do not share the Judge's view, it seems to me that when the paramount clause was incorporated, without any words of qualification, it means that all of the Hague Rules are incorporated ..."

Denning 勋爵也谈到法院不愿意判双方的明示条文因为不肯定而变无效,不管这不肯定是来自没有清楚的观念,或是没有意思,又或只是一个协议将来达成协议,说:"The court's reluctance to hold a provision void for uncertainty applies equally to cases where it is alleged that the provision discloses no clear concept; to cases where it is alleged that a provision is meaningless, and to cases where it is alleged that the agreement is no more than an agreement to agree."

笔者在同意上诉庭的判法之余,也可以再提出两个额外理由:一是上诉庭尊重订约双方的订约"目的"(purpose),即想在租约引进《海牙规则》;二是虽然市场上有多个不同版本的首要条文,但它们之间的内容并没有太大差异。

12.2.4 不肯定不是无效的案例之二:The "Tropwind"

The "Tropwind" (1982) 1 Lloyd's Rep. 232 CA 先例是无数同类案例中一个有关不准时或不足数支付期租合约下的租金而导致船东根据明示条文(NYPE 46 之第 5 条文)行使选择权撤船与终止租约的案例。在这个先例中的船东,因为租约的租金定得低,在运费市场高涨后一直找机会撤船。他已经在早一个先例中以承租人稍微迟延补偿加保费而撤船,但被判是无效:The "Tropwind" (1977) 1 Lloyd's Rep. 397。在本先例中,船东故技重施,虽然已经接近还船。当船舶抵达印度 Belikeri 港的同一天,承租人也准时支付了最后一期租金。在该租金内,承租人扣除了预估的还船燃油与估计的船东使费。这些金额都被仲裁庭确认为"善意与合理"(*bona fide* and reasonable)。这样看来,船东应该没有借口撤船。但船东还是根据租约的有关条文挑出好几个争议,该有关条文是第 56 条附加条文如下:"Clause 56: Should the vessel be on her voyage to the port of redelivery at the time when payment hire is due, said payment shall be made for such length of time as Owners or their Agents and Charterers or their Agents may agree upon as the established time necessary to complete the voyage. **Bunkers to be taken over by the vessel and estimated disbursement for Owners account before redelivery and difference shall be refunded by Owners or paid by Charterers as the case may be.**"(加黑部分是双方争议的一句)

上述条文对航运人士来说很熟悉,它允许承租人在最后的一、两期租金的支付中扣除估计的还船燃油与船东使费。没有这一条文,承租人要足数支付租金,否则会给船东借口去撤船。但上述条文有好几个地方引起争议。例如,第一句话是说"在航次中"(on her voyage)是否指在 Belikeri 港装了矿砂开航后,如果有支付租金才能适用,而当时船舶刚抵达还不能适用?这涉及合理解释的问题,毕竟"航次"一词可以有多个解释。在这里笔者针对的是另一个问题,上述条文的第二句写得太差劲。翻译成中文即是:"还船前将会被船舶接受的燃油与估计的船东应负责的使费,差额部分将视情况由船东退还或者承租人支付。"这一句漏了好几个字,如"燃油"一词前面应该加一个"估计",因为在事前无法知道准确的还船燃油。更大的问题是没有说明"可从该租金内扣除"(may be deducted from such hire payment),这一句只提到了估计船东的使费(这笔钱通常在期租合约是由承租人垫付或预支,稍后在租金的支付中扣除),但没有说应该怎么办。

结果在高院,Goff 大法官判这一句无效,因为太不肯定,说:"... I have particularly in mind the second submission of the owners, viz. that the charterers' right of deduction in respect of bunkers and disbursements was contingent upon agreement having been reached between the parties as to the established time necessary to complete the voyage. How that second submission is to be answered depends entirely upon how the second sentence of the clause is to be spelled out in full - which is, in this respect, a matter of pure speculation. In circumstances such as these the proper course is not (tempting though it may be) to invite the tribunal to make a guess at what the parties intended; the proper course is to have the charter rectified, to bring it in accordance with the fixture actually agreed before the charter was drawn up, and then to enforce the contract as rectified. Of course, **if no clear prior agreement was reached, then the charter cannot be rectified and the provision must be rejected as meaningless. In the present case, no claim for rectification having been made, the Court should not, in my judgment, speculate about the meaning of the second sentence of the charter, but should disregard it as meaningless.**"(加黑部分是笔者的强调)

但高院的判决被上诉庭推翻,认为这一条文的"目的"(purpose)十分明确,在租船市场上有大量这种相对拟定更好的条文可以比较,没有理由不给其任何解释。Denning 勋爵这样说:"The Judge rejected the second sentence of clause 56 altogether. He said that it was—... most defective, deficient even of a main verb ... the Court should reject it as meaningless. We have on a few occasions rejected a sentence as meaningless, as in *Nicolene v. Simmonds*, (1953) 1 Lloyd's Rep. 189; (1953) 1 Q. B. 543. But this is only when it is impossible to make sense of it. Rather than find it meaningless, we should strive to find out what was really intended - by amending the punctuation, or by supplying words, and so forth. In our present case much help can be found by looking at similar clauses of them. In order to bring this clause into line with them, all that is necessary is to omit the full stop and insert at that point ‘less estimated’. That is how the arbitrators read this clause. I think they were quite right to do so. To me the explanation is obvious. Someone in the trade wrote out the clause in handwriting, or dictated it. The typist got it down wrong. Her draft was never revised properly. So it got inserted in a defective form. It must obviously be put right. The Judge seems to have thought that it could not be done without rectification. That would indeed be making a mountain out of a molehill. We should trample down the molehill."

在笔者看来,上诉庭的判决肯定受欢迎,特别对英语与法律都不太精通的亚洲承租人或船东,合约条文拟订得不好时有发生。而且,以前上诉庭根据该条文的“目的”(purpose)解释也是符合今天的大精神与做法,就是“purposive approach to construction”。

12.2.5 不肯定不是无效的案例之三:Ashburn Anstalt v. Arnold

Ashburn Anstalt v. Arnold (1988) 2 W. L. R. 706 先例有关商铺租约,双方约定的不肯定内容是以下条文:“... in a prime position at the development with an area available for trading of approximately 100 square feet and with car parking facilities within the development for a term of 21 years and the rent in respect of such lease shall for the first seven years be 25 per cent less than the market rent."(加黑部分是笔者的强调)

法院判是上述条文/文字并非不肯定。其中“优质地段”(prime position)是地产界通用的术语,如果订约双方对提供的商铺是否为“优质地段”有争议,可以通过专家意见证据解决争议。另“大约”(approximately)一词也并非不肯定,可以给一个合理的百分比。

§13 合约记录错误的做法:合约变更与解释合约作出纠正

合约条文/文字经常有明显错误,通常在文书上,可以是拼写、文法、引错了名字(不论是个人或者机构)、漏了几个字或多写了几个字。在这种看来是合约错误记录的情况下,可以有不同做法,一种是申请“合约变更”(rectification),另一种是由法院/仲裁庭在解释合约的过程中作出“纠正”(correction)。合约变更并不容易成功,因为会有“重写”(rewrite)双方合约的危险,而且双方不一定在以前的谈判中对合约中的错误曾经同意过正确的条文/文字,并留下了有过这一真正订约意图的证据。至于通过解释合约对一些明显错误作出纠正,这是另一种做法,但这种做法只局限在“明显错误”(obvious mistake)。正如本书第一章 8.5 段所介绍的 The “Starsin” (2003) 1 Lloyd's Rep. 571 先例,提单中的一条喜玛拉雅条文在打印时漏掉一行共 17 个字,贵族院加上,这就是“纠正”的做法,Millett 勋爵说这做法是“解释合约而并非合约变更”(process was one of construction, not rectification)。以下分别介绍这两种做法。

13.1 合约变更

13.1.1 关于合约变更的权威说法

这可先节录《Chitty on Contracts》(第31版,2012年)一书之5-110段的总结如下:

"Rectification only applies to contracts which have been reduced to writing. It is a process by which the document is made to conform to what was actually agreed between the parties.

'... the remedy of rectification is one permitted by the Court, not for the purpose of altering the terms of an agreement entered into between two or more parties, but for that of correcting a written instrument which, by a mistake in verbal expression, does not accurately reflect their true agreement.'

Most of the cases involve what has been agreed by the parties having been wrongly recorded in the document without either party being aware of the mistake. These cases involve what may be termed rectification to correct a **common mistake.** Rectification may also be available when one party signed a written document which did not record his intentions correctly, and the other party knew of the first party's intentions[7]. In this case the court may rectify the document so that it reflects the first party's intentions. This may be termed a case of rectification to correct a **unilateral mistake.** There are some general principles which apply in both situations."(加黑部分是笔者的强调)

《Chitty on Contracts》(第31版,2012年)一书之5-130段针对变更的举证责任是说:"The burden of proof is on the party seeking rectification. He must produce 'convincing proof' not only that the document to be rectified was not in accordance with the parties' true intentions at the time of its execution, but also that the document in its proposed form does accord with their intention. It is essential that the extent of the rectification should be clearly ascertained and defined by evidence contemporaneous with or anterior to the contract. The denial of one of the parties that the deed as it stands is contrary to his intention ought to have considerable weight, and unless the other party can convince the court that the document does not represent his or both parties' intentions at the time of execution, rectification will only exceptionally be ordered. Indeed, it has been said that **it is not sufficient that the written contract does not represent the true inten-**

---

〔7〕 这种单方面的错误申请变更更加困难,需要达致"衡平法欺诈"(equitable fraud),这可看Denning大法官在Solle v Butcher (1950) 1 KB 671先例中举的一个例子:"one party, knowing the other is mistaken about the terms of an offer, or the identity of the person by whom it is made, lets him remain under his delusion and concludes a contract on the mistaken terms instead of pointing out the mistake."

tion of the parties; it must be shown that the written contract was actually contrary to the intention of the parties. Where it is sought to rectify a document in accordance with a prior agreement between the parties, it must be shown that the intention of the parties continued unaltered up to the time of the execution of the document."(加黑部分是笔者的强调)

至于一些权威先例中的说法,更加不少,以下节录一些最重要与较近期的说法。首先是 Mustill 大法官在 The "Olympic Pride" (1980) 2 Lloyd's Rep 67 先例中有关合约变更要符合五个条件的说法,这说法被视为充分反映了目前的法律地位:

"1. The remedy of rectification is available only for the putting right of a mistake in the terms of a document which purports to record a previous transaction. It is not an appropriate remedy where the mistake relates to the transaction itself rather than to the document which purports to record it.(变更的救济只适用在文件中错误记录了较早的约定。变更不针对交易中的错误。)

2. Rectification may be granted in two situations: (a) where there is a mistake common to both parties, the mistake being the belief that the document accurately records the transaction. (The fact that the mistake must be shared does not necessarily mean that it must arise in the same way on each side. Very often the mistake of one party occurs in the writing and of theother in the signing of the document, but the mistaken belief is common to both.); (b) where one party is mistaken as to the compliance of the document with the transaction and the other party knows of this mistaken belief but does nothing to correct it. The person seeking rectification in this situation must, in effect establish that his opponent was guilty of sharp practice. [变更适用于两种情况:(1)共同错误,双方误以为文件准确记录了他们之间的约定。(2)单方面错误,一方以为文件准确记录了他们之间的约定或订约意图,但对方实际上知道这一错误。但在这种情况下,申请变更的一方必须证明对方取巧或"不合情理"(unconscionable)。]

3. The prior transaction may consist either of a concluded agreement or of a continuing common intention. In the latter event, the intention must be objectively manifested. It is the words and acts of the parties demonstrating their intention, not the inward thoughts of the parties, which matter.(较早的约定可以是一个达成了的协议或是一个持续性的共同订约意图。在后者,订约意图必须是能够客观显示出来让法院/仲裁庭认定,不仅是双方内心的想法。)

4. The Court must be satisfied not only that the document fails to reflect the prior agreement or intention but also that there was a prior or common agreement (or intention) in terms which the Court can ascertain.(法院除了必须满足有关文件没有反映较早达成的协议或订约意图,也必须能够明确到底是什么协议或意图才能作出变更。)

5. The Court requires the mistake to be proved with a high degree of conviction be-

fore granting relief. There are sound policy reasons for this. The Court is reluctant to allow a party of full capacity who has signed a document with opportunity of inspection, to say afterwards that it is not what he meant. Otherwise, certainty and ready enforceability would be hindered by constant attempts to cloud the issue by reference to pre – contractual negotiations. These considerations apply with particular force in the field of commerce, where certainty is so important. Various expressions have been employed in the reported cases to describe the standard of proof required of the person who seeks rectification. Counsel in the present case were agreed that the standard can adequately be stated by saying that the Court must be 'sure' of the mistake, and of the existence of a prior agreement or common intention before granting the remedy."(必须有一个很高程度的证明,法院才会接受合约变更。原因是法院不愿意允许一方合约方在他有充分能力在签字前对有关的文件或合约作出检查的情况下,事后声称该文件或合约不代表他们之间的协议或意图。这会带来不肯定与合约不能马上履行。)

接下去对合约变更的权威说法是在贵族院的 Chartbrook Ltd v. Persimmon Homes Ltd (2009) UKHL 38 先例,其中在上诉庭 Lawrence Collins 大法官的说法,并且被贵族院认同是如下:

"There is no dispute on the applicable legal principles. The burden is on the party seeking rectification, and he must put forward convincing proof.

The court will rectify a contract if the evidence is clear and unambiguous that a mistake has been made in the recording of the parties' intention, what that intention was, and that the alleged intention continued in both parties' minds down to the time of the execution of the agreement: Swainland Builders Ltd v Freehold Properties Ltd [2002] 2 EGLR 71 at 74, [33].

The burden is particularly onerous where there have been prolonged negotiations between the parties eventually assuming the shape of a formal instrument on which they have been advised by skilled lawyers: Crane v Hegeman – Harris Co Inc [1939] 1 All ER 662 at 664 – 5; and also Snamprogetti Ltd v Phillips Petroleum Ltd [2001] EWCA 889 at [36].(申请合约变更一方的举证责任非常沉重,特别是涉及一个漫长的谈判后并在律师的协助下,双方签订了一份正式文件的情况。)

In cases where common mistake is alleged, it is necessary to establish not merely a continuing common intention, but also some outward expression of that prior accord: Joscelyne v Nissen [1970] 2 QB 86 at 97 – 98. The requirement of an outward manifestation of accord has been said to be an evidential factor rather than a strict legal requirement: Beasley v Munt [2006] EWCA Civ 370 at [36], per Mummery LJ. The claimant does not have to meet more than the civil standard of balance of probabilities, but convincing proof is required to counteract the cogent evidence of the parties' intention displayed by the instrument: Thomas Bates and Sons v Wyndham's Ltd. [1981] 1 WLR 505, 521 (CA).（这一段与较早Mustill大法官所说的一致，增加的只是虽然申请合约变更的原告有很重的举证责任，但在所有民事诉讼的举证责任还是平衡的可能性。）

Where only one party is mistaken, a species of equitable estoppel precludes a person who knows of the other party's mistake from resisting rectification: Snell, Equity, 31st ed 2005, para 14 – 15(2). Slade LJ described it as a 'drastic remedy' in The Nai Genova [1984] 1 Lloyd's Rep 353 at 365. In George Wimpey UK Ltd v VIC Construction Ltd [2005] EWCA Civ 77, [2005] BLR 135 Peter Gibson LJ referred to the 'exceptional jurisdiction to rectify for unilateral mistake' (para 51). The requisite knowledge is actual, including for that purpose 'blind eye', knowledge: Commissioner for the New Towns v Cooper (Great Britain) Ltd [1995] Ch 259; George Wimpey UK Ltd v VIC Construction Ltd [2005] BLR 135, per Blackburne J at [79] (close to dishonesty).（涉及单方面错误的合约变更，这可以说是"衡平法禁止反供"的一种，也就是对方或被告明知文件或合约错误记录了其订约意图，但刻意不提出并取巧。这等于原告需要证明被告实际上知道文件或合约错误记录，但不诚实而隐瞒。）

I should also emphasise at this point, because so much of the judge's conclusions rest on his assessment of the witnesses, that it has often been said that when a trial judge's estimate of a witness forms any substantial part of his judgment, his conclusions of fact should be left alone by the appellate court. It is only if satisfied that the trial judge has not taken proper advantage of having seen and heard the witnesses that an appellate court is justified in interfering: e. g. Assicurazioni Generali SpA v. Arab Insurance Group [2002] EWCA Civ 1642, [2003] 1 WLR 577 at [14] – [23], approved in Datec Electronic Holdings Ltd v United Parcels Services Ltd [2007] UKHL 23, [2007] 1 WLR 1325, at [46]."（合约变更经常涉及对事实证人的可信性评估，因为许多较早的谈判过程中会涉及口头证据。上诉庭对一审法院针对双方证人的可信性一般不应该质疑，除非一审法院在一些原则或程序上犯错。）

最后节录一个一审法院比较简短的说法，但也充分反映了目前的法律地位。这就是Steel大法官在Investec Bank (UK) Ltd v Zulman (2009) EWHC 1590 (Comm)先例中说：

"i) It is a form of relief for the purpose of correcting a written agreement because it does not reflect the terms of the true agreement at the time it was made.

ii) The true agreement need not have been a concluded and enforceable contract but there must have been a continuing common intention in regard to relevant provision reflected in an outward expression of accord down to the execution of the written contract.

iii) The failure to record the agreement must be as a consequence of a mistake: either

i. a mistake common to both parties whereby the written agreement does not record the terms as both intended; or

ii. a unilateral mistake in the sense that one party is mistaken as to the failure to incorporate the agreement in the documents and the other party aware of the mistake fails to draw attention to it.

iv) It must be established that the agreement, if corrected as claimed, would accurately represent the true agreement of the parties at the time of execution.

v) In that regard convincing proof is required to counteract the cogent evidence of the parties' intention as displayed by the contact itself: see The Nai Genova [1984] 1 Lloyd's Rep 353; Burroughs v. Abbott [1922] 1 Ch 86;. Joscelyne v. Nissen [1970] 2 QB 86; Thomas Bates v. Wyndham's Ltd [1981] 1 WLR 505."

以下进一步介绍上述权威说法的要点。

13.1.2 合约变更的救济适用的错误

在 David Hodge QC 所著的《Rectification》(2010 年)一书,针对这一方面是说:"Equity has the power to reform, or rectify, a written instrument which, by mistake, does not accord with the true agreement between the parties, so as to make it conform with that agreement; but it is a mistake in the way in which the agreement is expressed in writing that is rectified, and not a mistake in the agreement itself. Rectification is not an appropriate remedy where the mistake relates to the circumstances of the transaction itself, or its legal consequences, rather than the language, terms, meaning or effect of the document which purports to record it. Since the purpose of rectification is to enable the parties to correct mistakes in the way their transaction had been recorded in writing, it is no part of its function to enable them to change the substance of the transaction they have entered into, or to save one of the parties from the consequences of a mistake or from an improvident bargain. An erroneous assumption is not sufficient to justify rectification. The remedy of rectification does not extend to a case where the parties had no intention at all as regards some particular subject - matter, even though it can be clearly shown that they would have had some particular intention if the situation of that subject matter had been present to their minds. The doctrine of rectification cannot be invoked to re - write the course of history. Nor is rectification available where the parties specifically intend that the document should have the effect which it does have, even though they also mistakenly think that some other document has the same effect."

13.1.2.1 商业决定错误没有救济可言

这方面主要是已经多次提到文件或合约的变更只是针对错误记录双方已经达成的协议或共同/分享订约意图。但除了这种错误,还会有其他错误,这与合约变更的救济没有关系。例如,在2008年金融"海啸"之前,中国有很多钢厂与国外公司订立长达10至20年的买卖合约(煤炭或矿砂),或海上运输合约。但在2008年之后,市场(特别是航运市场)暴跌,中国公司作为买方或承租人根本无法履行,导致最终违约/毁约。

13.1.2.2 合约其他错误类别与不同救济

除了刚提到的一种极端错误,也会有其他法律作出救济的错误。这种错误涉及双方达成的协议或签订的合约本身有"严重与极端"(serious and radical)的错误(不论在事实或法律[8]方面),但这与合约记录错误无关,所以不涉及合约变更的衡平法救济,而是在普通法下这种错误可以回避合约,令其变为"空与无效的"(null and void)。这种可以获得救济的合约本身的错误有三类:一是双方共同错误;二是单方面错误;三是所谓的"合约并非是我所协议"(this is not my deed,或拉丁文的 *non est factum*)。但这三类错误都非常局限,也应该如此。关于这三类错误会在本章稍后的13.3小段进一步介绍。

13.1.3 申请合约变更不需要双方已经达成协议,共同/分享订约意图业已足够

在1970年前,普遍的理解是要成功申请合约变更,必须双方在较早时已经达成协议,只是最后在一份正式文件,也就是一份签署合约中记录错误。显然这十分局限,但在 Joscelyne v. Nissen (1970) 2 QB 86 先例,这方面有了改变。不需要双方已经达成协议,只要有证据显示双方在谈判时就有了共同/分享的订约意图,而这一意图被错误记录在后来的文件或合约中,就已经可以作出变更的救济。这方面的历史演变在 Chartbrook Ltd v. Persimmon Homes Ltd. (2009) UKHL 38 先例中,Hoffmann 勋爵有介绍说:"Until the decision of the Court of Appeal in Joscelyne v. Nissen (1970) 2 QB 86 there was a view, based upon *dicta* in 19th and early 20th century cases, that rectification was available only if there had been a concluded antecedent contract with which the instrument did not conform. In Lovell & Christmas Ltd v. Wall (1911) 104 LT 85, 88 Sir Herbert Cozens – Hardy MR said that rectification 'may be regarded as a branch of the doctrine of specific performance'. It presupposed a prior contract and required proof that, by common mistake, the final completed agreement as executed failed to give proper effect to the prior contract. In Jocelyne's case the Court of Appeal declared itself puzzled by the reference to specific performance, ... Since the decision in Joscelyne's case extended the availability of rectification to cases in which there had been no enforceable piror agreement, specific performance is plainly an inadequate explanation of the doctrine."(大致上是说在1911年的先例,曾经将合约变更视为履约指令的一种,而履约指令显然是指双方已经有了合约,法院才会下令双方必须履行。这带来了一贯以来的理解,即合约变更必须证明较早时有一个双方达成的协议。但这一理解

[8] Breenan v Bolt Burdon (2004) EWCA (Civ) 1017 先例。

在 Joscelyne v. Nissen 先例已经被改变。)

13.1.4 共同同意(a common accord)

在 David Hodge QC 所著的《Rectification》(2010 年)一书之 3-48 段,针对这一方面是说:"In order to found a claim for rectification for common mistake, the parties to document must share a common intention: a coincidence of intention is not sufficient; it must be a shared intention. Where it is sought to rectify a contract, it has been a matter of some academic controversy whether the law of rectification is concerned only with the objective manifestation of the intentions of the parties by communications 'crossing the line' between them, or whether the subjective intentions of the parties are also relevant to the decision whether the document should be rectified. When the English authorities have spoken of a common continuing intention, they have tended to refer to the intention that the parties have manifested by what they have said and done, rather than to their subjective intention. In Chartbrook Ltd v Persimmon Homes Ltd (2009) UKHL 38 the House of Lords has endorsed this objective approach to the terms of the parties' prior consensus, holding that, where the rectification of a contract is in issue, the question is what an objective observer would have understood the parties' intentions to have been, rather than their subjective intentions."(英国法律不是针对主观的意图,而是客观看双方有共同同意。这表示合约变更需要证明合约一方曾经有过通讯往来显示有这一共同/分享订约意图。)

这对双方较早已经达成的协议而言,是没有这方面的问题。因为如果已经有了一个有效的合约(通过口头或双方书信往来),肯定是双方有了"一致想法"(meeting of minds)。但如果申请变更只是根据双方在谈判时对记录错误的地方有了订约意图,就必须进一步证明这订约意图是双方共同/分享,而双方碰巧有相同的订约意图并不足以成功申请变更。要证明是共同/分享,就表示双方对这一要变更之处曾经有所交流,并且对方也表达了同样的订约意图。另外,这一共同/分享的订约意图必须根据证据由合理的人士(往往指法院或仲裁庭)客观判断是否存在,这也表示申请合约变更的一方必须能够提供证据。如果通过证人证言说其主观的订约意图与另一方一致,或如果在谈判时提出来对方肯定会接受,这不会被接受,毕竟到了诉讼时,对方肯定不会同意。

13.1.5 显露的共同同意(outward expression of accord)

在 David Hodge QC 所著的《Rectification》(2010 年)一书之 3-77 段,针对这一方面是说:"The requirement of an outward expression of accord originally referred to the perceived need for the party seeking rectification of a contract to point to something with the objective status of a prior agreement, even though it did not amount to a binding and concluded antecedent contract. Later judicial statement tended to treat the need for an outward expression of accord more as part of the requirement for convincing proof of the necessary common continuing intention (and thus as essentially an evidential factor), rather than as a strict legal requirement before rectification could be ordered. The decision of the House of Lords in Chartbrook Ltd v Persimmon Homes Ltd (2009) UKHL 38 almost certainly signals a return to the original position; and it is likely that the requirement now reflects the need for the party seeking rectification of a contract to establish a mistake in expressing the parties' prior consensus, as objectively construed, rather than what the parties subjectively believed that consensus to have been. In other words, the requirements of 'a common continuing intention' and 'some outward expression of accord' are not two separate conditions, but rather 'different sides of the same coin'."

这方面与上一小段所讲的道理一致,合约变更如果依赖双方在谈判时曾经有过共同/分享的订约意图,申请的一方就必须证明并让法院或仲裁庭客观作出判断是存在。而如果订约意图没有显露给对方,就难以证明双方有共同同意与分享。这方面也不是一个独立的法律要求或先决条件,必须满足才能成功申请合约变更。它与双方必须有一个共同与持续的订约意图这一先决条件是一回事。换言之,它被视为一个证据的问题,没有证据显露双方共同同意,就无法证明曾经有过共同/分享的订约意图。

至于怎样显露双方共同同意并分享某一个订约意图,当然最好是一方文书告知对方其订约意图,而对方文书回应说"我也有同样的意图"。但这种明确的情况很少,即使有,也不会涉及要花费律师费向仲裁庭或法院申请合约变更。这种显露可节录澳大利亚的 Ryledar Pty Ltd v Euphoric Pty Ltd (2007) NSWCA 65 先例说:"Caution is needed in evaluating the case law relating to whether or not an outward expression of accord is needed. That is because it is not clear how much (or how little) is involved in an assertion, or denial, of the need for an 'outward expression of accord'. It is not clear just what the phrase means. One possibility is that the parties have said 'we agree', or something similar, or performed an act like shaking hands or opening a bottle of champagne that is commonly recognised as an indication of a consensus having been reached. Another possibility is that each of the parties has in some fashion stated (though not to each other) his or her belief that an accord has been reached. Another is that the expression should be taken as performing the work that, in its context in Joscelyne v Nissen, it was designed to perform, namely of indicating that identical subjective intentions, of parties involved in a contractual negotiation, to use a word with a meaning different to its actual meaning is not enough to give rise to rectification unless those subjective intentions of the negotiators have not only become known to each other, but as well they have in some way stated that they propose to use the word with a meaning different to its actual meaning. There is no point in multiplying examples."

另在英国的 The "Aktor" (2008) 2 Lloyd's Rep 246 先例,Christopher Clarke 大

法官也有这方面的针对说:"Where one party has admitted that he had the same belief as the other, itself something of a rarity in a contested case, the likelihood is that the parties will have communicated that belief to each other in some way. Where such an admission is made it may be justifiable to infer that they did or to take the admission as accepting that. Further the requirement for an outward expression of accord may not require an express statement of the parties' agreement if it can be implied or is obvious from what occurred."(如果一方承认与对方有同样的订约意图,这就很明确,但很少案件会有这种情况出现,如果有,也往往不必诉讼了。更大的可能是双方交流了有关的订约意图并可以作出推断他们同意或分享。对显露的共同意图要求并不需要明示的双方同意,可以根据情况默示或是情况非常明显。)

曾经有说法是共同同意不一定需要显露,会有情况是十分明显双方有共同的订约意图,这样法院就可以默示有一个共同同意。在 JIS (1974) Ltd v MCP Investment Nominess I Ltd (2003) EWCA Civ 721 先例的一审中,Hart 大法官说:"... essentially directed to a question of evidence about the communication by one party to the other of his intention. A particular intention may be, as it seems to me, as a matter of the general nature of human discourse, be communicated by one party to another without express words necessarily being used. It may therefore sometimes be possible for the court to conclude that there was been sufficient outward evidence of the accord of the parties' intentions in relation to a particular term of their bargain without either party having actually spelled out to the other that term in so many words. It may be like an implied term in a contract, something which, in the context of the particular discourse, is so obvious that it need not be stated."

但这一先例去了上诉庭,被认为 Hart 大法官这一说法有"争论的余地"(room for argument)。但由于 Hart 大法官在第一审拒绝了合约变更的申请,所以也不存在上诉庭推翻与否。

也有其他先例说可以以其他的环境证据证明双方有一个显露的共同/分享与持续的订约意图。这在 Weeds v Blaney (1978) 2 E. G. L. R. 84 先例,Denning 勋爵说:"As to the two other cases which were cited this afternoon - Rose v Pim reported in (1953) 2 Q. B, 450 as qualified in Joselyne v Nissen (1970) 2 Q. B. 86. They show that there should be some outward evidence of the common intention of the parties. There is ample evidence here. The particulars of sale, the interview with the estate agent, the fence and the original plans, all offer ample evidence of the common intention of the parties. That is all that is needed."

而比较近期的有 Mace v Rutland House Textiles Ltd., Unreported November 22, 1999 (Chancery Div)先例,Peter Leaver QC 大法官说:"... the fact that there was no 'outward expression of accord' ... should not be fatal provided that there is convincing proof of the agreement or common intention."

总而言之,这一方面的要求只是证据方面,并非是申请文件或合约变更的先决条件。这表示从双方提供的证据(往往是口头证据)接受与否有一个显露的共同/分享与持续的订约意图还是要看法院或仲裁庭的判断,而这一方面无可避免是有偏差。至于这一点的权威说法,可以节录在 Munt v Beasley (2006) EWCA Civ 370 的上诉庭先例,Mummery 大法官说:"... the trend in recent cases to treat the expression 'outward expression of accord' more as an evidential factor rather than a strict legal requirement in all cases of rectification."

13.1.6　一个持续性的订约意图(a continuing intention)

这是一个重要的先决条件,正如 Hamblen 大法官在 Dunlop Haywards (DHL) Ltd v Barbon Insurance Group Ltd (2009) EWHC 2900 (Comm)先例所讲的:"... also important to bear in mind that rectification involves proof of mistake, in the present case common mistake. That requires proof that the difference between the prior and final agreement is due to a mistake made by both parties. This means that it is necessary to show that the parties in fact remained agreed on the (objectively determined) prior terms, or that their earlier (objectively determined) common intention was continuing at the date of the final contract, but by some mistake that prior agreement, or common intention, was not accurately expressed in the final contract."(必须能够证明双方在谈判中针对某一方面同意了或有共同/分享的订约意图必须持续不变直到签署合约的一刻。)

这是一个申请合约变更会遇上的困难,原因是双方在谈判时经常会改变或调整,如较早前双方已经就某个问题达成同意但谈判后期其中一方改变想法。举例而言,双方在订约前的几天已经明确同意了价格是 13000 人民币,但还在继续谈其余的条文。但在几天后双方签订的合约,记录的价格是 15000 人民币。期间没有任何证据他们的谈判再有涉及价格。这样如果是错误记录,也就是文书上有错误,显然应该把合约变更为 13000 人民币。但既然双方有争议,得利的一方就会说在后几天的谈判市场上涨,合约如果不反映这个上升的价格,也就是 15000 人民币,他就不会签署这份合约。谈判中途即使同意的地方被"重开"(reopen)也是常有的情况,涉及很多理由,如双方各自谈判的力量与谈判水平、市场的变化、环境的变迁(如有否新的竞争者加入)等。这样,法院或仲裁庭作出合约变更就必须肯定双方较早同意或有共同/分享订约意图持续直到签订合约(并被声称是记录错误)都没有任何改变。Cazalet 大法官在 Woolls v Powling, Unreported February 10, 1999 (CA)先例,说:"As to a continuing intention, any difference between the instrument and the terms previously agreed may be due not to mistake but to a decision by the parties to depart from those terms. A claim for rectification must therefore establish that the parties intended the instrument merely to carry out those terms and not to vary them."

这一方面证明不容易,特别是谈判双方都是有经验的合约方。例如,在国际贸易或国际航运,一般参与这些活动的人士都被认为有国际水平,就更加不容易被法院或仲裁庭接受是最后签署的合约有错误记录,而不是订约双方其中的一方改变想法。正如 Tuckey 大法官在 Snamprogetti Ltd v Phillips Petroleum Co UK Ltd (2001) EW-CA Civ 889 先例中说:"After months of negotiation experienced negotiators finally reduced their agreement into a detailed, lengthy document. The task of showing that this document did not represent the parties' intention was formidable."

当然,每一个案件的事实都不会一样,会有案件比较容易但也有更多的案件十分困难。例如,涉及漫长的谈判或谈判过程中有许多合约草稿不断作出修改并最后达致一份最终的正式文件。例如,在 Britoil plc v Hunt Overseas Oil Inc (1994) C. L. C. 561 先例,上诉庭的 Hobhouse 大法官就不肯接受看双方早期草拟的文件以认定双方的订约意图或达成的协议,说:"The process of negotiation and progressing towards a complete and formalized agreement is one which may contain many ambiguities. The purpose of the final document is to remove those ambiguities and to define authoritatively and clearly what the parties' respective rights and obligations are to be."

即使表面看来比较容易成功申请合约变更的案件,也不一定。在 The "Aktor" (2008) 2 Lloyd's Rep 246 先例,涉及二手船的买卖,双方在谈判中显示达成协议是以一份"要点重述"(Recap)确认双方已经同意的所有主要条文。但在后来拟定与签署的"正式合约"(Memorandum of Agreement)中,竟然记录不一样的内容。表面看来,申请合约变更应该相对容易。很多租约也会有同样的做法,通常双方交换并确认了一份电邮或传真的 Recap,就已经有了合约关系并开始履行。在很多短期的程租或期租合约,根本不会花时间与金钱另拟定一份正式合约。但在该先例,买方申请合约变更还是不成功,Christopher Clarke 大法官说:

"It is apparent from both judgments that, where parties have entered into a contract and that is followed by a further agreement, which is intended to reflect and not to vary the earlier agreement, a party will be entitled to rectify the later agreement if, on its true construction, it fails to carry the earlier agreement into effect. Moreover the court is markedly more likely to hold that there has been a mistake in such a case than it would be if a non-binding agreement is followed, after considerable negotiation, by a definitive binding one. Indeed such an entitlement will only be defeated if the parties have intended to vary their earlier agreement.

In the present case it was for the buyers to establish their entitlement to rectification and to do so convincingly. They were, however, at least halfway there in that it was common ground that the recap was a contract. ... The MOA does not bear the same meaning as the recap. Accordingly the buyers would be entitled to rectification if there was no intention on the part of the parties to vary the agreement. Since the onus of proof lies on the buyers I am prepared to accept that it was for them to establish that there was no intention to change. In practical terms that may be a light burden if, on the facts, no one suggested that there was any change involved.

But the arbitrators have held that, although there was a concluded agreement when the recap was sent out, that agreement was superseded by the final signed contract, ie the MOA, which was intended to record their final agreement: para 41 of the award. By that I take them to mean that the MOA was intended to be a complete replacement for the recap, to the exclusion of whatever had gone before, and so that the agreement between the parties was to be found within, and only within, the MOA. That is what they meant is apparent from their reference in para 31 of the award to their experience that, where a formal MOA is drawn up after termshave been agreed, the parties' intention is generally to record 'exclusively and comprehensively' the agreement between the parties, and in para 41 to the fact that that assumption was not rebutted in this case. As Rix LJ put it in HIH Casualty & General Insurance Ltd v New Hampshire Insurance Co [2001] Lloyd's Rep IR 596, page 619:

'Where. . . one contract has been intended to supersede an earlier contract, it must follow that the parties' contract must be found exclusively in the later contract. Thus the earlier contract cannot be used to add to, or modify the later contract.'

In the light of that finding of fact, rectification is not available to the buyers. The parties, on the arbitrators' findings, intended to agree what was in the MOA, even if it differed from what was in the recap."(加黑部分是笔者的强调)

13.1.7 合约变更后必须能够正确记录双方真正的共同/分享订约意图

针对这一方面,Simonds 大法官在 Crane v Hegeman – Harris Co Inc (1939) 1 All ER 662 先例说得十分清楚:"... the court can only act if satisfied beyond all reasonable doubt that the instrument does not represent(双方的)common intention and is further satisfied what their common intention was; for let this be clear that it is not sufficient to show that the written instrument does not represent their common intention unless positively also you can show what was their common intention."(也就是说,证明文件错误记录不足够,还必须说明怎样才是正确记录。)

在本章稍早的 13.1.1 小段,也已经提到 Mustill 大法官在 The "Olympic Pride" (1980) 2 Lloyd's Rep 67 先例中,条件之一是法院除了满足有关文件没有反映较早协议或订约意图,还必须明确到底协议或意图是什么,才能作出变更。

在 David Hodge QC 所著的《Rectification》(2010 年)一书之 3 – 132 段,针对这一方面是说:"The court must be satisfied that, if rectified as claimed, the document would accurately represent the true intention of the parties at the time it was executed. There is a necessary correlation between this requirement and the requirement that the document should fail to reflect the parties' true intention, because rectification exists to correct this state of affairs. It is a logical corollary to the requirement that there must be proof of the parties' true common intention so shown."

13.1.8 申请方的疏忽导致合约记录错误能否要求变更?

虽然文件或合约变更是衡平法救济,但救济不受申请方或其代表律师的疏忽导致错误记录的影响。这是因为合约变更的主要目的是不让另一方以这一错误记录不当得利,而不是追究谁疏忽。

在 Weeds v Blaney (1978) 2 E.G.L.R. 84 先例,Denning 勋爵说:"... there is a negligent mistake by the plaintiff or his solicitors, but that is no bar to rectification. It is indeed the very reason why rectification is granted. It is to correct that mistake and rectify the instrument so as to ensure that it expresses the common intention of the parties. So I find myself in agreement with the passage in Snell's Equity, 27th ed at page 613, on rectification: 'It is no defence that the plaintiff was careless, or that the plaintiff, being a solicitor, drafted the instrument himself.' So in this case, although the vendor's solicitor was negligent, that is no bar to the vendor getting the contract and transfer rectified. It was either a common mistake (as the judge found): or it was a mistake which the purchaser or his solicitors noticed (as they said) and said nothing. Their only right course would have been to have pointed out to the vendor's solicitors that they had made mistake. In any case these should be rectified."

更近期的澳大利亚 Pyledar Pty Ltd v Euphoric Pty Ltd (2007) NSWCA 65 先例,Campbell 大法官说:"It is because the avoidance of unconscientious taking advantage of the common mistake is the rationale of the remedy that it does not matter that the mistaken drafting of the agreement was carried out by the plaintiff, or that the plaintiff is a legal practitioner: Ball v Stories (1823) 1 Sim & St 210 at 219; 57 ER 84 at 88."

13.1.9 完整合约条文可否排除合约变更?

有关这一个课题在本书第十三章第 2 段有详论,并说明完整合约条文(entire agreement clauses)的本意就是为了排除合约内明示条文/文字以外的争议,如"附带保证/协议"(collateral warranty/contract)、"默示条文"(implied terms)、"误述"(misrepresentation)、"引导"(inducement)、"商业习惯做法/惯例"(custom/usage)、"侵权的共同责任"(concurrent liability in tort)等。这些争议都需要看外来证据/口头证据,所以有说法是完整合约条文也排除这些证据。在本段所针对的合约变更,真正是难逃必须看双方在签约前的谈判,看申请人能否明确证明双方已经达成协议或有共同/分享与持续的订约意图。换言之,涉及合约变更,必须看口头证据。这样,带来的疑问就是如果在双方签署的合约有一条完整合约条文,会否导致口头证据被排除,双方都失去了必须要依赖口头证据的合约变更的救济?

看来与其他的救济如误述不一样,合约变更的申请不影响仲裁庭或法院看双方谈判的口头证据，即使有关合约有一条完整的合约条文。这在 JJ Huber（Investment）Ltd v. The Private DIY Co. Ltd.（1995）NPC 102 先例有针对。案情涉及一个房屋租约被指是错误记录了"差饷"（rates）由房东支付，但在双方较早的协议是差饷由租客负责。该租约也有一条完整合约条文。Roger Cooke 大法官判是完整合约条文的作用是说明合约有哪些有效条文并在哪里（就是双方签署合约的四个角内）找得到。所以，这种条文并不能用来抗拒一个合约变更的申请。合约变更并非针对哪里找到双方同意的有效条文，而是针对双方签署的合约应该有什么准确的内容（that the purpose of an EAC was to define where the contractual terms were to be found. Such as clause was not a defence against a claim for rectification, which was not about finding contractual terms outside the four corners of the document, but rather about establishing what the document should contain...）。

在上诉庭的 Phillips Petroleum Co UK Ltd v. Snamprogetti Ltd（2001）EWCA Civ 889 先例，也有同样的判法，但 Tuckey 大法官补充说："... where there is an entire agreement clause this may tend to show that in fact no inconsistent governing intention has subsisted and that hence no basis for rectification has arisen because the parties have intended to be bound by the document in the material respects regardless of prior or other intentions."（合约如果有一条完整合约条文，这会强化双方不存在其他共同/分享的订约意图。）

在澳大利亚也有先例判完整合约条文不能用来抗拒合约变更的申请。在 Macdonald v. Shinki Australia Pty Ltd（1998）QCA 53 先例，McPherson J. A. 大法官判合约变更是合约外的救济，与口头证据规则无关，说："... well be impossible for the parties by means of any contractual provision, however artfully drawn, to escape the court's jurisdiction to order rectification in a matter calling for its exercise."

在同一先例，Davies J. A. 大法官也说："... Equitable relief for mistake ... is based on unconscionability; that it would be unconscientious of the party relying on the written instrument, to rely on it in the circumstances ... And it would generally be unconscientious of the party relying on the written instrument of contract to rely on it if it had been executed by the parties under the mistaken belief that it recorded the oral contract which they had made or their continuing common intention. Once that is seen to be the purpose of such equitable relief it can be seen also that it does not deny that, at law, the writing represents the entire agreement between the parties; but it prevents a party to that instrument from exercising any legal right arising thereunder because to do so would be unconscionable."

13.1.10　合约错误记录单方的订约意图能否要求变更？

较早所针对的是更常见与较早有这一衡平法救济的双方共同/分享的订约意图，但由于双方"共同错误"（common mistake）导致一份签署的文件或合约记录错误。

后来开始有了另一种可以有这一文件或合约变更的衡平法救济的情况,就是单方面错误。但显然单方面错误必须谨慎处理,因为一方(甲方)不知道对方(乙方)在签署合约时错误记录了其订约意图,但法院或仲裁庭还是作出合约变更,将合约改为乙方的订约意图,就会对甲方造成很大的不公道。如果订约时合约正确记录了乙方的订约意图,甲方可能不愿意签署。所以,单方面错误作出合约变更被指是一种"极端行为"(drastic action)。Blackburne 大法官在 George Wimpey UK Ltd v VI Construction Ltd (2005) EWCA Civ 77 先例中说:"It is drastic because recification for unilateral mistake has the result of imposing on the defendant a contract which he did not, and did not intend to, make and relieving the claimant from a contract which he did, albeit did not intend, to make."

所以,如果单方面的错误是由于自己不小心,是不会获得合约变更的救济。在早期的先例,作出变更的救济只是局限在"欺诈"(fraud)、"不恰当影响"(undue inference)或"信托责任"(fiduciary duty)。如在 Lovesy v Smith (1880) 15 Ch. D. 655 先例,涉及一位律师背景的男子不向他的未婚妻解释所草拟的婚前协议,特别是对男方的好处,也没有给她寻求独立法律意见的机会,在结婚当天的早晨要求她签署。法院以单方面错误去出文件或合约变更的救济。法院这样说:"... the doctrine that where there is a fiduciary relation between the parties the deed cannot stand, and is therefore liable to rectification, at the option of the party claiming, by merely omitting the provision complained of, unless the person against whom a trust is established has performed his duty in explaining in the clearest manner the effect of the transaction to the person standing in the position of the *cestui que trust*... The case is not put on the ground of fraud, but upon the ground of a departure from the clear duty of a person who has taken upon himself the position of adviser and conveyancer as (律师背景的丈夫) had done."

但上述的局限看来与商业合约关系不大,这在后来有进一步的放宽。首先,是在 A. Roberts & Co. Ltd. v Leicestershire County Council (1961) Ch. 555 先例,Pennycuick 大法官作出了合约变更并说可以在下列情况作出救济:"... a party is entitled to rectification of a contract upon proof that he believed a particular term to be included in the contract, and that the other party concluded the contract with the omission or a variation of that term in the knowledge that the first party believed the term to be included."

接下去在 Riverlate Properties Ltd v Paul (1975) Ch. 133 先例,上诉庭认同这一说法但加了一句说是另一方(抗拒合约变更的一方)"有一定程度的取巧"(Basically it appears to us that it must be such as to involve the lessee in a degree of sharp practice)。

再接下去在 Bates v Wyndhan (1981) 1 WLR 505 先例,上诉庭看来是认为另一方有否取巧也不重要,主要还是看是否除非作出合约变更的救济,否则另一方的行为会造成不公平。Buckley 大法官这样说:"Undoubtedly I think in any such case the conduct of the defendant must be such as to make it inequitable that he should be allowed to object to the rectification of the document. If this necessarily implies some measure of 'sharp practice', so be it; but for my part I think that the doctrine is one which depends more upon the equity of the position. The graver the character of the conduct involved, no doubt the heavier the burden of proof may be; but, in my view, the conduct must be such as to affect the conscience of the party who has suppressed the fact that he has recognized the presence of a mistake."

在 Bates v Wyndhan 先例,也明确了单方面错误的文件或合约变更是必须证明:(1)合约在签署时,由于申请合约变更方的错误而不准确记录了其订约意图(by mistake, the document did not represent his true intention at the time it was executed);(2)对方知道申请方的错误(the other party was aware of that mistake);(3)对方不告知申请方的错误(the non - mistaken party omitted to draw the mistake to the other party's notice);(4)这一错误导致对方得利或导致申请方蒙受损害(the mistake was one calculated either to benefit the non - mistaken party or [probably] to operate to the detriment of the mistaken party)。

在稍后的 Kemp v. Neptune Concrete Ltd (1989) 57 P. & C. R. 369 先例,也有成功申请合约变更必须证明四个先决条件的说法:"(1) a mistake whereby the claimant's subjective intention is not achieved by the document as executed (but in assessing such subjective intention, no *ex post facto* intention can be admitted); (2) that the other party was not mistaken; (3) that the other party was aware of the claimant's mistake at the time he executed the document; and (4) that it was unconscionable for the other party to stand by and let the claimant make the mistake."

13.1.11 对文件/合约变更的抗辩

由于合约变更是衡平法的救济,所以对这种申请的抗辩除了反驳申请方所提供的证据外,会以衡平法的理由为主。一是"怠慢"(laches)与"默许"(acquiescence);二是即使作出合约的变更,也不会有实际的作用。

针对第一个理由,可节录 David Hodge QC 所著的《Rectification》(2010 年)一书之5 - 06 段,如下:"It is doubtful whether mere delay, unaccompanied by any prejudice to the respondent, can ever disentitle an applicant to relief by way of rectification. However, the equitable doctrines of laches and acquiescence may operate to prevent a party from obtaining an order for rectification. 'Laches' is delay coupled with some form of relevant prejudice to the respondent; and time runs from the discovery of the mistake, rather than the execution of the document which it is sought to rectify. 'Acquiescence' arises where a party fails to insist upon his rights in circumstances which reasonably give rise to the assumption that he will never seek to do so. The touchstone of these equitable defences is unconscionability: whether, in all the circumstances, it would be unconscientious for the applicant to maintain his claim for rectification."

针对怠慢的说法,这是寻求所有的衡平法救济都需要尽快作出申请,否则就不会成功。例如,申请"履约指令"(specific performance)或"禁令"(injunction),一旦怠慢就会被法院拒绝申请,毕竟怠慢可能会带来对被告的不公平与损害。针对文件或合约的变更也不例外。但许多情况是合约错误记录了双方较早的协议或共同/分享的订约意图,往往是出了争议才会发觉。在这个时候,有关争议的原告或是被告才会申请合约变更,而这个时候往往与签署合约时会相隔很久。所以,针对这方面怠慢的说法,主要是看申请方在发觉文件或合约记录错误的时间与向法院或仲裁庭作出申请的时间是否有怠慢。如果有,法院就会拒绝作出变更:Turner v. Collins (1871) LR 7 Ch. App. 329 等先例。

针对第二个理由,可节录 David Hodge QC 所著的《Rectification》(2010 年)一书之 5 - 19 段,如下:"Rectification will be withheld **if it would serve no useful purpose or confer no practical benefit.** But even if the parties to a contract are no longer bound to render further performance of their primary obligations thereunder, the court will not withhold rectification (if it is otherwise appropriate) where issues still remain to be addressed between the contracting parties which would be affected by the order for rectification."(加黑部分是笔者的强调)

这一衡平法的抗辩是因为衡平法院一直以来是不会作出无谓与没有帮助的命令,这在 Udall v. Capri Lighting Ltd. (1988) QB 907 先例, Balcome 大法官说:"It is old and trite law that the 'court will not make any order in vain'."

这种情况主要适用在合约无法履行(如因为违约/毁约而终止)或合约的履行已经完成,这样往往对有关合约申请变更就没有意义或实际作用。但现在已经接受即使在这种情况下,如果对已经不存在履行的合约作出变更还是有一定用途,不影响申请或作出这方面的救济。这种用途可以是索赔损失,而合约虽然已经终止,但索赔的 6 年时效还没有届临。在 Trawl Industries of Australia Pty Ltd v. Effem Foods Pty Ltd. (1992) 27 NSWLR 326 的澳大利亚先例,Samuels 大法官说:

"... in the present case each of the parties accused the other of repudiation, which each asserted it had accepted....

... that the question of which of the parties repudiated its obligations under the contract cannot be determined until it is established whether or not the document they executed accurately contains the agreement they made; so that until the correct form of the agreement is established, the question of repudiation cannot be decided. If that is right, then it follows that it cannot be said that reformation of the contract is 'useless'. At all events, the position is such that I think that I am justified in assuming that the remedy of rectification remains open, and therefore in turning to the evidence to see whether it establishes some antecedentcommon intention absent from the writing."

看来会否作出这种救济主要看申请文件或合约变更的原因以及对方作出抗拒的理由,才能知道是否有用。在 Wright v. Robert Leonand Development Ltd. (1994) EGCS 69 先例,合约虽然不再存在,但还是被法院下令变更让买方可以向卖方索赔损失。另在 Toronto Dominion Bank v. Oberoi (2003) EWHC 3216 (Ch)先例,涉及合约如果不变更,就会带来一个可能会发生的争议,即合约支付的钱会以“复原”(restitution)的理由被要求归还。

13.1.12 合约变更的案例

以两个实际的案例来阐释。

第一个是英国上诉庭的 The “Nai Genova” (1984) 1 Lloyd's Rep 353 先例,涉及两艘意大利新造超级油轮的长达 10 年的“运输合约”(contract of affreightment)。在很多长期的合约,都会有一条“通货膨胀条文”(Escalation Clause),立下公式按照通货膨胀来调整将来的运费或租金。在 20 世纪 70 年代末 80 年代初,通货膨胀严重,至于怎样的公式可以准确反应实际的通货膨胀并不容易。在订约时,黄金的市场价格还在 1945 年“布雷顿森林体系”(Bretton Woods Regime)制定的 35 美元/盎司左右波动。但在该长期期租合约履行的后期,由于 1971 年 8 月美国单方面宣布美元与黄金脱钩,黄金的市场价格以数十倍的速度猛涨。这意味着该长期租约的租金需要调整至一个不可思议的金额,最后令一家著名的日本承租人要向香港船东哀求,说如果强制执行,它只能倒闭。最后这个案件是以和解而告终。至于 The “Nai Genova”先例的运输合约中的通货膨胀条文,是以 1980 年 1 月 1 日的船员与维修保养费用作为基数,而之后如果上涨,也就在每年要支付的运费中作出同样百分比的调整。在签署的合约中,这基数的费用是写下美元的数字,但后来承租人向仲裁庭申请合约变更,指双方在谈判中达成的订约意图是以意大利里拉为准,所以需要把合约中的美元改为里拉。这里所造成巨大差别显然是因为两种货币之间的汇率有了很大波动,意大利从 70 年代开始就出现了很严重的通货膨胀问题,意大利里拉对美元出现大幅贬值。

承租人申请合约的理据是有关的运输合约错误记录了其在签约前的谈判会议中的共同/分享的持续订约意图,“或是”(alternatively)至少有一个单方面错误(The escalation clause failed properly to reflect the continuing common intention of the parties, or alternatively, if the defendants [船东] did intend the agreement to be in such terms, they knew or must be taken to have been cognizant of the fact that the charterers' representatives engaged in concluding the agreement were mistaken as to the contents of this clause)。

针对有关谈判会议,参与的双方证人都作出证人证言与接受盘问,反正最后对事实的认定被一审法院总结为:“... It was Mr. Croce's (承租人的公司董事) contention that this figure was not merely discussed but agreed between the parties present. Mr. Rosina (船东的董事总经理) on the other hand would have it that there was no mention of the figure. Mr. Bocconcelli (承租人的海上运输主管) stood between the two, contending that the figure was mentioned but not discussed."

换言之,这就是一个双方的证人给了完全相矛盾的证言的典型情况,否则也不会涉及昂贵的诉讼了。谁真谁假难辨,而作为被告的船东证人,只要懂一点法律,也会坚持他没有这一共同/分享订约意图,更加不知道承租人有这一订约意图。法院或仲裁庭根据证据作出平衡的可能性的认定后,在法律而言就作为事实。在该先例,被认定的事实是中间的说法,即意大利里拉的基准有在会议中提出,但没有进一步的探讨。这认定的事实如下:"On 29th November 1974 the base figure in the escalation clause of 700,000,000 lire for repairs and maintenance was only mentioned without being discussed. It was not expected to constitute an impediment to a concluded agreement. Nor, on the other hand, was it so firmly established as a term of the clause that either party was justified in assuming, without confirming, that the escalation clause in any subsequent draft of the charter-party would be in a form which was not open to argument, or that the base figure included in it would necessarily remain the same."

特别要指出的是,法院也认定被告的船东不知道承租人在签署运输合约时有单方面的订约意图(以里拉为准)并被错误记录。结果承租人的申请失败,因为没有共同/分享的订约意图,也没有单方面错误。

第二个案例可介绍笔者曾经处理过的一个案件,案情在本书第二章之 8.4.1 段有详述,所以这里只简单介绍。只强调在伦敦仲裁的结果是中国承租人胜诉,但胜诉理由是该希腊船东把船舶从委内瑞拉开航去美湾,然后才发难向承租人要钱构成了"弃权"(waiver)或"禁止反供"(estoppel)。而如果该希腊船东在委内瑞拉卸港承租人命令船舶开往美湾时就发难,指出租约不允许去美国,承租人就会败诉。在此只说承租人的"主要依据"(primary case)是租约没有正确记录双方在谈判中共同/分享的理解与意图,即承租人将会从美湾装粮回中国后还船的计划。但这一主要依据,也就是要求变更合约并不成功。因为在该租约的谈判中,虽然证据显示了承租人明确告诉了船东其意图是准备去美湾装粮回中国,船东也没有异议,但这并不代表双方已经明确同意了或有共同/共享意图要去美湾装粮。毕竟承租人的意图也完全可以改变,因为在期租合约下,承租人可以去全球营运,除了租约明示规定的除外航区或像该租约中的油污条文中规定不去美国。既然双方没有同意或承租人只是显示了其意图去美湾装粮,也就谈不上租约错误记录了双方真正的约定或共同/分享与持续的订约意图,合约的变更也就不会成功。

从上述简单的案例可以看出,要成功变更合约并不容易。

13.2 通过解释合约纠正明显错误

13.2.1 合约变更与通过解释合约作出纠正的区别

这可节录 North Circular Properties Ltd. v. Internal Systems Organisation Ltd. Ch. D., unreported, October 26,1984 先例所说如下:"Of course the court will not lightly, as part of the construction process, tamper with the actual words used, particularly in a commercial document such as a lease. On the other hand the law is not such an ass as to compel the court to hold the parties to the actual words used when it is, as in my judgment it is in this case, **clear from the documents itself, without looking at extrinsic evidence, that such words were used only by virtue of a draftsman's blunder.** Such a process of correction of obvious drafting errors in the process of construction is of course distinct from the equitable doctrine of rectification. The former can only be adopted where the fact that a mistake has been made and the nature of the mistake can be ascertained with certainty from a consideration of the relevant instrument in the context of objective circumstances surrounding its execution. **Rectification, on the other hand will be appropriate in many other cases where the existence and nature of a mistake are apparent only from extrinsic evidence of the actual intention of the parties.**"(加黑部分是笔者的强调)

法院可对文件或合约中的"明显错误"(obvious mistake)作出纠正,而不必看任何外来证据/口头证据的说法很早已有,正如 St. Leonards 勋爵在 Wilson v. Wilson (1854) 5 H. L. Cas. 40 先例中所讲:"Now it is a great mistake if it be supposed that even a Court of Law cannot correct a mistake, or error on the face of an instrument; there is no magic in words. If you find a clear mistake and it admits of no other construction, a Court of Law, as well as a Court of Equity, without impugning any doctrine about correcting those things which can only be shown by parol evidence to be mistakes - without, I say, going into those cases at all, both Courts of Law and of Equity may correct an obvious mistake on the face of an instrument without the slightest difficulty."

在较近期的 East v. Pantiles (Plant Hire) Ltd (1982) 2 E. G. L. R. 111 先例, Brightman 大法官说到这种做法有两个先决条件,如果不能满足就只得通过合约变更的做法纠正合约记录错误了,说:"Two conditions must be satisfied: first there must be a clear mistake on the face of the instrument; secondly it must be clear what correction ought to be made in order to cure the mistake. If those conditions are satisfied, then the correction is made as a matter of construction. If they are not satisfied then either the claimant must pursue an action for rectification or he must leave it to a court of construction to reach what answer if can on the basis that the uncorrected wording represents the manner in which the parties decide to express their intention"

在更近期的权威说法是在 The "Starsin" (2003) 1 Lloyd's Rep. 571 先例,Bingham 勋爵说:"I take it to be clear in principle that the court should not interpolate words into a written instrument, of whatever nature, unless it is clear both that words have been omitted and what those omitted words were."

在同一案例,Millett 勋爵也说:"The clause does not make grammatical sense as it stands, and it is obvious that words have been omitted. The court must, therefore, supply the omission by implying at least the minimum necessary for the clause to make grammatical sense. This is what all the judges below did. But the authorities show that in a proper case the court will go further. Where it can see, not only that words have been omitted, but what those words are, then it is its duty to supply them. It is not necessary that the court should be certain precisely what words have been omitted; it is sufficient that it knows their gist. **The process is one of construction, not rectification**; this is evident from the fact that the Court of Chancery not infrequently supplied omissions in wills at a time when it had no jurisdiction to rectify them. "(加黑部分是笔者的强调)

13.2.2 案例之一

先介绍一个有关终止房屋租赁合约的1年通知的先例名为 Carradine Properties Ltd v. Aslam (1976) 1 W. L. R. 442。房东给房客的通知时为1974年9月,内中说明意图终止租约的日期是1973年9月。这是明显的错误,1973年应该是1975年。要注意在这种单方面作出的通知,不像合约还存在机会可以"变更"(rectification)。所以通过解释这一份文件对这一明显错误作出纠正是唯一的救济办法。Goulding大法官是这样说:"I think that a benevolent approach could be applied in this case as in (*Doe d. Duke of Bedford v. Knightley* [1796] 7 Durn & E. 63), because reasonably read by a reasonable tenant the mistake is obvious on the face of it, and there is no doubt what the mistake was. Therefore one interprets the notice as asserting an intention to determine in 1975. It is true that if whoever made the mistake had typed 1976 instead of 1973, the error would probably have been incurable because although the tenant might suspect there was a slip, it might be that the landlord did intend 1976, not knowing or understanding his right under the lease. In such a case the tenant would be entitled to disregard the notice but because a past date was given in the notice it is insensible and therefore an authority such as the *Duke of Bedford's* case is in point."

从上述可见,1975年写为1973年,明显是文件中有错误,但Goulding大法官说到,如果是1975年写错为1976年,这个错误就可能是致命的,因为法律对这种通知十分严格:Hankey v. Clavering (1942) 2 K. B. 326等先例。

13.2.3 案例之二

这是已经介绍过的The "Tropwind" (1982) 1 Lloyd's Rep. 232 CA先例,该租约的第56条文的第一句是:"Should the vessel be on her voyage to the port of redelivery at the time when payment hire is due, said payment shall be made for such length of time as Owners or their Agents and Charterers or their Agents may agree upon as the established time necessary to complete the voyage. ..."对租船了解的人士知道这一句是要求船东与承租人同意还要多长时间完成最后航次以满足支付足够的最后一笔租金。所以,很明显看到"established"一字应该是"estimated"的笔误。所以Denning勋爵简单作出纠

正说:“‘Established’ must be a mistake for ‘estimated’. That is obvious.”

13.2.4 案例之三

Fitzgerald v. Masters (1956)95 C. L. R. 420 先例涉及一个有关土地买卖的合约,其第 8 条文说“The usual conditions of sale ... shall so far as they are inconsistent herewith be deemed to be embodied herein.”

这应该也是明显的笔误,合并其他文件,当然是合并没有矛盾的内容,怎会是有矛盾的才合并。另外,订约双方好不容易谈判并同意了不少合约条文,怎会合并其他文件中有矛盾的内容,想把已经同意的条文推翻或挑起矛盾?所以“inconsistent”一字应该被纠正为“consistent”。澳大利亚的上诉庭是这样说:“There is a superficial difficulty in Clause 8 because it purports to incorporate a set of conditions so far as they are inconsistent with what has been specifically agreed upon. No real difficulty, however, is created. Words may generally be supplied, omitted or corrected, in an instrument, where it is clearly necessary in order to avoid absurdity or inconsistency. Here it would be indeed absurd to suppose that the parties having expressed their agreement on a number of special and essential matters, should intent to incorporate by reference a set of general conditions except that so far as they were inconsistent with what they had specifically agreed upon, and clause 8 must be read as it is said ‘consistent’ or ‘not inconsistent’.”

13.3 其他合约错误

在本章稍早的 13.1.2 段已经提到,除了商业决定错误(这是毫无救济可言)与本段针对的合约记录错误外,法律还会对三类错误作出救济。由于本书不是针对英国合约法,所以涉及合约本身的错误并且法律可能会作出救济,笔者不详论。只是先节录《Chitty on Contracts》(第 31 版,2012 年)一书之 5-001 段针对这 3 类错误的说法:

“Types of mistake. The doctrine of mistake in the law of contract deals with two rather different situations. In the first, the parties are agreed on the terms of the contract but have entered it under a shared and fundamental misapprehension as to the facts or the law. Cases in this category are now usually referred to as ‘common’ mistake, for normally the mistake is legally relevant only if both parties have contracted under the same misapprehension. In the second, there is some mistake or misunderstanding in the communications between the parties which prevents there being an effective agreement (for instance, if the parties misunderstand each other) or at least means that there is no agreement on the terms apparently stated (for instance, if one party in an offer states terms which the other party knows the first party does not intend, but nonetheless the other purports to accept). This second category is mistake, which can generally be referred to as ‘mistake in communication’, includes ‘mutual misunderstanding’, where each is mistaken as to the terms intended by the other, and ‘unilateral mistake’, where only one of the parties is mistaken, over the terms of the contract or the identity of the other party.

Non est factum. There is, however, a third type of mistake which might be seen as a viarant of unilateral mistake, but which for convenience will be placed in a separate category. It is peculiar to the law of written contracts, and it allows a party who has executed a document under a fundamental misapprehension as to its nature to plead that it is 'not his deed'. This is the defence of *non est facum.*"

13.3.1 错误(共同或单方面)的成因

造成这种错误的原因会是其中一方搞错,如对合约的标的,冒险不作出调查就订立合约。[9] 也可能作出了一些调查,但可能是调查不足、调查错误、错读调查报告等不同原因令他有了错误理解。这些成因有可能涉及他的疏忽或过错,也可能是完全无辜。他也可能在做法上完全合理,也可能不合理。例如,他应该作出调查但为了省钱或其他原因不作出,或是即使作出调查也是乱来。这样,有了一个重大的事实或法律错误是不会获得救济,因为不合理的做法导致错误不会有救济。

错误的另一个成因可能是其中一方从第三人得来的消息有误。在这种情况下,由于与合约的另一方完全无关,通常属于错误一方自己的风险,也不能令合约无效。至于错误的一方向第三人提出诉讼(通常是根据侵权,如疏忽或甚至是欺诈)就不是本小段要针对的方面。如果错误的一方查询的第三人是一个完全合理的渠道,也应该有准确的消息,如向有关当局调查但竟然发放的消息有误而导致错误,这可让错误的一方指他的做法完全合理。

错误的最后一个主要原因是对方的"误述"(misrepresentation),这一误述导致错误的一方订立合约会是对方无辜、疏忽或虚假所造成。这样,错误的一方会是有两种不同的救济,一种就是对方的误述导致合约的产生,这可让错误的一方也就是无辜方有权使合约"可令无效"(voidable)。这会在某些情况下比另一种以合约的错误令合约"空与无效"(null and void)的救济优胜,因为使合约可令无效就给了无辜方一定的主动权与其他救济。

13.3.2 错误(共同或单方面)令合约空与无效案例不多的原因

涉及错误要令合约变为空与无效的案例并不多,原因可从两方面分析。一是较早已经提到的与误述的关系,如一个无辜的误述会导致一个共同错误订立合约(如卖方向买方作出一个不正确的陈述,说他的货物存放在某处,但实际上当时已经发生火灾把该批货物烧毁,而双方根据这一无辜的误述订立合约)。已经简单提到,无辜方会更喜欢以对方的误述使合约可令无效。

第二个方面导致错误的案例不多,可对照性质上相同的合约"受阻"(frustration)

---

[9] McRae v Commonwealth Disposals Commission (1951) 84 CLR 377 先例,澳大利亚高院说:"... a party cannot rely on mutual mistake where the mistake consists of a belief which is, on the one hand, entertained by him without any reasonable ground..."

的说法。[10] 本来,合约受阻的情况与案例也是因为其成立的条件苛刻而不会太多,但相比起来错误出现的情况会比受阻更少。这里的原因可节录 Phillips 勋爵在 The "Great Peace" (2002) 2 Lloyd's Rep. 653 先例所说的:"Circumstances where a contract is void as a result of common mistake are likely to be less common than instances of frustration. Supervening events which defeat the contractual adventure will frequently not be the responsibility of either party. Where, however, the parties agree that something shall be done which is impossible at the time of making the agreement, it is much more likely that, on true construction of the agreement, one or other will have undertaken responsibility for the mistaken state of affairs. This may well explain why cases where contracts have been found to be void in consequence of common mistake are few and far between."(共同错误比合约受阻发生的更少。突发事件导致合约目的受挫通常没有任何一方有责任。但在订约时,即使已经存在一些令合约不能履行的情况,双方在合约中已经有明示或默示条文把责任/风险分摊给其中一方。这也解释了为什么共同错误令合约无效的案件不多。)

13.3.3 合约明示或默示分摊责任/风险是排除了错误的救济

双方在合约中已经通过明示或默示把有关的责任/风险(也就是共同错误之处)作出分摊的情况也不少,而这导致共同错误很少会成立的说法,可节录 Steyn 大法官在 Associated Japanese Bank (International) Ltd v Credit du Nord S. A (1989) 1 WLR 255 先例中说:"Logically, before one can turn to the rules as to mistake, whether at common law or in equity, one must first determine whether the contract itself, by express or implied condition precedent or otherwise, provides who bears the risk of the relevant mistake. It is at this hurdle that many pleas of mistake will either fail or prove to have been unnecessary. Only if the contract is silent on the point, is there scope for invoking mistake."

合约有明示条文分摊有关责任的近期先例有 William Sindall Plc v Cambridgeshire CC (1994) 1 WLR 1016 与 Standard Chartered Bank v Banque Marocaine du Commerce Exterieur (2006) EWHC 413 (Comm)。在前一个先例,上诉庭的 Hoffmann 大法官说:"In this case the contract says in express terms that it is subject to all easements other than those of which the vendor knows or has the means of knowledge. This allocates the risk of such incumbrances to the buyer and leaves no room for rescission on the grounds of mistake."

至于合约有默示条文分摊有关责任,可举货物买卖的例子,如根据 1979 年英国《货物销售法》,卖方有拥有货物所有权的默示责任(section 12),所以如果买卖双方对有关货物的所有权有共同错误,这方面的救济不通过共同错误,因为通过默示条文

---

〔10〕 关于合约受阻的说法,可看本书第十章之 4.2.2.4 段。

这一错误的风险已经分摊在卖方。这种默示责任的分摊也在其他方面,如买卖将来货物就必须符合合约对货物的描述(section 13)以及满意质量(section 14)等。

雷同的情况也出现在合约一方对一些重要的事实或法律有怀疑,但还是订立合约,这可以说是默示接受并承担有关错误的风险。正如 Hope 勋爵在 Kleinwort Benson Ltd v Lincoln City Council (1999) 2 AC 349 先例中说:"A state of doubt is different from that of mistake. A person who pays when in doubt takes the risk that he may be wrong - and that is so whether the issue is one of fact or one of law."

但怎样证明合约一方对错误之处有怀疑或没有怀疑,而前者就默示接受并承担风险?这可节录 Deutsche Morgan Grenfell Goup Plc v Inland Revenue Commissioners (2007) 1 AC 558 先例,Hoffmann 勋爵说:"... the circumstances in which a payment is made may show that the person who made the payment took the risk that, if the question was fully litigated, it might turn out that he did not owe the money. Payment under a compromise is an obvious example: see Brennan v Bolt Burdon [2005] QB 303. I would not regard the fact that the person making the payment had doubts about his liability as conclusive of the question of whether he took the risk, particularly if the existence of these doubts was unknown to the receiving party. It would be strange if a party whose lawyer had raised a doubt on the question but who decided nevertheless that he had better pay should be in a worse position than a party who had no doubts because he had never taken any advice, particularly if the receiving party had no idea that there was any difference in the circumstances in which the two payments had been made. It would be more rational if the question of whether a party should be treated as having taken the risk depended upon the objective circumstances surrounding the payment as they could reasonably have been known to both parties, including of course the extent to which the law was known to be in doubt."(这是针对一个和解协议能否因错误而变为空与无效。Hoffmann 勋爵说在和解协议下作出支付的一方要承担风险,即如果有关的争议诉讼到底,他会是胜诉并不需要支付对方任何金钱。Hoffmann 勋爵不接受作出支付一方对他有否责任有一定的怀疑就可以下结论是他愿意承担风险,从而拒绝作出错误的救济,特别是在对方不知道支付方有怀疑的情况下。否则就会造成支付方问了律师并提出了一些怀疑但最后还是决定作出和解。所以,更合理的做法是根据一方当事人作出支付时双方都应合理知道的客观情况,包括支付方有怀疑的法律层次,看他有否愿意接受与承担风险。)

13.3.4 错误(共同或单方面)主要权威先例的说法

有关错误的先例介绍,主要可看三个权威的普通法先例:Bell v Lever Bros Ltd (1932) AC 161; Associated Japanese Bank (International) Ltd v Credit du Nord S. A (1989) 1 WLR 255 与 The "Great Peace" (2002) 2 Lloyd's Rep. 653。

首先是在 Bell v Lever Bros Ltd 先例,Atkin 勋爵说:

"... the agreement of A. and B. to purchase a specific article is void if in fact the article had perished before the date of sale. In this case, though the parties in fact were agreed about the subject - matter, yet a consent to transfer or take delivery of something not existent is deemed useless, the consent is nullified. As codified in the Sale of Goods Act the contract is expressed to be void if the seller was in ignorance of the destruction of the specific chattel. I apprehend that if the seller with knowledge that a chattel was destroyed purported to sell it to a purchaser, the latter might sue for damages for non - delivery though the former could not sue for non - acceptance, but I know of no case where a seller has so committed himself. This is a case where mutual mistake certainly and unilateral mistake by the seller of goods will prevent a contract from arising. Corresponding to mistake as to the existence of the subject - matter is mistake as to title in cases where, unknown to the parties, the buyer is already the owner of that which the seller purports to sell to him. The parties intended to effectuate a transfer of ownership: such a transfer is impossible: the stipulation is *naturali ratione inutilis*...

Mistake as to quality of the thing contracted for raises more difficult questions. In such a case a mistake will not affect assent unless it is the mistake of both parties, and is as to the existence of some quality which makes the thing without the quality essentially different from the thing as it was believed to be. Of course it may appear that the parties contracted that the article should possess the quality which one or other or both mistakenly believed it to possess. But in such a case there is a contract and the inquiry is a different one, being whether the contract as to quality amounts to a condition or a warranty, a different branch of the law."

在之后的 Associated Japanese Bank (International) Ltd 先例,Steyn 大法官基本上是根据 Atkin 勋爵的权威说法,并列出了错误成立的五个条件,说:"The first imperative must be that the law ought to uphold rather than destroy apparent contracts. Secondly, the common law rules as to a mistake regarding the quality of the subject matter, like the common law rules regarding commercial frustration, are designed to cope with the impact of unexpected and wholly exceptional circumstances on apparent contracts. Thirdly, such a mistake in order to attract legal consequences must substantially be shared by both parties, and must relate to facts as they existed at the time the contract was made. Fourthly, and this is the point established by Bell v. Lever Brothers Ltd. [1932] A. C. 161, the mistake must render the subject matter of the contract essentially and radically different from the subject matter which the parties believed to exist. While the civilian distinction between the substance and attributes of the subject matter of a contract has played a role in the development of our law (and was cited in speeches in Bell v. Lever Brothers Ltd.), the principle enunciated in Bell v. Lever Brothers Ltd. is markedly narrower in scope than the civilian doctrine. It is therefore no longer useful to invoke the civilian distinction. The principles enunciated by Lord Atkin and Lord Thankerton represent the ratio decidendi of Bell v. Lever Brothers Ltd. Fifthly, there is a requirement which was not specifically discussed in Bell v. Lever Brothers Ltd. What happens if the party, who is seeking to rely on the mistake, had no reasonable grounds for his belief? An extreme example is that of the man who makes a contract with minimal knowledge of the facts to which the mistake relates but is content that it is a good speculative risk. In my judgment a party cannot be allowed to rely on a common mistake where the mistake consists of a belief which is entertained by him without any reasonable grounds for such belief: cf. McRae v. Commonwealth Disposals Commission (1951) 84 C. L. R. 377, 408. That is not because principles such as estoppel or negligence require it, but simply because policy and good sense dictate that the positive rules regarding common mistake should be so qualified."

最后可节录 Phillips 勋爵在近期的 The "Great Peace"先例的说法:"... the following elements must be present if common mistake is to avoid a contract: (i) there must be a common assumption as to the existence of a state of affairs; (ii) there must be no warranty by either party that that state of affairs exists; (iii) the non-existence of the state of affairs must not be attributable to the fault of either party; (iv) the non-existence of the state of affairs must render performance of the contract impossible; (v) the state of affairs may be the existence, or a vital attribute, of the consideration to be provided or circumstances which must subsist if performance of the contractual adventure is to be possible."[以下条件必须满足:(1)双方订约时共同假设有一个情况存在;(2)这一情况的存在并没有任何一方作出保证;(3)这一情况其实并不存在,也并非是其中一方的过错所致(如一栋房屋在交易成交前发生的火灾并非是其中一方疏忽或恶意造成);(4)不存在的情况导致合约无法履行;(5)这一情况是约因/对价的重要部分,或必须存在令有关合约的履行可以执行。]

13.3.5 普通法与衡平法的救济

以上介绍的是三个重要的普通法先例,但在很长一段时间,共同错误的救济也可以在衡平法下作出。而衡平法的好处是可以根据个别案情(特别是有关的共同错误造成对其中一方十分不公平的结果)作出有弹性的判决以及对错误的程度没有这么严格。衡平法救济的说法是上诉庭的 Denning 大法官在 Solle v Butcher (1950) 1 KB 671 先例提出,说:"A contract is ... liable in equity to be set aside if the parties were under a common misapprehension either as to facts or as to their relative and respective rights, provided that the misapprehension was fundamental and that the party seeking to set it aside was not himself at fault."

以上的说法看来与普通法区别不大。笔者也不会进一步节录 Denning 大法官其他显示普通法与衡平法的不同说法,如一个错误可能在"基本性重要"(fundamental importance)是不足满足普通法的考验,但可以满足衡平法的考验而令合约变为"可令无效"(voidable)。在以后的一些重要先例也有提到 Denning 大法官所说的不同之处,如在 Associated Japanese Bank (International) Ltd v Credit du Nord S. A (1989) 1 WLR 255 先例,Steyn 大法官说:"That brings me to the relationship between common law mistake and mistake in equity. Where common law mistake has been pleaded, the court must first consider this plea. If the contract is held to be void, no question of mistake in equity arises. But, if the contract is held to be valid, a plea of mistake in equity may still have to be considered..."

但这一针对共同错误的衡平法救济已经在 The "Great Peace" (2002) 2 Lloyd's Rep. 653 先例被贵族院推翻。Phillips 勋爵说:"... the premise of equity's intrusion into the effects of the common law is that the common law rule in question is seen in the particular case to work injustice, and for some reason the common law cannot cure itself. But it is difficult to see how that can apply here. Cases of fraud and misrepresentation, and undue influence, are all catered for under existing and uncontentious equitable rules. We are only concerned with the question whether relief might be given for common mistake in circumstances wider than those stipulated in Bell v. Lever Brothers. But that, surely, is a question as to where the common law should draw the line; not whether, given the common law rule, it needs to be mitigated by application of some other doctrine. The common law has drawn the line in Bell v. Lever Brothers. The effect of Solle v. Butcher is not to supplement or mitigate the common law; it is to say that Bell v. Lever Brothers was wrongly decided[11]."

单方面错误看来也是同样的命运,这在 The "Harriette N" (2008) 2 Lloyd's Rep 685 先例是说:"That case(The "Great Peace") was a common mistake case. The Court of Appeal reiterated the rule that a contract would only be held void at common law by reason of common mistake if the mistake of both sides concerned a fundamental assumption of a state of affairs (positive or negative) and the mistake rendered performance of the essence of the obligation impossible.

The Court of Appeal also considered whether there was any equitable principle which widened the circumstances in which a court could rescind a contract for common mistake when the common law would hold it was binding. The court declared that there was no jurisdiction to grant rescission of a contract on the ground of common mistake where that contract is valid and enforceable according to ordinary principles of contract law: para 157.

---

[11] 这可能指在贵族院的先例是以 3 比 2 的多数意见指公司错误的程度是不足够在普通法下获得救济,看来在 Denning 大法官的看法是这一错误程度在衡平法下足够。

. . . The Great Peace decision strongly suggests that there is no such jurisdiction in the case of a unilateral mistake. If there is no such jurisdiction in the case of a common mistake, I fear I am unable to see how, in logic, one can devise a rationale for an equitable jurisdiction in the case of a unilateral mistake, at least where there has been no misrepresentation by the other party. ”

错误失去衡平法的救济好坏与否有不同说法,显然有说法是支持,这包括 The "Great Peace"先例第一审的 Toulson 大法官说:

"... it could be held that Lord Denning's view about the jurisdiction of the court to set aside a valid contract on grounds of mutual mistake, in the absence of fraud, misrepresentation or unconscionable behaviour by the other party, was over – broad.

Despite the great respect due to Lord Denning, I would respectively adopt as correct the following statement of principle in Snell's Equity, 30th ed (2000), para 1 – 14: 'It is no part of the role of the court to dissolve or vary contracts thought to be harsh on the basis of so – called equitable principles. Its role is to prevent the defendant from insisting on his strict legal rights when, owing to his behaviour, it would be unconscionable or inequitable to allow him to do. '"(Snell's Equity 一书说衡平法不应该因为认为对其中一方太苛刻就终止或改变一份合约。衡平法院的职权只是当根据被告的行为让他坚持他的严格法律权利会是不合情理或不公平时,阻止他这样做。)

但持不同看法的也有不少,如在加拿大的 Miller Paving Ltd v B. Gottardo Construction Ltd (2007) 285 DLR (4th) 568 先例,Gouge 大法官说:"The loss of the flexibility needed to correct unjust results in widely diverse circumstances that would come from eliminating the equitable doctrine of common mistake would, I think, be a step backward. "

另在 Seddon 律师与 Ellinghaus 教授的《Cheshire and Fifoot's Law of Contract, Australian Edition》(第 9 版,2008 年)一书之 12. 3 段说:"Great Peace was a most unfortunate development, abandoning after over 50 years a doctrine that provided a flexible and sensible response to the problem of commom mistake ... until the High Court says otherwise, the doctrine of mistake in equity is part of the law of Australia. . . "

13.3.6 共同错误

双方共同错误局限在少数情况,如合约标的物的消失、对标的所有权有错误理解、合约或标的本质搞错、双方对合约的一个重大事实或法律假设错误。举例说,双方买卖一栋房屋,在双方都不知情的情况下,在签订合约时该房屋已经毁于火灾或地震。这样,这一刚签订的买卖合约就变为空或无效。而涉及的双方共同错误是在不知情的情况下订立合约,还以为这一栋房屋还是完好无损。可以说,如果这一栋房屋的摧毁发生在合约签订后,也会构成合约受阻而自动终止。这一普通法的地位也在 1979 年英国《货物销售法》之 s. 6 有所规定,说:"... that where there is a contract for the sale of specific goods and the goods without the knowledge of the seller have perished at the time when the contract was made, the contract is void."

这种双方共同错误的例子还有很多,如一个人寿保险的合约被判为无效,因为投保时保险针对的人士业已死亡:Scott v Coulson (1903) 2 Ch 249 先例。一家公司与两位员工达成协议,分别支付给他们20,000与30,000英镑的解雇金,但事后发现因为员工违反了职责,事实上公司有权不给任何解雇金而直接解雇,于是该公司以共同错误为由,要求拿回支付的解雇金:Bell v Lever Bros Ltd (1932) AC 161 先例。担保合约所涉及的4部机器从来不存在:Associated Japanese Bank (International) Ltd v Credit du Nord S. A (1989) 1 WLR 255 先例。订立土地买卖合约后发现该土地上有签约时双方没有意识到的"地役权"(easement):William Sindall Plc v Cambridgeshire County Council (1994) 1 WLR 1016 先例。双方根据一份由检验师作出的证明达成和解协议,但双方对该证明有一个基本性的错误理解或假设,这被法院判是和解协议空与无效:Grains & Gourrage v Huyton (1997) 1 Lloyd's Rep 628 先例。在一个有关海上救助/拖带的事件中,双方错误假设一个事实就是作为支援的另一艘商船"Great Peace"轮只离开遇险的船舶35海里,但实际的距离是410海里。在知道事实后遇险船舶的船东以共同错误宣称合约空与无效:The "Great Peace" (2002) 2 Lloyd's Rep 653 先例。

双方共同错误必须是根据双方提供的主观证据,客观来看十分"严重与极端"(serious and radical)或"基本性"(fundamental),双方根本没有订约意图,才能有合约无效的救济。在 Bell v Lever Bros Ltd 的贵族院先例,最后只是以3 : 2的多数判决不让公司与两位员工达成的协议变为无效,主要的原因就是认为这一错误并不足够严重。在本章之13.3.5段提到,这一错误程度在衡平法下可能足够。有不少其他的先例也有同样的结果,如在 William Sindall Plc v Cambridgeshire County Council 先例,就认为地役权不足够严重。

笔者最后一提的是针对合约标的错误必须是共同错误而不是单方面的错误。这在 Smith v Hughes (1871) LR 6 QB 597 先例,Cockburn 大法官说:"I take the true rule to be, that where a specific article is offered for sale, without express warranty, or without circumstances from which the law will imply a warranty—as where, for instance, an article is ordered for a specific purpose—and the buyer has full opportunity of inspecting and forming his own judgment, if he chooses to act on his own judgment, the rule caveat emptor applies. If he gets the article he contracted to buy, and that article corresponds with what it was sold as, he gets all he is entitled to, and is bound by the contract. Here the defendant agreed to buy a specific parcel of oats. The oats were what they were sold as, namely, good oats according to the sample. The buyer persuaded himself they were old oats, when they were not so; but the seller neither said nor did anything to contribute to his deception. He has himself to blame."

这一点也在近期的 The "Harriette N" (2008) 2 Lloyd's Rep 685 先例被确认,Aikens 大法官说:"That was the effect of the decision of the Court of Queen's Bench... in Smith v Hughes (1871] LR 6 QB 597 , see particularly at 603 per Cockburn CJ ... The correctness of that decision and the analysis in it has never been doubted."

13.3.7 单方面错误

单方面错误显然比双方共同错误会更加难成立,其不同之处在于只是一方对合约条文中的一个重要事实或法律有错误假设,但另一方并没有搞错,他完全知道他自己在做什么,而且知道对方错误而只是不主动提醒而已。这方面的法律可节录 Aikens 大法官在 The "Harriette N" (2008) 2 Lloyd's Rep 685 先例所说如下:"... The general rule at common law is that **if one party has made a mistake as to the terms of the contract and that mistake is known to the other party**, then the contract is not binding. The reasoning is that although the parties appear, objectively, to have agreed terms, it is clear that they are not in agreement. Therefore the normal rule of looking only at the objective agreement of the parties is displaced and the court admits evidence to show what each side subjectively intended to agree by way of terms. If it is clear from such evidence that there was not consensus, then there can be no contract, because the parties have not truly agreed on the terms. Some of the cases talk of such a contract being 'void', but I think it is clearer to say that there was never a contract at all."(加黑部分是笔者的强调)

13.3.7.1 单方面错误搞错对方身份

先介绍最著名的一种单方面错误就是搞错对方"身份"(identity)。这也与其他类别的单方面错误有一个不同之处就是他通常不是一条合约条文。在合约中,即使有条文针对公司董事局或委托人的授权,这也不是针对公司或委托人的身份。而合约方的身份是至关重要,如果搞错就根本谈不上双方有订约的意图。因为 A 是想与 B 订立合约关系,但结果不是 B 而是 C,A 怎样都谈不上有与 C 订约的意图。正如 Millett 勋爵在 The "Starsin" (2003) 1 Lloyd's Rep 571 先例中说:"The identity of the parties to a contract is fundamental. It is not simply a term or condition of the contract. It goes to the very existence of the contract itself. If it is uncertain, there is no contract."

把对方的身份搞错,在笔者涉及的航运与外贸也经常有。例如,曾经打过交道或对方看来是一家著名的大公司,就放心订立合约。例如,在十分近期的 Glencore Energy UK Ltd v Cirrus Oil Services Ltd (2014) 2 Lloyd's Rep 1 先例,就显示即使涉及金额庞大的石油买卖以及有经验的当事人,他们还是会先通过电邮谈妥合约的主要条文,后来(几天后甚至几周后)准备一份正式的文书合约时才向对方问公司全名。显然,如果期间市场价格有波动导致对方想从合约脱身,也有可能对方一直就是这样打算,就在被查问时指定/提出一家同名(或名字十分接近)的方便旗国家如巴拿马或利比里亚注册的公司。这样另一方如果不肯接受,就会带来这种争议。

这种情况往往也涉及搞错的一方疏忽，不问清楚对方的底细或稍作调查就很容易知道。所以，往往也不会有救济。但可以肯定地说，绝大部分搞错对方身份是来自对方的“欺诈性误述”（fraudulent misrepresentation）。也就是说，对方冒名欺骗搞错的一方。如在 Cundy v Lindsay（1878）3 App. Cas. 459 先例，涉及一个名为 Blenkarn 的骗子冒充一家著名公司 Blenkiron & Co. 向原告订购一批货物。原告对 Blenkiron & Co. 久闻大名，不以为意把货物给了骗子，以为交货给 Blenkiron & Co. 大可以放心。骗子取得货物后转卖给被告（无辜第三人或善意买方）。显然骗子不会支付货款给原告，这导致原告知道真相后向无辜第三人要回这批货物，因为骗子已经逃之夭夭。原告与被告之间的争议是原告与骗子所订立的买卖合约是否因为单方面的错误（对骗子的身份有单方面错误）而变为空与“无效”（void）。如果是，表示该批货物的“所有权”（title）从来没有从原告转移给骗子，因为从来没有过一份有效的合约。而骗子在没有所有权的情况下，当然也不能把该票货物的所有权再合法转移给被告。而被告作为一个善意与无辜的买方，反而变为侵占方，如果不马上归还该票货物，就要承担 1977 年《Torts（Interference with Goods）Act》立法下的“侵占”（conversion）的严格责任。

但如果原告与骗子的合约并不是在订立时已经空与无效，而只是因为欺诈性误述或后来骗子不付货款的违约可让原告“可令合约无效”（voidable），就表示只要骗子在合约终止前把货物转卖了给被告（骗子通常会把骗来的货物马上脱手），就是合法转移所有权，这批货物就变为属于善意的买方也就是被告。最后法院判是原告与骗子的合约空与无效，换言之，被告作为无辜与善意的买方可是冤枉，钱货两失。

像 Cundy v Lindsay 先例的案件经常发生，也是法律很难解决的问题，因为原告与被告都是无辜，而真正得利的骗子已经逃之夭夭。正如 Cairns 勋爵在该先例说：“My Lords, you have in this case to discharge a duty which is always a disagreeable one for any Court, namely, to determine as between two parties, both of whom are perfectly innocent, upon which of the two the consequences of a fraud practised upon both of them must fail.”

以前这种判法也可以理解，因为英国法律相比“合约权利”（contract right）更加重视“财产权”（property right），而无辜的买方充其量只有一个合约的权利，就是他与骗子订立的买卖合约。但近期的先例有一点倾向同情无辜与善意的买方。例如在 Shogun Finance Ltd v Hudson（2003）UKHL 62 先例，Nicholls 勋爵说：“As between two innocent persons the loss is more appropriately borne by the person who takes the risks inherent in parting with his goods without receiving payment.”

Millett 勋爵也说：“... someone has to bear the loss where there is fraud, but it is surely fairer that the party who was actually swindled and who had an opportunity to uncover the fraud should bear the loss rather than a party who entered the picture only after the swindle had been carried out and who had none.”

但在该先例,Nicholls 与 Millett 勋爵只是少数意见,多数的判决还是拒绝把单方面错误的搞错对方身份从合约是空与无效的法律地位变为可令无效,从而保护善意与无辜的第三人/买方。这一问题在现实生活中(不只是商业社会)很有影响,而且也与欧洲其他国家,如德国与法国的法律不一样。英国的"法律改革委员会"(Law Reform Committee)也早在20世纪60年代尝试作出改革,这是因为上诉庭的 Devlin 大法官在 Ingram v Little (1961) 1 QB 31 先例,就对这一问题提出了损失分摊的建议,也就是无辜的原告与被告各承担一半,说:"For the doing of justice, the relevant question in this sort of case is not whether the contract was void or voidable, but which of two innocent parties shall suffer for the fraud of a third. The plain answer is that the loss should be divided between them in such proportion as is just in all the circumstances. If it be pure misfortune, the loss should be borne equally; if the fault or imprudence of either party has caused or contributed to the loss, it should be borne by that party in whole or in part."

但这一建议在之后发表的法律改革委员会报告中被拒绝:Twelfth Report, Transfer of Title to Chattels, Cmnd. 2958 (1966), paras 9 to 12。在 Shogun Finance Ltd v Hudson 的贵族院先例后,又带来了对这一问题的探讨与批评。2005年,在法律改革委员会的第九个法律改革计划中,又加入了这一问题。这是在 Law Commission, Ninth Programme of Law Reform, Law Com. No. 293 (2005), paras 1.16, 3.51 – 3.57,说:"Transfer of title by non – owners is another area in which English law is markedly different to the laws of many of our continental neighbours and of some other common law jurisdictions. While this does not suggest that our law should be changed, it does suggest that we should review it to ensure that it does actually meet the needs of business and private citizens in the modern world."

但到了2008年,法律改革委员会认为政府与企业没有太大热情在这一问题作出改革,所以将计划押后至第十一个法律改革计划中看大形势会否有改变:Law Commission, Tenth Programme of Law Reform, Law Com. No. 311 (2008), paras 4.2 – 4.4。但到了2011年的第十一个法律改革计划中,还是没有改变:Law Commission, Eleventh Programme of Law Reform, Law Com. No. 330 (2011), paras 3.4 – 3.6。看来,这一英国法律历史悠久的问题还是会延续,也就是单方面错误的搞错对方身份会使合约从一开始就是空与无效,进而严重影响善意与无辜的买方。

最后一提的是,面对面交易与双方签订了一份正式合约与双方通过书面往来(如电邮)订立合约的情况有很大不同。针对面对面交易,法律有默示是一方合约方的意图就是与对方交易,不存在搞错对方身份,并且这个假设很难被驳倒:Shogun Finance Ltd v Hudson 先例。

13.3.7.2 其他的单方面错误

其他的单方面错误的法律地位在本章之13.3.7段有提到,也就是 Aikens 大法官在 The "Harriette N" (2008) 2 Lloyd's Rep 685 先例所说的必须是一方对合约条文有错误理解,并且对方知道这个错误。此外,这一错误也是"严重与极端"(serious and radical)或"基本性"(fundamental)。这些条件也可以理解,因为单方面错误实在太多,如较早前谈到的订约一方从第三人得来的消息有误甚至他理解错误,这与合约的另一方完全无关,就不可能作出救济让错误的一方从合约中脱身。例如,在商业上经常发生的就是向曾经与对方打过交道的朋友随口查问对方的商誉或财力,而朋友往往说应该可以或没有不好的消息。这种随口查问很难得到准确、反映现况与全面的真话。但还是有很多人为了方便与省钱这样做,然后订立一个可能非常昂贵的长期合约。但在订立的合约中,没有针对对方的商誉或财力的条文,对方也不会知道他有错误理解(如对方自己知道财力不足,但另一方也没有向他查问就以为对方并不在意)。所以这单方面的错误就不会有法律的救济。

单方面的错误也有不少被报道的先例是有关和解协议,但也很难有法律救济。如在 The "Ypatia Halcoussi" (1985) 2 Lloyd's Rep 364 先例,案情涉及一个期租合约的争议,双方律师最后达成和解协议。但其中一方忘了一笔款项,后来想起就希望以单方面错误推翻已经达成的和解协议。但这被 Bingham 大法官否定,因为对方不知道另一方忘了这一笔款项,所以不构成有法律救济的单方面错误。另在 OT Africa Line Ltd v Vickers Plc (1996) 1 Lloyd's 700 先例,涉及索赔金额是 70 万美元。在法院的审理中途,被告把 103,000 美元"支付法院"(payment into court)。原告反要约的金额是 185,000 美元加上 280,000 美元的诉讼费用。双方持续的谈判后,被告律师作出一个 150,000 英镑的要约,包括支付法院的一笔钱。但这里被告律师犯错,实际上被告愿意作出和解的是美元而不是英镑,但发传真时把"$"写成了"£"。被告以单方的错误要求法律救济也被法院否定,Mance 大法官说:"(原告)were ... not aware of, or in a position where they shut their eyes to, or responsible for or at fault in respect of any mistake made on(被告)side..."

在 OT Africa Line Ltd v Vickers Plc 先例,如果事实稍一变动就可能有不同结果。例如,原告提出和解的金额是 30 万美元,被告的反要约是 29 万英镑,折算为美元比 30 万更多。这样原告不可能不知道被告单方面的错误,如果取巧接受并坚持这一 29 万英镑的和解协议,法律就很有可能作出救济。

至于怎样的单方面错误有法律救济,典型的例子是新加坡上诉庭的 Chwee Kin Keong v Digilandmall. com Pte Ltd (2005) 1 SLR 502 先例。在该先例,卖方在他的网站上写错出售的镭射打印机价格,从原来的 3854 新加坡币写为 66 新加坡币。原告的买方看到就马上接受这一要约。但被告发觉自己的错误后拒绝交付镭射打印机。新加坡高院与上诉庭判有关的买卖合约由于单方面错误而空与无效。这显然正确,如果看双方提供的主观证据,卖方与买方都没有在一个最基本的买卖合约条文,也就是价格条文同意过或有订约意图。

另介绍近期的另一个单方面错误先例 The "Harriette N",案情涉及外贸与航运熟悉的装卸时间与滞期费的课题。该先例是一个 CIF 买卖合约,卸货港产生了滞期费,卖方(负责租船)向买方追讨滞期费。但卖方从船东取得的有关装卸文件(如准备就绪通知书、事实记录等)错读了卸货完毕的时间,以为是 2006 年 10 月 13 日。其实这只是其中一票货物卸下的时间,而真正卸货完毕是在 2006 年 10 月 24 日。这一误解导致卖方与买方对滞期费达成支付协议,金额是 103,527.84 美元。但后来卖方发觉自己单方面的错误,算出来的卸港滞期费是 539,360.96 美元,也就是还欠下差价的 435,833.12 美元。这就涉及了一个争议,即卖方单方面的错误可否令对滞期费的支付协议变为空与无效。

Atkins 大法官认为不可以,主要原因是:

1. 卸货港卸货完毕的时间,也就是卖方搞错之处,并非是该支付协议的条文。Atkins 大法官这样说:"Was it a term of this contract that this compromise was reached on the understanding that the discharge was completed on 13 October 2006? In my view it was not. It is true that Mr Rostrup(卖方) sent to Mr Hodge(买方) a hard copy of the calculation sheet, which showed that he had put in the information that 'laytime ended'[12] on 13 October 2006. It is also true that Mr Hodge saw this sheet and annotated it with his revised figures before the agreement was reached. But the date for the completion of discharge was not a term of the contract of compromise as to the amount of demurrage due on this sale contract."

2. 卖方搞错卸货时间涉及疏忽,所以即使除了普通法之外还有衡平法的救济,也不会作出。Atkins 大法官说:"The mistake was entirely the result of carelessness by Mr Rostrup, as he was constrained to admit in cross – examination. If I had held there was jurisdiction to grant rescission, I would have held, on the facts of this case, that it would not be just and equitable to grant it."

13.3.8 *non est factum*

至于第三种错误,也就是 *non est factum*,涉及订立合约的一方要求救济说其签错了合约。但这只能适用在一些十分局限也不会与商业合约有关系的情况,往往也是与签约方智力或精神上有缺陷或瞒骗等极端情况有联系。如在 Saunders v Anglia Building Society (1971) AC 1004 先例,涉及一位老妇人以为自己签的字是把房子作为礼物给她的侄子,但其实根本不是。所以在较早谈到的签了要命的合约的情况显然不适用这种 *non est factum* 的救济。甚至签一方不懂英语但签一个英文合约,或是愚昧无知,这也不适用 *non est factum*,因为"无知并不是一个抗辩的理由"(ignorance is no defence)。*non est factum* 适用的一些十分局限的情况可节录 Cartwright 教授在《Misrepresentation Mistake and Non – disclosure》(第 3 版,2012 年)一书之 13 – 56 段

〔12〕 卖方把 2006 年 10 月 13 日写为卸货时间终结,但如果是写为卸货完毕就至少可以争议说买方应该知道卖方的单方面错误。

所说："The plea of *non est factum* allows a party to say that, by reason of some disability, he could not understand the document. In the early law, this was applied to parties who were blind or illiterate, and so could not read it themselves and had to trust someone else to tell them what they were signing—and where they were misled about the document. In the modern law, however, this extedns also to other 'disabilities', whether from defective education, illness or innate incapacity. The disability may be permanent or temporary: the question is whether it rendered the party incapable of both reading and sufficiently understanding the deed or other document to be signed; that is, incapable of understanding it at least to be point of detecting the fundamental difference between the actual document and the document as he had believed it to be. It is not necessary that the other party to the document knew, or ought to have known, about the disability."

§14　私人字典

私人字典(private dictionary)是指一些条文/文字双方在谈判时同意了其代表的意思,这样,如果尊重双方的订约自由与双方订约意图,理论上就应该尊重它。

14.1　权威说法

可举一些权威的说法,首先是在 Lloyd v Lloyd (1837) 2 My. & Cr. 192 先例,Cottenham 大法官说:"If the provisions are clearly expressed and there is nothing to enable the court to put upon them a construction different from that which the words impart, no doubt the words must prevail; but if the provisions and expressions be contradictory, and if there be grounds, appearing from the face of the instrument, affording proof of the real intention of the parties, then that real intention will prevail against the obvious and ordinary meaning of the words. If the parties have themselves furnished a key to the meaning of the words used, it is not material by what expressions they convey their intention."

另在 Re Sassoon (1933) 1 Ch. 858 先例,Romer 大法官说:"Except in actions for rectification the Court has no power whatsoever of adding to or subtracting from the words of a written instrument. A testator or a settlor may, however, in the instrument itself indicate sufficiently plainly that he is using certain words or phrases in other than their literal and ordinary meaning. In such cases he is said to have provided his own dictionary, and the Court will construe such words and phrases in the light of that dictionary."(这就是私人字典的说法。)

在较近期的 Chartbrook Ltd v Persimmon Homes Ltd (2009) UKHL 38 先例,Hoffmann 勋爵说:"It is true that evidence may always be adduced that the parties habitually used words in an unconventional sense in order to support an argument that words in a contract should bear a similar unconventional meaning. This is the 'private dictionary' principle, which is akin to the principle by which a linguistic usage in a trade or among a religious sect may be proved."

私人字典的一般情况就是双方在订约的谈判时,对一些可能会起争议或有多种解释的文字有商讨并同意,这些文字如"利润"(profit)、某些"公式"(formula)或"计算"(calculation)等有多种解释或含糊之处。双方即使在书面合约中对这些文字有"定义条文"(definition clause)也不表示不会起争议,因为定义可能不清楚或没有充分反映双方在谈判中的商讨与同意。如在 Chartbrook Ltd v Persimmon Homes Ltd 先例,对有争议的"Additional Residential Payment"在合约的定义条文中有解释如何计算,但双方对这个解释有不同结论。另可举 Proforce Recruit case (2006) All ER (D) 247 先例中的"preferred supplier status",这是在一般的字典中也查不到的文字,变为看双方在谈判中所同意的定义或解释会是找出双方订约意图的唯一可行的办法。

14.2 私人字典属于共识性禁止反供的说法

私人字典的说法一个理据是与"共识性禁止反供"(estoppel by convention)有关,这就是双方在谈判时如果对合约的文字的意思有了共识,就不能在事后反悔。举一个极端的例子,如果双方在谈判时明确同意了合约中的"黑"是代表"白",并可以明确证明这一个不正常的私人字典,在解释合约时,也就只能把"黑"解释为"白"了。在 Vector Gas Ltd v Bay of Plenty Energy Co Ltd (2010) NZSC 5 的新西兰先例,Tipping 大法官说:"A private dictionary meaning is a meaning the words linguistically cannot reasonably bear. It is, nevertheless, open to a party to show that, despite that fact, the parties intended their words to have that special meaning for the purposes of their contract. This represents a consensual parallel with cases in which words have a special meaning by trade custom. It can also be regarded as a linguistic example of estoppel by convention. The estoppel prevents the accepted special meaning from later being disavowed. Estoppels can also arise in interpretation cases not involving a special meaning. They are then normally based on a common assumption or representation as to meaning... If parties wish, they may contract on the basis that black means white; albeit the unlikelihood of their doing so, without expressly saying so, will no doubt be a powerful factor when it comes to questions of proof. Whether the parties have adopted a private dictionary meaning must be determined objectively in the same way as other disputes as to meaning are determined."

14.3 谈判除外规则与私人字典的关系

寻找与证明私人字典,显然是无可避免要看双方谈判的证据。在本书第一章与第六章就已经详细介绍在最近的三、四十年已经对"外来证据/口头证据"(extrinsic/parol evidence)全面开放,即"口头证据规则"(parol evidence rule)基本上已经不存在。但这里还有剩余的限制,就是"谈判除外规则"(negotiation exclusion rule 或 prior negotiation rule),这可看本书第六章之2.5.1段。

这一条谈判除外规则可以先提及 Hoffmann 勋爵在 Investors Compensation Scheme v. West Bromwich Building Society (1998) 1 W. L. R. 896 先例中著名的解释合约的五大原则,其中第三个原则如下:"(3) The law excludes from the admissible background the previous negotiations of the parties and their declarations of subjective intent. **They are admissible only in an action for rectification.** The law makes this distinction for reasons of practical policy and, in this respect only, legal interpretation differs from the way we would interpret utterance in ordinary life. The boundaries of this exception are in some respects unclear. But this is not the occasion on which to explore them. "(加黑部分是笔者的强调)

换言之,目前解释合约条文/文字还是有两方面的口头证据是排除在外的,一是双方的谈判,二是订约方主观的愿望。至于背后的原因 Wilberforce 勋爵在 Prenn v Simmonds (1971) 3 All ER 237 先例中解释说:

"(i) The reason for not admitting evidence of these exchanges is not a technical one or even mainly one of convenience, (although the attempt to admit it did greatly prolong the case and add to its expense). **It is simply that such evidence is unhelpful.** By the nature of things, where negotiations are difficult, **the parties' positions, with each passing letter, are changing and until the final agreement, though converging, still divergent.** It is only the final document which records a consensus. If the previous documents use different expressions, how does the construction of those expressions, itself a doubtful process, help on the construction of the contractual words? If the same expressions are used, nothing is gained by looking back; indeed, something may be lost since the relevant surrounding circumstances may be different. And at this stage there is no consensus of the parties to appeal to. It may be said that previous documents may be looked at to explain the aims of the parties. In a limited sense it is true; the commercial, or business object, of the transaction, objectively ascertained, may be a surrounding fact.

(ii) **Far more, and indeed totally, dangerous is to admit evidence of one party's objective—even if this is known to the other party. However strongly pursued this may be, the other party may only be willing to give it partial recognition, and in a world of give and take, men often have to be satisfied with less than they want.** So, again, it would be a manner of speculation how far the common intention was that the particular objective should be realized.

(iii) In my opinion, then, **evidence of negotiations, or of the parties' intentions, ... ought not to be received, and evidence should be restricted to evidence of the**

factual background known to the parties at or before the date of the contract, including evidence of the 'genesis' and objectively the 'aim' of the transaction.〔13〕"(加黑部分是笔者的强调)

这样,私人字典是否受谈判除外规则的限制是不清楚。如果是,也就没有所谓私人字典这一说法了,这显然不对。但在一些权威的说法,如上述节录的 Hoffmann 勋爵在 Investors Compensation Scheme v. West Bromwich Building Society 先例的判决,唯一可以不受到限制的例外只是在"合约变更"(rectification)。

这方面可介绍几个案例,涉及为了寻找私人字典而引入订约双方的谈判证据。

14.3.1 不理会谈判除外规则的案例之一:The "Karen Oltmann"

The"Karen Oltmann" (1976) 2 Lloyd's Rep. 708 先例已经在本书第六章之 2.3.12 段有介绍,不重复。起争议的文字是"Charterers to have the option to redeliver the vessel after 12 months trading subject giving 3 months' notice"中的"after"的解释是"on the expiry of "或是"at anytime after the expiry of"? Kerr 大法官认为可以看双方在谈判中的明确订约意图,说:"However, on the basis that the word 'after' in clause 26 is capable of bearing two meanings as a matter of construction, **I do not think that there is any authority precluding the Court from examining the pre - charter - party exchanges in order to see whether the owners can make good their contention that the parties were in agreement in using this word in only one of its two senses, and having in effect both given it the same dictionary meaning to the exclusion of the other meaning.** Having then considered the pre - charter - party exchanges on this basis I find this contention is established. In these circumstances it seems to me that the charterers cannot now depart from this common meaning by asserting that this word has the opposite meaning in the charter - party. "(加黑部分是笔者的强调)

14.3.2 不理会谈判除外规则的案例之二:New Hampshire Insurance Company v. MGM Limited

在这一上诉庭先例 New Hampshire Insurance Company v. MGM Limited (1995) June 15, CA, Staughton 大法官十分清楚地说明这方面的做法如下:"**There is plain authority that evidence of negotiations is not admissible.** There are, of course, exceptions if it is said that the parties had reached an agreement or at any rate a common intention and by mistake this had not been recorded in the written contract. Then there can be rectification and evidence could be adduced for that purpose. **It was also said that evidence is admissible if agreement has been reached in the course of negotiations on the meaning of a particular term.** "(加黑部分是笔者的强调)

---

〔13〕 Wilberforce 勋爵在这里所讲的一些谈判除外规则的例外情况,在本书第六章之 2.5.1.2 与 2.5.1.3 段有介绍一些之后的发展与不同看法。

14.3.3 不理会谈判除外规则的案例之三:Nicholson v. Markham

Staughton 大法官在 Nicholson v. Markham (1997) 75 P. & C. R. 428 先例中接受了双方谈判的证据,但认为双方根本没有同意过起争议文字的解释,说:"Nothing that has been put before us by Miss Egan (被告代表大律师) comes anywhere remotely near showing an agreement by the parties on the use of particular words in this contract. It follows that evidence of negotiations was, in accordance with well established authority, inadmissible and could not be relied on."

14.3.4 不理会谈判除外规则的案例之四:Proforce Recruit case

Proforce Recruit case (2006) All ER (D) 247 先例涉及的"提供清洁服务合约"(service cleaning agreement)内有"preferred supplier status"一词,但没有给这一不常见的词组定义,上诉庭认为可看双方的谈判以找出双方采用该词的意图。Arden 大法官针对这一点,说:"In this case, the parties have used a very unusual combination of words ('preferred supplier status'). These words are undefined and they are not introduced or accompanied by any words of explanation. In those circumstances it is in my judgement reasonably arguable that on their true interpretation those words bear the meaning that the parties in common agreement. In admitting evidence as to those communications, the court would be hearing that evidence not with a view to taking the parties' subjective intent into account for the purpose of interpretation (a purpose precluded by the principle laid down by Lord Hoffman in (*Investors Compensation Scheme c. West Bromwich Building Society* (1998] 1 W. L. R. 896]) but for the purpose of identifying the meaning that the parties in effect incorporated into their agreement in circumstances where the court was satisfied that on their interpretation the terms of the agreement were to have this effect."

14.3.5 不理会谈判除外规则的案例之五:Jones v. Bright Capital Ltd

Jones v. Bright Capital Ltd (2006) EWHC 3151 (Ch)先例有关退休金的争议,Andrew Morritt C 大法官针对这一点说:"**In my view each of the letters in question is admissible on the issue of construction.** They show the genesis and subject matter of paragraph 38(3) of the defence which became a term of the compromise. They show the connection between the actuary's calculations and that paragraph and explain the figures and other terms which appear in it. None of them is relied on as indications of subjective intention and on the face of them they are not objectionable on that account. The mere fact that they were written in the course of inter – solicitor correspondence seeking to agree a redundancy package is not, in my judgement, a sufficient objection."

14.3.6 不理会谈判除外规则的案例之六:香港仲裁

在笔者处理的一个香港仲裁,也出现了"私人字典"(private dictionary)的争议。这是一个以中文进行的仲裁,涉及前后两份中文合约,这两份合约(并有明示规定两者如果有矛盾,后一份合约超越前一份)内有关的争议内容看来相同,但有细微差别。前一份文件中用的是一个“或”字串联起两件事情,而在后一份份量更重的合约中将其改为一个顿号“、”。双方争议的是这一改动是否使整个相关内容有了完全不同的意思,即顿号代表“与”的意思,变为两件事情都必须办妥。这样一个争议就涉及数亿港币的差别。其中涉及谈判的证据,一方反对仲裁庭接受此类证据(这证据主要在开庭前不久双方交换的证人证言内),而另一方持不同意见。仲裁庭考虑这一条文/文字有含糊,认为最好看双方在第一份合约后至第二份合约达成之间的谈判中到底如何约定,或是根本没有谈过这一点,只是一个笔误。结果,仲裁庭允许接受谈判的证据,也就是寻找私人字典的说法。仲裁庭也对双方当事人说明以 *de bene esse*〔14〕的做法处理,并要求反对接受此类证据的一方大律师设计反盘问对方证人,只要是涉及私人字典方面,因为仲裁庭会在裁决时一并考虑。这样提醒反对的一方是因为在开庭时他根本没有准备这一方面的外来证据/口头证据,也来不及,故此仲裁庭必须顾及对双方公平。

14.4 私人字典与合约变更的关系

私人字典与合约变更是十分接近的理念,但并不是同一码事。Kerr 大法官在 The “Karen Oltmann” (1976) 2 Lloyd’s Rep. 708 先例中对这两种做法的区分有说明如下:“Such (private dictionary) cases would not support a claim for rectification of the contract, because the choice of words in the contract would not result from any mistake. The words used in the contract would *ex hypothesi* reflect the meaning which both parties intended.”(私人字典不是合约变更,因为合约中的文字并不涉及错误记录双方的真正订约意图。只不过合约中的文字不能给他一般性的解释,否则不能反映双方在谈判时同意的解释。)

但显然这两种十分接近的做法都必须看谈判证据才能找得出答案,而在本章稍早的14.3段已经讲到合约变更是“谈判除外规则”(negotiation exclusion rule)唯一的例外。这样,私人字典这一做法也应该是谈判除外规则的另一个例外。

在 Chartbrook Ltd v. Persimmon Homes Ltd (2007) 1 All ER 1083 先例,高院曾经划了一条分水线,即如果争议的文字已经有了一条“定义条文”(definition clause)明示针对(如该先例中的相关合约所争议的“Additional Residential Payment”一词就有了定义),就不必看双方的谈判证据,也就是谈判除外规则适用。但这个案例上诉至贵族院,有了补充说是即使有定义条文,还是要看定义是否明确,而如果还是带来

---

〔14〕 如果法院/仲裁庭看了谈判证据后并没有发现私人字典,担心法院/仲裁庭看了双方谈判时的主观意愿并受影响或被“污染”而导致双方有另一新的争议,为了安全双方事先同意法院/仲裁庭可看这种他本来不该看的证据,但事后在作出判决/裁决时排除考虑这些见过或听过的证据,把它“置之脑后”(*de bene esse*)。通常,对证据法熟悉的法院/仲裁庭完全可以这样做。这方面内容与困难在《国际商务游戏规则——英美证据法》一书第二章之6.7.7.3.3段有涉及。

含糊与争议，就可从双方的谈判证据中寻找是否有私人字典。

§15　文字的排列与标点符号

文字的排列与标点符号（layout and punctuation）一般不是一个解释合约条文/文字的重要考虑，但还是经常在很多案子被提及。在一个比较早期的案件 Houston v Burns（1918）AC 337，贵族院有提到解释一份遗嘱必须考虑这一方面。Shaw 大法官是说："Punctuation is a rational part of English composition, and is sometimes quite significantly employed. I see no reason for depriving legal documents of such significance as attaches to punctuation in other writings."

但看来在近期的先例，这一方面的分量已经减低。在 Sammut and others v Manzi Jr（2009）2 All ER 234 先例，同样是解释一份遗嘱，枢密院就判是不考虑文字的排列与标点符号，说："That case（这是指 Houston v Burns 先例）concerned a will that was written in 1894, no doubt in manuscript. Their Lordships would not consider it safe in this case to attach significance to the formatting achieved by a word processor that may well have been operated by a secretary."

也有的其他近期先例指这方面的重量不大，如澳大利亚高院的 Chalmers Leask Underwriting Agencies v Mayne Nickless Ltd（1983）155 CLR 279 先例，说：".. the mere absence of a comma is of dubious worth as an aid to construction of a clause in which punctuation has plainly been a haphazard matter."

在 Scheldebouw BV v St James Homes（Grosvenor Dock）Ltd（2006）105 Con L. R. 90（TCC）先例，法院判是即使标点符号有关，也不能超越合约的明显意思，Jackson 大法官说："Although punctuation is relevant, the presence of certain full stops ... cannot override the obvious meaning of the clause."

但受到文字的排列与标点符号的一定影响的案例还是有，如 Sudbrook Trading Estate Ltd v Eggleton（1983）AC 444；The "Petr Shmidt"（1995）1 Lloyd's Rep. 202；BMBF（No. 12）Ltd v Harland and Wolff Shipbuilding and Heavy Industries Ltd（2001）EWCA Civ 862；BP Exploration Operating Co Ltd v Kvaerner Oilfield Products Ltd（2004）2 All ER（Comm）266；Emeraldian Ltd Partnership v Wellmix Shipping Ltd（2011）1 Lloyd's Rep 301 等先例。

在 Sudbrook Trading Estate Ltd v Eggleton 的贵族院先例，Diplock 勋爵说："The term 'valuer'（**with a capital 'V' at any rate**）is used nowadays to denote a member of a recognized profession comprised of persons possessed of skill and experience in assessing the market price of property, particularly real property."（加黑部分是笔者的强调）

但文字的排列与标点符号即使有关,一个好的判决往往还是有其他理由全面考虑。如在 The "Ioanna" (1978) 1 Lloyd's Rep. 238 先例中,租约中的第 13 条文如下:"13. General average & arbitration to be settled according to York - Antwerp Rules[15] 1950 in London..."

这被英国高院与上诉庭判是仲裁只针对船东与承租人在共同海损的争议要通过仲裁解决。但看来是一条仲裁条文被解释是不包括其他争议,所以在该案例中的滞期费争议就只能是由英国法院审理。

但到了 The "Petr Shmidt" 先例,高院在一个表面看来一样的条文却作出了不同的判决,有关条文是:"—General Average/Arbitration in London - English law to apply. —York - Antwerp Rules 1974 as Amended to Apply."(注意这条文文字的排列)

双方的争议是有关无单放货,但首先面临的问题是有否一条有效的伦敦仲裁条文,特别是有了上诉庭的 The "Ioanna" 先例。Potter 大法官判法是不一样,认为在 The "Ioanna" 先例的文字上的排列让高院与上诉庭认为只能有一个解释,即使订约方主观的意图不一样。Potter 大法官是这样说:"I do not gain substantial assistance from the decision in the *The Ioanna* because of the points of distinction already mentioned. It is plain that in that case the trial Judge and the Court of Appeal regarded the matter as so crystal clear that, despite the views of Mr. Justice Kerr(审理 The "Ioanna" 先例的大法官)as to the likely 'real' (i. e. subjective) intention of the parties, the wording could only admit of on construction."

但在 The "Petr Shmidt", Potter 大法官作出以下的区分与考虑:

1. 文字的连接符号与排列不一样,在 The "Petr Shmidt" 案例中是分开两句。第二句只针对共同海损,这就勉强能解释第一句既针对共同海损,也针对仲裁,都必须在伦敦进行是可以有一分为二的解释。

2. The "Ioanna" 先例是在一个金康租约内的附加条文,但 The "Petr Shmidt" 案例是解释一份电传的"重述要点"。在后者,简单与粗糙地记录双方所达成的协议可能性更大。

3. The "Petr Shmidt" 案例的"重述要点"中也合并了另一份著名的标准格式合约,名为 Vegoilvoy,格式内有独立的两条条文针对共同海损与仲裁,第 22 条针对共同海损的理算是在纽约,第 31 条针对仲裁也是在纽约。整体看这个租约,一定程度上表示是两种不同的事情。而且,如果电传中的一句"—General Average/Arbitration in London - English law to apply"只针对共同海损的争议去伦敦仲裁,,就超越了 Vegoilvoy 标准格式中的第 22 条,但不超越第 31 条,这一来岂非导致了共同海损的争议去伦敦而租约其他争议去纽约的不寻常安排。这显然不符合商业的合理性,正如 Bingham 大法官在 Ashville Investments Ltd v. Elmer Constructors Ltd (1988) 2

---

〔15〕 York - Antwerp Rules 是由国际海事委员会(CMI)拟定的针对共同海损的理算。

Lloyd's Rep. 73 先例中所说如下："... I would be very slow to attribute to reasonable parties an intention that there should in any foreseeable eventuality be two sets of proceedings."此外，Harbour Assurance Cp.（U. K）Ltd v. Kansa General International Insurance Co. Ltd.（1993）1 Lloyd's Rep. 455 先例中判有一个假设是只能去一个地方仲裁，Hoffman 勋爵说："The presumption in favour of one – stop adjudication."

4. 还有更重要的是，由于后一个案例有含糊之处，所以就更加要看合约的"背景/语境"(context)。这包括今天很少会发生共同海损，租船人士很少会关心这一方面的争议要怎样解决而需要在重述要点中针对。反而关心的是租约其他争议怎样解决。别说是 The "Petr Shmidt"的文字，就算是 The "Ioanna"的文字，笔者也认为订约方实际上是针对所有争议的仲裁而不只是针对共同海损的争议，只不过法院认为 The "Ioanna"只能有一个解释，就不管订约的背景/语境了，毕竟这也是当时比较早期的主流传统解释文书合约的做法。

最后一提的是在 The "Petr Shmidt"先例，由于与 The "Ioanna"先例同样是属于高院的判决，所以不存在可以推翻。虽然严格说高院之间的不同大法官也不需要受到先例的约束，但最好还是有为什么判决不同的理由。可以说在这一个案件，通过"区分"(distinguish)两个先例的文字的排列与标点符号作出了截然不同的判决。

第四章　其他内部解释合约的主要规则

§1　解释合约主要规则的作用

"解释合约的主要规则"(canons of construction)有好几十条,不少已经在本书其他章节提到。如在本书第三章之第1与第2段就介绍了一个十分重要的解释规则,即"整体与全面解释合约"(construing the document as a whole)并"给每一条文/文字都有一定的意思"(giving effect to all parts of a contract)。另在本书第七章之4.4.5段介绍了另一个重要的解释规则,即"明示条文超越默示条文"(express terms negative implied terms)。其他也是十分重要的解释合约规则,也在本章与本书其他地方都有谈到,如在第一章之8.5段介绍的The "Starsin"(2003)1 Lloyd's Rep. 571先例中,Bingham勋爵所总结的四条历史悠久与重要的解释合约规则。

但这些规则并非是法律,只是在解释个别合约/文件的时候起指导作用。这里可先举Wright勋爵在Luxor(Eastbourne)Ltd v. Cooper(1941)A.C. 108先例所说的:"I deprecate in general the attempt to enunciate decisions on the construction of agreements as if they embodied rules of law. To some extent decisions on one contract may help by way of analogy and illustration in the decision of another contract. But however similar the contracts may appear, the decision as to each must depend on the consideration of the language of the particular contract, read in the light of the material circumstances of the parties in view of which the contract is made."(我不赞成把解释合约的判决当作是法律的规定。在某一程度上,一份合约的判决可在另一个判决中类推与为例。但不论两份合约表面看来怎样相同,作出解释还是要根据个别合约的文字与其在订约时的重要环境/背景。)

在Hollier v. Rambler Motors(A.M.C.)Ltd(1972)2 Q.B. 71先例,Salmon大法官说:"解释合约的主要规则只是指引而不是我们的主人"(Rules of construction are merely our guides and not our masters)。

这表示在引用一些解释合约的主要规则,必须要灵活。而且在几乎每一种情况下,都能找到有两个相对的主要规则。举例说,一个主要规则是"如果语言是清楚无误,就应该给它效力"(if language is plain and unambiguous it must be given effect)。但马上就可以举一个相对的主要规则或反话,是"如果给与字义上的解释会带来可笑的后果或阻碍明显的订约目的则不适用”(not when the literal interpretation would lead to absurd consequences or thwart manifest purpose of the contract)。

再如“合约中的每一个字与条文都必须给其一定的意思”(every word and clause in a contract must be given meaning and effect to)的主要解释规则。但反话就是“如果条文/文字是不留心加入或者与合约其他部分起矛盾,就可以漠示/删除,当作是多余的话”(if inadvertently inserted or if repugnant to the rest of the contract, they may be rejected as surplusage)。

曾经有人统计过,发现有至少28个可以讲反话的例子。所以,在许多的解释合约主要规则中,在个别不同的合约条文/文字与背景/语境找出一个合情合理与有说服力(特别是接近的条文/文字已经有过不一致判决)的解释是一种艺术。

以下列出一些主要针对上述所讲的判例说法:

1. 在 Chandris v. Isbrandtsen – Moller Co Inc. (1951) 84 Ll. L. Rep. 347 先例中 Devlin 大法官所说的:“A rule of construction cannot be more than a guide to enable the court to arrive at the true meaning of the parties. ... To apply the rule automatically in that way would be to make it the master and not the servant of the purpose for which it was designed—namely to ascertain the meaning of the parties from the words which they have used.”

2. 在 Earl of Jersey v. Neath Union Rural Sanitary Authority (1889) 22 Q. B. D. 555 中 Lloyd 大法官说:“It is to be observed that the rule admits, as every rule of construction of documents must admit, as it is after all but a working canon to enable us to arrive at the meaning of the particular of document—it admits of being modified by the contents of the document itself, and there are classes of cases in which it is obvious that the rule will have to bend.”

3. 在 BCCI. v. Ali (2002) 1 A. C. 251 先例中 Clyde 勋爵说:“Such guides to construction as have been identified in the past should not be allowed to constrain an approach to construction which looks to commercial reality or common sense. If they are elevated to anything approaching the status of rules they would deservedly be regarded as impedimenta in the task of construction. But they may be seen as reflections upon the way in which people may ordinarily be expected to express themselves.”

4. Craighead 勋爵在 A. I. B. Group v. Martin (2001) U. K. H. L. 63 先例所说:“Like any other rule of interpretation, it is there to help to ascertain the objective meaning of the document in question. Like all such rules, it must be used with discrimination.”(如任何其他的解释合约规则,它只是帮助客观地找出文件的意思。好像所有解释合约规则一样,其使用必须是选择性的。)

5. 在 H. I. H. Casualty and General Insurance Ltd v. Chase Manhattan Bank (2001) C. L. C. 48 先例中 Aikens 大法官对此有所评论:“The court's task is still to discern

what the parties intended by the wording that they have agreed in the particular type of contract under consideration. But although 'rules' of construction are a guide to the intention of the parties, they are not the masters of the parties' intention."

本章接下只针对解释合约的一些其他在本书没有详尽探讨过的主要规则，并尽量避免重复。

§2 其余解释规则之一：标准格式的印本条件

标准格式合约/条文在商贸中使用得非常多，如租约、国际货物买卖、信用证、保单等。标准格式合约/条文通常由一些有关的商会拟定，以供其会员或行业其他人士在个别合约中使用。如国际商会（International Chamber of Commerce，简称ICC）就拟定大量的标准格式合约/条文，其中十分熟悉的标准格式条文就是适用与合并在信用证的UCP 600与在货物买卖合约的Incoterms。另一个重要与国际知名拟定大量标准格式合约/条文的商会就是世界最大的船东组织Baltic and International Maritime Council（简称BIMCO），其文件委员会已经有一百多年历史。BIMCO拟定的标准格式合约/条文多不胜数，如程租的金康租约（Gencon Charter - party）与大宗货买卖/航运最普遍使用的提单格式Congenbill。

2.1 标准格式合约的优点与缺点

标准格式合约通常都拟定的比较好与全面，毕竟这通常是有关商会花费大量时间与金钱成立一个专家工作小组仔细地拟定，整个过程往往涉及无数的草拟、商讨、争辩、市场调查、遇上疑点寻求大律师意见等，才会最终定稿。

但标准格式合约用在个别的交易中也有很多缺点。如合约方选用的标准格式合约并非对其交易十分配套，这导致双方需要对标准格式合约作出大量修改，并加上附加条文/文字。这样遇上有争议，标准格式内的条文/文字在解释时给的分量都比较轻。有关手写或打字的附加条文/文字分量都比标准格式的印本条文重的解释规则耳熟能详，这在本书第三章之5.2段有介绍。而且如果一个标准格式合约有太多的修改就会被视为双方"一次过"（one off）的合约[1]而失去法律对解释标准格式合约的一些好处。这些好处会在稍后的小段进一步分析，如尽量在解释合约条文/文字时不考虑案件的本质、背景与语境，并尽量跟从以前的先例或商业上普遍的理解，都是

〔1〕在Lewison大法官所著的《The Interpretation of Contracts》（第5版，2011年）一书第198页说："The dividing line between a contract which is a standard form with amendments and one which is not, may be difficult to define. Indeed in The Nema (1981) 2 Lloyd's Rep 239 (HL) itself, the basis of the charterparty was a standard form, but it had been so heavily amended that it was categorized as a 'one off' contract both by Lord Diplock and by Lord Roskill."

为了给商业有肯定性/可循性。

2.2 标准格式合约会有的倾向性

另一个缺点就是议定标准合约的商会都有其倾向性或/与自我保护。以属于船东组织的 BIMCO 为例,其以往的一些标准格式合约都会倾向保护船东而相对对承租人不利,这里最好的例子就是金康租约。但近期的标准格式合约,有不少是与"对手的商会"(counter – part organizations)磋商与同意后才定稿。显然这种标准格式合约就会持平得多,十分值得双方(通常是船东与货方)使用。但问题是精明的商业人士也不是追求持平,而是对自己是否有利。所以,在现实中经常见到使用一份持平的标准格式,还是被修改得面目全非,变为是一面倒保护其中一方。这样双方有了争议,法院会把该合约视为"一次过",反正不视为"一次过"也会在作出解释时依从一般的"解释规则"(rules of construction),不理会其本来是一份标准格式合约。在 The "Golden Victory" (2007) 2 Lloyd' s Rep 164 先例,Scott 勋爵说:"Certainty is a desideratum and a very important one, particularly in commercial contracts. But it is not a principle and must give way to principle. Otherwise incoherence of principle is the likely result. The achievement of certainty in relation to commercial contracts depends, I would suggest, on firm and settled principles of the law of contract rather than on the tailoring of principle in order to frustrate tactics of delay to which many litigants in many areas of litigation are wont to resort."(对商业合约而言,肯定性十分重要。但这不是一个原则,所以必须向解释合约的一些原则让步。否则,这会带来混乱。商业合约长期的稳定是根据一些明确与肯定的合约法原则。)

特定商会在拟定标准格式合约的倾向性/自我保护有很多例子,笔者只举两个。首先是大宗货买卖最普遍被使用的提单格式"Congenbill"为了避免船东与货方发生争议(最常见就是货损货差)时,船舶动辄就在卸港被扣押并被强迫卸港的国家法院应诉并会面对十分不利的地位,所以在 1994 年的格式加上了仲裁条文。该条文只是简单几个字说仲裁地点与做法是按照有关的租约,这通常是伦敦仲裁。这样就对货方不利,如中国的货方十分愿意在中国的海事法院提起诉讼,但要去伦敦仲裁就会有很大犹疑。另一个例子也是大宗货物的买卖合约,其中最著名的标准格式合约就是英国的两个商会 GAFTA(Grain and Feed Trade Association)与 FOSFA(Federation of Oils, Seeds and Fats Associations)所拟定的,并在国际上大量被使用。在这些标准格式合约,都规定了有争议是在英国的商会仲裁。而仲裁员名单中的仲裁员,大部分都来自国际贸易商。但这样国际贸易商是与中国货方作为对手,所以双方一有了争议,中国货方仲裁就会感到站在不利地位。在这种情况下,中国货方可以坚持把有关的仲裁条文改为贸仲或香港仲裁。

2.3 劳合社所拟定的标准格式保单——S. G. 保单的有趣历史

最后一提的是,即使是很高水平的商会或组织所拟定的标准格式合约,也会因为各种原因拟定得十分差劲。这里可举英国"劳合社"(Lloyd' s)所拟定的保单为例。

英国的劳合社很长一段时间(1779~1982年)以一份陈旧的劳合社保单标准格式,名为Lloyd's S. G. form of policy(简称S. G. 保单),承保水险。这份保单同时承保船舶与货物在海上运输的风险,其中"S"代表"船舶"(ship),"G"代表"货物"(goods)。而保单内所承保的风险类别是包括所有在200年前会面对的的水险与战争险。水险包括"peril of the sea"、"fire"、"jettisons"、"barratry of the master and mariner"等。战争险保的更多,如"enemies"、"letters of mart and countermart"、"surprisals"、"takings at sea"、"arrests"、"restrains and detainment of all kings、princes and people"等。这些所承保的风险都在同一标准格式保单内。这在200年前的外贸与航运做法是业已足够,因为当时船货往往是同一个人所拥有,货主很有可能就是船长或船长是他所雇用的。这样,投保就可以简单的以一份劳合社保单包括航次中面临的所有风险。但约五十年后,无线电令岸上与船舶可以进行通讯往来,船货开始变为由不同的人所拥有。需要作出承保的风险类别也越来越多,劳合社的保险人也开始专业化,如部分人承保水险,部分人承保战争险,部分人承保船舶,部分人承保货物等。

但劳合社为了尊重传统(毕竟S. G. 保单的标准格式保单在1906年《英国海上保险法》被作为附件一),加上已经有了大量的先例对其所有的条文/文字作出了权威性的解释,所以不愿意摒弃。劳合社针对行业的重大变化就是通过许多的标准格式条文以附件加在S. G保单。如针对船舶的承保就加上一系列标准格式条文只针对船舶的保险,针对货物的承保就加上同意的条文只针对货物保险。而承保水险但不承保战争险就更加麻烦了,加上一条所谓的"Free of Capture and Seizure Clause"(或简称F. C & S Clause)把劳合社保单内的战争险全部排除,变为承保的只剩下水险。而反过来只承保战争险但不承保水险,就把F. C & S Clause删除掉,然后加上一套专门针对战争险的标准格式条文。这样导致了不少的漏洞与著名的诉讼。

这种含糊的保单导致了联合国贸发局在1975年的大力抨击,并声称英国不肯随着时代的进步作出改变,准备拟订一份大家(特别是发展中国家)至少在条文/文字上都看得明白的保单:UNCTAD文件TD/B/C/14/1SL/27。

这方面英国法院自己的批评也不少,如Mocatta大法官在The "Anita" (1970) 2 Lloyd's Rep. 365先例中说:"It cannot be beyond the wit of Underwriters and those who advise them in this age of law reform to devise more straightforward and easily comprehended terms of cover."

另在Kuwait Airways v. Kuwait Insce (1999) 1 Lloyd's Rep. 803先例中,Hobhouse勋爵也有说:"An example of this approach in the marine market is the treatment of war risks. Historically the 'S. G' policy (as scheduled to the 1906 Act) covers war risks but these risks are then excluded by the F. C. & S. clause. This approach over the years gave rise to many disputes many of which could have been avoided had a more direct approach been adopted. The historical approach has been departed from in many sectors but its influence is still to be observed in the contracts which your Lordship's House has to consider on the present appeal."

以上的介绍已经过时,因为英国的保险市场很快就对联合国贸发局的批评给出一一回应,并在1982、1983年作出相应对策,拟订了专门针对不同种类保险的标准条文并且放弃使用S. G.保单。这被称为英国伦敦保险市场的一场"静默的革命"(silent revolution)。

2.4 标准格式合约条文/文字必须有肯定性/可循性的说法

商业上(特别是国际商业)使用的标准格式印本条文解释需要有肯定性/可循性,尽量不能受个别案件的本质与背景影响,这理念与解释立法的条文/文字一样,不能在不同案情的案件个别作出不同解释。这对商业活动尤其重要,如商务仲裁。这方面的权威说法多不胜数,可介绍部分先例如下:

1. 早在Dunlop & Son v. Balfour Williamson & Co (1892) 1 Q. B. 507先例,Esher M. R.勋爵就已经有说到:"It is a wholesome rule that has often been laid down that when a well - known document has been in constant use for a number of years, **the Court, in construing it, should not break away from previous decisions**, even if in the first instance they would have taken a different view, because all documents made after the meaning of one has been judicially determined are taken to have been made on the faith of the rule so laid down."(加黑是笔者的强调)

2. 在Atlantic Trading and Shipping Co v Louis Dreyfus & Co (1922) 2 AC 250先例,Dunedin勋爵说:"My Lords, in these commercial cases it is, I think, **of the highest importance that authority should not be disturbed**, and if your Lordships find that a certain doctrine has been laid down in former cases and presumably acted on in the framing of other contracts **you will not be disposed to alter that doctrine unless you think it is clearly wrong.**"(先例所定下的说法除非被认为是清楚错误,否则不应该被否定十分重要。)这里可一提的是,英国普通法有法院作出的判决对后来的判决有约束性,所谓的"stare decisis"大原则。但这不表示后来的判决不可以否定或是偏离。做法上有很多种,如上一级法院就不会受到下一级法院曾经作出过的判决约束,完全可以否定。而在高院这一个层次,也不受较早前判决约束,不同的大法官可以有不同的看法。但相比英国法院,香港在这方面是相对"保守",上诉庭作出的判决对之后的上诉庭判例是有约束力,只能由最高院推翻。而即使受到约束,法院/仲裁庭很容易通过不同案件的事实与较早前的先例作出"区分"(distinguish)以作出不同的决定。

3. Denning勋爵在The "Annefield" (1971) 1 Lloyd's Rep. 1先例讲得更明白,说商业人士如果不满意法院对一个标准格式合约的解释,他们可以更改标准格式:"Once a court has put a construction on commercial documents in a standard form, commercial men act upon it. It should be followed in all subsequent cases. If the business community is not satisfied with the decision, they should alter the form."

4. 在The "Nema" (1981) 2 Lloyd's Rep 239 (HL)先例,Diplock勋爵说:"..."

when contracts are entered into which incorporate standard terms it is in the interests alike of justice and of the conduct of commercial transactions that those standard terms should be construed and treated by arbitrators as giving rise to similar legal rights and obligations in all arbitrations in which the events have given rise to the dispute do not differ from one another in some relevant respect. It is only if parties to commercial contracts can rely upon a uniform construction being given to standard terms that they can prudently incorporate them in their contracts without the need for detailed negotiation or discussion. Such uniform construction of standard terms had been progressively established up to 1979, largely through decisions of the Courts upon special cases stated by arbitrators. In the result English commercial law has achieved a degree of comprehensiveness and certainly that has made it acceptable for adoption as the appropriate proper law to be applied to commercial contracts wherever made by parties of whatever nationality. "[当根据标准格式订立合约时,有关人士都希望仲裁庭在类似的争议会作出同样的裁决。只有标准格式合约会获得划一的解释,商业人士才会放心订立合约并避免过多与细节的谈判。在这些年来,通过仲裁庭"特殊案件"(special cases,这是在1950年英国《仲裁法》的做法,仲裁庭把双方争议的法律问题交给法院作出决定,这做法在1996年英国《仲裁法》已经被取消)的做法,已经对各种常被商业人士使用的标准格式作出了大量的案例,形成了划一的解释,并为英国商法奠定了很大程度的全面性与肯定性的根基。这导致全世界的商业人士,不论是什么国籍,都接受英国商法作为其合约的适用法。]

5. 在The "Chikuma" (1981) 1 Lloyd's Rep 371 先例,Bridge 勋爵说:"The ideal at which the Courts should aim, in construing such clauses, is to produce a result, such that in any given situation both parties seeking legal advice as to their rights and obligations can expect the same clear and confident answer from their advisers and neither will be tempted to embark on long and expensive litigation in the belief that victory depends on winning the sympathy of the Court. This ideal may never be fully attainable, but we shall certainly never even approximate to it unless we strive to follow clear and consistent principles and steadfastly refuse to be blown off course by the supposed merits of individual cases."(法院追求的理想就是解释标准格式合约条文/文字会导致一个结果,即在任何情况下有争议的当事人寻求有关他们的权利与义务的法律意见,他们都会取得同样的明确与肯定答案,导致他们根本不会企图通过一个漫长与昂贵的诉讼希望法院最后因为在个别案件的同情而判他们胜诉。所以法院这些年来都是追求清楚明确与肯定的原则,并抗拒根据个别案件的是非曲直而在原则上摇摆不定。)

6. 在更近期的The "World Symphony" (1991) 2 Lloyd's Rep 251 先例,高院的Hobhouse大法官说:"It is axiomatic in English commercial law that where certain contractual provisions have achieved an established and recognized meaning the Courts should not decline to follow earlier authorities in which that meaning is recognized unless

those previous authorities are clearly wrong. Without such a principle the certainty and continuity of commercial law is lost and there is a risk of frustrating rather than giving effect to the intentions of the parties. Parties must be able to contract on the basis of established decisions about the words they are choosing to use to express their contractual intention."（英国法院不应该偏离先例给标准合约条文/文字的解释，除非先例明显错误。没有这一个肯定性与持续性，带来的结果会是否定而不是支持双方的订约意图。合约方必须能够依据先例给有关的条文/文字的权威性解释，作出选择以表达他们的订约意图。）

笔者对上述的一些权威性说法十分认同，举例说在一些年代比较老的立法如1924年英国的《海上货物运输法》（这是根据《海牙规则》而立的法），里面的每一条条文/文字已通过判决而给予其一个解释，特别是贵族院定的调，就再也不会改变。如著名的"恪尽职责地适航"（due diligence to make the ship seaworthy），在贵族院的The "Muncaster Castle"（1961）1 Lloyd's Rep. 57先例定了调之后，再有的争议就是根据每一个案例不同的事实被认定后，然后套上The "Muncaster Castle"所给的解释，就能够得出判决的结果。这导致在许多货损货差涉及船舶是否适航的争议中，绝大部分都可以在有关证据披露后，双方对事实有了理解，就可以相当准确预测到诉讼到底会是怎样的结果，并可以达成成比例的和解。换言之，"恪尽职责地适航"的解释是肯定/可循的，不会再因个别合约的背景/语境而有所改变。

针对一些广泛被使用的标准格式合约如航运中的NYPE或金康租约或国际大宗货买卖的GAFTA/FOSFA合约，肯定性/可循性更加重要。因为它将会被许多人使用与依从，法律是不应该根据个别案件的不同情况，因为个别事件的公平合理而作出不同的解释。

而如果英国法院对标准格式合约/条文作出权威性的解释并不令部分商业人士满意，他们也不必怪责英国法律不公平或不现实。毕竟在订约自由下，双方完全可以更改有关的标准格式合约/条文，也就间接改变了英国法院曾经作出过的不满意判决。而如果是更普遍与大面积的不满意，有关的商会或组织更加可以把整个标准格式合约的版本作出更改。在BIMCO文件委员会，就密切关注英国法院的重要判例（因为航运与国际货物买卖普遍以英国法为适用法），一旦有英国判例对某一份标准格式合约/条文有批评或有不满意的判决，BIMCO文件委员很快就会成立小组作出新的版本。

2.5　解释立法条文/文字有同样的肯定性/可循性的重要性

英国也是不断有新的立法，在立法生效后往往解释有关立法的条文/文字的案例会不断出现。在过了一段时间后有关的立法几乎可能带来争议的每一句话或每一个字都有了法院的解释，这也表示整个立法就有了肯定性/可循性，就像1924年的《海上运输法》（也就是《海牙规则》）。这也解释了英国为什么不愿意动一些看来是十分古老、不完整与追不上时代的立法，如针对保险的唯一立法的1906年《海上保险法》,因为这会牵一发而动全身。

举例说,英国1996年的《仲裁法》被公认写得很好,很清楚明确与符合现代仲裁做法的立法。在生效后10年,英国政府委任的以 Bruce Harris 先生领导的工作小组作出检查,也认为没有任何需要改动/改善的地方。但即使是这样的立法,还是带来不少先例。举例说在 Cetelem SA v. Roust Holding Ltd (2005) 2 Lloyd's Rep. 494 先例,有关解释该立法之 Section 44 有关法院在仲裁庭还没有成立前作出“中间措施”(interim measure)的协助,到底能到什么程度。立法的条文是:

“44. (1) Unless otherwise agreed by the parties, the court has for the purposes of and in relation to arbitral proceedings the same power of making orders about the matters listed below as it has purposes of and in relation to legal proceedings.

(2) These matters are

(a) the taking of the evidence of witnesses

(b) the preservation of evidence

(c) making orders relating toproperty which is the subject of the proceedings or as to which any question arises in the proceedings

(i) for the inspection, photographing, preservation, custody or detention of theproperty, (对有争议的财产命令作出检查、拍照、保留等,这主要是协助保存证据以供将来仲裁使用。如在货物买卖的双方对提供的货物质量上有争议,就需要马上进行一个检查以防货物被处理后证据流失)or

(ii) ordering that samples be taken from, or any observation be made of or experiment conductedupon, the property

and for that purpose authorizing any person to enter any premises in thepossession or control of a party to the arbitration

(d) the sale of anygoods the subject of the proceedings(下令把货物出售)

(e) the gathering of an interim injunction or the appointment of receiver.

(3) If the case is one of urgency, the court may, on the application of a party or proposed party to the arbitral proceedings, make such orders as it thinks necessary for the purpose of preserving evidence orassets. (在紧急的情况下,法院可以作出他认为必须的命令保存证据或财产。)

(4) If the case is not one of urgency, the court shall act only on the application of a party to the arbitral proceedings (upon notice to the other parties and to the tribunal) made with the permission of the tribunal or the agreement in writing of the other parties.

. . .”

注意上述加黑的单词/文字针对的都可以翻译为“财产”,特别是“property”与“asset”之间看不出区别。在该先例,争议是这两个单词是否应该同义或是“asset”应该有更广泛的解释。在该上诉庭先例的案情是涉及法院是否在上述立法下,特别是根据 Section 44(3),有权禁止其中一方当事人处理或抛售他的公司股份。法院的这种中间措施权力根据该立法条文必须是为了"保留财产"(for the purpose of preserving assets)。但如果"asset"与"property"同义,法院就没有权力作出这种命令了。上诉庭认为立法故意在该条文选择一个不同的单词"asset"就显示了立法的意图是希望比较早的单词/文字"property"与"goods"有更广泛的解释,所以"asset"不仅是局限在"有形财产"(tangible assets)的保存,也包括了像本案例的公司股份,实际上是涉及一个"合约的权利"(contractual right)的无形财产。Clarke 大法官是这样说:

"However, the question is one of construction and freezing order as an order of the injunction of the language of section 44(3), construed in its context[2]. Can it fairly be said that an order of this kind could be necessary for the preservation of assets. I have reached the conclusion that it can.

Mr. Dunning(被禁止一方当事人的代表大律师) correctly accepts that 'assets' are not limited to tangible assets but include, for example, choses in action[3]. That is evident, both because section 44(2) refers to 'property' and 'goods', so that 'assets' must be wider than both and because the classic freezing injunction freezes bank accounts, which, when in credit, evidence choses in action. It seems to me that, **once it is accepted that 'asset' includes 'choses in action' there is no reason to limit them to particular types of chose in action.** There may be some other reason for limiting the operation of section 44(3) but **I do not see any reason why a contractual right should not be an 'asset' within the meaning of the subsection.** Further, given the fact that the purpose of section 44(3) is to permit orders for the preservation of assets, and given the limitations on the operation of the subsection, namely that it can only be invoked (a) when 'the case is one of urgency' and (b) when the judge thinks that it is 'necessary' to make the order, it seems to me that in this context there is **no good reason for construing the meaning of 'assets' narrowly.**"(加黑部分是笔者的强调)

2.6 标准格式合约条文/文字的解释应否考虑个别案件的本质说法

在 Glynn v Margetson (1893) AC 351 先例,Herschell 勋爵提到使用标准格式海上运输合约(在该先例涉及提单),印本条文是设计给各式各样的航次而不是某一个特定的航次,所以解释一条十分广泛的"绕航条文"(deviation clause)就不能漠视该特定航次与租约的本质与目的。

但说到在标准格式合约应否考虑个别案件的本质,Millett 勋爵在 A. I. B. Group (UK) v. Martin (2001) U. K. H. L. 63 先例中有很明确的说法:"A standard form is

---

〔2〕 这是根据本质来解释,但主要这里讲的"本质"是该文件的本质或是严格来说是该 Section 44(2)的内部本质或上下文,而不理会外来的背景或语境。

〔3〕 无形资产。

designed for use in a wide variety of different circumstances. It is not context - specific. Its value would be much diminished if it could not be relied upon as having the same meaning on all occasions. **Accordingly the relevance of the factual background of a particular case to its interpretation is necessarily limited.** The danger, of course, is that a standard form may be employed in circumstances for which it was not designed. Unless the context in a particular case shows that this has happened, however, the interpretation of the form ought not to be affected by the factual background."(加黑部分是笔者的强调)

Millett 勋爵的说法是标准格式合约的拟定是为了被用在广泛(或普遍性)但会各有不同的情况下。所以它根本不会也没有办法理会个别交易的本质。如果在不同本质/案件的事实下给出不同解释,会令这一份标准格式合约的价值减少甚至失去,因为肯定性/可循性肯定受到影响。故此解释标准格式合约在某一个特定案件,应该局限考虑背景/语境。但危险是一个标准格式合约会被使用在一个不是其设计适用的情况。除非是在某一个案件中这一种情况/本质能够被证明,否则解释一个标准格式合约是不应该受事实背景的影响。

从上述的说法中,可为 Glynn v. Margetson 先例自圆其说的解释是有关航次只是一个很短的航次与装运的货物是容易腐烂的橙子,但是标准格式的提单合约是设计普遍适用在不同航次(包括长航次)与不同货物(包括容易腐烂或不会腐烂的货物),印上了一条十分广泛的绕航条文,几乎可世界各地漫游后才卸港,是完全不适用。这可作为 Millett 勋爵所讲的例外情况,所以说法之间没有矛盾。

2.7 标准格式有肯定性/可循性先例下商业人士可以更改合约条文或行动补救的做法

在订约自由下,这种做法完全可以。这已经在较早前多次提及,不必再重复。这里的障碍又是同一个老问题,就是订约方(特别是来自发展中国家)往往没法通过订约自由更改(或抗拒更改)有关的合约条文/文字保护自己的利益。

针对一个对有关标准合约条文的解释不令人满意的先例更改合约条文的例子多不胜数,而且这是一个持续性的游戏。可先以一个船东与承租人士非常熟悉的情况作为例子,就是期租下的承租人不准时支付租金而导致船东有了选择权或自由终止合约与撤船。这是在著名与全球最广泛被使用的期租合约标准格式 NYPE 1946 的第 5 条如下:"otherwise failing the punctual and regular payment of the hire ... the Owners shall be at liberty to withdraw the vessel from the service of the Charterers ..."

首先解释"准时支付"(punctual payment)的"准时"。从一般的字义看,只要比最后的期限晚了 1 分钟也不算是准时。至于"支付"也在许多先例有了权威性解释,因为今天有各种不同的银行付款方式。例如,如果电汇一笔租金而其有效日期是要 4 天后船东才能动用这笔钱,这就不能算支付了:The "Chikuma" (1981) 1 Lloyd's Rep. 371 先例。接下 NYPE 1946 的第 5 条的"惯常支付"(regular payment)这一词也有权威性解释,这里包括了足数,即该付的租金是多少就应该付多少,承租人不能随便付1元钱就可以了事。

如果承租人做不到这一严格的承诺,船东就有了选择权或者自由可撤船。在航运市场波动十分厉害时,尤其是在航运市场不断高涨的年代,船东如果被一个廉价与租期较长的租约所束缚,可以说是每天做梦也希望承租人会"技术性违反"(因为承租人不会有意违反,这是一个对其有很大价值的租约)这一个承诺而给其机会可以撤船。英国有许多这方面的著名先例,都明确了法律为了追求肯定性/可循性而对这NYPE这一条条文作出严格的字面解释,也不会作出其他的救济,如"合约因轻微延误被没收财产/丧失合约的救济"(Relief against forfeiture)。[4] 笔者在这里介绍两个著名先例,第一个是有关准时支付的:The "Brimnes" (1974) 2 Lloyd's Rep. 241。在该先例租金应付的期限是1970年4月1日,承租人通过他的伦敦银行支付给船东在纽约的银行。该伦敦银行在纽约银行是有一个美元的账号,所以可以直接电汇支付船东的账号。但在出事情的一次,承租人的伦敦银行是通过其在纽约的关系银行另开了一张银行本票给船东的美国银行账号,这可被称为间接支付办法。但反正是直接或者间接支付,在该出事的一次就晚了一点时间,是在船东选择终止租船合约后的20分钟才支付到船东的账号。但上诉庭严格依照NYPE 1946的第5条作出解释认为没有准时支付租金而船东有权撤船。

第二个是贵族院的The "Chikuma"先例,看来对被终止租约的承租人更加不公平与不合理。案情是法院判定即使租金只少付了几十美元,亦不算是全数支付,船东仍有权撤回船舶。承租人原本已准时汇往船东银行,但由于双方银行均为意大利银行,它们之间有一个不为外人知道的协议,会把受益人可自由提款的日期推迟了几天。船东虽然当天亦可提取,但要支付约50美元的费用予银行。船东早就想撤船,就根据银行会扣约50美元的费用而指称承租人没有准时全数支付租金而撤船,如大部分这种的案例,这明显是船东的借口,因为市场大涨后希望从亏本或者赚得少的长期租约中脱身。事后,在仲裁庭判船东败诉,但最终的贵族院判船东胜诉,判决的不肯定明显可见。但贵族院既然讲了话,这就是先例也是最后一句话,就是该付的租金一点都不能少,没有所谓 *de minimis* 的优待。

在贵族院 Bridge 勋爵强调了肯定性(或者是可循性)的重要并引述了 Salmon 勋爵在 The "Laconia" (1977) 1 Lloyd's Rep. 315 先例的说法,如下:"Certainty is of primary importance in all commercial transactions."

接下来 Bridge 勋爵讲了一些重要的话,就是说船东与承租人之间有同等的谈判力量与水平,无法强迫对方做不愿意的事情。他们也有水平照顾自己的利益,也可不接受他们不愿意的合约条文。对一份普遍在使用的标准格式合约(这是指 NYPE 1946)来说,这肯定性/可循性是更加重要。法律有了清楚与肯定的合约解释,就可以

---

[4] 这方面可看本书第十章之6.2段。

让使用这些标准格式的商业人士知道自己的地位,有了争议寻求法律意见也可以很快与很准确地得到,甚至不必投身在一个漫长与昂贵的诉讼希望最终法院会是同情自己。所以,法院一定要坚持这些清楚与一致的大原则与合约解释,并拒绝根据个别案件的是非曲直东摇西摆。Bridge 勋爵的著名发言英文版已在本章较早的 2.4 段有节录,不再重复。

笔者认为这是一个非常正确的理念,因为对整个商业体系而言,有了这种明确而且对一方(承租人)不利的判决后,只要该方当事人是有谈判的力量与水平,就很快会发展出反击与保护自己的做法。这种做法就是在 NYPE 1946 的期租合约中作出更改,笔者马上就可以想得出 10 种以上的不同做法,如以下的例子:(1)将第 5 条文的一句,就是给船东有选择权或者是自由撤船删掉。(2)在第 5 条文针对船东有选择权或者自由撤船后多加一句说:"但必须是在船舶空载的时候。"(3)加上一条附加条文说:"本租约第 5 条文的'准时支付'是允许承租人在期限之后 3 天内支付。只要在 3 天后的期限支付了,本租约下也算是准时。"(4)加上一条附加条文说:"只要承租人准时支付了 90% 该付的租金,就当作是本租约第 5 条文的'惯常支付'。"

更加普遍的做法是承租人发展起来的以另一条附加条文作出针对,这就是要求船东遇上承租人没有作出准时与惯常支付租金时,就必须行使选择权,在撤船前先给出一个通知才能撤船。有了这个通知,承租人就不会在不知情的情况下被船东撤船,而且允许承租人根据通知作出及时补救。租船市场很快就接受了这种做法,导致今天的期租合约,不论是否以 NYPE 1946 为基础,都会加入一条名为"反技术取巧通知条文"(anti – technicality clause)。这也不仅是个别或多数承租人这样做,连 BIMCO 这种船东组织也拟定了类似的标准格式条文供大家使用。例如在 BIMCO Non – Payment of Hire Clause 的有关之处如下:"(b) The Owners shall notify the Charterers in writing within 24 running hours that the payment is overdue and must be received within 72 running hours from the time hire was due. If the payment is not received by the Owners within the number of running hours stated, the Owners may by giving written notice within 12 running hours withdraw the Vessel."

此外,NYPE 的新版本也已经作出了修改,这就是在 NYPE 1993 第 153 – 158 行订明了这一条反技术取巧通知条文,说:"At any time after the expiry of the grace period... while the hire is outstanding, the Owner shall, without prejudice to the liberty to withdraw, be entitled to withhold the performance of any and all of their obligations hereunder and shall have no responsibility whatsoever for any consequences thereof, in respect of which the Charterers hereby indemnify the Owners, and hire shall continue to accrue and any extra expenses resulting from such withholding shall be for the Charterers' account."

以上只谈到对个别或标准格式条文的更改对抗不满意的英国法院针对标准格式合约/条文解释的一些做法,承租人了解英国法律针对准时支付租金的严格性在行动上也可以作出恰当应对。例如,大可以在市场上涨时尽量提早支付,不要作出任何扣减以保证足数支付等。这样,承租人有不少武器来对付,又何愁英国法院在这一方面判得严格呢?难怪有说法是不肯定的法律是最不公平的法律。

所以可作出总结,即法院为了肯定性/可循性而严格解释 NYPE 1946 标准格式的第 5 条文看来是牺牲了个别案件的承租人,但很快商业社会或个别人士就会通过案例的公开报道知道英国法院定下的大原则与合约解释而作出相应对策,令这方面的不公道(对承租人而言)很快被消除。整个游戏规则的框架也是这样建立起来的。

§3 其余解释规则之二:整体解释商业合约的结果应该尽量合理

这一解释合约的主要规则也应该可以理解,即整体解释合约的结果应该尽量合理。这种情况特别是合约内的条文/文字有含糊之处,可以有两个或以上的解释。起点是因为订约双方应该被假设是希望达成一个公平合理的合约,而不会是一个可笑或荒谬的合约,这尤其是针对理性与现实的商业人士。这里可举以下的权威说法与个别案件的案情加深理解:

1. 在 Tillmanns & Co v. S. S. Knutsford Ltd (1908) 2 K. B. 385 先例,Farwell 大法官说:"In a mercantile document or a statute there is a presumption that business men do not intend to do anything absurd, which is some slight guïde; but in all cases it is a matter of construction."

2. 在澳大利亚的 Australian Broadcasting Commission v. Australian Performing Right Association Limited (1973) 129 CLR 99 先例,Gibbs 大法官说:"It is trite law that the primary duty of a court in construing a written contract is to endeavour to discover the intention of the parties from the words of the instrument in which the contract is embodied. Of course the whole of the instrument has to be considered, since the meaning of any one part of it may be revealed by other parts, and the words of every clause must if possible be construed so as to render them all harmonious one with another. **If the words used are unambiguous the court must give effect to them, notwithstanding that the result may appear capricious or unreasonable, and notwithstanding that it may be guessed or suspected that the parties intended something different.** The court has no power to remake or amend a contract for the purpose of avoiding a result which is considered to be inconvenient or unjust. **On the other hand, if the language is open to two constructions, that will be preferred which will avoid consequences which appear to be capricious, unreasonable, inconvenient or unjust**, 'even though the construction adopted is not the most obvious, or the most grammatically accurate', ... Further, it

will be permissible to depart from the ordinary meaning of the words of one provision so far as is necessary to avoid an inconsistency between that provision and the rest of the instrument. Finally, the statement of Lord Wright in Hillas & Co. Ltd. v. Arcos Ltd, that the court should construe commercial contracts ' fairly and broadly, without being too astute or subtle in finding defects', should not, in my opinion, be understood as limited to documents drawn by businessmen for themselves and without legal assistance."(法律明确就是法院在解释一份文书合约时的主要责任就是从双方用的文字中找出他们的订约意图。当然整份合约都需要整体考虑,也有部分的意图要看其他部分才能被发现。条文的每一个文字在如果可能的情况下都应该与其他合约的条文/文字协调,**如果文字不含糊,法院必须给其效力,即使解释的结果看来是反复无常或不合理,或法院估计或怀疑双方实际上有不同的意图但表达错误。但如果文字上可以有两个以上的解释,就必须选择一个结果是不会反复无常、不合理、不方便或不公平,即使其他的解释在文字或文法上更明显/准确。**但正如 Wright 勋爵所说,解释商业合约不要刻意挑毛病或含糊之处。)(加黑部分是笔者的强调)

3. Tito v Waddell (No. 2) (1977) Ch 106 先例是一个十分著名的案件,据说最终去了国际法院。涉及的案情很复杂,在这里只简单介绍与本小段有关的部分。案情涉及 1900 年在太平洋的 Banaba 小岛上发现了磷矿。当时该岛是英国的殖民地,于是英国政府给了一家英国公司采矿的专属授权。该公司之后又与小岛上的土著订立采矿的合约,相关合约有条文如下:"The company should return all worked - out lands to the original owners, and should replant such lands - **whenever possible** - with coconuts and other food - bearing trees, both in the lands already worked out and in those to be worked out."(英国公司会把所有采光了磷矿的土地还给原土地所有人,并会在**任何可以做得到的情况下**在该土地种植椰子树与其他有食用价值的树木……)

这一条文带来争议,代表土著利益的一方说"做得到的情况"(possible)字义上很清楚,但代表英国公司的一方说这一文字只代表"合理的可行"(reasonably practical)"合理的努力"(reasonably endeavour)。Megarry 大法官判是英国公司的解释被接受,说:

"I think that such phrases have to be construed in a reasonable sense when they are contained in business transactions intended to have legal effect. Today there are very many things which can be achieved, but only with a vast expenditure of time and effort and money. Because they can be achieved in this way they are literally ' possible'; but in a business document intended to have practical effect, the parties are unlikely to have contemplated an obligation to do something which is altogether outside the range of the practicable and reasonable merely because they use the word ' possible'."(Megarry 大法官认为这些文字要合理解释,特别是在一个商业的交易。在今天的科技,很多东西都可以做到,但会涉及大量的金钱与时间。这样在一个商业合约用上"做得到的情

况”,订约双方不大可能有订约意图就是不可行的也必须做得到。)

4. 在 The “Aragon” (1977) 1 Lloyd’s Rep. 343 先例,涉及一个期租租约,但是允许承租人营运的航区规定:“... always within Institute Warranty Limits East Coast Canada, **USA East of Panama Canal**, UK Continent Gibraltar - Hamburg Range, Mediterranean ...”

承租人要求船舶去美湾装粮去欧洲,但船东拒绝,理由是美湾港口如查尔斯顿、休斯敦与新奥尔兰等在经度上是在巴拿马运河以西,不是以东。但对航运了解的人士都把美国分为东岸与西岸,贯穿(东岸西岸或西岸东岸)就要经过巴拿马运河。对许多航运人士来说,虽然这不足成为习惯,巴拿马运河以东的港口应该是包括美湾。所以在美湾的查尔斯顿、休斯敦与新奥尔兰港口,都被视为在美国东岸的港口,也在租约的允许航区内。但对非航运的一般人来说,东或西是指经度。结果在英国高院与上诉庭,都判承租人胜诉,在经度而言是有点东西不分了。这里也反映了 Diplock 勋爵在 The “Antaios” (1985) A. C. 191 先例所说的,如果解释不符合商业合理性,就要排斥这种解释了。

当然,在订约自由下,如果在此案例中船东在订约时多加一句“以经度为准”,变为“USA East of Panama Canal, ... base on longitude”,而承租人也接受。这样,解释起来就应该是船东胜诉了,因为必须要给“以经度为准”一定的解释。

5. Diplock 勋爵在 The “Antaios”先例中说:“... if detailed semantic and syntactical analysis of words in a commercial contract is going to lead to a conclusion that flouts business common sense, it must be made to yield to business common sense.”(如果文字上的分析会带来一个结果是失去了商业常识,就必须屈从商业常识。)

6. Warner 大法官在 Datastream International Ltd. v. Oakeep Ltd (1986) 1 W. L. R. 404 先例中认为如果起争议的合约条文/文字可以有两个解释,一个比另一个更合理,就应该选择它,说:“Faced with that choice as to the meaning of the word, ... I prefer the meaning that does not produce an unreasonable and unfair result, ...”

7. 另在 Glofield Properties Ltd v. Morley (No. 2) (1989) 2 E. G. L. R. 118, CA 先例中 Nourse 大法官说:“... the question is whether [the judge] was also correct in deciding that the parties have clearly and unequivocally expressed an intention in the sense for which the plaintiff contends. If they have not, it is open to the court to construe their language in such a way as to produce the more sensible and realistic commercial result.”

8. 在 Laura Investment Co Ltd v. Havering London Borough Council (1993) 1 EGLR 124 先例,Hoffmann 大法官说:“This would be an uncommercial thing to do. It might be the consequence of the express language of the lease or the clear presumption of construction ... In a question such as this, however, where one has to deduce the intention of the parties from all circumstances ... I think one is free to assume that they in-

tended a fair and commercial result rather than an unfair one."

9. 在 Cargill International SA v. Bangladesh Sugar and Food Industries Corp. (1998) 1 WLR 461, CA 先例，Potter 大法官说："On the other hand, modern principles of construction require the court to have regard to the commercial background, the context of the contract and the circumstances of the parties, and to consider whether, against that background and in that context, to give the words a particular or restricted meaning would lead to an apparently unreasonable and unfair result."

10. Steyn 勋爵在 Society of Lloyd's v Robinson (1999) 1 All E. R. (Comm) 545 先例中说：

"Loyalty to the text of a commercial contract, instrument or document read in its contextual setting is the paramount principle of interpretation. But in the process of interpreting the meaning of the language of a commercial document the court ought generally to favour a commercially sensible construction. The reason for this approach is that a commercial construction is likely to give effect to the intention of the parties. Words ought therefore to be interpreted in the way in which a reasonable commercial person would have construed them and the reasonable commercial person can safely be assumed to be unimpressed with technical interpretations and undue emphasis on niceties of language."

11. 在 Kazakstan Wood Processors (Europe) Ltd v. Nederlandsche Creietverzekering Maatschappij NV (2000) CLC 822, CA 先例，Peter Gibson 大法官说："The court is entitled to look at those consequences because the more extreme they are, the less likely it is that commercial men will have intended an agreement with that result. But the court is not entitled to rewrite the bargain which they have made merely to accord with what the court thinks to be a more reasonable result, and the best guide to the parties' intentions remains the words which they have chosen to use in the contract."

12. 在 Hayward v. Norwich Union Insurance Ltd. (2001) 1 All ER (Comm) 545 先例，Peter Gibson 大法官说："It is always permissible to test whether words have a given meaning by considering whether they produce an unreasonable result if they have that meaning. The more unreasonable the result, the less likely it is that the parties intended the words to have that meaning."

13. 在 The "Resolute" (2009) 1 Lloyd's Rep 225 先例，案情涉及一艘渔船的保险。该保险合约有一条承诺性保证条文，说："Warranted Owner and/or Owner's experienced skipper on board and in charge at all times and one experienced crew member."（船东雇佣的有经验的船长所有时间都在船上负责，并加上一个有经验的船员。）

但在一次捕鱼回来船上的 4 个人包括船东自己都离开了船舶，让该渔船挂靠在泊位，并没有人看管。这种情况在渔船以及游艇经常发生，如果在期间出了意外会带来争议。该渔船在期间由于发电机继续运作而发生了火灾,保险公司以渔船船东违反了该承诺性保证条文而拒赔。上诉庭认为该条文有含糊之处:(1)该条文针对有经验的船长与有经验的船员,显然是针对渔船在海上航行的时间,而不是所有的时间,虽然条文是这样写;(2)含糊也包括了与合约其他条文一并解释,就是另有第26条文说明承保的范围或情况,这包括渔船在抛锚、靠泊、在允许航区内航行、在泊位搁浅、维修保养需要渔船在船厂被吊起与下水等。这样肯定在某些情况如搁浅或被吊起时,不可能有有经验船长与有经验船员在渔船上。所以有了含糊,Clarke大法官就以针对规则解释说:"In these circumstances, in accordance with the principles summarised above, the clause should be construed *contra proferentem*, that is against the insurer."

14. 在Barclays Bank Plc v. HHY Luxembourg SARL (2010) EWCA Civ. 1248先例,上诉庭的Longmore大法官说:"If a clause is capable of two meanings, as on any view this clause is, it is quite possible that neither meaning will flout common sense. In such circumstances, it is much more appropriate to adopt the more, rather than the less, commercial construction."

在这里顺便一提的是,读者会经常听到"免责条文"(exception clause)会受到比其他条文更严格的解释,这就是如果合约有两个解释,就会选择一个针对免责条款获利方的解释,而不是选择一个客观看比较合理的解释。免责条文会稍后在本章之第5段与本书第十二章之第1段进一步针对。

§4　其余解释规则之三:双方同意不合理事情必须用清楚无误的条文/文字

在订约自由下,双方可以约定完全不合理的事情,如通过一条不合理的"免责条文"(exception clause),无辜方反而要承担错误方(由于他或他的雇员的疏忽)所造成的损失。这种完全不合理的条文也可以出现在其他方面的条文,不一定只是免责条文。但由于这是不太可能的合约意图,双方必须以清楚无误与肯定的条文/文字表达才能支持这个解释。

4.1　权威的说法

正如Reid勋爵在Schuler (L) A. G. v. Wickman Machine Tool Sales Ltd (1973) 2 Lloyd's Rep. 53先例中所说:"The fact that a particular construction leads to a very unreasonable result must be a relevant consideration. The more unreasonable the result the more unlikely it is that the parties can have intended it, and if they do intend it the more necessary it is that they shall make that intention abundantly clear."(这是一条经常被引用的主要解释规则,说解释条文/文字会带来一个不合理的结果肯定是一个考

虑因素。越不合理的结果就表示越不可能是双方在订立合约时的共同订约意图。而如果这的确是他们的订约意图,就必须把这一意图写得清清楚楚。)

在该先例,Morris 勋爵也说:"Subject to any legal requirements, businessmen are free to make what contracts they choose but unless the terms of their agreement are clear a court will not be disposed to accept that they have agreed something utterly fantastic. If it is clear what they have agreed a Court will not be influenced by any suggestion that they would have been wiser to have made a different agreement."(商业人士完全自由订立他们选择的合约,但除非条文/文字十分清楚明确,法院不会接受他们同意一些十分荒谬的东西。而如果合约是清楚明确,法院不会受到双方应该更明智作出不同约定的说法的影响,毕竟法院不是订约方。)

在 Persimmon Homes (South Coast) Ltd. v. Hall Aggregates (South Coast) Ltd. (2008) EWHC 2379 (TCC)先例,Coulson 大法官说:"Where a particular construction may produce an unfair result, the court will often require clear words to support the construction in question."

在 Best Beat Ltd. v. Mourabt & Co Trustees Ltd (2008) EWHC 3156 (Ch)先例,Patten 大法官说:"there is, I think, a danger in attributing too easily to the parties a different intention from the one expressed in the language used in the interests of arriving at what (with the benefit of hindsight) may appear to be a commercially fair solution."(这是警告法院/仲裁庭不要为了表面看来是商业上比较公道,就轻易强加双方当事人一个与文字表达不一样的订约意图。)

在 Thompson & Anor v. Goblin Hill Hotels Ltd. (2011) UKPC 8 先例,Dyson 勋爵说:"... the plain and ordinary meaning of the words used ... can only be displaced if it produces a commercial absurdity."(只有在结果会带来商业上的荒谬时,才能否定合约文字的表面与一般性意思。[5])

最后一提的就是所谓的"红手规则"(red hand rule),但这个规则主要针对消费者。红手规则来自 Denning 勋爵在 J Spurling Ltd v. Bradshaw (1956) 1 WLR 461 先例中说:"... the more unreasonable a clause is, the greater the notice which must be

---

[5] 在 Lewison 大法官所著的《The Interpretation of Contracts》(第5版,2011年)一书第404页,认为这个要求太高。Lewison 大法官在该书的第五章说除了荒谬外,也可以根据内部矛盾(这可看本书第三章之第2段与第4段)或与合约目的相悖(这可看本书第十二章之1.7.4段)调整甚至否定合约文字的表面与一般性意思。这说法来自被称为解释合约的"黄金规则"(golden rule)与已经有超过150年历史的 Wensleydale 勋爵在 Grey v Pearson (1857) 6 H. L. Cas. 61 先例的说法:"... in construing ... all written instruments, the grammatical and ordinary sense of the words is to be adhered to, unless that would lead to some absurdity, or some repugnance or inconsistency with the rest of the instrument, in which case the grammatical and ordinary sense of the words may be modified, so as to avoid that absurdity and inconsistency, but no farther."

given of it. Some clauses which I have seen would need to be printed in red ink on the face of the document with a red hand pointing to them before notice could be held to be sufficient."

显然,这是法院敌视在针对消费者合约中不合理的条文/文字的一种做法。在1977年有了《不公平合约法》(《Unfair Contract Terms Act》)以成文法对消费者进行保护后,红手规则也就没有作用。针对商业合约中的不合理条文/文字主要或唯一的要求就是写得清楚无误,只能有一个解释。

4.2 什么是清楚无误/肯定的条文/文字会是法院/仲裁庭的印象

文字上清楚无误/肯定与含糊/不肯定已经提了不少,其中在本书第三章之第12段详细针对了怎样算是肯定与否的种类等。另在较早段节也说到这方面在解释合约的区别,包括含糊或不肯定应该找一个合理的解释。但如果清楚无误/肯定就应该给有关条文/文字所表达的意思,即使这会带来不合理的结果。但在一些"边缘"(borderline)的案件,区分什么是肯定与否的合约条文/文字并不容易。毕竟如果双方都有高水平的代表大律师,他们都有话说。所以在很多时候,这取决于法院/仲裁庭的主观印象。很有可能对一位仲裁员是清楚无误,但对另一位仲裁员是含糊。正如Sterndale勋爵在Ambatielos v Anton Jurgen Margarine Works (1922) 13 Lloyd's Rep. 357先例中,说:"... it is very difficult indeed to say what is ambiguous and what is not, and I do not think any test can be applied except that of the person who is dealing with it. If it does not seem ambiguous to him I am afraid he can only say 'It may seem ambiguous to others, but it does not to me."

也有许多其他的说法有关法院/仲裁庭的主观印象,如下:

1. 在Welsh v Greenwich London Borough Council (2001) 81 P & CR 12先例,Robert Walker大法官,说:"questions of construction are frequently a matter of impression and are not readily susceptible of precise explanation."

2. 在Designers Guild Ltd v Russell Williams (Textiles) Ltd (2000) 1 WLR 2416先例,Hoffmann勋爵说:"When judges say that a question is one of impression, they generally mean that it involves taking into account a number of factors of varying degrees of importance and deciding whether they are sufficient to bring the whole within some legal description. **It is often difficult to give precise reasons for arriving at a conclusion one way or the other** (apart from an enumeration of the relevant factors) and there are **borderline cases over which reasonable minds may differ.**"(加黑部分是笔者的强调)

3. 在Ashville Investments Ltd v Elmer Contractors Ltd (1989) QB 488先例,Balcombe大法官说:"As on any question of construction the issue is incapable of much elaboration: it is a matter of **how the words strike the reader.**"(加黑部分是笔者的强调)

4. 在 Norwich Union Life Insurance Society v British Railways Board (1987) 2 EG-LR 137 先例,Hoffmann 勋爵(他当时还是大法官)说:"The use of ordinary language to convey meaning often involves subtle discriminations which for most people are intuitive rather than capable of lucid explanation. An explanation of why ordinary English words in a particular context convey a given meaning is frequently more likely to confuse than to enlighten. Perhaps this is what judges mean when they say that questions of construction are often matters of impression."

5. 对一些特别困难作出解释的商业合约,对有商业背景/知识的法院或仲裁庭也经常会受到客观看有关的条文/文字所得出的第一个印象。在本书第六章之 2.3.12 段介绍的 The "Karen Oltmann" (1976) 2 Lloyd's Rep. 708 先例,案情涉及一个期租合约。Kerr 大法官这样说:"At this stage I am therefore left with my first impression, but without being able to pray in aid anything concrete or substantial which justifies my preference for this construction. I would expect it to be shared by brokers on the Baltic Exchange and by lawyers whose work brings them into frequent contact with charter-parties. On the other hand, others may equally firmly form the opposite impression..."

但在 The "Green Island" (2010) 2 Lloyd's Rep 1 先例,Neuberger 勋爵警告根据主观印象来解释可以是一件危险的事情,说:"First impression can be a dangerous guide to meaning: it is liable to be subjective, it is normally impossible to explain, and it not infrequently turns out to be wrong. However, as the purpose of interpretation is to work out what meaning the words in question convey, the initial impression they make on the tribunal charged with interpretation is often of relevance — not least in a case such as this, where the recipient of the document concerned will, in practice, read its provisions pretty quickly (if at all)."

4.3 解释"一次过"合约条文/文字的不肯定/不可预测

根据主观印象来解释合约,有可能会造成诉讼的结果不可预测,正如 McLauchlan 教授在《Contract Interpretation: What Is It About?》(2009) 31 Sydney Law Review 5 一文感叹说:"The outcome of interpretation litigation is notoriously difficult to predict. This is partly because questions of interpretation are often seen as 'matters of impression' or intuition, and inevitably the way in which judges mentally process language and apply it to the facts will vary according to their background and experience. Even so, the division of opinion that one finds in the cases is remarkable. Time and again judges will disagree on such elementary questions as whether particular words have a plain meaning and what is the 'commonsense' or 'commercially realistic' interpretation."(解释合约的诉讼经常会带来难以预测的结果。部分原因是解释也经常是涉及法官的印象或感觉,他们的思维方式显然会受到不同的背景与经验的影响而有不一样的结果。他们的不同意见在一些案件十分显著。经常不同的法官对一些很基本

的问题有疑义,如某一个文字是否有一个表面的意思或/与什么是符合常识或商业现实的解释。)

法官的主观印象在解释商业还有一个危险,就是他们不一定有这方面的经验或足够经验判断是否涉及"商业的荒谬"(commercial absurdity)或"商业常识"(commercial commonsense)。这种说法也有不少,在 The "World Symphony" (1992) 2 Lloyd's Rep 115 先例,上诉庭的 Donaldson 勋爵说:"... arguments based upon apparent commercial absurdity need to be regarded with caution not least because, whilst Judges of commercial experience are in a position to make some evaluation of the benefits and burdens of liberties and limitations contained in a charter - party, they are unlikely to be able to evaluate the countervailing burden or benefit of a particular rate of hire or length of charter, which depends upon current market conditions and because the alleged absurdity of a particular provision has to be judged in the context of the whole package. Maritime arbitrators in day to day contact with the market place are in a different position."

另是在 Skanska Rashleigh Weatherfoil Ltd v Somerfield Stores Ltd (2006) EWCA Civ 1732 先例,Neuberger 大法官说:"... it seems to me that the court must be careful before departing from the natural meaning of the provision in the contract merely because it may conflict with its notions of commercial common sense of what the parties may must or should have thought or intended. Judges are not always the most commercially - minded, let alone the most commercially experienced, of people, and should, I think, avoid arrogating to themselves overconfidently the role of arbiter of commercial reasonableness or likelihood."

正如 Donaldson 勋爵在上述节录中所说的最后一句话,仲裁员会对有关市场或商业做法有更大的认识,会比法院的主观印象更准确。这也是其他一些著名法官的说法,如 Denning 勋爵。但这也需要当事人对仲裁员的选择正确,现实中有不少当事人与他的代表律师挑选仲裁员还是退休法官或资深律师,根本不理会其对有关的商业是否熟悉。

这里的危险尤其是在"一次过"(one off)的合约的解释,已经在本章之第 2 段有过介绍,英国法院针对标准合约的解释要求尽量不要偏离已有的先例。但针对一次过的合约,有说法是解释时要考虑其不同的事实背景/语境,因此有不少英国法院的判决不鼓励对一次过的合约解释遵循先例,任由审理的法官自由发挥。这些权威说法也很多,只节录一个笔者认为有很明确说法的 Aspden v Seddon (1874) L. R. 10 Ch. App. 394 先例:"**No Judge objects more than I do to referring to authorities merely for the purpose of ascertaining the construction of a document; that is to say, I think it is the duty of a Judge to ascertain the construction of the instrument before him, and not to refer to the construction put by another Judge upon an instrument,**

perhaps similar, but not the same. The only result of referring to authorities for that purpose is confusion and error, in this way, that if you look at a similar instrument, and say that a certain construction was put upon it, and that it differs only to such a slight degree from the document before you, that you do not think the difference sufficient to alter the construction, you miss the real point of the case, which is to ascertain the meaning of the instrument before you. It may be quite true that in your opinion the difference between the two instruments is not sufficient to alter the construction, but at the same time the Judge who decided on that other instrument may have thought that that very difference would be sufficient to alter the interpretation of that instrument. You have, in fact, no guide whatever; and the result especially in some cases of wills, has been remarkable. There is, first, document A., and a Judge formed an opinion as to its construction. Then came document B., and some other Judge has said that it differs very little from document A.—not sufficiently to alter the construction—therefore he construes it in the same way. Then comes document C., and the Judge there compares it with document B., and says it differs very little, and therefore he shall construe it in the same way. And so the construction has gone on until we find a document which is in totally different terms from the first, and which no human being would think of construing in the same manner, but which has by this process come to be construed in the same manner."(加黑的部分是说没有其他的法官像 Jessel 法官一样反对解释合约要看其他先例。即其他法官怎样解释一份文件,即使该份文件是十分相似但不完全一样。这样解释合约只会带来混乱与错误。)

法官或仲裁员有太大灵活性与裁量权自由发挥作出合约解释带来的不肯定/不可预测也因为整个做法十分“矫揉造作”(artificial)。现实中往往是双方(或至少其中一方)在订约时根本没有想到或全面想到的问题,所以没有以清楚的明示条文/文字针对,并带来含糊。但法院/仲裁庭就硬要找出一个解释说是他们双方的订约意图,结果往往是胜诉方无所谓,败诉方就会说这根本不是他的订约意图,也肯定不是双方的订约意图。这方面可节录 Chadwick 大法官在 Bromarin v IMD Investments Ltd (1999) STC 301 先例中的说法:“It is not, to my mind, an appropriate approach to construction to hold that, where the parties contemplated event 'A', and they did not contemplate event 'B', their agreement must be taken as applying only in event 'A' and cannot apply in event 'B'. The task of the court is to decide, in the light of the agreement that the parties made, what they must have been taken to have intended in relation to the event, event 'B', which they did not contemplate. That is, of course, **an artificial exercise, because it requires there to be attributed to the parties an intention which they did not have (as a matter of fact) because they did not appreciate the problem which needed to be addressed.** But it is an exercise which the courts have been willing to undertake for as long as commercial contracts have come before them for construction. It is an exercise which requires the court to look at the whole agreement which the parties made, the words which they used and the circumstances in which they used them; and to ask what should reasonable parties be taken to have intended by the use of those words in that agreement, made in those circumstances, in relation to this event which they did not in fact foresee."(加黑部分是笔者的强调)

在伦敦仲裁,在1996年《仲裁法》与所谓The "Nema" Guideline下,仲裁庭对合约的解释,特别是一次过的合约条文/文字,几乎没有可能取得上诉的批文。这样,可以说伦敦仲裁员对一次过合约的解释会比法院更加可以自由发挥,因为法院的判决至少要公开。这样,也就可以明白在本书第六章之第14段介绍的针对中国船厂作出的不利裁决的解释,即有关造船合约[与日本造船格式(The Shipbuilders' Association of Japan,简称SAJ Form)十分相似,但肯定是有附加条文及其他更改导致有不同之处]的不可抗力条文中兜底的一句"or other causes beyond the control of the BUILDER or of its sub-contractors"是包括船东的过错与违约,虽然笔者无法认同,但也是无可奈何。

解释合约的不肯定与不可预测的问题也包括了在本书第一章与第六章谈到的解释合约的新趋势,即解释合约必须考虑"背景/语境"(background/factual matrix)。这表示要涉及大量的"外来证据"(extrinsic evidence)与事实的认定。这会导致法院/仲裁庭对合约的解释更加不肯定/不可预测,如双方争议的有关事实作出认定会无可避免地受到审理法官/仲裁员的偏向性、文化差异等的影响。由此可见,英国法律一直引以为傲的肯定性/可循性,真正分析只能说是局限在标准格式合约的解释与法律的默示(本书第七章之第3段),这在现实的情况中不多。

§5 其余解释规则之四:针对规则

针对规则(*Contra Proferentem*)是一个经常被适用的解释规则或解释合约的主要规则,其拉丁文写法是"*omnia praesumuntur contra proferentem*",英文的写法是"everything is presumed against the one who proffers",中文意思是"任何事情都是针对获利的一方来解释"。

5.1 适用的两种情况

在Youell v. Bland Welch & Co Ltd (1992) 2 Lloyd's Rep. 127先例,上诉庭的Staughton大法官说到这一解释规则会适用在如下的两种情况:"There are two well-established rules of construction, although one is perhaps more often relied on with success than the other. The *first* is that, in case of doubt, wording in a contract is to be construed against a party who seeks to rely on it in order to diminish or exclude his basic obligation, or any common law duty which arises apart from the contract. The *second* is that, again in the case of doubt, wording is to be construed against the party who proposed it for inclusion in the contract: it was up to him to make it clear. ”

另在 BHP v. British Steel (2000) 2 Lloyd's Rep. 277 先例,Evans 大法官说:“It is common ground that the rule of construction known as *Contra Proferentem* operates against the respondents for two reasons. *First*, they rely upon the clause to exclude or to limit the liability alleged against them, and *secondly*, they were responsible for introducing during the negotiating process the particular parts of the clause on which they now rely. This therefore is the first reason why the meaning of the words should be scrutinized with particular care before holding that they achieve either of these results. ”

这两种情况之一如果有任何含糊之处(如条文/文字有多个解释),就会针对想依赖它来减轻或豁免其基本合约义务或普通法责任(如疏忽的责任)的订约方[“获利方”(proferens)]解释。这种条文也就是一般所理解的“免责条文”(exception clause)。情况之二是如果有任何疑问,就要针对谁建议或拟定把有关条文/文字加在合约内的订约方(也会算是获利方),因为是他的责任说清楚。这也带来了一个说法就是谁拟定合约条文,就会在作出解释时针对他。正如 Binnie 大法官在 Co - operators Life Insurance Co v Gibbens, 2009 SCC 59 (Supreme Court of Canada)的加拿大先例中说:“Whoever holds the pen creates the ambiguity and must live with the consequences. ”

5.2 情况之一:免责条文的获利方

有关免责条文将会在本书第十二章之第1段有详细针对,在这里只做简单介绍。首先一提的是,传统针对免责条文的解释是有很大敌意,包括 Mitchell (George) (Chesterhall) Ltd v. Finney Lock Seed Ltd (1983) Q. B. 284 等先例中“扭曲解释”(strained construction),与先考虑免责条文以外的其他合约条文确立的是什么责任,然后才独立针对该免责条文看它是否能够对该责任提供一个抗辩:Rutter v Palmer (1922) 2 KB 87 等先例。但这种分开来解释免责条文的传统做法现在应是完全被否定,已经有无数的权威先例与说法是解释免责条文应该与其他合约条文一样,整个合约一并与总体解释:Swiss Bank Corporation v Brink's Mat Ltd (1986) 2 Lloyd's 79 等先例。主要的改变是自从保护消费者的1977年《不公平合约法》(《Unfair Contract Terms Act》)生效后,在 Photo Productions Ltd v. Securicor Transport Ltd (1980) 1 Lloyd's Rep. 545 先例敌视与扭曲解释免责条文的做法正式告终。其中 Diplock 勋爵认为1977年《不公平合约法》生效后已经可以保护英国法律希望保护的弱势群体(消费者),一般的商业合约由完全可以照顾自己利益的人士作出自我保护的谈判并达成一个都接受的合约。他们完全可以决定将来合约履行的风险应该怎样最好与最经济作出分摊。法院/仲裁庭不应该作出干预,对免责条文作出一个扭曲的解释。

但即使是现代对免责条文的解释方法,一旦有含糊之处,还是会根据针对原则作出针对获利方的解释。这可节录澳大利亚高院的 Darlington Futures Ltd v Delco Australia Pty Ltd (1986) 61 ALJR 76 先例(英国法律也是同样),如下:"... the interpretation of an exclusion clause is to be determined by construing the clause according to its natural and ordinary meaning, read in the light of the contract as whole, thereby giving due weight to the context in which the clause appears including the nature and object of the contract and, where appropriate, construing the clause *contra proferentem* in case of ambiguity."(这是说免责条文的解释与其他条文一致,就是根据条文/文字的自然与一般性意思并配合合约的语境与本质/目的整体解释。唯一不同之处是,如果免责条文有含糊之处,就会针对免责条文的获利方作出解释。)

举例说合约中经常会有的免责条文,如果想对一方当事人或他的雇员所造成的疏忽或过错免责,就必须写清楚,也就是相关的条文/文字只能得出一个自然与一般性的解释。例如,写明疏忽可以免责就是无可疑议的写得清清楚楚。但如果不清楚,也就是该条文/文字可以有两个解释,就会选择针对获利方的解释。如对"火灾"(fire)免责,这可以有两个解释,一是没有疏忽或过错而引起的火灾,二是疏忽或过错引起的火灾。这样,只写明"火灾"一词的免责条文是被解释为不包括获利方的疏忽或过错引起的火灾:Hollier v. Ramble Motors (A. M. C.) Ltd (1972) 2 Q. B. 71 先例。但如果文字上改成是"火灾,无论如何引致"(fire, howsoever/whatsoever caused),这就很可能包括依赖一方的疏忽或过错了。但更加肯定的写法是"火灾,即使是订约方的疏忽或过错所引致"(fire, even if it is caused by the negligence/default of the contractual party),这就完全明确包括依赖一方的疏忽或过错了。再否定的话,就变成违反本书第三章之第1段的另一个重要解释规则,即要给合约每一个双方约定的文字有一定的解释,这些文字就是"即使是订约方的疏忽或过错所引致"。有关这些方面会在本书第十二章之第1段有关免责条文有更详尽的针对。

5.3　情况之二:拟定合约条文/文字的获利方

在这种情况适用针对规则的原因有不少说法,首先可节录在 Houghton v Trafalgar Insurance Co Ltd (1955) 1 QB 247 先例,Somervell 大法官说:"If there is any ambiguity, **since it is the defendants' clause**, the ambiguity will be resolved in favour of the assured."(加黑部分是笔者的强调)

另是在 Tam Wing Chuen v Bank of Credit and Commerce Hong Kong Ltd (1996) 2 BCLC 69 先例,Mustill 勋爵说:"... the basis of the *contra proferentem* principle is that **a person who puts forward the wording of a proposed agreement may be assumed to have looked after his own interests**, so that if the words leave room for doubt about whether he is intended to have a particular benefit there is reason to suppose that he is not."(加黑部分是笔者的强调)

但看谁草拟的说法不适用在一些订约双方通过谈判共同草拟的合约条文/文字,换言之,不是看谁草拟第一稿,而要看整个过程是否你来我往地作出了大幅修改。这方面在 Kleinwort Benson Ltd v. Malaysia Mining Corporation Berhad (1989) 1 Lloyd's Rep. 556 先例,Hirst 大法官说:"... The rule that a document should be construed *contra proferentum* only applies where the wording is ambiguous. Here, for reasons explained below, I do not find this wording in any way ambiguous, so the question does not even arise. However, if it had, I should not have been prepared to hold here that the plaintiffs were the proponents. Originally it was proposed that the defendants should undertake the drafting, and although in the end the plaintiffs provided the first draft, this was in fact amended by the defendants before the wording reached its final form. **This was thus essentially a joint drafting effort.**"(加黑部分是笔者的强调)

问题是,这方面的轻重也不容易掌握。首先,如果太容易倾向针对草拟的订约方,就会带来一个问题——谁还肯草拟?另一个更重要的现实就是,双方只要有谈判,就几乎肯定会有一定程度的你来我往。非草拟方一句话也不说就全盘接受草拟方的合约条文/文字的情况绝无仅有。这样,会否已算是"共同草拟"(joint drafting effort)而变为不再适用针对规则?笔者可以介绍一个曾经经历过的仲裁案件。有关交易是由一家律师草拟所有的谈判中合约草稿,包括最后被双方签署的一稿。但该律师所是由订约一方所委任与支付所有费用,所以其效忠对象可想而知。另一方没有律师代表也没有人懂法律,但却相信草拟合约的律师所是一家香港著名的律师所,而且在谈判时双方关系良好。在谈判中,该没有律师代表的订约方也提出了对草拟合约的小部分内容的看法与更改,只是看来作用不大,并体现了一些粗糙甚至是错误理解。到出了争议,就有了针对规则是否适用的问题。反对的一方(也就是聘用律师的一方)认为签署的合约是共同草拟的结果。笔者只说在3人的仲裁庭内,大家看法也有很大不同。

还有的两个问题是:(1)这一情况会混淆谁是拟定合约方与谁是获利方,他们不一定相同;(2)在双方有争议谁是拟定合约方或双方共同草拟会需要看双方谈判证据,这又会涉及本书第三章之14.3段与第六章之2.5.1段介绍的"谈判除外规则"(negotiation exclusion rule)。针对第二个问题,在 Lewison 大法官所著的《The Interpretation of Contracts》(第5版,2011年)一书第364页说:"... may be countered by the argument that inquiry into the drafting process is being undertaken merely for the purpose of identifying an objective fact known to both parties, namely who drafted the clause. Such an inquiry does not therefore infringe the rule that evidence of negotiation is inadmissible for the purpose of identifying the subjective intentions of the parties."

还有更不明朗的情况是曾经有香港先例说非草拟的一方如果睁着眼睛签署,就不再适用针对规则。这是在 Mak Kee Ltd. v Sam Woo Bore Pile Foundation Ltd (HCSA 4/2002, 2002年5月15日)先例,委任大法官张举能的说法如下:"In the present case, there is no dispute that the confirmation letter was drafted by the Defendant. But in my judgment, this provides insufficient justification for allocating the risk of any ambiguity in the drafting to the Defendant. Whilst on the one hand the Defendant drafted the letter, on the other the Claimant signed it without making any alteration. In a sense, both parties were responsible for the resulting ambiguity in their agreement. If a party who drafts something should be careful with the words he uses, equally, so it seems to me, the party who chooses to sign something prepared by his counterpart should pay careful attention to the wording chosen by the other side before he writes his signature on the document."

这样会否代表"针对规则"的第二种情况根本在商业合约的现实中不多适用?合约拟定在许多的案件中都会存在不平衡的情况,如订约一方相对水平高与/或有律师代表,并草拟合约。但另一方水平有限(如部分中国公司)却也有对该草拟的合约提过少量修改,并最后出现在双方最后签署的合约内,会否因为是共同草拟或睁着眼睛签署令针对规则再也不适用?

最后一提的是,商业上常用的标准格式合约(没有大的更改),由于是有关商会而不是合约双方拟定,所以有说法是不适用针对规则。在 Tersons Ltd v Stevenage Development Corporation (1963) 2 Lloyd's Rep 333 先例,上诉庭的 Pearson 大法官说:"The General Conditions are not a partisan document or an 'imposed standard contract' as that phrase is sometimes used. It was not drawn up by one party in its own interests and imposed on the other party. It is a general form, evidently in common use, and prepared and revised jointly by several representative bodies including the Federation of Civil Engineering Contractors. It would naturally be incorporated in a contract of this kind, and should have the same meaning whether the one party or the other happens to have made the first mention of it in the negotiations."

5.4　适用在特定本质与类别的合约或订约方的身份的例子

根据以上所讲的两种适用情况,可以举一些因为"交易的本质与类别"(the nature or type of transaction)与"订约方的身份"(the status of the parties)会适用针对规则一个解释规则的例子。

5.4.1　例子之一:保险合约

这里可节录 Gerard McMeel 教授所著的《The Construction of Contracts—Interpretation, Implication and Rectification》(2007 年)一书之 6.27 段如下:"Contracts of insurance Insurance policies are traditionally drafted by the companies which issue them, and have often been strictly construed in favour of the insured. Indeed it has been said that the *Contra Proferentem* rule 'strongly applies' to such contracts. Contracts of life insurance are similarly construed *Contra Proferentem*, that is against the life office issuing the policy and in favour of the life assured."(保单传统是由保险公司拟定,所以要针对他们来解释。)

保险合约(contract of insurance)方面的先例有很多,如:

1. 在一个船舶保险合约的先例 Birrell v Dryer (1884) 9 App. Cas 345, Watson 勋爵说:"That the underwriters may be rightly held to be the proferentes with regard to many conditions in a policy I do not doubt; whether they ought to be so held depends, in each case, upon the character and substance of the condition. In the present case there are many considerations which lead to the inference that the clause in question is not one constructed and inserted by the appellants alone, and for their own protection merely. It was, in point of fact, inserted in the contract by the agent of the respondents; and it is in form a warranty by them that their vessel will not be navigated in certain waters, a matter which it was entirely within their power to regulate. These considerations point rather to the respondents themselves being the proferentes; but I think the substance of the warranty must be looked to; and that, in substance, its authorship is attributable to both parties alike."

2. 在 Cornish v Accident Insurance Co (1889) 23 QBD 453 先例, Lindley 大法官说:"In a case on the line, in a case of real doubt, the policy ought to be construed most strongly against the insurers; they frame the policy and insert the exceptions. But this principle ought only to be applied for the purpose of removing a doubt, not for the purpose of creating a doubt, or magnifying an ambiguity, when the circumstances of the case raise no real difficulty."

3. 另是在 Dodson v Peter H. Dodson Insurance Services (2001) 1 Lloyd's Rep 520 先例,案情涉及汽车保险, Mance 大法官说:"At the end of the day, and after some hesitation, we have come to the conclusion that it is more important to re - enforce the message that insureds are entitled to clear wordings and to the benefit of any ambiguity, than to force the present particular policy wording (and probably other policy wordings in future) into an artificial mould dictated by legal authority. If any insurer does not like our decision, it can for the future formulate its policies differently, provided that it makes its intention clear. Indeed, we would consider it desirable that motor insurers should in any event - and whatever such intentions may be - ensure that their intentions on the present point are made express in their wordings - to avoid yet further disputes and decisions in the series currently ending with this judgment."

5.4.2 例子之二:担保合约

有关"担保合约"(guarantee agreement)与"补偿合约"(indemnity agreement)的不同之处,本书第五章之6.6.1段有介绍。担保合约是受1677年《欺诈法》(《Statute of Frauds》)之 Section 4 管制,必须是文书形式并经过签署才有效。传统解释该文件是严格针对"债权人"(creditor)与善待"担保人"(guarantor),理由是担保合约只是一方获利:Nicholson v. Paget (1832) 1 C & M 48 先例。

目前在英国法律的地位看来也是相同,笔者可以节录《Law of Guarantees》(第6

版,2012年)一书之4-002段部分所说如下:

"There is a substantial body of authority which indicates that contracts of suretyship are to be construed in the same way as any other contract.[6] However, there are also numerous cases at the highest level which support a rule that contracts of this kind must be strictly construed so that no liability is imposed on the surety(担保人)which is not clearly and distinctly covered by the terms of the agreement. Thus in Blest v Brown (1862) 4 De G. F. & J. 367 at 376, Lord Campbell Stated:

'It must always be recollected in what manner a surety is bound. You bind him to the letter of his engagement. Beyond the proper interpretation of that engagement you have no hold upon him. He receives no benefit and no consideration. He is bound, therefore, according to the proper meaning and effect of the written agreement he has entered into.'[7]

Indeed, there are many judicial dicta which go so far as to suggest that guarantees are to be construed in favour of the surety: see for example, the observations of Bayley B. in Nicholson v Paget (1832) 1 Cr & M. 48 at 52, Donaldson J. in General Surety & Guarantee Co v Francis Parker Ltd (1977) 6 BLR 16 at 21, and Lord Oliver in Coghlan v SH Lock (Australia) Ltd (1987) 8 NSWLR 88. However this is probably not an independent rule of construction, but merely a reflection of the effect usually produced by the strict construction approach coupled with the application of the *contra proferentem* rule in cases of ambiguity. The usual result of the application of that rule is that the construction which is more favourable to the surety will be adopted, because in most cases, the terms of the contract will have been drafted by the creditor.[8] However, the *contra proferent-*

---

[6] 如 Mayer v Isaac (1840) 6 M. & W. 605; Wood v Priestner (1866) L. R. 2 Ex. 66; Eshelby v Federated European Bank Ltd (1932) 1 KB 254; Static Control Components (Europe) Ltd v Egan (2004) 2 Lloyd's Rep 429; ING Lease (UK) Ltd v Harwood (2007) EWHC 2292; Associated British Ports v Ferryways NV (2009) 1 Lloyd's Rep 595; Fairstate Ltd v General Enterprise & Management Ltd (2010) EWHC 3072 (QB)等英国先例。澳大利亚的类似先例有 Reid Murray Holdings Ltd (in liq) v David Murray Holdings Pty Ltd (1972) 5 SASR 386; SH Lock Discounts & Vredits Pty Ltd v Miles (1963) VR 656; Craig v Finance Consultants Pty Ltd (1964) NSWLR 1012 等。另可见新西兰的 Krtolica v Westpac Banking Corporation (2008) NZHC 1; Nlack v ASB Bank Ltd (2011) NZHC 703 等先例,与新加坡的 Standard Chartered Bank v Neocorp Ltd (2005) SGHC 43 等先例。

[7] 类似的先例还有 Straton v Rastall (1788) 2 Term Rep 366; Bacon v Chesney (1816) 1 Stark 192; Wheatley v Bastow (1855) 7 De G. M. & G. 261; Stamford, Spalding & Boston Banking Co v Ball (1862) 4 De G. F & J 310; Eshelby v Federated European Bank Ltd (1932) 1 KB 254; Eastern Counties Building Society v Russell (1947) 1 All ER 500 与澳大利亚的 Jones v Mason (1892) 13 NSWLR 157 等。

[8] 有许多类别的担保是由债权人拟定,如银行向个别客户作出借贷,就会要求他个人或他的亲人/朋友作出担保并作为担保人。

en rule will not be used to impose an interpretation on a contract which was clearly not intended. ”

5.4.3 例子之三:安抚函

经常会是一家集团背后的母公司向第三人作出一份安抚函(letter of comfort),并希望第三人会安心与它的子公司交易或作出信贷,如果在该安抚函有法律效力可以让第三人将来作出索赔,本质上就会与担保合约相似。在本书第二章之6.2段介绍过的 Kleinwort Benson v. Malaysia Mining Corporation (1989) 1 Lloyd's Rep. 556 先例,就是一个典型的例子,不重复。问题是如果担保合约的本质上是适用针对规则,则安抚函到底是何地位。笔者可节录 Gerard McMeel 教授的《The Construction of Contracts - Interpretation, Implication and Rectification》(2007年)一书之6.31段说:"In Kleinwort Benson v. Malaysia Mining Corporation the courts were faced with determining the status of a 'letter of comfort' furnished by a parent company to a bank which was providing finance to one of its subsidiaries. The original draft of the letter was prepared by the bank (although the bank had originally suggested that **the parent company undertake the drafting**). **The ultimate letter was the same in its essentials. The parent company submitted the resulting document should be strictly construed against the bank. This was rejected by Hirst J** who stated that the rule only applied where the words were ambiguous, which he did not think was the case. Furthermore, he thought the circumstances were more suggestive of a 'joint drafting effort'. **In contrast, the Court of Appeal did refer to the fact that the first draft was produced by the plaintiff bank**. A minor change in wording by the parent company was of no significance. **The principle of *contra proferentem* was applicable**, and if the bank required express words of promise it could have said so. In any event, the Court of Appeal would have reached the same conclusion were it a true joint effort. The remainder of the letter would have been superfluous had the crucial paragraph had the effect contended for by the bank."(MMC 争议说安抚函应该针对 KB 的银行解释,这在高院被拒绝,认为该文件的条文/文字没有任何含糊,所以针对规则不适用。加上高院认为该文件是双方都参与草拟,最后文件是属于双方努力的成果。但这在上诉庭被推翻,因为该文件草稿是先由 KB 提供给 MMC,然后 MMC 作出少量修改而已。如果 KB 希望 MMC 提供一个承诺而不是泛泛的安抚,就应该在文件中写清楚,所以上诉庭认为即使文件是双方努力的成果,仍要适用针对规则针对 KB 作出解释。)

5.4.4 例子之四:批地契约

在批地契约(deed of grant),法律一直十分明确是要针对"转让方"(grantor)作出解释。

在 Johnson v Edgware &c Railway Co (1866) 35 Beav 480 先例,Romilly 大法官说:"... It is to be observed, that all deeds are to be construed most strongly against the grantor."

在 Neill v Duke of Devonshire (1883) 8 App. Cas 135 先例,Selbourne 勋爵也说:"It is well settled that the words of a deed, executed for a valuable consideration, ought to be construed, as far as they properly may, in favour of the grantee."

另是在 Savill Brothers Ltd v Bethell (1902) 2 Ch. 523 先例,Stirling 大法官说:"It is a settled rule of construction that, where there is a grant and an exception out of it, the exception is to be taken as inserted for the benefit of the grantor, and to be construed in favour of the grantee."

5.4.5 例子之五:消费者合约

这种合约在本质上适用针对规则是因为有立法规定,这是在 1999 年英国《Unfair Terms in Consumer Contracts Regulations》中,说:"If there is a doubt about the meaning of a written term, the interpretation which is most favourable to the consumer shall prevail but this rule shall not apply in proceedings brought under regulations 12."

这条文实质上与针对条文十分类似,在 Peabody Trust Governors v Reeve (2008) 43 E. G. 196 先例,Gabriel Moss QC 大法官说:"This rule in the Regulation appears to be analogous to the domestic English law principle of *contra proferentem* which is normally to the effect that in the case of ambiguity a document is construed against the party putting it forward."

5.4.6 例子之六:特定合约条文

特定的合约条文也会适用针对规则作出解释,其中最著名的就是"免责条文"(exception clause),这会在本书第十二章之第 1 段详细针对。涉及免责条文的重要先例很多,近期就有 Amax International Ltd v Custodian Holdings Ltd (1986) 2 EGLR 111; Horwood v Land of Leather Ltd (2010) EWHC 546 (Comm); Steria Ltd v Sigma Wireless Communications Ltd (2008) BLR 79 等。

也会有其他的条文适用针对规则,如一条极端的条文对有关合约的本质作出了根本性的改变。S. I. A. T. v. Tradax (1978) 2 Lloyd's Rep. 470 先例有关一个 CIF 买卖,目的港是 Venice。在买卖合约中有一条由卖家拟定的针对文件的条文说:"If any document whatsoever required to be furnished by Seller is missing or in apparent contradiction with the clauses and conditions of the sale - contract and/or if such document contains errors or omissions of any kind, the Buyer must nevertheless perform and take up the documents ..."

看来这"文件条文"(documents clause)在 CIF 买卖是为了避免买方因市场下跌,以技术性理由指卖方交出的付运文件有缺陷而拒绝接受。针对上述条文,Donaldson 大法官指该条文是极端的,因为完全改变了 CIF 买卖是以文件进行买卖,必须严格针对必须提供有关付运文件的卖方解释,说:"The Tradax (卖方) documents clause is draconian. It is often said that whereas an f. o. b. sale of goods, a c. i. f. sale is a sale of documents. This is not wholly true, but it contains more than a grain of true. This clause alters the whole documentary basis of the contract. As such it is to be strictly construed."

另一种特定的情况是拟定合约条文的一方故意订得含糊。在 Commission for New Towns v. Cooper (Great Britain) Ltd (1995) Ch 259 先例中,Stuart – Smith 大法官说:"it had been deliberately and carefully drafted so as to be ambiguous."(该条文订立的不仅是含糊,而且是故意订得如此含糊。)

5.5　适用该解释规则只在条文/文字上有含糊的情况

首先是重复已经介绍过的,如果条文/文字上清楚无误,就不应该适用针对规则。这可节录 Roundell Palmer 大法官在 Birrell v. Dryer (1884) 9 App. Cas. 345 先例中所说的,如下:"I do not think that the evidence discloses any ambiguity or uncertainty, sufficient to prevent the application of the ordinary rules and the principles of construction... There does not appear to me to be any necessity for resorting to presumptions in favour of or against either party, whether founded on the rule *fortius contra proferentem*, or on the onus of proving an exception from the general affirmative terms of this contract."

另 Cohen 大法官在 Parkinson v. Barclay Bank Ltd (1951) 1 K. B. 368, CA 先例中说:"[Counsel] pressed us with the maxim that a deed must be construed *contra proferentem*. But if, applying the ordinary principles of construction, we arrive at a clear conclusion as to what the parties meant by the language which they used, I do not think that maxim comes in to action."

在 Mira Oil Resources of Tortola v Bocimar (1999) 2 Lloyd's Rep 101 先例,Colman 大法官说:"Further, this is not a case where the meaning of the words is so finely balanced that the *contra proferentum* rule should be applied in favour of the owners. If in the view of the Court one of two suggested meanings is significantly preferable to the other, as a matter of construction, it can safely be concluded that the former meaning reflects the mutual intention of the parties."

至于只在合约条文/文字有含糊的情况下(最典型就是条文/文字可以有两个或以上的解释),才能使用针对规则的权威说法也有不少。先介绍 London and Lancashire Fire Insurance Co Ltd v Bolands Ltd (1924) AC 836 先例,Sumner 勋爵说:"It is suggested further that there is some ambiguity about the proviso, and that, under the various well – known authorities, upon the principle of reading words contra proferentes, we ought to construe this proviso, which is in favour of the insurance company, adversely to them. That, however, is **a principle which depends upon there being some ambiguity** – that is to say, some choice of an expression – by those who are responsible for putting forward the clause, which leaves one unable to decide which of two meanings is the right one."(加黑部分是笔者的强调)

另有 St. Edmundsbury and Ipswich Diocesan Board of Finance and another v. Clark

(1975) 1 W. L. R. 468 先例,上诉庭的 Pennycuick 大法官说:"... [*contra proferentum*] *can only come into play if the court finds itself unable on the material before it to reach a sure conclusion on the construction of a reservation. The presumption is not itself* a factor to be taken into account in reaching the conclusion."

5.6　适用该解释规则要谨慎的说法

由于只是在条文/文字有含糊的情况下才适用针对规则,所以要求谨慎。可先介绍一些先例针对不一定真正存在含糊,而只是解释起来比较困难或/与根据其他一般性的合约解释规则就可以找得出答案的情况。首先是 London and Lancashire Fire Insurance Co Ltd v Bolands Ltd (1924) AC 836 先例,Sumner 勋爵说:"... In the present case it is a question only of construction. There may be some difficulty, there may be even some difference of opinion, about the construction, but it is a question quite capable of being solved by the ordinary rules of grammar, and it appears to me that there is no ground for saying that there is such an ambiguity as would warrant us in reading the clause otherwise than in accordance with its express terms."(现在的问题只是解释合约,这会有点困难,甚至审理的法官会有不同看法。但这是一个可以通过一般合约解释规则解决,就不应该说是有含糊并扭曲明确约定条文/文字的意思。)

另在 Direct Travel Insurance v. McGeown (2003) E. W. C. A. Civ 1606 先例,Auld 大法官警告不要太轻易与太早地认定条文的不明确以适用这个原则,他说:"A court should be wary of starting its analysis by finding an ambiguity by reference to the words in question looked at on their own. And it should not, in any event, on such a finding, move straight to the *contra proferentem* rule without first looking at the context and, where appropriate, permissible aids to identifying the purpose of the commercial document of which the words form part. **Too early recourse to the *contra proferentem* rule runs the danger of 'creating' an ambiguity where there is none.**"(加黑部分是笔者的强调,Auld 大法官是说太早适用针对规则会有危险是不自觉地在实际上并不存在含糊时制造含糊。)

另在 PNPF Trust Co Ltd v Taylor (2010) EWHC 1573 (Ch)先例,Warren 大法官说:"The fact that there are difficulties about a point of construction does not mean that there is a doubt or ambiguity of a type to which the *contra proferentem* rule may be applicable. If conventional canons of construction are capable of resolving the issue, they should be applied."(解释困难并不代表有含糊,如果传统的解释规则[在目前法律的地位下也包括考虑订约时的背景/语境]就可以解决,就不该适用针对规则。)

这带来很多英国先例的说法是只有在没有其他更适合的解释规则后,才能适用针对规则:The Olympic Brilliance (1982) 2 Lloyd's Rep 205, CA (usually a rule of, if not last, very late resort); Macey v Qazi, The Independent, January 13, 1987; Johnsey Estates Ltd v Webb (1990) 1 EGLR 80; McCann v Switzerland Insurance Australia

Ltd (2000) HCA 65; Sinochem International Oil (London) Co Ltd v Mobil Sales & Supply Corporation (2000) 1 Lloyd's Rep 339 (construction against the party putting forward a clause is a rule of last resort)等先例。

在上述提到 Johnsey Estates Ltd v Webb 先例,涉及担保合约。在本章较早的5.4.2段已经提到,担保合约的本质导致作出解释是针对债权人与善待担保人。在该先例,判是这不代表一开始就适用针对规则,而是应该先根据担保合约的一般条文/文字作出解释,也不善待担保人。针对规则只是最后才适用的办法。Millett 大法官这样说:"On the other hand the words have to be fairly construed in their context and in accordance with their proper meaning without in any way favouring the guarantor, who is not placed in any more favourable position in this regard than any other contracting party. The so-called rule of construction is very much a matter of last resort."

在英国以外其他的普通法国家也是有同样的说法,首先是澳大利亚的 McCann v Switzerland Insurance Australia Ltd 先例,Kirby 大法官说:"Courts now generally regard the *contra proferentem* rule (as it is called) as one of last resort because it is widely accepted that it is preferable that judges should struggle with the words actually used as applied to the unique circumstances of the case and reach their own conclusions by reference to the logic of the matter, rather than by using mechanical formulae."(针对规则是最后适用。普遍是接受法官应该尽量根据每一个不同案情的独特背景对有关合约条文/文字作出逻辑性的解释,而不是适用一条机械性的公式,也就是针对规则。)

另是一个香港先例 Mak Kee Ltd. v. Sam Woo Bore Pile Foundation Ltd (HCSA 4/2002, 2002年5月15日),委任大法官张举能说法如下:"Expressed shortly, the [*contra proferentum*] rule, which is applicable to the resolution of an ambiguity in an agreement that cannot be resolved by other principles of construction, is that the ambiguity is resolved against the party responsible for putting it forward or benefiting from its inclusion in the agreement. But as emphasized by the textbook authors, this is usually a rule of late if not last resort. The rule can only come into play if the court finds itself unable to reach a sure conclusion on the construction of the provision in question; and the rule is not a factor which may be taken into account in reaching that conclusion..."

一个不把针对规则作为最后适用的例外情况是在英国针对消费者的立法,即1999年的《消费者合约不公平条文条例》(《Unfair Terms in Consumer Contracts Regulations 1999》),根据 Regulation 7 解释消费者的交易时是强制性适用针对规则以保护消费者。

最后一提的是,即使在最后要适用针对规则,法院也提醒审理的法官/仲裁员不得扭曲有关条文/文字,不能只是为了针对获利方把合约内写的"黑"解释为"白"。这方面的先例有 North v Marina (2003) 11 BPR 21 与 Ravi v Logan Wines (2007) NSWCA 62。在前一个先例,Campbell 大法官说:"The role of the maxim is to enable the court to choose between alternative meaning of the document or clause in question, being meanings which are fairly open. It is not a legitimate use of the maxim to say that two meanings of a particular contractual provision are possible, and that the meaning unfavourable to the *proferens* should be chosen, if one of those alternative meanings is an unrealistic or unlikely construction of the contract."

§6　其余解释规则之五：解释合约尽量令它有效而不是无效

合约/条文如果不肯定或含糊，就会带来两个后果。可以导致无法判双方达成一个有效合约，也可以是双方有一个有效的合约，但漠视/删除不肯定/含糊的部分或条文/文字。显然，这种不肯定或含糊达致一个十分严重的地步，就是无法给其一个合理的解释。这可节录 Saville 大法官在 Vitol v Cie. Europeene (1988) 1 Lloyd's Rep 574 先例中的说法："The approach of the English law to questions of the true construction of contracts of this kind is to seek objectively to ascertain the intentions of the parties from the words which they have chosen to use. If those words are clear and admit of only one sensible meaning, then that is the meaning to be ascribed to them – and that meaning is taken to represent what the parties intended. If the words are not clear and admit of more than one sensible meaning, then the ambiguity may be resolved by looking at the aim and genesis of the agreement, choosing the meaning which seems to make the most sense in the context of the contract and its surrounding circumstances as a whole. **In some cases, of course, having attempted this exercise, it may simply remain impossible to give the words any sensible meaning at all, in which case they (or some of them) are either ignored, that is to say, treated as not forming part of the contract at all, or (if of apparent central importance) treated as demonstrating that the parties never really made an agreement at all...**"（加黑部分是笔者的强调）

至于决定是否是双方没有达成有效合约或只是漠视/删除部分主要看不肯定/含糊之处与一个可以有效的合约是否"能分开来"(severable)，如不肯定/含糊只是在一方有权选择之处就可以漠视/删除选择权的条文，但其余的合约或主合约还是有效与可执行。这些问题已经在本书第三章之第 12 段有针对，不重复。在这里只是针对另一条稍有不同的解释规则，就是在不肯定/含糊的情况下，即使十分极端，法院/仲裁庭还是应该尽量令有关/不肯定的合约或条文/文字有效而不是无效（*Ut res magis valeat quam pereat*）。这完整的解释规则的拉丁文写法是"*verba ita sunt interlligenda ut res magis valeat quam pereat*"，其英文写法是"the contract should be interpreted so that it is valid rather than ineffective"。

商业合约经常有不肯定/含糊,Wright 勋爵在 Hillas (W. N.) & Co v. Arcos (1932) 147 L. T. 503 先例中有解释原因说:“Business men often record the most important agreements in crude and summary fashion; modes of expression sufficient and clear to them in the course of their business may appear to those unfamiliar with the business far from complete or precise. It is accordingly the duty of the court to construe such documents fairly and broadly, without being too astute or subtle in finding defect; but, on the contrary, the court should seek to apply the old maxim of English law, *Verba ita sunt intelligenda ut res magis valeat quam pereat.*”

上述的原因也的确现实,许多商业上的协议非常粗糙。有不少商业人士觉得花太多的精力在合约的谈判与在文书合约中选用最恰当与准确的文字表达他们的订约意图是浪费时间。但这种情况不多,大部分的商业活动与最终达成合约是不会涉及律师的。而且,笔者认为 Wright 勋爵所说的只是部分原因,更大的原因是他们的水平。在商业活动,法院/仲裁庭理解合约有不肯定/含糊无可避免,应该尽量支持这种商业合约(特别是已经部分履行),判是有效而不是挑骨头并认为太不肯定/含糊而判是无效。

这方面权威的说法有不少,可介绍如下:

1. 在 Greater London Council v Connolly (1970) 2 QB 100 先例,Denning 勋爵说:“The courts are always loath to hold a condition bad for uncertainty. They will give it a reasonable meaning wherever possible.”

Pearson 勋爵说:“... the courts are always loath to hold a clause bad for uncertainty if a reasonable meaning can be given to it, and it seems to me easy to give a reasonable meaning to this clause.”

2. 在 Brown v Gould (1972) Ch. 53 先例,Megarry 大法官说:“No doubt there may be cases in which the draftsman's ineptitude will succeed in defeating the court's efforts to find a meaning for the provision in question; but only if the court is driven to it will it be held that a provision is void for uncertainty.”

3. 在 Cudgen Ruttle (No. 2) Pty Ltd v Chalk (1973) 49 AJLR 22 先例,Wilberforce 勋爵说:“In modern times the courts are readier to find an obligation which can be enforced even though some apparent certainty may be lacking as regards some term such as the price, provided that some means or standard by which that term can be fixed can be found.”

4. 在 The Tropwind (1982) 1 Lloyd's Rep 232 先例,Denning 勋爵说:“We have on a few occasions rejected a sentence as meaningless, as in Nicolene v Simmonds. But this is only when it is impossible to make sense of it. Rather than find it meaningless, we should strive to find out what was really intended by amending the punctuation, or by supplying words and so forth.”(有少数的情况法院要否定一条条文说是没有意思。

但这只会发生在无法给它任何解释的情况。法院应该尽量以各种办法如改变标点符号、增加一些文字等找出双方真正的意图,而不是认定它没有意思。)

5. 在 Dwr Cymru Cyfyngedig (Welsh Water) v Corus UK Ltd (2007) EWCA Civ 285 先例,Moor – Bick 大法官说:"Where many important terms have been left undecided and the contractual machinery for resolving disagreements is incapable of being operated, it may be impossible to avoid the conclusion that the agreement as a whole is unenforceable because the parties have failed to establish objective criteria capable of being applied by the court itself."(在许多重要的合约条文/文字没有明确作出决定下,是无法启动解释合约的机制来解决这个问题。这样无可避免得出结论是双方的合约整体而言不能执行,因为双方还没有同意一个客观的标准可让法院使用并找出其订约意图。)

6. 在 Whitecap Leisure Ltd v John H Rundle Ltd (2008) 2 Lloyd's Rep 216 先例,Moore – Bick 大法官说:"The conclusion that a contractual provision is so uncertain that it is incapable of being given a meaning of any kind is one which the courts have always been reluctant to accept, since they recognise that the very fact that it was included demonstrates that the parties intended it to have some effect."

接下来笔者可以提单合并进租约的例子来显示这一解释规则的大精神,这问题已经在本书第二章之 8.4.2 段有涉及。在不少短航次,船东与承租人以电文/电邮谈妥了租约后,船舶很快就会开航装港,甚至已经在装港附近等待。装完货物就要签发提单并合并租约条文让提单本身也拥有完整与配合租约的海上运输合约条文/文字,因为提单会稍后通过背书与交出给收货人并成为另一份独立的海上运输合约。但合并的做法往往就是靠在提单印本格式内简单的一句话,甚至从不考虑在提单印本格式的一句话中的空格(目的就是为了让船东与发货人填上合并的租约的日期以明确是哪一份合约)中填上他们想合并的租约。不考虑的原因是在现实中往往也做不到,因为在一些短航次,通常订立租约的时间与签发提单十分接近,普遍的情况是准备装货提单的发货人与签署提单的船长根本不知道关租约的日期与细节。

例如在 The "San Nicholas" (1976) 1 Lloyd's Rep 8 先例中的有关提单印本格式内的简单的一句话是:"This shipment is carried under and pursuant to the terms of the Charter dated ______ at ______ between ______ and ______ as Charterer."但这些空格都没有填上并带来争议是合并条文是否太不肯定/含糊而应该被漠视/删除。

同样的争议也出现在 The "SLS Everest" (1981) 2 Lloyd's Rep. 389 先例。有关提单印本格式内简单的一句是:"Freight and other conditions as per ______ including the exoneration clause."

这在今天船舶普遍转租频密的情况下,由于涉及太多份租约而带来提单中的"不完整"(incomplete)的合并条文更加不肯定/含糊。难怪有一些国家的判决认为没有填上空格明确被合并的一份租约的情况下是无效,如美国的 USA v. Cia Naviera

Continental SA (1962) AMC 2403 先例与 Southwestern Sugar & Molasses Co v. Eliza Jane Nicholson (1955) AMC 746 先例。但这样的判法就马上会面对另一个更大的难题，在这一个提单海上运输合约，双方（船东/承运人与提单持有人/收货人）发生争议时到底是以什么条件为准。毕竟，法律能作出默示十分有限，美国的1936年《海上运输法》（也就是1924年的《海牙规则》）只能针对货损货差的部分问题。船东与提单持有人其他许多的问题，如谁负责卸货、卸货时间与滞期费、留置权、安全泊位/卸港等都是无法解释，因为针对这些问题的明示条文/文字都只是在租约内才会有。

英国在早期的判例 Lignell v. Samuelson & Co Ltd (1921) 9 Lloyd's Rep. 361 中，判是承运人向收货人索赔"滞期费"（demurrage）败诉，因为程租租约（其中有滞期费的计算与费率）并没有被明确合并在提单内。但这个案例早已经被推翻，提单如果是作为船东与提单持有人之间的海上运输合约，就非要有条文/条件不可，否则难以解释他们之间的合约关系以及各自的义务/责任或权利。而且，如果有关双方想一想，在签发提单时合并一份有关租约也肯定是订约意图。所以在许多的案例中，都可以看到英国法院千方百计令提单的合并条文有一个解释，是有效而不是无效，正如本小段介绍的解释规则，如在 The "San Nicholas" (1976) 1 Lloyd's Rep. 8，The "Sevonia Team" (1983) 2 Lloyd's Rep. 641 等先例。其中 Lloyd 大法官在 The "Sevonia Team"先例中说："I turn now to the second main point in the case: which, if either, of the two charter - parties is incorporated in the bill of lading? Mr. Gilman (发货人代表大律师) submitted that the incorporation clause is **so vague and uncertain, that neither of the charters is effectively incorporated.** For that submission he relied on *Amidt v. Tiden* (1874) LR 9 QB 446. But, as the editors of Scrutton (这是当时最权威的海商法书籍) point out in a footnote, **a Court would nowadays hesitate long before reaching that conclusion.** In two recent decisions, the Court of Appeal has held that the bill of lading was effective to incorporate the terms of a charter, even though in each case there were two charters to choose from: see *The San Nicholas* and *The SLS Everest* [1981] 2 Lloyd's Rep. 389"（加黑部分是笔者的强调）

但这一严重的问题还是没有解决，因为今天一个航次与一艘船舶会因为转租而涉及多份租约，其中有不少是期租而不是程租。由于期租合约的条文/文字是针对租用船舶让承租人营运，通常不针对某一个特定航次的货物运输，所以内容完全不适合合并在提单内。在 The "SLS Everest"先例，上诉庭判是英国法律倾向接受提单所合并的租约是"第一份租约"（head - charterparty），因为这是签发或被授权签发提单的船长所知悉的一份。但如果该份租约是期租合约，由于内容不适合合并在一份提单，就会是合并的是"第二份的程租合约"（sub - voyage charterparty）。

但笔者的疑问是如果第二份的分租约也是期租呢？甚至整个租约链中都没有程租合约呢？毕竟，近年来的租船即使是针对一个特定航次的货物运输，也可以以期租方式进行，也就是所谓的"航次期租"（Time - Charter - Trip，或简称 TCT）。往往是这些 TCT 的内容，由于本质上是一个期租合约，也不适合合并在提单内。法院是否会被迫判提单的合并条文太不肯定与含糊，所以是无效？至少在权威的《Scrutton on Charter Parties and Bills of Lading》（第 20 版，1996 年）在 Article 38，Paragraph 1 就认为有这一个可能性，说："the court may conclude, on examining the facts, that the intention was to incorporate the sub – charter [and not the head charterparty]; or even, **in extreme cases, that the bill of lading is so ambiguous as to be void.**"（加黑部分是笔者的强调）

但在今天看来，英国法院/仲裁庭还是努力令提单的合并条文有效，而不是无效。这可以举近期的 The "Vinson" (2005) LMLN No. 677 先例，法院就合并了一个期租合约。而涉及的争议是货损（香蕉）的索赔。由于提单通常是强制性适用《海牙规则》或类似立法（中国就是《海商法》，英美就是《海上运输法》），所以货损的争议还是有默示条文可以解决。但如果换了另一种案情，涉及的争议是运费或滞期费/滞期损失，期租合约根本没有相关的条文/文字，提单合并了期租合约就会无法解释了。

再举第二个能够表达出该解释规则的大精神的例子就是已在本书第三章 5.5 段提过的 The "Saxon Star" (1958) 1 Lloyd's Rep 73 先例，并说明贵族院的判法就是根据这一个解释规则的精神。这就是一份租约中的"首要条文"（paramount clause）可以合并 1924 年《海牙规则》，这也是这一条条文的目的。但《海牙规则》的内容有许多与租约格格不入，甚至说明只适用在提单与不适用在租约。如在 Article 1 之定义条文，对海上运输合约的定义是说："applies only to contracts of carriage covered by a bill of lading or any similar document of title..."

显然租约并非是一份"物权凭证"（document of title）。而定义条文对谁是承运人是说："includes the owner or the charterer who enters into a contract of carriage with a shipper."

这也显然只适用在与发货人订立的海上运输合约，不论这承运人是船东或是承租人。但租约是船东与承租人之间作为订约方，与发货人毫无关系。

所以承认合并有效，就需要大量的篡改与删除不适用部分。贵族院就是这样做以支持订约方加上一条首要条文的明显订约目的（目的是希望针对提单与相关的航次租约在货损货差方面有一致的责任与权利，即都以《海牙规则》为准。这可以避免因为提单与相关租约的责任与权利并不一致，而导致船东与承租人之间需要进行昂贵与耗时的补偿诉讼），并且尽量避免判首要条文无效。

但要尊重本小段的解释规则，即尽量解释不肯定与含糊的约定是有效之余，也不要太过。一过了就会有"重写"（rewrite）双方合约的危险，这在 Hillas (W. N.) & Co v. Arcos 先例 Wright 勋爵有说明，如下："That maxim, however, does not mean that the court is to make a contract for the parties, or to go outside the words they have used, except in so far as there are appropriate implications of law, as for instance, the implication of what is just and reasonable to be ascertained by the court as matter of machinery where the contractual intention is clear but the contract is silent on some detail."

§7 其余解释规则之六:特别针对一件事情但不提其他同类事情

特别针对一件事情但不提其他同类事情(*Expessio unius*)这一解释规则的拉丁文完整写法是"*Expressio unius est exclusio alterius*",英文写法是"The expression of one thing is the exclusion of another"。其意思是如果合约对一些事情已经有特别针对,这就表示没有提到的同种类事情就排除在外。例如,在一个合约内有针对提出索赔一方的各种义务的条文(如及时作出通知,提供某些文件等),其中有一条或一句针对其中一种义务是规定属于先决条件,但其余义务就没有这样规定,这就应该解释为其余条文/义务并非是索赔的先决条件。

笔者可多举几个有关的案例以显示这一解释规则的大精神。第一个是期租合约的先例,名为 The "Tropwind" (1977) 1 Lloyd's Rep. 397。案情是承租人稍微迟延补偿加保费给船东,而因为当时航运市场高涨,船东就借此机会与借口撤船。租约中所针对的条文是 NYPE 46 标准格式之第 5 条文说:"... otherwise failing the punctual and regular payment of the hire, or bank guarantee, **or on any breach of this Charter Party**, the Owners shall be at liberty to withdraw the vessel from the service of the Charterers ..."(加黑部分是笔者的强调)

Kerr 大法官判船东败诉看来主要就是根据这一解释规则(虽然也会有其他考虑,如针对规则、按船东的解释会不符合商业常识[9]甚至对船东取巧的做法有不良印象等),因为这一句之中已经明确针对了不准时与足数支付租金船东就可以撤船,但没有针对同样是属于支付的加保费(或任何其他的费用)。所以即使迟延支付加保费是一种违约,但根据这一解释规则就表示被排除在明示允许船东撤船的条文外。Kerr 大法官是这样说:"It seems to me that the juxtaposition in a forfeiture clause of a reference to 'punctual and regular payment of hire' and the words 'or on any breach of the charterparty' requires the application of the rule of construction *expressio unius est exclusio alterius*... The latter words require to be construed restrictively in their context. They should be read so as to exclude breaches which only consist in delaying some payment beyond the time when it would otherwise be due, in particular when the charter prescribes no time for making the payment in question. The obligation to pay punctually,

[9] 如 Diplock 勋爵在 The "Antaios" (1985) A. C. 191 先例所说,如果解释不符合商业合理性,就要排斥这种解释了。否则从字面解释,租约的"任何违约"(any breach),不论轻重,都可以让船东在一个长期期租合约撤船,就会造成在现实中不可能会有真正的中长期租约了。

and therefore without any delay, is expressly dealt with in the preceding words and is confined to the payment of hire."

第二个先例是古老的 Hare v. Horton (1833) 5 B & Ad 715，这是有关一个"铸造厂"(foundry)与其两个"居住房屋"(dwelling – houses)的抵押合约。合约有说明抵押包括两个居住房屋内的壁炉、锅炉、钟与其他设施。之后双方有争议是铸造厂内的设施是否包括在合约内。Taunton 大法官判是不包括，说："But as the deed goes on to say 'together with all grates, boilers, bells and other fixtures in and about the said two dwelling houses' I think the mention of these fixtures excludes those in the foundry, on the principle '*expressio unius est exclusio alterius*'."

第三个是一个比较近期的案例 Amherst v. Walker (James) Goldsmith & Silversmith Ltd (1980) 254 E. G. 123，涉及一个房屋租赁合约。其一条"租金调整条文"(rent review clause)规定了三个步骤，一是由房东在某一天前给租客通知要调整租金；二是在某一天之前双方同意租金；三是在最后限期不能达成协议就由第三人(由 Royal Institute of Chartered Surveyor 的主席委任)决定是多少租金。其中第二与第三步说明了"时间规定是重要"(time to be of essence)，Bunge Corporation v. Tradax Export S. A. (1981) 2 Lloyd's Rep 1 与 Lombard Norton Central plc v. Butterworth (1987) QB 527 两个重要先例明确了这句话是可以把有关的时间规定提升为"条件条文"(condition)。[10] 双方的争议就是第一步的时间规定是否也属于条件条文，根据本段的解释规则答案明显是不属于，上诉庭的 David Cairns 大法官这样说："... where you have an agreement which specifies the time for doing three things and two of the three are stated to have a time limit which is of the essence of the contract and the other one is not, then it follows that in all probability, where it is not stated that it is to be of the essence, it is not intended to be of the essence. If the parties, when they wish something to be of the essence, say so in terms, then obviously it is of the essence they do say so and probability is that, where they do not say so, it is not intended to be of the essence."

最后一个案例是 London Borough of Dagenham & Barking v. Terrapin Construction Ltd (2000) B. L. R. 479, CA。案情有关一个建造合约，其中第 30 条文是针对建筑师签发的有关工程的"最后证明"(final certificate)。它包括一条 30. 8. 1 条文说该最后证明是针对雇主对材料质量与工艺水平的要求已经满足的结论性证明。但另一条 30. 9 条文说雇主作出支付不代表接受设计、工作、材料或东西是符合合约要求的结论性证明。双方争议的是有关"设计缺陷"(design defect)，而设计只在 30. 9 条提到但没有在 30. 8. 1 条文针对，所以判是 30. 8. 1 条文并不包括设计的缺陷，也就有了建筑师签发的最后证明也非针对设计缺陷的结论性证明。Otton 大法官说："The

〔10〕 针对这方面的详细介绍，可看本书第十章。

fact that within the same clause (clause 30) one sub - clause (30.9) refers to 'design' as a separate and additional category of contractual requirement (distinct from 'works' and 'materials') strongly suggests that the reference in the sub - clause to 30.8 to only the latter two contractual requirements, and the omission of 'design' was deliberate and reflected the intention of the parties."

在此也介绍笔者的一个仲裁,将在本书第十五章有节录。其一个争议是有关装卸时间如何计算,在航运市场高涨的当时,这是十分重要的课题。租约有一句是"假日与周日不算"(Sundays and holidays excluded)在固定的装卸时间,而承租人的主张是周六也不应该算,因为在上海装港周六是"周末假日"(weekend holiday)。但笔者判承租人败诉,其中一个重要理由就是根据本段的解释规则。试想想,如果周六也算是假日,周日就更加肯定是假日了。这样,何必再规定周日不算?笔者看来,解释双方的订约意图应该是假日只是指一些其他非周末的假日,如国庆或新年。

需注意的是,近期有一些说法是这一解释规则要小心适用,并指其好像"假设双方不会约定多余的内容"(presumption against surplusage)的解释原则[11]一样,没有太大帮助或分量。这可节录 Hoffman 勋爵在两个案例中的说法,第一个是 Beaufort Developments (N. I) Ltd v. Gilbert - Ash (N. I.) Ltd (1999) 1 A. C. 266 先例,他说:"This clause has itself been the subject of refined arguments of the *inclusio unius, expressio alterius* variety. ... In a contract such as this, such arguments are just as dangerous as the argument from redundancy, of which they are in truth merely a variety. ..."

第二个是 International Power plc v. Healy (2001) UKHL 20 先例,他说:"This is an argument of the *expressio alterius* variety. I think that such arguments are often perilous, especially when applied to a patchwork document like the pension scheme. The fact that a specific provision is made in one place may throw very little light on whether general words in another place include the power to do something similar. ..."

§8 其余解释规则之七:同类规则

同类规则(*Ejusdem generis*)是针对在一些特定事项的后面的"兜底性语言/文字"(general language/words)或"通称事项"(general item),该兜底性语言/文字会被视为特定事项的同类事项并给与一个局限性的解释,而不会是包罗万有。以下可先节录 Watson 勋爵在 Sun Fire Office v. Hart (1889) 14 App. Cas. 98 先例所讲的:"It is a well known canon of construction, that where a particular enumeration is followed by such words as 'or other', the latter expression ought, if not enlarged by the context, be

[11] 在本书第三章之第6段有详述。

limited to matters *Ejusdem Generis* with those specially enumerated."

这种情况经常会在免责条文中出现，就是有了一连串的特定免责事项后，加上一个兜底性语言/文字作为总结，如"或其他原因"(or any other cause)甚至一个简单的"et cetera"。但除了免责条文，也可以在其他条文出现。如期租合约下局限承租人可以装运的货物或营运的地区、停租条文，国际货物买卖与程租合约对装卸时间的停算事项条文，房屋的租赁合约包括房屋内的一些家具/电器设施，保险合约承保的范围或风险，许多不同类别合约中的不可抗力条文等。

8.1 支持同类规则的原因

支持同类规则的原因在于：

1."假设双方不会约定多余的内容"(presumption against surplusage)——这是一个主要支持的说法，即如果兜底性语言/文字不受局限，在其前面或后面列举的特定事项就变为多余的内容且没有任何意思了。但解释合约是要整体解释与给每一个订约方同意了的文字一定的解释。已经在本书第三章之第6段有介绍"假设双方不会约定多余的内容"的解释规则，是没有太大帮助或分量。这样看来，同类规则也会没有太大的分量。但它肯定还是存在有，上诉庭的Evans大法官在近期并涉及股权买卖合约争议的BOC Group Plc v Genteon LLC (1999) 1 All ER (Comm) 970先例说："Mr Strauss'(卖方的代表大律师)submission that there is no such thing as an *eiusdem generis* rule, particularly in the light of the ICS judgment, in my view goes too far. Admittedly the Latin ought to be replaced by English words and the interests of clarity may well be served by doing so. Maybe it is wrong to regard it as a rule. Sometimes it has been called a maxim or an aid to construction. What cannot be denied, in my view, is that the considerations which underlie it are ones which a reasonable man would take into account as a matter of commonsense. It is perhaps better now to refer to it as a factor which, when it is relevant, cannot properly be ignored."

2.局限解释应该比较接近订约意图——这里可节录Devlin勋爵在Chandris v. Isbrandtsen - Moller Co Inc. (1951) 84 Ll. L. Rep. 347先例所说："The so - called rule is, in short, really only a recognition of the fact that parties with their minds concerned with the particular objects about which they are contracting are apt to use words, phrases or clauses which, taken literally, are wider than they intend. ..."

3.一般认为兜底性语言/文字只是为了避免对特定事项的进一步区分——这可以节录The Thames and Mersey Marine Insurance Co Ltd v. Hamilton Fraser & Co (1877) 12 App. Cas. 484先例中，Macnaghten勋爵所讲的："to prevent disputes founded on nice distinctions. Their office is to cover in terms whatever may be within the spirit of the cases previously enumerated, and so they have a greater or lesser effect as a narrower or broader view is taken of those cases."

例如合约的不可抗力条文包括了下大雨与下大雪的事项，但遇上了雨夹冰雹，就怕有一些争议。如果不可抗力条文有兜底性语言/文字,即使同类规则适用,也可以避免。

8.2 排除同类规则的写法/做法

因为大原则是订约自由,所以如果订约双方不想局限兜底性语言/文字,也就是希望有关的条文有一个更加广泛的解释,把这一解释规则排除在外,最好是以文字说明,如"无论任何"(whatsoever)或"whether or not similar to the foregoing"等。这里可先节录 Devlin 大法官在 Chandris v. Isbrandtsen - Moller Co Inc. (1951) 84 Ll. L. Rep. 347 先例所说的,如下:"Legal draftsmen are all familiar with the existence of the rule, and familiar too with the proper signals to hoist if they do not want it to apply. Phrases such as 'whether or not similar to the foregoing' and 'without prejudice to the generality of the foregoing' are often employed in legal draftsmanship; and if the draftsman has read the report of *Larsen v. Sylvester & Co* he will know the addition of 'whatsoever' generally serves the same purpose."

另 Fry 大法官在 Earl of Jersey v. Neath Union Rural Sanitary Authority (1889) 22 QBD 555 先例中说:"... where you find the word 'whatsoever' following, as it does, upon certain substantives, it is often intended to repel, and in this case does effectually repel, the implication of the so - called doctrine of *ejusdem generis*..."

另在 The "Laconian Confidence" (1997) 1 Lloyd's Rep 139 先例,Rix 大法官说:"Those comments bring me back to consider the phrase 'any other cause' in the light of the authorities. In my judgment it is well established that those words, in the absence of 'whatsoever', should be construed either *ejusdem generis* or at any rate in some limited way reflecting the general context of the charter and clause..."

另一种明确的写法就好像是伦敦食糖商会拟定的买卖标准格式合约(Refined Sugar Association Contract)之第 17 条文的不可抗力条文如下:"*Force Majeure* Should EEC legislation, Government Intervention, ice, war, strikes, rebellion, political or labour - disturbance, civil commotion, fire, stress of weather, act of God or any cause of *force Majeure* (**whether or not of like kind to these before mentioned**) beyond the Seller's control prevent directly or indirectly within the delivery period stated in the contract:..."(加黑部分是笔者的强调)

另可介绍一种写法(有先例支持)是在有关的条文改变次序,就是把兜底性语言/文字放在特定事项的前面,而不是后面兜底。这样,就会有感觉是该兜底性语言/文字变为一句通称,起了主导作用,而后面的特定事项只是举一些例子。在 Ambatielos v Anto Jurgens Margarine Works (1922) 13 Lloyd's Rep. 357 先例,租约中的一条针对不算滞期费的特定事项条文是如下:"Should the vessel be detained by **causes over which the Charterers have no control**, viz., quarantine, ice, hurricanes, blockade, clearing of the steamer after the last cargo is taken over, etc., no demurrage is to be charged and lay days not to count."(加黑部分是笔者的强调)

法院判是同类规则不适用,上诉庭的 Sterndale 勋爵说:"The first difficulty that I feel in applying the doctrine of *ejusdem generis* to this case is that in this case, unlike any other which has been cited to us,... the specific words follow the general words and do not precede them."

针对这一点,贵族院的 Viscount Cave 大法官也说:"I know of no authority for applying that rule to a case of this kind, a case where, to begin with, the whole clause is governed by the initial general words, where, secondly, the expression to be so construed is the expression 'etc.,' and where, thirdly, there is no genus which comprises all the five cases specified other than the genus described in the general words."

最后一提的是排除同类规则,在订约自由的大原则下,可以是千变万化的写法。只是跟从有一些先例肯定的写法或做法,就会在有争议时可以有一些权威性的说法作为支持。正如 Watson 勋爵在 Sam Fire Office v Hart (1889) 14 App Cas 98 先例的说法:"The canon is attended with no difficulty, except in its application. Whether it applies at all, and if so, what effect should be given to it, must in every case depend upon the precise terms, subject - matter, and context of the clause under construction."

8.3　特定事项需要是"同类"才适用同类规则

合约的双方在通常约定一连串的特定事项后加上一个兜底性语言/文字,希望不会有遗漏,通常的原因是为了将来有争议,不会在一些接近的事项作出区分。正如在本章之 8.1 段节录的 Lord Macnaghten 勋爵在 The Thames and Mersey Marine Insurance Co Ltd v. Hamilton Fraser & Co (1877) 12 App. Cas. 484 先例的说法。笔者也觉得这是十分符合人性与商业做法,如双方在谈判与探讨什么情况下可以延误支付一笔钱时,列出了一连串的特定事项,并且这些事项都属于天灾人祸,就表示他们就是在想这类事情可以作为例外。这样如果这一连串的特定事项加上兜底性语言,就不能偏离与天灾人祸同类的事项。

8.3.1　权威说法

这方面有不少权威的说法,只说在 S. S. Magnhild v. McIntyre Brothers & Co (1920) 3 K. B. 321 先例,McCardie 大法官所说如下:"whether the specified things which precede the general words can be placed under some common category. By this [is meant] that the specified things must possess some common and dominant feature."(在兜底性语言/文字之前的特定事项是否属于同一类别,这表示各项特定事项之间一定要拥有一些共同与主要的特征。)

如果在兜底性语言/文字之前只有一项特定事项,这一解释规则仍然适用。在 Foscolo Mango & Co v. Stag Line Ltd (1931) 2 K. B. 48 这一航运十分重要的先例,是有关船舶绕航是否合理。有关的提单合约中允许船舶绕航的条文是:"liberty ... to call at any ports in any order, for bunkering or other purposes, ..."。换言之,唯一明示的特定事项是添加燃油,这通常是与该航次的履行有关的事项。在该先例的绕航是为了让两个在船上作出检查的岸上检验师离船,这与航次履行没有关系,所以不包括在"other purposes"的兜底性语言/文字,并构成不合理绕航。Slesser 大法官说:"On a strict application of the *ejusdem generis* rule it may be argued with some force that to construct a genus out of one species and undefined general words (which together with the species have gone to form the genus) in order to define the denotation of those general words is but a *petitio principii*, but however that may be, on the wider consideration of the intention and context there is ample authority for the view expressed by Hamilton J."

在 Anderson v Anderson (1895) 1 QB 749 先例,Esher 勋爵说:"... *prima facie* general words are to be taken in their larger sense, unless you can find that in the particular case the true construction of the instrument requires you to conclude that they are intended to be used in a sense limited to things *ejusdem generis* with those which have been specifically mentioned before."(起点是兜底性语言/文字是按照字义给其一个宽松的解释,除非在解释有关的文件/合约时得出结论,应该与较早特别针对的事情一并以同类规则作出解释。)

在近期的 BOC Group Plc v Genteon LLC (1999) 1 All ER (Comm) 970 先例,Evans 大法官说:"... with regard to the rule or maxim of *ejusdem generis*, it seems to me that that is a relevant factor in the present case. It might be summarised as follows. The meaning of general words, even 'whatsoever', may be limited by the context in which they appear."(这里重要的是说即使兜底性语言/文字有一个十分广泛的英文字"whatsoever",同类规则还是可以适用。)

8.3.2 什么是"同类"

"同类"(genus)一词是来自自然科学动植物分类中的"属",但在社会科学的层面,包括法律,有说法是不必分得这么精确,McCardie 大法官在 S. S. Magnhild v. McIntyre Brothers & Co (1920) 3 K. B. 321 先例中说:"The phrases of science deal with precise things. The phrases of law deal with matters of ambiguity and cross division."

在 BOC Group Plc v Genteon LLC (1999) 1 All ER (Comm) 970 先例,Evans 大法官对同类的看法也是宽松,说:"They may be used to refer to a class or category, a genus (or what Mr Pollock [买方代表大律师] called a tribe) of which some but not necessarily all the members are identified in the clause."

针对什么是同类,较早前已经有了不少介绍,特别是 Foscolo Mango & Co v. Stag Line Ltd (1931) 2 K. B. 48 先例更是很清楚地分析。在这里笔者只多举一个例子,就是在期租合约的"停租条文"(off – hire clause)。在期租合约,通常时间损失的风险是由承租人承担,因为他需要从交船一天到还船一天不断支付租金给船东。但期间会发生一些涉及船舶或船员的事故导致时间损失,而这些事故与船东的过错无关,所以不会构成违约可让承租人索赔损失。例如,船舶的正常进干坞维修保养、船长突然意外身亡令船舶无法航行直到有新的船长、海上事故等。承租人不愿意承担这些时间损失,所以期租合约都会有一条停租条文明确规定在这种涉及船舶或船员的事故导致时间损失,程租人可以停租。即使这一条停租条文除了针对一连串特定的事项外,还有一个兜底性语言/文字,但也是在许多先例被视为解释必须是按照同类规则。换言之,如果是一些与船舶或船员无关的"外来事项"(extraneous cause),通常不会是停租条文所包括,也就是承租人自己要承担风险。但有不少承租人在近年来都会坚持停租条文的兜底性语言/文字加上一个"whatsoever"以排除同类规则。这带来了不少令人困扰的判决,有兴趣的读者可参阅杨大明律师的《期租合约》一书。

在这里笔者只是针对近年来猖獗的索马里海盗所带来的问题,就是海盗劫持船舶后要收到赎金才会放船,中间的时间可能长达几个月甚至一两年,这段被劫持的时间是否停租?换句话说,被海盗劫持是否属于停租条文中的事项?这一问题带来了好几个仲裁与先例,包括在本章之8.2段提到的 The "Laconian Confidence" (1997) 1 Lloyd's Rep 139 先例与 The "Saldanha" (2011) 1 Lloyd's Rep 187 先例。这些争议都涉及了期租合约最普遍被使用的NYPE标准格式,其停租条文如下:"That in the event of the loss of time from default and/or deficiency of men including strike of Officers and/or crew or deficiency of ... stores, fire, breakdown or damages to hull, machinery or equipment, grounding, detention by average accidents to ship or cargo, dry-docking for the purpose of examination or painting bottom, **or by any other cause preventing the full working of the vessel**, the payment of hire shall cease for the time thereby lost ..."(加黑是笔者的强调)

在 The "Laconian Confidence"先例,Rix 大法官针对该停租条文的同类是说:"In my judgment it is well established that those words [ie, 'any other cause'], in the absence of 'whatsoever', should be construed either *ejusdem generis* or at any rate in some limited way reflecting the general context of the charter and clause ... A consideration of the named causes indicates that they all relate to the physical condition or efficiency of either vessel (including its crew) or, in one instance, cargo. There is, moreover, the general context ... that it is for the owners to provide an efficient ship and crew. In such circumstances it is to my mind natural to conclude that the unamended words 'any other cause' do not cover an entirely extraneous cause, ..."

在两个先例,都判是索马里海盗的劫持属于外来事项,时间损失与船舶或船员的事故无关,所以承租人不能停租。但也有说到是如果在兜底性语言/文字后加一个"whatsoever"就可能会有不同结果。在 The "Saldanha"先例,Gross 大法官是完全同意 The "Laconian Confidence"先例的判决。他也提到了承租人代表大律师的一些争议,部分节录如下:"Against this somewhat unpromising background, Mr Parsons'(承租人代表大律师) carefully constructed argument proceeded as follows. First, even without the additional word ‘whatsoever’, the wording ‘any other cause’ was a sweeping – up provision. That wording was there to prevent ‘disputes founded on nice distinctions’: see, Chandris v Isbrandtsen – Moller Co Inc [1951] 1 KB 240, at pages 246 and 247. Secondly and accepting that the sweeping – up provision was to be construed in some limited way reflecting the general context of clause 15, it was nonetheless not easy to identify any ‘genus’ which included all of the named causes in clause 15. The most that could be said was that they all related to the physical condition or efficiency of the vessel (including its crew) or, in one instance, cargo and did not include truly extraneous causes..."

但最后Gross大法官是判承租人败诉,认为海盗劫持是一个典型的外来事项,不存在与停租条文的特定事项作出区分,说:"With respect, I am unable to accept these submissions. Intuitively, as a matter of indelible impression and in agreement with the tribunal, I think that seizure by pirates is a ‘classic example" of a totally extraneous cause..."

8.3.3 特定事项不属于同类就不适用同类规则的说法

但如果在所有特定事项中找不出它们之间有共同与主要的特征,各有不同的针对,有说法是这同类规则不适用。Vaughan Williams大法官在Tillmanns & Co v S. S. Knutsford Ltd (1908) 2 KB 385 的上诉庭先例说:"if a common genus is not to be found the necessary consequence would be that the words ‘or any other cause’ could not be limited by the doctrine of *ejusdem generis*."

在同一个先例,Farwell大法官说:"Unless you can find a category there is no room for the application of the *ejusdem generis* doctrine."

但看来有一个说法就是即使在特定事项中找不出一个同类,同类原则还是有可能会适用。在Chandris v Isbrandtsen – Moller Co Inc (1951) 84 Ll. L. Rep. 347 先例,Devlin大法官说:"If the *ejusdem generis* principle is a rule of automatic application, it becomes of the first importance to determine exactly what the rule is. If it is merely, as I think, an aid to ascertaining the intention of the parties, no point of controversy need arise at all. If there is something to show that the literal meaning of the words is too wide, then they will he given such other meaning as seems best to consort with the intention of the parties. In some cases it may be that they will seem to indicate a genus; in others that they perform the simpler office of expanding the meaning of each enumerated item. If a genus cannot be found, doubtless that is one factor indicating that the parties did not intend to restrict the meaning of the words. **But I do not take it to be universally true that whenever a genus cannot be found the words must have been intended to have their literal meaning, whatever other indications there may be to the contrary.**"(加黑部分是笔者的强调)

在 Lewison 大法官所著的《The Interpretation of Contracts》(第5版,2011年)一书认为这是一个现代、正确与比较灵活的说法,在第391页说:"It has, however, the great merit of adopting a flexible approach to the interpretation of contracts, rather than a rigid application of prescriptive rules. Since the modern approach to the interpretation of contracts eschews rigid rules, it is thought that this is the right approach."

8.4 对同类规则不认同的说法

对同类规则也曾经有一些不认同或是不友善的说法,如在 Anderson v Anderson (1895) 1 QB 749 先例,Rigby 大法官说:"The doctrine known as that of *ejusdem generis* has, I think, frequently led to wrong conclusions on the construction of instruments."

另是在 Earl of Jersey v Neath Union Rural Sanitary Authority (1889) 22 QBD 555 先例,Fry 大法官说:"[The *ejusdem generis* principle] has often been urged for the sake of giving not the true effect to the contracts of parties, but a narrower effect than they were intended to have."

在笔者近期参与的伦敦的造船合约仲裁案件(这与本书第六章之第14段介绍的是同一类仲裁案件),也有对同类规则不认同或不友善的说法。原因是觉得同类规则太"咬文嚼字"(semantic)与不配合合约整体的解释。而针对合约整体的解释,仲裁员就会有很大的裁量权解释什么是双方的订约意图,正如本章之4.3段提到的仲裁员有了大量的弹性与裁量权会造成解释合约的诉讼经常会带来难以预测的结果。因为在伦敦仲裁的大量败诉给中国的造船业带来了巨大的影响,笔者再针对这一方面进行简单的介绍。简单地说,造船与其他工程一样,经常会发生延误。所以造船合约与工程合约一样,双方会约定一条不可抗力条文针对一些船厂无法控制的特定事项(通常就是一些天灾人祸)造成的延误。在该条文下,只要船厂作出准时与准确的通知,就可以相应延长交船的时间。这种延误通常被称为"允许延误"(permissible delay)。显然,延误也会是来自船厂自己的过错或原因,如工人不足、管理混乱、财政困难、分承建商/供应商的问题等。这些延误显然是不能相应延长交船的时间,而且造船合约通常会有条文约定如果是这些原因造成交船延误,每一天要支付的议定赔偿。这种延误通常被称为是"不允许延误"(impermissible delay)。

最后还会有一些延误是来自船东/买方的过错或原因,造船合约也会有明示条文针对允许延长交船日期与不必支付议定赔偿。但这些明示条文只会针对在造船合约经常会发生的船东/买方的过错或原因造成的延误,如提供的设备延误交付给船厂或延误支付分期预付船价等,而显然不可能也在订约时不可预见船东/买方造成的延误。这在2008年金融海啸后,航运市场暴跌90%,船东/买方想尽任何办法与不择手段从亏本的造船合约中脱身,就会有了一些订约时根本不可预见的非正常手段造成延误。

这带来的争议就是船东/买方的过错或原因造成延误,是否属于不可抗力的条文。船东/买方认为是包括在该条文的一个兜底性语言/文字,而由于船厂从来没有向船东作出延误通知说他错了与什么过错,等于是没有满足先决条文,也就不能依赖该条文延长交船日期。在伦敦仲裁,双方代表大律师都重点对这一同类规则作出争辩。

笔者不妨部分节录该不可抗力条文:"If, at any time before actual delivery, either the construction of the VESSEL, or any performance required hereunder as a prerequisite of delivery, of the VESSEL, is delayed due to war, blockade, revolution, insurrenction, civil commotions, riots, sabotage, lockouts, local temperature higher than 35 degree centrgrade, Acts of God or the public enemy, terrorism, plague or other epidemics, quarantines, prolonged failure or restriction of electric current from an outside source, freight embargoes, earthquakes, tidal waves, typhoons, hurricanes, storms **or other causes beyond the control of the BUILDER or of its sub - contractors**, as the case may be, the BUILDER shall not be liable for such delay and the time for delivery of the VESSEL under this Contract shall be extended without any reduction in the CONTRACT PRICE for a period of time which shall net exceed the total accumulated time of all such delays..."(加黑部分是笔者的强调)

对笔者而言,作为一条不可抗力条文以及该条文所针对的一连串特定事项都属于天灾人祸,以及船厂或船东都无法控制的事项。笔者认为可以找得出同类,所以兜底性的语言/文字(加黑部分)显然应该受到同类规则的适用。这样,列明事项明显与船东的过错不会是同类,甚至毫不相干。但其他两位仲裁员却认为不必理会特定事项是否同类,反正就是整体解释有关的造船合约并找出双方的订约意图,认为同类规则不适用,也就是双方没有意图把不可抗力的兜底性语言/文字局限在前面特定事项的同类。多数的裁决书是说:"However we were assisted by the statement of general principle at section 7.13 of Interpretation of Contracts (5th Ed) by Sir Kim Lewison. It is apparent from that text book that the *ejusdem generis* rule is one of construction. It is also apparent that, in the absence of an indication that the parties did not so intend, they are to be taken as having intended that, where particular words have some common characteristic which constitutes a genus, the general words which follow them ought to be limited to things of that genus. However, it seems to us to follow that if the language of the contract taken as a whole indicates that the parties did not intend that the general words which follow words of a particular genus should be limited to that genus, then effect must be given to the intention of the parties. We draw some support for this conclusion from the passage at page 388 of Interpretation of Contracts (5th Ed). It also seems to us to be an obvious one to draw as a matter of the general principle of how contracts are to be construed. Therefore for the reasons which we have given, we have concluded that the parties intended that delays 'due to default in performance by the BUYER' fall within Article VIII. 1 and we conclude that we must give effect to that intention in preference to a semantic analysis of the words used in Article VIII. 1 which pays no regard to the other terms of the Shipbuilding Contracts and the context in which Article VIII. 1 is set."

而针对造船合约整体解释,多数仲裁员也在裁决书的其他段节有说,这在本书第六章之14段有节录。大致是说多数裁决认为船东过错是属于不可抗力条文的事项并属于允许延误。如果船东过错不属于允许延误,船厂就无法获得交船日期的延长并且要支付船东议定赔偿。这并不合理,也不可能是双方订约时的共同意图。多数仲裁员认为双方在订约时一定是有一个共同意图是船东过错造成延误时可包括在不可抗力条文并可以让船厂延长交船日期与避免支付议定赔偿。需要船厂在船东延误时作出通知也在造船合约其他条文有所针对,多数仲裁员不能理解为什么针对船东的部分延误需要作出通知,但其他造成的延误就不必通知。显然,双方在订约时应该有共同的订约意图把所有不同类别的船东过错造成的延误都包括在不可抗力条文。

至于笔者的不同意见也在第六章之14段有节录,不重复。只针对本章所介绍的合约解释规则,笔者就觉得无法同意多数裁决。原因是:(1)在本章第3段介绍的解释规则要求解释结果尽量合理,商业合约也要符合商业常识。笔者觉得多数裁决做不到这一点,因为船东为了庞大的经济利益,过错可以是千奇百怪,完全意想不到。没有理由要求船厂在船东可能是杀人放火的过错作出通知(即使船厂能够马上知道)作为索赔的先决条件。(2)在本章之第7段介绍的另一条解释规则,就是如果合约对一些事情已经有特别针对,这就表示没有提到的同种类事情就排除在外。这样对船东的一些可能是轻微得多的过错,如迟延提供设备/物料、迟延批准图纸、延误支付预付船价等都有特定条文针对,就没有理由对其他同类但可能是严重得多的过错简单以不可抗力条文中的兜底性语言/文字全部包括。笔者认为其他的船东过错是排除在外,属于默示的普通法针对,也就是船东的违约可以让船厂索赔损失,这包括时间延误。不存在有多数裁决的担忧,就是船厂还是要向船东支付议定赔偿或不能延长交船日期。(3)在在本章之第4段介绍的越不合理的结果就越要写得清楚,笔者认为在这些造船合约是根本谈不上写得清楚。(4)在本小段所讲的同类规则,即使多数裁决认为不适用,也就是给与该条文的兜底性语言/文字(or other causes beyond the control of the BUILDER or of its sub – contractors)一般性的解释,笔者也不认为广泛到可以包括船东的过错。特别是在本章之第10段针对的一个重要合约解释规则是假设订约方不能从他自己的错误行为中获利,多数裁决真正是推翻了这个解释规则。

8.5 即使同类规则不适用,兜底性语言/文字还是应该受局限的说法

如果同类规则不适用,兜底性语言/文字就可以给它一般性的解释。但这里还是与其他条文/文字一样有一定的局限。在 The Thames and Mersey Marine Insurance Co Ltd v. Hamilton Fraser & Co (1877) 12 App. Cas. 484 先例,说是即使兜底性语言/文字在字义上是十分广泛与包罗万有,也受到同类规则与合约的本质与目的的局

限。所以,同类规则即使不适用,第二方面的局限仍然不会给它包罗万有的解释,Halsbury 勋爵说:"... Two rules of construction now firmly established as part of our law may be considered as limiting those words. **One is that words, however general, may be limited with respect to the subject matter in relation to which they are used.** The other is that general words may be restricted to the same genus as the specific words that precede them."(加黑部分是笔者的强调)

另是 Devlin 大法官在 Chandris v. Isbrandtsen – Moller Co Inc. (1951) 84 Ll. L. Rep. 347 先例所说的,如下:"... If a genus cannot be found, doubtless that is one factor indicating that the parties did not intend to restrict the meaning of the words, but I do not take it to be universally true that whenever a genus cannot be found the words must have been intended to have their literal meaning, **whatever other indications there may be to the contrary**..."(加黑部分是说其他会显示兜底性语言/文字即使不适用同类规则也要与其他合约条文/文字一并解释,其中包括了合约的本质与目的。)

有关解释任何合约条文/文字,包括兜底性语言/文字,是不能否定合约本质与目的。这也就是本书第十二章之 1.7.4 段所针对的"相悖理论"(doctrine of repugnancy),在此不重复。这一说法或解释规则很早就已经存在,这是早过"基本违约"(fundamental breach)的说法。在这里只介绍两个早期的案例,在第十二章之 3.4 段主要介绍一些相对近期先例所没有提及。这两个早期的案例涉及金康租约,其第 3 条文有关绕航所用的文字是十分广泛,说是"允许船舶为了任何原因可任何港口或多个港口,不论是顺着次序还是不按顺序"(The vessel has liberty to call at any port or ports in any order, for any purpose...)。这一条条文/文字以字义解释的话,船舶可以全球到处跑一两年再回来继续航次也没有问题。所以在 Leduc v Ward (1888) 20 QBD 475 先例中,贵族院就判上述广泛的文字只适用在租约航次中沿途的港口的绕航。另一个同样判法的重要先例是 Glynn v Margetson (1893) AC 351,这先例是第一个针对解释条文/文字必须配合有关合约的"目的"(object/purpose)。案情是一船橙子从西班牙的马拉加港装运去英国的利物浦,但提单合约以十分明确与广泛的文字允许绕航多处特定地方让船东做任何事情,说:"... with liberty to proceed to and stay at any port or ports in the Mediterranean, Levant, Black Sea or Adriatic, or on the coast of Africa, Spain, Portugal, France, Great Britain and Ireland for the purpose of delivery of coals, cargo or passengers or for any other purpose whatsoever."

在该案例,实际上船舶了离开利物浦卸港 350 海里的 Burriana 港,之后才回航去利物浦卸货。由于这一延误,船上的橙子全部烂掉。贵族院判根据上述十分广泛的绕航条文船舶也只能去一些沿途的港口作出轻微绕航,而且必须不能影响船上装运的橙子能够去利物浦完好的卸下。所以,解释就不能漠视该特定航次的本质与目的,Herschell 勋爵说:"My Lords, **the main object and intent**, as I have said, **of this charterparty is the carriage of oranges from Malaga to Liverpool.** That is the matter with which the shipper is concerned; and it seems to me that it would be to defeat what is the manifest object and intention of such a contract to hold that it was entered into with a power to the shipowner to proceed anywhere that he pleased, to trade in any manner that he pleased, and to arrive at the port at which the oranges were to be delivered when he pleased."(加黑部分是笔者的强调)

8.6　部分例子介绍

8.6.1　例子一:Wilson v. Whateley

先简单介绍一个早期有关房屋租赁合约的先例 Wilson v Whateley (1860) 1 Joh & H 436,其中有条文针对租约期满后租客要交还房子与交出里面的东西。这些东西是写在一个"明细表"(schedule),条文/文字是如下:"... together with all doors, wainscots, shelves, presses, dressers, drawers, locks, keys, bolts, bars, bells, staples, hinges, hearths, marble and other chimney - pieces, mantelpieces and chimney - jambs, foot - paces, slabs, covings, glazed windows, window - shutters, partitions, sinks, water - closets and cisterns, and things thereunto belonging, pumps, pipes, posts, pails and rails, water - tanks, and **other additions, improvements, fixtures and things which then were, or which at any time during the said term thereby granted should be anyways fixed or fastened to, or set up in or upon the said demised premises, or any part thereof**, in good order and condition."(加黑部分是兜底性语言/文字)

Page Wood 大法官认为在特定东西中找不出同类,其中有房东的"固定装置"(fixtures),但也有租客的固定装置。所以同类规则不适用。

8.6.2　例子二:The "Agios Nicolas"

在 The "Agios Nicolas"(1968) 2 Lloyd's Rep. 57 先例,案情是在有关的期租合约中,有一条文针对不允许承租人装运危险品,如下:"No live stock nor injurious, inflammable or dangerous goods (**such as** acids, explosives, calcium carbide, ferro silicon, naphtha, motor spirit, tar, or any of their produces) to be shipped."

争议是船舶装运了一票水分过多的"铁矿精"(iron ore concentrate),导致航次半途船舶倾侧而要紧急绕航最近的安全港口作出处理。船东事后向承租人索赔损失,指称承租人违约装危险品,这就涉及如何解释上述条文的争议。

注意是上述条文针对危险品的通称是在前面,之后针对特定的危险货物如硫酸、炸药等,这与本章之8.2段所讲有一定程度的相同。虽然在特定的明示危险货物中没有包括铁矿精或任何其他的"精矿"(concentrate),但解释该条文,如果视"危险品"(dangerous cargo)的通称是主导,这就包括所有危险品的同类货物。而后面的特定明示危险货物只是"为例"(for example),并非只局限在这几项。这样,只要水分过多的铁矿精是危险品(这是无法否认的事实,因为的确对船舶造成了危险),就包括在上述条文内。这显然就是提出索赔的船东说法,如下:"Mr. Davenport (船东大律师) submits that the words 'such as' mean 'for example', and he says that there is a general rule of construction that general words are *prima facie* to have their natural and larger meaning and are not to be restricted unless there is clear reason for so restricting them. He says that that rule is to be found in the judgement of Mr. Justice Devlin, as he then was, in *Chandris v Isbrandtsen – Moller Company, Inc.*, (1950) 83 LI. L. Rep. 385."

但承租人就希望是禁止装运的危险货物只局限在特定货物,即危险品的通称并不是主导,也不涉及同类规则,括号内的"such as"两个字应该被解释为"即是"(namely),令上述一句话变为"No live stock nor injurious, inflammable or dangerous goods (**namely** acids, explosives ...) to be shipped."如果这样解释,承租人就可以装铁矿精(或任何其他没有明示为不许装运的特定货物)。承租人争辩说,如果危险品的通称是主导并包罗万有,何必再麻烦地挑出一些特定货物作为例子。看来这是根据假设双方不会约定多余内容的合约解释规则,这在本书第三章之第6段有详述。

但 Donaldson 大法官不接受承租人的争辩,认为挑出一些特定的例子是从商业的角度让大家留心这些货物,不应该是双方有订约意图以这些例子作为对危险品的通称作出局限。Donaldson 大法官也认为承租人的争辩如果被接受,就根本不必在一开始规定危险品,干脆就直接列出特定被排除装运的危险货物会更清楚明了,写法是"No live stock or goods (such as acids, explosives, calcium carbide, ferro silicon, naphtha, motor spirit, tar, or any of their products) to be shipped"。

8.6.3 例子三:Reilly v. National Insurance & Guarantee Corporation Ltd

在 Reilly v National Insurance & Guarantee Corporation Ltd (2008) EWHC 722 (Comm)先例,案情涉及一个保险合约,其中有一条针对保险公司排除作出赔付的条文,如下:"This section does not indemnify the Insured in respect of any claim arising out of:... (ii) the failure of any fire or intruder alarm switch gear control panel or machinery to perform its intended function."

在该先例原告为客户安装灭火系统,包括火灾的报警设施在发出警告后,把罐装的二氧化碳经固定管道输送到发生火灾的地方。但之后发生火灾时系统的固定二氧化碳装置出现了问题,导致没有及时输送二氧化碳灭火而让火灾扩大并造成严重破坏。客户于是向原告提起索赔,双方最后以200万英镑庭外达成和解。而原告就向他的责任保险人要求在投保的保险合约"Tradesmen Insurance Policy"下获得补偿。但保险人根据上述的条文拒赔,认为发生火灾是二氧化碳装置的问题,属于被排除在外的"机械"(machinery),因为该文字应该有一个广泛解释,而且是独立的一个排除"设备"(equipment)。但原告认为该条文主要排除的是"any fire or intruder alarm"(火灾或盗窃的警报),这些是主导的文字,而其他跟从的开关设备、控制面板与机械应该是适用同类规则作出局限。

双方同意先以一个"预先争议"(preliminary issue)让法院对保单的有关条文作出解释,把昂贵的事实争议押后(如果有必要)。这样就需要对二氧化碳装置到底出了什么问题作出假设，也就是假设问题是以下的原因（真正原因将来审理证据后才作出认定），保险人是否要赔付。这两个原因是："(a) insufficient pressure in the master cylinder in the main CO2 system for（起火地点）, resulting either from the master cylinder having been incorrectly filled or pressurised or leakage from the discharge valve of the master cylinder; or(b) failure of the actuator piston on the cylinder valve of the master cylinder in the main CO2 system for（起火地点）to latch. As a consequence of this, CO2 escaped through the pilot orifice in the cylinder valve and not the main orifice. This in turn resulted in there being pilot pressure in the manifold but not full pressure and prevented the slave cylinder valves from opening."

在高院判是保险人胜诉，同类规则不适用，所以警报、开关设备、控制面板与机械都应该独立看待，作为不同设备。而二氧化碳装置的问题也就是机械的问题，所以被排除在赔付之外。但这一先例在上诉被部分改变。

首先是针对同类规则是否适用，上诉庭最终同意高院的判决。上诉庭认为该条文写得很含糊不清，如没有在每一个事项后加上一个逗号，这显然是加强了保险人的说法，就是应视为独立的设备。但由于保单其他条文也发生这种情况，没有加上逗号，所以这一考虑分量很轻。上诉庭也考虑到原告的说法，也就是警报是主导，后面应该适用同类规则局限解释，那么在正常情况下后面的设备都与主导的警报有关系。显然，控制面板与警报有关系，但开关装置与机械就没有关系。上诉庭不认为开关装置是一个简单的开关，而是根据牛津大字典应该被解释为一套高电压的装置。而机械一词虽然没有准确的定义，上诉庭的 Moore – Bick 大法官根据先例说："the word 'machinery' is capable of encompassing a wide range of devices which operate by means of physical movement to perform a particular function."（机械一词可以包括很多设备，只要是有物理移动完成某一样功能。）如"洒水器"(sprinkler)的水泵显然是机械。Moore – Bick 大法官也另举了一台电脑作为例子，电脑也有电子信号的移动，但这不是物理移动。所以电脑可以是一台"机器"(machine)，但不能是"机械"(machinery)。而警报谈不上有物理移动。

最后他也说如果原告的争议是正确，也就是警报才是主导，条文就应该只写这几个字，而不应该加上后来部分无关的设备。Moore – Bick 大法官认同针对保单的条文应该适用"针对规则"(*contra proferentum*)对保险人作出解释，但法院还是应该先尝试解释有争议的条文/文字并根据语境作出解释。

但对高院判二氧化碳装置的问题也就是机械的问题，上诉庭认为是简单化。因为机械需要有物理移动，但不是二氧化碳装置出的问题都涉及物理移动。如问题只是局限在气罐，如二氧化碳泄漏，这就说不上有任何物理移动。最后上诉庭对初步争议的答案或判决如下："(a) If the cause of the failure of the fixed CO2 system was insufficient pressure in the master cylinder resulting from the master cylinder having been incorrectly filled or pressured, **No**（这一原因造成二氧化碳装置的问题，保险人不能拒赔);(b) If the cause of the failure of the of the fixed CO2 system was insufficient pressure in the master cylinder resulting from leakage from the discharge valve of the master cylinder, **No**(这一原因造成二氧化碳装置的问题,保险人不能拒赔);(c) If the cause of the failure of the fixed CO2 system was the failure of the actuator piston on the cylinder valve of the master cylinder to latch, **Yes**(这一原因造成二氧化碳装置的问题,保险人可以拒赔)."

换言之,双方还是避免不了最后审理,就是根据证据对到底出了什么问题的事实认定。

§9 其余解释规则之八:分配解释

分配解释(*Reddendo singula singulis*)这一解释规则的英文写法是"by referring each to each",有说法这是一种"分配解释"(distributive construction),即把一个复数/多数(plural)作为单数(singular)后分配解释。

起争议的 AIB Group (UK) Ltd v Martin (2001) UKHL 63 先例,案情涉及两个生意上的合伙人向银行贷款,并签署了一份要求按时把所有银行贷的款项都要退还的还款合约。该合约有一条"解释条文"(interpretation clause)说明如果涉及多于一个抵押人/贷款人,他们的责任就是"共同与连带责任" (jointly and severally liable)。但问题是出在银行贷款包括其中一笔与合伙人生意没有关系而只是给其中的一位合伙人私人贷款的款项。在出了问题后,就存在另一位合伙人是否要对这一笔与他毫无关系的贷款负上共同与连带责任的争议。在贵族院,Millett 勋爵提到这一个解释规则,说:

"A distributive construction is commonly adopted when a plural subject is followed by a plural predicate and the plurals are broken down into their component singular. An example from every speech would be to say: 'A and B took their children to school'. *Prima facie* the word 'their' means 'belonging to both of them'. But this is not its only possible meaning, and if A and B are not married it is obviously not its meaning. In that case the word 'their' means 'of each of them'. But this means that A and B took their respective children to school, not each other's children. The children are distributed to the relevant parent. And it goes further than that. Although the word 'school' is in the singular, it may conceal a plural. If necessary, the sentence means that A and B took the children to their respective schools.

This is a well – established principle of construction. It often, and perhaps usually, gives the words their most natural meaning. It parades under a Latin name*Reddendo singula singulis*. This simply means that, when plurals are broken down, each singular component must be attributed to its respective singular and not to every other possible singular. It is a broad and general principle which departs from the literal and grammatical meaning and does not depend on the minutiae of language."

在该先例,如果分配解释规则适用,两位合伙人作为抵押人/贷款人会对银行给他们两位的贷款就要附上共同与连带责任,但对银行给他们个人的贷款就不必附上同样责任。但贵族院最后针对整个贷款协议的解释认为分配解释规则不适用,判银行胜诉,说:"... on a true construction of clause 2 of the joint mortgage read in conjunction with clause 1, the defendants had made one joint covenant making themselves jointly and severally liable to repay all sums of money advanced by the bank to the two of them together and to each of them separately; and that, accordingly, since they had both covenanted to pay the sums advanced by the bank to the first defendant alone as well as the sums advanced by the bank to the partnership, the second defendant(上诉的一位合伙人,他要为另一位合伙人的个人贷款负责)was liable for the shortfall arising from the first defendant's sole indebtedness."

§10 其余解释规则之九:假设订约方不能从自己的错误行为中获利

本小段所针对的是解释合约条文/文字就应该有这一假设。在本书第七章之10.3段会介绍法律在这方面也有同样的"默示"(implied by law),并会有更多相关的内容。法院在判决时往往并不会区分到底是根据合约条文/文字的解释或是根据默示条文,毕竟两者的关系十分密切。本小段与本书第十一章之第5段介绍的"妨碍原则"(prevention principle)与第十二章之第1段的"免责条文"(exception clause)也有密切关系,可以一并阅读。

假设订约方不能从自己的错误行为中获利(The presumption that a contracting party cannot take advantage of its own wrong)是一个非常重要的假设,适用在很多情况,如后续条件因为一方订约方的错误而无法满足而导致合约无效,这在本章之第10.5与10.6段有介绍。先介绍最明显受到影响的就是免责条文,代表犯错的一方或是其行为所导致的事故,即使在文字上清楚的规定是免责条文中的事项,但他还是有可能不能依赖免责,原因就是这一假设。简单的举一个例子,如果一份租约的免责条文说船舶搁浅可以免责,而有关船舶在礁石搁浅,这事故的发生也是免责条文针对的事项没有争议,但可以不让船东免责就与本条规则有关。因为搁浅是可以涉及或不涉及船员疏忽,如搁浅的礁石没有在海图显示,也不露出水面,船舶在出事故的时候也没有偏离航道或有任何不当之处,这样搁浅不涉及船员疏忽。但涉及船员疏忽而搁浅的事故经常发生,这样,解释免责条文针对的搁浅,可以给其一个宽泛的解释,即不论船员是否有疏忽,都包括在内。但一适用本段的合约解释规则,并作出假设,双方订约的意图是没有让有过错的一方获利,就可以得出结论是搁浅只应该解释为不涉及船员疏忽的搁浅。但这合约解释规则并非想干预订约自由,只是假设订约双方在正常的情况下不会接受对方可以从他或他的仆人的过错获利,变为自己一方要承担对方错误造成的后果。所以,免责条文需要以明示条文/文字明确说明获利方即使有疏忽或过错也可以依赖。这一假设也是与本章第4段双方同意不合理事情必须用清楚无误的条文/文字与第5段的针对规则是一致的精神。有一个可以排除这一假设的著名例子,在1924年的《海牙规则》中,Article IV Rule 2 (a)允许船东对船员的航行疏忽或过错免责。这种国际公约能够被通过也是有那个年代的特殊背景。读者也可比较一下一连串针对油污的国际公约或立法,都是将严格责任加于船东。难怪在《Aikens' Bills of Lading》(2006年)一书,在10.201段针对这一项免责说:"If anyone had to choose one commonly accepted exemption in maritime contracts which would cause most surprise to the man on the Clapham omnibus (这是英国的一个著名案例,指坐巴士的一般人士的看法), it would probably be that which exempts a carrier from liability if the master negligently steers the vessel into a rock or a lighthouse, with the result that the vessel and her cargo are lost. Not surprisingly this exception is construed strictly."

但这一假设也不只是针对免责条文,在其他不同针对的条文/文字也是同样。例如,和国际货物买卖与航运有十分密切关系的一个著名说法,"一旦滞期,永远滞期"(once on demurrage, always on demurrage)。这是因为货方或承租人一旦不能在固定装卸时间内完成作业,就已经违反承诺。违约的后果就是要向船东支付议定赔偿的滞期费,而要支付的是所有时间直到作业完毕。这所有时间包括本来在固定装卸时间不必计算的,如周末或坏天气。原因就是船舶继续在装港或卸港延误是货方或承租人违约或过错所导致,而这延误包括了周末或坏天气的时间。

10.1 权威说法

以下先介绍有关这一假设的主要权威说法:

1. 在Malins v. Freeman (1838) 4 Bing NC 395先例,Coltman大法官说:"It is so contrary to justice that a party should avoid his own contract by his own wrong, that unless constrained, we should not adopt a construction favourable to such a purpose."

2. 在Cheall v. APEX (1983) 2 A. C. 181先例,Diplock勋爵有经典的说法是:"... the well-known rule of construction that, except in the unlikely case that the contract contains clear express provisions to the contrary, it is to be presumed that it was not the intention of the parties that either party should be entitled to reply upon his own breaches of his primary obligations as bringing the contract to an end, i. e. as terminating any further primary obligations on his part then remaining unperformed. This rule of construction, which is paralleled by the rule of law that a contracting party cannot rely upon an e-

vent brought about by his own breach of contract as having terminated a contract by frustration, is often expressed in broad language as: 'A man cannot be permitted to take advantage of his own wrong'."

过错是在合约下针对另一方而言,而不是道德上的过错或是对第三人的过错。Diplock勋爵在该先例中也说:"... to attract the principle ... that a party to a contract is not permitted to take advantage of his own breach of duty, the duty must be one that is owed to the other party under that contract; breach of a duty whether contractual or non-contractual owed to a stranger to the contract does not suffice."

上述的说法是只有一方有过错,但如果双方都没有过错,这一假设就不适用了。在New Zealand Shipping v. Societe des Ateliers etc de France (1919) A.C. 1, HL先例中有说:"Each party is innocent; neither is in default: the conduct of neither has brought about the event, and in such a case the contract is interpreted with even and equal justice to both sides."

10.2 案例介绍之一:The "Afrapearl"

The"Afrapearl" (2004) 2 Lloyd's Rep. 305先例的有关案情是,该油轮在美湾装一船燃油去塞内加尔(Senegal)的达喀尔港(Dakar)与直布罗陀。油轮是在2001年7月10日抵达达喀尔并在15时递交了通知书,而卸货的计划是先在"海上泊位"(M'bao sea berth)通过长约3海里的"海底油管"(pipeline)卸一部分燃油,再挂靠码头卸其余部分。在海上泊位,油轮要以船缆挂上6个前后左右的浮筒以稳住船身,之后才把连接海底油管的16寸"橡皮管道"(hoses)由拖轮拉过来,再接上船上的"集管总管"(ship's manifold)。连接海底油管与橡皮管道之处,在海底也有一个集管总管,简称为PLEM。在该油轮抵达后不久,一位领航员上船准备海上泊位挂靠。当油轮开始接近海上泊位,船长看到有石油浮出海面,显示了连接PLEM的海底油管有破裂,但船长还是让船舶接上两条橡皮管道并看是否可卸货。卸货是在当天的22时45分开始,但不久就有大量的石油浮出水面。泊位当局叫停,时为23时。第二天有蛙人下去检查海底油管并试图修理。蛙人发觉裂缝是在海底油管最后一节的"凸缘"(flange)。但蛙人的暂时修理(主要是上紧凸缘的螺丝与使用速干水泥)并不成功,这导致该油轮在7月12日被下令离开海上泊位去锚地等待涉及更换管道的进一步修理。直到7月21日,油轮才被重新要求挂靠海上泊位卸货。但卸了约40分钟,又出现石油浮出海面。这样,油轮又在7月22日离开海上泊位去锚地等待。7月29日再挂靠,并只用一条橡皮管道以慢速卸货,总算让船舶在7月30卸完了海上泊位的这部分燃油。但这样就产生了大约50万美元的滞期费及其他损失,这就带来了争议,承租人想依据第8条文针对装卸时间(或/与滞期费)免算的事项之一"设备发生故障"(breakdown of equipment)。

上述案情涉及不同争议,与本段有关的是:(1)漏油是否涉及收货人的疏忽/过错而导致海底油管裂缝,如没有好好维修保养,会否影响承租人可依赖该租约的装卸时间免算条文的保障?(2)如果有关疏忽/过错是承租人自己而不是收货人,可否默示或假设不能依赖装卸时间免算条文的保障?判决的结果是如果承租人自己的疏忽/过错,如卸货的 M' bao sea berth 是承租人自己的私人泊位,其维修保养也是承租人自己负责,就不能依赖装卸时间免算事项的"设备发生故障"了,原因就是这一解释规则。但在本案例,M' bao sea berth 是属于收货人的私人泊位,疏忽/过错在缺乏维修保养也只是收货人的事,与承租人无关。这里要说明,收货人与承租人之间通常不会有代理协议,在很多 CIF 买卖中,承租人即使与收货人有合约关系,也是一个国际货物买卖合约。所以,不能要承租人承担收货人疏忽这一"转承责任"(vicarious liability)。最后的结果是承租人可在租约下依赖第 8 条文装卸时间免算条文中的设备发生故障这一事项。

10.3 案例介绍之二:伦敦仲裁

笔者在 2006 年作为仲裁庭成员之一的一个伦敦仲裁,案情是有关装运一船食糖去一个南亚国家卸货,该南亚国家在当时由于通货膨胀严重导致民意不满,所以临时豁免食用白糖的进口税,但黄糖仍需要征进口税。船舶卸货一半后,就被海关当局停止卸货。海关当局怀疑该船食糖并非白糖,而是黄糖,进口申报单填写白糖是故意逃税。收货人与海关当局在该南亚国家法院采取法律行动,经过 2 个月的延误,船舶在收货人提供银行担保的情况下把货物卸下海关仓库,船舶总算可以开航。但这 2 个月的滞期费就变为承租人与船东之间的争议,即在这个情况下可否停算卸货/滞期时间?

表面看来,船东很冤枉,有关货物的税务问题与船东毫无关系,这是"货物一方"的问题。但这里主要看双方约定的租约条文及解释风险由谁来承担,而即使不合理的也可以明示约定/规定(这在本章之第 4 段)。该租约是 Sugar Charter - party 1999 标准格式,有关免责/停算卸货时间条文有著名的特定事项,就是"政府干预"(government interference)所带来的时间损失或者延误可停算卸货时间与滞期费/滞期时间。此外,租约另有两条条文都把责任明确放在收货人,而与承租人无关。第一条是有关货物的税务是收货人负责。这一条经常出现的条文是说:"All taxes and/or dues and/or levies on vessel and/or freight at load/discharge ports to be for Owners account and all taxes and/or dues and/or levies on cargo to be for Shippers' account at load port(s) and Receivers' account at discharge port(s)."

这样,情况就对中国船东很不利,因为:(1)该南亚国家的海关当局明显就是政府,是作出了干预而导致船舶的严重延误。期间,海关当局不接受一些折中的解决办法,如把货物卸下海关仓库。另外,法院行动也比较缓慢。需注意的是,把船舶卸货叫停的是海关当局,不是法院。(2)收货人即使有错或者逃税,承租人也没有"转承责任"(vicarious liability),更何况租约有条文说明针对货物的税务只是收货人的事。(3)虽然收货人由于税务的问题导致了卸货中途被停止,而卸货时间一开始就会不断算在承租人,但免责/停算装卸时间条文的作用就是停算。而在本仲裁案件中的有关租约,正是有"政府干预"的停算事项。(4)即使是收货人的疏忽/过错导致停算事项的发生,也不影响承租人可依赖该停算装卸时间条文的保护。这方面在较早的有关"机器或者设备发生故障"的停算事项的 The "Afrapearl" (2004) 2 Lloyd's Rep. 305 上诉庭先例已经分析过。

笔者与其他两位伦敦仲裁员通过这些条文的分析,判中国船东败诉。即承租人可以依赖停算事项的"政府干预",即使干预是源自收货人可能的逃税。

看来,中国船东只能在以下情况胜诉:(1)中国船东能够证明承租人有涉及有关的逃税,当然这种证明证据很难取到,但也会有案件是承租人与收货人是同一家公司/集团可作出推断。如果能够证明,承租人就无法依赖停算条文的保护。因为在 The "Afrapearl"先例已经判过是有一个法律的假设或默示地位,就是承租人有过错就无法成功依赖卸货时间停算条文了。(2)另一个强而有力的原因是,逃税是一种欺诈行为,所以不管卸货时间停算条文说得怎样清楚,也起不了作用,因为"欺诈超越一切"(fraud unrivals all)。(3)如果中国船东是向南亚国家的收货人根据提单提出索赔滞期损失,机会就好得多。因为收货人再也不会有承租人提出的同样抗辩了,特别是收货人能够被证明确实有错甚至有逃税。但这里又会有另一个问题,南亚国家是一个发展中国家,所以除非提单合并了伦敦仲裁条文,可让中国船东向收货人提出伦敦仲裁,否则估计中国船东不敢去该国的法院向收货人提出诉讼或即使去也估计会面对严重的延误与不肯定。

总结而言,中国船东今后一些发展中国家(特别是著名麻烦的国家/港口)装卸货要小心接受政府插手/干预这种广泛的装卸时间停算条文。否则,出了事会困难重重。另一个更好的办法是在租约加一条条文说明承租人要对发货人/收货人的行为负责。

10.4 案例介绍之三:New Zealand Shipping v. Societe des Ateliers etc de France

造船工业中的合约也适用同一个解释规则,就是假设订约方不能从他自己错误的行为中获利。首先介绍本段一个著名先例 New Zealand Shipping v. Societe des Ateliers etc de France (1919) A. C. 1, HL,案情是有关一个造船合约下约定了完工日期是 1915 年 1 月 30 日。该造船合约另有约定是如果船厂无法在 18 个月内交船,合约就自动无效。该条文如下:"12. In case the Builders become bankrupt or insolvent or shall **fail or be unable to deliver the steamer within eighteen months** from the date agreed by this contract, thereupon **this contract shall become void...**"(加黑部分是笔者的强调)这与今天常见的造船合约的写法有点不一样,就是这一个所谓的"死亡日期"(drop dead date)或"销约期"(cancelling date)只是给买方一个选择权终止,他可以行使或不行使,这种条文显然对船厂不利。

在该先例,到了 1916 年 7 月 30 日,也就是刚过了 18 个月,双方有了争议。这就是船厂可否把合约视为无效,毕竟工程延误是船厂的事?贵族院判是船舶无法在约定的日期完成工程并非是船厂的过错,延误是由于第一次世界大战的战事(船厂是在法国)所造成,所以船厂可依赖该“后续条件”(condition subsequent)使合约无效或终止。在该先例中,Atkinson勋爵说:“If the contract shall be void on the happening of an event which one or either of them can by his own act or omission bring about, then the party, who by his own act or omission brings that event about, cannot be permitted either to insist upon the stipulation himself or to compel the other party, who is blameless, to insist upon it, because to permit the blameable party to do either would be to permit him to take advantage of his own wrong.”

今天的造船合约不大会有这种后续条件,造船工程有延误变为给船东选择权终止或不终止。但今天的造船合约也有另一条著名的后续条件,就是在订约后船厂需要尽快向政府取得批准,或/与向银行取得“还款担保”(refund guarantee)。由于不一定能取到,他们是以后续条件出现在一个造船合约。换言之,如果船厂无法在某一个约定的期限内取得批准或还款担保,该造船合约就自动变为无效。这条文有时被称为“Effective date of contract”。需要有这一后续条件是因为如果没有造船合约,船厂就不能向政府申请或向银行要求还款担保。所以这些申请都不能在双方仍在谈判的阶段作出或完成,变成非要先有了造船合约才申请,而申请不一定成功所以要有后续条件让合约可以自动变为无效。

这样根据New Zealand Shipping v. Societe des Ateliers etc de France先例,如果船厂合理(并留下文件证据证明合理)地向政府或者银行申请批准/还款担保,但在期限内被拒或者取不到,造船合约也就自动变为无效。相反,如果因为期间船价上涨或其他原因(如船厂与买方关系变坏),船厂不采取合理行动(或不留下文件证据证明)向政府和银行作出申请,这就是违约/毁约,因为是他的过错而导致这后续条件无法满足。

10.5 案例介绍之四:Cetelem SA v. Roust Holding Ltd

上述造船合约的安排在其他合约同样出现,如在著名的Cetelem SA v. Roust Holding Ltd (2005) 2 Lloyd's Rep. 494先例就涉及一个“股份买卖合约”(share purchase agreement)。该有关买卖的公司应该是俄罗斯背景,所以合约其中一条条文规定了向俄罗斯中央银行取得批准的后续条件。合约另一个条文说明是如果到了2005年1月31日取不到俄罗斯中央银行的批准,该合约就自动变为无效。

为了及时取得批准,被告要向俄罗斯中央银行提出申请批准与提供有关文件的最后期限是在2004年12月10日,但被告并没有这样做。结果等到2004年12月23日,原告向英国法院申请禁令/命令要求被告必须在12月29日前采取恰当的步骤以取得俄罗斯中央银行的批准。如果英国法院作出这样的命令,被告不严格执行就变为是藐视法院了。

这种“后续条件”(condition subsequent)在很多情况有,包括像二手船舶买卖会有上船检查:The “Merak” (1976) 2 Lloyd's Rep. 250先例。在国际货物买卖,也常会有申请出口证或进口证的条件。如果把它们作为“先决条件”(condition precedent),就代表只有成功申请到,才有约束性的合约。这样,在市场变动时就会有订约一方想取巧脱身,这完全合法。但如果以文字把它们作为后续条件,这就变为双方已经有了约束性的合约。如果市场有了变动,要负责申请出口证或进口证的一方就有可能在利益冲突下故意令申请不成功,或干脆不申请。但由于当时双方已经有了约束性的合约,所以本解释规则适用,也就是一方不能从他自己错误的行为中获利令合约终止。这方面在本书第八章合约的变数条件条文有详细介绍。

§11 其余解释规则之十:假设以清楚文字排除或改变法律地位

假设以清楚文字排除或改变法律地位(The presumption that clear words are required to exclude or modify remedies that arise by operation or law)又是一条重要与经常遇到的合约解释规则,但道理与本章之第4段的解释规则大同小异。第4段是指合约规定越不合理的事情就要越清楚与只能有一种说得过的解释(即使是不合理的解释)。原因是法律的地位通常被视为公平合理,虽然排除或改变法律地位也不一定不合理,但还是要写得清清楚楚才能达致这个效果。

这种法律地位,也就是所谓的法律默示地位,在本书第七章之第3段有详论。它可能来自立法(如《货物销售法》、《仲裁法等等),但也可能来自许多实际案例组织起来的普通法。通常明示地位可以超越默示地位,这正是本段所讲的合约解释规则。例外情况是在立法规定了不准以明示条文改变法律地位。而这种立法也越来越多,如《海上货物运输法》也就是《海牙规则》、《仲裁法》(在1996年立法明确规定了不少条文是属于"强制性"[mandatory],也就是不能排除或改变)、《不公平合约法》等都有这种规定。至于普通法的例外情况就是明示条文改变法律默示地位是违反"公共政策"(public policy),这样明示地位(即使写得清清楚楚)也不能改变默示地位。简单的例子是法律默示合法,但合约明示做违法的事情,这就不可能超越默示地位了。

以下介绍一些针对这一合约解释规则的权威说法,首先是在Gilbert - Ash (Northern) Ltd v. Modern Engineering (Bristol) Ltd (1974) A. C. 689先例,Diplock勋爵说:"... in construing such a contract one starts with the presumption that neither party intends to abandon any remedies for its breach arising by operation of law, and clear words must be used in order to rebut that presumption."

另在Stocznia v. Latvian Shipping (1998) 1 Lloyd's Rep. 609先例,Goff勋爵说:"... Considerations such as these lend added weight in this context to the familiar principle of construction that clear words are needed to rebut the presumption that a contracting party does not intend to abandon any remedies for breach of the contract arising by operation of law: . . . ”

11.1 例子一:排除《仲裁法》的默示地位

不妨就以1996年英国《仲裁法》为例,显示必须清楚才能排除或改变立法下的默示地位。该立法有一条重要的第44条文,给予英国法院作出中间措施(包括作出各种禁令、冻结财产等)的权力。但它也说明并非是强制性条文,订约双方可以用清楚无误的文字排除或改变该立法条文。至于怎样才算是清楚无误,就可参见笔者的《仲裁法——从1996年英国仲裁法到国际商务仲裁》一书第十章之2.2.1.1段。

11.2 例子二:排除抵销权利的 Gilbert – Ash (Northern) Ltd v. Modern Engineering (Bristol) Ltd

首先简单介绍普通法/衡平法下的“抵销”(set – off)[12]权利,这就是被告可以在欠下原告的债务中作出部分或全数的扣减,相等于抗辩的一种。这可节录Hanworth勋爵在Re a Judgment Debtor 1934中说的:“With regard to the word ‘set – off’, that is a word well – known and established in its meaning; it is something which provides a defence because the nature and quality of the sum so relied upon is a sum which is proper to be dealt with as diminishing the claim which is made, and against which the so demanded can be set – off. ”

这种情况在各种行业都会发生,如在期租合约就经常涉及承租人可在预付的租金中根据合约抵销或衡平法抵销扣减一些费用或索赔,船东不能以不足数支付租金为由撤船。在建筑业也知悉经常有承建商指控发展商要求支付约定的费用,发展商就会回应说:“因为你违反了合约,在工程或材料有不妥,所以你无权要求这笔费用,除非扣减了你违约所造成的损失。”这种说法实际上就是一种普通法抵销的“减少”(abatement)。这样,如果责任与赔偿金额已经明确,所谓是一种“议定赔偿”(liquidated sum),就至少可马上扣减并支付给债权人剩余的债务。但如果是否违约还要进行漫长的诉讼才能确定责任与赔偿金额,所谓是一种“非议定赔偿”(unliquidated sum),就会导致发展商(或承租人)明显欠下的费用(或租金)被拖欠,造成承建商(或船东)现金流动困难。但普通法的地位是不管是否议定赔偿,只要在该反索赔的本质上是允许抵销,就可作出善意与合理的估计金额的扣减:The “Nanfri” (1979) 1 Lloyd’s Rep. 201先例。所以在建筑合约,针对中间费用的预付,有一种做法就是由建筑师出“证明”(architect’s certificate)决定应付的金额后,发展商作出相应支付:Hanak v. Green (1958) 2 QB 9先例。这在一连串的上诉庭先例判是在有关合约的条文下,建筑师的证明可避免发展商作出进一步的抵销:Danways Ltd v. F G Minter Ltd (1971) 1 W. L. R. 1205先例。估计法院是看到这种争议发生太多与严重影响承建商或分承建商在进行工程中的现金流通,故此希望以这些判例作出避免。到了Gilbert – Ash (Northern) Ltd v. Modern Engineering (Bristol) Ltd (1974) A. C. 689

---

〔12〕 关于抵销,可看笔者的《损失赔偿与救济》一书第十一章之1.6段。

先例,上诉庭也是这样判法,即根据有关建筑合约的条文,欠下的费用只能扣减一些“成立或接受的议定赔偿”(established or admitted liquidated sums)。但这一先例与其他上诉庭同样判法的先例上诉至贵族院被一致推翻。Diplock 勋爵不接受该条文的一般性文字足够排除在争议中的金钱被善意抵销/减少,,说:“So when one is concerned with a building contract one starts with the presumption that each party is to be entitled to all those remedies for its breach as would arise by operation of law, including the remedy of setting up a breach of warranty in diminution or extinction of the price of material supplied or word executed under the contract. To rebut that presumption one must be able to find in the contract clear unequivocal words in which the parties have expressed their agreement that this remedy shall not be available in respect of breaches of that particular contract.”

据悉,该不受建筑业欢迎的贵族院先例的判决已经被后来生效的 1996 年英国《Housing Grants, Construction and Regeneration Act》与立法引进的“审裁”(adjudication)所改变。

有关条文是否足够明确排除普通法下抵销权利另可见本书第六章之第 12.5 段的 The BOC Group v. Centeon (Unreported April 29, 1999)先例,其中有大量内容针对合约怎样写才能够排除普通法下的抵销权利。

11.3 例子三:Stocznia v. Latvian Shipping

Stocznia v. Latvian Shipping (1998) 1 Lloyd's Rep. 609 先例是关于一个建造 6 艘冷藏船舶的造船合约,案情涉及船东没有支付造船厂两笔应在头两艘船舶安放龙骨时要预付的船价。船厂终止了造船合约并向英国法院申请“简易判决”(summary judgment),认为这两笔欠下的船价没有合理抗辩的余地。但该船东还是提出好几种抗辩,其中是根据造船合约之 5.05 条文的第二部分,如下:“In the event of such rescission by the Seller of this contract due to the Purchaser's default as provided for in this Clause, the Seller shall be entitled to retain and apply the instalments already paid by the Purchaser to the recovery of the Seller's loss and damage and at the same time the Seller shall have the full right and power either to complete or not to complete the Vessel and to sell the Vessel at a public or private sale on such terms and conditions as the Seller deems reasonable provided that the Seller is always obliged to mitigate all losses and damages due to any such Purchaser's default.”(如果因为买方/船东违约,造成卖方/船厂终止本合约,船厂有权扣留船东已经分期支付的船价并用来抵销船厂的损失。同时,船厂有权完成或不完成该船舶的建造,并以公开或私人方式转售该船舶,只要船厂是减少损失。)

船东的抗辩是,现在发生了船厂终止造船合约,船厂就必须先做上述条文规定(可称为结总账条文)的事情,因为该条文已经全面针对了发生这种情况应如何对待。这等于排除普通法下船厂(或任何债权人)可马上索赔已经欠下的债务的权利。

针对这一点,船厂与船东的争辩可节录 Goff 勋爵以下的说法:"I now turn to the impact of clause 5.05 on the yard's right to recover the keel – laying instalments in respect of vessels 1 and 2, its right having accrued before the date when the yard rescinded contracts 1 and 2 under clause 5.05(1). It was the submission of Mr. Glennie (船东代表大律师), for the buyers, that clause 5.05 provides **an exhaustive code** governing the yard's rights and remedies in the event of a rescission under the article for non – payment of an installment due under clause 5.02(b), (c) or (d); and that **the effect was to exclude what would otherwise have been the yard's right at common law to sue for such an unpaid installment as a debt.**"(加黑部分是笔者的强调)

贵族院判是上述的结总账条文根本没有清楚无误地剥夺船厂可索赔已经欠下的债务这一普通法的权利,也考虑上述条文主要针对船舶(建成或未建成)的出售,所得到的船价就要扣减已经支付的部分船价。但要知道在航运市场低潮时,船厂不一定能够很快成功出售。Goff 勋爵说:"I feel bound to say that I can find nothing in this provision inconsistent with the seller being entitled to enforce his accrued right to recover an unpaid instalment as a debt at common law ..."

§12 其余解释规则之十一:假设是合法

假设是合法(Presumption of legality)很容易理解,就是如果合约条文/文字只能有一个合理解释,但该解释是不合法。这样,看不合法的是什么方面,严重的话就会导致整个合约无效或如果分得开,把违法的条文作为部分无效。但如果有关的条文/文字可以有两个说得通的解释,这样,根据本小段的假设,就应该选择一个合法的解释而摒弃不合法的解释。除了这样的做法比较合理外,也会与其他的解释大原则一致,如本章之第6段介绍的"解释合约尽量令它有效而不是无效"(*Ut res magis valeat quam pereat*)。这方面的一些权威说法,首先是在 Lancashire County Council v. Municipal Mutual Insurance Ltd (1996) 3 All ER 545 先例,上诉庭的 Simon Brown 大法官说:"The only way in which public policy can properly be invoked in the construction of a contract is under the rule *ut res magis valeat quam pereat*: if the words are susceptible of two meanings, one of which would validate the particular clause or contract and the other render it void or ineffective, then the former interpretation should be applied even though it might otherwise, looking merely at the words and their context, be less appropriate."

另在 Global Network Services Pty Ltd v. Legion Telecall Pty Ltd (2001) N.S.W.C.A. 279 先例,Mason P 大法官所说如下:"The absolute construction contended for by Global involves the parties to the Contract promising in effect that one will act in a grossly uncommercial way that would involve unlawful activity on Legion's part and complicity on Global's part. Unless driven to such an outcome by intractable language, such a construction should be rejected having regard to the principle that, **where the words of a contract are capable of two meaning, one lawful and the other unlawful, the former construction should be preferred.**"(加黑部分是笔者的强调)

欧共体的合约法大原则也有同样的规定,这是在《The European Principles of Contract Law》之第5:106段,说:"An interpretation which makes the terms of the contract lawful, or effective, is to be preferred to one which would not."

12.1　例子之一:租约中有关无单放货的条文

这方面可举一些实际例子。由于现在出现大量的无单放货的情况,不少租约尤其是针对短航次会有一条明示条文强制船东必须在卸港无单放货,如:"In case original bills of lading cannot be made available at the discharge port, then vessel to release the cargo against Charterer's letter of indemnity in accordance to Owner's P&I Club wording."

这一条文所针对的可能合法,也可能不合法。合法的就是针对一些情况是提单在结汇的过程中发生延误,而不能及时抵达卸港。这样,采取折中的办法,就是在租约条文下通常以承租人给担保无单放货。本质上这与根据一流银行给的担保无单放货一样,不存在任何不合法。但如果提单还没有成功结汇,还在发货人手中,这表示该票货物的所有权还是在发货人。这样,再无单放货就是约定作出侵权行为,是"侵占"第三人拥有的货物(a tort of conversion)。这样,就变为非法,正如笔者所著的《国际商务游戏规则——英国合约法》第七章之4.4段有谈及,请参阅。这种案例已经有被报道过:The "Etalofos"(1995)。

这表示在这个假设是合法的大原则下,租约的这一条要求船东无单放货的条文在没有任何事实证明是非法的情况下应该判有效,因为它可以是合法的得到履行。例如,船东在同意了该条文后,之后改变心意。结果在被要求无单放货时,船东拒绝。这就是船东明显的违约并要负责所带来的赔偿,不能因为该条文有可能是不合法而说是无效。除非船东能够证明该承租人当时的特定要求本身不合法,就可以以非法作为抗辩。

这种情况也可以出现在另一种类似的情况,是在装港。承租人为了取得清洁提单,会在租约内加上条文要求船东必须签发清洁提单,并会加上说承租人或发货人会签发一封保函给船东。这样,这一约定又有很大可能是不合法而无效:Brown Jenkinson v Percy Dalton (1957) 1 Lloyd's Rep 31先例。但还会有可能是有关的约定完全合法,参阅笔者的《提单及其他付运单证》一书第六章之3.2.7.3段。

12.2　例子之二:需要符合法律要求才会是合法的合约

本小段是涉及合约可能不合法或非法履行的一个问题。众所周知,非法是违反公共政策,所以合约如果在订立时是双方有非法履行的订约意图,这就会带来严重后果。先简单节录《Chitty on Contracts》(第 31 版,2012 年)一书之 16 - 010 段:"**Both parties aware of legally objectionable features.** Neither party can sue upon a contract if:(a) both knew that its performance necessarily involved the commission of an act which, to their knowledge, is legally objectionable, that it is illegal or otherwise against public policy; or(b) both knew that the contract is intended to be performed in a manner which, to their knowledge is legally objectionable in that sense; or (c) the purpose of the contract is legally objectionable and that purpose is shared by both parties; or(d) both participate in perfoming the contract in a manner which they know to be legally objectionable."

有一些商业活动根据立法或有关国家的法律是属于非法,除非取得批准或允许等。而不获得批准或允许,有关的合约如果履行就是不合法了。但经常的做法会先订立合约,然后才试图取得批准或允许。英国法律对这一种有"后续条件"(condition subsequent)[13]的合约不持否定态度,关键只是看如果该后续条件满足不了,即没有符合法律的要求,该合约是否还要履行。如果是,这合约就涉及非法的问题而令合约被一开始就视为无效。这问题在 Pollock 大法官的《Principles of Contract》(第 13 版,1950 年)一书之第 263 段有提及并建议如何在这种情况下拟订一个合法并不会被视为无效的合约:"Whenever it is desired to contract for the doing of something which is not certainly lawful at the time, or the lawfulness of which depends on some event not within the control of the parties, the terms of the contract should make it clear that the thing is not to be done unless it becomes or is ascertained to be lawful."(如果订一个合约是准备履行一些在订约时是非法的事情,或者履行合法与否要根据将来订约方无法控制的发展,合约内的条文就应该写清楚合约内的事情是不会履行,除非在将来被明确了是合法。)

这一方面的法律并不明确,特别是在合约没有明确规定将来的履行要符合某一些立法规定为准,合约只是对这方面的要求沉默的情况。例如,在 R. A. Buckley 教授所著的《Illegality and Public Policy》(第 1 版,2002 年)一书中的 2.21 段就提到了英国法律不明确与一些矛盾的先例,说:"Should the law presume in favour of legality, so that conditional agreements will be effective in the absence of proof of a positive intention not to comply with the relevant provisions; or will the contracts be unenforceable in any event if they do not expressly provide that the statutory requirements are to be fulfilled? The former is the more able view. The older English authorities on the point are, however, conflicting. In *Swell v. Royal Exchange Assurance Co* (1813) 4 Taunt. 856 a question arose as to the legality of a voyage under charterparty whereby certain cargo was to be landed in England of a kind which required a statutory licence before it could be

[13] 有关变数条件条文可看本书第八章,本小段只针对合法或非法方面。

landed from the type of ship in question. Mansfield C. J. found in favour of the charterparty, and said that it was sufficient if the licence was obtained 'just before the act importation'. But in *Holland v. Hall* (1817) 1 B & Ald 53, decided shortly afterwards, and in which Sewell case was cited, a different result was reached. Abbott J. said:'If there be, on the face of the agreement, an illegal intention, is it too much to say, that the burden lies on the party who uses expressions *prima facie* importing an illegal purpose, to show that the intention was legal?'"(上述提到两个有矛盾的早期先例,1813 年的先例是有关一个航次是否合法,根据 1906 年《海上保险法》之 Section 41,有关的 S. G. 保单有一个承诺性保证承保的航次必须合法,因此如果不合法,保险人就不必作出赔付。该航次涉及是否合法的争议是因为船舶不是英国船,所以承保的"outward"航次从英国去外国就没有问题,但从外国装运货物进口去英国的"homeward"航次就当时的英国立法变为非法,除非取得政府的批准。Mansfield 大法官判该租约是合法,因为在进口英国之前取得批准就可以合法地履行。换言之,该租约可以被假设是合法履行,如船舶在没有抵达英国港口之前甚至在其他港口等待政府批准。但在后来的一个 1817 年的 Holland v. Hall 先例,作出了相反的判决。案情涉及一艘船舶的部分股份买卖[当时还没有通过有限公司拥有船舶,只是由自然人拥有,英国船舶登记允许一艘船可以有高达 64 股让同样数目的自然人共同拥有该船舶],而该船舶准备走一个航次运输军用物资去南美,但当时的法律需要取得政府批准才能走这一航次,否则不合法。法院认为合约表面看是有一个非法的订约意图,而如果合约方说是有合法的订约意图履行该合约,他有举证的责任。)

估计在 Holland v. Hall 先例,法院不相信订约双方会坚持在合法的情况下(取得批准)才会履行该合约。他们没有提供任何证据申请批准,法院认为他们不理会是否取得批准也照样履行,所以合约非法。在比较近期一点的可举加拿大上诉庭的先例 Maschinenfabrik Seydelmann K–G v. Presswood Bros (1966) 53 DLR (2d) 224,一审是判该合约非法,因为合约中没有任何显示履行是以符合有关立法要求为准。但上诉庭推翻了该判决,并提出了本段的假设,说:"...[the trial judge had] failed to take into account the well–settled presumption of law in favour of the legality of a contract; that if a contract can be reasonably susceptible of two meanings... one legal and the other not, that interpretation is to be put upon it which will support it and give it operation."

§13 其余解释规则之十二:如果是由律师草拟的文件假设有法律的定义

表面看来,是否有律师帮助合约双方草拟/拟定合约应该对整体合约的解释不应该有区别。毕竟现在有许多跨国公司草拟的合约恐怕在用字的严谨性比任何称职律师也毫不逊色。而如果一家跨国公司对另一家发展中国家公司订立的商业合约是一面倒,或是订约方只有一方花钱找称职律师帮助草拟/拟定合约导致他能够占尽先机,法院或仲裁庭解释合约也不会同情弱者而改写有关合约条文/文字。这样,本小段的问题主要就是涉及在解释合约内经常会有的"法律术语"(legal terms of art)。一个简单的法律术语,背后有许多含义。这样,到底是给它一个法律上的定义或是一般人从字面了解的意思?这些法律术语在合约中出现,可能来自行业上传统的写法,甚至是没有法律训练的合约方一知半解地随意滥用。正如在 Oxonica Energy Ltd v Neuftec Ltd (2008) EWHC 2127 (Pat)先例,第一审法院就提到这种滥用情况经常在知识产权的文件会出现,说:"... we quite often come across agreements that concern specialised legal subjects - and intellectual property licences fall into that category - which have been drafted by non - specialists. We can tell this from the way that technical expressions have been employed in the document. Sometimes those documents contain crucial ambiguities, not so much because of the misuse of the technical expressions, but because the draftsman had not enough understanding of the subject - matter to beware of the ambiguities that ought to be avoided. Such draftsmen, inspired by their word processors, are sometimes apt to cut and paste choice phrases and expressions where it was not necessary to do so."

但如果涉及有称职律师帮助草拟并用上了这些法律术语,解释就会给它一个法律上的定义的假设,并且不会考虑背景/语境。

在本书多处提到的著名的 Schuler (L) A. G. v. Wickman Machine Tool Sales Ltd (1973) 2 Lloyd's Rep. 53 先例,详细案情请看本书第五章之6.4段。该先例涉及合约中的"条件"(condition)一词,当时对"条件条文"(condition)与"保证条文"(warranty)两种不同违约的救济在1893年《货物销售法》有立法定义。这样如果假设适用,给该词一个法律的定义,"条件"就应该被解释为"条件条文",Wickman 作为独家经销商只要有任何轻微的违约都可让 Schuler 终止合约。但如果"条件"一词只是一般性的解释,就会只是代表合约的条文/条件(term)。例如,很多合约都会在抬头称为"合约条件"(Conditions of Contract),接下来的条文/条件各式各样并不一定涉及任何承诺(这就与违约与否毫无关系),如一条定义条文或适用法条文。在一些小的买卖,订货单与发票也经常会印上"条件请看背面"(for conditions see back)。最终没有被贵族院接受为条件条文,原因在本书第五章之6.4段有介绍。

另一个简单例子是近期的 Hayward v Norwich Union Insurance Ltd (2001) 1 All E. R. (Comm) 545 先例,案情涉及汽车保险合约。保险合约规定了"失窃"(theft)时车主把钥匙留在车上的情况不赔。显然,这是针对车主疏忽导致该投保的保时捷车轻易被盗。但在该先例的案情是,车主在加油站加油后走去付款时把钥匙留在车上,期间车子都在车主的视线范围内。显然大部分人会这样做,因为付了款就马上把车开走。但可能是车太抢眼,就被偷车贼上车开走。期间,车主试图阻拦,但由于有危险被撞而退开。这里涉及了一定程度的威胁与暴力，而这带来争议就是这种情况更接近"抢劫"(robbery)而不是盗窃，而保单并没有说抢劫不赔。这里只针对部分争议，就是车主争辩对一般人士，盗窃与抢劫被视为两码事。但最后高院与上诉庭都认为应该以法律定义解释这一词，1968 年《Theft Act》立法对盗窃与抢劫有不同定义，但根据定义，所有的抢劫都可以算盗窃。至于法院为什么以法律定义解释，案例中没有报告，但笔者估计是法院可能考虑到保单的一些标准条文通常由律师拟定，另加上其他因素，如保险行业需要肯定性。

这一条合约解释规则表面看来不太重要，但还是有很多先例，包括近期先例针对这一方面，如：Hallam Land Management Ltd v UK Coal Mining Ltd (2002) 2 EGLR 80; Sunport Shipping Ltd v Tryg – Baltica International (UK) Ltd (2003) 1 Lloyd's Rep 138, CA; Wooldridge v Canelhas Comercio Importacao E Exportacao Ltd (2004) Lloyd's Rep I. R. 915; Akici v LR Butlin Ltd (2006) 2 All E. R. 872; Castlebay Ltd v Asquith Properties Ltd (2006) 2 P. & C. R 22; Lymington Marina Ltd v MacNamara (2007) EWCA Civ 15; Walker v Kenley (2008) EWHC 370 (Ch); Lowe v National Insurance Bank of Jamaica (2008) UKPC 26; Oxonica Energy Ltd v Neuftec Ltd (2009) EWCA Civ 668; William Hare Ltd v Shepherd Construction Ltd (2010) EWCA Civ 283; Re Kaupthing Singer & Friedlander (2010) EWHC 316 (Ch); Durham v BAI (Run Off) Ltd (2011) 1 All ER 605 等。以下只节录一些权威的说法。

在 Sydall v. Casting Ltd. (1967) 1 QB 302 先例，Diplock 大法官说："... where a word or phrase which is a 'term of art' is used by an author who is not a lawyer, particularly in a document which he does not anticipate may have to be construed by a lawyer, he may have meant by it something different from its meaning when used by a lawyer as a term of art."

另在 Schuler (L) A. G. v. Wickman Machine Tool Sales Ltd (1974) A. C. 235 先例，Simon 勋爵说："The agreement was intended to have legal effect and was drawn up by lawyers. This raises a presumption that the words in the contract are used in the sense that they bear as legal terms of art, if they are reasonably capable of bearing such a meaning in their context."

在 Infiniteland Ltd v Artisan Contracting Ltd (2006) 1 BCLC 632 先例，上诉庭的 Carnwath 大法官说："In my view, **it is important in the interests of legal certainty** that such established distinctions should be respected, both by those drafting contracts, and by the courts in their interpretation. In the context of a professionally drawn legal document such as this, the court should start from a strong presumption that such expressions are used in their ordinary legal meanings."(加黑部分是笔者的强调)

在 Bedfordshire Police Authority v. Constable (2009) 2 All ER (Comm) 200 先例，Longmore 大法官说："This submission confuses two separate concepts. It may well be correct that 'liable as damages' has the comparatively technical meaning that an English lawyer would give to the concept of 'damages'. But if that is right it is then wrong to say that it must be construed against 'reasonably available background knowledge' so as to limit the technical sense of the phrase under the consideration. We are already outside the principle that **an ordinary term in a contract is to be construed against the commercial background or the 'aim and genesis' of the transaction. A technical phrase has been used and it must be interpreted in its technical sense without regard to reasonably available background knowledge.** If, therefore, the phrase 'legally liable to pay as damages' has connotations which a reasonably experienced layman might not appreciate or if the phrase leads to an inquiry which only a lawyer or a historian would be qualified to conduct, the concept of limiting this inquiry to background knowledge reasonably available to an insurance broker or an insurer must necessarily fade into the background."(加黑部分是说一般性的合约条文/文字要根据一般的商业背景/语境来解释,技术性术语[法律术语]就不应该根据背景/语境来解释。)

在澳大利亚上诉庭的 Phoenix Commercial Enterprises Pty Ltd v. Canada Bay Council (2010) NSWCA 64 先例,Campbell 大法官说:"If the document in question is drawn by a lawyer, is manifestly intended to effect a legal transaction, and uses an expression that is not an expression in common use but that has a meaning in an area of legal discourse that is relevant to the document in question, that in itself provides a basis for the reasonable reader concluding that **that expression is used in its special legal sense, unless there are other factors present that show it is not used in that special legal sense. So understood, the presumption is consistent with the current approach to construction.**"(加黑部分是笔者的强调)

§14 其余解释规则之十三:假设订约方不会不合理约定一些不可能做到的事情

会有一些不应该出现的情况,双方约定一些不可能做到的事情。这不是指一些沉重的履行责任,需要承诺方花很大的难度、费用与精力履行,这不是不履行合约承诺的合法理由。显然法院/仲裁庭解释合约,要避免作出一个结论是双方约定了一些不可能做到的事情,因为这并不合理。毕竟在商业合约,双方是为了履行合约并让双方得利才订立合约,不是为了约定不可能做到的事情。但现实中这种情况确有发生,其中很大原因就是乱订合约,不了解实际情况,导致作出一个承诺但最终是履行不了。这样,如果法院/仲裁庭只能作出这一解释,就只能判承诺方不能履行合约的"首要义务"(primary obligation),只能履行合约的"次要义务"(secondary obligation),也就是赔偿损失。有关合约首要义务与次要义务的说法在笔者的《损失赔偿与救济》一书第十一章之 1.1 段有简单介绍,首要义务就是其中一方承诺做一些事情。而次要义务就是指做出承诺的合约方违反了他做出的首要义务承诺而要作出金钱上的赔偿,让受害方可以回复到合约被履行的地位。详见 Diplock 勋爵在 Photo Production v Securicor (1980) 1 Lloyd's Rep 545 先例的著名说法。

这里可以介绍两个涉及国际货物买卖的先例,第一个是 The "Epaphus" (1987) 2 Lloyd's Rep. 215,另一个是 The "New Prosper" (1991) 2 Lloyd's Rep. 93。

14.1　案例一:The "Epaphus"

The "Epaphus" (1987) 2 Lloyd's Rep. 215 先例,有关的案情是一个 CFR 国际货物买卖,该船舶装了一船大米意大利。该 CFR 约定了目的地为"一个主要的意大利港口,在船舶经过苏伊士运河时由买方宣告"(one main Italian port to be declared on vessel passing Suez)。

结果买方宣告卸港是拉文纳(Ravenna),但该港水深不够,"Epaphus"轮根本进不了港。这导致船舶要先去安科纳(Ancona)卸下部分货物,才能回来拉文纳卸下其余货物。这样就涉及船舶延误与谁要承担滞期费的问题。买方认为卖方的船舶根本不适合所有的"主要意大利港口"(main Italian ports),而拉文纳无可争议是意大利的一个主要的港口。看来是,卖方应该在买卖合约局限买方可宣告的卸港为"all main Italian ports except Ravenna"。实际的情况是买卖合约明确让买方宣告任何主要的意大利港口为卸港,而拉文纳就是其中一个,船舶进不了等于是双方约定了(卖方承诺了)一些不可能做到的事情。

如果双方明确约定一些不可能做到的事情,如约定"at *any* one Italian port *however* small"(任何一个意大利港口,不论多小)或"*however* shallow"(不论水多浅),就只能这样解释了。反过来双方如果约定是"one Italian port"(一个意大利港口),这可解释为有一定合理的局限,也就是通过事实的默示,像 The "Moorcock" (1889) 14 P.D. 64 先例默示泊位必须是安全。[14] 例如,在船舶大小与水深方面有合理局限,毕竟意大利有太多小与水浅的港口。但在本案例,有关条文是双方的约定中已经对意大利港口加了限制,也是唯一的局限,就是"主要"(main)一词。这样,有了明示法律就不能再默示双方约定的主要意大利港口中还有其他合理局限。Donaldson 大法官是这样说:

"... , if this contract had provided in terms that the cargo would be delivered 'at one Italian port *however* small' or 'at any one Italian port', it would be impossible to construe this as a contract only to deliver at ports of sufficient size or draft limitation to permit the entry of the named vessel. The parties would, in effect, have listed all Italian ports and expressly agreed that the buyers could nominate any one of them. Nor could

---

〔14〕 这方面可看本书第七章之第 4 段。

any term to this effect be implied, since it would flatly contradict the express terms of the contract that the buyers' choice embraced *any* Italian port. On the other hand, if the contract had provided simply that the cargo would be delivered to 'at one Italian port' there would have been scope for considering whether the parties thereby intended in effect to list all Italian ports, however small, or only those Italian ports which were of a size or draft limitation suited to the vessel and a decision that the parties intended to refer only to the latter would have involved no contradiction of the express terms - only their construction...

However, in the instant case the parties have expressly chosen to limit the buyers' choice in a particular way, namely to *main* Italian ports. This cannot mean *some* main ports and the plain implication is that the parties were satisfied, albeit wrongly and even negligently, that the vessel could enter any main Italian port... In these circumstances it seems to me to be quite impossible in principle to construe 'main Italian port' as 'all main Italian ports except Ravenna' or to imply a term that, notwithstanding the express terms of the option, the buyers could not choose Ravenna or any main port with a draft limitation of less than the vessel's draft on arrival or hold..."

结果上诉庭判 CFR 卖方败诉,因为他用一艘船舶运载这批大米,根本是进不了买方有权宣告的卸港。在针对双方约定或其中一方合约方承诺一些不可能做到的事情方面,Donaldson 大法官给了一个很权威的说法,针对这种情况的法律后果,如下:"My starting point is that parties to any contract are free to agree upon any terms which they consider appropriate, including a term requiring one of the parties to do the impossible, although it would be highly unusual for parties knowingly so to agree. If they do so agree and if, as is inevitable, he fails to perform, he will be liable in damages. That said, any Court will hesitate for a long time before holding that, as a matter of construction, the parties have contracted for impossible, particularly in a commercial contract. Parties to such contracts can be expected to contemplate performance, not breach."(起点是订约方可以同意一些不可能做到的事情,虽然这在双方明知道的情况下会极少发生。如果他们真的这样约定,同意了但做不到的一方就要对损失负责赔偿。但法院应该有极大的犹豫,不应该轻易判是这个解释,特别是在商业合约。在这种商业合约中,订约方是考虑怎样履行,不是怎样违约。)

14.2 案例二:The "New Prosper"

The "New Prosper" (1991) 2 Lloyd's Rep. 93 先例又是涉及国际货物买卖合约,是一个 FOB 的买卖澳大利亚装 35,000 吨的散装大麦。在该合约中,装港是在第 37 条文如下:"Port(s) of Shipment: One or two ports at Seller's option out of Wallaroo, Port Lincoln, Port Pirie, Thevenard, Port Adelaide, Port Giles, Ardrossan in South Australia or Geelong and/or Portland (Victoria) or vice versa."

另有第 39 条文针对买方所指定装货的船舶必须符合的条件，如下："Nominated vessel(s) must comply with all South Australian and/or Victoria load port restrictions, i. e. LOA, Beam, SDW draft. However, before fixing vessel Buyers must obtain prior approval from Sellers."(买方指定的船舶必须符合所有装港的限制，如长度、宽度、吃水。在租船前买方必须先取得卖方的批准。)

这两条条文一并解释，对澳大利亚港口有认识的人士就马上得出一个结论是双方约定了一些不可能做到的事情。这是因为在约定的一连串列名装港中，有很多小港口是任何船舶如果装 35,000 吨散装大麦，都根本不够水深，如 Wallaroo, Port Pirie, Ardrossan 等。

这样，卖方可选择的装港就只能剩下了小部分列名港口，而要漠视/删除很多明示了的装港，这显然不是正确的解释合约做法。[15] 另一个可能的解决办法是作出事实的默示，即如果卖方将来选择了一些水深不够的装港，船舶就只装部分的货物，而不是约定的 35,000 吨了。但这样的事实默示也有极大的问题。因为卖方装不足货物可能会在买卖合约中违约或信用证结不了汇。也没有理由作出默示的同时，要求违反另一条明示条文，就是要装 35,000 吨大麦。此外，也很难推断说这就是双方的订约意图。看来，这一案例是比上一个更明显约定了不可能做到的事情。

案情涉及买方指定了"New Prosper"轮并告知了卖方。显然，如果卖方将来选择一些水深不够的港口，该轮无法装 35,000 吨大麦。卖方也就以这个理由拒绝了该船舶，这导致双方互相指责违约/毁约，并导致合约被终止。

买方的争辩是即使"New Prosper"轮将来不能去部分装港装 35,000 吨大麦，但这只是一个风险。将来"最后的卖方"(end seller)，也就是澳大利亚的"大麦局"(Barley Board)，如果选择一些水深足够的港口，问题也就不存在。而如果大麦局选择一些水深不够的港口，但允许超载，问题也可能解决。反之，这将来的风险是在买方，卖方不应该一开始就拒绝该轮。看来，仲裁庭接受这个说法，判卖方败诉。但这在高院被推翻。高院认为买方的争辩是商业上不能接受，因为这是限制大麦局的选择装港权利，而且违反了第 39 条文清楚写明买方指定的船舶必须符合所有的装港限制。结果，Phillips 大法官判是买方败诉，因为"New Prosper"轮不是一个有效的指定船舶。而说到该买卖合约同意了不可能做到的事情，Phillips 大法官说是只能让合约双方自己作出"适合的更改"(appropriate variation)。

§15　总结内部合约解释规则

在本书第三章与本章已经介绍了不少重要的合约解释规则，笔者可以在这里总

---

[15] 这可看本书第三章之第 1 段要整体解释合约与给每一条文/文字有一定解释。

结一下。首先节录 Lewison 大法官所著的《The Interpretation of Contracts》(第 5 版，2011 年)一书之第七章的标题讲到合约解释规则的作用说："The canons of construction are no more than pointers to ascertaining the meaning of a written contract. They are not to be slavishly applied, and where they point in different directions the court must select those which will produce a reasonable and just result."(合约解释规则只是指出方向确定一个文书合约的意思。不要盲目地适用这些规则，如果不同解释规则指向不同方向，法院就要找一些会提供合理与公平的结果的规则。)

另是在《Chitty on Contracts》(第 31 版，2012 年)一书之 12 - 045 段，说："Certain principles of construction have been formulated by the courts. Previously, these principles, referred to as 'rules', were applied somewhat rigidly and adhered to tenaciously (even though the application of one rule in preference to another might lead to an opposite result). However, it has been pointed out that the modern approach to construction is: '... to assimilate the way in which [contractual] documents are interpreted by judges to the common - sense principles by which any serious utterance would be interpreted in ordinary life.' As a result, most principles of construction are nowadays better regarded merely as guidelines or assumptions as to what the court may regard as the normal use of language and which assist judges to arrive at a reasonable interpretation of words used, though subject to examination of the relevant circumstances surrounding the transaction."

最后节录 Gibbs 大法官在 Australian Broadcasting Commission v. Australian Performing Right Association Limited (1973) 129 CLR 99 先例中针对了多条合约解释规则，总结了一个总体上的做法，如下："It is trite law that the primary duty of a court in construing a written contract is to endeavour to discover the intention of the parties from the words of the instrument in which the contract is embodied.〔16〕 Of course the whole of the instrument has to be considered, since the meaning of any one part of it may be revealed by other part,〔17〕 and the words of every clause must if possible be construed so as to render them harmonious one with another.〔18〕 If the words used are unambiguous the court must give effect to them, notwithstanding that with the result may appear capricious or unreasonable, and notwithstanding that it may be guessed or suspected that the parties intended something different.〔19〕 The court has no power to remake or amend a contract

---

〔16〕 这是早已确立的法律，就是法院解释一个文书合约的首要责任是根据合约中的条文/文字找出双方的订约意图。

〔17〕 当然要考虑整体的合约，因为其中部分内容的意思会被另一部分带出来。

〔18〕 如果可能，条文的每一个字都给其协调与统一的意思。

〔19〕 如果文字毫不含糊(即只有一个意思)，法院必须要给它这一个解释，即使这是不合理或是法官怀疑双方或其中一方可能有其他的主观订约意图。

for the purpose of avoiding a result which is considered to be inconvenient or unjust.[20] On the other hand, if the language is open to two constructions, that will be preferred which will avoid consequences which appeared to be capricious, unreasonable, inconvenient or unjust,[21] 'even though the construction adopted is not the most obvious, or the most grammatically accurate' to the used words from earlier authority cited in *Locke v. Dunlop* (1888) 39 Ch. D 387,[22] which, although spoken in relation to a will, are applicable to the construction of written instruments generally; see also *Bottomley's Case* (1880) 16 Ch D 681. Further, it will be permissible to depart from the ordinary meaning of the words of one provision so far as is necessary to avoid an inconsistency between that provision and the rest of the instrument.[23] Finally, the statement of Lord Wright in *Hillas & Co Ltd v. Arcos Ltd* (1932) 147 L. T. 503, that the court should construe commercial contracts 'fairly and broadly without being too astute or subtle in finding defects',[24] should not, in my opinion, be understood as limited to documents drawn by businessmen for themselves and without legal assistance.[25] (cf. *Upper Hunter County District Council v Australian Chilling and Freezing Co Ltd* [1968] 118 C. L. R. 429)"

---

〔20〕 法院是不可以只是为了避免一个不方便与不公平的结果而重写或者修改一个合约。

〔21〕 但如果文字可以有两个以上的解释,法院就会倾向避免一个看来变化无常、不合理、不方便与不公平的解释。

〔22〕 即使这一选择并不是最明显的与文法上准确的。

〔23〕 法院也可以偏离该文字一般性的解释,这是为了避免与合约条文/文字其余部分的不一致。

〔24〕 最后,正如 Wright 勋爵所说的那样,在解释商业合约要宽松而不要在文字上挑毛病。

〔25〕 这不限制商业人士在没有律师协助下所拟定的合约/文件。

第五章 有先例/立法作出过解释的条文/文字

§1 解释合约是法律问题

首先是简单说涉及双方争议，通常都有两个方面。一方面是“法律问题”(issue of law)的争议，另一方面是“事实问题”(issue of facts)的争议。前者是根据先例与一些权威的说法(如重要的法律书籍，普通法/英国法有太多先例，不容易寻找，很大程度就是靠这些书籍“编纂成书”[codify]，如大陆法编纂成法典)作出决定，后者是根据双方提供的证据(包括口头、文件与专家意见证据)以平衡的可能性作出认定。另一个重要的区分也在程序上，英国一直以来的公共政策就是法律问题不是仲裁庭说了算，而是双方当事人(通常是败诉方)可以把仲裁庭这一决定上诉至法院，让法院作出最后决定，并成为普通法的一个先例。但对事实问题的认定，就不存在上诉，法院也不会再度处理仲裁庭已经处理过的证据。而如果法院在考虑法律问题的上诉需要涉及事实问题，法院也必须接受仲裁庭的认定就是“事实”(facts)，不能“重开”(reopen)或质疑。

一直以来，英国的法律是把解释文书合约与文书文件视为法律问题。这可以先节录 Diplock 勋爵在 The “Nema” (1981) 2 Lloyd's Rep. 239 先例中所说的：“The answer must depend upon the true construction of the agreement between the parties; and in English jurisprudence, as a legacy of the system of trial by juries who might not all be literate, the construction of a written agreement, even between private parties, became classified as a question of law ... A lawyer nurtured in a jurisdiction that did not owe its origin to the common law of England would not regard it as a question of law at all ... Nevertheless, despite the disappearance of juries, literate or illiterate, in civil cases in England, it is far too late to change the technical classification of the ascertainment of meaning of a written contract between private parties as being ‘a question of law.’”

在 Carmichael v. National Power plc (1999) 1 W. L. R. 2042 先例，Hoffmann 勋爵也说：“In the 18th and 19th centuries the rule was maintained because it was essential to the development of English commercial law. There could have been no precedent and no certainty in the construction of standard commercial documents if questions of construction had been left in each case to a jury which gave no reasons for its decision.”(在

18 与 19 世纪,为了发展英国商法就有了这一规则。因为如果把解释合约视为事实的认定,并在每一个案件交给陪审团作出不必提供原因的决定,就无法建立一套先例,对商业的标准格式合约解释也就不会有任何肯定性。)

在近期的 Thorner v Majors (2009) 1 WLR 776 先例,Neuberger 勋爵说:

"(a) the interpretation of a purely written contract is a matter of law, and depends on a relatively objective contextual assessment, which almost always excludes evidence of the parties' subjective understanding of what they were agreeing, but (b) the interpretation of an oral contract is a matter of fact (I suggest inference from primary fact), rather than one of law, on which the parties' subjective understanding of what they were agreeing is admissible.

The reason for this dichotomy is partly historical. Juries were often illiterate, and could therefore not interpret written contracts, whereas they could interpret oral ones. But it also has a good practical basis. If the contract is solely in writing, the parties rarely give evidence as tothe terms of the contract, so it is cost - effective and practical to exclude evidence of their understanding as to its effect. On the other hand, if the contract was made orally, the parties will inevitably be giving evidence as to what was said and done at the relevant discussions or meetings, and it could be rather artificial to exclude evidence as to their contemporary understanding. Secondly, and perhaps more importantly, memory is often unreliable and self - serving, so it is better to exclude evidence of actual understanding when there is no doubt as to the terms of the contract, as when it is in writing. However, it is very often positively helpful to have such evidence to assist in the interpretation of an oral contract, as the parties will rarely, if ever, be able to recollect all the details and circumstances of the relevant conversations."

由于解释合约条文/文字在英国被视为法律问题,如果已经有先例对类似情况下的某些条文/文字作出解释,这应该是"约束性的先例"(binding precedent)。这种情况特别是在商业的标准格式合约或标准条文(如信用证的 UCP 600),因为肯定性与可循性在这些领域非常重要。许多著名大法官都有强调过,其中在本书第四章之 2.4 段有部分节录。在这里只一提是 Waller 大法官在 British Sugar plc v. NEI Power Projects Ltd (1997) 87 B. L. R. 42 的近期先例中说的:"... once a phrase has been authoritatively construed by a court in a very similar context to that which exists in the cases in point, it seems to me that a reasonable businessman must more naturally be taken to be having the intention that the phrase should bear the same meaning as construed in the case in point. It would again take very clear words to allow a court to construe the phrase differently."

总结以上所讲,将解释文书合约与文件视为法律问题的原因如下:

1. 在 18、19 世纪,英国法院对民事案件(包括商事案件)由陪审团审理,但由于当时不少陪审团成员是文盲,让他们解释文书合约/文件会有难度并且准确性也不令人放心,所以将解释合约/文件视为法律问题就可以由法官作出决定。

2. 现在更重要的原因是通过法院作出决定,就可以将一个个案件的判决编撰成书,让普通法/商法有机会发展与不断改善。但如果都当作事实问题处理,而每一个案件的事实背景都不一样,就发展不了一个制度。

3. 发展与建立一个制度也可以带来"肯定性"(certainty),而肯定性对商业活动尤其重要。让商业合约的双方事先知道什么该做与什么不该做等,就可以避免很多昂贵的诉讼。商业人士在谈判与达成合约时有这一法律背景就可以了解自己的地位,这也就带来了肯定。特别是在不少商业活动,如国际货物买卖与航运,都习惯使用已经有了不少先例作出法律解释的标准合约格式。

英国法律与大陆法不一样。例如在法国,解释文件是一个事实问题,所以法院管不了,这可见 B Nicholas 所著的《The French Law of Contract》(第 2 版,1992 年)一书第 47 页。虽然现在的趋势看来,英国法律也在向大陆法看齐,对解释文书合约这一方面也开始放开外来证据/口头证据,再也不是较早节录的 Thorner v Majors 先例中 Neuberger 勋爵说的,如果合约只是书面,双方当事人极少会需要提供证据让法院作出解释。看来,将解释合约作为法律问题,可以上诉至英国法院,真正的原因不是解释合约的本质,而是政策上发展英国商法。所以,有人认为将解释合约视为法律问题是程序上要这样对待。Diplock 勋爵在 The "Nema" 与 Antaios Compania Naviera SA v Salen Rederierna AB (1985) 1 AC 191 先例中说,解释一份私人文件/合约实际上是事实问题,虽然在程序方面被视为法律问题(如对裁决书中对合约条文/文字或书面文件的解释是可以在取得批文下上诉法院,而其他方面的事实认定就不能上诉)。

也有说法是解释合约混合了事实与法律问题,并且有两步程序。这在 Chatenay v Brazilian Submarine Telegraph Co Ltd (1891) 1 QB 79 先例,Lindley 大法官这样说:"The expression 'construction,' as applied to a document, at all events as used by English lawyers, includes two things: first, the meaning of the words; and, secondly, their legal effect, or the effect which is to be given to them. The meaning of the words I take to be a question of fact in all cases, whether we are dealing with a poem or a legal document. The effect of the words is a question of law."

即使在以前的说法也有许多本质上的例外,如解释一些普通在使用的英语/文字。Reid 勋爵在 Brutus v Cozens (1973) AC 854 先例说:"The meaning of an ordinary word of the English language is not a question of law. The proper construction of a statute is a question of law."

上述先例是针对立法,但在商业合约也适用。如在 Commonwealth Smelting Ltd and Another v Guardian Royal Exchange Assurance Ltd (1986) 1 Lloyd's Rep 121 先例,案情涉及"爆炸"一词的定义或解释,这是为了看一个在工厂发生的事故是否是属于承保的风险。Parker 大法官说:"It is of course trite law that the interpretation, whether it be of a statute or of a contract is a matter of law... If there is an ordinary English word used and it is not contended by either side that there is anything in the context which would result in it having a special meaning, then it is for the court to decide as a matter of fact. Whether the facts in the particular case are, or are not, within that ordinary meaning."

但不仅是普遍使用的英语/文字,"技术性的术语"(technical term)也是事实问题,法院需要证据作出解释。Westbury 勋爵在 Hill v Evans (1862) 4 DE G. P. & J 288 先例说:"It is true, as a proposition of law, that the construction of a specification (like the construction of all other written instruments) belongs to the Court; but the specification of an invention contains generally, if not always, some technical terms, some phrases of art, some description of processes which require the light to be derived from what are called surrounding circumstances. It is therefore an admitted rule of law, that the explanation of the words or technical terms of art, the phrases used in commerce and the proof and results of the processes which are described (and in a chemical patent, the ascertainment of chemical equivalents)—that all these are matters of fact upon which evidence may be given, contradictory testimony may be adduced, and upon which undoubtedly it is the province and the right of a jury to decide."

§2　不受先例约束的说法

但由于解释合约是要将合约全部条文一起综合解释与作出协调,而在订约自由下,即使是本质一样的合约使用了同样的文字或同一句话,由于其他条文不会一模一样,解释起来不一样是经常有的事。而且近年来解释合约的适当做法是必须要考虑订约时的背景/语境,而每一个合约都会不一样,所以有不少说法是解释合约不必理会先例作出过的解释。甚至有说法是上一层法院的解释不约束下一层法院,这可节录 May 大法官在 Ashville Investments Ltd v. Elmer Contractors Ltd (1988) 2 Lloyd's Rep. 73, CA 先例中所说:"This is not to say that the earlier decision on a given form of words will not be persuasive to a degree dependent on the extent of the similarity between the contracts and the surrounding circumstances in the two cases. In the interests of certainty and clarity a court may well think it right to construe words in an arbitration agreement, or indeed in a particular type of contract, in the same way as those words have been construed in another case involving an arbitration clause by another court. But in my opinion the subsequent court is not bound by the doctrine of *stare decisis* to do so."

上述的说法,在以前已经有了,如 Warrington 大法官在 Pedlar v. Road Block Gold Mines of India Ltd (1905) 2 Ch. 427 先例中所说的:"In a question of construction, no judge is bound by the decision of another judge. He is obliged to express his view of the meaning of the document which he has to construe, and in expressing that view, in my opinion, he is not bound by the view of somebody else. I remember hearing Sir George Jessel say that he should not regard himself as bound by the decision of a previous judge on the construction of the identical document and the identical passage of the document which he had to construe."

另外,Scrutton 大法官在 Westcott v. Hahn (1918) 1 K. B. 495 先例中也说:"A flood of authorities in and since the seventeenth century were poured out upon the Court, in which somewhat similar words to this covenant had received a construction from the Courts. In my view, however, the first thing to be done is to endeavour to ascertain from the words the parties have used in this case their actual intention. If they have used words which by a settled course of authority have acquired a technical meaning, the Court will give effect to those authorities; but, unless this is so, it appears to me very unprofitable to consider that Courts have thought that other words in other documents meant and to see which reported case has the least differences from the present."

另在 The "Mariasmi" (1970) 1 Lloyd's Rep. 247 先例,Mocatta 大法官说解释合约是一个由有经验的法官或仲裁员根据每一个不同案件的环境与所用的文字而得出的第一印象,如下:"Questions of construction are very often questions of first impression. They depend immensely upon the circumstances of each individual case and the precise words used in the contracts to be construed. ..."

在较近期的 Hawley v Luminar Leisure Ltd (2006) IRLR 817 先例,Hallett 大法官说:"... the caution which a court, seeking to identify the meaning of a word in a particular contract, must adopt when considering what assistance can be derived from either the word's acontextual meaning, or judicial decisions as to the meaning of the same word in a different contract. Because the contractual and commercial circumstances of each case are inevitably different, it can be positively dangerous to draw assistance from the acontextual meaning or from decisions of other courts as to the meaning, of a particular word, when context is so important on issues of interpretation. Of course, very different considerations may apply where a particular word or phrase has a specific well - established meaning in a certain type of contract."

另介绍 JHP Ltd v BBC Worldwide Ltd (2008) EWHC 757 (Ch)先例,Norris 大法官说:"The process of construction is the ascertainment of the meaning which the document would convey to a reasonable person having all background knowledge which would reasonably have been available to the parties in the situation in which they were at the time of the contract. **In this process reported decisions on the meaning of the same or similar words in other documents are of very little assistance (unless the words have**

a technical meaning in formal documents which the draftsman may be taken to have known), save for pointing up occasions on which the point may have arisen before and alerting the Court to the arguments then advanced. **That is in part because the factual background known to the parties will invariably differ from document to document.**"(加黑部分是笔者的强调)

最后是在 Enterprise Inns Plc v The Forest Hill Tavern Public House Ltd (2010) EWHC 2368 (Ch)先例,Morritt 大法官说:"Plainly such a decision cannot be conclusive as to the interpretation of other contracts made at different times, between different parties and in different circumstances even though both are questions of law. But a decision on the interpretation of a contract may be persuasive as to the interpretation of another contract using similar language by parties involved in a similar trade and in similar circumstances, particularly where knowledge of the previous decision may be imputed to the parties."(虽然解释合约是一个法律问题,但以前的判决对后来的合约解释不是结论性,毕竟不同的合约是在不同的时间订立,涉及不同的订约方与处于不同的环境/背景。但在后来另一份合约使用了同样的条文/文字并在同样的行业与同样的环境/背景,先例的解释会有一定的说服力,特别是双方在订立合约时知道有这一先例。)

这也是在本书第四章之4.3段(与其他地方)提到的"一次过"合约(而涉及中国公司的绝大部分合约都是一次过合约)的解释是不可预测。

§3　标准格式合约的解释应该受先例约束的说法

有一些行业经常使用标准格式合约,这样如果某行业有拟订得好与完整的标准格式合约,使用方即使要作出修改或增加附加条文,也会是少量。这主要是外贸、航运、保险等行业。它们都涉及同业的组织或商会,因为需要有这种组织拟定标准格式合约并推广使用。至于一些个别的商业合约,如公司收购或合资,虽然合约会加入一些常见的"惯用条文"(boilerplate clause),但主要的一些条文/文字还是以订约双方自己的语言,不涉及标准格式合约。

看来针对一些著名的标准格式合约的解释与上一段有不同的说法,就是必须依从先例。这主要考虑在肯定性与可循性的方面,比一般的合约条文/文字优先,因为使用的人很多,每一次使用都会涉及不同背景。但为了肯定,必须让他们在使用时就能知道法律的地位,从而作出明智的谈判与知道订约后应该怎样履行。这与订约方自己以自己的条文/文字表达订约意图的解释是两码事,因为他们所选择的文字未必准确。很多著名的大法官都有提到过,重要的一些例子已经在本书第四章之2.4段有介绍,在这里不重复。笔者只节录小部分没有重复的权威说法如下。

1. Staughton 大法官在 The "Radauti" (1987) 2 Lloyd's Rep. 276 先例中说:"In

the shipping world, as in some other fields of commercial activity, once a particular clause, phrase or word has received an authoritative interpretation from the Courts, it is thought right to follow that interpretation in other cases in the belief that the parties to subsequent contracts will have had it in mind when concluding their bargains, or at least their legal advisers will have considered it when deciding whether to pursue a dispute subsequently."

2. 在 The "Kalliopi A" (1988) 2 Lloyd's Rep. 101 先例,Staughton 大法官也是有同样的说法如下:"As is usual in such cases we were referred to quite a number of decisions on different contracts containing different wording. It must, I suppose, be accepted that the interpretation of a charter – party cannot be conducted solely on the basis of the ordinary English meaning of the words which the parties have used in their contract. Regard must be had to what the same words or phrase have been held to mean in the past. Once a particular clause, phrase or word has received an authoritative interpretation on other cases in the belief that the parties to subsequent contracts will have had it in mind when concluding their bargains or at least their legal advisers will have considered it when deciding whether to pursue a dispute subsequently."

3. 在 British Sugar Plc v NEI Power Projects Ltd (1997) 87 BLR 42 先例,Waller 大法官说:"... once a phrase has been authoritatively construed by a court in a very similar context to that which exists in the case in point, it seems to me that a reasonable businessman must more naturally be taken to be having the intention that the phrase should bear the same meaning as construed in the case in point."

即使是近三十年来有了偏离传统解释文书合约的做法,Hoffmann 勋爵也在 Mannai Investment Co Ltd v. Eagle Star Life Assurance Co Ltd (1997) A. C. 749 先例说明解释标准格式合约或条文不能与一般合约的条文/文字相提并论,并以信用证的 UCP 500 为例,说:"There are documents in which the need for certainty is paramount and which admissible background is restricted to avoid the possibility that the same document may have different meaning for different people according to their knowledge of the background. Documents required by bankers' commercial credits fall within this category. Article 13(a) of the Uniform Customs and Practice for Commercial Credits (1993 revision) says that the documents must 'upon their face' appear to be in accordance with the terms and conditions of the credit. But the reasons of policy which require the restriction of background in this case do not apply to notices given pursuant to clauses in leases."

§4　法院长期作出肯定解释的条文/文字应该受先例约束的说法

在《Chitty on Contracts》(第31版,2012年)一书之12－053段,有如下说法:"**Established judicial construction**. Where the same words or contractual provisions have for many years received a judicial construction, the court will suppose that the parties have contracted upon the belief that their words will be understood in the accepted legal sense."

这种情况不严格不是针对标准格式合约,而是针对一些长期以来法院有延续性对一些商业上常用的条文/文字的解释,应该受先例约束。例如,在国际货物买卖合约,不论是否使用标准格式合约,只要订约双方用上了CIF或FOB一词,英国法律的所有有关先例就应该适用,并对下一级的法院有约束力。在航运的租约,如果订约双方用上了"抵达船舶"(arrived ship)一词,也应该有同样的对待。这样,有水平的商业人士用上了这些条文/文字就有了肯定性与可循性。

§5　先例约束性对解释合约的有效性成疑

在本书第四章之4.3段有提到,解释合约的不肯定与不可预测,虽然针对的是一次过的合约条文/文字,但显然是针对商业上经常使用的标准格式合约的解释,至少是在理论上,就相对肯定与可循得多,这也是英国感到非常自傲的。但在现实中,特别是在航运,即使是使用一些著名的标准格式合约,如金康租约或NYPE,也往往会被修改得面目全非或/与有好几十条甚至上百条的附加条文,其中很多都是属于"一次过"(one－off)的条文。这是否还属于一个标准格式的合约不无疑问,如在The "Nema"(1981) 2 Lloyd's Rep. 239先例,虽然有关的租约也是一份标准格式合约的C. Ore 7,Diplock勋爵与Roskill勋爵仍是将其归类为"一次过"条文的合约。这在本书第四章之2.1段也有提到。

就算是没有大改动,合约仍可以归类为标准格式的合约,但只要有一定数量的修改与附加条文,个别法官/仲裁员往往很容易挑出与先例不同之处作出"区分"(distinguish),并作出不同的解释。

还有一种情况是在标准格式合约把一些文字作出了有必要甚至没有必要的改动,但本质上换汤不换药。这样,严格说是先例可以不再约束,因为文字上有所不同。但在这种情况还是不容易作出有说服力的区分,并会影响肯定性与可循性,所以不值得鼓励与可能不被上级法院认同。

另一个问题是解释合约在一些本质上看来是换汤不换药的合约条文/文字,有太多不同的说法导致有许多不同方向的先例。这令后来的案件无所适从。Staughton 大法官在 The "Kalliopi A" (1988) 2 Lloyd's Rep. 101 先例所说如下:"Proliferation of *obiter dicta* in this field will not necessarily be of assistance to shipowners and charterers, or their brokers, when drawing up their contracts; nor will it necessarily help their legal advisers when they are deciding whether to litigate. But what it certainly will do is add a further tier to the great edifice of authority with which arbitrators and Judges are confronted in a case on the interpretation of a charter – party."

另在 Wuhan Guoyu Logistics Group Co Ltd v Emporiki Bank of Greece (2014) 1 Lloyd's Rep 266 先例,Longmore 大法官说:"It is a problem of our system of precedent, that as more and more cases get decided, it seems to be necessary for judges at first instance to consider each case and determine how near or how far the document in question differs from the document construed in each past case. The commercial community deserves better than this, if better can be done. The judge did not find this case particularly easy and neither do I. The difficulty, as so often in these cases, is that there are pointers in different directions."

§6 先例作出解释的单词介绍

从上述所讲,可以见到这里又涉及法律肯定性/可循性的考虑。所以,一些有明确先例作出解释的文字,在个别合约中出现(不论是在标准格式合约或在一次过的条文),又无法有说服力地(如根据合约的其他相关条文)与先例区分,通常法院/仲裁庭还是参照先例作出解释。以下介绍极少数一些有关时间计算与其他单词的例子。

6.1 例子之一:月

在各种合约常见的文字就是"月"(month)。这在期租合约有条文会说明租期是几个月或者每个月或半个月要支付或者预付租金,在岸上的房屋租赁合约会有条文说明房租是每个月预付或者到付,贷款合约会有条文说明每一个月或者每 3 个月归还一部分贷款,有其他各种合约会规定在几个月内必须做一些事情,如行使合约的选择权等。这样,"月"怎样计算或者解释就至关重要,双方必须明确才知道自己的承诺是什么与如果迟延会有什么责任。毕竟准时履行合约是"重要"(of the essence)。[1] 这看来是一个简单的问题,但其实也有许多不明朗之处。如有阳历与阴历的月份,也有月份是 31 天和 28 天之分,等等。这通过一连串的先例定下了大原

---

〔1〕 这可见本书第十章。

则，商业人士就按规则行事。

在英国，1926年之前的说法是“月”指“阴历月”（lunar month），后来才变为普遍接受“月”指“日历月”（calendar month）。但为了避免争议或者不肯定，有不少合约甚至是立法会给其明示的定义。例如，在1979年英国《货物销售法》中Section10（3）说：“In a contract of sale ‘month’ *prima facie* means calendar month.”在1925年的英国《财产法》（Law of Property Act），当时的解释更加不肯定，故此在该立法的Section 61有一个解释，说：“‘Month’ means calendar month.”

这样，从一个月到下一个月的计算办法就是以两个月的同样日子为准，如3月30日后的一个月就是指最后期限为4月30日。如果下一期的期租租金或者是房租是4月30日后的一个月，而5月是一个长月，最后支付期限是5月30日而不是5月31日。但如果遇上短月，如1月31日之后的一个月，就会是2月28日（或者在闰年就是2月29日了）。Diplock勋爵在Dodds v Walker（1981）1 WLR 1027先例，说：“... when the relevant period is a month or specified number of months after the giving of a notice, the general rule is that the period ends upon the corresponding date in the appropriate subsequent month, ie the day of that month that bears the same number as the day of the earlier month on which the notice was given.”

这样的计算被称为“对应日期规则”（corresponding date rule），这在较近期的一个香港终审法院的Far East Drug（BVI）Co Ltd v First Pacific Co Ltd（2006）2 HKLRD 157先例也有适用。

这就是英国法律定下大原则与文字的解释。订约当事人如果不满意，可以以明示条文作出改变，只要能够清楚表达，法院/仲裁庭一定会尊重双方当事人的订约意图。例如，说明一个月在本合约是指60天，虽然这有点不可理喻，但写清楚了，也无可非议。另可以索性避免用“月”这个文字，如在一个期租合约改为更加容易计算的期租租金每15天或者30天预付一次。

6.2　例子之二：天

很多合约都会涉及天（day），因为要计算时间做各种各样的事情，如在多少天内向对方作出通知或金钱上的支付等。例如，在国际货物买卖合约或程租合约，会规定多少天作出各样的通知（如要求FOB买方在船舶抵达装港前10天或8天不等的时间预先向卖方作出通知），或规定多少天内作出支付（如支付货价或运费），或规定多少天内采取一些行动（如要在卸完货后30天内提出索赔），或规定多少天内完成任务（最常见的是规定负责装或卸的一方在多少天内完成作业，否则要赔偿给派船一方或船东滞期损失/滞期费）。

因为有订约自由，以双方在租约或买卖合约所使用的固定装卸时间的文字为例，就有了千奇百怪的写法，不熟悉的人很容易上当。实务中往往会见到不同的写法，如仅这“天”字就会被写作“days”，“calendar days”，“running days”，“consecutive days”，“conventional days”，“working days”，“weather working days”，“weather permitting days","working days of 24 hours","working day of 24 consecutive hours","weather permitting working days",等等。这样,它的意思是否一样,是否给与同一解释?或是应该不同,并且如何不同解释?笔者不在此逐一解释其区别,有兴趣的读者可看笔者的《装卸时间与滞期费》一书。以下只举一些例子介绍这方面带来的争议。

6.2.1 天或日历天

众所周知,一天有24个小时。通常这24小时是指一个子夜到下一个子夜,这是字典对"天"的解释之一,也是在一些商业规则中的定义,如用作计算装卸时间指引的《Charterparty Laytime Definition 1980》对"天"的定义为:"'DAY'—means a continuous period of 24 hours which, unless the context otherwise requires, runs from midnight to midnight."

但据悉一个"太阳日"(solar day)与一个"天文日"(astronomical day)是从一天中午起算到另一天中午,但这应该与商业的关系不大。这样,可以说"天"(days)是等同"日历天"(calendar days)。

6.2.2 子夜规则

"日历天"是以日历算多少天。例如,今天是8月7日周四,今天就是一个日历天。明天是8月8日周五,这就是第二个日历天。所以,日历天可以说是从"一个子夜到另一个子夜"(midnight to midnight)。这就带来了著名的"子夜规则"(midnight rules)。例如,其中的订约一方有在某一天之前必须做某件事的义务,他就有直到子夜的一整天可履行,要过了子夜,对方才可以指责他违约。这种案件在期租合约下的准时支付租金很多,而且涉及庞大的金额。在期租合约,有明示条文允许船东在承租人不准时支付租金的情况下撤船,而船东在运费高涨时无时无刻不在等待承租人不准时支付租金的一刻。但经常见到船东在到期支付租金的一天,在银行下班时还没有收到租金,就急不可待地撤船或给出"反技术取巧通知"(anti - technicality notice)。从一个现实的角度看来,银行下了班的确是不再可能让承租人准时支付租金。但法律上,由于该付租金的一天还没有到子夜,还不到时间说承租人没有准时支付。这方面可以看贵族院先例The "Afovos" (1983) 1 Lloyd's Rep. 335与杨大明律师所著的《期租合同》一书第十八篇。

如果想避免这一"子夜规则",可以以明示条文规定必须在有关日子"下班前"(close of business)或干脆"下午5点前"(before 5 pm)等履行合约承诺否则就是违约,现实中也确实经常有这种做法。

6.2.3 法律不理会一天的部分时间

这一法律地位已经有很多说法,如早在Pugh v. Duke of Leeds (1777) 2 Cowp. 714先例,Mansfield勋爵就说法律没有一天的部分这个概念:"'Date' does not mean the hour or the minute, but the day of delivery; and in law there is no fraction of a day."

另在Lester v. Garland (1808) 15 Ves. 248先例,William Grant M. R.大法官也

说:"Our law rejects fractions of a day more generally than the civil law does. The effect is to render the day a sort of indivisible point; so that any act, done in the compass of it, is no more referable to any one, than to any other, portion of it; but the act and the day are co - extensive; and therefore the act cannot properly be said to be passed, until the day is passed."

还有在 Cartwright v. MacCormack (1963) 1 W. L. R. 18 先例,Harman 大法官也说:"... generally speaking, when a day is mentioned from which the time is to start running, fractions of a day ought to be disregarded and time should run from midnight."

这表示会有两个结果,一是把部分时间当作一整天计算,或是计算时不理会部分的时间。换言之,或者不算,或者就算一天。这是 Rigby 大法官在 Re North Exp. Hashuck (1895) 2 Q. B. 264 先例中所讲的:"It is said that the law takes no account of fractions of a day; but that is not a correct statement, if it means that the law will never inquire at what time a particular event took place; for instance a difference of five minutes in the registration of two deeds in the Middlesex Registry would be sufficient to determine a question of priorities, and the time of their respective registrations would, as a matter of course be looked at. If the doctrine is cut down to the proposition that in the computation of time the law takes no account of fractions of a day, then it means one of two things: either that the fraction of a day is to be taken as one whole day, or that it is to be excluded altogether from the calculation; it does not help us to determine in any particular case whether the part is to be left out or kept in."

这在笔者的《装卸时间与滞期费》一书第十二章之 3.1 段也有清楚介绍。

但又是在订约自由下,双方可以以明示条文改变上述的默示地位,经常也有人这样做,把一天的部分时间也加入计算。

6.3 例子之三:现金

商业合约离不开金钱,所以"现金"(cash)一词经常在合约中出现。随着世界的改变,很难想象商业合约下的支付还是像中古时代那样,由支付方用麻包袋装了现金交给另一方。随着银行体系的建立与通讯技术的改进,支付的办法已有多种,如电汇、银行本票、汇票等。

由于在一些古老的标准格式合约还印上了"现金"一词,如航运最普遍被使用的期租合约格式 NYPE 46,所以法律解释这一词要符合"商业合理性"(commercial commonsense),正如已经多次提到的 Diplock 勋爵在 The "Antaios" (No. 2) (1984) 2 Lloyd's Rep. 235 先例所说的:"... if a detailed semantic and syntactical analysis of words in a commercial contract is going to lead to a conclusion that flouts business common sense, it must be made to yield to business common sense."

所以法律的解释开始配合现代的商业做法。首先是在 The "Georgios C." (1971) 1 Lloyd's Rep. 7 先例,判是"现金支付"包括了"汇款"(transfer)、"银行本票"(bank draft)、"银行付款单"(banker's payment slip)。到了 The "Brimnes" (1972) 2 Lloyd's Rep. 465 先例,Brandon 大法官对"现金支付"一词给了更明确的定义,说:"In my view these words must be interpreted against the background of modern commercial practice. So interpreted it seems to me that they shipowners contend, have a wilder meaning, comprehending any commercially - recognised method of transferring funds, the result of which is to give the transferee the unconditional right to the immediate use of the funds transferred."(这文字的解释需要考虑现代商业做法的背景。在 Brandon 大法官看来,现金包括任何商业上认可的汇款办法,只要达到一个结果是给收款人一个无条件的权利可马上使用这笔钱。)

6.4 例子之四:条件

条件(condition)这一单词在合约中经常出现,但与许多其他文字一样,有很多不同的解释。Stoljar 教授在他的《The Contractual Concept of Condition》(1958) 69 LQR 485 一文中给出了十二个不同的意思。但针对一般的合约而言,它是有三个主要的不同"用途"(usage),如下:

1. 它只是指合约的"条文/条件"(terms)。例如,很多合约都会在抬头称"合约条件"(conditions of contract)。在一些小金额的买卖,订货单与发票也经常会印上"条件请看背面"(for conditions see back)。这种做法也会出现在其他许多不同的情况,如火车票或渡轮票等。这表示"条件"一词在这样的情况下使用没有什么特别的技术上或法律的重要性,主要是要求对方做出一些履行的承诺,可称为"承诺性条件"(promissory condition),在本段稍后会详细介绍。

2. 立法上将其视为基本性的条文。这是指 1979 年的英国《货物销售法》,特别是 Section 11 到 Section 15。这一立法的前一个版本是在 1893 年,也是这个立法把合约条文分为"条件"(condition)与"保证"(warranty),导致不少人认为合约条文只有这两大分类。其实,该立法只是针对货物买卖。1979 年的《货物销售法》在 Section 11(3) 区分了条件与保证以及它们的不同救济,如下:"Whether a stipulation in a contract of sale is a condition, the breach of which may give rise to a right to treat the contract as repudiated, or a warranty, the breach of which may give rise to a claim for damages but not to a right to reject the goods and treat the contract as repudiated, depends in each case on the construction of the contract; and a stipulation may be a condition, though called a warranty in the contract."

立法条文是说明违反条件的救济有三种,包括拒绝货物,将买卖合约视为违约/毁约终止与索赔损失。但违反保证就只有索赔损失的一种救济方法。接下来,该立法在 Section 12 至 Section 15 列出一连串的条文针对货物主权、将来货物必须符合货物的描述或样品、货物的满意质量与适合买方的用途等,并把它们列为条件,这通常被称为"默示条件"(implied condition)。

3. "先决条件或后续条件"(condition precedent or condition subsequent)。简单

说,先决条件是指除非它被履行,否则双方没有合约关系。至于后续条件是指如果它后来发生,该合约就会自动终止或变为无效。关于这方面的课题在本书第八章变数条件条文有详细介绍。

在英国普通法任何违约都可以索赔损失,但肯定不是每一种违约都可以让受害方不必进一步履行合约(这包括暂时停止受害方在合约下的履行义务或永久终止合约)。在英国法律,能够终止合约基本上只有四种情况:(1)与《货物销售法》的说法相近的,就是对方违反了一个条件条文;(2)对方违反了一个中间条文并产生严重后果;(3)对方以文字或者行动显示了他不愿意继续履行合约,这是属于一种“违约/毁约行为”(repudiatory conduct),受害方可以接受并终止合约;(4)根据合约的明示条文所给与的终止合约权利,这种权利不一定与对方是否违约有关系。

普通法将合约中作出各种承诺的条文区分为三大类:(1)“条件条文”(condition);(2)“中间条文”(intermediate/innominate terms);(3)“保证条文”(warranty)。条件条文的违反(即使是轻微的违反)可以导致受害方终止合约并索赔损失,而保证条文的违反,受害方只能索赔损失。至于中间条文就要看每一个案件的不同本质与事实,如果违反后果严重,其救济与违反条件条文的一样。今天的合约条文绝大部分属于中间条文,而不会归类为条件条文或保证条文。这是有几个重要原因,如英国法律尽量支持合约的履行而不支持合约的终止。另在现实中有许多合约条文的违反可轻可重,非要在每次事件中看它会造成的后果严重性才能决定恰当的救济。例如,在确立中间条文的重要贵族院先例 The “Hongkong Fir” (1961) 2 Lloyd's Rep 478,针对的是船舶适航问题到底是条件条文或是保证条文,结果在该先例中贵族院创立出一种新的中间条文。它的合理性 Scarman 勋爵在 Bunge Corporation v. Tradax Export S. A. (1981) 2 Lloyd's Rep 1 先例有解释说:“... In the *Hongkong Fir* case the term in question provide for the obligation of seaworthiness, breach of which it is well known may be trivial (e. g. one defective rivet) or very serious (e. g. a hole in the bottom of the ship). It is inconceivable that parties when including such a term in their contract could have contemplated or intended (unless they expressly say so) that one defective rivet would entitle the charterer to end the contract or that a hole in the bottom of the ship would not. I read the *Hongkong Fir* case as being concerned as much with the construction of the contract as with the consequences and effect of breach. ...”(船东对适航的承诺如果违反可以有很大轻重的差别,可以轻至一颗螺丝钉的小毛病,或重至船底有个大洞,一开航就会沉没。双方订约方不可能把不论轻重的不适航都视为条件条文,允许承租人终止租约。)

多数合约条文现在属于中间条文,这也带来了坏处,就是不肯定。受害方在对方违约后(特别是有时间规定的承诺)[2],很难掌握到底能否终止合约,即使是客观认

〔2〕 这方面在本书第十章有更详尽的介绍。

为对方的违约十分严重。有少数的判例会把某一种延误的违约归属于条件条文,如在 The “Mihalis Angelos” (CA) (1970) 2 Lloyd's Rep. 43 先例中,判租约中的“估计可装货日期”(expected readiness to load)是条件条文。

为了肯定与减少中间条文带来的不肯定,在 Bunge Corporation v. Tradax Export S. A. 与 Lombard Norton Central plc v. Butterworth (1987) QB 527 两个重要先例,贵族院明确了商业合约(主要是商品买卖,特别是涉及一连串买卖的合约)中针对时间的承诺(如付运期、买方开出信用证的期限、指定装港或卸港的期限、派船的期限等),都属于条件条文。在后一个先例 Diplock 勋爵的说法如下:“In some stipulations in commercial contracts as to time when something must be done by one of the parties or some event must occur, time is of the essence; in others it is not. In commercial contracts for the sale of goods *prima facie* a stipulated time of delivery is of the essence, but *prima facie* a stipulated time of payment is not (Sale of Goods Act 1893).”

至于其他类别的合约(甚至是商业合约/买卖合约),订约方经常为了肯定在合约以明示条文规定某些条文是条件条文。其中一种安全的写法是说明某些条文是“重要”(of the essence),特别是针对准时支付合约下的款项或完成交易。

在合约中通过明示条文把承诺提升为条件条文,由于后果严重(受害方可以终止合约),所以要写得特别清楚,正如 Reid 勋爵在 Schuler AG v. Wickman Machine Tool Sales Ltd (1973) 2 Lloyd's Rep. 53 先例所说的名言:“The fact that a particular construction leads to a very unreasonable result must be a relevant consideration. The more unreasonable the result the more unlikely it is that the parties can have intended it, and if they do intend it the more necessary it is that they shall make that intention abundantly clear.”(越不合理的结果,就越不像订约双方有这个意图。如果他们真的有这个订约意图,会更加需要把这个意图说得更加清楚。)

该先例的案情是英国公司 Wickman 与德国生产商 Schuler 签订了合约,Wickman 从而获得 Schuler 产品在英国的独家销售权,产品是汽车工业所用的 panel presses。合约第7(b)条文如下:“It shall be a condition of this agreement that Wickman shall send its representatives to visit the six firms whose name are listed in the Schedule hereto at least once in every week for the purpose of soliciting orders for panel presses.”(为了招揽 panel presses 的订单,Wickman 必须派遣营业代表每周走访6家工厂,这是本合约下的条件。)

注意在上述条文是明示规定了 Wickman 的承诺“条件”,至于6家工厂是英国最大的6家汽车生产商。另合约的第11条文说明合约期是4年半,之后双方可以给12个月通知终止合约。这表示在合约最初的4年半,Wickman 必须派两位指定营业代表的其中一位走访在英国的6家工厂共1400次。如果第7(b)条文是条件条文,Wickman 只要少了1次走访,Schuler 就可以违反条件条文终止合约。另外,该合约也没有针对指定营业代表如果死亡、退休或者生病不能走访应该如何履行才不算违约。换言之,如果把第7(b)条文当作是条件条文,就看来太不合理,因为合约将会太容易被 Schuler 终止,正如 Reid 勋爵所说:“If the parties gave any thought to the matter at all they must have realised the probability that in a few cases out of 1, 400 required visits a visit as stipulated must be impossible.”

结果贵族院的多数否定了第7(b)条文可解释为条件条文,认为“条件”(condition)这个词除了其“法律上专门的意义”(strict legal sense)之外,还有很多其他意思。所以,虽然第7(b)条文确有很“强烈表示”(strong indication)“提升”为条件条文,但仍不够清楚订明这一十分不合理的解释。

但贵族院持相反意见的 Wilberforce 勋爵认为这是一个双方约定的条件条文,说:“... for my part, to call the clause arbitrary, capricious or fantastic, or to introduce as test of its validity the ubiquitous reasonable man (I do not know whether he is English or German) is to assume, contrary to the evidence, that both parties to this contract adopted a standard of easygoing tolerance rather than one of aggressive, insistent, punctuality and efficiency.”[Wilberforce 勋爵认为把第7(b)条文说成是独断独行、反复无常或荒谬,或以一个到处存在的合理人士(不论是英国人还是德国人)来作出一个考验,都是与证据不符地假设该合约下双方可以允许一种悠闲的与容忍的履约标准,而不是要求一个有闯劲的、坚持、准时与高效率的履约标准。]

看来,在该案件中的外来证据/口头证据显示了 Schuler 与 Wickman 在谈判中同意了严格的走访这6家工厂,是 Wilberforce 勋爵认为的双方所约定的一个“有闯劲的、坚持、准时与高效率”(aggressive, insistent, punctuality and efficiency)的履约标准。这样,根据订约时的背景/语境,第7(b)条文应该解释为条件条文。但 Wilberforce 勋爵是唯一持不同意见的大法官。在该著名的案例中可以见到把重点放在合约条文/文字与把重点放在“背景/语境”(background/factual matrix)作出解释会带来不同结果,而这种分歧在1973年或更早已经存在。在贵族院或最高院近期的大量判例如 Charter Reinsurance Co Ltd v. Fagan (1997) A. C. 313 与 Investors Compensation Scheme v. West Bromwich Building Society (1998) 1 W. L. R. 896 等后,解释合约新趋势是重视订约背景/语境,这可看本书第一章与第六章。如果这一案例在现在审理,Wilberforce 勋爵的不同意见可能会受到更大支持。

6.5 例子之五:保证

保证(warranty)这一单词也有几个不同的解释,决定哪一个是准确的解释要看相关的“语境”(factual matrix)。一个广泛的定义就是一个承诺,这承诺可以针对承诺当时“存在的事实”(existing fact)或者是一个“延续的情况”(continuous state of affairs)。这承诺也可以针对被要求提供的财产或者服务的质量。这种承诺会在谈判中出现,如在一个公司收购的交易中,卖方向收购方保证他的公司赚钱(这是存在的事实),并保证他的公司前景非常好(这是一个延续的情况)。这种承诺或保证如果不正确,会根据不同的事实构成欺诈、疏忽或无辜的“误述”(misrepresentation)。在

1967 年《误述法》之前,由于普通法不承认疏忽误述,但欺诈误述不容易证明,所以需要"附带保证"(collateral warranty)的说法作出救济。也就是承诺方不论是任何类别的误述,只要作出过保证,就算没有明示在有关的合约,也会像受到另一个附带合约的约束。[3] 这正是"保证"一词的其中一种常见用法。

这种承诺除了谈判外也通常出现在合并收购的合约,卖方会作出一连串的保证。在这些公司收购交易中所作出的保证,在本质上十分重要。如在 Eurocopy plc v. Teesdale (1992) BCLC 1067 先例中就有一份独立的"披露信函"(Disclosure Letter),内容是全面的披露收购公司的财产、债务与其他业务上与经济上的状况。另在第 3.3 条文说:"The Warranties are given subject to the matters set out in the Disclosure Letter ... but no other information relating to the Company of which the Purchaser has knowledge (actual constructive or imputed) shall preclude or affect any claim made by the Purchaser for breach of any of the Warranties or reduce any amount recoverable."

另一个有关"保证"这一词的解释是在 1979 年《货物销售法》与普通法, 被视为一个比较不重要的承诺性条文,对它的违反只会导致损失赔偿。但在普通法,合约条文的承诺性会被视为保证条文的也不多,多数还是被视为中间条文。

另一个有关保证的很不同解释是,如果这一个字出现在保险合约,如在一个船舶保险的保单中是"warrant class",就变为保证船舶有认可的船级。而如果在受保期内船级被撤销,即使是看来无害的短暂时间,也可能有严重后果。这是因为 1906 英国《海上保险法》对保单内的这种保证必须完全依照,有非常严格的立法解释。对其违反带来的严重后果是接近甚至超越条件条文,但又不完全相同,如它会自动导致保险人的赔付责任在违反保证的一天终止。这是在 1906 年英国《海上保险法》之 Section 33 (3),说:"(3) A warranty, as above defined, is a condition which must be exactly complied with, whether it be material to the risk or not. If it be not so complied with, then, subject to any express provision in the policy, the insurer is discharged from liability as from the date of the breach of warranty, but without prejudice to any liability incurred by him before that date."

6.6 例子之六:补偿(indemnity)

补偿(indemnity)这一单词也是在合约中有至少两个不同的解释,这可节录 Staughton 大法官在 The "Eurus" (1998) 1 Lloyd's Rep. 351 先例中所说如下:"The word 'indemnity' is likewise used in two senses. It may mean simply damages awarded

---

[3] 针对附带保证,《Chitty on Contracts》(第 31 版,2012 年)一书之 12 - 033 段说:"Undertakings may be given that are collateral to another contract. they may be considered to be independent of that other contract either because they cannot fairly be regarded as having been incorporated therein, or because rules of evidence hinder their incorporation, or requirements of form or is made between parties other than those by or to whom the undertaking is given. Such undertakings are often referred to as collateral contracts, or 'collateral warranties'."

for tort or breach of contract. ... Alternatively the word ' indemnity ' may refer to all loss suffered which is attributable to a specified cause ... "

一般而言,补偿条文通常是规定如果一方(被补偿方)因为履行合约而有了对第三人的责任,他可以从另一方(补偿方)得到对该责任带来的损失补偿。

6.6.1　补偿与担保的区分

事实上,现实中大量存在的"补偿保险"(indemnity insurance)就是补偿条文的一种,在受保人对第三人有责任时,由保险人对其作出补偿。但在一般非保险的合约,补偿条文试图在一些特定情况下把"主要责任"(primary responsibility)从一方(被补偿方)转移另外一方(补偿方),并可令被补偿方免受损失(如要先作出赔偿,会导致经济上破产)。这里,先要解释普通法与衡平法的不同对待。

在 Johnston v. Salvage Association (1887) 19 QBD 458 先例中,Lindley 大法官是这样说:"In equity a contract to indemnify can be specifically enforced before there has been any such breach of contract as would sustain an action at law. In equity the plaintiff need not pay and perhaps ruin himself before seeking relief. He is entitled to be relieved from liability."

Goff 勋爵也在 The "Fanti" and "Padre Island" (1990) 2 Lloyd's Rep. 191 先例中说:"I accept that, at common law, a contract of indemnity gives rise to an action for unliquidated damages, arising from the failure of the indemnifier to prevent the indemnified person from suffering damage, for example, by having to pay a third party. I also accept that, at common law, the cause of action does not (unless the contract provides otherwise) arise until the indemnified person can show actual loss ... This is, as I understand it, because the promise of indemnity is simply a promise to hold the indemnified person harmless against a specific loss or expense. On this basis, no debt can arise before the loss is suffered or the expense incurred; however, once the loss is suffered or the expense incurred, the indemnifier is in breach of contract for having failed to hold the indemnified person harmless against the relevant loss or expense. There is no condition of prior payment ... It is for this reason that equity felt that it could, and should, intervene. ... Equity does not mend men's bargains; but it may grant specific performance of a contract, consistently with its terms, where the remedies at law are inadequate, this is what has happened in the case of contracts of indemnity, as a general rule, 'Indemnity requires that the party to be indemnified shall never be called upon to pay' ... "

在同一个先例,Brandon 勋爵也说:"There is no doubt that before the passing of the Supreme Court of Judicature Acts 1873 and 1875, there was a difference the remedies available to enforce an ordinary contract of indemnity (by which I mean a contract of indemnity not containing any express 'pay to be paid' provision) at law on the one hand and in equity on the other. At law the party to be indemnified had to discharge the liability himself first and then sue indemnifier for damages for breach of contract. In equity an ordinary contract of indemnity could be directed to be specifically performed by ordering that the indemnifier should pay the amount concerned directly to the third party to whom the liability was owed or in some cases to the parties to be indemnified... **There is further no doubt that since the passing of the Supreme Court of Judicature Acts 1873 and 1875 the equitable remedy has prevailed over the remedy at law.**"(加黑部分是现在的法律地位。)

笔者可以在这里简单解释上述说法,就是在普通法的地位,补偿是要被补偿方先承担损失,也就是支付给第三人后,才能证明他有实际损失可向补偿方要求补偿。但这样会带来困难,如被补偿方无法先承担一大笔损失。如果先要支付出才能寻求补偿就会来的太晚,被补偿方可能因此而破产或倒闭。所以衡平法就在这种情况下作出一些救济,如作出"履约指令"(specific performance),强制补偿方在补偿合约下直接向第三人作出支付,让被补偿方不必先作出支付。

这可以是生死之别,如船东经常会面临无单放货的要求,而用来交换的就是一份收货人或/与银行所作出的"补偿承诺"(Letter of Indemnity)。它被通称为保函,但文字上并不是一个"担保"(surety)。[4] 上述无单放货的补偿承诺更会明确地写明说:

"In consideration of your complying with our above request, we hereby agree as follows:

1. To indemnify you, your servants and agents and to hold all of you harmless in respect of any liability, loss, damage or expenses of whatsoever nature which you may sustain by reason of delivering the cargo in accordance with our request.

2. In the event of any proceedings being commence against you or any of your servants or agents in connection with the delivery of the cargo as aforesaid to provide you or them on demand with sufficient funds to defend the same.

3. If, in connection of the delivery of cargo as aforesaid, the ship or any other ship or property belonging to you should be arrested or detained or if the arrest or detention thereof should be threatened to provide on demand such bail or other security as maybe required to prevent such an arrest or detention or to secure the release of such ship or property and to indemnify you in respect of any liability, loss, damage or expense caused by such arrest or detention or threatened arrest or detention whether or not such arrest or detention or threatened arrest ordetention may be justified. ...

7. This indemnity shall be governed by and construed in accordance with English

〔4〕"担保合约"(Suretyship or contract of guarantee)下,作为担保人只是承担损失或债务的"次要责任"(secondary liability),被担保人才承担主要责任。这是补偿合约与担保合约最主要的不同。

law..."

这一个补偿承诺在一船货物的价格动辄就几百万或几千万美元的今天十分重要。如果在无单放货后，船东被提单持有人扣船并很快从法院取得简易判决，船东就面临支付这一笔巨款或是船舶被法院拍卖并宣布破产。如果手中只是有一份担保，担保人（不论是收货人或银行）就可以说："船东你先支付了，再来找我，否则我也不能明确你是有责任赔付与赔付多少！"但如果是一份补偿合约（也就是较早说的保函），船东就可以要求补偿人（如银行）马上作出支付，如果补偿人拒绝，船东可向法院申请履约指令。

其他的分别是补偿条文/承诺不受1677年英国《欺诈法》的管制，即不要求补偿人的文书签字。这也是为什么很多合约中，包括租约中，都有补偿条文，但租约并不需要补偿人签字才能令这一补偿条文有效。但担保合约就受1677年《欺诈法》的管制，需要担保人签字。

最后一提的分别是担保合约必须与主合约共存，但补偿合约下由于补偿人变为要承担主要责任或成为"主债务人"（principle debtor），就没有合约共存的说法。换言之，担保合约只是"附带"（accessory）在一个主合约。而如果作为主债务人的被担保方因为各种合法理由不必对第三人负责，担保人也不必负责。

6.6.2　补偿是否是一种损失赔偿？

补偿条文/合约下的索赔到底是否是"损失赔偿"（claim in damages）？毕竟，要补偿所针对的特定情况不一定与任何违约有关。如果被补偿方的索赔是损失赔偿，被补偿方就会有许多其他针对损失的原则要考虑，如损失是否"遥远"（remoteness），这包括可否"合理预见"（reasonably foreseeable）与因果关系有否被打断，以及受害方有否"减少损失"（mitigation）等。例如，在无单放货下，船东向收货人或/与银行所作出的保函提出索赔并要求补偿，收货人或银行就会说："你应该自己先提供担保放船并委任律师对无单放货的索赔作出抗辩，因为你应该减少损失如船期的延误。"如果船东的索赔并非是损失赔偿，这说法就不正确，因为被补偿人没有减少损失的义务。

这正是在本书第三章之6.2.4段所介绍的The "Eurus"（1998）1 Lloyd's Rep. 351先例的主要争议，因为在该先例，尼日利亚到了8时之后装完货才能出该天提单的不为双方订约时知悉的习惯做法所带来的损失太遥远，承租人以损失赔偿的救济方法就不能成功向船东索赔。但该先例认为，如果有关的租约是有一条有效的补偿条文，要追究的只是"因果关系"（causation）有没有被打断。如果没有，补偿人就要赔偿，不存在损失遥远的说法。

6.6.3　补偿下因果关系的中断

补偿条文只是追究特定情况（如无单放货）与产生对第三人责任（提单持有人扣船提出侵占货物的索赔）之间的直接的"因果关系"（causation），而因果关系会被打断的主要原因是被补偿人自己的疏忽。

在期租合约，由于承租人有权在全球营运船舶，会对船舶带来各种各样的危险，如不安全港口/泊位、不安全货物、签发提单带来额外责任等。所以,法律对期租合约是有默示的补偿责任,不少期租合约中也有明示的补偿条文,被补偿方是船东而补偿方是承租人。在这种经常出现的案件中,因果关系是否有中断是主要的争议,也是承租人重要甚至唯一的抗辩。这一课题可参见杨大明律师所著的《期租合同》之第二十四篇之24.4.3段。

接下来介绍一些期租合约外的重要先例,首先是 Canada Steamship Lines Ltd v. R. (1952) 1 Lloyd's Rep. 1 的枢密院先例,案情涉及加拿大政府出租一个在蒙特里尔的码头货棚给有关的船公司,在出租合约中,有一条补偿条文,要求该船公司补偿出租人的所有损失等,条文非常广泛,如下:"That the lessee shall at all times indemnify and save harmless the lessor from and against all claims and demands, loss, costs, damages, actions, suits or proceedings by whomsoever made, brought or prosecuted, in any manner based upon, occasioned by or attributable to the execution of these presents or any actions taken or things done... by virtue hereof, or the exercises in any manner of rights arising hereunder."

出租合约也涉及出租人(加拿大政府)要进行该码头货棚的修理,但不幸在修理期间,由于出租人的工人疏忽使用喷灯而导致火灾。把属于第三人的价值超过50万加元的货物烧毁,这导致第三人纷纷向加拿大政府提出索赔。而加拿大政府也就以出租人身份向该船公司要求补偿。

在枢密院,判是补偿条文虽然十分广泛,但还是不足以说明出租人的工人所造成的损失不论是如何重大,都需要承租人的船公司承担主要责任。Morton 勋爵说:"Such a liability for the negligence of others must surely be imposed by very clear words, if it is to be imposed at all."

接下的 Smith v South Wales Switchgear Ltd (1978) 1 WLR 165 先例,Viscount Dilhorne 是这样说:"When considering the meaning of such a clause one must, I think, regard it as even more inherently improbable that one party should agree to discharge the liability of the other party for acts for which he is responsible."(在考虑一条补偿条文时,应该视为是潜在性不大可能是补偿方愿意对被补偿方自己要负责的行为作出补偿并免了他的责任。)

在同一个先例,Keith 勋爵根据 Canada Steamship Ltd v The King (1952) AC 192, PC 的枢密院先例也说:"While they apply to the construction both of a clause bearing to exempt from certain liabilities a party who has undertaken to carry out contractual work and of a clause whereby such a party has agreed to indemnify the other party against liabilities which would ordinarily fall upon him, they apply a fortiori in the latter case, since it represents a less usual and more extreme situation."

换言之,解释补偿条文与一条免责条文一样,要针对获利方严格解释。而免责条文是明确需要明示"疏忽"(negligence)或类似的文字才能对疏忽免责:Cillespie

Brothers Ltd v Bowles (Roy) Transport Ltd (1973) QB 400 先例。所以,补偿条文也是有同样的要求。

最后介绍一个被补偿方涉及疏忽而中断因果关系的判决,是在英国著名的 Piper Alpha 钻油平台事件带来的案例。这是一个北海的海上油井发生爆炸与火灾,最终导致 165 个油井工人死亡。该案例名为 E E Caleonia Ltd v Orbit Value Co Ltd (1994) 1 WLR 1515, CA,案情涉及该油井经营人在灾难后支付了一笔钱给死亡工人的家属作为庭外和解,然后根据与被告的工程公司(他雇用了该死亡的工人)的合约中的补偿条文要求补偿。因为事故涉及该油井经营人的疏忽,所以补偿条文的因果关系也被打断。

6.7 例子之七:必须与可能

从字义来看,上述两个词应该清楚明了,“必须”(shall)应该是强制性,而“可能”(may)是允许性。但会有情况是看了合约的上下文,协调解释就会有不同的结论。首先是在本书第三章之 2.4 段的 PCCW Global Ltd v. Interactive Communications Service Ltd (2006) Civil Appeal No. 18 先例,香港高院在解释一条美国纽约州法院的管辖权条文时,就是将“必须”一词解释为“可能”。

至于把“可能”解释为“必须”,可简单节录《Black's Law Dictionary》所说如下:“Although normally used a verb to express a possibility, courts not infrequently construe ‘may’ as ‘shall’ or ‘must’ to the end that justice is not the slave of grammar. However, as a general rule, the word ‘may’ is not treated as a word of command unless there is something in the context or subject - matter as to indicate that it was used in such a sense.”

这可看本书第六章之 13.2 段介绍的澳大利亚最高院的 Royal Botanic Gardens and Domain Trust v South Sydney City Council (2002) 240 CLR 45 先例。在该先例,澳大利亚最高院根据相关的背景/语境,认为合约条文中的“may”一词应解释为“only”。

§7 先例作出解释的条文介绍

这一小段与上一小段稍微不同之处是不针对个别单词,而是针对经常被适用且可能在标准格式合约的条文,是否受到长期作出肯定解释的先例约束或可根据个别文字上的改动而偏离。笔者以下举两个例子。

7.1 例子之一:程租与买卖合约下的装卸时间与滞期费停算条文

传统的说法是装卸时间一开始,就会不断计算在承租人(或国际货物买卖下的非派船方)。这道理十分简单,因为在程租合约或国际货物买卖合约下,承租人或非派船方(如 FOB 卖方或 CIF/CFR 买方)作出了承诺在固定的装卸时间内完成作业。

而英国法律下合约的承诺是严格,不存在合理与否。所以,承租人或非派船方就必须要以明示条文规定在一些他们无法控制的情况下(通常是所谓的不可抗力事件,如政府干预、动乱、罢工等)停算装卸时间。没有这一条装卸时间停算条文,这些不可抗力事件导致装卸作业延误的风险还是在承租人或非派船方。

固定装卸时间完毕,但作业还没有完成,承租人或非派船方就违反了他的承诺。这一违约就带来赔偿的责任,而由于这种情况经常发生,程租合约或国际货物买卖合约为了避免复杂与昂贵的损失计算,都会事前约定"议定赔偿"(liquidated damages)的金额,也就是"滞期费"(demurrage)。滞期费一开始,也是不断计算在承租人或买卖合约下的非派船方。这是根据另一个原则,就是承租人或非派船方的违约,也就是不能在固定装卸时间内完成作业导致了船舶滞期,不能开航。这样,即使固定装卸时间会有免算条文,或约定的固定时间排除一些周末假期或不能装卸的坏天气,也不再适用在滞期费的计算了。这带来了一句十分著名的说法:"一旦滞期,永远滞期(once on demurrage, always on demurrage)。"但根据同样道理,清楚无误的明示条文可以超越这一法律默示的地位。所以,如果有一条滞期费停算条文(也可以与装卸时间停算条文写在一起),就可以改变这一著名说法的地位。但由于这是客观看不合理,承租人或非派船方的违约导致船舶被滞期,竟然还要在船东或派船方没有任何错误的情况下停算。但这是订约自由,法院/仲裁庭的责任只是解释合约。唯一要记得Reid勋爵在Schuler (L) A. G. v. Wickman Machine Tool Sales Ltd(1973) 2 Lloyd's Rep. 53先例中说的越不合理的结果就越需要双方以清楚无误的明示条文/文字显示他们的订约意图。

停算滞期费时间也涉及另一个解释原则,就是订约方不能以自己的错误行为来获利,这方面请看本书第四章之第10段与本书第七章之10.3段。正如Diplock勋爵在Cheall v. APEX (1983) 2 A. C. 181先例中所说的:"... the well known rule of construction that, except in the unlikely case that the contract contains clear express provisions to the contrary, it is to be presumed that it was not the intention of the parties that either party should be entitled to rely upon his own breaches of his primary obligations ..."

但问题是在订约自由下可以有许多不同表达的条文/文字说明承租人可以停算装卸时间与滞期费,这就带来一些著名的案例是高水平的高院大法官也认为这些条文/文字十分广泛与十分明确,可达到停算装卸时间与滞期费的目的,即使没有针对性说明滞期费停算。但随后这些案件上诉至上诉庭,就往往被改变。

第一个案例是The "Kalliopi A" (1988) 2 Lloyd's Rep. 101,其有关条文是一条免责条文,其中文字上并没有说明有关的免责事项可停算装卸时间与滞期费,只是说这些免责事项是双方(船东与承租人)都可依赖。但请注意停算装卸时间与滞期费只是承租人需要依赖与得利,与船东无关,而免责条文通常是针对双方都可以在一些特定的事项中免责。在该先例的租约,第36条文如下:"The act of God, restraint of

Princes and Rulers . . . and all and every other unavoidable hindrances which may prevent the . . . discharging . . . during the . . . voyage always mutually [excepted]."

在卸港,船舶受到严重的延误,原因就是港口拥挤。有关港口拥挤是上述免责条文中的一个特定事项之"unavoidable hindrances"所包括在内:Larsen v Sylvester (1908) 96 LT 94; The Radauti (1988) 2 Lloyd's Rep 416 等先例。所以关键的争议点还是在这一条文说明这免责事项如果"阻止了卸货"(prevent the discharge),承租人就可以免责是否足够清楚让承租人不必作出滞期费的损失赔偿。如果仅是从字面看而不管先例与解释原则(如免责条文不明确会针对获利方解释),笔者恐怕也觉得足够清楚,免责就是免了赔偿损失,即不必支付滞期费。这正是第一审高院的 Evans 大法官所持的看法,说:

"The central issue is whether clause 36 operates so as to exclude the charterers' liability for demurrage. To have that effect the clause must be clearly intended to do so. Short of identifying 'demurrage' by name, the words are clear: 'unavoidable hindrance (sc. congestion) which may prevent the . . . discharging . . . always mutually [excepted]'. This must be commercial shorthand for 'neither party to be liable for the consequences of', and the charterers' liability for the consequences if discharging is prevented is measured in terms of demurrage. So the clause purports to exempt charterers from their liability for what will be put forward as a demurrage claim. . . .

Clause36 in my judgement exempts the charterers from liability for demurrage in respect of the period when congestion prevented discharge and delivery from taking place. This conclusion gives effect to the words of the clause without infringing the undoubted rule that any demurrage exception must be clearly worded."

但这一判决到上诉庭,被 Staughton 大法官为首的上诉庭一致推翻了,理由是解释合约不能仅依据条文/文字的一般性解释,而必须考虑一贯以来的先例对承租人如果不想对他的违约(违反在固定时间内卸货的承诺)作出赔偿的责任,也就是支付滞期费,就必须有针对性地写得清清楚楚,而不能只是一条一般性的免责条文。

在不久之后的另一个先例 The "Lefthero" (1992) 2 Lloyd's Rep. 109,情况与 The "Kalliopi A"几乎是一致。当然有关的租约条文第 28 条在文字上又有所不同,如下:"28. Neither the vessel nor the Owners nor Master not the Charterers/Shippers/Receivers shall be responsible for any loss or damage or delay or failure in performing hereunder, arising or resulting from . . . restraint of princes . . ."

在该先例中也发生了严重的船舶延误,可以说是因为政府禁令所导致,应该包括在"restraint of princes"的政府干预的免责事项内。而上述的第 28 条文明确说明承租人/发货人/收货人不必为这一免责事项所导致的"延误"(delay)负责。这样从文字的表面看来,没有理由要承租人赔偿船东滞期费(真正是针对船舶延误)的损失,这又是第一审高院 Evans 大法官的看法。但他的判决又再度给不同大法官的上诉庭所一致推翻,背后的原因与 The "Kalliopi A"先例一样。Lloyd 大法官这样说:"On the face of it, the words of clause 28 are wide enough to cover delay by the charterers in discharging the vessel, where the delay arises or results from restraint of princes. If the charterers are not so protected, then the clause is, as the Judge said, very one – sided[5]. But it has long been the law that to protect a charterer against liability for demurrage, the language of the exceptions clause must be clearly worded to that effect."

在目前看来,在程租合约或国际货物买卖合约,如果承租人或非派船方想把滞期费在一些他们也无法控制的特定免责事项下停算,就必须针对性地说明,如像 The "Angelia" (1972) 2 Lloyd's Rep. 154 先例的有关条文是在约定了一连串不同的免责事项后,加了一句如下:"... neither Charterer nor Shippers shall be liable for any loss or damage resulting from any such excepted causes and time lost by reason thereof shall not count as lay days or days on demurrage."

7.2 例子之二:程租合约下的中止条文

再下一个例子也可以说是同一个理念,就是在程租合约(特别是一些标准格式)经常会有一条"中止与留置条文"(cesser and lien clause)。如 C (Ore) 7 的程租合约标准格式的第21 条文如下:"All liability of Charterer shall cease on completion of loading and payment of advance, if any, Owner having lien on Cargo for freight, dead freight, and demurrage."(承租人的所有合约责任在装完货物与支付了任何预付的费用[指预付部分的运费作为费用让船东有资金完成航次,因为普通法的地位是船东完成了航次才能赚取运费。但在现代的做法是可指支付了预付与双方约定赚取的运费]后,就必须终止,船东对船上的货物在将会赚取的运费、亏舱费、滞期费有一个留置权。这也表示船东有了这个留置权就不必再找已经说明所有合约责任被终止了的承租人。)

这一条条文与 CIF(或 CFR)买卖是十分配套。有不少 CIF/CFR 卖方,作为承租人以程租合约租进一艘船舶,把他出售的货物付运,在装了货物与取得了运费预付的提单后,通常就可以对 CIF/CFR 买方开出的信用证结汇,并取得全部货款。之后,CIF/CFR 卖方显然不想继续承担合约的责任,甚至不想再理会付运之后的事情。这在买卖合约应该如此,因为他对买方的承诺基本上在货物付运后已经履行完毕。但在租约下,CIF/CFR 卖方作为承租人还不能脱身,所以加上一条中止条文就显然希

---

[5] 这是因为如果相互对延误免责,船东在船舶造成延误的违约下,只要是免责事项所造成,船东可依赖相互免责条文,如对交货造成延误,甚至是对易腐的货物造成严重损害。但在同一条文下,承租人几乎唯一需要依赖的就是装卸货物所造成延误的违约,必经在程租合约下承租人没有太多其他的承诺。这样如果承租人还是不能依赖这免责条文,而需要另外一条特定的条文,看来对承租人不公平合理。这也导致相互免责条文这样解释便变成一面倒,只是船东才会依赖。这也是 Evans 大法官在两个先例中第一审的看法,所以不是说没有理由。但上诉庭根据一直以来的先例还是坚持承租人需要另一条特定条文才能停算滞期费。

望能够做到这一点。在订约自由下，虽然是不合理，也很难想象任何精明的船东会同意程租合约才履行了一半就可以让承租人脱身，但也并非有公共政策阻止双方以清楚无误的文字作出这样的约定。正如在 Anglo – Oriental Navigation Co Ltd v T & J Brocklebank Ltd (1927) 27 Ll L Rep 359 先例，Roche 大法官说："... it is possible for parties to provide by their contract in absolute terms that at a certain point the liability of the charterers shall cease, and that nothing shall keep it open..."

在现实中与英国法律的地位，海上运输的风险（包括船东/承运人的违约）是在 CIF/CFR 买方。例如，运输中发生的货损货差买方是要向保险人而不是卖方要求补偿，而保险人也会代位向船东/承运人索赔。而卸货的作业也不是 CIF/CFR 卖方所能控制，买卖合约下会规定由买方负责卸货，而买方也不会不卸货/提货。唯一会给 CIF/CFR 卖方带来责任与麻烦就是经常在卸港会产生延误与滞期费，将来船东会根据租约的规定向他（作为承租人）提出索赔，而作出质疑就需要向买方查询与取得证明到底在卸货作业中发生了什么事情，并需要在支付滞期费给船东后根据买卖合约相应的条文买方追讨等。所以，理想的安排就是通过租约强制船东在卸港对卸货作业所造成的延误与滞期费通过留置货物（所有或部分）向收货人直接结算与收取。这也是程租合约中有留置条文的成因。留置是指"扣住第三人的货物/财产作为对方履行合约承诺的担保的权利"（the right to hold property of another as security for the performance of an obligation）。在普通法下，船东/承运人有权针对欠下的运费、共同海损的分摊、与救助费用留置货物。但这不包括卸港的滞期费与亏舱费，这种费用本质上是承租人违约的损失赔偿。所以让船东/承运人对这些费用作出留置货物，这权利就必须来自合约。这也是一条留置条文的原因，而承租人合约的留置条文通过把租约条文合并在提单中，就可以让船东/承运人面对买方（也是收货人与提单持有人）也有了合约的留置权。

但由于中止条文与留置条文通常写在同一条条文，一直以来也被一并作出解释，这就带来了不能仅看中止条文的文字说是让承租人的所有合约责任半途中止（如上述 C [Ore] 7 标准格式条文），而是必须看上下文进行合理与符合商业的解释。即假设船东愿意让承租人半途中止所有的租约责任，就必须换取到船东有其他的替代救济。也就是船东能够有有效的货物留置权，在这个程度上就可以让承租人中止他的责任。这也是这两条条文一并解释所带来的"共存原则"（co – extensive principle）。这方面可先节录这重要说法的先例 Hansen v Harrold Brothers (1894) 1 QB 612 (CA)，Esher 勋爵 MR 说："... where the provision for cesser of liability is accompanied by the stipulation as to lien, then the cesser of liability is not to apply in so far as the lien, which by the charterparty the charterers are enabled to create, is not equivalent to the liability of the charterers. Where, in such a case, the provisions of the charterparty enable the charterers to make such terms with the shippers that the lien which is created is not commensurate with the liability of the charterers under the charterparty, then the cesser clause will only apply so far as the lien which can be exercised by the shipowner is commensurate with such liability."

在 Anglo – Oriental Navigation Co Ltd v T & J Brocklebank Ltd 先例,Roche 大法官说:"... the true construction of the cesser clause, although it may be apparently absolute in its terms, having regard to the other provisions of the document and particularly to the nature and scope of the clause or clauses conferring liens for liabilities, may be that its operation is correlative and coextensive with the operation of the clause or clauses which confer a lien. That is to say, liability ceases if and so far as a lien is conferred, and does not cease if a lien is not conferred."

不多举许多先例的同样说法,只多节录一个比较近期的 The "Sinoe" (1971) 1 Lloyd's Rep 514 先例,Donaldson 大法官说:"Cesser clauses are curious animals because it is now well established that they do not mean what they appear to say, namely that the charterers' liability shall cease as soon as the cargo is on board. Instead, in the absence of special wording which is not present in this charter, they mean that the charterers' liability shall cease if and to the extent that the owners have an alternative remedy by way of lien on the cargo."

在简单解释了中止条文与留置条文的共存原则后,应该很容易推算到承租人在程租合约下的许多在卸港的承诺都不涉及留置权,所以承租人在租约下的责任也中止不了。如对承租人有很大风险的安全港口/泊位责任,装卸工人作业不当对船舶造成损坏,多使用了卸货泊位等。例如在 The "Aegis Britannic" (1987) 1 Lloyd's Rep. 119 先例,有关的程租合约有以下的中止与留置条文(在该租约是分开的条文,但这不应该有什么影响),如下:"20. Owners shall have a lien on the cargo for freight, deadfreight and demurrage. Charterers shall remain responsible for deadferight and demurrage incurred at loading port. Charterers shall also remain responsible for freight and demurrage incurred at discharging port.... 35. Charterers liability under the charter – party to cease upon being shipped except as regards payment of freight, deadfreight and demurrage incurred at both ends."

这中止条文(第 35 条)明示了承租人的租约责任在货物付运后中止,在文字上对中止的责任只针对运费、亏舱费与滞期费。在本先例,在卸港发生的问题与滞期费无关,而是涉及卸货工人疏忽导致了货损,令船东被迫对收货人作出赔偿。但在租约,是承租人要负责卸货与承担有关的风险,所以船东向承租人提出索赔。这是根据租约的第 5 条文,如下:"5. Cargo to be brought to, loaded and stowed... discharged at the expense and risk of shippers/charterers... receivers/charterers."

但承租人就认为根据第 35 条文他的租约责任已经中止。在高院,Staughton 大法官这样说:

"If I am entitled to construe the charter – party in accordance with the meaning of ordinary English words I would hold that by clauses 20 and 35 (i) the owners are to have a lien for freight, dead freight and demurrage, (ii) the charterers are to remain liable for freight, dead freight and demurrage, and (iii) otherwise their liability shall cease upon shipment... the ordinary meaning of clause 35, the cesser clause as I shall call it, suggests to me that the charterers have a good answer to this claim.(如果只是根据租约的终止与留置条文/文字作出解释,承租人的说法是对的,可以对船东的索赔作出一个好的抗辩。)

Unfortunately, the problem is not as simple as that. There is a long line of authority to show that the cesser clause has a special and limited meaning."(但不幸的是,问题并非这么简单,有一贯以来的权威先例显示了终止条文有一个特殊与局限的解释。)

结果,Staughton 大法官判是承租人不能中止这一租约的责任。显然是因为卸货工人疏忽导致了货损造成的损失,船东并没有其他替代救济,如留置货物向收货人收取。去了上诉庭,也是有同样的结果,Dillon 大法官说:"A charter-party ought not to be construed as imposing a liability on charterers and taking away that same liability in the same breadth unless the Court was driven to that conclusion; the cesser clause had usually been construed as applying only where the charter provided the owners with an alternative remedy, a remedy which was not only effective in theory but also effective in practice."

英国法律看来在这一共存原则是多年来一致与肯定的判法,但解释个别合约还是有很多疑问与新问题。例如,如果一个标准格式的程租合约的中止与留置条文,留置部分被删除而只剩下了中止部分,这样会否给中止条文字面上广泛的解释或是不给任何解释?又或是,保障船东的 1994 年"金康租约"标准格式为了让船东有更广泛的留置货物权利,已经可以留置任何其他的损失与租约欠下的钱。其措辞如下:"The Owners shall a lien on the cargo and on all sub-freights payable in respect of the cargo, for freight, dead-freight, demurrage, **claims for damages and for all other amounts due** under this Charter Party including costs of recovering same."(加黑部分是笔者的强调)

金康租约是没有一条中止条文,但如果把这种措辞的留置条文以附加条文的形式加在好像 C(Ore)7 的中止条文,或是把 C(Ore)7 的中止条文加在金康租约,会否在共存原则下有不同的解释,也就是承租人可以把卸港的其他责任,如不安全港口/泊位、卸货工人作业不当对船舶或货物造成损害等也中止,毕竟留置条文已经包括了损失(即违约的金钱损失),在理论上也希望实际上给了船东一个替代救济?

§8 约束性先例有所改变带来的不肯定

英国法律虽然非常强调肯定性/可循性,特别是在商法,但不表示普通法,也就是法院所建立的法律,不会随着时代作出改变。只要这改变是有秩序与在深思熟虑下所作出的平衡,也无可厚非,正如 Sir Roy Goode 教授在 The Hamlyn Lectures 上的《Commercial Law in the Next Millennium》一文中所说的:"What does cause concern is not change in itself but change which is made too readily or too frequently. Long – established principles should not lightly be given up. It is confusing if courts one year move in one direction, the next in another and in the third return to their starting position. But if change is properly controlled, the world of commerce will normally have little to fear."

但即使是有秩序的改变,还是会带来短暂的不肯定。因为商业人士(包括他们的律师)明确知道先例一贯对某些条文/文字的解释,所以在订约时采纳并使用。但结果有了争议诉讼,法院就作出改变,这显然带来了不肯定。如果以后的判例是保持一致,或者这改变是来自最高的贵族院,这不肯定应该只是短暂的。但高院的不同法官之间的判决并不相互约束,如果他们之间作出的判法不一致甚至有完全不同判法,又或者判法总在改变,就会对商业人士带来极大的不肯定与无所适从。

这种有秩序的与深思熟虑下的改变可举笔者熟悉的国际货物买卖合约与程租合约下的装卸时间为例。承租人或者非派船的买卖方承诺在一个固定时间完成装卸,就会想到坏天气是影响其无法履行此承诺而要造成船舶延误并赔偿滞期费的因素之一。所以针对坏天气一直以来有两种写法,一种写法是把承诺的天数描述为"好天气工作天"(weather working days)。如果约定是 5 天装完货,这样每一天都要计算,因为这是指日历天,不管天晴还是下雨。但如果约定是 5 个"好天气工作天",这就对承租人保障较好了。至于某一天是否有其他原因导致本来也不会进行装卸作业或者船舶仍在锚地待泊,只要该天是"坏天气工作天"(non – weather working day),还是不算在固定装卸时间。这样,"好天气工作天"一贯被解释为对承租人承诺的是怎样的固定装卸时间,是一种对承诺的"描述"(descriptive)。

但另有一种写法是把承租人承诺的固定装卸时间写为"天气允许"(weather permitting),这在很长一段时间都不被视为对承诺的描述,而被当作一种"免责"(exceptive)。也就是与本章之 7.1 段介绍的装卸时间停算条文的本质一样,而坏天气也相当于停算条文中的其他特定事项,如暴动或罢工。这样坏天气就必须与是否有真正不允许装卸作业有因果关系,如果有直接关系或影响才可以不算在固定装卸时间。这样,如果承租人没有计划或不能装卸货物(如船舶仍在锚地待泊),不允许装卸作业的坏天气是不影响固定装卸时间的计算。

这样,"好天气工作天"与"天气允许"这两句十分接近的话却一贯被解释为很不一样，尤其是在船舶在锚地等待泊位装卸时间的计算。在这些时间中遇上坏天气，写作“好天气工作天”的固定装卸时间可不包括在内，写作“天气允许”的固定装卸时间则不可以停算。这是表面看来不合理的解释，因为两个不同用字但对一般商业人士看来十分接近的措辞竟然会有这么差异与“可笑”（absurd）的解释。正如 Donaldson 大法官在 The “Vorras” (1983) 1 Lloyd' s Rep. 579 先例所举的例子如下：“The construction can lead to a very surprising result. Assume that two tankers arrive on successive days and each has a laytime of 72 running hours whether permitting. The first gets into the berth and bad weather prevents loading for the next 21 days, after which she loads in 72 hours. Her charterers will neither pay demurrage nor receive dispatch. The second, which arrived next day, has to wait 20 days for the weather to improve and then three days for the other vessel to load. She then herself loads in three days. Her charterers are liable to pay 23 days' demurrage. Yet for only three of those days did it matter that she could not get into the berth. If she had been able to do so, she could not have loaded because of the weather. One would have expected the second tanker to be liable for three days' demurrage, not 23 days.”

本来，“天气允许”一词并非明确无误，唯一结果只能作出这样不合理的解释。但问题是 Brandon 大法官在 The “Camelia” and The “Magnolia” (1978) 2 Lloyd' s Rep. 182 先例作出了这样的解释。而 Brandon 大法官是依从另一个更早的先例 Stephens v. Harris (1887) 57 L. J. Q. B. 203。反正一直以来，商业人士（不论是国际货物买卖或者是航运）都接受了“天气允许”与“好天气工作天”有很不同的解释。但到了 The “Vorras”先例，法律就被上诉庭改变过来，也就是推翻 Brandon 大法官的先例，说他是误解了 Stephens v. Harris 先例。Donaldson 大法官这样说：“In the absence of authority, other than the decision of Mr. Justice Brandon which was, I think, based upon a misreading of *Stephens v. Harris*. I have to construe the words used in their natural meaning. . . . I would construe '72 hours, weather permitting' as meaning '72 hours when the weather was of such a nature as to permit loading'.”

这样的解释还有一个合理之处，就是“天气允许”通常与固定装卸时间的描述写在同一句，如：“5 天，天气允许，周末与假日除外”（5 days, weather permitting, Sundays and holidays excluded）。这样，“5 天”与“周末与假日除外”毫无疑问是属于对固定装卸时间的“描述”（descriptive），但同一句内的“天气允许”却被解释为“免责性”（exceptive），这看来有点说不通。所以 Donaldson 大法官这样说：“*Prima facie*, any clause defining laytime is descriptive and any clause providing that time shall not count against laytime so defined is exceptive. If it matters, I would classify the expression '72 running hours, weather permitting' as descriptive.”

看来，这个法律的改变是肯定而且带来更合理的结果，虽然也会给商业人士带来短暂的不肯定，但英国商法作出这种有秩序与深思熟虑的改变与完善应该还是受到欢迎。

§9 合约的定义条文

在一些比较复杂的文书合约中,经常会有一条非常详尽的条文针对有关合约中的文字作出解释或定义,故该条文可被称为"解释条文"(interpretation clause)或"定义条文"(definition clause)。条文的作用是简化合约所有其他条文的拟定并减少重复,而针对一些技术性/专业的文字,更会是字典上查不到与没有权威性的先例针对过,合约中的定义条文就会有帮助。这可节录 Millett 勋爵在 AIB Group (UK) Ltd v Martin (2001) UKHL 63 先例中说:"... The purpose of such a clause is twofold. It shortens the drafting and avoids unnecessary repetition; and it enables the form to be used in a variety of different situations. It is not the purpose of such a clause to enlarge the parties' rights and obligations beyond those provided by the operative provisions by imposing, for example, a secondary liability as surety in addition to a primary liability as principal debtor."

例如,在笔者作为仲裁员所见到的一份技术转让合约,第 1 条文就是一条"definition clause",它有长达 3 页纸的定义(现实中也不算长),可部分节录如下:

"Section 1 – Definitions

Words that are not capitalized as employed in this Agreement shall have their dictionary meaning. The terms 'herein' 'hereunder' and 'hereof' unless specifically limited, shall have reference to the entire Agreement. The words 'shall' and 'will' are mandatory, the word 'may' is permissive, the word 'or' is not conclusive, the words 'includes' and 'including' are not limiting, the singular includes the plural and, unless otherwise specified, 'day' is a calendar day. Reference to 'Section' and Section number are to the 'Section' and Section number in this Agreement.

The following capitalized terms shall have the below described meanings:

'CHANGE OF CONTROL' shall mean, with respect to A 公司, one (1) transaction or a series of related transactions which results in a third party that competes either with the COMPANY, a SUBSIDIARY or any of the COMPANY's direct or indirect parent or affiliate companies obtaining, directly or indirectly, (i) thirty percent (30%) or more of the ownership of the outstanding voting shares or other ownership interest of, or (ii) CONTROL of A 公司.

'CONTROL' shall mean the power to direct the affairs of a PERSON by reason of ownership of voting stock, by asset acquisition, contract or otherwise.

'LICENSED TECHNOLOGY' shall mean a) the LICENSED DOCUMENTATION listed in Appendix A or b) additional technical information transferred or otherwise disclosed orally or in writing by COMPANY to A 公司 in providing technical assistance pursuant to Section 3.

'PERSON' shall mean any individual, corporation, partnership, joint venture, trust, business association, governmental entity or other entity.

'SUBSIDIARY' shall mean a corporation, company or other entity:

1) more than fifty percent (50%) of whose outstanding shares or securities (representing the right to vote for the election of directors or other managing authority) are, now or hereafter, owned or controlled, directly or indirectly, by a party hereto, but such corporation, company or other entity shall be deemed to be a SUBSIDIARY only so long as such ownership or control exists, or

2) which does not have outstanding shares or securities, as may be the case in a partnership, joint venture or unincorporated association, but more than fifty percent (50%) of whose ownership interest representing the right to make the decisions for such corporation, company or other entity is, now or hereafter, owned or controlled, directly or indirectly, by a party hereto, but such corporation, company or other entity shall be deemed to be a SUBSIDIARY only so long as such ownership or control exists.

'TERM' shall mean the period of time this Agreement is in effect which shall commence on the EFFECTIVE DATE and expires at 11:59 P. M. on June 30, 2003, unless terminated pursuant to Section 7."

另在 Sinochem v. Mobil (2000) 1 Lloyd's Rep. 339 先例中,也有一条定义或解释条文,其中提到了集团公司,而双方当事人都是庞大的集团,与许多公司有千丝万缕的关系,所以美孚石油拟定条文时就给了何谓"集团公司"一个明示定义:"'Affiliate' for the purposes of this agreement means a company which directly or indirectly controls, is controlled by, or is under common control with, a party hereto. For this purpose, 'control' means the right to exercise more than 50% of the voting rights at a shareholders' meeting."

有不少近期的先例已经明确说定义条文对有关的文字作出的解释必然超越了该文字的传统解释,也不应该受到订约时的背景/语境影响作出改变。这里可先介绍 Anglo Continental Educational Group (GB) Ltd v Capital Homes (Southern) Ltd (2009) EWCA Civ 218 先例,有关的条文是说:"the following words and expression shall have the following meanings for all purposes."

上诉庭的 Arden 大法官说:"Accordingly the possibility of defined terms being excluded by the context is ruled out."

另在 T & N Ltd (in administration) v Royal & Sun Alliance Plc (2003) 2 All ER (Comm) 939 先例,案情涉及一份对雇员的责任保单。保单排除了"尘肺病"(pneumoconiosis)的赔偿责任,另也有一条针对"尘肺病"一词的定义条文。Lawrence Collins 大法官说:“I do not consider that there is any legitimate process of interpretation which can yield the meaning for which the Royal contends, either on the basis of an appeal to the idea of something having gone wrong with the words, or on the basis of an appeal to the **factual matrix.** The exclusion contains its own specific definition of ‘pneumoconiosis’ and there is no permissible basis for ignoring that express definition. **I accept T&N's case that any attempt by the Royal to widen the factual matrix for the purpose of putting a different, wider meaning on the word ‘pneumoconiosis’ will plainly be not for the purpose of explaining the words used, but rather for the purpose of contradicting them**, i. e that ‘white is black and that a dollar is fifty cents’.”(加黑部分是笔者的强调)

在 JIS(1974)Ltd v MCE Investment Nominees I Ltd(2003)EWCA Civ 721 先例,Carnwath 大法官说:“‘Demised premises’, for the purposes of the break clause, are defined as including the shop units. To put it beyond doubt, the schedule says that they are excluded only for the purpose of the rent review. **That is what the language says, and no amount of background evidence will change that stark fact.**”(加黑部分是笔者的强调)

所以,如果合约有一条定义条文,除非涉及“合约变更”(rectification)或“禁止反供”(estoppel)的救济,双方谈判的证据不被接受否定或改变定义条文所作出的定义,即使有一方声称双方谈判时同意了一个不同的解释:Chartbrook Homes Ltd v Persimmon Homes Ltd(2009)UKHL 38 先例。在 Lewison 大法官所著的《The Interpretation of Contracts》(第 5 版,2011 年)一书第 246 页有同样的说法:“If a contract contains an express definition, then in the absence of a claim for rectification or a plea of estoppel, evidence of the negotiations is not admissible for the purpose of contradicting the definition, even where it is alleged that the parties negotiated on the basis of an agreed meaning.”

另是不少合约通常会有“序言”(recital),有先例判是序言如果与定义条文有冲突,定义条文的分量会更重:Brookfield Construction(UK)Ltd v Foster & Partnership Ltd(2009)EWHC 307(TCC)先例。

看来,对定义条文作出解释会否定或作出改变唯一的情况是按照双方定义解释会带来商业上可笑的结果。[6] 这在 City Inn(Jersey)Ltd v Ten Trinity Square Ltd(2008)EWCA Civ 156 先例,Jacob 大法官说:“It is obviously a strong thing to say that where a draftsman has actually defined a term for the purposes of his document that in some places (but not others) where he uses his chosen term he must have intended some other meaning. It is not impossible, however. If, approaching the document through the

---

〔6〕 可笑的结果是可以偏离在本书多处有提及,包括第一章之第 5 段的“黄金规则”(golden rule)。

eyes of the intended sort of reader (here a conveyancer), the court concludes that notwithstanding his chosen definition the draftsman just must have meant something else by the use of the term, it will so construe the document. Such a conclusion **will only be reached where, if the term is given its defined meaning the result would be absurd, given the factual background, known to both parties, in which the document was prepared. Nothing less than absurdity will do** — it is not enough that one conclusion makes better commercial sense than another."(加黑部分是笔者的强调)

在 Lewison 大法官所著的《The Interpretation of Contracts》(第 5 版,2011 年)一书第 250 页也说:"In the author's opinion ... Even where the contract contains an apparently comprehensive definition, it is thought that the court could depart from it if the application of the definition produced an absurd result. In Chipsaway International Ltd v Kerr (2008) EWHC 1887 (Ch) the court departed from a defined term, because application of the definition would have produced a nonsense."

但定义条文怎样的写法会带来争议,因为该条文并不一定写得清楚与不含糊。例如,定义条文是写为"包括"(including)了一些情况。这样定义条文就会被扩展包括一些其他根据合约本质或上下文相同的情况:Adelphi (Estate) Ltd v Christie (1984) 1 EGLR 19 先例。在 Lewison 大法官所著的《The Interpretation of Contracts》(第 5 版,2011 年)一书第 247 页说:"Where a term is defined as 'including' certain things, the definition is not exhaustive, and anything which falls within the natural meaning of the term in the context of the particular contract will also be held to fall within the defined term."

另也经常见到定义条文加上一句说"如果本质/语境允许"(where the context so admits),这显然也会带来定义条文的分量减轻:Franklins Pty Ltd v Metcash Trading Ltd (2009) NSWCA 407 先例。这一句也带来了含糊,如本质/语境到底是指整个合约订立的本质/语境,或只是该合约中的上下文:Phillips v Rafiq (2007) 1 WLR 1351 先例? 在 Lewison 大法官所著的《The Interpretation of Contracts》(第 5 版,2011 年)一书第 248 页说:"The use of the phrase 'unless the context otherwise requires' may itself be ambiguous. The context may mean the context in which the contract is made, in other words, the whole background or the matrix of fact. It may, however, be that the relevant contract is the context in the contract itself, in other words the context in which the word is used from time to time and place to place in the contract. In most cases this will not matter, but context will not usually be allowed to contradict an express definition. In *Hammonds v Jones* (2009) EWCA Civ 1400 Lloyd L. J. said: 'The definitions in the Partnership Deed apply 'unless the context otherwise requires'. This does enable the definition to give way to the context if necessary.'"

在本书第四章之第 9 段所介绍的"分配解释"(*Reddendo singula singulis*)规则提

到的 AIB Group (UK) Ltd v Martin 贵族院先例,多数决定也很大程度受到有关合约中的一条解释条文/定义条文的影响。在两个生意上的合伙人向银行贷款的合约中,抵押人/贷款人(mortgagor)是被解释为:"If the expression 'the mortgagor' includes more than one person it shall be construed as referring to all and/or any one of those persons and the obligations of such persons hereunder shall be joint and several."

Millett 勋爵说:"The fact that the question concerns the application of an interpretation clause is also significatnt... The application of such a clause is not merely a question of construction. If it is capable of being applied to the operative provisions in more than one way, it should be applied in a way which serves its purpose rather than in a way which extends the parties' obligation beyond those contemplated by the operative provisions. Of course, an interpretation clause may have this effect; but if so it should do so plainly and unambiguously."

在 Phillips v Rafiq 先例,案情是涉及一个车祸中死亡的乘客的遗孀向驾驶疏忽的司机与 Motor Insurers' Bureau(简称"MIB")的两位被告索赔损失。事发时,车祸中的死者把他的汽车交给疏忽的司机/朋友驾驶,而该司机没有投保第三人责任险。至于死者自己的汽车所投保的第三人责任险也刚过期,并没有续保。换言之,在该车祸中,原告的死者遗孀没有任何保险公司作出赔偿。而作为第一被告的司机即使有责任作出赔偿,也可能没有钱赔。这也是原告把 MIB 也加进来作为第二被告的原因。

这也需要简单介绍 MIB 的背景,就是在 1930 年英国《Road Traffic Act》强制要求所有的汽车与驾驶人都需要投保第三人责任险。但这里有一个漏洞需要填补,如果疏忽或其他原因漏了或忘了作出投保,就会有危险导致在交通意外中伤亡的第三人得不到赔偿。所以 1946 年就成立了 MIB 在这种情况下对第三人作出赔偿。MIB 的经费来自英国投保第三人责任险的保险公司,他们都必须是 MIB 的会员,而他们收取的保费有部分要交出给 MIB。换言之,MIB 的经费间接还是来自一般的市民。而 MIB 作出怎样的赔偿是通过与英国运输部的一个协议,最早的协议是在 1946 年,而在本案例有关的协议是 1999 年的"Motor Insurers' Bureau (Uninsured Drivers) Agreement"。该协议的第 1 条文是定义条文,它对原告一词所作出的定义如下:"In this agreement, **unless the context otherwise requires**, the following expression shall have the following meaning: 'claimant' means **a person who has commenced or who proposes to commence relevant proceedings and has made an application under this agreement in respect thereof.**"(加黑部分是笔者的强调)

协议也在一些情况排除了赔偿的责任,其中有关的一条是第 6(e)条文如下:"(e) a claim which is made in respect of a relevant liability described in paragraph (2) by a claimant who, at the time of the use giving rise to the relevant liability was voluntarily allowing himself to be carried in the vehicle and, either before the commencement of his journey in the vehicle or after such commencement if he could reasonably be expected to have alighted from it, knew or ought to have known that ... (ii) the vehicle was being used without there being in force in relation to its use such a contract of insurance as would comply with Part VI of the 1988 Act ... "

这带来一个看来矛盾的情况，就是车祸中的死者如果只是受伤，他想向 MIB 要求赔偿就会有问题，因为第 6(e)条文所排除的情况正是他身处的情况。但问题是本案例的原告是死者的遗孀，她对死者身处的情况毫不知情。在高院与上诉庭的判决，最后 MIB 都败诉。这里解释有关协议是看背景/语境，包括成立 MIB 的一些文件与 MIB 与英国运输部的协议的修改，认为没有对死者的遗孀作出同样的排除。而在本先例，死者的遗孀是完全符合第 1 条的定义条文中对原告的定义。MIB 的代表大律师说第 1 条有"unless the context otherwise requires"的一句话给了一定程度的弹性。但这也被法院拒绝，其中上诉庭的 Ward 大法官说："Mr Worthington（MIB 代表大律师）relies, of course, on the flexibility of the new definitions in 1999 because 'claimant' means the person who commences the proceedings unless the context otherwise requires. In considering what that means, another issue of construction may possibly arise in that the words 'in this agreement, unless the context otherwise requires' may be ambiguous. The context may mean, as Mr Worthington contends it does, the context in which the agreement is made, in other words, the whole background or the matrix of fact. It may, however, be that the relevant context is the context in the agreement itself, in other words the context in which the word is used from time to time and place to place in the agreement. For my part this does not seem to matter much. The word 'claimant' must of course be looked at in the context of the sentence or paragraph in the agreement in which it is placed to see how it fits in with the agreement read as a whole. "

§10　立法对文字作出定义

有一些有关商业的立法给了文字定义协助解释。其中最著名的就是英国 1925 年的《财产法》(《Law of Property Act》)。它在 Section 61 有一些著名的定义，它们不只适用在有关财产交易的合约，也适用在所有其他的合约或文件。

一是有关"人"(persons)，定义是说明除非合约另有不同意图，这一个字包括了自然人与法人，如公司、组织与合伙(Unless the contrary intention appears 'person' includes companies, unincorporated associations and partnerships)。但即使有了上述定义，在个别合约的解释还是要顾及不同本质与背景。如在 Deutsche Genossenschaftsbank v. Burnhope (1995) 1 W. L. R. 1580, HL 这一贵族院先例，合约是银行的保单中针对受保风险是如被"人"盗窃或假冒等。结果银行是被一个客户(一家公司)欺骗,贵族院多数(Steyn 勋爵持不同意见)判是在受保风险范围内,因为在保单中的“人”应该只针对自然人而不是法人,《财产法》的定义不适用。

二是有关“单数与复数”(singular and plural),《财产法》的定义是除非合约另有不同意图,单数包括复数与复数包括单数(Unless the contrary intention appears the singular includes the plural, and vice versa)。这样看来,难怪以前见过一位英国著名的仲裁员对 ICC 坚持要删除裁决书中的原告与被告(claimants and respondents)中的“s”,理由是原告与被告都是一家有限公司。

三是有关性别的“男性与女性”(masculine and feminine),《财产法》的定义是除非合约另有不同意图,提到一个性别就包括了所有性别(Unless the contrary intention appears reference to one gender shall include all genders)。

此外,《财产法》也有针对“月”的定义,这已经较早在本章 6.1 段介绍过,不重复。

另一个立法是英国 1979 年《货物销售法》(《Sale of Goods Act》),内中 Section 61 也有许多对文字的定义,这里就不一一介绍,只一提这些文字包括像“货物”(goods)、“买卖”(sale)、“买卖合约”(contract of sale)、“消费者合约”(consumer contract)、“卖方”(seller)、“买方”(buyer)、“特定货物”(specific goods)、“将来的货物”(future goods)、“物权凭证”(document of title to goods)、“交付”(delivery)、“保证”(warranty)、“过错”(fault)等。

立法在 Section 61 也在一开始说明这些定义在解释合约时适用,“除非本质或标的另有不同要求”(unless the context or subject matter otherwise requires)。

§11 正本文件与最佳证据规则

例如,有关的文件是否必须是正本。在英国,在最佳证据规则(Best Evidence Rule)被否定后,已经没有这种要求了。这方面先可举 R v. Governor of Pentonville Prison, ex parte Osman (1990) 1 WLR 227, DC 先例,Lloyd 大法官说:“As to his first submission, this court would be more than happy to say good bye to the best evidence rule. We accept that it served an important purpose in the days of parchment and quill pens. But since the invention of carbon paper and, still more, the photocopiers and the telefacsimile machine, that purpose has largely gone. Where there is an allegation of forgery the court will obviously attach little, if any weight to anything other than the original; so also if the copy produced in court is illegible. But to maintain a general exclusionary rule for these limited purposes is, in our view, hardly justifiable. So we would, if we could, be happy to accept Mr. Nicholls'(申请把最佳证据规则判死刑的被告大律师) first submission. But although the little loved best evidence rule has been dying for some time, the recent authorities suggest that it is still not quite dead."

但在之后的一个上诉庭先例,就正式判了最佳证据规则死刑,案例名为 Masquerade Music Ltd v. Springsteen (2001) EWCA Civ 513。该先例涉及著名歌星 Bruce Springsteen 先生。他向英国法院申请了一个禁令,禁止 Masquerade Music Ltd 这一家公司侵犯他在 20 世纪 70 年代所灌录歌曲的版权。但面对的其中一个要求是 Bruce Springsteen 要证明他的确享有版权。根据英国的 1956 年《版权法》,版权的转让必须是文书形式,并有转让人的签字。Bruce Springsteen 无法提供一部分的转让版权文书,就向法院申请接受"次佳的证据"(secondary evidence),这是一个美国律师给的口头证据,他是有关版权转让交易中的法律顾问。Ferris 大法官认为只需要合理、透彻寻找最佳证据,如有一定困难,就可以接受次佳的证据。到上诉庭,更是正式宣布最佳证据规则的死亡。Jonathan Parker 大法官是这样说:"In my judgment, the time has now come when it can be said with confidence that the best evidence rule, long on its deathbed, has finally expired. In every case where a party seeks to adduce secondary evidence of the contents of a document, it is a matter for the court to decide, in the light of all the circumstances of the case, what (if any) weight to attach to that evidence."

Jonathan Parker 大法官在检讨了 18 与 19 世纪的有关最佳证据规则的先例后,说:"... an increasingly fact – based and flexible application of that rule, in which the court's inquiry as to what has become of the original document is directed at establishing not so much that the best evidence is before the court as that the party seeking to rely on secondary evidence of the contents of the document genuinely does not have the original document available to him: in other words, that no improper purpose is involved and that there are no grounds for viewing the secondary evidence with suspicion."

最后,Jonathan Parker 大法官说到曾经要提供全面搜查最佳证据的做法再也不需要了,如下:"... there was no obligation on the respondent to make an exhaustive search, or indeed any search at all. The only requirement was for him to provide a reasonable explanation for his non – production of the minutes, in the sense that unless he did so the court would almost certainly decline to admit secondary evidence. Given that there was no allegation by the appellants of impropriety or bad faith against Mr. Springsteen and his advisers, and that there was nothing in the evidence to suggest that such attempts as were made on Mr. Springsteen's behalf to find the assignments were other than wholly genuine attempts, the judge was entitled to take as the appropriate yardstick the 'without any difficulty' test adopted by the Divisional Court in *Osman*."

总结而言,如果正本文件已经灭失,则不再要求证明已经尽了所有办法搜索但不成功。甚至一个合理的搜索也不再需要。在一般情况下,只要说明曾经搜索过与采取过一些手段搜索或只要能够讲得出有关文件是如何灭失的,就已经足够。

这里唯一的例外是涉及欺诈或其他不当行为的指控,就会需要提供有争议的正本文件,只要该文件仍在有关当事人的手中。这是因为有可能该文件的"鉴定"(authentication)会涉及专家证人。根据英国的《民事诉讼规则》,Part 31 要求对方提供正本文件是需要提前给通知。但这些与本书针对的合约解释没有什么关系,所以略过不谈。

最后一提的是《Phipson on Evidence》(第 18 版,2013 年)一书之 7 - 37 段说:"The maxim that 'the best evidence must be given of which the nature of the case permits' was once treated as expressing the great fundamental principle upon which the law of evidence depends ... But although this maxim played a conspicuous part in the early history of the subject, today it is of little practical importance. Indeed, the Divisional Court has described it as having gone by the board long ago, and one modern text refers to it as an 'evidentiary ghost.'"

第六章　外部解释合约——订约时的背景/语境

§1　序　言

1.1　传统解释看来是双方接受的完整文书合约条文/文字的做法

传统法院的做法解释文书合约/文件是尽量给一个"文字上"(literal)的意思,即"一般性"(ordinary)、"自然"(natural)、"平易"(plain)、"通用"(popular sense)的解释。如果不只是一个词而涉及一份文书合约/文件内不同的条文/文字,传统法院的做法就是根据本书介绍的解释合约的规则给其一个综合的解释。解释合约只是在一份看来是双方接受的完整文书合约(典型的例子就是双方签署[1]了的一份合约)的"四个角内"(four corners of the contract)的条文/文字,除了在一些十分例外的情况是必须看合约以外的证据才能解决争议(如涉及"合约变更"[rectification],"附带保证/协议"[collateral warranty or contract],"误述"[misrepresentation]等),不论有关双方订约时的背景、理解些什么或为什么使用起争议的语言等。

这传统解释合约的做法与可接受外来证据的十分例外的情况在 Lovell and Christmas Ltd v. Wall (1911) 104 LT 85 的上诉庭先例中 Cozens - Hardy MR 大法官有说明如下:"If there is one principle more clearly established than another in English law it is surely this: it is for the court to construe a written document. It is irrelevant and improper to ask what the parties, prior to the execution of the instrument, intended or understood. What is the meaning of the language that they have used therein? That is the problem, and the only problem. In saying that, I do not mean to assert that no evidence can be admitted. Indeed, the contrary is clear. If a deed relates to Black Acre, you may have evidence to show what are the parcels. If a document is in a foreign language, you may have an interpreter. If it contains technical terms, an expert may explain them. If, according to the custom of a trade or the usage of the market, a word has acquired a secondary meaning, evidence may be given to prove it. A well - known instance is where in a particular trade 1000 rabbits meant 1200. But unless the case can be brought within some or one of these exceptions, it is the duty of the court, which is presumed to under-

---

〔1〕 英国有所谓的"签字规则"(signature rule),可看本书第十三章之第2段。

stand the English language, to construe the document according to the ordinary grammatical meaning of the words used therein, and without reference to anything which has previously passed between the parties to it."(大致上是说解释合约不允许提供证据,除非是十分例外的情况,如合约涉及外文,或技术性的术语,或贸易习惯用语,才可以引进证据以协助法院解释合约。)

上述说法可以说是与一个不懂法律人士的思维方式很不一样,后者会马上想到如果解释一个合约的真正订约意图,最简单的办法就是把订约双方请来,要求他们作出解释。但这其实也不简单,因为他们有了争议就肯定会是作出对自己有利的解释,变为接受这种主观的订约意图只会令争议更加复杂与无所适从。这在 G Dworkin 先生的《Odgers' Construction of Deeds and Statutes》(第 5 版,1967 年)一书中有提及:"To a layman, the easiest way to answer this question might seem to be to call the parties before the court and ask them what they meant. In that case, the parties would not only usurp the function of the court, but would probably hold entirely different opinions as to what was meant by the words used."

这样,这两种截然不同的思维方式孰优孰劣,可探讨一下。不懂法律的人士接受在争议中的订约双方提供合约解释的证据,有几方面问题:(1)英国法律一直以来坚持根据合约中双方约定的文字客观解释,由订约双方提供证据就变为有危险接受主观解释了。(2)这种证据不可避免对证人自己有利,而且可能解决争议与订约的时间相隔较长,真实性值得怀疑,尤其是口头证据。(3)双方在争议中提供两个不同的版本通常不会对法官/仲裁员对合约的解释有真正帮助,反而会带来混乱。(4)双方在谈判中经常会改变立场,甚至在每一封来往的信函中讨价还价,这种改变只有到了最后订约的一刻或签署合约双方"认命"时才会停止,所以看谈判过程往往也找不出双方最后定局的真正订约意图。

上述的一些问题 Wilberforce 勋爵在 Prenn v. Simmonds (1971) W. L. R. 1381 先例中有提到,说:"On principle, the matter is worth pursuing a little, because the present case illustrates very well the disadvantages and danger of departing from established doctrine and the virtue of the latter. There were prolonged negotiations between solicitors, with exchanges of draft clauses, ultimately emerging in clause 2 of the agreement. The reason for not admitting evidence of these exchanges is not a technical one, or even mainly one of convenience (though the attempt to admit it did greatly prolong the case and add to its expense). It is simply that such evidence is unhelpful. By the nature of things, where negotiations are difficult, the parties' positions, with each passing letter, are changing and until the final agreement, though converging still divergent. It is only the final documents which records a consensus. If the previous documents use different expressions, how does construction as an expression, itself a doubtful process, help on the construction of the contractual words? If the same expressions are used, nothing is gained by looking back; indeed, something may be lost since the relevant surrounding circumstances may be different. And at this stage there is no consensus to the parties to appeal to. It may be said that previous documents may be looked to explain the aims of the parties. In a limited sense this is true: the commercial, or business object, of the transaction, objectively ascertained, may be a surrounding fact ... and if it can be shown that one interpretation completely frustrates that object, to the extent of rendering the contract futile, that may be a strong argument for an alternative interpretation, if that can reasonably be found. But beyond that it may be difficult to go: it may be a matter of degree, or of judgment, how far one interpretation, or another, gives effect to a common intention: parties, indeed may be pursuing that intention with differing emphasis and hoping to achieve to an represent a formula which means different things to each side, yet may be accepted because that is the only way to get 'agreement' and in the hope that disputes will not arise. The only course can then be try to ascertain the 'natural' meaning. Far more common, and indeed, totally dangerous is to admit evidence of one party's objective—even if this known to the other party."

1.2 文字表达的不足之处

但这一传统解释合约做法受到批评,原因之一就是文字上的表达可以有好几个不同的解释,甚至也不能简单说它们之间有合理与否之分。再以"consideration"一字为例,Webster 字典就给了四个十分不同的解释:一是"考虑"(deliberation);二是"尊重他人或为他人着想"(respect for others, thoughtful regard);三是"一个行动的原因"(a motive for action, reason);四是"报酬/支付"(remuneration, payment)。可以说,在一些商业或与法律有关的文件中,只有第四个解释才比较适用,可视为合约中的约因或对价。所以,转看《Oxford Law Dictionary》对"consideration"一字的解释就只有针对第四个解释,如:"Consideration may be a promise to do or forbear from doing something, or some loss or detriment suffered at the request of the promisor. It is normally a payment, transfer of goods, doing of services or surrender of another legal claim. It cannot be anything which the promisee is already under an obligation to do. It must be of some value, but not necessarily value equivalent or adequate to the promise."

这表示解释合约文字,除了看字典的一般性与"传统解释"(conventional meaning),还要看合约的"语境"(context)与双方对有关条文/文字的意图。这在澳大利亚的 Byrnes v Kendle (2011) 243 CLR 253 先例与贵族院的 Chartbrook Ltd v Persimmon Homes Ltd (2009) UKHL 38 先例都有提到:"The question is not what the words meant but what these parties meant."

原因之二是每一个合约在订立时都有其独特与双方了解的"背景事实"(background facts)与合约的"目的"(purpose),但最后在拟定合约时双方所表达的条文/文字与可能是不协调的有关条文并不能清楚反映这些背景与目的。这样,要看双方在订约时的背景事实与目的才能更加准确地掌握双方所用的条文/文字应该代表或综合代表什么解释,即该合约的"事实背景"(factual circumstance)或"语境"(factual matrix)。[2] 这些背景往往就是在双方的谈判过程中,其中会显示双方对合约的某一条文/文字的共同理解等。而这样做倒不是合理与否的问题,而是这才代表了双方订约时用某一些文字的真正意图。

举例说明,如果合约涉及一个保函并由第三人"加签"(countersign),就会带来争议第三人签字是作为担保人或只是作为见证合约方签订了保函。但如果合约的措辞不够明确,法院或仲裁庭可以看双方的谈判,就可能有证据显示提供保函的合约方曾经不同意第三人作为担保人,但被对方拒绝导致最后让步。这一背景事实就显示了双方订约的意图在针对"加签"一词是要第三人作为担保人。

1.3 目前解释看来是双方接受的完整文书合约条文/文字要考虑的三个方面

所以现在有关解释合约条文/文字的法律地位应该要考虑三个方面:一是合约本身,包括其他所有的条文以作出全面、完整与协调的解释,这是涉及合约内部的解释,在本书第三章至第五章有详论;二是合约的本质,如涉及保险、货物买卖、航运或建筑的不同本质;三是订约时的背景,这包括事实与法律两个方面。

1.3.1 合约的本质

"语境"(factual matrix/context)包括了合约的本质与订约的背景,反正他们之间也没有太大区别。针对合约的本质,解释合约时要加以考虑的例子在本书很多地方有提到。例如,在本章稍后的4.4段介绍的The "Oakwell" (1999) 1 Lloyd's Rep. 249先例,船东互保协会的担保的本质就是为了避免船舶被扣押。

另一个较早的例子是合伙人协议的本质上可以随时终止,除非合约有明示作出不同规定。Cairns勋爵在Llanlli Railway and Dock Co v L. N. W. R. (1875) L. R. 1 App. Cas. 550先例是这样说:"With regard to contracts of partnership they also are already ruled and settled, by law, to be capable of termination at any moment unless a definite limit is prescribed upon the face of them. And, the law being well settled, when you have a contract of that kind, you apply the understood law, and you hold that the parties, knowing what the law was, must be supposed to have intended entering into a partnership which could at any time be terminated, if they did not provide upon the face of their contract that it should be a continuing partnership."

又如在航运的期租合约,承租人需要承担时间损失,在解释一些相关的条文,如停租条文或免责条文等时,也需要了解这一本质。Donaldson勋爵在The "World Symphony" (1992) 2 Lloyd's Rep 115先例,说:"... it is for the parties to give expression to the terms of their bargain and this has always to be done against a background of general law and accepted principles, such as that prima facie the risk of loss by delay in

[2] "factual matrix"直译过来应是"事实矩阵",在本书意译为"语境",希望对读者来说更容易理解。

performance under a time charter – party falls upon the charterer. ”

最后可一提是在 Rainy Sky SA and others v Kookmin Bank (2012) 1 Lloyd's Rep 34 的最高院先例,有关合约的本质是造船合约的“还款担保”(refund guarantee),作用就是为了在造船合约被买方合法终止时,能够有银行作出担保让买方在船厂不作出支付时向银行取回他所预付的造船价格。

1.3.2 订约的背景

影响合约解释的订约时的背景包罗万有,也在本书很多地方有提到。这些背景涉及事实与法律。

1.3.2.1 事实背景

涉及事实的背景很好的例子就是在本章之 12.2 段介绍的 The “Diana Prosperity” (1976) 2 Lloyd's Rep. 621 先例,有关的背景就是订约时双方都理解或应该理解日本造船厂的做法。什么算是有关的事实也没有理念上的限制,仅有的三个限制可节录 Burton 大法官在 Durham v BAI (Run Off) Ltd (2009) 2 All ER 26 先例中的说法:“The first is relevance ... The second is knowledge: the facts in question ‘should have been reasonably available to the parties’. ... The third qualification is objectivity, so as not to introduce by a side wind evidence of the subjective intention of the parties, but subject ... to a certain degree of flexibility ...”(对事实背景的证据仅有三个限制:一是有关与否;二是双方都可以合理知道有关的事实;三是客观性,也就是涉及双方各自主观的意图必须排除,只有针对客观事实背景的证据才被接受,这方面也有一定程度的伸缩性。)

针对上述的三个限制,只一提的是第二个,就是一个澳大利亚的近期先例,名为 The Movie Network Channels Pty Ltd v Optus Vision Pty Ltd (2010) NSWCA 111,指出在今天的互联网时代,双方订约时可以合理取得的事实背景资料是无限的。所以针对这一限制,也就是双方可以合理知道的有关事实,应该只是双方真正知道的事实才能协助解释合约条文/文字。但目前在英国还没有这个说法。

以下可多举一些这方面的近期先例:

1. 在 R v Clowes (No. 2) (1994) 2 All E. R. 316, CA 先例,投资者申请购买一本小册子中描述的投资计划,该小册子被判是可以被接受作为帮助解释合约的外来证据。

2. Matthew Hall Ortech Ltd v Tarmac Roadstone Ltd (1997) 87 BLR 96 先例,在解释一份标准工程合约时,一份草拟合约时有考虑的指南被判是可以接受的外来证据。

3. 在 Association of British Travel Agents Ltd v British Airways Plc (2000) 1 Lloyd's Rep 169 先例,国际航空运输协会的票务手册只在其中一方的办公室中有,双方在谈判很少提到该手册,也不是另一方合约方可以合理接触到。因此该手册被判是不能被接受作为帮助解释相关的代理合约的外来证据。但双方都可以合理取到的航空界通用的术语被判是可以被接受。

4. 在 Holding & Barnes PLC v Hill House Hammond Ltd (2001) EWCA Civ 1334 先例,案情涉及写字楼租赁。法院接受解释有争议的租赁合约可以接受双方同时订立的另外 7 个租赁合约作为外来证据。

5. 在 Khan v Khan (2008) Bus. L. R. D73 先例,案情涉及两个兄弟合伙做生意但后来因为意见不合而闹翻。双方之后在一个家庭会议中达成和解协议,包括如何分配一些财产/物业。但事后双方对分配有了争议,上诉庭在考虑该和解协议的解释包括是否达成协议判是可以接受有关不同文化背景(这两兄弟出身回教家庭)的外来证据。据知,该先例是第一个有关接受文化背景解释合约的先例。

6. 在 Crema v Cenkos Securities Plc (2010) EWCA Civ 1444 的上诉庭先例,法院在解释合约接受了有关市场做法的专家意见证据,即使市场做法并非是"贸易习惯"(trade custom),但显然市场做法是双方订约时知道或可以合理知道的事实。

7. 在 Pink Floyd Music Ltd v EMI Records Ltd (2010) EWCA Civ 1429 的上诉庭先例,案情涉及音乐唱片的"许可协议"(license agreement),争议是相关的条文/文字是否包括网络音源与手机铃声买卖。上诉庭在解释该许可协议时接受了音像产业市场做法的专家意见证据。

最后可简单介绍两个在 Investors Compensation Scheme v. West Bromwich Building Society (1998) 1 W. L. R. 896 先例之前的有关保险的高院先例,它们对是否接受保险市场的专家证人提供有关市场做法的外来证据有完全不同的看法。可以说在有了 Investors Compensation Scheme v. West Bromwich Building Society 先例的指引,加上上述介绍的两个上诉庭先例 Crema v Cenkos Securities Plc 与 Pink Floyd Music Ltd v EMI Records Ltd,这种不同看法不应该再在高院或仲裁庭出现。

第一个是 The "Leegas" (1987) 1 Lloyd's Rep 471 先例,案情涉及劳合社与英国保险市场的做法,这在本书第七章之 5.2.1 段的 Roar Marine v. Bimeh Iran Insurance (1998) 1 Lloyd's Rep. 423, QBD 先例也有介绍。这就是涉及一个昂贵的船舶保险,保险经纪首先会为船东找一位"带头保险人"(leader),希望他接受承保并开出合理的保费率。这种在伦敦市场被其他保险公司尊重与愿意跟从的带头保险人很多是劳合社的一些"保险小组"(Syndicate)的"保险人"(underwriter)。带头保险人接受承担某一百分比的风险后,他就会在一份"承保单"(slip)签署他的名字。之后保险经纪会找其他的保险人或保险公司将百分百的船价作出投保。但之后还有不少工作会要跟进,如有关的保单需要作出更改,或索赔需要决定是否赔付或拒赔等。显然,要每一个保险人/保险公司个别作出决定就太耗时、昂贵与不肯定。所以保单通常有一条文说明是"跟从带头保险人"(follow the leader clause),也就是带头保险人作出的决定对其他跟从的保险人或保险公司有约束。在 The "Leegas"先例,有关的条文是:"Any amendments additions deletions including new and or managed and or chartered notice of assignment ratings and alterations of any description to be agreed by Leading Underwriter and to be binding on all others hereon."

在承保的期间,除了两次的更改有带头与跟从保险人/保险公司的签字外,有许多其他对保单的更改都只有带头保险人作出决定与签字。这些更改包括各方面,如把船东另外的一条姐妹船也加入保单,多次延长保险期限,批准船舶开往某一些港口或航次等。但不幸的是,1986 年 4 月 17 日"Leegas"轮在两伊战争中于波斯湾被飞弹击沉。这显然属于战争险,而带头保险人也根据他所承保的百分比作出赔付。但跟从保险人/保险公司就以出事是在其没有参与而只是带头保险人作出决定的延长保险期限内为由拒赔。而船东就在英国法院向跟从保险人/保险公司提起诉讼,原因是在跟从带头保险人条文下,带头保险人的决定是对其有明确约束的。作为被告的跟从保险人/保险公司要求引入外来证据,就是伦敦保险市场对这一条文的理解。特别是跟从保险人/保险公司一般不会在该条文下授权带头保险人延长保险期限,因为一般保险人/保险公司都不会接受无限期的延长。被告也希望引入一个劳合社保险人协会的协议,其中说:"We hereby agree not to underwrite War Risks insurance or re-insurance for a period exceeding 12 months."

但 Hirst 大法官拒绝接受这些外来证据,理由是该跟从带头保险人条文写得清清楚楚,一般保险人/保险公司不接受无限期的延长只属于主观意图,而劳合社保险人协会的协议不是船东能够合理知道的事实背景等。根据有关条文,Hirst 大法官以简易判决判船东胜诉。看来,该先例如果在今天审理,对外来证据的接受与否就应该有不同做法,即使最后的判决还是船东胜诉。毕竟接受外来证据的引入与根据外来证据对有关条文的解释不同。

第二个是同期的一个再保险案例,名为 Phillips and Stratton v Dorintal Insurance Ltd (1987) 1 Lloyd's Rep 482。在该先例,高院的 Steyn 大法官有不同看法,并接受总共 3 位专家证人有关再保险市场做法的外来证据。Steyn 大法官最后是这样说:"It will be obvious that without the aid of expert evidence I have come to the conclusion that the plaintiffs' interpretation of the critical contractual documents is correct. If (contrary to my view) the contractual documents are ambiguous, I hold that the expert evidence decisively tilts the balance in favour of the plaintiffs' interpretation. But, if I am wrong to the extent that without expert evidence the first defendants' construction ought to be preferred, I nevertheless find on the evidence as a matter of fact that the relevant provisions of the three contractual documents have been impressed with a customary meaning, or a settled meaning by the universally understood usage and practice of the London insurance market, which overrides any contrary interpretation. Insofar as it may be relevant, I find proved as a fact a customary meaning in the London market in the strict sense of that expression."

1.3.2.2　法律背景

至于法律方面,特别是在本书第七章之第 3 段所讲的法律默示地位,显然是重要背景。毕竟有水平的合约双方都应该知道这些法律默示地位才进行谈判与最后拟定一份文书合约。法律是重要的订约背景，有许多权威的说法可节录如下：

1. 在 Winter Garden Theatre (London) Ltd v Millennium Productions Ltd (1948) AC 173 的贵族院先例，Porter 勋爵说："... there are very few, if any, contracts which can be construed without taking into consideration a long background of gradual development and the implication of customary provisions, and I do not think that the meaning of a licence can be reached by considering the matter, as it were, in the air: its incidents have a long history behind them."

2. 在 Toomey v Eagle Star Insurance Co Ltd (1994) 1 Lloyd's Rep 516, CA 先例，Hobhouse 大法官说："It is also necessary that the Court should have regard to previous decisions of the Courts upon the same or similar wording. Parties to a commercial contract are to be taken to have contracted against a background which includes the previous decisions upon the construction of similar contracts."

3. 在 Oxonica Energy Ltd v Neuftec Ltd (2008) EWHC 2127 (Pat) 先例 Peter Prescott QC 大法官说（他的判决也被上诉庭确认）："The background knowledge that the neutral, reasonable person employs when understanding a commercial document can include a knowledge of the relevant law ... Indeed a person could not properly understand the Licence Deed in this case unless he had a good general knowledge of patent law and international practice in that regard. The problem is that the more of that knowledge he had the more he might be baffled by the document."

1.3.3　根据合约语境（本质与背景）解释有关条文/文字的案例

先举一个显示根据合约"语境"（factual matrix/context）作出的解释，是 The "Zeus V" (1999) 1 Lloyd's Rep. 703 先例，其中对受保游艇的"检验"（survey）是获得保单保障的先决条件。但明示条文并没有详尽说明检验包括什么。本来，"检验"只是非常一般性与通用的文字，对游艇随便看看可以是检验，对游艇在干坞花上好几天时间全面检查也可以是检验，所以在该先例应该给这一文字什么解释呢？要求赔付的游艇船东当然希望检验的解释尽量宽松，因为他的确进行了简单的检验，而且这检验也不包括要把检验的结果在风险产生前交出给保险商。但不想赔付的保险商自然希望"检验"一字有严格解释，包括针对适航、乘客的安全、船舶要进干坞（表示对船底也要检验）、要打开主机、进行海上"试航"（sea trial）、船舶重心测验等，同时这个检验不可以由不同的检验师进行且任何不妥之处全部要修复等。在这些对"检验"一字的不同解释中，Colman 大法官根据订约时的事实背景与保险合约的本质判这检验是投保这种风险的保险商通常所要求的范围，具体包括什么则要靠专家证人的意见证据了。而判决的结果认为该简单检验不足以满足合理的保险商要求，所以不必作出赔付。

Colman 大法官这样判：

"... a condition survey should have been satisfactory in the sense that it gave rise to no defects or recommendations in respect of seaworthiness or passenger safety; and whereas it was not a precondition of the continuance of the cover that underwriters would be provided with a report and that they should approve it, nevertheless the assured would have to provide such report for the purpose of evidencing compliance with the subject condition;

The subject condition was not to be construed as necessarily imposing on the assured a requirement that there should be an out of the water survey or the opening up of machinery or sea trials or stability tests after completion of the refit and before the commencement of the in commission period; the nature of the survey required, on the proper construction of the condition was one which was to be no more stringent than in all the circumstances would reasonably be necessary to satisfy the underwriters of the vessel' s seaworthiness and safety; only if it were inadequate for this purpose would the underwriter be entitled to treat themselves as off risk once the period of commission had started;

The subject condition required any condition survey and valuation to be entirely conducted and the results recorded by the same independent qualified surveyor and not partly by an anonymousgovernmental surveyor in respect of some aspects of the vessel and partly by another surveyor engaged by the assured in respect of other aspects of the vessel; the fact that the SVL report referred to what was stated to be the results of the MMM inspections ashore and afloat did not amount to a survey report in respect of those results; the survey conducted by SVL was insufficiently comprehensive to satisfy the reasonable requirement of an underwriter for the purpose of the subject condition; it followed that the condition was not complied with and the underwriters were not at risk at the time of the loss;"

所以,在最近的三四十年,英国法律有许多重要案例强调解释合约必须先考虑订约时的"背景"(background)才能理解文字或条文的本质,这背景可被称为"语境"(factual matrix 或 context)。虽然早在 River Wear Commissioners v. Adamson (1877) 2 App Cas 743, HL 先例中 Blackburn 勋爵就已经提到这一方面说:"But, from the imperfection of language, it is impossible to know what that intention is without inquiring farther, and seeing what the circumstances were with reference to which the words were used, and what was the object, appearing from those circumstances, which the person using them had in view, for the meaning of words varies according to the circumstances with respect to which they were used."

1.3.4 传统与新趋势在解释合约时对证明合约语境的外来证据态度的改变

但以前的传统解释合约做法,即基本上避免考虑语境,也不接受证明语境需要的文书合约以外的"外来证据"(extrinsic evidence),有很大不同。"语境"也发展到以往遇上合约中有"含糊"(ambiguity)或"不肯定"(uncertainty)之处,才考虑至目前即使合约中清楚明确的表达,也会考虑语境。目前的地位可节录上诉庭在 Static Control Components (Europe) Ltd v. Egan (2004) 2 Lloyd's Rep. 429 先例中所说的:"... in principle, all contracts had to be construed in the light of their factual background, that background being ascertained on an objective basis; accordingly, the fact that a document appeared to have a clear meaning on its face did not prevent, or indeed excuse the Court from looking at the background; the judge had been correct to look at the background to the signing of the guarantee."

从 Hoffmann 勋爵在 Investors Compensation Scheme c. West Bromwich Building Society (1998) 1 W. L. R. 896 先例所说要求丢掉以前解释合约的大部分"思维包袱"(intellectual baggage),也可见到这个变化。

看来,新趋势应该是在贵族院的 Investor Compensation Scheme v West Bromwich Building Society 先例有了定论,其中只节录 Hoffmann 勋爵所说的如下:"The meaning which a document (or any other utterance) would convey to a reasonable man is not the same thing as the meaning of its words. The meaning of words is a matter of dictionaries and grammars; the meaning of the document is what the parties using those words against the relevant background would reasonably have been understood to mean. ..."(一份文件[或者任何讲的话]会给一个合理人士带来与内中文字不一样的意思。文字的意思是由字典与语法得来,但一份文件的意思是订约方合理理解的他们根据当时的背景所采用的文字的意思。)

但这个变化也不代表"背景/语境"这一说法以前并不存在与现在被全盘接受。时至今日,没有被全盘接受是因为考虑语境的确会带来各种问题,如仍存在的所谓"谈判除外规则"(negotiation exclusion rule 或 prior negotiation rule),这在本书第三章之 14.3 段与本章之 2.5.1 段有介绍。也有质疑这个变化到底是否有重大改变,或只是强调方面有不同侧重,或是以前先看文书合约的文字,但现在先看背景/语境再看文书合约的文字。这里可节录 Evans 大法官在 The BOC Group v. Centeon (1999) 1 All E. R. (Comm) 970 先例中所说的:"The old intellectual baggage has been discarded but the courts are not traveling light. The cabin trunks have been replaced by airline suitcases; the contents are much the same, though they are expressed in more modern language."

即使合约有清楚无误的明确规定,法院或仲裁员还是需要看双方订约时的背景/语境才能够肯定:Rainy Sky SA and others v Kookmin Bank (2012) 1 Lloyd's Rep 34 先例。可以说,Investors Compensation Scheme c. West Bromwich Building Society 先例所带来的新趋势的确导致了本来相对简单的解释合约诉讼(虽然是有机会错判了双方真正的订约意图)变得十分昂贵与耗时,因为要处理大量的外来证据以了解背景/语境。

针对目前英国法律对解释合约的新趋势,最安全还是节录权威的《Chitty on

Contracts》(第31版,2012年)一书之12-118段,在总结上述提到过的先例与大量其他的先例后,说:"The modern view, however, is that the words do not have to be vague, ambiguous or otherwise uncertain before extrinsic evidence will be admitted. Since the purpose of the inquiry is to ascertain the meaning which the words would convey to a reasonable person against the available background of the transaction in question, the court is free (subject to certain exceptions) to look to all the relevant circumstances surrounding the transaction, not merely in order to choose between the possible meanings of words which are ambiguous but even to conclude that the parties must, for whatever reason, have used the wrong words or syntax. So the court is entitled (and, **indeed, bound**) to enquire beyond the language of the document and see what the circumstances were with reference to which words were used, and the object appearing from those circumstances which the person using them had in view. The court must place itself in the same 'factual matrix' as that in which the parties were."(新趋势是条文/文字不需要含糊不清才能接受外来证据。除了一些例外情况,法院完全自由看所有的合约事实背景/语境,不仅为了在有关条文/文字可能有的多个不同解释中作出选择,甚至可以得出结论就是当事人错误选择了文字或句法。所以法院有权[甚至**是必须**]对文书文件以外的事实作出查询,以确定双方当事人在怎样的情况与目的下使用有关条文/文字。法院必须把自己处在双方当事人同样的背景/语境作出解释。)

同样与更明确的说法也在Lewison大法官所著的《The Interpretation of Contracts》(第5版,2011年)一书之3.1.7段的标题,说:"In construing any written agreement the court is entitled to look at evidence of the objective factual background known to the parties at or before the date of the contract. **This principle applies even if the contract appears to be unambiguous.** There is no conceptual limit to background. It can include anything relevant which would have affected the way in which the document would have been understood by a reasonable person. However, this does not entitle the court to look at evidence of the parties' subjective intentions; nor to ascribe to the words of the contract a meaning that they cannot legitimately bear."(解释任何文书合约,法院有权看订约时客观的事实背景的证据。**这一大原则在合约看来是不含糊的情况也适用。**针对何为背景没有理念上的局限,包括任何会影响一个合理人士对有关文件理解的事情。但法院不应该看双方的主观意图的证据,也不能给合约中的条文/文字说不通的解释。)

这方面最后可先介绍在近期的Persimmon Homes (South Coast) Ltd v Hall Aggregates (South Coast) Ltd (2008) EWHC 2379 (TCC)先例,Coulson大法官说:"It is always necessary for the court to consider the factual background to a commercial contract even if the wording of that contract might be regarded as unambiguous or sensible."

§2 口头证据规则

要进一步探讨语境,先要介绍解释合约条文/文字可以接受什么证据的问题,包括了口头证据(parol evidence rule)。口头证据是指一些在订约前双方谈判的记录与过程,不论是口头或是文件。这包括合约的草稿(Miller v. Travers [1832] 8 Bing. 244; Ingris v. Buttery [1878] 3 App. Cas. 552; National Bank of Australasia v Falkingham & Sons [1902] A. C. 585 等先例),初步协议(Leggott v. Barrett [1880] 15 Ch. D. 306; Youell v. Bland Welch & Co Ltd [1992] 2 Lloyd's Rep. 127)等先例与谈判来往信函(Mercantile Bank of Sydney v. Taylor [1893] A. C. 317 等先例)。

2.1 什么是口头证据

口头证据规则包括三个方面:(1)不接受一些次要的证据,即今天已经不存在的最佳证据规则(Masquerade Music Ltd v. Springsteen [2001] E. W. C. A. Civ 513; [2001] C. P. L. R. 369; [2001] E. M. L. R. 25)。对一个已经签署的合约,这是双方订约意图最佳的证据,以一些以前谈判的次要口头证据帮助解释合约条文/文字就是违反最佳证据规则。(2)不容许提供文书合约以外的证据以改变、推翻或增加该文件的条文/文字。(3)一直以来,法官通常只局限在文书合约的四角内作出解释,不能接受与考虑有关背景的外来证据。

2.2 不接受口头证据/合约以外的外来证据的原因

按理说,英国法律将解释文书合约条文/文字视为法律问题,就应该不存在证据的问题:Carmichael v. National Power plc (1999) 1 W. L. R. 2042, HL;The "Nema" (1981) 2 Lloyd's Rep. 239 等先例。这也是传统解释合约的做法,就是只客观看合约本身书面的内容。至于其他的证据(材料),特别是订约前的一些谈判或背景,或是订约后双方的履行,被视为"外来证据"(extrinsic evidence),尽量要拒绝接受,即使它们对解释合约条文/文字有一定帮助,但更大的可能是带来混乱。这方面权威的说法是早在1878年,Blackburn勋爵在Inglis v John Buttery & Co (1878) 3 App Cas 552先例中说:"the formal contract shall supersede all loose and preliminary negotiations... there shall be no room for misunderstandings which may often arise, and which do constantly arise, in the course of long, and it may be desultory conversations, or in the course of correspondence or negotiations during which the parties are often widely at issue as to what they will insist on and what they will concede."

接下Morris勋爵在Bank of Australasia v. Palmer (1897) A. C. 540先例中说:"Parol testimony cannot be received to contradict, vary, add to or subtract from the terms of a written contract, or the terms in which the parties have deliberately agreed to record any part of their contract."(不能接受口头证据否定、改变、增加或减低文书合

约的内容，毕竟这是双方有意识地同意以文书合约记录他们的约定。）

另在 Jacobs v. Batavia & General Plantation Trust (1924) 1 Ch 287 先例也有同样说法："firmly established ... rule of law that parol evidence cannot be admitted to add to, vary or contradict a deed or other written instrument."

显然，排除口头证据只适用在一种情况，就是能够假设双方已经把他们之间所有的约定记录在一份文书的合约内，通常就是一份签署了的合约。其合理性是为了尊重双方记录在案的合约，进而避免一些不方便与麻烦的争议（great inconvenience and troublesome litigation in many instances）：Mercantile Agency Co Ltd v. Flitwick Chalybeate Co (1897) 14 T. L. R. 90 先例。其也有其他十分重要的好处，包括"肯定性"（certainty），这是在商业社会特别重要的考虑。例如，商业人士如果有了争议，可让订约方的律师或者法律顾问安心的根据记录在案的文书合约给出法律意见，而不必把谈判过程从头到尾取证才敢讲话。除了律师外，更重要的是一份文书合约会被第三人依赖，如银行根据一份签署的合约给与贷款或作出担保。这些方面在本书第一章之 4.3 段有详论，不重复。

2.3　例外情况下可接受外来证据/口头证据

但显然上述的假设在很多情况不能成立，所以排除口头证据已经很早就有了许多例外。例如，只要能证明一份文书合约并非是双方所有的约定，而只是部分内容。如双方的约定一部分记录在文书，另一部分在口头：这方面请看本书第二章之 13 段。Russell 勋爵在 Gillespie Bros. & Co v. Cheney, Eggar & Co (1896) 2 Q. B. 59 先例说："... although when the parties arrive at a definite written contract the implication or presumption is very strong that such contract is intended to contain all the terms of their bargain, it is a presumption only, and it is open to either of the parties to allege that there was, in addition to what appears in the written agreement, an antecedent express stipulation not intended by the parties to be excluded, but intended to continue in force with the express written agreement."

"附带保证/协议"（collateral warranty/contract）的说法也属于这一类文书合约只包括了部分内容的情况，通常是订约一方为了吸引另一方同意而作出的承诺，但该承诺并不记录在文书合约内，法律就会把该合约外的承诺视为附带协议，正如 Denning 勋爵在 Dick Bentley Productions Ltd v. Harold Smith (Motors) Ltd (1965) 1 W. L. R. 623 先例中对附带协议有解释如下："... it seems to me that if a representation is made in the course of dealing for a contract for the very purpose of inducing the other party to act upon it, and actually inducing him to act upon it, by entering into the contract, that is *prima facie* ground for inferring that it was intended as a warranty. It is not necessary to speak of it being collateral. Suffice it to say it was intended to be acted upon and was in fact acted on."

另一种例外情况是在合约的有效性受到争议，如显示的文书合约被指称有错误或违反立法,这可节录《Chitty on Contracts》(第 31 版,2012 年)一书之 12 - 106 段:"No Contract. Extrinsic evidence is admissible to show that what appears to be a valid and binding contract is in fact no contract at all. Thus evidence may be admitted to show that one or both parties contracted under a mistake, or that a person who signed the document was under a misapprehension as to the real nature of the transaction into which he had entered so that it was 'not his deed' in law. Also it may be shown that the writing was not intended by the parties to give rise to contractual obligations or that the contract is void for non - compliance with a statute."

这种例外的情况可以伸延去合约的有效性受到其他方面的争议的情况,如"非法"(illegality)[3]、"误述"(misrepresentation)[4]等会导致合约变为"无效"(void)。在这种争议,就非要看口头证据了,如双方在谈判时提到合约或其中的条文为了欺骗第三人。而即使合约有效,也会有相关条文解释涉及其他争议,如"合约变更"(rectification)[5]、"避免做出可笑的解释"(avoid absurd result)[6]、"货物买卖之有关法律默示要求卖方提供货物的质量是适合买方用途"(implied terms about fitness for a particular purpose)[7]等,都涉及需要看口头证据。

概括而言,在《Chitty on Contracts》(第 31 版,2012 年)一书中 12 - 096 段至 12 - 133 段就罗列出了 19 种例外情况可接受口头或外来证据。另在 Gerard McMeel 教授的《The Construction of Contracts—Interpretation, Implication and Rectification》(2007 年)一书中列举了如下 11 种例外情况。

2.3.1　例外一:文件并非是被订约双方意图当作完整的合约

一份文件如一份已签署的合约会被假设是双方意图当作完整合约(document not intended to be whole contract)的记录。但这只是假设,可以被推翻,如已经介绍过的法院接受部分书面部分口头合约,或是附带协议的情况。明确是被当作完整的合约看来只有一种情况,就是文件中有一条非常广泛的"完整合约条文"(entire agreement clause)。有了这一个条文,就有可能在绝大部分的情况下排除外来证据/口头证据,

---

〔3〕 Imperial Chemical Industries Ltd v Shatwell (1965) AC 656; Tinsley v Milligan (1994) 1 AC 340 等先例。

〔4〕 Hedley Byrne & Co Ltd v Heller and Partners Ltd [1964] AC 465; Avon Insurance v Swire [2000] 1All ER 573; Cassa di Risparmio della Repubblica di san Marino SpA v Barclays Bank Ltd (2011) EWHC 484 (2011) 1 CLC 701 等先例。

〔5〕 Re Butlin's Settlement Trusts (1976) Ch. 251; Co - operative Insurance Society Ltd v Centremoor Ltd (1983) 268 EG 1027 等先例。

〔6〕 Tillmanns & Co v. S. S. Lnutsford Ltd (1908) 2 K. B. 385; Fitzgerald v Masters (1956) 95 CLR 420; Watson v Philpps (1985) 63 ALR 321; Westpac Banking Corp v Tanzone Pty Ltd (2000) 9 BPR 17; Dockside Holdings Pty Ltd v Rakio Pty Ltd (2001) 79 SASR 374 等先例。

〔7〕 Gillespie Bros & Co v Cheney Eggar & Co (1896) 2 QB 59 等先例。显然买方用途会否告知卖方并依赖卖方的知识做出判断,往往只是在口头证据内。

只能以该合约的四个角内的条文/文字为准。虽然针对本章所讲的新趋势解释合约，如果引进外来证据/口头证据只是为了解释这一份完整合约内的条文/文字，看来与一条一般目前写法的“完整合约条文”本意没有冲突，所以能否成功排除还是有一定疑问。但完整合约条文的文字/措辞是来自订约自由，个别的条文写法也很不一样。所以如果想绝对排除外来证据/口头证据扭转本章所讲的新趋势，也应该可以。

2.3.2　例外二：附带保证/协议

已经简单介绍过，附带保证/协议（collateral warranties or contracts）通常是订约谈判时一方为了吸引对方而作出了一些承诺或陈述，如在买卖合约中卖方“卖花赞花香”，但这些承诺或陈述并没有记录在文书的合约内。这些陈述可能是由于疏忽而导致不正确，但在1967年《误述法》生效前，由于普通法只将误述区分为两种，一种是“欺诈性误述”（fraudulent misrepresentation），另一种是“无辜性误述”（innocent misrepresentation），这意味着“疏忽的误述”（negligent misrepresentation）除非其严重性能够提升到欺诈性误述，否则往往令受害方得不到索赔损失的救济。这样，法院为了公正，就经常将这种疏忽的误述当作另一个合约或保证，可名为“附带保证/协议”。显然要证明有这个合约或保证的存在，是在文书合约以外，就要看双方谈判的口头证据了。

举一个例子是 City of Westminster Properties Ltd v. Mudd (1959) Ch 129, Ch D 先例，案情是一个店铺的租约，订约谈判时房东知道租户是要租用该店铺同时用作一个古董店与居所，但租约明示不准店铺用作住宅。在续约的签署前，房东代理口头告诉租户不会反对他继续居住。后来房东反悔，但法院认为房东是受到他在签约前这个承诺的约束。

另一个例子就是 Esso v. Mardon (1976) 2 Lloyd's Rep. 305 先例，案情有关 Esso 石油公司建造了一个加油站，并出租给一位 Mardon 先生，在谈判时，Esso 的一位当地经理告诉 Mardon 先生说，估计该加油站能够一年出售20万加仑汽油。但后来的销量与这个数字差得很远，因为当地的规划部不批准 Esso 让加油站直接面对大街，而需要从边道才能进出。但 Esso 把加油站出租给 Mardon 先生时并没有把原先的20万加仑汽油销售量往下作出调整。结果一审法院判是没有这个附带保证/协议，但这被上诉庭推翻，Denning 勋爵说：“... there was a breach of a collateral warranty that the forecast as to the throughput had been made with reasonable care and skill and was sound.”

要证明一个附带保证/协议，并非容易。因为许多在谈判中作出的所谓保证并非是保证或承诺，而只是吹嘘或给一些主观的“意见”（opinion）。早在 Heihut Symons v. Buckleton (1913) A. C. 30, HL 先例，Moulton 勋爵就对附带保证/协议的成立有指引如下：“It is evident, both on principle and on authority, that there may be a contract the consideration for which is the making of some other contract. ‘If you will make such and such a contract I will give you one hundred pounds,’ is in every sense of the word a complete legal contract, but each has an independent existence, and they do not differ in respect of their possessing to the full the character and status of a contract. But such collateral contract must from their very nature be rare... Such collateral contract, the sole effect of which is to vary or to add to the terms of the principle contract, are therefore viewed with suspicion by the law. They must be proved strictly. Not only the terms of such contracts but the existence of an *animus contrahendi* on the part of all the parties to them must clearly be shewn. Any laxity on these points would enable parties to escape from the full performance of the obligations of contracts unquestionably entered into by them and more especially would have the effect of lessening the authority of written contracts by making it possible to vary them by suggesting the existence of verbal collateral agreements relating to the same subject - matter."

在 Inntrepreneur v. East Crown (2000) 2 Lloyd's Rep. 611,Lightman 大法官对怎样才能成功构成一个附带保证/协议的各项要求有一个很完整的总结如下:"(1) a pre - contractual statement will only be treated as having contractual effect if the evidence shows that parties intended this to be the case. Intention is a question of fact to be decided by looking at the totality of the evidence;(2) the test is the ordinary objective test for the formation of contract: what is relevant is not the subjective thought of one party but what a reasonable outside observer would infer from all the circumstances;(3) in deciding the question of intention, one important consideration will be whether the statement is followed by further negotiations and a written contract not containing any term corresponding to the statement. In such a case, it will be harder to infer that the statement was intended to have contractual effect because the *prima facie* assumption will be that the written contract includes all the terms the parties wanted to be binding between them;(4) a further important factor will be the lapse of time between the statement and the making of the formal contract. The longer the interval, the greater the presumption must be that the parties did not intend the statement to have contractual effect in relation to a subsequent deal;(5) a representation of fact is much more likely intended to have contractual effect than a statement of future fact or a future forecast."

上述案例的案情也可以略为介绍,涉及一个在伦敦酒吧的 30 年租赁,租赁合约中有一条文要求租客向一些房东指定的啤酒供应商购买啤酒。开始时,在 1996 年,租客购买了 280 桶啤酒。但之后急跌,到了 1998 年 4 月后,租客根本停止了向指定供应商购买啤酒,显示租客是通过其他渠道购买。房东法院申请禁令,试图禁止租客这样做。租客的抗辩是在签约前,房东曾经口头答应说到了 1998 年 3 月,就会放开对租客这些购买啤酒的约束,这构成了附带保证/协议。但根据证据,Lightman 大法官不认定房东曾经作出过这样的承诺或保证。而且,对租客更致命的是该租赁合约中有一条"完整合约条文",排除了附带保证/协议。

笔者认为,在1967年《误述法》生效后,立法承认了疏忽误述,并且可给受害方救济,法院已经对附带保证/协议的说法有所收紧。如在Esso v. Mardon先例的一审判是证据并不显示有一个附带保证/协议,但有一个疏忽的误述可给与救济。

另也可以不说是有一个附带保证/协议,而将合约说成部分书面部分口头的形式,而所谓的口头附带保证/协议,实是文书合约的口头部分。这是在J Evans & Sons (Portsmouth) Ltd v. Andrea Mezario (1976) 1 W. L. R. 1078, CA先例,案情是在集装箱运输的早期,由于有一些非专门设计的集装箱船舶装运,把集装箱放在甲板就有较大危险被冲下大海。所以在该案例中,货方要求他进口的机器不要装在甲板,而负责运输的"无船承运人"(non－vessel operation common carrier,或简称NVOCC)向货方口头保证该集装箱不会装在甲板,但结果并非如此而且出事了。但在有关的运输合约中,有明示条文允许无船承运人完全自由怎样装载。但上诉庭判是运输合约不管是怎样写法,无船承运人的口头承诺与保证有约束力,是整个运输合约的一部分。Roskill大法官是这样说:"In such a case the court does not require to have recourse to lawyer's devices such as collateral oral warranty in order to seek to adduce evidence which would not otherwise be admissible. The court is entitled to look at all the evidence from start to finish in order to see what the bargain was that was struck between the parties."

2.3.3　例外三:合约变更

与上一小段针对的附带保证本质上一样的是合约的变更(rectification),前者指签字的合约没有完整记录双方在谈判中所达成的其他方面的协议,后者指签字的合约没有准确并且是相反记录了双方在谈判中所达成的协议或"共同与分享的订约意图"(common/shared intention)。举一个变更合约的例子,合约写的是"东",但如果看双方谈判中所同意或订约意图是"西",如果法院能够从外来证据/口头证据明确双方真正的约定,而合约只是错误记录,法院就会作出变更。变更是最常见让法院或者仲裁庭接受与仔细考虑外来证据/口头证据的例子。当然这并不代表双方谈判后整理出一份合约让双方签字可以很随便,因为变更错误记录的合约除了要花费昂贵的律师费用(除非对方同意),法院或仲裁庭一般也不会善待这种申请,除非是口头证据能够完全明确双方真正的约定或订约意图与合约中记录的是相违背。只要有任何疑点,法院或仲裁庭就不敢变更合约。关于合约变更在本书第三章之13.1段有详细介绍。

2.3.4　例外四:对文字有怀疑或解释困难下才看周围环境

这也就是订约背景或语境(surrounding circumstances),只是在以前的解释合约中不被重视与只能局限在文书合约条文/文字不明确或解释起来有困难的情况。但并非以前没有这个说法,如在本章之1.3.3段曾节录的Blackburn勋爵在River Wear Commissioners v. Adamson (1877) 2 App Cas 743, HL先例中的重要说法。这里可节录《Chitty on Contracts》(第31版,2012年)一书之12－118段所说:"But under the older restrictive view expressed in this statement, and endorsed in a number of subsequent cases, extrinsic evidence is admissible only where the sense and meaning of the words of the written instrument is doubtful or difficulty arises when it is sought to apply the language of the instrument to the circumstances under consideration. If the words have a clear and fixed meaning, not capable of explanation, extrinsic evidence would not be admissible to show that the parties meant something different from what they would have written."

2.3.5 例外五:合约标的或订约方身份

在这种情况下,可接受合约以外的外来证据让法院能够明确合约标的或订约方身份(subject matter or identity)是什么,早在 Shore v Wilson (1842) 9 Cl & F 355, 525;4 ER450,HL 先例,Parke B 大法官就有提到如下:"... every material fact which will enable the Court to identify the person or thing mentioned in the instrument, and to place the Court, whose province is to declare the meaning of the words of the instrument, as near as may be in the situation of the parties to it."

早在 Macdonald v Longbottom (1859) 1 E&E 977 先例,法院已清楚地表明在谈判中双方都知道的事实会被接受确定合约标的究竟是什么。在该先例,涉及的争议是买卖合约中的"你的羊毛"指的只是原告自己农场里的,还是也包括原告从别的农场收购的。看来这一约定不像一般的买卖合约会说明买卖的数量或重量。这样,如果订约后市场价格有所改变,就会有争议"你的羊毛"到底包括了什么。法院判是两者都包括,因为原告在订立合约前曾经告诉过被告的代理人他的羊毛来自这两个渠道。

该判决也被 Bank of New Zealand v Simpson (1900) AC 182 先例跟从,Davey 勋爵引用了 Campbell 勋爵在 Macdonald v Longbottom 先例的判决,如下:"I am of opinion that, when there is a contract for the sale of a specific subject – matter, oral evidence may be received, for the purpose of showing what that subject – matter was, of every fact within the knowledge of the parties before and at the time of the contract."

本书第一章有介绍法院拒绝看外来证据的古老先例,如 In re Fish; Ingham v. Rayner (1894) 2 Ch. 83 先例,在该先例的遗嘱是把住所给遗嘱订立人的侄女名为"Eliza"。但遗产订立人没有一个合法的侄女叫 Eliza,但有一个曾侄女名为 Eliza。证据显示他还有一个非法的曾侄女名为 Eliza,看来大家感情非常好,并且住在一起,应该明确是想把住所给她。但上诉庭判是住所应该给合法的 Eliza,因为拒绝看外来证据。这显然也不是正确的判法,因为扭曲或否定了遗嘱订立人真正的订约意图。可以说在今天,这种严格排除外来证据的解释再也不会被接受。

相反,在澳大利亚的 Hope v RCA Photophone of Autstralia Pty Ltd (1937) 59 CLR 348 先例,Latham 大法官是说:"Latent ambiguity exists when a description, evidently meant to apply to only one person or thing, is shown equally applicable to more than one person or thing; for example, a legacy 'to my nephew John', where the testator had two nephews of that name. In such a case the ambiguity is raised by extrinsic evidence and it is allowed to be removed by similar evidence."

在该先例,Latham 大法官举了一个例子就是一份遗嘱上写着"给我的侄子 John",但是遗嘱订立人有两个侄子都叫 John。这时候就需要外来证据判断到底遗嘱订立人是想把遗产留给哪一个侄子。例如,其中一个侄子 John 和遗嘱订立人关系很好,甚至住在一栋房子里,但另一个侄子 John 是十年才见一次面,那么毫无疑问遗嘱订立人所指的侄子 John 应该是关系很好的那一个,也是作出馈赠的意中人。

最后介绍的是 J W Carter 教授在 2013 年在《Journal of Contract Law》发表的《Context and Literalism in Construction》一文中的一个例子,就是 A 与 B 达成协议出售 A 的马匹。但事实上 A 有两匹马,一匹是骏马,另一匹是老马。这样如果双方有争议哪一匹马才是双方的买卖合约的标的,就非要接受双方谈判的证据。这些谈判的证据会是 B 的订约意图/想法,并告知了 A,甚至会得到 A 的同意或至少没有反对。如 B 告诉 A 他愿意出高价,因为他想买一匹骏马将来出赛。这样,显然就可以相对准确对"A 的马匹"一词作出符合双方订约意图的解释。

同样是根据证据找出双方订约的标的也可以得出不同的后果,就是双方心目中的标的根本不同,这会导致双方以为达成协议,但实际上根本没有"一致想法"(meeting of minds),所以不存在有效的合约。

同样道理适用在有关订约方身份的方面,这可节录《Chitty on Contracts》(第 31 版,2012 年)一书 12 – 122 段如下:"Identity of parties. The identity of parties may be established by extrinsic evidence where it is not clear from the written instrument to whom it refers. So, where a landlord handed to his tenant a letter addressed 'Dear Sir' in which he promised to renew a lease, extrinsic evidence was admitted to identify the proposed lessee, even though no mention of his name appeared in the agreement. Extrinsic evidence will also be admitted to show in what capacity the parties contracted, e. g. to show which party was the buyer and which the seller, or to correct a misnomer."

2.3.6　例外六:技术与科学性用语

技术与科学性用语(technical or scientific language)经常会碰到,法官/仲裁员只是根据一些常识或字典上对这些用语的一般性解释并不足够,更有可能字典上根本找不到,而是需要合约以外的外来证据(包括专家意见证据)才能安全地作出解释。在这种情况下可作出解释一早在 Shore v. Wilson (1842) 9 Cl. &F. 355 先例已经被确认。在 Baldwin—Francis Ltd v. Patents Appeal Tribunal (1959) 1 Q. B. 105 先例,法院被要求解释合约中的"规格或技术性条件"(specification),双方大律师各自解释有关的技术性用语,上诉庭认为没有进一步的证据无法作出解释。在上诉庭,Reid 勋爵这样说:"... Technicalities crop up in a great variety of cases and, when the parties are not in dispute about them they are often explained without evidence. Counsel give explanations and by doing so they are not giving anything away; if they were not in agreement evidence would be led. But in a case where it is not competent to lead evidence counsel could not, in my view, properly be asked to help in this way unless there is some other way for the court to get the necessary information. If the court find that there is a genuine dispute and real doubt about any technical matter, then I do not think that it can proceed farther without evidence."

同样的说法也可见在 Cooper (Max) and Sons Pty Ltd v. Sydney City Council (1980) 54 A. L. J. 234 先例,案情有关在一个建筑合约中"pay loadings"一词的解释。Diplock 勋爵说:"it is not an expression that is used in ordinary speech; without extrinsic evidence from a witness experienced in the building industry and familiar with the technical terms used in it, a judge could only speculate as to the meaning."(这不是一个日常可以见到的用语,没有一个对建筑合约有经验的证人提供外来证据,法官只能臆猜这一词的解释。)

2.3.7 例外七:商业习惯做法/惯例或术语

这一方面的问题已经在默示条文的本书第七章之第5段中有详细提及,包括商业习惯做法/惯例(trade usages or terms)可改变合约明示条文/文字的解释。这就需要外来证据确定是否接受这种商业习惯做法/惯例。这外来证据可被接受早在 Shore v. Wilson (1842) 9 Cl. & F. 355 先例被提到。另在 Bowes v. Shand (1877) 2 App Cas 455 先例,Cairns 勋爵也有提到说:"That of course would, according to the well-known rule of law, which admits parol evidence not to contradict a document, but to explain the words used in it, supply as it were, the mercantile dictionary in which you are to find the mercantile meaning of the words which are used. That would be a legitimate and well-known mode of construing the document."

2.3.8 例外八:年代久远的文件

年代久远的文件(ancient documents)可见在 Shore v. Wilson (1842) 9 Cl. & F. 355 先例中 Gurney B 大法官所说的如果随着时间的流逝与环境的改变,用字含义变得不清楚,外来证据可被接受用来帮助解释。同一个案例中 Coleridge 大法官也说:"But in proportion as we are removed from the period of which an author writes we are not sure of the meaning of the words he has used; we are not sure that at that period the primary meaning of the words was the same as now, for by the primary is not meant the etymological, but that which the ordinary usage of society affixes to it. We are also equally uncertain whether at that period the words did not bear a technical or conventional sense; and whether they were not so used by the writer. When, therefore, we are called on to construe deeds of the years 1704 and 1707, it seems to me that we are not only at liberty, but are bound, to inquire what at that time was the meaning of the phrase used in them; not taking for granted, because they bear a certain clear meaning now, that they did so then."

还是在同一个案例,Tindal 大法官也说在这种情况下外来证据可以接受:"where by the lapse of time and change of manners, the words have acquired in the present age a different meaning from which they bore when originally employed."

近期一点的先例有 Earl of Lonsdale v. Att - Gen (1982) 1 W. L. R. 887。

2.3.9　例外九:外语

如果一个合约内有外语(foreign language),法院可以接受外来证据对该合约作出翻译,这是在 Shore v. Wilson (1842) 9 Cl. & F. 355 被确认。

另一个较近期的先例是 Glymn (Covent Garden) Ltd v. Wittleder (1959) 2 Lloyd's Rep. 409。有关一个买卖德国土豆的 CIF 合约,合约是部分德语、部分英语。判是英国买方只是受德语被翻译为英语的部分条文/文字的约束。

2.3.10　例外十:不是被告所意向订的合约的有关事实以及损害合约成立的事实

例外十是不是被告所意向订的合约的有关事实以及损害合约成立的事实(*non est factum* and vitiating factors)。*Non est factum* 的概念早在 16 世纪开始适用在一些与欺诈无关的案件,如涉及盲人、文盲与一些"无能力人士"(incapacity)所订的合约。但它不能适用在一些疏忽或不小心的情况,正如 Reid 勋爵在 Saunders v. Anglia Building Society (1971) A. C. 1004 先例所说的:"The plea cannot be available to anyone who was content to sign without the trouble to try to find out at least the general effect of the document."

至于一些损害合约成立的事实,如欺诈、非法、误述、错误或胁迫等,也是非得看合约以外的外来证据才能够认定是否有这种事实存在。这在《Chitty on Contracts》(第 31 版,2012 年)一书之 12 - 112 段如下:"**Fraud**, **illegality**, etc. Extrinsic evidence will always be admitted to defeat a deed or written contract on the ground of fraud, illegality, misrepresentation, mistake or duress. Also in the application of equitable remedies such as specific performance or the refusal thereof, rectification, or rescission, extrinsic evidence will be admitted to prove the grounds upon which relief is sought."

2.3.11　例外十一:合约归类或假局的合约

由于不同合约会受不同立法管辖,这些立法会带来不同的特权或严格责任。这是由法院根据所有的证据将该有关合约归类(characterization)。这方面可节录 Gerard McMeel 教授的《The Construction of Contracts—Interpretation, Implication and rectification》(2007 年)一书第 25.36 段如下:"Many statues either confer privileges or attach onerous obligations on one or both parties to transactions which fall into particular legal categories or concepts (and often leave it to the judge to define or describe with precision the boundaries of those concepts). For example, does an interest in a flat create a lease or license for the purpose of statutory rights of tenure or (when applicable) rent control? Such questions arise commonly in the tax and insolvency contexts. As we observed in Chapter 1 the resulting questions are not pure questions of construction."

"假局的合约"(sham)是指一个合约假装为一个有法律后果的协议。这种并非善意产生法律关系的合约经常涉及欺诈,但并不一定是有欺诈才会被归类为假局的合约。这可节录《Chitty on Contracts》(第31版,2012年)一书之2-189段如下:"Other cases. The cases in which there is no intention to create legal relations cannot be exhaustively classified. Contractual intention may, for example, be negatived by evidence that 'the agreement was a good agreement ... made without any intention ... of creating legal relations,' that it was a sham, made with 'no intention ... to create *bona fide* legal relations,' that it formed part of a course of conduct that was 'just an act or a role-play', and that the parties had not yet completed the contractual negotiations. Many other disparate factors can lead to the same conclusion: for example, where an agreement was made that a landlord would not enforce an order for possession against a tenant who had fallen into arrears with her rent, it was held that this agreement did not create a new tenancy as the parties 'plainly did not [so] intend': the agreement merely had the effect of turning the tenant into a 'tolerated trespasser.'"

海事经常有这种案例,船东为了逃避债务,防止船舶被扣押,或是船价市场上涨后想从原来的长期租约或较早订立的买卖合约脱身,可把船舶以更高价转卖给另一个买方等原因,就安排一个内部船舶买卖。反正在方便旗国家注册与改名十分容易与快捷,结果只是更换了船名与船旗。往往这样做也没有法律禁止,但这并非是善意产生法律关系的船舶买卖合约,显然是假局的合约。有关的先例很多,如在笔者的《海事法》一书中有提到的 The "Maritime Trader"(1981) 2 Lloyd's Rep. 153,The "Saudi Prince"(1982) 2 Lloyd's Rep. 255,The "Evpo Agnic" (1988) 2 Lloyd's Rep. 411,The "Mawan" (1988) 2 Lloyd's Rep. 459,The "Tjaskemolen"(1997) 2 Lloyd's Rep. 465 等先例。

为了调查与证明一个合约是否是假局的合约,就要涉及接受外来证据,这包括订约前的口头证据与订约后的行为。这在 A G Securities v. Vaughan (1990) 1 A. C. 417 先例中 Jauncey 勋爵说:"... although the subsequent actings of the parties may not be looked at for the purpose of construing the agreements they may be looked at for the purpose of determining whether or not parts of the agreements are a sham in the sense that they were intended merely as 'dressing up' and not as provisions to which any effect would be given."

如果法院从证据认定了有关的合约是一个假局的合约,就会要归类(如属于另一个种类的合约)或宣告该表明合约其实不存在。

2.3.12 例外十二:合约文字有一种以上解释,而其中一方指出双方谈判时有约定的解释

这一方面,其实已经在本书第三章之14段的"私人字典"(private dictionary)有

过详论。但笔者在这里再多作补充并尽量不重复,以显示针对所谓的口头证据规则的例外有很多并包括这一个。这是在 The "Karen Oltmann" (1976) 2 Lloyd's Rep. 708 先例,案情是有关一个两年的期租合约,但其中有一条附加条文给了承租人在 12 个月的营运后还船的"选择权"(option),只要提前 3 个月告知船东,说:"Charterers to have the option to redeliver the vessel after 12 months trading subject giving 3 months' notice. "(加黑是起争议的文字)

但承租人在船舶交船后营运了 19 个月之后才给 3 个月通知要还船。船东指选择权只是在 12 个月营运后才还船,而 3 个月通知就是要在交船后 9 个月时作出,而只要承租人没有这样选择,该选择权就失效或弃权,承租人必须完成两年租约期才能还船。换言之,承租人对附加条文的"after 12 months trading"的解释为"at any time after the vessel had traded for 12 months",即 12 个月营运后所有的时间内都可以行使还船的选择权。但船东对附加条文的解释为"When the vessel has traded for 12 months"或"on the expiry of 12 months trading"。看来,承租人与船东的不同解释都说得通。

在该先例中,船东声称承租人在合约谈判时曾经针对这个选择权作出过陈述,希望是两年租约期但有选择权变为 12 个月。结果是 Kerr 大法官看了双方谈判租约时的电传往来,并同意船东的说法,判船东胜诉。至于接受口头证据(特别是谈判证据),Kerr 大法官有这样的解释:"... If a contract contains words which in their context are fairly capable of bearing more than one meaning, and if it is alleged that the parties have in effect negotiated on an agreed basis that the words bore only one of the two possible meanings, then it is permissible for the Court to examinc the extrinsic evidence relied upon to see whether the parties have in fact used the words in question in one sense only, so that they have in effect given their own dictionary meaning to the words as the result of their common intention. Such cases would not support a claim for rectification of the contract, because the choice of words in the contract would not result from any mistake. The words used in the contract would *ex hypothesi* reflected the meaning which both parties intended. "

这一例外也在后来的先例中被接受,可见 Hoffmann 勋爵在 Carmichael v. National Power plc (1999) 1 W. L. R. 2042, HL 先例所说的:"The evidence of a party as to what the terms he understood to have been agreed is some evidence tending to show that those terms, in an objective sense, were agreed. Of course the tribunal may reject such evidence and conclude that the party misunderstood the effect of what was being said and done. But when both parties are agreed about what they understood their mutual obligations (or lack of them) to be, it is strong thing to exclude their evidence from consideration. "

这说法与下级法院的 Ward 大法官所说的"What they thought they had achieved

is of no importance"截然不同。

这也可见 Gerard McMeel 教授在《The Construction of Contracts—Interpretation, Implication and Rectification》(2007 年)一书第 3.04 段所说的:"... In the context of contractual interpretation, where the parties have a shared understanding of the meaning of significance of particular words which differs from their conventional meaning, the parties' own understanding prevails."

2.3.13 总结对口头证据规则的例外

由于有太多例外,难怪 1996 年英国"法律委员会"(Law Commission)有关"口头证据规则"(The Parol Evidence Rule)所作的报告认为只是在普通法发展过程中历史遗留下来的,并建议废除,说:"We have now concluded that a parol evidence rule ... which on occasion may have been applied to exclude or to deny effect to relevant evidence, no longer has either the width or the effect once attributed to it. In particular, no parol evidence rule today requires a court to exclude or ignore evidence which should be admitted or acted upon if the true contractual intention of the parties is to be ascertained and effect given to it."

2.4 支持口头证据规则的说法

但与"最佳证据规则"(Best Evidence Rule)的正式被判死刑不同(Masquerade Music Ltd v. Springsteen [2001] E. W. C. A. Civ 513; [2001] C. P. L. R. 369; [2001] E. M. L. R. 25),口头证据规则(Parol Evidence Rule)没有正式被判死刑,而且最近还有法院作出支持口头证据规则的说法。

第一个例子是在 AIB Group (UK) Ltd v. Martin (2001) 1 W. L. R. 94 先例中 Hutton 勋爵所说的:"It is a general rule in the construction of deeds that the intention of the parties is to be ascertained from the words used in the deed and that, with certain limited exceptions, extrinsic evidence cannot be given to show the real intention of the parties. On occasions this rule may lead to the actual intention of the parties being defeated but the rule is applied to ensure certainty in legal affairs. In *Mallan v. May* Pollock CB stated: 'We must apply the ordinary rules of construction to this instrument; and though, by so doing, we may, in some instances, probably in this, defeat the real intention of the parties, such a course tend to establish a greater degree of certainty in the administration of the law.'"(我们必须以一贯性的规则解释合约,虽然会有情况双方真正订约意图没有获得支持,但这是为了让释法的过程带来更大程度的肯定性。)

另一个例子在 Shogun v. Hudson (2004) 1 A. C. 919 先例,Hobhouse 勋爵也是以商业合约的肯定性为由拒绝了口头证据证明订约方的身份(虽然这应该是例外之一),说:"The rule that other evidence may not be adduced to contradict the provisions of a contract contained in a written document is fundamental to the mercantile law of this country; the bargain is the document; the certainty of the contract depends on it ... This rule is one the great strengths of English commercial law and is one of the main reasons for the international success of English law in preference to laxer systems which do not provide the same certainty."

Hobhouse 勋爵的说法难免受到批评，如在《Lloyd's Maritime and Commercial Law Quarterly》中 Gerard McMeel 教授的文章中说："Lord Hobhouse treats the parol evidence rule as being a conclusive presumption, which it was never said to be in the classic discussions. This is a much more stringent rule than England has ever had. With respect to the late Lord Hobhouse, this approach is deeply unsound."

2.5 目前剩下不被接受的外来证据

目前看来还剩下的不被接受的"外来证据"(extrinsic evidence)主要还有两种，虽然仍是有很有限的例外情况。

2.5.1 不被接受的外来证据之一：谈判除外规则

这是在订约前的谈判与有关订约方的"主观意图/想法"(subjective intension)的证据还是不被接受，这方面已经在本书第三章之 14.3 段有提到过。再次强调就是这一种证据是 Hoffmann 勋爵在 Investors Compensation Scheme v. West Bromwich Building Society (1998) 1 W.L.R. 896 中总结的 5 条解释合约规则的第三条。另多举一些有关先例的说法，一是在 The "Rio Assu" (1999) 1 Lloyd's Rep. 115 先例，上诉庭的 Waller 大法官这样说："The negotiations of a contract can often be a compromise. It is dangerous to make the assumption that one party intended to have something supplied or provided for by the contract, or that the other party intended to have something supplied or provided by the contract. Contracts are negotiated and ultimately each may think that he has what he wishes, but it is for the Court to interpret the language of the contract. There is no doubt about the correctness of the principle."

另是一个近期的香港先例，显示了香港法律是完全依从英国的做法：Ng Chun Kong Calvin trading as Ko and Co. v. First Star Development Limited (CACV No. 81 of 2006)。上诉庭郭美超大法官说："There is no conceptual limits to what can be regarded as background. It includes absolutely anything which would have affected the way in which the language of the document would have been understood by a reasonable man and which he would have regarded as relevant **save that previous negotiations of the parties and their declarations of subjective intent are excluded.**"(加黑部分是笔者的强调)

2.5.1.1 不接受谈判证据的原因

简单说，不接受谈判证据的原因除了在本书第三章之 14.3 段节录 Wilberforce 勋爵在 Prenn v. Simmonds (1971) 1 WLR 1381 先例中的说法，也就是这些谈判的证据对解释合约不会有帮助。其他的原因可节录 Lewison 大法官所著的《The Interpretation of Contracts》(第 5 版，2011 年)一书第 92 页所说如下："Other reasons that have been advanced to justify the rule are: that it reduces uncertainty and unpredictability in the resolution of disputes; that it prevents unfairness to third parties who may be unaware of the course of negotiations; and that **the admission of evidence about the course of negotiations would subvert the objective approach to the interpretation of contracts that is the bedrock of the English approach.** "(加黑的一句应该指英国法律下解释双方的合约是客观看,这样如果接受双方谈判的主观证据并加以考虑就有了直接的冲突。)

2.5.1.2　谈判除外规则的例外之一:订约时的背景

对谈判除外规则有批评或有保留意见的也不少,其中一点就是谈判证据不能用来协助解释合约,但可以接受作为谈判时背景/语境的证据并间接协助解释合约。这方面先可节录在新西兰的 Yoshimoto v Canterbury Golf International Ltd (2001) 1 NZLR 523 先例,Thomas 大法官说:"I would also reiterate that, for the purposes of this case, I am not seeking to entirely abrogate the rule that evidence of prior contractual negotiations is not receivable to ascertain the meaning of a contract. What I am suggesting is that the rule should not be treated as an absolute and rigid rule to the point where the court is called upon to impose an interpretation which does not accord with the parties' actual intention. The objective basis would remain. But that basis would be enhanced by approaching the task of determining what the contract would convey to a reasonable person without artificially restricting the background knowledge available to the parties at the time they completed the contract. Subject to the caution which I will shortly stress, that background knowledge should be able to include reference to matters that might otherwise come under the general heading of negotiations where such a reference would undoubtedly assist to ascertain the true meaning of the parties' contract..."

另在新西兰的 Vector Gas Ltd v Bay of Plenty Energy Ltd (2010) NZSC 5 先例,Tipping 大法官说:

"The vice in admitting subjective evidence of negotiations, is that doing so would be inconsistent with the objective basis on which interpretation issues are resolved. As already seen, evidence of a party□s subjective intention is not relevant to an objective resolution of interpretation issues. Although the common law takes the view that it is only the final written contract which records the ultimate consensus of the parties, the way that consensus is expressed may be based on an agreement as to meaning reached during negotiations.

There is no problem with objective evidence directed to the context, factual or linguistic, in which the negotiations were taking place. That kind of evidence can properly inform an objective approach to meaning. Whereas evidence of the subjective content of negotiations is inadmissible on account of its irrelevance, **evidence of facts,**

circumstances and conduct attending the negotiations is admissible if it is capable of shedding objective light on meaning. It is often said in contract interpretation cases that evidence of surrounding circumstances is admissible. Circumstances which surround the making of the contract can operate both before and after its formation. In either case irrelevance should be the touchstone for the exclusion of evidence. I do not consider there are any sufficiently persuasive pragmatic grounds on which to exclude evidence that is relevant."(加黑部分是笔者的强调)

但看来在英国法律,贵族院的 Chartbrook Ltd v Persimmon Homes Ltd (2009) UKHL 38 先例重申了这一条证据除外规则。而针对谈判证据可以帮助了解订约时的背景/语境,Hoffmann 勋爵看来不认同并区分与其他从外来证据所认定的背景/语境,说:"But pre-contractual negotiations seem to me capable of raising practical questions different from those created by other forms of background. **Whereas the surrounding circumstances are, by definition, objective facts, which will usually be uncontroversial, statements in the course of pre-contractual negotiations will be drenched in subjectivity and may, if oral, be very much in dispute.** It is often not easy to distinguish between those statements which (if they were made at all) merely reflect the aspirations of one or other of the parties and those which embody at least a provisional consensus which may throw light on the meaning of the contract which was eventually concluded. But the imprecision of the line between negotiation and provisional agreement is the very reason why in every case of dispute over interpretation, one or other of the parties is likely to require a court or arbitrator to take the course of negotiations into account."(加黑部分是笔者的强调)

2.5.1.3 谈判除外规则的例外之二:合约双方的目的

这一本质上差不多的例外说法可节录 Sales 大法官在 Investec Bank (Channel Islands) Ltd v The Retail Group Plc (2009) EWHC 476 (Ch)先例说:"... in interpreting a contract, regard may be had to the content of the parties' negotiations to establish 'the genesis and object' of a provision. This seems to me to be a relevant part of the factual matrix, since if the parties in the course of their negotiations are agreed on a general objective which is to be achieved by inclusion of a provision in their contract, that objective would naturally inform the way in which a reasonable person in the position of the parties would approach the task of interpreting the provision in question."

另在 Scottish Widows Fund and Life Assurance Society v BGC International (2012) EWCA Civ 607 先例,在上诉庭的 Arden 大法官看来是不反对谈判证据协助找出订约双方的目的,但必须小心对待这种证据会有主观性,说:

"Mr McGhee(被告代表大律师)relies on the parties' pre-contractual negotiations as evidence establishing that the common object of the transaction was that SW should give BGC the equivalent of a reverse premium of £ 10m and that BGC should then take over the Barings lease. I accept that the objective fact of the common aim of the parties in entering into the Relevant lease and the supplemental agreement would be part of the background admissible on interpretation. ... Mr McGhee submits that pre – contractual negotiations can be prayed in aid of the objective fact of the aim of a transaction.

This is a difficult area: see generally, for instance, my judgment in Square Mile Partnership v Fitzmaurice McCall Ltd [2007] 2 BCLC 23 at paragraphs 59 to 63. The judge rightly held that negotiations could not be used to support detailed points of interpretation (judgment, paragraph 17(vii)). Pre – contractual negotiations rarely descend into detail on every point; the negotiations are unlikely to throw any light on the detailed points of interpretation that generally arise after execution.

However this does not necessarily mean that the pre – contractual negotiations should be accepted as evidence even as to the general object of the transaction. **Statements made in the course of negotiations are often no more than statements of a negotiating stance at that point in time, thus shedding more heat than light on issues as to interpretation of the final deal. ...**

These factors mean that judges **should exercise considerable caution before treating as admissible communications in the course of pre – contractual negotiations relied on as evidencing the parties' objective aim in completing the transaction.** "(加黑部分是笔者的强调)

这一问题也带出其他问题,其中很难在谈判证据中作出区分可接受与否的证据。在 Excelsior Group productions Ltd v Yorkshire Television Ltd (2009) EWHC 1751 (Comm)先例,Flaux 大法官说:"It seems to me that there is a very fine line between looking at the negotiations to see if the parties have agreed on the general objective of a provision as part of the task of interpreting the provision and looking at the negotiations to draw an inference about what the contract meant (which is not permissible), a line so fine it almost vanishes."

2.5.1.4 谈判除外规则的例外所带来的问题

在较早时所提到的谈判除外规则的两种例外(还不能说是明确),其他已经明确了的例外还有在本书第三章提到的合约"变更"(rectification)与"私人字典"(private dictionary)。此外,针对消费者的合约也是一种例外,因为在 1999 年的《Unfair Terms in Consumer Contracts Regulations》之 Regulation 5 是说:"A contractual term which has not been individually negotiated shall be regarded as unfair if, contrary to the requirement of good faith, it causes a significant imbalance in the parties' rights and obligations arising under the contract , to the detriment of the consumer."

但接受谈判证据,也带来不少问题。第一个问题就是很难区分哪些谈判证据是

“可以接受”(admissible)或“不能接受”(inadmissible),后者显然是谈判双方的一些主观意图。第二个问题是法院或仲裁庭在诉讼中哪一个阶段作出谈判证据是否可以接受的决定。第三个问题是审理的法院或仲裁庭在考虑了谈判证据,包括一些不能接受的口头或书面证据后,很难事后在解释合约条文/文字时不受影响。

2.5.1.4.1　问题之一:难以区分哪些谈判证据可以接受或不能接受

现实中,要区分订约前哪些口头证据/谈判证据是可被接受(有关订约的背景)与哪些不可以被接受(订约方之间的谈判与主观意图)并不清晰。看来,前者如谈判过程中的共同理解、所针对的行业与市场、合约的本质/目的、商业习惯做法等客观事实。例如,在 The “Diana Prosperity” (1976) 2 Lloyd's Rep. 621 先例就涉及日本造船业中习惯做法的背景证据,应该十分明确是属于订约时的事实背景/语境,有关的证据完全可以接受。但这些证据通常是通过外来证据。这些可被接受的外来证据并需要专家证人,所以不存在订约双方谈判证据。至于不可以被接受的证据会是双方所交换的“合约草稿”(draft contracts)或有了一份文书合约后,之前的谈判文书/电文往来。以租船合约为例,这包括所有“在达成协议前的所有谈判”(pre – fixture negotiation)与“来往的电文”(fixture telexes/emails)等。

但笔者认为,进一步细分/区分谈判证据中订约方的主观意图/想法与客观事实背景还十分困难与不清晰。例如,一方订约方的证人给了一份证人证言,说明他的公司一贯的政策是只与大公司订立合约,与 BVI 或皮包公司订约就必须要有母公司或银行担保才会接受,而对方正是一家 BVI 公司。特别是,这一政策没有在谈判时告知对方,但认为对方根据以前的交往也应该知道。这显然是该订约方的主观意图/想法,特别是对方的证人证言否认知道有这一政策。而另一个极端是该订约方在谈判过程中的证据显示了他公司的政策,并坚持对方提供母公司或银行担保,否则就拒绝谈判。但这被对方拒绝后,该订约方最后还是继续谈判并与对方也是一家 BVI 公司达成协议。这样,被拒绝提供母公司或银行担保的事实就变为一个事实背景/语境,如果合约中有不明确之处就不应该解释为母公司或银行愿意提供担保。但如果是介于两者中间的情况,如该订约方正式告知对方其公司的意图或是坚定不移的政策,并要求对方提供母公司或银行担保,但另一方不置可否,既没有明确同意,但也没有拒绝。而双方就继续谈下并达成协议,这就很难区分到底是主观意图/想法或是事实背景。看来,告知是公司的意图就有很大可能是主观意图,但告知是公司坚定不移的政策就看来是事实背景/语境。而即使是前者,作出告知的一方将其订约意图/想法已经传达给了对方,是一个“传达了的意图”(communicated intention),会否也被视为双方共同知道的背景/语境?另是,该订约方在提出要求或作出告知与对方作出反应所用的条文/文字也有关系,如坚持或决绝。

由于双方的谈判会是一个漫长与不稳定的过程,听这些证据(特别是口头证据)后,经常会无所适从。而且,也会给审理的法院或仲裁庭有了更大的空间解释什么是事实背景与语境。例如,订约一方说他的草拟合约给了对方而对方并没有反对有关内容,但这代表了什么? 或是,对方在草拟合约(但不是一份标准格式)中作出了一些没有实质重要性的修改,这又代表了什么? 这只不过是谈判中一个过程,对方到了后期改变主意并无不可,更不用说当时不反对并不足够成为对有关内容的约定。再举一个例子是一方回应对方大律师的盘问时,说对方"应该"已经同意了他的订约意图。但换了对方的证人,就坚决认定对方"肯定"同意了另一个订约意图。难道就凭这样的细微差别给回答"肯定"的一方证人多一点份量? 又或是,反而给回答"应该"的一方证人多一点份量,因为事隔多年,这样的说法比较可信? 这种经历令笔者想起最早时口头证据不被接受的原因的确是有一定道理,就是不可靠与通常会带来混乱,并且令一份双方签订的合约失了不同程度的肯定性,正如本章之2.2段所讲。所以也有不少人对英国法院近三四十年来在解释合约(特别是商业合约)或文书/文件方面,从传统的"字面解释"(textual interpretation),变为越来越走向"背景/语境解释"(contextual construction),有很大意见。这方面会在本章的结论时谈到。

针对这一个问题,可节录一些先例的说法。在 Oceanbulk Shipping and Trading Sa v TMT Asia Ltd (2011) 1 Lloyd's Rep 96 先例,Clarke 勋爵说:"Trial judges frequently have to distinguish between material which forms part of the pre-contractual negotiations which is part of the factual matrix and therefore admissible as an aid to interpretation and material which forms part of the pre-contractual negotiations but which is not part of the factual matrix and is not therefore admissible. This is often a straightforward task but sometimes it is not."

在澳大利亚的 Secured Income Real Estate (Austrilia) Ltd v St. Martins Investments Pty Ltd (1979) 144 CLR 596 先例也有类似的争议与问题,Mason 大法官是说:"This was said to be evidence of surrounding circumstances to which recourse could be had in interpreting the contract. In truth the evidence is not evidence of surrounding circumstances; it is evidence of the antecedent oral negotiations and expectations of the parties and as such it cannot be used for the purpose of construing the words of a written contract intended by the parties to comprehensively record the terms of the agreement which they have made."

2.5.1.4.2　问题之二:哪一个阶段作出谈判证据是否可以接受的决定

如果双方合约方有其中一方想依赖谈判证据,问题就是在什么时候作出决定到底是否可以接受。毕竟文件披露的程序通常在诉讼中来得比较早。在 Standard Life Assurance Ltd v Oak Dedicated Ltd (2008) 1 CLC 59 先例,Tomlinson 大法官说是在中间阶段,法官很难决定到底谈判证据是否可以被接受,这一问题更好是由审理的法官决定。在 Beazer Homes Ltd v Stroude (2005) EWCA Civ 265 先例,上诉庭的 Mummery 大法官也同意这个说法,说:"In general, disputes about the admissibility of evidence in civil proceedings are best left to be resolved by the judge at the substantive hearing of the application or at the trial of the action, rather than at a separate preliminary hearing. The judge at a preliminary hearing on admissibility will usually be less well informed about the case. Preliminary hearings can also cause unnecessary costs and delays."

另是在 Anglo Continental Educational Group (GB) Ltd v Capital Homes (Southern) Ltd (2009) EWCA Civ 218 先例,上诉庭的 Arden 大法官说:"Time and costs should not be unnecessarily spent on evidence about communications before an agreement is made. If a party is served with a witness statement which it considers may contain material which is inadmissible on a question of interpretation, it should seek to establish from the other party the basis on which the evidence is said to be admissible. If he is dissatisfied with the answer, he may in appropriate circumstances make an application to exclude the evidence before replying to it. Another course would be to issue an application to be heard at trial, but this may lead to increased costs and a diversion of the time available for trial to this subsidiary issue. Yet another course would be for the court at the case management conference to direct the parties to identify in writing the precise point which they say the evidence establishes and why they say that that evidence is admissible. This may shorten the time spent at trial on any application to exclude it. At all events, the court should not allow the focus of a case about interpretation to be distorted by a detailed enquiry about material that plays a minor role, if any, in resolving the case."

看来怎样才是最恰当的做法还有很多不同说法。以上的先例都是针对法院,但仲裁庭也同样会面对这个问题。

2.5.1.4.3 问题之三:事后解释合约条文/文字会受影响

简单说,谈判证据如果被接受,不论是涉及合约变更、私人字典、误述或任何其他原因,但事后不成功,法院之后解释合约条文/文字时不应该受到这些谈判证据的影响。正如 Denning 勋爵在 Arrale v Costain (1976) 1 Lloyd's Rep 98 先例中的说法:"In my opinion, therefore, a judge ought not to be influenced by evidence of negotiation and discussions beforehand. Whenever it is admitted for another purpose (which fails) then, when the judge turns to his remaining task of construing the written contract itself, he should put the evidence on one side and not be influenced by it."

换言之,这也是本书第三章之 14.3.6 所提到的"置之脑后"(*de bene esse*)。但在现实中,这也不容易做到。这可看 Denning 勋爵的《The Discipline of the Law》一书之 55 页与 Attorney - General v Dreux Holdings (1996) 7 TCLR 617, NZCA 先例。

2.5.2 不被接受的外来证据之二:订约后双方的行为

这是"订约后双方的行为"(subsequent conduct),如在履约时双方表现出来对合约条文/文字的理解。表面看来,这也是很好的表现了双方真正的订约意图,否则不会这样理解并作出相关行为。但它又有问题,如双方或作出行为的一方理解错误,合约解释不能因此被扭曲。这可以有其他说法针对,如"共识性禁止反供"(estoppel by convention),但不应影响较早时订立了的合约的解释。有关这一种证据,在下一段会更加详尽地分析。

在这一种的“外来证据”(extrinsic evidence)以协助解释一份含糊的文书合约条文/文字,曾经有先例对它的接受性持宽松态度。这可举 Watcham v. Attorney – General of the East African Protectorate (1919) A. C. 533, PC 先例为例,在此案例中,Atkinson 勋爵说:“The principle of the above – mentioned decisions, so far as it is based on the probability of a change during the lapse of time in the meaning of the language used in an ancient document, cannot of course have any application to the construction of modern instruments, but even in these cases extrinsic evidence may be given to identify the subject – matter to which they refer, and where their language is ambiguous the circumstances surrounding their execution may be similarly proved to show the sense in which the parties used the language they have employed, and what was their intention as revealed by their language used in that sense.”

Denning 勋爵也在 AIP v. Texas Bank (1982) Q. B. 84 先例有非常善待的说法:“For many years I thought that when the meaning of a contract was uncertain you could look at the subsequent conduct of the parties so as to ascertain it. That seemed to me sensible enough. The parties themselves should know what they meant by their words better than anyone else.”

但在 20 世纪 70 年代,贵族院就有了两个重要先例严格排除订约后双方的行为的外来证据协助合约条文/文字的解释,除非是共识性禁止反供或“行为的更改合约”(variation by conduct)。这两个先例就是 James Miller & Partners Ltd v. Whitworth Street Estates (Manchester) Ltd (1970) A. C. 583, HL 与 Schuler v. Wickman (1973) 2 Lloyd’s Rep. 53, HL。更改合约等于是另一个协议或是第二个合约,并需要约因/对价的支持与双方同意。至于共识性禁止反供,简单的例子是一方同意另一方做一件事,如在租约下同意装运一种原本不允许装运的危险品。这同意可能是出于承诺方对租约条文的误解或自己根本没有查看,或是想表示友好合作。但几天后承诺方反悔说是租约条文明示规定不准装运危险品。这就会给被承诺方造成损害,因为他已经依赖承诺方几天前的承诺而作出安排。所以,承诺方会被禁止反供”(estopped),衡平法不允许他反悔。但这并不会改变租约的条文就是不准装运危险品的解释,条文也不会因为这一航次的禁止反供而有所改变,这毕竟不是合约更改。所以在以后的航次中,被承诺方还是必须严格遵守合约条文,不准装运危险品。

可以说英国法律在这一方面已经稳定,这在 Schuler v. Wickman 的贵族院先例后,特别是 Nicholls 勋爵的说法。

但这也不是说所有其他普通法国家都有同一个看法,如在新西兰最高院的 Gibbons Holdings Ltd v Wholesale (2008) 1 NZLR 277 先例,就判订约后双方行为的证据可以被接受帮助解释合约。

2.5.2.1　排除订约后双方的行为的证据的案例一：James Miller & Partners Ltd v. Whitworth Street Estates (Manchester) Ltd

James Miller & Partners Ltd v. Whitworth Street Estates (Manchester) Ltd (1970) A.C. 583, HL 这一贵族院先例，涉及一个苏格兰的建筑工程，但双方当事人使用的合约标准格式是英国的 1963 年版本的 Royal Institute of British Architects (RIBA)。它的内容中没有适用法，而有一条仲裁条文，但没有说明仲裁地点与依照什么仲裁法，只是规定仲裁员由 RIBA 主席委任。在这之后，双方出现争议，在 RIBA 主席的委任下，一位苏格兰人被委任为仲裁员，之后整个仲裁都在苏格兰进行。但在作出裁决书前，被告根据英国的 1950 年《仲裁法》要求仲裁员以"特殊事项"(case stated 或 special case)的做法要求英国法院对法律问题作出判决(这方面的课题在笔者所著的《国际商务仲裁》一书的第二章 2.2.3 段有详论)。这就带来一个问题，就是这一仲裁到底是苏格兰仲裁还是英国仲裁？另一个类似的问题是适用法与仲裁的程序法到底是苏格兰法还是英国法？

有关双方在订约后的行为，即是他们在苏格兰进行的仲裁，可否协助解释该建筑合约中的仲裁条文，Reid 勋爵说："I must say I had thought it was now well settled that it is not legitimate to use as an aid in the construction of the contract anything which the parties said or did after it was made. Otherwise one might have the result that a contract meant one thing the day it was signed, but by reason of subsequent events meant something different a month or a year later."(我以为法律已经明确下来，不能以订约后双方所说与所做的事情协助解释合约。否则就会造成一个情况是合约有不同解释，一个是在订约的一天，另一个是一个月或一年后根据双方的行为。)

Wilberforce 勋爵说："Reliance on subsequent conduct seems to have had considerable influence on the opinions expressed and, I would respectfully think, led the members of the court to attribute insufficient importance to the fact that the building site, and so the place of performance, was in Scotland. In my opinion, once it was seen that the parties had made no express choice of law, the correct course was to ascertain from all the relevant contemporary circumstances including, but not limited to, what the parties said or did at the time, what intention ought to be imputed to them on the formation of the contract. Unless it were found an estoppel or a subsequent agreement, I do not think that subsequent conduct can be relevant to this question."

2.5.2.2　排除订约后双方行为的证据的案例二：Schuler v. Wickman

Schuler v. Wickman (1973) 2 Lloyd's Rep. 53, HL 先例案情为 Wickman 与 Schuler 签订了合约，Wickman 从而获得 Schuler 产品在英国的独家销售权。合约第 7 条文订明，Wickman 的两位指定代表的其中一位必须在每一周走访 6 家工厂。这一规定被说明是"条件"(condition)。但后来 Wickman 没有完全这样做，Schuler 于是终止了合约。Schuler 认为，合约的第 7 条文已约定为条件条文，故而尽管 Wickman 只是轻微地破坏,Schuler 仍然有权取消合约。英国贵族院否定了这种观点,认为"条件"(condition)这个词除了"法律上专门的意义"(strict legal sense)之外还有很多其他的意思(如有些商业人士纯指"条文")。所以,虽然第 7 条文确有很"强烈表示"(strong indication)"提升"第 7 条文为条件条文,但仍不够清楚订明这一十分苛刻与不合理的说法。不合理之处是只要是多达 1400 次的走访中少了一次,Schuler 即可以终止合约。

与本章有关的是双方在贵族院有提出有关订约后双方的行为可否协助解释合约中的"条件"(condition)一词。这订约后的行为是双方在履约时曾经两次见面,其中有提到如果 Wickman 没有足够的走访,他们可以在 60 天内作出补救。反正就是在双方的交谈中显示了双方认为合约的第 7 条文并不被视为现在 Schuler 在法院所争辩的立场,即没有被视为合约的条件。这方面被贵族院拒绝,笔者也完全同意。这种情况其实经常发生,就是当事人曾经一度对合约条文/文字有了错误理解,最后找律师时才被纠正,所以正式诉讼,所争辩的立场与以前双方当事人接触时理解的不一致。除非较早的错误理解造成了一些禁止反供,否则不应该让这些行为扭曲对合约条文/文字的客观解释。其中 Reid 勋爵说:"I must add some observations about a matter which was fully argued before your Lordships. The majority of the Court of Appeal were influenced by a consideration of actings subsequent to the making of the contract. In my view, this was inconsistent with the decision of this House in *Whitworth v. Miller*, [1970] 1 Lloyd's Rep. 269. We were asked by the respondent to reconsider that decision on this point and I have done so. As a result I see no reason to change the view which I expressed in that case."

另 Wilberforce 勋爵也就这一点表示同意,说:"In my opinion, subsequent actings ought not to have been taken into account. The general rule is that extrinsic evidence is not admissible for the construction of a written document; the parties' intentions must be ascertained, on legal principles of construction, from the words they have used. It is one and the same principle which excludes evidence of statements, or actions, during negotiations, at the time of the contract, or subsequent to the contract, any of which the lay mind might at first sight seem proper to receive..."

§3 口头合约与部分口头部分文书合约的不同对待

要强调的是,以上所讲的有关外来证据不被接受解释合约只针对看来是双方接受的完整文书合约,但针对口头合约(oral agreement)或部分口头合约部分文书合约(partly oral, partly written agreement)并不适用。这里涉及的大原则是解释文书合约条文/文字是法律问题,但找出口头合约包括的内容与意思,这是事实问题。所以针对口头合约，所有的相关证据都应该被接纳与考虑，分别只在给与不同的分量，而这也包括订约后双方的行为与整个口头证据（即谈判的过程）。这里有不同对待的一个重要原因是口头合约是根据口头证据，这方面的肯定与可靠性就完全比不上文书合约这一份文件了。

这里可介绍一个有关先例，就是 Maggs (trading as BM Builders) v Marsh (2006) EWCA Civ 1058。案情有关一个承建商提供一个装修的估价给屋主，之后工作就开始进行，但双方只是达成口头协议加上部分文书协议（估价部分）。在履行时，屋主要求承建商做其他的工作。在第一审，法院的 Recorder 不允许订约后双方的行为协助解释合约。但上诉后，这一个判决被推翻，认为这种外来证据可协助解释一个部分文书部分口头协议。Smith 大法官是这样说："Was the recorder wrong to exclude this evidence? In my view, he plainly was. The recorder properly directed himself that his task was to decide what the parties agreed at the time of the original contract in March 2003. He very properly said that that was ascertainable at the time. Of course it was ascertained. The parties did not write down what they had agreed. No complete record was made. Accordingly, the only way was to decide what had been agreed then was to hear evidence about it at the trial, two or three years later. The accuracy of the parties' recollections was mutually disputed. In those circumstances, it is plain to me, as a matter of general principle, that, for the purpose of testing the accuracy of those recollections, it is highly relevant to hear evidence about what the parties had said and done about the disputed matters in the meantime. . . . In my judgement it is clear that the principle set out in Miller's case, does not apply to an oral contract. Determining the terms of an oral contract is a question of fact. Establishing the facts will usually, as here, depend upon the recollections of the parties and other witnesses. The accuracy of those recollections may be tested and elucidated by things said and done by the parties or witnesses after the agreement has been concluded. Receiving evidence of such words or actions does not mean that the judge is losing sight of his task of deciding what the parties agreed at the time of the contract. It is simply helping him to decide whose recollection is right. It is not surprising to me that the editor of Lewison should observe that there is nothing in the authorities to prevent the court from looking at post contract actions of the parties. As a matter of principle, I can see every reason why such evidence should be received."

§4 放开外来证据/口头证据的缺点与批评

无论如何，今天解释合约难免在绝大部分情况下是要把订约从头到尾的相关文件（特别是背景/语境的文件证据）都接受，唯一排除的只是谈判证据，特别是过程中如订约方一些单方面的“主观想法”(subjective thinking),因为这对解释合约条文/文字是没有帮助。

关于这种放开的做法,也有不少的问题与抱怨。有一些问题是想得到,如文书合约的肯定性会减少(正如 Hobhouse 勋爵所说),律师根据文书合约给法律意见会更小心,第三人难以安心依赖一份看来是双方接受的完整文书合约,诉讼费用昂贵等。这里可先参见笔者早在 1998 年的《国际商务游戏规则——英美证据法》一书第七章 1.1.3 段提到的一个仲裁案件并批评放开口头证据。以下,笔者详细介绍。

4.1 批评之一:令诉讼费用昂贵与时间延长

在 Investors Compensation Scheme Ltd v. West Bromwich Building Society (1998) 1 W. L. R. 896 先例,Hoffmann 勋爵说要扔掉解释合约的“旧包袱”,所有一个合理第三人觉得会影响合约条文/文字解释的证据都可以接受,说:“... the admissible background included absolute anything which would have affected the way in which the language of the document would have been understood by a reasonable man...”

这是一句很多人知道的名言,显示了英国法院正式走向解释合约的新趋势。但也不是所有的著名大法官认同,Phillips 勋爵针对 Hoffmann 勋爵旧包袱的说法,在 The Tychy (No. 2) (2001) 2 Lloyd's Rep 403 先例中说:“With respect to Lord Hoffmann, we are inclined to think that a little intellectual hand luggage is no bad thing when approaching the task of construing a contract.”

而在 NLA Group Ltd v. Bowers (1999) 1 Lloyd's Rep. 109 先例,Timothy Walker 大法官也提到追求背景/语境可能会带来大量证据,这导致已经昂贵的诉讼费用更加昂贵,另加上诉讼时间的延长。因为针对这些口头/外来证据,会有大量的文件披露、开庭审理、对有关证人的反盘问等。这与一直以来可简单处理文书合约解释的争议做法,如在法院或仲裁中作为一个快速与简短的“预先争议”(preliminary issue)审理并作出一个“宣告判决或裁决”(declaratory judgement/award),会截然不同。

在 Wire TV Ltd v. CableTel (UK) Ltd (1998) C. L. C. 244 先例中 Lightman 大法官说他花费大量时间处理没用的证据:“A very large part of the flood of evidence in this case on the factual matrix in which the agreement was to be construed was legally inadmissible and the greater part of the remainder was totally unhelpful. I had to spend over half a day hearing argument as a prelude to strike out the bulk of the witness statements before me as containing material ... which should never have been or remained there.”(这里涉及开庭前法官要删除大量证人证言的内容,估计是因为涉及谈判与谈判过程中的一些主观意图,所以不可接受。)

另 Staughton 大法官也在 Scottish Power plc v. Britoil (exploration) Ltd, The Times, 1 December 1997 先例提到:“it is often difficult for a judge to restrain the enthusiasm of counsel for producing a great deal of evidence under the heading of matrix, which on examination is found to contribute little or nothing to the true understanding of the parties' contract. All, or almost all, judges are now concerned to the huge cost of litigation. I have to say that such a wide definition of surrounding circumstances, background or matrix seems likely to increase the cost, to no very obvious advantage."

Staughton 大法官在《How do the courts interpret commercial contracts?》(1999) CLJ 303 一文中说根据合约背景/语境解释的方法无疑给商业争议带来了大量费用,而 Investors Compensation Scheme v. West Bromwich Building Society 也是英国历史上带来诉讼费用昂贵最重要的先例。

可以 NLA Group Ltd v. Bowers 先例显示诉讼费用的高昂,只为了解释有 7 个字的清楚明确的条文,原告提供了 5 个证人,再加上另传召了 2 个证人,以及提供专家证据与大量文件,其中一份有关劳合社的报告名为"Lloyd's: A Route Forward",不包括附录也有超过 200 页纸,说这些证据都显示了订约时的背景/语境。但最后 Timothy Walker 大法官认为没有任何帮助,说:"... I have given the seven words at issue in this case what I regard as their unambiguous and sensible meaning in their immediate commercial context. I look no further than that. In *National Bank of Sharjah v. Dellborg and Others*, (unreported: C. A. July 9, 1997, from New Law Online Cases Digest) Lord Justice Saville (as he then was) said this in a judgment with which both of the other members of the Court expressly agreed: [Saville 大法官所讲的话可见本章之 4.3 段的节录]. I respectfully agree with those observations, particularly the reference to the costs and delays of litigation and arbitration. I should add as a footnote that at the end of his judgment Lord Justice Saville referred to the *West Bromwich* case, a copy of the speeches having been supplied to the Court of Appeal after the argument; he said it made no difference to his conclusions."

所以有说法是 Hoffmann 勋爵自己的态度也在 Investors Compensation Scheme Ltd v. West Bromwich Building Society 后的 BCCI v. Ali (2001) U. K. H. L. 8 先例中有所收紧,重新考虑了他针对"语境"(factual matrix)的解释合约的第二个原则的适用范围,他强调自己只是说订约语境的定义没有限制,并不是说任何证据全部都要考虑。特别是一份正规的合约,不应该轻易接受订约方会在用语上犯错,他绝对不鼓励挖出所有的背景/语境来看双方订的合约是否准确表达与记录他们的订约意图。他说:"... I was merely saying that there is no conceptual limit to what can be regarded as background. It is not, for example, confined to the factual background but can include the state of the law (as in cases in which one takes into account that the parties are unlikely to have intended to agree to something unlawful or legally ineffective) or proved common assumptions which were in fact quite mistaken. **But the primary source of understanding what the parties meant is their language interpreted in accordance with conventional usage: '... we do not easily accept that people have made linguistic mistakes, particularly in formal documents.' I was certainly not encouraging a**

trawl through 'background' which could not have made a reasonable person think that the parties must have departed from conventional usage."(加黑部分是笔者的强调)

这不再是传统解释合约只严格地找出文书合约"文字上的传统意思"(conventional meaning)的做法也无可避免影响了在香港或伦敦的仲裁。在仲裁中解释合约经常可以文件审理或以一个"预先争议"(preliminary issue)简单地处理掉,这也是法律问题,如果涉及的解释是影响较深远的合约条文,可以在1996年英国《仲裁法》之section 69下取得批文后上诉法院做最后决定。但现在解释合约也可以引进大量证据,将其视为法律问题就有可商榷之处。至于导致仲裁费用昂贵,在目前的大环境下,仲裁员可以事后在费用上作出惩罚。如在作出大量文件披露后,事后发觉有关背景/语境的证据对解释合约条文/文字没有帮助,下令披露的申请方承担有关费用,不论最终的胜负。但不管是谁付这笔费用,均是浪费,也令诉讼/仲裁背上了昂贵的恶名,更不用说诉讼时间上的延误不存在任何补救办法。有关费用的惩罚,可举NLA Group Ltd v. Bowers (1999) 1 Lloyd's Rep. 109先例为例,Timothy Walker大法官让大量提供背景/语境证据的原告支付以"补偿标准"(indemnity basis)为准的费用给胜诉的被告的判决。。

另可举例子是2005年笔者在一个香港仲裁中被要求解释一个期租合约的租约期长短条文,船东的代表律师提供了大量有关谈判租约的通信往来,说这是解释订约时的背景/语境。笔者也无法拒绝以免被指称违反自然公正。笔者觉得租约期长短条文清楚明确,这些证据毫无帮助,结果笔者的确惩罚了胜诉船东承担这一部分的费用。有关这一点的仲裁裁决可节录如下:"With the above in mind, I must conclude that I have difficulty accepting the Owners' arguments of *factual matrix*. To start off, the relevant words used by the parties such as '*minimum/maximum*' are exceedingly clear and unambiguous to people in the chartering business. There is no imperfection of language which I need to enquire further. Furthermore, there were many rounds of offers and counters, part of which is being cited by me from Paragraphs 9 to 17 above. I cannot find any factual background 'known to the parties' or 'special circumstances' that could lead to the construction or 'manipulation' of '*minimum* 34/*maximum* 38 *months time charter*' as meaning the same as '3 years' or '36 months'. Indeed with several counters back-and-forth in narrowing or expanding the '*minimum/maximum*' period (such as, in Paragraph 14, the Owners countered with '*minimum* 35/*maximum* 37 *months*' against Charterers' last of '*minimum*34/*maximum*38 *months*'), I have difficulty in accepting all the different descriptions of the precise time charter periods used by the parties can all be taken to mean '3 years'. In any event, I find the Owners (and indeed the Charterers) are very experienced and knowledgeable in that they know precisely what was meant by the use of the description of '*minimum/maximum*' for the time charter period at the time of negotiations.

Therefore, I reject the Owners' argument of *factual matrix*. As mentioned, it has taken up a lot of time in this reference. In today's environment of awarding costs based on success and failure of different issues, I have a feeling that if I am asked to deal with costs later by the parties, I will take this matter into account."

另一个例子是在2013年,案情十分简单,虽然争议金额庞大,涉及高达数亿人民币的股权买卖。买方已经支付了这笔钱,合约清楚明确地规定如果卖方控制的公司在某一天还无法在香港证券交易所上市,卖方在买方要求下就必须在一个期限内退还买方这笔钱,另加上高达20%的复息。结果公司上不了市,买方要求卖方退还支付了的钱并加上利息。但卖方迟迟不付并两次哀求买方延期归还,而买方也同意了。但最后还是没有退还的情况下,买方开始了仲裁,笔者被委任为独任仲裁员。

在双方的文书请求中,卖方没有提出实质的抗辩,只是提出管辖权的质疑。但这个质疑也很难站住脚,就是指股权买卖合约才有一条香港仲裁条文,但后来双方同意延期归还的口头与通信往来的协议中并没有香港仲裁条文,所以双方的争议不应该受到仲裁的管辖。这显然是一个法律问题,看来没有事实问题的争议。但经过不断的程序上延误,在大家同意开庭前两个月左右,卖方突然申请提供好几个证人的口头证据,因为双方同意延期归还这一笔钱是通过双方见面会谈,而后来的通信往来所记录的必须要看双方在会谈中的谈判才能有正确的解释。买方作为原告显然大力反对。对笔者而言,如果允许这些外来证据,显然会导致原来安排的1~2天开庭时间不足够而需要延期。幸亏笔者是独任仲裁员,安排另一开庭时间相对容易,所以这不是重要的考虑。笔者反而关心仲裁费用的大幅提高(如从1~2天的开庭变为5~6天的开庭),而最关心的就是会对买方不公平,因为不知道卖方要提供何种口头证据。如在文书请求的抗辩书中,卖方指控在最后一次的见面会谈,买方的代表曾经同意有需要可无限期延迟归还这一笔钱,或是曾经同意不必支付利息,又或是本金只需归还一半等。而买方也在文书请求的答辩书中否认这种指控。这样就的确需要有关的证人出庭接受盘问,而最后由笔者决定是否相信这些指控。但由于在文书请求中并没有实质的抗辩,如果允许卖方提供口头证据,买方就很容易受到"突击"(ambush),因为不知道卖方证人会讲什么,无法准备自己的证人或其他有帮助的文件(如在两次会谈见面后都有向公司作出完整的文书记录)。所以,最后笔者拒绝卖方提供口头证据并在卖方拒绝参与开庭后很快作出裁决书。

但这不影响卖方向香港国际仲裁中心质疑笔者的"不当与不公正"程序的处理,否定了买方提供有关证据的权利。最后由香港仲裁中心委任的一个由三位国际仲裁员成立的"小组"(Sub - committee)作出了决定,认定笔者并没有犯错。其中可节录部分内容如下:

"**Mr. Yang's Position**

Mr. Yang takes a similar view. His position is two - fold: (i) first that the issues which fall to be determined in these proceedings are, on the whole, legal issues, for which fact evidence is not required; and (ii) second, thatthe Respondent repeatedly failed, despite requests to do so, to inform him of what specific issues of fact needed to be dealt with and by which witnesses of the Respondent.

Mr. Yang has also expressed his concernthat without identifying the specific issues of fact which the Respondent wanted to cover in witness evidence, he was faced with the possibility of there being adduced very general and broad – scope evidence, which would not be relevant or material to the issues in dispute, and which would cause him to lose 'complete control' over the proceedings.

Sub – committee analysis

In the Sub – committee's view, the record shows that Mr. Yang repeatedly requested the Respondent to indicate precisely what interlocutory orders and witness evidence were required, and yet the Respondent either did not, or was unable to, indicate this and / or was unable to persuade Mr. Yang that the identified issues in dispute required factual evidence for their resolution.

In the circumstances, the Sub – committee is satisfied that Mr. Yang acted within hisdiscretionary authority in declining to grant the Respondent's applications for discovery and witness evidence and considers that the Respondent has not proven its allegation of bias in this respect."

4.2 批评之二:有危险法官/仲裁员重写合约或错判

这会鼓励法官或者仲裁员以考虑了背景/语境为由,对一个有争议的合约"重写"(rewrite)或是自由演绎。这严重违反了基本的大原则,即他们不是订约方,应该只是解释原告与被告之间订立的合约内容。当然,这不是放开口头证据规则与接纳语境的本意,也不是所有其他的合约解释规则的本意。但是法官或仲裁员必须小心,也经常看到在这方面作出警戒的权威说法。如在 Skanska Rashleigh Weatherfold Lts v Somerfield Stores Lts (2006) EWCA Civ 1732 的上诉庭先例,Neuberger 大法官说:"... **the surrounding circumstances** and commercial common sense **do not represent a licence to the court to re – write a contract merely because its terms seem somewhat unexpected, a little unreasonable, or not commercially very wise.** The contract will contain the words the parties have chosen to use in order to identify their contractual rights and obligations. At least between them, they have control over the words they use and what they agree, and in that respect the words of the written contract are different from the surrounding circumstances or commercial common sense which the parties cannot control, at least to the same extent."(加黑部分是笔者的强调)

至于有更大危险的错判是因为多接受了大量的外来证据/口头证据,法官/仲裁员在这些方面的裁量权会有更多与更大错判的危险。如受到订约方的一些订约意图/想法的影响，而这是不对的，正如 May 大法官在 Plumb Brothers v. Dolmac (Agriculture) Ltd (1984) 271 E. G. 373, CA 先例中说："There is the danger, if one stresses reference to 'the factual matrix', that one may be influenced by what is in truth a finding of the subjective intention of the parties at the relevant time, in stead of carrying out what I understand to be the correct exercise, namely determining objectively the intent of the parties from the words of the documents themselves in the light of the circumstances surrounding the transaction. It is not permissible, I think, to take into account a finding of fact about what the parties intended a document to achieve when one is faced with a problem some five, 10 or many years later of construing it."

根据文书合约条文的文字/措辞严格解释也固然会有错判的危险，但对一个比较严格与仔细拟定的商业合约，机会相对来说就低得多。这种传统的严格解释如果错判也可能有救济(通过上诉)。而且这种错判的风险也是双方当事人比较容易预测及预防，如将一个金额庞大的商业合约在最后签订前先交给一个有能力的律师仔细审阅。这错判的危险曾见过一个说法可节录如下："A court's conclusions on the social context of a commercial agreement may be impressionistic at best, despite hearing testimony of witnesses and experts. One reason for drafting comprehensive documents is to provide a more reliable source of evidence than witnesses, who are more likely to give evidence of their states of mind and subjective intent, along with the 'context'."(法院根据事实与专家证人的证言对一个商业合约的背景/语境作出的结论至多只是凭感觉。原因之一在于，花大量的精力与时间拟定详尽的合约文件就是为了提供更可靠的证据证明双方同意了什么，这比证人证言可靠的多，他们往往会把主观想法混杂在背景/语境的证据。)

4.3　批评之三：合约涉及第三人的疑惑或/与不公平

这会给非订约方的第三人带来疑惑或/与不公平，因为所有涉及有关合约的第三人不会知道订约时的背景/语境，他们纯粹看一份合约的条文/文字。但目前解释合约的新趋势是过分强调订约方在谈判时想同意什么，而不是最后实际上同意了什么，正如 Bingham 勋爵在《A new thing under the sun? The interpretation of contracts and the ICS decision》(2008) 12 Edinburgh LR 374 一文所说的："excessive emphasis on what the parties wanted to agree and too little on what they actually did agree."

举例说，有关或受到影响的第三人问律师意见，律师也只能看有关的文件特别是一份合约作出客观的法律意见。Saville 大法官在 National Bank of Shajah v. Dellborg, unreported, Court of Appeal, 9 July 1997 先例，也针对这个新趋势提出了两个反对意见，第一个是增加诉讼费用，这已经提到过而不重复。另一个反对意见就是影响第三人，Saville 大法官是这样说：

"It is difficult to quarrel with the general proposition that when interpreting an agreement the court is trying to work out what the parties intended to agree, rather than analyzing words in a vacuum. Thus where the words the parties have used are ambiguous or, read literally, are meaningless or nonsensical, the surrounding circumstances must be considered in order to select the appropriate meaning or to give the words meaning or sense. However, where the words used have an unambiguous and sensible meaning as a matter of ordinary language, I see serious objections in an approach which would permit the surrounding circumstances to alter that meaning. (无法异议是在解释合约时法院想找出双方意图同意些什么,而不是在一个真空内分析合约的文字。所以如果双方使用的文字含糊、毫无意义或不可理喻,订约时的背景/语境就应该考虑以找出双方对这些文字的解释或意思。但如果双方使用的文字可以按照其一般意思得出清楚与合理的解释,我觉得要严重反对一个趋势就是允许背景/语境改变这些文字的一般解释。)

Firstly, such an approach would seem to entail that even where the words the parties have chosen to use have only one meaning, and that meaning is not self - evidently nonsensical, the Court will not be allowed to adopt that meaning without an examination of the surroundingcircumstances, which could involve discovery, cross - examination and the like; for a party seeking to challenge that meaning could assert with great force that until the circumstances are fully examined, it is impossible to decide whether or not they should override the plain words of the agreement. This would do nothing but add to the costs and delays of litigation and indeed of arbitration, much of which is concerned with interpreting agreements. (这一段是指目前解释合约的新趋势带来诉讼的昂贵与延误。)

Secondly, the position of third parties (which would include assignees of contractual rights) does not seem to have been considered at all. They are unlikely in the nature of things to be aware of the surrounding circumstances. Where the words of the agreement have only one meaning and that meaning is not self - evidently nonsensical, is that third party justified in taking that to be the agreement that was made, or unable to rely on the words used without examining (which is likely to be difficult or impossible for third parties to do) all the surrounding circumstances? If the former is the case, the law would treat the agreement as meaning one thing to the parties and another to third parties, hardly a satisfactory state of affairs. If the latter is the case, then unless third parties can discover all the surrounding circumstances and are satisfied that they make no difference, they cannot safely proceed to act on the basis of what the agreement actually says. This again would seem to be highly unsatisfactory. (加黑部分强调的就是目前解释合约的新趋势影响到第三人)

To my mind there is much to be said for the simple rule that where the words the parties have chosen to use have only one meaning, and that meaning is not self - evidently nonsensical, the law should takethat to be their intended agreement and should not allow the surrounding circumstances to override what (*ex hypothesi*) is clear and obvious. This would enable all to know where they stand without the need for further investigations, and for the court to provide the answer, where the point is contested, without undue delay or expense. The law of rectification provides the means for correcting the agreement where the parties have made a mistake in writing it down. To my mind what appears to be the present law does no service to the international or domestic commercial community, let alone others, such as those entering into lease and the like.

For these reasons it seems to me that what appears to be the latest approach requires qualification, if norreconsideration."

另是在 Chartbrook Ltd v Persimmon Homes Ltd (2009) UKHL 38 先例,高院对这一点有极大的反响,说:

"... Most modern commercial contracts are to greater or lesser extent assignable, such that the benefit or burden of the obligations therein contained can be, and often is, transmitted to third parties who took no part in the negotiation of the contract, and who may therefore be assumed to be wholly ignorant of what took place. Some types of commercial contracts, such as long leases of land, commonly give rise to transmission or rights and obligations long after the contract negotiators have died. Others, such as the agreement in this case, are of a more limited duration, but it is common ground that the agreement was understood and intended to be capable of assignment by way of security to a bank, and indeed was so assigned. Furthermore, even in the absence of assignment, the rights and obligations created by a commercial contract may form an important part of the auditing of its financial health may be dependent upon a proper understanding of its items, again by persons with no participation in, or knowledge of, its negotiation.

If the parties' negotiations were, to the extent 'helpful', to be routinely admissible as an aid to contractual construction, then no such third parties reading, dealing with or having transferred to them rights or obligations under the contract could make any safe assumptions about its meaning without themselves carrying out an inquiry as to those negotiations, so as to put themselves in the same state of knowledge as the parties to the contract. Furthermore, since ambiguity is no longer (after the Investors Compensation Scheme case) a prerequisite for recourse to the admissible background, a third parties' appreciation of the apparently unambiguous meaning of a word, phrase or term could be subverted by reference to the original parties' negotiations, without which no secondary meaning was even capable of being guessed at."

需要注意的是,一份文书合约影响第三人的情况十分普遍,如提单被转让,合约权益被转让,银行依据文书合约作出贷款或担保等。还有这方面的立法如 1999 年的

《Contracts (Rights of Third Parties) Act》,该课题在笔者所著的《损失赔偿与救济》一书的第七章之第6段有介绍。所以,这是放开口头证据其中的一个重要批评/缺点。

4.4 批评之四:已经有明确先例作出解释或明确做法的合约条文/文字

背景/语境是否能够适用在一些情况也颇有疑问,如一些条文/文字已经有了非常明确的先例作出了解释。这样会有看法是双方当事人订约时选择这些条文/文字,双方已经应该有共同的意图与了解,特别是双方在订约时有律师的协助,这在订约时的法律理解与协助毕竟也是背景/语境的一部分。如在 British Sugar plc v. NEI Power Projects Ltd (1997) 87 BLR 42 先例,起争议的条文/文字是"consequential loss"(间接损失),Waller 大法官就是不同意看订约时的事实背景/语境以协助解释,说:"Once a phrase has been authoritatively construed by a court in a very similar context to that which exists in the case in point, it seems to me that a reasonable businessman must more naturally be taken to be having the intention that the phrase should bear the same meaning as construed in the case in point. It would again take very clear words to allow a court to construe the phrase differently."

另在 The "Oakwell" (1999) 1 Lloyd's Rep. 249 先例,案情涉及海事的货损货差索赔的一般做法,就是有一批燃油在海上受到海水的污染,这导致船东互保协会提供给提单持有人与承租人一个担保以避免船舶被扣押。该互保协会担保的内容是市场上惯常见到的条文/文字,其中说明如下:"... we undertake that we will, within 14 days of the receipt from you of a request to do so, instruct solicitors to accept on behalf of the ship - owner service at your option of *in personam* or *in rem* proceedings brought by the cargo - owners in the English High Court of Justice and to file acknowledgment of the service thereof."

在取得互保协会担保后,该船舶被船东出售拆废铁。代表货方的律师也不以为意,反正他认为已经有了互保协会担保,就不足为虑。不久,货方律师代表提单持有人法院作出"告船告票"(*in rem* writ)。但互保协会就提出了一个了解海事诉讼的人士才会理解的技术性争议,即根据英国法律的《Supreme Court Act 1981》之21(4)段,作出告船告票时,有关船舶必须是由有个人责任的船东所拥有。唯一的例外就是告船告票的索赔本身是一个"海事优先权"(maritime lien),这才是不必理会到底有关船舶的船东是否对索赔有个人责任。这样,在本案件互保协会指称提单持有人在作出告船告票时,该船舶已经是拆了废铁,再也不是有个人责任的船东所拥有了,所以英国海事法院根本没有《Supreme Court Act 1981》所赋予的管辖权。互保协会声称错误是在提单持有人,他应该在取得互保协会担保后马上作出告船告票。但问题这并非是市场的一般做法,有了互保协会担保后,通常是船方(通过互保协会)与货方谈判和解,不会贸然多花律师费用作出告票甚至推进诉讼。有很多货损货差就是这样通过谈判和解而解决,现实中也有很多金额不大的索赔要避免昂贵的律师费用。

结果该案中双方都提供了专家意见证据,这些专家都是对货损货差索赔很有经验的律师。但 Timothy Walker 大法官认为不需要这些外来证据的协助,因为互保协会担保本身已经写得非常清楚,而且是标准的条文/文字与一些惯常做法,说:"In reality, the plaintiffs did not need any expert evidence to establish their case, and the proper construction of the agreement emerges clearly without any external aids, simply from the words used and the obvious commercial purpose of a club undertaking."

Timothy Walker 大法官认为互保协会是无条件在担保中同意接受告船告票的送达,如果互保协会现在要在担保中加入一个条件,就是有关船舶在作出告票时仍是同一船东所拥有,应该在订约时在担保中加上。如果互保协会要在订约时加上这一条件,也肯定提单持有人不会接受。

看来,在这一案例中看订约时的环境并引入昂贵的专家意见证据又是一次劳民伤财的行为。

4.5　批评之五:带来法律的不肯定

考虑订约时的事实背景/语境一个严重的不妥之处是带来法律不肯定,毕竟要不同法官或仲裁员接受大量的证据已经会对事实背景有不同的认定或演绎,这已经是一方面的不肯定。而争议双方提供在这方面的证据也会像本章之 4.2 段提到的往往会在背景/语境的证据中混杂其主观想法,这又是另一方面的不肯定。这也表示法官或仲裁员需要很小心区分双方在谈判时在某一方面达致充分的协议或理解可以对双方后来发生的合约解释争议有帮助,与更多会发生的在谈判中作出"自我保护"(self - serving)或"渴望"(aspirational)的陈述。而经常是不容易区分,不少法官或仲裁员也不一定是作出准确演绎的适合人选。这些因素加起就带来相比传统解释合约的做法,即简单看合约内容,新趋势会是更不肯定的结果。这是 Hoffmann 勋爵自己承认,他在 Chartbrook Ltd v Persimmon Homes Ltd (2009) UKHL 38 先例说:"the more one allows conventional meanings or syntax to be displaced by inferences drawn from background, the less predictable the outcome is likely to be."

例如,在最早作出定论的三个主要先例,贵族院的 5 位大法官持不同意见,都是以多数意见为准。在 Mannai Investment Co. Ltd v. Eagle Star Assurance Co. Ltd (1997) AC 749 的贵族院先例中,以 3 比 2 的多数为判决。另在 Investors Compensation Scheme Ltd v. West Bromwich Building Society (1998) 1 W. L. R. 896, Deutsch Genossenschaftabank v. Nurnhope (1995) 1 W. L. R 1580 与 BCCI v. Ali (2001) UKHL 8 先例,都是以 4 比 1 的多数通过判决。看来全面看了订约时背景/语境的大量证据后,大家反而更加糊涂。有说法是倒不如用传统的做法解释合约的文字,恐怕更容易得出一致的意见。

肯定性对商业合约尤其重要,这早在 Vallejo v Wheeler (1774) 1 Cowp 143 先例中, Mansfield 勋爵就说:"certainty is the great object of mercantile law."这些年来有无数的大法官强调肯定性对商业合约的重要,并可以让知道法律地位的商业人士很快与有信心依照合约的规定以及有针对性的先例作出决定,如可否终止合约。比较近期一点的是 Hobhouse 勋爵在《International conventions and commercial law: The persuit of uniformity》一文中说:"It could be thought relevant to consider first what are actually the needs of the commercial community. The first and paramount requirement is the achievement of certainty as far as that is possible ... most importantly, to provide a means of definitively identifying and crystallizing the bargain that has been struck and, almost as importantly, to create a clear allocation of risk between the parties. International trade is sophisticated; it takes place in a competitive and usually fluctuating market; it involves risks; it needs enforceable rights and liabilities. The parties must also be able to make their own bargain for themselves, using if they so choose one of the standard contractual schemes available in their trade ... The law is simply a tool which enables [the commercial man] to conduct his commercial activity effectively and efficiently. It is not an instrument of state policy, as is for instance consumer protection, nor should it be seen as an opportunity for paternalism."

众所周知,英国的商法是在全球空前成功的产业,给英国带来无法估量的经济与非经济的利益,也是美国这一首屈一指的经济强国自认没有办法竞争的领域。在绝大部分跨国的商业合约中,如果订约方想加上一条针对适用法的条文,都会想到英国法。而英国法其中一个重要的卖点就是肯定性与法院或仲裁员不会改写双方拟定的合约。但正如在 Ewan McKendrick 教授在《English contract law: A rich past, an uncertain future?》(1997) 50 Current Legal Problems 25 一文中说:"The creep of contextualism, discretion and regulation threatens that reputation."(这种解释合约的新趋势威胁到了英国商法的声誉。)也有不少其他要求扭转这一新趋势的呼吁,如在 Jonathan Morgan 博士在 2013 年剑桥大学出版的《Contract Law Minimalism —— A formalist restatement of Commercial Contract Law》一书中的结论说:"The trend is in the wrong direction. It is increasingly believed that a flexible contextual approach is required to meet commercial expectations. However, as we have argued, sophisticated contractors prefer clear rules to resolve disputes... A return to practical formalism is well overdue."

在其他普通法国家的法院,也有强烈提出批评,特别是针对带来不肯定的方面。加拿大 Alberta 省的上诉庭在 Gainers Inc v Pocklington Financial Corporation 2000 ABCA 151 先例中说:"If hindsight, implication, unspoken thoughts, and unwritten statements could have so pivotal a role as they appear to have had here, **then written contracts would become a mere trap for the credulous. Almost all commercial certainty would evaporate**, and commercial litigation becomes a swearing contest. A suit on a commercial contract, no matter how carefully drafted, would become a long historical investigation of an insoluble mystery. Often who said what to whom by telephone 15 years ago is impossible to unravel. A formal written contract should not rise or fall with such mysteries."(加黑部分是笔者的强调)

4.6　批评之六:订约方会对文书合约的拟定怠慢

英国法律一直以来,都是要求订约方小心文书合约的拟定,特别是在有充分订约自由的商业合约,更加需要小心约定与审查。现在放开外来证据/口头证据的趋势会带来订约方对这一方面的怠慢。

估计将来的商业合约中会越来越多见到"完整合约条文"(entire agreement clause)作为相对比较"高水平/复杂"(sophisticated)的商业人士对英国法律这个新趋势的对策。虽然这种完整合约条文,在目前广泛的语境解释合约的新趋势下能否成功排除所有的外来证据/口头证据还有疑问,这可看本书第十三章之第2段。

4.7　对批评的总结

照理说合约的条文/文字足够或相对明确无误,如在本章稍早的4.1段介绍的笔者作为独任仲裁员的香港仲裁案件,就不应受订约时背景/语境的扭曲,也不应该在这方面花费大量的金钱与时间。正如Park大法官在Breadner v. Granville - Grossman (2001) Ch 523先例中说,如果订约方并不像是用字错误,就应该根据这些所用的文字作出一般性的解释:"It is of course true that Lord Hoffmann was mainly concerned to bring out that there are circumstances where it is appropriate to depart from the natural and ordinary meaning of words, but he had partially in mind cases where it was realistic to acknowledge that the draftsman had made a 'linguistic mistake', In this case... I do not think that the draftsman... made a linguistic mistake. He said what he intended to say. So why should not the 'natural and ordinary meaning' of his words be adopted?"

但问题是一份合约能够被称为明确无误、毫无瑕疵的情况不多。毕竟解释合约条文,一般也不会只针对一条条文,往往是整个合约有关条文的综合解释。现实中,双方的代表律师如果是高水平,都能够在表面看来是清楚无误的合约条文挑出疑点。这表示大部分的情况下,在目前解释合约的新趋势,还是免不了争议的订约方要求提供证据以显示订约时的事实背景/语境。但笔者估计现实中不少香港或伦敦的仲裁员受传统解释合约的做法影响太深,所以感觉上就是争议双方即使花费了大量金钱与时间提供证据并争辩订约时的背景/语境,但最后的判法还是照合约中的条文/文字一般性解释。情况就好像Park大法官所说的:"Although I appreciate that the modern approach to construction of a legal document has loosened to quite some degree from a formal syntactical approach... it remains the case that the starting point, and usually the finishing point as well, is to identify the natural and ordinary meaning of the words which the draftsman has used ..."

如果合约条文之间有冲突,目前的新趋势也只是多给仲裁员以他的感觉或印象进行自由的演绎。但不论好坏,估计英国法律也不会走回传统做法,因为这本来就是世界的潮流(会在本章稍后的5.1段介绍),不是英国法律可置身其外。

§5 支持放开外来证据/口头证据的说法

针对上述介绍的各种批评,也有一些相反的说法针对部分的批评,并且表示支持,原因如下。

5.1 支持原因之一:与国际接轨

主要原因之一是英国法律要尽量吻合欧共体的法律与国际做法。在《Principles of European Contract Law》第5-102条文,它是这样说:"In interpreting a contract, regard shall be had, in particular, to:(a) the circumstances in which it was concluded, including the preliminary negotiations;(b) the conduct of the parties, even subsequent to the conclusion of the contract;(c) the nature and purpose of the contract;(d) the interpretation which has already been given to similar clause by the parties and the practices they have established between themselves;(e) the meaning commonly given to terms and expressions in the branch of activity concerned and the interpretation similar clauses may already have received;(f) usages; and(g) good faith and fair dealing."

看来,欧洲大陆法所涉及的面更广,远不止在订约的背景/语境范围内。像(a)、(b)与(g)都是英国法律所不予考虑的。在笔者眼中,根据欧洲合约法的原则解释条文/文字,有危险是把法律问题变为事实问题来判。

另在国际上,如在联合国的《United National Convention on Contracts for the International Sales of Goods》(或简称CISG)就有了明示条文第8条要求解释合约考虑订约方的意图,特别是要考虑双方的谈判与之后的行为,说:"(1) For the purpose of this Convention statements made by and other conduct of a party are to be interpreted according to his intent where the other party knew or could not have been unaware what that intent was. (2) If the preceding paragraph is not applicable, statements made by and other conduct of a party are to be interpreted according to the understanding that a reasonable person of the same kind as the other party would have had in the same circumstances. (3) In determining the intent of a party or the understanding a reasonable person would have had, due consideration is to be given to all relevant circumstances of the case including the negotiations, any practices which the parties have established between themselves, usages and any subsequent conduct of the parties."

另在《UNIDROIT Principles of International Commercial Contracts》的第201条文,也有同样的明示条文有关外来证据:"§201 Whose Meaning Prevails(1) Where the parties have attached the same meaning to a promise or agreement or a term whereof, it is interpreted in accordance with that meaning. (2) Where the parties have attached different meanings to a promise or agreement or a term thereof, it is interpreted in accordance with the meaning attached by one or them if at the time the agreement was made (a) that party did not know of any different meaning attached by the other, and the other knew the meaning attached by the first party; or (b) that party had no reason to know of any different meaning attached by the other, and the other had reason to know the meaning attached by the first party. (3) Except as stated in this section, neither party is bound by the meaning attached by the other, even though the result may be a failure of mutual assent."

例如对于第201(2)(a)条文规定,J W Carter教授在2013年在《Journal of Contract Law》发表的《Context and Literalism in Construction》有说:"Under § 201(2)(a), context provides a basis for the conclusion that one party has manifested an intention to the other, and did not know that the other party had a different understanding. The first party's understanding prevails - notwithstanding the subjective views of the other. It does not matter whether that meaning is the same as that which a reasonable person would give to the contract, without the benefit of the evidence."(如果根据证据认定了订约一方曾经表达了一个订约意图给另一方,但不知道另一方对此条文/文字有不同理解。这样前者的订约意图或理解超越了另一方不同的主观理解。这也不考虑对这一事实背景不了解的合理第三人对该条文/文字上是否会有不同理解。)

另一个重要的公约是1969年《Vienna Convention on the Law of Treaties》(1980年生效),其中Article 31也规定了一般的解释协议规则,如下:"1. A treaty shall be interpreted in good faith in accordance with the ordinary meaning to be given to the terms of the treaty in their context and in the light of its object and purpose. 2. The context for the purpose of the interpretation of a treaty shall comprise, in addition to the text, including its preamble and annexes: (a) any agreement relating to the treaty which was made between all the parties in connexion with the conclusion of the treaty; (b) any instrument which was made by one or more parties in connexion with the conclusion of the treaty and accepted by the other parties as an instrument related to the treaty."

另在Article 32针对解释的补充方法,说:"Recourse may be had to supplementary means of interpretation, including the preparatory work of the treaty and the circumstances of its conclusion, in order to confirm the meaning resulting from the application of article 31, or to determine the meaning when the interpretation according to article 31, or to determine the meaning when the interpretation according to article 31: (a) leaves the meaning ambiguous or obscure; or (b) leads to a result which is manifestly absurd or unreasonable."

英国作为欧共体的成员,与欧洲法律在解释合约不同之处可以结合上述所讲并节录Hoffmann勋爵在Chartbrook Ltd v Persimmon Homes Ltd (2009) UKHL 38先例所说如下:"Supporters of the admissibility of pre – contractual negotiations draw attention to the fact that continental legal systems seem to have little difficulty in taking them into account. Both the UNIDROIT Principles of European Contract Law (1999) provide that in ascertaining the ‘common intention of the parties’, regard shall be provide that in ascertaining the ‘common intention of the parties’, regard shall be had to prior negotiations: arts 4(3) and 5(102) respectively. The same is true of the United Nations Convention on Contracts for the International Sale of Goods (1980). But these instruments reflect the French philosophy of contractual interpretation, which is altogether different from that of English law... English law ... mixes up the ascertainment of intention with ... rules of law by depersonalising the contracting parties and asking, not what their intentions actually were, but what a reasonable outside observer would have taken them to be. One cannot in my opinion simply transpose rules based on one philosophy of contractual interpretation to another, or assume that the practical effect of admitting such evidence under the English system of civil procedure will be the same as that under a continental system."

即使是其他的普通法国家,也与英国看法不一样。如新西兰已经将 CISG 立法为 1994 年《Sale of Goods (United Nations Convention) Act》。而在美国,根据《Uniform Commercial Code》的 Article 2 - 208 与 1979 年《Restatement (2nd) ‘Contracts’》[8]的 Section 202 (4)也与英国传统解释合约的做法有完全不同的改变,立法明确规定了解释合约可以考虑外来证据,包括订约后双方的行为。在美国的权威书籍《Corbin on Contracts》(1960 年)提到客观解释合约并不意味着法院就只能看合约的条文/文字的字面意思,而不考虑可能显示订约方对此有不同解释的证据。因此,如果 A 与 B 订立了合约,并且有证据显示 A 对合约的某些条文/文字有特定意思,而 B 对此也知情,则即使一个对 A 的特定意思不知情的合理第三人会对合约中的条文/文字有不同解释,知情的 B 也不能否定 A 原来特定的意思。针对 1979 年《Restatement (2nd) ‘Contracts’》之 Section 202,立法解释(b)中说:“The meaning of words and other symbols commonly depends on their context; the meaning of their conduct is even more dependent on the circumstances. In interpreting the words and conduct of the parties to a contract, a court seeks to put itself in the position they occupied at the time the contract was made. When the parties have adopted a writing as a final expression of their agreement, interpretation is directed to the meaning of that writing in the light of the circumstances... The circumstances for this purpose include the entire situation, as it appeared to the parties, and in appropriated cases may include facts known to one party of which the other had reason to know.”

---

〔8〕 1979 年《Restatement (2nd) ‘Contracts’》与 1932 年《Restatement of the Law of Contracts》的相关规定有很大不同。

针对 1979 年《Restatement (2nd) 'Contracts'》之 Section 212(1)，立法解释(b)认为要考虑合约背景/语境不局限在合约的条文/文字含糊的情况(not limited to cases where it is determined that the language used is ambiguous)。另是 Section 214(c)规定如下："Agreement and negotiations prior to or contemporaneous with the adoption of a writing are admissible in evidence to establish ... the meaning of the writing, whether or not integrated."

最后介绍美国的 Pacific Gas and Eletric Co v G W Thomas Drayage v Rigging Co Inc 69 Cal 2d 33; 442 P 2d 641 (1968)先例，在第一审法院拒绝接受外来证据改变被视为清楚无误的合约条文/文字，但去了上诉庭，这不被接受，其中 Traynor CJ 大法官认为不论有关的文件是用字含糊或是清楚无误，都不影响要将背景/语境与本质加以考虑。他是这样解释："If words had absolute and constant referents, it might be possible to discover contractual intention in the words themselves and in the manner in which they were arranged. Words, however, do not have absolute and constant referents ... The meaning of particular words or groups of words varies with the '... verbal context and surrounding circumstances and purposes in view of the linguistic education and experience of their users and their hearers or readers (not excluding judges) ... A word has no meaning apart from these factors; much less does it have an objective meaning, one true meaning'. ([A L] Corbin, 'The Interpretation of Words and the Parol Evidence Rule' (1965) 50 Cornell LQ 161 at 187)."

5.2　支持原因之二：可以通过案件的管理控制外来证据

针对放开外来证据有令诉讼昂贵的批评，因为为了协助合约条文/文字的解释可能需要引入大量证据。这也有相反的说法就是在英国法院，现在有了 Civil Procedural Rules 的民事诉讼程序改革，法院可通过案件的管理限制文件的披露。这可见在 Egan v. Static Control Components (Europe) Ltd (2004) 2 Lloyd's Rep. 429 先例中 Arden 大法官说所说的："When the principle in the Investors Compensation Scheme v. West Bromwich Building Society (1998) 1 W. L. R. 896, HL (ICS) case were first enunciated, there were fears that the courts would on simple questions of construction of deeds and documents be inundated with background material ... speaking for myself, I am not aware that the fears expressed as to the opening of the floodgates have been realized. The powers of case management in the Civil Procedural Rules could obviously be used to keep evidence within proper bounds. The important point is that the principles in the ICS case lead to a more principled and fairer result by focusing on the meaning which the relevant background objectively assessed indicates the parties intended."

在仲裁中，也有说法是仲裁员可以通过限制文件披露与是否接受专家证据针对这一批评。当然，理论与现实不一定是同一回事。仲裁员在面对一方当事人坚持要提供有关订约前的外来证据/口头证据，并坚持这一方面的披露，不知道内情的仲裁员恐怕不容易坚决抗拒,毕竟要顾及自然公正。正如在稍早的4.1段解释的笔者作为独任仲裁员的案件,笔者不接受被告提供的外来证据/口头证据,结果被被告挑战笔者作为仲裁员的公正与独立。在仲裁机构甚至是法院没有作出决定前,对这种挑战仲裁员毕竟是会感到不安与疑虑。

5.3 支持原因之三:有关口头证据的规则已经不成规则与太多例外

这方面已经在本章之2.3段探讨过,总而言之就是许多有关商业与合约法的争议与不同理论都要法官/仲裁员看口头证据或订约后行为的外来证据,如合约是否成立或有效、授权问题、合约变更、共识性禁止反供等。而且在一个诉讼中,经常会有订约一方作出这些方面的"替代争辩"(alternative argument),导致这些外来证据经常被抖出来。这样,如果进一步把这些外来证据协助解释合约条文/文字,也增加不了费用与延误。这在《The Construction of Contracts—Interpretation, Implication and Rectification》(2007年)一书之5.133段有提到说:

"The existence of escape routes from the current rules in the shape of rectification for prior negotiations and estoppel by convention for subsequent conduct (together with other less clear exceptions) further demonstrates the incoherence of the current English position. This is especially so given the tendency of counsel to make these alternative pleas and therefore ensure that the prior negotiations or subsequent conduct are included in the relevant trial bundle. This argument also refutes the counter - argument that the current rule shortens litigation, is more efficient, and requires a less tedious judicial exercise.

The prior negotiations and subsequent conduct rules are further inconsistent with neighbouring bodies of commercial and contractual doctrine, such as the requirement that the courts sit through negotiations to determine whether a contract has been formed, and the broad approach to the evidence taken in cases attempting to ascertain whether an agent has apparent authority to contract on behalf of a principal. These examples can be multiplied."

但只要法官或仲裁员还是可以决定是否接受外来证据/口头证据这一说法而不是全面开放,就会给了法官或仲裁员一定的裁量权在有些情况下拒绝接受。如明确无误的合约条文/文字就可以排除口头证据,只是在含糊不清或作出字面的解释会带来可笑结果时才需要引入口头证据,法官或仲裁员就可以在拒绝接受口头证据的同时声称有关的合约条文合约/文字明确无误。毕竟,对一位看来含糊或可笑但对一位看来是明确无误的情况的确存在,如在Investors Compensation Scheme v. West Bromwich Building Society (1998) 1 W. L. R. 896, HL先例,Lloyd勋爵的少数意见认为合约条文不会带来可笑的结果。

5.4 支持原因之四:有不少情况确有帮助找出真正订约意图

这方面已经在本章讲了很多,如在2.3.5段就给了不少例子,笔者也可以介绍自己的一次印象深刻的经历,虽然案件本身涉及的金额并不高。这是一个伦敦仲裁案件,在 LMLN 386 有报道。有关期租合约说明是跑一个从美国装散粮中东的航次,第 7 条文说明/承诺承租人可以全权使用船舶的装货地方/甲板与所有的载重量("the full reach of the vessel's holds, decks, and usual places of loading")。但是,附加条文有一条明显是特殊条文的第 59 条:"Owners have the right to bunker at loading port ... about 800 metric tons Intermediate Fuel Oil and about 100 metric tons Marine Diesel Oil without affecting charterers' operations."((在不影响承租人的作业的情况下,船东有权在装港添加约 800 吨燃油与约 100 吨柴油。)

在美国装港,船东作出加油安排,但承租人拒绝,说这样会令他少装货物(少装 900 吨散粮),这明显是影响他的作业(charterers' operations),这在第 59 条附加条文中说明是例外,所以船东不能行使权利加油。船东争辩说不影响承租人作业只是指实际装货作业不受影响,如加油驳船不阻挡装货的驳船,或是船东为加油要在装货半途移船到另一个装油泊位。船东说,这个租约明确是装散粮,而不是装棉花,如果船东有权加油就与装货在载重方面有冲突,必须要给第 59 条文一个综合与更重分量的解释。既然该条文是明确了船东可添加 900 吨燃油,给这特殊的规定一定的解释就免不了承租人要少装 900 吨散粮,不能让承租人说这影响了承租人作业而否定了整条第 59 条文,特别是否定这细致明确的添加 900 吨燃油的一句话。

但仲裁庭判"作业"(operations)一词应作广泛解释,而承租人少装货肯定是其中的一种,所以船东败诉。这样判,也表示第 59 条文(毕竟是附加条文)配合这航次期租合约说明是去美湾满载散粮,就变得毫无作用与意思。到底这样解释有关条文与判法是否正确有争议,笔者也有很大保留。因为一个基本原则以传统方法解释合约是尽量协调每一条文,给与双方当事人所约定的文字有一定与全面的意思,而不是否定(这方面请看本书第三章 1 至 6 段)。如果能够局限地解释"作业"(operations)一词,不否定整条第 59 条文的意思,这应比较符合公道。即船东可在不影响实际装货作业的情况下自己添加燃油,承租人当然要少装 900 吨货物,但这是在订立租约时让步并接受了第 59 条文时同意的。

在该案件,如果仲裁庭能够接受并一并看双方谈判的口头证据后才作出合约条文/文字的解释,就更加明确应判船东胜诉。过程是船东与承租人在第一回合的谈判中,船东要求在装港允许添加约 900 吨燃油,这是因为美湾燃油价格相对十分便宜,而在中东与远东就价格昂贵。所以船东要考虑在中东卸货之后还船,船舶仍有足够的廉价燃油可走下一航次或返回远东。但承租人拒绝,结果双方就再不接触,船东找另外的生意,而承租人找另外的船舶。但时间过了一个星期,该承租人又回来找船东,而该船舶刚好还没有定下其他的租约,这带来第二回合的谈判。在谈判中,显然承租人让步,所以有了这第 59 条文。如果这些口头证据都抖出来,估计任何有一点点头脑的仲裁员都不会判船东败诉,完全否定该第 59 条文与漠视订约的事实背景/语境。

但可惜由于金额不高,加上承租人律师抗拒提供外来证据/口头证据,并且受到仲裁庭的支持。结果就造成这种不公平与偏离双方订约意图的结果,因为仲裁庭仅机械式地解释租约中第59条文的“作业”(operation)一词。

以下再总结或重复一下针对外来证据/口头证据的重要方面,然后对一些重要案例做比较详细的介绍,让读者可以更好掌握。

§6 外来证据/口头证据与合约本身起冲突时的证据分量

由于目前的趋势是可接受口头/外来证据,以协助解释合约条文/文字,这就存在如果两方面起冲突时,应该给哪一方面更重的分量? Steyn大法官在《Interpretation: Legal Texts and their Landscape》一文中说:“The mandated point of departure must be the text itself. It does not mean that contextual material in aid of the interpretation of a text must be ruled out or downgraded. After all, a statement is only intelligible if one knows under what conditions it was made. **But extrinsic materials are subordinate to the text itself.** The primacy of the text is the framework of reference for the judge considering a point of interpretation. But all legal text must be construed against the contextual setting in which they come into existence. Taking full account of such aids to construction the judge must concentrate on the different meanings which the text is capable of letting in. What falls beyond that range of possible meaning will not be a result attainable by interpretation.”(加黑部分是指外来证据必须在次位,而合约的条文/文字有更重的分量)

在 Arbuthnott v. Fagan (1996) LRLR 135 先例有同样的说法,就是外来证据不应该超越合约本身清楚明确的条文/文字,因为后者才是有关订约方的真正意图最肯定的指引。Bingham大法官说:“Courts will never construe words in a vacuum. To a greater or lesser extent, depending on the subject matter, they will wish to be informed of what may variously be described as the context, the background, the factual matrix or the mischief. To seek to construe any instrument in ignorance or disregard of the circumstances which gave rise to it or the situation in which it is expected to take effect is in my view pedantic, sterile and productive of error. **But that is not to say that an initial judgment of what an instrument was or should reasonably have been intended to achieve should be permitted to override the clear language of the instrument, since what an author says is usually the surest guide to what he means. To my mind construction is a composite exercise, neither uncompromisingly literal nor unswervingly purposive**: the instrument must speak for itself, but it must do so in situ and not be transported to the laboratory for microscopic analysis.”(加黑部分也是说清楚无误的合

约条文/文字应该有更重的分量，毕竟订约方作为该文件的作者把有关的写法视为最肯定的指引显示他们的想法。Bingham 大法官认为解释合约是一个综合性的做法，既不能是毫不妥协作出严格的字面上的解释，也不能坚定不移地作出订约目的的解释。）

上述虽然讲到分量还是文书合约的条文/文字为重，尤其是在合约条文/文字清楚无误的情况下，但在一些判例，笔者也不觉得一成不变。会有情况是一些明显与重要的订约目的/背景被确定后与合约条文/文字有矛盾，但法院判是前者超越了后者，如本书第一章提到的 Charter Reinsurance Co Ltd v. Fagan（1997）AC 313，HL 与第一章之 8.3 段及本章之 12.3 段的 Investors Compensation Scheme v. West Bromwich Building Society（1998）1 W. L. R. 896，HL 等先例。

§7　外来证据/口头证据的背景/语境须是订约时双方都知道或能合理知道

这方面已经在本章多处提及，但在此可强调并节录 Gerard McMeel 教授《The Construction of Contracts—Interpretation，Implication and Rectification》（2007 年）一书第 5.69 段如下："A critical restriction is that background must be reasonably available to both parties. But that is also an objectively judged requirement. Actual knowledge or ignorance is irrelevant. It is critical that the information is reasonably available to both parties. As Brennan J opined in *Codelfa Construction Prop Ltd v. State Rail Authority of New South Wales*（1982）149 C. L. R. 337：'an extrinsic fact known only to one of the contracting party can shed no light upon the meaning with which that word or phrase was used by the other or others."

这在 Scottish Power plc v. Britoil（Exploration）Ltd（The Times，December 12，1997）先例，Staughton 大法官认为订约背景应该只局限在订约双方订约时所想得到的与当时在旁边发生的一些事情（"surrounding circumstances" should be confined to what the parties had in mind，and what was going on around them at the time when they were making the contract.）。

针对订约时"双方都知道或能合理知道的事实"（mutually known facts）能够协助解释合约并不是新鲜的理念，以前也在局限的情况下被接受，如在本章之 1.1 段提到的技术性术语等描述性条文。但现在双方都知道或能合理知道的事实协助解释合约被进一步放开，成为确定合约的背景/语境的重要准则。这可看 J W Carter 教授的《The Construction of Commercial Contracts》（2013 年）中提到说："'mutual knowledge' as a sufficient criterion for context as a whole."

§8 订约方单方面的主观意图不被接受

在本书第一章之4.3段已经提到过,解释合约不接受订约方的“主观意图”(subjective intention),因为这对客观解释合约条文/文字毫无帮助。笔者经常听到一些关于诉讼的技巧,经常出现的一条就是盘问对方证人在订下有争议的条文/文字时到底在想什么。这盘问经常会被证人一方的律师反对,也往往会被仲裁员认定不该问,也与这个道理有关。

在新趋势解释合约,是接受订约时的背景/语境的证据以找出真正的订约意图,但要注意的是,这是指客观与合理看双方一致并反映在他们所拟定的合约条文/文字的订约意图而不是看单方面的主观意图。单方面的主观意图一直被抗拒接受,除非是违背了法官/仲裁员要客观解释有争议的合约条文/文字外,接受主观意图还会带来其他大问题。如会造成不公平,因为订约一方的主观意图往往不为对方所知道或接受,如果被法律支持,就有可能造成对对方不公平。另外,会有情况导致整个合约的无效,因为各为其说就谈不上订约时有“一致想法”(meeting of minds),正如Donaldson大法官在Summit Investment Inc. v. British Steel Corp (1987) 1 Lloyd's Rep. 230先例所说的:“... their actual intentions are happily irrelevant, since, were it otherwise, many, and perhaps most, disputes upon points of construction would be resolved by holding that the parties were not *ad idem*.”

最近三四十年所改变了的解释文书合约做法只是先假设双方约定的合约条文/文字表达了他们的订约意图,但文字表达出来的有两个层面。第一个层面也就是传统解释合约所重视的,语文上/文法上的解释(这会在字典中找到)与对合约中的条文作出综合解释(这根据本书所介绍的多条解释合约规则)。但另一个层面就是订约双方在订约的“背景”(background)、“语境”(factual matrix 或 context)下所想表达的意图。把这个背景/语境找出来一并考虑,这就会在一些案件中达致更准确与商业上合理的解释,在本章之5.4段所介绍的笔者败诉的一个伦敦仲裁案件,就是一个非常典型的例子。这也就是现在被肯定的正确做法。

对上述所讲可介绍Hoffmann勋爵在Mannai Investment Co Ltd v. Eagle Star Life Assurance Society Ltd (1997) A. C. 749先例所说的:

“It is of course true that the law is not concerned with the speaker's subjective intentions. But the notion that the law's concern is therefore with the 'meaning of his words' conceals an important ambiguity. The ambiguity lies in a failure to distinguish between the meaning of words and the question of what would be understood as the meaning of a person who uses the words. The meaning of words, as they would appear in a dictionary, and the effect of their syntactical arrangement, as it would appear in a grammar, is part of the material arrangement which we use to understand a speaker's utterance. But it is only a part; another part is our knowledge of the background against which the utterance was made. It is that background which enable us, not only to choose the intended meaning when a word has more than one dictionary meaning but also, in the ways I have explained, to understand a speaker's meaning, often without ambiguity, when he has used the wrong words.

When, therefore, lawyers say that they are concerned, not with subjective meaning but with the meaning of the language which the speaker has used, what they mean is that they are concerned with what he would objectively have been understood to mean. This involves examining not only the words and the grammar but the background as well."

但笔者看来的一个问题是,如果一位法官或仲裁员接受了外来证据/口头证据后才区分双方的订约意图与单方面的主观意图会是不容易,特别是在本章之2.5.1.4.1段提到的"告知过对方的意图"(communicated intention)。另外,如果看了单方面的主观意图的证据再试图排除,也可能会受到影响。这也是"特权证据"(privilege evidence)被视为公共政策,绝对不让法官或仲裁员看(除非当事方弃权),以免受到污染或影响的道理。

§9 如何以外来证据/口头证据协助解释合约条文/文字

有一个说法就是以这种外来证据/口头证据"直接使用"(direct use)在解释合约是不允许,但"间接使用"(indirect use)就允许。这两个不同的使用可下述图表作为进一步的介绍。

直接使用:

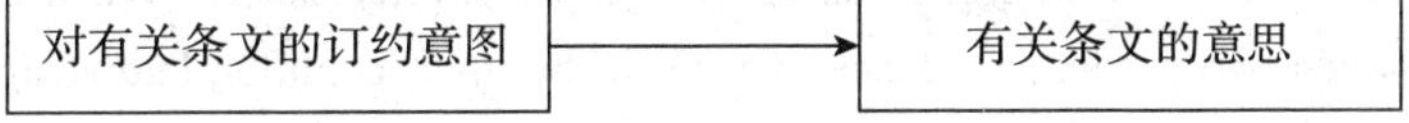

间接使用:

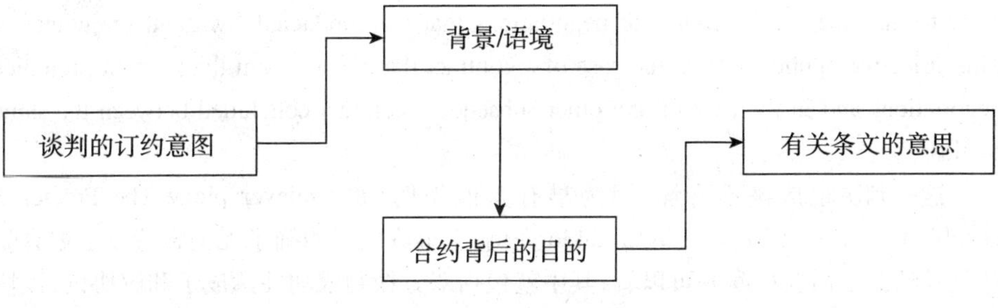

但现实中,往往直接使用与间接使用还是有很多不明确与重叠,笔者感觉是有很多案例也不理会到底是直接或是间接依赖或使用外来证据/口头证据协助解释合约条文/文字。

笔者的理解是,如果合约条文/文字有明确针对,就不能以外来证据/口头证据直接协助解释,因为这实际上是以双方在谈判的订约意图或目的试图否定他们在合约中的条文/文字,除非涉及合约变更。这也符合本章之第6段所讲的原则。但针对间接使用,就会在合约中的条文/文字有两个可能的解释下找出双方订约的背景/语境与合约的目的,作出协助。举例说,如果双方在谈判中提到甚至接受有关工程合约的目的之一是必须及时完工,而合约中的有争议条文/文字(可能涉及时间方面或工程的进度)有两个可能的解释,就会根据合约的背景/语境在解释条文/文字时偏向为时间是重要的解释。

§10 外来证据/口头证据与无损害特权

众所周知,"特权证据"(privilege evidence)根据公共政策不能被要求披露,包括双方有争议后谈判希望达成和解的有关文件与资料,名为"无损害特权证据"(without prejudice evidence)。在 Oceanbulk Shipping v. TMT Asia (2011) 1 Lloyd's Rep. 96 先例,案情涉及一个"远期运费协议"(forward freight swap agreement 或简称 FFA)的争议,并且双方事后达成了和解。双方承认这一和解合约存在,但对内容的解释有争议。其中 TMT 声称对方在谈判时曾经有一些对事实的陈述,这构成了背景/语境解释该和解协议的第5条。但对方反对,并指这些谈判时的背景/语境可以享有特权。TMT 在第一审获得高院的支持,但在上诉庭被多数意见判是败诉,而最后在最高院又获得胜诉。判决由 Clark 勋爵作出,但笔者只节录 Phillips 勋爵所说如下:"The principle to be derived from this appeal can be shortly stated. When construing a contract between two parties, evidence of facts within their common knowledge is admissible where those facts have a bearing on the meaning that should be given to the words of the contract. This is so even where the knowledge of those facts is conveyed by one party to the other in the course of negotiations that are conducted 'without prejudice'. This principle applies both in the case of a contract that results from the without prejudice negotiations and in the case of any other subsequent contract concluded between the same parties."

这一判决也应该不奇怪,因为早有其他先例,如 Unilever plc v The Procter & Gamble Co (CA) (2000) 1 WLR 2436 先例,上诉庭已经明确了无损害特权证据有哪些例外情况是需要披露并可以看,其中就包括双方谈判成功并达成了和解协议,该协议与较早时谈判的往来文件或资料就不再享有特权,说:"(1) ... when the issue is whether without prejudice communication have resulted in a concluded compromise agreement, those communications are admissible...（2）Evidence of the negotiations is also admissible to show that an agreement apparently concluded between the parties during the negotiations should be set aside on the ground of misrepresentation, fraud or undue influence. Underwood v Cox（1912）4 DLR 66, a decision from Ontario, is a striking illustration of this..."

所以英国最高院的判决,可以接受外来证据解释和解合约条文/文字也就理所当然了。

§11　对放开外来证据/口头证据的展望

在这方面的展望,一是估计将来会有更多案例令大量外来证据/口头证据中订约背景/语境与订约方主观意图之间的分界线更加清晰,以及"直接使用"(direct use)与"间接使用"(indirect use)的区分等。David McLauchlan 先生在《The Contract that Neither Party Intends》(2012）29 JCL 26 一文中说,什么证据应该可以接受与协助解释合约的意思的争议继续存在(The issue therefore remains: what evidence ought to be available to determine the meaning of a contract?)。二是在解释合约的案件中"肯定性"(certainty)会减低,毕竟外来证据多了,就已经难肯定了。笔者感觉是仲裁员解释合约有了太多自由与裁量权,会比认定"事实争议"(issue of facts)更加不肯定,也更会受到其他无可避免的外来因素影响。如除了事实认定,现在连合约解释的法律判决也更大程度受到法官或仲裁员文化背景的差异所影响。

在此想探讨另一个展望,就是由于开放外来证据会影响无辜第三人,导致将来会否在政策上禁止一些文件/文书合约以外来证据的语境来协助解释有关条文/文字。这方面可节录 Hoffmann 勋爵在 Mannai Investment Co Ltd v. Eagle Star Life Assurance Co Ltd（1997）A. C. 749 先例所说如下:"There are documents in which the need for certainty is paramount and in which admissible background is restricted to avoid the possibility that the same document may have different meaning for different people according to their knowledge of the background."(有一些文件肯定性是至关重要,所以要局限接受有关背景的证据以防止同一份文件会根据不同人士是否知道有关背景/语境而有不同解释。)

这些文件/文书合约可能如银行的信用证,银行要根据有关的付运文件作出一笔付款,但银行不会对这些文件的背景有任何了解,也不会有相关的商业知识。如在 J H Rayner & Co Ltd v. Hambro's Bank Ltd（1943）K. B. 37, CA 先例,作为银行就不会知道一份文件中的"Cornamdel groundnut"与"machine - shelled groundnut kernels"是同一样货物。这里也可重复节录 Hoffmann 勋爵也在 Mannai Investment Co Ltd v.

Eagle Star Life Assurance Co Ltd 先例所说的有关解释信用证的 UCP 500 不应该看订约背景,说:"Documents required by bankers' commercial credits fall within this category. Article 13(a) of the Uniform Customs and Practice for Commercial Credits (1993 revision) says that the documents must 'upon their face' appear to be in accordance with the terms and conditions of the credit. But the reasons of policy which require the restriction of background in this case do not apply to notices given pursuant to clauses in leases."

另一种文件/文书合约应该有不同对待是标准格式合约,因为在市场上有许多人在使用,不应该是任由个别案件的不同背景而扭曲条文/文字的解释,这会带来不肯定。这在 AIB Group (UK) Ltd Martin (2001) UKHL 63, (2002) 1 W. L. R. 94 先例,Millett 勋爵说:"A standard form is designed for use in a wide variety of different circumstances. It is not context – specific. Its value would be much diminished if it could not be relied upon as having the same meaning on all occasions. Accordingly the relevance of the factual background of a particular case to its interpretation is necessarily limited. The danger, of course, is that a standard form may be employed in circumstances for which it was not designed. Unless the context in a particular case shows that this has happened, however, the interpretation of the form ought not to be affected by the factual background."

但这里可以说明的是,在外贸与航运业务中,当事人使用标准格式合约绝少是没有修改与加上或多或少的附加条文。这样,仲裁员可以扭曲个别合约的标准格式合约条文,说是与其他附加条文一并根据订约背景/语境考虑,就有了不同的解释。

再另一类文件/文书合约是一些被法律要求是文书形式的,如在 1986 年的《财产法》(《Law of Property [Miscellaneous Provision] Act》)之 Section 2 就规定土地买卖的合约必须是文书形式。Gibson 大法官在 Firstpost Homes Ltd v. Johnson (1995) W. L. R. 1567, 1571, CA 先例有针对这一规定说是为了简化法律与避免争议,所以要求整个合约是记录在一份文件,并有双方签署:"... [section 2 of the 1989 Act was] intended to simplify the law and to avoid dispute, the contract now being in a single document containing all the terms and signed by the parties. Thereby it has been sought to avoid the need to have extrinsic evidence as to that contract."

最后介绍的一种文件/文书合约是提单,这是在国际货物买卖经常要以背书转让的文件,而无辜买方会根据提单上的明示条文/文字而付出数以百万美元。银行也是同样情况,把提单作为质押作出融资。所以,提单的肯定性至关重要,正如 Diplock 勋爵在 The "Miramar" (1984) 2 Lloyd's Rep. 129 先例所说的:"The word in the Exxonvoy bill of lading upon which this appeal turns are the same irrespective of whether it is issued in respect of a complete or part of a cargo, received on board at the first or any subsequent loading port for carriage to and discharge at the last or any previous discharging port. There must be ascribed to the words a meaning that would make good commercial sense if the Exxonvoy bill of lading were issued in any of these situations, and not some meaning that imposed upon a transferee to whom the bill of lading for goods afloat was negotiated, a financial liability of unknown extent that no business man in his senses would be willing to incur."事实上,已经有案例是在本质上不允许在提单的文书内容增加口头证据,可参见笔者的《提单与其他付运单证》一书第四章2.2.4段。

§12　有关放开外来证据/口头证据协助解释合约条文/文字的英国先例

这种先例有不少,仅看《Chitty on Contracts》(第31版,2012年)一书,英国就已经有:Prenn v. Simmonds (1971) 1 W. L. R. 1381; Moschi v. Lep Air Services Ltd (1973) A. C. 351; Reardon Smith Line Ltd v. Yngvar Hansen – Tangen (1976) 1 W. L. R. 989; Bunge v. Kruse (1977) 1 Lloyd's Rep. 492; Harmony Shipping Co SA v. Saudi – Europe Line Ltd (1981) 1 Lloyd's Rep. 377; Shell Tankers (UK) Ltd v. Astro Comino Armadora SA (1981) 2 Lloyd's Rep. 40; Wace v. Pan Atlantic Group Inc. (1981) 2 Lloyd's Rep. 339; Perrylease Ltd v. Imecar A. G. (1988) 1 W. L. R. 463; Vitol BV v. Compagnie Europeenne des Petroles (1988) 1 Lloyd's Rep. 574; Shearson Lehman Hutton Inc. v. Maclaine Watson & Co Ltd (1989) 2 Lloyd's Rep. 570; Forsikringsaktieselskapet Vesta v. J. N. E. Butcher, Bain Dawes Ltd (1989) 1 Lloyd's Rep. 330; Anangel Atlas Compania Naviera SA v. I. H. I. Co Ltd (1990) 2 Lloyd's rep. 526; Bankers Trust Co v. State Bank of India (1991) 2 Lloyd's Rep. 443; Levett v. Barclays Bank (1995) 1 W. L. R. 1260; International Fina Services AG v. Katrina Shipping Ltd (1995) 2 Lloyd's Rep. 344; Cresspark Ltd v. Wymering Mansions Ltd (1996) E. G. C. S. 63; Mannai Investment Co Ltd v. Eagle Star Life Assurance Ltd (1997) A. C. 749; Investors Compensation Scheme Ltd v. West Bromwich Building Society (1998) 1 W. L. R. 896; Don King Productions Ltd v. Warren (1998) 2 Lloyd's Rep. 176; Ringway Roadmarking v. Adbruj (1998) 2 B. C. L. C. 625; NLA Group Ltd v. Bowers (1999) 1 Lloyd's Rep. 109; The "Rio Assu" (1999) 1 Lloyd's Rep. 115; Eridania SpA v. Rudolf A Oetker (2000) 2 Lloyd's Rep. 209; Canterbury Golf International Ltd v Yoshimoto (2001) N. Z. L. R. 525; Bank of Credit and Commerce International v Ali (2002) 1 A. C. 251; Aqua Design & Play International Ltd v Kier Regional Ltd (2002) EWCA Civ 797; P&S Platt Ltd v Crouch (2003) EWCA Civ 1110; NBTY Europe Ltd v Nutricia International BV (2005) EWHC 734 (Comm); Beazer

Homes Ltd v Stroude (2005) EWCA Civ 265; Profoce Recruit Ltd v Rugby Group Ltd (2006) EWCA Civ 69; Dornoch Ltd v Mauritius Union Assurance Co Ltd (2006) 2 Lloyd's Rep 475; Nearfield Ltd v Lincoln Nominees Ltd (2006) EWHC 2421 (Ch); ING Lease (UK) Ltd v Harwood (2007) EWHC 2292 (QB); Pratt v Aigaion Insurance Co SA (2009) 1 Lloyd's Rep 225; Anglo – Continental Educational Group (GB) Ltd v Capital Homes (Southern) Ltd (2009) EWCA Civ 218; Oceanbulk Shipping and Trading SA v TMT Asia Ltd (2011) 1 Lloyd's Rep 96; Ted Baker Plc v AXA Insurance UK plc (2012) EWHC 1406 (Comm)。

值得一提的是,接受外来证据/口头证据协助解释合约条文/文字也被香港法院[Jumbo King Ltd v. Faithful Properties Ltd (1999) H. K. C. F. A. R. 279 先例],以及新西兰法院所采纳[Boat Park Ltd v. Hutchinson (1999) 2 N. Z. L. R. 74; Yoshimoto v. Canterbury Golf International Ltd (2001) 1 N. Z. L. R. 523 等先例]。但澳大利亚法院说是采取了更谨慎的态度来对待,如 Royal Botanic Gardens and Domain Trust v. South Sydney City Council (2002) 240 CLR 45 先例,但也有大量的先例还是跟随新趋势解释合约。

笔者先挑少数重要或有趣的英国先例作为介绍,然后会介绍几个澳大利亚与新加坡的先例,因为这些国家的法律都无可避免受到了新趋势解释合约的影响。

12.1 英国案例之一:Prenn v. Simmonds

第一个重要先例就是贵族院的 Prenn v. Simmonds (1971) W. L. R. 1381,争议是有关双方一个"盖章合约"(sealed contract)中的"利润"(profits)一词的解释。案情有关一个协议中约定只要公司利润在有关的年份中超过 300,000 英镑,Simmonds 博士就可以行使一个认股权。但仅局限在有关的公司看,利润达不到这个数字。但如果包括所有附带公司,利润就超出了这一数字。这一词有争议是利润到底只局限在有关的公司,或是包括整个集团公司(包括附带公司)的利润。Wilberforce 勋爵作出了唯一的判决原因,根据该合约的商业背景与其客观目的对"利润"一词作出解释,也警告"英国法律不能被孤立在一些严格字义解释的荒岛"(English law was not 'left behind in some island of literal interpretation'.)。用上"孤立"一词是由于英国在这一方面的立场与世界不配合,Wilberforce 勋爵说:"In order for the agreement of July 6, 1960, to be understood, it must be placed in its context. The time has long passed when agreements, even those under seal, were isolated from the matrix of facts in which they were set and interpreted purely on internal linguistic considerations. There is no need to appeal here to any modern, anti – literalist tendencies, for Lord Blackburn's well – known judgment in *River Wear Commissioners v. Adamson* (1877) 2 App Cas 743, 763 provides ample warrant for a liberal approach, we must, as he said, inquire beyond the language and see what the circumstances were with reference to which the words were used, and the object, appearing from those circumstances, which the person using them had in view. Moreover, at any rate since 1859 (*Macdonald v. Longbottom* 1 E &E 977) it has been clear enough that evidence of mutually known facts may be admitted to identify the meaning of a descriptive term."

该案例在上诉庭,Denning 勋爵也有同样的判法,说:"The judge put a literal construction on the word 'profits' holding that it meant the separate profits of the holding company: but then, finding that that literal construction was contrary to the intention of the parties, he had to resort to rectification to put is right. We think that he was wrong to give the word a literal construction: and that he should, in the circumstances have construed it as meaning 'consolidated profits'. So there is no need to rectify the agreement ..."(高院给"利润"一个严格的解释……这严格解释是与双方订约意图不符,要把文书合约变更。我认为给这一词一个严格的解释是错误的,高院大法官应该根据整个订约环境作出解释,而不必变更合约。)

12.2　英国案例之二:The "Diana Prosperity"

接下的一个重要贵族院先例是 The "Diana Prosperity" (1976) 2 Lloyd's Rep. 621。涉及 1972 年日本的"新光"油轮(Sanko)建造 50 艘 8 万吨油轮然后转租出,而在出租时,该油轮还没有开始建造,不会有船名,所以唯一能够"认定"(identify)是哪一艘船只能依靠造船合约所提供的"船壳号码"(hull number)。Sanko 是把该船舶长期期租给一家欧洲公司名为 Hansen,而 Hansen 再把该船舶背靠背转租给英国的 Reardon Smith 公司。这两份租约中对船名都是写作"... to be built by Osaka Shipbuilding Co. Ltd. and known as Hull no. 354 until named and shall have a deadweight of about 87,600 tons."

Sanko 是用一家名为 Sculptor 的利比里亚公司向 Sumitomo(日本著名的商社)订购这艘新油轮,而 Sumitomo 再向大阪船厂(Osaka)下订单,并取得了这一 Osaka hull no. 354。但大阪船厂本身无法建造一艘 8 万吨的油轮,所以它就把真正建造有关油轮的工程给了同集团下距离大阪 300 英里的一个名为 Oshima 的新船厂。并有了另一个船壳号码为 Oshima hull no. 004。也可以说,该船舶现在有了两个船壳号码并出现在有关文件中。另要一提的是,Oshima 船厂是由大阪船厂控股 50%,而 Sumitomo 拥有大阪船厂与 Oshima 船厂另外 50% 的股份。Oshima 船厂由大阪船厂监督,并且有关的管理层来自从大阪船厂。这也是日本造船业通常的做法,就是由一些大商社如三井、三菱揽造船合约,然后分给集团下的各大小船厂建造。无可争议的事实是 Oshima hull no. 004 就是 Osaka hull no. 354,也就是最后建成下水名为 The "Diana Prosperity"的船舶。这是订约时的整个背景。

到船舶建成下水要交船时,英国的 Reardon Smith 公司拒绝接船,因为当时运费市场(1976 年)与几年前订下租约与造船合约的 1972 年相比,严重下挫。Reardon Smith 就是以租约的船舶是要在大阪船厂建造,而如果 The "Diana Prosperity"不符合这个描述,这属于违反英国的《货物销售法》(当时是 1893 年版本)中对货物要符合描述的默示条件条文。

但承租人这个说法被贵族院拒绝,认为本案例是租约而并非是买卖合约,合约“语境”(context)不一样。Wilberforce 勋爵并引述了 Roskill 大法官在 The “Hansa Nord” (1975) 2 Lloyd's Rep. 445 所说:“In principle it is not easy to see why the law relating to contracts for the sale of goods should be different from the law relating to the performance of other contractual obligations, whether charterparties or other types of contract. Sale of goods law is but one branch of the general law of contract. It is desirable that the same legal principles should apply to the law of contract as a whole and that different legal principles should not apply to different branches of that law.”

但对本书重要之处在于,The “Diana Prosperity”就是租约中约定的 Osaka hull no. 354,而作出这个解释,正是根据双方订约时的背景/语境,即大家都对日本造船工业的习惯性运作模式有了解。在该案例中确实也有大量的事实证据证明日本造船工业的运作模式是有习惯性的做法,以协助法院作出解释。Wilberforce 勋爵是这样说:“It is less easy to define what evidence may be used in order to enable a term to be construed. To argue that practices adopted in the shipbuilding industry in Japan, for example as to sub - contracting, charter - party contract between two foreign shipping companies, whether or not these practices are known to the parties, is in my opinion to exceed what is permissible. But it does not follow that, renouncing this evidence, one must be confined within the four corners of the document. No contracts are made in a vacuum: there is always a setting in which they have to be placed. The nature of what is legitimate to have regard to is usually described as ‘the surrounding circumstances’ but this phrase is imprecise: it can be illustrated but hardly defined. In a commercial contract it is certainly right that the Court should know the commercial purpose of the contract and this in turn presupposes knowledge of the genesis of the transaction, the background, the context, the market in which the parties are operating. . . .”

12.3 英国案例之三:Investors Compensation Scheme c. West Bromwich Building Society

这是一个十分重要的贵族院先例,可以说是为放开口头证据寻找“语境”(factual matrix)的趋势定了调。该先例已经在本书第一章 8.3 段有提到,以下详细介绍并且避免重复。有关 Investors Compensation Scheme v. West Bromwich Building Society (1998) 1 W. L. R. 896 先例中的案情对中国读者(包括是笔者)不容易理解,因为它纯是涉及英国本土的房屋问题。英国有不少一般家庭的老人拥有自己的房屋,这恐怕就是他们唯一的贵重资产,并且也是非常值钱的资产。但由于他们没有什么积蓄,也早已退休而没有收入,就会有各种动脑筋的人想出“方案”(scheme)。本先例的方案是把房屋抵押,而把抵押得来的钱投资在一个“与股票挂钩的债券”(equity - linked bond),这在股市兴旺时会为屋主带来很高收益的利息/回报。在本先例中,方案名为"home income plans",作出抵押的 Housing Society(等于银行)可简称为 WBBS(即被告 West Bromwich Building Society),想出这个方案的投资顾问名为 Fisher Prew - Smith,另有许多律师所参与。

另也要解释的是英国有一个立法名为《Financial Services Act 1986》,在该立法下,英国政府成立了一个可简称为 ICS(即原告 Investors Compensation Scheme)的机构管理一笔赔偿基金给一些在这种被批准的投资方案中蒙受损失的屋主(可称为是投资者或 Investor)。这显然是保持社会稳定的做法与福利的一部分,虽然它也并非全额赔偿这方面的损失。每当 ICS 收到申请赔偿时,就会要求 Investor 签一份"索赔表格"(claim form),其中包括同意在收到赔偿后,Investor 就把所有向投资顾问、有关律师或所有其他可能有责任的第三人的"索赔权利"(chose of action)"转让"(assign)给 ICS。这是在表格的 Section 4 如下:"1. I/we agree that my/our rights against the participant firm in respect of the claim shall pass to Investors Compensation Scheme Ltd ('ICS') on payment of compensation pursuant to Financial Service (Compensation of Investors) Rules 1990 ('the rules') . . . 6. I/we hereby assign absolutely to ICS **each and every third party claim** and the benefit thereof. . . "

但本案例的表格另有 Section 3(b)针对抵押银行 WBBS 作出了例外情况,说明如下:"ICS agrees that the following claims shall not be treated as a 'third party claim' (as defined in Section 4 of this form) for the purpose of this agreement and that the benefit of such claims shall enure to you absolutely: **Any claim (whether sounding in rescission for undue influence or otherwise) that you have or may have against the WBBS in which you claim an abatement of sums which you would otherwise have to repay to that society in respect of sums borrowed by you from that society in connection with the transaction and dealings giving rise to the claim (including interest on any such sums).**"

而起争议的就是上述加黑的"Any claim (whether sounding in rescission for undue influence or otherwise)"。ICS 说应该被理解为"Any claim sounding in rescission (whether for undue influence or otherwise)",但持相反意见的 WBBS 认为应该被理解为"Any claim",而不必理会括号内的内容。区别是前者把索赔的种类局限在房屋抵押的废除,而后者就广泛的多,可包括所有的索赔。进一步解释,因为 Section 3(b)是作为转让诉权的例外,就是前者的解释表示 ICS 有权向 WBBS 索赔(如果他也有责任,如参与投资顾问对 Investor 的误述或作出错误投资意见),只除了是房屋抵押的废除。但如果是后者的解释,就表示所有向 WBBS 索赔的权利是作为例外,依然保存在 Investor 手中,并没有转让给 ICS。

但这里还存在一个更复杂的问题,就是只有一个诉权,不能部分拆开来转让,因为会带来太大的不肯定。这样,如果是后者的解释,表示诉权在 Investor 手中,而 Investor 向 WBBS 起诉,很有可能 WBBS 会向法院申请把其他参与的投资顾问与律师一并拉进来作为共同被告，一次过审理。这样，就表示 ICS 可以通过 Section 4 的转让向投资顾问与律师索赔，但会令整个转让的安排变得十分混乱，因为损失是同样的损失，需要法院有很好的管理才能判几个被告谁要负责些什么与赔付给哪一个原告。

在该案例中，重要的是投资顾问已经破产，所以转让对他的诉权没有价值。但一个针对 WBBS 的诉权就有价值了，虽然这还要看 WBBS 是否有责任。

在上诉庭与贵族院的 Lloyd 勋爵（少数意见），认为解释 Section 3（b）应该是从一个不懂法律的 Investor 眼中看。他看 Section 3（b）时，会以为所有能向 WBBS 的索赔，只要减轻抵押的款项，诉权都在 Investor，毕竟他并非从 ICS 获得所有损失的赔偿。Lloyd 勋爵也认为括号内的内容，尤其是第一个字“不论”（whether）与最后的字“or otherwise”并没有什么意思而并非为了局限在前面的广泛文字“any claim”，说：“It is said that the plain meaning would make the words in brackets otiose. So indeed it would. But words in brackets are often otiose, especially brackets in the format ‘(whether . . . or otherwise).’ They show that the general words which precede the parenthesis are not limited to any particular kind of claim, but cover all claims so long as they are claims for reduction of sums due.”

Lloyd 勋爵也说到括号内的内容可能是在拟定文件时只想到因为不当影响（undue influence）而让 Investor 废除抵押。但这订得很奇怪，因为废除不仅是只有这个原因，如 WBBS 曾经有过误述也会有这个后果。Lloyd 勋爵在这一方面是说：

“The objection to the plain meaning is the inclusion of the words ‘for undue influence’ after ‘rescission’; for any lawyer would know that there are other grounds on which the investor might claim rescission, for example, on the ground of misrepresentation. Why, therefore, should the draftsman have specifically included one of the grounds on which the investor might claim rescission, but not others?

We do not know the answer to this question. It may be that if one had access to the preliminary drafts of the claim form, or to the mind of the draftsman himself, the answer would emerge clearly enough. It may be that a claim for rescission on the ground of undueinfluence was, for some reason, uppermost in the draftsman's mind; so he put the words in. but we cannot go into the draftsman's mind. We have nothing to go on but the words he has used. The inclusion of undue influence is odd, but not so odd as to obscure the meaning. ‘Or otherwise’ must relate back to ‘whether sounding in rescission’. Any other construction would leave ‘whether’ hanging in the air. So ‘or otherwise’ covers claims in contract and tort. It is not limited to other grounds for claiming rescission. The drafting is slovenly. But I do not have any great difficulty with the meaning.”

最后一提的是 Lloyd 勋爵不接受解释合约可以有一个做法是将括号内的文字搬出来而局限括号前的“any claim”，说：“I know of no principle of construction which would enable the court to take words from within the brackets, where they are clearly intended to underline the width of ‘any claim’, and place them outside the bracket where they have the exact opposite effect.”

但 Lloyd 勋爵并非反对新趋势,而是亦支持新的解释合约做法找出订约双方的真正意图或目的,只不过在本先例他不觉得按文件的条文/文字按字义来解释有“可笑的结果”(absurdity)。这是因为 ICS 只是赔了 50% 或稍微较多的众多 Investors 的损失,所以后者不把诉权全部转让给 ICS 也可以理解。他说:“Purposive interpretation of a contract is a useful tool where the purpose can be identified with reasonable certainty.”

反正 Lloyd 勋爵的结论就是 Investor 保留了对 WBBS 起诉的权利,ICS 只拥有起诉投资顾问与除 WBBS 外第三人的权利,他这样说:“So the position would be that he, the investor, would retain his right to sue WBBS for a reduction of the mortgage debt, but ICS would obtain the right to sue Fisher Prew – Smith and ‘third parties’ other than WBBS...”

至于分开诉权(Investor 有诉权告 WBBS,ICS 有诉权告投资顾问与律师),而损失只有一个并且会合并审理,Lloyd 勋爵觉得在良好的案件管理下应该问题不大。

现在看贵族院多数的意见,他们认为所有的索赔权利都已经转让给了 ICS,Investor 再也没有对 WBBS 的诉权,仅有的例外就是有权废除抵押。看来,多数贵族院成员的说法不是针对 Section 3(b)文字上的解释,而是看背景与整体的合理性。Hoffmann 勋爵有以下的几方面说法(只部分解释与节录):

1. 从 Claim Form 整体看,包括它有一个专门给 Investors 这种不懂法律的人士看的“解释注脚”(explanatory note),只说到:转让的诉权是针对一些对 Investors 的损失要负责与作出的赔偿(You also agree that ICS should be able to use any rights which you now have against anyone else in relation to the claim. Examples might be directors of the firm or other persons also responsible for causing the loss for which you are being compensated. You give up all those rights and transfer them to ICS.)。Hoffmann 勋爵认为,如果在这种文字下可被解释是向 WBBS 的索赔权利仍是保留在 Investors 手中,这解释注脚就会严重误导或错误。

2. Hoffmann 勋爵也认为 Section 3(b)只针对一种情况,就是不懂法律的人士可能不视为一种索赔,即废除抵押后并“扣减”(abatement)欠下的债务,但这不是涉及向 WBBS 索取任何金钱,只减少归还。

3. Hoffmann 勋爵也认为重要的是只有对抵押废除的权利并不是一种可以转让的权利。转让的“chose of action”是指一个索赔金钱的诉权。但废除抵押不是这种权利,因为它与房屋的拥有是不可分割的。ICS 根本对房屋抵押废除或不废除没有发言权与不感兴趣。Hoffmann 勋爵是这样说:

“Now it is important to notice that a claim to rescission is a right of action but can in no way be described as a chose in action or part of a chose in action. It is a claim to be relieved of a mortgage, and such a claim can be made only by the owner of the mortgaged property. The owner cannot assign a right to rescission separately from his property because it would make no sense to acquire a right to have someone else's property relieved of a mortgage. Likewise, the possibility of an abatement of the debt as part of the process of rescission is not a chose in action which can be assigned. It is simply part of the process of rescission, which is a right attached to the ownership of the house itself.

It can therefore be seen that in reserving to the investor any claim to an abatement of the mortgage debt consequent upon rescission, section 3(b) was not cutting down the scope of the chose in action which was assigned to ICS."

4. Hoffmann 勋爵也认为这是非常奇怪的事情,即向 WBBS 索赔损失的权利还是给 Investor。并且在拟定时要想想这样的做法在理念上是否行得通。在常识看来, ICS 或者有索赔权利的转让,或者没有,而不会这样分开各有各的诉权,但损失只有一个,并在将来出事情时看谁动得快。Hoffmann 勋爵这样说:"... any lawyer would think it extremely odd for ICS to take an assignment of the investor's claim for damages against the solicitors and leave the investor with a claim for the same damage against WBBS. He would be likely to wonder whether this was conceptually possible and, as I shall explain, I think that his doubts would be well founded. The investor and ICS could not between them recover more than the loss which the investor had actually suffered. As a matter of common sense, one would therefore expect that ICS either had a right to the damages or it did not. It would seem eccentric to leave this question to be decided (if such a thing were possible) by a race to judgment."

总而言之,贵族院的大多数解释 Section 3(b)方法正是 Lloyd 勋爵所不认同的,就是把括号内的部分内容搬去局限括号前的"any claim",变为"Any claim sounding in rescission (whether for undue influence or otherwise)",也只有这一种权利为 Investor 所保留。

其中最重要的是 Hoffmann 勋爵把英国当今的法律在解释文件/文书合约归纳了五个著名原则如下:

"(1) Interpretation is the ascertainment of the meaning which the document would convey to a reasonable person having all the background knowledge which would reasonably have been available to the parties in the situation in which they were at the time of the contract.

(2) The background was famously referred to by LordWilberforce as the 'matrix of fact', but this phrase is, if anything, an understated description of what the background may include. Subject to the requirement that it should have been reasonably available to the parties and to the exception to be mentioned next, it includes absolutely anything which would have affected the way in which the language of the document would have

been understood by a reasonable man.

(3) The law excludes from the admissible background the previous negotiations of the parties and their declarations of subjective intent. They are admissible only in an action for rectification. The law makes this distinction for reasons of practical policy and, in this respect only, legal interpretation differs from the way we would interpret utterance in ordinary life. The boundaries of this exception are in some respects unclear. But this is not the occasion on which to explore them.

(4) The meaningwhich a document (or any other utterance) would convey to a reasonable man is not the same thing as the meaning of its words. The meaning of words is a matter of dictionaries and grammars; the meaning of the document is what the parties using those words against the relevant background would reasonably have been understood to mean. The background may not merely enable the reasonable man to choose between the possible meanings of words which are ambiguous but even (as occasionally happens in ordinary life) to conclude that the parties must, for whatever reason, have used the wrong words or syntax (see *Mannai Investment Co Ltd v. Eagle Star Life Assurance Co Ltd* [1997] A.C. 749)。

(5) The'rule' that words should be given their 'natural and ordinary meaning' reflects the commonsense proposition that people have made linguistic mistakes, particularly in formal documents. On the other hand, if one would nevertheless conclude from the background that something must have gone wrong with the language, the law does not require judges to attribute to the parties an intention which they plainly could not have had. Lord Diplock made this point more vigorously when he said in *Antaios Cia Naviera SA v. Salen Rederierna AB*, *The 'Antaios'* (1985) A.C. 191: '... if detailed semantic and syntactical analysis of words in a commercial contract is going to lead to a conclusion that flouts business common sense, it must be made to yield to business common sense.'

This is now, the starting point for a consideration of principles of interpretation. In *B.C.C.I. v. Ali* (2001) U.K.H.L. 8; (2001) 1 A.C. 251 Lord Bingham of Cornhill summarised them as follows: 'To ascertain the intention of the parties the court reads the terms of the contract as a whole, giving the words used their natural and ordinary meaning in the context of the agreement, the parties' relationship and all the relevant facts surrounding the transaction so far as known to the parties. To ascertain the parties' intention the court does not of course inquire into the parties' subjective states of mind but makes an objective judgment based on the materials already identified."

以上 Hoffmann 勋爵的重要原则可以概述如下:(1)解释合约是为确定在订约时一份文件/合约对一个拥有双方订约时所知道的背景的合理的人士所传达的意思。(2)这些背景与知识被 Wilberforce 勋爵称为"订约的语境"(matrix of fact),包括任何可以影响合约文字会被一个合理的人士所理解,限制只是在订约时双方合理了解的以及如第(3)点所述。(3)法律对于有关背景/语境的理解(证据)的接受只排除了订约方在以前的谈判证据与过程中宣告他们的"主观意图"(subjective intention),它只在"合约变更"(rectification)的情况下可被接受。法律对此的区分是为了实际操作,解释合约与解释日常生活的讲话不一样。(4)合约传递给一个合理人士的信息与其本身文字表面的意思并不一定相同。文字表面的意思来自于字典和语法。合约传递的意思是订约方利用文字加上背景理解所要表达的意思。(5)文字应该被给与其"自然与通常含义"的原则反映一个常识,就是法院不容易接受订约方犯下文字错误,特别是在正式的文件中。另一方面,如果还是从背景/语境的理解中推断合约中条文/文字肯定是词不达意,法律并不要求法官强加给订约方一个他们明显没有的真正订约意图。

12.4　英国案例之四:NLA Group Ltd v. Bowers

NLA Group Ltd v. Bowers(1999) 1 Lloyd's Rep. 109 是一个有关劳合社受保伤亡与失业保险(disable and unemployment insurance)的先例,投保的是 Birmingham Midshire Building Society(简称 BMBS),保的是向 BMBS 贷款买房屋的家庭,如果他们遇上伤亡或失业无法还款就要保险来赔付了。之后,BMBS 把保险赔付转让给 NLA Group Ltd,NLA 就是以受让人的身份起诉劳合社"保险小组"(syndicate)的 Bowers,要求赔付。

案情是在 1993 年,BMBS 已经向 Bowers 等 7 个劳合社保险小组投保。在 1994 年度,保险被更新,再续保一年。保单中承诺支付 BMBS 所有保费的 25% 作为基本佣金,而且保单中加了一条条文答应另支付利润佣金的 60% 说:"**Subject to renewal with Lloyd's market** Profit Share Commission payable to Assured of 60 per cent ... Profit Share commission deficits are carried forward until extinction."(在前面加黑部分就是争议的 7 个字,表面的字义看是加了一个支付利润佣金的先决条件,就是要继续跟劳合社投保)。

到了 1995 年,BMBS 换了保险人,虽然保险带头人仍是劳合社,但是另一个名为"Cassidy and Others"的保险小组。而带头保险人所占的风险是 27.5%,其余的 72.5% 就分别由其他非劳合社的保险公司分摊。

这样就带来争议是 Bowers 应否支付佣金给 BMBS 或更正确的是 NLA 这一受让人。这争议表面看来很简单,就是看上述的案情下是否符合支付佣金的先决条件。NLA 当然说是,因为 1995 年的保险带头人仍是劳合社成员。由于争议看来简单,所以是以一个"预先争议"(preliminary issue)的方式向法院提出,要求法院解答以下问题:"Did the obtaining by BMBS of the insurance for the 1995 policy year referred to in paragraph 6 of the Point of Reply amount to 'a renewal with the Lloyd's market' by BMBS within the meaning of that phrase as contained in the 1994 Policy, so as to entitle BMBS to receive from the Defendant Profit Share commission pursuant to the terms of the 1994 Policy?"

本来,这一先决条件就是要求 BMBS 与原来的保险人续保,这才要支付 60% 利润佣金作为吸引。而如果换了其他保险人/保险公司,原来的保险人根本没有诱因要支付这笔庞大的利润佣金。所以,在正常情况下,应该很快作出判决。Timothy Walker 大法官是这样说:"It is the first seven words of that clause that I have to construe. It is absolutely apparent both from the way the 1993 cover was operated and from the words of the 1994 clause itself (with its express reference to 'renewal') that the substantial profit commission of 60 per cent. payable in addition to the basic commission of 25 per cent. of premium was a bonus or, to use a more pejorative word, an inducement to the assured to renew the insurance. The aim of the transaction was in this respect to get further business for the underwriters subscribing to the cover. There was no sense in the underwriters agreeing to pay profit commission unless they received something in return, namely renewal with them. Further, the percentage and calculation of the profit commission in 1994 were identical to the percentages and calculation of the profit commission in 1993. In addition, the provisions for deficits to be carried forward to extinction in both cases envisaged a continuing relationship. Thus the relevant Lloyd's market identified in the 1994 slip policy was the underwriters subscribing to it. In simple terms the clause was saying: 'If you stay with us again next year, we will pay you profit commission again for this year'."

看来这么简单的问题,原告 NLA 却引进了很多有关订约时背景/语境的证据,但最后还是改变不了败诉的命运。这些方面已经较早时在本章之 4.1 段有涉及。

12.5 英国案例之五:The BOC Group v. Centeon

The BOC Group v. Centeon (1999) 1 All E. R. (Comm) 970 的上诉庭先例是有关一个股票买卖合约的解释,有关的解释是条文是否明示禁止普通法下的"抵销"(set-off)。该第 2.7 条文是如下:"**Obligations Concerning Payments.** The Purchaser agrees that the Initial Consideration and any Further Consideration shall be paid on the dates specified for payment herein, time being of the essence. The purchaser's obligation to make payment of the deferred installments of the Initial Consideration and (subject to the express terms thereof) the **Further Consideration shall be absolute and unconditional** and shall not be affected by any transfer of any of the equity interest in Delta, the transfer of any or all of Delta's assets or business, the dissolution of Delta, the termination of the business of Delta (or any part thereof), the success or failure of any research projects undertaken by Delta, the future commercialization or otherwise of any products Delta's further business prospects or technological or technical successes or by any other matter whatsoever. For the avoidance of doubt, nothing in this Agreement shall impose any obligation on Purchaser or Delta either to commence or to continue to manufacture, distribute or sell any of the products. ”（加黑的部分就是主要争议的几个字，是说买方的付款必须绝对与无条件，争议是这几个字是否代表了禁止抵销）。

案情是买卖一家名为 Delta 的公司，它的业务主要是在生物学，特别是有关基因的科技。但看来该公司还比较新，估计收入最少要 2 年以上，所以看来购买这些未经考验的公司有相当的风险。BOC 在这一案例中是卖方，它把 Delta 股票卖给 Centeon，作价 4500 万美元，分三次支付，每一次付 1500 万美元，第一期是在订约/成交时，第二期是一年后，而第三期是在 2 年后。到了要支付第三期的 1500 万美元时，Centeon 拒付，说是他因为 BOC 的误述与其他违约而错误购入了一家毫无价值的公司，所以要提出比 1500 万美元更高的反索赔。这种反索赔与股票买卖的支付关系密切，所以根据普通法应该可以抵销，这是双方当事人都接受的法律地位。

为什么能否抵销这么重要？答案是如果不能抵销而只能提出反索赔，Centeon 就需要马上筹这笔到期要支付的 1500 万美元，否则 BOC 很容易去法院拿到一个简易判决强制支付。由于没有抵销的权利，Centeon 没有对这笔钱的支付有任何抗辩。而且，如果 Centeon 在付了这 1500 万美元后，继续推进他的反索赔，这肯定是一个庞大、漫长与昂贵的诉讼，即使 Centeon 胜诉也恐怕在好几年之后才收得回这笔钱。

对任何收款人如卖家，为了避免收的钱会被支付人抵销，就通常以明示条文否定这个普通法的权利。所以，经常有看到明示条文说明要支付的一笔钱不准抵销。如果没有这么清楚的写法，不用“抵销”一词而用“扣减”（deduction）一词，结果会是如何曾在一个案例中有过判决，Waller 大法官认为是足够。这是 Marubeni Corp v. Sea Containers Ltd（17/05/1995），有关条文说：“... without any deduction or withholding whatsoever. ”。但这判法与较早的 Connaught Restaurants Ltd v. Indoor Leisure Ltd（1994）1 W. L. R. 501 先例中的同样用词（without any deduction）不一致。可见要改变或否定普通法的地位，明示条文要写得很清楚，甚至最好有针对性地说明是不能抵销。

上诉庭在本先例中，判是上述的第 2. 7 条文并不清楚明确否定普通法的抵销权利。一些主要的原因包括该股票买卖合约的拟定是双方通过律师，而这些律师应该对普通法的抵销权利非常了解，也应该了解否定抵销必须用字清楚明确。另一个原因是双方的谈判中与后来显示在第 2. 7 条文是 Centeon 必须作出支付，约定不论后来 Delta 发生什么，如公司解散、公司业务中止、公司业务失败等，都不影响支付责任。但这些事项只涉及 Delta 公司将来的进展或失败，与 Centeon 所说的反索赔（即买了一家没有价值的公司）无关。所以不像是在订约时双方有意图去排除 Centeon 公司抵销的权利。但笔者看来，本案例虽然有多处提到订约时的背景/语境，但实际的判决其实与这些也没有太大关系，因为仅看第 2. 7 条文就已经可以得出同样的答案。

关于合约条文/文字意图排除普通法下抵销权利的先例亦可见本书第四章之 11. 2 段的 Gilbert – Ash（Northern）Ltd v. Modern Engineering（Bristol）Ltd（1974）

A. C. 689 先例。

12.6　英国案例之六：The "Rio Assu"

The"Rio Assu"（1999）1 Lloyd's Rep. 115 这一先例涉及航运的货损货差索赔，船东（实际上是光船承租人）在船舶被扣押后由互保协会给了担保。担保在文字上只是针对该光船承租人如果最后在英国法院被判是有责任，互保协会就会作出支付。但不久后，该光船承租人不再存在，而公司的责任与资产被另一家公司继承。这就带来一个争议互保协会是否还要负责任。货方显然认为解释该担保，针对光船承租人的名字 LB 应该被解释为"LB or its successors"，因为货方扣船以及互保协会为了放船提供担保都是为了给货方足够的保障，好像船东没有互保协会提供担保就会要把担保的金额存放在法院，否则船舶就会被法院拍卖。所以足够的保障就表示包括光船承租人后来发生清盘、合并、继承等变化，虽然在订约当时大家没有以明示条文针对这个变化。但互保协会反驳说如果太注重考虑这方面，就会带来以后的担保无论拟定的怎么差劲，都没有影响。换言之，双方所争的是"字面"（textual）或是"语境"（contextual）解释。笔者看来，如果是传统根据文件的四个角作出严格解释，担保只写 LB 就会只针对这一家公司。但如果接受外来证据并广泛考虑，就会得出不同结论，正如该案例的高院与上诉庭判决。法院考虑到许多方面，除了提供担保也就是订约时双方都应该有共同意图提供足够保障给货方，也包括如互保协会的规则是如果 LB 被清盘，并不表示该公司不存在，互保协会还是要根据它的担保作出支付。这样，如果不是清盘而是合并或继承，互保协会就可以不必支付会很奇怪。所以高院的 Clark 大法官（被上诉庭支持）是判："Mr. Cooke（互保协会代表大律师）submits that that is not what the wrds say, I have, however, reached the conclusion that if the words are construed in their context having regard to all the circumstances, including the commercial purpose of the agreement, they are properly to be construed as submitted by Mr. Kendrick（货方代表大律师）, even though if considered by themselves（指担保的文字）they more naturally have the meaning given to them by Mr. Cooke."

12.7　英国案例之七：Canterbury Golf International Ltd v. Yoshimoto

Canterbury Golf International Ltd v. Yoshimoto（2002）UKPC 99 这一先例是从新西兰法院一直上诉到英国的枢密院，案情又是涉及一家公司的股票买卖合约。该公司是为了在新西兰拥有一块土地而成立并想将该土地开发成一个高尔夫球场。该公司本来是由 Yoshimoto 先生所拥有，后来因财政问题要出售，就开始与 Canterbury Golf International（简称 CGI）讨价还价，但一直谈不拢。该土地市值 300 万新西兰元以上，Yoshimoto 先生不肯减价。结果 CGI 想出一个办法，就是先在签约时即时支付 200 万新西兰元，这是第一期。但之后的 100 万新西兰元的支付就有一个先决条件，这在该合约的第 6.3 条文说明是 CGI 要在 12 个月内取得开发高尔夫球场的所有批文："It shall be a condition precedent to the Vendor's right to demand payment ... of NZ $ 1 million that [CGI] obtain **all necessary ... consents** to the Development within twelve months of the date of this Agreement."

CGI 说服 Yoshimoto 先生接受,说是在要发展一个高尔夫球场的大前提下,要取得批文才可以完全肯定。所以届时支付这 100 万新西兰元表示 Yoshimoto 先生可以全数得到 300 万新西兰元的价值。Yoshimoto 先生的公司在当时已经向当局提出申请,估计没有问题,在几个月内就应该取得批文,所以就答应了。

但这第 6.3 条文是对 Yoshimoto 先生十分不利的条文,因为申请批文的是 CGI。CGI 大可以做手脚而导致这一先决条件不能满足,从而逃避这笔钱的支付。虽然该合约中有其他条文要求 CGI 合理取得这些批文,但 CGI 如果没有这样做,恐怕 Yoshimoto 先生也不容易取得支持违约的证据。而后来的事实也正是如此,就是欠缺了一份名为"资源批准"(resource consent)的批文,它是在合约的 12 个月后再晚了 5 个月才拿到。这就给了 CGI 理由不支付,说是先决条件根本没有满足。如果 CGI 能够成功赖掉支付第二期的 100 万新西兰元,他就把一块值 300 万以上的土地以 200 万买下来。Yoshimoto 先生同意这么不利的条文是新西兰上诉庭的 Thomas 大法官也觉得不可思议,说:"On the face of it, the arrangement was a recipe of disaster. Making every allowance for the exigencies of the time, unknown facts or factors, and the beneficent perception of hindsight, it is difficult to understand how Mr Yoshimoto or his legal advisers ever came to contemplate accepting the format which was adopted. The $1m was only payable if and when planning approval for the development was obtained. But responsibility for obtaining that planning approval was vested in the purchaser, CGI, and a strict finite time was fixed within which that approval had to be obtained. If the necessary approvals, which were under the control of CGI, were not obtained within that time CGI stood to save $1m, roughly a third of the value of the land if the development was to proceed. The very oddness of the arrangement suggests that there is more to it than meets the eye."

双方的争议是,该先决条件中的"all necessary ... consents"是否包括这一份资源批准批文。在新西兰的上诉庭,Thomas 大法官认为要考虑四个方面,一是合约的其他部分;二是商业的目标;三是语境;四是外来证据。在外来证据方面,Thomas 大法官考虑了双方在谈判中所交换的"草拟合约"(draft contract)。而其中有一份在有关的段节中针对批文曾经加上"现在正在申请的"(presently applied for)的限制,但这一句后来被删掉。Thomas 大法官在其间看不到有证据显示双方曾经改变过主意,所以判是 Yoshimoto 先生胜诉,因为在订约时还没有申请"资源批准"的批文。

接下来是上诉庭根据案例的背景/语境,判 CGI 败诉。但该先例最后被上诉到枢密院,该上诉庭的判决被改变,枢密院认为不应该代订约方"重写"(rewrite)合约。而有关能否考虑双方在谈判时所交换的草拟合约,在新西兰上诉庭的审理中,法院接受了 5 个草拟合约来帮助解释最后的合约。但枢密院说不可以接受这种有关谈判的证据,因为没有帮助。Hoffmann 勋爵这样说:"In a separate section of his judgment,

Thomas J expressed the view that his construction was supported by two provisions in earlier drafts of the contract. He said that the normal rule which excludes evidence of pre – contractual negotiations, authoritatively stated by Lord Wilberforce in *Prenn v. Simmonds* . . . should be relaxed or departed from. Their Lordship do not think that this is a suitable occasion for re – examining the law because they consider that in this case the evidence is, as Lord Wilberforce predicted, unhelpful."

这看来有一点讽刺,因为新西兰的上诉庭推翻第一审的判决并认为要重点考虑背景/语境,其中一个主要原因是解释合约应与英国看齐,因为最终的决定权在枢密院。这一个案例也带来了警惕,就是合约订得差劲也不是说在目前的解释合约时考虑背景/语境的新趋势下就可以乐观地认为会作出救济。另外,也可以看到目前解释文书合约的新趋势下所带来的不肯定的判决。

顺便一提是,新加坡的上诉庭也有同样判法的一个案例,就是双方在谈判时草拟的合约不能用来协助解释最后达成的文书合约:The Management Corporation Strata Title Plan No 1933 v. Liang Huat Aluminium Ltd (2001) BLR 351 先例。

看来,谈判时草拟合约的证据不被接受为订约时背景/语境,主要是在它本质上涉及了订约方单方面的"主观意图"(subjective intention)与是谈判证据的一部分,这方面在本章之第 8 段有详及。而且,它的内容不代表决定性,充其量只是代表讨价还价的其中一个阶段。

12.8 英国案例之八:Static Control Components (Europe) Ltd v. Egan

Static Control Components (Europe) Ltd v. Egan (2004) 2 Lloyd's Rep. 429 的先例,有关一家公司董事所作出的个人担保。该公司名为 TBS,向 Static Control 长期买零件。为此,Static Control 要求 TBS 董事 Egan 先生作出个人担保。第一个担保是在 1998 年 2 月签署,但担保有效期只是 6 个月并在金额上限制为 75,000 英镑。这之后陆续签了总共 3 个个人担保,条文基本上一样。这些担保虽然有效期是 6 个月,但没有索赔的时效。到了 1999 年 9 月,TBS 欠下了 Static Control 共 143,000 英镑的货款,这导致 Static Control 十分关心。在之后的谈判中,达成了一个协议,就是 Egan 先生提供了另一个更高限额的担保(第四个个人担保)以取代以前已经过期的担保,从 75,000 英镑提高至 150,000 英镑,而 Static Control 答应 TBS 继续供应零件,但金额限制在每周 12,000 英镑与付款时间缩短为收到发票后 45 天,另对已经欠下的 143,000 英镑作出分期摊还。

大半年后,时为 2000 年 5 月份,TBS 宣布破产,在那一刻欠 Static Control 的金额共是 111,883.82 英镑。在这大半年期间,事实上 TBS 对 Static Control 的大量零件供应都有作出准时支付。而且,对原来欠下的 143,000 英镑也有作出小部分的摊还。所以,在破产的一刻所欠的 111,883.82 英镑大部分属于原来欠下的余款,而新的欠款(即从第四个个人担保至 TBS 破产这段时间内的供应)只涉及 14,000 英镑。

争议是作出个人担保的 Egan 先生认为第四个担保在文字上只是针对担保以后

的零件供应,所以只要支付 14,000 英镑。该担保的文字是说:“Now I Paul Egan of TBS Cygma plc AGREE that: 1. I shall be responsible to you for the price of all trade goods that **you may supply** to the trader but so that my liability to you shall be in respect of **the whole debt** but shall in no event exceed the sum of £ 150,000. 2. This guarantee is a continuing guarantee and security and my liability under it shall not be affected by your giving time or any other indulgence to the trader.”

Egan 先生依赖的是前三个加黑的字“你会供应”(you may supply)中的“may”一字,明确针对将来的零件供应才需要负上个人责任。但 Static Control 依赖的是后三个加黑的字“所有债务”(the whole debt)。看来,在同一句中的内容相互矛盾,双方在争议中各取所需。

在一审与上诉庭,都是判 Egan 先生败诉。上诉庭说是在考虑了双方订立第四个担保的所有背景/语境后,可以得出以下的结论:(1)独立来看,“你会供应”的一句的确是针对将来的零件供应。(2)但“我对你的责任是所有债务”(my liability to you shall be in respect of the whole debt)就可以有两种解释,一是只针对将来的债务,二是也可包括给担保时已经存在的债务。(3)在订立第四个担保的一天(1999 年 9 月 2 日),Static Control 手中有 Egan 先生已经作出的个人担保,只是在金额上只有 75,000 英镑,不足全数支付当时欠下的债务。但如果第四个担保只针对将来的债务,Static Control 没有理由放弃这些担保,而换这第四个担保。(有关判词是:“As at Sept. 2, 1999 Static Control already had a valid and binding guarantee for the first £ 75,000 of the pre – existing debt and there was no conceivable commercial reason why they should agree to forego the protection of that guarantee. It is true that under the new guarantee the ceiling was increasing to £ 150,000, but that increase would be of no expected benefit to them if the new guarantee related only to future sales, since credit on future sales was not expected to exceed about £ 72,000.”)(4)第四个担保唯一改变的是提高担保金额至 150,000 英镑,这如果只针对将来的零件供应是没有意思。因为将来的供应已经约定了每周供应不超过 12,000 英镑,而且必须在 45 天内支付。显然,如果过了时间不支付,Static Control 就会停止供应与在担保中要求支付。所以放帐的最高金额应该只是约 72,000 英镑,何须 150,000 英镑的担保?但如果 150,000 英镑的担保是为了针对在订约时已经欠下的 143,000 英镑,这就完全是说得通。(有关判词是:“So, to increase the ceiling at the same time as limiting the guarantee to future sales makes no commercial sense. But there is obvious commercial sense in increasing the ceiling if the exiting debt is already around £ 143,000 and future sales would continue.”)

(5)所以对一个合理与客观的人士,在知道了所有订约时的背景,会认为担保是为了已经欠下与将来会欠下的债务。

笔者觉得这个案件挺有趣,除了类似情况经常发生,也显示了背景/语境的威力。因为仅根据第四个担保的文字上作解释,看来是 Egan 先生胜诉的机会大得多(这可看上述结论一与二),但一考虑订约时的背景/语境,就有了相反的结论。

12.9 英国案例之九:GE Frankona Reinsurance Ltd v. CMM Trust No 1400

GE Frankona Reinsurance Ltd v. CMM Trust No 1400 (2006) EWHC 429 这一个先例是很有趣的,因为涉及了合约中的条文/文字清楚无误,但法院还是看背景/语境。它所涉及的是一艘名为"The Newfoundland Explorer" 的游艇,其价值高达 300 万美元并较长期的停泊在美国一个游艇会的泊位。船东为该船投保,是以 Institute Time Clauses Hulls Port Risks 的标准保单条文为准,保单中还有一个保证为"Warranted vessel fully crewed at all times."(保证游艇在所有时间都有全套船员)。

案情是该游艇上发生了严重火灾,火灾由发电机过热而引起,但当时没有人在游艇上。船东为该游艇雇佣了一名船长,但船长回家了,他的住所离开游艇的泊位约 15 公里或 30 分钟的路程。

保险公司拒赔,因为船东破坏保证。而 1906 年英国《海上保险法》对保证的定义十分严厉,比一般合约的条件条文有过之而无不及。这样,双方的争议就是在对这一保证的解释,因为船东认为他没有违反这个保证。他的解释是"全套船员"(fully crewed)只针对"雇佣"(employment),但不针对他们所处的"位置"(location)。而在该先例,船东的确有雇佣船长,只不过他在发生意外时没有在游艇上。

针对这表面看来清楚无误的保证(Gross 大法官也认为只有一个解释),双方也对其解释有很多争议:

1. 保单是保一段长时间,在这个期间,该游艇会做很多不同的事情,如开航走一个远洋航次,或只是走一个沿岸的航次,或游艇没有动力挂靠在泊位,又或游艇开动发电机挂靠在泊位等。显然在上述不同的情况下需要的船员数量都不一样,所以应该怎样解释保证中要求的"全套船员"(fully crewed)的数量?

2. 如果保证中的"所有时间"(at all times)是指 24 小时,怎样解释一些无可避免的船员需要离开游艇的情况,如有紧急事故如炸弹警报而需要船员撤离?又或是该船员因疫病而被送医院?或在较正常的情况下他需要到岸上调整缆绳、给船旁上油漆或到附近购买粮食及游艇的补给?是否这样的情况一发生就是违反保证,可让保险公司拒赔?

Gross 大法官判是:

(A)针对保证中需要"全套船员",他认为游艇在挂靠泊位时,也最少有一个船员必须在游艇上。他这样说:"In terms of crew numbers, whether a vessel is 'fully crewed' or not must depend on what she is doing; manifestly, a vessel undertaking an ocean voyage will have different crewing requirement to a vessel laid up alongside a berth. However, as already discussed (and exceptional instances apart), a vessel will not be crewed, let alone 'fully crewed' if no crew members are on board. Accordingly, 'fully crewed' must mean at least one crew member on board the vessel, whatever she is doing. . . ."

(B)针对保证中的“所有时间”,一般与正常的解释就是 24 小时,因为“所有”这一词清楚无误。但这一般性的解释也必须受到背景与商业合理性的约束,正如 Diplock 勋爵在 The “Antaios” (1984) 2 Lloyd’s Rep 235 先例所说:“... if detailed semantic and syntactical analysis of words in a commercial contract is going to lead to a conclusion that flouts business common sense, it must be made to yield to business common sense.”所以这一方面的保证需要受到限制,如上述所讲的紧急情况与唯一看守游艇的船长需要上岸办事。Gross 大法官这样说:“However, as foreshadowed, it seems to me that considerations of commercial commonsense also point to the need for some qualification of the literal meaning of the wording ‘at all times’. So: (i) Emergencies can arise, requiring the evacuation of the vessel or even the area. Take for instance, a bomb scare or similar alert. It is inconceivable that the parties are to be understood as intending that the absence of crew from the vessel for the duration of such an emergency could place the defendant in breach of warranty. (ii) It may be necessary for certain crewing duties to be performed ashore or otherwise than on board the vessel. For instance, adjusting moorings, working on a fouled propeller, or painting the outside of the hull. Given the claimant’s acceptance that a one – man crew would be sufficient while the vessel was laid up alongside a berth, it could not sensibly be said that the absence of any crew member on board the vessel while such duties were performed would result in a breach of warranty. (iii) On the premise that a one – man crew suffices, the context tells against certain other situations resulting in a breach of warranty. By way of example, consider the purchase of food or other supplies for the vessel. Necessarily, the single crew member will be absent while undertaking such tasks. I am not inclined to think that the parties could realistically have intended that in these circumstances there would have been a breach of warranty... I am unable to accept that such temporary departures *must* be within the vicinity of the vessel; could it, for example, make all the difference to insurance cover that the chandlery was in one part of the marina or another? To my mind, it is the purpose of the departure, rather than the distanced travelled from the vessel, which is critical.”换言之,“所有时间”这清楚无误的一词解释就被上述所讲的情况约束与限制了。

(C)至于船东的争议指保证只要求船员的雇佣而不理会其所在的位置,Gross 大法官完全不能接受。考虑到这一案件的背景是为一艘非常昂贵的游艇投保,保险公司要求这一保证以期望游艇上不断有人看管完全可以理解。他也推理说该游艇在保期内可能会开航,或者开航时船东只要雇佣了船员但他们不需要在游艇上而只留在家里,可以让她无人驾驶在海上漂流,这不可能是保险人的意图。至于说游艇靠泊时与游艇开航时有不同对待,这是保单中短短的一句保证完全看不出来的内容。这内容也不是必须,所以不可能是默示。Gross 大法官说:“To confine the warranty to matters of employment is, with respect, unreal. A warranty solely focused on employment does not begin to meet the commercial purpose underlying this contractual provision. ... If once however it is accepted that the warranty is not confined to questions of employment, then it seems inevitable that its true focus must relate to the *location* of the crew; save for the qualification already discussed, that location must be on board the vessel at all times. For completeness, this construction makes good practical sense, whether the vessel is laid up alongside a berth (the situation with which the contract is primarily concerned) or undertaking the other limited activities additionally contemplated by the contract; for example, it is difficult to envisage how the vessel could be 'fully crewed at all times' when at sea, if the crew were anywhere other than on board the vessel."

总结上述先例,Gross 大法官虽然认为保单的保证清楚无误,而且曾经有过类似的 Brownsville Holdings Ltd v. Adamjee Insurance Co Ltd (2000) 2 All ER (Comm) 803 先例,但还是针对与考虑案件的本质与背景/语境才对保单条文/文字作出解释。这包括像游艇价值的高昂,游艇挂靠在泊位的一些正常活动等。其中还提到了在将来全面审理时会需要专家证人。但在考虑后,Gross 大法官认为本质与背景/语境的考虑只加强了他对保证条文/文字所表达的一般性解释的信心。

§13 其他普通法国家法院的先例与看法

可以说,在 60 年前,英国的法律也就是所有普通法国家的法律。毕竟普通法国家如澳大利亚、加拿大、新西兰、新加坡、马来西亚与香港地区的最后上诉都是英国的"枢密院"(Privy Council)。但现在已经不是这种情况,所以普通法的国家法院虽然还是会尽最大的努力统一,但恐怕还是难免有分歧之处。这也带来了呼吁就是法院,特别是更高的法院作出判决时,应该尽量考虑与采纳其他普通法国家法院的先例与看法。这可节录 Collins 勋爵在 Jones v Kaney (2011) UKSC 13 先例所说:"**It is highly desirable that at this appellate level, in cases where issues of legal policy are concerned, the Court should be informed about the position in other common law countries.** This Court is often helped by being referred to authorities from other common law systems, including the United States. It is only in the United States that there has been extensive discussion in the case law of the policy implications of removal of immunity for actions by disappointed clients against their experts. On this appeal the appellant did not rely on the United States material, although it is helpful to his case. The respondent's counsel drew attention to some of the United States cases on the basis of research which (it was said) was 'slightly hampered by the renovation of the Middle Temple's American room.' But there is an outstanding collection of United States material in the Institute of Advanced Legal Studies in London University, and (provided the barristers or solicitors concerned are prepared to make the expenditure) all of the material is readily available on line. Lord Wilberforce said in Buttes Gas & Oil Co v Hammer (Nos 2 &3) [1982] AC 888, 936 – 937: 'When the judicial approach to an identical problem between the same parties has been spelt out with such articulation in a country, one not only so closely akin to ours in legal approach, the fabric of whose legal doctrine in this area is so closely interwoven with ours, but that to which all the parties before us belong, spelt out moreover in convincing language and reasoning, **we should be unwise not to take the benefit of it.' This is not, of course, as that case was, litigation between the same parties in the two countries, but the principle is the same.**"(加黑部分是笔者的强调)

这也带来了今天不论是法院或是仲裁庭,即使有关合约是约定适用英国法,也会遇到双方当事人的代表律师提供其他普通法国家的判决。

在本书第一章与本章所针对的合约解释近年来的新趋势,特别是在著名的 Investors Compensation Scheme Ltd v West Bromwich Building Society (1998) 1 W. L. R. 896 先例所带来的"from text to context"解释文件/合约,也就无可避免冲击了其他普通法的国家。M P Furmston 教授在 2013 年 5 月之"Future Development of Contract Law and the Relationship between the Contract Laws of the Commonwealth"会议中发表的《A Study of Contract Law in the Major Commonwealth Jurisdictions》一文有提到几个普通法国家对英国法律在解释合约的趋势是否有跟从。他首先提到了新加坡基本上是同一趋势,这是在 Zurich Insurance (Singapore) Pte Ltd v B – Gold Interior Design & Construction Pte Ltd (2008) 3 SLR 1029 先例。另是在新西兰的 Vector Gas Ltd v Bay of Plenty Energy Ltd (2010) NZSC 5 先例,最高院的 5 个法官看来有一些不同说法,但多数意见是判对外来证据/口头证据全面开放,不要求显示合约条文/文字有"含糊"(ambiguity),这也是本章之 2. 3. 4 段所指的对文字有怀疑或解释困难的情况。换言之新西兰也是接受英国法律在解释合约的趋势。

但在澳大利亚,有点不明确。在"最高院"(High Court)的 Royal Botanic Gardens and Domain Trust v South Sydney City Council (2002) 240 CLR 45 先例,看来还是要求有关文件/合约有含糊之处才会接受外来证据/口头证据。

以下对一些上述提到或没有提到的先例做进一步的介绍。

13.1 澳大利亚案例之一:Pacific Carriers Ltd v. BNP Paribas

第一个澳大利亚先例是 Pacific Carriers Ltd v BNP Paribas (2004) 218 CLR 451, 案情是船长在印度卸港"无单放货"(delivery of cargo without bill of lading)。有关的货物是豆荚,卖方是澳大利亚公司,买方是印度公司。承运人是新加坡的 Pacific Carriers。在这次无单放货的事件中,Pacific Carriers 预先取得了两份保障,是由澳大利亚卖方签发的"保函"(letter of indemnity),再由 BNP Paribas 的法国银行加签。事后无单放货导致 Pacific Carriers 作为船东真正的提单持有人以侵占货物起诉并作出赔偿,之后 Pacific Carrier 向法国银行要求补偿,法国银行与签字的女职员声称只是为了"公证"(authenticate)或"证明"(witness)澳大利亚卖方的签字。但在澳大利亚最高院,判是法国银行加签是作为"补偿人"(indemnifier)。最高院的判决是根据订约时的周边环境与谈判中的事实背景,如 Pacific Carriers 曾经拒绝印度买方所提供的保函,原因是没有可信赖的银行加签承诺补偿。此外在澳大利亚卖方与 Pacific Carriers 的谈判中,后者也明确了其目的是取得一家可被接受银行作为补偿人。后者的证据看来也可被视为 Pacific Carriers 的主观订约意图,但这已经告知了对方,而且曾经拒绝印度买方所提供的保函本身是事实背景。

13.2 澳大利亚案例之二:Royal Botanic Gardens and Domain Trust v. South Sydney City Council

第二个澳大利亚先例是 Royal Botanic Gardens and Domain Trust v. South Sydney City Council (2002) 240 CLR 45。案情有关一个在悉尼 Domain Parkland 的土地的长期租赁合约,而租这块土地的主要目的是建造一个公众停车场,订约双方也是公共机构,而不是想谋利的商业机构。有关的争议涉及租赁合约的租金调整条文,说:"... in making any such determination, the Trustees **may** have regard to additional costs and expenses which they may incur in regard to the surface of the Domain above or in the vicinity of the parking station and the footway and which arise out of the construction operation and maintenance of the parking station by the Lessee."(调整租金时,出租人可以增加由于承租人建造、营运与保养停车场而带来需要配合平整附近的人行道等所花费的使费。)

而双方的争议是出租人能否在调整租金时把其他的因素也考虑在内。显然仅看有关的条文,他所用的文字是"may",也没有其他的说明是出租人只能考虑这一有关使费的因素,所以没有理由局限。这也是最高院中持少数意见的 Kirby 大法官的看法,说:"The language of para (iv) is strongly against the proposition advanced by the council(承租人). That paragraph is expressed in terms of what the trustees 'may have regard to'... Had it been proposed to confine the trustees(出租人)to having regard only to the costs and expenses mentioned in para (iv) ... this would have been expressly stated. It was not."

也就是说如果合约条文/文字只是说"may",就没理由加以局限并把"可以"一字改写为"只能"。

但多数意见认为"may"一字"含糊"(ambiguous),需要根据订约时的背景/语境协助解释,并认定了两个事实背景。一是双方在谈判时很想保护出租人不会因为这一租赁,有任何经济上的不利。而双方唯一在谈判中针对会对出租人造成经济不利的就是条文中所针对的额外费用,所以有争议的条文/文字不能被解释为出租人能在调整租金时把其他特别是商业的因素一并考虑。所以多数判决这样说:"Clause 4

(b) read as a whole contained a statement of the totality of the matters to be taken into account in fixing the successive rent determinations."

13.3 澳大利亚案例之三:Secured Income Real Estate (Australia) Ltd. v. St. Martins Investments Pty. Ltd

第三个澳大利亚先例是 Secured Income Real Estate (Australia) Ltd. v. St. Martins Investments Pty. Ltd (1979) 144 CLR 596,案情涉及商业办公大厦的买卖。买卖合约规定如果卖方无法租出一定数量的单位,就要减低出售价格。结果卖方没有在期限前租出规定数量的单位,导致出售价格会大幅度下调。卖方于是提出自己"回租"(lease back)一些单位以达到售价不会有任何扣减的目的。但显然买方不同意卖方的提议,理由是卖方只是短期回租这些单位以达到不扣减售价的目的,这意味着买方失了拥有足够数量的长期租客的利益。这导致双方对合约中有关出租与售价调整条文解释的争议,该条文 1(c)这样说:"In the event that ... the Vendor shall not be in a position to provide to the Purchaser evidence to the reasonable satisfaction of the Purchaser that the aggregate rental payable per annum under leases in respect of the subject premises does not amount to $227,900.00 then in such case the balance purchase moneys payable in Clause 1 (a) (iii) hereof shall be reduced..."(加黑部分是有争议的一词,中文可解释为"租约")

卖方的争议显然是有关条文中的租约一词没有任何局限,也没有规定租期的长短,所以没理由不包括卖方短期回租的租约。但买方坚持这租约一词只局限在"商业租约"(commercial lease)并提供双方在谈判时的证据,显示了曾经告知卖方有关这一要求以及他购买这一商业办公大厦的目的是长期投资。

但澳大利亚最高院判是不接受买卖合约中的"租约"(lease)一词只局限为出租给第三人或一个真正的"商业租约"。的确也没有理由排除如果卖方真正是向买方回租部分单位继续营运。但最后买方还是胜诉倒是因为该买卖合约另有一条条文 1 (d),可节录如下:"After the date of execution of this Contract all leases of the subject premises shall be first approved by the Purchaser. Such approval shall not be capriciously or arbitrarily withheld..."

澳大利亚最高院判是买方可以拒绝批准卖方只为了避免售价的下调的短暂回租,而这样做并不是"任性"(capriciously)与"武断"(arbitrarily)。

13.4 澳大利亚案例之四:Franklins Pty Ltd v. Metcash Trading Ltd

最后介绍南威尔士上诉庭的 Franklins Pty Ltd v. Metcash Trading Ltd (2009) 76 NSWLR 603 先例。案情涉及供应商与超级市场的商品买卖,其中有争议的合约条文是针对批发价格,说:"Wholesale Price of a Product means Metcash's 'Wholesale 5' price for that Product, being the Supplier's Wholesale list price for that Product... less **all** allowances and **discounts** (**such as** trade discounts, distributor allowances, warehouse allowances, bulk buy allowances and cash discounts) provided to Metcash by that Supplier."（加黑部分是起争议的文字，字义上是指所有折扣都要从批发价格中扣除。）

双方的争议是在有关的条文下，供应商是否需要在批发价格中扣除来货的所有折扣。这种折扣包括两种，一种是"公布了或大家都知道的折扣"（published discounts），另一种是个别供应商所取得的"机密折扣"（confidential discounts）。显然，后者的折扣不是每一位供应商都可以取得，也不会大家都知道。如果按照有关的合约条文看，所用的文字是"所有折扣"（all discounts），另括号内"举例"（such as）了一些折扣，说明还有其他不知名的折扣。这样看来，应该是机密折扣也应在批发价格中扣除。但上诉庭在解释有关的条文中很受双方谈判的证据，特别是双方订约时所知道的情况（显然超级市场不知道机密折扣）影响，说："matters of the understanding, belief or intention of the relevant executives of Franklins or Metcash."

对笔者来说，这一判决也不无争议之处，特别在英国的 Rainy Sky SA and others v Kookmin Bank（2012）1 Lloyd's Rep 34 先例后，也就是合约有明确规定的，就不应该受到谈判证据的影响重写合约条文/文字，除非上诉庭在看了这些证据后觉得合约规定并不明确。这在本书第一章之 8.6 段有介绍。

13.5　新加坡案例：Zurich Insurance（Singapore）Pte Ltd v. B – Gold Interior Design & Construction Pte Ltd

在 Zurich Insurance（Singapore）Pte Ltd v. B – Gold Interior Design & Construction Pte Ltd（2008）3 SLR 1029 先例，新加坡上诉庭详细分析了《Evidence Act》立法中针对外来证据/口头证据可否被接受的部分，并明确该立法可以支持英国与其他普通法国家在解释合约接受外来证据/口头证据的新趋势。

该案例的案情是一个工程的承建商 B – Gold 投保施工的责任险，这在较早的工程合约中雇主 MediaCorp 有明确要求 B – Gold 投保的范围。事后发生火灾，原因是 B – Gold 的一个分承建商 Regius 的工人在施工时抽烟并留下烟头。这导致 MediaCorp 要求 B – Gold 赔偿财产损失，而 B – Gold 则根据保单向保险公司 Zurich 要求补偿。但 Zurich 拒绝并认为有关损失不在其保单承保范围内。这就涉及 B – Gold 抖出投保也就是订约时的事实背景证据，如向保险经纪人提供一份工程合约并要求保险公司提供 B – Gold 所需要的保险范围。但这些证据被法院判是不能清楚或明显显示了订约时的事实背景或"语境"（context）。

13.6　香港案例：Jumbo King Ltd v. Faithful Properties Ltd & Ors

香港也有一个重要的终审法院 Jumbo King Ltd v. Faithful Properties Ltd & Ors（1999）2HKCFAR 279 先例经常被提到与引用，案情涉及一幢在香港尖沙咀的多层式大厦的某些商业单位的买卖合约。这些单位包括 2 个天台与 4 个杂用房。但双方有了争议，买方拒绝成交。争议之一尽管原来的发展商已经保留对天台与杂用房的独有占用权，但该大厦公契没有明示，所以买方认为这些地方变为是共用部分，发展商不能有效把这一个独有占用权转让给卖方。在第一审，高院判买方胜诉并有权终止该买卖合约。但了上诉庭被推翻，而最后在终审法院也是卖方胜诉。法院在考虑订立该大厦公契的事情与法律背景,以及它希望达致的实际目的解释该大厦公契的整体内容,认为是有意而且在事实上给予发展商该天台与杂用房的独有占用权。要争辩说那些地方由开始就没有被分配的公用地方是不合实际的。终审法院的 Hoffmann 勋爵对文件/合约解释的指引可总结如下:"(a) Where a contract is embodied in a document, the whole of the document must be considered. (b) The object of the exercise of construction is to ascertain the meaning which that document would convey to a reasonable person having all background which would reasonably have been available to the parties in the situation they were at the time of contract, and which would have affected the way in which the language of the document would have been understood by a reasonable man, excluding the parties' actual negotiations. (c) Words in a contractual document should be given their natural and ordinary meaning so as to reflect the common sense proposition that people producing such document do not usually make linguistic mistakes. Nonetheless, the meaning which a document would convey to a reasonable person is not the same thing as the meaning of its words. The meaning of a document is what the parties using those words against the relevant background would reasonably have been understood to mean. (d) The starting point must be the words and phrases which the parties have chosen to use. It is not a permissible method of construction to propound a general or generally accepted principle for sharing commercial risks between the parties or seeking in the abstract to determine a reasonable allocation of risk between them and then to seek to force the provisions of the charter into the straitjacket of that principle or into that concept of reasonableness. (e) As part of the interpretative process, regard should be had to the consequences of rival constructions, bearing in mind that it is generally presumed that reasonable businessmen intend to produce reasonable results rather than bizarre or unreasonable results. Semantics should not generally triumph over commercial common sense. (f) If there is true ambiguity (not a forced or contrived ambiguity) such ambiguity is normally resolved against the party seeking to enhance his protection if at least he was principally the draftsman of the ambiguous clause."

§14 中国船厂在伦敦仲裁的中间裁决

2008 年金融海啸后,航运市场暴跌而导致外国船东纷纷从较早时以高价订购船舶的造船合约中脱身,并在随后的 5、6 年为伦敦仲裁带来 2000 个以上的造船合约争议,每个争议都涉及数以百万或上千万美元以上的金额,中国船厂是全军覆没。这种案件的案情类别主要是中国船厂完工/交船日期过了造船合约的死线,也就是"死亡日期"(drop – dead date)或"销约期"(cancelling date)。造成延误的原因可能是订约时中国船厂对交船日期过分乐观或者是对工程的管理不好等，但往往也涉及外国船东的不合作与造成妨碍所带来的延误。这方面的问题在本书其他章节有提到，如有关"同类规则"的第四章，有关有关"对于时间的规定"的第十章，有关"延误"与"妨碍原则"的第十一章与有关"专家决定条文"的第十四章，在此不再重复。而这一小段所针对的是大约在2013年开始，有外国船东以另一种手段加快对付中国船厂的抗辩，以避免可能的漫长的开庭处理，中国船厂指称外国船东的不合作与造成障碍并带来延误。这一种手段就是暂时不理会双方争议的证据（因为证据的处理才会带来漫长的开庭），而是只尽快以一个"中间裁决书"（partial award）对一些"预先争议"（preliminary issue）作出宣告与决定。预先争议也包括如果外国船东胜诉，船厂（与作出"还款担保"[refund guarantee]的银行）就需要马上退还预付了的船价并加上合约约定的利息。这样，外国船东如果胜诉，就可以避免在漫长的开庭完结后并且由仲裁庭作出"最后裁决书"（final award）才能要求退还预付船价。

这些预先争议是先假设船东的确有"过错"（default），并造成船舶建造的延误。但由于船厂没有向船东作出通知（这是双方所同意的事实，也明显不过），所以即使是船东过错也不能延长交船日期或死亡日期。所以，外国船东是合法终止了造船合约并且船厂必须马上退还预付船价并加上约定利息。而针对这些预先争议，全部涉及对有关造船合约（基本上是大同小异）中的条文作出解释。换言之，这不涉及争议的事实证据，只是看有关合约的四个角内的内容。也没有任何一方提出本章所讲的要根据合约的背景/语境与本质进行解释，所以也没有涉及任何谈判的证据。

笔者涉及三个伦敦仲裁，据悉在伦敦至少有二三十个同类仲裁案件，并且中国船厂全部败诉。在涉及的三个仲裁，笔者对有关造船合约的解释与其他伦敦仲裁员不一致，持的是少数意见。

在进一步介绍有关案件前，可先节录有关造船合约的条文如下：

"ARTICLE VIII - DELAYS & EXTENTION OF TIME FOR DELIVERY（延误与交船日期延长）

1. CAUSE OF DELAY（延误原因）

If, at any time before actual delivery, either the construction of the VESSEL, or any performance required hereunder as a prerequisite of delivery, of the VESSEL, is delayed due to war, blockade, revolution, insurrection, civil commotions, riots, sabotage, lockouts, local temperature higher than 35 degree centigrade, Acts of God or the public enemy, terrorism, plague or other epidemics, quarantines, prolonged failure or restriction of electric current from an outside source, freight embargoes earthquakes, tidal waves, typhoons, hurricanes, storms or other causes beyond the control of the BUILDER or of its sub-contractors, as the case may be, the BUILDER shall not be liable for such delay and the time for delivery of the VESSEL under this Contract shall be extended without any reduction in the CONTRACT PRICE for a period of time which shall net exceed the total accumulated time of all such delays, subject nevertheless to the BUYER's right of cancellation under Paragraph 3 of this Article and subject however to all relevant 'provisions of this Contract which authorize and permit extension of the time of delivery of the VESSEL. [这里针对的事项都是本书第十一章针对工程合约所提到的第一类延误,也就是针对一些外来(如高温、台风等)或第三人(战争、动乱、恐怖行为等)所造成的延误。这种延误通常也被视为所谓"不可抗力"事项。实际上中国船厂涉及的造船合约,基本上都是按照日本造船格式(The Shipbuilders' Association of Japan, 简称 SAJ Form)的同一条文,除了针对的事项有一些轻微变动外,就是条文的抬头在 SAJ Form 有明确说明不可抗力:"DELAYS & EXTENTION OF TIME FOR DELIVERY (force majeure)"。这在多数的裁决书也变为对中国船厂不利的一点,稍后会针对。]

2. NOTICE OF DELAY

Within seven (7) days from the date of commencement of delay on account of which the BUILDER claims that it is entitled under this Contract to an extension of the time for delivery of the VESSEL, the BUILDER shall advise the BUYER by telefax or email confirmed in writing, of the date such delay commenced, and the reasons therefore.

Likewise within seven (7) days after such delay ends, the BUILDER shall advise the BUYER in writing or by telefax or email confirmed in writing, of the date such delay ended, and also shall specify the maximum period of the time by which the date for delivery of the VESSEL is extended by reason of such delay. Failure by the BUYER to acknowledge the BUILDER's notification of any claim for extension of the DELIVERY DATE within thirty (30) days after receipt by the BUYER of such notification, shall be deemed to be a waiver by the BUYER of its right to object to such extension.

In the event that the BUILDER shall not comply with the notices required to be sent under this clause, they shall not be entitled to any relief claimed. (这条文是针对船厂需要作出延误通知,并在最后一句说明船厂没有作出通知就不能有任何救济,这主要是延长交船日期的救济。)

3. RIGHT TO CANCEL FOR EXCESSIVE DELAY

If the total accumulated time of all delays on account of the causes specified in Paragraph 1 of the Article aggregate to two hundred an twenty five (225) days or more, ... in any circumstances, excluding delays due to arbitration as provided for in Article XIII hereof or due to default in performance by the BUYER, ... hereof, permit extension or postponement of the time for delivery of the VESSEL, then in such event, the BUYER may in accordance with the provisions set out herein cancel this Contract... [这条文是说如果上一条文所针对的不可抗力事项并允许延长交船日期造成了总共 225 天的延

误(从约定的交船日期起算),排除了因为根据第13条文有关仲裁带来的延误与买方的过错……买方有权终止合约。]

ARTICLE X CANCELLATION, REJECTION AND RESCISSION BY THE BUYER

……

3. Upon such refund by the BUILDER to the BUYER, all obligations, duties and liabilities of each of the parties hereto to the other under this Contract shall be forthwith completely discharged.(如果船厂作出了预付船价的还款给买方/船东,本合约的所有承诺与责任全部终结。)

ARTICLE XI - BUYER'S DEFAULT(买方过错)

1. DEFINITION OF DEFAULT(过错的定义)

The BUYER shall be deemed in default of this obligation under the Contract if any of the following events occurs:(如果发生了下列的情况,买方被视为是有过错)

(a) The BUYER fails to pay any instalment of the CONTRACT PRICE to the BUILDER when any such instalment becomes due and payable under the provisions of Article II hereof provided the BUYER shall have received the BUILDER'S demand for payment in accordance with Article II hereof and futher provided that a refund guarantee has been issued executed and received by the BUYER in respect of those instalments before delivery; or (买方没有按照合约作出预付船价)

(b) The BUYER fails to deliver to the BUILDER irrevocable and unconditional Letter of Guarantee to be issued by [(船东一家巴拿马公司)背后的母公司] within the time specified in accordance with Paragraph 6 of Article II hereof;(买方没有按照约定提供给船厂其母公司的保函。有这一需要是因为大部分的买方都是方便旗国家的单船公司,而在没有接收有关的船舶前,是一家典型的皮包公司。)

(c) The BUYER fails to take delivery of the Vessel, when the VESSEL is duly tendered for delivery by the BUILDER in accordance with the Contract and under the provisions of Article VII hereof.(买方拒绝接收按照合约准时可以交船的船舶)

2. NOTICE OF DEFAULT

If the BUYER is in default of payment or in performance of its obligation as provided hereinabove, the BUILDER shall notify the BUYER to that effect by telefax or email after the date of occurrence of the default as per Paragraph I of this Article and the BUYER shall forthwith acknowledge by telefax or email to the BUILDER that such notification has been received. In case the BUYER does not give the aforesaid telefax or email acknowledgement to the BUILDER within three (3) calendar days it shall be deemed that such notification has been duly received by the BUYER..."(针对上述的买方过错,船厂要求作出通知)

简单而言,外国船东主要的争议是它的过错(假设存在),如不合作与造成妨碍,这应该属于 Article VIII. 1 内的事项,也就是包括在兜底的"or other causes beyond the control of the BUILDER or of its sub - contractors"。因为该造船合约会导致交船日期延误不外就是两类,一类是所谓的"允许延误"(permissible delay),也就是 Article VIII. 1 所针对的延误事项。在这种延误事项下,只要船厂根据 Article VIII. 2 作出了通知并证明或同意了有关事项造成的延误,就可以延长交船日期,也不存在每天因为延误而需要支付的议定赔偿。但另一类是所谓的"不允许延误"(inpermissible delay),这一类延误事项千变万化,也不需要在造船合约中规定。这是船厂自己需要承担的延误。这种延误不需要向船东作出通知,也不存在可以延长交船日期,而每天的延误需要向船东支付议定赔偿。

但根据本书第十一章提到工程合约的延误还有第三类,也就是买方/船东的过错,通常不会在工程合约中规定。根据英国"一般法律"(general law),在这种情况下约定的延误交船(或完工)日期就变为"无限期"(at large),这也是所谓的"妨碍原则"(prevention principle)。但也有先例说如果相关的工程或造船合约对这种延误有明示条文针对,这一默示的妨碍原则也就不适用:Multiplex v Honeywell (2007) EWHC 447 (TCC); Adyard Abu Dhabi v SD Marine Services (2011) EWHC 848 (Comm)等先例。这也表示如果解释这个造船合约并得出的结论是船东的过错包括在 Article VIII. 1 内,妨碍原则也就不适用。

但根据 Article VIII. 2,针对 Article VIII. 1 的延误事项必须作出通知,否则船厂根本不能获得任何救济,这包括延长交船日期(与相应的死亡日期)的救济。

笔者所知道的伦敦仲裁员在解释有关造船合约都得出一个结论,就是船东过错包括在 Article VIII. 1 内,所以船厂没有作出通知,也就是什么救济都不会有。至于笔者涉及的三个仲裁裁决,由于是不同仲裁员,虽然结论一致,但原因都不同。笔者只部分节录其中一个裁决中的多数意见,如下:

"Our view that the parties intended that '*delays due to default in performance by the BUYER*' fall within the expression '*other causes beyond the control of the BUILDER or its sub - contractors*' and is therefore a permissible delay within Article VIII. 1 as well as an excluded delay under Article VIII. 3 is supported by a number of other factors: - (多数意见也就是裁决结果认为船东过错属于 Article VIII. 1 的事项并属于允许延误。)

(a) If '*delays... due to default in performance by the BUYER*' do not fall within Article VIII. 1 with the result that the Builders would not be entitled to an extension of the Delivery date, this would mean that if the Buyers' default resulted in a delay of more than 30 days, after the contractual Delivery date, the price would be reduced by US $7,000 per day under Article III. 1(b). It seems to us that an intention that a reduction in the Vessel's price should result from a default by the Buyers, is such an unlikely result that the parties cannot have intended it. We therefore consider that the parties must have intended that a default by the Buyers should be included in the delays to which Article VIII. 1 applies so that in the event of '*delays. . . due to default in performance by the BUYER*', the Delivery date could be extended by the Builders under Article VIII. 1 and a reduction in the Contract price as a result of the Buyers' default avoided. (如果船东过错不属于允许延误,船厂就无法获得交船日期的延长。而如果船东错误带来了 30 天的延误,就根据 Article III. 1(b)在船价中每天扣减 7,000 美元的议定赔偿。这并不合理,也不可能是双方订约时的共同意图。多数仲裁员认为双方在订约时一定有一个共同意图,在船东过错造成延误时可包括在 Article VIII. 1 并可以让船厂延长交船日期与避免支付议定赔偿。)

(b) The Builders are entitled to an extension of the Delivery date in the event of the Buyers' default under other articles than Article VIII. 1. For example, under Article V. 4 the Delivery date may be extended '*Should the BUYER fail to deliver to the BUILDER such items within the time specified, ... provided such delay in delivery of the BUYER's supplied items shall affect the delivery of the VESSEL*'. It may also be extended in the event of a Buyers' default as defined in Article XI. 1 by virtue of Article XI. 4(a). In the event of such a default by the Buyers a notice must be given under Article VIII. 2 because it provides that such a notice should be given in the event of '*any delay*'. It is difficult to see why the parties should intend that a builder should be entitled to an extension of the Delivery date (provided it gives the appropriate notice) in respect of some types of default by a buyer but not others. We conclude therefore that this was not the intention of the parties and they intended all types of default by the Buyers not specifically covered by other articles which permit an extension of the Delivery date, to fall within Article VIII. 1. (需要船厂在船东延误时作出通知也在造船合约其他条文有所针对,如 Article V. 4 规定船东供应的物料如果交货发生延误,船厂要作出通知。多数仲裁员不能理解为什么针对船东的部分延误需要作出通知,但其他造成的延误就不必通知。显然,双方在订约时应该有共同的订约意图把所有不同类别的船东过错造成的延误都包括在 Article VIII. 1。)

Accordingly, unless we are driven by authority to reach the opposite conclusion, we would conclude as a matter of construction that the parties intended or if they had addressed the question would have intended that a delay '*due to default in performance by the BUYER*' should fall within Article VIII. 1 because it is a cause '*beyond the control of the BUILDER or its sub – contractors*' which would entitle the Builders to an extension of the Delivery date under Article VIII. 1 as well as an extension of the Cancelling date under Article VIII. 3. "(除非有先例作出相反的解释,这就是多数仲裁员的裁决,也就是船东胜诉。)

代表中国船厂的大律师也有提出一些非常有关的先例,特别是针对类似 Article

VIII. 1 的解释。其中最重要的就是 The "Kriti Rex" (1996) 2 Lloyd's Rep 171 先例,Moore - Bick 大法官是这样说:"In general I think it fair to approach such clauses with the presumption that the expression force majeure is likely to be restricted to supervening events which arise without the fault of either party and for which neither of them has undertaken responsibility."(不可抗力只应该局限在一些外来的事项,不涉及任何合约方的过错与没有一方需要承担合约规定的责任。)

但多数仲裁员与上述先例只作出了简短与没有太大说服力(对笔者而言)的区分,主要是指本造船合约与 SAJ Form 不一致,后者是加上了"不可抗力"字样。裁决书这样说:"We would not dissent from that view but we note that the expression *force majeure* is not used in Article VIII. 1. more importantly, for the reasons which we have given, in our view the other provisions in the Shipbuilding Contracts rebuts any such presumption."

笔者觉得没有说服力的地方就是英国法律在解释合约时,重视的是内容而不是一个简短的抬头。没有加上"不可抗力条文"的抬头就导致一条同样内容的条文变为不是这种条文,这有一点说不通。[9] 至于该造船合约其他的条文,笔者也看不出有任何地方可以有足够分量与 The "Kriti Rex"先例区分。加上,在本书第十三章之 1.7 - 1.11 段介绍的解释不可抗力条文的一般规则,都与笔者认为 Article VIII. 1 是没有包括船东的错误相符合。

至于多数仲裁员所关心船厂的一点,也就是如果船东过错不包括在 Article VIII. 1 内,船厂岂非不能延长交船日期(与相应的死亡日期)并需要支付议定赔偿,笔者也认为很简单。如果多数仲裁员不接受该造船合约的延误只分两类,而是笔者认为的三类,也就是船东因妨碍而造成的延误,可以让船厂根据一般法律向船东索赔损失并且令造船合约的交船日期变为无限期。换言之,如果 Article VIII. 1 不包括船东过错造成的延误,就会是除了该造船合约已有明示条文针对的小部分船东延误,包括在 Article V. 4 针对的船东供应的物料交货发生延误,或 Article XI. 1 所针对的三类船东延误(没有支付预付船价、不提供母公司担保与拒绝接船)是必须按照明示规定办,如作出通知,其他类别没有以明示条文针对并造成了延误的船东过错在笔者看来都应该适用"妨碍原则"(prevention principle)。在妨碍原则下,英国法律也没有要求无辜方作出通知的先决条件。毕竟作出正确的 Article VIII. 2 通知并非易事,这方面可看本书第十一章之 4.1.2 与 4.1.3 段。

在巨大的经济利益下,船东可能做出一些不可思议的过错。毕竟,能够找到理由终止涉及庞大金额的造船合约,对个别中小型的船东更是有生死区别。在航运低潮时,有不少被报道的船东"凿沉船舶"(scuttling)骗保险公司的案件,包括 The "Gold Sky" (1972) 2 Lloyd's Rep 187; The "Michael" (1979) 1 Lloyd's Rep 55; The

---

〔9〕 这可看本书第二章之 12 段。

"Captain Panagos D. P." (1986) 2 Lloyd's Rep 470; The "Grecia Express" (2002) 2 Lloyd's Rep 88 等著名先例。问题是,如果这种在订立造船合约时应该双方都没有考虑过的事项(因为当时航运市场高涨)是多数仲裁员认为根据订约时的背景/语境或/与综合解释,造船合约所有条文应该包括在 Article VIII. 1,并需要根据 Article VIII. 1 作出通知,就会使无辜的船厂面对一种不可能做到的情况。因为这种船东极端的过错都十分隐蔽,船厂不可能在发生时很快能知道并作出通知。

在这里笔者也可以根据造船与一般的知识解释,多数仲裁员认为既然有明示条文针对部分船东过错需要作出通知,就没有理由对其他船东过错所造成的延误不必通知。笔者认为,针对船东过错如供应物料交货延误与迟延支付预付船价,需要船厂作出通知是因为这些事项都要通过船东需要负责的第三人执行。例如,供应物料是船东通过供应商交货,支付预付船价是通过银行。所以,如果发生延误,船厂不作出通知船东是不会知道并可以作出补救。这与期租合约通常要求准时与足数支付租金,否则船东可以撤船,但经常有一条"反技术取巧条文"(anti - technicality clause)要求船东撤船前必须作出通知,让承租人可以作出补救(如承租人的银行疏忽没有把租金汇出或搞错了收款人)的情况类似。

多数仲裁员认为即使是船东过错造成延误,但为了"肯定"(certainty)必须能知道这一过错造成了多长的延误,否则就不知道在哪一天才可以有权终止造船合约,而实际造成的延误只有船厂才知道。但笔者认为肯定固然重要,但除了明示条文针对的船东过错,如果是其他错误,特别是一些极端的过错,就没理由把一个不可能做到的通知责任加在船厂。

笔者也关心这样解释 Articlc VIII. 会带来严重后果,因为条文的内容毕竟是与 SAJ Form 一致,而 SAJ Form 是造船合约中用的最普遍的格式合约。在分析 SAJ Form 最著名的 Simon Curtis 律师所著的《The Law of Shipbuilding Contracts》一书,即使是在 2013 年的第 4 版,也是半句也没有提到 SAJ Form 的 Article VIII. 1 不可抗力条文是包括船东过错。这导致笔者作出少数的不同意见,这在三个裁决书中,内容也完全不一样,有长有短。以下只节录最短的一个裁决书的不同意见,如下:

"The second issue is the construction/interpretation of Article VIII. 1 & VIII. 2. Namely, whether "buyer's defaults" are included in Art. VIII(1) as "or other causes beyond the control of the Builder. . . ", which call for yard's prior notice as a pre - condition?

I agree on reasonableness or business common sense, the Builder should not be allowed to keep delay "up its sleeve" and to produce at a convenient moment as a defence to a claim that the right to cancel the Contracts had arisen. Therefore, the Builder should give prior notice as the Buyer would not know the schedule or critical path of construction. I also appreciate the importance of certainty in commercial contracts.

But in the Preliminary issues before me, I believe my decision is limited only to the interpretation/construction of this Contract. Structurally, this Contract is no different with the standard SAJ form. So it is very much a decision concerning the construction of SAJ Form.

Could it be the intention of the drafters of the SAJ form, which has been long reputed to be a form favourable to shipbuilders? I must admit that I have some doubts because 'buyer's defaults' can be far-fetched and extreme when huge sums are involved. The types of 'buyer's defaults' I have in mind are for instance, a secretive arson or sabotage. Or, to unduly entertain or to bribe the classification surveyor. I can visualize causes of such delays, which are subtle in nature, would not be immediately ascertainable by the Builder. In those cases, it will be difficult, if at all possible, for the yard to serve notice in strict compliance to Article VIII. 2, such as within 7 days from the date of commencement of delay and to state the precise reason(s).

It is true that even in a delay by Buyer's defaults, the Buyer still would not know the impact, as it has no direct knowledge of the critical path. But unless it is clearly stated in the Contract so much so the Builder has committed to do the impossible when it comes to notice of 'buyer's defaults', I am reluctant to so hold. The majority's decision may also be too generous to the defaulting Buyer in the name of certainty, at the expense of the innocent Builder.

I have carefully considered the majority's reasons set out in paragraph 44 (and others). But I am unable to form a view or impression that other provisions in the Shipbuilding Contracts have persuasively and clearly rebutted the presumption in that the general words in Article VIII. 1 should not included 'buyer's defaults'."

最后一提 Article X. 3,也就是简单的一句说如果船厂作出了预付船价的还款给买方/船东,本合约的所有承诺与责任全部终结。对笔者而言,这明显表达了双方订约意图是要算总账之后才会涉及船厂需要归还预付船价(船厂不支付就可以向作出还款担保的银行要这笔钱)。本来有这一条文,外国船东在中间裁决书几乎肯定败诉。但船东在笔者涉及的仲裁案件中,外国船东都在开庭前放弃了这一权利(有关放弃合约条文的权利在本书第八章变数条件条文之 7.1 段有针对,但 Article X. 3 并不是船东单方面有利,能否有效弃权有疑问,只是船厂代表律师没有争议)。船东的弃权就说明船厂或银行即使退还了预付船价,造船合约的承诺与责任并不终结,船厂还可以在另一个最后裁决书索赔其指控的船东过错造成的延误与损失。但船厂不可能对一个巴拿马的皮包公司持续昂贵与漫长的开庭,这是典型的"good money chase after bad"。笔者还有一个更大的考虑,也就是船东即使事后放弃了他在该条文的权利,这会否影响造船合约的解释。毕竟,解释是根据双方订约时的意图以及当时的背景/语境。但可惜船东的代表大律师与多数仲裁员都没有给笔者说法,更谈不上满意的解释。这导致笔者只能在这一条文也作出少数意见,加上一条简短的意见说:"In

Article X.3 of the Contract, I am of the view that a subsequent waiver by the Buyer should not affect its clear meaning when it comes to construction/interpretation."

看来笔者上述所讲的疑虑也部分反映在不同意见中,答案要看英国法院会有什么解释了。反正笔者在这里想指出的是,对事实的认定(如对一些重要证人相信与否)固然不好掌握,但看来对合约的解释即所谓的"法律观点"(issue of law)也不好掌握或不肯定。特别是目前仲裁员有了更大的空间可以广泛考虑订约时的背景/语境,加上解释合约的规则实在太多并且往往相互冲突,导致怎样决定都可以自圆其说。如在这三个伦敦仲裁案件中,笔者感觉多数仲裁员有自己偏向性认为的重点,并在合议中非常强调双方订约时重视"肯定"(certainty),也是他们的共同/分享订约意图。所以即使是船东过错造成延误,也只有船厂才知道这些延误是不是在"关键路径"(critical path),也就是船东过错是否造成了工程的延误与延误程度。根据这一思路考虑,就会对同样一份造船合约作出与笔者十分不同的解释。

§15　总　结

可以说从上述与第一章所介绍的案例,合约有关的条文是否明确不再是能否看订约时的语境的一个考虑。在今天解释合约的新趋势下,再也不局限在传统的例外情况(如技术性术语、含糊或可笑)才能对大量(如果涉及漫长的谈判或其他外来的事实背景)的外来证据/口头证据开放。这表示任何涉及经常遇到的解释合约条文/文字的争议,法院或仲裁庭从一开始就可以或应该接受外来证据/口头证据,这可看 Hoffman 勋爵在 Investors Compensation Scheme Ltd v West Bromwich Building Society (1998) 1 W. L. R. 896 先例与 Chartbrook Ltd v Persimmon Homes Ltd (2009) UKHL 38 先例的说法。现实中,传统解释合约条文/文字在字义上清楚无误就不能接受外来证据/口头证据带来的区别也不太大,原因是有了争议,通常是表面看来明确的条文或文字,双方的代表律师都有理有据。至于含糊与否,准则也不是太高。通常只要是"解释有一定困难"(difficulty in interpretation)或"解释有一定的疑问"(interpretation that is for any reason doubtful)就已经足够让法院或仲裁庭接受外来证据/口头证据。但现在是全面开放订约时的外来证据/口头证据去协助解释合约,看来仲裁员想通过案件管理减少诉讼费用与时间,会比"认定事实"(finding of facts)所需要披露的文件证据更加困难。在后者的情况,至少仲裁员有更大的裁量权拒绝披露或不接受一些无关与不重要的证据。

新趋势无可否认存在许多问题,笔者不重复,只提两个重要的方面。一是诉讼费用变得昂贵,因为本来相对简单与廉宜的解释合约(在仲裁通常不需要开庭,以一份文件往往就是合约加上双方的文书争辩即可作出裁决)变为需要开庭处理可能是大量的双方谈判背景/语境与本质。这甚至可以被一些精明的被告律师利用为一种借口拖延诉讼,有理有据要求对大量的谈判与背景文件作出全面披露(这与仲裁的程序企图尽量减少或避免披露正好背道而驰)与提高费用,甚至进一步要求原告提供高昂的"费用担保"(security for costs)逼使原告作出让步。

另一个问题是律师(与其他第三人)要更加小心,他们再也不能只看合约文件的"四个角"(four corners),而要小心作出法律意见,如在本章之13.4段介绍的案例,律师如果看到合约条文/文字写的是"all",就不要说死"all means all"。而涉及金额高昂的合约,合约方可能需要一开始谈判就委任称职律师从旁密切参与,这是因为谈判的外来证据/口头证据也变为解释合约的根据,所以需要内行人保证这些证据是自我保护以及与最后拟定的合约相配合。但这样,显然会导致商业活动与订立合约的成本更加高昂。

看来,对英国法院(与其他普通法国家法院)而言,还在找出一个恰当的平衡。就是节省诉讼费用与商业法律必须肯定等相对简单以合约的四个角内作出解释,但无可避免会有部分案件错判了双方订约的意图,或是继续全面开放外来证据/口头证据的新趋势。

第七章 默示条文

§1 序 言

解释合约的大精神还是要从合约文件本身寻找、确定订约方的订约意图。法院/仲裁庭在解释合约时不能随意增删或改变合约的内容,他的职能只是解释而不是“重写”(rewrite)合约。但由于知识水平、订约能力、行业惯例与现实等种种原因,经常可见合约条文并不完整。在这种情况下一旦双方对合约没有写明的内容有了争议,法院/仲裁庭该怎么办呢?鉴于解释合约的最终目标是为了客观地寻找合约双方当事人的意图,出于政策性或必须性的考虑(因为合约中所遗留的一个不完整之处必须有一个说法才能补这个漏洞让合约得以顺利履行),是允许法院/仲裁庭给合约增加一些其原本没有明示的内容,这就是我们通常所指的“默示条文”(implied terms)(或称为隐含条文)了。所谓默示条文,就是订约时双方从来没有写明或提到,而由法院/仲裁庭根据有关法律地位或有关合约的特定事实或习惯做法等而引入合约的条文。在一定程度上就把此当作是订约双方“假设的订约意图”(presumed contractual intention)或至少不是与订约意图有矛盾。

由于这类条文无需写进合约也构成合约的内容,从而对合约方构成约束,因此出于商业的肯定性,法律对其限定的条件也是较为严格的,这特别是针对“事实的默示”(implied in fact),一直以来都是需要满足一些“考验”(tests)才会作出默示。根据 BP Refinery (Westernport) Pty Ltd v The Shire of Hastings (1977) 180 CLR 266 先例,想要成功作出事实默示将一条隐含条文加进一份特定的文件/合约,就必须满足一些先决条件或考验如:(1)合理与公平;(2)是合约的“商业效力”(business efficacy)所“必须”(necessary),如果缺少此隐含条文合约仍能运作,则不会作出默示;(3)在订约时可以假设双方会理所当然或异口同声地同意这隐含条文的所谓“好事第三人”(officious bystander)的考验;(4)隐含条文可以被清楚地表达;(5)不能与合约明示条文起冲突[(i) it must be reasonable and equitable; (ii) it must be necessary to give business efficacy to the contract, so that no term will be implied if the contract is effective without it; (iii) it must be so obvious that “it goes without saying”; (iv) it must be capable of clear expression; (v) it must not contradict any express term of the contract.”]

§2 默示条文的性质与分类

默示条文主要可分为两种,一种是"法律的默示"(implied by law),另一种是"事实的默示"(implied in fact)。Wright 勋爵在 Luxor (Eastbourne) Ltd v. Cooper (1941) A. C. 108 先例是这样说:"The expression 'implied term' is used in different senses. Sometimes it denotes some term which does not depend on the actual intention of the parties but on a rule of law, such as the terms, warranties or conditions which, if not expressly excluded, the law imports, as for instance under the Sale of Goods Act and the Marine Insurance Act. But a case like the present is different because what it is sought to imply is based on an intention imputed to the parties from their actual circumstances."(默示条文有不同的类别,有时并不根据双方的真正订约意图,而是根据法律地位,如《货物销售法》或《海上保险法》内的条文、保证或条件。只要没有被明示条文否定,就会被默示适用。但本案例的情况不一样,申请默示是根据假设双方在订约时的意图,换言之这就变为事实的默示。)

在后期的案件,Wright 勋爵的这个分类开始引人注意,Simonds 子爵与 Tucker 勋爵在 Lister v. Romford Ice and Cold Storage Co Ltd (1957) A. C. 555 先例也有提到。但这个两分法真正发展起来是在 Liverpool City Council v. Irwin (1977) A. C. 239 先例,贵族院的 Cross 勋爵对这两种默示有区分如下:"When it implies a term in a contract the court is sometimes laying down a general rule that in all contracts of a certain type—sale of goods, master and servant, landlord and tenant, and so on—some provision is to be implied unless the parties have expressly exclude it. In deciding whether or not to lay down such a *prima facie* rule the court will naturally ask itself whether in the general run of such cases the term in question would be one which it would be reasonable to insert. Sometimes, however, there is no defined type but what the court is being in effect asked to do is to rectify a particular—often a very detailed—contract by inserting in it a term which the parties have not expressed. Here it is not enough for the court to say that the suggested term is one the presence of which would make the contract a better or fairer one; it must be able to say that the insertion of the term is necessary to give — as it is put — business efficacy to the contract and that if its absence had been pointed out at the time both parties — assuming them to have been reasonable men—would have agreed without hesitation to its insertion."[作出默示条文,法院会在一些不同类别的合约(如货物买卖、雇佣合约、租赁合约等)默示一些隐含条文,认为在所有这种类别的合约都合理应该适用,除非在个别合约被双方约定的明示条文所否定。但会有情况是不涉及合约的类别而是法院被要求对一个十分详细的合约加上隐含条文。在这种情

况下,法院不能说引入隐含条文对该合约会更好与更加公平合理,因为这是改写合约。法院必须能够说引入隐含条文是必须,而且欠缺了这隐含条文,如果在订约时提醒双方,他们会毫不犹豫同意在合约中加上。]

这两种不同默示条文的区别如下：

区别	法律的默示	事实的默示
其他的名称[1]	General default rules(这名称也显示它一般适用在某一个类别的合约,而且是在没有明示条文针对的情况下)	*Ad hoc* gap – fillers(这名称也显示了它是随意填补个别合约中的漏洞,随意也表示不是一般适用而只是在个别合约中的不同情况)
适用	普遍适用在某种类别的合约关系,如货物买卖(1979 年《货物销售法》与一些普通法的默示)或是房东与住客之间(Liverpool City Council v. Irwin [1977] A. C. 239 等先例),仲裁协议的机密(Ali Shipping Corporation v. Shipyard Trogir [1998] 1 Lloyd's Rep 643 等先例)	根据双方的订约意图但没有在合约内明示规定或针对的情况,法院/仲裁庭必须小心不改写合约,而只是满足一些严格的考验才作出默示。这只能是适用在个别的合约而不能普遍性的适用在同样类别的合约关系
考验标准	不是根据双方的订约意图,也不要求"必须"(necessary)[2]令个别合约有"商业效力"(business efficacy)[3],而是根据一些较"广泛的考虑"(wider consideration)如政策考虑或从整体看是合理。通常订约方如果不喜欢这某一个法律默示的条文,可以明示条文否定或超越	要求"必须"(necessary)增加这一事实默示才能令合约有一个完整的说法与可以顺利履行,即给予"商业效力"(business efficacy)。仅是合理或不合理不足以作出这一种默示
案例	Eichholz v. Bannister (1864) 144 ER 284; Liverpool City Council v. Irwin (1977) A. C. 239 等	The "Moorcock" (1889) 14 P. D. 64 等

以下的段节会进一步详细介绍。

---

[1] Equitable Life Assurance Society v Hyman (2002) 1 AC 408 先例中的说法。

[2] 上诉庭的 Dyson 大法官在 Grossley v Faithful & Gould Holdings Ltd (2004) EWCA Civ 293 先例中说:"It seems to me that, rather than focus on the elusive concept of necessity, it is better to recognize that, to some extent at least, the existence and scope of standardised implied terms raise questions of reasonableness, fairness and the balancing of competing policy consideration."

[3] 贵族院的 Bridge 勋爵在 Scally v Southern Health and Social Services Board (1992) 1 AC 294 先例说:"A clear distinction is drawn in the speeches of Viscount Simonds in Lister v. Romford Ice and Cold Storage Co. Ltd. [1957] A. C. 555 and Lord Wilberforce in Liverpool City Council v. Irwin [1977] A. C. 239 between the search for an implied term necessary to give business efficacy to a particular contract and the search, based on wider considerations, for a term which the law will imply as a necessary incident of a definable category of contractual relationship."

§3 默示类别之一:法律的默示

首先是法律的默示,这种默示可来自两个方面,“立法”(statute)或“普通法/案例法”(common law)。在上述 Wright 勋爵的判词中就提到了两个立法,一是 1893 年的《货物销售法》(《Sale of Goods Act》)(这一立法已经被 1979 年的立法替代);二是 1906 年的《海上保险法》(《Marine Insurance Act》)。显然,这两个立法分别针对货物买卖合约与保险合约的不同类别合约。而普通法的默示也是以案例针对不同类别的合约作出各种不同的默示条文。换言之,两种法律的默示都是针对不同类别的合约。这也解释了为什么有些争议涉及有关的合约到底是属于哪个类别,而对笔者熟悉的造船合约,表面看来应该属于“工程合约”(construction contract),但法律已经明确属于“买卖合约”(sale contract)。Diplock 大法官在 McDougall v Aeromarine of Emsworth Ltd (1958) 2 Lloyd's Rep 345 先例中说:“... it seems well settled by authority that, although a shipbuilding contract is, in form, a contract for the construction of the vessel, it is in law a contract for sale of goods...”这也表示《货物销售法》内所有的默示条文如建造与交出的船舶必须有“所有权”(title)出售,船舶必须“符合合约的描述”(correspond with description),“满意质量”(satisfactory quality)等,这方面可看杨大明律师的《国际货物买卖》一书。

3.1 法律默示的考验标准

这一方面在稍早的图表已经有简单介绍,在本段会进一步介绍。首先在 Liverpool City Council v. Irwin (1977) A. C. 239 先例之前,英国法院对法律默示与事实默示的区分看来并不明确。事实上,在该先例的上诉庭,Denning 勋爵也被认为是混淆了两者。这在贵族院的 Cross 勋爵的判词中(在本章之第 2 段已经有节录)可以看到,其中认为“好事第三人”(officious bystander)的考验只适用在事实的默示。Cross 勋爵继续并谈到法律默示的考验标准说:“To say, as Lord Reid said in Young & Marten Ltd. v. McManus Childs Ltd. [1969] 1 A. C. 454 , 465, that '... no warranty ought to be implied in a contract unless it is in all the circumstances reasonable' is, in my view, quite different from saying that any warranty or term which is, in all the circumstances, reasonable ought to be implied in a contract. I am confident that Lord Reid meant no more than that unless a warranty or term is in all the circumstances reasonable there can be no question of implying it into a contract, but before it is implied much else besides is necessary, for example that without it the contract would be **inefficacious, futile and absurd.**”(Reid 勋爵在较早的先例说是必须在所有的情况下是合理才能默示,在 Cross 勋爵看来合理并不足够,默示是需要如果不作出这个类别的合约就会无效、无意义与可笑。)

另在 Scally v. Southern Health Board（1992）1 A. C. 294 先例：“A clear distinction is drawn in the speeches of Viscount Simonds in Lister v Romford Ice and Cold Storage Co Ltd（1957）AC 555 and Lord Wilberforce in Liverpool City Council v. Irwin（1977）A. C. 239 between the search for an implied term necessary to give business efficacy to a particular contract and the search, based on **wider considerations**, for a term which the law will imply as a necessary incident of a definable category of contractual relationship.”（在较早的两个先例，找出一个明确的区分，分别为了某一特定合约的商业效力作出默示条文与为了更广泛的考虑对某一明确类别的合约关系作出法律默示。）

上述所讲到的“广泛的考虑”也可以说是政策上的考虑，这可节录上诉庭的 Dyson 大法官在 Crossley v Faithful & Gould Holdings Ltd（2004）EWCA Civ 293 先例说：“It seems to me that, rather than focus on the elusive concept of necessity, it is better to recognize that, to some extent at least, the existence and scope of standardized implied terms raise questions of reasonableness, fairness and the **balancing of competing policy consideration.**”（加黑部分是笔者的强调）

最后节录的是 Elizabeth Peden 的《Policy Concerns Behind Implication of Terms in Law》（2001）117 LQR 459 一文中说法律默示是：“because of the nature of the contract, rather than the supposed intentions of the parties.”

以下笔者可以总结法律默示的考验标准如下：

1. 法律默示必须合理，这也与事实默示必须合理一致。这与明示条文完全不一样，因为在订约自由下双方完全可以自由同意一些完全不合理的条文或合约。这与大陆法十分强调的“善意”（good faith）也有一定关系，这在本书第九章中有介绍，英国是没有善意的说法，其中也举了许多重要的先例，认为这会带来英国法律的不肯定与不符合现实，因为在一个商业合约是各自谋利、勾心斗角，特别是在谈判时基本上处于“对抗”（adversarial）的地位。但通过法律的默示必须合情合理，也就是要求双方善意，就可以与英国普通法假设合约双方站在对抗地位相配合。举例说，如果法律默示货物买卖的出售的货物必须不能“货不对版”，虽然有订约自由可以否定或排除这一默示条文，但这样卖方就遇上困难，因为要获得买方的同意就不会容易甚至会大幅度减价等才能获得对方同意一条很不合理允许卖方“货不对版”的明示条文。

2. 仅是合理还不足够，还需要法律不作出默示有关类别的合约（而不是个别合约）就会无效、无意义与可笑。至于怎样会导致无效或可笑，在接下所介绍的先例会更加明确显示。在这里只举一个涉及货物买卖的例子。如果卖方出售的货物是他没有“所有权”（title），可能是他借回来或只是托管，这样，无辜的买方在给了货款之后，买到的东西也是一场空，因为只要真正拥有货物的当事人一知道，就可以把货物要回，毕竟在英国法下财产权比合约权更高。而即使买方向卖方追讨这笔已支付的货款，卖方也可以理直气壮说要“买方自己小心”（*caveat emptor*）。这样岂非是令该买卖合约无效或可笑,除非法律作出默示,要求卖方出售的货物有所有权。

3. 法律默示是在广泛的考虑与政策下作出,也就是对某一类别的合约整体的考虑。例如,在过去三四十年就有许多法律的默示通过先例针对雇佣合约,正如 Slynn 勋爵在 Spring v Guardian Assurance (1995) 2 AC 296 先例说:"the changes which have taken place in the employer/employee relationship with far greater duties imposed on the employer than in the past, whether by statute or by judicial decision, to care for the physical, financial and even psychological welfare of the employee."

4. 由于法律默示不是针对个别合约,所以事实默示的一些考验,主要是好事第三人不适用。

3.2 立法默示

3.2.1 针对合约类别之一:货物买卖与《货物销售法》

1979 年英国《货物销售法》中有很多默示条文。而这一立法或其前身在 1893 年的立法其实是把较早前所判的先例收集起来"立法化"(codify)。其中最重要的例子是卖方对出售的货物有一个默示条文,即他拥有所有权出售该有关货物,货物也没有债务与押记,及买方可宁静地占有该货物等。这是在第 12 条文,可部分节录如下:

"12. Implied terms about title, etc. (1) In a contract of sale, other than one to which subsection (3) below applies, there is an implied (term) on the part of the seller that in the case of a sale he has a right to sell the goods, and in the case of an agreement to sell he will have such a right at the time when the property is to pass. (2) In a contract of sale, other than one to which subsection (3) below applies, there is also an implied (term) that -(a) the goods are free, and will remain free until the time when the property is to pass, from any charge or encumbrance not disclosed or known to the buyer before the contract is made, and (b) the buyer will enjoy quiet possession of the goods except so far as it may be disturbed by the owner or other person entitled to the benefit of any charge or encumbrance so disclosed or known..."

有关卖方必须对有关货物拥有所有权的先例,也可以是最早确认法律默示的做法,名为 Eichholz v. Bannister (1864) 144 ER 284,其中上诉庭的 Byles 大法官的判词针对当时英国法律对这方面是说:"It has been said over and over again that there is no implied warranty of title on the mere sale of a chattel. But it is certainly, as my Lord has observed, barren ground; not a single judgment has been given upon it. In every case, there has been, subject to one single exception, either declaration or conduct. Chancellor Kent, 2 Com. 478, says: 'In every sale of a chattel, if the possession be at the time in another, and there be no covenant or warranty of title, the rule of *caveat emptor* applies, and the party buys at his peril;' for which he cites the dicta of Lord Holt in Medina v. Stoughton, 1 Salk. 210, 1 Ld. Raym. 523, and of Buller, J., in Pasley v. Freeman, 3 T. R. 57, 58. 'But,' he goes on, 'if the seller has possession of the article, and he sells it as his own, and not as agent for another, and for a fair price, he is understood to warrant the title.' Thus the law stands that, if there be declaration or conduct or warranty whereby the buyer is induced to believe that the seller has title to the goods he professes to sell, an action lies for a breach."(在此案例之前没有说法在出售货物是有一个对所有权有默示保证,唯一买方可以有救济的情况是卖方在出售时,曾经宣告或以行动显示他对有关货物有所有权并误导了买方。否则英国法律的地位是要买方自己小心。)

该先例概括说:"In the case of goods sold in an open shop or warehouse, there is an implied warranty on the part of the seller that he is the owner of the goods: and, if it turns out otherwise,—as, where the goods are claimed by the true owner, from whom they have been stolen,—the buyer may recover back the price as money paid upon a consideration which has failed."(货物如果在一个公开营运的商店或货仓出售,法律对卖方有一个默示,就是他保证他拥有这批货物。如果事后有第三人声称他才是有关货物的主人,货物只是被偷取,买方有权向卖方取回这一笔货款。)

另是针对"将来的货物"(future goods),《货物销售法》之第 13 条文是说:"(1) Where there is a contract for the sale of goods by description, there is an implied [term] that the goods will correspond with the description."

这一条立法默示条文是来自 Gardiner v Gray (1815) 4 Camp. 144 与 Jones v Bright (1829) 5 Bing 533 先例。两个先例都涉及 Ellenborough 勋爵,他在前一个先例是说:"the purchaser has a right to expect a saleable article answering the description in the contract. Without any particular warranty, this is an implied term in every such contract. Where there is no opportunity to inspect the commodity, the maxim of *caveat emptor* does not apply. He cannot without a warranty insist that it shall be of any particular quality or fineness, but the intention of both parties must be taken to be, that it shall be saleable in the market under the demonination mentioned in the contract between them."(买方有权希望买到货物与合约的描述一致,即使卖方没有作出任何保证,他也应该在该买卖合约有一个默示条文或承诺。如果买方在订立买卖合约时没有机会检查有关货物,"买方自己小心"的大原则不适用。)

笔者不多介绍 1979 年《货物销售法》其他法律的默示条文,如"满意的质量"(satisfactory quality)[这是一个新的立法(《Sale and Supply of Goods Act 1994》)]改动,不涉及先例,在 1893 年的立法是"可销售质量"[merchanable quality])与"货物适合买方用途"(fit for the purpose of the buyer)(这涉及一些先例,如 Jones v Bright; Wallis v Russell [1902] 2 IR 584; Preist v Last [1903] 2 KB 148 等)。除了 1979 年《货物销售法》外,另有雷同默示条文并扩大针对"租购合约"(hire - purchase contract)与"货物及服务混在一起的合约"(contract for work and material)的相关立法:《Supply of Goods (Implied Terms) Act 1973》与《Supply of Goods and Services Act

1982》。

笔者只简单介绍这些立法的默示条文如何操作。举例说,在一个船舶买卖合约下,买方在接受船舶后才发觉船舶以前留下了大量债务,导致船舶在一些港口不断被扣押。这样,买方或新船东的损失显然可以向卖方索赔。但要成功索赔首先在责任方面要证明卖方违反买卖合约的条文。如果双方的买卖合约是以一些拟定得严谨的标准格式合约,如 1993 年挪威格式,它是有一条明示条文针对卖方不能遗留债务,这是第 9 条文如下:"9. Encumbrances The sellers warrant that the Vessel, at the time of delivery, is free from all charters, encumbrances, mortgages and maritime liens or any other debts whatsoever. The sellers hereby undertake to indemnify the Buyers against all consequences of claims made against the Vessel which have been incurred prior to the time of delivery."

在这个情况下,买方很容易证明卖方违反了买卖合约的第 9 条明示条文,接下来只是计算赔偿损失的金额。但不难想到有一些同类的合约没有这么正规的情况,如游艇或内河船舶的买卖,买卖双方根本不知道也不会使用挪威格式。这样,订约双方没有想到也自然漏掉如上述的挪威格式第 9 条文的可能性就很大了,这正是 Steyn 勋爵在近期的 Equitable Life Assurance Society v. Hyman (2002) 1 A. C. 408, HL 先例所说的"一般性的遗漏"(general default)的情况。这样,无辜的买方买下了一艘留下许多债务的船舶难道就没有救济了吗?显然,这并不公道。而且这种情况会很普遍,而并非只局限在某一艘船舶或某一个买卖合约,因为《货物销售法》适用在所有种类货物的买卖包括船舶。所以,为了公平、政策或避免这种类别的合约变为"无效、无意义与可笑"(inefficacious, futile and absurd)的需要,有了立法强加这些默示条文,这是稍早有节录的《货物销售法》第 12(2)(a)与(b)条文。这样,买方向卖方索赔损失,如果卖方说:"我从来没有对你作出任何承诺说该船舶没有余下的债务。"买方就可以回答说:"就算是没有明示条文作出这种承诺,但《货物销售法》有默示条文要求该船舶没有债务与可以让我作为买方享有宁静的占有,但你做不到,所以违反了默示条文。"

当然,即使是立法的默示条文,如果不是像 1924 年《海牙规则》之 Article 3(8)或 1977 年《不公平合约法》(《Unfair Contract Terms Act》)之 s. 6(1)(b)规定不准以明示条文改变的话,也不影响双方的订约自由。所以默示条文应该屈服于明示条文,如上述船舶的卖方以明示条文说明该船舶有一笔债务,而买方也接受了并承诺将来自己承担后果,这样《货物销售法》的有关默示条文就在此方面不适用了。

3.2.2 针对合约类别之二:保险合约与《海上保险法》

Wright 勋爵在 Luxor (Eastbourne) Ltd v. Cooper (1941) A. C. 108 先例提到的另一个立法就是 1906 年《海上保险法》,这里面也有大量的默示条文。最广为人知的是第 17 条文说明保险合约要"绝对善意"(utmost good - faith)。再多举一个例子是立法的第 39 条文针对"航次保险"(voyage policy),受保人的船东有一个在航次开始前必须令船舶绝对适航的“默示保证”(implied warranty)。这种默示保证在《海上保险法》有5条,如船舶/货物必须“中立”(warranty of neutrality)、船舶/货物在投保与作出保证的一天“安全”(warranty of good safety)、“投保的航次合法”(warranty of legality)。而众所周知,保险法的“保证”是一种“承诺性保证”(promissory warranty),并不是一般合约的保证条文。而且受保人如果违反,后果会比违反合约的条件条文更严重,因为第33(3)条文有说明后果:“(3) A warranty, as above defined, is a condition which must be exactly complied with, whether it be material to the risk or not. If it be not so complied with, then, subject to any express provision in the policy, the insurer is discharged from liability as from the date of the breach of warranty, but without prejudice to any liability incurred by him before that date.”

除了“保证”外,《海上保险法》还有其他的“默示条件”(implied condition),如船舶在投保的航次会尽快起航、不可以“绕航”(deviation)、不可以保险合约规定外的港口、不得在航次中延误等。

这些默示条文的操作如上述例子,笔者不多介绍。至于以保险合约明示条文否定或更改立法的默示条文,针对“绝对善意”就少会出现,但不是没有。例如,绝对善意的要求带来了订约前受保人的披露与不能误述责任就会在保单以明示条文否定或超越,如在 HIH v. New Hampshire (2001) 2 Lloyd's Rep. 161 先例中的保单有第8条文如下:“To the fullest extent permissible by applicable law, the Insurer hereby agrees that it will not seek to or be entitled to avoid or rescind this Policy or reject any claim hereunder or be entitled to seek any remedy or redress on the grounds of ... non-disclosure or misrepresentation by any person or any other similar grounds. The Insurer irrevocably agrees not to assert and waives any and all defences and rights of set-off and/or counterclaim (including without limitation any such rights acquired by assignment or otherwise) which it may have against the Assured or which may be available so as to deny payment of any amount due hereunder in accordance with the express terms hereof.”

另是有针对航次保险必须适航的默示保证,就更多见到有明示条文作出改变以否定或超越对船舶的绝对适航责任。对船东的做法而言,由于“定期保险”(time policy)在海上保险法没有保证绝对适航责任,所以这已经是国际船东普遍的做法。至于在货物保险,由于这种保险也是受1906年《海上保险法》的管辖,就有一条标准条文可简称为“确认适航条文”(Seaworthiness Admitted Clause)通过“合约弃权”(contractual waiver)放弃这一默示责任,因为今天的现实中货方根本管不了船舶是否适航。如在1982年的“伦敦保险学会货物条文(A)”(Institute Cargo Clauses [A]),就有第5.2条文说:“The underwriters waive any breach of the implied warranties of seaworthiness of the ship and fitness of the ship to carry the subject-matter insured to destination, unless the Assured or their servants are privy to such unseaworthiness or unfitness.”。

3.3 普通法默示

除了立法外,普通法也通过案例大量增加默示条文在每一个不同类别的合约。正如Cross勋爵在Liverpool City Council v. Irwin (1977) AC 239先例中说:"When it implies a term in a contract the court is sometimes laying down a general rule that in all contracts of a certain type - sale of goods, master and servant, landlord and tenant and so on - some provisions is to be implied unless the parties have expressly excluded."

法院肯作出默示条文的考验标准在本章稍早的3.1段已经有介绍。在很大的程度上,立法默示也是通过把普通法的默示立法化。数百年来,英国法院特别是加上其他普通法国家所判的案例已经多不胜数,如果需要更深入了解对某一类别的合约有什么普通法/案例法作出的默示条文,就必须阅读针对该类别合约的专题的书籍。笔者也认为,在任何一个行业熟悉业务都必须理解该行业的法律默示条文很重要。英国法律已经有了大量的先例针对不同类别行业所作出的法律默示,已经形成了一套完整、合理、逻辑性强、现实可行与实际在使用中的游戏规则。而在任何一个行业订立一份自我保护的合约,熟悉了什么是默示条文才能把一个合约订好。如对自己不利的默示地位,就会要求加入明示条文作出改变。但如果对自己十分有利的默示地位,就不要额外增加明示条文,以免在双方讨价还价后反而会写得不伦不类而引起争议。

以下简略介绍一些合约类别,如雇佣合约与房屋租赁合约。

3.3.1 类别之一:雇佣合约

雇佣关系是社会上一个很大的问题,所以涉及雇佣合约应该作出什么的法律默示条文很早就有先例,而在近三四十年更是有了大量先例针对雇佣合约并作出了各式各样的默示条文,特别是对雇主增加了责任。正如Hoffmann勋爵在Johnson v Unisys Ltd (2001) UKHL 13先例中说:"... over the last 30 years or so, the nature of the contract of employment has been transformed. It has been recognised that a person's employment is usually one of the most important things in his or her life. It gives not only a livelihood but an occupation, an identity and a sense of self-esteem. The law has changed to recognise this social reality."

先介绍一个早期的先例Robb v Green (1895) 2 QB 315,案情涉及雇员从雇主的订单中抄下了顾客名单,准备将来自立门户抢这批客人,看来这涉及雇员的效忠问题。

在上诉庭,判是在雇佣合约有默示条文要求雇员对雇主有善意。其中Esher勋爵引用了Bowen大法官在Lamb v Evans (1893) 1 Ch. 218先例的判决说:"The common law, it is true, treats the matter from the point of view of an implied contract, and assumes that there is a promise to do that which is part of the bargain, or which can be fairly implied as part of the good faith which is necessary to make the bargain effectual. What is an implied contract or an implied promise in law? It is that promise which the law implies and authorizes us to infer in order to give the transaction that effect which the parties must have intended it to have, and without which it would be futile."

但这一判法看来是受到批评,因为雇佣合约一般不会防止雇员将来作出生意上的竞争,而涉及专业人士的雇佣合约更加会有共识是雇员迟早会离开,并以他在雇佣期间所学到的专业知识、经验与人脉作出竞争。所以很难说雇佣合约会变为"无意义"(futile)。至于从雇主的订单中抄下了顾客名单是否"大逆不道",也存在疑问,一位记忆力好的雇员不必抄下也会在他的雇佣期间全部记下为将来使用。后来就有了改变,在 Wessex Dairies Ltd v Smith (1935) 2 KB 80 先例,案情涉及一个派牛奶的雇员自立门户并招揽雇主的客户,而且被告的雇员也太心急,在他仍在雇佣的最后几天就已经开始招揽客户。这被上诉庭判是不被允许,但看来上诉庭认为将来作出竞争是允许的,除非有关的雇佣合约有明示条文(这种被称为 restrictive convenant 条文会后详)。Maugham 大法官说:"First, after the employment terminates, the servant may, in the absence of special stipulation, canvass the customers of the late employer, and further he may send a circular to every customer. On the other hand, it has been held that while the servant is in the employment of the master he is not justified in making a list of the master's customers, and he can be restrained, as he was in Robb v. Green, from making such a list, or if he has made one, he will be ordered to give it up. But it is to be noted that in Robb v. Green the defendant was not restrained from sending out circulars to customers whose names he could remember. Another thing to be borne in mind is that although the servant is not entitled to make use of information which he has obtained in confidence in his master's service he is entitled to make use of the knowledge and skill which he acquired while in that service, including knowledge and skill directly obtained from the master in teaching him his business. It follows, in my opinion, that the servant may, while in the employment of the master, be as agreeable, attentive and skilful as it is in his power to be to others with the ultimate view of obtaining the benefit of the customers' friendly feelings when he calls upon them if and when he sets up business for himself. That is, of course, where there is no valid restrictive clause preventing him doing so."

同样的法律默示地位在接下的 Faccenda Chicken Ltd v Fowler (1987) Ch. 117 先例有了进一步的明确,这一著名先例在笔者与杨大明律师合著的《禁令》一书有介绍。

从先例中所作出的默示地位就可以看到雇佣合约中的明示条文的目的。一是明示条文针对什么会是雇主认为的商业机密/秘密,加强成为第三类资料的可能性。二是明示条文就是"限制商贸/就业契约/条文"(restraint of trade clause),这种条文涉及公共政策,包括人权的考虑。正如在 Petrofina Ltd v Martin (1966) Ch 146 先例,Denning 勋爵说:"Every member of the community is entitled to carry on any trade or business he chooses and in such manner as he thinks most desirable in his own interests, so long as he does nothing unlawful: with the consequence that any contract which interferes with the free exercise of his trade or business, by restricting him in the work he may do for others, or the arrangements which he may make with others, is a contract in restraint of trade. It is invalid unless it is reasonable as between the parties and not injurious to the public interest."(社会上每一个人/公司都可自由选择做任何行业/商贸,只要合法。任何合约条文干预这种自由,如不准进行某种商业活动,或是不准被雇用,都属这种合约条文,即表面看来是法院不予协助执行。除非是条文合理公平,而且不损害公众利益。)

法律对这种限制商贸/就业契约/条文(这种条文也不只是出现在雇佣合约,也包括其他方面如买卖或收购一盘生意、供应货物或/与服务、公会与雇主组织、独家代理商或独家经销商、土地使用等)有敌意是可以理解,可举一个极端例子说明:在一个雇佣合约,雇员被迫接受了一个合约条文说明如果一旦他离职,今后 50 年不准在全球做任何性质的工作谋生。但该雇佣合约涉及的工作性质也非是全球性,并且只针对一种专门的工作。这样,有关条文根本不像是合理保护雇主的合法利益,而是像要逼死雇员,永远要屈膝在雇主下做奴隶。看来对这条文的敌视与看待是与"惩罚性条文"(penalty clause)一致,都会被视为"阻吓违约的一方"(in terrorem of the offending party)。

但英国法律也理解在今天竞争激烈的商业社会,以这种条文在一定程度限制雇员有必要。所以取得平衡,法院是作出默示有关条文是合理保护雇主的合法利益,该条文就被法院承认/接受。至于怎样才算是合理,这可节录《Chitty on Contracts》(第 31 版,2012 年)之 16-093 段所说:

"While all restraints of trade of which the doctrine applies are *prima facie* unenforceable, all, whether partial or total, are enforceable if reasonable. As was said by Lord Macnaghen in Nordenfelt v Maxim Nordenfelt & Co:

'It is a sufficient justification, and indeed it is the only justification, if the restriction is reasonable—reasonable, that is, in reference to the interests of the parties concerned and reasonable in reference to the interests of the public, so framed and so guarded as to afford adequate protection to the party in whose favour it is imposed, while at the same time it is in no way injurious to the public.'

In determining reasonableness the court 'is entitled to consider whether or not a covenant of a narrower nature would have sufficed for the convenantee's protection'.(考虑是否合理,法院会考虑是否可以有一条条文是比较狭窄但已经足够保护雇主。)

Even if the restraint is unlimited in time or in space it will be upheld if it is reasonable, although the absence of such a limit 'is a remarkable feature*prima facie* needing justification'. Worldwide restrictions have passed muster in the courts, but only where the restrictions to be reasonably effectual had to be worldwide...”(有关条文在雇主想保护的地区范围以防止前雇员限制不利的竞争,与限制竞争期限的长短都是重要的考虑。)

除了条文本身对限制的内容是否合理外,合理还要看:(1)有关的“约因/对价”(consideration)是否与条文限制的程度成正比;(2)双方在订立合约时,相对的谈判力量是否一面倒。由于本小段不是主要针对这一方面,就略过不再细谈。

其他普通法在个别案例对雇佣合约作出法律默示条文的部分先例有:

1. 在 Lister v. Romford Ice and Cold Storage Co Ltd (1957) A. C. 555 先例,案情涉及在雇佣合约中,雇员履行职务时有疏忽或没有尽责的情况下带来民事责任,雇主是否可以要求雇员分摊责任。该先例涉及雇员开货车时疏忽碰伤了人。

2. 在 Jones v Manchester Corporation (1952) QB 852 先例,判是雇员如果涉及非法行为,是否有默示责任补偿雇主的损失。

3. 在 Harmer v Cornelius (1858) 5 C. B. N. S. 236 先例,案情涉及一位画匠的雇佣合约,他被发觉不称职,并非他所说的有这方面的手艺。Willes 大法官针对一个有技术的雇员是说:“When a skilled labourer, artizan, or artist is employed, there is on his part an implied warranty that he is of skill reasonably competent to the task he undertakes, *Spondes peritiam artis*. Thus, if an apothecary, a watch - maker, or an attorney be employed for reward, they each impliedly undertake to possess and exercise reasonable skill in their several arts. The public profession of an art is a representation and undertaking to all the world that the professor possesses the requisite ability and skill. An express promise or express representation in the particular case is not necessary.”

4. 在 Sim v Rotherham M. B. C (1987) Ch. 216 先例,属于专业的雇员有一个默示责任与他的同事合作来恰当地履行专业。如一个学校,如果有另一个老师休假,作为老师的雇员有默示责任依从校长的合理安排代课。

5. 在 Scally v Southern Health and Social Services Board (1992) 1 AC 294 的贵族院先例,判是如果合约中有一条条文并非是与雇员本身谈判,而是通过与代表团体或工会等谈判达成,雇员不会合理知道这条文带给他的合约权利,除非雇主告知,在这种情况下雇主就有告知的默示责任。

6. 在 Mahmud v. Bank of Credit and Commerce International SA (1998) AC 20, HL 的贵族院先例,再度确认了雇佣合约中有一个默示条文就是双方有一个“相互信任的关系”(trust of confidence)。如果雇主做一些不诚实与腐败的事情,导致雇员在银行倒闭后难以寻找工作,前途受损,前雇主的银行要作出赔偿。贵族院说:“... the bank was under an implied obligation to its employees not to conduct a dishonest or corrupt business. This implied obligation is no more than one particular aspect of the portmanteau, general obligation not to engage in conduct likely to undermine the trust and confidence required if the employment relationship is to continue in the manner the

employment contract implicitly envisages. . . . I do not accept the liquidators'（被告银行/雇主的清盘人）submission that the conduct of which complaint is made must be targeted in some way at the employee or a group of employees. No doubt that will often be the position, perhaps usually so. But there is no reason in principle why this must always be so. The trust and confidence required in the employment relationship can be undermined by an employer, or indeed an employee, in many different ways. I can see no justification for the law giving the employee a remedy if the unjustified trust – destroying conduct occurs in some ways but refusing a remedy if it occurs in others. The conduct must, of course, impinge on the relationship in the sense that, looked at objectively, it is likely to destroy or seriously damage the degree of trust and confidence the employee is reasonably entitled to have in his employer. That requires one to look at all the circumstances."

3.3.2 类别之二:房屋租赁合约

这方面可先介绍 Miller v Hancock（1893）2 QB 177 先例,案情涉及一位火车公司的雇员向一个名为 Gwynne & Co 的客户收回欠款,但他在造访时,在该客户租用的办公楼的楼梯摔倒。这一先例就从一个人身伤害的案件发展到一个 Gwynne & Co 与房东的争议,就是谁负责对楼梯维修保养,让它可以安全使用。而楼梯并非属于出租办公楼的部分,双方的合约也没有明示针对,这就涉及是否作出默示。上诉庭的 Bowen 大法官是这样说:"It appears to me obvious, when one considers what a flat of this kind is, and the only way in which it can be enjoyed, that the parties to the demise of it must have intended by necessary implication, as a basis without which the whole transaction would be futile, that the landlord should maintain the staircase, which is essential to the enjoyment of the premises demised, and should keep it reasonably safe for the use of the tenants, and also of those persons who would necessarily go up and down the stairs in the ordinary course of business with the tenants; because, of course, a landlord must know when he lets a flat that tradesmen and other persons having business with the tenant must have access to it. It seems to me that it would render the whole transaction **inefficacious and absurd** if an implied undertaking were not assumed on the part of the landlord to maintain the staircase so far as might be necessary for the reasonable enjoyment of the demised premises."（加黑部分显示这是一个法律的默示）

但接下来贵族院在 Fairman v Perpetual Investment B. S.（1923）AC 74 先例,改变了 Miller v Hancock 的上诉庭先例,判房东只是对隐蔽的危险有责任。这方面后来也有了立法,就是《Occupier's Liability Act 1957》,就此略过。

接下来在著名的 Liverpool City Council v. Irwin（1977）A. C. 239 贵族院先例,也涉及类似问题,但面对不是访客,而是针对租客。该先例涉及一栋在利物浦的公屋,楼高 15 层,有 70 个单位。在该大楼,公用地方经常被破坏,电梯与楼梯的照明经常时好时坏,垃圾槽经常堵塞。这导致住在 9 楼与 10 楼的 Leslie Irwin 与 Maureen Irwin 拒绝支付租金,于是政府(房屋委员会)作为房东通过法律程序要赶走他们,而他们就反告房屋委员会违反租约中的默示条文。贵族院同意在一个高层大楼的出租,如果房东对公用地方保留了控制,他就有一个默示责任做出合理的维修保养。贵族院最后挑出了7个默示责任,增加给房屋委员会,如下:"(1) an implied letting giving the tenant the right of exclusive possession;(2) an implied covenant of quiet enjoyment;(3) an implied easement for tenants and their licensees to use the stairs;(4) a right in the nature of an easement to use the lifts;(5) an easement to use the rubbish chutes;(6) an obligation on the landlord to exercise reasonable care to keep in reasonable repair and usability the common parts (including the lifts and chutes);(7) where the nature of the structure required artificial light an obligation to take reasonable care to maintain adequate lighting."

但在该先例的案情,认定房屋委员会对公用地方是有做出合理的维修保养,问题是经常被破坏。

3.4 法律默示下不同性质合约的分类

这就带来了下一个问题,即如何把有争议的合约分类,因为它们有不同的法律默示条文。这方面通常十分容易分类,如 FOB 或 CIF 买卖就肯定是国际货物买卖合约,受《货物销售法》的管辖并会引进该立法下的法律默示条文。

但看来还是有局部困难,如目前在英国法律下电脑软件的买卖是否属于1979年《货物销售法》管辖或属于1982年《货物与服务提供法》管辖还不明朗:St Albans City and District Council v. International Computers Ltd (1996) 4 All E. R. 481, CA 先例。同样的不明朗也出现在造船合约,虽然已经有一连串先例判其属于买卖"将来货物"(future goods)的合约。要知道一个货物买卖合约与工程合约有各自不同的法律默示条文,所以必须能够分类。Diplock 大法官在 McDougall v. Aeromarine of Emsworth Ltd (1958) 2 Lloyd's Rep. 345 先例说:"... it seems well settled by authority that, although a shipbuilding contract is, in form, a contract for the construction of the vessel, it is in law a contract for the sale of goods ..."

确定合约的定性/分类是解释合约的工作:Wong Mee Wan v. Kwan Kin Travel Service Ltd (1996) 1 W. L. R. 38, 42, PC 先例。在确定合约分类时,可考虑双方之前的交易,合约订约的背景/环境等事实。

§4 默示类别之二:事实的默示

在本章之第2段的图表显示了在 Equitable Life Assurance Society v. Hyman (2002) 1 A. C. 408, CA, HL 先例,Steyn 勋爵把事实的默示称为"*ad hoc* gap fillers",从"随意"(*ad hoc*)一词我们也可看出事实默示的特点。它是针对个别合约,往

往也没有任何直接的先例或立法针对,而判了之后也不会可适用在将来的类似合约。这是因为每一个合约在订约自由下都会有不大相同的写法,也往往有不同的“背景/语境”(background circumstance/factual matrix),导致很容易作出区分并给予不同的解释。由于解释合约条文是一个法律问题,而法律问题在伦敦仲裁可以上诉至法院,但由于在“Nema Guideline”(The “Nema” [1981] 2 Lloyd’s Rep. 239 先例)有所收紧,上诉是要先取得上诉批文,而在“一次过”(one - off)的案件,可以说不会有取得上诉批文的希望。这就可以得出一个结论,大部分的“*ad hoc* gap fillers”,特别只是影响个别的合约与相关的当事人,都会是“一次过”的案件。相反,在较早时针对的法律默示就会是影响面广,上诉就会机会大得多了。

有关事实的默示先举一个简单的例子,就是订约双方同意在一条明示条文支付一笔钱(或做一件事)。如果双方的合约完整,就应想到也应约定付钱的期限。这样,如果有明示约定付钱必须准时在某一天,或“立即”(immediately)/“马上”(forthwith)等措辞,解释起来就十分容易了。但如果双方的合约根本没有提到任何时间规定,加上双方有了争议,如收款人说是在订约后的第二天就应该支付,但付款人说是订约后 1 年才需要支付,就存在怎样在双方的两个极端之间认定付款的时间了。注意是由于没有明示条文,所以只有靠默示条文。而且,必须要有一个说法,否则该合约就有了一个大漏洞,不填补的话,订约双方根本无法履行付款的一步。这样,法院/仲裁庭就会作出一个合理时间必须付钱的默示条文。“合理”(reasonable)是因为默示条文本质上必须合理,因为这是假设双方都合理:请看本书第四章之第 3 段与第十章之 4.2.1 段。另是可肯定双方在订约时都不会提出异议的,当然就只能是对大家都合理。这合理就要看该合约的其他明示条文与背景,如该笔钱虽然是美元,但付款人所在地是中国大陆,收款人是在外国。这样,考虑到中国大陆有外汇管制,再加上收款人所在地可能不方便与有关的时间碰巧又是长假期,法院/仲裁庭会在这种环境下认定付款的合理时间是在订约后的两个星期内,既不是收款人所说的第二天,更不是付款人所说的 1 年。

从上述的例子也可以看到在另一个合约,有类似的情况出现,但事实上有一点改变如有关的付款人与收款人都是在香港的公司,金额也不大,这样默示的合理时间可能只有一两个银行工作日,而不再是两个星期了。

4.1 事实默示的权威先例:The “Moorcock”

英国在事实默示的第一个著名先例是 The “Moorcock” (1889) 14 P. D. 64,案情是被告拥有泰晤士河畔的一个码头,他将此码头租用给原告“Moorcock”轮的船东,当时双方都知道船舶在低潮期间肯定要搁浅来作业的,结果因为河床凹凸不平而导致船舶损坏。但船东与码头所有人之间的租用合约没有明示条文保证卸货码头安全,所以要依赖默示条文,就是码头所有人保证船东卸货码头安全。上诉庭的 Bowen 大法官说:“Now, an implied warranty, or, as it is called, a covenant in law, as distinguished from an express contract or express warranty, really is in all cases founded upon the presumed intention of the parties, and upon reason. The implication which the law draws from what must obviously have been the intention of the parties, the law draws with the object of giving efficacy to the transaction and preventing such a failure of consideration as cannot have been within the contemplation of either sides; and I believe if one were to take all the cases, and there are many, of implied warranties or covenants in law, it will be found that in all of them the law is raising an implication from the presumed intention of the parties with the object of giving to the transaction such efficacy as both parties must have intended that at all events it should have."(这一默示的保证是假设双方订约时的共同意图,并给双方的交易一个效力。)

上诉庭决定默示码头所有人有责任采取"合理小心"(reasonable care)肯定泊位安全(并非是很多后来解释指该先例要求泊位所有人必须提供一个安全泊位)。

Bowen 大法官的判词就提出了一个"合约效力"(efficacy to contract)与"必须"(necessary)的说法,这可节录《Chitty on Contracts》(第 31 版,2012 年)一书之 13 - 006 段如下:"A term will be implied if it is necessary, in the business sense, to give efficacy to the contract... In this situation, although here is an apparently complete bargain, the courts are willing to add a term on the ground that without it the contract will not work or because an implication is necessary to give effect to the reasonable expectations of the parties."

4.2 The "Moorcock"先例带来大量的同类案例

The "Moorcock"先例后带来了大量的同类案例,在《Implied Terms in English Contract Law》(2011 年)一书提到,仅是被报道并引用 The "Moorcock"先例的就有大约四百个。至于引用同一原则但没有提到该先例,以及没有被报道的先例更加多不胜数。这方面也可节录《Chitty on Contracts》之 13 - 007 段所说:"The principle laid down in *The Moorcock* has been approved and applied many times. For example, a term has been implied into a contract for the use of a wharf that it was safe for a ship to lie at the wharf;[4] into a contract for a Turkish bath that the couches for reclining on were free from vermin;[5] into a charterparty that the charterer would not order the ship to proceed to a port impossible of access[6] and would indemnify the shipowner against loss incurred in complying with the charterer's orders;[7] into a contract of bailment, the purpose of which was the use of the goods by the bailee, an authority to do in relation to the

---

〔4〕 The Moorcock (1889) 14 PD 64 先例。

〔5〕 Silverman v Imperial London Hotels Ltd (1927) 137 LT 57 先例。

〔6〕 Aktieselskabet Olivebank v Dansk Svolsyre Fabrik (1919) 2 KB 162 先例。但 Eurico Spa v philippe-Brothers (1987) 3 Lloyd's Rep 215 有相反的判决。

〔7〕 Triad Shipping Co v Stellar Chartering & Brokerage Inc (1994) 2 Lloyd's Rep 227 先例。

goods all things reasonably incidental to their reasonable use;[8] into a contract for printing of banknotes that the plates should not be allowed to get into the hands of unauthorized persons;[9] into a father's contract to pay such school bills of his son as should be approved by him, that such consent should not be unreasonably withheld;[10] into a contract between a 'pop group' and their personal manager, that the latter would not do anything which he could reasonably foresee would destroy the mutual confidence which was required to exist between them;[11] into a contract to provide a package holiday that reasonable care and skill would be used in rendering the services which the tour operator had contracted to provided, whether these were carried out by the tour organizer or others;[12] into a contract for driving lessons that the vehicle provided would be covered by insurance;[13] into a contract of agency that the principal would not deprive the agent of his commission by committing a breach of the contract between himself and a purchaser which released the purchaser from his obligation to pay the purchase price;[14] into insurance contracts between underwriters and insureds that documents previously shown to the underwriters by the insureds' brokers, and in the possession of the brokers, should be made available to the underwriters;[15] into a contract between architects and a construction company that the architects would carry out their design work in such time as would enable the company to complete its contract with its client;[16] into a towage contract that the tug would proceed with all reasonable despatch;[17] into a contract of sale of goods, where defective goods had been returned to the seller for repair, that the seller would inform the buyer of the nature of the defect and what had been done to repair it;[18] into contracts between landowners and developers that one party had to tell the other that a Town and Country Planning Act 1990 s. 106 agreement could not be obtained[19] or that

---

〔8〕 Tappenden v Artus (1964) 2 QB 185 先例。

〔9〕 Banco de Portugal v Waterlow & Sons Ltd (1932) AC 452 先例。

〔10〕 Addison v Brown (1954) 1 WLR 779 先例。

〔11〕 Page One Records Ltd v Britton (1968) 1 WLR 157 先例; Denmark Productions Ltd v Boscobel Productions Ltd (1969) 1 QB 699 先例。

〔12〕 Wong Mee Wan v Kwan Kin Travel Services (1996) 1 WLR 38 先例。

〔13〕 British School of Motoring Ltd v Simms (1971) 1 All ER 317 先例。

〔14〕 Alpha Trading Ltd v Dunshaw - Patten Ltd (1981) 1 Lloyd's Rep 122 先例。

〔15〕 Goshawk Dedicated Ltd v Tyser & Co Ltd (2006) 1 Lloyd's Rep 566 先例。

〔16〕 CFW Architects v Cowlin Construction Ltd (2006) EWHC 6 (TCC) 先例。

〔17〕 Ease Faith Ltd v Leonis Marine Management Ltd (2006) 1 Lloyd's Rep 673 先例。

〔18〕 J C Ritchie Ltd v Lloyd Ltd (2006) UKHL 9 先例。

〔19〕 Yewbelle Ltd v London Green Developments Ltd (2007) EWCA Civ 475 先例。

the landowner was not free to sell the property while the agreement was in force[20];into a mooring contract, an obligation to take reasonable care to see that the layerage was safe[21]; into an estate agent's contract that, in order to earn its commission, the agent had to be the effective cause of the purchase[22]; into a construction contract that, where one party had paid money to the other in compliance with a decision of an adjudicator, that party was entitled to have the dispute finally determined by legal proceedings and, if the dispute was finally resolved in its favour, to have the money repaid to it[23]; into a letter of credit transaction that the issuing bank was obliged to act in accordance with the disposal statement in its art. 16 UCP notice[24]; into a contract of guarantee that the creditor would provide a Lloyd's decision within a reasonable time frame form the receipt of a notice of dispute.[25]"

笔者不分别介绍这些根据 The "Moorcock"先例带来的大量先例,只简单介绍三个重要与被经常提到的先例:Reigate v Union Manufacturing (1918) 1 KB 592; Shirlaw v. Southern Foundries (1926) Ltd (1939) 2 K. B. 206 与 Philips Electronique Grand Public DA & Anor v British Sky Broadcasting Ltd (1995) EMLR 472。

4.3　另一个事实默示考验之"好事第三人"先例:Reigate v. Union Manufacturing 与 Shirlaw v. Southern Foundries (1926) Ltd

Reigate v Union Manufacturing (1918) 1 KB 592 先例涉及"商业代理人"(commercial agent),案情涉及 Reigate 先生被 Union Manufacturing 有限公司委任为英国与英国殖民地的独家代理,并可以在他招揽到的生意中赚取佣金,Reigate 先生同时也入资该公司。该独家代理合约为期 7 年并在 7 年后自动延期,但任何一方可以给 6 个月通知终止该代理合约。之后该公司经营困难并要求 Reigate 先生增加入资,在被拒绝后,公司自动清盘,而最终该公司被出售。事后 Reigate 先生起诉该公司并指控被告违反该 7 年的合约并索赔损失。上诉庭的 Scrutton 大法官针对该代理合约的明示条文表达的意思是:"Turning to this contract, what have the parties expressed? In consideration of the plaintiff (Reigate 先生) investing £ 1,000 in the capital of the company the company appoint him as their sole agent for the sale of certain goods for seven years, payment to be by a commission on goods delivered on his orders and paid for; and the company are to accept and execute all orders sent by the plaintiff unless they have rea-

---

[20] Berkeley Community Villages Ltd v pullen (2007) EWHC 1130 (Ch)先例。

[21] George v Coastal Marine 2004 Ltd (2009) 2 Lloyd's Rep 356 先例。

[22] MSM Consulting Ltd v Republic of Tanzania (2009) EWHC 232 (QB)先例。但 Glentree Estates Ltd v Favermead Ltd (2010) EWCA Civ 1473 先例有相反的判决。

[23] Jim Ennis Construction Ltd v Premier Asphalt Ltd (2009) EWHC 1906 (TCC) 先例。

[24] Fortis Bank SA/NV v Indian Overseas Bank (2010) 2 Lloyd's Rep 641 先例。

[25] Ostfriesische Volksbank EG v Fortis Bank (2010) EWHC 361 (Comm) 先例。

sonable grounds for refusal."

但是否有一个默示条文要求被告 Union Manufacturing 的有限公司继续经营7年让该代理合约持续有效,Scrutton 大法官不同意作出默示说:"Is that a necessary implication? If this matter had been mooted at the time when the contract was being negotiated, I expect that the parties would at once have disagreed as to what the position was. Unless we are satisfied that it is an implication which must necessarily have been in the minds of both parties, we cannot imply a term which they have not expressed, especially when I see that they have thought sufficiently about the matter to express two conditions on which the agreement is to be determined, first, the obvious one on the death of the agent; and, secondly, by six months' notice after the expiration of the seven years."(如果这一问题在双方谈判时被带出来,Scrutton 大法官估计他们会不同意在怎样的情况下可让被告的有限公司终止营运。法院不能在双方没有明示条文的情况下默示条文,特别是考虑到双方应该在谈判时已经想到两种情况可以导致代理合约的终止,一是 Reigate 先生的死亡,二是7年后通过6个月的通知终止合约。)

上诉庭最后也是判被告违约/毁约,因为他没有钱履行并通过自动清盘令合约被终止。

这个先例重要的是 Scrutton 大法官讲了以下一段话说:"These principles, however, have been clearly established: The first thing is to see what the parties have expressed in the contract; and then an implied term is not to be added because the Court thinks it would have been reasonable to have inserted it in the contract. A term can only be implied if it is necessary in the business sense to give efficacy to the contract; that is, if it is such a term that it can confidently be said that if at the time the contract was being negotiated some one had said to the parties, 'What will happen in such a case,' they would both have replied, 'Of course, so and so will happen; we did not trouble to say that; it is too clear.' Unless the Court comes to some such conclusion as that, it ought not to imply a term which the parties themselves have not expressed."

这一段话被视为是带来了事实默示的另一个考验,也就是"好事第三人考验"(officious bystander test),这被视为与 The "Moorcock"的考验并不相同:The "Manifest Lipkowy"(1989) 2 Lloyd's Rep 138 先例。至于好事第三人的名称,倒是在另一个 Shirlaw v. Southern Foundries (1926) Ltd (1939) 2 K. B. 206 先例被提出来。该先例是一个公司与其常务董事之间的一个10年雇佣合约,签约3年后公司被收购,新的母公司重写了其公司章程,使其有权解雇任何董事。上诉庭多数判是这一10年的雇佣合约内有默示条文该公司不能事后改变公司章程以影响或改变该合约。上诉庭的 Mackinnon 大法官说:"I recognize that the right or duty of a Court to find the existence of an implied term or implied terms in a written contract is a matter to be exercised with care; and a Court is too often invited to do so upon vague and uncertain grounds. Too often also such an invitation is backed by the citation of a sentence or two from the judgment of Bowen L. J. in The Moorcock. ... For my part, I think that there is a test that may be at least as useful as such generalities. If I may quote from an essay which I wrote some years ago, I then said: '*Prima facie* that which in any contract is left to be implied and need not be expressed is something so obvious that it goes without saying; so that, if, while the parties were making their bargain, **an officious bystander** were to suggest some express provision for it in their agreement, they would testily suppress him with a common 'Oh, of course!' 'At least it is true, I think, that, if a term were never implied by a judge unless it could pass that test, he could not be held to be wrong."(加黑部分是笔者的强调)

4.4 默示条文必须满足五个条件的先例:BP Refinery v. Shire of Hastings

在 Philips Electronique Grand Public DA & Anor v. British Sky Broadcasting Ltd (1995) EMLR 472 先例,案情涉及著名的飞利浦(Philips Electronique Grand Public DA)与 British Satellite Broadcasting(简称 BSB)订立合约,为 BSB 提供 D-MAC 标准的卫星信号接收器。但 BSB 在市场份额竞争不过使用 PAL 标准的 Sky(英国的天空卫星电视),并在之后为了减少损失,被迫与 Sky 合并。合并之后的 British Sky Broadcasting 使用的是 PAL 标准,并在过渡期把在使用 D-MAC 标准的客户转使用 PAL 标准,这导致飞利浦指控 BSB 违反它们之间的生产与供应 D-MAC 标准的卫星信号接收器合约。在该十分详尽的合约,有明示条文针对如果 BSB 违约要求其他制造商提供卫星信号接收器,就会要赔偿飞利浦。但没有条文针对 BSB 如果这一业务或宏图大计出了大问题最后被迫要与 Sky 合并的情况,也没有要求 BSB 作出明示承诺购买一定数目的 D-MAC 标准的卫星信号接收器。这表示飞利浦要胜诉,就必须先要求法院作出一些默示条文。飞利浦提出的是该合约英国有 6 条默示条文,如下:

"(1) the defendant would do nothing of its own motion which would, or might, have the effect of frustrating the commercial purpose of the Agreement;(被告不可以它的行为导致合约的商业目的受阻)

(2) the defendant would do nothing of its own motion which would, or might, have the effect of putting an end to and/or changing the circumstances under which the Agreement would be and remain operative;(被告不可以它的行为令合约的履行终止或情况改变)

(3) the defendant would not commit any act which would tend to impede or render impossible the marketing of the Receivers and/or to render the Receivers useless or unmarketable;(被告不可以做任何事情导致妨碍或不能在市场销售接收器)

(4) the defendant would use its best endeavours to continue to broadcast by direct satellite a service which would be receivable by members of the general public in the U-

nited Kingdom by means of the receiving equipment manufactured by the plaintiffs until 31 December 1992 and for a reasonable period thereafter;(被告应尽最大的努力继续广播并通过使用原告生产与提供的接收器,直到 1992 年 12 月 31 日[合约终止的时间]与之后的一段合理时间)

(5) the defendant would do nothing of its own motion which would, or might, have the effect of causing it to cease or curtail the broadcasting by direct satellite of a service which would be receivable by members of the general public in the United Kingdom by means of the receiving equipment manufactured and supplied by the plaintiffs until 31 December 1992 and for a reasonable period thereafter;(被告不可以它的行为导致原告生产的接收器停止或减少被公众使用的后果)

(6) the defendant would not, alternatively would not without the prior approval of theplaintiffs, make any announcement prior to 31 December 1992, nor for a reasonable period thereafter, that it would, or alternatively might, cease or curtail its broadcast by direct satellite of a service receivable by members of the general public in the United Kingdom by means of the receiving equipment manufactured and supplied by the plaintiffs."(被告要在 1992 年 12 月 31 日前向英国公众宣布它将停止或减少使用原告生产的接收器,就必须事先取得原告的批准)

看来这 6 个默示条文或保证有很大程度的重复,但反正最后是被法院拒绝作出默示,也表示飞利浦败诉。上诉庭的 Bingham 认为如果在双方订约时,有好事第三人向他们提出 BSB 的宏图大计如果出大问题,合约加上明示条文针对这一大问题会有怎样的结果。可以估计,双方对怎样分摊这一个风险会有很多不同看法,也会谈出很多不同结果,反正飞利浦会希望分担越少风险越好,但 BSB 也不会愿意承担过多的风险。这样,就根本很难作出默示。

至于飞利浦提出的 6 条默示条文,Bingham 大法官认为第 1 条与第 2 条太广泛(默示应该尽量狭窄),而且估计双方在谈判时特别是 BSB 不会接受。至于第 3 条默示条文,Bingham 大法官怀疑 BSB 会否愿意这么早就放弃经营的自由。至于第 4 条与第 5 条,基本上是同意默示,Bingham 大法官认为对飞利浦没有价值,因为 BSB 实际上在与 Sky 合并后的过渡期还是继续以 D - MAC 标准广播。最后第 6 条涉及欺骗大众也因为不合理与不公平作出默示,也谈不上是商业效力所必须。

上诉庭的 Bingham 大法官引用了 Simon 勋爵在 BP Refinery (Westernport) Pty Ltd v the President, Councillors and Ratepayers of Shire of Hastings (1978) 52 ALJR 20 的枢密院先例中所讲的对事实默示的五个条件,说:"Their Lordships do not think it necessary to review exhaustively the authorities on the implication of a term in a contract which the parties have not thought fit to express. In their view, for a term to be implied, the following conditions (which may overlap) must be satisfied: (1) it must be reasonable and equitable; (2) it must be necessary to give business efficacy to the contract, so that no term will be implied if the contract is effective without it;（3）it must be so obvious that ‘it goes without saying’;（4）it must be capable of clear expression;（5）it must not contradict any express term of the contract.”[这五个条件是:(i)合理与公平;(ii)合约的商业效力所必须,如果缺少此条文合约仍能运作,则不会默示;(iii)在订约时可以假设双方会理所当然或异口同声地同意这个说法;(iv)可以被清楚地表达;(v)不能与合约明示条文起冲突。]

这五个条件会分别在接下的段节做进一步的介绍。

4.4.1　事实默示条件之一:默示的条文一定要合理

默示条文必须客观合理可见 Reid 勋爵在 Young and Marten Ltd v. McManus Childs Ltd（1969）1 A. C. 454 先例中说的:“No warranty ought to be implied in a contract unless it is in all the circumstances reasonable.”

另是 Salmon 勋爵在 Liverpool City Council v Irwin（1977）AC 239 先例说:“... unless a warranty or term is in all the circumstances reasonable there can be no question of implying it into a contract, but before it is implied much else besides is necessary...”

Simon 勋爵在 BP Refinery（Westernport）Pty Ltd v the President, Councillors and Ratepayers of Shire of Hastings（1978）52 ALJR 20 先例中也说,默示条文的第一个条件就是必须合理与公平。

最后可节录的是 Hoffmann 勋爵在 Attorney General of Belize v Belize Telecom Ltd（2009）2 All ER 1127 先例中的说法:“... it is not enough for a court to consider that the implied term expresses what it would have been reasonable for the parties to agree to. It must be satisfied that it is what the contract actually means.”

针对事实的默示,合理性可以分两个方面:一是先解释有关合约的明示条文看是否有需要作出默示条文。二是在认定了需要默示,被默示的条文本身与加了默示条文后的结果必须合理,正如 Beazer Homes Ltd v County Council of Durham（2010）EWCA Civ 1175 先例中说的“The implication of an unreasonable term is of course impossible”。毕竟,这是假设双方在谈判时的订约意图,如果有被双方遗漏了的事情,但有一位好事第三人提出,显然需要对双方都十分合情合理才会异口同声地接受。不合理的条文(主要是对其中一方不利)当然经常出现,但这只局限在明示条文。而在约定这种不合理条文的过程中,也可以想得到双方会经历过艰苦的谈判而最终其中一方作出让步,或是由于心急达成协议,也或是谈判水平与知识差劲以致签了“卖身契”也不自知等原因,这是法律管不了。

“合理”一词在默示条文时经常出现,无论是在合约履约时间没有明示就会有“合理时间”(reasonable time)履行承诺的默示,还是合约对货物价格没有明示而要以“合理价格”(*quantum meruit* price)的默示。

但仅是合理与否并不足够作出默示,所以法官与仲裁员经常要警觉,不要为了把一个有缺陷的合约变为更好、更合理与更平衡作出默示。

这是笔者认为经常引起误解的地方,特别是对英国法律不了解的人士。他们一遇上对其不利、不明朗或不希望发生的情况,而且没有明示条文针对时,就想求助默示条文,理由是他们认为这样做才合理。但这是完全说不通的,且不说他们认为的合理通常只是主观上的合理,更重要的是默示其实是相当严格的,因为这一做法是与"订约自由"(freedom of contract)与"合约的相互关系"(privity of contract)起严重的冲突。法院/仲裁庭并不是合约的一方,他们只是解释该合约中产生的争议,所以无权增加或删除该合约明示了的条文。而增加默示条文正是做这种有严重冲突的行为,除非是完全符合法律的严格要求,而其中就是能够肯定假设默示的部分正是双方订约的意图。正如 Steyn 大法官在 The "Damodar General T. J. Park" (1986) 2 Lloyd's Rep. 68 先例中所说的:"It is not permissible to imply a term simply because the court considers it to be reasonable. To do so would amount to be a process of rewriting contracts."

除了合理是不足以默示,另在 Shirlaw v. Southern Foundries (1926) Ltd (1939) 2 K. B. 206 先例,McKinnon 大法官也提到法院经常以不肯定与含糊的理由被要求作出默示(... a Court is too often invited to do so upon vague and uncertain grounds),这显然是法院/仲裁庭需要抗拒的。

早在 Re Comptoir Commercial Anversois and Power Son and Co (1920) 1 KB 868 先例,Scrutton 大法官就已经说到合理不足够作出默示并举了一种情况说:"The Court... ought not to imply a term merely because it would be a reasonable term to include if the parties had thought about the matter, or because one party, if he had thought about the matter, would not have made the contract unless the term was included; it must be such a necessary term that both parties must have intended that it should be a term of the contract, and have only not expressed it because its necessity was so obvious that it was taken for granted."(不能法院认为合理就作出默示,因为会有情况是其中合约一方如果在订约时确实有考虑这一看来是合约的漏洞,他会拒绝签订这一份合约。)

也是在同样的理由下,默示是有潜在的危险干预双方订约自由,在订约双方或其中一方选择不在订约时加入明示条文针对,但法院或仲裁庭却事后作出默示。Bingham 大法官在 Philips Electronique Grand Public S. A. v. British Sky Broadcasting Ltd (1995) E. M. L. R. 472 先例中在这一点说得很清楚:"The court's usual role in contractual interpretation is, by resolving ambiguities or reconciling apparent inconsistencies, to attribute the true meaning to the language in which the parties have themselves expressed their contract. The implication of contract terms involves a different and altogether more ambitious undertaking: the interpolation of terms to deal with matters which, *ex hypothesi*, the parties themselves have made no provision. It is because the implication of terms is so potentially intrusive that the law imposes strict constraints on the excise of this extraordinary power ... "

Scrutton 大法官更早在 Reigate v. Union Manufacturing Co（Ramsbottom）Ltd（1918）1 K. B. 592, CA 先例说："The first thing is to see that the parties have expressed in the contract; and then an implied term is not to be added because the court thinks that it would have been reasonable to have inserted it."（首先看订约双方有否在合约中的明示，之后才考虑是否默示。但不该只因为法院认为这样做合理，就增加默示条文。）

另在 Liverpool City Council v. Irwin（1977）A. C. 239 先例，Edmund – Davies 勋爵也有说："The touchstone is always necessary and not merely reasonableness."

4.4.2 事实默示条件之二：合约有商业效力所必须

这也是作出默示条文的其中一个最主要的条件，即"商业效力"与"必须性"的要求。"商业效力"（business efficacy）一词应该来自 Bowen 大法官 The "Moorcock"（1889）14 P. D. 64 先例，说："In business transactions such as this, what the law desires to effect by the implication is to give such business efficacy to the transaction as must have been intended at all events by both parties who are businessmen . . ."

至于"必须性"（necessity 或 necessary），Wilberforce 勋爵在 Liverpool City Council v. Irwin（1977）A. C. 239 先例说："In my opinion such obligation should be read into the contract as the nature of the contract itself implicitly requires, no more or less: a test, in other words of necessity."（作出默示是必须，而默示条文应该不多不少，也就是要尽量狭窄。）

另 Steyn 勋爵在 National Commercial Bank Jamaica Ltd v Guyana Refrigerators Ltd（1998）53WLR 229 先例中的说法："The implication put forward is not one that can be implied by law; it is not an incident to be annexed by law to a standardized contract. It is a term implied in fact; if it is sustainable, it must be derived from the particular terms of the special instructions. It is not enough that such an implied term would be a reasonable and sensible one. The touchstone requires no citation of authority; it is always strict necessity."（事实默示与法律默示不一样，针对的不是一份标准格式合约，而是根据特定的合约作出默示。仅是合情合理并不足够，而是必须严格需要。）

Steyn 勋爵在 Equitable Life Assurance Society v. Hyman（2002）1 A. C. 408 先例中也说了同样一句话："The legal test of the implication of such a term is a standard of strict necessity."（标准是严格必须才能默示）

有关"必须"的标准是严格或是合理，特别是事实的默示与法律的默示是否在标准方面有所不同，会稍后另段详及。

关于这个条件或考验的评论，可见 Scrutton 大法官在 Reigate v. Union Manufacturing Co（1918）1 K. B. 592 先例所说的："A term can only be implied if it is necessary in a business sense to give efficacy to the contract; that is, if it is such a term that it can be confidently said that if at the time the contract was being negotiated someone had said to the parties ‘What will happen in such a case?’, they would have replied: ‘Of course, so and so will happen; we did not trouble to say that; it is too clear.’”

从上述 Scrutton 大法官的话中可看出,要默示一条条文似乎要同时满足“商业效力的必须”与“好事第三人”这两个考验。

另是 Denning 勋爵在 Shell UK Ltd v. Lostock Garage Ltd (1976) 1 W. L. R. 1187 先例中也有同样的说法:“Such an imputation is only to be made when it is necessary to imply a term to give efficacy to the contract and make it a workable agreement in such manner as the parties would clearly have done if they had applied their mind to the contingency which has arisen. These are the ‘officious bystander’ type of case.”(只有在必须这样做才能令有关的合约有效力并且可以履行,并且只要双方在订约时曾经考虑到如果出现这种变数,他们明显会是这样约定的情况下,才应该作出默示。这是一个“好事第三人”的考验。)

但看来现在的法律地位发展趋势是只要其中一个考验得以满足,就可以默示。笔者在本章较早的4.3段已经提到这两个考验不完全相同。这方面在下一小段先介绍了“好事第三人”的条件或考验后才详及,这里只节录 Bingham 大法官在 The “Manifest Lipkowy” (1989) 2 Lloyd's Rep. 138 中说的:“I take it to be well - established law that a term will be implied only where it is necessary in a business sense to give efficacy to a contract, or where the term is one which the parties must obviously have intended.”(法律已经十分明确,默示条文只适用在一种必须给一个合约有商业效力,或是双方订约时明显有这一意图。)

4.4.3 事实默示条件之三:订约时可以假设双方理所当然或异口同声地同意这个说法

已经在4.3段提到这一“好事第三人”(officious bystander)考验在 Reigate v Union Manufacturing (1918) 1 KB 592 先例先提出,但正式登场是在 Shirlaw v. Southern Foundries (1926) Ltd (1939) 2 K. B. 206, CA 先例。McKinnon 大法官是说:“*Prima facie* that which in any contract is left to be implied and need not be expressed is something so obvious that it goes without saying; so that, if, while the parties were making their bargain, an officious bystander were to suggest some express provision for it in their agreement, they would testily suppress him with a common ‘Oh, of course’.”

“好事第三人”的考验只适用在事实的默示而不适用在法律的默示,因为前者才需要假设双方都会在订约时异口同声地同意。但对这一考验也有不少批评。

4.4.3.1 批评之一:问题怎样设计会影响答案

这一考验本身也受过不少批评,这也可以理解。毕竟,假设订约双方会否异口同声同意好事第三人的问题很大程度依赖问的是什么问题。这一批评可节录 Aicken 大法官在澳大利亚的 Codelfa Construction Pty Ltd v State Rail Authority of New South Wales 先例中说:“The first problem is that the manner in which the officious bystander formulates his question will often determine the answer which the parties give ... One may formulate another query – must the officious bystander be satisfied with the first response or may he pose a second question, and if not, why not?"

好像 The "Moorcock" (1889) 14 P. D. 64 先例,假设如果有一位第三人问订约双方的问题是:"码头所有人了解他的码头状况,是否他应该承担码头的安全,毕竟船东对该码头一无所知?"看来订约双方异口同声同意的机会就颇大。但假设问题改为:"如果河道浅会有危险导致船舶搁浅会受损,码头所有人是否保证安全?"(undertaken to see that the bottom of the river is reasonably fit, or at all events that they have taken reasonable care to find out that the bottom of the river is reasonably fit for the purpose....),Treitel 教授相信订约双方不会异口同声说"是",至少码头所有人不大可能这样说。再假设问题是:"是否码头所有人应该承担码头的安全,不论是否有过错或疏忽,都要绝对/严格负责船舶安全与作出损失赔偿,不论这个损失多大?"看来更加可以相信订约双方,特别是码头所有人,不会异口同声同意。估计最有可能会发生好像在 Bank of Nova Scotia v. Hellenic Mutual War Risks Association (Bermuda) Ltd (1989) 2 Lloyd's Rep. 238 先例,得到的答案是"需要问过律师才能回答",这带来的后果就是不能作出事实的默示条文。

在 Spring v National Amalgamated Stevedores and Docker Society (1956) 1 WLR 585 先例,涉及被告的公会声称原告作为会员,应该有默示条文允许公会与其他组织订立合约与会员将会受到公会合法与恰当订立的合约约束。案例涉及一个名为 Bridlington 协议,管制会员从一个公会转另一个公会。Leonard Stone 大法官针对是否作出被告所说的默示条文适用了好事第三人考验,说:"If that test were to be applied to the facts of the present case and the bystander had asked the plaintiff at the time he paid his five shillings and signed the acceptance form, 'Won't you put into it some reference to the Bridlington Agreement?', I think (indeed, I have no doubt) the plaintiff would have answered 'What's that?' In my judgment, that is sufficient to dispose of this case... "(如果原告在支付 5 先令加入公会的时候被好事第三人问,你是否需要针对 Bridlington 协议? 法官认为原告会毫无疑问回答说:"这是什么东西?"这一答案就足够否定作出默示条文。)

但这一判决受到批评,认为这样问可以说只会有这一个答案。如果问题设计比较中立,如问原告作为公会会员是否应受到合法并恰当的协议约束,答案就会不一样。而且,Hoffmann 勋爵稍后在 Attorney General of Belize v Belize Telecom Ltd (2009) 2 All ER 1127 先例有说是合约方如果要求好事第三人进一步解释他的问题,这是完全正常,说:"In such circumstances, the fact that the actual parties might have said to the officious bystander 'Could you please explain that again?' does not matter."

所以在《The Interpretation of Contract》(第 5 版,2011 年)一书的第 301 页认为 Spring v National Amalgamated Stevedores and Docker Society 先例判错,说:"it is considered that Spring v National Amalgamated Stevedores and Docker Society would not be decided in the same way today."

总结而言,如果设计的问题十分中立,估计会得到双方一个满意的答案支持作出默示条文就机会大。相反,如果设计的问题比较针对一方面或有敌意,得到满意的答案机会就低多了。所以,设计问题要十分有技巧,这通常是由申请增加默示条文的一方当事人先提出建议。

4.4.3.2 批评之二:问题越复杂就越难假设订约双方会简单同意

另一个批评是假设的问题如果越复杂,就越不容易得到订约双方异口同声的同意。本来要主张默示的当事人设计一个或多个适合的问题已经不容易,因为要在问题内满足合理性与必须性并在同时令对方无法坚持订约时不会同意,才可以说服法院/仲裁庭作出默示。在 Ashmore v. Lloyd's (1992) 2 Lloyd's Rep. 620 先例,案情涉及英国劳合社在20世纪80年代所出的经济问题,即许多加入"劳合社"(Lloyd's)作为会员面对大量索赔(其中是来自美国的"石棉"[asbestos]索赔)而面临破产,因为他们根据当时的英国传统是要个人承担无限责任。这些面临困境的会员部分起诉劳合社,指称它没有好好监督负责承保的"保险小组"(syndicates)管理代理人。但由于双方的合约(包括在劳合社章程与申请表格)没有相关的明示条文,起诉的会员必须依赖默示条文,其中包括像劳合社对有关的风险有责任预先警告会员与监督保险小组管理代理人。而他们律师所设计的问题有两条。第一个问题是:"... if at the [劳合社] meeting to admit a new Member, an officious bystander had interrupted the proceedings and said, 'You Lloyd's are asking this applicant underwriting member to engage in a high risk business and, in effect, entrust his entire personal fortune to an underwriting agent approved by you with whom he is not to interfere, and whom you know he relies on and is by the system you impose forced to rely on: [Question] what if something professionally discreditable is or becomes known to Lloyd's about the underwriting agent which might prejudice the member's underwriting interests, other than matters which in Lloyd's reasonable opinion are not capable of being seriously prejudicial to the member's underwriting interests, would you Lloyd's be obliged to take reasonable steps to alert the applicant, if thought necessary, in confidence, and tell the underwriting agent within a reasonable time thereafter what you have done?"

第二个问题是:"Alternatively, the question (within the same introduction) would be ... what if something professionally discreditable is or becomes known to Lloyd's about the underwriting agent, in the following categories: (a) any disciplinary measures concluded against the underwriting agent or any of its officers or employees; (b) the findings of an investigation resulting in any such disciplinary measures; or (c) an embargo imposed by Lloyd's on new Names joining the syndicate or syndicates of the underwriting agent due to a lack of confidence in the abilities of the underwriting agent or its staff, which might prejudice the members' underwriting interests, other than matters which in Lloyd's reasonable opinion are not capable of being seriously prejudicial to the members' underwriting interests, would you Lloyd's be obliged to take reasonable steps to alert the applicant, if thought necessary, in confidence, and tell the underwriting agent within a reasonable time thereafter what you have done?"

Gatehouse 大法官认为问题过于复杂,就算双方能马上回答,答案也不会是一个简单的"同意"(Oh, of course),他说:

"To start with, I find it impossible to contemplate an officious bystander at the [劳合社] being capable of think up so complex a question; one which has taken a team of skilled lawyers so long and so many attempts to formulate. Even if he could, the answer of both parties would certainly not be, 'Oh, of course! That is something that is so obvious that it goes without saying'.(劳合社的好事第三人不会想得出这么复杂的问题,这些问题是由一群高水平的律师用很长时间设计出来,答案也不会是一个简单的同意。)...

Themore complicated the question, the less obvious it becomes.(越复杂的问题也就变得更加不明显,可假设为双方会简单地同意。)

In summary, the original way in which the implied 'duty to alert' was pleaded was too wide to be reasonable, let alone a matter of necessary. This was recognized by the Plaintiffs' Counsel and successive attempts were made to overcome these difficulties. These inevitably made the term progressively more complex and less likely to satisfy the simpleofficious bystander test. There is no possibility of both parties answering the question posed (assuming the bystander could construct it) with an immediate, 'Yes of course, that is so obvious that it goes without saying."(总结而言,所谓的默示要求劳合社有责任作出警告是太广泛而变得不合理,更加谈不上必须。)

问题太过复杂也带来了另一个可能的后果,就是答案先要问他的律师,这在稍早的4.4.3.1段的 Bank of Nova Scotia v. Hellenic Mutual War Risks Association (Bermuda) Ltd (1989) 2 Lloyd's Rep. 238 先例已经提到。

4.4.3.3　批评之三:问题可否一直问

另一个批评是,如果第一个问题回答得不满意,能否再问下?如果不能,为什么不能?如果能,迟早会有一个问题是双方合约方都不会抗拒或不同意。在 Little v. Courage Ltd (1994) 70 P. & C. R. 469, CA 先例,上诉庭认为订约双方对好事第三人的问题的第一反应可能是你不必问这种傻问题,但法院也说到"好事第三人"不仅仅要"好事",也要有耐心继续问。

这里涉及一种技巧就是问题或一连串问题可以精心设计,进而掌握到会有什么答案。这本来就是民意调查的惯常手法,在诉讼就涉及精明的律师作出设计了。

大概也是上述的原因,虽然"好事第三人"的考验还存在,但看来这并非一个简单的考验,而且会严格。可能更多的默示条文是以较早介绍的另一个稍有不同的考验,即"商业效力"(business efficacy)需要作出默示令合约能够顺利履行或运行。特别是现在有说法放宽,如在 Equitable Life Assurance Society v. Hyman (2002) 1 A. C. 408 先例,Steyn 勋爵指默示实质上是为了给予"双方合理期望效果"(The implication is essential to give effect to the reasonable expectations of the parties)。看来他的侧重点已经不是以默示条文"填补个别合约漏洞"(*ad hoc* gap filler)而让合约顺利履行,而是能否按照双方合理期望来运行。这带来了另一个问题,就是默示的"必须性"是否要同时通过"商业效力"与"好事第三人"两个考验,或只要其中一个。这会在下一段探讨。

4.4.3.4 默示条文是否要同时满足"商业效力"与"好事第三人"两个考验?

增加默示条文就必须通过两个条件或考验,一是"商业效力"(business efficacy)的考验,二是"好事第三人"(officious bystander)的考验。在 Bank of Nova Scotia v. Hellenic Mutual War Risks Association (Bermuda) Ltd (1989) 2 Lloyd's Rep. 238 先例,案情涉及船东为了节省高昂的战争险加保费而不在进入战争险的波斯湾前根据保单的要求告知战争保险人(在该先例是一个战争险互保协会),这导致船东在船舶被战争险摧毁得不到赔偿而影响作出融资的银行。该先例涉及银行指控战争互保协会与他们之间的合约关系(主要是互保协会向银行作出的一封保函)虽然没有明示条文,但有默示条文或责任要求互保协会提前警告银行这种船东不诚实的行为会影响银行的担保。上诉庭说"好事第三人"与"商业效力"是同一个考验:"it is necessary to be clear upon what basis Hobhouse J. (一审大法官) proceeded. The first was by implicit requirement from the nature of the contract. The second was based upon the proposition that the parties if asked by the officious bystander would have responded that it was obvious 'that the club should notify the bank.' The second basis, which Hobhouse J. applied by way of confirmation of the first, is that also known as 'business efficacy'..."

但近期有更多说法是这两个考验其实并不一样,也不需要同时通过两个考验才能够默示。在 Associated Japanese Bank (International) Ltd v. Credit du Nord S. A. (1989) 1 W. L. R. 255 先例,Steyn 勋爵对这两种默示的情况有更详细的分析说:"In the present contract such a condition may only be held to be implied **if one of two** applicable tests is satisfied. The first is that such an implication is necessary to give business efficacy to the relevant contract ... In other words, the criterion is whether the implication is necessary to render the contract ... workable. That is usually described as the *Moorcock* test.... But there is another type of implication, which seems more appropriate in the present context. It is possible to imply a term if the court is satisfied that reasonable men, faced with the suggested term which was *ex hopothesi* not expressed in the contract, would without hesitation say: yes, of course, that is 'so obvious that it goes without saying'.... Although broader in scope than the *Moorcock* test, it is nevertheless a stringent test, and it will only be permissible to hold that an implication has been established on this basis in comparatively rare cases ..."

还有 Bingham 大法官在 The "Manifest Lipkowy" (1989) 2 Lloyd's Rep. 138 先例中说的:"I take it to be well – established law that a term will be implied only where it is necessary in a business sense to give efficacy to a contract, or where the term is one which the parties must obviously have intended."(法律已经十分明确,默示条文只适用在一种必须的情况,给一个合约商业上的效力,或是双方订约时明显有这一意图。)

另在 Ashmore v. Lloyd's (1992) 2 Lloyd's Rep. 620 先例,高院的 Gatehouse 大法官明确了这是两种不同的考验,虽然它们经常重叠。而有不少增加默示条文的案件是根据其中一个考验,说:"The first two tests (这就是指'商业效力'的第一个考验与'好事第三人'的第二个考验) will often overlap and, indeed, have in the past been regarded as single test embodying both aspects. See, for example, Lord Tucker's speech in *Lister* at page 594. But they are in fact distinct tests with the result that **a term may sometimes be implied on the basis of one but not the other.** A striking example is the decision of Mr. Justice Steyn in (The "Damodar General T. J. Park" [1986] 2 Lloyd's Rep. 68). Whichever of the ... tests the Court is considering, **implication is a matter of necessity**, and the necessity test is a stringent one."(加黑部分是笔者的强调)

4.4.4 事实默示条件之四:默示条文必须能够清楚地表达

这个条件其实与上一个条件有重复或类似的地方,如果不能清楚地表达,也就谈不上订约双方可被假设异口同声地同意与接受了:R. v. Paddington and St Marylebone Rent Tribunal Ex p. Bedrock Investments Ltd (1974) K. B. 984 先例。在 Shell UK Ltd v. Lostock Garage Ltd (1976) 1 W. L. R. 1187 先例,就是由于默示条文过于含糊,不能清楚表达而被拒绝。另在 Sethia (K. C.) (1944) Ltd v. Partabmull Rameshwar (1950) 1 All E. R. 51 先例,Jenkins 大法官也有类似说法。

在一方主张一条默示条文时,要注意不要有太多可选择的默示条文,选择余地越大,越不明显是理所当然:Trollope & Colls Ltd v. North Western Metropolitan Regional Hospital Board (1973) 1 W. L. R. 601 先例。在《The Interpretation of Contracts》(第5版,2011 年)一书第302 页也说:"In asserting the existence of an implied term, it is also important not to argue for a wide variety of alternative implications. The more possibilities there are, the less anyone of them is obvious."

类似在 Philips Electronique Grand Public S. A. v. British Sky Broadcasting Ltd (1995) E. M. L. R. 472 先例,Bingham 大法官说:"And it is not enough to show that had the parties foreseen the eventuality which in fact occurred they would have wished to make provision for it, unless it can also be shown either that there was only one contractual solution or that one of several possible solutions would without doubt have been preferred."

在 Chantry Estates (South East) Ltd v Anderson (2008) EWHC 2457 (Ch)先例, Morgan 大法官说:"The court is not here to re – write the contract and select from an a la carte menu of possibilities the one which the court thinks might have been more even-handed for the parties to have agreed."

先介绍贵族院的 Trollope & Colls v North West 先例,涉及工程合约的延误与延长。十分粗略的案情是工程分几个阶段,但后来的第三个阶段并没有明示条文针对第一阶段的延误,而第一阶段涉及"允许延误"(permissible delay)与"不允许延误"(non – permissible delay),并且双方有争议发生的延误到底是否允许。由于没有明示条文,承建商主张默示。表面看来公道,但问题是作出怎样的默示条文。这里会有四五个选择,如只默示第一阶段的允许延误(即使双方有争议)在第三阶段延长工程完工日期,或是默示第一阶段的所有延误都可以延长,或是双方应该仲裁并认定允许延误后延长这一段时间。最终被贵族院判是太不明显,所以无法作出默示。其中 Cross 勋爵说:"There is something to be said for and against each of these possible ways of dealing with the problem and one cannot say that the parties had they directed their minds to the question would, as reasonable people, at once have agreed that one of the ways was obviously the right way. If they had reached agreement on this point at all it would probably only have been after a process of negotiation in which the pros and cons of the various possibilities were canvassed in detail."

Cross 勋爵也说到在有太多选择的情况下,法院不应该平衡并找出最公平的方法重写该合约条文:"Moreover if, **contrary to my opinion**, it is for the court in a case such as this to select what it considers to be on balance the fairest way of re – writing this clause..."

另一个例子是笔者熟悉的海事案例 The "Badagry" (1985) 1 Lloyd's Rep. 395。案情有关一个 8 年的期租,约定的租金相比出事时的市场高得多。所以,船东千方百计保持这个值钱的期租合约,因为出事到租约期届满还有 4 年之久。船舶出的事故是该船舶在一个航次中发生火灾,结果船舶被拖去巴西的里约热内卢。由于损坏太大,船舶被保险人接受为"推定全损"(constructive total loss),而船东递交给保险人的"弃船通知"(notice of abandonment)是在 1977 年 10 月 13 日。双方没有争议的是在该天之后,由于"Badagry"轮已经确定全损,正常情况下租约应该在这个时间或更早在发生火灾的时间已是"受阻"(frustration)。但已经提到过船东想保持这个期租,做法就是以另一艘同类型的船舶作为替代船舶。原因在于,租约第 33 条文赋予了船东选择权,条文如下:"Owners have the option to substitute the vessel with a similar vessel type/size during the period of this charter – party."

该先例主要是针对租约受阻并自动终止,就不存在船东还可以行使第 33 条文的选择权。但该租约还有另一条条文是 3(d),针对船舶如果发生推定全损,租金停付,说:“... If the vessel should become a constructive total loss hire shall cease at the time of the casualty resulting in such loss...”

这看来是一条停租条文,显示在船舶推定全损后,后果只是停租。这带来船东对默示条文的请求,就是停租后总会有重新支付租金的一天。但问题是,如果默示船东还是有选择权指定一艘替代船舶,根据第3(d)条文说明租金在推定全损事故后停付,而船东可以在两三个月后以另一艘“Bonny”轮作为替代船舶,租金怎么计算?如何重新开始(迟至12月1日[替代船舶能够交船的一天]或较早的合理时间内替代)?在哪里交船给承租人(船东说“Bonny”轮在里约热内卢交船,但到了12月1日,承租人几乎肯定不会有货物在那里待装,进而不会想在该港交船)等?注意是这些问题全部没有在第3(d)条文有针对,都要依赖默示条文,并假设这许多不同的可能性都是订约双方的意图。上诉庭拒绝作出默示,其中Lloyd大法官说:

“For if cl. 33 had been intended to apply in the case of a total loss as well as a partial loss, there would surely have been some cross – reference to cl. 3 (d), so as to provide for the recommencement of hire. I use the word “recommencement” rather than “resumption”, in order to underline the contrast between cl. 3 (d) and the off hire clause.

Mr. Boyd(船东代表大律师)argued that a term as to the recommencement of hire can be implied; he conceded there might be some dispute as to what that term should be, but he said that that dispute could be resolved without difficulty by any commercial arbitrator.

I cannot accept that solution. Before a term can be implied in a commercial contract, it must not only be necessary that a term should be implied in order to give the contract business efficacy; but the term to be implied must also be capable of being defined with reasonable precision. Since it is impossible to say with any precision at all what term should be implied in the case of a total loss, I am driven to the conclusion that the parties never did intend cl. 33 to apply to such a case.”

4.4.5 事实默示条件之五:默示条文不能与明示条文起冲突

默示条文是假设双方的订约意图,如果双方在合约里已经有明示条文针对,这假设不能成立,因为明示条文代表了双方真正的订约意图。笔者可在几方面谈谈这一重要的事实默示条件:(1)默示条文不能与明示条文起冲突,即明示超越默示;(2)进一步,就是已经有明示条文针对某一方面“内容”(subject matter),就不应该作出默示条文,即使不会与明示条文起冲突;(3)一个越详尽与全面的合约就应该避免作出默示条文;(4)双方在谈判时已经涉及但没有谈拢的条文是应该作出默示。

就第一个方面详尽的评论可见Parker大法官在Tamplin (F. A.) Steamship Co Ltd v. Anglo – Mexican Petroleum Products Co Ltd (1916) 2 A. C. 387先例所说的:“It is, of course, impossible to imply in a contract any term or condition inconsistent with its express provisions, or with the intention of the parties as gathered from those provisions. The first thing, therefore, in every case is to compare the term or condition which it is sought to imply with the express provisions of the contract, and with the intention of the parties as gathered from those provisions, and ascertain whether there is any inconsistency."

另可介绍 Evershed 大法官在 Lynch v. Thorne (1956) 1 W. L. R. 303 先例中所说的:"... a term *prima facie* to be implied must, according to well established principle, always yield to the express letter of the bargain."

另有 Steyn 勋爵在 Equitable Life Assurance Society v. Hyman (2002) 1 A. C. 408 先例中说的:"This principle is sparingly and cautiously used and may never be employed to imply a term in conflict with the express terms of the text."

在 Johnson v Unisys Ltd (2003) 1 AC 518 先例,Hoffmann 勋爵说:"... any terms which the courts imply into a contract must be consistent with the express terms. Implied terms may supplement the express terms of the contract but cannot contradict them. Only Parliament may actually override what the parties have agreed."

在 Anders & Kern UK Ltd v CGU Insurance Plc (2008) 2 All ER (Comm) 1185 先例,Toulson 大法官说:"you cannot imply a term which contradicts an expressed term, because the parties cannot have intended that."

在 Autoclenz Ltd v Belcher (2009) EWCA Civ 1046 先例,Aikens 大法官说:"Once it is established that the written terms of the contract were agreed, it is not possible to imply terms into a contract that are inconsistent with its express terms. The only way it can be argued that a contract contains a term which is inconsistent with one of its express terms is to allege that the written terms do not accurately reflect the true agreement of the parties."

进一步,就是合约内已经有明示条文针对某一方面"内容"(subject matter),法院/仲裁庭就不会就相关内容作出默示,即使这默示条文并不会与明示约定实际上起冲突。这道理也很容易理解,就是法院/仲裁庭不能通过默示使合约变得更好或更平衡。毕竟双方如果已经针对了某方面的内容,即使客观看来还是有遗漏,明示条文也很可能代表他们关于这个内容所能同意的订约意图。在 Broome v. Pardess Co-operative Society of Orange Growers (Est. 1900) Ltd (1940) 1 All E. R. 603 先例,Mackinnon 大法官说:"Where the parties have made an express provision as regards some matter with regard to the contract, it is, and must be, extremely difficult for either of them to say in regard to that subject-matter, as to which there is an express provision, that there is also an implied provision or condition in the contract."

另是 Coulson 大法官在 Persimmon Homes (South Coast) Ltd v Hall Aggregates (South Coast) Ltd (2008) EWHC 2379 (TCC)先例中说:"An express term in a contract excludes the possibility of implying any term dealing with the same subject - matter as the express term."

这可以带来另一个说法,一个非常详尽与包罗万有的合约,如一些大型合作协议,就应该尽量避免作出默示。因为明示条文没有直接或间接地涉及的"内容"(subject matter)恐怕不会太多,甚至没有。这些详尽的合约,很可能有多条明示条文针对有争议的一方面内容,往往把所有这些条文合并起来解释就可以找出双方订约的真正意图,这样就不应该再增加任何默示条文假设他们的订约意图。这方面的说法有不少先例,如一个合约看上去是双方谈判结果有了全面体现,真正的明示订约意图就越加明显:Duke of Westminster v. Guild (1985) Q. B. 688;Broome v. Pardess Co - operative Society of Orange Growers (Est. 1900) Ltd (1940) 1 All E. R. 603;Philips Electronique Grand Public S. A. v. British Sky Broadcasting Ltd (1995) E. M. L. R. 472, CA 等先例。

另 Mason 大法官在 Codelfa Construction Pty Ltd v. State Rail Authority of New South Wales (1982) 149 C. L. R. 337 先例也有说:"For obvious reasons the courts are slow to imply a term. In many cases, what the parties have actually agreed upon represents the totality of their willingness to agree; each may be prepared to take his chance in relation to an eventuality for which no provision is made. **The more detailed and comprehensive the contract the less ground there is for supposing that the parties have failed to address their minds to the question at issue.**"(加黑是笔者的强调)

反之,如果一份合约明显不完整,法院/仲裁庭就比较愿意来填补漏洞令合约可以"有效"(efficacy)与"可行"(workable):Liverpool City Council v. Irwin (1977) A. C. 239 先例。

最后探讨的情况就是如果订约双方在合约谈判中明确拒绝部分内容,会否对默示条文有影响呢? 答案应该是明显,这种情况在今天根据 Investors Compensation Scheme v. West Bromwich Building Society (1998) 1 W. L. R. 896 先例可以披露"口头证据"(parol evidence)的大环境下,显然不能作出默示与假设订约双方有这样的订约意图,因为证据显示了他们在谈判中根本没有。

§5 默示类别之三:惯例/商业习惯做法/过往行为的默示

5.1 惯例/商业习惯做法

这种默示条文与较早介绍的法律的默示与事实的默示不一样,可称为第三种但也是次要与较少见的默示。它是针对一些主要"惯例"(custom)或"商业上习惯做法"(trade usage)达致两方面的目的:一是协助解释合约内的明示条文(这表示习惯做法/惯例是背景/语境[factual matrix]的一部分);二是增加默示条文。惯例或商业上习惯做法通常被视为一码事,但如果要区分,可以说前者是针对地点,而后者针对商业做法。

惯例/商业习惯做法带来的默示条文,特别在商业合约,已经有很悠久的历史。这可节录 Parker B 大法官在 Hutton v Warren (1836) 1 M. & W. 466 先例说:"It has long been settled, that, in commercial transactions, extrinsic evidence of custom and usage is admissible to annex incidents to written contracts, in matters with respect to which they are silent. The same rule has also been applied to contracts in other transactions of life, in which known usages have been established and prevailed; and this has been done upon the principle of presumption that, in such transactions, the parties did not mean to express in writing the whole of the contract by which they intended to be bound, but a contract with reference to those known usages."

对国际外贸与航运人士所熟悉的"提单"(bill of lading),其中一个最重要的作用作为"物权凭证"(document of title),就是通过一个古老的英国先例 Lickbarrow v Mason (1782) 2 T. R. 63 承认在地中海港口进行的货物买卖的商业上习惯做法。

至于惯例/商业习惯做法的默示的案件肯定相比法律的默示与事实的默示在数量上无法相提并论,但还是会遇到,甚至也有说法是有不少。例如,Lloyd 勋爵在 Baker v Black Sea & Baltic General Insurance Co Ltd (1998) 1 WLR 974 先例中说:"it is very common in mercantile contracts, where there is an established market usage, to add a term to an otherwise complete bilateral contract, on the grounds that it is what the parties would unhesitatingly have agreed. This was indeed the fabric out of which much of the modern commercial law was created in the 18th and early 19th centuries."

但也有说法是比较少成功,这可节录 Staughton 大法官在 The "Litsion Pride" (1985) 1 Lloyd's 437 先例中说:"It is rare in modern times to find that a contract is varied or enlarged by custom."

可以肯定的就是证明惯例/商业习惯做法并被法院/仲裁庭接受与作出相关的默示条文非常不容易,这要严格满足一些条件,会在接下的段节介绍。

这种默示条文会对一个合约内明示条文的解释带来极大冲击,甚至会作出与合约明示条文显示的订约意图完全不一样的结论,必须严格对待。这可见 Produce Oil Brokers Co Ltd v. Olympia Oil and Cake Ltd (1917) 1 K. B. 320 先例所说的:"The contract construed without the custom will be different from what it is if construed with the custom, and in that sense every admission of custom varies the written contract."

举例在 Smith v. Wilson (1832) 3 B & Ad 728 先例,涉及的是合约明示了价格是"60 英镑每一千只兔子"。但法院接受在有关地方(英国的 Suffolk)的惯例是把"一千"(thousand)视为 1200。

另一个例子是 The "Eurus" (1998) 1 Lloyd's Rep 351 先例,案情涉及一艘油轮尼日利亚装 32,000 吨原油。该船舶估计在 1992 年 1 月 31 日凌晨抵达装港并可递交“通知书”(notice of readiness)。但早在1月23日,承租人知道2月份的油价比1月份的油价低,需要取得2月份的提单,因为对他作为FOB买家有利。承租人命令船长不要在1月31日11时之前递交通知书给发货人/炼油厂。承租人这个命令在接下去几天不停被重复,可见对承租人是一件十分重要的事。船舶在1月31日0时30分抵达装港并马上挂靠装货泊位并在6时36分开始装货。承租人发觉后,想尽办法减低装货速度,最后货物是在2月1日1时30分装完。从这些事实看来,船长可签发2月份的提单应该理所当然,但承租人与船东都不知道在尼日利亚的习惯做法是要到2月1日8时后装完原油才会签发2月份的提单,在这个时间之前仍是签发1月份的提单。结果这就带来了差价达70万美元的争议。只说法院接受了尼日利亚港口的这一惯例。

5.2 能够被接受为惯例/商业习惯做法的条件

这方面权威的说法可先节录《Chitty on Contracts》(第31版,2012年)一书之13-019段,如下:“If there is an invariable, certain and general usage or custom of any particular trade or place, the law will imply on the part of one who contracts or employs another to contract for him upon a matter to which such usage or custom has reference a promise for the benefit of the other party in conformity with such usage or custom; provided there is **no inconsistency** between the usage and the terms of the contract. To be binding, however, the usage must be **notorious**, **certain** and **reasonable**, and **not contrary to law**; and it must also be something more than a mere trade practice. But when such usage is proved, it will form the basis of the contract between the parties.”(加黑部分是笔者的强调)

在Fox-Bourne v. Vernon & Co. Ltd. (1894) 10 T. L. R. 647的早期先例的说法是:“... a uniform practice so well defined and recognised that contracting parties must be assumed to have had it in their minds when they contracted.”(一个非常明确与受到承认的习惯的做法,可以假设订约双方在订约时就有这些惯例/习惯做法在他们的脑海中。)

在比较近期的先例Danowski v Henry Moore Foundantion (1996) CLY 1282先例,上诉庭的Nourse大法官依据《Chitty on Contracts》一书说:“To be binding, however, the usage must be notorious, certain and reasonable, and not contrary to law; and it must also be something more than a mere trade practice.”

在更近期的Durham v BAI (Run Off) Ltd (2009) 2 All ER 26先例,Burton大法官说:“I must be astute to ensure that such usage as is alleged and relied upon: (i) existed at the date of the relevant contract; (ii) does not contradict the terms of the contract or clause; (iii) is certain, notorious and universal; (iv) is binding, in the sense that it is not simply a usage which parties choose from time to time to follow.”

最后要节录的是一个澳大利亚的先例Con-Stan Industries of Australia Pty Ltd v

Norwich Winterthur Insurance (Australia) Ltd (1986) 160 CLR 226,最高院在考虑了普通法国家的权威先例后作出以下总结,说:"(1) The existence of a custom or usage that will justify the implication of a term into a contract is a question of fact... (2) There must be evidence that the matters relied on are so well known and acquiesced in that everyone making a contract in the situation can reasonably be presumed to have imported a term embodying them into the contract... (3) A term will not be implied into a contract on the basis of custom where it is contrary to the express terms of the agreement... (4) A person may be bound by a custom notwithstanding the fact that he had no knowledge of it. Historically the courts approached this question in a rather different way. It was said that, as a general rule, a person who was ignorant of the existence of a custom or usage was not bound by it. To this rule there was a qualification that a person would be presumed to know of the usage if it was of such notoriety that all persons dealing in that sphere could easily ascertain the nature and content of the custom. It would then be reasonable to impute that knowledge to a person, notwithstanding his ignorance of it: see Halsbury's Laws of England, 4th ed. vol. 12, pars. 467 – 468; Jones v. Canavan. In this way, the issue of notoriety discussed in (2) above came to be co – extensive with the question of imputed knowledge. The achievement of sufficient notoriety was both a necessary and sufficient condition for knowledge of a custom to be attributed to a person who was in fact unaware of it. The result is that in modern times nothing turns on the presence or absence of actual knowledge of the custom; that matter will stand or fall with the resolution of the issue of the degree of notoriety which the custom has achieved."

总结以上权威说法,可以说能够被英国法律接受为惯例/商业习惯做法,就需要满足如下条件:(1)"肯定"(certain);(2)"出名"(notorious);(3)"合理"(reasonable);(4)"普及"(universal)而不是部分人士随意遵从与否的一些做法,甚至"一贯做法"(practice)也不足够成立为习惯做法;(5)惯例/商业习惯做法在订合约的一天就已经存在;(6)不得与明示条文有直接冲突;(7)即使是不知道惯例/商业习惯做法也受到约束;(8)合法。

上述的条件会有重叠,如肯定与普及。如果有一个惯例/商业习惯做法是部分业内人士遵从,但另一部分的业内人士不遵从甚至有其他很不同的做法,这样就很难说有一个肯定的习惯做法,也更加谈不上普及。而出名这一条件又会是与合约方即使不知道惯例/商业习惯做法也受到约束有重叠之处。至于合理这一条件也会不得与明示条文有直接冲突与合法有重叠之处,因为很简单,如果与明示条文有直接冲突或不合法,就不可能是合理。以下的段节针对上述的一些条件进一步探讨。

5.2.1 条件之一:肯定与普及

对惯例/商业习惯做法的肯定性的要求可见 Mance 大法官在 Roar Marine v. Bimeh Iran Insurance (1998) 1 Lloyd's Rep. 423, QBD 先例中所说的:"For there to be any relevance in custom or practice, whether in a strict or informal sense, it must be possible to identify the particular custom or practice with certainty."

该先例的案情可作出介绍,让大家更明白这个说法。涉及一艘船舶名为"Daylan",船东与受让人(贷款银行)向一些在世界各地的保险公司索赔其各自承保的百分比。该船舶主机的曲轴发生损坏/破裂而需要修理。船壳保险虽然涉及多家保险公司,但带头承保的是劳合社一个保险小组(Syndicate 724)。修理后该带头保险人接受事故是出自船员疏忽的受保风险,并对他所承保的部分作出赔偿。但其余的保险公司拒付,虽然保单有一条文说明是"跟从带头保险人"(follow the leader clause),如下:"It is agreed with or without previous notice to follow leading British underwriters in regard to ... settlements in respect of claims ... [the follow the leader clause]."(本书第六章之1.3.2.1段 The "Leegas" (1987) 1 Lloyd's Rep 471 先例有大同小异的案情)

这样,船东与受让人在英国法院起诉这些保险公司,并认为保单有这种条文下,后者在带头保险人已经作出赔付的情况下就没有可争议的,所以向法院申请"简易判决"(summary judgement)。这些拒赔的保险公司的主要抗辩之一是声称伦敦市场有一个习惯做法,即使有这一种条文的保单,每一个保险公司还是可以个别质疑索赔,即使带头保险人已经作出赔付。至于证据方面,代表这些保险公司的业务律师Dowling 先生与几位保险公司与劳合社人士查问后作出了一个"宣誓书"(affidavit),其中内容可小部分节录如下:

"4. Most parties stated that they considered an obligation to follow only in relation to legitimate claims. They were adamant that co – insurers would not pay a claim if they had serious doubts as to the validity of the claim, and that in practice in such a situation assureds, through their brokers, habitually treat the co – insurers as entitled to proof of the validity of the claim, independent of the leader's decision on it. I was advised that the only situation in which the decision of a leader underwriter would be treated as final and binding was where urgent temporary repairs were carried out. On the other hand, some stated that it was their view that an obligation to follow was a strict obligation which applied in all circumstances.

5. I was advised that it was not unusual for following underwriters to demand further evidence, information or documents relating to a claim in order to satisfy themselves that the claim was validly made. When such a demand is made, the follower is invariably given the further information and documents requested and makes his own decision as to settlement. The following underwriter will, of course, be under considerable commercial pressure to settle a claim which has been settled by a lead underwriter, so as to avoid gaining a reputation as a difficult underwriter. Nevertheless the advice I received was that, in a case where there was a genuine concern as to the legitimacy of a claim, the follower

would refuse to follow.

6. Additionally, it was maintained that, in order for a leader underwriter's evaluation of a claim to be considered satisfactory, the leader would have to have made a proper investigation of the claim in which all contemporaneous records and documents relating to the claim were examined and the claim itself was supported by expert advice. It was not considered acceptable for a leader underwriter simply to rely on an adjustment document. Any refusal or prevarication on the part of an insured to produce documents and evidence would be viewed with a good deal of suspicion and would increase the likelihood of the follower refusing to follow."

这一宣誓书的证据大受 Mance 大法官的批评,并指出即使是接受 Dowling 先生的说法,他自己也在第 4 段承认是伦敦市场在这一方面没有肯定的习惯做法,只不过是部分的保险人士是一个做法,而另一部分人士是另一个做法。而即使是有大部分保险人的做法是如 Dowling 先生所讲,这也不足够构成习惯做法可令保单的"follow the leader clause"根据他们的做法作出与字面相异的解释。Mance 大法官是这样说:

"Here, Mr. Dowling himself acknowledges at the end of paragraph 4 (and in the comment made through Counsel about 'both sides of the debate') that there is no such certain or identifiable custom or practice. If 60, 70, 80 or even 90 per cent. of the market behave in one way, but 40, 30,20 or only 10 per cent. of the market behave in another, there is still no reason to assume that any particular contract is to be read in the way in which the former group behaves, rather than the latter. Even in a case (unlike the present, in my view) where the wording of a particular clause could, respectably, be interpreted in alternative ways, the proper interpretation cannot be determined by majority vote. The mere fact that the behaviour or attitude of one group of market practitioners may have been tolerated does not mean that it is right, particularly when there is a significant, even though minority, group viewing the position and acting differently.

In all these circumstances, the contention that there is any legally binding custom or practice which could affect the construction of the present 'follow the leader' clause is hopeless. The contention that there is any relevant market behaviours or attitude which could in any way shape the proper construction is equally untenable."

换言之,惯例/商业习惯做法不被接受,因为伦敦市场的保险人/保险公司对跟从带头保险人的做法并不一致,换言之无法明确一种做法是肯定与普及。这样就不被接受可改变保单中的跟从带头保险人的明示条文的解释。

再举另外一个有关石油买卖的先例:The "Mathraki"(1990) 2 Lloyd's Rep. 84。案情有关装在"Mathraki"轮的一批北海石油,涉及 31 个买卖合约链,其中夹在当中的是该先例的原告(Vitol)与被告(Phibro Energy)。他们之间根据标准条文 Inco Term 1980 其中有一条要求原告作为卖方给买方至少 3 个工作天的指定通知:"Sellers to give to buyers minimum 3 working days' notice of nomination together with vessels demurrage rates"

Vitol 在 1987 年 11 月 10 日(周二)16 时 58 分(伦敦时间)收到上一个卖方(Marc Rich)的指定通知后,就马上转给下一个买方 Phibro Energy,后者是在同一天的 18 时 3 0 分(瑞士时间)收到该电传。但后者随即拒绝该错误通知,认为已经太晚,并非是至少 3 个工作天。至于他为什么这样做,很大可能就是市场下跌。但如果该指定通知是将 11 月 10 日也算作一天,因为作出通知时还没有过子夜,其实算到最后交货日是足 3 个工作天,Phibro Energy 无权拒绝。但 Phibro Energy 声称指定通知是在第二天的 11 月 11 日上午 9 时才收到,从该天起算 3 个工作天就不足了,令 Phibro Energy 有权拒绝。

按理说,根据明确的先例是"一天的部分也算是一天"(the rule that part of a day is to be treated as a day)。这可看笔者的《装卸时间与滞期费》一书第十二章第 3 段,特别是 Devlin 勋爵在 Vancouver Strikes Cases (1963) 1 Lloyd's Rep. 12 先例的说法中就包括了上一句话。这里也可看本书第五章之 6.2.3 段。所以,仅看 Inco Term 1980 有关条文的写法,Phibro Energy 应该无权拒绝该买卖合约,因为 11 月 10 日也算一天,子夜还没有过。但 Phibro Energy 说是在该北海石油的市场有一个习惯做法是在任何一个工作天,只算到 17 时为止,因为之后大家已经下班。但根据双方提供的专家意见证据,说法各异并有证据显示在市场中通常有指定通知晚过 17 时,毕竟这是涉及广泛地区的石油商的行业。

这样,Evans 大法官判是有太多与太不肯定的不同意见,无法显示有一个习惯性的做法在该行业可作出默示条文。他说:"The mere existence of these divergent opinions enabled the plaintiffs to submit that there could not be, given the difference of opinion among independent expert witnesses, any such uniform practice or usage of the trade as could give rise to the alleged implied terms."

5.2.2　条件之二:出名与订约时不知道也会受到约束

这一条件完全可以理解,因为如果一个惯例/商业习惯做法不是出名的,就无法合理假设双方在订约时脑海中有这样的惯例/商业习惯做法。没有足够程度的出名,就有可能一方或双方都不知道有这种所谓习惯做法。正如较早曾介绍的澳大利亚的先例 Con – Stan Industries of Australia Pty Ltd v Norwich Winterthur Insurance (Australia) Ltd (1986) 160 CLR 226,最高院的判词中提到必须十分出名才能假设合约方订约时知道有这种惯例/商业习惯做法(that a person would be presumed to know of the usage if it was of such notoriety that all persons dealing in that sphere could easily ascertain the nature and content of the custom)。最高院也提到说惯例/商业习惯出名的程度也决定了是否假设其中合约一方受到约束,即使他真正不知道(the achievement of sufficient notoriety was both a necessary and sufficient condition for knowledge of a custom to be attributed to a person who was in fact unaware of it)。

目前的英国法律也是同样地位,如果惯例/商业习惯做法能够成立,也表示有足够的出名,即使双方订约时实际上有一方(因为是水平低或无知等原因)并不知悉,仍要受其约束。这可见 Ungoed – Thomas 大法官在 Cunliffe – Owen v. Teather & Greenwood (1967) 1 W. L. R. 1421 先例中所说的:"A party to a contract is bound by usages applicable to it as certain, notorious and reasonable, although not known to him. If the practice, though certain and notorious is unreasonable, it of course follows that it cannot constitute a usage which the court will enforce as a usage. Nevertheless if a party knows of such a practice and agrees to it, then though unreasonable, he is bound by it ..."

请注意上述先例中节录的最后一句是说到,如果双方在订约时有证明知道一些不合理的惯例/商业习惯做法(如其中一方在谈判时告诉另一方有这种习惯做法),这样他还是同意订约,就会受到约束。看来,这可能是唯一一种例外情况惯例/商业习惯做法,即使不合理仍是适用。

最后要注意的是,订约双方如果不是有关商业领域的从业人员,很难假设他们在订约时脑海中已经想到有关的惯例/商业习惯做法,也会在这种比较罕见的情况下不适用:Holt & Co v. Collyear (1881) 16 Ch D 718, Ch D 先例。

5.2.3 条件之三:合理

惯例/商业习惯做法的合理性包括了商业习惯不能不合理,毕竟所有类别的默示条文都必须合理,不合理的只能是一些明确无误的明示条文,这是双方的订约自由,法院/仲裁庭管不到。但在上一小段也提到了一种十分例外的情况,就是双方在谈判时被对方告知一些不合理的习惯做法,但仍接受就会受到约束,但这是接近明示条文而不是默示条文的领域,可能更适合的救济是"合约变更"(rectification)。

合理与否可分几方面来看,如针对一些基本的法律大原则与相比订约双方已经同意了的明示条文。以下探讨。

5.2.3.1 基本法律大原则或规则下不合理

在 Anglo – African Merchants Ltd v. Baylay (1970) 1 Q. B. 311, QBD 先例与 North and South Trust Co v. Berkeley (1971) 1 W. L. R. 470, CA 先例,案情有关劳合社市场的经纪人的做法,他们的身份是作为被保险人的代理人劳合社市场寻找愿意承保的"保险小组"(syndicates)。但后来劳合社市场发展出来一种习惯做法,就是如果出了事故,这些经纪人也代保险小组调查有关的保险索赔是否在承保范围内,这就导致他们手中有一些有关的报告如"检查报告"(survey report)。在有关的两个先例,经纪人拒绝把这些报告披露给被保险人,虽然后者是前者的"委托人"(principal)。这种劳合社市场的习惯做法被判是不合理,与"代理人的基本法律"(law of agency)大原则背道而驰,涉及在同一时间为两个有利益冲突的雇主服务。Megaw 大法官在 Anglo – African Merchants Ltd v. Baylay 先例说:"Even if it were established to be a practice well known to persons seeking insurance—not merely to insurers and brokers—I should hold the view, in conformity with the passage which I have cited from *Bowstead*（这是一本权威书籍有关代理人法律）, *that a custom will not be upheld by the courts of this country if it contradicts the vital principle that an agent may not at the same time serve two masters—two principals—in actual or potential opposition to one another: unless, he has the explicit, informed, consent of both principals.*"

在后一个先例，Donaldson 大法官同意 Megaw 大法官的说法，认为这种商业做法"完全不合理"（wholly unreasonable），不能成为惯例/商业习惯做法。

另一个先例是 London Export Corp Ltd v. Jubilee Coffee Roasting Co Ltd（1958）1 Lloyd's Rep. 197，有关一个商会仲裁（Incorporated Oil Seed Association）的惯例。该商会仲裁有两个层面，先是由 2 位当事人委任的仲裁员审理，他们如果不同意，就由一位"公断人"（umpire）作出决定。第二个层面是上诉，上诉由一个上诉委员会决定。在该案例中，争议由第一层面的公断人裁决后，被上诉至上诉委员会。但原先的公断人也是上诉委员会的一份子，一并裁决，说是该商会的习惯做法。这样，违反了该商会仲裁规则，说明是不准第一层面审理的公断人参与上诉。而且，这也在一定程度上违反了自然公正。所以，高院与上诉庭判是该商会仲裁的这种习惯做法不合理。

5.2.3.2 合约明示条文或架构下不合理

在 Humfrey v. Dale（1917）1 K.B. 320，DC 先例中有说明要把此惯例/商业习惯做法当作合约条文来看待是需要不会非理性并且与合约其他明示条文不起冲突才能被默示："To fall within the exception, therefore of repugnancy, the incident must be such as if expressed in the written contract would make it insensible or inconsistent."

为了更好表达，笔者又要比较详尽地介绍一个先例，这是 Kum and Another v. Wah Tat Bank Ltd.（1971）1 Lloyd's Rep. 439。这一先例是唯一一个承认大副收据可以有提单作用的先例，依据的就是在该有关航次中的商业习惯做法。案情是有一票货物（橡胶）从马来西亚沙捞越去新加坡的短航线，总共签发了好几份大副收据。这些大副收据被用作"质押"（pledge）向一家沙捞越的银行融资。但之后发生了无单放货（无单是指大副收据，因为根本没有提单签发），银行就在新加坡法院向船东起诉，指称船东"侵占了他的货物"（conversion of goods），这一案例最终上诉到英国枢密院。其中一个争议是沙捞越往返新加坡的班轮航线的习惯做法是只签发大副收据，根本没有提单，所以大副收据可被视为"物权凭证"（document of title）。但这在高院被拒绝，说："... no amount of customs as that described in this case can change the character of this document so as to confer any additional rights and thus make the mate's receipt equivalent to documents of title. A local custom however strong can never achieved this effect."

但这在上诉后被推翻并接受这一在沙捞越往返新加坡航线中的习惯做法。证据显示了沙捞越去新加坡所运载的货物有 90% ~95% 只签发大副收据，而新加坡去沙捞越是大约 75% ~80%。至于会签发提单的，可能是一些要转运的货物，如从新加坡转运到其他港口/国家的国际运输。枢密院认为,证据显示这一商业习惯做法足够肯定,做法上也没有不合理,可以把大副收据视为“物权凭证”(document of title),毕竟这只是一份文件的称呼/名字而已。Devlin 勋爵认为商业人士可以有自由怎样做,没有要求他们必须严格使用某一种表格,普通法并不是官僚主义:“The function of commercial law is to allow, so far as it can, commercial men to do business in the way in which they want to do it and not to require them to stick to forms that they may think to be outmoded. The common law is not bureaucratic.”

但在该先例无法把该大副收据视为物权凭证反而是因为在大副收据上印上了“不能转让”(non – negotiable)一词,Devlin 勋爵认为这样有了明示的印章,惯例/商业习惯做法就必须靠边站了,他说:“There are well established rules of construction which permit the Court to disregard printed words when they are inconsistent with written words or with the paramount object which the document appears from its language to be designed to achieve. But these rules can be used only when there is conflict between one part of the document and another or between the effect of a part and the effect of the whole. They are rules for reconciling different expressions in or of the document itself. They cannot be used to introduce into the document, either by implication or by force of custom, what is outside it. The rule is plain and clear that inconsistency with the document defeats the custom. If this document had ‘Negotiable’ printed in the right hand corner and ‘not negotiable’ in the left, the argument could begin. But if the right – hand corner is blank, custom cannot be used to fill it. Whichever way the argument for the respondents is put, it amounts in the end to a submission that the force of custom should expel from the document words that are on it: this is not permissible by law.”

顺便一提的是,在本章稍早的 5.2.1 段提到的 Roar Marine v. Bimeh Iran Insurance (1998) 1 Lloyd’s Rep. 423, QBD 先例,看来也是与明示条文的跟从带头保险人条文有冲突。但在该先例,被告的保险公司是以英国保险市场的惯例/商业习惯做法作为外来证据协助“解释合约”(construction of contract),希望回避这一不得与明示条文起冲突的条件。这一方面也不被 Mance 大法官接受,说:“I consider that the defendants’ primary case on construction also fails for a further reason. **The defendants are in reality seeking not to construe but to contradict the wording of the ‘follow the leader’ clause. That is illegitimate in the context of custom and practice in the strict legal sense.** It is a fortiori impermissible in so far as they seek to rely on the weaker conception of a suggested matrix of usual attitudes or behaviour. The only matrix of any real relevance in the material before me is, in my view, to be found in the obvious commercial purpose of the clause in simplifying administration and claims settlement. The defendants’ construction undermines that purpose to a very fundamental extent.”(加黑部分是笔者的强调)

5.3 过往行为的默示

过往行为的默示往往出现在合约双方有口头合约的情况下，如果双方之前已经有过好几次交易，并且双方曾经交换过一些文件是包含了一些条文，法院/仲裁庭就可能会根据双方过往的行为作出默示有同样效力的条文。

在 Hollier v Rambler Motors (AMC) Ltd (1972) 2 QB 71 先例，原告 Hollier 先生打电话给被告的车房，并与被告车房的经理探讨汽车漏油需要修理的问题。被告车房的经理表示如果原告能将汽车送到车房，被告可以进行修理。双方在电话中没有提到其他方面，更谈不上达成任何协议。之后汽车被送到了被告车房，但由于被告的疏忽，汽车被烧毁。原告提出索赔损失，并指被告作为托管人疏忽与没有小心谨慎的责任，这被第一审法院支持。但被告试图依赖在它的标准条文中的一条免责条文。显然在这一次的修理，被告没有与原告谈过标准条文的议题。但在双方过往的 5 年交往，曾经有好几次的汽车维修，其中估计有两次原告甚至签了一份发票的文件，而发票是印上了车房的标准条文。上诉庭的 Salmon 大法官判是双方过往的交易太少，不足够让他作出默示，说："Mr. Tuckey（被告证人）says that there was a course of dealing which constituted the three or four occasions over five years - that is, on an average, not quite one dealing a year - from which it is to be implied that what he called 'the condition' at the bottom of the contract should be imported into the oral agreement made in the middle of March 1970. I am bound to say that, for my part, I do not know of any other case in which it has been decided or even argued that a term could be implied into an oral contract on the strength of a course of dealing (if it can be so called) which consisted at the most of three or four transactions over a period of five years."

这方面也可以节录《Chitty on Contracts》（第 31 版，2012 年）一书之 13 - 023 段说："**When implied from previous course of dealing.** It is, however, clear that a term may be implied in any given case from the circumstances of the parties having consistently on former and similar occasions adopted a particular course of dealing. Thus, a covenant to pay interest or to allow interest to be added to principal at stated periods and to pay interest on the whole, has been held to be implied form the fact that on former occasions the accounts between the parties have been stated and settled on that footing.[26] And it has been held that an oral contract between the buyer and seller of goods incorporated by a long course of dealing conditions printed on the back of 'sold notes' as condi-

〔26〕 Calton v Bragg (1812) 15 East 223; Bruce v Hunter (1813) 3 Camp 467; Newal v Jones (1830) 1 Moo. & M. 449; Re. Lloyd Edwards (1891) 65 L. T. 453; Re Marquisof Anglesey (1901) 2 Ch. 548 等先例。

tions of sale, in so far as a condition was appropriate to the oral contract.[27]"

§6 法律的默示与事实的默示对"必须性"的不同要求

法律曾经十分明确,即任何默示条文在必须的情况下才给予,正如 Edmund – Davies 勋爵在 Liverpool City Council v. Irwin (1977) A. C. 239, HL 先例中说:"The touchstone is always necessity and not merely reasonableness."

但近年来涉及"事实的默示"(implied in fact)与"法律的默示"(implied by law)对"必须性"的要求程度有不同,所以需要另段探讨。在事实的默示对"必须性"的要求是严格应明确,在本章之4.4.2 段已经提到 Steyn 勋爵在 National Commercial Bank Jamaica Ltd v Guyana Refrigerators Ltd (1998) 53WLR 229 先例与 Equitable Life Assurance Society v. Hyman (2002) 1 A. C. 408 先例都说事实默示必须"严格必须"(strict necessity)。

在必须性的要求下,也带来另一个说法就是作出默示要尽量狭窄,正如 Wilberforce 勋爵在 Liverpool City Council v. Irwin 先例也说:"In my opinion such obligation should be read into the contract as the nature of the contract itself implicitly requires, **no more or less**: a test, in other words of necessity."(作出默示是必须,而默示条文应该不多不少,也就是要尽量狭窄。)

另 Lightman 大法官在 Robin Ray v Classic FM (1998) F. S. R. 622 先例说:"In short a **minimalist approach** is called for. An implication may only be made if this is necessary, and then **only of what is necessary and no more.**"(加黑部分是笔者的强调)

这可以解释贵族院在拒绝对房东作出有一个对出租的多层大厦的公众地方维修保养的"绝对责任"(absolute obligation)的默示,而只肯默示有一个合理的责任,并改变了上诉庭的判决。

但 Liverpool City Council v. Irwin 先例涉及法律的默示,现在有很多说法是法律的默示对"必须"的要求不能太严格,因为在许多情况下做不到,所以应该有更多的

---

〔27〕 J. Spurling Ltd v Bradshaw (1956) 1 WLR 461; Cockerton v Naviera Aznar SA (1960) 2 Lloyd's Rep 451; McCutcheon v David MacBrayne Ltd (1964) 1 WLR 125, HL; Henry kendall& Sons v William Lillico & Sons Ltd (1969) 2 AC 31; Transmotors Ltd v Robertson Buckley & Co Ltd (1970) 1 Lloyd's Rep 224; Hollier v Rambler Motors (AMC) Ltd (1972) 2 QB 71; Eastman Chemical International A. G. v N. M. T. Trading Ltd (1972) 2 Lloyd's Rep 25; Roberts v Elwells Engineers Ltd (1972) 2 QB 586; Gillespie Bros & Co Ltd v Roy Bowles Transport Ltd (1973) QB 400; S. I. A. T. di del Ferro v Tradax Overseas SA (1980) 1 Lloyd's Rep 659; F. R. Lurssen Werft GmbH & Co KG v Halle (2011) 1 Lloyd's Rep 265 等先例。

其他考虑,包括"合理的必须"(reasonably necessary)或政策方面的合理等。在 Lewison 大法官所著的《The Interpretation of Contracts》(第 5 版,2011 年)一书第 6.02 段就提到这一个说法:

"**Where the court is asked to imply a term as a legal incident of a particular legal relationship, the strict test of necessity need not be satisfied. The court is concerned with broader questions of policy.**

As has been seen, the court has recently isolated a special category of implied terms, namely those where the court is asked to imply a term as a legal incident of a particular relationship, as a default rule which will apply unless specifically excluded. These kinds of implied term are not based upon the intention of the parties, actual or presumed, in a given instance, although the provenance of a particular term may well have been the commonplace use of such a term in earlier times in contracts of that type, so establishing what later would become the default rule."(法院在近年来把一种默示条文独立对待,也就是法律的默示。这种默示不根据订约双方的真正或假设订约意图,而是关注一个更广泛的政策考虑,而严格的必须考验也不必满足。)

简单的举例说,仲裁协议的机密性是在最近十几年才兴起的说法,在 Dolling Banker v. Merret (1990) 1 W. L. R. 1205 先例以前并不存在。这是默示条文,即双方不必在仲裁条文明示规定也要保密。从这一近期的变化,就已经可以看出仲裁的机密性并非是严格的必须性,否则难以解释以前可以不必须。这一默示显然是为了鼓励仲裁而带来的政策性改变与政策性地认为这样才是在今天的商业环境下合理。

除了 Lewison 大法官所著的《The Interpretation of Contracts》(第 5 版,2011 年)一书,可列举一些其他著名的书籍中的有关说法。在 Atiyah 教授的《An Introduction to the Law of Contract》一书(第 5 版,1995 年)中的第 207 页说"严格的必须性"要求是不现实的,合理性亦应多加考虑,最后发展趋势可能只是需要"合理的必须性"就可以默示,如下:"... the difference in opinion between the judges on this point seems, however, to have been somewhat unreal. For it is evident that the formula that implications can only be made when necessary is not to be taken too literally. It is not necessary to have lifts in blocks of flats ten stories high (indeed high rise buildings existed long before lifts were invented), though it would no doubt be exceedingly inconvenient not to have them. So 'necessary' really seems to mean 'reasonably necessary', and that must mean, 'reasonably necessary having regard to the context and the price'. So in the end there does not seems to be much difference between what is necessary and what is reasonable."。(Atiyah 教授认为"必须"不应该太死板。如一个 10 层高的楼房应否默示必须有电梯[或对电梯保持良好状态],虽然在电梯没有发明之前就已经存在很高的楼房了。显然,电梯并不是必须,只不过是对住在高层的住户极不方便罢了。所以,如果要默示,就应该根据一个说法是"合理的必须"而无法说成是严格的必须,特别可

以考虑作出决定当时的情况[如电梯已经十分普及]与房屋的价值或管理费。这表示必须性与合理性有一定关系,甚至看不出两个考验的区别。)

而这个观点也被 Ewan McKendrick 教授在 2005 年的旧版《Contract Law—Text, Cases and Materials》一书中接受,他在分析著名的 Liverpool City Council v. Irwin 先例时说到要求可能是这个“合理的必须性”而非“严格的必须性”,在第 388 页说:“The case is generally regarded as an authority on terms implied by law, on the basis that the term that ... Where then did the decision of the House of Lords in *Liverpool City Council v. Irwin* leave the law? In the first place it re - affirmed that the test to be applied when deciding whether or not to imply a term is based on necessity and not simply on reasonableness. But it left some uncertainty in relation to terms implied in law because the terms implied into the tenancy contract did not seem to be necessary ingredient of all contracts of this type. It might have been ‘reasonably necessary’ but not ‘necessary’. **That the test for the implication of terms as a matter of law might be slightly less stringent than that applicable to terms implied in fact** is evidenced by the fact that Lord Cross concluded that a term was not to be implied on the basis of the officious bystander test but that it was nevertheless appropriate to imply a term as a matter of law into all contracts of this type.”(加黑部分是笔者的强调)

而在 Gerard McMeel 教授 2007 年旧版的《The Construction of Contracts—Interpretation, Implication and Rectification》一书第 10.03 段说虽然有些针对法律默示的判决建议“必须性”的要求适用,但实际操作中法院还是适用一些较广泛的“合理的必须”,并对案件事实情况加以考虑:“At bottom the implication of terms in law is a matter of public policy, and despite occasional judicial statements suggesting that the test is one of necessity in practice broader standards of reasonableness and an analysis of competing factors will determine whether or not the courts will recognize a new implied term in law.”

Elizabeth Peden 女士则感叹这方面法律缺少学术研究导致法律的不明确,她在《Law Quarterly Review》的分析认为法院应考虑许多因素,包括商业惯例、法律(法规与侵权法)默示责任之间的关系、哪一方合约方更适合承担损失或应该对风险投保、订约双方各自的谈判地位和商业规模、双方的责任可能受标准格式管辖以及与普遍大原则的协调、对社会的影响和公正性。

上述一些著名法律学者的说法明显对英国法院有一定影响力,在 Crossly v. Faithful & Gould Holdings Ltd (2004) EWCA Civ 293 先例,Dyson 大法官建议“合理性的问题、公平与政策考虑的冲突与平衡”(questions of reasonableness, fairness and balancing of competing policy considerations)比“必须性”(necessary)的要求更为重要。而在较早所节录的 Lewison 大法官所著的《The Interpretation of Contracts》(第 5 版,2011 年)一书,更加明确了法院近年来对法律默示的“必须性”所作出的改变。

§7 默示条文近期的一些重要改变、说法与做法

7.1 其他有关默示条文分类的说法

已经介绍了三种主要的默示条文,但还有许多其他对默示条文分类的说法,如 Glanville Williams 教授在《Language and the Law》(1945) 61 L. Q. R. 71 一文第 401 页将默示条文分为三种:(1)双方订约时可能想到但没有费力写明的(terms that the parties probably had in mind but did not trouble to express);(2)不管订约双方当时有没有想到,如果有人提出,他们会写明的(terms that the parties, whether or not they actually had them in mind, would probably have expressed if the question had been brought to their attention);(3) 不管订约双方当时有没有想到,也不管他们如果预见到困难会否写明,只要法院为了公平或政策或法治的需要,就可以默示(terms that, whether or not the parties they had them in mind or would have expressed them if they had foreseen the difficulty, are implied by the court because of the court's view of fairness or policy or in consequence of rules of law)。

他指出,(1)是为了努力找出双方的真实意图;(2)是努力通过假设来找出双方的假定或有条件的意图,即如果双方预见到会有此困难就会有的意图;(3)不关心订约双方的订约意图也要默示,除非双方可以用明示条文来排除这种默示的情况。

至于在先例的说法,首先是在 Liverpool City Council v. Irwin (1977) A. C. 239 先例之第 253 页 Wilberforce 勋爵将默示条文分为四大类(但其实只同意有三类),其中第一类是商业惯例的默示,第二类是事实的默示,第三类是被他以不合传统而否定的由 Denning 勋爵倡导的合理性的默示,第四类就是法律的默示,而它们之间就是一个"连续光谱上的图案"(shade on a continuous spectrum)的关系,说:

"To say that the construction of a complete contract out of these elements involves a process of 'implication' may be correct; it would be so if implication means the supplying of what is not expressed. But there are varieties of implications which the courts think fit to make and they do not necessarily involve the same process.

[1] Where there is, on the face of it, a complete, bilateral contract, the courts are sometimes willing to add terms to it, as implied terms: this is very common in mercantile contracts where there is an established usage: in that case the courts are spelling out what both parties know and would, if asked, unhesitatingly agree to be part of the bargain.

[2] In other cases, where there is an apparently complete bargain, the courts are willing to add a term on the ground that without it the contract will not work—this is the case, if not of*The Moorcock* ... it self on its facts, at least the doctrine of the Court of Appeal, a strict test—though the degree of strictness seems to vary with the current judi-

cial trend—and I think that they were right not to accept it as applicable here.

[3] There is a third variety of implication, that which I think Lord Denning MR favours, or at least didfavour in this case, and that is the implication of reasonable terms. But although I agree with many of his instances, which in fact fall under one or other of the preceding heads, I cannot go so far as to endorse his principle; indeed, it seems to me, with respect, to extend a long, and desirable, way beyond sound authority.

[4] The present case, in my opinion, represents a fourth category, or I would rather say a fourth **shade on a continuous spectrum.** The court here is simply concerned to establish what the contract is, the parties not having themselves fully stated the terms. In this sense the court is searching for what must be implied."(加黑部分是笔者的强调)

另在 The "Damodar General T. J. Park" (1986) 2 Lloyd's Rep. 68 先例,Steyn 大法官将默示条文也分为三类,除了法律默示与事实默示,第三类则是任何一个合理人士看来"再明显不过"(go without saying)的默示,他说:"Sometimes it is said that a term is implied into the contract when in truth a positive rule of law of contract is applied because of the category in which a particular contract falls. Another type of implied term is a term in order to give business efficacy to the contract. The basis of such an implication is that the contract is unworkable without it. There is, however, another form of implication.... It is possible to imply a term, if the court or arbitrator, as the case may be, is satisfied that reasonable men, faced with the suggested term which *ex hypothesi* was not expressed in the contract, would without hesitation say: 'yes, of course that is so obvious that it goes without saying.'"

在 Bratton Seymour Service Co Ltd v Oxborough (1993) BCLC 693 先例,上诉庭的 Steyn 大法官还提到了另一种默示,就是仅根据文件/合约的"解释默示"(construction implication),说:"I will readily accept that the law should not adopt a black-letter approach. It is possible to imply a term purely from the language of the document itself: a purely constructional implication is not precluded."

7.2 "一个连续光谱上的图案"的说法

不同类别的默示条文之间的区分看来也不是那么严格与明确的。正如 Wilberforce 勋爵所说法院的默示只是"一个连续光谱上的图案"(shades on a continuous spectrum),即有重叠模糊地带,并不是黑白分明那么简单。可举一个简单的例子,在本书第十章之 4.1 段提到"商业合约"(mercantile contract)的明示或默示时间规定都很重要。这方面有很多先例,可以说这些案例起初会是根据事实的默示而作出这样的决定,也就是根据个别案件的案情认为时间规定重要。但随着时间流逝,这方面的判决已经变为被广泛接受与权威性的原则,同类合约但不同案情的案例都依从,就会令该原则变为一个法律的默示。

例如在 The "Moorcock" (1889) 14 PD 64, CA 先例,Treitel 教授在《The Law of

Contract》一书中就指出了该先例并不明确是否是事实或是法律的默示，虽然一般的说法是该先例是第一个有关事实的默示。这两者之间主要的区别之一就是事实的默示必须在订约时要通过一个"好事第三人"的考验，这才可以假设双方有这一订约意图。但较早在4.4.3.1段有谈到，第三人的问题怎样设计就会带来双方不同的反应。这表示在The "Moorcock"先例设计双方不会异口同声说"是"的问题并不困难，也就表示双方并没有这一订约意图而不能算是事实的默示了，只会是一个法律的默示。当然，这方面的区分在The "Moorcock"先例并不重要，反正法院肯作出默示就已经足够。在那个年代，也没有细化到默示条文的分类。但法律发展下，肯定会有情况这方面的区分是重要，因为法律的默示并不是随便就能作出，而一作出它的适用面也会广泛，所以作出前必须要对如上一小段提到的Crossly v. Faithful & Gould Holdings Ltd (2004) EWCA Civ 293先例中建议的"合理性的问题、公平与政策考虑的冲突与平衡"(questions of reasonableness, fairness and balancing of competing policy considerations)作出深思熟虑。

这"连续光谱"的分类困难问题，一个明显的例子可见仲裁的机密性，在《仲裁法——从1996年英国仲裁法到国际商务仲裁》一书第十三章2.1段有提到，它到底是根据每一个案件不同情况来看的事实默示还是对所有仲裁协议划一的法律默示？在Dolling Baker v. Merrett (1990) 1 WLR 1205先例，上诉庭判是由于仲裁的私人性质，理应有一默示责任约束仲裁当事方要对仲裁的文件保密。Parker大法官在判词中说："... As between parties to an arbitration, although the proceedings are consensual and may thus be regarded as wholly voluntary, their very nature is such that there must, in my judgment, be some implied obligation on both parties not to disclose or use for any other purpose any documents prepared for and used in the arbitration, or disclosed or produced in the course of the arbitration, or transcripts or notes of the evidence in the arbitration or the award, and indeed not to disclose in any other way what evidence had been given by any witness in an arbitration, save with the consent of the other party, or pursuant to an order or leave of the court. The qualification is necessary, just as it is in the case of the **implied obligation of secrecy** between banker and customer."

但Parker大法官上述的讲话没有清楚说明这"保密的默示责任"(implied obligation of secrecy)是根据事实默示、习惯默示还是法律默示，而只是把它等同银行与客户之间的保密责任：Tournier v. National Provincial and Union Bank of England (1924) 1 K.B. 461先例。若该责任是事实默示，则每一个仲裁都必须要考虑事实上是否需要有此默示条文。要构成事实的默示要通过两个考验或其中一个，一是从商业意义上看，默示引入机密是否必须"赋予仲裁条文完整的效力"(give efficacy to the arbitration clause)；二是要满足"好事第三人"(officious bystander)的考验。如果属于习惯默示，则要考虑是否仲裁都有保秘这一习惯做法。如果属于法律默示，有关的默示条文的存在是由于仲裁条文的本质，根据"更广泛的政策考虑"(wider consideration)而需由法律硬性规定。

在 Hassneh Insurance Co. of Israel and others v. Steuart J. Mew (1993) 2 Lloyd's Rep 243 先例,高院的 Colman 大法官对 Parker 大法官在 Dolling Baker v. Merrett (1990) 1 WLR 1205 先例所指的默示责任有以下的看法:

"... Such an obligation can exist only because it is implied in the agreement to arbitrate and like any other implied term must be capable of reasonably precise definition. The implication of the term must be based on custom or business efficacy.

If the parties to an English law contract refer their disputes to arbitration they are entitled to assume at the least that the hearing will be conducted in private. That assumption arises from a practice which has been universal inLondon for hundreds of years and, I believe, undisputed. It is a practice which represents an important advantage of arbitration over the Courts as a means of dispute resolution. The informality attaching to a hearing held in private and the candour to which it may give rise is an essential ingredient of arbitration, so essential that if privacy were denied by an officious bystander, I have no doubt that, in the case of practically every arbitration agreement, both the parties would object."

Colman 大法官认为私下开庭,不许外人旁听是英国仲裁的一贯做法,而这亦是支持他对仲裁所提供的的证据/资料及仲裁裁决书予以保密的原因,这也是相当于习惯做法的默示。Colman 大法官接下来也认为仲裁的机密十分重要,如果有好事第三人提出,仲裁双方是不会有异议,这也是说可以以事实的默示作出机密的责任。

在之后出了一个与英国说法唱反调的澳大利亚最高院的先例:Esso Australia Resources Limited v. Plowman (1995) 183 CLR 10,不认为仲裁协议是有机密的默示,因为有太多的例外情况,如仲裁往往会有保险公司在背后所以要向它披露,作为当事人的公司向税局报税需要对会计师披露,公司上市需要披露仲裁的资料,公司收购也有同样的需要等。这表示如果有个别仲裁需要有机密(如涉及知识产权或商业机密),当事人双方就需要在他们的仲裁协议加上明示条文。

这导致英国在接下来的一个重要先例中要衡量与决定英国法律应该对仲裁的机密性采取的立场与依据的说法。这就是在上诉庭的权威案例名为 Ali Shipping Corporation v. Shipyard Trogir (1998) 1 Lloyd's Rep 643,Potter 大法官认为这默示条文不是来自习惯做法或商业效力的考虑,而应属于法律上的默示条文,从仲裁过程不受公众注目之政策的考虑而推断仲裁的机密性,

说:"... I consider that the implied term ought properly to be regarded as attaching as a matter of law. It seems to me that, in holding as a matter of principle that the obligation of confidentiality (whatever its precise limits) arises as an essential corollary of the privacy of arbitration proceedings, the Court is propounding a term which arises 'as the nature of the contract itself implicitly requires'... As Lord Bridge observed in *Scally v. Southern Health Board*, [1992] 1 A. C. 294 at p. 307, a clear distinction is to be drawn –

.... Between the search for an implied term necessary to give business efficacy to a particular contract and the search, based on wider considerations, for a term which the law will necessarily imply as a necessary incident of a definable category of contractual relationship.

In my view an arbitration clause is a good example of the latter type of implied term.

While acknowledging that the boundaries of the obligation of confidence which thereby arise have yet to be delineated (cf. *Hyundai Engineering & Construction Co. Ltd. v. Active Building & Civil Construction Co. Ltd.* [unreported], 9 March 1994, per Phillips J.), **the manner in which that may best be achieved is by formulating exceptions of broad application to be applied in individual cases, rather than by seeking to reconsider, and if necessary adapt, the general rule on each occasion in the light of the particular circumstances and presumed intentions of the parties at the time of their original agreement.**"(加黑部分是笔者的强调)

在上述判词中的最后一段,可见到上诉庭 Potter 大法官选择不事实默示而选择法律默示,显然是为了对仲裁的更广泛的政策考虑。这方面也可从该先例的案情中进一步了解,它涉及 6 家公司向同一造船厂订下造船合约建造 6 艘船舶。这 6 家单船公司的成立主要是与造船厂个别签约与作为将来新船的船东,他们背后由一家控股公司拥有,并透过该控股公司拥有的另一家船公司作为代理人及经理人,一直在与造船厂联系。这是典型航运公司的营运模式,可以说,他们全是一家人。

由于造船厂未能按其中一份合约依期完成建造船舶(Hull 202),合约的单船船东,亦即本案的原告,终止合约后并向造船厂提起伦敦仲裁与索赔损失。在该 Hull 202 仲裁,造船厂辩称它为原告造船的责任是把所有造船合约一并对待,但其中三个合约(Hulls 204 – 206)船东没有支付首期款项。Hull 202 仲裁中独任仲裁员不接受造船厂的论点,他认为尽管另三个造船合约没有按时付款是违反合约,但毕竟是不同的合约与不同的船东(单船船东)。结果是判造船厂要对原告的损失负责,金额高达 3400 万英镑另加诉讼费用。

这样,可想而知的是造船厂马上向另外三个船东(Hulls 204 – 206)提起伦敦仲裁,追讨合约欠款/损失。估计造船厂希望在 Hull 202 的败诉仲裁裁决书能够被执行前,Hulls 204 – 206 的三个仲裁判下来就有机会对冲。为了支持他能尽快向后来的仲裁庭成功申请并取得"中间裁决书"(interim arbitration award),造船厂希望向该仲裁庭披露在先前与原告针对 Hull 202 仲裁时提供的材料(主要是船东的证人证言)及仲裁裁决书,其中内容有认定船东没有支付在 Hulls 204 – 206 首期款项。这可对三个单船船东的抗辩作出强而有力的反驳,造船厂并指出有关争议已在先前的仲裁处理了,属"一事不再理"(issue estoppel)。原告知悉造船厂披露的意图后(他当然知道,因为这些公司本来就是一家人),就"单方面"(*ex - parte*)向法院申请禁令禁止造船厂在后来的仲裁披露 Hull 202 仲裁的资料,因为破坏了仲裁的机密性。这被法院支持,但之后在"双方出庭"(*inter - parte*)的聆讯中,高院的 Clarke 大法官解除禁令。但船东取得上诉的批准,并获上诉庭推翻高院的判决与恢复禁令。这表示上诉庭认为仲裁必须机密的立场不变,也不受到澳大利亚先例的影响。

至于根据的是哪一类的默示,Potter 大法官认为 Hull 202 仲裁中认定 Hulls 204 - 206 没有支付首期款项的违约,并不构成"一审终局"(*Res judicata*)或构成"一事不再理"(issue estoppel),因为它们之间是不同的造船合约,另加上仲裁裁决书不是法院先例,不会有这样的效果。所以要披露 Hull 202 仲裁的资料与裁决书,达不到"合理必须保护合法利益"(reasonable necessary for the protection for the legitimate interests)的法律要求,上诉庭也因此恢复解除了的禁令。Potter 大法官也说如果在 Hull 202 仲裁中的证人证言,与 Hulls 204 - 206 仲裁中同一批证人(船东)出现矛盾与不一致的证言时,才会达到合理必须披露,但目前还没有这种情况出现。这表示根据该不同而且会不断有变化的事实作出默示机密,就每次都要按照不同事实考虑。这会变得十分困难、不稳定与昂贵。比较容易的做法就是根据公共政策判仲裁协议必须机密的大前提,也就是作出这一法律默示,然后根据个别案件的不同事实看是否需要作出例外的判定(如一个例外就是为了合理必须保护仲裁当事方的合法利益)。这就是 Potter 大法官在上述判决中的最后一段话的意思。

总结上述案例,英国普通法承认仲裁的机密性是源自当事方订立的仲裁条文中,有一个对仲裁保密的默示责任,这默示责任是法律默示的条文,硬性引入于仲裁条文中,不需再明示。仲裁的机密性不再需要考虑订约意图或商业效力与好事第三人的考验。

7.3 Belize 先例带来对默示条文、合约解释与合约变更的重大改变

7.3.1 默示条文与合约变更的关系

合约的默示条文(特别是事实的默示)与"合约变更"(rectification)[28]之间的关系密切,两者都是为了找出合约双方的订约意图与目的,在 Liverpool City Council v. Irwin (1977) A. C. 239 先例中 Cross 勋爵说:"Sometimes, however, there is no question of laying down any *prima facie* rule applicable to all cases of defined type but what the court is being in effect asked to do is to rectify a particular—often very detailed—contract by inserting in it a term which the parties have not expressed."

默示条文与合约变更有一致之处是都涉及合约本身有缺陷或漏洞,不是它记录错了双方真正达成的协议,就是有所遗漏令合约无法产生效力(或商业效力)而必须有一个说法。前者的情况是通过合约变更来纠正记录的错误,并反映双方真正的订

---

〔28〕 这可看本书第六章之 2.3.3 段。

约意图。而后者的情况是通过各种考验假设双方应该有的订约意图,并引入默示条文反映这一意图。唯一的差异是默示条文只是“假设”(presume)双方的订约意图,但合约变更就涉及申请人必须举证变更是反映双方在谈判时“真正”(actual)与持续的“共同/分享”(common/shared)订约意图。也是这个不同导致合约变更的申请不容易成功,也不是这么频密,但相比默示条文的申请就频密得多了。毕竟,一个合约不论是否签署,只要有所遗漏,或明示条文不够明确或全面,难逃就有默示条文之争。

这在 Codelfa Construction Prop Ltd v. State Rail Authority of New South Wales (1982) 149 C. L. R. 337 先例,Mason 大法官有说:“The implication of a term is to be compared, and at the same time contrasted, with rectification of a contract. In each case the problem is caused by a deficiency in the expression of the contractual agreement. A term which should have been included has been omitted. The difference is that with rectification the term which has been omitted and should have been included was actually agreed upon; with implication the term is one which it is presumed that the parties would have agreed upon had they turned their minds to it—it is not a term that they have actually agreed upon. Thus, in the case of the implied term the deficiency in the expression of the consensual agreement is caused by the failure of the parties to direct their minds to a particular eventuality and to make explicit provision for it. **Rectification ensures that the contract gives effect to the parties' actual intention; the implication of a term is designed to give effect to the parties' presumed intention.**”(加黑部分是笔者的强调)

默示条文与合约变更还有其他不同之处,如默示条文不能与合约的明示条文起冲突,而合约变更是可以“重写”(re – write)合约,毕竟就是为了改写被证明是纪录错误的明示条文。

7.3.2　默示条文与解释合约的关系

作出默示(特别是事实默示)与解释合约之间也是有密切关系,两者(与合约变更一样)都是为了找出合约双方的订约意图与目的。正如 Steyn 勋爵在 National Commercial Bank Jamaica Ltd v Guyanna Refrigerators Ltd (1998) 53 WLR 229 先例说:“The processes of construction and implication of terms are closely linked, but as a matter of legal analysis they need to be kept separate.”(两种做法十分密切,但作为法律分析,它们需要分开。例如,解释合约是客观找出订约双方以文字所表达的订约意图,但默示条文的事实默示是要满足一些如必须性满足商业效力或/与好事第三人等的考验。)

在 The “Rio Assu” (1999) 1 Lloyd's Rep. 115 先例,有关的案情在本书第六章之 12.6 段有介绍,就是一个典型的案件法院同时以解释有关文件/合约(根据背景/语境作出广泛的解释)与事实的默示条文(通过好事第三人的考验)都得出了同样的结果。

但一直以来有争议是这两种做法会否是同一码事。这在 Lewison 大法官所著的

《The Interpretation of Contracts》(第 5 版,2011 年)一书之 6.03 段有说:"There has been debate in the past on the question whether the implication of a term is truly a question of interpreting the contract. In Trollope & Colls Ltd v North West Metropolitan Regional Hospital Board, Lord Pearson said that it had been convenient to contrast a 'construction point' with an argument on the implication of a term: 'without prejudice to the question whether as a matter of strict theory the implication of a term may properly be considered as an aspect of the construction of the contract."

在现在被普遍接受的三种或是更多类别的默示是一个连续光谱上的图案的说法,暗示了至少在某个阶段默示条文属于解释合约。在 Lewison 大法官所著的《The Interpretation of Contracts》(第 5 版,2011 年)一书之 6.01 段说:

"In addition, the image of 'shades on a continuous spectrum' (which comes from the speech of Lord Wilberforce in Liverpool City Council v Irwin) itself suggests that at least at some points on the spectrum, the process of implication is a facet of that of interpretation. At one end of the spectrum the court is doing no more than stating the logical corollary of a term expressly agreed. This is clearly part of the process of interpretation. Towards the middle of the spectrum the court is making explicit that which is implicit, not in a logical sense, but in a practical or commercial sense, in the parties' bargain. And at the other end of the spectrum the court is filling gaps in the bargain as expressed.

However, there are unresolved tensions in the notion of the 'continuous spectrum'. In construing the express terms of a contract the court often stresses the importance of the reasonableness of the construction selected or of the result achieved. By contrast, in discussing the circumstances in which a term is to be implied, the court repeatedly stresses that the touchstone is necessity, not reasonableness. If the implication of terms is part of a continuous spectrum beginning with the construction of express terms, it would seem to follow that at some point in the spectrum there is a radical change in approach. The location of that point is uncertain. Hence some judges do not draw a rigid distinction between the process of interpretation and the process of implication. Thus in Chaffe v Kingsley, Sedley LJ said:

'The distinction between the construction of documents and the implication of terms, which at the start seemed likely to occupy much of the argument, is often a mare's nest. Attempting the latter inevitably provokes the true but unhelpful response that words are being artificially introduced into a document; attempting the former almost as inevitably provokes the response, equally true and equally unhelpful, that the terms relied on are not visible. It has been helpful, therefore, to be conducted directly on the search for meaning.'"

Lewison 大法官认为这个连续光谱的一端是法院根据双方的明示条文作出一个

合理的解释,这显然就是解释合约,光谱的中间部分是法院是作出实际与商业上需要的默示(这看来是针对法律默示与惯例/商业习惯做法默示),而光谱的另一端是填补双方合约中的漏洞(这看来是针对事实默示)。这当然也有说不通的地方,就是默示条文的考验是必须性,而合约解释是根据合理性,在这个连续光谱的哪一点要作出改变完全不肯定。

7.3.3 Attorney General of Belize v. Belize Telecom Ltd 先例

但这一方面可以说在英国法律已经明确了默示条文本质上是属于解释合约条文,为了客观找出订约双方的订约意图:Attorney General of Belize v. Belize Telecom Ltd (2009) 2 All ER 1127 先例。在该枢密院先例,Hoffmann 勋爵说:

"Before discussing in greater detail the reasoning of the Court of Appeal, the Board will make some general observations about the process of implication. The court has no power to improve upon the instrument which it is called upon to construe, whether it be a contract, a statute or articles of association. It cannot introduce terms to make it fairer or more reasonable. It is concerned only to discover what the instrument means. However, that meaning is not necessarily or always what the authors or parties to the document would have intended. It is the meaning which the instrument would convey to a reasonable person having all the background knowledge which would reasonably be available to the audience to whom the instrument is addressed: see Investors Compensation Scheme Ltd v West Bromwich Building Society [1998] 1 WLR 896, 912 - 913. It is this objective meaning which is conventionally called the intention of the parties, or the intention of Parliament, or the intention of whatever person or body was or is deemed to have been the author of the instrument. (法院没有权利解释文件/合约而把它变得更好,也不能引进条文令它变得更公平与合理。法院只是找出有关文件/合约的意思。但这一意思并不一定是文件撰写人的意图,而是一个合理第三人在知道所有有关的背景客观认为是什么意思。这一客观的意思也是传统被称为双方订约意图。)

The question of implication arises when the instrument does not expressly provide for what is to happen when some event occurs. The most usual inference in such a case is that nothing is to happen. If the parties had intended something to happen, the instrument would have said so. Otherwise, the express provisions of the instrument are to continue to operate undisturbed. If the event has caused loss to one or other of the parties, the loss lies where it falls. (默示条文的问题会出现在一份文件没有明示规定了某些情况如果发生应该怎么办。最普遍的推断是没有什么要办,否则文件会有说明。)

In some cases, however, the reasonable addressee would understand the instrument to mean something else. He would consider that the only meaning consistent with the other provisions of the instrument, read against the relevant background, is that something is to happen. Theevent in question is to affect the rights of the parties. The instrument may not have expressly said so, but this is what it must mean. In such a case, it is said that the court implies a term as to what will happen if the event in question occurs. But the implication of the term is not an addition to the instrument. It only spells out what the instrument means."(但会有情况是一个合理第三人[往往由法官或仲裁员代表]会认为文件/合约想有所针对,这样才可以与合约的其他条文配合。文件/合约虽然没有明示规定,但这肯定是该文件/合约的意思。这样,法院会默示引进条文针对发生了某种情况应该怎么办。但默示条文并不是为了增加内容,只是解释有关文件/合约到底是什么意思。)

Hoffmann 勋爵早在《The Intolerable Wrestle with Words and Meanings》(1997) 114 SALJ 656 一文就已经说道:"In fact, of course, the implication of a term into a contract is an exercise in interpretation like any other. It may seem odd to speak of interpretation when, by definition, the terms has not been expressed in words, but the only difference is that when we imply a term, we are engaged in interpreting the meaning of the contract as a whole. For this purpose, we apply the ordinary rule of contractual interpretation by which the parties are depersonalized and assumed to be reasonable."(默示条文是解释合约。这说法看来奇怪,因为如果该条文根本没有明示,怎样解释合约条文?这里的区别只是作出默示,是整体解释一份合约的意思。所以应该适用一般合约解释的规则,并且不理会合约双方的个人意图并假设他们是合理。)

Attorney General of Belize v Belize Telecom Ltd 先例可以说是已经普遍被后来的很多先例接受。[29] 只一提的是,上诉庭的 Aikens 大法官在 Crema v Cenkos Securities Plc (2010) EWCA Civ 1444 先例对 Hoffmann 勋爵在该先例的说法进行了总结。另上诉庭的 Arden 大法官在 Stena Line Ltd v Merchant Navy Ratings Pension Fund Trustees Ltd (2011) EWCA Civ 543 先例说:"**The Belize case constitutes an important and recent development in the principles of interpretation, which the courts are probably still absorbing and ingesting.** It is appropriate to take the statement of princi-

---

[29] Benedetti v Sawiris (2009) EWHC 1330 (Ch); CDV Software Entertainment AG v Gamecock Media Europe Ltd (2009) EWHC 2965 (Ch); INTA Navigation Ltd v Ranch Investments Ltd (2010) 1 Lloyd's Rep 74; Mediterranean Salvage and Towage Ltd v Seamar Trading and Commerce Inc (2010) 1 All ER (Comm) 1; ENE Kos 1 Ltd v Petroleo Brasileiro SA (No. 2) (2010) 1 All ER (Comm) 669; AET Inc Ltd v Arcadia petroleum Ltd (2010) 2 P & CR 19; Gregory Projects (Halifax) Ltd v Tenpin (Halifax) Ltd (2010) 2 All E. R. (Comm) 646; Rutherford v Seymour Pierce Ltd (2010) IRLR 606; Chantry Estates (Southeast) Ltd v Anderson (2010) 130 Con. L. R. 11; PNPF Trust Co Ltd v Taylor (2010) EWHC 1573 (Ch); Re Agrimarche Ltd (2010) EWHC 1655 (Ch); Crema v Centros Securities Plc (2010) EWCA Civ 1444; KG Bominflot Bunkergesellschaft fur Mineraloele mbH & Co v Petroplus Marketing AG (2010) All ER (D) 174; Societe Generale, London Branch v Geys (2011) EWCA Civ 307; Garratt v Mirror Group Newspapers Ltd (2011) EWCA Civ 425; North Shore Ventures Ltd v Anstead Holdings Inc (2011) 1 All ER (Comm) 81 等先例。

ples in it in more detail since it is directly relevant to the issue that I am considering in this case. In Belize, the Privy Council analysed the case law on the implication of terms and decided that the implication of terms is, in essence, an exercise in interpretation. This development promotes the internal coherence of the law by emphasising the role played by the principles of interpretation not only in the context of the interpretation of documents simpliciter but also in the field of the implication of terms. Those principles are the unifying factor. The internal coherence of the law is important because it enables the courts to identify the aims and values that underpin the law and to pursue those values and aims so as to achieve consistency in the structure of the law."(加黑部分是笔者的强调)

7.3.4 对 Belize 先例不同看法的说法与判例

正如 Arden 大法官所讲,还是有少部分不同的判法,如在英国的 Groveholt Ltd v Hughes (2010) EWCA Civ 538 先例,上诉庭是说传统对默示条文的考验并没有任何改变。笔者也有看到对这一方面改变的批评或质疑,其中可节录新加坡首席大法官 Sundaresh Menon 在 2013 年 5 月之"Future Development of Contract Law and the Relationship between the Contract Laws of the Commonwealth"会议中发表的《Contract Law from the Trenches – A Former Litigator's Perspective》一文所说:

"In Belize, Lord Hoffmann stated that the preferred approach towards the implication of terms was to ask 'whether such a provision would spell out in express words what the instrument, read against the relevant background, would reasonably be understood to mean'. In other words, whether a term should be implied into a contract becomes an aspect of contractual interpretation. On this basis, the traditional tests referring to 'business efficacy' or the 'officious bystander' might well be displaced. Moreover, the criterion of 'necessity' has been tempered, with 'reasonableness' taking its place. Although Belize was a decision of the Privy Council, some later English cases have accepted Lord Hoffmann's approach in Belize. (Hoffmann 勋爵在 Belize 先例的说法令默示条文变为合约解释,这会导致商业效力与好事第三人的传统考验被替代。也令必须性的考验被合理性所替代。虽然 Belize 先例只是枢密院的决定,不严格是英国法律,但后来已经有很多英国先例接受了这一说法。)...

It appears that these developments too may have been a result of civil law influence. Under Art 6:102 of the Principles of European Contract Law, implied terms may stem from, inter alia, the 'intention of the parties' and the 'nature and purpose of the contract'. These same touchstones are used in the process of contractual interpretation described in Art 5:101 and 5:102. There is no separate doctrine of rectification and there is no need for such a doctrine because contractual interpretation is a question of fact. Lord Hoffmann's use of contextual interpretation as a means to account for implication as well as rectification brings English common law appreciably closer to the civil law.(这里的变化看来是受到大陆法的影响,而英国普通法是想与大陆法接近。)

In relation to implication, the Singapore Court of Appeal in MFM Restaurants Pte Ltd v Fish& Co Restaurants Pte Ltd (MFM Restaurants) observed in obiter that the uncertainty generated in the area of interpretation would apply equally in the area of implied terms. In the later case of Foo Jong Peng v Phua Kiah Mai, the court rejected the Belize approach because the process of implication involved tests that were specific and different from those which operated in relation to the interpretation of express terms in a contract. The Belize approach did not shed light on how a particular term ought to be implied - there were supplied by the 'business efficacy' and 'officious bystander' test.(新加坡法院看来没有接受,在第一个先例,新加坡上诉庭认为这一说法会带来不肯定,而默示条文传统的考验相对肯定。在第二个先例,新加坡法院拒绝跟从 Belize 先例,认为传统的考验是明确而且与解释合约的明示条文不一样。Belize 先例的说法/做法无法帮助找出应该默示怎样的条文,但通过传统的商业效力与好事第三人的考验就可以提供。)

While the concepts of interpretation and implication might be 'closely linked', on the other hand, as Lord Steyn had observed, 'as a matter of legal analysis they need to be kept separate'. Broadening the traditional requirement from 'necessity' in order to imply terms, to 'reasonableness' further adds to the uncertainty brought about by collapsing the hitherto separate concepts of implication and interpretation. . . .

I suggest that the difficulties caused by the blurring between interpretation, implication and rectification can be quite serious as they are not only conceptual but also very practical in nature. From the perspective of a practitioner on one side of a dispute, it will be easy and even attractive be plead all three as alternatives so that evidence that might otherwise be inadmissible for the purposes of interpretation or implication might nonetheless be admitted ostensibly for the purposes of rectification[30]. From the perspective of a practitioner on the other side of that dispute, this can be most unsatisfactory and even smack of cynicism. This highlights the need for specific guidelines or tests that distinguish one concept from the other and that are clear about what evidence may be admissible in each instance. Alternatively, one might choose to embrace a complete merger of all three accompanied by some adjustment to the threshold of admissibility but this will potentially have quite significant implications for how we conceptualise these issues and, at a practical level, how we litigate them."(新加坡首席大法官认为解释合约、默示条文与合约变更的区分变了是模糊与带来困难。这会是对诉讼律师带来十分严重的后

---

〔30〕 有关合约变更的救济才是"谈判除外规则"的例外,这方面可看本书第三章之 13.1 段与 14.3 段。

果。如作出请求,会是更安全把解释合约、默示条文与合约变更都包括在内〔31〕,这也会带来大量的证据是本来没有必要。)

§8　默示条文与证据

法院/仲裁庭在决定是否作出默示条文时,可接受的证据与解释合约的"明示条文"(express terms)大致上一样。例如,可以接受有关"背景/语境(surrounding background/factual matrix)"的证据。另是在涉及惯例/商业习惯做法的默示,更是一直以来都可接受这方面的证据,正如 Parke B 大法官在 Hutton v. Warren (1836) 1 M & W 466, 150 E. R. 517 先例中所说的:"It has long been settled that in commercial transactions, extrinsic evidence of custom and usage is admissible to annex incidents to written contracts in matters with respect to which they are silent. The same rule has been applied to contracts in other transactions of life, in which known usages have been established and prevailed; and this has been done upon the principle of presumption that, in such transactions, the parties did not mean to express in writing the whole of the contract by which they intended to be bound, but a contract with reference to those known usage."

与解释合约的明示条文可能有不同的反而是在双方谈判时的证据,所谓的"谈判除外规则"(negotiation exclusion rule 或 prior negotiation rule),这方面还是不可接受协助解释明示合约条文/文字,这可看本书第三章之 14.3 段与第六章之 2.5.1 段。虽然这方面的法律也有例外情况,如一个例外是"合约变更"(rectification),这就是申请的一方要证明双方真正在谈判时达成的持续性的共同/分享的订约意图与签署的合约并不一致,后者有一个文书或记录上的错误。这方面的举证责任非常沉重,所以申请合约变更并非易事,这也在本书第三章之 13.1 段与第六章之 2.3.3 段有提及。第二个例外是"私人字典"(private dictionary),这在本书第三章之 14 段也已有介绍,不重复。但笔者在这里多举一个例外情况可允许看双方谈判时的证据,这就是考虑是否作出默示条文。举一个简单的例子,如果在谈判中双方曾经提到过这个问题,甚至有一方草拟了有关的条文但被另一方拒绝,最后双方对这个问题就不了了之并达成与签署合约。这样,如果双方事后有了应否默示的争议,而要默示的问题恰恰就是双方在谈判时已经探讨过并且放弃的,看来就不应该默示,等于强加一个假设的订约意图但实际上有证据证明他们并没有这个意图。

这一方面的说法,可节录 Gerard Mcmeel 教授的《the Construction of Contracts—Interpretation, Implication and Rectification》(2007 年)一书有关内容如下:

---

〔31〕 这已经是常见的做法,如在较早的 7.3.2 段提到的 The "Rio Assu" (1999) 1 Lloyd's Rep. 115 先例。

"**Evidence that the parties rejected a particular draft provision**

Where the prior negotiations of the parties evidence the consideration by both of a particular draft term or proposed formulation of a provision which is then rejected the courts will consider such material. In effect the rejection of a particular term or formulation should preclude any later argument that a term should be implied akin to the discarded provision.

In*Codelfa Construciton Prop Ltd v. State Rail Authority of New South Wales* (1982) 149 C. L. R. 337, Mason J tentatively suggested that this might be the case: There may perhaps be one situation in which evidence of the actual intention of the parties should be allowed to prevail over their presumed intention. If it transpires that the parties have refused to include in their contract a provision which would give effect to the presumed intention of persons in their position it may be proper to receive evidence of that refusal. After all, the court is interpreting the contract which the parties have made and in that exercise the court takes into account what reasonable men in that situation would have intended to convey by words of the contract a meaning which the parties have united in rejecting? It is possible that evidence of mutual intention, if amounting to concurrence, is receivable so as to negative an inference sought to be drawn for the surrounding circumstances."

§9 默示条文与完整合约条文的关系

"完整合约条文"(entire agreement clause)在本书第十三章之第2段有介绍,其危险(或优点)是肯定合约本身的明示条文就已经包罗万有,不再存在有其他订约前的"陈述"(representation)、"保证"(warranty)、"附带协议"(collateral agreement)等争议(不管是否存在)。主要是看该条文的写法是否广泛,如果够广泛的话,可以排除其他方面如"惯例/商业习惯做法"(custom or trade usage)的默示。

在 Exxonmobil Sales and Supply Corp v. Texaco Ltd (2004) 1 All E. R. (Comm) 435 先例,合约有一条完整合约条文说明合约:"contains the entire agreement of the parties ... and there is no other promise, representation, warranty, **usage or course of dealing** affecting it."(加黑部分是笔者的强调)

Nigel Teare 大法官判是这完整合约条文可以排除有关惯例/商业习惯做法的默示,但同时也强调有关其他种类的默示条文(即法律与事实的默示)就不是这么容易排除:"It seems to me arguable that where it is necessary to imply a term in order to make the express terms work such an implied term may not be excluded by the entire agreement clause because it could not be said that such a term is to be found in the document or documents forming part of the contract. The same cannot be said of an implied term based on custom or usage."

完整合约条文的文字通常不足够排除立法或普通法的法律默示,如1906年《保险法》下的"绝对善意"(utmost good - faith)。要想排除这种法律的默示,就要靠明确的明示条文了。更不用说有一些立法的法律默示,更加是不准以明示条文排除,如1924年《海牙规则》的适航责任。更加明确的是,完整合约条文不足够排除那些对合约商业效力有"必须性"的事实默示,因为不默示一个说法该合约就会履行或运行不了。

§10　法律/事实默示条文的例子

笔者最后在许多不同的默示条文挑选少量的例子简单介绍。这些例子包括了法律与事实的默示,而针对普通法的默示,也不局限在本章之3.3段介绍的法律默示大量针对不同特定类别的合约,而是包括了一些针对或适用在所有的合约类别的默示。

10.1　默示条文例子一:履约需要对方先给通知

在任何一个合约,往往都有双方各自应履行的各种义务,这不需要对方提醒。所以如果不准时(合约明示规定的时间或法律默示的合理时间)履行,即会是违约,而且后果可大可小(这可见本书第十章)。但会有情况是在履行前,必须要有对方提供恰当的资料或作出通知,才能进行。这样,即使没有明示条文的规定,法院/仲裁庭也会作出这方面的默示。

举一个简单的例子,如果一个合约规定了合约一方必须在某一个时间内准时支付对方一笔钱,但合约没有针对付款办法,法律会作出默示就是对方作为收款人必须提前告知支付方他的银行帐号,否则支付方无法准时履约。如果付款办法是有明示条文规定,但针对收款人的银行只是说"另被通知"(to be advised)。但收款人没有提前告知支付方银行资料,这样针对"另被通知"的解释也是应该必须在支付方履约前作出。

这方面要作出默示条文,很早已有先例 Vyse v. Wakefield (1840) 5 M. & W. 442 说:"Where a party stipulates to a certain thing in a certain specific event which may become known to him, or with which he can make himself acquainted, he is not entitled to any notice, unless he stipulates for it; but where it is to do a thing which lies within the peculiar knowledge of the opposite party, then notice ought to be given to him."(如果一方在合约中承诺在特定情况下做一件事,他无权要求对方作出通知,这等于不需要对方提醒才履约,除非合约有明示规定。但如果他做的一件事是对方才会知道,法律就默示对方必须要向承诺方作出通知。)

在这一默示条文下,就可以带出在国际货物买卖与程租合约下的派船一方(FOB

买卖下的买方)或船东在抵达第一个装港时必须要通知对方有关船舶抵达与备妥装货,也就是所谓的“准备就绪通知书”(notice of readiness)。否则对方(也就是货方)没有责任履行合约责任,即提供货物与装货,并开始起算装卸时间。试想,如果没有通知,货方不一定容易知道船舶已经抵达装港。即使抵达与否可以看得见或向港务局查得到,货方也没办法知道船舶真正的状况是否已经备妥,如上一票货物是否已经卸清、货舱是否清洁、装卸设备是否有故障、舱盖能否打开等。当然,普通法的地位只是要求派船方/船东发出通知,没有对该通知作出形式上的要求,如口述的通知业已足够,看来这也是本章之第6段所讲的法律作出的默示要尽量狭窄,不多强加不必要的责任。航运与外贸通常对准备就绪通知书有很形式上的要求,如必须是文书形式、递交的对象、递交的时间等,这都来自明示条文,法律的默示没有。这样,针对约定的要求必须严格遵守,否则就会导致准备就绪通知书无效,这又显示了明示条文比默示条文分量更重。

10.2 默示条文例子二:双方必须给予协助/合作让对方顺利履行合约

有不少合约的履行,履约方是需要对方给予协助/合作方能成事,这样,就会有必须作出一个法律的默示条文,除非合约已经有明示条文针对。这与本书第四章之第10段“假设订约方不能从他自己错误的行为中获利”有十分相同的精神,但该小段是针对“解释规则”(rules of construction),而本小段是针对默示条文,这也反映了本章之7.3.2段介绍的默示条文属于解释合约这一说法。这方面在大陆法系由“善意”(good faith)的理论针对,在英国法律就是默示的说法了。

这默示地位可以明示条文超越,因为有订约的自由。但现实中很少会出现,而如果有的话,这种明示条文也会严格被解释,因为通常在平等地位下谈判有一定知识水平的订约方都不会同意这种条文,让其中一方可以不合作或是作出妨碍或是通过自己错误而获利。

英国法律通常不愿意插手双方在一个合约中的一般性合作,以顺利履行。合约没有特定规定的一般性合作,这通常是一个事实问题。这是双方订约方自己的事情,哪些方面需要双方合作所涉及面亦十分广,加上合作的准则不容易确定,法律也不容易管。这可见 Devlin 大法官在 Mona Oil Equipment & Supply Co Ltd v. Rhodesia Railways Ltd (1949) 2 All E. R. 1014 先例中所说的:“It is, no doubt, true that every business contract depends for its smooth working on co - operation, but in the ordinary business contract, apart, of course, from express terms, the law can enforce co - operation only in a limited degree—to the extent that it is necessary to make the contract workable. For any higher degree of co - operation the parties must rely on the desire that both of them usually have that the business should get done.”

这表示一些经常遇到的情况,就是合约其中一方向对方作出各种要求协助/合作,是没有在合约内规定的。这种要求千变万化,包括要求金钱上如加价/减价,或是要求提供一些文件或资料,或是要求做合约没有要求做或甚至与合约不符的事情

(可见 North Sea Energy Holdings N. V. v. Petroleum Authority of Thailand [1999] 1 Lloyd's Rep. 483 先例)等。国际货物买卖合约与程租合约中的要求也是各种各样,如船舶发生延误,船东要求承租人或货方的合作延长销约期或其他的期限,或是要求允许做一些事情,如承租人要求上船检查,而这并非是该租约下必须或明示允许的检查等。

本来提出要求没有问题,也不会是违约/毁约,除非在提出要求的同时加上非法的威胁。现实中经常会见到被要求的合约方如果对自己的法律地位不了解(即可否根据合约或法律地位拒绝),加上怕事或一厢情愿地合作,甚至认为英国法律下必须协助/合作,就会贸然答应,但事后又反悔而造成可能是"弃权"(waiver)或"禁止反供"(estoppels)甚至是违约/毁约的行为。遇上这种情况,被要求方很重要的一点就是了解根据该合约下的明示或默示条文,是否必须提供对方提出的要求协助/合作。如果不是,法律不会要求必须要这样做。即使是同意合作,也必须先与对方谈条件,要求对方作出其他方面相应让步。这里可节录 Hirst 大法官在 Siporex Trade S. A. v. Banque Indosuez (1986) 2 Lloyd's Rep. 146 先例所说如下:"I do not for a moment doubt that in the world of everyday commerce such co-operation frequently occurs, nor do I doubt that it is highly desirable, especially where important matter are left outstanding. But proof of mere normality of practice, or even of a high degree of desirability, falls far short of establishing the existence of a contractual duty owed by the buyer to be implied as a contractual term. See *Liverpool City Council v. Irwin*, [1977] A. C. 239—a case which is particularly helpful in the present context as showing that the stringent business efficacy test applies even where the Court is being asked to insert implied terms in an incomplete contract..."(Hirst 大法官说他从来不怀疑在商业世界这种双方的合作经常发生,这也是好事,特别是双方没有在合约中作出规定。但如果想证明这是正常的商业行为,即使是加上了这行为是一个高程度的好事,还是很难让该先例的买方作出该买卖合约中有一个合作的默示条文。在 Liverpool City Council v. Irwin 先例有关住客与房东谁有责任维护/维修公共区域的先例,可以清楚看到在一个不完整的合约没有针对某种情况下,要求法律加入一条默示条文针对是十分困难的。)

但法律还是在一些方面对订约双方必须协助/合作作出默示,这方面在上一小段的 Vyse v. Wakefield (1840) 5 M. & W. 442 先例就已经提到,可另介绍在 Mackay v. Dick (1881) 6 App. Cas. 251 先例,Blackburn 大法官也有大同小异的说法:"... where in a written contract it appears that both parties have agreed that something shall be done, **which cannot be effectually done unless both parties concur in doing it**, the construction of the contract is that each agrees to do all that is necessary to be done on his part for the carrying out of that thing, though there may be no express words to that effect."(加黑部分是笔者的强调)

在现实的合约履行中,一方的履行需要对方合作才能进行的情况经常发生。简单的例子是其中一方需要在一个期限前付出一笔金钱(不论是租约的租金或者是运费,或房屋买卖的一笔定金),就需要对方的合作提供银行账号。再如,如果甲雇用乙来为他画像,就有默示条文是需要甲本人的配合提供造型。在这种情况下的协助/合作,就有了法律的默示。例如,在前面已经提到,国际货物买卖合约与程租合约中会要求船长向发货人递交准备就绪通知书,尽管一般合约中会有明示条文针对,但即使没有的情况下,法律也会默示船东有这样的责任协助/合作。这是因为只有船长递交准备就绪通知书后,发货人才能安心安排装货。但前面提到的其他要求,如延误方要求对方合作延长期限,或是要求允许检验,因为这不是合约一方的履行必须要有对方作出相应的合作/协助,法律不会有这样的默示,而对事实的默示仅是"必须性"(necessary)已经相当困难(如没有对船舶做出检查,承租人还是可以在船长确认备妥后装货),所以这种要求必须要有明示条文来针对。

这些案例大量存在笔者熟悉的国际外贸与航运,以下对少部分作出介绍。先是有关油脂的一个 CIF 买卖,名为 Siporex Trade S. A. v. Banque Indosuez (1986) 2 Lloyd's Rep. 146 先例。案情简单的介绍是由于买方没有准时开出准确的信用证而构成违约/毁约,结果买卖合约被卖方终止。买方声称卖方有一个法律默示责任协助买方完成信用证的条文与解决问题,因为在该案例中的买卖合约有许多不明朗的地方,如有关信用证的最后有效期。买方也声称这种协助/合作在国际贸易是十分普遍的做法,并提供专家意见。但 Hirst 大法官拒绝默示卖方需要协助买方开出信用证,认为没有这个必须性,而且默示这种责任会带来严重的后果,说:"In my judgment, under the normal well established principles of letters of credit, it is for the buyer to establish the letter of credit as required by the contract. If the contract terms are themselves incomplete, and unresolvable by reference to custom, the supposed duty to cooperate would in effect be no more than an agreement to agree, which is not a workable contractual term. Moreover, the scope of the proposed duty in any given case would be impossible to define with the degree of precision necessary for a workable term. In these circumstances Mr. Hallgarten(买方大律师)'s proposed implied term fails the business efficacy test and I am not prepared to hold that there is any legal duty imposed on the seller to cooperate with the buyer..."。

下一个是 The "Aello" (1960) 1 Lloyd's Rep. 623 先例,船舶抵达布伊诺斯艾利斯装运玉米,但进不了港,因为承租人/发货人必需先向阿根廷的散粮部提出申请一份名为"Giro"的文件,船舶才会被允许进港。这样,即使程租合约没有作出任何规定,法律也默示承租人有这个提供协助/合作的责任。

同样的道理在 The "Atlantic Sunbeam" (1973) 1 Lloyd's Rep. 483 先例,船舶是加尔各答港卸货,又是需要一份文件名为"jetty challan"才进得了港口并能够递交通知书。但这一份文件是收货人的责任向港口当局取得,船东自己做不来。法院又是判承租人有这个默示责任"合理快速"(reasonable despatch)取得这份文件。

在 The “Timna” (1970) 2 Lloyd's Rep. 409 先例,承租人被要求在合理时间内指定第一个卸港让船舶可抵达卸货,不能让船舶在海上漂流不知道往哪里开,船东也无法履行他卸港卸货的承诺。

另在 The “World Navigator” (1991) 2 Lloyd's Rep. 23 先例,涉及是一个 FOB 买卖合约。这样,就是买方派船,但买方派的“World Navigator”轮去了阿根廷的罗萨里奥就无法进港靠泊,因为发货人有一些文件还没处理好。这种困难的情况也会出现在发货人货物没有备妥。这对买方会带来极严重的后果,除了对船舶延误会要承担滞期费或滞期损失外,更会造成付运的延误。在该先例,高院的 Philips 大法官判卖方有一个提供协助/合作的默示条文或责任,他说:“... the evidence demonstrated that *World Navigator* could not berth without the co – operation of the sellers in providing appropriate loading documentation and **it was common ground that it was necessary to imply into the f. o. b. contract a term requiring the sellers to provide that co – operation**; there was an implied obligation on the sellers to act with reasonable dispatch and in accordance with ordinary practice in doing those acts which were necessary to enable the buyers to present their vessel for loading at the berth; if availability of goods sold was necessary to enable the buyers' vessel to berth there was an absolute obligation on the sellers to have the goods available when the vessel arrived provided 15 days' notice had been given; it might be that this obligation could be extended to cover the procurement of documentation if this was something solely within the control of the sellers.”(加黑部分是笔者的强调)

上诉庭也同意了这一默示责任,而且无法说死是哪些事情要提供协助/合作,因为要根据不同的案件与当时的背景/环境作出默示:“... there was an obligation to do all that was necessary to enable the vessel to berth on the expiry of the 15 days' notice; it was probably impossible and undesirable to define the precise ambit of the obligation for in all cases what was to be implied would or might be dependent both on the terms of the contract and the surrounding circumstances.”

10.3 默示条文例子三:合约一方不能通过自己的错误获利

这一小段与本书第四章之第 10 段“假设订约方不能从他自己错误的行为中获利”比上一小段关系更加密切,甚至可以说是同一码事。第四章之第 10 段是针对“解释规则”(rules of construction),而本小段是针对法律默示条文,也更加鲜明反映了本章之 7.3.2 段介绍的默示条文属于解释合约这一说法。在许多有关的先例,法院是把这一默示地位与合约明示条文的解释混为一谈,以下等于补充第四章之第 10 段所讲的内容。

针对这方面的先例也有不少,首先是贵族院的Alghussein Establishment v. Eton College, (1988) 1 WLR 587 先例,法院是说:“The principle that in the absence of clear express provisions in a contract to the contrary it was not to be presumed that the parties intended that a party should be entitled to take advantage of his own breach as against the other party was not limited to cases where a party was relying on his own wrong to avoid his obligations under the contract but applied also where a party sought to obtain a benefit under a continuing contract on account of his breach."(大意是说如果合约中没有明示条文显示订约双方有相反意图,那么不能假设订约双方有意图让其中一方有权通过他自己的违约而获利。双方有这种订约意图会十分奇怪与不正常,在订约自由下,他们可以这样做,但必须要用明确无误的文字/措辞表达。这一原则不仅适用在一方依赖他自己的错误来避免合约责任的情况,也适用在一方在一个持续的合约下要求通过他自己的错误获利的情况。)

在Doe d Bryan v. Bancks (1821) 4 B & Ald 401 先例,在一个长期煤矿租约中有附带条文如下:"Provided also, and it is mutually agreed between the parties hereto, that the aforesaid works should commence and begin within one year from the date thereof, and **if the same should stop or cease working at any time two years, this lease shall be deemed void** to all intents and purposes."(加黑部分是笔者的强调)

Bayley 法官说:"I am of opinion, that the true construction of the proviso in this lease, 'that it shall be null and void to all intents and purposes upon a cesser of two years' is, that it shall be voidable only at the option of the lessor, and that it does not lie in the mouth of the lessee, who has been guilty of a wrongful act, in omitting to work in pursuance of his covenant, to avail himself of that wrongful act, and to insist, that thereby the lease has become void to all intents and purposes."(大意是说 Bayley 法官认为煤矿租约的附带条文[即如果停止工作两年,租约就会失效]虽然没有说明谁有权令租约无效,但真正的解释应该只有出租人有选择权。而如果矿场的租用人错误或不作为停止工作两年,他是没有权令租约无效,因为他不能因为自己的错误而得利。)

在上诉庭的 New Zealand Shipping Co. v. Societa des Ateliers et Chantiers de France (1919) AC 1 先例,Viscount Reading 大法官说:"Unless the language of the contract constrains the Court to hold otherwise, the law of England never permits a party to take advantage of his own default or wrong... Unless there are clear words to the contrary, a clause making a contract void must be read subject to the condition that the party who is seeking to set up the invalidity is not himself in default."(除非合约的文字约束法院必须给出相反的判决[因为有订约自由],否则英国法下从不允许一方因为自己的错误而从合约获利……除非有清楚的文字显示合约有相反意图,否则使合约无效的条文必须解释为主张合约无效的一方自己并无过错。)

Scrutton 大法官也说:"I think that clause 12 and all other clauses are to be read subject to an overriding condition or proviso that the party shall not take advantage of his own wrong, and therefore is stopped from alleging invalidity of which his own breach of contract is the cause."(Scrutton 大法官认为合约的第 12 条文与其他条文的解释要遵

循一个最重要的条件或者附带条文,即合约的一方不能因为他自己的错误而获利,因此他禁止主张因为自己的违约而使合约无效。)

之后在贵族院,Finlay LC 勋爵说:"Questions of this sort have often arisen in case of provisions that a lease should be void on non - payment of rent or non - performance of covenants by the lease. It has always been held that the lessee could not take advantage of his own act or default, to avoid the lease, and the expression generally employed has been that such proviso makes the lease voidable by the lessor, or void at the option of the lessor. The decisions on the point are uniform, and are really illustrations of the very old principle laid down by Lord Coke that a man shall not be allowed to take advantage of a condition which he himself brought about."(这类问题经常发生在房屋租赁合约中有条文规定如果不付租金或者不履行租赁合约,租赁合约就变为无效。一直以来,法院的判决都是租客不能利用他自己的行为或过失来使租赁合约无效。这措辞一般被解释为这种附带条文让房东可使合约无效,或者说房东有令合约无效的选择权。关于这一点的判决是统一的,也正是由 Coke 勋爵确立的一个非常古老的原则,即任何人不应该被允许利用他自己造成的原因获利。)

Cheall v Association of Professional Executive Clerical and Computer Staff (1983)2 AC 180 先例根据 New Zealand Shipping Co. v. Societa des Ateliers et Chantiers de France 先例重申了这一原则并提到会有两方面的影响。一是已经提到的默示地位,二是解释明示条文时也尽量避免作出这种解释,因为按常理说双方的订约意图是不会想让对方通过他的错误让自己获利。Diplock 勋爵是这样说:"In the course of the speeches, which are not entirely consistent with one another, reference was made by all their Lordships to the well known rule of construction that, except in the unlikely case that the contract contains clear express provisions to the contrary, it is to be presumed that it was not the intention of the parties that either party should be entitled to rely upon his own breaches of his primary obligations as bringing the contract to an end, i. e. as terminating any further primary obligations on his part then remaining unperformed. This rule of construction, which is paralleled by the rule of law that a contracting party cannot rely upon an event brought about by his own breach of contract as having terminated a contract by frustration, is often expressed in broad language as: 'A man cannot be permitted to take advantage of his own wrong.'"

最后回本段较早已经提到的 Alghussein Establishment v. Eton College 先例,显示了即使有明示条文针对"故意过错"(willful default),但由于有关条文与合约其他的条文一并解释有不明确,所以贵族院判是并非完全明确超越了法律的默示,也就是解释有关条文还是适用一方不能通过自己的错误获利的原则。该先例的案情涉及伦敦一块土地的所有人与一家开发商订立合约,合约包括开发商开发这块土地,以及将土地与建完后的建筑租给开发商 99 年。该合约的第 3(a)条文规定开放商必须尽最大努力获得开发的相关批准,而第3(b)条文如下:"as soon as is reasonably practicable following all necessary licences permissions consents and approvals having been obtained as aforesaid to use its best endeavours to commence and proceed diligently with the development in accordance with such licences permissions consents and approvals and complete the development to the reasonable satisfaction of the surveyors..."

接下来的第4条文针对的是99年的租约,文字/措辞上就有点莫名其妙,说:"Upon the proper issue of the certificate of practical completion... the landlords will forthwith grant and tenant shall forthwith accept and execute a counterpart of the lease provided that if for any reason due to the willful default of the tenant the development shall remain uncompleted on the 29th day of September 1983 the lease shall forthwith be granted and completed as aforesaid but without prejudice to the provisions of clause 3 hereof."

第4条文在字面上是说建完后并发出证明/证书,土地所有人就会给予一个租约。这显示了租约是在建筑完成后才开始,为期99年。但第二句就莫名其妙,说如果是开发商(也将会是租客)的故意过错导致建筑在1983年9月29日不能完成,土地所有人就应该马上给予一个99年的租约。但这样土地所有人就惨了,等于把一块没有被开发的土地以低的不能再低的租金被对方绑死,失去了土地被开发后的利益与租金。

但开发商因为在1978年订约后的伦敦地产环境下建造会亏本,迟迟没有开始工作。这显然是开发商违反了第3条文,也由于是故意,应该属于故意的过错。在1984年10月23日,土地所有人通过他的律师通知开发商因为开发商违约/毁约,合约被终止。这从第4条文的字面看来土地所有人完全没有按照合约办事,因为第4条文是要求他给予一个99年的租约。开发商于是向法院申请"履约指令"(specific performance),要求土地所有人履行合约,土地所有人则反申请要求颁令土地的占有权。

该先例主要的争议是,开发商能否依赖合约的第4条文要求土地所有人给予租约。一审法院认为开发商不能依赖合约的第4条文,上诉庭和贵族院也都支持了一审法院的判决。贵族院的Jauncey勋爵认为第4条文写得十分奇怪并且与第3条文不符。根据合约的第3条文,开发商必须尽最大努力完成开发。但根据合约的第4条文,开发商在开发完成后才能获得租约,除非因为他的故意过错导致开发在1983年9月29日前无法完成。这就会导致一个十分怪异的结果,也就是开发商故意拖慢进度甚至根本不开始开发,他可以在1983年9月29日获得这一十分有利的租约。但如果开发商尽了最大努力进行工程,但在1983年9月29日还没有完工,他反而不能获得这一租约。由于这一矛盾,Jauncey勋爵判是尽管第4条文提到了开发商的故意过错,但并没有明确写明双方同意让开发商可以通过自己的过错获利。因此不能取代解释合约的默示地位,也就是合约一方是不能通过自己的过错获利。贵族院的判决如下:"the well known rule of construction, that there was a presumption that a party to a contract could not be permitted to take advantage of his own wrong as against the other party, applied, in the absence of an express provision to contradict the presumption, as much to a party who sought to obtain a benefit under a continuing contract on account of his breach, as it did to a party who relied on his breach to avoid a contract and thereby escape his obligations; that the terms of the proviso to clause 4 were not apt to displace that rule of construction and that, therefore, the plaintiffs were not entitled to invoke the proviso to obtain the grant of the lease."

10.4 默示条文例子四:经纪人的佣金合约

涉及经纪人的佣金合约,好像其他类别的合约一样,普通法对这种合约关系有不少的法律默示条文。有过一些重要的先例说明在一些情况下有默示条文及在另一些情况下就不适用。第一种情况是判有默示条文就是"委托人"(principal)如果与第三人通过经纪人达成一宗交易,该经纪人在合约履行时就有权收取佣金。

第二种情况是委托人不能因为他的违约/毁约而导致合约无法履行,进而剥夺了该经纪人的佣金。这方面即使没有明示条文说明,法律也会作出默示:Alpha Trading Ltd v. Dunnshaw – Patten Ltd. (1981) 1 Lloyd's Rep. 122 先例。事实上还有更早的先例,主要是适用在保障房屋买卖的经纪人。例如在 Luxor (Eastbourne) Ltd. v. Cooper (1941) A. C. 108 先例,贵族院的 Wright 勋爵说:"The vendor is then no longer free to dispose of his property. Though the sale is not completed the property in equity has passed from him to the purchaser. If he refuses to complete he would be guilty of a breach of agreement vis – à – vis the purchaser. I think, as at present advised, that it ought then to be held that **he is also in breach of his contract with the commission agent, that is, of some term which can properly be implied.**"(加黑部分是笔者的强调)

但在许多其他情况,就不会有默示条文保障经纪人的佣金。在这种情况,在航运涉及金额庞大的佣金,经纪人在赚取后如果怕失去,就会投保这方面的风险。

如在 Luxor (Eastbourne) Ltd. v. Cooper 的贵族院先例,就判委托人如果自己另有渠道把房屋卖掉给其他人,即使他在与经纪人的合约中同意如果由后者促成的买卖成功就会给予佣金,也不默示委托人要保障赚不到佣金的经纪人。所以,如果经纪人希望委托人只能通过他出售有关的房屋,就必须以明示条文在他们之间的合约规定出售必须通过他作为"独家代理"(exclusive agent)。该先例中这样说:"Where an agent is promised a commission only if he brings about the sale which he is endeavouring to effect there is no room for an implied term that the principal will not dispose of the property himself or through other channels or otherwise act so as to prevent the agent earning his commission."

在另一个情况,委托人如果不涉及违约而与合约对方同意终止合约,进而剥夺了经纪人部分佣金(因为佣金是按期支付),法律也不默示委托人要赔偿给经纪人少赚的部分佣金。有关先例是一个 18 个月的期租合约,规定支付给经纪人的佣金是在租金支付后才付。在履行了 4 个月后,船东把船舶卖给承租人,租约也随之终止。法院判是船东没有违反任何默示条文:French (L.) and co Ltd v. Leeston Shipping Co Ltd (1922) 1 A.C. 451 先例。看来,这与租约履行了 4 个月船舶因船东没有过错(或租约是免责)的事故而沉没并导致租约受阻的道理一样。这样,经纪人还没有赚取的佣金也泡汤,除非他买了保险。这会带来疑问,委托人会否与合约另一方提前终止合约并另订立新合约,进而剥夺前一份合约要支付给经纪人的佣金?可能在这种情况,除了经纪人可起诉委托人,法律会有其他的救济,其中包括经纪人可以"经济侵权"(economic tort)之"阴谋"(conspiracy)起诉合约另一方。所以这种情况也不太会发生。

在 The "Manifest Lipkowy" (1989) 2 Lloyd's Rep. 139 先例,案情又涉及另一种情况。有关船舶的买卖,卖方与经纪人达成了一个协议支付佣金,并明确规定了佣金将会在支付船价时授权买方银行扣起。但之后由于交船延误并错过了销约期,买方乘机终止买卖合约。这就带来经纪人向卖方起诉要求赔偿佣金,说是在这种情况下有一个默示条文。这种案情又是与较早的先例不一样,首先它不涉及卖方(也就是委托人)的违约,而即使交船晚了涉及违约,终止买卖合约也不是卖方的行为,而是对方买方行使选择权。结果是上诉庭拒绝作出这样的默示,特别是加上市场的做法就是船舶买卖最终不成交是通常不支付佣金,这也涉及本章稍早的第 6 段介绍的默示条文要尽量狭窄,只是在必要的情况下才作出法律默示。Bingham 大法官这样说:"... it was well established law that a term would be implied only where it was necessary to give business efficacy to a contract or where the term was one which the parties must obviously have intended; there was nothing in the agreement to suggest that the parties intended the plaintiffs to be remunerated if there were never, because of the defendants' default, any sale proceedings from which the commission could be deducted; the contract as made was wholly workable without the implied term and the appeal would be dismissed."

10.5 默示条文例子五:合约期限的默示

当合约没有明示写明何时期满或终止,法院或仲裁庭可以作出一个事实的默示该合约在一个合理期限届满通过作出合理通知终止。默示的原因是假设双方不会有意图任何情况下也要把该合约履行下去。特别是考虑到一些合约会直接与严重受到如通货膨胀、环境改变等影响,更加不可能是订约双方意图无限期地履行该合约。所以可能性应是在双方对合约的期限在订约时有所遗漏较大,法律可根据事实与背景/环境作出默示填补这个漏洞。

有关的先例很早就已经有说法,这在 Llanelly Railway and Dock Co v L. N. W. R (1875) L. R. 7 App. Cas 550 先例,Selborne 勋爵就说:"... an agreement *de futuro*, extending over a tract of time which, on the face of the instrument, is indefinite and unlimited, must (in general) throw upon any one alleging that it is not perpetual, the burden of proving that allegation, either from the nature of the subject, or from some rule of law applicable thereto."

到了 Australia Blue Metal Ltd v Hughes (1963) AC 74 先例,Devlin 勋爵就第一次提到不论是解释合约或是作出默示条文,可以通过作出通知终止这种合约,说:"It is true that it does not require very much to induce a court to read into an agreement of a commercial character, either by construction or by implication, a provision that the arrangements between the parties, whatever they may be, shall be terminable only upon reasonable notice."

在 Re Spenborough Urban District Council's Agreement (1968) CH. 139 先例,Buckley 大法官解释在怎样的情况下法院愿意作出事实的默示条文,说:"Authority establishes that, where an agreement does not in terms confer on the parties or one of them a power to determine the agreement, whether such a power should be inferred is a question of construction of the agreement to be determined in accordance with the ordinary principle applicable to such a question. ... An agreement which is silent about determination will not be determinable unless the facts of the case, such as the subject matter of the agreement, the nature of the contract or the circumstances in which the agreement was made, support a finding that the parties intended it to be determinable, but there is in my judgment, no presumption one way or the other."

10.5.1　允许作出合理通知终止合约的先例

这方面的案例与笔者见过的案件有不少,可见即使涉及很高的金额,很多商业人士在订立合约的时候还是十分不小心,对这么重要的事情竟然遗漏。以下简单介绍一些先例被判是可以通过合理通知终止合约:

1. Credition Gas Co v. Crediton Urban District Council (1928) 1 Ch. 17 先例,涉及一家石油公司与当地政府订约,石油公司承诺负责当地一切公共照明,从9月1日开始,直到来年的5月1日,"每年有效",判是合约可通过合理通知终止。

2. Martin－Baker Aircraft Co Ltd v. Canadian Flight Equipment Ltd (1955) 2 Q.B. 556 先例,案情涉及一家公司与另一家公司订约,给予后者生产弹射座椅的授权,而回报是后者支付前者专利使用费。合约没有关于如何终止的规定,McNair 大法官判是可以合理通知终止,说:"I have little doubt that the law merchant would regard a contract for sale of a hundred tons of coal monthly at a fixed price, no period being specified, as a contract determinable on reasonable notice."

3. 在 Kores Manufacturing Co Ltd v. Kolok Manufacturing Co Ltd (1957) 1 W.L.R. 1012 先例,两家公司订约同意相互之间不雇佣对方5年内雇佣过的人,合约本身没有规定期限,判是可以通过作出12个月的通知终止。

4. 在 Milner（JH）& Son v Bilton（Percy）Ltd（1966）1 WLE 1582 先例，一家律所被聘用为一个地产开发项目及完工后建筑租赁的长期法律顾问。相关合约中没有规定期限，判是可以通过作出合理的通知终止。

5. 在 Re Spenborough Urban District Council's Agreement（1968）Ch 139 先例，案情涉及政府当局与工厂订立合约，约定可以排放进公共的下水管道的工业废水数量，被判是可以通过作出合理的通知终止。

10.5.2 怎样才算是“合理”的通知？

可以作出合理通知终止没有明示规定期限的合约，涉及怎样才算是合理与有效的提前通知。首先，针对合理与否是看作出通知时，而有关的考虑是合约的本质、双方已经履行了的时间、有关业务的性质、合约对合约双方的重要性等。所以，每一个案件都会有它特定的情况并会导致通知所需要的合理时间都不一致。有关的先例可看：Martin - Baker Aircraft Co Ltd v. Canadian Flight Equipment Ltd（1955）2 Q. B. 556（12 个月）；Decro - Wall v Practitioners in Marketing Ltd（1971）1 WLR 361（12 个月）；Alpha Lettings Ltd and Neptune Research and Development Inc（2003）EWCA Civ 704（4 个月）；Jackson Distribution Ltd v Tum Yeto Inc（2009）EWHC 982（QB）（9 个月）等先例。

10.5.3 合约期限有含糊不清的明示规定能否作出默示？

在不少案例，涉及一个最大的问题就是在本章之 4.4.5 段所讲的如果合约有了“明示条文”（express terms），就只涉及解释该条文，但不能再作出默示条文。因为明示条文已经真正反映了双方订约意图，不存在可以作出假设。在这些案例，涉及一些对合约期限的写法不明确，这样就会存在不同的法院/仲裁庭会认为该合约有或是没有明示条文。如果合约期限的写法明确，如 1000 年，即使是完全不合理也不存在法院可以作出默示条文。例如在 Kirklees Metropolitan Borough Council v. Yorkshire Woolen District Transport Co Ltd（1978）77 L. G. R. 448 先例，涉及两家当地权力机构与一家公司签订了 99 年的交通服务合约，作为回报此公司将给予两机构一个利润的百分比。但后来公司的继承人意图通过作出通知将该合约终止，结果被判是默示条文不成立，Walton 大法官说“by no stretch of the imagination（could such a term be implied）”。

先介绍一些有关合约期限写得不明确的先例。首先是 Staffordshire Area Health Authority v. South Staffordshire Waterworks Co（1978）1 W. L. R. 1387 先例，案情涉及一个供水合约，由供水商与一家医院在 1929 年订立，说明“今后所有时间”（at all times hereafter）由前者供水给后者，而费用是每 1000 加仑 7 便士。到了 1971 年，食水的价格已经上涨到每 1000 加仑 55 便士。这样，供水商就给了医院一个 6 个月的合约终止通知。在高院，先是判“今后所有时间”应被解释为“永久”（forever or in perpetuity），供水商败诉。但该先例到了上诉庭，该判决被推翻，认为供水商有权在合理通知后终止该供水合约。Goff 大法官认为即使合约期限有明示为“今后所有时间”,这一句话的合理解释可以是“今后所有时间只要本合约继续存在”(at all times hereafter during the subsistence of this agreement)。这不影响可以以该合约没有说明期限作出事实的默示条文,也就是供水商有权作出合理通知后终止该合约。

但有一个新西兰的 Gore District Council v. Power Co Ltd (1996) 1 N. Z. L. R. 58 案例是在同样的合约文字/措辞下作出相反的判决,案情是一家电力公司在 1927 年同意以一个固定价格为当地政府提供电力。到了 1995 年左右,当地政府每年支付的电费只是 16,639 新西兰元,但由于通货膨胀与耗电量大增,根据市场价格应该支付 204,529 新西兰元。这样,在 1995 年 2 月 28 日,电力公司向地方政府作出了 15 个月的通知要终止合约。该合约内写明有关合约期限是与 Staffordshire Area Health Authority v. South Staffordshire Waterworks Co 先例一致的“for all time thereafter”,却被判是合约不能以合理通知终止。

新西兰法院也仔细考虑过 Staffordshire Area Health Authority v. South Staffordshire Waterworks Co 这一英国先例,并对两个案件的不同作出区分。笔者看来也不觉得这些区分十分显著与有说服力,估计最重要的还是新西兰法院认为双方已经有了明示条文就不应该默示,并认为该明示条文写得十分明确,说:“The words of the agreement are clear. It is difficult to imagine a clearer way a drafter could impose a permanent obligation than to say ‘*the provisions of this Deed shall be binding on* [*the parties*] *for all time hereafter*’. Had the parties wished to make the agreement determinable on reasonable notice, it is safe to assume that they would have said so.”

在一个比较近期的英国先例 Harbinger UK Ltd v. GEI Information Services Ltd (2000) 1 All ER (Comm) 166,案情涉及提供电脑软件与服务支持合约,其中第 10 条文说:“(Harbinger 作为提供服务方) will provide support and maintenance in perpetuity in return for an annual payment, as specified in Schedule One, and subject to the following conditions...”(加黑部分是笔者的强调)

合约是在 1996 年 8 月下旬签订,但到了 1998 年 12 月 30 日,Harbinger 作出通知于 1999 年 12 月 31 日终止合约。上诉庭推翻了高院的判决,并认为“永久”(in perpetuity)一词在本案例的整个案情下看是足够明确的明示合约期限。但由于该合约只是单方面合约,所以这一明确的合约期限只是约束 Harbinger,而对 GEI 而言,电脑软件更新换代很快,不可能是永久,所以它可以在不需要 Harbinger 继续提供服务支持时终止合约。Evan 大法官说:

“The words ‘in perpetuity’ in clause 10 make it clear that the support and maintenance obligation extends beyond termination of the Agreement under clause 3. Equally clearly, they do not impose any time limit on the existence of that obligation. ‘In perpetuity’ is inconsistent with a time limit, and the words mean, in my judgment, that the obligation is to continue ‘without limit of time’.

This does not mean literally ‘for ever’ or ‘until the crack of doom’. The contractitself—meaning the unilateral contract under which the obligation to provide support and maintenance arises—will not live forever. The time will come when the technology is superseded and the software is outdated. As a result, customers will require a change in the software (and no doubt in the hardware) which they use and they will no longer make the annual payments in return for which the services are provided. No one can predict definitely when this will occur. But until it does, the contract and the obligation both survive.

'In perpetuity' in my judgment emphasises this negative aspect. There is nothing in the clause 10 contract which imposes a time limit, and the obligation continues as long as the contract survives. Perhaps because the appellants have sought to give the words a positive meaning, the judge was able to reject their construction as uncommercial, and both he and the respondents tried to seek out some other positive meaning. Hence the respondents' alternative suggestion of a reasonable time and judge's contractual timetable which he devised in order to place a time - limit on the operation of the clause; but the words themselves provide expressly that there is no time - limit. Both of these attempts founder, in my judgment, on the plain fact that the express words 'in perpetuity' are inconsistent with any time - limit on the operation of the clause."

最后一提的是,也涉及有明示条文就不作出默示条文的原则下,但明示条文并不针对合约期限而是针对什么情况终止合约的明示条文,也会令作出合约默示条文变得困难:Re Berker Sportscraft Ltd's Agreements (1947) 177 L. T. 420;Colchester and East Essex Co - operative Society Ltd v. Kelvedon Labour Club and Institute Ltd. (2003) EWCA Civ 1671 等先例。

10.6 默示条文例子六:关于价格的默示

虽然在现实中这种情况不经常出现,但当合约没有明示约定一个价格(不论是买卖价格或是服务的费用),这会带来两个结果。一个结果是如果在很早期时,就会更好是理解为双方还没有谈妥,合约不能成立,毕竟价格是任何商业合约中至关重要的条件。但另一个结果是无法说双方之间没有合约,虽然价格没有明示约定,因为双方已经履行了或甲乙双方都异口同声承认有一个合约关系。这样,法院/仲裁庭只能根据双方已经达成的合约条文与当时的背景/环境默示该合约的价格为合理价格。这方面可见 Denning 勋爵(那时仍是大法官)在 British Bank for Foreign Trade Ltd v. Novinex Ltd (1949) 1 K. B. 623 先例中所说的(这原则或说法被上诉庭肯定):"The principle to be deduced from the cases is that if there is an essential term which has yet to be agreed and there is no express or implied provision for its solution, the result in point of law is that there is no binding contract. In seeing whether there is an implied provision for its solution, however, there is a difference between an arrangement which is wholly executory on both sides and one which has been executed on one side or the other. In the ordinary way, if there is an arrangement to supply goods at a price 'to be agreed' or to perform service on terms 'to be agreed', then although, while the matter is still executory, there may be no binding contract, nevertheless, if it is executed on one side, that is, if the one does his part without having come to an agreement as to the price or the terms, then the law will say that there is necessarily implied, from the conduct of the parties, a contract that, in default of agreement, a reasonable sum is to be paid."（从先例可以得出的原则是在一个尚未履行与一个已经开始履行的交易有区分。如果合约尚未履行，价格没有同意就会被视为有效的合约还没有达成。但如果一个已经开始履行的交易，但双方还没有同意价格，法律就只能根据双方的行为默示已经有一个合约并需要作出合理价格的支付。）

另在 Sykes (Wessex) Ltd v. Fine Fare Ltd (1967) 1 Lloyd's Rep. 53 先例中 Denning 勋爵也说了同样的话："In a commercial agreement the further the parties have gone with their contract, the more ready are the Courts to imply an reasonable term so as to give effect to their intentions. When much has been done, the Courts will do their best not to destroy the bargain. When nothing has been done, it is easier to say that there is no agreement between the parties because the essential terms have not been agreed. But when an agreement has been acted upon and the parties, as here, have been put to great expense in implementing it, we ought to imply all reasonable terms so as to avoid any uncertainties."

在这方面先介绍一个权威先例 Foley v. Classique Coaches Ltd (1934) 2 K. B. 1，双方在一个汽油供应合约中写明"价格待定"(at a price to be agreed)，汽油随后事实上被提供了。由于汽油已被供应与接受，法院判应支付的是默示的合理价格。

另一个有关的先例是 Voest Alpine Intertrading GmbH v. Chevron International Oil Co Ltd (1987) 2 Lloyd's Rep. 547，是有关原油买卖的合约链约定价格调整根据进一步谈判来解决，判是有默示条文如果双方不能达成一致，就要由一个独立裁判人来确定（这要看合约本身同意了什么形式的争议解决机制）。

在一个更近期的先例 Mamidoil - Jetoil Greek Petroleum Co SA v Okta Vrude Oil Refinery AD (2001) 2 Lloyd's Rep 76，涉及一个 10 年的合约在希腊的 Salonica 处理/储存/提炼原油，双方只对前两年所收取的费用有约定，具体的案情可看本书第九章之 5.2.3 段。上诉庭推翻了一审的判决认为余下的 4 年（因为有 4 年双方已经达成协议）所收取的费用就是以合理价格为准，并作出指引有关如何确定合理价格。Rix 大法官这样说："In my judgment, the 1993 contract should be viewed as a contract for a fixed period of at least 10 years and a term should be implied that in the absence of agreement reasonable fees should be determined for the period after 1994. I would seek to put the matter in the following way. . . . (vi) There is no evidence that the resolution of a reasonable fee would cause any difficulty at all. On the contrary, the evidence is the other way... Although it is not possible to say that there was a market or list price for the handling service, nevertheless Jetoil was not a monopoly, nor, I would infer, was the refinery the only customer of the facilities at Salonica. In the absence of evidence to the contrary, I would infer that it was perfectly possible to derive from the agreements of price and price increases over the years objective criteria for working out a reasonable fee. Thus, although it is true to say that the contract itself contained no mechanism or guidance (other than the arbitration clause) as to how a reasonable fee would be derived, I do not consider that the contract should fail on that ground. Contractually derived criteria or guidance may be of assistance in finding an implied term for a reasonable price: but the authorities indicate that the Courts are well prepared to make the implication even in their absence."(没有证据显示决定合理价格会有困难,证据反而显示了不难作出决定。虽然是没有市场价格或标准价格针对处理/储存/提炼原油的费用,但原告并不是在当地垄断,也不是只有这一个客户。除非有明确的证据,Rix 大法官认为完全可以从其他所约定的费用以及每年的费用增加客观计算出什么是合理费用。虽然该合约是没有机制或指引[除了有仲裁条文]关于怎样拟定合理费用,Rix 大法官不认为合约就因此被视为不能执行而终止。虽然合约如果有机制或指引就有很大帮助,但权威先例已经显示了法院完全有能力在没有这方面的帮助的情况下也可以决定默示的合理费用/价格。)

这种价格没有明示约定的情况在一些行业中倒是常见,如保单就常会有规定"保费是稍后约定"(premium to be arranged)或救助合约的救助奖金要由仲裁员来厘定。这也不影响已经有了有效的保单(或救助合约),只是保费要根据合理价格,除非双方能够稍后同意。

10.7 默示条文例子七:履行合约标准的默示

法律对履行合约的标准根据不同的行业与情况会作出不同的默示。例如,在货物买卖,本章之 3.2.1 段已经介绍过各种默示条文,包括像卖方拥有该有关货物的所有权,买方可宁静地占有该货物等。在商品制造合约(包括建筑),有默示条文是被制造的商品将会合理"符合其用途"(fit for the purpose)。这些默示条文都会是严格责任。

在服务性合约,也有立法针对,这是在 1982 年的《货物与服务提供法》(《Supply of Goods and Services Act 1982》)的 Section 13:"carry out the service with reasonable care and skill."

这样的文字明显不是严格责任,但该立法在 Section 16(3)(a)保留了任何法律会对供应商强加一个更严格责任:"any rule of law which imposes on the supplier a stricter duty."

这带来了服务性合约会是有可能既有严格责任,如服务的同时也提供了零件/配件,因为这样就会带来零件/配件需要符合其用途或达到预期的效果。但看来如果只纯粹是提供服务,法律的默示地位只是服务方提供的服务是有合理的小心与技术业已足够,一般不会对服务结果的好坏作出默示。虽然,在例外情况下(这方面会在本小段稍后针对专业人士的服务探讨)也会有默示条文是要求服务会达到所期望的效果。另也会有默示条文提升到绝对/严格的责任,如在普通法下对船舶对货方提供海上运输的服务在开航前的适航是绝对责任,虽然这一普通法责任已经被国际公约/立法的 1924 年《海牙规则》减轻到"恪尽职责"(due diligence)。

针对提供的商品要合理符合其用途或达到预期的效果,早在 Francis v. Cockrell (1870) L. R. 5 Q. B. 501 先例,Kelly C. B. 大法官就说:"I do not hesitate to say that I am clearly of opinion, as a general proposition of law, that when one man engages with another to supply him with a particular article or thing, to be applied to a certain use or purpose, in consideration of a pecuniary payment, he enters into an implied contract that the article or thing shall be reasonably fit for the purpose for which it is to be used and to which it is to be applied."

在提供工作的合约与材料供应合约,也有默示是工作要有"良好的工艺"(good and workmanlike),"材料的质量要良好"(good and proper materials):Stewart v. Ravell's Garage (1952) 2 Q. B. 545 等先例。另在 Miller v. Cannon Hill Estate Ltd (1931) 2 K. B. 113 先例,案情是有关房屋买卖,而卖方也是该房屋的建造商。法院判卖方有三个默示责任,一是建造的房屋要有良好的工艺;二是建造的房屋材料质量要良好;三是房屋要合理适合自然人的居住。但情况一变,在一个没有装修好的房屋的租赁合约,因为本质不同,就没有房屋要适合自然人居住的这个默示条文了:Hart v. Windsor (1844) 12 M. & W. 68;Sleafer v. Lambeth Borough Council (1960) 1 Q. B. 43;Duke of Westminster v. Guild (1985) Q. B. 688(实质上没有备妥);Edler v. Auerbach (1950) 1 K. B. 359;Hill v. Harris (1965) 2 Q. B. 601(法律上没有备妥)等先例。

较早时已经提到过,专业人士纯粹服务性合约有不同标准,通常不会有默示是提供服务的专业人士要达致客户预期的效果,只会默示他要有"合理的小心与技术"(reasonable care and skill)。例如,医生不保证医好病人,律师不保证赢案子。原因很简单,由于变数太多与结果不稳定,所以提供服务的人士也保证不了一定有满意的结果。在 Thake v. Maurice (1986) 1 All E. R. 497, CA 先例,上诉庭只认同医生有合理的小心与技术的服务标准,但不保证什么,因为动手术的结果无法预测,而且人体状况各异。Nourse 大法官说:"general knowledge in medical science all things, or nearly all things, are uncertain."

这一判法与 Eyre v. Measday (1986) 1 All E. R. 488 先例一致,这与 Thake v. Maurice (1986) 1 All E. R. 497, CA 两个先例都是有关绝育手术。在后一个先例,是一个女士做了绝育手术之后仍然怀孕,而根据医学上的统计,绝育手术的确没有办法 100% 保险,而只能到 99%。法院判:

"Counsel for the plaintiff(怀孕女士的大律师), in the light of the passage in cross – examination which I have just read and in the light of all the other background of the case to which I have referred, submitted that if someone had said to the parties, 'Is it intended that the defendant(被告的医生)should warrant that the operation will render the plaintiff absolutely sterile? ', the answer of both parties must have been, 'Yes.' This, he submitted, is really the only possible inference from what had been said on both sides in the defendant's consulting rooms. He particularly drew attention to the question that he had put to the defendant, 'Would it have been reasonable for her to have gone away from your consulting rooms thinking that she would be sterilised and that would be the end of the matter? ', To which the defendant had replied, 'Yes, it would.' Counsel for the plaintiff submitted that the defendant himself was thus acknowledging that the reasonable inference would have been as he suggested.

Applying *The Moorcock* principles, I think there is no doubt that the plaintiff would have been entitled reasonably to assume that the defendant was warranting that the operation would be performed with reasonable care and skill. That, I think, would have been the inevitable inference to be drawn, from an objective standpoint, from the relevant discussion between the parties. The contract did, in my opinion, include an implied warranty of that nature. However, that inference on its own does not enable the plaintiff to succeed in the present case. She has to go further. She has to suggest, and it is suggested on her behalf, that the defendant, by necessary implication, committed himself to an unqualified guarantee as to the success of the particular operation proposed, in achieving its purpose of sterilising her, even though he were to exercise all due care and skill in performing it. The suggestion is that the guarantee went beyond due care and skill and extended to an unqualified warranty that the plaintiff would be absolutely sterile.

On the facts of the present case, I do not think that any intelligent lay bystander (let alone another medical man), on hearing the discussion which took place between the defendant and the other two parties, could have reasonably drawn the inference that the defendant was intending to give any warranty of this nature. It is true that in cross – examination he admitted that it would have been reasonable for the plaintiff to have gone away from his consulting rooms thinking that she would be sterilised. He did not, however, admit that it would have been reasonable for her to have left his consulting rooms thinking that he had given her a guarantee that after the operation she would be absolutely sterile; this, I think, is the really relevant point. She has to say that this would have been the reasonable inference from what he said to her and from what she and her husband said to him. **But, in my opinion, in the absence of any express warranty, the court should be slow to imply against a medical man an unqualified warranty as to the re-**

sults of an intended operation, for the very simple reason that, objectively speaking, it is most unlikely that a responsible medical man would intend to give a warranty of this nature. Of course, objectively speaking, it is likely that he would give a guarantee that he would do what he had undertaken to do with reasonable care and skill but it is quite another matter to say that he has committed himself to the extent suggested in the present case."(加黑部分是笔者的强调)

如果医疗是不肯定,难以默示会达到病人的预期效果,法律的诉讼结果就更加不肯定了,没有理由要代表律师保证诉讼的结果。但注意在一些例外情况也会有默示条文是专业人士的服务会要求达致预期效果。在 Greaves & Co (Contractors) Ltd v. Baynham Meikle (1975) 1 W. L. R. 1095 先例,是有关一个设计可供叉车作业的仓库有问题,设计的工程师是否有默示责任达至预期效果。在该先例,上诉庭判是设计的工程师违反了合理小心与技术的默示责任,也违反了设计要达至预期效果的另一默示责任。但可节录 Denning 勋爵曾提到达至预期效果的默示条文法律上仍是不明朗,他说:

"Apply this to the employment of a professional man. The law does not usually imply a warranty that he will achieve the desired result, but only a term that he will use reasonable care and skill. The surgeon does not warrant that he will cure the patient. Nor does the solicitor warrant that he will win the case. But, when a dentist agrees to make a set of false teeth for a patient, there is an implied warranty that they will fit his gums: see Samuels v Davis (1943) 1 K. B. 527.(针对专业人士的雇佣,法律通常不会默示他会保证达到一个预期的效果,他只需要合理的小心与技术作出服务。医生不保证他会医好病人,律师不保证他会胜诉。但如果一个牙医为他的病人提供了一副假牙,这就会带来一个默示责任该副假牙是达致预期效果。这显然是因为牙医提供的商品要合理符合其用途。)

What then is the position when an architect or an engineer is employed to design a house or a bridge? Is he under an implied warranty that, if the work is carried out to his design, it will be reasonably fit for the purpose? Or is he only under a duty to use reasonable care and skill? This question may require to be answered some day as matter of law. But in the present case I do not think we need answer it. . . . "(这样如果一个建筑师或工程师被雇佣设计一栋房子或一座桥梁,之后按照他的设计建造。这样他是否有一个默示责任保证该房子或桥梁必须合理符合其用途,或他只是有一个合理小心与技术的责任?这一方面还需要法院有一天作出解答。显然,法律如果不明朗,有关的当事人永远可以明示条文把他们同意的责任分摊在合约中作出规定。)

§11　默示合约

本章以上段节针对的是一个合约中的默示条文,本段是针对同样的大原则适用在一个默示的合约(implied contract)。众所周知,能够构成一个合约,是有一些基本要求,在《国际商务游戏规则——英国合约法》一书第二章有详论。笔者在这里只说合约必须是双方同意了一些"主要条文"(essential terms),而同意的形式可以通过文书、口头或行为达成。有关合约的主要条文,如订约方、价格或/与标的,通常要求双方约定,尽量不要依赖默示条文。因为默示条文并不能令一个没有达成协议变为一个有效合约或填补不完整之处令其变为有效合约。这方面可节录 Aotearoa International Ltd v. Scanmcarrie A/S (1985) 2 Lloyd's Rep. 419 先例中 Roskill 勋爵所说的:"... the first question must always be whether any legally binding contract has been made, for until that issue is decided a court cannot properly decide what extra terms, if any, must be implied into what is *ex hypothesi* a legally binding bargain work. It is not correct in principle, in order to determine whether there is a legally binding bargain, to add to those terms which alone the parties have expressed, further implied terms upon which they have not expressly agreed and then by adding the express terms and the implied terms together thereby create what would not otherwise be a legally binding bargain."

至于达成合约的形式,会发生罕有的情况是双方从来没有接触过,无法说成是有任何文书、口头或行为上的接触达成任何合约,但他们之间发生的争议又非要是合约关系才说得通,毕竟民事诉讼除了合约外主要只有侵权,而侵权的关系在争议中是说不通的。这样,就出现了默示合约的说法。但大道理与默示条文一样,它必须十分严谨才能把双方硬说成是有一个合约关系,而且也必须要这样做不可。笔者稍后介绍一些实例后读者就会更加明白为什么必须要有默示合约的说法了,在此先介绍在怎样的情况下才可作出事实的默示指双方有一个合约。这方面大道理是一样,即首要条件是"必须"(necessary)这样做,与有"商业效力"(business efficacy),这两样本来就是同一码事。Bingham 大法官在一个著名的提单先例 The "Aramis" (1989) 1 Lloyd's Rep. 213 CA 说:

"These cases may be said to decide no more than that whether a contract is to be implied is a question of fact and that a contract will only be implied where it is necessary to do so ... Whether on such facts ... a contract may be implied must be considered in the light of ordinary contractual principles.

Most contracts are, of course, made expressly, whether orally or in writing. But here, on the evidence, nothing was said, nothing was written. So regard must be paid to the conduct of the parties alone. The questions to be answered are, I think, twofold:(1) Whether the conduct of the bill of lading holder in presenting the bill of lading to the ship's agent would be reasonably understood by the agents (or the shipowner) as an offer to enter into a contract on the bill of lading terms. (2) Whether the conduct of the ship's agent in accepting the bill or the conduct of the master in agreeing to give delivery or in giving delivery would be reasonably understood by the bill of lading holder as an acceptance of his offer.

I do not think it is enough for the party seeking the implication of a contract to obtain 'it might' as an answer to these questions, for it would, in my view, be contrary to principle tocountenance the implication of a contract from conduct if the conduct relied upon is no more consistent with an intention to contract than with an intention not to contract. It must, surely, be necessary to identify conduct referable to contract contended for or, at the very least, conduct inconsistent with there being no contract made between the parties to the effect contended for. Put another way, I think it must be fatal to the implication of a contract if the parties would or might have acted exactly as they did in the absence of a contract.

If this approach is correct, I think it is impossible to imply a contract on the bare facts of this case. Nothing that the shipowners or the bill of lading holders did need have been different had their intention been not to make a contract on the bill of lading terms. Their business relationship was entirely efficacious without the implication of any contract between them. Although the bill of lading holders had no title to any part of any undivided bulk cargo they had a perfectly good right to demand delivery and the shipowners had no right to refuse or to impose conditions."

这一问题最早与最大规模出现在提单,因为提单被转让一些第三人的收货人手中,或是被质押给银行,而银行最终需要提货。这些收货人都不会是原来与承运人订约的一方,也往往从来没有接触过。但很多时候他们之间(收货人与承运人)需要有合约关系才在一些争议说得通,仅是侵权关系完全不足够。例如,在一些货损货差索赔、运费或滞期费的索赔等。合约关系最终还是要靠立法解决,英国的立法先是1855年的《提单法》,后来是1992年的《海上货物运输法》。但在立法之前,遇上这种情况要硬把收货人与承运人说成是有合约关系,就有了默示合约的说法。即使在1855年立法之后,由于适用的情况比较局限,还是不断有一些案件不能适用该立法而要继续以普通法的默示合约解释。希望是到了1992年的立法后,扩大了适用面,这方面的问题会比较更好解决。有关这些方面在笔者的《提单及其他付运单证》一书有详论,不重复。

当然默示合约的说法也不只是适用在提单,而是在所有其他方面。其中,如果双方没有达成任何协议就已经履行,变为需要有一个合约关系的说法,就已经可以归纳为一个默示的合约，虽然在这种情况会有其他的说法解释一个合约关系，如双方以行动的形式达成合约。这里的先例可举 G Percy Trientham Ltd v. Archital Luxfer Ltd.（1993）1 Lloyd's Rep. 25，CA 先例，案情有关一个岸上的承建商与分承建商，分承建商要提供与安装铝窗。在工程完毕与支付后，发展商投诉工程有缺陷。但当承建商向分承建商追索时，后者声称双方从来没有达成过协议。到高院，看来是对分承建商的狡辩不满，结果是在双方的通信往来中硬说成双方实际上已经达成了合约。但了上诉庭，认为在双方的通信往来中实在没有办法说成双方已经达成合约，但认为通过双方的履行而有一个合约，这估计可以说成是默示合约或双方以行动达成合约，而行动就是履行。

另举一个更明确的默示合约的先例，也是双方事前从来没有接触过，这是 Brown & Davis v. Galbraith（1972）1 W. L. R. 997。案情有关一位车主在出了车祸后，需要对车辆进行修理。修理厂与保险公司之间直接谈判与达成协议，包括对修理的估价及保险公司接受估价与授权进行修理等方面。保险公司也向修理厂确认了他会支付修理费并要求修完后给保险公司发票，但需要扣除 25 英镑由车主自负的修理费（这应该是免赔额），修理厂应直接向车主收取。但在修理完毕后，保险公司还没有作出支付前就倒闭。这就导致修理厂要直接向车主索赔，但他们之间可以说几乎没有接触过，难以把他们之间说成有合约关系。在第一审，法官判是他们之间有一个默示合约，就是支付所有的修理费用。但了上诉庭，推翻了一审的判决。上诉庭认为除了保险公司与修理厂之间的明示修理合约要支付除了 25 英镑外所有的修理费用，另有一个默示合约是在车主与修理厂之间。但在这一默示合约，车主所要支付的只是 25 英镑。

第八章　合约的变数条件条文

§1　承诺性条件与变数条件的不同

1.1　什么是承诺性条件

英国法律下的订约自由大原则下，只要不违反公共政策，双方同意的条文不论是否合理，都会获得承认与执行。而且履行合约是绝对或严格责任，[1]否则就要赔偿对方的损失让他恢复到合约被履行的地位。这些简单的说法都表示在国际的商业社会，订立一份自我保护的合约是至关重要，否则会是“签了要命的合约”（sign your life away in the contract）。在本章，笔者会介绍许多合约的谈判或是在已经生效的合约，订约一方或双方会加上各种有关合约履行的“条件”（condition）。这些条件会是要求对方作出一些履行的承诺，可称为“承诺性条件”（promissory condition）。这样，如果对方做不到，就等于违约。至于这种承诺性条件是否严重至合约的条件条文，可让受害方终止合约并索赔损失，显然也不是在合约中把该承诺形容为“条件”就足够把该承诺提升为条件条文，因为“条件”一词实际上十分滥用。这方面在主要的先例 L Schuler AG v Wickman Machine Tool Sales Ltd（1973）2 Lloyd's Rep 53 中，Reid 勋爵说：“In the ordinary use of the English language ‘condition’ has many meanings, some of which have nothing to do with agreements. In connection with an agreement it

---

〔1〕 合约下作出的承诺早在 Paradine v Jane（1647）82 ER 897 先例被判是绝对责任，不论是什么理由造成无法履行都属于违约。所以，这种合约被称为“absolute contract”。但后来，主要是来自海事案例，发展出一些十分局限的可以免责的情况，其中主要是“天意”（act of God）与“英皇敌人”（King's enemy）：Coggs v Bernard（1703）92 ER 109 先例；另是英国法律导致合约履行变为非法：Brewster v Kitchel（1679）90 ER 995 与 Baily v De Crespigny（1869）LR 4 QB 180 先例。所以也可以把合约的承诺称为严格责任，但英国法律的默示免责情况还是比其他大陆法国家所承认的不可抗力要狭窄得多。而英国法律也不承认其他国家法律导致合约履行变为非法的情况可以免责：Blight v Page（1801）127 ER 163 先例。因此，如果合约的适用法是英国法，而不是其他大陆法国家的法律，就不能以不可抗力免责，除非有明示规定：Chartered Mercantile Bank of India v Netherlands India Steam Navigation Company（1883）122 ER 1135 先例。注意是这一个法律地位比“合约受阻”（frustration）的说法早得多，合约受阻的说法最先出现在 Taylor v Caldwell（1863）122 ER 309 先例。但很早就已经承认合约可以有两种，一种就是较早所讲的“absolute contract”，而另一种就是本章所针对的有先决条件或后续条件的“conditional contract”：Cutter v Powell（1795）101 ER 573；Boyd v Siffkin（1809）170 ER 1172；Barret v Dutton（1815）171 ER 106 等先例。

may mean a precondition: something which must happen or be done before the agreement can take effect. Or it may mean some state of affairs which must continue to exist if the agreement is to remain in force. The legal meaning on which Schuler(被告)relies is, I think, one which would not occur to a layman; a condition in that sense is not something which has an automatic effect. It is a term the breach of which by one party gives to the other an option either to terminate the contract or to let the contract proceed and, if he so desires, sue for damages for the breach."

1.2 什么是变数条件

上述所讲有关承诺性条件在本书第五章之6.4段有针对,但本章并非是针对承诺性条件,也不是针对违约方到底是"违反条件条文"(breach of condition),或只是"违反保证条文"(breach of warranty),或是近期更加被重视与广泛适用的"违反中间条文"(breach of intermediate/innominate term)。本章是针对谈判或订约双方约定合约的生效或是履行需要根据一些将来会发生或不会发生的"变数"(contingency)成熟与否而定,往往双方也会规定一个时限。这种约定通常被称为合约的"先决条件"(condition precedent)或是"后续条件"(condition subsequent)。变数通常会是针对外来的事情(如国际货物买卖会涉及能否取得出口证或进口证、金额庞大的投资会涉及能否融资成功、造船合约涉及船厂能否取得银行的还款担保或船东取得履约担保、许多国际性合约会涉及政府当局的批准等),不涉及任何一方的合约承诺保证有关变数必定会成熟,所以也不涉及违约。这种条件通常被称为"变数条件"(contingent condition)或"变数先决条件"(contingent condition precedent),即使它在本质上是一个后续条件:Total Gas v Arco British (1998) 2 Lloyd's Rep 209 等先例。显然,变数先决条件也像承诺性条件一词经常被滥用。有许多不同类别的合约都经常会有变数先决条件的出现,而且对这些变数先决条件的写法也往往不太明确,所以带来了许多先例。大原则是,合约中的变数先决条件的解释完全是根据订约自由以及适用本书所讲的各种解释合约规则。所以有一些变数先决条件的写法会是在条件没有成熟之前合约不会生效,那么这可以说是"合约成立的先决条件"(可称为"contingency impacts on contract formation")。但会有更多变数先决条件在条件没有成熟之前合约的主要责任不必开始履行,这可以说是"合约履行的先决条件"(可称为"contingency impacts on contract performance")。这表示双方已经有了合约关系,受到约束,双方也不能因为其他原因,如市场突变,单方面从合约中脱身。也有一些变数先决条件会对合约其中一方明示或者默示要求他作出部分履行,例如,这一变数会是向有关政府申请批准,而合约会明示要求一方当事人向政府作出申请并取得批文,这就会带来争议需要履约的一方应该承担什么程度的责任。另也会有一些变数条件的满足是以其中一方的满意与否为准,这就会带来争议这一满意与否到底是主观或是客观的考验或准则。本章会在以下的段节探讨这些问题,也可指出在订约自由下,完全可用清楚与全面的明示条文针对这些问题以保障自己的利益,这在本章结束前会举一条拟定的比较完整的合约条文针对。

1.3　商业社会为什么需要变数条件

商业上的合约经常会有变数先决条件的要求,可以举几个典型的例子。第一就是有关当局或银行等第三人通常不会花心思与时间为一个仍在谈判中的交易作出批准或是允许融资或提供担保。所以,商业合约往往谈妥后,如果一方或双方当事人需要银行融资或提供担保,银行才会真正考虑有关的申请。但这里也有风险,因为就算银行曾经在原则上愿意提供融资或担保,也会事后改变主意。这样,如果一方当事人融资不成功或提供不了担保,会导致他无法完成交易。但如果这一交易已经有了最后与约束性的合约(因为谈判已经完结),他就会变为违约/毁约,除非在该合约中加上了一个变数条件作为合约履行的先决条件,这就是"subject to finance"或类似的用语所需要起的作用,而变数就是是否取得融资或担保。

第二个例子,就是在许多买卖交易,买方需要对有关的标的作出检验,并感觉满意后才完成交易。如果在本土的买卖(如房屋买卖),对有关的标的作出检验会相对方便与便宜,那么买方可以在检验后再进行谈判,谈不拢也无所谓。但如果有关的标的是远在他方,而且检验十分复杂并需要专业人士进行,买方就不会愿意在花了不少钱的检验满意后再进行谈判。这是因为卖方会改变主意不出售,或是敲竹杠,或是把有关标的在买方检验的期间已经卖了给第三人。因此买方需要对卖方作出一些约束,因为进行检验需要时间。其中最普遍被使用的办法就是在双方谈妥的合约加上一个变数先决条件,如"subject to satisfactory inspection"或类似的用语,而变数就是检验是否满意。

再举一个例子,有许多合约会有关联的合约,但它们都没有办法在同一个时间内敲定,这导致了它们之间的时差会有风险。例如,一个承建商向雇主作出有关工程的报价,最后被雇主接受,双方就有了合约关系。但该承建商的报价是根据与综合了有关工程的分承建商或供应商较早提供的报价作出。显然,承建商不敢在被雇主接受报价前无条件接受分承建商或供应商的报价,因为这变为一个有约束性的合约关系。雇主如果不接受报价而把工程合约给了另一位第三人,该承建商就会被夹在当中。但不接受分承建商或供应商的报价带来的恶果就是有了雇主的合约后,再找分承建商或供应商希望以合约明确下来,他们或个别会改变主意,如要提高报价甚至说原来的报价算错了(如在 Holman Construction Ltd v Delta Timber Co Ltd [1972] NZLR 1081 先例)。这样,承建商本来可以赚取微利的工程合约就变为还没开始进行就要亏本。看来,安全的做法是与分承建商或供应商根据他们的报价敲定一个合约关系,不让他们可以脱身,但在这些有关的合约中加上一个变数先决条件,如"subject to the contractor securing the main contract",而变数就是能否取得雇主的工程合约。

1.4　变数条件通常的用语

通常的用语或是文字表达一个变数先决条件会是"subject to"(以……为准)、"condition on"(取决于)或"condition precedent",但只要清楚表达了这一订约意图,文字/措辞可以千变万化。例如在 North Sea Energy Holdings N. V. v. Petroleum Authority of Thailand (1997) 2 Lloyd' s Rep 418 先例,变数先决条件是在一个"附函"(side letter),措辞是:"In consideration of our agreement to enter into an agreement ... with MSH ... for the supply of oil we confirm our agreement as a condition precedence for effectiveness of Agreement that **before the nomination of the first Load** MSH will provide to PTT (Petroleum Authority of Thailand) **official confirmation from original supplier that the oil may be supplied without restriction to the Buyer in Thailand** ... where the Buyer has processing facilities."(加黑部分是变数先决条件)

至于在造船合约,有关的条文往往被称为"合约生效日期条文"(effective date of contract clause)。这在中国船厂普遍使用的造船合约(SAJ 标准格式)条文是:"This Contract shall become effective as from the date of execution hereof by the BUYER and the BUILDER. However, in the event that (这里会是针对特定的变数,通常是不能在多少天内取得还款担保或签发出口证) days from the date of this Contract, then, in such case, this Contract shall automatically become null and void, unless otherwise mutually agreed in writing between the parties hereto, and the both parties hereto shall be immediately and completely discharged from all of their obligations to each other under this Contract as though this Contract had never been entered into at all."

§2　变数先决条件不同类别的权威说法

变数先决条件可先节录权威书籍《Chitty on Contracts》(第 31 版,2012 年)一书之2－153 段,如下:"**Effects of agreements subject to contingent conditions precedent: in general.** Where an agreement is subject to a contingent condition precedent, there is, before the occurrence of the condition, no duty on either party to render the principal performance promised by him: for example, a seller is not bound to deliver and a buyer is not bound to pay. Nor, in such a case, does either party undertake that the condition will occur. But an agreement subject to such a condition may impose some degree of obligation on the parties or on one of them. Whether it has this effect, and if so what degree of obligation is imposed, depends on the true construction of the term specifying condition."(如果合约有一个变数先决条件,就会是在发生这一变数前双方当事人都不需要履行他们的承诺:如卖方不需要交货,而买方也不需要作出支付。在这种情况下,双方也没有对有关的变数会否成熟作出任何责任的承诺或保证。但会有在合约中对有关的变数要求一方或双方当事人承担一些责任,有否这一责任与程度就要在个别的案件解释有关的变数与合约条文的文字/措辞。)

2.1 《Chitty on Contracts》有关变数先决条件的不同类别

接下去《Chitty on Contracts》(第 31 版,2012 年)一书在 12 - 028 段解释根据合约不同的写法,这变数先决条件可以分为三大类:"**Conditions precedent.** The liability of one or both of the contracting parties may become effective only if certain facts are ascertained to exist or upon the occurrence or non - occurrence of some further event. In such a case the contract is said to be subject to a condition precedent. The failure of a condition precedent may have one of a number of effects. It may, in the first place, suspend the rights and obligations of both parties, as, for instance, where the parties enter into an agreement on the express understanding that it is not to become binding on either of them unless the condition is fulfilled. Secondly, one party may assume an immediate unilateral binding obligation, subject to a condition. From this he cannot withdraw; but no bilateral contract, binding on both parties, comes into existence until the condition is fulfilled. Thirdly, the parties may enter into an immediate binding contract, but subject to a condition, which suspends all or some of the obligations of one or both parties pending fulfillment of the condition. These conditions precedent are, however, normally contingent and not promissory, and in such a case neither party will be liable to the other if the condition is not fulfilled."(直到某些将来的变数的发生或不发生确定之后,一方或双方合约方的合约责任才生效。在这种情况下,合约是以一个变数先决条件为准。先决条件的变数如果没有成熟,根据合约的写法可能会有三种不同的后果。第一,双方明确理解直到有关变数成熟,双方不受到订立的合约约束。第二,合约一方马上单方面受到约束,但以一个先决条件为准。直到有关的变数成熟或不成熟,他不能从合约中单方面脱身,而期间合约并非对双方都有约束。第三,双方可以订立一个马上约束双方的合约,但以一个变数条件为准。期间双方所有或部分合约责任的履行被暂时中止,直到变数条件成熟。由于变数先决条件是针对变数,而不属于承诺性条件,变数不成熟通常没有任何一方合约方需要承担责任或赔偿损失。)

进一步分析以上所讲的三种不同(通过解释有关合约条文的文字/措辞)变数先决条件,可以说第一种就是双方都可以随时脱身,令一个文书的合约变为"根本不是一个合约"(not an agreement at all):Pym v Campbell (1856) 6 E & B 370 先例。

第二与第三种的变数先决条件看来都属于后续条件,如果该变数先决条件不成熟,双方就可以从合约中脱身。这样,所谓的变数先决条件本质上等于一个后续条件,这是《Chitty on Contracts》(第 31 版,2012 年)一书在 2 - 155 段所说:"... However, if it becomes clear that the condition has not occurred, or that it can no longer occur, within the time specified in the contract, the parties will be under no further obligation under the contract. In such a case, the effect of the non - occurrence of the condition is that the parties are 'no longer bound' by the contract, or that the contract is 'discharged'. What the parties have called a 'condition precedent' can thus operate as, or have the effect of, a condition subsequent. ”(会是明确如果在合约约定的期限内,先决条件没有发生,或不可能发生,双方当事人就不必继续履行有关的合约。在这种情况下,实际上是说双方当事人再也不受到合约的约束,或是合约已经被解除。双方当事人在这种情况下所说的先决条件在本质上是一个后续条件。)

2.2 Masters v. Cameron 澳大利亚先例有关“以签署合约为准”的变数先决条件的不同类别

在 Masters v. Cameron (1954) 91 CLR 353 的重要先例,澳大利亚高院判是“subject to contract”(但同样的道理也适用在任何其他的“subject to”)有三种可能的解释双方的订约意图,如下:

“Where parties who have been in negotiation reach agreement upon terms of a contractual nature and also agree that the matter of their negotiation shall be dealt with by a formal contract, the case may belong to any of three classes. It may be one in which the parties have reached finality in arranging all the terms of their bargain and intend to be immediately bound to the performance of those terms, but at the same time propose to have the terms restated in a form which will be fuller or more precise but not different in effect. (第一种可能的解释,就是双方完全谈妥合约并马上受到约束履行合约,只是同时想把谈妥的条文进一步完整与精确订立正式合约[这个工作通常是交给律师完成,但在航运的租约会是交给经纪人完成],但无意再有任何更改。看来在这种可能的解释,是把履行合约与整理一份正式合约当作是两件不同的事,可以同时进行。) Or, secondly, it may be a case in which the parties have completely agreed upon all the terms of their bargain and intend no departure from or addition to that which their agreed terms express or imply, but nevertheless have made performance of one or more of the terms conditional upon the execution of a formal document. (这是第二种可能的解释,就是双方完全谈妥合约,无意再有任何更改或补充双方同意了的明示或默示条文,但对合约或只针对部分条文的履行是取决于签署一份正式文件) Or, thirdly, the case may be one in which the intention of the parties is not to make a concluded bargain at all, unless and until they execute a formal contract. (这是第三种可能的解释,就是双方意图是没有一个谈妥的交易直到双方签署一份正式合约,这也表示双方的意图是在合约签署之前都停留在谈判的阶段,没有受到合约的约束。)

In each of the first two cases there is a binding contract: in the first case a contract binding the parties at once to perform the agreed terms whether the contemplated formal document comes into existence or not, and to join (if they have so agreed) in settling and executing the formal document; and in the second case a contract binding the parties to join in bringing the formal contract into existence and then to carry it into execution. Of these two cases the first is the more common. (上述的第一种与第二种可能的解释,都表示双方已经订立了一个有约束性的合约,特别是在写得不明确的情况下,第一种

可能的解释更为普遍。)

Cases of the third class are fundamentally different. They are cases in which the terms of agreement are not intended to have, and therefore do not have, any binding effect of their own... The parties may have so provided either because they have dealt only with major matters and contemplate that others will or may be regulated by provisions to be introduced into the formal document... or simply because they wish to reserve to themselves a right to withdraw at any time until the formal document is signed. (上述第三种可能的解释完全不同,显示双方在签署正式合约之前,还会有可能增加其他条文或规定,甚至可以自由撤离还没有生效的合约关系) These possibilities were both referred to in Rossiter v Miller [(1878) 3 App Cas 1124]. Lord O'Hagan said [(1878) 3 App Cas 1124 at 1149]: 'Undoubtedly, if any prospective contract, involving the possibility of new terms, or the modification of those already discussed, remains to be adopted, matters must be taken to be still in a train of negotiation, and a dissatisfied party may refuse to proceed. But when an agreement embracing all the particulars essential for finality and completeness, even though it may be desired to reduce it to shape by a solicitor, is such that those particulars must remain unchanged, it is not, in my mind, less coercive because of the technical formality which remains to be made'. (O'Hagan 勋爵说如果一个初步的合约,涉及可能会有新的条文或对已经讨论过的条文进行修改,毫无疑问双方还停留在谈判阶段,事后对谈判不满意的一方可以撤离。但是如果一个协议包括了所有重要细节,显示这已经是终局,双方再也没有什么好谈的,那么尽管双方协议中要求律师整理出一份正式的合约,而没有显示对谈妥的细节有所改变,这样签署一份正式合约只是一个技术性的例行公事。) And Lord Blackburn said [(1878) 3 App Cas 1124 at 1152]: 'parties often do enter into a negotiation meaning that, when they have (or think they have) come to one mind, the result shall be put into formal shape, and then (if on seeing the result in that shape they find they are agreed) signed and made binding; but that each party is to reserve to himself the right to retire from the contract, if, on looking at the formal contract, he finds that though it may represent what he said, it does not represent what he meant to say. Whenever, on the true construction of the evidence, this appears to be the intention, I think that the parties ought not to be held bound till they have executed the formal agreement'. (Blackburn 勋爵说双方当事人经常进行谈判时的意图是当他们已经达成一致意见时,这一结果将会记录在一份正式的合约。如果双方认同这一份合约就是他们在谈判中所同意的,就会签署令该合约对双方有约束力,但保留认为该正式合约不是他在谈判中所说的话,或是并不代表他心里所想说的话时,就可以抽身的权利。如果根据个别案件的证据显示双方确实有这一想法或意图,就应该判是双方没有受到合约的约束,直到他们签署一份正式合约。) So, as Parker J said in Von Hatzfeldt - Wildenburg v Alexander [(1912) 1 Ch

284 at 289] in such a case there is no enforceable contract, either because the condition is unfulfilled or because the law does not recognize a contract to enter into a contract."

这一澳大利亚先例的法律地位在近期的《Contract Formation: Law and Practice》(2010年)一书的9.17到9.18段被总结如下:

"In summary, in the first category the agreement is a binding contract and must be performed when the time for performance accrues. In the second category there is a binding contract but the parties are not required to perform until a formal contract is executed. When expressing the existence of the first two categories, the court emphasized that the word 'subject to contract' do not in all cases mean that the parties are still in negotiation.(总结而言,第一类的谈判结果是有了一个有约束力的合约,双方在履行的时间届临时必须履行。第二类的谈判结果是有了一个有约束力的合约,但双方不必履行,直到有一份正式的合约被签署。针对这两种解释,法院强调"以签署合约为准"并非在所有的案件都代表双方仍在谈判阶段。)

They said: Throughout the decisions on this branch of the law the proposition is insisted upon which Lord Blackburn express in Rossiter v Miller[(1878) 3 App Cas 1124] when he said that the mere fact that the parties have expressly stipulated that there shall afterwards be a formal agreement prepared, embodying the terms, which shall be signed by the parties does not, by itself, show that they continue merely in negotiation. His Lordship proceeded: '... as soon as the fact is established of the final mutual assent of the parties so that those who draw up the formal agreement have not the power to vary the terms already settled, I think the contract is completed' [(1878) 3 App Cas 1124, 1151].(澳大利亚法院同意 Blackburn 勋爵在 Rossiter v Miller 先例中的说法,双方写明以后来一个正式的合约为准,本身并不代表他们还在谈判。只要是认定了事实双方要谈的已经有了约定,特别是后来准备正式合约的人[如律师]没有改变合约的权利,合约就已经完成了。)

In the third category there is no binding contract until a formal contract is executed. Often such an agreement is characterized as an unenforceable agreement to agree."(第三类的谈判结果是直到双方签署了一份正式合约,合约双方之间没有一个有约束力的合约。这一类是属于没有法律效力的"协议将来达成协议"。)

2.3 North Sea Energy Holdings N. V. v. Petroleum Authority of Thailand 英国先例有关变数先决条件的不同类别

针对变数先决条件不同类别与带来不同后果的说法,也有不少英国先例。笔者可以节录其中的一个较近期的 North Sea Energy Holdings N. V. v. Petroleum Authority of Thailand (1997) 2 Lloyd's Rep 418 先例。Thomas 大法官说:"What effect a condition will have upon an obligation depends upon the construction of the agreement. As was made clear by Lord Justice Denning in Trans Trust SPRL v Danubian Trading Co

Ltd (1952) 1 Lloyd's Rep 348 at p 355, col. 2; (1952) 2 QB 297 at p 304, sometimes an obligation is a condition precedent to the formation of a contract; in that case, it is a condition which must be fulfilled before any contract is concluded at all. In other cases, the contract is concluded, but the condition is a condition precedent to an essential term of the contract. Professor Treitel has helpfully discussed four possibilities at pp. 59 – 61 of The Law of Contract(先决条件到底会带来什么后果是根据合约的解释。这可以是一个合约成立的先决条件,也可以是一个合约履行的先决条件。Treitel 教授在他的《The Law of Contract》一书中总结说,变数先决条件有四种可能的结果):(1) Before the event occurs, each party is free to withdraw from the agreement(第一种可能的解释是在针对的变数发生前,任何一方合约方可以随意从合约中撤离). (2) Before the event occurs, the main obligations have not accrued; but so long as the event can still occur, one or both of the parties can not withdraw(第二种可能的解释是在变数发生前,主要的合约履行还没有开始,但只要这个变数仍然会发生,一方或双方合约方不能从合约中撤离,也表示合约的履行只是暂停).[2] (3) Before the event occurs, the main obligations have not accrued; but in the meantime neither party must do anything to prevent the occurrence of the event(第三种可能的解释是在变数发生前,主要的合约履行还没有开始,但在期间任何一方合约方都不能做妨碍这一变数发生的事). (4) Before the event occurs, the main obligations have not accrued, but one of the parties undertakes to use reasonable efforts to bring the event about (without absolutely undertaking that his efforts will succeed)."(第四种可能的解释是在变数发生前,主要的合约履行还没有开始,但其中一方合约方承诺以合理努力令特定的变数发生[但并非有严格责任保证会成功令变数先决条件成熟]。)

2.4　早期对不同类别的变数先决条件不明确判法的先例

在一些还算比较早期的先例,如 The "John S. Darbyshire" (1977) 2 Lloyd's Rep 457 先例,针对变数先决条件到底属于什么类别在判决并不明确,毕竟后续条件

---

〔2〕 这看来是变数先决条件如果不成熟,但有机会成熟,特别是有关的合约如果没有定下一个期限,就会有危险是即使合理时间已过,也只被解释为合约"暂停"(suspend),但还是有效,双方也不能终止合约。这一判法的先例不多,有 Charles H. Windschuegl Ltd v Alexander Pickering & Co Ltd (1950) 84 Ll L Rep 89, Smallman v Smallman (1972) Fam. 25 与 De Oleaga & Co v West Cumberland Iron and Steel Co (1879) 3 QBD 472。变数先决条件的后果是只暂停合约或是终止合约,在 Total Gas v Arco British (1998) 2 Lloyd's Rep 209 的贵族院先例有充分针对。看来,如果合约没有暂停的用语,或是其他特别的原因,法院是不愿意判变数条件如果不成熟,只会暂停合约。因为这会对合约当事人的一方甚至双方带来不肯定,而合约可能是受阻才会停止暂停而自动终止。

在早期甚至是近期也经常被称为先决条件。[3] 该租约的变数条件是“subject to satisfactory trial voyage”的用语，显示承租人要试用船舶后感到满意才会较长期或多航次地租进有关船舶。在本案，由于涉及了承租人租用船舶是为了专门运载“淀粉浆”（starch slurry），承租人关心船舶是否适合这一种十分特殊的运输，所以在电传中双方订立1年期租说明：“Subject to satisfactory completion of two trial voyages John S. Darbyshire from Koog to Woolwich, Charterers accept your offer of Aug. 11 except... Duration minimum of 6 months with option to cancel thereafter providing 3 months' notice to cancel is given on both sides. Expect duration 10 to 11 months...”

但在两个试用航次跑完后，承租人告诉船东由于经济原因（因为承租人有其他渠道购买淀粉浆，价格有变动），所以终止租约。这导致船东向承租人提出索赔，逼使承租人在这一诉讼向英国法院作出宣告就是期租合约有否订立。看来，法院对这一“subject to satisfactory trial voyage”用语的解释，没有明确判是先决条件或后续条件，而是把租约分为两个部分，首先就是两个试用的航次有约束力并且履行了，但针对接下的1年期租，这用语是合约成立的先决条件。Mocatta大法官是这样说：“It seems to me entirely understandable, and to be anticipated, that before binding themselves to a time charter for a minimum of nine months or 12 months at £ 325 per day, the plaintiffs should insist on a satisfactory completion of two trial voyages. To my mind the case clearly falls in the category where there is a '**condition precedent to contract**'.”（加黑部分是笔者的强调）

但Mocatta大法官在他的附带意看来更像是说这条文/文字是后续条件或是合约履行的先决条件。他说在该两个试用航次，承租人如果不满意，必须是局限在有关货物的装运中的技术问题（而不是其他原因，如航运市场有所波动），说：“However, the case may go higher, and in deference to the arguments of Counsel, I briefly express my views upon them... I think the words 'subject to satisfactory completion of two trial voyages' should be construed 'subject to *bona fides*'... The subject matter of satisfactory completion must, however, be limited to the technical aspects of the venture, namely the successful loading, unloading and agitation of the cargo and navigation of the vessel. I do not think changes of price at which the plaintiffs could buy starch from their parent – company in Holland are relevant.”

如果承租人不满意受到法院所讲的局限，这看来是像一个后续条件多于一个先

---

[3] 早在Charles H. Windschuegl Ltd v Alexander Pickering & Co Ltd (1950) 84 Ll L Rep 89先例，Devlin大法官就说：“whether it is regarded as a condition precedent, or condition subsequent, does not matter very much, I think, as a matter of law or as a matter of business.”另是Steyn勋爵在Total Gas v Arco British (1998) 2 Lloyd's Rep 209先例里说的：“'condition precedent' is sometimes used in the sense of a condition subsequent. That is not so surprising. The question is condition precedent to what? And in this case the question can then only receive the answer: the operation of the contract.”

决条件，因为在先决条件下，双方基本上还没有约束性的合约关系，根本不存在承租人以什么理由（甚至没有理由）撤离。

2.5　法院或仲裁庭近期倾向解释一个变数先决条件是合约履行的先决条件而不是合约成立的先决条件

近期的英国或其他普通法法院或仲裁庭有比较普遍的心态就是商业人士一般的意图是订立合约，所以会是更愿意解释双方经过漫长与昂贵的谈判后达成一个约束性合约，而不会让其中一方以解释起来模棱两可的“subject to”逃避合约关系。所以有许多“subject to”会被解释为 Masters v Cameron（1954）91 CLR 353 先例中的第二种解释。这也表示针对这方面的早期先例要小心看待，不一定会被依从。而且，解释每一个不同事实的合约中的“subject to”，也会是可以自由发挥不存在受到先例的约束。这可节录《Contract Formation：Law and Practice》（2010 年）一书的 9.41 段：“In more recent times, the courts have become reluctant to allow a party to escape a contract on the basis that it is void by reason of a condition precedent. This reflects that the courts are aware of how commercial parties transact and expect obligations to arise out of transactions that in the past would be held void for uncertainty and incompleteness. Indeed the whole process of entering into preliminary agreements reflects such methods of transacting. It is therefore not surprising that today many more cases are being held to fall within the second category of Masters v Cameron.”

在澳大利亚的 Perri v Coolangatta Investments Proprietary Ltd（1982）149 CLR 537 先例，Mason 大法官说：“Generally speaking the court will tend to favour that construction which leads to the conclusion that a particular stipulation is a condition precedent to performance as against that which leads to the conclusion that the stipulation is a condition precedent to the formation or existence of a contract. In most cases it is artificial to say, in the face of the details settled upon by the parties, that there is no binding contract unless the event in question happens. Instead, it is appropriate in conformity with the mutual intention of the parties to say that there is a binding contract which makes the stipulated event a condition precedent to the duty of one party, or perhaps of both parties, to perform. Furthermore, it gives the courts greater scope in determining and adjusting the rights of the parties. For these reasons the condition will not be construed as a condition precedent to the formation of a contract unless the contract read as a whole plainly compels this conclusion.”（一般而言，法院喜欢的解释是有关的变数先决条件只是针对合约的履行，而不是针对合约的成立。在大部分的情况下，说双方同意所有的细节但还是没有一个有约束性的合约，除非发生一个特定的变数是有一点矫揉造作。这样判的话，也给了法院更大的空间决定与调整双方的权利，这是因为变数先决条件如果针对合约的成立，法院变得只能判变数不成立就没有合约关系。所以，变数先决条件会被判是针对合约的成立必须有明确的文字/措辞逼使法院作出这一结论。）

§3 后续条件

3.1 后续条件的定义

已经提到过《Chitty on Contracts》(第31版,2012年)一书之2-155段说有很多变数的先决条件本质是后续条件,换言之,合约双方在等待变数的发生或成熟,已经受到合约的约束,不能单方面随意脱身。后续条件在《Chitty on Contracts》中的权威定义是在12-030段如下:"The obligation of one or both parties may be made subject to a condition that it is to be immediately binding, but if certain facts are ascertained to exist or upon the occurrence or non-occurrence of some further event, then either the contract is to cease to bind on one or both parties are to have the right to avoid the contract or bring it to an end. In such a case the contract is said to be subject to a condition subsequent. An example is provided by the case of Head v Tattersall (1871) LR 7 Ex 7 where A bought a horse from B which B warranted to have been hunted with the Bicester hounds. If it did not answer its description, A was to have the right to return it by a certain day. The horse did not answer its description and A accordingly returned it before the day. In the meantime, however, the horse had been injured without A's fault. It was held that the injury did not cause A to lose his right to return the horse and he could recover the purchase price paid."(合约马上约束双方,但其中一方所作出的合约承诺是以一个条件为准,如果该条件的事实或变数被确认是不存在或是一些将来变数应该会发生但没有发生,合约就变得不再约束双方或双方有权避免该合约的履行或取消合约。一个著名的先例是Head v Tattersall,案情涉及A向B购买一匹马,说它有经验与猎犬一起打猎。并且合约说明了如果该匹马并没有这方面的经验,A就有权在某天前把它退还给B。结果该匹马并没有这种打猎的经验,A就马上把它退还给B。但该匹马在期间受了伤,而受的伤并非是A的过错引致[如果A有过错就可能不适用,因为合约已经存在,或是A作为该匹马的托管人,至少有赔偿损失的责任]。法院判A有权退还该匹马并取回已经支付的钱,也不必对马匹受伤负责。)

3.2 如何认定是先决条件或是后续条件

如果变数先决条件所针对特定的变数是合约成立的先决条件,那么直到先决条件得到满足,双方的任何一方可以从"谈判"(negotiatio n)中撤离或重启谈判已经谈妥了的条文。原因是有约束性的合约还没有成立,所以任何一方均不受到任何约束。这也就是在本章之2.1段中《Chitty on Contracts》(第31版,2012年)一书之12-028段提到的三种不同后果中的第一种。

先决条件也可以是针对已经存在了的合约履行,即这一先决条件如果没有得到满足,就会导致合约的终止或在其中订约一方的选择下可取消。在这一意义上,这种先决条件本质上就是后续条件。

另有一个生动的说法有关它们的区别，就是先决条件是产生合约责任的条件，而后续条件是毁掉合约责任的条件（a condition precedent is a condition attached to the creation of an obligation while a condition subsequent is a condition attached to the destruction of an obligation）：Head v Tattersall （1871） LR 7 Ex 7；Thompson v ASDA – MFI plc （1988） Ch 241 等先例。

双方如果在这方面有争议，法院或仲裁院一般也会是第一步考虑变数条件是否是合约成立的先决条件，如果不是，第二步就会考虑这一后续条件所针对的变数是什么以及是否有满足。

也有一个说法是先决条件（这只是指合约成立的先决条件）所要针对的是双方有否“订约意图”（intention to contract），但后续条件是针对变数的条文/文字来“解释合约”（construction of contract）。这样，法院或者仲裁庭认定有关事实方面所依赖的证据也有所不同。例如《Contract Formation：Law and Practice》（2010 年）一书之 9.09 段所说，对前者的事实认定可参考更广泛的证据：“However, it needs to be kept in mind that generally the evidence available to determine whether a contract has been formed is wider than the evidence available to construe and determine the meaning and legal effect of the terms of a contract.”

而后者由于已经有合约关系，认定事实（包括看双方订约的背景/语境）主要是更明确了解双方所用文字/措辞的真正意图，特别是有关的文字/措辞有含糊之处：Rainy Sky SA and others v Kookmin Bank （2012） 1 Lloyd's Rep 34 先例。否则，主要还是看双方明确约定的文字/措辞并根据合约解释的规则（本书所针对的各种规则）客观找出有关条文的意思。正如 Steyn 勋爵在 Total Gas v Arco British （1998） 2 Lloyd's Rep 209 先例中说：“But as in the case of all contracts, loyalty to the contractual text viewed against its relevant contextual background is the first principle of construction.”

在每一个不同的合约或合约的谈判中，订约双方在来往的通讯中针对变数条件所用的文字/措辞以及有关案件的背景/语境，可能被解释为一个约束性合约的先决条件或是后续条件，甚至有可能什么都不是（如双方在谈判结束时说明某一个变数［如领导或董事局批准］，但这只是例行手续），并会因此带来截然不同的后果。这会是在双方谈判中很明确的规定，如说明变数是合约成立的先决条件，就表示直到“条件已经成熟”（lift subject/condition），双方仍是在谈判的阶段。这有好处也有坏处，好处是还没有约束性的合约关系，其中一方要走就走。但这也可能变为坏事，特别涉及航运市场或其他会大幅度波动的市场。如果合约中已经清楚写明变数条件是合约成立的先决条件，那么双方是不应该有争议。但是大多数情况下，合约并没有明确写明是先决条件还是后续条件，这就需要客观解释每一个案件中不同“subject to”或“condition to”用词以针对一个变数的订约意图，看看有关的变数是什么性质，订约方或谈判双方到底在想什么等。这在很多案件中也不容易,经常会涉及上一级法院推翻下一级法院的例子。当然会有十分明确的情况,如已经提到过的领导或董事局批准,但只是例行手续。或是有关的变数条件是双方已经签订了的合约的其中一条条文,甚至双方在该合约中已经履行了部分承诺,这变数条件明显是后续条件。

已经提到过在解释变数条件是否是合约成立的先决条件时,法院或者仲裁庭可以参考更广泛的证据,以认定双方有否订约意图。找出这个意图,显然双方的接触与谈判都会是重要的证据,另也包括了其他“外来证据”(extrinsic evidence):Pym v Campbell (1856) 6 E & B 370, Air Great Lakes Pty Ltd v KS Easter (Holdings) Pty Ltd (1985) 2 NSWLR 309 等先例。另是,在声称双方已经有合约关系后的行为(如有否一方开始履行)也会是重要证据:Australian Broadcasting Corporation v XIVth Commonwealth Games Ltd (1988) 18 NSWLR 540 先例。但如果这是涉及解释一个有约束力合约的条文,这种证据都受到局限或被排除,特别是在该合约中有关的条文写得十分明确的情况下。

至于判断双方的订约意图时要考虑哪些方面,在 Mississippi & Dominion S. S. Co. v. Swift 86 Me. 248, 29 A. 1063 (1894)先例,美国法院就有提到一些,说:“In determining which view is entertained in any particular case, several circumstances may be helpful, as whether the contract is of that class which are usually found to be in writing, whether it is of such nature as to need a formal writing for its full expression, whether it has few or many details, whether the amount involved is large or small, whether it is a common or unusual contract, whether the negotiations themselves indicate that a written draft is contemplated as the final conclusion of the negotiations. If a written draft is proposed, suggested, or referred to during the negotiations, it is some evidence that the parties intended it to be the final closing of the contract.”(在考虑每一个案件订约双方的订约意图时,有几个方面的情况可以参考,如合约是否属于一般情况下都会有书面合约的类型,合约的性质是否是正式书面合约才能有完整的表述,合约细节的多少,涉及金额的大小,合约是一般性还是不常见的合约,双方谈判时有没有表示一份书面草稿就算是双方谈判的结束。如果一份书面草稿在谈判时被提议、建议或提到,这在一定程度上可以证明双方意图把这份草稿当作谈判的结束。)

笔者可以对 Mississippi & Dominion S. S. Co. v. Swift 这一早期美国先例做进一步的介绍,案情涉及双方谈判租用 3 艘船舶的部分舱位,并加装冷藏设备以运输“带骨肉”(dressed meat),双方文书/电报的往来中提到要签署一份正式合约。这带来双方的争议,就是在没有签署合约的情况下,双方是否有一个约束性的合约关系。Emery 大法官说:“From these expressions of courts and jurists, it is quite clear that, after all, the question is mainly one of intention. If the party sought to be charged intended to close a contract prior to the formal signing of a written draft, or if he signified such an intention to the other party, he will be bound by the contract actually made, though the signing of the written draft be omitted. If, on the other hand, such party neither had nor signified such an intention to close the contract until it was fully expressed in a written instrument, and attested by signatures, then he will not be bound until the signatures are affixed. The expression of the idea may be attempted in other words: If the written draft is viewed by the parties merely as a convenient memorial or record of their previous contract, its absence does not affect the binding force of the contract. If, however, it is viewed as the consummation of the negotiation, there is no contract until the written draft is finally signed."（这看来是针对双方的订约意图）

下一个案例是涉及土地买卖的 Von Hatzfeldt – Wildenburg v Alexander (1912) 1 Ch 284 先例，Parker 大法官针对双方约定中的"subject to contract"用语是这样说："It appears to be well settled by the authorities that if the documents or letters relied on as constituting a contract contemplate the execution of a further contract between the parties, it is a question of construction whether the execution of the further contract is a condition or term of the bargain or whether it is a mere expression of the desire of the parties as to the manner in which the transaction already agreed to will in fact go through. In the former case there is no enforceable contract either because the condition is unfulfilled or because the law does not recognize a contract to enter into a contract. In the latter case there is a binding contract and the reference to the more formal document may be ignored."（根据先例，有关的文件或书信往来能否构成一份约束性的合约，即使双方有想到签订另一份合约，是要根据有关的文件或书信所用的文字/措辞与其他方面解释双方要签订另一份合约是否是一个先决条件[这样就是双方还没有约束性的合约关系，因为法律不承认一份将来订立合约的合约]。但如果只是表达了双方希望已经同意了的交易要以这样的方式明确下来，就表示双方已经有一个约束性的合约，而他们希望有一份正式文件的表示可以不加理会。）

再下一个是 Trans Trust SPRL v Danubian Trading Co Ltd (1952) 1 Lloyd's Rep 348 先例，案情涉及货物买卖合约。有关合约有"subject to the opening of a credit"的用语，但买方没有开出信用证。上诉庭的 Denning 大法官针对开出信用证这一变数说是可以是合约成立的先决条件，也可以是合约履行的先决条件（这等于是后续条件），说："Sometimes it is a condition precedent to the formation of a contract, that is, it is a condition which must be fulfilled before any contract is concluded at all. In those cases the stipulation 'subject to the opening of a credit' is rather like a stipulation 'subject to contract'. If no credit is provided, there is no contract between the parties. In other cases a contract is concluded and the stipulation for a credit is a condition which is an essential term of the contract. In those cases the provision of the credit is a condition precedent, not to the formation of a contract, but to the obligation of the seller to deliver the goods. If the buyer fails to provide the credit, the seller can treat himself as discharged from any further performance of the contract and can sue the buyer for damages for not providing the credit. ”

最后介绍一个近期名为 The “Pacific Champ” (2013) 2 Lloyd’s Rep 320 的租船先例。案情涉及船东(韩国的 HMM)与承租人(Americas Bulk Transport,简称 ABT)到底有否达成一个航次期租租约。在一个重要的有关电邮中,看来已经把同意的重要条文(包括交船与还船地点、每天的租金、交船与还船燃油数量与价格、适用法与仲裁条文等)列出。而有关的航次是去委内瑞拉的奥里诺科河与美湾并装运一批属于危险品的“直接还原铁”(direct reduced iron)。双方的电邮中另有一条争议的 12 项说:“12. SUBJECT REVIEW OWNERS HEAD CHARTER PARTY BTB.”(以查阅船东原租约背靠背为准)

也一提的是第 8、9、11 项与第 13 项也有关,可节录如下:

“8. ILOHC – BTB

9. VICTUALLING, ETC – BTB...

11. HOLD CONDITION CLAUSE ASPER HEAD C/P....

13. SUBJECT CHARTERERS RECONFIRMATION CLOSE OF BUSINESS NY TIME FEB 12, 2008.”

这就带来了双方的争议,其中 HMM 所坚持的是双方还没有合约关系,第 12 项是一个先决条件。HMM 也需要这一先决条件,因为 Pacific Champ 轮实际上是光租回来,HMM 必须肯定期租一个航次给 ABT 装运的危险品与航行地区是光船租约中原船东所允许与两份租约的有关条文是“背靠背”(BTB 或 Back – to – back),否则 HMM 作为二船东就会夹在当中。而事实上在查阅后,原租约的光租虽然没有禁止装运直接还原铁,但的确是不允许委内瑞拉的奥里诺科河。换言之,在查阅原租约后,与航次期租合约在航行地区的条文不是“背靠背”,也就是先决条件没有满足而没有有效的租约。但 ABT 坚持双方已经有合约关系,第 12 项只是一个后续条件,而查阅的原租约是指 HMM 曾经提供的一份以 NYPE 标准格式合约为基础的“租约范本”(proforma charter – party)。[4] 毕竟双方意图订立的是一份航次期租合约,有关条文/文字与原租约的光船租约格格不入。至于 BTB 是把该租约范本的条文/文字在“合逻辑的修改”(logical amendment)后合并进他们之间的期租合约。所以如果是后续条件,就表示只有 ABT 到了 2008 年 2 月 12 日的纽约下班前不再确认接受租约范本的 BTB,如第 8 项的 ILOHC 在租约范本的相关条文支付给 HMM 的一笔费用太高,双方才是没有合约关系。

表面看来,HMM 的争议有一定的说服力。毕竟谈到原租约,也就只有一份光船

---

〔4〕 期租合约的谈判会涉及上百条条文,使用一份双方已经达成与履行过的租约或承租人惯用的期租合约作为范本,只在双方认为需要的地方作出修改,可以大大地减少工作量,不需要逐条进行重新谈判。

租约。在租船业务中,熟悉业务的人士都不会把“head charter – party”与“proforma charter – party”混在一起,它们根本是两份不同的文件。但仲裁庭与高院在全面考虑有关的背景/语境后,判是 ABT 胜诉,部分理由可节录 Eder 大法官所说如下:

“In my view, the proper starting point is to seek to identify what is being referred to as the ‘... Head CP BTB ...’. In one sense, these words are the high point of Mr MacDonald Eggers QC’s(HMM 代表大律师)case, viz in truth there was only one ‘head charterparty’ ie the Bareboat Charterparty. However, in context, it is relatively plain to me (as it was to the arbitral tribunal) that this cannot be the case for the following reasons. First, the references in the second recap to the particular terms which were to be ‘BTB’ (ie Items 8 and 9) and also to the hold condition clause ‘as per Head C/P’ in Item 11 are, in my view, more naturally to be read as referring to the Pro forma Charterparty[5] – although I accept that there is no perfect alignment. Secondly, although I accept Mr MacDonald Eggers QC’s general entreaties that, consistent with the authorities cited above, I should focus on the words used by the parties, it would be wrong, in my view, to exclude the relevant factual matrix. In particular, it seems to me that this includes the fact that the parties were both aware of the Pro forma Charterparty and, indeed, a copy was, of course, sent by Mr Baek(HMM 证人)to Mr Song(ABT 证人)on the morning of 12 February. If Mr MacDonald Eggers QC is right on his construction of the second recap, this would have been irrelevant and unnecessary. Further, as noted above, it is one of the curious features of this case that the Pro forma Charterparty was a very old unsigned draft which named HMM as the charterer. In such circumstances, I can well understand the parties referring to this document as the ‘head charterparty’. Such a description was, of course, inaccurate because it was not in truth at that time, ie in 2008, a head charterparty at all. However, although out of date and unsigned, it identified HMM as the charterer and, in such circumstances, I can understand why the parties might loosely have described it in such terms. ...

Against that background, it seems to me that the proper construction of Item 12 becomes clear, ie as held by the tribunal and submitted by Mr Davey(ABT 代表大律师),

---

〔5〕 这一原因可向对租船业务不了解的读者稍做解释,就是第 8 项的“ILOHC”代表“in lieu of hull cleaning”,这经常发生在期租合约还船前最后的一个航次卸完货,承租人需要把船舱清洁后,如同交船时的情况一样,才能还船。但这样会延误还船时间,表示承租人要多支付租金。另一个更大的麻烦会是在最后的一个卸港,可能找岸上工人清洁船舱是一个昂贵或难以安排的作业。所以,承租人一般都会争取给船东一笔费用,作为让船东自己在还船后安排清洁船舱。这会可以在空放下一个装港的航次中通过船员清洁,而清洁后的杂物/货物残余可以抛进大海。看来,本先例的第 8 项的“BTB”就是合并一个租约范本,因为这也是一份期租合约。但合并 HMM 与船东的原租约的一份光船租约就不配合了。同样的道理也在第 9 项与第 11 项。

the document being referred to was the Pro forma Charterparty, that the acronym 'BTB' had the effect of incorporating the Pro forma Charterparty into the fixture between HMM and ABT subject only to review by ABT and reconfirmation by 09.00 on 13 February ....”

另是 Eder 大法官也有针对第 12 项的写法到底是一个先决条件或是后续条件,说:“Ultimately, this conclusion does not, in my view, depend upon any general principle but rather a proper construction of the parties' agreement: see, eg, Chitty on Contracts, volume 1, para 2-153; also, Lewison, The Interpretation of Contracts, 5th Edition, para 16.04 and the cases there cited including Varverakis v Compagnia de Navegacion Artico SA (The Merak) [1976] 2 Lloyd's Rep 250 and Ee v Kakar (1979) 40 P & CR 223. Although it is, of course well established that terms such as “subject to details” generally preclude the existence of a binding contract, the legal effect of a term as contained here in Item 12 taken together with Item 13 is, in my view, of a type as referred to in Chitty on Contracts, volume 1, para 2-155 and described in London Arbitration 18/06 (2006) 702 LMLN 3 as follows: '... If the only subject had been charterers' reconfirmation, then the tribunal would have been in no doubt that the charterers would be entitled to succeed. In that event, there would have been a concluded contract already ..., a contract that was subject to a condition subsequent, ie a reconfirmation within the time specified. The owners would not have been able to back out of that until the time for reconfirmation had gone. Provided the charterers reconfirmed within time, the owners would be bound to perform on the terms agreed up to then. Similarly, if between the time of the 'subject' fixture and reconfirmation the owners had sought to change something such as the description or a part of it, they would not have been entitled to do so...'”

3.3 后续条件下法律默示的合约责任

如果合约中的变数条件是后续条件,由于双方已经有了合约关系,只不过是一个“有条件合约”(conditional contract),双方就有了合约的责任,如受到合约履行的一些重要原则约束,如任何一方不得做一些事情妨碍合约履行的“妨碍原则”(prevention principle)以及有过错的一方不能在有关的后续条件取巧。这表示必须根据后续条件的变数与写法,并在订约方没有任何妨碍行为与过错下,这个条件无法满足才能终止合约。看来,后续条件下的“变数条件”(contingency condition)也有了“承诺性条件”(promissory condition)的意味,可以导致违约与损失的索赔。

3.3.1 需要履行部分责任的合约方必须诚实、善意、采取合理步骤

后续条件的成熟有时需要其中一方合约方履行部分责任。需要履行部分责任的一方有一个必须诚实、善意并采取合理步骤让后续条件成熟的默示责任。在 Marten v Whale (1917) 2 KB 480 这一较早的先例,有关土地买卖的合约有一个“subject to purchaser's solicitor's approval of title and restrictions"。上诉庭的 Scrutton 大法官强调原告的买方有一个默示责任委任一位律师并善意向他咨询，而该律师也必须提供诚实的法律意见，因为这一"subject to"不是买方的选择权，该合约是有后续条件的合约。而且原告不得在妨碍原则下令所针对的变数得不到满足。Scrutton 大法官说："The plaintiff was under an implied obligation to appoint a solicitor and ... consult him in good faith, and that solicitor shall give his honest opinion... That is not an option; it is a conditional contract."

3.3.2　根据案件的实际情况确定合理步骤

这方面可举一个有关国际货物买卖的 Brauer & Co (Great Britain) Ltd v James Clark (Brush Materials) Ltd (1952) 2 Lloyd's Rep. 147 先例，案情涉及"巴西粽叶纤维"(Bahia piassava)的 CIF 买卖，而合约中的第 9 条不可抗力条文中有约定："This contract is subject to a Brazilian export licence"。通常这是一个后续条件，否则作为买卖合约中的条文之一会说不通。有关的变数就是能否取得巴西出口证，而巴西出口证显然是由卖方作出申请。但后来可能是有关货物的市场价格上涨，巴西银行的有关部门规定了有关货物的最低 FOB 价格是 180 英镑/吨才给予出口证。这表示有关合约的价格偏低，必须提高才可以申请到出口证。这导致卖方对买方说："你有三个选择，一个是让合约终止，另一个是接受新的价格，最后一个是仲裁解决问题。"最后买方没有作出任何选择，而卖方也没有付运货物，毕竟没有取得出口证。问题是卖方能否以后续条件没有满足从该买卖合约撤离。英国上诉庭判是卖方如果想依赖这一后续条件，他必须证明已经采取了合理步骤但依然得不到出口证。而在这一先例，第一审曾经认定了一个事实，就是卖方如果愿意多付一点钱给巴西的供应商，就会取得出口证。换言之，卖方没有合理这样做，所以判是卖方败诉。这个判决也得到了上诉庭的支持，其中 Denning 勋爵也谈到如果要卖方多支付 100 倍的货价才能取得出口证，这就变为不合理的要求，结果也应另当别论。Denning 勋爵这样说："There is a specific finding that an export licence could have been obtained if the seller had been prepared to pay a higher price for the goods to his Brazilian associates——a price which higher, that is, than the price at which he had contracted to resell them. Was that a step which he could reasonably be expected to take? This depends on how much was the price he had to pay to get the licence. If it was, to take the Judge's illustration, one hundred times as much as the contract price, that would be 'a fundamentally different situation' which had unexpectedly emerged, and he would not be bound to pay it... But if the price he had to pay was only the current market price, as we told it was, then he ought to have paid it so as to get the licence."

3.3.3　双方需要合作与不能有过错令后续条件不成熟

由于在后续条件的情况下双方已经有了合约关系，不论是需要履行部分责任或是需要合作的合约方都必须这样做令后续条件成熟，不能有过错，也不能取巧令后续条件得不到成熟。这方面的默示责任已经在本书第七章之10.2段有介绍。合约方会不合作或是取巧往往是因为市场有了变化,而导致其中合约一方希望脱身。例如,他需要向当局或者银行提出申请批准或担保,但拒绝或延误这样做,希望在合约规定的时限届临,可以因为后续条件不成熟解除合约。会有情况更是不等待时限届临,就威胁对方说除非肯更改有关合约的条件,如对已经约定好的价格加价或减价,否则不会履行他的责任令后续条件成熟。这实际上是违约/毁约,可以被对方接受并索赔损失。

首先有关双方必须合作的法律默示地位,有关的先例有:A. V. Pound & Co Ltd v M. W. Hardy & Co. Inc (1986) AC 588; Metro Meat Ltd v Fares Rural Co Pty Ltd (1985) 2 Lloyd's Rep 13; Phoebus Kyprianou v Vyprus Textiles Ltd (1958) 2 Lloyd's Rep 60; North Sea Energy Holdings N. V. v. Petroleum Authority of Thailand (1997) 2 Lloyd's Rep 418。例如,如果变数涉及申请批文/批准,申请一方往往需要另一方提供资料,另一方就必须合作尽快提供。在 Mackay v Dick (1881) 6 App. Cas 251 先例,Blackburn 勋爵说:"I think I may safely say as a general rule, that where in a contract it appears that both parties have agreed that something shall be done, which can not effectively be done unless both concur in doing it, the construction of the contract is that each agrees to do all that is necessary to be done on his part for the carrying out of that thing, though there may be no express words to that effect."

另在 A. V. Pound & Co Ltd v M. W. Hardy & Co. Inc 先例,Harrow 勋爵说:"There might be a license system based not on destination but on the proportion of a manufacturer's product to be sent out of the country. In such a case, the facts necessary to be stated would be known to the producer and not to the buyer. It would seem obvious that in such a case it would be for the seller to apply. There may well be cases in which each party must be ready and willing to cooperate. If in the present case, sellers had written to the buyers; told them the licensing scheme; told them the suppliers' names and asked them to give the name of the destination and the ship to the suppliers, there might well have been an obligation on the buyers to do these things. The appellants invited your Lordships to lay down some general rules. There can be no general rule."

接下来是有关双方合约方不能有过错令后续条件不成熟导致合约被终止的法律默示责任,这方面权威先例有不少,笔者只简单介绍几个重要先例与权威说法。第一个是 New Zealand Shipping Co. Ltd v Societie Des Ateliers et Chantiers de France (1919) AC 1 先例,案情有关一个造船合约中后续条件说明如果延误交船超出原来约定的日期18个月,合约就变得无效。在贵族院,Atkinson 勋爵认为不能因为一方的过错或行为导致另一方不能依赖后续条件终止合约(如船厂故意延误导致合约无效)说:"If the ... contract shall be void on the happening of an event which one or either of them can by his own act or omission bring about, then the party, who by his own act or omission brings that event about, cannot be permitted either to insist upon the stipulation himself or to compel the other party, who is blameless, to insist upon it, because to permit the blamable party to do either would be to permit him to take advantage of his own wrong."

第二个是 Cheall v Association of Professional Executive Clerical and Computer Staff (1983) 2 AC 180 先例,案情涉及公会和会员之间的合约。Diplock 勋爵说:"... the rule of construction [is] that, except in the unlikely case that the contract contains clear express words to the contrary, it is to be presumed that it was not the intention of the parties that either party should be entitled to rely upon his own breaches of his primary obligations as bringing the contract to an end..."(除非是在不寻常的情况下,就是合约中另有不同的明确规定,否则就应该假设订约双方不会有意图允许一方可以依赖他自己的违约或者过错令合约终止。)

另一个也是一脉相通的默示责任是,双方合约方都不能做任何事情对该变数先决条件的成熟造成障碍,这也是众所周知的"妨碍原则"(prevention principle),可参阅本书第十一章之第5段。在《Chitty on Contracts》(第31版,2012年)一书之2-156段中写到:"A third possibility is that, before the event occurs, the main obligations have not accrued; but that in the meantime neither party must do anything to prevent the occurrence of that event..."

这通常会发生在一些变数涉及双方都需要做一点事情才能令该变数成熟的情况,但由于市场变化而希望从合约中脱身的一方不尽快做他该做的事情,使对方也动不了,最终导致期限届满时后续条件还不成熟。

§4 常见的变数先决条件例子之一:subject to contract

"Subject to contract"这一变数先决条件最常见就是在土地买卖的合约,但也经常会在其他类型的合约出现。笔者最近在一个香港仲裁中就涉及一个买卖合约的双方达成了和解协议,和解协议是针对中国买方合法拒货后,卖方愿意减价改变原来的合约。但在双方谈判电邮往来中,中国买方就说明是"subject to contract by respective lawyers"。在该香港仲裁,仲裁庭一致判双方已经达成了一个有约束力的和解协议,不存在中国买方的代表律师可以事后增加要求。

有关"subject to contract"的先例很多,主要涉及土地买卖,这包括了较早的2.2段所介绍的 Masters v Cameron (1954) 91 CLR 353 先例。通常在土地买卖,都被视为这一用语是表示双方没有合约关系直到正式合约被签署与交换,这方面先例有:Winn v Bull (1877) 7 Ch D 29; Farmer v Honan (1919) 26 CLR 183; Thompson & Son Ltd v The King (1920) 2 IR 365; Copper v Ridout (1921) 1 Ch 291; Sinclair Scott

& Co Ltd v Naughton (1929) 43 CLR 310; Raingold v Bromley (1931) 2 Ch 307; Eccles v Bryant (1948) Ch 93; Zimin v Wentworth Properties Pty Ltd (1958) 59 SR (NSW) 101; D'Silva v Lister Development Ltd (1971) Ch 17; Allen v Carbone (1975) 132 CLR 528; Carruthers v Whitaker (1975) 2 NZLR 667; Bridle Estates Pty Ltd v MyerRealty Ltd (1977) 15 ALR 415; Derby & Co Ltd v ITC Pension Trust Ltd (1977) 2 All ER 890; Shell Oil New Zealand Ltd v Wordcom Investments Ltd (1992) 1 NZLR 129; Marek v Australasian Conference Association Pty Ltd (1994) 2 Qd R 521; New Selangor Plantations SDN BHD v Talam Management Services SDN BHD (1996) 4 CLJ 94; Fitzwood Pty Ltd v Unique Coal Pty Ltd (in liq) (2001) 188 ALR 566 等。

在 Chillingworth v Esche (1924) 1 Ch 97 先例,Sargant 大法官也提到在土地买卖的合约,这一用语已经有一个肯定性接近国际货物买卖的 FOB 或 CIF 买卖的解释说:"In the context of real estate contracts, these words have acquired a definite ascertained legal meaning—not quite so definite a meaning perhaps as such expressions as fob or cif in mercantile transactions, but approaching that degree of definiteness."

在 Smissaert v Chiodo 330 P 2d 98 (1958)的美国先例,案情涉及房产买卖。原告以定金的形式向被告发出购买房产的要约,并签发了一张标准定金收据。被告在接受原告的要约时加上了一个附录,如下:"It is further mutually understood and agreed by and between the parties to this agreement that the validity of said proposed agreement is subject and conditioned upon the parties agreeing upon and reducing to writing all terms and conditions necessary and incidental to the validity of said proposed agreement; and that seller shall pay total real estate commission of 5% upon completion of said sale."(加黑部分是笔者的强调)

这可以说是一个十分详尽与明确的变数先决条件,原告也在这份附录签了名。之后双方继续对价格与被告之后租回这套房产的担保进行谈判,但是谈判最后破裂。原告声称已经存在买卖合约,并向法院申请履约指令。

加州上诉法院的 Bray 法官判说这个变数条件的意思取决于对双方意图的客观解释。尽管收据很可能包括了一个有效合约的所有要素,但包括了一条变数条件的附录显示了双方在有一个正式的书面合约前都不受合约约束的意图。Bray 法官说:"Even though the informal agreement might have contained all the essential elements of a contract, the addendum conditioned validity on a formal document which would contain all the incidental terms."

§5 常见的变数先决条件例子之二:subject to details

这是在航运的租船业务中经常有的变数先决条件,已经有很多的先例明确了这是一个合约成立的先决条件。换言之,在这一个变数没有成熟前,双方还没有合约关系。在租约的洽谈,特别是短航次经常非常匆忙,往往在租约谈判时不分昼夜,给对方的要约或反要约也常常需要对方在15分钟甚至10分钟之内给予回复,否则就会失效。而谈判的做法上也是双方先谈租约的"主要条文"(main terms),这在程租合约是运费、装卸港口、货物品种、装卸时间与滞期费、仲裁条文等。显然,如果双方在主要条文也谈不拢,就不必再花时间进一步谈判租约的细节。而双方如果在主要条文谈得拢,才值得花时间谈判租约的进一步细节,如如何签发提单、船舶适航/适货方面问题、船员的协助以及奖金等。英国法律认为即使双方已经就租约的主要条文达成了一致,在"subject to details"的情况下表示双方的意图是租约并没有成立,因为当事人在细节条文还需要达成一致。也不能说主要条文重要,但细节条文不重要。即使有一些细节条文客观看来无关重要,但重要与否是双方当事人自己决定,法律不能强加说双方不同意也受到合约约束。即使双方同意使用金康格式的程租合约,同样也不意味着可以解决所有细节问题:Samos Shipping Enterprises Ltd v Eckhardt & Co KG (The "Nissos Samos") (1985) 1 Lloyd's Rep 378; Star Steamship Society v Beogradska Plovidba (The "Junior K") (1988) 2 Lloyd's Rep 583; Atlantic Marine Transport Corp v Coscol Petroleum Corp (The "Pina") (1992) 2 Lloyd's Rep 103; CPC Consolidated Pool Carriers GmbH v CTM CIA Transmediterranea SA (The "CPC Gallia") (1994) 1 Lloyd's Rep 68; Granit SA v Benship International Inc (1994) 1 Lloyd's Rep 526; Ignazio Messina & Co v Polskie Linie Oceaniczne (1995) 2 Lloyd's Rep 566; Henderson v Amadio Pty Ltd (No. 1) (1995) 140 ALR 391; Thoresen & Co (Bangkok) Ltd v Fathom Marine Co Ltd (2004) 1 Lloyd's Rep 622等先例。可以说,这是一个相对容易理解的变数先决条件显示双方仍在谈判,无意让主要条款谈妥就有了租约的约束。

§6　常见的变数先决条件例子之三:subject to logical amendments/alterations

"subject to logical amendments/alterations"是差不多的用语,就不会被视为合约成立的先决条件,也不会是后续条件。这也是租船业务洽谈中比较常见的用语,因为绝大多数租约的洽谈都是以某一份标准格式或更常见是根据双方不久前已经履行完毕的租约为基础进行的,这可以大大地减轻双方谈判的工作量。虽然没有有关先例,这一变数条件会被视为什么都不是,根本不会影响有效租约的存在。这是因为双方已经局限了只对已经履行完毕的租约作出"逻辑性"(logical)的修改,什么是逻辑性可以由仲裁庭客观作出判断,这不像"subject to details"中所针对的细节条文,其中一方当事人完全可以坚持他对某一细节条文的主观要求甚至看来是不合理的立场,无需第三人异议。《Voyage Charters》(第 4 版,2014 年)一书之 1. 20 段是说 :“Whilst there is no decisive authority on the meaning of such expressions standing alone, there is no reason to hold that they prevent the existence of a binding contract. Their effect, unlike ‘subject to details’, is not to permit either party to raise for negotiation any matters of detail which he wishes, and the only amendments permissible are those which follow logically and inevitably from the terms agreed, and thus can be determined objectively.”

§7 常见的变数先决条件例子之四:subject to finance

许多商业合约都会有这一变数先决条件,虽然它们的写法都不一样。原因是许多涉及庞大金额的交易都会需要银行融资或提供担保。如果合约仍是在谈判阶段,需要银行融资或提供担保(在造船合约就通常要求船厂提供银行的“还款担保”[refund guarantee])的一方不会与他的银行敲定(这也是订立另一个合约),而他的银行也不会理睬,毕竟任何合约的谈判都不能肯定会成功或谈出什么条件。所以,商业合约往往谈妥后,需要银行融资或提供担保的一方才能与他的银行敲定。但这里也有风险,因为就算银行曾经在原则上愿意提供融资或担保,也可能事后改变主意。这样,如果一方当事人融资不成功或提供不了担保,会导致他无法完成交易。但如果这一交易已经有了最后与约束性的合约(因为谈判已经完结),他就会变为违约/毁约,除非在该合约中加上了一个变数条件作为先决条件,这就是“subject to finance”或类似的用语所需要起的作用,而变数就是能否取得融资或担保。

但这一变数条件也带来许多不明朗之处,除非在订约自由下有明示条文针对。首先就是合约如果有了这个变数条件,会否导致合约太不肯定而无法生效?看来这一说法应该在今天的普通法下很难站得住脚,这可节录一个澳大利亚高院的 Meehan v Jones (1982) 149 CLR 571 先例,案情涉及土地买卖,相关条文规定:“This contract is executed by the parties subject to ... (b) The Purchaser or his nominee receiving approval for finance on satisfactory terms and conditions in an amount sufficient to complete the purchase hereunder; And should either of the above conditions not be satisfied on or before 31st July, 1979 (or such extended time as the parties may agree upon) then this Contract (other than for the provisions of this Clause) shall be null and void and at an end and all monies paid hereunder by the Purchaser shall be refunded in full.”

买方在 7 月 30 日通知卖方他已经取得了融资,但在这一天前,卖方就已经把土地卖给了第三人。卖方称合约因为不肯定而无效,但法院判是这个变数条件不会使合约不肯定,Mason 大法官说:“To say that clauses of this kind are void for uncertainty is to ignore the traditional doctrine that courts should be astute to adopt a construction which will preserve the validity of the contract. Moreover, it is a draconian solution—

one which is best calculated to frustrate the expectations of the parties, because in an increasing number of cases purchasers depend on the provisions of finance in order to complete."

下一个不明朗与富争议之处是这一变数条件到底是针对合约成立或是针对合约履行的先决条件？换言之，如果是后者，就变为一个后续条件。看来在目前的法律地位下，通常这一变数条件会被视为后续条件。英国枢密院的 Graham v Pitkin (1992) 1 WLR 403 先例，案情也是涉及房屋的买卖。买卖合约中有条文写明"subject to the purchaser obtaining a mortgage from the Victoria Mutual Building Society of £ 19,000 for 10 years."但买方并没有成功取得这笔抵押贷款，卖方想要以此终止合约。买方表示她愿意以现金付清余款，但卖方拒绝。显然当时的房价涨了，所以卖方想脱身，但买方想履行。买方于是向法院申请履约指令强制卖方完成交易。枢密院判这个变数条件是后续条件而不是合约成立的先决条件，也不认为这一变数条件会令这个买卖合约不肯定而变为无效。

7.1 变数先决条件或后续条件是对买方单方面有利或买卖双方都有利？

在刚刚提到的 Graham v Pitkin (1992) 1 WLR 403 先例，也带来了另一个重要的课题，就是这一变数条件到底是对单方面有利或是双方都有好处？这是因为对单方面有利，也就是只对买方有利，他可以选择"放弃权利"(waiver)。在该先例，买方无法成功获得融资，也等于不能满足这一后续条件而导致该房屋买卖合约终止。但如果当时的房屋价格上涨，买方想完成交易并且可以不通过向银行融资也可以自己支付给卖方，他就会想这样做。但反过来卖方就希望合约终止，就可以把价格上涨了的房屋以更高的价格卖给第三人。这就带来了争议，而买方能够保住这一买卖合约完成交易唯一就是靠这一变数条件只是单方面给买方的权利，他可以放弃，也表示这一后续条件不再存在。这也是英国枢密院在 Graham v Pitkin 先例中的判法。

但这说法也并非是肯定，因为有看法认为这一个变数条件对另一方，也就是卖方有一定好处。这就是这一个变数条件可以约束买方除了这一个原因外不能以其它理由逃避合约责任，Mason 大法官在 Meehan v Jones (1982) 149 CLR 571 先例中说："Although the primary object of the condition is to protect the purchaser, it is perhaps difficult to assert that the clause is for his benefit exclusively when it states that the result of non-performance is that the contract shall be null and void, rather than null and void at the option of the purchaser."

显然如果变数条件是对双方都有好处，就轮不到一方当事人随意放弃。看来如果买方希望只有他可以从这一变数条件中得利，在合约条文中就要写得更清楚。例如好像 Mason 大法官说这一后续条件如果不成熟，买方有选择权可终止合约。或是，写明这一后续条件"只是买方得利"(for the sole benefit of the buyer)。通常，法院或仲裁庭也是看合约条文以确定一个变数条件(任何的变数条件)是否只是让一方当事人得利。在 Heron Garage Properties Ltd v Moss (1974) 1 WLR 148 先例，Brightman 大法官说:“Without seeking to define the precise limits within a contracting party seeking specific performance may waive a stipulation on the ground that it is intended only for his benefit, it seems to me that in general the proposition only applies where the stipulation is in terms for the exclusive benefit of the plaintiff because it is a power or right vested by the contract in him alone... or where the stipulation is by inevitable implication for the benefit of him alone... **If it is not obvious on the face of the contract that the stipulation is for the exclusive benefit of the party seeking to eliminate it, then in my opinion it cannot be struck out unilaterally.**”(加黑部分是笔者的强调)

7.2　变数先决条件或后续条件涉及单方面的满意是主观或客观的考验

再下一个不明朗之处就是合约变数条件如果不成熟,也就是买方无法取得银行的融资,往往是由于与银行之间的条件谈不拢,如在融资的利率或年期方面。同样的问题在卖方要提供担保时也会存在,如在造船合约,船厂作为卖方要提供还款担保,它也会由于与银行之间条件谈不拢,被银行拒绝作出还款担保。换言之,一方当事人无法取得“满意”(satisfactory)的融资或担保。有许多这种变数条件甚至会说明,如在上述的 Meehan v Jones (1982) 149 CLR 571 先例的相关条文就会更明确与详尽的说明“subject to ... finance on satisfactory terms and conditions in an amount sufficient to complete the purchase”,这样就会带来一个争议就是满意与否是一个主观或客观的考验。这十分重要,因为属于主观考验,就会对合约另外一方很不利。如在土地买卖,市场价格如果下跌,主要得利的买方就可以利用这一“subject to finance”甚至说明是“subject to satisfactory finance”从合约中脱身,也就是在正常情况下应该满意的融资条件,买方也可以说主观上不满意。如果属于客观考验,就再也不是以买方自说自话为准。看来,这方面的不明朗也可以明示条文提高肯定性,如写明“买方的满意”(subject to satisfaction of the buyer),这就有较大机会被解释为买方主观的考验。总体而言,多数有关先例都会把这一融资的变数是否满意视为买方主观的考验,对买方唯一的约束就是他这一满意与否必须诚实与合理。显然,买方是否诚实与合理很难证明,除非涉及十分极端的案件,如有关银行几乎是无条件送钱上门,但该当事人的买方还是拒绝接受。

其中 Meehan v Jones 先例认为一般针对融资或担保的变数条件只是主观的考验,而不是一个合理第三人(合理第三人一般是在诉讼时由法官或者仲裁员假设他就是该第三人),Gibbs 大法官是这样解释:“A cautious purchaser might be satisfied only with finance which was repayable over a long term and at comparatively low rates of interest, whereas a more adventurous purchaser might wish to proceed with the sale even though the term of the loan was short and the rate or interest high. It would be strange if an adventurous purchaser, having obtained finance on terms which were satisfactory to him, but at which a reasonable man might cavil, could be told by the vendor that the sale would not proceed, although the vendor was to be paid out in full and would have no interest in the purchaser's financial situation thereafter. Equally it would hardly seem likely that the parties would intend that a purchaser would be bound to complete if he honestly regarded the terms and conditions on which finance was available as unsatisfactory, notwithstanding that a court might take a different view. The intention of such a clause in my opinion is to leave it to the purchaser himself to decide whether the terms and conditions on which finance is available are satisfactory. The condition prevents a purchaser from being obliged to go through with a sale when he does not believe that he can raise the necessary funds. **Such a condition is generally entirely for the protection of the purchaser, and it is the satisfaction of the purchaser, not that of some hypothetical reasonable man, that will satisfy the condition.** No doubt it may be implied that the purchaser will act honestly in deciding whether or not he is satisfied. However, it does not seem to me necessary, in order to give business efficacy to a contract, that a condition should be implied that the purchaser will make reasonable efforts to obtain finance. The parties may expect that he will, but he does not contract to so do."（加黑部分是笔者的强调）

针对这一个先例，Furmston 教授在《Subject to Finance》（1983）3 OJLS 438 一文中也认为是主观的考验，说："Since the commercial purpose of the 'subject to satisfactory finance' provision was to give the purchaser an opportunity to raise finance, the natural inference was that the finance must be satisfactory to him and not to some hypothetical reasonable purchaser."

这方面的先例另可以介绍 Fast Ferries v Ferries Australia（2000）1 Lloyd's Rep 534，有关条文明确说明融资条件必须让买方满意。该先例同时也有提到，除非买方犯错或阻碍这个后续条件，否则会以买方满意为准。案情涉及建造两艘"双体船"（catamaran），其中建造船舶的融资来自一家名为 Debis 的财务公司。由于受到压力，就是船厂有其他船东在谈判，导致船厂没有空泊位，所以在 1995 年 2 月 20 日双方就签了造船合约。该合约的变数条件在第 27 条文，如下："This agreement is condition upon Debis agreeing to provide finance for the vessel on terms and conditions which are **satisfactory to the purchaser** and builder.

The above condition shall be met before the 28th February 1995 for this agreement to become effective."

之后，船东支付了 5% 的船价作为定金，而 Debis 与船东/船厂有关融资的谈判也继续。到了 5 月 18 日，船东不接受 Debis 新提出的条件而终止了融资谈判，并要求船厂归还定金。但船厂拒绝归还，并指称船东应该接受 Debis 的条件，而不这样做是犯错，根据 New Zealand Shipping Co. Ltd v Societie Des Ateliers et Chantiers de France（1919）AC 1 先例，应该有一个默示条件不能让船东自己犯错，令后续条件得不到满足而终止造船合约。但高院拒绝船厂这个说法，认为船东没有必要接受新的融资条件,Steel 大法官说:"... it is important to bear in mind that the [shipbuilding] contract had been conditional on the provision of finance by Debis on terms which were satisfactory to [the buyer and the builder] ... While a term could readily be implied that neither party would prevent approval [of the financing] being given on the terms offered (e. g. by withdrawing the application), there is no basis ... for implying any term to the effect that either party was under an obligation to accept different finance terms."

Steel 大法官支持是以一个主观的考验为准(但要小心在这个先例,合约中是写明要买方与船厂都满意),说:"The assessment of what were to be regarded as satisfactory terms was by definition to be an entirely subjective matter from each party's perspective."

但要小心也有一些先例看来是以一个合理第三人的客观考验为准,如 Martin v Macarthur (1963) NZLR 403 先例,Richmond 大法官认为这一后续条件的举证责任是在买方,证明他无法取得融资。另有一些美国先例更加明确以客观的考验为准,如 Mattei v Hopper 330 P 2d 625 (1958);Misano di Navigazione v United States of America 968 F 2d 273 (1992)等。在后一个先例是说:"Where a contract conditions performance upon the satisfaction of one party and is ambiguous as to the applicable standard of satisfaction, courts generally require performance to the satisfaction of a reasonable man, particularly when a definite objective test of satisfaction is available."(如果一个合约有后续条件是以一方合约方的满意为准,但合约对什么是满意的标准含糊,法院通常要求以一个合理第三人的满意为准,特别是有办法明确这一客观的考验。)

在这一先例也依赖了美国的《Restatement (2d) Contract》之 s. 228,如下:"S. 228 Satisfaction of the Obligor as a Condition When it is a condition of an obligor's duty that he be satisfied with respect to the obligee's performance or with respect to something else, and it is practicable to determine whether a reasonable person in the position of the obligor would be satisfied, and interpretation is preferred under which the condition occurs if such a reasonable person in the position of the obligor would be satisfied."

撇开主观或客观的考验,普通法对这一后续条件的要求还是明确,这就是享有这一变数的一方当事方必须合理、诚实与善意行事,当然证明这一点困难重重。这里有很多说法,如在 Meehan v Jones 先例,Mason 大法官说:"The limitation that the purchaser must act honestly, or honestly and reasonably, takes the case out of the principle that: '... where words which by themselves constitute a promise are accompanied by words which show that the promisor is to have a discretion or option as to whether he will carry out that which purports to be the promise, the result is that there is no contract on which an action can be brought.' ... The judgment of the purchaser as to what constitutes finance on satisfactory terms is not an unfettered discretion—it must be reached honestly, or honestly and reasonably."

英国的 Lee – Parker v Izzet（1971）3 All ER 1099 先例，案情涉及房屋买卖。合约第 5 条文说："The completion date shall be（on or before）the . . . day of . . . 1969 or within twenty – eight days of . . . arranging for the（买方）a satisfactory mortgage or mortgages for the balance of the purchase price outstanding . . . ."

Goff 大法官判是融资必须让一个合理的买方满意。Slade 大法官在 Janmohamed v Hassam（1976）126 NLJ 696 先例也有类似说法。该先例案情也是涉及房屋买卖，合约中有条文规定如果买方无法在 1 个月内取得让他满意的银行抵押贷款，合约就会被撤销。Slade 大法官判合约中有一个默示条件就是不满意不能是不合理的，即 Slade 大法官要求买方的不满意必须是诚实与合理的。

已经在本小段一开始提到过，造船合约中通常有一个变数条件是银行需要提供给买方还款担保。在航运市场高涨的年代，曾经多次见到一些船厂在签了造船合约后仍在等待还款担保这一变数的成熟时，对船东说："船价在上一个月涨了，你必须加 100 万美元的船价，否则我就不继续申请还款担保，终止合约。"这就构成了一个愚蠢的违约/毁约，船东可以向法院索赔损失。因为船厂普遍不了解这是一个变数先决条件或后续条件，申请还款担保并不是船厂的选择权。但是如果船厂有证据证明银行拒绝提供还款担保或条件不令人满意，船厂就可以合法从合约中脱身，而这里船厂是有很大的灵活性可以合法逼船东提高船价。

看来，最安全的做法还是在有关合约中以明确的条文作出规定，如在较早提到过的"subject to finance"加上"to the buyer's sole satisfaction"等用语。更加有合约会以详尽的明示条文针对一方当事人对变数条件所要作出的行为准则，如在 Total Gas v Arco British（1998）2 Lloyd's Rep 209 先例，在该供应 14 年北海天然气的一个高昂金额合约中涉及了几个变数先决条件，其中包括取得英国商务部与其他部门/单位的批准，与卖方成功加入一个对经过处理的天然气进行分配的协议（party to allocation agreement），有明示条文明确了卖方需要承担的责任，如下：

"The Seller shall use its reasonable endeavours to obtain the approvals and consents and become party to the Allocation Agreement referred to in Clause 2.8.1 above by 1st March 1996. In using its reasonable endeavours to become a party to the Allocation Agreement, the Seller shall not be obliged to accept onerous contractual obligations and/or make an unusual or excessive payment（or payments）with（a）all other parties to the Allocation Agreement do not or would not have to accept and/or make; and/or（b）a Reasonable and Prudent Operator would not accept and/or make.（卖方必须合理努力取得批准与成为分配合约一份子，但卖方不需要在分配合约接受苛刻的合约条文以及要支付不正常或超额的费用，如果其他分配合约的用家不会接受与/或一个合理与谨慎的营业者不会接受这种条件。）

If the approvals and/or consents are not obtained by 1 March 1996, either the Seller or the Buyer may terminate this Agreement at any time thereafter...（如果在 1996 年 3 月

1 日前还没有取得批准或成为分配合约一份子,本合约可以任由卖方与买方终止。)”

§8 常见的变数先决条件例子之五: subject to satisfaction of . . .

这一变数在上一小段的“subject to finance”已经有十分详尽地探讨过,特别是满意与否到底是一个客观还是主观的考验。显然,如果是一个主观的考验,就很容易给一个可以决定满意与否的当事人操纵,变得十分危险。但满意与否的变数客观存在,这也不仅是在“subject to finance”(虽然这方面的先例很多),而是也会发生在许多其他的变数条件,如在许多买卖合约中会出现的“subject to survey”,对一个特定标的作出检验后买方感觉满意才会有约束性的合约,或是买方如果不满意可以从一个约束性的合约脱身。例如,在二手船舶买卖对船舶作出检验,或是在公司并购对有关的公司作出尽职调查等,都会说明买方必须满意。针对这主观或客观考验的困难可以看 Mason 大法官在 Meehan v Jones (1982) 149 CLR 571 先例说:

“In this case it is not necessary to decide whether the purchaser, in deciding whether finance is on satisfactory terms, is bound to act honestly or whether he is also bound to act reasonably. The cases already mentioned appear to support the first rather than the second alternative. And there is some ground for thinking that the parties contemplated that the question was to be left to the honest judgment of the purchaser rather than to the judgment of a court as to whether the purchaser acted reasonably in the circumstances. (本案不需要考虑买方在取得合理条件的融资是否需要诚实行事或是合理行事,前者代表主观考验,而后者代表客观考验。有关的其他案例看来支持前者的考验,这也有一定道理就是让买方诚实作出判断到底融资条件是否能被接受,而不是事后让法院决定买方有否在当时的情况下合理行事。)

On the other hand, it has been said that a condition of this type imports an obligation or promise on the part of the purchaser to act honestly and reasonably. . . The reasoning which underlies the decisions of this Court upholding the implication of an obligation on the part of a party to a contract to do all that was reasonable on his part to obtain a statutory consent applies with equal force here. . . (但另一方面,也有说法是这种先决条件下买方应该诚实与合理行事,也就是要同时满足主观与客观的考验)

Here the expressed intention of the parties was that the purchaser would obtain finance; his obtaining of finance on satisfactory terms was necessary to give the transaction its intended efficacy. The consequence would be that he had an obligation to do all that was reasonable on his part to obtain that finance. It would make for greater consistency to say that, if the purchaser is bound to act reasonably in seeking to obtain finance, he is bound to act reasonably as well as honestly in deciding whether the finance was satisfactory. So I understood the special condition would preserve an even balance between the vendors and the purchaser. However, I have no need to decide the question. Here it makes no difference whether the purchaser was under an obligation to act honestly or honestly and reasonably in deciding whether the terms of an offer were satisfactory."

在航运,经常会在租约出现,而肯定在二手船买卖的谈判中出现是"subject to survey"或是"subject to satisfactory survey",这一用语在 Astra Trust v Adams (1969) 1 Lloyd's Rep 81 先例看来没有明确这是合约成立的先决条件或合约履行的先决条件。Megaw 大法官判决的总结如下:"(1) that there was no simple distinction between a sale of land and sale of a ship; that 'satisfactory' did not add to or subtract from what would have been the meaning and effect in law in absence of that word; and that, accordingly, there was no binding contract; (2) (obiter) (i) that, if there was a legally binding contract, it was conditional upon a survey satisfactory to plaintiffs; that it was an implied term that dissatisfaction must be *bona fide*; and that, on the evidence, plaintiffs' dissatisfaction was *bona fide*; (ii) that, even if an objective test applied, plaintiffs were not unreasonable in taking view that survey report was not satisfactory. Judgment for plaintiff."[(1) Megaw 大法官认为是否加满意这个字在法律上是没有区别,双方没有约束性的合约;(2)(附带意见)(i)即使是有一个法律约束性的合约,也有一个先决条件就是原告的买方必须有一个满意的检验,满意与否法律默示是必须善意,而根据证据来看,原告的不满意是善意的;(ii)就算是根据一个客观的考验,原告也没有不合理之处认为检验报告不满意。]

看来,Megaw 大法官也没有明确交代满意的检验到底是客观或是主观的考验,只要求或默示买方必须善意或诚实。但已经在较早时提到过,问题是主观的考验不论是善意或者诚实通常很难证明。

在另一个稍后先例 The "Merak" (1976) 2 Lloyd's Rep 250,有关二手船买卖合约,第 2 条文要求买方先支付 10% 船价的定金后才能作出检验,而买方也给了这笔定金。接下去的履约是买方派员上船做表面检验,如果满意,就必须在 48 小时内通知卖方,该买卖也就完全肯定。这一上船做的表面检验通常的用语是"subject superficial inspection afloat at port/dates to be agreed",这是二手船买卖的习惯性做法。检验满意后并及时向卖方作出确认,可以说"变数条件成熟"(subject lift),买卖也就算是"清洁"(clean)。双方再接下去的履约步骤就是各自安排在一个适当的港口(这要根据船舶实际的营运与双方的方便)交接船舶。在 The "Merak"先例,由于船价市场在支付订金但买方还没有上船检验期间急涨,卖方想从买卖合约中脱身,认为让买方上船检验是一个合约成立的先决条件。由于还没有合约的关系,卖方拒绝让买方上船检验,估计卖方同时想把船舶以更高的价格卖给其他买方,或是向原买方要求加价。但英国高院与上诉庭都判这一个上船检验的变数条件不是合约成立的先决条

件,而只是合约履行的先决条件,也就是一个后续条件。Denning 勋爵是这样说:

"In my opinion, the telexes, with those clauses incorporated, form a binding contract. The parties are bound by contract to provide for and make inspection. The buyer has then an option whether to go on, or not. The word: '... should the vessel be refused this contract shall be considered null and void' do not mean that it was null and void from the beginning. They mean as from the date of refusal the buyer is acquitted of any obligation.

So it seems to me that on those clauses, which are incorporated into this sale - and - purchase agreement, there was a binding contract. The seller was bound to go ahead and provide the opportunity for inspection. When he refused to go ahead, that was a breach."

需注意的是,Denning 勋爵说买方有一个"选择权"(option)接受或者拒绝该检验结果,看来也不完全正确,因为在上面已经提到,针对这一变数先决条件或是后续条件,买方至少有主观甚至是客观的考验,也就是必须诚实、善意与合理。笔者就想起多年前曾经处理过的案件,涉及在订立二手船买卖后还没有上船检验的期间,船舶市场价格大跌。笔者的朋友作为买方十分坦率地向希腊船东的卖方说:"船价市场大跌,我不要花钱检验,我不买这艘船了。"幸亏该希腊船东作为卖方并没有马上掌握机会接受违约/毁约,终止合约,没收 10% 的定金并在其余的差价向买方索赔,而以强硬的态度要求买方履约。而买方也及时委任笔者,笔者第一件事就是马上向希腊船东撤回违约/毁约的说法,并向希腊船东保证买方会履约并上船检验。这样,正如 Asquith 大法官在 Howard v Pickford Tool Co Ltd (1951) 1 KB 417 先例中所说,之前没有被接受的预期违约就好像"没有发生过的镜花水月"(a thing writ in water)。接下来希腊船东也知道不妙,回电要求买方保证不会以上船检验不满意为由终止合约。笔者的回应是这不能保证,大家完全要按合约办事。不久后,船舶在新加坡进行上船检验,笔者代买方委任了一位新加坡的验船师上船检验,在电文的委任中完全符合一贯的做法,包括要求验船师尽快作出一个专业与客观的报告,以便在 48 小时内作出决定。但私下给了他一个电话,简单说买方对该船舶兴趣不大,估计不需要太仔细与昂贵的检验。该外籍验船师看来十分精明,他上船检验时间不长,收费也相对便宜,但报告把该船舶讲得情况很恶劣(也可能是真实情况)。这样买方在 48 小时内取消该二手船买卖。希腊船东十分生气,拒绝退还 10% 的定金,并最终导致要去伦敦仲裁。显然仲裁的结果是买方胜诉,因为该希腊船东无法证明买方不诚实、恶意甚至不合理。他至多指出买方在以前的违约/毁约已经显示了想从合约中脱身,但这离开证明还不足以证明不诚实与恶意,甚至是客观的不合理。毕竟在市场下跌时,任何一个正常的买方都希望从以前订下的不利合约脱身,这不代表他们不诚实与恶意。在该案件,即使根据客观的合理标准,买方也足以根据该检验报告证明他的合理。

§9　常见的变数先决条件例子之六：subject to approval/permission

合约中也经常有"subject to approval/permission"，也就是以认可/批准为准。这批准可以是来自董事局（subject to board approval）或是其他人士或当局（如在中国大陆所出的担保就需要外汇局的批准）。在租船业务与国际货物买卖的合约，就经常需要一些有关单位（如政府或有关政府部门、发货人、收货人、大石油公司或董事局等）认可/批准船舶（往往是有关船舶的技术描述方面，如是否接受一艘超龄的船舶，但也可以是针对船东的声誉），双方就可以因为合约成立的先决条件或后续条件（这要看是针对什么变数与双方使用的条文/文字）不成熟而终止租约。《Voyage Charters》（第4版，2014年）一书之1.26段有说到另一种程租合约常见的董事局认可/批准为准，说："Another 'subject' occasionally encountered in charter negotiations is 'subject to board approval', and the effect of this expression must also be to negative contractual intent until approval has been obtained."

但笔者对这个说法也有一定的怀疑，特别经常在租船业务中见到在这一种"subject to"，会加上一句"只是例行手续"（which is formality）。这样这一"subject to"就会是什么都不是。看来，如果董事局认可/批准对受影响的一方的确事关重大，在没有批准之前不能有一个约束性的合约，最安全的做法就是把话说得更清楚而不要仅以"subject to"这一模棱两可的用语。

在《Contract Formation：Law and Practice》（2010年）一书的9.24段也有针对"subject to approval"说："On one view, where a 'subject to' clause requires the formal contract to be approved by the parties or their solicitors or some other third party, this is a strong indicator that any legal obligations are only to arise in the future. However, every case depends on its facts. It is equally arguable that an approval or satisfaction provision is merely intended to suspend performance or is a mere formality and is not intended to impact on performance or formation."

这种"subject to"如果是针对律师的认可/批准，在一些涉及金额较高与比较复杂的合约谈判中经常出现，也就是最后版本的合约需要让当事人的律师认可/批准（或类似用语）。估计是在律师认为合约没有严重缺陷后，当事人才签署。这样又要看每一个案件决定到底是一个先决条件、后续条件或什么都不是。例如，在一种情况是要求"subject to"的一方从来没有见过对方提供的标准合约，这样"subject to"他的律师认可/批准该标准合约的条款，就完全可以料想到他会在有些方面要求作出改变，这就表示这一"subject to"会是合约成立的先决条件。在美国的Southern Bell Telegraph Co v John Hancock Mutual Life Insurance Co 579 F Supp 1065（1982）先例，Forrester 大法官说:"The facts suggest that prior to [the withdrawal to the] offer on April 16, Southern Bell did not demonstratively assent to enter into an immediate bargain. The language 'subject to the review of the contract by our legal counsel' in... [the]... letter of April 14 cannot be said to encompass a context of the parties' settled expectations, especially in light of the fact that prior to the writing of this letter, no one at Southern Bell had ever seen or reviewed a copy of the GIC. Whether ... the 'subject to review' clause [was] tantamount to a rigorous examination or a cursory evaluation by Southern Bell's counsel of the specimen contract, future actions by Southern Bell were anticipated."

但换一种情况是双方当事人已经有了十分充分的谈判,根本不像还有进一步的内容需要双方同意。这样同样的"subject to"就会是后续条件或者什么都不是。也是在美国的 Arnold Palmer Golf Co v Fuqua Industries Inc, 541 F 2d 584 (1976)先例,上诉庭推翻了高院的判决,认为一条"subject to approval by the respective counsel of Palmer and Fuqua of all legal matters"至多是后续条件,所以被告单方面从合约中撤离构成了违约。其中两个主要的考虑因素在于,一是双方已经有了十分充分的谈判,没有进一步的内容需要同意;二是被告曾经在报纸作出通告说订立了这一合作协议。

§10 常见的变数先决条件例子之七:租船与国际商品买卖的 subject to stem

在程租合约(与国际商品买卖合约)中也经常会有"subject to cargo stem",也就是以货物备妥装船为准。这是经常在大宗的干散货的租船业务中出现的变数先决条件。如涉及煤炭,就是给供应商从矿场把煤炭运到装港泊位,可以及时装船。如果供应商告诉承租人无法及时把煤炭备妥装船,承租人就可以及时向船东告知"stem failed"并从程租合约中脱身。有些时候,"subject to stem"更加是表示承租人要找到货物装船,这在《Time Charters》(第 6 版,2008 年)之 1.29 段说:"'Sub stem' is a phrase normally seen only in voyage charters. It means that the contract is conditional upon the charterer being able to find a cargo."

这一变数条件看来本质上十分重要。在 Kokusai Kisen Kabushiki Kaisha v Johnson (1921) 8 Ll L Rep 434 先例中,法院认为"subject to stem"是先决条件,Rowlatt 大法官判是直到租约约定的限期(是在周五)之前,承租人不受到约束。他判是这一变数条件的实质意思是承租人告诉船东:"We have arranged this charter - party, but I am not in a position to tell you if I can undertake to load this ship until I have found out whether I shall have a stem on Friday."

Rowlatt 大法官不同意船东的争辩,就是承租人不能仅说"我无法安排货物装船",而是需要承担责任备货,并且需要证明他有采取合理行为备货,但不成功(Defendant's[承租人] duty to arrange a stem, and he could only excuse himself for non-performance on proving that he took reasonable steps to arrange a stem and failed)。但在一个近期被报道的伦敦仲裁 LMLN No. 702 (2006) 18/06 中,这一变数先决条件被归类为后续条件。

§11　常见的变数先决条件例子之八：不取决于双方当事人的变数

在《Voyage Charters》(第4版,2014年)一书之1.26段也有提到一些完全不取决于双方当事人的变数,如果在限期前这外来的变数不再影响租约(也可以是其他类型合约)的履行,这变数条件就变为什么都不是,根本不影响一份有效合约的履行,说:"Where, however, the 'subject' is some event outside either party's control or opinion (e.g., 'subject to removal of embargo on shipment of wheat within 14 days') the conclusion is more likely to be that each party is bound, and must perform if the condition is fulfilled, failing which the contract lapses."

§12　变数先决条件条文的例子

对变数先决条件拟定的比较完整的例子还是经常看到。笔者最近的一个香港仲裁案件,案情涉及公司的收购,有关合约中有条文是这样规定:

"4CONDITIONS PRECEDENT(先决条件)

4.1The parties hereby agree that Completion of this Agreement is conditional upon the following occurring and remaining satisfied on or before the Long Stop Date (or waived by the investor pursuant to Clause 4.2):(双方同意这一合约的完成是取决于以下变数在限期前的成熟,除非投资方对有关的先决条件弃权)

(A)(被投资方的A公司) having confirmed that there being no fact or circumstance (including legal, financial or changes in regulations) which would materially and adversely affecting the legal, financial and business operations or standing or continued existence of Company or its ability to continue to carry on its ordinary business;(A确认没有任何事实或情况会重大与不利地影响有关目标公司的正常营运与业务)

(B)A公司 having completed the matters to be done prior to Completion in relation to all of the covenants and agreements required to be performed by it under this Agreement;

(C)The approval of the board of directors and/or the general meeting of shareholder

(s) of the Investor being obtained for this Agreement and the transactions contemplated under this Agreement;

(D)The approval of the board of directors and/or the general meeting of shareholder(s) of A公司 being obtained for the new share issuance under this Agreement; (A公司董事局在股东大会中批准并发行新股)and

(E)All other necessary consents, if any, being granted and not withdrawn or revoked by third (including without limitation, government bodies, and other relevant authorities having jurisdiction over the transactions contemplate under this Agreement) and if such consents are obtained subject to any conditions and where such conditions affect any of the Parties, such conditions being acceptable to the Party concerned and, if such conditions are required to be fulfilled before Completion, such conditions being fulfilled before Completion.

4.2The conditions herein are for the benefit of the Investor and the Investor may waive all or any of such conditions in Clause 4.1 at any time by notice in writing to A公司.(本条文的先决条件只是由投资方得利,投资方可以对任何的变数条件作出弃权[针对这一方面可看本章之7.1段])

8Termination

8.1If the conditions set out in Clause 4.1 shall not have been fulfilled (or waived by the Investor in accordance with Clause 4.2) on the Long Stop Date the provisions of this Agreement shall (other than this Clause...) from such date *ipso facto* cease and determine and none of the Parties shall have any claim against the other for costs, damages, compensation or otherwise save in respect of any antecedent breach of this Agreement and the right of the Investor pursuant to the undertaking of A公司 in Clauses 6.2."

第九章　善意谈判协议与条文

§1　不肯定不予解释的典型:善意

在讨论“善意”(good faith)这个课题前,首先一提的是,合约如果太不肯定,就会有危险法院或仲裁庭不给予解释,也就是合约无效。这方面已经在本书第三章之12段有详尽解释,不重复。只是说普通法一直以来十分抗拒“善意”这个概念,一个重要的原因就是会给商业合约带来不肯定。英国合约法还是严格依照订约自由与必须严格履行同意了的合约条文的大原则,不存在因为善意的要求就可以或多或少地改变合约的履行。反映这种精神的英国案例数之不尽,许多期租合约下租金只要少付或晚付了一点,船东在航运市场高涨时就会撤船。这是因为期租合约都规定了承租人要准时支付租金并在承租人没有做到时允许船东有选择权撤船与终止租约。这些案件都不存在善意或船东这样取巧是“不合情理的”(unconscionable)争议,即使有也不会被法院接受,反正租约条文是这样写,那就这样判。同样精神的著名案例也有很多,如在《Chitty on Contracts》(第31版,2012年)一书针对善意主题的1－040段就介绍了 Union Eagle Ltd v Golden Achievement Ltd (1997) AC 514 先例,买卖房屋的买方晚了10分钟(如堵车或等电梯等琐碎的延误)支付完成交易的价款就被卖方终止合约,这是因为土地价格上涨,卖家借这个小小的延误取巧不卖,并且可以没收订金。这是因为合约规定了完成交易的时限是“合约的精要”(essence of contract),也就是代表双方同意这时限是条件条文。买方向法院申请救济,要求法院对卖方作出履约指令交出土地,但这最终被贵族院拒绝。在 Hoffmann 勋爵的判词中,就提到了考虑善意或不合情理就会导致商业合约不肯定,说:“The principle that equity will restrain the enforcement of legal rights when it would be unconscionable to insist upon them has an attractive breadth. But the reasons why the courts have rejected such generalizations are founded not merely upon authority... but also upon considerations of business. These are, in summary, that in many forms of transaction it is of great importance that if something happens for which the contract has made express provision, the parties should know with certainty that the terms of the contract will be enforced. The existence of an undefined discretion to refuse to enforce the contract on the ground that this would be 'unconscionable' is sufficient to create uncertainty.”

但这个抗拒在近年来已经不断减弱,这是由多个原因造成。第一个是政治上的考虑,因为英国与大部分的大陆法国家不同,这方面可节录 Bingham 大法官在 Interfoto Picture Library Ltd v Stiletto Visual Programms Ltd (1989) QB 433 中的说法:"In many civil law systems, and perhaps in most legal systems outside the common law world, the law of obligations recognizes and enforces an overriding principle that in making and carrying out contracts parties should act in good faith. This does not simply mean that they should not deceive each other... ; its effect is perhaps most aptly conveyed by such metaphorical colloquialisms as 'playing fair'; 'coming clean' or 'putting one's cards face upwards on the table'. It is in essence a principle of fair and open leading... English law has, characteristically, committed itself to no such overriding principle, but has developed piecemeal solutions in response to demonstrated problems of unfairness."

这与中国《合同法》的规定不同,中国《合同法》第 6 条、第 42 条与第 60 条均有对诚实信用的规定,这应该与善意的说法是同一回事。另在欧盟的合同法《Lando Commission's Principles of European Contract Law》的 Article 1.106 也规定了善意,而且不准试图以合约条文对这善意的要求作出改变:"(i) In exercising his rights and performing his duties each party must act in accordance with good faith and fair dealing. (ii) The parties may not exclude or limit this duty."

这也是反映了几个重要欧盟国家有关这方面的法律,如德国 BGB 民法典的 Section 242,法国民法典的 Article 1134 与意大利民法典的 Article 1377、1366 与 1375。在这些国家,善意延伸至合约的履行与执行。

理所当然,英国涉及欧共体的法律经常有善意的责任。如在《Unfair Terms in Consumer Contract Regulation 1999》,有贵族院的先例 Director General of Fair Trading v First National Bank plc (2002) 1 AC 481 判是合约条文要公平合理不违反善意是要求在订约的程序上与实体上都公平合理。另一个例子是《Commercial Agents Directive》(1986/653/EEC),要求代理人对他的委托人必须尽责任与善意。其他有要求善意的法条有《Financial Services Distance Marketing Directive》(2002/65/EU)、《Unfair Commercial Practices Directive》(2005/29/EU)与在提议中并且明示不允许排除善意的《Regulation of the European Parliament and of the Council on a Common European Sales Law Com》([2001] 635 final, Annex I, CESL Proposal, Annex I, art 2 CESL)。这些法律显然影响英国,因为它也是欧盟成员国之一。

英国甚至与同是普通法的美国与澳大利亚也有所不同,这在《Chitty on Contracts》(第 31 版,2012 年)一书之 1 – 041 段有说:"As Lord Brown – Wilkinson has observed: '... throughout the common law world it is a matter of controversy to what extent obligations of good faith are to be found in contractual relationships', and other common law systems have taken varying positions as to the relevance of good faith in the creation or the performance of contracts. Perhaps the most extensive use is taken by lawyers in the

United States, the Restatement (Second) of Contracts requiring that 'every contract imposes upon each party a duty of good faith and fair dealing in its performance and enforcement'. In Australia too, courts and writers are generally quite open to the use of good faith, holding that an agreement to negotiate in good faith may be contractually enforceable, an willing to find implied terms requiring co-operation in performance, if not always good faith, between the parties."

第二个原因会是商业的现实,其中有一些十分重要的标准格式合约对善意有所规定。如第一份针对衍生品合约的标准格式合约,由 International Swaps and Derivatives Association(简称 ISDA)的组织在 1992 年推出的 ISDA Master Agreement。该标准协议中有许多善意条文,如要求双方善意达成关于汇率价值的协议[第 6(f)条],要求双方善意达成关于公平合理市场价格的协议[第 9(h)(i)(ii)条],善意选择银行等(第 14 条)。有关 ISDA Master Agreement 在笔者《损失赔偿与救济》一书的第十九章中有详论,在此不重复。

另一份重要的标准格式合约是建造合约,New Engineering Contract(NEC)之第三版标准格式合约有规定说:"The Employer, the Contractor, the Project Manager and the Supervisor shall act as stated in this contract and in the spirit of mutual trust and co-operation."

一般由合约双方拟定的非标准格式的合约中也有越来越多的合约条文要求双方善意,这方面会稍后介绍。所以,近期的英国法院越来越愿意接受给善意一定的解释。Arden 大法官 2013 年 4 月 26 日在新加坡法律学院(Singapore Academy of Law)所发表的名为《Coming to Terms with Good Faith》的文章中就显示出这个趋势。

§2 为何抗拒善意

在英国商法发展的早期,对善意并没有抗拒。将以前判例法典化的 1906 年英国《海上保险法》对海上保险合约就有善意的要求。Mansfield 勋爵也曾经想把海上保险合约的善意原则延伸至所有其他的合约。他在 Carter v Boehm (1766) 3 Burr 1905 说:"the governing principle is applicable to all contracts and dealings. Good faith forbids either party by concealing what he privately knows, to draw the other into a bargain, from his ignorance of that fact, and his believing the contrary. But either party may be innocently silent, as to grounds open to both, to exercise their judgment upon."

到了 19 世纪末 20 世纪初,英国法院的最高大原则是尊重订约自由与"当事人自治"(party autonomy),法院唯一插手私人合约的就是解释合约条文。但严格解释双方的合约条文就会有机会带来苛刻的结果,这令英国以外的不少国家通过立法将善意责任的要求加入合约中,以期找到一个比较公平合理的平衡。在这种立法下,法院就可把善意作为诠释的工具解释双方之间的合约条文。法院也可以把善意当作一个实质的责任,把不合作的一方视为违约。但英国法律的发展不一样,是通过一些比较细化与有针对性的说法针对这一问题,如一些在本书有提及的双方必须给予协助/合作以让对方顺利履行合约,不能妨碍对方履约与不能因为自己的错误获利等默示要求。正如 Hope 勋爵在 R (European Roma Rights) v Prague Immigration Office (2005) 2 AC 1 中所说:"The preferred approach in England is to avoid any commitment to over – arching principle, in favor of piecemeal solutions in response to demonstrated problems of unfairness."(英国不喜欢一些至高无上的原则[如善意或是要做好人],而是倾向于个别针对一些不公平合理的问题。)

另一提是 Steyn 勋爵 2000 年在"The Clifford Chance Millennium Lectures"讲座上说:"Thus the continental systems recognize an overarching duty of good faith in the performance of contracts. The common law achieves similar results by a resort to implied terms, rectification and estoppel."(不像大陆法承认善意责任在合约的履行中至高无上的地位,普通法凭借默示条文、[1]合约变更[2]与禁止翻供等更有针对性的理论达到同一个目标。)

根据许多针对善意的先例,可以总结英国法院抗拒这一大原则的原因如下:

1. 善意与英国合约法下的订约自由、承认每一方有权合法为他自己谋取合约利益以及谈判双方处于敌对地位的现实与大原则在法理上有基本矛盾,看来也是与英国公共政策相抵触。这可介绍贵族院在 1992 年的先例,名为 Walford v. Miles (1992) 2 AC 128。该案是关于一个"互锁合约"(lock – out agreement),合约的内容是在收购一家公司及其办公地点的交易中买方有独享的谈判权利。互锁合约没有约定谈判的期限。买方在谈判时出价 200 万英镑,但卖方以同样的价格卖给了第三方。买方私下有内幕消息知道该收购的标的价值 300 万英镑,但卖方自己却不知道。所以,买方向卖方索赔 100 万英镑的损失,因为卖方违反了互锁合约。买方也指卖方在该合约下,应该默示有善意与他谈判的要求,而不应该背后找第三方。但贵族院判是英国法律对谈判没有善意的要求,因为这是"与谈判地位有本性上的矛盾"(inherently inconsistent with the position of a negotiating party)。在本案例,贵族院质疑如果谈判有善意的默示要求,买方自己也有问题了,因为他应该将私下的内幕消息告诉卖方说明他的开价偏低了,毕竟善意应该是互相的。

其中贵族院的 Ackner 勋爵是这样说:"[The] concept of a duty to carry on negotiations in good faith is inherently repugnant to the adversarial position of the parties when

---

〔1〕 例如,在本书第七章默示条文之 10.2 与 10.3 段针对的双方必须给予协助/合作让对方顺利履行合约与合约一方不能从自己的错误中获利。虽然默示条文可以被明示条文排除,但正常的合约方都不会同意明示条文规定一方可以阻碍另一方的履行或是可以从他自己的错误中获利。

〔2〕 在本书第三章之 13.1 段有针对。

involved in negotiations. Each party to the negotiations is entitled to pursue his (or her) own interest, so long as he avoids making misrepresentations ... A duty to negotiate in good faith is as unworkable in practice as it is inherently inconsistent with the position of a negotiating party."

2. 善意的说法非常空泛与不肯定,很难说它在各谋其利的商业合约中应该令谈判双方受限制或约束达到什么程度。善意是针对一个道德标准,但说不清楚的就是这个道德标准是什么。如果没有最低标准作出衡量,就会有很大的不稳定与无数争议,如善意是针对订约方自己主观的看法或者是有一个客观的标准。还有是善意是否包括不能利用机会(non - opportunities),不占对方便宜,不论合约条文怎么写都不应该剥削对方(non - exploitation),或不推卸责任(non - shirking),等等?在英国一个著名的名为 Hamlyn 的系列讲座(基金在 1949 年成立,第一讲的讲者是 Denning 勋爵),1997 年由 Roy Goode 教授主讲的"Commercial Law in the Next Millennium"中就善意这一问题说到在英国法律,遇上涉及善意的问题,通常可以适用其他更加有针对性的原则(如默示条文、弃权与禁止翻供等),达到同一个结论。但如果找不到其他有针对性的原则而适用善意,就很难找到一个标准衡量什么才是善意。这会带来不肯定,而商业关系中最重要的就是肯定性及可预测性。举例说明善意会带来的不肯定,这就是德国民法典有一条要求善意,这看来相对无害甚至令人安心的一句话,在德国却带来了无数的诉讼,仅在《Staudinger's Kommentar zum Burgerlichen Gesetzbuch》这一本权威书籍,就有 500 页来分析这一方面。以下节录上述提到的 Roy Goode 教授发言中所讲的话:"We are, in my view, right to be cautious about adopting a general requirement of good faith in contracts, even though this is enshrined not only in civil law but in the American Uniform Commercial Code and jurisprudence and has powerful supporters in England. (see for example, Lord Steyn, 'Contract Law: Fulfilling the Reasonable Expectations of Honest Men' [1997] 113 LQR 433). Very often one finds that recourse to the concept of good faith is used to bolster a conclusion that can easily be arrived at through the application of other, more specific, principles. Where this is not the case it can prove very difficult to give a definable content to the good faith standard and to predict the outcome of commercial disputes in which one party has sought to do no more than enforce the terms of a contract freely negotiated. For convincing evidence of this we need go no further than section 242 of the German Civil Code, which provides that: 'The debtor is obliged to perform in accordance with the requirements of good faith, regard being had to ordinary usage'. This innocuous - looking general clause, which has a contractual counterpart in section 157, has generated a mass of litigation to which more than 500 pages of detailed analysis have been devoted in the leading commentary on the BGB (Staudinger's *Kommentar zum Burgerlichen Gesetzbuch* [13th ed., 1995]). This is not to deny the benefits of a concept that the civilians have forged

into a weapon of remarkable power and that also features strongly in the Unidroit *Principles of International Commercial Contracts Art.* 1. 7 and in the *Principles of European Contract Law Art.* 1. 106 prepared by the Commission on European Contract Law. **But the stability of financial and commercial transactions is of especial importance for the world's leading financial centre; hence the preference of English law for party autonomy in the defining of substantive rights** and for confinement of equitable relief to situations involving procedural unfairness. It is possible that this will change when the courts have become accustomed to applying the good faith test embodied in the Unfair Terms in Consumer Contracts Regulations 1994. But the courts already apply a more protective standard to consumer contracts and may see no reason to extend a general concept of good faith to commercial dealings."(加黑部分是笔者的强调)

3. 即使是善意有了最低标准或准则,如根据订约方自己主观但诚实的看法,问题是怎样认定他脑袋里想些什么。一些有关善意的文章强调善意是要看某一个行动的原因是什么。但问题是这一原因是任由被质疑缺乏善意的订约方自己提供,而对方往往没有办法否定或质疑,因为他的脑袋里怎么想的只有他自己知道。例如,在 Walford v. Miles 先例,卖方不理会互锁协议中断谈判,可能是因为经济利益,也可能是因为市场有了变化,又或是卖方认为他与买方的谈判成功机会很低,对继续谈判不乐观。这样,如果第一个原因是不善意,但第二个原因是善意,法院或仲裁庭怎样才能区分?如果任由卖方提供证据,他肯定会坚持是因为第二个原因或其他善意的原因才中断谈判。在现实中,一个重要的行动,如中断谈判,更加会是有太多原因,而内中是包括了善意的或不善意的,很难作出区分。看来,这又是与不肯定的问题有密切关系。

另可以节录上诉庭的 Longmore 大法官在 Petromec Inc v Petroleo Brasileiro SA Petrobras (No. 3) (2006) 1 Lloyd's Rep 121 先例中差不多是同样道理的一段话:"The traditional objections to enforcing an obligation to negotiate in good faith are (1) that the obligation is an agreement to agree and thus too uncertain to enforce, (2) that it is difficult, if not impossible, to say whether, if negotiations are brought to an end, the termination is brought about in good or in bad faith, and (3) that, since it can never be known whether good faith negotiations would have produced an agreement at all or what the terms of any agreement would have been if it would have been reached, it is impossible to assess any loss caused by breach of the obligation."(传统抗拒执行一个要求善意谈判的合约是因为太不肯定,如果谈判中断是没办法明确中断是由于善意或恶意,也没有办法明确即使是善意的谈判会否谈得出结果以及会是什么样的结果。这样就根本没有基础计算出由于违反这一善意责任所造成的损失。)

§3　善意适用之一:裁量权

3.1　行使合约裁量权必须善意并考虑对方的利益与公平合理

但英国法院也不是对善意这一原则或说法完全陌生,一种情况就出现在裁量权(discretion)。这就是要求有权作出裁量权的一方必须有类似善意的说法行使权力,如必须考虑受影响的对方的利益与公平合理等。

3.1.1　先例之一:Tillmanns & Co. v. SS. Knutsford Ltd

第一个介绍的先例是 Tillmanns & Co. v. SS. Knutsford Ltd (1908) 2 K. B. 385, 涉及租约中有一条条文,就是如果船长认为卸港不安全,他有权在其他安全港口或地点卸下货物。针对船长这一个裁量权,Farwell 大法官说:"I am not satisfied in this particular case that the captain did surrender the discretion that was given his under clause 4 to discharge at some other safe port of place; but I may add that, as at present advised, I think he was bound to exercise that discretion fairly as between both parties, and not merely to do his best for the shipowners, his masters, disregarding the interests of the charterers."

3.1.2　先例之二:Weinberger v. Inglis

接下来的先例是 Weinberger v. Inglis (1919) AC 606,涉及一个在德国出生但已经取得英国公民身份的人士申请重新成为伦敦交易所会员,但被拒绝。根据交易所的章程,委员会有权根据他们认为适合与否(shall think proper)接受或拒绝会员。针对这一裁量权,贵族院的 Atkinson 勋爵说:"... that they have acted bona fide and honestly for the furtherance, in their belief, of the interests they were bound to protect [- asserted -] that in order to vitiate the exercise of their powers it must be shown by evidence that their action was arbitrary and capricious."(委员会是善意与诚实做出决定,如果想阻止他们行使权力,必须有证据显示这一决定是武断与任性的。)

3.1.3　先例之三:Government of The Republic of Spain v. North of England S. S. Co., Ltd.

再接下来是 Government of The Republic of Spain v. North of England S. S. Co., Ltd., (1938) 61 Ll. L. Rep 44 先例,涉及船长或船东在租约中的战争条文下可以行使的裁量权(如拒绝进入装港或卸港)。Lewis 大法官针对这一裁量权是说:"No '*mala fides*' is suggested, but it is said, and I think with truth, that discretion must not be exercised in an arbitrary and unreasonable manner, and in this case there was really no exercise of discretion at all as the matter was not considered or no full or sufficient inquiry was made."(不提升到恶意这么严重,这裁量权还是不能武断或不合理行使。如果没有清楚考虑或作出全面/足够的查询前就作出决定,这根本不是行使裁量权。)

3.1.4 先例之四:The "Vainqueur Jose"

在 The "Vainqueur Jose" (1979) 1 Lloyd's Rep 557 先例,案情涉及互保协会行使它的裁量权,Mocatta 大法官说:"To the exercise of such discretion the common law principle must apply and these undoubtedly include fairness, reasonableness, bona fides, and absence of misdirection in law."(行使裁量权在普通法的要求是公平、合理、善意与不能误解法律。)

3.1.5 先例之五:The "Product Star"

另在 The "Product Star" (1993) 1 Lloyd's Rep 397 先例,也是涉及租约中的战争条文,在租约订立的一天,即 1987 年 4 月 6 日,当时两伊战争已经开始(1980 年 9 月开战)。由于它是一艘油轮,所以租约规定是一些波斯湾的港口,其中包括阿拉伯联合酋长国的 Ruwais。但走了 4 个航次从 Ruwais 装石油产品去孟加拉后,估计由于战争局势突然吃紧,船东/船长行使对租约战争条文的裁量权而拒绝前往 Ruwais。结果承租人接受船东的违约/毁约终止租约。高院与上诉庭都是判船东/船长在行使合约裁量权时必须诚实、善意,不可以任性、武断与不合理。上诉庭的 Leggatt 大法官说:"The essential question always is whether the relevant power has been abused. Where A and B contract with each other to confer a discretion on A, that does not render B subject to A's uninhibited whim. In my judgment, the authorities show that not only must the discretion be exercised honestly and in good faith, but, having regard to the provisions of the contract by which it is conferred, it must not be exercised arbitrarily, capriciously and unreasonably. That entails a proper consideration of the matter after making any necessary inquiries."

其中行使裁量权是否合理,法院也强调了必须看租约订立时的背景与租约的其他条文。高院的 Diamond 大法官认为如果事发时 Ruwais 的战争风险在本质上并非与订约一天有很大改变的情况下让船东行使裁量权就不公平了:"... it would be inequitable to permit the owners to rely on clause 40 unless the danger in reaching Ruwais was different from that which existed at the date of the charter."

而上诉庭的 Leggatt 大法官也提到了将租约其他的条文如订约时的背景也一并考虑是否合理,说:"... for the purpose of construing 'dangerous' in clause 40 the common intention that the vessel should trade to UAE ports was relevant to the reasonableness of refusal by the owners to proceed there; clause 10 gave the charterers the right to order the vessel to Ruwais; although at the time when the charter was made the whole of the Gulf including UAE water constituted a war risk zone the owners were, by the combination of clauses 10, 40(2) and 50 accepting that in the circumstances prevailing at the date of the charter the risks of proceeding to UAE ports and loading there were not such as they would consider dangerous so as to render the discretion under clause 40(2) exercisable..."

3.1.6 先例之六:Gan Insurance Co Ltd v. Tai Ping Insurance Co Ltd (No. 2)

在 Gan Insurance Co Ltd v. Tai Ping Insurance Co Ltd (No. 2) (2001) 2 All ER (Comm) 299 先例,Tai Ping 是一家台湾地区的保险公司,它与第三方订立了保险合约,并将其中一部分风险向 Gan 再保。再保条文中有一条规定 Tai Ping 与第三方达成的任何和解协议都必须经过 Gan 的批准,否则 Gan 对此和解协议不负责。之后第三方的工厂发生了火灾,Tai Ping 与第三方达成了和解协议。Gan 其中一个争辩就是 Tai Ping 与第三方达成的和解协议没有经过 Gan 的批准,因此 Gan 对此不负责任。上诉庭判是 Gan 在再保协议中有不批准 Tai Ping 提议的和解协议的合约裁量权,但他有一个默示义务不能武断或任性行使这个裁量权,行使该裁量权必须要善意。Mance 大法官说:"In summary, the right to withhold approval was, here, Gan's, and no one else's. It is a right to be exercised in good faith after consideration of and on the basis of the facts giving rise to the particular claim, and not with reference to considerations wholly extraneous to the subject – matter of the particular reinsurance or arbitrarily. It is to be exercised by considering the claim as a whole. The court cannot substitute its own view of the reasonableness of a reinsurer's decision to withhold approval under subcl. (c)."

3.1.7 先例之七:Paragon Finance plc v. Nash 与 Paragon Finance plc v. Pender

Paragon Finance plc v. Nash (2002) 1 W. L. R. 685, CA 先例涉及住宅房屋的抵押,而还款的利息是浮动,争议涉及抵押银行规定利率的权利是否受默示条文的限制。这在较早的 Lombard Tricity Finance Ltd v. Paton (1989) 1 All E. R. 918 先例中,被判是没有默示条文的限制。但在本案例,上诉庭判是抵押银行的裁量权是受到限制,并提出了订约方合理期望的说法,Dyson 大法官说:"I would hold that there were terms to be implied in both agreements that the rates of interest would not be set dishonestly, for an improper purpose, capriciously or arbitrarily. I have no doubt that such an implied term is necessary in order to give effect to the reasonable expectations of the parties."

在该案例中也提到了一些被认为是不合理的做法,如因为贷款人头发的颜色而有歧视性对待或对一些麻烦的贷款人提高利息至他所不能承受的程度。但上诉庭拒绝默示银行不能订立不合理的利率(除非是高到一个没有其他银行会这样订立的程度,这就可能违反了其他的默示条文,如不能独行独断与反复无常)。上诉庭不接受与英国最大的抵押银行的利率进行比较后而指称该案中银行确定的利率为不合理利率。看来,这也是法院要做出的分水线,一方面要对银行的裁量权作出合理限制,另一方面又要顾及银行必须要有营运的自由。这在下一个有同样判法的案件 Paragon Finance plc v. Pender (2005) EWCA Civ 760,上诉庭的 Jonathan Parker 大法官说:"I do not understand him to be saying that a lender may not, for a genuine commercial reason, adopt a policy of raising interest rates to levels at which its borrowers generally, or a particular category of its borrowers, may be expected to consider refinancing their borrowing at more favourable rates of interest offered by other commercial lenders. Save as otherwise expressly agreed with its borrowers, a commercial lender is in my judgment free to conduct its business in what it genuinely believes to be its best commercial interest. ”。

3.1.8 先例之八：Equitable Life Assurance Society v. Hyman

Equitable Life Assurance Society v. Hyman (2002) 1 A. C. 408, HL 先例的重要性是在以前许多先例要求行使裁量权时要善意的准则基础上，又多加了一个可被称为“订约双方的合理期望”(the reasonable expectations of the parties)的准则。首先可简单介绍该重要贵族院先例的案情，有关 Equitable Life 的相互人寿保险公司(mutual life assurance society)在市场推销一种保单是有“保证年金率”(guaranteed annuity rate，简称 GAR)，它是保证保单持有人有最低的一笔年金。此外，保单持有人也与其他人寿保单持有人一样享有利润奖金，包括每年的奖金(annual bonus)与高额的最后奖金(final bonus)。在当时，Equitable Life 有大约 9 万个保单持有人享有 GAR，另有 29 万保单持有人不享有 GAR，而基金的金额高达 2100 亿英镑。到了 1998 年 9 月，由于市场的年金率下跌，它比 GAR 要低 25%。这使 Equitable Life 在支付 GAR 保单时有点吃不消，董事局于是想出一个办法，就是在最后奖金部分动手脚，即给 GAR 保单的持有人一个更低的金额，平衡两种不同保单的最终结果。根据保单的条文与公司章程，董事局是有没有限制的管辖权决定发放多少奖金及是否给与，说：“... they shall apportion the amount of such declared surplus by way of bonus among the holders of the participating policies on such principles , and by such methods, as they may from time to time determine. ”

为了避免面对 9 万个 GAR 保单持有人的集体诉讼，Equitable Life 挑了有代表性的 Hyman 先生去法院要求宣誓判决，看看董事局能否行使这个裁量权。在高院的一审，Equitable Life 胜诉。但去了上诉庭与贵族院，判是 GAR 保单持有人胜诉。贵族院判是行使这种裁量权与整个 GAR 的结构不一致。Steyn 勋爵说：“It cannot be seriously doubted that the provision for guaranteed annuity rate was a good selling point in the marketing by the society of the GAR policies. It is also obvious that it would have been a significant attraction for purchasers of GAR policies. The society points out that no special charge was made for the inclusion in the policy of GAR provisions. So be it. This factor does not alter the reasonable expectations of the parties. The supposition of the parties must be presumed to have been that the directors would not exercise their discretion in conflict with contractual rights. These are the circumstances in which the directors of the Society resolved upon a differential policy which was designed to deprive the relevant guarantees of any substantial value. ”

3.1.9 先例之九：Ying Ho Co Ltd & Others and Secretary for Justice

Ying Ho Co Ltd & Others and Secretary for Justice (2004) 7 HKCFAR 先例的案情是有关华懋地产公司想建造的一栋办公楼。华懋公司在 1991 年投标得到一块在荃湾的土地,计划建造一幢世界第一高楼。在投地时,还没有新机场的计划,所以不存在对荃湾的楼宇有高度限制。但在华懋公司根据投地条件把建造计划交给香港政府批准时,就产生这一高度限制的问题。代表华懋公司出面投地的原告发展商起诉香港政府,声称这一高度限制的裁量权是适用贵族院在 Equitable Life Assurance Society v. Hyman (2002) 1 A. C. 408, HL 先例中的默示条文,即合约的裁量权必须不能违反订约方合理与合法的期望。在香港的终审法院,Ribeiro 大法官认为该贵族院的先例涉及 Equitable Life 董事局与保单持有人之间有一个诚信责任(fiduciary duty),但政府与地产开发展商之间没有这个责任。而且,Ribeiro 大法官也不认为贵族院的先例对裁量权的默示限制是对所有的商业合约都广泛适用,说:"... it seems to me very doubtful whether the House of Lords was actually seeking to lay down any principle of the breadth suggested. Indeed, I find it difficult to envisage how a court is to ascertain, in the context of a commercial contract, the parties' legitimate expectations as opposed to ascertaining what they must be taken to have intended by construing that contract on orthodox principles. The Equitable Life case appears perfectly explicable on the basis that the contractual discretion in question had to be construed so as not to undermine the express and implied contractual rights conferred on policyholders by the policy."。

Ribeiro 大法官认为默示的局限只适用在政府行使裁量权会损害发展商的明示或默示的合约权利的情况。

3.1.10 先例之十:Lymington Marina Ltd v. MacNamara

在 Lymington Marina Ltd v. MacNamara (2007) Bus LR Digest D29 先例,Lymington Marina 公司有一个可供小游艇停靠的码头,MacNamara 先生的父亲从 Lymington Marina 公司得到了可以在该码头停靠游艇的授权。授权中有一条条文规定 MacNamara 先生的父亲只要获得了 Lymington Marina 公司的批准,就可以把该授权转让给第三人,但 Lymington Marina 公司对是否批准转让有"绝对裁量权"(absolute discretion)。授权中也规定说只要 Lymington Marina 公司批准,MacNamara 先生的父亲可以对其他人进行附属授权(sublicense)。关于附属授权的批准,并没有规定说 Lymington Marina 公司有绝对裁量权。MacNamara 先生从他父亲那里继承了这个授权,并试图对他的两个兄弟进行附属授权。Lymington Marina 公司拒绝批准这个附属授权,理由是附属授权只适用授权人(也就是 MacNamara 先生)不在时偶尔使用码头的情况。而在该案中,Lymington Marina 公司认为附属授权人(也就是 MacNamara 先生的两个兄弟)会经常使用码头,所以不批准这一附属授权。上诉庭判是 Lymington Marina 公司对是否批准附属授权没有绝对裁量权,不批准的理由只限于反对附属授权人使用码头。而在一般的批准或不批准的情况,Lymington Marina 公司有默示责任善意行使裁量权,而不能武断地不批准附属授权。

3.1.11 先例之十一:Socimer International Bank Ltd v. Standard Bank London Ltd

在 Socimer International Bank Ltd v. Standard Bank London Ltd (2008) 1 Lloyd's

Rep 558 先例,上诉庭认为:"It is plain from these authorities that a decision - maker's discretion will be limited, as a matter of necessary implication, by concepts of honesty, good faith, and genuineness, and the need for the absence of arbitrariness, capriciousness, perversity and irrationality. The concern is that the discretion should not be abused."

3.1.12 先例之十二:JML Direct Ltd. v. Freesat UK Ltd

在 JML Direct Ltd. v. Freesat UK Ltd (2010) EWCA Civ 34 先例,案情涉及 Freesat 作为电子节目单的供应商有权决定 JML 的两个频道的位置前后。根据规定,Freesat 应该客观考虑,并必须考虑双方订约的时间、电视观众的方便与期望等。但 JML 对 Freesat 最后决定的位置不满意,认为不够突出,并起诉 Freesat 要求履约指令或违约的金钱赔偿。Freesat 承认它没有考虑双方订约的时间,而对于电视观众的方便与期望方面则是依赖了市场调查。第一审与上诉庭拒绝了 JML 的指控,并认为 Freesat 在做决定时对双方订约时间不给予任何分量以及依赖市场调查并没有违反合约的规定,也没有武断或/与非理性行使裁量权。上诉庭 Moore - Bick 大法官提到行使裁量权必须善意说:"Such an obligation(善意的责任) is likely to be implicit in any commercial contract under which one party is given the right to make a decision on a matter which affects both parties whose interests are not the same."

3.1.13 先例之十三:Compass Group UK and Ireland Ltd v. Mid Essex Hospital Services NHS Trust

在 Compass Group UK and Ireland Ltd v. Mid Essex Hospital Services NHS Trust (2013) EWCA Civ 200 先例,具体案情会在稍后的 6.4 段介绍,这里只节录上诉庭的 Jackson 大法官说:"An important feature of the above line of authorities is that in each case the discretion did not involve a simple decision whether or not to exercise an absolute contractual right. The discretion involved making any assessment or choosing from a range of options, taking into account the interests of both parties. In any contract under which one party is permitted to exercise such a discretion, there is an implied term. The precise formulation of that term has been variously expressed in the authorities. In essence, however, it is that the relevant party will not exercise its discretion in an arbitrary, capricious or irrational manner."

3.2 合约履行选择权/裁量权与真正或绝对选择权的分别

在这里一提的是,合约中的裁量权通常是一种"合约履行的选择权"(performance option),这种选择权要与另一种"真正或绝对选择权"(true or absolute option)作出区分。后一种选择权不需要考虑对方的利益,正如 Bowen 大法官在 Tharsis Suphur and Copper Co Ltd v Morel Brother & Co and others (1891) 2 QB 647 先例中所说:"The option is given for the benefit of the person who has to exercise it. He is bound to exercise it in a reasonable time, but is not bound in exercising it to consider the benefit or otherwise of the other party."

后一种选择权在其他方面也与前一种选择权有所不同,如享有选择权的一方必须在合约规定的时间或没有明示规定就必须在合理时间内告知对方自己作出的选择,否则将被视为"弃权"(waiver)。而前一种的合约履行选择权就往往不必告知对方,只需要直接作出履行。这方面可介绍 The "Aspa Maria" (1976) 2 Lloyd's Rep 643 先例,案情涉及租期6个月加延长6个月选择权的期租合约。另还有条文允许船舶可以加减30天还船的选择权,这种条文在期租合约通常会有,因为最后航次能够完成并还船的时间经常不能严格掌控。显然,允许承租人延长6个月租期的选择权应是一个真正或绝对选择权,但加减30天还船的选择权却是前一种的合约履行的选择权。至于是否需要告知对方自己作出的选择,Denning 勋爵说是有所不同:"There is another point I would mention. It seems to me that the phrase '30 days more or less at charterers' option' was not a true option. It did not have to be exercised by express notice or declaration such as Lord Devlin said would be necessary for a true option: see the Reardon Smith case, (1963) 1 Lloyd's Rep 12; (1963) A. C. 691. The charterer could properly redeliver the vessel within the 30 days more or less so long as he gave the proper notice of redelivery, which would be 30 days in this case. It would not be necessary for him to do anything more by way of exercising an option."

另要注意是后一种选择权,也就是一个真正或绝对的选择权下作出的告知必须清楚与肯定,这可节录在 The "Trado" (1982) 1 Lloyd's Rep 157 先例,Parker 大法官说:"Those who have options in their favour must, if they wish to exercise them, exercise them in words which are not really capable of doubt."

而一旦通过告知作出选择就将会是最终与有约束力,好像原来的合约就是这样明示规定,选择方再也不能反悔。Parker 大法官在 The "Trado" 先例说:"It is clear law that if a charterer has an option as to port, berth, method of loading and so on that option, once exercised, is binding and is as if written into the charter party as to the port, berth or means of loading, as the case may be."

总结而言,这两种选择权的不同可介绍 Vancouver Strike Cases (1963) 1 Lloyd's Rep 12 先例,该案例涉及几艘船舶由于温哥华严重罢工而无法装载小麦。船东要求承租人装载租约中其他可供选择的替代货物,因为装载这些货物就不受罢工影响。但由于承租人只是准备付运小麦,显然不能接受船东的要求,双方产生了争议。在有关的租约中,涉及小麦与其他替代选择货物的写法是在第1条文如下:"... the said vessel ... shall receive on board ... a full and complete cargo ... of WHEAT in bulk ... and/or BARLEY in bulk, and/or FLOUR in sacks as below... Charterer has the option of loading up to one - third cargo of BARLEY in bulk ... [and] up to one - third cargo of FLOUR in bags ..."

这案例一直打到了贵族院,贵族院同意上诉庭的判决认为第1条文的写法/措辞是代表一个“真正与没有局限的选择权”(true and unfettered option),承租人没有必要行使装载其他替代货物的选择权。这又是一个与合约履行的选择权的不同之处,因为这种选择权涉及合约履行,有权的一方如果不选择就会令合约无法履行下去。贵族院是判:“The primary obligation on the charterers under the charter – party was to provide a cargo of wheat only; that the exceptions clause covered delay in shipping of wheat; and that there was no obligation on charterers to lose that protection by exercising their option to provide another kind of cargo which was not affected by a cause of delay, even assuming that such a cargo was readily available.”

在这一先例,有十分详尽地分析不同文字/措辞会产生不同的选择权,其中 Devlin 勋爵是这样说:

“My Lords, ‘option’ in its widest interpretation means simply choice or freedom of choice. An obligation in a contract can frequently be performed in a large number of ways and the party under obligation can choose any one of the ways he likes. A contract may, for example, provide for September/October shipment and the shipper may then select any one of the 61 days which he likes. I doubt if in such a case the shipper would, in the ordinary use of language, be described as having 61 options. But when a contract itself limits and enumerates the obligations, as when it obliges the shipper to ship wheat or barley or flour, it is quite sensible and natural to talk of his having an option to ship any one of these three commodities. There is, however, a narrower sense in which the word can be used and that is to confer a right of choice specially granted to the holder of the option and to be used solely for his own benefit. It is in this sense, I think, that the word is generally used in the business world. (合约中选择权一词可以被广义解释为作出选择的自由。履行方经常能以很多不同方法履行合约中的承诺,这往往不是商业社会认为的真正或绝对的选择权。例如,一个买卖合约允许卖方/发货人在 9/10 月作出付运,这表示他可以在两个月间的 61 天中的任何一天作出付运。很难按照字面把它解释为卖方有 61 个选择权并需要通知买方与选择在任何一天作出付运。如果合约中对某一承诺作出了局限与列举了不同的履行方法,如买卖合约要求卖方/发货人付运小麦或大麦或面粉,就表示卖方只需要根据他自己的利益行使选择权付运这三种商品的其中任何一种即可。)

At first sight this appears to be a distinction without a difference. When a party under obligation selects between various alternatives, is he not considering simply his own benefit and convenience? A shipper who ships on Sept. 4 and not on Sept. 5 has chosen that date because it suits him better than the other. The difference arises when for some reason or another the pursuit of one alternative is temporarily or permanently barred. Where there is no option in the business sense, the consequence of damming one channel is simply that the flow of duty is diverted into the others and the freedom of choice thus restricted. If then a shipper cannot ship wheat, he must ship either barley or flour. The width of the alternatives is in the contract for the benefit of both parties and it can be a liability as well as a benefit for the shipper.（表面看来上述不同写法的选择权没有实质区别，反正有权选择的一方总是会根据自己的利益或方便作出选择。一个卖方/发货人选择在9月4日而不是在9月5日付运显然是他认为前者的时间更加符合他的利益或方便。不同选择权的区别体现在当他做出选择的权利被暂时或永久禁止时，拥有合约履行选择权的一方就不得不按照其他替代的选择履行，否则就会构成是违约/毁约，这实际上令他失去了真正选择的自由。如卖方/发货人不能付运小麦，他就必须付运大麦或面粉，否则就是违约/毁约。从这个角度来看，这种写法的履约选择权与其包括的各种替代选择履行方法对双方都有好处，而卖方/发货人既有在这三种商品中作出选择的好处，同时又有必须作出一种选择让合约获得履行的责任。这不像一个真正或绝对的商业上选择权，因为合约本身已经有一个主要履行的方法，其他替代的方法只供选择。卖方往往可以不作出选择，但如果卖方选择了付运大麦，这将会是最终与有约束力，好像原来的买卖合约只约定了付运大麦，既没有小麦也没有面粉。）

But where there is a ‘business option’ the legal position is quite different. There is not then one contractual obligation to be performed in alternative ways, but one obligation to be performed in one way, unless the option holder chooses to substitute another way and does so by the effective exercise of his option. In exercising the option, which he has acquired solely for his own advantage, the holder is not bound to consider the convenience or the interest of the other party. If the obligation is to ship a full and complete cargo of wheat with the option to change to barley or flour and the shipment of wheat is impeded, he is not obliged to change to barley or flour simply because that is the only way in which he could ship a full and complete cargo. So the question here is whether the contractual obligation on the charterer is correctly expressed as an obligation to ship a full and complete cargo of wheat, barley or flour in proportions which can, subject to the specified limits, be selected by the charterer; or whether it is an obligation to ship a full and complete cargo of wheat with an option to the charterer to substitute for that cargo a mixed one."（在一个真正或绝对的商业上选择权，法律地位就很不一样。享有选择权的一方在这种选择权中没有责任以替代的选择履行合约，而合约的履行只是根据一个约定的方法直到享有选择权的一方纯粹是为了他自己的利益行使了选择权并令替代方法取代了原有约定的方法。而这样做，享有选择权的一方根本不需要考虑对方的方便与利益。显然在本先例，租约中规定承租人的首要责任或履行方法只是满载一船的小麦，而不是在小麦、大麦、面粉中选择一个作为替代履行。或是，如果是6个月加延长6个月租期的选择权的期租合约，承租人没有及时行使延长6个月租期的选择权，在6个月后就必须还船。但如果承租人及时作出了延长6个月的选择，该

期租合约的租期就从6个月变为1年。)

3.3 订约自由下针对选择权/裁量权的用字/措辞

在上述对两种选择权或裁量权的区别作出介绍后,笔者可以说在大部分的情况下区分这两种选择权并不困难。但如果有必要划分,就要小心地使用文字/措辞。从Vancouver Strike Cases (1963) 1 Lloyd's Rep 12先例就已经可以看到,如果承租人只是主要为了装小麦,而万一装运小麦有了阻碍(不论是可以令承租人违约/毁约或是租约[或买卖合约]可以免责甚至有关的阻碍构成了合约的受阻),这时租约如果使承租人有真正与绝对选择权装运其他替代货物如大麦或面粉,承租人就有了一定的自由可避免违约/毁约(这是上述所讲的障碍中唯一需要作出金钱损失赔偿的)或可以在运费市场上涨时取巧,即选择装大麦或面粉并及时告知船东。如果承租人自己没有这种货物,他可以转租给其他有大麦或面粉的分承租人并赚取运费差价。但如果运费市场下跌,而原来装运小麦的计划有了阻碍(如出口变为非法),承租人就可以以受阻终止租约并且不存在赔偿任何金钱的损失,因为船东无法迫使他行使一个真正的选择权。但如果承租人租船时还没有决定装小麦、大麦或面粉,他在租约约定选择这三种货物的其中一种,这就变为合约履行的选择权。但承租人如果不想履行也不想赔偿船东损失,受阻或可以免责的情况就必须是同时发生在这三种货物上,这显然不容易。如果承租人订约时还没决定装什么货物,只是最大的可能就是小麦,他还是可以用本段提到的第一种情况的写法,也就是给自己一个真正的选择权,达到同样的目的。反正真正选择权可以单方面行使或不行使,所以只有好处。

在订约自由下,如果怕对这两种选择权的规定不清楚而令行使选择权或裁量权时被解释为要考虑对方的利益,可以以文字/措辞加以改变。例如,在一个合约履行的选择权,有裁量权或选择权的一方完全可以像Lymington Marina Ltd v. MacNamara (2007) Bus LR Digest D29先例中一样写上"absolute discretion"或"the discretion is final and not open to challenge"。

§4 善意适用之二:投标

做出"投标的邀请"(invitation to tender)并不是一个要约,只是一个"邀约"(invitation to treat)。"投标人"(tenderer)所做出的标书是"要约"(offer),而最后接受与否是"邀请人"(invitor)的自由。也只有在邀请人接受或进一步谈判成功后,才会产生一个合约,如工程合约。所以在投标的标书中,邀请人有完全的自由接受其中一份标书并拒绝其他标书,甚至拒绝所有标书:Spencer v Harding (1869-70) L. R. 5 C. P. 561先例。"拍卖"(auction)也是一个邀约,不过是公开的,而不是像投标那样接受暗标:Payne v. Cave (1789) 3 Term Rep. 148。每一个拍卖中的出价(不论是通过行动还是语言)才是一个要约。

投标人在邀请人有完全自由决定是否接受标书的情况下变得十分被动。毕竟准备标书尤其是针对一个大工程的标书,会花费不少人力、物力与金钱,但最后结果很可能只是一场空。这倒是次要,毕竟投标会有其他竞争者,但主要怕是自己的标书根本没有被邀请人公平合理地考虑,甚至没有看过。正如 Nolan 大法官在 Fairclough Building Ltd v Port Talbot Borough Council (1992) 62 BLR 82 先例说:"A tenderer is always at risk of having his tender rejected either on its intrinsic merits or on the ground of some disqualifying factor personal to the tenderer. Provided that the ground of rejection does not conflict with some binding undertaking or representation previously given by the customer to the tenderer the latter cannot complain. It is not sufficient for him to say however understandably that he regards the ground of rejection as unreasonable."

4.1　公共工程合约之附带协议

近年来法律上有了保护投标人的做法,出现了"附带协议"(collateral contract)的理论。约束邀请人必须按照公布的投标程序做并善意考虑投标人的标书。其中针对公共工程的合约,更加有立法规定的《Public Work Contracts Regulations》(SI 1991/2680)。至于针对私人工程的合约,就会取决于邀请人在发出投标邀请时有否作出承诺或陈述,如会按照一些国际上标准的投标程序。显然投标人如果需要花费大量金钱与时间制作标书,在邀请人没有任何承诺或陈述的情况下就不会愿意投标。

接下来介绍针对公共工程合约的一些先例。在 Harmon CFEM Facades (UK) Ltd v The Corporate Officer of the House of Commons (2000) 67 Con L. R. 1 先例, Humphrey Lloyd 大法官说:" Implied from the procurement regime required by the European directives ... whereby the principles of fairness and equality form part of a preliminary contract ... It is now clear in English law that in the public sector where competitive tenders are sought and responded to, a contract comes into existence whereby the prospective employer impliedly agrees to consider all tenderers fairly."

在该先例,原告作为投标人提供的一份标书是最低价格,但被告的邀请人接受了另一份第二低价格的标书,理由是实际上价钱更划算(better value for money)。但成功的标书是根据另一个不同的设计,无法与原告的设计作出比较。原告也指称被告考虑另一个不同的设计,而原告无法针对该另一个设计作出竞争。法院也在被告的内部文件中找不出任何有关原告标书实际有任何不妥的证据,并认定了被告对原告不友善是因为原告国籍的理由。法院最后判原告胜诉并可以向被告取回损失,这包括所有浪费了的费用以及利润损失。

在较早另一个涉及公共工程投标的著名先例 Blackpool and Fylde Aero Club v Blackpool Borough Council (1990) 1 WLR 1195,案情十分明确与简单,邀请人根本没有拆开投标人的标书,更加谈不上加以考虑。这被法院认为在有一个附带协议的情况下,明显就是邀请人违反了这一协议。上诉庭的 Stocker 大法官说:"this obligation would not preclude or inhibit the council from deciding not to accept any tender or to award the concession, provided the decision was *bona fide* and honest, to any tenderer."

这在另一个类似先例 Fairclough Building Ltd v Port Talbot Borough Council (1992) 62 B. L. R. 82, Michael Davies 大法官说:"The duty of the defendants was to act in good faith - not to issue a sham invitation to the plaintiffs or anyone else, for example, which here they did not do. Then it was the duty... honestly to consider the tenders of those whom they had placed on the shortlist, unless there were reasonable grounds for not doing so."

在这一先例,投标人的一个董事与被告的邀请人的公司的一个总建筑师在投标期间结婚,被告为了怕有任何表面看来的利益冲突,拒绝考虑投标人的标书。这被法院判是合理,也不违反附带协议。

4.2 私人工程之附带协议

至于私人工程的投标,先可介绍贵族院的 Harvela Investments Ltd v. Royal Trust Co of Canada Ltd (1986) AC 207 先例。该先例明确了如果邀请人在邀请投标同时作出了一些承诺,如说将会接受最高投标,这就会带来不同后果,即邀请人会被视为受一个附带协议的约束。该贵族院先例的案情是被告 RTC 拥有一家公司的股份,并准备出售。而该公司中两位股东都对 RTC 准备出售的股份有兴趣,因为谁买下就变成大股东。RTC 在邀请投标时,估计是为了吸引他们都作出高价投标,说明他将接受最高的投标价格。结果是原告 H 投了标,标价是 2,175,000 美元。而另一个有兴趣的股东 O 也投了标,但标价是:"2,100,000 美元或是 RTC 收到的投标最高价格如果不是 O,O 就比该最高价格多加 101,000 美元"。这显示了如果 O 的做法可以被接受,这控制性股票就是他囊中之物了。反正是该案件发展下,H 向法院申请禁令阻止 RTC 把股份卖给 O,说是 RTC 在邀请投标的时候承诺了最高投标价格就会被接受,而 H 的标价正是最高投标价格。贵族院判 H 胜诉,认为采取暗标的做法主要是不让投标方知道对手出的价格。所以,O 的标价说是多加 101,000 美元不是一个正确做法,贵族院认为 RTC 不应该接受,而应该接受最高投标标价的 H。至于 RTC 较早的承诺必须出售给最高标价的一方,贵族院根据的理论是 RTC 对投标有兴趣的人士作出了"单方合约"(unilateral contract),所以受到约束,这等于是附带协议的说法。

接下来一个是介绍 J&A Developments Ltd v Edina Manufacturing Ltd (2006) N. I. Q. B. 85 先例,显示了法院也会执行明示附带协议。在该先例,被告在投标的邀请中有一条明示条文说:"tendering procedure will be in accordance with the principles of the Code of Procedure for Single Stage Tendering 1996."

原告的标书是最低价格,但依然超过了雇主的预算。根据 Code of Procedure for Single Stage Tendering 1996 的 7.1 - 7.3 段,遇到这种情况,雇主应该先与最低价格的投标人谈判是否同意改变规格或工作量来减低价格。只有当与最低价格的投标人谈判失败后,才能与价格第二低的投标人谈判。而在该先例,雇主既没有告诉原告他的预算金额,也没有试图与之谈判能否改变规格或工作量,只是要求原告减价,在被原告拒绝后，就把这个工程给了同意减价的价格第二低的投标人。这被法院视为雇主违反了附带协议，需要赔偿原告投标浪费的费用与预期利润。

§5　合约之善意

这是本章主要针对的话题，首先可以分为两大类，第一类是“善意谈判合约”（good faith negotiation contract），第二类是“善意谈判条文”（good faith negotiation clause）。大致上第一类是双方还没有合约关系，但是订立一个合约要求双方善意谈判或尽最大努力谈判，最后达成一个合约。第二类是双方已经有了合约关系，但有很多东西无法在订约时说死，留待将来谈判并达成协议。条文会明示规定双方必须善意谈判，或是没有明示也会有默示。

5.1　善意谈判协议

这种协议存在的背景就是双方还没有任何的合约关系，只是在谈判希望达成一个合约，或是还有变数条件令双方还没有有效的合约。在谈判期间，双方约定谈判必须是双方善意或类似的要求，如有诚意或是尽最大努力。英国法院对这种“协议将来达成协议”（agreement to agree）的做法一直以来都有很大敌意，这方面已经在本书第三章之12.1.3段提到，不重复。但这种做法被区分为“双方根本不存在有任何合约关系”与“双方已经有合约关系而对合约相关的一些将来才会发生的事情约定一个协议将来达成协议”看来在较近期的一个重要先例中才有显示。这就是Courtney & Fairburn Ltd v Tolaini Bros (Hotels) Ltd (1975) 1 WLR 297先例。在该先例，双方同意原告（承建商）向被告（雇主）介绍融资的渠道以发展一些地产项目，而回报就是被告雇佣原告进行有关的工程。而这些工程的费用双方同意是在工程成本的估算上加5%的利润，并在文书的往来中同意由测量师谈判一个公平合理的工程价格（to instruct your Quantity Surveyor to negotiate fair and reasonable contract sums）。原告为被告介绍了融资渠道后开始谈判，但谈不拢，之后被告就自己委任了其他承建商进行工程。上诉庭判是双方文书往来所达成的协议只是一个“协议将来达成协议”（agreement to agree），没有法律效力，而且双方因为没有同意费用也不存在有任何合约关系。双方的文书往来只是约定由测量师谈判一个公平合理的价格，而测量师也的确被指定了，只不过最后还是谈不拢。结果上诉庭判被告是可以委任其他承建商，因为英国法律不承认这一种双方还没有合约关系的协议。Denning勋爵说：

“But then this point was raised: even if there was not a contract actually to build, was not there a contract to negotiate? In this case Mr. Tolaini（被告）did instruct his quantity surveyor to negotiate, but the negotiations broke down. It may be suggested that the quantity surveyor was to blame for the failure of the negotiations. But does that give rise to a cause of action? There is very little guidance in the books about a contract to negotiate. It was touched upon by Lord Wright in Hillas & Co. Ltd. v. Arcos Ltd. (1932) 147 L. T. 503, 515, where he said: 'There is then no bargain except to negotiate, and negotiations may be fruitless and end without any contract ensuing; yet even then, in strict theory, there is a contract (if there is good consideration) to negotiate, though in the event of repudiation by one party the damages may be nominal, unless a jury think that the opportunity to negotiate was of some appreciable value to the injured party.'

That tentative opinion by Lord Wright does not seem to me to be well founded. If the law does not recognise a contract to enter into a contract (when there is a fundamental term yet to be agreed) it seems to me it cannot recognise a contract to negotiate. The reason is because it is too uncertain to have any binding force. No court could estimate the damages because no one can tell whether the negotiations would be successful or would fall through: or if successful, what the result would be. It seems to me that a contract to negotiate, like a contract to enter into a contract, is not a contract known to the law." (Denning 勋爵说在本案例,被告有委任测量师谈判价格但结果谈不拢,即使谈不拢是因为测量师的过错,但原告会否有一个英国法律承认的诉因?这方面英国法律没有针对性的先例,但 Wright 勋爵在 1932 年的 Hillas & Co. Ltd. v. Arcos Ltd. 先例曾经说:"双方只有一个谈判的协议,这个谈判可能是一场空。但严格说,只要这一协议有约因,双方还是有需要谈判的协议。即使有一方违约/毁约拒绝谈判,也只会带来名义损失,除非陪审团认定违约方导致无辜方有实质损失。"这表示 Wright 勋爵还是承认这一种协议将来达成协议,但这说法在本案例被上诉庭否定,Denning 勋爵认为英国法律不承认一个只是约定谈判希望将来达成一个合约的协议,因为太不肯定。)

而 Diplock 勋爵也明确说明 Wright 勋爵的说法是不正确的法律,说:"I agree and would only add my agreement that the dictum, for it is no more, of Lord Wright in Hillas & Co. Ltd. v. Arcos Ltd., 147 L. T. 503, 515, to which Lord Denning M. R. has referred, though an attractive theory, should in my view be regarded as bad law."

看来该先例之后是明确英国法律不承认善意谈判协议,但在今天的商业社会,这种协议的必要性越来越明显。这出现在公司并购的谈判期间,买方会需要花费金钱与时间做出"恪尽职责"(due diligence)的调查等。这样,如果卖方根本不受约束,可以随时终止谈判,买方就不会愿意投入金钱与时间参与这一可能漫长与艰巨的谈判过程。这样一来,在涉及公司并购的谈判,双方会先签订一份善意谈判协议。这种协议通常被称为"互锁协议"(lock – out agreement),内容主要是捆绑双方必须善意谈判,在谈判期间卖方不得与其他人士/公司如与另一个买方磋商或洽谈。显然如果这是一个法律承认与愿意执行的合约,在违反卖方时,买方就可以马上去法院申请禁令阻止卖方这样做。这种互锁协议符合近代商业社会的现实需要,所以十分务实的英国法院在原则上承认其有效:Pitt v. PHH Asset Management Ltd. (1994) 1 WLR

327, CA 等先例。但在本章之第 2 段已经提到的 Walford v. Miles (1992) 2 AC 128 先例,因为互锁合约中没有谈判的期限,被视为太不肯定而令贵族院判其无效。这也可以理解,就是双方没有明示规定谈判的期限,就有危险让买方可以慢慢地谈判,甚至拖延。而如果卖方心急出售公司,希望套现却被一个没有期限的互锁合约锁死,这对卖方会是致命。在该先例,贵族院也拒绝默示任何期限,因为默示必须合理,但何为合理期限根本说不准。另外,默示是要满足在订约时可以假设双方理所当然或异口同声地同意这个说法,但这显然不可能。关于这方面可看本书第七章之 4 段。

但 Walford v. Miles 的贵族院判决受到很多的批评,如在 Petromec Inc v. Petroleo Brasilerio SA Petrobras (2006) 1 Lloyd's Rep 121 先例,上诉庭的 Longmore 大法官说:"It is not irrelevant that it is an express obligation which is part of a complex agreement drafted by City of London solicitors ... It would be a strong thing to declare unenforceable a clause into which the parties have deliberately and expressly entered. I have already observed that it is of comparatively narrow scope. To decide that it has 'no legal content' to use Lord Ackner's phrase would be for the law deliberately to defeat the reasonable expectations of honest men ... Lord Steyn hoped that the House of Lords might reconsider *Walford v. Miles* with the benefit of fuller argument. That is not an option open to this court. I would only say that I do not consider *Walford v. Miles* binds us to hold that the express obligation to negotiate as contained in clause 12.4 of the Supervision Agreement is completely without legal substance."

其他的批评可参阅一些重要的评论文章如 P Neill QC 的《A Key to Lock – out Agreements》(1992) 108 LQR 405 与 Steyn 勋爵的《Contract Law and the Reasonable Expectations of Honest Men》(1997) 113 LQR 433 等。另也可节录《Chitty on Contracts》(第 31 版,2012 年)一书之 2 – 140 段的部分内容,如下:"In *Walford v. Miles* the principal agreement was not legally binding because it was subject to contract, and the lock – out agreement was not legally binding because it specified no dates. The case does not exclude the possibility that a different conclusion may be reached where the parties have reached agreement on all essential points so as to show that they do intend to be legally bound by the agreement, but have left other points open. The court may then imply a term that they are to negotiate in good faith so as to settle outstanding details which are to be incorporated in the formal document setting out the full terms of the contract between them."

这种善意谈判协议在其他领域中的适用也被逐渐放宽,如 Smith v Morgan (1971) 1 W. L. R. 803,案情涉及一块土地的买卖,合约中有约定卖方同意在 5 年内不卖另一块相邻的土地,而之后如果要卖,买方也有第一选择权买,价格另议。相关的条文说:"the first option of purchasing . . . at a price to be agreed upon"。这虽然是一个有效合约中的条文,但本质上还是针对将来买卖另一块土地的交易。法院判是该针对另一块土地的协议不会因为太不肯定而变为无效。这并非是一个协议将来达成协议,而是在卖方身上加了一个要先与原买方谈判并且报价不能超过他想卖的价格的责任。这看来与 J&A Developments Ltd v Edina Manufacturing Ltd (2006) N. I. Q. B. 85 先例中投标的附带协议的说法有一点相近。

最后是在本章之第 4 段提到的投标的附带协议,本质上也是属于这种要求善意谈判的协议。

总结而言,英国法院会在两种情况下才愿意执行要求善意谈判的协议。第一种情况是明确显示双方有"订约意图"(intention to contract)达成这种善意谈判的协议。在英国法律下,看有否订约意图,通常是看有否"约因/对价"(consideration)。这在上述提到的先例都不难找出这一订约的意图。但在本质上,如果双方谈判一个合约还没有谈得拢或是另有变数条件,本身就显示了双方没有订约意图。所以,如果订约意图不明显或是在灰色地带,估计英国法院就不愿意支持一个要求善意谈判协议的有效性。

第二种情况是这种协议的内容必须"肯定"(certain),否则即使有订约意图,也会因为不肯定而被英国法院认为无效。这种情况发生在 Walford v. Miles 与 Barbudev v Eurocom Cable Management Bulgaria Eood (2012) EWCA Civ 548 先例。Walford v. Miles 先例已经介绍过,只说该互锁协议无效与不被执行只是因为它没有一个谈判的期限而被视为太不肯定。换言之,贵族院是接受互锁协议这种协议将来达成协议的做法,只要该协议有一段明确的谈判期限。

Barbudev v Eurocom Cable Management Bulgaria Eood 这个近期先例,也涉及公司的并购,原告是将被收购公司的大股东,而被告是收购方,被告计划在成功收购原告的公司后,将原告的公司与另一家不久前也被其收购的公司合并。谈判时双方设想是给原告一个选择权,让其在将来合并后的新公司投资 10% 的股份。于是双方的股权买卖协议中规定,要完成该股权买卖协议的先决条件是被告与原告签订一个投资协议。但在股权买卖协议中接着规定,任何一方都可以书面通知的方式放弃这个先决条件。原告对被告也有权放弃这个先决条件表示关心,因为这意味着他有可能无法获得新公司的 10% 的股份。因此双方又签订了一份"附函"(side letter),被告同意在双方签署股权买卖协议后的合理时间内提供给原告一个投资新公司的机会,相关条文会在将来同意。并且双方会善意谈判一个投资协议。附函内容如下:"In consideration for you agreeing to enter into the proposed transaction and to sign the Transaction Documents, the Purchaser [i. e. ECMB] hereby agrees that, as soon as reasonably practicable after the signing of the Agreement by all Parties, we shall offer you the opportunity to invest in the Purchaser on the terms to be agreed between us which shall be set out in the Investment Agreement and we agree to negotiate the Investment Agreement in good faith with you. . . . "

之后被告确实放弃了签订投资协议这个先决条件,股权买卖协议完成。双方对投资协议进行了谈判,但最后没有达成一致。原告起诉被告没有遵守附函上的条文。

上诉庭判是该附函由律师草拟,附函中的条文及其用字都证明了双方确实有订约意图。但仅有订约意图并不足够,该附函只是一份协议将来达成协议。附函清楚地显示双方没有就投资的条文达成一致,只是同意将来会进行谈判。虽然该附函中有较为详细的条文在一般的协议将来达成的协议中不会出现,但这些条文本身也并不肯定,如附函中说原告同意投资不少于165万欧元,也就是说有可能原告可以投资多于这个数目。这可能就会涉及双方对原告可以投资的股票数目或股价需要进行进一步的谈判并最后达成一致。因此,上诉庭认为该附函太不肯定而判无效。

5.2　善意谈判条文

5.2.1　与善意谈判协议不同

善意谈判条文与上段所针对的善意谈判协议本质上完全不同,虽然在表面看来都是一个"协议将来达成协议"(agreement to agree),但是直到 Courtney & Fairburn Ltd v Tolaini Bros (Hotels) Ltd (1975) 1 WLR 297 先例,才对这两者严格作出区分。善意谈判条文与善意谈判协议最大的不同就是前者已经有了一个对双方都有约束性的合约,只不过针对某一些将来才会发生的问题,双方约定以一个条文说明将来发生时再善意谈判。这样,本质上不像善意谈判协议会与英国的一些公共政策有冲突,如在一个合约谈判中,双方完全有自由合法为自己谋利与各自在一个"敌对的地位"(adversarial position),所以 Denning 勋爵所讲这种善意谈判协议是"unfamiliar in English law"。但在一个有订约意图与约束力的合约关系,一条善意谈判条文本质上是要求双方"共同努力"(work together)或"合作"(cooperate),没有与公共政策有任何冲突。看来只要该条文足够肯定,就没有理由不给它一个解释并且执行。但看来英国法院还是与对待善意谈判协议一样,对善意谈判条文也同样有敌意。这里可简单节录《Chitty on Contracts》(第31版,2012年)一书之1-047所讲:"**Express term to negotiate in good faith.** In the case of good faith, the validity of such a term remains doubtful owing to the view expressed by Lord Ackner in Walford v Miles that a duty to negotiate in good faith as an (unenforceable) agreement to agree."

这方面是在 Petromec Inc v Petroleo Brasileiro SA Petrobas (2006) 1 Lloyd's Rep 121 先例才有了改变,上诉庭的 Longmore 大法官明确把善意谈判条文与贵族院先例 Walford v. Miles (1992) 2 AC 128 针对的善意谈判协议作出区分,说:"I doubt, however, if any of these objections would be good reasons for saying that the obligation to negotiate in good faith contained in clause 12.4 is unenforceable in this particular case .... **The main distinction between ... [*Walford*] and this case was that in that case there was no concluded agreement at all since everything was 'subject to contract'; there was, moreover, no express agreement to negotiate.** The good faith negotiation clause in this case is not a bare agreement to negotiate. It is not irrelevant that it is an express obligation which is part of a complex agreement drafted by City of London solicitors ... **It would be a strong thing to declare unenforceable a clause into which the parties have deliberately and expressly entered.** I have already observed that it is of comparatively narrow scope. To decide that it has 'no legal content' .... Would be for the law deliberately to defeat the reasonable expectations of honest men ... Lord Steyn hoped that the House of Lords might reconsider *Walford* ... with the benefit of fuller argument. That is not an option open to this court. I would only say that I do not consider that *Walford* ... binds us to hold that the express obligation to negotiate as contained in clause 12.4 of the Supervision Agreement is completely without legal substance."(加黑部分是笔者的强调)

接下来有许多作出同样判法的先例,包括近期的 Gold Group Properties Ltd v. BDW Trading Ltd. (2010) EWHC 1632 先例,也是将善意谈判条文与善意谈判协议作出区分。

另在 Butters v BBC Worldwide Ltd (2009) EWHC 1954 先例,Peter Smith 大法官说:"I do not accept that *Walford* has any relevance to a clause to be found in an existing agreement."

5.2.2 合约中协议将来达成协议的条文在以前的情况

在一个完全有效与有约束性的合约中有一条协议将来达成协议的条文(不论条文有没有进一步明示双方必须善意谈判或是"尽最大努力"[best endeavor]等类似的规定)并不是最近才出现的问题,这方面可以进一步探讨。

首先要指出一个有效与有约束性的合约,前提是双方必须对所有他们希望谈妥的条文都达成协议。这涉及合约的"全面性"(completeness),也就是指所有双方要谈妥的"重要条文"(essential terms)都必须完全同意了才会有一个合约。至于什么是重要条文,则完全由双方决定。但如果双方没有显示出哪些是他们视为的重要条文而必须要同意才会有合约关系,就需要法院或仲裁庭作出客观判断了。这判断会是根据不同的行业,习惯的做法与解释每个案件中不同的文件与行为等。但通常是只要有足够的重要条文达成协议可让合约得以履行,双方就已经有可能被视为有了合约关系,任何一方不能逃避合约的产生。这方面最著名的先例就是 Pagnan SpA v Feed Products Ltd (1987) 2 Lloyd's Rep 601,该先例涉及双方在谈判一个农产品的 FOB 买卖,其中双方对货物数量、质量、价格与付款办法等都已经有了一致的意愿或想法。但买卖双方当时还没有同意装港的装货率与滞期费率等许多其他条文。之后,双方在装港的装货率与滞期费率等条文谈不拢,买方坚持这是自己认为的重要条文,必须与卖方同意后才能有合约关系。但卖方声称双方已经同意了足够的重要条文,所以已经有了合约关系。至于有了合约继续磋商一些其他方面履行的细节,不论是否能同意补充已经存在的合约,不影响双方已经有了合约关系并已经同意了足够履行的重要条文。至于是否同意装货率与滞期费等条文,完全不足以影响该买卖合约的履行,因为法律针对没有约定装货率就会默示合理的装货时间,如果卖方超出了合理时间,也根据普通法地位默示要赔偿滞期损失。所以,根本不存在需要对装货率与滞期费达成协议才能履行合约。在该先例,英国法院同意卖方的说法。在国际商贸中经常涉及漫长的谈判过程,一不小心很容易出问题。例如,经常会发生中国卖方或买方在价值高昂的国际商品买卖中采取简单做法,只与对方同意了价格、数量与付运日期等,就觉得谈判成功。但实际上还有很多内容根本没有提出,更不用说谈妥,中方以为可以留待稍后再把其他方面挖出来陆续与对方谈,如好像 Pagnan SpA v Feed Products Ltd 先例〔3〕的情况。这样,对方如果精明,就会有几种情况出现,一是中方提出要谈的问题对他不利,他就会坚持双方已经有了合约,他无须答应任何东西。二是对方不想履行该合约(如商品市场价格有了波动),他就会借助中方提出要谈的问题作出反要约,然后借机会终止谈判,从合约脱身。

防止这种情况的发生,就是要自己清楚谈判与达成合约的分水线,并以文字明确。这种做法可以有很多,如一开始在要约或反要约时,把自己认为必须谈妥才能有合约的重要条文清楚地列出来。在一个比较复杂的国际买卖合约,这可能会是多达二三十条或更多。这样,对方没有同意任何一条,法院与仲裁庭都不会判双方已经过了谈判阶段并达成了合约。另一种做法是在向对方作出相对简单(如只针对价格等少数几项重要条文)的要约或反要约时,同时附上一份自己喜欢或惯用的合约格式。这表示对方就算马上接受而令合约产生,这一合约的基础还是按照附上的合约格式。再一种常见的做法干脆在作出的要约、反要约或接受对方的要约时用文字写清楚,说明"以其他细节为准"(subject detail)显示还在谈判的阶段。

但需注意的是,有关合同的全面性并不表示事无大小必须同意,因为怎样严密的合约总会有某些方面是双方想留待将来同意。这可能是因为这些方面不一定发生,双方也就没必要花太多精力谈判。也会是这些方面很难在订约时约定,双方也就把这个麻烦留待将来才同意。例如,在一个长达 5 年或 10 年的供货合约,订约时双方只同意了第一年的价格,之后的价格就以条文规定逐年另议。这条文甚至会规定双方必须善意谈判达成协议。只要在订约时清楚显示了双方同意把某一些方面留待将来同意,这不会影响一个合约的有效性。很多时候,双方更加会是已经开始履行,变为更加不存在对合约的有效性有任何疑问。这样针对有关的条文,虽然只是"协议将来达成协议"(agreement to agree),或是一条善意谈判条文,英国法院还是要作出解释,否则合约可能无法继续履行,至于是否有效并可以执行,只取决于它是否足够肯定。

总结上述所讲,笔者或者可以节录《Benjamin's Sale of Goods》(2010 年,8th edn)之 2-046 段(该书只针对货物买卖合约),说:"**Price to be agreed.** If the price is left to be agreed upon subsequently between the parties, there will ordinarily be no binding contract, on the grounds of uncertainty, unless and until they later reach agreement on a

---

〔3〕 针对该先例与本自然段接下去提到的情况与本书第二章之第 2 段有密切关系。

price. Moreover, an agreement to leave the price open to further negotiation will normally exclude any inference that the price should be a reasonable price in accordance with the provisions of s.8(2)(这是指1979年英国《货物销售法》的条文，在下一段有进一步介绍). But, in accordance with the principle that the courts will endeavour to uphold bargains which the parties believe themselves to have concluded especially in the case of executed or partially executed contracts, it may sometimes be possible either to infer an intention that at any rate a reasonable price should be paid if no price is later settled, or to have regard to other circumstances, such as the course of dealing between the parties. Where an approximate price has already been agreed, the inference that the sale shall be at a reasonable price near the sum or within the range mentioned may readily be drawn."

5.2.2.1　以合约的价格为例

在商业合约，显然价格是一条重要条文，也往往是双方进行谈判最先涉及的方面。如果谈不拢，这个谈判往往就无法继续进行。如果有一方坚持说双方已经达成合约，因为双方已经同意了部分的重要条文并足够履行，估计也仍十分困难说服法院这是个全面的合约。在英国法院，也有一些先例显示了双方没有同意价格就往往还没有越过谈判与合约之间的分水线。针对货物买卖合约，可介绍May & Butcher Ltd v. R (1934) 2 KB 17先例。该先例中双方同意了货物买卖的"价格双方时常同意"(prices to be agreed upon from time to time)，贵族院判是双方还没有越过分水线，受到有效合约的约束。贵族院认为不应该越俎代庖，为双方对有关价格作出决定说这就是默示的合理价格。在该先例中，双方也同意了一条仲裁条文，但贵族院认为如果判双方没有合约关系，该仲裁协议也无效，不能通过仲裁令一个合约变得"全面"(complete)。同样的判法也在King's Motors (Oxford) Ltd v. Lax (1969) 3 All ER 665先例。

在Courtney & Fairburn Ltd v Tolaini Bros (Hotels) Ltd (1975) 1 WLR 297先例，涉及工程合约，Denning勋爵也说到这一点：

"Now the price in a building contract is of fundamental importance. It is so essential a term that there is no contract unless the price is agreed or there is an agreed method of ascertaining it, not dependent on the negotiations of the two parties themselves. In a building contract both parties must know at the outset, before the work is started, what the price is to be, or, at all events, what agreed estimates are. No builder and no employer would ever dream of entering into a building contract for over £200,000 without there being an estimate of the cost and an agreed means of ascertaining the price.

In the ordinary course of things the architects and the quantity surveyors get out the specification and the bills of quantities. They are submitted to the contractors. They work out the figures and tender for the work at a named price: and there is a specified means of alteringit up or down for extras or omissions and so forth, usually by means of an architect's certificate. In the absence of some such machinery, the only contract which you might find is a contract to do the work for a reasonable sum, or for a sum to be fixed by a third party. But here there is no such contract at all. There is no machinery for ascertaining the price except by negotiation. **In other words, the price is still to be agreed. Seeing that there is no agreement on so fundamental matter as the price, there is no contract.**"(加黑部分是笔者的强调)

但现实中还经常会有双方订立有效合约,但价格将来才作出决定,不论是否需要通过双方的谈判决定或是按照将来的市场价格。早在 1893 年英国《货物销售法》与更新的 1979 年《货物销售法》,就有 Section 8(2)说:"Where a contract has been validly concluded but does not expressly or impliedly fix or make provision for determining the price, the parties are considered in the absence of any indication to the contrary, to have impliedly made reference to the price generally charged at the time of the conclusion of the contract for such goods sold under comparable circumstances in the trade concerned."

另在 1980 年《维也纳货物销售公约》之 Article 14 也有类似说法:"sufficiently definite and indicates the intention of the offeror to be bound in case of acceptance. A proposal is sufficiently definite if it indicates the goods and expressly or implicitly fixes or makes provision for determining the quantity and **the price.**"

这些立法虽然没有说价格将来由双方通过谈判来决定,但实际做法就通常会是如此。而如果双方谈不拢,就会由法院或仲裁庭(如果有关买卖合约有仲裁条文)决定什么是合理价格。反正重要一点就是价格在订约时没有同意不代表一定会影响有效的合约产生,只要双方在谈判中表达清楚他们的意愿。

有不少先例针对合约价格还没有同意但双方明确同意一条协议将来达成协议的条文并不影响一个有约束性与有效合约的产生。在 Foley v. Classique Coaches Ltd (1934) 2 KB 1 先例,上诉庭判是一个有关供应汽油的合约有效,虽然在价格上的约定是"将来同意"(prices to be agreed)。在该先例,汽油也已经供应了达 3 年之久,表示已经在履行,而且双方的合约中也有一条全面的仲裁条文。法院认为在这种情况之下,双方不能同意将来的价格就可以让仲裁庭作出决定。在这个先例,显然双方已经作出部分履行是一个重要的考虑因素,因为上诉庭很难说双方是在没有合约关系的约束下履行的。

另 Queensland Electricity Generating Board v. New Hope Collieries Pty Ltd (1989) 1 Lloyd's Rep. 205 先例涉及一个长达 15 年的煤炭供应合约。双方在合约内针对前 5 年的价格同意了一个基本价格与一条详尽的根据通货膨胀情况对价格作出调整的条文。但针对接下来 10 年,合约说明另同意价格及调整。Queensland Electricity 这一方在履行完了前 5 年的合约,就认为合约完结了,因为之后 10 年的价格只是一个协议将来达成协议,没有法律效力。但英国枢密院不同意,认为之后 10 年的价格如果双方通过谈判不能同意,可以根据一条广泛的仲裁条文仲裁然后由仲裁庭判什么是合理价格。枢密院的 Robin Cooke 爵士说:"At the present day, in cases where the parties have agreed on an arbitration or valuation clause, in wide enough terms, the courts accord full weight to the manifest intention to create continuing legal relations. Arguments invoking alleged uncertainty, or alleged inadequacy in the machinery available to the courts for making contractual rights effective, exert minimal attraction."(在今天,如果双方同意了一条广泛的仲裁条文与估价条文,法院会大力支持这个明显的订约意图令双方继续有合约的关系。一些主张不肯定或定价机制不足够的说法在今天是不大有吸引力。)

在 Wenning v. Robinson (1964) 64 SRNSW 157 先例,有关的条文说价格是"根据估价"(at valuation),这被判有效而价格就是一个公平合理的价格。

另在 Sudbrook Trading Estate v. Eggleton (1983) 1 AC 444 先例,房东给了租客一个选择权买下房屋,但价格是由双方各自指定一位的两位估价师来同意,而如果他们不能同意估价结果,就由他们委任一位公断人来做决定。这里的机制好像就是一个委任仲裁庭的机制。反正在该先例,当租客行使选择权时,房东说是该条文因为价格没有同意而变得太不肯定,所以无效并拒绝指定估价师。贵族院判该合约的价格可以根据条文规定的机制确定,并作出履约指令。这等于是房东必须要指定估价师,否则是藐视法院。

5.2.2.2 以合约的货物数量为例

这里可以简单介绍一个著名先例 F. & G. Style (Wessex), Ltd v. Fine Fare Ltd (1967) 1 Lloyd's Rep. 53,该案涉及一个5年的买卖冻鸡的协议,供应的数量第一年说明是每周最少3万只,最多8万只,到了第二年及以后,供应的数量就是要双方同意。该条文是如下:"(a) To give to [plaintiffs] at least twenty six weeks previous notice in writing of the numbers of broiler fowl required by [defendants] for processing for the week commencing with the expiry of such notice Provided that any numbers of broiler fowl referred to in a notice given under these provisions shall (i) be not less than Thirty thousand per week nor more than Eighty thousand per week (except by agreement between the parties hereto) during the first year of this Agreement and **thereafter such other figures as may be agreed between the parties hereto** and (ii) continue to apply from week to week until a further notice in writing is given varying the numbers of broiler fowl required."

被告 Fine Fare 在履行了一年之后就终止合约,说是接下来的货物数量还没有达成协议。但这被上诉庭拒绝,认为接受被告的说法等于是把5年的协议变为1年协议,这不可能是双方订约的意愿。Denning 勋爵这样说:"I would just say this. In a commercial agreement the further the parties have gone on with their contract, the more ready are the Courts to imply their intentions. When much has been done, the Courts will do their best not to destroy the bargain. When nothing has been done, it is easier to say there is no agreement between the parties because the essential terms have not been agreed. But when an agreement has been acted upon and the parties as here, have been put to great expense in implementing it, we ought to imply all reasonable terms so as to avoid any uncertainties. In this case there is less difficulty than in others because there is arbitration clause which, liberally construed, is sufficient to resolve any uncertainties which the parties have left. Bearing those principles in mind, I am quite satisfied that this phrase '[after the first year] such other figures as may be agreed between the parties hereto', does not introduce such uncertainty into the contract as to render it no contract. Effect can be given to this agreement by saying that in default of agreement, the number as may be ascertained by an arbitrator under the arbitration clause. You can either imply a term that, in default of agreement, the number shall be a reasonable number, with a subsequent provision that in case of any dispute as to what is reasonable, it should be determined by arbitration: or, alternatively, run the two terms together and say 'such reasonable figures as the arbitrator may determine'. Whichever is adopted, it all comes to the same thing. The provision that figures were to 'be agreed' does not nullify the contract. It can be made certain by reasonable figures being ascertained by an arbitrator."

5.2.3　协议将来达成协议或善意谈判条文必须肯定

这一点十分重要并已经在较早时提到,以下介绍 Mamidoil – Jetoil v. Okta (2001) 2 Lloyd's Rep. 76 先例。涉及一个从1993年开始的长达10年的处理与提炼进口原油的合约。在合约已经被履行的6年,1993年至1995年的费用约定在4美元/吨,而如果每年处理的原油多于50万吨,就会有一个每吨0.5美元的折扣。1995年12月,双方同意以同样的费用针对1996年进口的原油。到了1997年6月,双方对1997年的费用问题也达成了同样的协议。1998年5月也有同样的约定,期间直至1999年12月31日。争议是从2000年1月1日起,双方是否仍有合约关系。原告认为合约不会因此终止,而有关的费用应是一个合理费用。虽然双方在合约中只约定了第一年的费用,但之后的费用就应该是一个合理费用,并且双方如果不能同意,就可让仲裁庭来决定。但一审的 Thomas 大法官认为双方如果谈不拢,有关合约就在2000年1月1日后变为无效。这带来不肯定(uncertainty)的原因如下:(1)该案中涉及的处理与提炼原油的费用没有类似的市场价格可以作为基础进而找出合理金额,而合约中或双方以前的交易也没有显示出有可决定合理费用的机制,这样让仲裁庭作出决定也恐怕没有依据;(2)除了每吨的费用要同意外,这里还涉及其他方面如该费用要维持多久(一年? 两年? 剩余的合约有效期?)与怎样针对费用扣减与处理的原油数量(因为数量大就可以有折扣)之间的关系。Thomas 大法官是这样说:

"... there are no universal principles of construction and each case must be decided on the construction of the particular document. It is clear in my view on the construction of the 1993 agreement, at the end of the initial period for which the price was agreed, the parties had to agree not only the new price but also the period for which the new price was applicable; the parties did not provide any mechanism for the fixing of these matters in default of agreement. Although the contract contained an arbitration clause, it was accepted by Jetoil that this was different to a clause which the parties agreed to refer the matter to a Court; in other words there was nothing distinctive about the choice of arbitration. **I do not therefore regard the contract as containing any special mechanism for the fixing of the price or the period for which it was to apply. This is an important consideration.**

Moreover the agreement leaves at large questions as to whether the rate is to be affected by the volume of oil manipulated or whether if the price is fixed for a longer period, whether the price should be higher or lower. If a price was to be fixed by an arbitrator in default of agreement, some guidance would be expected as there would be no obvious market price for such work; for example, in long term pipeline contracts, provision is something made for the price to be fixed by reference to the rate of return on the investment in the facility.

In my view, when the parties provided for the agreement to be valid for 10 years, they fixed the maximum period for which it was to apply. They envisaged that the parties would, after the initial period for which the price was agreed, try and agree a new price and the period for which that subsisted; however, the continued subsistence of the agreement was dependent on that agreement being reached; **they never envisaged the price payable to be a reasonable one, but a price to be reached by agreement.** "(加黑部分是笔者的强调)

一审的判决被上诉庭推翻,主要是上诉庭认为合理费用在该合约下可以决定,这在本书第七章之10.6段有介绍。

另一提 Mallozzi v. Carapelli SpA (1976) 1 Lloyd's Rep 407 先例,案情涉及一个CIF买卖合约,其中针对意大利卸港的条文是“... CIF Free out one safe port West Coast Italy - excluding Genoa. First or second port *to be agreed* between Sellers and Buyers on the ship passing the Straits of Gilbraltar”。买方最后是要船舶去 Naples 卸港。有关的船舶实际上还装了卖方自己的货物,准备 Genoa 卸货。这样就涉及先 Naples 港或先 Genoa 港,这也在条文中有所规定,即在船舶经过直布罗陀海峡时,由买卖双方同意。但实际上他们无法达成一致,因为当时两个意大利港口都十分拥挤,为了减少(或多收取)滞期费,大家都希望船舶先去对方的港口,而稍后在自己的港口没那么拥挤时,才去自己的港口。由于没办法达成协议,显然是控制船舶的 CIF 卖方有了主动权,结果船舶先去了 Naples 港并产生了一大笔滞期费。买方因为这笔钱与卖方产生争议。在第一审,Kerr 大法官判买方胜诉,认为该协议将来达成协议是有法律效力,双方必须“善意谈判”(bona fide negotiate)试图达成协议。但根据有关证据,CIF 卖方一路坚持先去 Naples 港,根本看不出有任何善意进行谈判,所以判卖方违约。但 Kerr 大法官同意这个违约有可能只是赔偿名义损失。但上诉庭推翻一审的判决并认为该协议将来达成协议无效。这主要是在上诉的期间有了 Courtney & Fairburn Ltd v Tolaini Bros (Hotels) Ltd (1975) 1 WLR 297 先例,它虽然是针对善意谈判协议,但上诉庭的 Denning 勋爵还是很明确否定了所有协议将来达成协议在法律上的有效性,说是“not a contract known to the law”。但在笔者看来,即使是判协议将来达成协议在政策上有效,也会因为该条文本身不肯定而无法执行。这可看 Roskill 大法官所说:“One has to look at this clause and see whether or not, on its true construction, in the context in which it appears in this contract, it is susceptible of being an enforceable provision a failure to comply with which will sound in damages, whether nominal or substantial ... I do not think it is susceptible of legal enforcement, and for this reason: it simply provides that the parties *may* agree on first or second port. It does not provide that they *must*. ”(加黑部分是笔者的强调)

5.2.4 协议将来达成协议不明示善意是否能默示?

如果一个有效与有约束力的合约中有一条“协议将来达成协议”(agreement to agree)条文或类似条文如“要求双方合作条文”(cooperation clause),但并没有明示双方必须善意的文字,英国法律会否做出默示?在本章开始,就已经节录了 Bingham 大法官在 Interfoto Picture Library Ltd v Stiletto Visual Programms Ltd (1989) QB 433 先例中明确英国法律并没有这一善意的责任,这也表示没有默示的要求。甚至在十分近期的 Yam Seng Pte Ltd v. International Trade Corp Ltd (2013) EWHC 111 (QB)先例,Leggatt 大法官也明确了这一点说:

“**An implied duty of good faith**?

As pleaded in the particulars of claim, it is Yam Seng's case that there was an implied term of the agreement that the parties would deal with each other in good faith.

The subject of whether English law does or should recognise a general duty to perform contracts in good faith is one on which a large body of academic literature exists. However, I not am aware of any decision of an English court, and none was cited to me, in which the question has been considered in any depth.

The general view among commentators appears to be that in English contract law there is no legal principle of good faith of general application: see Chitty on Contracts (31st edn), Vol 1, para. 1 – 039....

Three main reasons have been given for what Professor McKendrick has called the ‘traditional English hostility’ towards a doctrine of good faith: see McKendrick, Contract Law (9th edn) pp. 221 – 2. The first is the one referred to by Bingham LJ in the passage quoted above: that the preferred method of English law is to proceed incrementally by fashioning particular solutions in response to particular problems rather than by enforcing broad overarching principles. A second reason is that English law is said to embody an ethos of individualism, whereby the parties are free to pursue their own self - interest not only in negotiating but also in performing contracts provided they do not act in breach of a term of the contract. The third main reason given is a fear that recognising a general requirement of good faith in the performance of contracts would create too much uncertainty. There is concern that the content of the obligation would be vague and subjective and that its adoption would undermine the goal of contractual certainty to which English law has always attached great weight."

换言之,在一般合约的关系,如果希望能够以善意约束双方不论是在将来的谈判或是合作,应该以明示条文做出,才会有机会被法院执行。

但在有些类别的合约,法律是默示有善意的要求,如"合伙人"(partnership)之间的合约:O'Neill v. Phillips (1999) 1 WLR 1092。这显然是因为这种合约需要双方合作无间,否则履行不了。虽然这种合约经常也有这种明示条文,但即使没有明示,法律也还是会作出默示。这方面也可节录 The "Star Sea" (2001) 1 Lloyd's Rep 389,Hobhouse 勋爵说:"... having a contractual obligation of good faith in the performance of the contract presents no conceptual difficulty in itself. Such an obligation can arise from an implied or inferred contractual term. It is commonly the subject of an express term in certain types of contract such as partnership contracts."

另一种重要类别的合约就是保险合约,众所周知在 1906 年英国《海上保险法》之 Section 17 就明确规定了保险合约是基于双方善意,而如果违反就令该保险合约无效:"A contract of marine insurance is a contract based upon the utmost good faith and, if the utmost good faith be not observed by either party, the contract may be avoided by the other party."

换言之,保险合约的善意来自立法,是属于"法律的默示"(implied by law)。虽然该立法名为《海上保险法》,但这个善意的默示地位适用在其他所有保险合约。

第三种重要类别的合约是"商业代理"(commercial agent)合约,在 1993 年的《The Commercial Agents (Council Directive) Regulations》中,商业代理是指作为货物买卖代理人的自雇人士(但不包括不收取佣金的代理人或只涉及商品买卖的代理人)。可能根据欧盟不同国家,会延伸"服务"(service):United Antwerp Maritime Agencies (Unamar) NV v Navigation Maritime Bulgare (2014) 1 Lloyd's Rep 161。该立法之 regulation 3 与 4 明确规定了善意的要求。

最后一提的重要合约类别是雇佣合约,也有法律默示的善意要求,这是在《The Employment Rights Act 1996》之 section 43G(1)(a)。即使是普通法也有这一雇主与雇员之间类似善意的要求,在贵族院的 Malik v Bank of Credit and Commerce International SA (1998) A. C. 20 先例是说:"... employer will not, without reasonable and proper cause, conduct itself in a manner likely to destroy or seriously damage the relationship of confidence and trust between employer and employee."

有关的先例还有不少，如 Scally v Southern Health and Social Services Board (1992) 1 AC 294; Street v. Derbyshire Unemployed Workers' Centre (2004) EWCA Civ 964 等。

其他还有一些针对性的合约类别也会有个别的先例默示善意的要求。如早在 Trego v Hunt (1896) AC 7 先例，涉及买卖商誉的合约，贵族院判有一个默示要求是卖方不能向该业务以前的客户拉生意，Macnaghten 勋爵说："not an honest thing to pocket the price and then to recapture the subject of sale"。而近期一些的是 Training in Compliance Ltd v Dewse (2004) EWHC 3094 先例，案情涉及一个"合资业务"(joint business venture)，涉及两个提供专业服务的公司合作为金融企业提供合规方面的专业服务，这看来与合伙人之间的合约有一点相似。

但在 Bedfordshire CC v Fitzpatrick Contractors Ltd (1998) 62 Con. L. R. 64 先例，法院就拒绝对一个特许经营合约作出善意的默示，Dyson 大法官认为这种合约关系更接近商业关系而不是雇佣关系，说："much closer to an ordinary commercial relationship, than one between employer and employee."

§6　近期判明示善意要求条文是有效的案例

近期有不少合约有明示善意谈判条文都获得法院的承认与执行的先例。这些先例做出的救济会涉及金钱赔偿或履约指令（案情适合作出该救济，特别是在金钱赔偿并非是一个妥善的救济情况下，如只是涉及名义损失）。如已经在较早提到的 Petromec Inc v Petroleo Brasileiro SA Petrobras (No. 3) (2006) 1 Lloyd's Rep 121; Butters v BBC Worldwide Ltd (2009) EWHC 1954; Gold Group Properties Ltd v. BDW Trading Ltd. (2010) EWHC 1632 等先例。

接下来会简单介绍部分先例以及其他有同样针对的先例，让读者充分了解这方面。

6.1　案例之一：Berkeley Community Villages Ltd v. Pullen

在 Berkeley Community Villages Ltd v. Pullen (2007) EWHC 1330 先例，案情涉及一个发展商与农场主或土地所有人之间的一个合约。在谈判的过程中，发展商曾经出价 1.2 亿英镑收购这块土地，但最后没有成事。最后双方达成的合约是发展商用它的专业知识发掘有关土地的最大潜力，并向当局申请"规划许可"(Planning Consent)。在取得规划许可后，估计该土地的市场价格也会大升，发展商可以从出售土地的收益中收取 10% 的费用。在该合约有一条针对善意的明示条文，说："... in all matters relating to this Agreement the parties will act with the **utmost good faith** towards one another and will act reasonably and prudently at all times."(加黑部分是笔者的强调)

合约达成之后,发展商十分积极的履行以及申请规划许可,也估计会顺利取得。而在该期间,农场主却试图把该土地出售给第三人,因为第三人出价高达3.5亿英镑。发展商知悉后,向英国法院紧急申请禁令,阻止这一买卖,认为农场主违反了善意的要求。法院同意这是违反,Morgan大法官说:"... a contractual obligation to observe reasonable commercial standards of fair dealing in accordance with their action which related to the Agreement and also required faithfulness to the agreed common purpose and consistency with justified expectations of the developer."

法院也认为发展商已经投入大量的时间与努力让该土地价格上升,所以不是农场主愿意给一笔合理或补偿性费用就可以了事。在该合约,双方同意的共同目标与发展商的合法期望是在规划批准后,出售土地的价格中收取费用。所以,法院同意向农场主作出禁令。

6.2 案例之二:CPC Group Ltd. v. Qatari Diar Real Estate Investment Co

在CPC Group Ltd. v. Qatari Diar Real Estate Investment Co (2010) EWHC1535 (Ch)先例,CPC(一家英国地产商)与Qatari Diar(简称QD,是卡塔尔的主权基金)成立了一家合资公司,买下了切尔西军营的土地进行重新开发(CPC出资200万英镑,其余9.57亿英镑都是QD支付),并提交了规划申请。之后CPC与QD订立了一份买卖合约,CPC把它在合资公司的所有利益卖给QD。价钱分为两部分,先支付37,917,806英镑的"初始款"(initial consideration),再主要根据将来获得规划许可的进度支付总计不超过8,100万英镑的"迟付款"(deferred consideration)。有关买卖合约中有争议的重要条文,可节录如下:

"7.1 [QD] and [CPC] shall **both act in the utmost good faith** towards each other in relation to the matters set out in this Deed and in Schedule 4 and [QD] **shall use all reasonable but commercially prudent endeavours** to enable the achievement of the various threshold events...

5(f) The Planning Application shall not be withdrawn unless:(不能撤回规划申请除非:)(i) the City Council have prepared an officer's report recommending that the Planning Application be refused or the Mayor has indicated that he intends to exercise his power to direct the City Council to refuse the Planning Application or call in the Planning Application for his determination (if applicable) or the Secretary of State has issued a holding objection (a "Deemed Refusal"); **and** (ii) the Planning Consultant recommends to [QD] and [CPC] jointly that a revised Planning Application stands a better chance of delivering a Planning Permission than the pursuit of an Appeal of the previous planning application."

提交申请的重建规划遭到了查尔斯王子与伦敦市长的强烈反对,原因是重建规划会破坏伦敦的城市面貌。QD 在此压力下撤销了规划申请,并准备了一个新的建筑方案大纲,但这意味着 CPC 拿到的迟付款会减少。于是,CPC 开始起诉 QD,指它撤销规划申请违反 Schedule 4 之 5(f)条文。

该案的主要争议有三个:(1)QD 撤销规划申请是否违反合约;(2)QD 撤销申请的行为是否违反最大善意行事的合约责任,或违反它要用合理与商业谨慎的努力来保证可以达成支付迟付款条件的合约责任,或/与它不能设计"阴谋"或借故避免或减少迟付款支付的合约责任;(3)QD 则声称 CPC 采取了一系列的行为只是为了可以尽快拿到钱(迟付款),CPC 的这些行为是否违反了尽最大善意行事的合约责任。

第一个争议与本章内容关系不大,不详细介绍,Vos 大法官判是 QD 撤销申请并不符合合约 Schedule 4 之 5(f)条文规定的两个必须同时出现的情况,违反了合约。针对第二个争议中的尽最大善意行事,Vos 大法官说:"It seems to me that the content of the obligation of utmost good faith in the SPA (买卖合约) was to adhere to the spirit of the contract, which was to seek to obtain planning consent for the maximum Developable Area in the shortest possible time, and to observe reasonable commercial standards of fair dealing, and to be faithful to the agreed common purpose, and to act consistently with the justified expectations of the parties. I do not need, it seems to me, to decide whether this obligation could only be broken if QD or CPC acted in bad faith, but it might be hard to understand, as Lord Scott said in Manifest Shipping how, without bad faith, there can be a breach of a 'duty of good faith, utmost or otherwise'."(看来合约中明示对最大善意的要求是希望符合合约的精神:一是尽快取得规划批准,并且可以有最大的发展面积;二是双方遵守公平交易的合理商业标准;三是忠实对待双方同意的共同目的;四是按照双方的合理期望行事。我不需要决定到底这个合约要求是否只是在其中一方有恶意行为才算是违反,但正如 Scott 勋爵在 Manifest Shipping Co v. Uni – Polaris Shipping Co [2003] 1 AC 469 先例中说,如果没有恶意,怎么能说是违反善意。)

而针对合理与商业谨慎努力,Vos 大法官这样说:

"The obligation to use 'all reasonable endeavours' does not always require the obligor to sacrifice his commercial interests. In this case, the matter is, however, clearer, because the contract itself, as I have already said, contains other indications that QD was not to be required to sacrifice its commercial interests. Indeed the words of clause 7.1 itself make that clear by using the added words 'but commercially prudent' in the phrase 'all reasonable but commercially prudent endeavours'. (7.1 条文所用的文字是以"合理与商业谨慎努力"履行以达到合约目的,这显示了 QD 不需要牺牲自己的商业利益履行)

Lord Grabiner accepts that the words 'but commercially prudent' provide a brake on the lengths to which QD had to go in using 'all reasonable endeavours'. But in my judgment, his acceptance does not go far enough. Clause 7.1 and paragraph 5(a) are not equivalent to a 'best endeavours' obligation, and they do not require QD to ignore or forego its commercial interests. Instead, they allow QD to consider its own commercial interests alongside those of CPC, and require it to take all reasonable steps to procure the Planning Permission, provided those steps are commercially prudent. In the context of the facts of this case, this distinction is important, because when QD came to consider how to respond to the Prince of Wales's intervention, it was, in my judgment, permitted to consider its own commercial interests in deciding how to respond. The clauses do not, as it seems to me, allow QD to consider its own political interests, insofar as they are different from its commercial interests or insofar as they require commercially imprudent measures."(有关合约条文并不要求 QD 妄顾或牺牲商业利益,而且完全允许 QD 这样做,以取得规划批准。在这个案件的事实,涉及 QD 要怎样回应查尔斯王子的干预,法院认为 QD 是完全可以考虑怎样回应才符合自己的商业利益。该合约条文看来是不允许 QD 在政治利益与商业利益不同时,因保护政治利益而做出不符合商业利益或商业上不恰当的行为)

在本先例,法院判 QD 在十分困难的政治情况下已经尽力做到最好,以保证能尽量在最短时间内拿到规划批准。法院也判 QD 撤销申请并不是它自己想或故意这么做,也不是为了阻止 CPC 拿到钱。因此,QD 没有违反合约下最大善意行事的责任以及以合理与商业谨慎做出努力的责任。

至于第三个争议,尽管 Vos 大法官认为 CPC 确实采取了一系列行为试图尽快拿到钱,但 QD 无法证明这些行为是恶意,或者有任何实质影响,所以不能说 CPC 违反了最大善意行事的合约责任。最后的结果就是双方都没有违反合约中有关善意的要求。

6.3 案例之三:Gold Group Properties Ltd v. BDW Trading Ltd

在 Gold Group Properties Ltd v. BDW Trading Ltd.(2010)EWHC 1632 先例,Gold 是土地所有人,BDW 是开发商。双方订立合约约定 BDW 在 Gold 的土地上建造住宅,并在之后将这些住宅卖掉与 Gold 分享收益。该合约规定了住宅的最低售价与怎样进行利益分配,并且第 11 条文明示规定了双方要善意行事,说:

"The parties mutually covenant and agree that:

11.1 during the continuance of this Agreement all transactions entered into between the parties shall be conducted in **good faith** and on the basis set out in this Agreement or if not provided for herein on an arm's length basis;

11.2 each of them shall at all times act in **good faith** towards the other and use all reasonable endeavours to ensure the observance by themselves of the terms of this Agreement and the agreements referred to in, or contemplated by this Agreement; and

11.3 neither will seek to increase its profit or reduce its loss at the expense of the other."

因为房产市场下跌,BDW 没有开发这块土地,于是被 Gold 起诉要求 BDW 赔偿因为违约/毁约而造成的损失。BDW 反索赔 Gold 违反了合约中对善意的明示规定,因为 Gold 拒绝重新谈判或改变合约中的利益分配条文并坚持合约中的最低售价条文,而不降低售价,这房子在当时的市场是卖不出去的。

在该先例,BDW 实际上做出了两个要约给 Gold,一是延迟工程两年,二是修改利益分配条文。显然延迟工程两年对 Gold 没有任何好处,而如果按照 BDW 的要求修改合约,Gold 的利益更会减少约 280 万英镑。客观看来,等于 BDW 从 Gold"夺取"了 280 万英镑来增加它的利益或减少它的损失,这是合约第 11.3 条文所明确禁止的。因此,Stephen Furst 大法官认为 Gold 不接受延迟工程两年与修改利益分配条文甚至拒绝进行谈判,不能说是违反了善意的责任。Stephen Furst 大法官说:

"In particular there is a helpful review of authority in Automasters Australia Ptv Ltd v Bruness Ptv Ltd [2002] WASC 286. In that case Hasluck J cites the observation of Barrett J in Overlook v Foxtel (2002) Aust Contract R 90 – 143 at [65 – 67]:

'It must be accepted that the party subject to the obligation is not required to subordinate the party's own interests, so long as pursuit of those interests does not entail unreasonable interference with the enjoyment of a benefit conferred by the express contractual terms so that the enjoyment becomes (or could become) ... 'nugatory, worthless or, perhaps, seriously undermined' ... the implied obligation of good faith underwrites the spirit of the contract and supports the integrity of its character. A party is precluded from cynical resort to the black letter. But no party is fixed with the duty to subordinate self – interest entirely which is the lot of the fiduciary ... The duty is not a duty to prefer the interests of the other contracting party. It is, rather, a duty to recognise and to have due regard to the legitimate interests of both the parties in the enjoyment of the fruits of the contract as delineated by its terms.'

Thus good faith, whilst requiring the parties to act in a way that will allow both parties to enjoy the anticipated benefits of the contract, does not require either party to give up a freely negotiated financial advantage clearly embedded in the contract."

但 Stephen Furst 大法官也认为如果 BDW 只是要求 Gold 谈判住宅最低售价条文,否则在当时市场无法出售,而如果 Gold 拒绝,就有可能是违反合约的善意要求,说:"it would seem that a revision in the minimum prices might well have had to be agreed in order for the units to be sold. Had Gold refused to negotiate or agree a reduction in the minimum prices it might well have been in breach of the obligation to reach agreement on the schedule of minimum prices and the obligations to act in good faith since such a reduction would not have affected Gold's profit from the development but might have been necessary to permit the Agreement to be performed as envisaged."

但在该先例,BDW 没有向 Gold 提出重新谈判最低售价条文,因此不能说 Gold 违反了善意的责任。

6.4 案例之四:Compass Group UK and Ireland Ltd v. Mid Essex Hospital Services NHS Trust

在 Compass Group UK and Ireland Ltd v. Mid Essex Hospital Services NHS Trust (2013) EWCA Civ 200 先例,原告与被告订立了7年的合约,向两家医院提供伙食与清洁服务。根据合约,原告的服务要不断的受到医院当局的评估,如果服务不达标(合约的附件中有十分详尽的标准),就会被扣分与扣减支付服务的费用。而如果扣分扣到了某个程度,医院当局就有权终止合约。在合约开始履行不久后,医院当局对原告作出了十分苛刻的评估,并且被指是乱扣分与乱扣减费用。最后该合约也被原告终止,理由是医院当局违约/毁约。有关争议的重要条文,可节录如下:

"3.5 The Trust (医院当局) and the Contractor (提供服务的原告) will co - operate with each other in **good faith** and will take all reasonable action as is necessary for the efficient transmission of information and instructions and to enable the Trust or, as the case may be, any Beneficiary to derive the full benefit of the Contract. At all times in the performance of the Services, the Contractor will co - operate fully with any other contractors appointed by the Trust or any Beneficiary in connection with other services at the Location. . . .

5.8 The Trust or any Beneficiary shall ascertain whether the Contractor's provision of the Services meets the performance criteria as specified in the Service Level Specification or, if the criteria are not so specified, meets the standards of a professional provider of the Services. Where such performance criteria or standards have not been met by the Contractor in the performance of the Services then the Trust shall be entitled to levy payment deductions against the monthly amount of the Contract Price payable to the Contractor in accordance with the terms of the Payment Mechanism. . . . "

双方在法院的争议集中在两个方面,一是根据上述的第5.8 条文,医院当局是否在行使扣减费用的裁量权时,有不能武断、任性与非理性的默示责任;二是第3.5 条文的善意明示规定。法院认定医院当局是针对一些小问题做出了过多的扣分以及扣减费用,如对过了最佳食用日期一天的巧克力慕斯扣了84,540 镑。第一审法院判医院当局败诉,认为医院当局破坏了第3.5 条文有关善意的明示规定,并且违反了第5.8 条文的默示责任,而武断、任性与非理性的行使裁量权。所以,医院当局构成了违约/毁约。但到了上诉庭,这两方面都被推翻。首先针对第5.8 条文,上诉庭认为有关的文字显示了这是绝对裁量权。而且,医院当局乱扣分与乱扣减费用,本身就是违反了第5.8 条。所以不能也没有必要再默示一个不得武断、任性与非理性行使的责任。至于针对第3.5 条文,善意的要求只是针对合约在两方面的主要目的:一是有效的提供消息与指示(efficient transmission of information and instructions);二是让医院当局能够取得所有的合约利益(to derive the full benefit of the Contract)。虽然医院当局乱扣分与乱扣减费用(虽然多扣的部分金钱已在合约终止前退还),并搞坏双方关系,但完全没有影响到这两方面的主要目的。双方的履行还是有提供消息与指示的合作,而医院当局也取得了所有合约的利益,也就是原告一直提供伙食与清洁服务。此外,第一审也没有认定或区分医院当局乱扣分与乱扣减费用是由于不诚实,或只是根据一个复杂的合约条文计算有误才得出。所以,上诉庭判是医院当局并没有违约/毁约。

6.5　案例之五:HSBC Institutional Trust Services (Singapore) Ltd v. Toshin Development Singapore Pte Ltd

HSBC Institutional Trust Services (Singapore) Ltd v. Toshin Development Singapore Pte Ltd (2012) 4 SLR 738 是一个新加坡的上诉庭先例,案情涉及 HSBC 与 Toshin 在新加坡的地标建筑义安城中的六层楼的租约。该租约长达 20 年,并且 Toshin 有延长 12 年的选择权。租约规定每三年租金调整一次,调整机制可节录如下:

"(c) (i) Prior to the commencement of each Rental Term (other than the first), the Lessor and the Lessee shall in **good faith endeavour** to agree on the prevailing market rental value of the Demised Premises (excluding service charge payable and disregarding the value of all fixtures and fittings installed by the Lessee) for [the] purpose of determining the New Annual Rent for the relevant Rental Term.

(ii) If by three (3) months (time being of the essence) before commencement of the relevant Rental Term the parties have not reached agreement on the New Annual Rent, the parties shall appoint three international firms of licensed valuers (the "licensed valuers") on the basisthat each of the licensed valuers shall proceed to separately determine the prevailing market rental value of the Demised Premises. The licensed valuers shall be nominated by agreement between the Lessor and the Lessee or in the absence of agreement by the parties on any one of the licensed valuers by a date ten (10) weeks (time being of the essence) before commencement of the relevant Rental Term, such of the licensed valuers as have not been agreed upon shall be nominated by the President for the time being of the Singapore Institute of Surveyors and Valuers (or its successor institute) on the application of either the Lessor or the Lessee. If the said President is not available or is unable to make such nomination at the time of [the] application, the nomination may be made by the Vice – President or the next senior officer of the said Institute then available and able to make such nomination. All costs and expenses of and in connection with the appointment of the licensed valuers shall be borne by the Lessor and the Lessee in equal shares. The licensed valuers shall act as experts and not as arbitrators and their respective decisions shall be binding and conclusive on the parties..."(大致是说每

三年租金调整,如果双方在调整前三个月无法达成协议,就交给三家在新加坡的国际注册估价师事务作出估价,并以他们的平均租金为准。如果双方无法同意哪三家,就由新加坡测量与估价师学会的会长作出决定。)

Toshin 在租约调整之前,私下花钱聘请了新加坡所有 8 家符合资格的注册估价师国际事务所对六层楼进行估价。双方对租价进行谈判,无法达成一致意见,需要同意 3 家进行估价。尽管 Toshin 已经获得了新加坡所有 8 家符合资格的国际注册估价师事务所的估价,但它并没有将这件事披露给 HSBC。HSBC 偶然得知 Toshin 之前单方面进行的估价,认为合约中的调整机制不再可行,并向法院申请这样的宣告。高等法院驳回了 HSBC 的申请,HSBC 上诉至上诉庭,理由之一是 Toshin 违反了租约中的善意责任。针对这个争议,上诉庭认为可分成四个问题:一是租约中明示的"善意"一词是否有效?二是如果有效,善意责任的范围是什么?三是 Toshin 是否违反了善意责任?四是 Toshin 违反了善意责任是否导致调整机制不再可行?

V K Rajah 大法官将该案例与 Walford v. Miles (1992) 2 AC 128 先例进行了区分(也就是善意谈判条文与善意谈判协议的区别),说:"As a preliminary observation, we are of the view that a valid distinction can be drawn between the pre – contractual negotiations in Walford and the 'negotiations' between the Parties under the Rent Review Exercise in the present case. We would hesitate to characterise the position of the Parties as being strictly 'adversarial'. While they obviously do not have identical interests and, to that extent, may not see eye to eye, they have committed themselves to a mechanism to resolve how the new rent for (*inter alia*) the Last Rental Term is to be set. Unlike parties who are merely in pre – contractual negotiations, the Parties are not free to simply walk away from the negotiating table for no rhyme or reason."

V K Rajah 大法官接着说:"... as part of a wider existing contractual framework, there is a clause obliging the parties to negotiate certain contractual modalities in good faith, such negotiations need not necessarily be adversarial and hostile, but call instead for a consensual approach to resolve the identified matters as part of the performance of the broader existing agreement. This is also part of the wider contractual duty to co – operate to implement the contract. The parties are, of course, certainly not disentitled from having regard to their own commercial self – interests in the course of the negotiations so long as their conduct does not involve bad faith."

看来 V K Rajah 大法官是支持合约中明示的"善意"一词有效,针对第二个问题,V K Rajah 大法官对善意的范围有很详尽的说法,如下:

"At its core, the concept of good faith encompasses the threshold subjective requirement of acting honestly, as well as the objective requirement of observing accepted commercial standards of fair dealing in the performance of the identified obligations. This encompasses a duty to act fairly, having regard to the legitimate interests of the other party.

(要求双方诚实,并在客观看来是按照一般商业准则进行公平交易,并履行合约中明确了的承诺或责任。公平履行只需要照顾到合约另一方的合法利益)...

In the present case, the obligation to'in good faith endeavour to agree' on the new rent for each new rental term after the first rental term is both certain and capable of being observed by both of the Parties. It is an obligation that requires the Parties to co – operate fully to facilitate the determination of the new rent. It is not difficult to ascertain what reasonable commercial standards of fair dealing require in such a context. (在本案件,双方对善意的承诺同意新的租金可以履行,这就要求双方全面合作按照调整机制对新的租金作出决定。确定什么是一般的合理商业准则进行公平交易也没有任何困难,笔者估计是因为这种做法在房屋租赁市场比较普遍)...

Both of the Parties are required to faithfully co – operate with each other to achieve this common purpose. Faithfulness to the common purpose incorporates an obligation during the course of negotiations not to attempt to unfairly profit from the known ignorance of the other. (双方需要真诚合作,这表示在双方谈判时,其中一方不能因为对方不知情而不公平获利)...

Accordingly, when the Parties entered into negotiations on the new rent for the Last Rental Term, reasonable commercial standards of fair dealing must necessarily dictate the disclosure of all material information which could have an impact on the negotiations and/or the ultimate determination of the new rent."(所以双方进行谈判,按照合理商业准则进行公平交易就表示双方必须披露所有重要资料,只要这些资料会对谈判与最后新租金的决定有影响。)

上述所讲显然对第三个问题给出了答案,也就是 Toshin 的确是违反善意。它私下先联系新加坡所有的国际注册估价师事务所,并偷偷作出估价,知道谁高谁低。之后与 HSBC 的谈判中,如果需要选择 3 家国际注册估价师事务所进行估价,Toshin 就心里有数,而 HSBC 却被蒙在鼓里,双方谈判同意的 3 家显然会对 HSBC 不利。

这带来第四个问题,就是 Toshin 的违约后果。显然,因为 HSBC 及时知道这一消息,并向新加坡法院申请调整机制不再可行的宣告,就表示 HSBC 还没有蒙受任何金钱上的损失,不存在金钱的救济。然后就是该调整机制是否不可行,答案是"否"。原因在于,该条文明确如果双方无法同意选哪三家国际注册估价师事务所(不论是何原因,包括其中一方违反善意),则由新加坡测量与估价师学会的会长作出决定。显然该会长作为第三人没有内幕消息,所以他选的 3 家可能对 Toshin 有利,也是它想选的,但也完全有可能是 3 家 Toshin 最不想选的。反正,有了这个进一步的机制委任国际注册估价师事务所,就表示该条文的调整机制完全可行。

§7 善意——如何掌握轻重与适用于实际案件

看来英国法律针对善意的问题已经如对"不可抗力"(*force majeure*)一样,虽然原本自己的体系中没有这一理念与说法,但英国法院在面对现实与顺应潮流的情况下已经完全接受双方有明确订约意图约定的对善意的要求,特别是针对善意谈判或合作的条文。剩下来主要的问题是,怎样掌握轻重并建立一套指引(为了有"可循性"[predictability])适用在千变万化的实际案件,毕竟一直以来最主要反对协议将来达成协议的原因就是太不肯定。

这个问题并不容易,但正如Longmore大法官在Petromec Inc v Petroleo Brasileiro SA Petrobras (No. 3) (2006) 1 Lloyd's Rep 121先例中批评Walford v. Miles (1992) 2 AC 128先例所讲的:"The difficulty of a problem should not be an excuse for the court to withhold relevant assistance from the parties by declaring a blanket unenforceability of the obligation."(解决问题的困难并不能作为干脆全面不承认与不执行这种条文的理由。)

以下总结在近期先例中可以看到的指引。

7.1 双方谈判主观或客观

近期的先例中对到底是以"客观考验"(objective test)或是"主观考验"(subjective test)为标准衡量是否有善意有不同或不清楚的说法。例如,在本章之第2段提到的Petromec Inc v Petroleo Brasileiro SA Petrobras (No. 3) (2006) 1 Lloyd's Rep 121先例,Longmore大法官说:"... it is difficult, if not impossible, to say whether, if negotiations are brought to an end, the termination is brought about in good or in bad faith..."

这是把善意与恶意对立起来,而中间没有灰色地带。他也说到了没有欺诈,就不大可能认定恶意,说:"If fraudulent representations as to the intention to continue negotiations were made, the obligation to negotiate in good faith is likely to fall away as a separate obligation; if there was no fraudulent representation, it is perhaps less likely that there will have been bad faith in terminating negotiations but it will not be particularly difficult to tell whether there was or not."

在本章之6.2段介绍过的CPC Group Ltd. v. Qatari Diar Real Estate Investment Co (2010) EWHC1535 (Ch)先例,Vos大法官也说:"it might be hard to understand, as Lord Scott said in Manifest Shipping how, without bad faith, there can be a breach of a 'duty of good faith, utmost or otherwise'."

这些说法看来是主观考验,也显示了如果不能证明被指是违反善意的一方"主观不诚实"(subjective dishonesty),就无法证明违约。但如果是这样的说法,就会太狭窄,现实中也太难证明主观不诚实或欺诈。考虑到有不少涉及公共政策或合约本质需要双方紧密合作的合约(如本章之5.2.4段介绍的雇佣合约、合伙人合约等),法律也会是默示善意,这表示如果只是给明示善意条文太狭窄的解释,看来就没有太多意思。

支持客观考验的先例也不少,包括 Berkeley Community Villages Ltd v. Pullen (2007) EWHC 1330;Compass Group UK and Ireland Ltd v. Mid Essex Hospital Services NHS Trust (2013) EWCA Civ 200;Yam Seng Pte Ltd v International Trade Corp Ltd. (2013) EWHC 111 (QB)等。

考虑到在本章之第3段介绍的裁量权的考验是"主观诚实"(subjective honesty)与"客观理性"(objective rationality),看来同样的考验也应该适用在明示善意条文。例如,在 The "Product Star" (1993) 1 Lloyd's Rep 397 先例,Leggatt 大法官说:"In my judgment, the authorities show that not only must the discretion be exercised **honestly** and in good faith, but, having regard to the provisions of the contract by which it is conferred, it **must not** be exercised **arbitrarily, capriciously and unreasonably.**"(加黑部分是笔者的强调)

显然,要求诚实作出裁量权是主观考验,而不能武断、任性、不合理是客观理性的考验。

这在新加坡的 HSBC Institutional Trust Services (Singapore) Ltd v. Toshin Development Singapore Pte Ltd (2012) 4 SLR 738 先例,也可以看到涉及 Toshin 有否隐瞒与不披露重要的资料给 HSBC 的主观考验,以及什么是进行公平交易的合理商业准则的客观考验。

7.2 善意不要求合约一方牺牲利益

这方面在澳大利亚的 Overlook v. Foxtel (2002) Aust Contract E 90 – 143 先例中,Barrett 大法官说:"It must be accepted that the party subject to the obligation is not required to subordinate the party's own interests, so long as pursuit of those interests does not entail unreasonable interference with the enjoyment of a benefit conferred by the express contractual terms so that the enjoyment becomes (or could become) ... 'nugatory, worthless or, perhaps, seriously undermined' ... the implied obligation of good faith underwrites the spirit of the contract and supports the integrity of its character. A party is precluded from cynical resort to the black letter. But no party is fixed with the duty to subordinate self – interest entirely which is the lot of the fiduciary ... The duty is not a duty to prefer the interests of the other contracting party. It is, rather, a duty to recognize and to have due regard to the legitimate interests of both the parties in the enjoyment of the fruits of the contract as delineated by its terms."

这句判词也被 Stephen Furst 大法官在 Gold Group Properties Ltd v. BDW Trading Ltd. (2010) EWHC 1632 先例中认同与引用,说:"Thus good faith, whilst requiring the parties to act in a way that will allow both parties to enjoy the anticipated benefits of the contract, does not require either party to give up a freely negotiated financial advantage clearly embedded in the contract."(善意要求双方合作让大家都可以享有合约所预计的利益,但不要求其中一方牺牲他在合约中的经济好处。)

这样的判法也很有道理,因为商业合约中双方都是为了牟利。所以,善意要求双方尽最大的努力合作并尊重对方的合法利益,但并不表示要求其中一方牺牲他的经济或合约权益。这表示合约中如果有明示的善意条文,也可以知道自己合作的底线。例如,在一个国际货物买卖合约,即使有善意条文,如果遇上卖方有困难要求买方延长提供货物的付运期,甚至只需要延长一两天,买方不同意也不会违反该合约中的善意条文。买方可能因为市场下跌想取巧,但买方也很容易说付运期是合约明示条文,也是他的合约权益。

7.3　不诚实、隐瞒、误述等行为显然违反善意

如果涉及了不诚实、隐瞒、误述等行为,这显然是违反合约中明示善意条文的要求。这些方面已经在上述先例中有详尽介绍,不重复。

7.4　法院什么时候介入

善意条文通常要求双方谈判并最后达成对某些事项的协议,这表示法院即使作出执行,也尽量不要自己做出决定,因为这不是双方的约定,有越俎代庖的意味。例如,在新加坡的 HSBC Institutional Trust Services (Singapore) Ltd v. Toshin Development Singapore Pte Ltd (2012) 4 SLR 738 先例,法院最后的判决是调整机制依然可行,而不是根据证据自己决定什么是合理的租金。至于法院在何时需要介入决定什么是最后合理价格,可节录 Henry Hoskins 大律师在《Contractual obligations to negotiate in good faith: faithfulness to the agreed common purpose》L. Q. R. 2014, 130(Jan)一文中说:"Given that the parties provided for the costs to be decided, at least in the first instance, by negotiation, it is unlikely that they intended that a court could review their negotiations at the request of a dissatisfied party merely because the court would have arrived at a slightly different figure for the 'reasonable costs'. At the other extreme, the point made above that a test of mere subjective honesty would often be redundant applies with even greater force in the context of negotiation, where much protection against dishonest representations is already provided by the tort of deceit. It is more likely that the parties intended a middle – way between these two extremes, the courting intervening only if the parties did not negotiate honestly and rationally within the framework provided by the agreement."

这是说法院只能在双方不诚实与不理性的按照合约的机制进行谈判时才会介入。

7.5　合约如果有其他针对性的条文

在本章开始时,提到 Union Eagle Ltd v Golden Achievement Ltd (1997) AC 514

先例显示了英国法律为了商业的肯定性会严格解释合约条文。买方迟延10分钟支付房屋买卖价款以完成交易就被卖方终止合约,并蒙受重大的经济损失。那么,如果合约中有一条广泛的针对履行合约必须善意的条文,情况会否有所不同?笔者认为不会,其中的道理与笔者在本章之7.2段所举的要求延长国际货物买卖的付运期的例子一样。这也显示了追求商业合约肯定性的英国法律与重视善意的大陆法系的不同之处。笔者认为,如果合约中有明确针对性的条文,英国法院或仲裁庭不会认为因为有了善意条文,就可以默示或扭曲该针对性条文。但以中国《合同法》第54条规定为例,在订立合同时显失公平的合约,当事人一方有权请求人民法院或者仲裁机构变更或者撤销。

§8 仲裁条文中的协议将来达成协议

今天的商业合约,特别是国际性的合约都会有一条仲裁条文。在亚洲,合约方普遍的做法就是在仲裁条文中加上在仲裁开始之前,双方必须友好谈判和解或进行调解。这种条文可被称为是"Escalation Clause"或"Multi - tier Arbitration Clause"。显然,合约方认为这样写比较符合商业友好,也配合双方在订合约时相对友好的气氛。但现实中如果事后出了争议,所谓的"先决条件"(condition precedent)通常没有用。往往是一方开始仲裁向另一方施压,而另一方如果承受不了压力就会很快作出让步。也有可能另一方不向压力屈服,但也不想面对仲裁,往往会对管辖权提出质疑(challenge to jurisdiction)。就是在这种仲裁条文下,必须先走第一步友好谈判以期达成和解或进行调解,才能走第二步的仲裁,而没有走第一步就走第二步不符合仲裁条文的规定,令仲裁庭没有管辖权。

传统英国法律的说法是这第一步的所谓先决条件,是一个协议将来达成协议,法院不予执行。如The "Jing Hong Hai" (1989) 2 Lloyd's Rep 522,Steyn大法官说:"The submission by the charterers that it was a condition precedent to the submission to arbitration that the parties would be unable to reach amicable settlement would be rejected."

换言之,多年来的做法就是精明的原告根本不会理睬这个所谓的前提条件,直接开始仲裁,而仲裁员也从来不怀疑管辖权有问题,因为先决条件只是一个无效的协议将来达成协议。但随着英国法律对协议将来达成协议态度的改变,特别是在一个有效合约中的条文(仲裁条文),近期的案例也有了很大改变。现在再也不是一口否定协议将来达成协议的有效性,即使最后判无效,也往往是根据"不肯定"(uncertain)的理由。例如,如果只是简单的一句写着双方必须先"友好和解"(amicable settlement)后才仲裁,就有很大的可能是被法院或仲裁庭视为不肯定而无效。换言之,这种条文需要写的更加明确,包括在和解的谈判中,双方要做的什么以及谈多久与怎么样终止这一步等。

针对这方面,在笔者的《仲裁法——从 1996 年英国仲裁法到国际商务仲裁》第一章之 1.20 段有针对,不全部重复。在 Tang Chung Wah and anorv Grant Thornton International Limited and ors (2012) EWHC 3198 (Ch)先例,有这方面的指引。案情涉及 Grant Thornton 这家会计师事务所的合伙人之间的协议,合约中有一条伦敦国际仲裁院(London Court of International Arbitration,简称 LCIA)的仲裁条文。但在仲裁开始之前,有条文清楚列出了和解/调解的先决条件,如下:

"Section 14.3

(a) Any dispute or difference as described in Section 14.2 shall in the first instance be referred to the Chief Executive in an attempt to settle such dispute or difference by amicable conciliation or an informal nature. The conciliation provided for in this Section 14.3 shall be applicable notwithstanding that GTIL may be a party to the dispute or difference in question.

(b) The Chief Executive shall attempt to resolve the dispute or difference in an amicable fashion. Any party may submit a request for such conciliation regarding any such dispute or difference, and the Chief Executive shall have up to one (1) month after receipt of such request to attempt to resolve it.

(c) If the dispute or difference shall not have been resolved within one (1) month following submissions to the Chief Executive, it shall be referred to a Panel of three (3) members of the Board to be selected by the Board, none of whom shall be associated with or in any other wayrelated to the Member Firm or Member Firms who are parties to the dispute or difference. The Panel shall have up to one (1) month to attempt to resolve the dispute or difference.

(d) Until the earlier of (i) such date as the Panel shall determine that it cannot resolve the dispute or difference, or (ii) the date one (1) month after the request for conciliation of the dispute or difference has been referred to it, no party may commence any arbitration procedures in accordance with this Agreement."

该先例涉及 Grant Thornton 与香港合伙人之间的争议,发展到要赶走香港合伙人。显然在这个争议,因为利益冲突,上述十分详尽的友好和解/调解机制根本无法启动。首先,首席执行官因为利益冲突而无法走第一步,在 1 个月后也无法走第二步找出 3 位董事组成调解庭。这导致 Grant Thornton 直接去 LCIA 开始仲裁,但香港合伙人认为没有先走第一步的先决条件,所以仲裁庭没有管辖权。这一管辖权争议最后根据 1996 年英国《仲裁法》之 section 67 诉至高院,Hildyard 大法官判是该先决条件太不肯定而无效。特别是条文没有针对在两个月后如果调解庭明确没有办法成立,任何一方应该怎么办才能以仲裁解决争议,并且不会构成违约。

即使这一条一般人看来已经非常详尽的条文仍被法院视为不够肯定。笔者认为,英国法院也是非常实际与肯想办法解决问题。因为在该先例,不是 Grant Thornton 是否愿意走第一步的先决条件,而是走不了。这样,如果 Grant Thornton 不能直接提起 LCIA 仲裁,就等于要无限期搁置争议,这显然不是英国法院想要看到的结果。但如果该案的案情不是因为利益冲突 Grant Thornton 走不了第一步,而是明明可以走第一步却不愿意并直接提起 LCIA 仲裁,判法可能就会有所不同而变为会判是该条文肯定,而 Grant Thornton 没有完成该条文的先决条件,所以仲裁庭没有管辖权。

最后 Hildyard 大法官也给了一个针对这类条文的指引,说:"In the context of a positive obligation to attempt to resolve a dispute or difference amicably before referring a matter to arbitration or bringing proceedings the test is whether the provision prescribes, without the need for further agreement, (a) a sufficiently certain and unequivocal commitment to commence a process (b) from which may be discerned what steps each party is required to take to put the process in place and which is (c) sufficiently clearly defined to enable the Court to determine objectively (i) what under that process is the minimum required of the parties to the dispute in terms of their participation in it and (ii) when or how the process will be exhausted or properly terminable without breach."

另在一个更近期的先例 Emirates Trading Agency LLC v Prime Mineral Exports Private Limited (2014) EWHC 2014, Teare 大法官认为如果需要法院(或仲裁员)强制执行要求双方必须先进行友好谈判和解或进行调解的仲裁条文,在写法上必须是:"(a) A sufficiently certain and unequivocal commitment to commence a process; (b) From which may be discerned what steps each parties require to take to put the process in place; and which is (c) Sufficiently clearly defined to enable the court to determine objectively (i) what under that process is the minimum required of the parties to the dispute in terms of their participation in it and (ii) when or how the process will be exhausted or properly terminable without breach."

Teare 大法官也提到法院怎样强制双方必须要谈判或调解与怎样判定其中一方是否违约,说:"Whilst it may be difficult in some circumstances to establish a breach of the obligation there will be other circumstances in which a court is likely to be able to identify conduct, if it exists, which departs from the conduct expected of parties who have agreed to seek to resolve contractual disputes by friendly discussions. For example, a party who refused to discuss his claim at all could easily be shown to have breached the obligation to seek to resolve his claim by friendly discussion. Difficulty of proof of breach in some cases does not mean that the clause lacks real content."(有时候会不容易确定是否违约或只是双方真正的谈不拢,但也会有情况是法院可以在行为中肯定其中一方是否违约。例如,有一方拒绝谈判就可以很明确的显示违反友好谈判的承诺。部分案件中比较困难证明是否违约并不代表有关条文的写法没有实质内容。)

另外 Teare 大法官提到如果有一方违反友好谈判的承诺会有什么救济,说:"If a party were to seek damages for breach of the obligation it might be difficult to establish what the outcome of the discussions would have been but in such a case damages could, in appropriate cases be awarded for **loss of a chance.**"(加黑部分是笔者的强调)

有关"机会损失"(loss of chance)的金钱赔偿救济,在笔者的《损失赔偿与救济》第六章之4-7段有详述。这是近年才发展起来的一种金钱损失赔偿:Allied Maples Group Ltd v Simmons & Simmons (a firm) (1995) 1 WLR 1602 先例。笔者也在该章4.5段提到机会损失的核算是完全依照法院或者仲裁庭的裁量权,所以有很大的不肯定性,而且双方当事人可以不凭证据任意发挥。而且,核算的办法也不科学,往往会令机会损失的金额变得很大。

这表示在这种仲裁条文或争议解决条文下,当事人要十分小心对待友好谈判或调解。即使对方不提出,自己一方也应该提出,反正不要留下证据将来让仲裁员或法院认为是不友好。即使无意作出任何让步,只要在实质的谈判中寸步不让或只是象征性退让,也很容易令对方知难而退。虽然友好善意谈判往往表示必须是"诚实"(honest)与按照一般商业上合理的做法,但即使是内心不诚实也不想与对方谈判,表面上也要做得诚实地想与对方谈判,并留下文书证据。

§9 总结协议将来达成协议与善意条文的原则

在 Mamidoil - Jetoil v. Okta (2001) 2 Lloyd's Rep. 76 先例,Rix 大法官总结了很有帮助的大原则如下:

"In my judgment the following principles relevant to the present case can be deduced from these authorities, but this is intended to be in no way an exhaustive list:

(i) Each case must be decided on its own facts and on the construction of its own agreement. Subject to that:

(ii) Where no contract exists, the use of an expression such as 'to be agreed' in relation to an essential term is likely to prevent any contract coming into existence, on the ground of uncertainty. This may be summed up by the principle that 'you cannot agree to agree'.

(iii) Similarly, where no contract exists, the absence of agreement on essential terms of the agreement may prevent any contract coming into existence, again on the ground of uncertainty.

(iv) However, particularly in commercial dealings between parties who are familiar with the trade in question, and particularly where the parties have acted in the belief that they had a binding contract, the Courts are willing to imply terms, where that is possible, to enable to be carried out.

(v) Where a contract has once come into existence, even the expression 'to be agreed' in relation to future executory obligations is not necessarily fatal to its continue existence.

(vi) Particularly in the case of contracts for future performance over a period, where the parties may desire or need to leave matters to be adjusted in the working out of their contract, the Court will assist the parties to do so, so as to preserve rather than destroy bargains, on the basis that what can be made certain is itself certain. *Certum est quod certum reddi potest.*

(vii) This is particularly the case where one party has either already had the advantage of some performance which reflects the parties' agreement on a long term relationship, or has had to make an investment premised on that agreement.

(viii) For these purposes, an express stipulation for a reasonable or fair measure or price will be sufficient criterion for the Courts to add on. But even in the absence of express language, the Courts are prepared to imply an obligation in terms of what is reasonable.

(ix) Such implications are reflected but not exhausted by the statutory provision for the implication of a reasonable price now to be found in Section 8 (2) of the Sale of Goods Act, 1979 (and, in the case of services, in Section 15 (1) of the Supply of Goods and Services Act, 1982).

(x) The presence of an arbitration clause may assist the Courts to hold a contract to be sufficiently certain or to be capable of being rendered so, presumably as indicating a commercial and contractualmechanism, which can be operated with the assistance of experts in the field, by which the parties, in the absence of agreement, may resolve that dispute."

根据上述重要结论,第一,每个案件一定要依照它的事实解释,除非是:第二,如果还没有达成合约,双方以“进一步同意”的措辞针对一条重要的条文(如价格)是可能会令合约不存在,原因是不肯定。这原则就是不能协议将来达成的协议。第三,同样的,即使双方没有说明“进一步同意”,但一条重要的条文还没有达成协议,也可以令合约不存在,原因也是不肯定。第四,但是,在有经验的商业人士之间,特别是他们在相信已经有一份有约束力的合约的基础上行事的情况下,法院愿意尽量在双方没有约定的方面以默示条文加以补充,以便让双方履行该合约。第五,如果一个有效合约已经达成,即便针对将来尚未发生的事情有“进一步同意”的措辞,也不一定会对合约的继续存在与有效性有致命的影响。第六,特别是针对一个比较长期的合约,双方希望或需要把一些问题留待将来调整或通过谈判同意,法院会尽量帮助双方,以保证双方的交易被保留而不是被破坏。第七,尤其是其中一方已经在该合约下取得了一些好处，或其中一方已经根据该合约作出了一些投资/投入。第八，为了支持合约，如果有条文规定公平合理的做法或价格，法院就已经足够可以作出协助。但就算没有明示条文，法院也可以默示什么是合理或公平。第九，这种默示的做法在立法也有部分反映，如1979年《货物销售法》之8.2条说："Where the price is not determined... the buyer must pay a reasonable price"。第十，如果双方已经同意了一条仲裁条文，法院就更加会判已经足够肯定有一个合约或已经有机制令尚未同意的部分变得肯定，因为有了仲裁员作为相关领域的专家，双方对没有同意的争议可以通过仲裁员的帮助解决。

英国法院在近期案例中作出的解释看来会受中方当事人的欢迎，因为中方当事人特别喜欢强调善意。例如，中国的造船案件在伦敦仲裁中大量败诉，几乎全军覆没。中国船厂极可能感觉西方买方的不善意或恶意，因为西方买方是在2008年金融海啸航运市场暴跌的情况下逃避一些高价的造船合约。伦敦仲裁庭判西方买方胜诉就显示了根本不考虑善意。所以，如果英国法律改变一贯的立场支持善意条文的有效性，会否如果在将来的造船合约加上一条广泛的善意条文就会令目前全面败诉的情况有所改变，伦敦仲裁庭会否有不同的决定？笔者认为不会，正如在本书多处提到，英国法律还是重视合约尤其是商业合约的肯定性，不会像中国《合同法》下法院或仲裁庭可以改变或撤销合约。如果合约中有条文明示针对，如在造船合约中的"死亡日期"（drop dead date）或"销约期"（canceling date）条文，则过了这个时间船厂还交不了船，买方或船东就可以选择终止合约并拿回已付的分期预付款及利息。即使有这一条广泛的善意条文，法院或仲裁庭也不会漠视或扭曲特定明示条文的规定。但如果延误导致在死亡日期前交不了船是因买方或船东的不合作或阻挠所造成，通常在造船合约中也会有其他的明示条文（如针对买方延误支付分期预付款等）或默示条文（如本书第七章之13段的介绍）针对某些特定的情况。

但这并不是说摆这一广泛的善意条文毫无用处，如本书第十一章之第5段介绍的"妨碍原则"（prevention principle），就有可能在因买方或船东的行为导致延误的情况下适用。但在 Adyard Abu Dhabi v SD Marine Services （2011） EWHC 848 先例，Hamblen 大法官说如果造船合约中有明示条文针对，妨碍原则的默示地位或条文就不适用。而中国船厂在伦敦仲裁中，经常提出妨碍原则作为诉因或抗辩，也经常败诉，原因是大部分伦敦仲裁员认为造船合约已经有明示条文针对（即通常被称为不可抗力条文中的兜底的一句"any other causes beyond the control of the shipyard"）的情况下妨碍原则不适用，但笔者并不认同这样的解释。〔4〕如果船东的妨碍也是不可抗力条文中的事项之一，中国船厂必须要作出通知，才能享有延长交船日期的权利。但中国船厂通常不会作出通知，特别是船东可能会作出千变万化的妨碍行为，船厂更

〔4〕 笔者的少数意见或看法应该已经受到英国法院的支持，虽然还是在其他方面判中国船厂败诉，这可看本书第六章之第14段。

加无从通知。这样,如果另有一条善意条文,中国船厂就可以通过买方违反该条文的替代诉因要求同样的救济,估计买方或船东就很难以 Adyard Abu Dhabi v SD Marine Services 先例中的理由开脱。

但要证明买方或船东违反善意条文,还是要满足他是主观不诚实与客观不理性的要求。所以,还是避免不了有证据甚至是非常充分的证据(特别是文件证据)说服仲裁庭。证据是中国船厂甚至大部分中方当事人的弱项,就算能证明对方违反了善意条文,下一步还要证明对方违约所造成的后果,如有否造成延误与延误多久。这又涉及另一个问题,就是中国船厂很少有详细的全局计划,更不用说有"关键路径分析"(critical path analysis)。[5] 所以,解决这个困局的正途还是普遍提高中国船厂的管理水平与加强对英国法律的理解(毕竟是同意了伦敦仲裁)。

---

〔5〕 这方面可看本书第十一章之4.7段。

第十章 时间规定重要

§1 概述与历史

合约“时间规定”(time provision)在履行合约十分重要,因为很大部分的违约实际上就是涉及延误。这延误可能短暂也可能漫长,有时更会经年累月也不履行。但直到延误方向无辜方以文字或行动说明不再履行,可以说延误方的违约在本质上还是停留在延误。英国法律针对合约履行中的时间规定是否属于“保证条文”(warranty)或是“条件条文”(condition)是十分重要与复杂的问题。如果是前者,违约方如果错过了规定时间,履行后果往往并不严重,如延误支付一笔金钱就会有利息损失,这在今天低息的环境下,要违约方赔偿这笔利息不会是太大的阻吓力。事实上,很多不同的延误都不会带来损失而只带来不便,或是有严重损失(如延误支付导致无辜方无法完成另一个交易)也很难证明与被视为“遥远”(remoteness)。损失难以证明也是很多合约中喜欢约定以“议定赔偿”(liquidated damages)针对某种特定的延误的原因,如在国际货物买卖合约与程租合约中就普遍约定“滞期费”(demurrage)针对装卸货物对船舶延误的赔偿。但如果是后者的条件条文,违约方如果错过了规定时间履行会构成“违约/毁约”(repudiation),除了会带来金钱损失索赔外,有关合约也会被无辜方终止。这往往是一个强而有力的阻吓力,因为不少违约方(针对一些合约中可能有许多承诺的履行以及它们的明示/默示时间规定)实际上并不想让该合约终止。而这个额外的权利(就是可以选择终止合约)对无辜方却经常会有莫大的好处,也就是可以合法在一个合约中脱身。这种情况经常会出现,如无辜方再也不想与违约方打交道,因为找到更好的机会或对象。这种情况更加会出现在十分波动的市场,就是如果市场在订立合约后上扬,甚至没有上扬但普遍对市场的长短前景看好,都会导致无辜方想从较早订立的合约中合法脱身。

在英国普通法院与衡平法院还没有根据《Supreme Court of Judicature Act 1873》合并之前,两个法院对合约中时间规定有不同的看法与对待。简单说,合约(尤其是土地买卖合约)中对时间的规定一般来说会被普通法院视为条件条文,必须严格遵守。但衡平法院对此有不同的看法(如判抵押品在超过合约规定的偿还日期后仍可以赎回)。合并两个法院的原因之一,就是希望避免这种分歧。这在United Scientific Holdings Ltd v Burnley BC (1978) AC 904先例,Simon勋爵的判决中有介绍,说:

“This can only be interpreted by bearing in mind that the object of Section 25 of the Supreme Court of Judicature Act 1873 was to reconcile the differences between common law and equity so that the two systems (together with the admiralty, testamentary and matrimonial) could form a single coherent code.”

看来普通法院与衡平法院合并后是衡平法院的观点占上风。在《Supreme Court of Judicature Act 1873》之 Section 25 (7) 就是针对所有法院对时间规定要统一,说:“Stipulations in contracts, as to time or otherwise, which would not before the passing of this Act have been deemed to be or to have become of the essence of such contracts in a Court of Equity, shall receive in all courts the same construction and effect as they would have heretofore received in equity.”

这立法条文已经被《Property Act 1925》之 Section 41 所替代,说:“Stipulations in a contract, as to time or otherwise, which according to the rules of equity are not deemed to be or to have become of the essence of the contract, are also construed and have effect at law in accordance with the same rules.”

在普通法院与衡平法院合并后,英国法律对合约的时间规定还是继续在发展,而且变得十分精细与复杂,并开始适用在所有的合约关系中。这一过程在 United Scientific Holdings Ltd v Burnley BC 先例,Simon 勋爵有提到说:“But the fused law has continued to evolve since 1875; and it has developed a more sophisticated approach to contractual terms: see Wallis, Son & Wells v. Pratt & Haynes [1910] 2 K. B. 1003, 1012; Hongkong Fir Shipping Co. Ltd. v. Kawasaki Kisen Kaisha Ltd. [1962] 2 Q. B. 26, especially the judgment of Diplock L. J.; Wickman Machine Tool Sales Ltd. v. L. Schuler A. G. [1974] A. C. 235, 264 – 265. The law may well come to inquire whether a contractual stipulation as to time is (a) so fundamental to the efficacy of the contract that any breach discharges the other party from his contractual obligations ('essence'), or (b) such that a serious breach discharges the other party, a less serious breach giving a right to damages (if any) (or interest), or (c) such that no breach does more than give a right to damages (if any) (or interest) ('non – essential'). If this sort of analysis falls to be made, I see no reason why any type of contract should, because of its nature, be excluded.”

Simon 勋爵也同意《Halsbury's Laws of England》(第 4 版,1973 年至 1987 年)对这方面的总结,说:“In my view the modern law in the case of contracts of all types is correctly summarised in Halsbury's Laws of England, 4th ed., vol. 9, para. 481, p. 338: 'Time will not be considered to be of the essence unless: (1) thc parties expressly stipulate that conditions as to time must be strictly complied with; or (2) the nature of the subject matter of the contract or the surrounding circumstances show that time should be considered to be of the essence; ...'”(这是说针对时间规定的现代法律地位,在

《Halsbury's Laws of England》一书的总结就是时间不视为重要,除非:合约规定是重要;合约的性质与周边环境显示时间是重要。)

§2 目前英国法律对合约中时间规定的地位

这一重要的问题可以先节录权威的《Halsbury's Laws of England》(第5版,2008年至2012年)与《Halsbury's Laws of Hong Kong》(第2版,2011年)中对目前英国法律地位的同样总结写法:"The current law, in the case of contracts of all types, may be summarized as follows. Time will not be considered to be of the essence unless: (1) the parties expressly stipulate that conditions as to time must be strictly complied with; or (2) the nature of the subject matter of the contract or the surrounding circumstances show that time should be considered to be of the essence; or (3) a party who has been subjected to unreasonable delay gives notice to the party in default making time of the essence."[时间规定不被视为是重要,除非:(1) 合约明示规定时间必须严格遵守;(2) 合约的本质或周边的环境显示了时间规定应该被视为重要;(3) 一方当事人面对对方不合理的延误作出了通知给违约的对方,规定一段合理时间说明是重要与必须遵守。](可以看到这与上一段引用的第4版《Halsbury's Laws of England》是一致说法。)

换言之,时间规定的延误是否是违反条件条文让无辜方有权终止合约主要是看该时间规定是否"重要"(of essence)。而只有三种办法可以令时间规定变为重要,一是"明示"(express words),二是"默示"(by implication),三是通过作出通知使得时间变为重要。

上述显示了英国普通法的起点再也不是把合约的时间规定视为重要,也就是大部分的规定都不会被视为条件条文,一旦违反(也就是延误履行合约的承诺)就可以让无辜方终止合约。无辜方如果贸然终止合约,反而会构成违约/毁约。介绍一个著名的上诉庭先例 Decro – Wall International SA v Practitioners in Marketing Ltd (1971) 1 WLR 361,案情涉及经常会起纠纷的争议,也就是被告多次迟付账单长达3个星期,但法院判是这并不能让原告终止合约。因为一般性的延误作出支付不被视为重要,即使违反了无辜方也只能向违约方索赔损失,这损失往往就是一些在今天低息的环境下微不足道的利息。

简单介绍,上述总结的第一种情况就是通过订约自由双方明确在合约中约定时间必须严格遵守,条文甚至会把不遵守的后果写明。这种明示条文作出规定的例子不胜枚举,对航运界人士十分熟悉的就是期租合约的租金支付,这是船东十分关心的大事,承租人必须准时作出支付。但由于现代法律的地位,就需要以明示条文针对。在著名与最广泛使用的标准格式 NYPE 有关条文是规定一旦迟延支付,船东就可以撤船:"Failing the punctual and regular payment of the hire,... or on any breach of this charterparty, the owners shall be at liberty to withdraw the vessel from the service of the charterers, without prejudice to any claim they [the owners] may otherwise have on the charterers."

有了这样的明示规定,就不必理会法律的默示地位,也就是承租人迟延支付租金到底是违反保证条文或是条件条文的区分再也不重要。毕竟,法律的地位总比不上合约明示条文的肯定,虽然近期有了 The "Astra" (2013) 2 Lloyd's Rep 69 先例说准时支付租金是条件条文,但这只是第一审,加上 Flaux 大法官判的理由会有争议性,所以该先例的权威性与约束性还要看进一步的发展。

在一个期租合约还涉及租金以外的其他支付,如承租人要补偿船东因船舶被指令战区或冰封地区的额外保费,这会是一笔数额颇大的金钱。但已有一些先例说明 NYPE 的有关条文只针对租金的准时支付,而没有明确针对期租合约其他的支付。在 The "Tropwind" (No.1) (1977) 1 Lloyd's Rep 397 先例,Kerr 大法官说:"But in my view any businessmen reading this clause, while of course realizing that any delay in paying the hire gives rise to the right of withdrawal, would be astonished to be told that any delay in making some other payment which might become due is also covered by these general words. If this had been the intention, then the requirement of punctual payment could easily have been widened so as to include all sums which might become due, as well as the payment of hire."

这个问题后来也有另一个上诉庭先例 The "Laconia" (1977) 1 Lloyd's Rep 315 的多数意见是认同 The "Tropwind"先例的观点。也表示了一般性的支付,如果没有明确的明示条文针对,延误不会重要,违反的也只是保证条文。

第二种情况也是要看法律的默示地位,如合约的本质如果是"商业合约"(mercantile contract),就为了商业的肯定性(让商业人士在出事情时明确知道他的法律地位与怎样做才是安全)与有关的市场经常会是有快速与激烈的波动,时间规定就往往被视为重要,也就是条件条文,履约双方必须严格遵守。这也在《Halsbury's Laws of Hong Kong》(第2版,2011年)一书之115.298段有说明:"Apart from express agreement or notice making time of the essence, the court will require precise compliance with stipulations as to time wherever the circumstances of the case indicate that this would fulfill the intention of the parties. Broadly speaking, time will be considered of the essence in 'mercantile' contracts and in other cases where the nature of the contract or of the subject matter or the circumstances of the case require precision compliance."

除了合约的本质,还要看有关时间规定的周边环境决定它是否重要。这种例子也有不少,如针对提供担保或定金。这种条文即使没有明确规定它是条件条文,也明显很重要。往往是为了给另一方也就是无辜方对合约将来的履行一定的保障或让他安心,这个重要因素没有办法以金钱量化。如果违约方延误提供担保或定金,无辜方也无法索赔任何损失。因为如果最终交易完成,违约方较早时有否提供担保也变得无关重要。这样,对违约方不及时提供担保或定金唯一可以产生阻吓力的就是把它视为条件条文,一旦违约就会导致无辜方有权终止有关合约。这种先例有不少,如在涉及二手船舶买卖的 The "Selene G" (1981) 2 Lloyd's Rep 180 先例,Goff 大法官判是不提供 10% 的保证金是违反了条件条文,属于违约/毁约,说:"It seems to me quite plain that, in accordance with what I understand to be the ordinary effect of a requirement in a contract for payment of a deposit, the intention was that the payment of the deposit should be made within 48 hours, and if that was not done the seller, would not have got the security for the buyers' performance to which he was entitled. And not having received that security for performance of the contract, he would be entitled to say: 'I can now call this transaction off and let my ship be sold elsewhere'. So I hold that the construction of the contract for which the sellers contend is right."

之后在 The "Blankenstein" (1985) 1 Lloyd's Rep 93 先例,上诉庭的 Fox 大法官说:"支付保证金在一份约束性合约是基本条文"(payment of the deposit... was in my view a fundamental term of a concluded contract)。

同样的情况也出现在针对索赔时效的规定,一旦错过,就会导致丧失索赔的权利。针对这种条文,以前会有比较严格的要求,以保障想提出索赔的合约方不会轻易错过这个时间规定(特别会有不少时间规定是一段很短暂的时间),这种写法最好的代表就是 1924 年《海牙规则》之 Article 3(6),说:"In any event the carrier and the ship shall be discharged from all liability in respect of loss or damage unless suit is brought within one year after delivery of the goods or the date when the goods should have been delivered."

也就是必须说明错过时效或时间规定的严重后果。但近期的先例已经趋向宽松解释,认为双方在订约时约定条文针对提起索赔的时效,只能是为了这一后果,不可能再会有其他解释。这表示任何想提起索赔的合约方必须对这种条文十分警觉,否则一旦错过就后果严重。

第三种情况针对两个方面,第一方面是合约对时间的规定只属于保证条文,但对方延误履行他的承诺,导致无辜方变得十分被动。即使他能够索赔损失,但证明不了或在今天的低息环境下不会有太多损失,而诉讼的延误与费用都不值得。第二方面合约对时间的规定属于条件条文(不论明示或默示),但无辜方面对违约方的违约做出了弃权的言行。这种情况经常会发生,如属于商业合约中的国际货物买卖,针对支付货款往往是通过信用证并通常会规定买方必须开出信用证的时间,这时间的规定(不论明示或者默示)明确属于条件条文。但买方的这种违约,也就是延误履行他开出信用证的承诺,往往是发生在有关的市场下挫,导致买方不愿意履行的情况。既然是条件条文,无辜方的卖方就有了比保证条文多的一个权利,就是索赔损失外还可以终止合约。但卖方通常不愿意贸然终止合约,而会想尽办法说服或威胁买方履行,即使已经错过了时间规定。这种言行往往被法律视为卖方弃权,也就是放弃了可以终止合约的权利,毕竟他说服或威胁买方履行的言行与终止合约的意图相违背。买方的确也有可能被说服或吓倒履行并开出信用证。但如果买方不被说服或吓倒,而市场还是不断下挫,总会到卖方觉得无望或是找到其他的替代买方的地步,决定终止合约。但这样,卖方就要十分小心,他如果想恢复原来拥有但已经被放弃了的权利,也就是终止合约,他就必须先向违约的买方作出通知,否则变为他自己违约/毁约。这方面在本章第5.3段有介绍。

本章以下会对这三种情况分别进行更详尽的介绍。

§3 第一种情况:合约明示时间规定重要(expressed to be of essence)

3.1 对时间规定解释的大原则

在订约自由下,双方显然可以把他们在一个合约中针对哪些他们认为重要或者比较重要的履行约定为"重要"(of essence),是属于条件条文。由于每个合约都会有不同的写法(除非只使用一些标准格式并且没有作出任何改动),所以还是避免不了会有争议。大道理还是法院或者仲裁庭会根据本书的合约解释的大原则客观作出解释以找出双方的"订约意图"(contractual intention)。所以在本书第一章所讲的一些近期的先例如 Charter Reinsurance Co Ltd v. Fagan (1997) AC 313;Mannai Investments Co Ltd v. Eagle Star Life Assurance Co Ltd (1997) A. C. 749;Investors Compensation Scheme v. West Bromwich Building Society (1998) 1 W. L. R. 896;BCCI v. Ali (2001) 1 UKHL 8, (2002) 1 AC 251;The "Starsin" (2003) 1 Lloyd's Rep. 571 与 Rainy Sky SA and others v Kookmin Bank (2012) 1 Lloyd's Rep 34 都适用。

为了方便阅读,不妨再部分重复一些经典的说法。在 Bentsen v Taylor Sons & Co (1893) 2 QB 274 先例,上诉庭的 Bowen 大法官说:"There is no way of deciding that question except by looking at the contract in the light of the surrounding circumstances, and then making up one's mind whether the intention of the parties, as gathered from the instrument itself, will best be carried out by treating the promise as a warranty sounding only in damages, or as a condition precedent by the failure to perform which the other party is relieved of his liability."

另在 BCCI v. Ali 先例,Bingham 勋爵是这样说:"To ascertain the intention of the parties the court reads the terms of the contract as a whole, giving the words their ordinary meaning in the context of the agreement the parties' relationship and all the relevant facts surrounding the transaction as far as known to the parties. To ascertain the parties' intentions the court does not of course enquire into the parties' subjective states of mind but makes an objective judgment based on the materials already identified."

最后是 Rainy Sky SA and others v Kookmin Bank 先例,Clarke 勋爵说:"Where the parties have used unambiguous language, the court must apply it."

这表示如果双方能够做到以清楚无误,不能有另一种解释的文字显示双方的订约意图,说明某个时间规定是重要,法院或仲裁庭也就只能这样解释,不应该再质疑或猜测双方的订约意图。但问题是在一个复杂的合约中不容易做到,特别是解释合约时法院或仲裁庭还需要整体看,表示即使针对时间规定的文字清楚无误,也会与合约的其他条文有矛盾而导致订约意图受到质疑甚至是"歪曲"(distort)的判决/裁决。

还有一些解释合约的精神也需要掌握,特别是针对延误。一是法院或仲裁庭一般的倾向是支持合约的有效性,不会想太容易让合约终止。在 The "Hansa Nord" (1975) 2 Lloyd's Rep 445 先例有一句名言:"Contracts are made to be performed and not to be avoided"。这表示只要能够找到一个合理解释回避(即使是表面看起来清楚明确的规定),有不少法官或仲裁员不愿意把时间规定视为条件条文。而且,已经在《Halsbury's Laws of England》(第 5 版, 2008 年至 2012 年)中介绍过,目前英国法律地位针对时间规定的起点是假设时间规定并非重要(time will not be considered to be of the essence, unless...)。

第二是解释合约,通常是太广泛与太苛刻的条文不会获得支持。例如,合约有一条条文说明"本合约的准时履行视为重要",通常都不会获得支持。这是因为一个复杂的合约双方会有无数完全不同性质的承诺要履行。这些履行即使没有明示的时间规定,也免不了有默示规定(合理时间)。很难想象双方会有一个订约意图就是让该条文把每个明示或默示的时间规定都视为重要,一旦有轻微的延误,就可让其中一方从一个昂贵的合约中脱身。Harman 大法官在 Bovis Homes Inc. v. Oakcliff Investment Corp., Ch D, 30 March 1994 先例中说:"In considering whether time is of the essence of a term in a contract the Court must bear in mind the nature of the obligations imposed by the term. If the term requires a single act to be done it is easier to conclude that the time for doing the required act may be of the essence of the term."

第三是理解明示或默示的时间规定的本质,这是与合约其他的承诺很不一样。原因是两个方面,第一方面就是在较早时已经提到履行的延误与其他的承诺被违反很不一样,就是很难或比较难作出补救与量化为金钱损失。正如,西方人所讲的一句话"you cannot turn the clock back"。举一个例子,在笔者的《损失赔偿与救济》一书第十五章之 3.1 段有介绍国际货物买卖中常见的恶行,就是 CIF/CFR 卖方错过了最后付运期(这是条件条文),但通过"倒签提单"(back - dated bill of lading)瞒骗买方他的付运是准时按合约履行。这种倒签通常不会涉及很长的时间,往往只有一两天。由于本质上倒签提单就是涉及对付运期规定的延误,所以损失往往也只是这一两天市场价格的差别。但在这么短暂的时间有许多市场往往不会有波动,也表示了这个延误的违约虽然是欺诈性与严重,但没有给买方带来任何的实质损失。这正是 Taylor v Bank of Athens (1922) 27 Com Cas 142 先例的判法。但到了 Finlay (James) & Co v Kwik Hoo Tong Handel Maatschappij (1929) 1 KB 400 先例,总算找到了另一个缺口,判卖方倒签提单不只是延误付运,还有另一个诉因是剥夺了买方可以拒绝这套付运单证(如果没有倒签)的权利。这样,损失就可能很大而不仅是倒签的一两天的市场差价,并带来了一定程度的公平公正针对这种恶行。

相比延误的违约,其他性质的承诺被违反,作出补救与量化为金钱损失就相对容易得多。例如,违约方对无辜方造成财产(不论是货物、房屋、船舶等)的损坏,无辜方的补救就是修复损坏并索赔修理的费用与时间损失。如果损坏严重而需要市场购买或建造另一个替代,补救的办法与计算金钱的损失也是相对容易。

第二个方面是时间规定不像其他性质的合约承诺,违约的后果只有一个,就是造成延误。但其他的合约承诺的违约会带来千变万化的后果,这样针对其他性质的合约承诺,就比较难解释一经违反,不论是如何轻微与没有造成什么后果,都可以让无辜方终止合约。这样,加上第一方面的原因也就是金钱损失很难计算,就会导致有倾向接受时间规定的违反唯一恰当的后果就是允许无辜方终止合约。否则很难接受双方约定一些针对特定合约承诺履行的时间规定,但同时是没有意图在违约时获得救济。

这也可以解释国际货物买卖合约与租约经常有的一条条文,就是要求 FOB 买方或船东派遣一艘"适航"(seaworthy)的船舶装港并在某一天"备妥装货"(ready to load)。但同一句话内的两个承诺需要船东履行,针对前者的履行法院判并非是条件条文而是中间条文,[1]而针对后者的履行则判是条件条文。[2]

这表示有关合约的条文只要相对明确约定时间规定是重要,加上延误造成金钱损失不易计算,无辜方会比其他类别的违约更容易说服法院或仲裁庭有关规定的恰当解释应该是属于条件条文,可让无辜方终止合约。

3.2　不同写法的明示规定

以下逐一针对合约中惯常的写法,虽然也只能是看很片面的部分,因为还可能会涉及整个合约整体的解释。

3.2.1　时间规定重要

合约中如果对时间规定明示是重要,看来是万无一失,会被解释为条件条文。如果其中一方合约方迟延履行,另一方就可以视为违反了条件条文,并接受对方的违约/毁约终止合约。无辜方无须理会到底迟了多少时间,因为条件条文不会再区分轻

---

〔1〕在 The "Hongkong Fir" (1961) 2 Lloyd's Rep 478 先例,贵族院判船舶适航的违反只是违反了中间条文,无辜方不能终止合约。

〔2〕这方面有许多先例,只一提比较近期的著名先例 The "Mihalis Angelos" (1970) 2 Lloyd's Rep 43。该先例中租约说明船是"now trading and expected ready to load about 1st July",另外订有销约期是 7 月 20 日。这 7 月 1 日的估计可装货日期根本是错的,船实际上 7 月 7 日才抵达装港。注意此时销约期仍未过,但承租人没有货可装,所以终止租约。高院判这估计可装货日期只是中间条文,但上诉庭不同意,认为是条件条文,承租人可因此终止租约,即使销约期未过。

微或严重。Mustill 大法官在 Lombard North Central plc v Butterworth (1987) QB 527 先例中说:"A stipulation that time is of the essence, in relation to a particular contractual terms, denotes that timely performance is a condition of the contract. The consequence is that delay in performance is treated as going to the root of the contract, without regard to the magnitude of the breach... A clause expressly assigning a particular obligation to the category of condition is not a clause which purports to fix the damages for breaches of the obligation, and is not subject to the law governing penalty clauses."

另作出主要判决的 Nicholls 大法官说:"I must now consider a further submission advanced by the plaintiffs that, time of payment having been made of the essence by this provision, it was open to the plaintiffs, once default in payment of any one instalment on the due date had occurred, to treat the agreement as having been repudiated by the defendant, and claim damages for loss of the whole transaction, even though in the absence of this which arises is one of construction: on the true construction of this clause, did the 'time of the essence' provision have the effect submitted by the plaintiffs? In my view, the answer to this question is 'Yes'."

但在较早时也已经提到,如果广泛说是合约内针对任何性质承诺的时间规定都是重要,就往往不会获得法院或仲裁庭的支持。因为这不大像是双方的订约意图让任何轻微的延误都可以终止合约。Browne – Wilkinson 法官在 British & Commonwealth Holdings Plc v Quadrex Holdings Inc (1989) Q. B. 842 先例中说"合约内的时间规定重要"(time being of the essence of the contract)的说法有误导性,应该只是针对某个特定的时间规定才会是重要。Browne – Wilkinson 大法官的说法可节录如下:"The basic question is whether the failure to comply with a contractual provision within the time limited by the contract constitutes a repudiation of the contract i. e. is time of the essence of that contractual provision. The phrase 'time is of the essence of the contract' is capable of causing confusion since the question in each case is whether time is of the essence of the particular contractual term which has been breached... There is therefore no general concept that time is of the essence of a contract as a whole: the question is whether time is of the essence of a particular term in question."

例如在本章之第 2 段已经提到在期租合约下,根据英国法律的默示地位准时支付租金并不重要,所以 NYPE 标准格式期租合约要明示加上承租人延误支付租金会给船东撤船的选择权。但在 The "Mahakam" (2012) 1 Lloyd's Rep 87 先例,该光租租约有条文明示规定准时支付租金是"重要"(shall be of essence)。这导致 Eder 大法官判是针对这一特定的履行(也就是支付租金)的时间规定,被提升为条件条文,承租人延误支付构成违约/毁约。

3.2.2 时间规定是条件条文

这也会是经常见到的写法,但比较危险与不可靠。原因是英文的"condition"在文件/合约中会有很多解释,也经常被滥用。例如,有许多合约会在抬头写"terms and conditions",甚至只写"conditions",然后写下一大堆条文根本与承诺性条件条文甚至是保证条文毫无关系。另外更重要的是在本书第五章之6.4段讲到的L Schuler AG v. Wickman Machine Tool Sales Ltd (1973) 2 Lloyd's Rep. 53先例,简单重复一下在该先例中代理合约有第7(b)条文如下:"It shall be a condition of this agreement that Wickman shall send its representatives to visit the six firms whose names are listed in the Schedule hereto at least once in every week for the purpose of soliciting orders for panel presses."(Wickman必须派遣营业代表每周走访6家工厂,目的是招揽panel presses的订单,这是本合约下的条件。)

贵族院判是如果把第7(b)条文当作是条件条文,Wickman只要少了1次走访,Schuler就可以终止合约太不合理,因为合约太容易被终止了。毕竟,该合约也没有其他条文针对指定营业代表如果死亡、退休或者生病,或交通、天气等妨碍而不能走访应该如何履行才不会导致合约被终止。

L Schuler AG v. Wickman Machine Tool Sales Ltd先例虽然不是针对时间规定而是其他方面的合约履行,但可想而知仅仅把时间规定写作"condition"并希望被接受为条件条文,是不安全与不可靠的。

另也可以节录The "Varenna" (1983) 2 Lloyd's Rep 592先例,Donaldson大法官也说这一个文字好像变色龙,根据周边不同的环境而有不同的解释(a chameleon - like word which takes on its meaning from surroundings)。

3.2.3 写明违反时间规定的后果

这看来是比较安全与可靠的写法,也经常在合约中见到与在无数的先例中被接受。毕竟,如果以一句话而不是简单的一两个字说明违反的后果,即使是怀有敌意的法院或仲裁庭,也无法为这句话找出另一个可以说得通的解释,除非漠视(但这是英国法律所不接受的,因为双方的约定必须要给一个合理解释),变为唯一的选择就是给这一句话字面表达的解释。

3.2.3.1 写明有选择权可终止合约

通常的做法是规定如果发生某种延误的违约,甚至不严格是违约的某种情况,另一方有 可终止合约的"选择权"(option)。

例如在租船合约中,就经常会有一条"销约期条文"(cancelling clause)说明船舶如果不在某一天,也就是销约期之前抵达装港,承租人可以终止租约。例如,在中国大陆经常被使用的程租合约标准格式Gencon 1994之第9条规定:"Should the Vessel not be ready to load (whether in berth or not) on the cancelling date... the Charterers shall have the option of cancelling this Charter Party."

在期租合约,针对租金准时的支付也有一条明确的写明违反的后果条文,这在本章较早前也已经提到。这个条文在NYPE标准格式中在较早时节录过,这里就不再重复。这里可以节录另一份油轮经常使用的标准格式Shelltime 4,其中在第9条文有同样精神但写法不同:"In default of such proper and timely payment:(a) Owners shall notify Charterers of such default and Charterers shall within seven days of receipt of such notice pay to Owners the amount due, including interest, failing which Owners may withdraw the vessel from the service of Charterers without prejudice to any other rights Owners may have under this charter or otherwise; ..."

这种写法是明确说明发生延误情况的后果,而延误会是涉及违约与否:More v The Demise Charterers of the Ship "Jotunheim" (2005) 1 Lloyd's Rep 181。例如,延误在销约期之前抵达装港,原因会是船舶不适航导致装港的航次中发生事故、或船舶不合理"绕航"(deviation)等违约的原因所造成。但也可能是其他不涉及违约的原因,如坏天气、船舶碰撞或搁浅(这种航行疏忽在租约中往往是可以免责)等原因造成延误。同样的道理也适用在承租人延误支付租金,如果是承租人自己资金的问题或员工疏忽,这显然是违约造成延误。但如果是有关政府的干预或严重天灾导致汇款延误,这又会是不涉及违约的原因。这方面的问题在本章之3.2.3.6段讲的"分叉原则"(The Bifurcated Principle)有进一步探讨,换言之是无辜方可以根据合约对发生延误情况的后果终止合约,但如果有额外的损失想向延误方索赔,就必须根据普通法先证明延误方的延误是违约的原因所造成。

3.2.3.2　造船合约中写明延误的后果

在造船合约(与其他的工程合约)会涉及无数合约承诺要履行,针对其中重要的履行,也会有条文明确规定延误的后果。在中国大陆普遍适用的日本标准造船合约格式(SAJ Form),就有条文说明如果在约定交船时间后的一段期限(180天、210天不等,完全看双方谈判),船厂还不能交船,卖方有权终止合约,也就是拒船。这一段期限的最后一天也通常被称为"死亡日期"(drop dead date)或销约期。这在SAJ Form中是Article VIII:

"**4. Right to Rescind for Excessive Delay** If the total accumulated time of all delays on account of the causes specified in Paragraph 1 of this Article, excluding delays of a nature which under the terms of this Contract permit postponement of the Delivery Date, amounts to Two Hundred and Ten (210) days or more, then, in such event, the BUYER may rescind this Contract..."

另是更近期的2007年NEWBUILDCON标准造船合约格式,第39条文写的更明确,说:"... The Buyer shall have the right to terminate this contract forthwith upon giving notice in the event that: ... the delivery of the Vessel is delayed by more than 180 days..."

造船合约对另一个重要承诺的延误履行的后果也有了明确,这就是买方的分期付款(预付船价)。显然,"现金流"(cashflow)对船厂十分重要,因为在建造船舶的过程中,有大量使费需要支付,包括工人的工资、物料/设备等的购买等。所以在SAJ Form中,针对买方如果在规定时间后15天内支付,只需要加上利息。但如果超过15

天，有关的条文是："If any default by the BUYER continues for a period of fifteen (15) days, the BUILDER may, at its option, rescind this Contract by giving notice of such effect to the BUYER by cable confirmed in writing. Upon receipt by the BUYER of such notice of rescission, this Contract shall forthwith become null and void and any of the BUYER's Supplies shall become the sole property of the BUILDER. In the event of such rescission of this Contract, the BUILDER shall be entitled to retain any Installment or Installments therefore paid by the BUYER to the BUILDER on account of this contract."

最后一提是这样的写法也可以显示了造船合约（或其他工程合约）没有同样针对的时间规定（明示或默示）是不会被视为重要。这也是解释合约的其中一条规定（rules of construction），就是拉丁语的 *Expressio unius exclusio alterius*，而英文就是"A canon of construction holding that to express or include one thing implies the exclusion of the other, or of the alternative"。

3.2.3.3　写明延误作出滞期费通知的后果

在国际货物买卖合约，也经常有时间规定要求另一方作出通知。在本章多处提到，在国际货物买卖合约中针对通知或指定的时间规定通常或起点是视为"重要"（of essence）或条件条文。笔者在这里与下一小段针对两种经常会引起争议的通知的要求。

第一种就是涉及滞期费的索赔，这显然会发生在国际货物买卖合约（或程租合约），有关的条文就是要求派遣船舶的卖/买方（或租约下的船东）在一个时间规定内向对方提出滞期费的索赔，并附上有关的文件支持。由于时间规定通常十分短暂与提出索赔的形式或附上的文件要求也十分严格，往往是陷阱重重导致派遣船舶方（或船东）防不胜防。例如像 The "Yellow Star" (2000) 2 Lloyd's Rep 637 先例的一个"船旁交货"（ex - ship）的买卖合约中的有关条文："(1) Any demurrage is due provided owners actually claim it. (2) Pro Rata quantity loaded if part cargo. (3) Rate as per charter - party. Rate AFRA to apply if vessel owned or t/c. (4) **Any claim barred if not notified duly supported by relevant documents (whereof copy of charter - party and copy of owner's demurrage claim and invoice) within 90 days from bill of lading date.**"（加黑部分是笔者的强调）

这种时间规定条文在 20 世纪 80 年代首先出现在油轮租约，时至今天已经在很多的程租合约（与国际货物买卖合约）中出现。承租人的理由是船东必须尽早通知对滞期费提出索赔并提供完整的资料与文件，这可以让承租人，往往是货方（可以是卖方或是买方）马上在有关的港口作出调查或向买卖的对方提出同样的索赔或要求补偿。而如果时间拖长了，就会令承租人面对困难。这种条文也后来扩展到干货轮的程租合约（与国际货物买卖合约）中的装卸时间与滞期费条文。

这种写得十分明确与苛刻的条文导致了大量这种案例，如 The "Oltenia" (1982) 1 Lloyd's Rep 448; The "Pera" (1985) 2 Lloyd's Rep. 103; The "Medusa" (1986)

2 Lloyd's Rep. 328; OK Petroleum v. Vitol (1995) 2 Lloyd's Rep. 160; The "Bow Cedar" LMLN No. 656 (2005), The "Sabrewing" (2008) 1 Lloyd's Rep. 286; The "Eternity" (2009) 1 Lloyd's Rep. 107; The "Eagle Valencia" (2010) 2 Lloyd's Rep. 257(CA); The "Abqaiq" LMLN No. 812, 7 January 2011 等与无数的仲裁案件。

这种条文也有不少看法是有一定的商业理由,正如 Bingham 法官在 The "Oltenia" 先例中所说:"The commercial intention underlying the clause seems to me plainly to have been to ensure that claims were made by the owners within short period of final discharge so that the claim could be investigated and if possible resolved while the facts were still fresh... This object could only be achieved if the charterers were put in possession of the factual material which they required in order to satisfy themselves whether the claims were well – founded or not. I cannot regard the expression 'all available supporting documents' as in any way ambiguous: documents supporting the owners' claim on liability would of course be included, but so would a document relating to quantum only, just as a doctor's bill would be a document supporting a claim for personal injury. The owners would not, as a matter of common sense, be debarred from making factual corrections to claims presented in time... nor from putting a different legal label on a claim previously presented, but the owners are in my view shut out from enforcing a claim the substance of which and the supporting documents of which (subject always to *de minimis* exceptions) have not been presented in time."

另在 The "Sabrewing" 先例,Gloster 大法官也说:"An important commercial purpose of the demurrage time bar clauses in this case was to ensure the charterers were presented with a package of documents by owners that was sufficient in itself for them to consider (without the need for collateral investigation and, therefore, without the need to make any check of other documents received from third parties) in order to evaluate each and every part of owners' claim. .... The authorities show that parties are obliged to comply carefully and strictly with demurrage time bar clauses of this sort, which are well known within the industry."

在 The "Eagle Valencia" 先例,上诉庭的 Longmore 大法官说:"It is not unreasonable for charterers to require such a notice nor is it unreasonable to expect owners to supply it."

这种条文一般都写得十分明确,特别是没有在时间规定内作出通知的后果。正如 Longmore 大法官所说这种条文有合情合理之处,是船东(或派遣船舶的买/卖方)自己要小心不要答应太苛刻的条文(如时间规定或时效太短暂)与抓紧提出索赔。但在下一小段针对另一种的通知就会有情况是即使小心也无法及时作出。

3.2.3.4 写明延误作出货损货差通知的后果

针对货损货差也经常有国际货物买卖合约加上条文,要求买方如果在卸港发现货物损坏并向卖方提出货损货差,就必须在一个很短暂的时间规定(几天、1 个月或2 个月不等)通知卖方,否则就丧失索赔货损货差的权利。这里又涉及条文有明确规定了延误作出通知的严重后果,至于对买方会带来的困难程度要看有关的条文怎样写,特别是时间规定从什么时候起算。商品经常会在海上转卖,所以在卸货与交货后,能够发现货物损坏并需要提出货损货差索赔的经常是最后的买方或收货人。但许多中间贸易商也在其中一个合约是买方,要求他们在短暂的时间规定内向卖方提出货损货差的索赔会造成困难,因为直到最后的收货人提出前,他们并不会知道。特别是如果条文写得不好,短暂的时间规定从船舶抵达卸港或船舶卸完货就开始计算,而不是买方(中间商)知道了货损货差才起算,问题会更加严重。

此外,会有货损货差是在卸货甚至交货后较长的一段时间才会发觉。这可介绍著名的 The "Ocean Dynamic" (1982) 2 Lloyd's Rep 88 先例,案情涉及 50 吨的美国樱桃经海路运往英国,用作制作馅饼。货物包装适用箱子,不完全密封,每箱装有 30 磅的樱桃。货物装上一艘名为"Ocean Dynamic"的冷藏船,被堆装在第二货舱的底层。该船自美国开行后,先去法国的 Le Havre 卸货,再去英国的 Harwich 卸货,并把樱桃卸下。这批樱桃在 1976 年 9 月 12 日卸下,寄存在码头的冷藏库。9 月 17 日,部分的樱桃开始用冷藏货车运给收货人分销的买方的冷藏库。9 月 20 日,分销的买方开始生产。9 月 22 日,在生产线上首次发现碎玻璃。之后,发现碎玻璃越来越多,而且有很大片的,印有"Johnnie Walker"威士忌的招牌纸,显示碎玻璃来自碎酒瓶。这导致生产被迫停止,所有货物被销毁,生产线要重新清理后才能恢复生产。分销的买方损失惨重。

船东否认事故是发生在船舶运输的过程中,指卸货时如有玻璃片应可以从表面看见。而在船上时第二货舱并没有其他货物,不会有威士忌酒堆装在一起。在装卸时,也很难想象会有人故意将威士忌空酒瓶掉进第二货舱。这样,收货人就要对整个运输存储与作业过程作出调查与举证,看有否可能在其中某个环节中发生了事故。首先是在装港,船东也承认不可能在装船前已发生这种事故,只因未被发觉才签发了清洁提单。而从卸下船舶至交到生产的工厂,有几个环节:船上卸下,寄存在码头的冷藏库,冷藏货车运分销的买方的工厂。在考虑了所有的举证后,Goff 大法官根据"平衡的可能性"(balance of probability)作出判断,认为事故不是在这些环节中发生。

十分幸运的是,调查中发现了其中一块碎片附有 Johnnie Walker 威士忌的招牌纸,这提供了重要线索,经追查,这是来自一批 1974 年卖给汉堡船舶供应商的威士忌。换言之,酒瓶来自船上。此外,收货人也派人去过"Ocean Dynamic"轮的姐妹船观察它的卸货情况,发觉装卸工人在船上喝酒,边喝酒边干活,对此也有证人出庭作证。这一切综合起来,Goff 大法官根据平衡的可能性判是船员向装卸工人提供/出售廉价的免税威士忌,装卸工人在卸货时喝酒(因为带不走),之后到处乱丢空酒瓶而导致此次事故。

结果船东要负责,因为收货人举证证明了货物自船舶卸下时已发生货损。显然,在这一事实的认定下,船东是违反了《海牙规则》要求妥善与小心卸货,为此船东也没有免责条文可以依赖。

在笔者的《损失赔偿与救济》一书第十七章之7.2.3段,介绍了一个较近期的香港仲裁案件,有关的FOB买卖合约有一条条文说:"Quality discrepancy claim should be filed by the buyer within 45 days after arrival of the goods at the port of discharge. . . . "(买方应该在货物抵达卸港的45天内作出货物质量问题索赔的通知。)

在该案件,中国买方是在船舶抵达卸港后50天才通知卖方有关货物质量的问题。买方本人并没有任何拖延,因为他转售货物后是从"分买方"(sub - buyer)处得到通知后,才能马上转告卖方。这样,在后来的质量问题索赔中,卖方主要的抗辩之一就是过了45天的时效或时间规定。上述条文对买方很不利,45天是从货物抵达卸货港的一天开始计算,但这一天不代表货物是从船舶卸下。换言之,遇上卸港拥挤的情况下,可能过了45天货物还是在船舱内,买方根本没有机会对货物的质量作出检查。另一个不利之处就是买方明知道货物会转售(尤其是不少商品会多次转售),所以最后对货物的质量检查往往是来自最终的分买方,因为他才会对货物作出检查。最后笔者是判该条文并不重要,延误了5天并不影响买方的索赔货损货差权利,原因包括:(1)针对45天所用的文字是"应该"(should),这个字并非是足够决绝或肯定,这也是笔者作出买方胜诉的裁决的主要原因。(2)上述条文针对45天只要求买方作出质量问题的通知,没有要求这45天内提起仲裁等措辞。这种措辞通常会在时效条文中出现。(3)上述条文也没有说到错过45天,会有什么后果。(4)笔者也有考虑到这个延误在案件是不影响其他有关合约或一连串的合约,所以没有必要默示这个时间规定是重要。

总结本小段,中国的买方或是中间商对这个经常会面对的条文怎样拟定要很小心,要么抗拒这种条文,要么在条文的措辞是肯定自己能做到,如只需要在自己知道会要索赔货损货差后"尽快"(as soon as possible)通知卖方。

3.2.3.5　其他类别合约中写明延误的后果

在货物(包括二手船)买卖的合约中还有不少这种案例,如 NF Lantis & Co Ltd v. Kyoda Shoji (UK) Ltd (1956) 2 Lloyd's Rep 176 先例(条文说明"如果派船或交付货物受到任何原因造成的延误"[should despatch shipping or delivery of the goods or any part thereof be delayed prevented or prohibited for any cause whatsoever]卖方有权终止合约,但这条文由于太广泛而受到法院的敌视,判是卖方必须自己先拥有有关的货物,才能适用这个条文);The "Solholt" (1983) 1 Lloyd's Rep 605 CA 先例(案情涉及二手船买卖,条文针对交船的销约期,Donaldson 大法官说:"As we have already accepted as being trite law, the buyers had an unfettered right in the circumstances of this case to affirm the original contract of sale or to cancel it.");The "Al Tawfiq" (1984) 2 Lloyd's Rep 598 先例(案情与 The "Solholt"先例类似)等。

涉及土地/房屋租赁合约的先例有:Hudson v. Bartram (1818) 3 Madd 440; Doe d Dixon v. Roe (1849) 7 CB 134; Hill v. Kempsall (1849) 7 CB 134; Hughes v. Metropolitan Rly (1877) 2 App Cas 439 (HL); Birmingham and District Land Co v. London and North Western Rly (1888) 40 Ch D 268 (CA)等。

涉及租购合约的先例有: Financings Ltd v. Baldock (1963) 2 QB 104 (CA); Brady v. St. Margaret's Trust Ltd (1963) 2 QB 494 (CA); Charterhouse Credit Co v. Tolly (1963) 2 QB 683 (CA); United Dominions Trust (Commercial) Ltd. v. Ennis (1968) 1 QB 54 (CA)等。另属于保护消费者的立法《Consumer Credit Act 1974》之Sections 87 – 104 针对租用人的违约有十分详尽的规定,包括违反时间规定作出支付。

涉及土地买卖的先例有:Hudson v. Temple (1860) 54 E. R. 735; Barclay v. Messenger (1874) 43 LJ Ch 449; Mayson v. Clouet (1924) AC 980 (PC); Harold Wood Brick Co v. Ferris (1935) 2 KB 198 (CA)等。另可看《Barnsley's Conveyancing Law and Practice》(第4版, 1996年)一书第423页。

涉及建造合约的先例有:Baker v. Gray (1856) 25 LJCP 161; Re Garrud ex parte Newitt (1881) 16 Ch D 522 (CA); Hoshua Henshaw & Sons v. Rochdale Corp (1944) KB 381 (CA); Stoczia Gdanska SA v. Latvian Shipping Co (2002) 2 Lloyd's Rep 436等。另可看《Hudson's Building and Engineering Contracts》(第11版, 1995年)之第十二章与《Keating on Construction Contracts》(第8版, 2006年)之10.001 – 10.007段。

3.2.3.6　写明以选择终止合约为后果带来的分叉原则(The Bifurcated Principle)

最后一提的是,有部分合约条文写着违反时间规定的后果是让无辜方有选择权终止合约但没有同时说明(或说得不清楚)时间规定是重要提升为条件条文,就有危险是被视为终止合约纯粹是来自无辜方的选择权,毕竟原来的时间规定不是重要的条文。这对于终止合约是没有影响,但对索赔损失就会有很大的影响。这是因为在终止合约后如果还继续产生损失,就会有危险造成损失的"原因/近因"(proximate cause)或"因果关系"(causation)被指不是来自违约方违反时间规定(因为没有提升为条件条文是不足够终止合约),而是由于无辜方自己根据合约权利选择终止合约。

这个原则的先例有不少是与"租购合约"(hire – purchase contract)有关,第一个简单介绍的先例是 Overstone Ltd v Shipway (1962) 1 WLR 117,该先例涉及一辆汽车的租购合约。租方支付了73镑的定金后,以汽车有缺陷为由拒绝支付分期付款。车主取回汽车后,以265镑将转卖了汽车,并向租方索赔转卖的差价。一审法院拒绝了车主的索赔,认为车主的损失不是因为租方的违约,而是因为他自己选择取回汽车并以便宜的价格转卖。然而上诉法庭多数意见支持了车主的上诉,认为在该先例,租方不仅仅是迟付分期付款,而是清楚地表明他不会继续履行合约。因此,车主唯一合理的行动就是取回汽车并以可能的最高价格卖出。Holroyd Pearce 大法官也说,如果租方只是稍微延迟支付，但没有任何证据显示他会拒绝继续履行合约，那么车主的损失就有可能是由于他取回汽车并转卖，而不是由于租方违约/毁约。

这一点在之后的 Financings Ltd v Baldock (1963) 2 QB 104 先例有进一步发展。该先例涉及一辆小货车的租购合约，合约中明确如果有一期分期付款迟延了 10 天以上支付，车主可以选择终止合约。租方支付了定金，但没有支付前两期分期付款。当车主准备取回小货车时，租方要求多给他一点时间，并表示他很快就可以付款。事后证明租方无法很快支付这两期的分期付款，于是车主终止了合约并将小货车转卖，之后向租方索赔差价。一审法院根据 Overstone Ltd v Shipway 先例的随口意见，驳回了车主的索赔，认为在该先例的情况下车主终止合约并取回小货车的行为不合理。接着，上诉庭驳回了车主的上诉，但是根据的是不同的理由。上诉庭认为能否获得赔偿的考验并不是终止合约是否合理，关键在于在该先例租方并不存在违约/毁约，而只是车主行使了合约明示规定的终止合约的权利。在这种情况下，车主不能获得全部赔偿，而只能获得合约终止前被延误支付的分期付款。Denning 勋爵说："It seems to me that where an agreement of hiring is terminated by virtue of a power contained in it, and the owner retakes the vehicle, he can recover damages for any breach up to the date of termination but not for any breach thereafter, for the simple reason that there are no breaches thereafter."

Diplock 大法官在该先例的判决中，提到了他几年前在 The "Hongkong Fir" (1961) 2 Lloyd's Rep 478 先例的判决，讲明有选择权终止合约并不代表一定可以索赔损失，说："As I ventured to point out in Hongkong Fir Shipping Co Ltd v Kawasaki Kisen Kaisha Ltd, parties to a contract may incorporate in it provisions which expressly define the events, whether or not they amount to breaches of the contract, which are to have this result. But such a provision may do no more than define an event which of itself, or at the option of one or other of the parties, brings the contract to an end and thus relieves both parties from their undertakings further to perform their obligations thereunder. Whether it does more than this and confers any other rights or remedies on either party on the termination of the contract, depends on the true construction of the relevant provision. If it does not, then each party is left with such causes of action, if any, as had already accrued to him at the date the contract came to an end, but acquires no fresh cause of action as a result of the termination."

这方面的先例也有不少出现在航运的期租合约，船东按照租约对承租人延误支付租金所规定的后果终止租约，也就是撤船。但往往撤船时船上还有货物，需要开去卸港把它卸下。船东也不能推搪这一责任，因为租约外（这方面履行的责任已经消失），还有另一份不同对象的运输合约责任，就是承租人代表船东较早前所签发的提单（往往是运费已付提单）。如果船东不履行卸下船上的货物，就会被提单持有人的收货人起诉与扣船。这样，完成航次甚至要安排在卸港卸下货物，可能是一大笔费用。船东如果向承租人索赔,往往在因果关系方面成问题。因为如果船东不撤船,承租人肯定按照租约要继续承担有关费用(包括昂贵的燃油费、港口卸货费用等)完成航次。而承租人迟付租金的救济只是让船东索赔延误的损失,也往往就是利息。而这笔费用或损失,船东要蒙受的真正原因就是船东自己选择撤船,不存在承租人的违约(会有情况承租人迟付租金的"违约"是由租约内的免责条文的事项所造成)或违约并非是条件条文。

这方面要介绍的先例首先是 The "Tropwind" (1982) 1 Lloyd's Rep 232,Denning 勋爵针对这个问题发表了他的个人意见说:"But, if they allow the vessel to remain in the service of the charterers, fulfilling contracts of carriage which the charterers have made and the bills of lading that have been already issued, it means that those contract still subsist: and the vessel has not been withdrawn from the service of the charterers, especially when as here the owners are going half – shares in any profit made by the sub – charterers. Even if the notice of withdrawal were effective by itself without more, I cannot see any basis on which the shipowners could recover any sum from the charterers. **The charterer who is a few minutes late or pays a few dollars too little is not thereby guilty of a repudiation of the charter. The damages for such a breach would be trifling.** If there is cargo on board at the time of the notice of withdrawal – and the shipowner carries it to its destination – he does so by way of fulfilling the original charter or bill of lading – and not by way of any new request by the charterer. So he cannot recover the market rate either on a *quantum meruit* or otherwise."(加黑部分是笔者的强调)

著名的《Time Charters》(第6版,2008年)一书在分析了之前的先例后,总结说:"Despite these dicta, it is thought the better view is that the obligation to pay hire is by nature an intermediate term, so damages for the loss of the charter are recoverable only where the failure to pay hire by the due date can be shown to be repudiatory. It may be that the judicial remarks recorded above should not be understood as meaning that Clause 5 is a condition, but only that its draftsman, by adding an option to withdraw to that obligation to pay hire, has given to that obligation one characteristic of a condition, namely that any breach gives a right of termination. But uncertainty will remain until the House of Lords has shed more light on this important question."

《Time Charters》一书说较好的看法是准时支付租金属于中间条文,船东能够索赔损失就必须能证明承租人不准时支付租金是违约/毁约。最后一句是希望贵族院能够对这个重要的问题讲最后一句话,这个机会的确也很快来到。接下来就可以介绍 The "Kos" (2010) 1 Lloyd's Rep 87 先例的第一审,Andrew Smith 大法官也作出对因果关系有同样看法的判决,说:"In these circumstances, I cannot accept that the owners' claim is recoverable as damages for the failure to pay hire. I agree with the charterers' submission that, once the breach is not said to be repudiatory, it is an answer to the claim that the loss was not effectively caused by their failure to pay hire on time because the owners' decision to withdraw the vessel breaks the chain of causation."

但这个先例到了最高院被改变过来,虽然这只是多数意见,Sumption 勋爵不是针对因果关系造成损失,而是判该期租合约的"补偿条文"(indemnity clause),足够广泛针对由于承租人签发提单所带来的履行时间与费用,不论这些花费是产生在撤船前或撤船后。此外,即使是撤船,由于货物还是装在船上需要卸下,船东作为没有合约关系的"托管人"(bailee),也有权取回托管与卸下的时间与费用向委托人(也就是承租人)。他这样说:"The loss claimed by the owners was the consequence of the charterers' order to load the parcel of cargo which was on board the vessel when it was withdrawn. The need to discharge the cargo in the owners' time arose from the combination of two effective causes, namely: (i) the fact that the cargo had been loaded; and (ii) the withdrawal of the vessel. The cargo which the charterers had ordered the vessel to load was still on board when the charterparty came to an end. On any realistic view, that was because the charterers had put it there. It was true that it was only because of the withdrawal that the subsequent discharge of the cargo at Angra dos Reis had to be done in the owners' time and without earning contractual hire. But that was the very reason why the detention of the vessel fell within the indemnity. The need to discharge the cargo in their own time and at their own expense was not an ordinary incident of the chartered service and was not a risk that the owners assumed under the contract. It arose after the chartered service had come to an end in accordance with the withdrawal clause in the contract... The owners were also entitled to recover the sums claimed as non – contractual bailees of the cargo after the withdrawal of the vessel. The cargo had been originally bailed to the owners under a contract which came to an end while the cargo was still in their possession. As a matter of law the owners' obligation to look after the cargo continued notwithstanding the termination of the charterparty, and the owners had a correlative right to charge the charterers with the expenses reasonably incurred in so doing. The only reasonable or practical option open to the owners once the charterparty had come to an end was to retain the cargo until it could be discharged at the port where the vessel was then located."

最后一提的是,已经在本章之第 2 段提过 The "Astra" (2013) 2 Lloyd's Rep 69 先例说准时支付租金是条件条文,但这只是第一审,所以权威性与约束性还要看后续发展。在该先例,Flaux 大法官认为明示条文要求准时支付租金并加上了一条"反技术取巧条文"(anti – technicality clause,这条文是要求船东撤船之前必须通知承租人没有及时或足数收到租金,并让承租人在一个期限内作出补救),整体解释起来就会令时间变为重要,承租人延误支付租金就是违反条件条文。但笔者认为这个理据颇有争议性,因为反技术取巧条文是为了保护承租人,也是在承租人的坚持下才会加入期租合约，说是反而会导致准时支付租金本来不重要变为重要，提升为条件条文是说不通。针对分叉原则，也就是船东撤船的同时能否索赔损失，Flaux 大法官也有说是当前运费市场下跌，船东并非像 70、80 年代的一些著名先例是因为市场高涨取巧撤船，所以，如果不能索赔损失是不公平。但把延误支付租金作为违反条件条文，这个问题就不存在，也与分叉原则无关了。但实际上只要在期租合约把有关条文从允许船东有选择权撤船，改为 The "Mahakam" (2012) 1 Lloyd's Rep 87 先例中准时支付租金是"重要"（shall be of essence）的写法，就可以解决这个分叉原则的问题了。

总结本小段说在合约中针对不重要或不是条件条文的延误，以针对性条文加上给无辜方一个选择权终止合约，并不能明确把该延误提升为条件条文。如果发生违约，无辜方根据明示的选择权终止合约没有问题。但另想索赔终止合约所带来的损失，由于不明确是条件条文，加上因果关系的说法，就会有危险无辜方的损失就没有办法取回。

3.2.4 写明另一方的履行是取决于对方依照规定时间履行

这种写法在一些早期的先例已经有，如 Clarke v Gurnell (1611) 1 Bulst 167（写明一方支付运费是取决于准时开航的"先决条件"[condition precedent]）；Tidey v Mollett (1864) 16 CB (NS) 298（案情涉及买方约定会接受一栋房屋，但原告必须在某天之前完工，这被判是原告如果延误被告就不必接受）；Leeds and Hanley Theatre of Varieties v Broadbent (1898) 1 Ch 343（一份抵押协议约定本金在 3 年后才需要归还"但每半年支付一次的利息必须准时支付"[if in the meantime every half – yearly payment of interest shall be punctually made]，判是"if"这个字代表"取决于"，所以如果有任何延误支付利息，对方可以提早要求归还本金）。

还有其他的写法，如"subject to"（Caney v Leith [1937] 2 All ER 532; Koedding v Slaughter 634 F 2d [1980] [USCA] 等先例）与"provided that"（Kennedy v Jenkins [1909] 28 NZLR 1073 等先例）。还有一种写法是"on condition"，但近期的 Dun & Bradstreet Software Services (England) Ltd v Provident Mutual Life Assurance Association (1998) 2 EGLR 175 先例与 North Hertfordshire DC v Hitchin Industrial Estate Ltd (1992) 2 EGLR 121 先例有不同判法。所以总结而言，这种写法也是有不肯定之处。

3.2.5 其他的写法

这里还会有许多不同的写法，但不是写得完全清楚明确，就会带来各种不肯定的法院或仲裁庭判决/裁决。有许多对某个特定承诺的履行的写法被判是不足够显示时间规定是"重要"（of essence）。如"立即"（immediately）：Leech v Lamb (1855) 11 Ex 437; Alexiadi v Robinson (1861) 2 F & F 679; Re Todd and McFadden's Contract (1908) 1 IR 213 等先例。或是"马上"（forthwith）：Simpson v Henderson (1829) Mood & M 300; Staunton v Wood (1851) 16 QB 638; Roberts v Brett (1865) 11 HLC 337; King v Chamberlain (1871) 40 LJCP 273; Hudson v Hill (1874) 43 LJCP 273;

Owens v Upham (1909) 39 NBR 198 (Supreme Ct of New Brunswick); R v Cuthbertson (1949) 4 DLR 369 (Exchequer Ct of Canada)等先例。或是“尽快”(as soon as possible):Attwood v Emery (1856) 1 CB NS 110; Hydraulic Engineering Co Ltd v McHaffie Goslett & Co (1878) 4 QBD 670 (CA); Wigan Coal & Iron Co v Eckersley (1910) 103 LT 468 (HL); King's Old Country Ltd v Liquid Carbonic Canadian Corp (1942) 2 WWR 603; Vines v Djordevitch (1955) 91 CLR 512 (High Ct of Australia)等先例。或是“付运时间关键”(Delivery dates are material):Aries Powerplant Ltd v. ECE Systerms Ltd (1996) 45 Con LR 111 等先例。

3.2.5.1 写法被视为显示重要的先例之一:Gill & Duffus SA v. Societe pour l' Exportation des Sucres SA

在 Gill & Duffus SA v. Societe pour l' Exportation des Sucres SA (1985) 1 Lloyd's Rep 621 先例,案情涉及食糖的 FOB 买卖,合约中规定卖方最迟在 1983 年 11 月 14 日指定装港(port to be specified by the Sellers at latest Monday 14.11.83)。这时间规定在一审被认为是条件条文。之后上诉法院也支持了这个判决:Gill & Duffus SA v Societe pour l' Exportation des Sucres SA (1986) 1 Lloyd's Rep 322。Leggatt 大法官说:“There are no words in the English language by which a deadline can be appointed more concisely, more precisely and with more finality than the words 'at latest'; and I hold that they mean what they say.”

3.2.5.2 写法被视为是显示重要的先例之二:Harold Wood Brick Co Ltd v. Ferris

在 Harold Wood Brick Co Ltd v. Ferris (1935) 2 KB 198 先例,案情涉及的土地买卖合约约定的完成日期是 1935 年 8 月 31 日。合约中的另一条文规定如果合约延误履行,购房款要存入买卖双方律师的联名户口,但是交易无论如何不应迟于 1935 年 9 月 15 日完成,否则卖方可以终止合约并没收定金:“if for any reason the actual completion of the purchase is delayed beyond August 31, 1933, then nevertheless on that date the purchase money ... shall be placed on deposit ... but the purchase **shall in any event actually be completed not later than** September 15, 1933. ... Should the purchaser fail to complete the said purchase in accordance with this agreement any deposit paid by the purchaser shall be forfeited to the vendors who may rescind the sale and resell the property.”

上诉庭判是合约的措辞显示了在 9 月 15 日前完成交易是合约的条件条文。

但在 Touche Ross & Co v Secretary of State for the Environment (1983) 46 P. & C.R. 187 先例,合约条文规定:“... the question of what is a fair market rack rental of the demised premises shall **as soon as practicable and in any event not later than three months** after the service of the said notice be referred for decision to a surveyor...”

这看起来和 Harold Wood Brick Co Ltd v Ferris 先例中的写法差不多,但上诉庭认为这时间规定不是条件条文。Dillon 大法官说:"If the clause had simply said that 'the question shall as soon as practicable be referred for decision to a surveyor' there would be no doubt that time was not of the essence. Equally, in the light of United Scientific Holdings Ltd. v. Burnley Borough Council if the clause had simply said that 'the question shall within three months after the service of the landlord's notice be referred' time would not have been of the essence. *Prima facie*, therefore, it seems to me somewhat hard to deduce, from the running together of those two alternatives into the composite phrase 'shall as soon as practicable and in any event not later than three months after service of the notice be referred,' that time is to be of the essence and that the parties are concerned to show that this is not just ordinary use of language to indicate a desire that the matter should not be unduly protracted; they are concerned to show that the time limit is obligatory and really means what it says, unlike any mere time limit in a rent review clause."

所以这写法还是不能算是肯定能够被视为重要。

3.2.5.3　写法被视为是显示重要的先例之三:The "Seaflower"

再接下来介绍的是一个航运的案例名为 The "Seaflower"(2001) 1 Lloyd's Rep 341 (CA)。案情涉及一艘油轮的期租合约,其中第 46 条文如下:"Vessel is presently MOBIL ... CONOCO ... BP ... and SHELL acceptable. Owners **guarantee** to obtain within 60 (sixty) days EXXON approval in addition to present approvals ... If for any reason, Owners would lose **even one** of such acceptances they must advise Charterers at once and they must reinstate same within 30 (thirty) days from such occurrence failing which Charterers will be at liberty to cancel charter party."(加黑部分是笔者的强调)

有关上述条文的背景可以先简单介绍,就是油轮的租约中经常可以看到有类似条文规定油轮必须得到一些主要石油公司对油轮全面的检查后作出的许可或批准,因为这样承租人才能营运该油轮,如把该油轮转租给主要石油公司,或是被允许使用它们的泊位与设施。

在该先例船东在相关合约中的第 46 条文前半部分"保证"(guarantee)说在 60 天内取得 EXXON 这家世界上最大的石油公司的批准,但并没有说如果船东有延误,无法在 60 天内取得批准,承租人就可以终止租约。但第 46 条文后半部分规定,如果船东失去了某家石油公司的批准,必须在 30 天重新取得,否则承租人就可以终止租约。在该先例,案情涉及船东无法在规定的 60 天内取得 EXXON 的批准,这样就涉及第 46 条文的解释,也就是它是否是条件条文或针对前半部分只是保证条文,后半部分才是条件条文或已经明示把后果写清楚。

上诉庭推翻了一审法院的判决,认为这个承诺是合约的条件条文,一旦明确船东不可能在 60 天内取得 EXXON 的批准,承租人就可以终止租约。上诉庭没有采纳船东的争辩说第 46 条文的后半部分明确给予承租人终止租约的权利,但前半部分没有给予承租人同样的权利,显示了双方的订约意图是承租人并不能因为船东没有在 60 天内取得 EXXON 的批准而终止租约。船东的争辩看来是根据本书第四章之第 8 段所介绍的合约解释规则之一的"特别针对一件事情但不提其他同类事情"(*expressio unius est exclusio alteius*)。但上诉庭认为,第 46 条文整体看是重要,即在前半部分也有了"保证"(guarantee)一词强调了它的重要性,而后半部分有"even one"一词,显示了对所有列名的主要石油公司的批准的重要性。

3.2.6 合约整体的解释

根据合约解释的一般原则,法院或仲裁庭会看整个合约的内容。这有许多权威的说法,只简单节录一个较早期的先例 Calico Printers' Association v Barclays Bank Ltd (1931) 145 LT 51,Scrutton 大法官针对免责条文不能独立针对而要看整个合约说:"First of all, in my view, you do not take part of the document and consider it by itself; **you are to construe the whole document.** The parties have used a set of words to express their legal relations to each other and it is no good saying: 'Here I find in sentence A clear words, so I need not trouble about sentence B, because sentence B, if it contradicts sentence A, I will reject as repugnant, and I will ... assume that these parties used these words not meaning anything by them, and therefore I need not trouble about them because they do not use clear language in sentence A'."(加黑部分是笔者的强调)

在更近期的先例有 Clarke 大法官在 National Westminster Bank v Utreche – America Finance Co (2001) 3 All E. R. 733 (CA)说:"like any clause, clause 8.2(d) must be construed in its context and **in the context of the contract as a whole** having regard to its factual matrix or surrounding circumstances."(加黑部分是笔者的强调)

另 Hoffmann 勋爵在 HIH Casualty and General Insurance Ltd v Chase Manhattan Bank (2003) 2 Lloyd's Rep 61 先例说:"The question, as it seems to me, is whether the language used by the parties, **construed in the context of the whole instrument** and against the admissible background, leads to the conclusion..."(加黑部分是笔者的强调)

最后是 Bingham 勋爵在 Dairy Containers Ltd v Tasman Orient Line CV (2005) 1 WLR 215 先例说:"This clause must be construed in the context of the contract as a whole."

合约的时间规定(如付款)也不例外,决定对特定时间的规定是否是合约重要或根本性的条文,还要看整体的合约。这是最麻烦与困难的事情,因为仅是写好了针对特定履行的时间规定还不足够,而是要看其他的合约条文。一个复杂的合约会有上百条甚至好几百条条文,精明的律师经常可以挑出合约中有其他的有关条文显示了时间规定并非是重要。

3.2.6.1 例子之一:L Schuler AG v. Wickman Machine Tool Sales Ltd

在著名的 L Schuler AG v. Wickman Machine Tool Sales Ltd (1973) 2 Lloyd's Rep. 53 先例,除了是判"condition"一字不够明确显示是条件条文外(这在本章之

3.2.2 段已经有介绍），贵族院作出这样的判决的另一个重要原因是合约中有另外一条条文针对合约的终止，说明一方如果严重违反合约承诺，另一方需要文书作出通知并在对方没有在 60 天内作出补救的情况下才能终止合约。这样一个争议就是写着"condition"的条文即使被解释为条件条文能否独立于另一条针对合约终止的条文，可让 Schuler 不必作出通知就终止合约？或是，即使 Wickman 违反了条件条文，合约的终止还是按照另一条文的做法？贵族院显然不愿意支持太容易让合约一方终止合约，也不认为这是一个合情合理的解释，而是倾向支持两条条文必须一并解释。其中 Reid 勋爵是这样说："There is much force in this criticism. But on any view the interrelation and consequences of the various provisions of this agreement are so ill – thought out that I am not disposed to discard the natural meaning of the words which I have quoted merely because giving to them their natural meaning implies that the draftsman has forgotten something which a better draftsman would have remembered. If the terms of clause 11（这是要求作出通知的条文）are wide enough to apply to breaches of clause 7（这是写着 condition 的条文）then I am inclined to hold that clause 7 must be read subject to the provisions of clause 11. "

3.2.6.2　例子之二：The "Luxmar"

较近期的先例可以介绍 The "Luxmar"（2007）2 Lloyd's Rep 542，案情涉及一船的汽油买卖，其中合约中针对交付货物的条文如下：

"7. DELIVERY

FOB 1 SAB REFINERY NORTH SITE（PRIOLO TERMINAL – AUGUSTA BAY）IN A SINGLE LOT BY M/T "TBN"/SUBS TO BE NOMINATED BY BUYER AND TO BE ACCEPTABLE TO SELLER IN THE PERIOD 27 – 30/05/2004.（这是 FOB 买卖，交货地点是一个安全锚地或泊位，在意大利 Augusta 港的一个炼油厂。付运的是一船的货物，船舶将会由买方指定但需要被卖方接受，时间是在 2004 年 5 月 27 日至 30 日。）

BUYER WILL NARROW SUCH PERIOD TO A TWO DAY LAYCAN LATEST BY 21/05/2004 COB ITALIAN TIME.（买方将最迟在 5 月 21 日意大利办公时间内缩短这 4 天的期限至 2 天，作为 Laycan。）

THE LAYCAN IS AN ESSENTIAL ELEMENT OF THE CONTRACT, IN FAVOUR OF SELLER.（Laycan 是本合约的重要元素，由卖方得利）"

在该买卖合约中还有其他条文针对装货时间与滞期费的支付。

该先例的案情是买方在 5 月 17 日指定了 Luxmar 轮装该票货，并在 5 月 21 日准时把 Laycan 缩短为两天，也就是 5 月 29 日与 30 日。但实际上船舶早到，是在 5 月 28 日早上 10 点钟，并且船长递交了"准备就绪通知书"（notice of readiness）。但由于技术故障，卖方没有办法装货，直到 6 月 3 日。但装货之前买方就宣告合约被终止（背后原因是汽油市场下跌），因为卖方不在付运期间装货，违反了条件条文。但卖方指有关的第7条文并非针对付运,只要卖方能够在装货的时间内完成装货,就算是履行了合约。而即使是超出了允许的装货时间,后果也只是索赔“滞期费”(demurrage)。所以买方终止合约拒绝装货是违约/毁约。

这里就涉及两方面需要进一步解释,一是国际货物买卖合约的付运期,一般被视为条件条文。在现实中,如果卖方不能在付运期内装货,卖方也往往不能取得符合付运期的单证银行结汇。这也是众所周知带来倒签提单恶行的根本原因。但在同样的道理下,指定船舶的FOB买方也必须配合,能够租一艘船舶装港并允许卖方在付运期内装货。显然,这也应该是一条条件条文。所以,如果该买卖合约的第7条是针对付运,5月27日至30日应是条件条文。这一点在该先例也被高院与上诉庭确认,其中Longmore大法官是这样说:“There can be little doubt that, if the first paragraph of the delivery clause stood on its own, it would be treated as a condition of the contract, see Benjamin's Sale of Goods, 7th end, para 20 – 029 and the cases there cited, particularly Yelo v S M Machado & Co [1952] 1 Lloyd's Rep 183 and Tradax Export SA v Italgrani di Francesco Ambrosio [1986] 1 Lloyd's Rep 112 at page 17 per Kerr LJ.”

但问题是这个先例的第7条,双方约定的不仅是第一段,而是加上了第二与第三段。后两段是针对Laycan,这一词在租约中常见。Laycan是指一个期限,在本案例是两天。第一天是指Layday,也就是指承租人没有责任要在该天之前装货,而装货时间也不会起算。对船东而言,也表示他不会想早到,因为早到也无法要承租人提早装货并起算时间。在今天昂贵的燃油下,船东经常会要求船长减速以节省燃油,因为比Layday更早抵达装港没有意义。至于这个期限的最后一天是指“销约期”(Cancelling date),也就是船舶抵达装港晚于该天,承租人就可以终止合约。这两天一前一后,合并起来就是Laycan的期限。换言之,对船东而言,船舶最好就是在Laycan之间的时间抵达,没必要提早,更不能晚于销约期。租约也经常会像本案例一样,有条文要求船东收窄Laycan。这可以让承租人备妥装货的时间缩短,进而方便与省钱(如仓库费用)。而船东在更近付运的时间由于会是已经租了船并更好掌握船期,知道船舶抵达装港的准确时间,往往也比较能够收窄这个Laycan。这种条文在租约而言已经被明确属于条件条文,在The “Niizura” (1996) 2 Lloyd's Rep 66先例,Mance大法官说:“Both authority and principle in my judgment support charterers' case that compliance with the laycan narrowing provision is a condition precedent to delivery .... The provision regarding delivery and the commencement of time are of considerable practical significance to parties to a time charter, Certainty about their ambit is important, and, in a mercantile contract of this nature, there is not the same reluctance as there may be elsewhere about recognizing provisions relating to time as conditions upon which further performance depends; ...”

这个租约的惯用词也越来越多用在FOB买卖。会是承租人的角色就换为FOB卖方,而船东的角色就换为派船的FOB买方。这样,如果买方派遣的船舶晚于销约期抵达装港，就表示卖方有权拒绝接受。

但 Laycan 所针对的重要之处之一是“装货时间”（fixed laytime for loading）的计算，而规定的装货时间如果延误，这延误也往往有一条议定赔偿的条文针对，也就是滞期费条文。换言之，违反装货时间规定只被视为保证条文，不被视为条件条文。这样判法当然还有其他合理的考虑，如果装货时间被视为重要，一旦延误，就让无辜方的船东有权终止租约，会带来严重的后果。因为届时往往会是装了一半的货，不上不下，船东如果可以终止合约，就可以狠狠敲承租人一笔钱才肯“回”（reinstate）终止了的租约。所以，对装货时间的延误必须要达致“受阻延误”（frustration delay），船东才可能终止租约。

再看本先例，就是第 7 条的第一段的 4 天时间是付运期的条件条文，但第二段的两天是 Laycan，这不是条件条文，即使是销约期，也只是给承租人或 FOB 卖方一个选择权终止租约/买卖合约，与违约无关。而第三段说明 Laycan 至关重要。这样的一条条文不伦不类，要把他们合并起来作出解释不容易。而该先例的买方终止合约的理由是卖方因为技术故障6 月 3 日才能装货，过了付运期，违反了条件条文。但卖方指称买方终止合约是违约/毁约，因为第 7 条文只是主要针对 Laycan，即使是错过也只是违反保证条文，唯一的救济就是支付滞期费。至于受阻延误，显然在6 月 3 日才能装货完全不能说成是受阻。

在高院与上诉庭，都判是卖方胜诉。其中上诉庭的 Longmore 大法官是这样说：“It was these considerations that led the judge to hold that the concept of the laycan in the second paragraph of the delivery clause was an essential part of the clause as a whole and that the word ‘delivery’ had to be construed accordingly. The use of a laydays/cancelling provision in the contract (particularly a provision entitling a vessel to present at any moment up to the end of the delivery period) makes the contract a non – traditional fob contract in that time of delivery has become an obligation which is not of the essence of the contract. That is not a surprise, since traders are constantly adapting and even changing traditional fob contracts in the course of their business. If they want to rely on delivery obligations as they have been traditionally construed, they may well be advised not to employ cancelling provisions but that is, as always, a matter for them.”（最后一句 Longmore 大法官是说如果买卖双方想依赖交付日期是重要，是条件条文，就最好不要同时加上销约期条文，导致整个条文不伦不类，并且会作出并非传统的 FOB 买卖的解释。）

§4 第二种情况:合约默示时间规定是重要(implied to be of essence)

这里就涉及合约的本质与周边环境显示了时间规定是重要而作出默示,这与本书所针对的解释文件/合约的条文/文字是否代表了双方的订约意图基本上是同一码事。默示条文在本书第七章有详细的解释,其中第3段就针对"法律的默示"(implied by law),第4段针对"事实的默示"(implied in fact),第2段的图表显示了两者的主要区别。其中事实的默示是根据订约双方的意图并"假设"(assume)双方在订约时都会同意,但没有在合约内明示规定或针对的情况。此外,也必须是作出这样的默示才能令合约有"商业效力"(business efficacy)。这种苛刻的要求在法律的默示是不必要的。近期也另有说法是默示条文也是属于解释合约的一种做法广泛解释有关的文件/合约:Attorney General of Belize v Belize Telecom Ltd (2009) UKPC 10 先例。正如《Chitty on Contracts》(第31版,2012年)一书之13-005段说:"... the principles that traditionally govern the implication (or non-implication) of terms and which are set out in the paragraphs which follow should now no longer be regarded as 'tests' to be applied to determine whether or not a term should be implied but rather as guidelines to assist the court to answer the single question: Is that what the instrument, read as whole against the relevant background, would reasonably be understood to mean?"

4.1 法律默示时间规定是否重要

法律默示会来自立法,如在1979年英国《Sale of Goods Act》之 Sections 12-15,就有几个著名的默示条文而且都被视为"条件条文"(condition),如针对货物的所有权,货物不能货不对版与质量必须令人满意等。

至于在普通法的地位,已经有无数的案例提到"商业合约"(mercantile contract)的明示或默示时间规定都是重要。主要原因之一是为了"肯定"(certainty),这也是英国法律一直引以为傲的,并广泛为国际商业社会接受。这方面有许多先例,[3]可以说这些案例起初是根据事实的默示而作出这样的决定,也就是根据个别案件的案情认为时间规定是重要。但后来,这方面的判决已经变为被广泛接受与权威性的原则,不同案情的案例都依从,就会令该原则变为法律的默示。

这就带来几方面的问题需要进一步探讨,如英国法律对肯定性的重视、什么是商业合约、其他非商业合约的时间规定是否不重要。

4.1.1 英国法律对肯定性的重视

英国法律一贯以来十分重视肯定性,这在无数的先例都有强调。其中一个最重要的肯定就是双方有了看来是全面与最终的合约,英国法院就严格按照双方的约定(这显示在合约的条文/文字中)解释与执行。这尤其是在"商业合约"(commercial 或 mercantile contract),因为可以假设订约双方都是有一定的水平与经验在合约中作出自我保护。所以,在一个没有瑕疵(如不涉及误述、欺诈、非法、错误、胁迫等)与经过双方谈判最终被接受的合约,英国法院通常不会作出任何干预。英国法院或仲裁庭会把一些在中国法律可能认为没有问题的做法,如改写双方的合约,或是以善意等大原则扭曲双方约定的合约条文等,视为大逆不道。

由于先例太多,在这里只介绍一个涉及明示的时间规定有了延误的权威先例。在 Bunge Corporation New York v Tradax SA (1981) 2 Lloyds Rep 1 先例,相关的 FOB 买卖合约是一连串的货物买卖合约中的一部分。合约中有一条条文规定买方必须至少提前 15 天通知卖方船舶的预计备妥日期与要求装运的货物的预计数量,下一步就是卖方决定装港并通知买方让后者派遣船舶该港口装货。贵族院判这个时间规定是条件条文,所以在买方延误作出提前 15 天的通知,卖方可以终止买卖合约。

---

[3] 如船舶在特定一天备妥可以装货是条件条文:Corkling v Massey (1873) 8 CP 395; Sanday v Keighley Maxsted & Co Ltd (1922) 27 Com Cas 296 (CA); Re Empire Shipping Co and Hall Bryan Ltd (1940) 1 DLR 695; The "Mihalis Angelos" (1970) 2 Lloyd's Rep 43; The "Mavro Vetranic" (1985) 1 Lloyd's Rep 581; The "Baleares" (1993) 1 Lloyd's Rep 215 等先例。FOB 买卖中买方指定派遣船舶的时间是条件条文:Bunge Corp v Tradax Export SA (1981) 2 Lloyds Rep 1 等先例。如果合约明确规定货物已经或者将在特定时间付运,但货物在不符合规定的时间付运,买方可以拒货:Bowes v Shand (1877) 2 App Cas 455; Montague L Meyer Ltd v Travaru A/B H Cornelius of Gamleby (1930) 46 TLR 553; Cobec Brazilian Trading Co Ltd v Toepfer (1982) 1 Lloyd's Rep 528; Bergerco USA v Vegoil Ltd (1984) 1 Lloyd's Rep 440; The "Golden Rio" (1990) 2 Lloyd's Rep 273 等先例。货物买卖合约中交付货物的日期一般被视为条件条文:Alewyn v Pryor (1826) Ry & M 406; Harrington v Brown (1917) 23 CLR 297; Hartley v Hymans (1920) 3 KB 475; Finagrain SA Geneva v P Kruse Hamburg (1976) 2 Lloyd's Rep 508; The "Eurometal" (1981) 1 Lloyd's Rep 337; The "Naxos" (1990) 1 WLR 1337; The "Honam Jade" (1991) 1 Lloyd's Rep 38 等先例。同样,CIF 合约下,卖方履行合约责任的时间规定一般也被视为条件条文:The "Mihalis Angelos"; Bremer v Vanden (1978) 2 Lloyd's Rep 109; Toepfer v Lenersan - Poortman BV (1980) 1 Lloyd's Rep 143 等先例。尽管支付货价的时间规定不是重要,但支付定金或提供担保的时间规定是条件条文:The "Selene G" (1981) 2 Lloyd's Rep 180 等先例。

Lowry 勋爵列举了在这个先例中影响他决定的一些因素,如下:

"(1) There are enormous practical advantages in certainty, not least in regard to string contracts where today's buyer may be tomorrow's seller. (肯定是在现实中有莫大的好处,特别是在一连串的合约下。)

(2) Most members of the string will have many on - going contracts simultaneously and they must be able to do business with confidence in the legal results of their actions. (一连串合约下每一位合约方是买方也同时是卖方,他们就有信心知道采取的行动会有什么法律后果。)

(3) Decisions would be too difficult if the term were innominate, litigation would be rife and years might elapse before the results were known. (如果有关时间规定的条文只被视为中间条文,[4]就需要在进行大量与漫长的诉讼后,才会知道自己采取的行动到底有什么后果。)

(4) The difficulty of assessing damages is an indication in favour of condition... (时间规定有了延误的违约也很难计算金钱损失,如在本案中买卖合约所规定的 15 天通知,如果买方是晚了一天才作出通知,卖方到底会有什么金钱损失也很难预测,而往往只是给卖方带来不便。所以把这视为违反条件条文,就会对卖方有更大的实际意义,他有权终止合约。)

(5) One can at least say that recent litigation has provided indications that the term is a condition. Parties to similar contracts should (failing a strong contra - indication) be able to rely on this... (如果先例明确了这时间规定是条件条文,在同样的合约条文下,合约方就可以依赖并采取相应的行动。)

(6) To make 'total loss' the only test of a condition is contrary to authority and experience, when one recalls that terms as to the date of sailing, deviation from a voyage and the date of delivery are regarded as conditions, but that failure to comply with them does not always have serious consequences. (看是否是条件条文并非只看后果是否严重,已经有明确的先例判是条文规定船舶开航的一天,在航次中不得不合理绕航与交

---

〔4〕 中间条文是在贵族院的 The "Hongkong Fir" (1961) 1 Lloyd's Rep 478 先例后的说法,换言之是除了条件条文与保证条文之外,还多了一个中间条文。中间条文的违约后果是要看个别事件所带来的后果是否严重。如果严重,除了允许受害方索赔损失之外也允许他终止合约,换言之,这是与条件条文法律地位一致。但如果不严重,受害方只能索赔金钱损失,这是与保证条文法律地位一致。在决定违约的后果是否严重到允许受害方终止合约,就会要考虑很多因素,其中重要的是考虑金钱的赔偿对无辜方是否为足够的救济。另也要看整体的公平与否,如无辜方因为延误而受到实际的影响,如果是条件条文就会带来技术性违约让无辜方有了取巧的机会,如违约方只是延误了 10 分钟:Union Eagle Ltd v Golden Achievement Ltd (1997) AC 514 (PC)。换言之,中间条文不像条件条文或保证条文,是追求公平合理,但最终作出决定还是个别的法官或仲裁员。而且有了争议双方都会有理由,这就导致对中间条文下是否合法终止合约或违约/毁约的整个考虑最后得出的判决或裁决不肯定,显然是违反了追求肯定的期望。

货日期都属于条件条文,但这种违约也通常不会带来严重的后果。)

(7) Nor need an implied condition pass the total loss test: see (6) above.

(8) If the consequences of breach of condition turn out to be slight, the innocent party may treat the condition as an innominate term or a warranty.

(9) While the sellers could have made time of the essence, if it were not so already, this wouldrequire reasonable notice, which might well not be practical either in a string contract or at all.(卖方可以以明示条文在该买卖合约明确时间规定是重要,也就是提升为条件条文。卖方也可以作出通知使得时间规定变为重要,但这种做法在一个“背靠背”的一连串合约会是不现实。)

(10) In Tarrabochia v Hickie, (1865) 1 H. &N. 183; 156 E. R. 1168, upon which the appellants strongly relied, Baron Bramwell said: 'No doubt it is competent for the parties, if they think fit, to declare in express terms that any matter shall be a condition precedent, but when they have not so expressed themselves, it is necessary for those who construe the instrument to see whether they intend to do it. Since, however, they could have done it, those who construe the instrument should be chary in dong for them that which they might, but have not done for themselves.' But in that very case both Chief Baron Pollock and Baron Bramwell, without the benefit of any express term, said that, where the agreement was that a ship should sail on a particular day, that was a condition precedent.

(11) To accept the argument that conditions ought not to be implied 'because the parties themselves know how to describe a term' would logically condemn the entire doctrine of implied terms.(条件条文不能通过默示而必须让双方在合约中明示是否定了整个默示条文的说法。)

(12) Arbitrators and courts might if the term were innominate, give different answers concerning the effect of a breach in very similar transactions, and parties could never learn by experience what was likely to happen in a given situation. So – called string contracts are not made, or adjudicated on, in strings."(如果时间规定的条文是中间条文,即使是同类的交易,仲裁员与法院也会根据违约的后果作出不同的决定。这表示一连串合约在最后得出的判决并非是一连串的同样结果。而当事人也无法从经验学到到底怎样的做法才是正确。)

在该先例,其他的大法官也有强调肯定对商业合约的重要性,其中节录 Wilberforce 勋爵所说:“... clearly essential that both buyer and seller (who may change roles in the next series of contracts, or even in the same chain of contracts) should know precisely what their obligations are, most especially because the ability of the seller to fulfil his obligation may be totally dependent on punctual performance by the buyer... It would expose the parties, after a breach of one, two, three, seven and other numbers of days to an argument whether this delay would have left time for the seller to provide the goods. It would make it, at the time, at least difficult, and sometimes impossible, for the supplier to know whether he could do so. It would fatally remove from a vital provision in the contract that certainty which is the most indispensable quality of mercantile contracts, and lead to a large increase in arbitrations."

Roskill 勋爵也说:"I agree with counsel that in a mercantile contract when a term has to be performed by one party as a condition precedent to the ability of the other party to perform another term, especially an essential term such as the nomination of a single loading port, the term as to time for the performance of the former obligation will in general fall to be treated as a condition."

总结说,在商业合约中对时间规定(特别是明示的时间规定)通常会被假设是条件条文。这可节录《Chitty on Contracts》(第31版,2012年)一书之12-037段说:"In mercantile contracts, where it is of importance that the parties should know precisely what their obligations are and be able to act with confidence in the legal results of their actions, the courts will readily construe a stipulation as to time as a condition of the contract."

这就带来了下一小段要针对的问题,什么是商业合约,而如果非商业合约有时间规定是否重要等问题。

4.1.2 什么是商业合约

上一小段已经提到过,在 Bunge Corporation New York v Tradax SA (1981) 2 Lloyds Rep 1 的贵族院先例,明确了商业合约的时间规定,即使没有明示说明它是"重要"(of essence),也被视为重要,任何轻微的违反都会导致严重的后果。至于什么是商业合约,看来历史最悠久也是最无可争议的应该就是货物买卖合约。至于与国际货物买卖有密切关系的不同合约类别,如租船合约、信用证、保险合约等,看来也应该是商业合约。但有权威的说法是商业合约实际上十分广泛,如在 International Asset Control Ltd (t/a IAC Films) v. Films Sans Frontieres SARL (1999) EMLR 268 (CA) 先例,有关合约是涉及电影的发行,上诉庭的 Waller 大法官说:"This is not my understanding of the word 'Mercantile' and nor would I think it to be the understanding of those who named the Business Courts the 'Mercantile Lists'. 'Mercantile' is simply another word for Commercial Trading or Business, and a contract relating to the distribution of films is as 'Mercantile' as any other business contract."

Wilberforce 勋爵在 The "Diana Prosperity" (1976) 2 Lloyd's Rep 621 先例也有说:"... I would respectfully endorse what was recently said by Lord Justice Roskill in The "Hansa Nord" (1975) 2 Lloyd's Rep. 445: 'In principle it is not easy to see why the law relating to contracts for the sale of goods should be different from the law relating to the performance of other contractual obligations, whether charter-parties or other types of contract. Sale of goods law is but one branch of the general law of contract. It is desirable that the same legal principles should apply to the law of contract as a whole and that different legal principles should not apply to different branches of that law. ' "

至于为什么商业合约会被单独列出来认为时间规定通常被默示为重要,会是商业合约通常都会涉及英国法律默示时间规定是否重要的一些考虑。例如,在 Bunge Corporation New York v Tradax SA 先例已经提到与强调的肯定性、一连串买卖等。此外,在货物买卖的“商品”(commodity)市场价格波动很大与很快,也是一个重要的考虑。这些考虑会稍后进一步介绍。

相对其他的合约,如房屋租赁的“租金调整条文”(rent review clause)〔5〕中的时间规定,就有许多的先例包括贵族院的重要先例 United Scientific Holdings Ltd v Burnley BC (1978) AC 904 都不默示为重要。

在笔者熟悉的国际货物买卖与航运,英国法律对时间规定默示是重要,一有违反就是违反了条件条文的先例很多。只针对四个方面举例如下:

1. 程租合约(或是 FOB 买卖合约)承诺的有关船舶(或派遣的船舶)“估计装货日期”(expected ready to load)是条件条文:Corkling v Massey (1873) 8 CP 395; Sanday v Keighley Maxsted & CO Ltd (1922) 27 Com Cas 296 (CA); Re Empire Shipping Co and Hall Bryan Ltd (1940) 1 DLR 695 (Supreme Ct of British Columbia); The “Mihalis Angelos” (1970) 2 Lloyd's Rep. 43; The “Mavro Vetranic” (1985) 1 Lloyd's Rep 581; The “Baleares” (1993) 1 Lloyd's Rep 215 (CA)等先例。

2. 买卖合约中的交货日期是条件条文:Alewyn v Pryor (1826) Ry & M 406; Wimshurst v Deeley (1845) 2 CB 253; Plevins v Downing (1876) 1 CPD 220; Harrington v Brown (1917) 23 CLR 297; Hartley v Hymans (1920) 3 KB 475; Aron & Co Inc v Comptoir Wegimont (1921) KB 435; Berg & Sons v Landauer (1925) 42 TLR 142; Finagrain SA Geneva v P Kruse Hamburg (1976) 2 Lloyd's Rep 508; The “Eurometal” (1981) 1 Lloyd's Rep 337; The “Naxos” (1990) 1 WLR 1337 (HL); The “Honam Jade” (1991) 1 Lloyd's Rep 38 (CA)等先例。

3. 国际货物买卖合约虽然有估计高达 80% 的结算(也就是买方向卖方支付货价)还是以“往来账户”(open account),但仍有一定的比例是买方向卖方开出银行的

---

〔5〕 例如在 United Scientific Holdings Ltd v Burnley BC (1978) AC 904 的贵族院先例,其中一个房屋租赁合约的租金调整条文针对调整机制与时间规定说:“The market rent may be determined and notified to the lessees in the manner following: (a) the proposed rent shall be specified in a notice in writing ('the lessors' notice') served by the lessors ... on the lessees not more than 12 months nor less than six months prior to the review date; (b) the lessees may within one month after service of the lessors' notice of the proposed rent serve on the lessors a counter notice ('the lessees' notice') either agreeing the proposed rent or specifying the amount of rent which the lessees consider to be the market rent for the period in question..."

"信用证"(letter of credit)作为支付办法，特别是涉及中国的买卖，这更加是普遍的做法。买卖合约通常对买方开出信用证的时间有明示规定。但如果没有明示规定，英国法律的默示合理时间看来是根据合约付运期或实际付运日期，而后者日期是在CIF与FOB买卖合约分别由卖方或买方决定，所以这方面是有一点复杂。[6] 在《Benjamin on Sale of Goods》(第18版,2010年)一书之23-051至23-058段有详论。但明确的是，明示或默示开出信用证的时间规定都是条件条文。如Dexters Ltd v Schenker & Co (1923) 14 Lloyd's Rep 586; Lindsay (AE) & Co Ltd v Cook (1953) 1 Lloyd's Rep 328; Ets Chainbaux SARL v Harbormaster Ltd (1955) 1 Lloyd's Rep 303; Garcia v Page & Co Ltd (1936) 55 Ll LR 391; Trans Trust SPRL v Danubian Trading Co Ltd (1952) 1 Lloyd's Rep 348等先例。

4. 在信用证的操作下，卖方在付运货物后作为信用证的受益人向银行递交付运文件结汇(或直接向买方递交收取货款)，时间规定也同样重要，一有延误就会导致买方可以拒绝有关文件(也等于是拒货与终止买卖合约)：Toepfer v. Lenersan - Poortman NV (1980) 1 Lloyd's Rep 143等先例。

这种同类的案例是多不胜数，如针对股票买卖(Hare v Nicoll [1966] 2 QB 130与British and Commonwealth Holding plc v Quadrex Holdings Inc [1989] QB 842等先例)，租船合约(The "Tres Flores" [1973] 2 Lloyd's Rep 247; The "Brimnes" [1974] 2 Lloyd's Rep 241; The "Laconia" [1977] 1 Lloyd's Rep. 315等先例)与货物买卖合约(Bowes v Shand [1877] 2 App Cas 455; Sharp v Chrismas [1892] 8 TLR 687; Ian Stach Ltd v Baker Bosley Ltd [1958] 1 Lloyd's Rep. 127; Transpetrol Ltd v Transol Olieprodukten Nederland NV [1989] 1 Lloyd's Rep 309等先例)。

总结而言，即使是涉及最典型的商业合约，也就是买卖合约，也不是每个时间规定都是重要或是条件条文。例如，买方支付货款表面看来重要(至少是对卖方而言)，但在1979年立法也有一点意外地默示支付货款如果有延误，这违约并不重要，只是属于"保证条文"(warranty)，换言之卖方对这个违约只能索赔损失，通常也就是利息。Section 10(1) - (2)是这样说："(1) Unless a different intention appears from the terms of the contract stipulations as to time of payment are not of the essence of a contract of sale. (2) whether any other stipulation as to time is of the essence of the contract or not depends on the terms of the contract."

但较早前已经提到与买方支付货款密切相关的开出信用证的时间规定，就是条件条文。在本章之第2段也已经提到与买方支付货款有密切相关的提供保证金，在

[6] Pavia & Co SpA v. Thurmann - Nielsent (1951) 2 Lloyd's Rep. 328; Sinason - Teicher v. Oilcakes and Oilseeds Trading Co. (1954) 2 Lloyd's Rep. 327; Plasticmoda SpA v. Davidsons (Mancester) Ltd. (1952) 1 Lloyd's Rep. 527; Ian Stach Ltd. v. Baker Bosly Ltd. (1958) 1 Lloyd's Rep. 127等先例。

SCCMO（London）Ltd v Societe Generale de Compensation（1956）1 Lloyd's Rep 299；The"Selene G"（1981）2 Lloyd's Rep 180 与 The"Blankenstein"（1985）1 Lloyd's Rep 93 等先例被判是条件条文。另一个不被视为是条件条文的先例是在本章之 3.2.6.2 段介绍的 The"Luxmar"（2007）2 Lloyd's Rep 542 先例。

所以，英国法院会更愿意假设商业合约的时间规定是重要，而在商业合约的时间规定也会比其他类别的合约更加有机会被解释为重要或条件条文，但说到底还是看是针对什么承诺。

4.2　默示有关时间规定的两个方面

针对时间规定的默示，有两方面要针对。一是合约中对履行没有明示的时间规定（如某一天或 7 天内等），就需要法律根据每个不同案件的事实作出事实的默示到底什么是"合理时间"（reasonable time）。有了这一合理时间，也就是有了默示的时间规定需要承诺方必须作出履行。二是有了明示时间规定或是默示时间规定，如果在有关的合约中没有像本章第 3 段所讲的明示规定时间是重要或是条件条文，就需要进一步默示在该合约下，这个时间规定是否重要，是属于条件条文。

4.2.1　默示之一：考虑合理时间的因素

不少订得仔细的合约都会对一些重要的履行有明确的时间规定。例如，国际货物买卖合约会有交货时间、FOB 买方通知派船时间、卖方通知买方准确装港时间、卖方交单时间、卖方允许的"装货时间"（loading laytime）、CIF/CFR 买方允许的"卸货时间"（discharge laytime）等。但即使是订得仔细，也会对一些履行没有作出明确的时间规定，更不用说是一份粗糙的合约。例如，会在有关的买卖合约中有条文允许买方参与装港的货物检查，但没有说明卖方最迟在什么时间通知买方让他有时间参与。这样，通常的说法就是卖方必须在合理时间内作出通知。此外，立法也会针对部分的履行在没有明示时间规定的情况下作出合理时间的默示。例如，在 1979 年英国《货物销售法》之 Section 29（3）与 Section 37 都有对合理时间的规定。另是《Supply of Goods and Services Act 1982》之 Section 14（1）可节录如下："Where, under the contract for a supply of a service by a supplier acting in the course of a business, the time for the service to be carried out is not fixed by the contract, left to be fixed in a manner agreed by the contract or determined by the course of dealing between the parties, there is an implied term that the supplier will carry out the service within a reasonable time."

显然这个合理时间必须根据每个不同案件的事实而认定，在英国以前民事诉讼还有陪审团的时候，这个问题是由陪审团而不是由法官决定：Alexiadi v Robinson（1861）2 F & F 679 先例。在今天显然是要由法官或者是仲裁员作出这个事实的认定，这里笔者是探讨应该有怎样的考虑。

4.2.1.1　订约时存在的因素与周边环境

在 Ellis v Thompson（1838）3 M & W 445 先例，Alderson 大法官说："It seems to me the correct mode of ascertaining what reasonable time is in such a case as this, is by placing the Court ... in the same situation as the contracting parties themselves were in at the time they made the contract: that is to say, ... all those circumstances which were known to both parties at the time when the contract was made, and under which the contract itself took place."

另在 Pearl Mill Co Ltd v Ivy Tannery Ltd (1919) 1 KB 78 先例,McCardie 大法官也说:"Reasonable time is of course a matter which depends on the nature of the contract, its terms, the class of the goods, the practice of the trade, and the general circumstances of the case."(合理时间是要看合约的本质、合约的条文、货物的类别、有关贸易的做法与案件的一般情况/环境。)

这两个先例都是针对货物买卖中卖方交货的合理时间,但同样的原则可以被使用在其他合约履行的合理时间。显然与其他解释合约的大原则一样,法院或仲裁庭应该客观考虑而不会理会其中一方主观的想法或愿望(如承诺方/履约方希望慢慢来,但对方对尽快履行有期望)。

这就带来了另一个考虑,双方的谈判中有否针对履约期待的快慢。虽然在传统的解释合约通常不考虑谈判的证据(口头证据[parol evidence]),但认定合理时间是可以加以考虑:Ellis v Thompson 先例。这一点在许多美国的先例也有针对:Stange v Wilson 17 Mich 342 (1868) (Michigan); Zone Co v Service Transport Co 137 NJL 112 (1948) (New Jersey); Jay Clutter Custom Digging v English 393 NE 2d 230 (1979) (Indiana)等。

如果如上述所讲承诺方希望慢慢来或被承诺方希望尽快履行是曾经在谈判中告诉了对方,对方也没有提出反对,这显然会影响认定什么是合理时间的决定。在 Jonathan Wren & Co Ltd v Microdec plc (1999) 65 Con LR 157 先例,原告订购了某个"专业版电脑软件"(specialist computer software package)并说明希望在 1996 年 7 月底就可以使用,而供应商也没有表示他赶不及这个时间。之后原告终止该合约,原因之一是该电脑软件不适合他的用途,另一个原因是根据《Supply of Goods and Services Act 1982》已经过了合理时间。法院在考虑什么是合理时间时,认为可以考虑供应商早知道客户急着需要这套电脑软件。

在谈判中或在订约时也会涉及双方对要履行的合理时间的理解以及在其他方面的"知识"(knowledge)。这在一定的程度上类似损失"遥远性"(remoteness),就是在 Hadley v Baxendale (1854) 9 EX 341 先例中作出区分的一般损失与特别损失。前者是订约时双方可以料想得到违约会带来的损失类别,后者是需要对方作出通知才知道违约可能造成这种特别损失。针对合理时间,前者的先例有 Carlton SS Co Ltd v Castle Mail Packets Co Ltd (1898) AC 486,涉及在一个租约下承租人延误装货,但延误是由于港口的特殊情况而造成,而这种情况是双方订约时就应该知道。

至于后者的先例,第一个有 Charnock v Liverpool Corp (1968) 1 WLR 1498,案情涉及一个车房用了 8 个星期修理原告的车子,这被判是太长与超出了合理时间,一般这种修理只需要5个星期,所以车房要赔偿原告因为延误造成的损失。车房对延误的理由是人手短缺与其他紧急的工作需要赶,但这些理由都不被接受,因为都是作为顾客的车主在订约时不知道的车房困难,不能包括在合理时间内。另一个先例是Foster v Heintzmann (1923) 4 DLR 166,涉及一架钢琴的买卖。订购是在9月初,到了圣诞节还没有交货。但卖方并不需要承担延误的责任,因为他不知道买方是意图把这架钢琴作为圣诞礼物,所以他有较宽松的合理时间。

相反是在Panalpina v Densil Underwear (1981) 1 Lloyd's Rep 187先例,涉及一批在11月订购的衬衣空运去尼日利亚。但承运人有延误,衬衣运抵尼日利亚的日期是12月18日与12月21日,已经赶不及圣诞节的销售,买方于是拒货并导致托运的卖方蒙受损失。事后承运人向卖方索赔运费,但卖方以承运人的延误反索赔一笔更加庞大的利润损失(因为被买方拒货)。在该先例是承运人败诉,原因是法院相信卖方在托运时曾经告诉承运人,该批衬衣必须在圣诞前抵达并赶上圣诞节的销售。Fay大法官是这样说:"I have already found that I accept Mr. Ram's evidence to the effect that he informed Mr. Fagin that the purchaser in Lagos wanted the goods before Christmas, for the Christmas market, and that he told because the purchaser insisted he wanted them for Christmas. That seems to me, accepting it as I do, to bring the defendants' claim within the second rule in Hadley v Baxendale."

但会有情况是即使没有通知,承运人(或是买卖合约的卖方)也应该知道买方需要赶上圣诞节的销售,如有关的货物是圣诞灯饰或者是圣诞树。

较早提到的Jonathan Wren & Co Ltd v Microdec plc先例也带出了另一个问题,有关"履行通常需要多久"(time normally required for performance)。在该先例,法院考虑了该电脑软件已经有存货,安装并不太困难,并在短时间内就可以让客户使用。这方面的考虑也在其他先例有涉及,如在Nelson v Patrick (1846) 2 Car & Kir 641先例,涉及原告指被告延误收回装水泥的桶,但法院认为被告应该有一个宽松与合理的时间履行。Wilde大法官说:"A tradesman, who has to send his goods to all parts of the country, must necessarily require a considerable time to get back the casks from his customs."

可以想得到,如果收回的桶是在外国,特别是一些遥远的国家,这一合理时间恐怕会需要更长了。如果双方有了一个规定的明示时间,即使是短暂得不现实,无法履行,被告还是违反时间规定,因为明示了的情况下就不存在合理与否的说法,必须严格履约。

在考虑履行通常需要的合理时间时,也应考虑订约时合约双方是否已经可以预见履行时会遇上延误。例如,在较早时已经提到的Carlton SS Co Ltd v Castle Mail Packets Co Ltd先例,相关港口的特殊情况就是船舶需要搁浅在泊位装货(这种情况在河道的港口经常会发生,搁浅通常也不会对船舶有危险,因为河床是软泥),但有关的租约规定了船舶不允许搁浅(always afloat),这导致船舶在低潮时无法靠泊而带来装货严重延误。但这种情况是双方订合约的时候预见得到的。

这种道理可以适用在许多其他的情况,如国际货物买卖合约或程租,如果涉及一个航次是冬季横跨大西洋,可以合理预见会遇上坏天气的延误。合理抵达卸港的时间显然就不能与夏季横跨大西洋甚至不必越洋的航次相提并论。

双方在订合约时所针对的标的或者事情,也是计算合理时间的考虑之一。例如,在货物买卖或货物运输,涉及“易腐”(perishable)货物,如水果,显然履行的合理时间就会更短暂。如果涉及波动激烈的市场,也会是有同样的考虑,这可看 Jaslow v Waterbury Co (CCA 2nd Circuit), 296 F363 (1924)先例。

最后一提的是,如果履行的时间有贸易习惯,这也是考虑的因素之一。这方面有爱尔兰的 Ross Brothers v Shaw (1917) IR 367 先例,美国的 Rochester Distilling Co v Geloso 92 Conn 43 (1917)先例。英国这方面的先例是 FC Bradley and Sons Ltd v Colonial Continental Trading Ltd (1964) 2 Lloyd's Rep 52,案情涉及英国著名的 Covent Garden 蔬果超市的贸易习惯是土豆应该可以立即运送,因此上诉庭判在该先例合理的运送时间是 72 小时。

4.2.1.2 合约履行时存在的因素与周边环境

这可以先节录 Seymour 大法官在 Astea UK Ltd v Time Group Ltd (2003) EWHC 725 先例中说:“... a broad consideration, with the benefit of hindsight, and viewed from the time at which one party contends that a reasonable time for performance had been exceeded, of what would, in all the circumstances which are by then known to have happened, have been a reasonable time for performance. That broad consideration is likely to include any estimate given by the performing party of how long it would take him to perform; whether that estimate has been exceeded, and if so, in what circumstances; whether the party for whose benefit the relevant obligation was to be performed needed to participate in the performance, actively, in the sense of collaborating in what was needed to be done, or passively, in the sense of being in a position to receive performance, or not at all; whether it was necessary for third parties to collaborate with the performing party in order to enable it to perform; and what exactly was the cause, or were the causes, of the delay to performance. The list is not intended to be exhaustive.”(这是一个广泛的考虑,并且可以“事后诸葛亮”地考虑所有双方知道已经发生了的情况,决定什么是履行有关承诺的合理时间。这广泛的考虑包括履约方曾经作出过的需要的时间的估计;如果超出这个估计时间是什么原因造成以及这原因是否可以包括在合理时间内;被承诺方是否需要参与这有关的履行,如要提供合作;履约方是否需要第三方的合作才能履行等。)

显然履行的“承诺方”(promisor)的实际行为与态度都会是考虑合理时间的因素。履约方/承诺方如果能证明他是尽最大的努力履行,就会有较大可能被视为在需要的合理时间内。但如果证据是显示了履约方懒散,就会有不同的判决。在第一个美国的 Jay Clutter Custom Digging Co v English 181 Ind App 603, 393 NE 2d 230 (1979) (Indiana)先例,考虑到承诺方两次向被承诺方保证会在几天后完工,但依然没有完成,法院判是承诺方没有在合理时间内履行合约。另一个美国先例是 Mizell v Burnett 49 NC249, 69 Am Dec 744 (1857) (North Carolina),案情涉及木材的买卖,卖方被判是可以拒绝买方太迟的付运要求,因为有证据显示买方故意浪费时间希望看看市场会否上涨。

这方面也涉及承诺方有否采取合理的步骤履行。在 Hales v London and North Western Railway (1863) 4 B & S 66 先例,被告同意用货运火车送一批货去 Sunderland 附近的目的地。因为目的地不通火车,被告根据惯常做法,先把货送往 Newcastle,几天后由运输公司送往目的地。法院判是被告没有在合理时间内履行合约。被告本可以先通过火车将货物从 Newcastle 送到 Sunderland,然后再通过运输公司送往目的地,这样货物就可以提前几天送达。被告没有采取合理的步骤保证货物送达的速度,导致法院得出了被告没有在合理时间内履行合约的结论。由此可见,如果承运人有自己惯常的做法(但这不一定是最快捷的),最好在合约中写明路线,或至少明示规定时间,而不要依赖默示的合理时间。

“被承诺方”(promisee)的实际行为与态度也是考虑合理时间的因素,特别是一个十分积极与不断催促对方履行的被承诺方,就会有更大可能说服法院或仲裁庭对方没有在合理时间内履行。这方面的先例有 Wigginton v Dodd (1862) 2 F & F 844 与美国的 US v 476 Acres of Land 86 F Supp 632 (1949) (Pennsylvania)等。

接下来一个十分重要的考虑因素就是在履行的过程中是否发生了一些不可预见的也是承诺方“无法控制事项”(supervening event)。这种无法控制事项甚至可能会导致合约的受阻,但后者在延误程度上就需要高得多,需要达致双方订合约时所知道或应该知道的合约目的再也无法达到的程度。但如果履行中遇上无法控制事项只带来延误,通常只是会延长合理的时间。在 Hick v Raymond and Reid (1893) AC 22 先例,案情涉及提单下要求收货人负责从船上卸货,但没有规定时间。卸货因为码头工人罢工被中断了几个星期,争议就是收货人是否要对延误造成的损失负责。这就又涉及什么是合理时间的问题,Watson 勋爵是这样说:“The rule is not confined to contracts for the carriage of goods by sea. In the case of other contracts the condition of reasonable time has been frequently interpreted; and has invariably been held to mean that the party on whom it is incumbent duly fulfils his obligation, notwithstanding protracted delay, so long as such delay is attributable to causes beyond his control, and he has neither acted negligently not unreasonably.”

从 Watson 勋爵最后的一句话中可以见到,在履行过程中如果受到不可预见又无法控制的外来事项,只要的确是无法控制的原因造成,履约方/承诺方没有疏忽或不合理之处,就谈不上是违约,或是合理时间也需要相应的延长。而如果是明示的时间规定,规定的时间就必须严格依照,不存在合理与否的说法。这也要看合约怎样写,如有没有针对性的免责条文或是不可抗力条文。否则,这方面的延误风险是属于承诺方,因为合约的履行是严格责任,而遇上这种外来事项导致延误的风险也是属于承诺方要承担的。

4.2.2 默示之二:考虑时间规定是否重要的因素

如果在合约没有明示约定有关的时间规定是否是"重要"(of essence),就会需要法院或仲裁庭作出决定。这通常是一个非常重要的决定,牵连的金额往往也比较大,因为通常会涉及终止合约的问题。也就是如果违反时间规定(不论是明示或默示)是重要,无辜方就可以极轻微的延误终止合约,而他这样做往往是市场的变动使得终止合约对他十分有利。相反,如果违反时间规定是不重要,只是保证条文,无辜方终止合约也就变为自己违约/毁约。

相对其他类别的违约,英国法律更愿意把违反时间规定视为重要。原因主要是两个方面:第一,延误通常不会带来金钱损失或即使有金钱损失也很难计算,所以为了对延误的违约有一定的救济与阻吓违约方不要轻视时间规定,让无辜方有权终止合约显然是有效的办法。第二,延误的违约只会是一个方式,就是比时间规定晚了。但其他类别的违约会有许多方式,其中程度轻重会很不一样。这样针对其他类别的违约,就不会把它视为条件条文,否则一个程度很轻的违约也会带来合约的终止就有点太过。

考虑时间规定是否重要的其他因素会在以下进一步的探讨。

4.2.2.1 考虑之一:合约承诺的本质是什么

已经提到过贵族院的 Bunge Corporation New York v Tradax SA (1981) 2 Lloyds Rep 1 先例明确了如果合约的本质是商业合约,就有更大可能把时间规定视为是重要。但背后的原因不外是为了肯定,国际货物买卖经常涉及一连串的买卖/转卖与其他关联合约(即涉及合约链),商品市场往往有很大与很快的波动导致"价格变化"(fluctuation in value),甚至会涉及"合约标的的寿命不长"(subject matter of wasting nature)等。

商业合约经常被提到的一个特点是某个特定的合约可能只是一连串合约中的一部分,不能准时履行一个合约造成的后果会顺着这一连串的合约传下而导致严重后果。例如,在 CIF/CFR 买卖合约下卖方需要作出"划归通知"(notice of appropriation)(这通知主要是向买方说明有关的货物是装在什么船舶上与哪一天签发的提单),而准时作出划归通知的重要性可参见杨大明律师的《国际货物买卖》一书之第 323 页。

而除了划归通知,国际货物买卖合约还会有许多其他的"通知"(notification)或"指定"(nomination),如 FOB 买方指定船舶与通知卖方有关预计抵港日期,FOB 卖方指定装港或 CIF/CFR 买方指定卸港,买方指定银行收取付运文件。对这些通知或指定的时间规定通常是条件条文,因为除了会涉及一连串买卖合约外,还会涉及被通知的一方是在收到通知后才能采取下一步的行动。例如,FOB 卖方不准时指定装港,FOB 买方作为承租人就无法在程租合约下向船东宣港。这可能会带来一连串的影响,如船舶会因此赶不上租约的销约期,严重的更会是船东把承租人不宣港视为违约/毁约等。

问题是有其他类别的合约也会有同样的特征,所以有人认为并不应该把商业合约与非商业合约区别对待。在一些非商业合约中,对肯定性的要求与商业合约一样重要。如房屋买卖也常常涉及一连串的合约,其中一个合约的延误也会影响合约链的履行。从这个角度上看,很难说两者有区别。因此,Treitel 教授在他的《Treitel on the Law of Contract》一书中认为,更好的做法是所有的合约都根据延误履行会带来什么潜在后果来决定是否是条件条文。看来,Treitel 教授认为在没有明示条文说明的情况下,应把所有合约的时间规定都当做"中间条文"(innominate term)。

有先例判是货物买卖如果只是买方自用,不涉及其他合约,时间规定就不被视为重要:Paton v Payne (1897) 35 SLR 112; Re Simoco Digital UK Ltd (2004) EWHC 209 (Ch)等先例。而在本章之 4.1.2 段曾经提到 1979 年英国《货物销售法》把支付货款的延误不视为重要,也是因为这一笔金钱不会与其他合约有牵连:Martindale v Smith (1841) 1 QB 389 先例。相反,准时开出信用证被视为重要,除了其他原因外,也因为这会涉及其他合约,如中间贸易商需要该信用证向下一个卖方开出信用证,或者是以"背靠背"(back - to - back)或者是以"转让"(transfer)的方式。

有关合约如果涉及市场有很大与很快的波动,或是合约标的的寿命不长,也会导致在本质上时间规定会被视为"重要"(of essence)或条件条文。这方面也可看 Salmon 勋爵在 United Scientific Holdings Ltd v Burnley BC (1978) AC 904 先例中说:"In commercial transactions, provisions as to time are usually but not always regarded as being of the essence of the contract. They are certainly so regarded where the subject matter of the contract is the acquisition of **a wasting asset** or of **a perishable commodity** or is something likely to **change rapidly in value.** In such cases if, e. g. the seller fails to deliver within the time specified in the contract, the buyer may well be seriously prejudiced."(加黑部分是笔者的强调)

例如在 Re Schwabacher (1908) 98 L. T. 127 先例,Parker 大法官说:"With regard to contracts for the sale of shares, I think that time is of the essence both at law and in equity. Shares continually vary in price from day to day, and that is precisely why courts of equity have considered such a contract to be one in which time is of the essence of the contract, and not like a contract for the sale and purchase of real estate, in which time is not of the essence of the contract."

另是在 Grant & Ors v Lapid Developments Ltd & Anor (1996) B. C. C. 410 先例,案情也是涉及股票买卖,法院判是公司股票在 5 年间价值波动很大导致转让的时间规定是重要。这类先例还有 British and Commonwealth Holdings plc v Quadrex Holdings Inc (1989) QB 842 (CA)与香港的 Sun Lee Kyoung Sil v Jia Weili HCA 1768/

2009 等。

合约标的的寿命不长的先例看来不多与年代久远,有涉及“年金保险”(life annuity)的 Withy v Cottle (1823) Turn & R 78;涉及较短房屋租赁合约的 Hudson v Temple (1860) 54 E. R. 735, Tilley v Thomas (1867) L. R. 3 Ch. App. 61 与 Pips (Leisure Productions) Ltd v Walton (1982) 45 P. & C. R. 415;涉及营业中业务的买卖的 Cowles v Gate (1871) L. R. 7 Ch. App. 12 与 Lock v Bell (1930) Ch. 35 等。

4.2.2.2 考虑之二:时间规定所针对的承诺尺度

时间规定如果是针对一个特定或局限的承诺(如支付一笔钱或交出某些文件)就有更大的机会被视为“重要”(of essence)。相反,如果一个合约(即使是商业合约)有针对许多不同轻重的承诺的时间规定,并且另有条文说明本合约的所有时间规定都是重要,就很难会被解释或是默示为所有合约内的时间规定都是重要。这里的精神是与 The “Hongkong Fir” (1961) 1 Lloyd's Rep 478 先例带来的中间条文的说法是一致的。

Bovis Homes Inc v Oakcliff Investment Corp, Ch D, 30 March 1994 先例涉及房屋建造工程的完工日期是否是重要的争议。合约对于完工的时间规定是 3 年,但完工也包括了很多其他的承诺,如材料必须优质,工艺必须达标,必须符合所有有关的批准与规定等。这表示承建商在这样的承诺下可以有许多不同方式的违约,而且是本质上与时间规定的延误无关。这被法院判 3 年的时间规定并非是重要或条件条文,Harman 大法官说:“In considering whether time is of the essence of a term in a contract the Court must bear in mind the nature of the obligation imposed by the term. If the term requires a single act to be done it is easier to conclude that the time for doing the required act may be of the essence of the term.”

在稍后的 Etzin v Reece (2002) All ER (D) 405 先例也有同样的说法。该先例涉及复杂的房屋买卖,其中合约的第 1 条文涉及支付费用(包括按比例的房价、律师费用、印花税等)与第 3 条文要求“勤力与尽快”(diligently and promptly)的作出有关安排。Etzin 先生(只是联手买下该房屋的租客之一)延误支付他按比例应该支付的费用与房价,这被 L. Henderson QC 大法官判是违约,并导致完成交易时把他排除。有关第 1 条文与第 3 条文的违约,是说:

“The obligation on the lessees in clause 1 of the May Agreement to pay the purchase price and other costs referred to in the Second Schedule **'as and when the same fall due'** is in my judgment to be construed as requiring them to contribute their percentage shares when payment is legally due, and by necessary implication to make their contributions available in sufficient time to enable the costs to be paid on the due date. In the case of the purchase price payable on completion, I accept the submission for the Defendants that this means putting the nominee purchaser's solicitors in funds in sufficient time to enable completion to take place on the date agreed ...

This obligation is then reinforced by clause 3, which obliges each of the lessees **diligently and promptly** to do all things necessary or desirable to further the success of the application and the acquisition of the freehold. . . .

Adopting this approach, it seems to me plain beyond argument that Mr Etzin was in serious and repeated breach of his obligations under both clause 1 and clause 3 of the May Agreement."

但针对这个涉及延误的违约是否"重要"(of essence),L. Henderson QC 大法官说:"Attractively thought these submissions were advanced, I am unable to accept them. The principal difficulty, in my judgment, is that **the obligations under both clauses** 1 **and** 3 **embrace a wide variety of matters, ranging from the critically important to the relatively trivial.** For example, under clause 1 the obligation to pay the lessee's share of the purchase price when it falls due is obviously crucial, but the obligation to pay the lessee's share of stamp duty, or of professional fees or disbursements, may be much less significant, especially in the absence of any machinery for ascertaining exactly when the payments fall due. So too under clause 3 the things that are necessary or desirable to further the success of the application and the acquisition of the freehold will vary enormously in importance, and in my view it is impossible to impute to the parties a common intention that any failure to do any of those things diligently and promptly, however insignificant the breach and however trivial the consequences, is to be treated without more as a repudiatory breach of an essential term. **In my judgment both clauses are classic examples of intermediate or innominate contractual terms, where the legal consequences of a breach will depend on the particular circumstances.**"(加黑部分是笔者的强调)

4.2.2.3 考虑之三:与合约其他条文或其他相关合约责任的关系

这在较早4.2.2.1段已经有提到,如在国际货物买卖合约中的条文,如果针对"通知"(notification)或"指定"(nomination)的时间规定通常是条件条文:Busk v Spence (1815) 4 Camp 329; Tsakiroglou & Co Ltd v Transgrains SA (1958) 1 Lloyd's Rep 562; The "Al Hofuf" (1981) 1 Lloyd's Rep 81; Gill & Duffus SA v Societe pour L'Exportation des Sucres SA (1986) 1 Lloyd's Rep 322 (CA); Warde v Feedex International Inc (1985) 2 Lloyd's Rep 290 等先例。原因是除了会涉及一连串买卖合约或其他相关合约外,还会涉及被通知方是在收到通知后才能采取下一步行动。但如果在比较少见的情况下不会有这方面的影响,就会作出不一样的判决。例如,Kidston v Monceau Ironworks (1902) 77 Com Cas 82 先例涉及了 CIF/CFR 合约。而 CIF/CFR 合约如果约定几个可能的卸港或是面积比较广泛的卸货区域,就通常会有明示或默示条文要求买方准时向卖方作出通知有关他最后选择的卸港。通常这一时间是合约的条件条文,卖方有了这个通知才可以租船以及确定货物装船后签发提单的卸港,因此这时间规定显然是重要。但在该先例的少见情况是买方延误通知不影响卖方租船与准时作出付运,时间规定被判是不重要。

同样的原则也适用在其他类别的合约,毕竟解释合约是要整体对待。这里先介绍在本章4.1.2段提到的房屋租赁的"租金调整条文"(rent review clause)。英国房屋租赁合约通常会是年代很长,在 United Scientific Holdings Ltd v Burnley BC (1978) AC 904 先例涉及的两个租约,一个长达21年,另一个长达99年。在21年的租约,第一个7年约定的租金是每年117,340英镑,但余下的两个7年就适用租金调整的机制。根据不同写法,这种条文的调整机制往往是先要房东在一个时间规定内向租客作出通知要求增加的新租金,之后是租客在一个规定时间内向房东作出一个反通知,也就是像一个反要约,说明他愿意支付的租金。而之后如果双方无法达成协议,条文会规定由第三人,如英国测量师学会的会长,作出决定。该租金调整条文也会多加一句被称为"break clause",如果最后决定的租金仍是租客认为承担不起,他就有在规定时间终止租约的选择权。

针对租金调整条文中的时间规定到底是否"重要"(of essence)有很多争议。如果重要(不论通过明示或默示),就会对房东造成很大不公平。他可能由于短暂的延误作出通知而失了增加租金的机会,导致接下来的一段长时间(如7年)还是只能收取租客原来的与偏低的租金。简单而言,在贵族院的 United Scientific Holdings Ltd v Burnley BC 先例,已经明确了这些时间规定并不重要。但有先例判是同一个租约下如果有一条"break clause"并规定了时间,就会是不一样:Richards & Son v Karenita (1971) 221 EG 25; Coventry City Council v J Hepworth & Son Ltd (1983) 46 P & CR 170 (CA); Legal and General Assurance (Pension Management) Ltd v Cheshire CC (1983) 46 P & CR 160 等先例。否则可以想到的结果就是房东如果延误启动调整租金机制,可能会导致租客即使行使他在 break clause 的选择权终止租约也是太迟。例如,房东在第8年才启动租金调整机制,之后英国测量师学会的会长决定的租金是租客负担不起。即使租客根据 break clause 马上选择终止租约,还是要补回这一年大幅上涨的租金差价,因为租约是明示规定在第一个7年后的租金就适用调整后的租金,这显然对租客不公平。但如果没有这一条 break clause,看来就会有不同的判法:Touche Ross & Co v Secretary of State for the Environment (1983) 46 P & CR 187 先例。

4.2.2.4 考虑之四:对无辜方有否其他救济

如果把时间规定视为重要,显然就给了无辜方从有关合约中脱身的机会。在现实中,无辜方想从合约中脱身往往与违约无关或只有很少关系,除非延误十分严重。例如,无辜方是一批货物的卖方,如果市场下跌,他就会尽量容忍买方的各种延误,即使这些都是属于条件条文,如准时开出信用证,准时派遣船舶装港等。但如果反过来市场猛涨,他就会毫不犹豫在买方稍有延误的情况下终止买卖合约。显然,英国法律不鼓励太容易让任何一方终止合约,正如 Roskill 大法官在 The "Hansa Nord"

(1975) 2 Lloyd's Rep 445 先例中说:"In principle contracts are made to be performed and not to be avoided according to the whims of market fluctuation and where there is a free choice between two possible constructions. I think the Court should tend to prefer that construction which will ensure performance and not encourage avoidance of contractual obligations."

这就解释了如果在有关合约已经有了救济的办法针对某类的延误违约,或是可以有一个后果比较不严重的解决办法,法院或仲裁庭也就不会把这种延误视为重要。由于延误的损失很难计算,不少合约针对延误会以违约方向无辜方赔偿每天多少钱的"议定赔偿"(liquidated damages)。在国际货物买卖合约,就经常会有这种条文。如卖方无法在付运期内作出付运,这本来是违反条件条文,但会有条文说是卖方可以向买方作出通知延长付运期若干天,并以货价打折作为对价。这样,只要卖方作出通知延长付运期,就不存在违反条件条文的说法了。也会有条文要求卖方在某规定的日期交货,而如果有延误,就会每5天或10天赔偿一定金额的议定赔偿。但显然,在买卖合约最常见的时间规定,就是在FOB合约下卖方承诺在固定装货时间完成装货与CIF/CFR合约下买方承诺在固定卸货时间完成卸货。但众所周知,这方面的时间规定并非是条件条文,因为双方通常会同意装卸货如果有延误,违反承诺的卖方或买方需要支付"滞期费"(demurrage)。同样的固定装卸时间与滞期费条文也在相关的程租合约出现,这时间规定也不是条件条文,违约唯一的救济就是支付滞期费:Aktielskabet v. Arcos Ltd (1927) 1 KB 352 (CA); Suisse Atlantique v N. V. Rotterdamsche (1966) 1 Lloyd's Rep 529 等先例。

所以在买卖合约,不存在无辜方(不论是FOB买方或CIF/CFR卖方)可以在固定装卸货时间届满但没有装货或卸货时终止合约,或指令船舶离开装港或卸港,或私下去其他卸港卸货。问题是如果延误装卸十分严重,仅靠滞期费的支付不足赔偿损失,或是对违约方的经济状况不了解导致无辜方对将来取回滞期费信心不足,就有疑问到底延误装卸到什么程度才能终止合约,或是因为有了滞期费作为救济就根本不会有这样的一天?简单的答案就是要等到该合约的“受阻延误”(frustration delay)。[7] 这恐怕是要无辜方等太久,而且不肯定到底是多久才是安全声称合约自动终止。这样,不想依赖普通法的受阻延误,就只能靠自己在合约中加上明示条文说明在装卸港发生延误,无辜方怎样保护自己。在装港,特别是在一些供应货物不稳定的港口(如在亚洲的印尼港口就经常有这种问题),无辜方(这会是 FOB 买卖合约的买

---

〔7〕 合约受阻的理念是相对比较后期才发展起来,以前的普通法是合约必须“绝对履行”(absolute performance):Paradine v Jane (1647) 82 ER 897 先例。合约受阻是直到 Taylor v Caldwell (1863) 122 ER 309 先例才开始出现。合约受阻的经典说法是 Radcliffe 勋爵在 Davis Constractors Ltd v Fareham UDC (1956) AC 696 先例中说:“... Frustration occurs whenever the law recognizes that without default of either party a contractual obligation has become incapable of being performed because the circumstances in which performance is called for would render it a thing radically different from that which was undertaken by the contract. *Non haec in foedera veni*. It was not this I promised to do.”至于什么程度的延误会构成受阻延误可令合约自动终止,可节录 Baihache 大法官在 Admiral Shipping Co v Weidner Hopkins Ltd (1916) 1 KB 429 先例中的说法:“... by it the fulfillment of the contract in the only way in which fulfillment is contemplated and practicable is so inordinately postponed that its fulfillment when the delay is over will not accomplish the only object or objects which both parties to the contract must have known that each one of them had in view at the time they made the contract and for the accomplishment of which object or objects the contract was made.”这是说延误的程度达致双方订合约时所知道或应该知道该合约的目的再也无法达到的程度。受阻延误也有其他大同小异的说法,如“goes to the root of the matter”,“deprives the charterer of the whole benefit of the contract”,“entirely frustrates the object of the charterer in chartering the ship”等。到底延误多久才达致受阻延误要看个别案件的不同事实,但显然是需要十分严重的程度。著名的期租合约先例 The “Hongkong Fir” (1961) 2 Lloyd's Rep 478 与 The “Hermosa” (1982) 1 Lloyd's Rep 570 就是典型的教训,该两艘船舶都涉及进行修理的漫长延误,船舶状况显然极差,停租的时间比履行的时间长得多,但两个先例的承租人都被判是违约/毁约,因为在还没有受阻延误前就终止租约。但不同案情也会使得表面看来很短的时间就构成了受阻延误。如在 Poussard v Spiers (1876) 1 QBD 410 先例,案情涉及一个戏剧歌手与剧院的雇佣合约,但在表演的第一天,该歌手生病而无法演出,而在 3 天后才病愈要求复工,但被剧院拒绝,这被法院接受,认为第一天的表演是该合约的基础目的。这里也可以一提是受阻延误与“违约/毁约延误”(repudiation delay)在不同案件中对延误的程度会一致,这在 The “Hermosa”先例有针对。它们唯一的区别就是涉及合约一方的违约/毁约延误,只有无辜方才有终止合约的选择权,因为本来是保证条文的延误严重至违约/毁约可让无辜方接受终止合约。但不涉及违约/毁约的受阻延误是自动令有关的合约终止,而终止是双方合约方都有的权利。针对受阻延误需要多久的延误,是不能事后在审理时看最后造成了多久延误。这在仲裁法律著名的 The “Nema” (1981) 2 Lloyd's Rep 239 (HL)先例有针对,该先例涉及独任仲裁员 Donald Davis 先生判是有关的租约因为装港的罢工而受阻,但事后显示仲裁员的决定作出后,罢工很快在一周内结束。但贵族院支持上诉庭的 Templeman 大法官的判法:“In the present case there is one circumstance which in my judgement disqualifies the court from insisting that ... it would have reached a conclusion different from that of the arbitrator. That circumstance is that the court inevitably considers the matter with hindsight, that is to say with knowledge that the strike ended on 5 October. On 26 September the arbitrator was driven by both parties to make a decision without knowing whether or when the strike would end.”针对合约受阻另可看本书第十三章之 1.1 段与第十五章之第 3 段。

方或程租合约的船东)会加上一条明示条文说明在装港等了15天或20天不等,但还没有开始装货,FOB买方或程租合约的船东就有权终止合约并保留索赔的权利。这种条文通常被称为"Jupiter条文"(条文的名称是由于在20世纪80年代曾经出过这种大事,而承租人就叫Jupiter)。

Jupiter条文的一种写法可以是如下:

"Owners' option of cancelling:

If for reasons not attributable to the vessel and/or owners (a) Charterers fail in their duty to furnish voyage instructions or loading orders in accordance with Cl. 2, and such failure has lasted for not less than 10 days, or (b) Loading has not commenced and 20 days have passed after valid notice of readiness has been tendered, owners shall have the option of cancelling this charter party.

If such option is exercised and the delay is attributable to owners, they shall not be liable for loss of charterers. Whether or not owners exercise this option no claim they may have on charterers for loss of time or otherwise shall be prejudiced thereby."

在其他类别的合约也是有同样的精神,如在涉及租金调整的United Scientific Holdings Ltd v Burnley BC (1978) AC 904贵族院先例,以及后来的一些案例如Metrolands Investments Ltd v. Dewhurst Ltd (1986) 3 All ER 659 (CA)与Chancery Lane Developments Ltd v. Wade's Departmental Stores Ltd (1987) 53 P & CR 306 (CA)等,由于法院认定房东与租客均可以启动租金调整的机制,就没有必要把房东准时作出通知要求调整租金视为重要,而让租客在对方轻微延误的情况下取巧,甚至在某些合约采取严重的手段终止租约。

在同样的精神下,如果延误或违反时间规定不存在有任何其他的救济,这就会加强认定时间规定是重要,因为除了让无辜方有权终止合约外,就等于违约方的延误根本没有救济可言。这种情况会发生在某些类别的合约如"担保"(guarantee),因为延误只会带来无辜方的担忧与失去保障,而这无法量化为金钱:SCCMO (London) Ltd v Societe Generale de Compensation (1956) 1 Lloyd's Rep 299; The "Selene G" (1981) 2 Lloyd's Rep 180等先例。更明显的情况是发生在"单方面合约"(unilateral contract)或"选择权"(option),这在下一小段会探讨。

4.3 单方面合约/选择权

"合约的选择权"(contractual option)经常会遇到,这在本书第九章之3.2段有详论。它并非是上述所讲的"承诺性条文"(promissory condition),而是属于一种"单方面合约"(unilateral contract),也就是拥有选择权的一方在规定的时间内行使后,才变为对双方有约束的"新合约"(new contract)。如在一个租购合约,允许一方在一个规定时间内作出选择是否购买,而如果他行使了这一选择权,就会从一个租用合约变为一个买卖合约了。

法律明确如果有选择权的一方没有严格按照有关条文的规定行使权利,这包括时间规定,无辜方就不再受到约束:Hare v Nicoll (1966) 2 QB 130; United Dominions Trust (Commercial) Ltd v Eagle Aircraft Services Ltd (1968) 1 WLR 74 (CA); Millers Wharf Partnership Ltd v Corinthian Column Ltd (1991) 61 P & CR 461; Di Luca v Juraise (Springs) Ltd (1998) 79 P & CR 139 (CA); Valentines Properties Ltd v Huntco Corp Ltd (2001) UKPC 14; Credit Lyonnais SA v Russell Jones & Walker (2002) EWHC 1310 (Ch); Haugland Tankers AS v RMK Marine (2005) 1 Lloyd's Rep 573 等先例。

显然行使合约选择权的时间规定,视为是"重要"(of essence)。如果违反,带来的后果是失了这一选择权或被视为"弃权"(waiver)。根本原因是这种延误与上述的承诺性条文的延误不一样,它不涉及"违约"(breach),所以也不存在有权选择的一方延误行使选择权会面对金钱损失的索赔,因为双方还没有新合约的约束。例如,在 Nicholson v Smith (1882) 22 ChD 640 先例,案情涉及租客可以在规定时间内选择续租。显然租客必须在规定时间内作出是否续租的选择,否则会让房东不知道或不肯定是否应该尽快寻找新的租客,从而可能会带来无法量化的麻烦与损失。另在较近期的 Millichamp v Jones (1983) 1 All ER 267 先例,案情涉及买地的选择权。这又是买方或者潜在买方(因为他可能选择不买)延误行使其选择权会带来对卖方的严重不公平,毕竟房屋价格可能波动,卖方在买方延误的期间会错失了其他的机会。例如,被迫拒绝其他出更高价格的买方,但这方面的损失并不能向还没有合约关系的延误方索赔。在商业合约中,也经常有延误行使这种合约规定的选择权的先例,如在 The "Avisfaith" (1969) 2 Lloyd's Rep 257 先例,涉及承租人延误行使延长租约的选择权,Roskill 大法官判是违反了一条重要的条文,说:"First, the option is created in favour of the charterers. It is their option. Secondly, the only condition attaching to the exercise of that option by them is that they have to declare whether they are going to exercise it and declare that not later than a stated date. It is axiomatic contract law that parties are entitled to know their right and that if one party has a right which he can exercise unilaterally in his absolute discretion. Then he must exercise that right either, if no time limit is provided, within a reasonable time, or, if a time limit provided, then within the time limit so provided. Otherwise uncertainties introduced into business transactions whereas certainty is an essential prerequisite to the efficient conduct of business."

合约选择权在这方面明确的法律地位曾经为房屋租赁合约的租金调整机制带来了一个非常复杂的问题,这是在 Samuel Properties (Developments) Ltd v Hayek (1972) 1 WLR 1296 先例,有关的租金调整条文把房东这个可以调整租金的权利明示为"选择权"(option)。这导致上诉庭判房东如果没有严格按照时间规定行使这一选择权,就失去了调整租金的权利。这个先例也带来其他同样判法的先例,如 Stylo Shoes Ltd v Wetherall Bond Street W. 1 Ltd (1974) 237 E. G. 343 与 Mount Charlotte Investments Ltd v Leek and Westbourne Building Society (1976) 1 All E. R. 890。但同时也有唱反调的先例,如 Bailey v Memorial Enterprises Ltd（1974）1 WLR 728（CA）与 Kenilworth Industrial Sites v EC Little & Co Ltd（1975）1 WLR 143（CA）,认为整个租金调整的机制与选择权无关,所以时间规定并不重要。这方面的混乱最后是在 United Scientific Holdings Ltd v Burnley BC（1978）AC 904 的贵族院先例有了明确。首先明确了租金调整机制并非只是给房东利益的一个单方面合约,而是双方均有利益。因为没有租金调整条文,房东就不会愿意以订约时的合理租金长期出租给租客,因为避免不了将来会有通货膨胀的问题。这表示租金调整的时间规定并不重要,也没有商业上原因必须在规定的一天确定调整。而且房东延误启动调整租金,租客如果觉得自己会受损,可以主动要求租金调整或向屋主作出通知使得时间规定变为重要(这在本章之第5段有详论)。反正在 United Scientific Holdings Ltd v Burnley BC 先例后,法律应该是明确了这方面的时间规定并不重要,但这是一个假设,而假设可以被其他方面否定或改变。这其他方面包括:一是合约条文是否有不同的显示,如明确写明时间规定是重要;二是租金调整条文有否与房屋租赁合约中的其他合约承诺相反的规定;三是周围的环境。

4.4　中国船厂在造船期间发生不可抗力事项的延误通知

针对不可抗力条文在本书第十三章之第1段有详细的介绍,这里只局限针对没有在规定时间内作出"延误通知"(notice of delay)会带来的后果。在实践中,许多条文会明确说明如果没有在规定时间内作出通知的后果,也就是不能依赖不可抗力事项,可以说及时作出通知是依赖不可抗力事项的"先决条件"(condition precedent)。如在 BIMCO Standard Shipbuilding Contract 2007(简称 NEWBUILDCON)的相关条文中说:"The Builder shall notify the Buyer **within [five (5)] running days** of when the Builder becomes aware of the occurrence of any event of delay on account of which the Builder asserts that it may be entitled to claim an extension of the Delivery Date. **A failure to so notify shall bar the Builder from claiming any extension to the Delivery Date.**"(加黑部分是笔者的强调)

这种明确的文字/措辞也在个别造船合约中出现,如在 Finance for Shipping Ltd v Appledore Shipbuilding Ltd（1982）Com L. R. 49 先例中的有关条文的最后一句是说:"Failure on the part of the Builders to provide the Purchasers with the dates of the commencement or end of any delay as aforesaid within the time stipulated herein shall disentitle the Builders from any extension of the delivery date in respect of the event for which the extension shall be claimed."

在 Adyard Abu Dhabi v SD Marine Services（2011）BLR 384 先例,相关合约的不可抗力条文的文字/措辞也是明确了及时通知是先决条件,说:"Failure of the builder to notify in the manner set out above shall disentitle such delay to be considered a permissible delay under the terms of contract."

如果合约中明确写明,没有或延误作出通知的后果再也不能依赖不可抗力事项,那么时间规定是重要或是先决条件是没有争议。这对造船合约(或其他岸上工程合约)会带来的后果就是发生了不可抗力事项,船厂(或承建商)由于没有或延误作出通知而导致不能以该事项延长交船(或完成工程/建筑)日期。而该事项所造成的延误也变为“不允许的延误”(non - permissible delay),导致船厂(或承建商)需要为这种延误赔付“议定赔偿”(liquidated damages),也不能延长交船日期、销约期/死亡日期。

但如果条文没有明确规定是否是先决条件或是“中间条件”(innominate/intermediate term),就经常会带来争议是在没有及时作出通知的情况下可否仍依赖不可抗力事项。而在时间规定是中间条件的情况下只允许被通知方索赔收不到及时通知所导致的损失,而这在通知迟延半天/一天作出的情况下,损失很可能是零。这里也要说明依赖不可抗力事项的一方要作出通知(在造船合约就是船厂给买方/船东通知)的原因,才可以理解为什么稍晚的通知通常不会有损失。

这原因首先可以节录《The Law of Shipbuilding Contracts》(第4版,2012年)一书第164页所说:“Most shipbuilding contracts contain strict time limits within which the builder’s claims for postponement of the Delivery Date must be notified to the buyer. This is primarily designed to afford the buyer an immediate opportunity to investigate the circumstances of the delay and, where appropriate, to challenge the builder’s claim. The time limit provisions are, however, also of significance in permitting both parties to maintain an accurate running total of the builder’s claims for extension of the Delivery Date; this may be needed (*inter alia*) to establish the date of accrual in the buyer’s favour of rights to rescind the contract for delay.”(大部分造船合约有严格的时间规定要求船厂在期间作出有关交船延误的通知。这主要的原因是让买方有机会马上调查有否发生相关的不可抗力事项与即使发生不可抗力事项,有否造成船厂所通知的延误,以便将来对船厂的延期作出质疑与反证的准备。这通知的时限也会在其他方面重要,如让双方都明确知道延误后的新交船日期[毕竟买方要安排接船是需要时间作出准备,或可能会有订下租约或运输合约的销约期或安排,或向融资银行作出通知等]。如果涉及买方想以错过销约期/死亡日期为由终止合约,就更加需要知道船厂延误了多久以计算新的销约期/死亡日期。)

在 Multiplex Construction (UK) v Honeywell Control System (2007) BLR 195 先例中,Jackson 大法官针对作出准时通知的重要性也说:“Contractual terms requiring a contractor to give prompt notice of delay serve a valuable purpose; such notice enables matters to be investigated while they are still current. Furthermore, such notice sometimes gives the employer the opportunity to withdraw instructions when the financial consequences become apparent.”(这也是提到同样的原因,就是允许被通知方及时对通知中的不可抗力事项与造成的延误作出调查,否则会随着时间的流逝而令取证变得困难。此外,通知也给了雇主[在造船合约即是买方/船东]考虑经济后果并撤回一

些指令的机会[例如,在造船合约如果船厂通知交船的延误,而买方的船东订了一个非常赚钱的长期租约但销约期开始紧张,在这种情况下,买方的船东就可以撤回一些指令,如需要延长交船时间的船舶规格的变更或改进,或是放弃一些单方面对买方有利的条文如不要求船舶的试航或修妥]。)

虽然有以上堂而皇之的原因,但最后决定有关的延误通知的时间规定是先决条件或是中间条文还是取决于对条文以及有关合约整体的解释,因为法律在这一方面看来并不明确。所以最好还是采用像 NEWBUILDCON 这种明确的写法,虽然它会对船厂必须准时作出延误通知增加了很多压力,但至少双方能肯定他们之间的法律地位与可以避免将来昂贵的诉讼。这方面法律的不明确可以节录《The Law of Shipbuilding Contracts》(第 4 版,2012 年)一书第 165 页所说:"The legal effect of non – compliance with such a time – limit is unclear. On one view, breach by the builder of his obligation to notify in time sounds only in damages; the builder remains entitled to assert his claim for postponement, although he is liable to the buyer in damages for any loss sustained as a result of the late notification. Given, however, the primary purpose for which a time – limit for notification is incorporated in standard form contracts (i. e. , to afford the buyer an immediate opportunity to investigate and, if necessary, challenge the claim), the better view is that failure to notify in time bars the claim completely."

中国船厂在 2008 年金融海啸之后,涉及数以千计的伦敦仲裁,绝大多数案件都是惨败。可以说,中国船厂越希望保住合约、顺利交船,外国买方就越容易从高价的造船合约中脱身。中国船厂败诉的重要原因之一(其他原因请看本书第四章之第 8 段,第六章之第 14 段,第十一章之第 4 段与第 5 段,第十四章之 2. 5. 2 段与 2. 6. 2 段)是经常不给通知,即使在有关造船合约中的不可抗力条文明确写明及时通知是先决条件(像 NEWBUILDCON 的标准格式合约),中国船厂还是置之不理。虽然有更多造船合约的不可抗力条文并没有明确规定及时通知是先决条件或条件条文甚至写得十分含糊,但以笔者所知道,在伦敦仲裁中都把该时间规定视为重要。虽然部分中国船厂会聘用大律师争辩这一点,如说是如果被视为先决条件,双方在订约时为什么不用 NEWBUILDCON 类似的文字/措辞,但这种争议没有用(请看本书第三章之第 9 段)。伦敦仲裁员的普遍看法在《The Law of Shipbuilding Contracts》(第 4 版,2012 年)一书之第 165 页也有反映,说:"the better view is that failure to notify in time bars the claim completely. . . . Although the existence of a chain of sale contracts would be very unusual indeed in a shipbuilding context, it is submitted that the same principles ought to apply and that, in order to avoid 'commercial confusion' between the parties, the right to claim '*force majeure*' extensions should normally be held conditional upon the builder giving timely notices of the events on which he seeks to rely. This was the approach adopted in a shipbuilding context in *Adyard*, where the High Court held that the builder's claim for a permissible delay extension failed because he had not given timely notice of the 'cause of delay' under standard shipbuilding contract *force majeure* provisions."(虽然一连串买卖合约在造船合约中不常见[在 Bremer v Vanden [1978] 2 Lloyd's Rep. 109 等先例,[8]贵族院把该买卖合约是一连串的合约视为判通知的时间规定是条件条文的十分重要的原因,因为延误作出通知会无可避免导致对方在另一个"背靠背"的合约有同样的违约,而后果可大可小],但同样的原则[贵族院的 Bremer v Vanden 先例]依然适用,就是为了避免商业上的混乱[指双方不知道有延长交船日期或销约期与延长多久的混乱],通常判是船厂作出准时与准确的通知是依赖不可抗力事项延长完工日期的先决条件。这看来也是 Adyard 先例的看法[虽然这不是该先例的主要针对]。)

即使没有好 NEWBUILDCON 标准格式的有关不可抗力条文一样,把延误通知这么明确地写明是可依赖相关不可抗力事项的先决条件或条件条文,任何合约方想依赖不可抗力事项(特别相关条文有明示时间规定或用了一些肯定的文字,如"必须"[shall]),都应该把有关条文的通知要求视为先决条件,并严格执行。除非是该条文明确写明有关的延误通知不是先决条件而只是保证条文或中间条文。虽然在这种争议,双方代表律师通常还是依据 Bremer v Vanden 先例作出争辩,但现实中笔者觉得已经有一定的偏离。这就是在 Mamidoil – Jetoil Greek Petroleum Co SA v. Okta Crude Oil Refinery AD (2003) 2 Lloyd's Rep. 635 先例与 Steria Ltd v Sigma Wireless Communications Ltd (2008) BLR 79 先例,虽然合约条文写得比较含糊,没有明确的时间规定(在 Bremer v Vanden 的贵族院先例说有时间规定作出通知是解释为先决条件的重要一点),但法院还是判准时作出延误通知是先决条件。如在 Mamidoil – Jetoil Greek Petroleum Co SA v. Okta Crude Oil Refinery AD 先例,条文的文字是"必须尽快作出通知"(shall give prompt notice),看来"必须"一词导致法院解释为先决条件。

特别是在造船合约,笔者参与的伦敦仲裁,其他伦敦仲裁员普遍都会同情买方/船东,认为中国船厂没有准时甚至完全没有作出通知对船东太不公平。在没有准时通知的情况下,往往就会剥夺了买方调查取证的机会,特别是对中国船厂想依赖的不可抗力事项与声称所造成的延误都抱有怀疑。而在没有作出延误通知的情况下,往往造成的情况是买方在销约期届临后终止合约,中国船厂就声称有发生过可以根据造船合约延长交船日期或销约期的不可抗力事项。这样,如果只把没有或延误作出通知视为保证条文或中间条文,让中国船厂证明有关的不可抗力事项与所造成的延误,可以说中国船厂只要成功延长一天,就已经足以把买方在销约期刚届临就终止合约的行为从合法变为违约/毁约。这被伦敦仲裁员普遍视为完全不可以接受的不合理与不公平。在这种想法下,本来把时间规定条文视为中间条文也会提升至条件条文,让买方可成功抗拒中国船厂依赖不可抗力事项延长交船日期或销约期。

---

[8] Wilberforce 勋爵在该先例作出的三条指引,可看本书第十三章之 1.3.2.4 段。

虽然也有个别案例说是如果通知是“无效果”(futile)、“无用”(useless)与“不必要”(unnecessary),即使有关的要求是先决条件也可以不必作出:Barrett Bros (Taxis) Ltd v Davies (1996) 1 WLR 1334; The “Mozart” (1985) 1 Lloyd' s Rep 239; The “Ailsa Craig” (2008) 2 Lloyd' s Rep 384 先例。但这种先例的通知都是相对简单,可以理解是如果船长亲自看到了装货设备故障或知悉在哪里还船,就何必再给船长通知。但涉及造船合约,对通知的内容都会有更复杂的明示要求,除了是不可抗力事项开始的一天,也包括结束的一天。另是船厂还要通知船东工程延误的时间。这样,即使船东有总管在船厂监督造船,会知道部分内容,如开始的一天或/与结束的一天,也不会知道全部内容。或是,他即使知道也会否认,这也很容易被仲裁庭相信。所以,船厂不作出通知而指称船东的总管已经知道,恐怕不会容易。

§5　第三种情况:通知使得时间变为重要(notice making time to be essence)

5.1　序言

本章一开始就已经谈到,有一些合约的履行针对时间规定(不论是明示或是默示)属于保证条文,并且提到这些违反会对违约方没有严重后果与阻吓力,这样显然最好的阻吓力就是这个保证条文能够提升为条件条文,通知违约方知道如果不马上或及时履行,就会失了这个最后的机会,所谓的“last chance saloon”。这种类似做法在一些大陆法系国家也有,如德国的民法,具体可见 Tony Weir 翻译的《An Introduction to Comparative Law》(第 3 版, 1998 年)一书。在英国部分的立法中也有类似规定,如《Property Act 1925》之 Section 146 与《Consumer Credit Act 1974》之 Sections 87、88。笔者也可以节录有同样立法条文的《Sale of Goods Act 1979》之 Section 48 (3)如下:“(3) Where the goods are of a perishable nature, or where the unpaid seller gives notice to the buyer of his intention to re – sell, and the buyer does not within a reasonable time pay or tender the price, the unpaid seller may re – sell the goods and recover from the original buyer damages for any loss occasioned by his breach of contract.”

显然这是因为在同样的立法中之 Section 10(1)规定了货物买卖中的买方不准时支付货款并非是重要的条文,换言之,充其量只是保证条文,说:“(1) Unless a different intention appears from the terms of the contract, stipulations as to time of payment are not of the essence of a contract of sale.”

所以就有 Section 48(3)针对,卖方不必守着这批货,漫漫无期地等待买方付款,而是可以作出通知说他有意图将货物转卖给别人。而如果买方依然没有在规定的合理时间内付款,卖方就有权终止有关买卖合约,转卖这批货。这做法等于通过一份通知,把本来是属于保证条文提升为条件条文。

但上述所讲的只是个别立法的规定,做法上只是针对非常局限的情况,并非普遍适用在所有合约关系的普通法。而在普通法的大原则下,显然行不通,因为不存在一种说法是合约的一方可以单方面改变合约条文与本质,包括把本来属于保证条文(或中间条文)单方面提升为条件条文。这方面的先例有 Green v Sevin (1879) 13 Ch D. 589; Raineri v Miles (1981) AC 1050 (HL); Behzadi v Shaftesbury Hotels (1992) Ch 1 (CA);Re Olympia & York Canary Wharf Ltd (No. 2) (1993) BCC 159 等。

所以有必要详细介绍这个以作出通知把时间规定提升为合约重要条文,也就是可让无辜方终止合约的做法,以及该做法怎样在普通法可以自圆其说。

5.2 通知使得时间变为重要的做法来自衡平法院

首先针对这种做法的历史,最早出现在《Supreme Court of Judicature Act 1873》之前,也就是在普通法院与衡平法院还没有合并时的衡平法院。已经提到过,当时的普通法院与衡平法院对时间规定一般是否被视为合约的"重要条文"(of essence)有不同看法与对待。前者通常把一般合约对时间上的规定(包括土地买卖合约)假设为重要条文,但衡平法院就有不同看法与对待(如作出救济,特别是对违约方作出"履约指令"[specific performance])。虽然两个法院都有例外,但还是存在重要的不同。如衡平法院在 Stickney v Keeble (1915) AC 386 (HL)先例,Parker 勋爵有说如果双方明示规定有关时间规定是重要条文,或者在本质上或周边的环境显示应该是重要条文,衡平法院也是接受。但还有一种情况衡平法院会判无辜方可以终止合约是衡平法院认为针对不重要时间规定的延误已经达到了十分严重的程度,显示了违约方已经放弃了有关合约。在当时还没有合约受阻与十分严重的延误导致合约的本质有了改变或无法再履行而令合约自动终止的所谓"受阻延误"(frustration delay)的说法。这种严重程度的延误显示已经放弃有关合约有各种不同的称呼,如在 Lloyd v Collett (1793) 4 Bro CC 469 先例中,说是"inordinate delay, laches or gross negligence","evidence of an abandonment of the contract",或是在 Harrington v Wheeler (1799) 4 Ves J 685 先例中的"such a refusal to perform an agreement, as would amount to a complete abandonment; so that the contract would be gone in equity as well as at law"。

显然,到底怎样才算达到足够显示违约方放弃有关合约的严重程度,还是十分不明确。这就带来了一种做法,无辜方向违约方作出一个通知,说明如果违约方不在合理时间内履行,无辜方就会把有关合约视为被放弃。这种做法在早期的一些衡平法院先例中有报道:Reynolds v Nelson (1821) 6 Madd 18;Heaphy v Hill (1824) 2 Sim & St 29;Watson v Reid (1830) 1 Russ & My 236;Taylor v Brown (1839) 2 Beav 180 等。而在 Taylor v Brown 先例,这种做法的合法性或认受性被明确下来。Langdale 勋爵是这样说:"Now as I have before stated, where the contract and the circumstances are such that time is not in this Court considered to be the essence of the contract - in such case, if any unnecessary delay is created by one party the other has a right to limit a reasonable time in which the contract shall be perfected by the other. It has been repeatedly so considered in this Court; and where the time has been thus fairly limited, by a notice stating that within such a period that which is required must be done or otherwise the contract will be treated as at an end, this Court has very frequently supported that proceeding; and bills having been afterwards filed for the specific performance of the contract, this Court has dismissed them with costs."

这也就带来了大家熟悉的"通过作出通知使得时间变为重要"(notice making time of the essence)的说法与做法。

5.3　通知使得时间变为重要的做法使用的两种情况

这种做法普遍被使用在两种情况:

第一,有时间规定的合约条文不是条件条文或合约的重要条文,或者是不能确定是否是条件条文,就可以这样做以明确自己(也就是无辜方)的法律地位,令后来的行动,也就是终止合约变得更加安全。如相对近期的 British and Commonwealth Holdings plc v Quadrex Holdings Inc (1989) QB 842 (CA),案情涉及一家私人公司的股票买卖。合约中双方对交接日期(也就是卖方交出股票与买方作出支付)并没有明确规定。事后买方无法提供足够的资金支付,卖方作出通知并在规定时间届临后终止合约。但买方认为时间规定不是合约的条件条文,声称卖方的终止合约是违约/毁约。上诉庭的 Brown – Wilkinson 大法官说:"although the contract specified that completion was to take place as soon as reasonably practicable after certain preliminaries had been fulfilled, no date had been fixed or was capable of precise determination from the contract and, therefore, time was not originally of the essence of the completion of the agreement; but that the commercial nature of the contract was such that if time had been specified for completion, it would have been of the essence and, in those circumstances, the plaintiff, if an innocent party, was entitled to make time of the essence by serving on 25 January 1988 a reasonable notice to complete even though the defendant had not been guilty of improper or undue delay."(虽然合约没有对完成交易的日期有规定,这显示了时间并不重要。但根据合约的本质,如果有明示规定完成交易日期,这就会是重要或是条件条文。这样,原告作为无辜方有权在 1988 年 1 月 25 日通过作出合理通知给被告,令完成交易日期变得重要。)

第二,时间规定的合约条文本身是明示或默示的条件条文或合约的重要条文,但由于被无辜方"弃权"(waiver),导致终止合约的权利失去。这样,弃权所导致的合约权利有可能是永久失去,因为再也恢复不了合约原来的地位,如对"合约选择权"(contractual option)的权利被放弃。在这种情况下,作出通知也没有用,因为改变不了什么。但也有不少的弃权只是属于暂时性,而弃权并非更改合约条文,完全可以恢复原来的地位,也就是通过通知要求对方按合约条文办事。例如,无辜方对违约方延误或不作出其中一笔金钱的支付作出弃权,甚至不再收取,不表示对将来合约中要求作出的支付也失去了权利。这种事情在船舶或房屋的租赁就经常发生。例如,船舶的期租合约中针对租金的支付,通常通过明示条文规定是重要条文,如果承租人延误作出支付会让船东有权终止租约,也就是撤船。现在更有了 The "Astra" (2013) 2 Lloyd's Rep 69 先例说即使合约中没有明示规定,迟付租金也属于违反了条件条文。但在航运市场低潮时,船东不会想终止合约,所以对承租人的延误支付(或者是不足的支付)不理会,这往往就会构成弃权或禁止翻供。如在 The "Petrofina" (1948) 82 Ll. L Rep 43 先例就是这种情况,严格说是属于一种"共识性禁止翻供"(estoppel by convention)。这样,船东如果在航运市场开始复苏时想按合约的规定履行(准时支付足额的租金,而且是重要条文),就需要通过作出通知恢复他原来的地位了。否则,贸然终止合约,也就是撤船,船东会是麻烦大了,因为在没有恢复原来地位之前这样做就是违约/毁约。

在本章稍早的第 2 段有提到另一种经常发生的情况,也是中国公司必须要重视的,就是在国际货物买卖合约,如果订约后市场下挫,经常会发生的情况是买方不在明示规定的时间或是默示的合理时间开出"信用证"(letter of credit)。这明确是违反条件条文,卖方作为无辜方可以终止合约。但由于市场下挫,卖方通常不会这样做,而会施压或说好话要求买方开出信用证。这样,延误作出选择终止合约就会明显构成了弃权与禁止翻供。如果市场继续下挫,而买方还是不予理睬,也不开出信用证,卖方就会感到对挽救这一票买卖无望,想终止合约。但卖方要小心的是,他终止合约的选择权会是已经被暂时放弃或禁止翻供。所以安全的做法是卖方先向违约的买方作出通知,并在通知的合理时间过了后才终止合约。

《Halsbury's Laws of Hong Kong》(第 2 版, 2011 年)之 115.301 段有这方面的说法,可节录如下:"**In cases where time is not originally of the essence of the contract**, ***or*** **where a stipulation making time of the essence has been waived**, time may be made of the essence, where there is unreasonable delay, by a notice from the party who is not in default fixing a reasonable time for performance and stating that, in the event of non-performance within the time so fixed, he intends to treat the contract as broken. The time so fixed must be reasonable having regard to the state of things at the time when the notice is given, and to all the circumstances of the case. Such a notice (at least where the completion of the contract can only be given effect by both parties discharging their outstanding obligations) is as binding on the party giving it as on the party receiving it."(加黑部分是笔者的强调)

5.4 通知使得时间变为重要的做法被视为对方违约/毁约的证明

至于这种说法/做法怎样在普通法的大原则下自圆其说,也就是较早时提到的合约方不能单方面改变合约条文的本质,把保证条文提升为条件条文。在《Contractual Duties: Performance, Breach, Termination and Remedies》(2011 年)一书之 11 - 001

段认为,这样的通知并不能使时间规定变为条件条文,相反它只能提供证据反映出无辜方希望违约方尽快履行合约。只有当违约方没有在通知的合理时间内履行的行为已经严重到属于影响合约根基的“违约/毁约”(repudiation),或者违约方持续性的不履行已经接近暗示他放弃履行合约时,无辜方才能终止合约。相关段节可节录如下:“Such a notice does not have the effect of rendering the time stipulation a condition. Instead, it merely provides evidence of the notifying party's expectation that performance must be accomplished speedily. The innocent party will acquire the right to terminate for failure to satisfy the notice period only if the breach can be characterized as a repudiation which goes to the root of the contract or if his continuing default discloses an implicit renunciation.”

另是 Simon 勋爵在 United Scientific Holdings Ltd v Burnley BC (1978) AC 904 先例也说:“The notice operates as evidence that the promisee considers that a reasonable time for performance has elapsed by the date of the notice and as evidence of the date by which the promisee now considers it reasonable for the contractual obligation to be performed. The promisor is put on notice of these matters. It is only in this sense that time is made of the essence of a contract in which it was previously non – essential. The promisee is really saying, 'Unless you perform by such – and – such a date, I shall treat your failure as s repudiation of the contract'.”

换言之,作出通知并不能单方面改变合约条文的本质,但可以作为证明违约方违约/毁约,也就是不再履行有关合约的证据。这样,通知所规定的时间一旦届临,无辜方就可以接受违约方的违约/毁约终止合约。但这里也会有很多变数,不像是条件条文这么简单。因为如果在所规定的时间届临前,违约方回应说“请你再给我一点时间,我就会履行”,这就带来了变数。如果所规定的时间是条件条文(如上述第二种情况的弃权后要恢复原来地位),无辜方可以不理会违约方的回应。反正规定的合理时间一届临,就是违反了条件条文,无辜方可以终止合约。但如果所规定的时间本质上只是保证条文,而违约方的回应是想履行,只不过需要多一点时间,这就很难以较早的通知作为违约方违约/毁约的证明。看来,安全的做法是无辜方只能延长并规定另一个合理时间,并通知违约方。但这也难保违约方不会再重新用这个手段,导致无辜方为了安全需要再延长并作出另一个通知。

最后一提的是,United Scientific Holdings Ltd v Burnley BC 先例的说法也没有新意,这种“通过作出通知使得时间变为重要”的做法最早在衡平法院就是为了证明对方“放弃”(abandon)有关的合约,这已经在较早时提到。

上述提到延误履行的时间规定属于保证条文,才需要这种作出通知的做法,而本身属于条件条文的时间规定,由于一违反就可以让无辜方有权终止合约,所以不存在作出通知的做法,除非涉及弃权或禁止翻供。但要一提的是,不是任何时间规定的保证条文都可以这样做,毕竟违约/毁约的说法也是只针对一些有一定重要性的条文或承诺。这可以先简单节录《Chitty on Contracts》（第31版，2012年）一书之24－018段针对"违约/毁约"（Renunciation）的第一句话："A renunciation of a contract occurs when one party by words or conduct evinces an intention not to perform，or expressly declares that he is or will be unable to perform，his obligations under the contract **in some essential respect.**"（加黑部分是笔者的强调）

这表示无辜方不能把小事向违约方作出通知施加压力，甚至为自己创造终止合约的机会，因为违约方即使拒绝履行该小事，也构成不了违约/毁约。这可以节录 Eshun v Moorgate Mercantile Credit Co（1971）1 WLR 722（CA）先例，案情涉及一辆汽车的租购合约，租方没有支付两期的分期付款，车主向他作出通知，规定了不在9天内支付就会被视为违约/毁约。但在上诉庭，判是在《Hire Purchase Act 1965》立法下该通知无效，原因是这种违约不能构成违约/毁约。Denning 勋爵是这样说："The owner says in effect to the hirer：'If you do not pay we shall assume that you are terminating by repudiation and will enforce our rights accordingly.' The owners had no right to make any such assumption. The mere non－payment of one or two instalments does not amount to repudiation ... [The notice] ... seeks to put upon the hirer a repudiation when he had never repudiated ... It is inaccurate and misleading. It is defective and insufficient. It is not a good notice of default."

5.5 如何作出正确的通知使得时间变为重要

接下来要探讨的是，怎样作出正确的通知使得时间变为重要，这问题涉及三个重要的方面：一是通知的时间；二是通知的内容；三是通知的效力。

5.5.1 重要方面之一：通知的时间

这一重要的方面涉及两点，一是无辜方自己必须能够、备妥与愿意（able、ready and willing）履行他在该有关合约下的承诺；二是对方已经造成了延误的违约。

针对第一点，考虑到这个做法原来是来自衡平法，就表示无辜方必须自己是"干净"才能寻求衡平法的救济。这种英文的说法有多种，如"He who comes to equity must do equity"，或是"one must come with a clean hand"等。这就表示如果无辜方自己也不能够履行他在有关合约下的承诺，就无法作出有效的通知，要求对方履行。这种早期先例很多，都是涉及土地/房屋的买卖。如 Eagleview Ltd v Worthgate Ltd Ch D，14 July 1998 先例，案情涉及有关的买卖合约有条文要求租客搬走，房屋是空置才交出给买方。但在卖方作出通知的一天，实际上他不能让租客搬走，所以无权作出通知。当然这方面会是有千变万化的情况，如在新西兰 Adamson v Barton（1981）2 NZLR 690 先例，十分接近的案情就判作出的通知有效，因为在该天，租客虽然还没有搬走，但卖方知道也明确了租客会在房屋"交接一天"（completion date）前会搬走。

这方面也涉及无辜方的合作与否的问题，如在 Cole v Rose（1978）3 All ER 1121 先例，涉及卖方的律师被买方查问到底"地税"（land charge）付清了没有，这属于卖方的责任或承诺。事实上在卖方作出通知时，该笔钱已经付清，但卖方律师不合作，不愿意告诉与保证买方他已经支付。法院判是有关的通知无效,因为买方在收到这个通知时,无法知道当时的情况,也就不能肯定应否在通知规定的时间内履行并完成交易。

这方面还涉及了另一个困难,即"能够、备妥与愿意"的程度,这会是适用"极微小"(*de minimis*)原则。如在 Van Reesema v Giameos (No 2) (1978) 17 SASR 353 的澳大利亚先例,停车场里还有一些只需要花费 213 澳元的小工程没有完成,法院判这不影响通知的有效性。比较近期的先例也有不少,如 Adamson v Barton(房屋中留有垃圾,桌椅没有搬走),Gogard Pty Ltd v Satnaq Pty Ltd (1999) NSWSC 1283(邻近的土地上还有些小障碍物)等,都判是不会影响通知的有效性,也不代表卖方不"能够、备妥与愿意"履行他的承诺交出土地/房屋。

针对第二点,对方或违约方造成延误,这就带来违约方的延误到何种程度才能作出通知。首先,如果延误合约规定的时间本身是条件条文或先决条件,就根本不存在需要作出通知才令时间规定变为重要。此外,如果延误的严重程度达致普通法的"受阻延误"(frustration delay),也不存在需要先作出通知才可以让合约终止。在以前的衡平法针对可以作出通知的延误程度,有许多不同的说法,如在 Mathuen v Andrews (1936) 3 Sol 200 先例中说是"gross, vexatious, unreasonable or unnecessary",在 King v Wilson (1843) 6 Beav 124 先例中说是"great and improper delay",在 Taylor v Brown (1839) 2 Beav 180 先例中说是"unnecessary delay",在 Pegg v Wisden (1852) 16 Beav 239 先例中说是"improper delay"等。从字面上看,对于有一定重要性的保证条文,并非合约规定的时间一过,无辜方就可以作出通知,违约方必须有一段时间的"不合理延误"(undue delay)。有说法是这段时间应该介于合约明示或默示规定的时间与受阻延误之间,这就有很大的不肯定。

这方面在近期的 Behzadi v Shaftesbury Hotels (1992) Ch. 1 先例有了明确,上诉庭是判土地/房屋买卖中,无辜的卖方在买方违约后(即使违反的不是条件条文)就可以作出通知使得时间变为重要。Nourse 大法官在他的判决中也对合约规定作出了区分,一种是"open contract",也就是对履行的时间没有明示规定,如买卖合约下根本没有对卖方什么时候交付货物作出规定,这样就必须等待法律默示的"合理时间"(reasonable time)届临,才存在有了延误的违约。这也会包括一些空泛或含糊的时间规定,如"尽快"(as soon as possible):Hydraulic Engineering Co ltd v McHaffie (1878) 4 QBD 670; Verelst's Administratrix v Motor Union Insurance Co Ltd (1925) 2 KB 137 等先例,或是"马上"(forthwith):Hyde v Watt (1843) 12 M & W 254; Hudson v Hill (1874) 43 LJCP 273 等先例。这种规定也会以法律默示的合理时间为准。

另一种是履行时间有明确规定的合约,这个规定可以是某个特定的日期或是一个时间段(如 7 天内)。这样,该天届临但承诺方没有履行就已经是违约,没有必要再押后无辜方作出通知的权利,看来再也不需要无辜方等待一段更长的不合理延误(但不必长至受阻延误)才作出通知。

5.5.2 重要方面之二:通知的内容

这个重要的方面也涉及两点,这可看澳大利亚的 O'Brien v Dawson (1941) 41 SR (NSW) 295 先例。一是通知内的时间规定必须合理;二是通知必须明确写明对方或违约方需要做些什么,以及没有履行会有什么后果。

针对第一点,什么是“合理时间”(reasonable time)完全看每个案件的不同事实:Ajit v Sammy (1957) 1 AC 255 (PC)先例。这完全是“合理”,因为合理有很大的幅度,对每种情况都会得出不同的合理时间。例如,违约方作出一笔金额不大的支付,看来是举手之劳。这样无辜方向违约方作出通知可能只需要给一个短暂的时间,如一两个银行工作日。这对一家香港公司可能完全合理,但如果违约方是一家大陆的公司,即使金额不大但由于涉及外币,就会因外汇管制有很多手续要处理,这样合理时间就可能会长得多。所以,有许多先例涉及不同的时间规定,判是合理与否,都不必太操心,因为它们都涉及不同的案情。例如在 Crawford v Toogood (1879) 13 Ch D 153 先例,无辜方通知中的 5 个星期被判是不合理;在 Re Barr's Contract (1956) Ch 551 先例,无辜方通知中的 28 天也被判是不合理。但在 Macbryde v Weekes (1856) 22 Beav 533 先例,法院判 1 个月的时间是合理。另在 Stickney v Keeble (1915) AC 386 先例,法院判只有 14 天的时间也是合理。而在 Ajit v Sammy 先例,枢密院更加认为 6 天的时间是合理。

决定什么是合理时间时必须考虑的因素,重要因素之一显然是针对要求对方做什么,也就是违约方延误的是什么合约承诺的履行。显然,如果是一件简单的事情,如较早时提到的支付一笔小钱,这合理时间就可以短得多。但如果要求对方做的是一件重要的事情,如支付一大笔钱,可以合理估计到违约方需要集资,甚至向银行融资,这合理时间就会相应长得多。毕竟向违约方作出通知就是为了给他最后的机会履行合约,所以现实是不足够的时间显然不合理。

其他的因素有无辜方自己的行为,如他自己过去的履行也是经常延误,就会影响他在通知中要求违约方在很短的时间内履行合约的权利:Freeman v Jacobs (1980) 1 BPR 9273;Fiske v Sterling Investment Co Pty Ltd (1977) 3 ACLR 158 等先例。如果无辜方被法院认为是他自己经常延误履行,但通过作出通知给违约方一段很短暂的时间履行合约,目的只是为了想从这个亏本的合约中脱身,就更加不会被善待:Green v Sevin (1879) 13 Ch D 589 先例。如果无辜方以前对违约方的延误有过默认或忍受,也会是需要在通知中给予较长的时间:Adams v Quasar Management Services Pty Ltd (2002) QSC 223 先例。

相反是无辜方不断向违约方施加压力,要求尽快履行合约,或是时间规定本来是条件条文,但因为弃权或禁止翻供暂时被中止行使权力,就会被允许通知违约方并给他一个比较短暂的时间履行:Charles Rickards Ltd v Oppenhaim (1950) 1 KB 616 先例。

另是在 Peregrine Systems Ltd v Steria Ltd (2005) EWCA Civ 239 先例,判是合理

时间应该是一个广泛的考虑,并且可以事后来看什么才算是合理(a broad consideration which can include the benefit of hindsight)。

可以说,决定合理或不合理时间的因素还有很多,而且不稳定。将来在法院或仲裁庭,也往往是让法官或是仲裁员随意决定,所以,在通知中规定的合理时间最好保守一点,即比较长一点。此外,在通知中向违约方加一句说:"如果你愿意履行,但我给的时间不足够,请尽快告诉我,让我考虑延长。否则你就必须严格依照通知中的时间履行。"而违约方并没有回应,有这句话在通知中会对法院或仲裁庭有影响,就是通知中规定的时间是合理。

通知的内容除了合理时间外,还必须包括要求违约方做什么,以及不做的后果。在澳大利亚高院的 Neeta (Epping) Pty v Phillips (1974) 131 CLR 286 先例,通知是要求违约方支付土地买卖的款项加上利息,但合约并不允许收取利息,这通知被判是无效。针对这方面通知的内容要完全正确与明确:Hanson v Cameron (1949) 1 DLR 16;Charles Investments Pty Ltd v Karakis (2002) NSWSC 1213 等先例。看来,安全的做法是在通知中重复有关的合约条文,说明对方是什么违约,并要求他在规定的时间内履行。

至于针对违约方如果不履行的后果,曾经有一些早期的先例要求通知明确说明如果对方不履行合约,该合约将被终止。这些早期的先例在澳大利亚的 Balog v Crestani (1975) 132 CLR 289 先例中有提到。但看来近期的先例没有这么严格,毕竟违约方如果不在通知的合理时间内履行,无辜方也不一定非要终止合约,他还是有终止与否的选择权。所以,没有理由要求无辜方在作出通知时就事先作出选择。而且,万一通知被判是无效,无辜方把后果说的太死就有危险被指控为违约/毁约。这些方面的问题在 Laurinda Pty Ltd and others v Capalba Park Shopping Centre Pty Ltd (1989) 166 CLR 623 的澳大利亚先例有充分针对。所以,近期的先例只要求有关的通知能够清楚地向违约方表明如果通知的要求与时限没有被依从,有关合约会有可能被终止:Balog v Crestani; Laurinda Pty Ltd and others v Capalba Park Shopping Centre Pty Ltd; Morris v Robert Jones Investments Ltd (1994) 2 NZLR 275; Wilde v Anstee (1999) NSWSC 612 等先例。

针对不足够明确说明后果也有不少先例,如通知只说明无辜方会"执行有关合约"(enforce the contract):Lenneberg v McGirr (1919) 19 SR (NSW) 83 先例;或说无辜方会"按情况处理"(act accordingly):Reynolds v Nelson (1821) 6 Madd 18 先例;或说无辜方会"依赖他在合约中的权利"(rely on his rights under the contract):Smith v Hamilton (1951) Ch 174 先例,除非是同时把终止合约的权利也明确包括在内:Balog v Cresani 先例。

即使通知说明后果是会"使得时间现在变为重要"(time is now of essence),看来是依足了以前衡平法院与普通法院对时间规定是否重要的说法,也会是不安全。原因是违约方可能被法院或仲裁庭接受是没有受过法律的训练,所以不知道这句话的意思。此外,也有先例判这句话会带来混乱:British & Commonwealth Holdings Plc v Quadrex Holdings Inc (1989) Q. B. 842 先例。所以为了安全,就算是在通知中说明"使得时间现在变为重要",最好也强调如果没有依照通知要求履行,无辜方保留终止合约的权利。

5.5.3 重要方面之三:通知的效力

有效通知的后果显然是在合理时间届满后,违约方还是没有履行,无辜方就可以终止合约。而且这是属于违约/毁约,所以无辜方如果蒙受其他金钱的损失,也可以向违约方提出索赔。也已经提到,即使违约方不依照通知,无辜方还是有不终止合约的选择权。但如果将来有这个必要,无辜方可以另给一个通知,并规定另一个合理时间要求违约方必须履行合约:Charles Rickards Ltd v Oppenhaim (1950) 1 KB 616; Afford v Till (1990) 35 EG 56; Electcoms Sdn Bhd v Internet Technology Asia Ventures Sdn Bhd (2002) 481 MLJU 1 等先例。

此外,也必须理解通知是令一个本来不是条件条文的延误变为重要,显然,通知合理时间届满的一天变为重要对双方都有约束力。如果届时无辜方或作出通知的一方拒绝履行或无法履行,就会导致接受该通知的原违约方变为无辜方与有权终止合约。此外,这种通知的效力也表示了对合约履行的"确认"(affirmation),所以作出通知的无辜方不能不给对方依照通知履行合约的合理机会。而如果无辜方突然想终止合约,如明确了违约方原先的延误是违反了条件条文,而加上市场突然暴升/暴跌,导致无辜方想尽快终止合约以防止违约方按照通知履行合约,这就会构成违约/毁约。

通知的效力也会受到其他的影响,如在澳大利亚的 Legione v Hateley (1983) 152 CLR 406 先例,相关土地合约规定的时间已经错过,于是卖方作出通知,要求违约的买方在合理时间内支付余下土地买卖的价格,而买方没有做到。但该先例涉及的案情很复杂,而且当时法院面对买方的"履约指令"(specific performance)申请。结果是澳大利亚高院同意作出履约指令,也就是命令双方必须履行合约,这表示卖方不能按照通知终止合约。该先例复杂的案情是有关买卖的土地虽然还没有交接,但已经允许买方占有,并在土地上建造了一栋房屋。显然,法院认为在这种情况下,让卖方终止就会同时接管这栋房屋而造成"不当得利"(unjust enrichment)。此外,在通知的合理时间届满后没有几天时间,买方就已经可以作出支付,并完全是备妥与愿意完成交接。还有一个因素是买方错误理解了卖方律师对他作出的承诺,就是可以迟延几天才完成交易,但实际上卖方律师没有明确的承诺,所以构成不了承诺性禁止翻供。

5.6 通知使得时间变为重要是否适用于其他合约或商业合约

读者会注意到绝大部分先例,特别是早期衡平法院的先例,都是针对土地/房屋买卖。这就带来了一个疑问,在《Supreme Court of Judicature Act 1873》立法后,衡平法院与普通法院合并在一起,通知使得时间规定变为重要这个做法能否适用在其他合约,尤其是商业合约。这方面有三个重要的先例:Harley v Hymans (1920) 3 KB

937；Charles Rickards Ltd v Oppenhaim（1950）1 KB 616 与 United Scientific Holdings Ltd v Burnley BC（1978）AC 904。

在第一个先例 Harley v Hymans，涉及买卖棉花的合约，约定了分批的交货日期，并规定了开始付运的时间是 1918 年 11 月 15 日。但卖方延误交货，买方接受了延误的交货并且不断地催促卖方交付其余的货物。直到 1919 年 3 月 13 日，买方突然拒绝接受延误的交货，这种情况发生的背后原因有很多，如市场价格下挫。英国高院的 McCardie 大法官判是交货时间本来是条件条文，但由于买方的行为构成了弃权或禁止翻供，所以买方不能突然终止合约。McCardie 大法官也提到，买方如果作出一个合理时间的通知，情况就会不一样了，说："I do not doubt that the defendant would have been entitled in March, 1919, to give a notice fixing a reasonable time within which the plaintiff was required to supply the undelivered balance of the contract goods."

第二个 Charles Rickards Ltd v Oppenhaim 先例，合约涉及原告建造与交付一辆车子给被告，约定的时间是"6 个月或最迟 7 个月"（six, or at the most seven months），这个明示时间规定被判是条件条文。但原告延误作出交付，而被告的买方也放弃了他终止合约的权利，只是不断催促尽早交付。到了 1948 年 6 月 28 日，被告通知原告必须在 7 月 25 日交付，因为他准备出国并需要使用该辆车子。但到了 7 月 25 日，车子还是没有作出交付，被告于是终止合约。原告指控被告的买方违约/毁约，并对较早的 Harley v Hymans 先例作出区分，指该先例是针对货物买卖，但本案例针对的是汽车的建造合约。但这一个争辩被上诉庭拒绝，其中 Denning 大法官是这样说："In my view it is unnecessary to determine it was a contract for the sale of goods or a contract for work and labour, because, whatever it was, the defendant was entitled to give a notice bringing matters to a head. It would be most unreasonable if the defendant, having been lenient and waived the initial expressed time, should, by so doing, have prevented himself from ever thereafter insisting on reasonably quick delivery. In my judgment he was entitled to give a reasonable notice making time of the essence of the matter."

到了这个阶段已经很明确，通知这种做法也可以使用在其他合约，包括商业合约。但这两个先例所针对的只是第二种情况，也就是时间规定本来是合约的条件条文，只不过由于弃权或禁止翻供，无辜方需要以通知恢复原来的地位。而针对第一种情况，也就是原来合约中的时间规定只是保证条文，能否以通知使它变为重要还是不明确。但也有一些权威的说法说可以，如在《Halsbury's Laws of England》（第 2 版，1932 年至 1941 年）vol 3 之 380 段，针对建造合约、工程师与设计师，Singleton 大法官就认同了以下一段话："In cases where time has not been made of the essence of the contract, *or* where, although time originally was of the essence of the contract, the time so fixed for performance has ceased to be applicable by reason of waiver or otherwise, the employer has still a right by notice to fix a reasonable time for the completion of the work, and in case the contractor does not complete by that time, to dismiss the contractor just as a vendor would be entitled to rescind the contract in case of a contract for the sale of land."

再接下来要介绍的是贵族院的 United Scientific Holdings Ltd v Burnley BC 先例。案情涉及房屋租赁的租金调整条文的时间规定。已经在本章较早的 5.4 段提到过,Simon 勋爵在该案中说这个通知是"违约/毁约的证据"(evidence of repudiation),也明确了这种通知的有效性与作用。

在本章开头节录的《Halsbury's Laws of England》(第 5 版,2008 年至 2012 年)也可以看出,通知使得时间规定变为重要的做法适用于"所有类别的合约"(contracts of all types)。

§6 合约因轻微延误被没收财产/丧失合约的救济

由于时间规定被视为重要而导致相对轻微的延误或违约被无辜方根据合约条文"没收财产/丧失合约"(forfeiture),会在个别案件造成不成比例的不公平。这带来了一个问题就是衡平法能否在这种不公平的案件中作出救济,如无辜方想终止合约,但衡平法院作出"履约指令"(specific performance)。看来,衡平法这样做会是与双方约定的合约条文唱反调,不应该轻易作出这种救济,否则就等于视合约的约定如无物。以下可以探讨在哪些情况下以前的衡平法院或现在的英国法院(已经一并处理普通法与衡平法)会作出这种衡平法救济。

6.1 救济之一:立法

这种救济主要针对房东与租客,因为有不少租约会将时间规定(如支付租金)视为重要。但严格执行会对租客十分不利,因为租约的终止或丧失会导致租客被赶出屋门,如果在房价高涨时出现大量这种案件会造成社会不安定。在《Common Law Procedure Act 1852》之 Sections 210 – 212 规定是如果租客长达 6 个月没有支付租金,房东才可以采取行动驱逐租客。但如果租客在开庭审理前支付了欠下的租金与有关诉讼费用,这个诉讼就必须中止。

涉及房屋租赁的合约也可能会有其他类别的违约,在《Law of Property Act 1925》的立法之 Section 146(1),规定了房东要重新进入被出租的房屋并终止合约,必须要先给租客一个明确的通知,然后才能执行。这个通知也必须讲明:(1)到底指控的是什么违约;(2)要求租客作出补救,只要是补救可以做到;(3)要求租客补偿违约造成的损失。

6.2 救济之二:衡平法的管辖权

衡平法院有相关的管辖权已经历史悠久,在衡平法院觉得可以通过其他办法对无辜方作出救济(如不准时支付一笔钱可以赔偿利息作为替代而不必让无辜方终止合约),就可能会作出所谓"没收财产/丧失合约的救济"(relief against forfeiture)。但这种救济会到什么程度是到了 Hill v Barclay (1811) 18 Ves J 56 先例才有了明确。在该先例,Eldon 勋爵判是这种救济只局限在两种情况:(1)合约以没收财产/丧失合约保证(或是威胁)对方准时支付一笔钱:Shiloh Spinners Ltd v Harding (1973) AC 691 (HL)等先例;(2)违约涉及了欺诈、错误或惊讶等,如 Harries v. Bryant (1827) 4 Russ 89; Elliot v. Turner (1843) 13 Sim 477; Hughes v. Metropolitan Rly (1877) 2 App Cas 439 (HL); Atkin v. Rose (1923) 1 Ch 522 等先例。显然在这个说法下,"没收财产/丧失合约的救济"十分狭窄。

但到了 1973 年,贵族院在 Shiloh Spinners Ltd v. Harding 先例中扩大了这种救济的适用性。其中 Wilberforce 勋爵说:"... it remains true today that equity expects men to carry out their bargains and will not let them buy their way out by uncovenanted payment. But it is consistent with these principles that we should reaffirm the right of courts of equity in appropriate and limited cases to relieve against forfeiture for breach of covenant or condition where the primary object of the bargain is to secure a stated result which can effectively be attained when the matter comes before the court, and where the forfeiture provision is added by way of security for the production of that result. The word 'appropriate' involves consideration of the conduct of the applicant for relief, in particular where his default was willful, of the gravity of the breaches, and of the disparity between the value of the property of which the forfeiture is claimed as compared with the damage caused by the breach."(衡平法院有权在恰当与尽量局限的情况下作出救济,而"恰当"涉及申请救济方或违约方的行为,特别是他的过错是否是故意以及违约的程度[这里涉及衡平法的一个大原则,就是申请救济方如果是自己的过错所造成,就往往不能获得救济],与有关被终止或丧失的合约标的价值与该违约造成的损失是否成比例。)

但更重要的是 Simon 勋爵十分宽松的说法:"... equity has an **unlimited and unfettered jurisdiction** to relieve against contractual forfeitures and penalties. What have sometimes been regarded as fetters to the jurisdiction are, in my view, more properly to be seen as considerations which the court will weigh in deciding how to exercise an unfettered jurisdiction."(衡平法有一个没有局限与没有约束的管辖权针对合约丧失或被惩罚作出救济。)

这也就带来一些对航运界非常熟悉的先例。已经在本章之第 2 段提到,期租合约中通常都会有条文明示规定承租人必须准时支付租金,否则船东可以撤船。由于航运市场有十分大的波动,市场如果上涨,船东就会根据这个条文取巧。也就是在承租人万一疏忽、或者支付的租金稍有欠缺(如银行多扣了汇款的手续费)、或者银行疏忽延误汇出等,船东会毫不犹豫马上撤船。显然这对承租人造成很大的困境,丧失了一艘以便宜租金金额租进的船舶固然是损失严重,更会是承租人在船东撤船时已经作出了其他安排,并因为船东撤船而带来进一步的损失。这样,承租人显然就会想到有否可能像岸上的房屋买卖或租赁合约一样,寻求这种救济。这带来了一个上诉了贵族院的 The “Scaptrade” (1983) 2 Lloyd’s Rep 253 (HL)先例。在高院与上诉庭,承租人都无法成功说服法院给予这种衡平法救济。高院认为承租人无法解释为什么延误支付租金,所以违约是他有过错,纯粹是涉及金额很大或损失很大与违约程度不成比例并非是给予衡平法救济的理由。在上诉庭,Robert Goff 大法官也是拒绝给予这一衡平法救济,认为期租合约等商业合约需要肯定性(这显然是指合约怎样写,就应该怎样解释与执行)。而且双方当事人,包括承租人自己应该有足够的知识水平在订约时保护自己的利益,如加进一条“反技术取巧条文”(anti – technicality clause)(这条文是要求船东撤船之前必须通知承租人没有及时或足数收到租金,并让承租人在一个期限内作出补救),或是在操作上尽量提早支付租金。Robert Goff 大法官是这样说:“Indeed, when we come to consider the nature of a contract such as a time charter, and circumstances in which it is likely to be made, we see the most formidable arguments against the proposed extension of the equitable jurisdiction. In the first place, a time charter is a commercial transaction in the sense that it is generally entered into for the purposes of trade, between commercial organizations acting at arm’s length. It is for the parties to bargain about the terms of the contract. They can bargain not only about the form of charter to be used; they can also bargain about any amendments to the standard form, and about the rate of hire to be paid having regard to the other terms of the contract agreed between them. Parties to such contracts should be capable of looking after themselves: at the very least, they are capable of taking advice, and the services of brokers are available, and are frequently used, when negotiating terms. The possibility that shipowners may snatch at the possibility to withdraw ships from the services of time charterers for non – payment of hire must be very well known in the world of shipping; it must also be very well known that anti – technicality clauses are available which are effective to prevent any such occurrence. If a prospective time charterer wishes to have any such clause included in the charter, he can bargain for it: if he finds it necessary or desirable to agree to a charter which contains no such clause, he can warn the relevant section of his office, and his bank, of the importance of security timeous payment.”

贵族院也判是承租人败诉,Diplock 勋爵(其他4 位大法官也完全同意)也是拒绝给予这种衡平法救济。贵族院把这种救济视为与履约指令是同一码事,即命令船东不准撤船。但期租合约是一个“提供服务的合约”(service contract),而英国法律针对履约指令在传统上是不会向提供服务的合约作出:Lumley v Wagner (1852) 1 DE G M & G 604 与 Warner Brothers Pictures Inc v Nelson (1937) 1 KB 209 等先例。这方面可看笔者的《损失赔偿与救济》一书第十二章之 6 段的详细介绍。针对衡平法院以前对以没收财产/丧失合约威胁对方准时支付作出救济的情况,Diplock 勋爵除了区分期租合约下预付租金的作用并不一致外,也说明以前衡平法院针对的往往是涉及土地/房屋的租赁,本质上与期租合约不一样。

看来,这个衡平法救济的管辖权并不太广泛,而只能涉及"转移财产"(transfer of proprietary)或"占有权"(possessory right)的情况,而不是所有合约都会适用。这也不代表这个衡平法的救济只适用在土地/房屋的合约,仍可以适用在航运,如"光船租约"(demise/bareboat charter)就涉及承租人通过他所雇用的船长对船舶有占有权,正如Diplock勋爵在说到期租只是提供服务说:"A time charter, **unless it is a charter by demise**, with which your Lordships are not here concerned, transfers to the charterer no interest in or right to possession of the vessel; it is a contract for services to be rendered to the charterer by the shipowner through the use of the vessel by the shipowner's own servants, the master and the crew, acting in accordance with such directions as to the cargoes to be loaded and the voyages to be undertaken as by the terms of the charter – party the charterer is entitled to give to them."(加黑部分是笔者的强调)

有关光船租约涉及没收财产/丧失合约的救济的近期先例有 More v The Demise Charterers of the Ship "Jotunheim" (2005) 1 Lloyd's Rep 181,将在本章稍后的6.4段有详细介绍。

6.3 衡平法对土地/房屋买卖的没收财产涉及买方已经做了工作的救济

有关这种衡平法救济,在另一种涉及土地/房屋买卖的合约有很大问题。传统的看法是,如果双方当事人明示了时间规定是重要,衡平法律就没有管辖权给予救济:Steedman v Drinkle (1916) 1 AC 275 与 Brickles v Snell (1916) 2 AC 599 (PC)等先例。但经常会出现的情况是买方在卖方允许下,会在买卖完成之前已经在有关的土地/房屋上做了一些工作。这样,如果卖方根据合约没收财产/终止合约,如由于买方迟延支付,就会造成看来是比上述期租合约的撤船更不公平的情况。如在 Re Dagenham (Thames) Dock Co, ex p Hulse (1873) LR 8 Ch App 1022 先例,案情涉及土地买卖,买方是用来建造一个"干坞"(dry dock)并事先被允许占有该土地与开始工作。合约另规定土地买卖的价格分两期支付,一半预付,另一半在买卖完成才支付,也规定了时间是重要,并允许卖方在买方违约时可以重新占有土地与任何已经进行了的工作。之后买方没有支付后一笔的土地价格,但卖方被拒绝重新占有土地与进行了的工作。法院认为这样做等同支持一条"惩罚性条文"(penalty clause),因为卖方既可以终止合约,又可以取回土地与已经进行了的工作,还可以把买方已经支付了的一半土地价格没收。

在接下来的 Kilmer v British Columbia Orchard Lands Ltd (1913) AC 319 (PC)先例,案情也是大同小异,卖方由于买方延误支付分期的土地价格,就根据有关合约中的"丧失一切条文"(forfeiture clause)把买方已经支付的预付款没收,并终止合约。这被枢密院判是有关的条文等同于惩罚性条文而无效。

6.4 没收财产/丧失合约的衡平法救济在近期的先例看前景

这方面一直有很多的同类案例,只先介绍一个近期的重要先例 Union Eagle Ltd

v Golden Achievement Ltd (1997) AC 514 (PC)。案情涉及香港的一套房屋的买卖,有关的合约规定了“合约完成日期”(completion date)与在该天的下午 5 点之前完成(显然是因为 5 点前才是办公时间)。合约也规定了时间是重要,而且卖方在买方违约的情况下有权终止合约并且没收预付的定金。买方晚了 10 分钟(可能是交通问题)才抵达合约完成的地点,也就是卖方的律师所。这给卖方根据有关的条文终止合约并没收定金的机会,可以想得到当时的房价也应该在上涨。但在枢密院,判是衡平法也不适用在这种合约,其中 Hoffman 勋爵拒绝区分土地买卖合约与一般的商业合约(如上述介绍的期租合约),并认为土地买卖合约一样需要肯定性,说:“The principle that equity will restrain the enforcement of legal rights when it would be unconscionable to insist upon them has an attractive breadth. But the reasons why the courts have rejected such generalisations are founded not merely on authority ... but also upon practical considerations of business. These are, in summary, that in many forms of transaction it is of great importance that if something happens for which the contract has made express provision, the parties should know with certainty that the terms of the contract will be enforced. The existence of an undefined discretion to refuse to enforce the contract on the ground that this would be ‘unconscionable’ is sufficient to create uncertainty. Even if it is most unlikely that a discretion to grant relief will be exercised, its mere existence enables litigation to be employed as a negotiating tactic. The realities of commercial life are that this may cause injustice which cannot be fully compensated by the ultimate decision in the case.”(衡平法对一些不合情理的情况下禁止行使合约权利有吸引力。但在很多交易,如果合约有明示条文针对,合约方必须能够肯定有关条文会获得执行。如果有一个不明确的衡平法裁量权,可以令合约的明示条文不能获得执行,就会带来不肯定,合约双方均会感到无所适从。就算是衡平法的裁量权通常不会作出,也足够导致合约双方会提起诉讼或作为谈判的筹码。这反而会带来对整体商业社会的不公平,是这种衡平法救济会在个别案件带来的公平并不足以补救的。)

Hoffman 勋爵也认为,在 Re Dagenham (Thames) Dock Co, ex p Hulse (1873) LR 8 Ch App 1022 等先例的不公平情况,卖方把买方在有关土地所做的工作也一并没收的“不当得利”(unjust enrichment)问题最好还是以“复原法”(law of restitution)处理,而不是让违反一条明示为重要条文的买方通过这种救济来保留合约的利益。

接下来在澳大利亚高院的 Tanwar Enterprises Pty Ltd v Cauchi (2003) 201 ALR 359 先例,也是涉及买方由于无法得到银行的融资而无法支付最后的房价完成交易,被卖方取消合约与没收预付的定金。买方向法院申请这种衡平法的救济以及履约指令要求卖方完成交易。显然买方在一审、上诉庭与高院都不成功,高院更是说明在这种同类的案件,衡平法只会插手在一些涉及了无辜的卖方本身有一些行动造成买方无法完成交易,导致让卖方行使合约权利变为“不合情理”(unconscionable)的情况。

总结而言,针对土地买卖,英国衡平法的救济还是明确的存在:Shiloh Spinners

Ltd v. Harding (1973) AC 691 (HL)。但看来并不是一剂“万灵药”,有可能会像澳大利亚的先例一样,要求对方有一些不合情理的言行,才会作出救济。

最后也介绍一个与商业有更密切关系与更近期,涉及光船租约的 More v The Demise Charterers of the Ship “Jotunheim” (2005) 1 Lloyd's Rep 181 先例。在本章之6.2段已经提到期租合约(也包括程租合约)由于只是服务合约,是不会有这个没收财产/丧失合约的救济,但“光船租约”(demise/bareboat charter)是例外。在该先例,涉及一个船东以 BIMCO 标准格式的 Barecon 89 把“Jotunheim”轮光船租给承租人48个月,租约也规定了在租期届满后,有关的船舶是归承租人所有,换言之,这是一个“租购合约”(hire – purchase agreement)。根据租约的约定,租金是每个月要预付而且必须足数。其中第32条文是说:“It is hereby agreed between sellers and buyers that in case of buyers' default for non – payment of hire monies due to owner or non – performance of any of the agreed terms within the realm of this agreement the vessel will return back to the sellers free of all expense, fuel invoices and with the remaining fuel on board free of costs to the sellers.”

在2003年年底交船后,承租人在第一期租金的支付就已经有延误而且是小量不足数(因为银行收费)。而船东就一直在催促承租人,如在2004年2月15日要支付的租金,船东在1月30日就已经开始催促并要求原来支付的两期租金不足之数也要在下一次支付补足。承租人一直对延误表示歉意,说是等到收到下一笔运费就马上支付,并说船舶因为需要修理以满足“港口管制”(port state control)而造成了一定的延误。到了2月24日,船东通过他的经纪人提醒承租人支付在2月15日欠下的租金,并威胁如果不在该天支付,船东就会撤船。到了2月25日早晨,船东通知承租人撤船,而承租人也是在2月26日才支付。

双方的争议涉及没收财产/丧失合约的救济与本章所介绍的所有议题,首先是这准时与足数支付租金是否是该光船租约“条件条文”(condition)或是“重要”(of essence)。承租人的争辩是租约并没有这样写明,所以并不重要。但 Cooke 大法官说是第32条文已经把延误与不足数支付租金的严重后果写得清清楚楚,所以根本不需要理会有否明示这方面是重要与否。此外,由于船东在2月24日已经给了承租人最后的警告,这通知足以令时间规定变为重要(可见本章之第5段)。Cooke 大法官是这样说:“There is no need for the charter to specify that time of payment is ‘of the essence’, since the clause itself sets out the specific consequences of failure to make any payments due. The parties have specifically agreed in a commercial contract what is to occur in these circumstances. It, therefore, matters no that the clause makes no express reference to ‘punctual’ or ‘punctual and regular payment’ or hire because the terms of the agreement are clear on this point. Moreover, even if this were not so, the owners, by their ultimatum of Feb. 24, could be said to have effectively made time of the essence for the purpose of this clause.”

第二个争议是涉及船东是否对较早的两期延误支付有默认/忍受,导致"弃权或禁止翻供"(waiver or estoppel)。但由于船东不断在催促承租人,所以 Cooke 大法官完全不同意涉及任何弃权,说:"Therefore, the constant pressing for hire, coupled with the threat of withdrawal, cannot mean that a reasonable time has passed, with the result of the loss of right to withdraw, if, following the threat, no payment is made and the right is then exercised. That is what occurred here and in such circumstances the demise charterers cannot succeed in showing waiver."

第三个争议也是与没收财产/丧失合约的救济有密切关系,就是这种救济是否适用在该先例。Cooke 大法官是肯定适用,说:"It is accepted by the owners that the Court is, in principle, entitled to grant relief from forfeiture of a contract such as this, provided that the object of the transaction and of the insertion of the right to forfeit for non - payment of money or is essentially to secure the payment of that money or is security for the attainment of a specific result which can be achieved through the Courts. If the contract provides for a right to retain possession of a chattel so long as the conditions of the agreement are performed, together with the right to purchase the chattel by payment of the instalments provided for by the contract, relief from forfeiture is available provided that the right of forfeiture is for either of these purposes."

但在肯定后,下一个问题就涉及 Cooke 大法官的裁量权看该先例的案情是否恰当作出这个衡平法的救济。这些因素包括了多方面,包括对承租人有利或不利之处。例如,对承租人有利是绝大部分欠下的租金已经是支付,不足够的金额微不足道,船舶已经装运了货物(100 多辆车子)并签发了 33 份提单而对第三人(货方)有了合约责任,承租人也花了一些钱(但不多)对船舶作出了修理。而对承租人不利是承租人延误支付租金涉及"故意行为"(a deliberate flouting)与"一定程度的乱来"(a degree of cavalier disregard for the strict obligations of the contract)。此外,撤船发生在较早期,承租人所支付的定金与修理费用加起来的金额远远比不上租期 48 个月(减去已支付租金的 3 个月)余下要支付的租金(都会面对延误的风险)。看来,Cooke 大法官认为法律的肯定性特别是对双方谈判后并同意的条文必须获得执行是至关重要,所以拒绝作出这个衡平法的救济,说:"Ultimately, I conclude that this is not one of those limited cases where it is appropriate for the Court to grant relief. The commercial character of the freely negotiated contract, including in particular the form of the clause with no provision for days of grace, militates against the granting of any relief in the present case. There is a need for certainty in the commercial context and this means that the limited hardship to the demise charterers which will ensue because of the lost opportunity to purchase the vessel, the wasted payments and potential exposure to third parties should lie with them that being the risk which they undertook, and in part expressly undertook under cl. 32, to bear, when they chose not to pay the hire due after receiving the owners' ultimatum. In my judgment, therefore, this is not an appropriate case for relief from forfeiture and I refuse to grant it."(这是一个自由谈判而达成的商业合约,为了肯定,就表示对承租人有限的困境,如失了购买船舶的机会、花费了的费用、与对第三人的合约责任都只能由承租人承担,也是他接受租约第32条文所要冒的风险。毕竟承租人自己选择不支付租金,即使是在2月24日收到了船东的最后警告。所以在本先例的案情,Cooke大法官不认为是一个适当的案件作出衡平法的救济。)

第十一章　延　　误

§1　延误定义

"延误"(delay)一词看来明确,但实际上是一个不肯定的词。对延误的定义有不少,在 Cable (William) Ltd v Trainor (1957) NZLR 337 先例,新西兰上诉庭的 Shorland 大法官说:"The dictionary meaning of the noun 'delay' is the 'the putting off' or 'the deferring'. These latter words, in our opinion, in their ordinary meaning connote **postponement of performance of some act or step beyond the point of time when the act or step should have been performed.**"(字典的定义是推迟了一些需要履行的行为或步骤,导致超过了原定计划的时间。)

这个看来明确的定义就会有不明朗或有争议之处。例如,什么是需要履行的"行为"(act)或"步骤"(step)? 举一个生活中的例子,如要赶一班飞机去北京开会。安排了的的士可能晚到或堵在路上或办理登机时产生延误,但只要最后勉强能赶得上这班飞机,对真正需要履行的行为,也就是赶这班飞机北京,并没有造成延误。但在复杂的商业合约,有时候要履行的行为或步骤是什么并不明确。而且,对任何一个特定合约的解释是要根据它的"语境"(context),这在本书第一章与第六章有详论。这表示每个合约的行为或步骤,以及什么是时间损失或延误,都不可以统一地解释。

例如,在一个期租合约,船舶在一个上海空放去印尼装港的航次半途发生主机故障,导致损失了 3 天。这对该航次而言,船舶的确是比原定计划延误了 3 天才抵达印尼装港,看来承租人可以把这 3 天的时间损失停租。而如果主机故障涉及船东违约,如不适航,承租人还可以向船东索赔其他延误带来的损失。但如果船舶到了印尼装港,由于港口拥挤或其他原因封港,显示船舶即使按照原定计划抵达,也靠不了泊装货。换言之,航次中延误了 3 天或没有延误对该船舶的装货而言并没有任何区别。这样对承租人能否停租,即船舶有没有对期租合约要履行的行为造成时间损失或延误,就有了不同看法。看来对什么是该船舶要履行的行为也有可争议之处,到底应该是准时抵达印尼装港等待装货,还是准时完成整个装卸的航次(特别是期租只针对单一航次时)。

另一个在工程合约下会是不明朗或可争议之处是什么才是原定计划的时间。显然,工程合约的本质就是要求承建商准时完成合约工程,如果涉及时间损失或者延误,就是指工程的延误。但如果从来没有任何计划,也谈不上有任何时限完成履行有关的行为或步骤,也就不存在延误,因为根本没有比较的基准。而即使是有计划的时间,还会涉及计划是否合理与现实。显然,如果完全不合理或过度乐观的计划,作为衡量有否延误与延误程度的基准,就会是不准确与不能被接受。这个问题在一些复杂工程特别严重,而中国公司涉及越来越多这种涉外工程,如建设工厂、造桥、修建铁路、造船等。如果中国公司在订约时只是凭乐观与主观臆猜承诺一个完工日期,就会有很大危险导致违约。而如果是对方违约导致延误,中国公司也没有可信赖的基准证明到底造成了什么延误以提出索赔。

中国公司如果没有合理与现实的事先计划,就无法证明是什么延误与延误程度。这种延误在工程合约中来自三个方面。一是通常以一条"不可抗力"(*force majeure*)条文针对的一些外来或第三人所造成的延误,如天气、动乱、政府干预等。这种延误通常在工程合约会允许延长完成履行的时间,但到底延长多久甚至是否延长就涉及受影响的中国公司作为承建商或是船厂需要证明是什么延误与延误程度。二是对方(工程合约的雇主)的过错所造成的延误,如不合作甚至造成障碍。但在这方面,受影响的中国公司即使证明了责任(如证明了对方过错甚至故意造成延误),也需要证明是什么延误与延误程度,否则等于没有办法证明损失。三是中国公司作为承建商或船厂自己造成的延误,如工人不足够或是分包商或分供应商造成的延误。这样,延误通常也不存在可以延长完成履行的时间,也不可以向雇主索赔损失(特别是时间的损失),等于是后果自负。但中国公司还是需要知道是什么延误与延误程度,因为在很多方面还是必要。例如,向自己的分包商或分供应商提出索赔,或是知道后可以通过其他的办法做出补救,把失去的时间争取回来,以达到准时完成工程或交船的目的。

因为一个工程涉及的步骤很多,时间上的计算也十分复杂,如果没有合理、清晰、全面、详尽、客观与现实的事先"计划"(programme)与组织,作为承建商或是船厂的中国公司就谈不上有良好的管理。一旦发生了争议,也会被置于非常不利的地位,如证明不了是什么延误与延误程度。如今普遍被承建商或船厂选择的规划工程的方法是"关键路径方式"(critical path method),这在接下来的段节会有详细介绍。

2008 年金融海啸以来,航运市场暴跌 90% 。外国船东作为买方在这个时间之前所订立的造船合约中船舶的价值马上跌了一半以上。外国船东于是采用各种办法拖延,如总管不合作,不及时回复船厂的查询(如配件供应、规格变更等),对图纸的审批拖拖拉拉等。一旦拖过了"死亡日期"(drop dead date),也就是"销约期"(canceling date),外国船东就选择终止合约,然后根据还款担保银行拿回已经支付的分期付款及利息。中国船厂一方面是文件证据不足以证明船东的过错或违约,另一方面由于没有在管理上应用详尽的建设计划,如采用关键路径方式,也就没有可以说服仲裁员的基准考量船东方面的过错或违约造成了什么延误与延误程度。

§2 期租合约——什么是停租事项带来的时间损失或延误?

在期租合约下,众所周知是承租人要承担租期内时间的损失。这是因为承租人在船东“交出”(delivery)船舶直到“还船”(redelivery)是要不断给船东支付每天的租金(通常15天一期,而且是预付),而期租合约也通常有条文规定如果承租人不准时与足数支付租金,船东就可以撤船或/与采取其他的相应行动,如启动仲裁、留置货物或暂停履行船东在租约内的承诺等。上述的安排都在一些著名的标准格式期租合约(如“NYPE”)内有所规定。

但也不代表承租人是绝对需要或愿意承担任何原因造成租期内的时间损失,第一类原因就是上述所讲的,对方过错造成的延误,这对方也就是指船东与他的雇员/船长。所以,期租合约会需要有很多明示条文要求船东作出严格的合约承诺,如承诺要合理甚至绝对维修保养船舶以供承租人营运的需要;船长在履行承租人的命令时必须“速遣”(utmost despatch);提供给承租人“习惯做法的协助”(customary assistance);船长必须合理依从承租人合法的“营运指令”(employment order or direction)等。有了这些明示承诺,如果有所违反,如因为船长或船员在岸上喝酒而致使船舶卸完货也无法开航,或承租人指令船东往东开但船长不理会或不合理延误等情况,导致承租人蒙受时间损失(以及其他金钱上的损失)就可以根据英国的“一般法律”(general law)证明船东违约并索赔损失。

第二类造成时间损失的事项属于船东并没有过错或违约(租约没有针对性承诺),所以根据一般法律无法成功指控船东违约并索赔损失,但事项的原因与船东/船舶有关,所以承租人并不愿意承担时间损失。这种类别的事项的典型代表是船舶要定期维修保养并要进船坞清洁船底等,这不能说是船东违约,船东实际上是在履行他在期租合约中的承诺维修保养船舶以供承租人营运的需要。这样,承租人无法根据一般法律把这段时间的损失转移给船东,但也不甘心自己承担。所以唯一的应对办法就是根据订约自由加上一条条文说明在这种情况下,承租人可以停止支付租金。另一个典型代表的事项是船舶在航行中遇上海难(如碰撞或搁浅),这往往会带来严重的时间损失或延误。但承租人也无法以一般法律指控船东违约或有过错,因为租约中船东不会承诺船舶不会遇上海难,而即使发生海难且船东实际有过错,他也因为租约中普遍存在的航行疏忽免责条文(包括在1924年《海牙规则》内并普遍把该立法以首要条文合并在租约内)而不必承担责任。这也带来了一条众所周知的“停租条文”(off - hire clause)。显然根据双方的订约自由以及双方不同的谈判力量与水平,停租条文会是千变万化。但停租条文所针对的事项越少,对船东就越有利。相反,停租条文所针对的事项越多,甚至加上了一些十分广泛的兜底文字,如“无论任何”(whatsoever)就会对承租人越有利。在订约自由下,如果船东答应了一条明示条文说明承租人如果找不到生意或是遇到不可抗力事项的情况下也可以停租,就能把本来应该由承租人承担的时间风险转移给船东。

承租人在原则上要承担时间的损失可以简单的例子说明。例如,承租人由于找不到生意(下一个分租约)而需要船舶停在某个地方等待下一个航次的命令,承租人还是要向船东支付租金,找不到生意要等待的时间损失显然是承租人要承担的营运风险。又如一些性质上属于不可抗力的事项造成延误,如由于坏天气或大雾,本来3天的航次变为5天,或是船舶装/卸完了货无法马上开航,这又是承租人自己承担,因为延误的期间还是要向船东支付租金。

承租人在上述的两类原因造成的事项想把相关时间损失或延误的风险转嫁给船东,会需要证明两个方面。第一个方面是责任,就是根据一般法律下证明船东违约,这就表示船东有了责任。而接下来第二个方面是损失,包括违约造成的时间损失或延误。而如果根据期租合约中的停租条文,承租人就需要证明发生了停租条文内所明示的事项或情况。而进一步(根据停租条文的文字/措辞),承租人就要证明该停租事项对他造成的时间损失或延误。这种条文可被称为“净时间损失”(net loss of time)条文。但由于停租条文不是一般法律,而是根据双方订约自由。所以也经常会有少数的停租条文(特别是出现在双方私下自己拟定的附加条文)并不针对停租事项有否造成时间损失,这种条文可被称为“时间段停租”(period off - hire)。净时间损失表示需要证明停租事项所造成的延误程度,著名的NYPE标准格式合约的停租条文就是典型写法:“15. That **in the event of the loss of time** from deficiency of men or stores, fire, breakdown or damages to hall, machinery or equipment, grounding, detention by average accidents to ship or cargo, dry docking for the purpose of examination or painting bottom, or by any other cause preventing the full working of the vessel, **the payment of hire shall cease for the time thereby lost**; and if upon the voyage the speed be reduced by defect in or breakdown of any part of her hall, machinery or equipment, the time so lost, and the cost of any extra fuel consumed in consequence thereof, and all extra expenses shall be deducted from the hire.”(加黑部分是笔者的强调)

至于后者的时间段停租,在以前的停租条文经常有,但现在比较少见,在双方当事人自己拟定的针对某特定事项停租的附加条文才会出现,而原因可能是他们根本不知道有这些微妙的区别。例如,如果承租人想在船舶被索马里海盗劫持的时间段停租,会在附加条文与船东同意写为:“如果船舶被海盗劫持,该时间段承租人不必支付租金”。显然,在这样的写法下,只要证明发生了被海盗劫持的事项,从一开始直到终结,都可以停租。至于在这个时间段实际上承租人没有时间损失或受到延误,如由于航运市场差而找不到生意,也不影响承租人停租。而如果承租人时间的损失远不止被海盗劫持的这段时间,他也不能多向船东停租。因为这不是一般的法律所管,被海盗劫持也谈不上是船东的过错或违反船东在租约内的承诺(不可能会有明示条文要船东承诺船舶不会受到海盗劫持)。如果没有一条附加条文停租,这时间损失或延误本来是承租人自己要承担的风险。所以,只能按照该条文的规定停租,也就是船舶被海盗劫持这个时间段停租。

但如果该附加条文的写法稍有变动为:"如果船舶被海盗劫持,造成的时间损失或延误承租人不必支付租金"。在这样的写法下,除了要证明被海盗劫持的事项(这不会是困难),承租人还要进一步证明造成了什么时间损失或延误。要证明时间损失或延误就可能困难得多,这也是本段接下来要讲的内容。

"净时间损失"(net loss of time)条文与"时间段停租"(period off – hire)条文的区别可节录 Goff 大法官在 The "Pythia" (1982) 2 Lloyd's Rep 160 先例中说:"Now it is customary to draw a distinction between what have been called 'period' off – hire clauses and 'net loss of time' off – hire clause. Historically some time charters have contained period clauses under which in certain specified circumstances the ship goes off – hire for a certain period. The difficulty with such clauses has however been that the ship might be put off – hire during a period when by reason of a specified event her performance was impaired despite the fact that during such period she was partially capable of performing and did so perform the services required of her ... However, there are also, perhaps because of possible injustices of this kind, net loss of time clauses, under which the ship is only put off – hire for the 'time loss hereby', so that the time charterers cannot escape all liability for hire in respect of time for which they have at least some use of the vessel for the services immediately required of her."

停租条文一针对有否造成时间损失(或同义的"净时间损失"[net loss of time])或真正的延误,就会带来了一个富有争议的大问题,即所针对的延误到底只是针对停租事项造成的向承租人提供即时服务要求的延误(charter service immediately required),或是对整个航次甚至整个租约期(租约期会涉及多个航次或只是单一航次)造成了整体的延误(charter service overall),或是两方面的延误都要兼顾才能停租?在前者,会有停租事项并不造成任何延误,简单的例子是主机故障并需要修理,但有关的时间船舶是在靠泊卸货,根本不需要用主机。换言之,船舶既没有造成 charter service immediately required(因为发生故障当时承租人要求的服务只是卸货)的延误,也没有造成 charter service overall 的延误,所以承租人不可以停租。而后者的例子是可以假设一艘船舶在海上航行发生停租事项(主机故障而失去动力),在 3 天之后才修复,表面看来是造成了 3 天的延误,这是针对 charter service immediately required 而言。但如果把需要考虑的"行为"(act)拉长,也就是看是否有 charter service overall 的延误,就最起码要考虑该船舶所需要港口进行的装卸作业是否也受到同样 3 天的延误。例如,该港口发生事故如航道因较早的一个意外堵塞,船舶即使早到 3 天也进不了港。或是,要装的货物由于公路或车皮的问题而一直无法拉到港口范围。换言之,停租事项对整个航次或至少装港装货而言并没有造成真正的延误。

情况也会是另一种,如该船舶没有在海上的 3 天延误,如果准时抵达下一个港口,就可以进港。而碰巧也是在第二天该港口才发生事故导致进不了港,航道需要在 10 天后才能清除堵塞,让船舶重新进港。这样,停租事项对承租人造成的真正延误感觉上是 10 天,而不仅是 3 天。

表面看来,针对整个航次的延误来考虑对承租人造成了什么时间损失会比较公平合理。但找出如果没有发生停租事项有关的航次会提早多久可以终结,也就是省多少时间,经常会涉及大量的查询与臆猜性的假设。以上述的例子来看,即没有海上的 3 天延误,准时抵达下一个港口就可以进港,但是否没有这 3 天的主机故障,船舶就一定能够准时抵达?如早 3 天的天气很坏,甚至有台风在附近。或是这准时抵达下一个港口是只能早不能晚,即使是晚一两个小时,因为另有一艘船舶也是在同时抵达,进港挂泊的优先权会给另一艘稍微早到的船舶抢去。又或是,在停租事项后承租人才宣港,他完全可以选择另一个港口是早到也不管用等。

这种问题在杨大明律师的《期租合同》第三十五篇之 35.7.5 段有针对,但在近期有了一个英国先例名为 The "Athena" (2013) 2 Lloyd's Rep 673。案情涉及船舶从俄罗斯的新罗希克斯港运小麦去叙利亚。但在叙利亚的塔图斯港,收货人因为小麦被污染而拒货。根据叙利亚的法律不能转卖,必须返回原装港。2010 年 1 月 16 日,船舶离开塔图斯港,名义上是返回新罗希克斯港。期租租约的承租人也就是卖方为了减少损失,命令船东开去利比亚的班加西港。但船东考虑到提单与叙利亚法律的问题,并没有根据承租人的命令开去班加西港,而是在 1 月 19 日到 30 日期间在海上漂流,直到 2 月 18 日才完成卸货。承租人认为根据租约的第 62 条文,承租人有权改港并重发提单。船长不听从承租人的指令是违约,而船长的违令属于租约的停租事项。仲裁庭的多数意见是判船东不应该在海上漂流而不开往班加西港,并且不接受船东的争辩说,即使船舶直接驶往班加西港也不能提早卸货,因为还没有重新签发提单,所以对整个租约或 charter service overall 而言(整个航次包括了班加西港的卸货)并没有造成任何时间损失或延误。仲裁庭的多数裁决是船东败诉,但之后船东提起上诉,第一审的 Walker 大法官判是承租人只能针对 charter service overall 的净时间损失停租并推翻裁决书。但后来上诉庭又推翻了 Walker 大法官的判决,认为仲裁庭多数的裁决是正确的,Tomlinson 大法官说:"The judge's view is unjustified by the wording of the clause, inconsistent with the conventional approach to the clause, which approach is here underscored by typed language additional to that in the printed form, inconsistent with hallowed authority and could moreover lead to the need for 'the most intricate and speculative enquiries as to the course which events would have taken' if full working of the vessel had not been prevented... Such enquiries could typically not be conducted, or at any rate finalised, before the charterers come under an obligation to pay their next monthly or semi-monthly instalment of hire from which they would ordinarily expect to deduct accrued off-hire. The judge's view could also lead to the bizarre outcome that a vessel might be off – hire under a head charterparty yet on – hire under a sub – charterparty on terms materially identical save as to the period of the charter."(指第一审的判法不正确,因为针对整个行为的时间损失或延误,会带来要对一些没有发生过的事情作出大量的查询与臆猜性的假设。它也会导致了承租人无法在预付的租金扣除停租,因为需要等待所有的后遗症都出现才能知道是否有时间损失。另也会造成在同样一个停租事项下,在主租约是停租,但分租约就不能停租。)

有关上述判决的最后一句,也就是有同样的文字/措辞的停租条文下,会造成主租约与分租约不同对待,笔者想到的一种情况是两份期租合约的租期长短不一样。例如,分租约在卸完货马上就要还船,这样船舶在卸港如果发生了停租事项而导致了3天的时间损失,往往还船日期也会受到相同的延误,这3天就无可质疑应该停租。但由于主租约的租约期较长,承租人在卸完货后通过努力仍没能找到下一个分租约,导致需要船舶在卸完货停留在卸港外等待下一航次的指令。这样,船东就会可争辩说,在卸港的停租事项并没有对整个租约或 charter service overall 造成3天或任何时间损失或延误。

§3 国际货物买卖与程租合约——装卸时间与滞期费

在国际货物买卖(international sale)与航运业务,装卸时间与滞期费是最常见的争议。这首先要明白是涉及国际货物(主要是针对大宗的商品)买卖,就免不了需要航运,也往往代表买卖双方其中的一方需要以承租人的身份租船,传统的做法与现在还是经常会有的做法是以"程租"(voyage charter)而不是上一段所讲的期租租船。在上一段的一开始提到在期租合约下,众所周知是承租人要承担租期内时间的损失。但在程租,程租期间也就是有关航次内的时间损失却是要船东自己承担。这道理也很简单,因为承租人在程租下是支付一笔固定的"运费"(freight),承租人主要甚至唯一的要求就是船东承诺把有关货物从特定的装港运到特定的卸港。至于运输的时间多长或多短,承租人(特别是 CIF 卖方)通常不关心,固定的运费也不会因此而有所调整。而对船东而言,显然在收取一笔固定的运费下,尽快完成航次就表示每天的收益有所增加,所以船东通常都会希望速遣。除非有其他经济的因素导致不同的考虑,如燃油价格高会导致船东在运费不高(因为航运低潮)的日子减速以节省燃油。

在上一小段曾经讲到一些性质上属于不可抗力的事项造成延误,如由于坏天气或大雾,本来3天的航次变成5天,或是船舶装/卸完货无法马上开航,在期租下是承租人自己承担,但在程租下就反过来是船东自己要承担这一时间损失或延误的风险。

但在程租合约的航次中,有一段时间可能甚至经常发生延误,船东非常不愿意承担这一风险,这就是在港内的装卸货时间。主要的原因就是在这一段时间船东无法控制,大部分的工作也是承租人做而与船东无关。这样,为了把这一段延误时间从船东转移给承租人,简单的办法就是在程租合约内以订约自由加上条文要求承租人作出承诺在某一段固定的时间内完成装卸,也是所谓"固定装卸时间"(fixed laytime)的说法。而如果承租人不能在承诺的一段时间内完成装卸,就构成违约并且要赔偿船东的损失。而如果没有这一约定,鉴于程租合约下的时间损失或者延误的风险是在船东,装卸作业发生延误是要船东自己承担,除非能够在上述所讲的"一般法律"(general law)下成功证明承租人违约(如怠慢报关、不安排装卸工人或卡车等)并索赔损失。

而由于近年来港口拥挤与造成装卸货作业延误的原因会很多,这种违约经常发生,所以为了减轻要证明损失的困难,双方习惯在程租合约内约定固定装卸时间的同时,也约定一个每天延误要支付的议定赔偿,也就是众所周知的"滞期费"(demurrage)。

程租合约下的固定装卸时间与滞期费也影响了国际货物买卖,道理也很简单。在 FOB 买卖,买方负责租船与派船装港装货。在程租合约下,FOB 买方作为承租人显然难逃在装卸港发生延误要对船东支付滞期费的赔偿。在卸港发生延误,FOB 买方也很可能是收货方,只能怪自己并要承担这一风险。毕竟他也可以有一定程度的控制,如在程租合约下要对船东支付高昂的滞期费,为了想减少就会尽量加快速度卸货,如安排工人加班等。但问题是针对装港,FOB 买方是无法控制,装货作业是由 FOB 卖方或发货人控制。这样 FOB 买方就不愿意承担责任,更不愿意被夹在当中面对船东在程租合约下有固定装货时间的承诺,但没有获得卖方作出的同样承诺。所以,在 FOB 买卖合约针对装港,买方会要求加上一条对自己有利的固定装货时间条文(有利就尽量把时间订得短)与滞期费(有利就尽量把议定赔偿的金额提得高)。

至于在更普遍的 CIF 买卖,就由卖方租船把货物运到约定的卸港,这方面的考虑与做法就反了过来。所以 CIF 买卖合约就必须有固定卸货时间与滞期费条文针对卸货作业,以保障 CIF 卖方。这一方面在 CIF 比 FOB 买卖合约更加重要,因为通常在卸港发生延误的可能性与程度大大超出了装港。

以上简单介绍了程租合约与国际货物买卖合约针对装卸作业与延误的基本框架,接下来就针对在固定装卸时间的承诺下,如果发生了时间损失或延误,承租人如何把本来要承担的风险转嫁给船东。如果读者希望更深入研究这个方面,请看笔者的《装卸时间与滞期费》一书。

在程租合约下,如果装港或卸港航次完结并开始计算装卸时间,就表示时间损失或延误的风险从船东转移到了承租人。显然这个分水线十分重要并且不容易认定,也经常引起争议。英国法律的地位(可称为法律默示地位),也就是合理看怎么样划这一条分水线,认为装卸时间就是承租人承诺在这一段时间内装卸完毕,否则要赔偿滞期费。所以开始计算,显然船舶是抵达租约约定的港口内一个能够装卸的地点,并且船舶备妥。还有是这两个条件,所谓"抵达"(arrived)与"备妥"(ready)也必须通知承租人,让承租人可以马上或尽快装货(或卸货)。这通知也就是通常所说的"准备就绪通知书”(notice of readiness),而如果承租人在船东递交了有效通知书之后还迟迟不装货或卸货,这是他自己的问题,装卸时间还是照算并且在固定时间届满就要开始支付滞期费。英国法律也因为时代的改变而有所调整,如由于在 20 世纪 60 年代后港口十分拥挤,导致船舶经常要在港外待泊,而港外锚地通常是不能装卸地点,所以谈不上船舶在港外锚地已经抵达。这导致在 The “Johanna Oldendorff” (1973) 2 Lloyd's Rep 285 先例规定只要船舶到达了港区范围,就算是航次完结,船舶抵达,时间损失或延误的风险也就可以转移到承租人。这延误明显包括了在港外锚地等待泊位的时间以及其他各种原因所造成的延误,如航道堵塞、等待拖轮、领航员罢工等。但英国贵族院也不愿意进一步扭曲船舶必须到达在租约中约定的装卸港,所以如果港外锚地或船舶等待泊位的地点是不在约定的港口管辖范围,英国法律还是认为船舶没有抵达:The “Maratha Envoy” (1977) 1 Lloyd's Rep 217 先例。例如,船舶约定去上海装货,但上海港拥挤,船舶需要在长江口等待 10 天后才能进港。英国法律的地位下就认为船舶还没有抵达,因为长江口不属于上海港区的范围。这样,如果船东不愿意承担这 10 天时间的损失或延误,就只能以明示条文超越英国法律的默示地位。也就是加一条条文,如说船舶在长江口抛锚就算是抵达,并可以向承租人递交通知书。

本章最主要还是针对在固定的装卸时间已经开始计算的情况下,并且装卸作业造成时间损失或延误的风险是由承租人承担的大前提下,承租人怎样把部分的风险转移给船东。首先是整个装卸作业十分顺利,也没有任何来自船东或第三人造成的延误,这样按道理说承租人可以履行在固定装卸时间内完成作业的承诺,往往也不必涉及滞期费的支付。但第一类的时间损失或延误会来自船东,显然如果这涉及船东或雇员的违约/过错,承租人就可以根据“一般法律”(general law)向船东索赔损失(包括时间损失)。例如,船长或船员要求承租人先给红包才肯打开舱盖允许装货或卸货。船东有否违约/过错,有时也不容易认定。而如果没有造成对承租人任何延误,违约/过错也往往不能把延误风险转嫁到船东,虽然这方面也有不同与富争议的判法:The “Stolt Spur” (2002) 1 Lloyd's Rep 786 先例。但这不同的判法也受到质疑,如在 John Schofield 的《Laytime and Demurrage》(第 6 版,2011 年)一书的 4.18 段,作者有针对船东违约/过错方面说:“It is well established that, whilst a charterer's obligation to complete loading or discharging within the prescribed lay days is unconditional, nevertheless laytime or time on demurrage thereafter will not run whilst here is a delay caused by the fault of the shipowner or those for whom he is responsible. This is sometimes referred to as the rule in Budgett v Binnington. This raises two questions. What is meant by fault? And for whom is the shipowner responsible? Unfortunately the answers given by the courts to these questions have not always been as clear and separate as they might have been. The converse of this is that, if the shipowner is 'prevented' form carrying out his part of cargo operations by the acts of persons over whom he has no control, he is not responsible for the consequent delay."

第二类的时间损失或延误会来自一些外来事项或第三人行为,如坏天气、动乱、政府干预等。这也可以算是"不可抗力"(*force majeure*)事项,本来是应该承租人在固定装卸时间的承诺下需要承担的风险。但一些精明的承租人往往不愿意,做法就只能通过明示条文把这些事项所造成的时间损失的风险或延误转嫁船东。而一般而言,针对坏天气的风险承租人通常会要求装卸时间必须是"好天气工作天"(weather working day),这表示坏天气的时间损失或延误由于不算装卸时间,风险就从承租人转移到船东。除了坏天气以外的外来或第三人原因造成延误,承租人就会希望通过一条"停算装卸时间(与滞期费)的除外条文"(laytime [demurrage] exclusion/exception clause)把风险转移到船东。本质上与期租合约的"停租条文"(off – hire clause)一样,承租人在条文中把这些停算装卸时间事项写得越广泛,就对承租人越有利。相反,没有或极少明示停算事项的除外条文的租约就对承租人不利。例如,对船东十分有利的"金康租约 1994"(Gencon 1994),标准格式内根本谈不上有一条停算装卸时间(与滞期费)的除外条文。这表示发生了任何第二类的时间损失,风险都是在承租人,装卸时间照算与滞期费照付,即使承租人在期间由于一些外来或第三人的事项导致根本无法进行装卸作业。

在一些对船东不利的标准格式程租合约,就往往有一条包括十分广泛事项的停算装卸时间(与滞期费)的除外条文。如在 Sugar Charterparty 1999,第 28 条文是说:"**Strike and *Force Majeure*** In the event that whilst at or off the loading place or discharging place the loading and/or discharging of the vessel is prevented or delayed by any of the following occurrences: strikes, riots, civil commotions, lockouts of men, accidents and/or breakdowns on railways, stoppages on railway and/or river and/or canal by ice or frost, mechanical breakdowns at mechanical loading plants, government interferences, vessel being inoperative or rendered inoperative due to the terms and conditions of employment of the Officers and Crew, time so lost shall not count as laytime or time on demurrage or detention."

上述停算装卸时间的除外条文就以一些十分广泛的文字/措辞包括许多外来或第三人造成的时间损失或延误,如"意外"(accidents)或"政府干预"(government interferences)。这种广泛的条文也经常引起争议,毕竟在有关事项造成严重的延误时,涉及庞大金额的滞期费,双方会对谁应该承担时间损失或延误的风险争辩。这种案例在笔者的《装卸时间与滞期费》一书之十五章有详述。

会有一种经常发生的情况,就是装卸作业需要使用船上的吊杆或装卸设备,相比其他事项造成时间损失或延误会有一些独特的问题。一是由于装卸设备经常会发生故障,造成的延误也不严重,不值得花时间与金钱找出每次故障的真正原因。这种原因会是承租人自己要负责的装卸工人在作业中疏忽/过错导致装卸设备故障,显然这种延误应当由承租人自己承担。但如果船上的装卸设备故障与承租人无关,是设备本身的问题,就有可能会是来自船东的违约(因为程租合约往往有条文要求船东承诺装卸设备是在良好的工作状况),但也会可能是与违约无关或可以免责,如故障是天气或设备的内在缺陷所造成。另一个问题是船舶有几个舱,有大有小,如果需要使用船舶装卸设备卸载的是小舱,即使中途发生故障造成小舱的卸载发生短暂的延误,很有可能对整个船舶卸货的时间(往往最大的船舱完成卸货才是整个作业完结)不会有任何影响。因此金康格式(其他承租合约也有类似条文)直接规定说:“All such equipment to be in good working order. Unless caused by negligence of the stevedores, time lost by breakdown of the Vessel's cargo handling gear or motive power - pro rata the total number of cranes/winches required at that time for the loading/discharging of cargo under this Charter Party - shall not count as laytime or time on demurrage.”

以上第一句就是船东承诺装卸设备是在良好的工作状况的条文。接下来就是除非承租人的装卸工人疏忽所造成的故障(这一方面也经常有争议,但船东相对比较容易证明),装卸设备在作业中的故障按比例停止计算装卸时间/滞期费。换言之,假设一艘船舶有5个船舱与5套独立的装卸设备,如果其中有1套装卸设备发生故障,就应当停算1/5的装卸时间/滞期费,也就是承租人把这时间损失的风险转嫁给了船东。这也与上段针对期租合约所介绍的“时间段停租”(period off - hire)道理一样,文字/措辞只针对发生故障这一段时间,而不理会对整个停算装卸作业是否最后造成了延误,这写法明显与一般的停算装卸时间(与滞期费)的除外条文有所区别。这对船东也没有不公道,因为发生故障的船舱/装卸设备可能是船舶上最大的一个,最后对承租人造成的真正延误(指装卸作业完结)是5/5而不是1/5。

§4 工程合约/造船合约的时间损失或延误

工程合约(也包括造船合约)的双方总会约定一个完工日期,在造船合约中也就是交船日期。对雇主而言,他会要求承建商作出这一严格的承诺,也就是要求在某个日期前完工,而不会让承建商任意按照他自己认为合理的速度来进行重要的工程。很多工程都是与一些重要而紧迫的计划联系,例如,为了下一届奥运会或者足球世界杯而建造运动场馆、酒店、公路、桥梁、地铁/高铁等。就是造一艘船舶,也往往是船东对中长期的航运市场看好或自己的营运有需要才会订下造船合约,如果由船厂按任意速度建造,可能会比船东期望的时间晚得多而且不肯定,船东一定不会接受。这导致造船合约也避免不了需要船厂作出严格的承诺会在某个日期前完工并交船。上述也是一般的工程合约或造船合约中条文/文字的背景/语境或本质。

至于在谈判时如何约定这一完工或交船日期,显然有经验与谨慎的承建商(或船厂)就不会随便承诺一个很乐观的日期预测,让雇主(或船东)在订约时高兴,但事后自己却做不到。承建商会凭他的经验以及特定工程的需要作出一个尽量合理、清晰、全面、详尽、客观与现实的计划，相对准确地估计完工日期后，才会在工程合约中以明示条文作出承诺。否则，承建商对工程的延误可能会承担十分严重的后果，因为这是违反了承诺，就要面对雇主的损失作出赔偿（每天的议定赔偿），甚至导致工程合约被终止。

即使是一位很有经验与谨慎的承包商通过十分客观与详细的计划作出完工日期的估计，并将其写入工程合约（造船合约）内，也不表示该承建商实际上可以准确无误地在约定的日期内完工。因为在工程的进行中，往往会出现一些意外与无法事先针对的事项导致时间损失或延误。这种事项的原因就是上文提到过的三类情况，即第一类是类似不可抗力，如坏天气、火灾、战争等外来因素导致的工程的延误；第二类是雇主（或船东）或他的雇员（如监督造船的总管）的过错、不合作或造成障碍导致工程的延误；第三类是承建商（或船厂）自己要承担的时间损失风险，如由于工人不足、财政问题、自己的分承建商/供应商造成各种延误、承建商自己的怠慢等。

4.1　不可抗力事项的延误

在工程合约通常会有条文针对上述不同类别的延误。在第一类的延误，工程合约往往有一条"不可抗力"（*force majeure*）条文，规定发生了这些事项导致工程延误，就可以相应延长完工的日期。这显然十分公道，因为即使承建商承诺一个十分客观甚至是保守的完工日期，还是控制不了在施工时遇到这些不可抗力的事项会造成延误。但往往有关的条文会同时要求，一旦发生了不可抗力事项，承建商就需要及时向雇主作出"延误通知"（notice of delay）。

4.1.1　要求承建商作出延误通知

这一延误通知的目的就是让雇主知道并有机会马上作出调查以确定是出现了列明的不可抗力事项并造成工程的延误。这方面可以节录 Duncan Wallace 教授在《Hudson on Building Contracts》一书中所说："Contractual terms requiring a contractor to give prompt notice of delay serve a valuable purpose; such notices enables matters to be investigated while they are still current. Furthermore, such notice sometimes gives the employer the opportunity to withdraw instructions when the financial consequences become apparent. If *Gaymark* is good law, then a contractor could disregard with impunity any provision making proper notice a condition precedent. At his option the contractor could set time at large."

如果承建商没有在时间规定作出通知，通常的后果就是不能按照不可抗力条文延长完工（或交船）日期。换言之，准时与正确作出通知是承建商可延长完工日期的"先决条件"（condition precedent）。这个后果会在一些标准工程合约中有明示规定，如 FIDIC "Silver Book" Sub – Clause 20.1 如下："If the Contractor fails to give notice of a claim within such period of 28 days, the Time for Completion shall not be extended, the Contractor shall not be entitled to additional payment, and the Employer shall be discharged from all liability in connection with the claim."

近期的先例为了给这要求承建商作出延误通知的条文一定的意义,导致了即使是有关条文没有明确写明是先决条件,甚至对延误通知的时间规定比较含糊,也通常都会判是同样的结果。如在 Steria Ltd v. Sigma Wireless Communications Ltd (2008) BLR 79 先例,相关的条文不是针对不可抗力,而是针对在特定的情况下分承包商可以延长完成工程合约的时限,并可以不必为这种延误支付每天的议定赔偿。针对通知的 6.1 条文是说:"... by reason of a variation to the Subcontract Works, or by reason of any breach by [Sigma](承建商), [Steria](分承建商) shall be delayed in the execution of the Subcontract Works, then in any case provided the Sub – Contractor shall have given within a reasonable period written notice to the Contractor of the circumstances giving rise to the delay..."

Stephen Davies 法官认为条文写的很明确,不需要再明示延误作出通知的后果,如不能依赖所针对的事项延长工程的完成时间。如果分承包商没有在合理时间内作出通知,就不能再要求延长时限,说:

"In my judgment the phrase 'provided that the sub – contractor shall have given within a reasonable period written notice to the contractor of the circumstances giving rise to the delay' is clear in its meaning. What the sub – contractor is required to do is give written notice within a reasonable period from when he is delayed, and the fact that there may be scope for argument in an individual case as to whether or not a notice was given within a reasonable period is not in itself any reason for arguing that it is unclear in its meaning and intent. In my opinion the real issue which is raised on the wording of this clause is whether those clear words by themselves suffice, or whether the clause also needs to include some express statement to the effect that unless written notice is given within a reasonable time the sub – contractor will not be entitled to an extension of time.

In my judgment **a further express statement of that kind is not necessary.** I consider that a notification requirement may, and in this case does, operate as a condition precedent even though it does not contain an express warning as to the consequence of non – compliance. It is true that in many cases (see for example the contract in the Multiplex case itself) careful drafters will include such an express statement, in order to put the matter beyond doubt. It does not however follow, in my opinion, that a clause — such as the one used here — which makes it clear in ordinary language that the right to an extension of time is conditional on notification being given should not be treated as a condition precedent. This is an individually negotiated sub – contract between two substantial and experienced companies, and I would be loathe to hold that a clearly worded requirement fails due to the absence of legal 'boilerplate'."(加黑部分是笔者的强调)

即使不是工程合约而是其他类别的合约,近期的案例也是有同样的判法。在 Mamidoil – Jetoil Greek Petroleum Co SA v. Okta Crude Oil Refinery AD (2003) 2

Lloyd's Rep. 635 先例，也判是不可抗力条文中的准时通知是先决条件或条件条文，虽然它并没有明确的时间规定，如 7 天或 10 天不等。该条文是说：

"The party invoking *force majeure*, shall give **prompt notice** to the other party by fax, telex followed by registered letter stating the kind of *force majeure*."（加黑部分是笔者的强调）

而由于这个条文没有明确到底迟延给通知是"先决条件"（condition precedent）或是"中间条文"（innominate term），双方又有了常见的争议。原告认为立即给通知是被告可以依赖不可抗力事项的先决条件，被告没有立即通知就不能再依赖不可抗力事项。但被告声称这只是中间条文。高院的 Aikens 大法官判是如果没有给通知，不可抗力事项就不能依赖，这等于说把这个条文视为条件条文，或是想依赖不可抗力事项的先决条件，说："I would have been inclined to hold that notice provision in the 1993 contract is a condition precedent. The form of the notice provision is imperative; a party 'invoking *force majeure* shall give prompt notice to the other party'. The implication behind that imperative is that if the party does not then it cannot rely on *force majeure*. The reason for requiring notice to be given must be that the '*other party*' can then investigate the alleged *force majeure* at the time. It can challenge whether it does prevent performance or delay in performance by the party invoking *force majeure*. Alternatively it can see if there are other means of enabling performance to be continued. Lastly, if the notice provision is only an innominate term, then I find it difficult to see when the innocent party could allege it had suffered additional damage as a result of not being told promptly of the *force majeure* event other than the very damages that it would wish to recover for the first party's failure to perform the contract at all. These factors would all lead me to conclude that the parties intended the notice provision to be a condition precedent."

中国船厂在 2008 年金融海啸后的大量伦敦仲裁败诉案件，原因在本书已经有多处涉及，包括本书本章之第 5 段的妨碍原则，第四章有关同类原则，第六章有关造船合约条文解释的中间裁决，第十章有关对于时间的规定与第十四章有关专家决定条文，在此不再重复。其中有不少案件也涉及这一没有或延误作出不可抗力条文下的延误通知给船东/买方，导致丧失了权利。造船合约显然属于工程合约（虽然本质上被视为买卖合约[1]）的一种，这方面也有近期的相关案例，如 Adyard Abu Dhabi v SD Marine Services (2011) BLR 384 先例，在本章之第 5 段针对"妨碍原则"（prevention principle）有介绍。该先例涉及造船合约的买方是否可以合法终止合约，主要是

---

〔1〕 Diplock 大法官在 McDougall v Aeromarine of Emsworth Ltd (1958) 2 Lloyd's Rep 345 先例中说："... it seems well settled by authority that, although a shipbuilding contract is, in form, a contract for the construction of the vessel, it is in law a contract for sale of goods..."。

针对妨碍原则而不是针对在时限内作出通知,但 Hamblen 大法官在他的判决的附带意见中看来也是把准时作出延误通知视为先决条件,说:“On the construction of the contract which I have held to be correct the contract provides for an extension of time in the events which happened through article VIII and article II, clause 3.3. However, any claim for such permissible delay fails due to the lack of an article VIII, clause 2 notice.”这些案件中显示了中国船厂没有按照造船合约条文作出通知的意识,导致在明确发生了不可抗力事项的情况下也无法延长交船日期或死亡日期,从而进一步导致手握高利润的造船合约却只能眼看船东合法脱身,这是极其可惜的。

4.1.2 准时作出延误通知的困难

要求中国船厂准时作出“延误通知”(notice of delay)在现实中或操作中十分困难。第一个困难是不可抗力条文所针对的事项通常很多,这些事项会针对大事件,也会针对一些小事。在后者的事项,它们会造成的工程延误经常不会是一开始就明显,往往是不断累积才最后造成一段比较可观的时间的延误。这样针对前者的大事件,如早期的日本大地震或强力台风袭击上海,一发生就明显造成工程停顿,工人上不了班,不少有水平与有经验的船厂会向船东准时作出延误通知。后者的小事如“工人短缺”(labor shortage)或“劳工争议”(labor disturbance)、“正常计划外的其他天气情况”(other weather conditions not included in normal planning)、“延误运输”(delays or failure in transportation)、“材料短缺”(shortage of materials)等,这些事情造成的延误往往一开始不明显,不容易作出通知,就算有水平与有经验的船厂也很少会准时作出通知。

第二个困难是来自造船合约中不可抗力条文针对时限的文字/措辞。如笔者见到很多涉及中国船厂的造船合约中规定:“Within (若干天) from the date of **commencement of any delay**... the BUILDER shall advise the BUYER by telefax or E-mail confirmed in writing, of the date such delay commenced, and the reasons therefor.”(加黑部分是笔者的强调)

注意这是从开始延误的一天起算若干天(3 天、5 天、7 天或 10 天不等),而通知必须明确写明延误开始的一天与造成的原因。这往往很难做得到,特别是一些船厂不会马上知道的不可抗力事项,如来自供应商或分承建商的延误(不可抗力事项针对延误运输、材料短缺、厂房或设备的损坏与意外等,往往延伸至供应商与分承建商,因为有很多工程会分包给他们)。如在 Finance for Shipping Ltd v Appledore Shipbuilding Ltd (1982) Com L. R. 49 先例,延误就来自建造船舶主机的分承建商。所以中国船厂必须要抗拒这种条文的文字/措辞。这里可以引用《The Law of Shipbuilding Contracts》(第 4 版,2012 年)一书之第 166 页谈到:“It should be noted that time runs in each case from the date of commencement or cessation of the alleged *force majeure* event, rather than from the date on which the builder first learns of the same; the builder may therefore be unable to give the required notice in time if the event has its immediate impact outside the shipyard, perhaps by affecting a subcontractor or supplier rather than the builder directly. **The SAJ Form wording is for this reason often amended to provide that time shall run only from the date on which the builder first learns of the *force majeure* event in question.**"(加黑部分是笔者的强调)最后一句是说,日本标准造船格式(SAJ Form)的文字/措辞经常被改为这个若干天应从船厂第一次知道相关的不可抗力事项开始计算。这样就不必担心分承建商在出了事情之后10天才通知船厂他的厂房发生了事故,导致船厂马上通知船东也已经错过时间规定。

4.1.3 准确作出延误通知的困难

对中国船厂第二个困难是"延误通知"(notice of delay)除了要及时作出之外,也必须准确,这包括有关不可抗力条文对通知内容的明示要求,如什么不可抗力事项造成延误与延误程度。不准确通知的地位与从来没有作出是一样的。这个法律地位在针对"准备就绪通知书"(notice of readiness)的先例很明确,如 The "Mexico 1" (1990) 1 Lloyd's Rep 507 先例等。另在 Christensen v Hindustan Steel Ltd (1971) 1 Lloyd's Rep 395 先例,Donaldson 大法官说:"... the general rule that a notice of readiness is wholly ineffective if ... the vessel is not... ready when it is given."

有关航次租约中对准备就绪通知书的严格性在笔者的《装卸时间与滞期费》一书第九章与第十章都有详论,并强调现实中会出现太多无效通知书的情况。虽然在造船合约的延误通知会在本质上有一点不同,但估计船厂作出不准确的通知恐怕不会在今天被伦敦仲裁员宽待,所以船厂必须小心。例如,在造船合约中常常会要求延误通知中写明造成延误的原因,如果船厂给的原因不准确就会带来问题。而如果原因写得太详细,可能会导致只能依赖通知中列明的原因造成的延误,而不能依赖其他事项造成的延误。所以在保证准确的基础上,应该把造成延误的原因写得尽量宽泛。另一个危险会是在准备就绪通知书以前,有很多通知都属于"初步通知"(inchoate 或 prospective notice),但在 The "Mexico 1"先例已经明确下来初步通知是无效的,等于从来没有给过通知。这表示在造船合约的延误通知,也会有这个危险,这在 Finance for Shipping Ltd v Appledore Shipbuilding Ltd (1982) Com. L.R 49 先例出现。这种通知会是在船厂出了不可抗力事项后,不知道将来会否对交船日期或销约期延误,先向买方作出一个通知。

为了避免延误通知的有效性将来受到质疑,中国船厂最好在他们的造船合约中加上一条条文针对船东在接到延迟通知后的若干天(可以是5天或10天不等)内必须告知船厂他是否反对,否则就被视为同意或弃权,这种放弃反对的权利的条文在法律是被视为"合约弃权"(contractual waiver)。条文的文字/措辞可以是:"Failure of the BUYER to object to the BUILDER's claim for postponement of the Delivery Date within (若干天,这是让船东/买方对延误通知调查后决定接受或反对,显然对船厂而言,这个期限越短越好) after receipt by the BUYER of such notice of claim shall be deemed to be a waiver by the BUYER of its right to object such postponement of the Delivery Date."

如果船东不在规定的时间内告知船厂他质疑延误通知有缺陷,船东就被当作"放弃"(waiver)了反对延迟交船日期的权利。在 Finance for Shipping Ltd v Appledore Shipbuilding Ltd 先例,上诉庭判是船东给船厂模棱两可的回复就给了船厂一个抗辩指船东放弃了质疑延误通知无效的权利。造船合约如果有这种合约弃权的条文,中国船厂更加应该尽量准时与准确作出延误通知。而只要给了延误通知,即使有缺陷(因为有争议时船东会对延误通知的内容挑剌),也可以多一个争辩说船东弃权。而如果中国船厂从来都没有作出过延误通知,就连这个争辩都欠缺。

4.1.4 延误通知有关延误程度

上一小段已经提到"延误通知"(notice of delay)要准确,其中包括通知内容需要告知船东或雇主有关不可抗力事项延误。如在中国不少造船合约,明示条文会规定延误通知其中一项内容是由于该不可抗力事项造成对交船日期最长的延误(shall specify the maximum period of time by which the date for delivery of the VESSEL is extended by reason of such delay)。这是对中国船厂(或承建商)一个更大的困难,因为涉及本章接下来会谈的内容,即往往通过"关键路径分析"(critical path analysis)才能估计到对交船或工程完工造成了什么延误。固然,船东/雇主会对声称造成的延误有疑义,而且在有关工程合约如果有条文造成了合约弃权,必须准时提出质疑。这样,双方的争议最后还是需要仲裁解决,而仲裁员也会根据关键路径分析看待这个问题。但关键是,如果明示条文对中国船厂或承建商有要求,它就必须对有关延误的程度作出合情合理的估计,才能作出准确的延误通知。

这方面的困难涉及怎样证明是否有延误与延误的程度。例如,发生了不可抗力的事项,如坏天气,可能对整个工程造成延误,但也有可能根本不受影响。例如,其中一天下大雨,并且有明确的证明(如天文台的记录)显示工地受影响。但这不代表有关的工程受到延误,因为可能是有关的建筑已经封顶,在进行的都是室内工作。这样,大雨就不会造成"关键路径延误"(critical path delay)。[2] 但如果坏天气是大雨造成泛滥,交通瘫痪而导致工人无法上班,那么就有很大可能是造成了关键路径延误。又如,下大雪虽然导致工人无法上班,但如果有关船舶已经基本完工,只是需要安排试航,而试航并不受下大雪的影响,此时就显然没有造成工程的延误。另外,承建商如果没有一个客观与详细的文书计划,也就无法通过对比,证明有关的不可抗力事项对原来的计划造成了什么延误。又或是在一家酒店的建造中,地毯是由雇主提供,但供应商的提供发生了延误。这是否影响关键路径要看地板是否已经平整,而地板能否平整又要看地下的水管或电线有没有铺设完毕。只有在这些关键路径的工程都已经按计划的时间做妥,雇主提供的地毯发生延误才是造成了关键路径延误。但

〔2〕 这在稍后会进一步详尽介绍。

通过不同的合约写法与措辞,也可以回避要证明真正造成了什么延误的困难。本章之第2段提到的租约中“某时段停租”(period off - hire)的条文,就是很好的例子。工程合约其实也可以这样做,如针对不可抗力事项,说明只要发生列明的不可抗力事项,直到该事项完结,有关的时间段就可以相应延长完工(或交船)日期,根本不提及该事项有否对工程造成延误或延误程度。这样的写法看起来比较不公道,但优胜之处就是对承建商(或船厂)相对简单,不必证明该事项所造成的真正延误。

4.2 雇主或其雇员的延误与妨碍原则

在第二类的延误也就是雇主(或船东)或其雇员过错造成的延误,承建商(或船厂)往往可以根据“一般法律”(general law)向雇主提出索赔,包括时间损失。很少工程合约会对雇主的过错有明示规定,原因之一就是订约时很少会预计并以明示条文针对对方的过错或违约。另一个原因就是雇主(或任何人士)的过错会是千变万化,根本无法尽录。在造船合约,会有条文针对船东作为买方的过错,如船东没有提供在合约中承诺的母公司或银行的履约担保、准时支付分期造船预付款、拒绝在交船时接收船舶、船东延误提供他的设备等,并会像本章之4.1段提到的不可抗力条文一样规定相关事项造成的延误可以延长交船日期。但显然船东可以犯的过错或违约远远不止这两三项,船东有时甚至会为了从亏本的造船合约中脱身偷偷安排犯罪分子放火,使建造中的船舶被损坏或烧毁,[3]装作是船厂自己的问题导致无法及时交船甚至永远交不了船。显然,订立造船合约时不会想到这种极端的过错。所以,只要在造船合约中没有明示条文针对,如果真的发生就只能依赖一般法律。这一般法律就是在本章稍后的第5段所讲的“妨碍原则”(prevention principle),不在此重复。

承建商即使在责任方面证明了雇主有过错或违反妨碍原则的默示条文,还要进一步证明他的损失,也就是对这个工程合约的行为(显然就是及时完工)带来了什么时间损失或延误。这又回到了上文提到过的困境,即如果承建商没有客观与详细的计划作为基准,就无法提供证明雇主(或船东)的过错对原来的计划造成了什么延误,也就是证明不了时间损失。涉及中国船厂的仲裁案件,反而是外国船东经常通过向船厂要求文件披露而获得一些船厂并不完整的文件记录,如年度工作计划、[4]设备订单、工人名单等,并通过分析这些文件所显示的有关船舶与其他建造中的船舶的里程碑日期指出中国船厂的整个工程混乱,往往还没有开始建造就已经有了严重与

---

[3] The “Ikarian Reefer” (1995) 1 Lloyd’s Rep 455 先例;另可看在航运低潮时有大量涉及船东凿沉船舶骗保险公司的案例,如 The “Gold Sky” (1972) 2 Lloyd’s Rep 187; The “Michael” (1979) 1 Lloyd’s Rep 55; The “Captain Panagos D. P.” (1986) 2 Lloyd’s Rep 470; The “Grecia Express” (2002) 2 Lloyd’s Rep 88 等。

[4] 这并非是本章之4.7段所讲的关键路径方式,而只是船厂整体的年度计划,包括所有在建造或会建造的船舶。但仍会针对有关的个别船舶显示了一些里程碑日期,如什么时候切割钢板、安放龙骨或钢结构、安装主机、试航等。船东/买方支付分期付款的时间往往根据造船合约的规定与这些步骤完成的时间相配合,显然其中许多里程碑日期如果有延误会造成关键路径延误。

无可避免的延误。即使中国船厂在责任方面胜诉,也无法证明任何真正的损失或延误,因为即使没有船东的妨碍,船厂也无法在销约期前交船。这也可能涉及“同步延误”(concurrent delay)的问题,这在本章之5.6段有介绍。

4.3 承建商(分承建商/供应商)或其雇员造成的延误

第三类的延误就是承建商(或船厂)或其雇员所造成的延误,但也可以包括没有被包括在第一类的不可抗力条文中的外来事项或第三人的行为造成的延误。承建商自己就要承担这方面的时间损失或延误的风险。毕竟,他们作出了严格的承诺在某一日期完工(或交船),也承诺在死亡日期或销约期还是不能完工,对方就可以终止合约,所以要承担这个风险也理所当然。当然在订约自由下,承建商永远可以通过订约自由把尽量多与广的事项加在工程合约内的不可抗力条文,让他只要作出通知与证明延误就可以延长完工日期。但一般对不可抗力条文,雇主会大力抗拒承建商加入后者可以有一定程度控制的事项(如工人不足或罢工或材料短缺),而只会接受承建商完全不能控制的事项(包括第三人的行为,如政府干预或动乱等)。但只要是在承诺完工日期不能完工,而又是由这第三类的延误所造成,就往往在工程合约会约定承建商每一天的延误(即使发生在缓冲时间内)都是违约,并要对雇主作出金钱赔偿。但因为计算工程延误的损失不易,双方往往在工程合约内会同意每一天的延误承建商要支付特定金额的“议定赔偿”(liquidated damages)。这样,虽然在这第三类的延误,承建商不需要向雇主证明有关事项造成了工程的延误,但为了自己更好地管理工程,而第三类的延误又常常与其他类别的延误有密切关系,承建商还是逃避不了需要证明是否对整个工程有延误以及延误的程度。例如,如果发生延误的事项初步看来是容许延长完工日期的不可抗力事项,但由于证明不了或不可抗力条文订得不够广泛,就会导致该事项最后会是属于这第三类的延误,要承建商自己承担延误的风险。

4.4 销约期

工程合约(或造船合约)通常还会约定一个销约期(或造船合约的死亡日期),有关的条文通常是给雇主(或船东)可以终止有关合约的选择权。销约期与承诺的完工(或交船)日期之间往往有一段缓冲时间,如造船合约就通常有180天或210天不等的缓冲时间。换言之,如果发生在这一段缓冲时间的延误,即使是属于本章之4.3段介绍的第三类延误,雇主对承建商的违约所能取得的救济也只是索赔每天的议定赔偿。但问题是,如果发生十分严重的延误(可以是第一类不可抗力事项的延误或第三类承建商需要承担风险的延误),甚至严重至工程可能不会完工,如承建商经济发生严重困难,雇主就会面临一个抉择,是否需要中途更换承建商以继续完成工程。这样,雇主必须先终止原工程合约,才可以与新承建商订立另一个工程合约。但由于延误(甚至是严重延误)本身不一定构成条件条文,而且工程合约针对延误已经有了约定的救济办法,也就是支付议定赔偿。所以为了有权终止原工程合约,就必须要有这一销约期的明示条文。

但还会有一个变数是一些外来或第三人造成的延误(这可以是不可抗力事项,但也可以是承建商要承担),如工程(例如建造酒店)的地点发生动乱。这会导致雇主根本不在乎工程什么时候完工,反正完工后也无法经营,而承建商又是一个实力雄厚的公司,雇主乐得根据工程合约把每天的延误向承建商索取议定赔偿。这样,即使有销约期条文,雇主也不行使终止工程合约的选择权。工程合约应该对承建商需要支付的议定赔偿有一个限额。

近年来,中国船厂转向订立一些复杂与时间性十分重要的海工造船合约(主要针对海上钻探的钻油平台或相关船舶)。这些造船合约会规定每个工序的完成时间,甚至会进一步让船东在船厂跟不上工序时有终止造船合约的选择权,并把该建造了一半的船舶给其他船厂尽快与尽好地完成工程,然后向违约的船厂索赔所有的损失。这种造船合约显然对船厂十分危险,因为这不是关心交船日期与死亡日期这么简单,也不是仅靠支付议定赔偿就可以解决问题。所以船厂在同意这种条文之前,必须在约定的每个工序的完成时间上有深思熟虑的计划并且能够严格遵守。在 Pacific Ocean Shipping Corp v. Sembawang Corp Ltd (No. 1) (1998) Commercial Court 4 June 1998 先例中,该造船(改装)合约就有这种条文。在合约的第 5 条文规定了一连串的工序的开始日期与完工日期,即有了许多的“里程碑日期”(milestone),另加上了船舶总完工与交船的日期,就是 1995 年 8 月 16 日。另合约有一条 17.1 条文把这些时间提升至条件条文,说:“PARTIES expressly agree that time is of the essence for the WORK.”

另外加上一条更加明确的条文说明如果船厂无法在工程的进展速度上让船东合理满意工序完工日期与总完工与交船的日期,船东有权在建造的任何时间内终止造船合约。该条文是第 37.1(e)条文,如下:“The OWNERS shall have the right, without prejudice to any of its other rights or remedies under, or in, or arising from, or in connection with the CONTRACT or at law, by giving NOTICE to the BUILDER to terminate the CONTRACT if the BUILDER: - - (e) fails, neglects, refuses or is unable during the course of the WORK to provide sufficient materials, equipment, services or labour to perform the WORK at the quality specified and at a progress rate deemed sufficient by the OWNERS to provide a reasonable assurance that the WORK shall be completed in accordance with the CONTRACT provisions.”

该新加坡船厂接受了上述苛刻条文的严重后果就是被船东在建造/改装的中途终止合约外,还要面对 2.5 亿英镑的巨大损失索赔,并且在花费高额诉讼费用后败诉。看来中国船厂的转向要被迫或自愿接受这种危险性更高的海工造船合约(危险性包括苛刻的合约条文、高昂的船舶价格与索赔金额、投机性的买方、油价下跌、船东/买方弃船后难以转卖等),必须要有警惕。

4.5　承建商向分承建商/供应商索赔

上述第三类延误如果来自分承建商/供应商的过错或违约,导致整个工程的延误并需要向雇主支付议定赔偿或被雇主终止工程合约,就会带来承建商要向分承建商/供应商索赔损失的问题,因为他们之间也是有独立的合约关系。这样,承建商就需要证明"因果关系"(causation),即后者的违约或过错造成的延误是承建商对整个工程延误的原因,并导致要向雇主支付议定赔偿或被终止合约。

例如,笔者不久前处理过一个造船合约的仲裁案件,就是中国船厂向韩国主机制造商订购一台主机,但该主机有一个表面检查不出来的内在缺陷,导致在试航时主机严重损坏并需要更换。该韩国主机虽然实质上是船东要求与指定,但造船合约的规定主机供应商属于船厂的供应商,该主机损坏与需要更换的事项也没有包括在不可抗力条文内,所以仲裁庭判时间的损失由中国船厂承担。由于延误刚好超过了该造船合约的死亡日期/销约期,也就给外国船东从这个造船合约中脱身的机会。但接下来就会涉及中国船厂向韩国主机供应商索赔这一损失,当然能否成功索赔与赔偿金额还要看有关供应合约的条文,如有否免责条文或赔偿金额限制条文。但中国船厂难逃要证明有关事项是否对工程造成延误以及延误的程度,虽然在这个明显的案件证明不困难,因为该主机的损坏与更换明显是关键路径延误。

接下来进一步介绍承建商(或船厂)为了良好管理工程(或造船)与发生争议时证明延误所需要的合理、清晰、全面、详尽、客观与现实的工程计划,也就是上文数次提到的关键路径分析。

4.6 工程计划

复杂的工程合约,往往可以分割成不同的工序,如一个造船合约就会包括安放龙骨或装配"分段预制船体"(pre - fabricated blocks)、安装主机、船舶出坞、其他许多机件/配件的装配等。其中,为了计划上的方便,将一些继续分割意义不大的工序称为"项目"(activity)。而每个项目的设定都应该有一个预计完成的日期,而且这个预计必须是现实与根据"承建商"(contractor)(在造船合约中则为船厂)的人力物力做得到。

现代的工程合约,由于其本身的复杂性,或者是涉及特殊专业工程,或是有时需要国际供应商的参与,在开工的过程中会有很多需要多方互动与各个承建商、分承建商之间合作的内容。因此,建造过程中的任何"事项"(event)均需要一个有效的方式来衡量该事项对整个建造工程的影响。普遍应用的方式就是为工程合约设计一个"计划"(programme)。

计划包含很多的类型。首先开始设计的是"投标计划"(tender programme),这是一个简单的计划,仅仅为了有关工程"投标"(tender),并不一定包含详实的项目规划。投标计划经过设计项目间的先后顺序以及确定各个项目的前置要求,就可以称为"总进度计划"(master programme)。总进度计划在工程的最开始表现为粗略的"基准计划"(baseline programme),其后在经过完善、调整与更新后,即可以制定"预定计划"(as - planned programme),用以模拟长期工程中所有项目的先后完成顺序。在整个工程的进行过程中,对工程进度是否达到要求的衡量,需要依赖预定计划进行。而且一旦发生项目的变更(如取消或更改有关项目)或其他有影响的事项出现,这些事项对于总工程的实际影响,如额外的花费、完工日期的延误等也需要有预定计划的内容才能一目了然,并且如果有需要的话,作出合适的应对。

预定计划或总进度计划有三个目的:(1)预计理论上最早能够完成工程的日期;(2)考量“里程碑日期”(milestone)或阶段完成日期的设立在逻辑顺序上的合理性;(3)考量由于材料、厂房、人力资源的限制所导致的工程时段上的合理性。然而部分承建商并不倾向于编制一份完善的预定计划,这往往是因为担忧制定一份计划后却不能按详细的计划日期完成。而且,如果要根据关键路径方式制定一份完善的预定计划,则需要对有关工程有丰富经验的人士通过调研与分析,以获得具体与准确的数据,这些数据有时需要从“分承建商”(sub - contractor)处获得。如果只是粗糙与不准确的数据,整个计划就没有意义。

编制一份预定计划看似会增加承建商的成本以及在建造过程中需要完成计划的压力,但事实上,如果有一份完善的预定计划,承建商或实际建造人员能够有计划地对工程中的人事作出安排,反而能够高效地完成工程。更重要的是,有了这份预定计划,承建商可以清楚了解工程进行中的每一个行为、每一个改动会对整个工程所造成的影响,一旦发生延误争议,工程双方也会有基准来解决争议,可以节省下大量的诉讼费用。重要的好处可总结如下:(1)在工程合约中,设定出一个计划最基本的好处之一就是可以对里程碑日期有一个预定的规划,从而把有关工程管理好。这个重要的日期往往包括应当开工的日期、应当获得有关当局批文的日期、测试日期、完工/交船的日期等。有了这个里程碑日期,各方的承建商、分承建商以及雇主就有了合作的大框架。(2)可以有效监管建造的进度和预计后续的变化。例如,预定计划会对每个项目都有应当完成的时间限定,若是在该限定内没有完成,则可以明显看出属于延误,后续的相关项目则可能就会发生需要推迟进行而产生连锁反应。在有一个详细的计划的前提下,各个项目的进度以及如何要求后续项目进行配合就会一目了然。(3)一旦发生延误,如何在后续的项目中进行应对/补救措施也体现了预定计划的优越之处。有这样一个计划,在后续的项目之间如何见缝插针,在何时可以有时间和人力进行补救才能有效率以及有实效地进行规划。(4)如果因工程合约延误导致了损失,没有预定计划,就无从判断由哪个项目造成的延误最终导致损失,也就无法评定承建商和雇主之间对时间损失或延误风险的责任归属,又或是在双方都有造成延误的情况下,哪方的延误真正导致损失,或是如何计算这一延误造成的时间损失都会是无法肯定。

如果需要设计一个合理、清晰、全面、详尽、客观与现实的预定计划,就需要对项目工程“时段”(duration)等数据进行调研以及分析其内在的逻辑顺序,应用一定的方法来对计划中的各个项目进行编排。如在 Kitson Sheet Metal Ltd v. Matthew Hall Mechanical & Electrical Engineers Ltd (1989) 47 B. L. R. 82 先例中,工程的计划在建造工程中变动了多次,但均没有数据和逻辑顺序分析的支持,法院认为此时的工程计划最多不过是对建造意图进行了陈述,并非是一个真正意义上可以依赖的计划。

工程延误与不能及时完工往往也不是雇主所愿意见到,所以为了避免盲目依赖承建商所提供的完工日期,一些建造的标准合约已经在条文内会加入一条要求承建商对工程作出计划,甚至进一步规定“陈述整个计划所采纳的方式”(method statement)。如建造合约中的 JCT80 合约第 5. 3. 1. 2 条文要求承建方:“... provide the CA... with 2 copies of this master programme for the execution of the Works and within 14 days of any decision by the (CA) under clause 25. 3. 1 or 33. 1. 3 with 2 copies of any amendments and revisions to take account of that decision...”

又如在 Norwegian Standard Form Shipbuilding Contract 之 Article V (1)的第一句,就是要求船厂尽快在造船合约订立后给一个详细的工程计划,说:“As soon as possible after the Date of Contract the Builder shall put forward a proposed detailed building schedule, including a schedule for testing. The Buyer shall make its comment on the schedule as soon as possible and the latest within 7 days. The schedules shall be issued by the Builder in writing not later than 30 days after the Date of Contract.”

4.7 关键路径方式

在 20 世纪 60 年代,为了更好管理与控制工期并控制费用,开始出现“关键路径方式”(critical path method)。在 Haney v. United States, 676 F. 2d 584 (1982)先例中,关键路径方式被描述如下:“Essentially, the critical path method is an efficient way of organizing and scheduling a complex project which consists of numerous interrelated separate small projects. Each Sub – project is identified and classified as to the duration and precedence of the work (e. g. one could not carpet an area until the flooring is down and the flooring cannot be completed until the underlying electrical and telephone conduits are installed). The data is then analysed, usually by computer, to determine the most efficient programme for the entire project. Many sub – projects may be performed at any time within the given period without any effect on the completion of the entire project. However, some items of work are given no leeway and must be performed on programme; otherwise, the entire project will be delayed. These latter items of work are on the ‘critical path’. A delay or acceleration of work along the critical path will affect the entire project...”(关键路径方式是一种把无数的相关大小工序有效组织起来并做出时间表的办法。通过关键路径方式,需要明确每个项目的内容、所需要的时间以及项目之间的先后顺序。再用电脑对这些数据进一步分析,并找出对整个工程最有效的计划。有不少项目可以在工程中任何时间进行,根本不影响工程的最后完工日期,但有些项目就绝对不能延误,并必须按照计划完成,否则就会造成对整个工程的延误。也就是说,这种项目就是在关键路径上的项目,一有延误就会造成对整个工程完工日期的真正延误。)

另在 K/S Stasupply A/S v Dae Dong Shipbuilding Company Ltd 23 October 1986,

QBD, unreported 先例, Hobhouse 大法官也引用了仲裁员对关键路径分析的定义如下:"The Buyer was well aware that the vessel's construction had, as is usual, been programmed with a critical path; this involved that *force majeure* delay affecting any particular item of supply or aspect of construction would not necessarily have a correspondingly great effect upon the overall construction of the vessel."Hobhouse 大法官接着说:"That is a convenient statement by the arbitrator, but it is just a statement of the obvious: if a whole sequence of acts are having to be performed and they are being performed in a complex way, then some of those acts and some of those performances are critical to the completion of the job on time; others are not. The critical path is merely an analysis which identifies the way in which and the extent to which individual items will be causative of delay in the completion of the job."

在一个复杂与漫长的工程,承建商要证明某个事项(不论是不可抗力事项或是来自雇主的问题,如妨碍行为)造成了整个工程的延误以及延误程度,并非容易。这里涉及复杂与细微的对因果关系的分析,而且需要十分完整的证据,如承建商或是船厂原来的工程计划、工作进度等。还会经常涉及专家证人,即所谓的"延误专家"(delay expert)对仲裁庭做出协助。

应用关键路径方式时,首先需要将整个工程项目分为单独的项目,而这些项目会是数以百计甚至数以千计。之后,通过调研后的数据与过往经验以确定每个项目的预计工程时段。然后通过项目与项目之间完成的先后逻辑关系将所有的项目相连,这样,就会出现一个从工程起始到工程完成的项目路径。由于项目数量很多,项目与项目之间的逻辑关系也往往千变万化,如假定 B 项目和 C 项目是可以同时进行的项目,而只有完成了 B 项目以及 C 项目才能开始进行 A 项目的工作。此时对于完成 A、B 以及 C 三个项目的时间上的总花费来说,就会存在两个方式的算法或者叫两条"路径",一条是计算"A + B"的时间,一条是计算"A + C"的时间。

可以想到的是,整个工程的工期显然应当由所有路径中最长的一条决定,而这条路径就是所谓的"关键路径"。如在上述的例子中,如果 B 项目需要 3 周,而 C 项目需要 1 周,则 A + B 的路径就是关键路径,此时可以认为 B 项目就是处在关键路径上。所谓的"关键",指的是在这条路径上的项目必须按照计划完成,否则工程一定会延误。

而如果一个项目并不在关键路径上,此时这个项目所在的路径中就有一段可以"浮动"(float)的时间,提早或稍晚对工程的最终完成并不会造成影响。如上述例子中的 C 项目,只需要在 B 项目需要花费的 3 周时间以内完成即可,在 B 项目和 C 项目同时开始的情况下,即使 C 项目的完成时间超出预定的 1 周,只要不超过 B 项目将要花费的 3 周时间,就不会对最终的工程完成产生任何影响。也有其他情况是一些项目在整个工程中很多阶段都可以进行,只要挑选一个方便的阶段进行项目就可以,不必限定在某个特定阶段进行或完成,这些项目显然也不是在关键路径上。

因此,如果需要分析工程出现延误的原因,尤其是针对每个单独项目的延误(如雇主的问题)对工程的影响,或者是突发事件(如坏天气)对工程的影响时,采用了关键路径方式的预定计划就提供了比较的基准。

由于关键路径方式对整个工程完工的时间作出预计是需要大量的前期投入,包括较早时提到的需要有关工程有丰富经验的人士通过调研与分析,获得具体与准确的大量数据。而整理与分析这些数据涉及大量的计算,包括最初的路径编排和后续的项目更新都需要通过计算机来完成。但在早期计算机仍然处于高端并未普及民用的阶段,虽然应用这一方式普遍能够带来相对完备的计划,但对于一般的工程而言,与传统的手工绘图制定计划相比,采用这一关键路径方式制定计划带来的好处并不明显。因此在早期,关键路径方式并没有被工程/建造行业大量应用,只是在超大型的工程才会采纳。直到90年代电子计算机技术的兴盛后,通过计算机程序计算的成本大大降低,使得关键路径方式被承建商普及到了大部分的工程中,也有应用在关键路径方式的软件可以买到。但要强调的是,在这个软件里输入上百甚至上千的数据,从而得出一个合理、清晰、全面、详尽、客观与现实的计划才是关键。之后在工程的进行中,不少承建商还会派专人监控,不断看工程是否有延误以及延误是否在关键路径或会有相互影响。

4.7.1 应用关键路径分析的例子

以下是一位顾问工程师朋友梁永强教授提供的一个有关岸上工程的简单例子,希望能够把这方面的计算说得更明白:

在现今商业/工程项目中,"网络工作计划图"(programming),尤其是"关键路径分析"(critical path analysis),是一个十分重要的管理工具,关键路径的基本概念可以容易理解。

试举一建筑工程项目,其中一部份网络工作计划图(为方便解释,这里只节录5个工作程序):

工序①: 地基开挖围护设计及审批,总承建商聘请顾问公司设计,及提交业主/雇主审批,所需时间为20天,其中包括业主与总承建商同意的5天业主审批时间。

工序②: 地盘平整工程,总承建商聘用分包商施工,所需时间为30天。

工序③: 地基设计及审批,总承建商聘请顾问公司设计,及提交业主审批,所需时间为20天,其中包括业主与总承建商同意的5天业主审批时间。

工序④: 地基开挖围护施工,总承建商施工,所需时间为15天。

工序⑤: 地基施工,总承建商施工,所需时间为45天。

根据合约条文,工序①必需在工程第30天完成,工序③地基设计及审批,正常情况下需在地基开挖围护设计审批后才能开始,以减少废置工作。另外,合约条文包括如发生了没有在正常计划中的洪水及风暴,工期可顺应延长。

如上所述，网络工作计划图如下图所示：

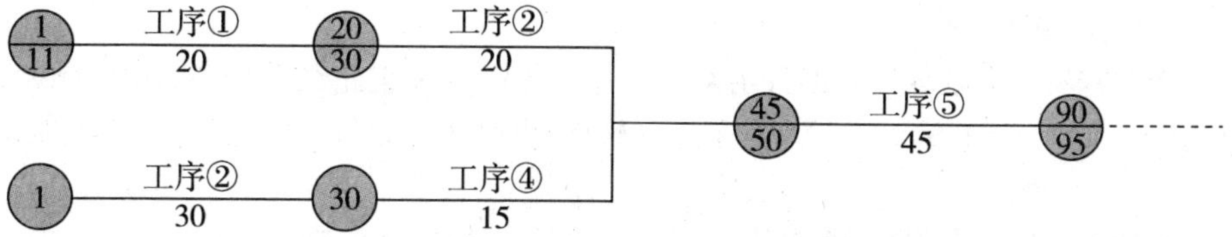

工序①，最早开始时间为工程项目第1天，因其所需工期为20天，最早完工时间便是第20天，就合约条文，工序①最晚完工时间为第30天，其相应最晚开始时间便是第11天。因此，本工序浮动时间（最晚完工时间－最早开始时间－工期）是30－1＋1－20＝10天。

工序②，本工序没有浮动时间，这是一个关键路径，不能有延误。

工序③，与工序④有关连，因为工序⑤开始时，工序③及④必须已经完成，就工序③独立而言，最早开始时间就是工序①最早完结之时（第21天），工期需时20天，因此，其最早完工时间为第40天。工序③最晚开始时间为第31天，相应最晚完工时间为第50天，但是，对工序④而言，因为前一个工序②是在关键路径并且没有浮动，它的最早开始时间及最晚开始时间皆为第31天，其所需工期为15天，因此它的最早及最晚完工时间都是第45天，基于上述考虑，工序③及工序④的最早及最晚完工时间应为第45天及第50天。工序③独立考虑的最早完工时间第40天在加入工序④因素后予以放弃，因为即使工序③能于第40天完工，工序⑤还是未能展开，因为工序④还未完工。

在工程进行期间，假如工序①受到延误，因业主审批需时10天，不是原先同意的5天，如果设计提交是在第20天或之前，那么整个工序还是可以在第30天或以前完成，对整个工程没有延误，它的完工期仍是在最晚完工时间或以前，就关键路径分析而言，工期便不应延长。

但是，如果设计提交是在第21天至第25天期间，如果业主是按原来协议用5天审批，整个工序还是可以在第30天或以前完成，现在因为业主需时10天，那么工期便在关键路径分析而言，得到延长。

当然，如果设计提交是在第25天以后，总承建商自己已经有延误了。

举另外一个情形，如果在第30天，工序①及工序②都顺利完成，工序③工序④便可以继续展开，其间如有洪水及风暴共10天，对工序③而言，是没有受到影响，但对工序④而言，它的施工便受到阻延，原来这工序是有50－30－15＝5天浮动，现在不只没有浮动，更加需要总工期延长5天，以确保工序能在第55天完成。

以上讨论旨在就网络工作计划图及关键路径分析作一介绍，希望读者了解其基本原理，在今天的商业项目中，像建筑工程、造船工程等，工序十分繁多，关系也错综复杂，要认明哪些是关键路径以及其他工序的浮动期等，需要仔细分析，很多时候需要电脑的协助，这些网络图及关键路径其实也十分适合电脑程式操作。因为他们依赖的原理并不复杂,需要的是有系统的逻辑思维及调研、分析,从而得出关键路径及网络工作计划图。

现在有不少电脑软件协助订出网络工作计划图及关键路径等资料,像 Microsoft Timeline 和 Oracle Primavera 等,有了这些软件,可以减少分析时间,提高准确性及减少错误运算。例如,在一个地下铁路车站的建造中,其中一项重要程序是基坑开挖,就是在地面开挖一个深坑,从而建造一个地下车站,假如这个地下车站是在一个空地上建造,是一个比较简单及直接的项目,但只是开挖程序已经要考虑以下环节,这些环节必须具备,才有条件进行基坑开挖工序:(1)土地是否已经回收,并已经交付给承建商为工地。(2)土地是否有管道,如地下雨水渠、污水渠、电线及电缆、煤气管道等,需要改道或迁移,或需要临时支撑方便开挖。(3)开挖程序及基坑维护与支撑是否已经设计完成及呈交有关部门审批,施工执照是否已经办妥。(4)开挖期间临时交通安排,泥土运出的路径是否已经与交通部门及区议会沟通及获得认可。(5)泥土运出到堆填区的许可证是否已经办妥。(6)开挖及基坑维护与支撑工程的物料及机械什么时间到位,它们的安排及定购时间需要多久等。

从以上可见,只是一个工序,已经与不少其他工序有关系,每个工序都可以输入就有关的计划什么时候可以完成,从而得到开挖工序最早可以在什么时候开始。在以上的举例中,开挖工序有 6 个条件,都不可缺少,那么开挖最早进行的时间便是以上 6 项条件中最迟完成的那一天。

在大型开挖工程,很多时候都会把开挖面积分区,方便运作及计划,如把这个地下车站开挖简单分为左右两区,这开挖工序所需的时间也牵涉不少因素及环节:(1)机械及工人的数量,在这里,开挖机、运泥车、工人每天出土量也要估算,通常承建商都有自己的资料数据,这样就可以很快估算投入的机械及工人的每天开挖出土量。(2)在开挖区内的场地布置及临时通道,包括运泥车坡道,车子出入口位置等,都可以影响出土数量。(3)如果工地是在市区内,很有可能出土有时间限制,那么,临时泥土存放区在开挖地区内有可能成为临界点,影响整个开挖工序的时间。(4)香港在夏季雨量也十分大,工地施工尤其是基坑开挖会受到天气影响,承建商也要在天气这一环节上作出估计及预备,使开挖工序的时间能够减少误差,从而影响整个项目程序。

在这些不同的因素及条件下,承建商对开挖的出工量作出评估,得出整个工序所需时间,把它输入至软件。有些时间,承建商也可以作风险评估,把最低出产量、最高出产量及最可能出产量分别输入,从而观察工序对整个工程的影响。有了开挖这个工序的时间,受这工序影响的其他运作也可以相应输入:(1)在开挖期间,基坑支撑工程也要配合,在开挖至某个深度,基坑支撑必须进行以确保开挖能继续下。(2)在基坑开挖范围外的沉降监察,地下管理的测量及观察,也必须配合。(3)其他往后的工序,如平整底部,对开挖底部进行土力测试,开始布置钢筋及灌筑混凝土等,也可以为了争取时间分成部分进行或在开挖整个工序完成后进行,这些工序的开始期会是依赖开挖工序的进度,与开挖工序息息相关,更是不可缺少的先决条件。

从以上可以看到,只是一个在空地里开挖的工序,能够开始所需要的条件,在进行期间所需的时间及与其他往后相关工序的关系是千丝万缕,有很多考虑、元素及相互关系,电脑软件如 Primavera 或 Time Line 便可以把以上资料收集后通过程式成立网络工作计划图及关键路径。这些软件根据输入资料,分析后完成流程图,横轴是时间,纵轴是不同的工序,每个工序的开始及完成时间都可以一目了然,它们与其他工序的关系也可以清楚看见,关键路径更加会突显,方便确认及注意。

在一个大型项目中,网络工作计划图的工序数以千计,把这个网络打印出来往往是十尺以上长度,通过这个十分全面的网络,所有的工序及相互关系就可以了如指掌。Primavera 及 Time Line 这些软件更可以把这些网络分门别类,就不同的工种抽出以便分析他们对整个项目的贡献及其流程。另一方面,对管理层而言,他们需要宏观整个项目,这些软件也可以归纳整个流程,浓缩到数十个工序使管理层能够有概括的认识,就不同重要的里程碑的完成时间以及各个阶段所需时间及其关系有所了解。

当然,关键路径分析也是十分重要的功能,在这上千以上的工序找出哪些是关键工序,肯定是需要软件如 Primavera 或 Time Line 的帮助,有了这些关键路径及工序,项目管理、资源分配、施工监察等也可以相应进行,使项目能在工期内顺利完成。在今天项目/工程管理中,关键路径分析已是必须的步骤,不能或缺。

除了关键路径分析功能外,一些先进及强大的电脑软件,如 Primavera,更可以在其他非关键路径的工序上展示出这工序与其他工序的关系,它与这些工序的浮动时间是多少。在复杂的项目上,这样的功能往往也十分重要。因为除了关键工序以外,也有不少工序十分重要,稍有迟误便会成为关键路径,对整个项目的进度及完工期有所影响。能对这些工序及早计划,作出准确认识及应变措施是十分重要与必须的。

除了网络工作计划图及关键路径分析外,Primavera 或 Time Line 这些电脑软件更可以分析所需材料,如在建造地下车站项目中,如果在各个工序中也输入所需的钢筋数量,包括地下护土墙的建造、地下车站基础建造、地下车站的建造、车站上盖的建造等,电脑软件便可以把这些不同工序所需要的钢筋,作出分析及归纳:(1)整个项目的钢筋数量;(2)不同工序钢筋的需求,相应计算出要采购的时间;(3)存储钢筋的数量及所需空间。

同样地,如果在各个不同的工序中也输入人力资源、所需机械等基本资料,电脑软件也可以作出分析及归纳。在人力资源计划上,这是十分有用及重要,通过这个软件不同工种的人员,包括管理人员(如项目经理、分区经理、工人管工等)、技术人员(如工程师、工程测量师、经济师等)、工程人员(如机械师、木匠、水喉匠、技工、普通杂工等)的需求及就位时间也可以一目了然。

Primavera 软件是这样介绍自己的:

"Oracle Primavera P6 Enterprise Project Portfolio Management (P6 EPPM) is a robust and easy - to - use integrated solution for globally prioritizing, planning, managing, and executing projects, programs, and portfolios. It optimizes role - specific functionality to satisfy each team member's needs, responsibilities, and skills. It provides a single solution for managing projects of any size, adapts to various levels of complexity within a project, and intelligently scales to meet the needs of various roles, functions, or skill levels in your organization and on your project team.

Thousands of companies rely on P6 EPPM to:

> Plan, schedule, and manage the right strategic mix of projects

> Make informed project, cost, and resource management decisions

> Enhance team collaboration and workflow productivity

> Maximize each project contributor's skills and responsibilities

> Track progress and optimize capacity for maximum profitability

> Deliver programs and projects on time and within budget

> Share data with human capital, financial management, and enterprise resource planning systems

Actual deployments require a variety of databases, servers, applications, and supporting technologies. P6 EPPM also integrates with many other optional solutions such as Primavera Contract Management, Oracle Primavera Risk Analysis, Oracle PPM, and Primavera Earned Value Management."

这些电脑软件的确大大地协助了项目/工程管理,所以很多大型的工程,如香港地下铁公司的各种项目,或迪士尼乐园的建造工程,都指定需要运用 Primavera 软件作项目管理,更要求承建商定期作出网络工作计划图修正,更新关键路径,把资源及人力的资料定时汇报方便业主/雇主作出监察。

但我们必须谨记,电脑软件只是一个程式,其作用是绝对需要依赖输入的数据。如果输入的数据错误或不完整,则电脑分析出来的结果也是枉然。如果程序的关系是错误的,那么网络工作计划图的作用便没有了。如果工序的时间是错误的,那么关键路径也会有误差。除此之外,项目/工程管理是一个经常更新的运作,在项目开始前,可以计划及订立网络工作计划图及关键路径,项目进行中,各个工序很多时候都不是按原先计划进行,其原因数不胜数,可能是外在因素,如天气情况、物料及人力供应误差,也可能是内在因素,如资金问题、人才流失等。网络及关键路径必须定时更新,在大型工程项目中,往往是每月更新,只是网络及关键路径更新便是一份厚厚的文件。在流程图上,每个工序的快慢都可以看到,并量化其延误或加速,对项目管理及进度监察十分有用。

在整个项目中,承建商及业主/雇主需要一整队人员全职负责网络工作计划图及关键路径分析,也需要各个部门定时更新资料及进度,以求得到最好效果,从 Primavera 或 Time Line 得到宝贵资料来作出有效的项目/工程管理。

4.7.2 "平行的关键路径"上的延误分析

单独一个事项有机会只是对关键路径产生延误,此时则导致总工期的延误;也有可能只导致了非关键路径的延误,此时则不会对总工期产生影响。再进一步分析延误的后果时就要结合工程合约看这些事项的性质,能否延长合约的完工日期要看是否属于"可以延长完工日期的延误"(excusable delays),以及能否获得雇主的赔偿则要看是否属于"可以赔偿的延误"(compensable delay),进而得出雇主和承建商双方对延误的风险如何分担的结论。

而由于工程项目非常复杂,可能会有很多不同,如果在同一关键路径上的同一时间,发生不同性质的事项同时导致延误,在考虑后果的时候就会产生问题。类似性质的也可以是不同的事项在"平行的关键路径"(concurrent critical path)上同时发生产生延误。所谓平行的关键路径,指的是在同时进行的多条路径中,最长的不只一条,此时这几条最长的关键路径就可以将他们称为平行的关键路径。如果有两种不同性质的事项同时发生在两条平行的关键路径上就可能带来一些问题,这也是在建筑/工程合约经常会发生的争议。例如,假设有两条平行的关键路径,一条称为 A 路径,另一条称为 B 路径。在 A 路径上由于雇主问题造成的可以延长完工日期并且可以赔偿的事项带来了 10 天的延误;在 B 路径上的同一时间由于不可以延长完工日期也不可以获得赔偿的事项(如承建商自己的工程有瑕疵需要完工前补救等)也造成了 10 天的延误。此时就产生了问题,两个事项均带来关键路径 10 天的延误,承建商是否可以要求延长完工日期与获得赔偿呢? Keith Pickavance 先生的《Delay and Disruption in Construction Contracts》(2005 年)一书里给出这样的回答:"the position in regard to damages would have been no different if the neutral event had in fact been attributable to C's (承建商) own malfeasance, say, for example, time taken up in repairing defective work. So far as damages are concerned, both are at C's risk. Thus, where one of the parallel delays is the responsibility of C, say, correcting defects, whilst the other gives him an entitlement to an EOT (Extension of Time) and compensation for loss and expense, say late instructions, C will be entitled to an EOT and be relieved from LADs (议定赔偿). However, he will not be able to recover the prolongation and disruption costs arising from the non-compensable event which occurred at the same time but will only be able to recover the prolongation and disruption costs flowing from the compensable event."(如果平行延误是由于不包括在不可抗力条文内的外来事项与承建商自己的问题所造成,如工程有瑕疵需要完工前补救,这带来的损失都是承建商要承担的风险。但如果平行延误一边是承建商自己的问题所造成,另一边是雇主的问题[如迟延作出指示或批准]所造成,而后者是承建商可以延长完工日期与获得有关赔偿。这样,承建商有权延长完工日期,也不必支付他本来因为自己的问题所造成的延误的议定赔偿。在这种情况下,承建商可以向雇主索赔由于雇主的问题带来的延长费用,但不能索赔由于自己的问题所带来的损失。)[5]

---

[5] 但针对在雇主与承建商的错误或行为同时造成延误的情况,也可看本章稍后的 5.6 段。

4.8 总结

工程合约(与造船合约)的完工日期延误是几乎每个工程都无可避免会出现的争议,这有一点像本章之第3段在国际货物买卖合约与程租合约的装卸港延误与滞期费,也是同样的频密。而且这些争议都十分复杂且涉及昂贵的诉讼,毕竟证明时间损失或延误并且是在关键路径不容易。即使承建商有了一个看来合理、清晰、全面、详尽、客观与现实的计划或关键路径,但一有了诉讼就难免对方会挑错,往往也可以在个别工序或事项中挑出问题。

笔者对近年来中国船厂在伦敦仲裁的大量案件也深有感触,也考虑到底有何办法可以避免与不要延伸至其他工程合约。笔者想到针对不可抗力等事项的第一类延误,或者中国船厂在有强大谈判力量时可以改写有关条文,不再针对交船日期的延误,而是类似在本章较早的第2段谈到的说明是只要发生列明的不可抗力事项,直到该事项完结,有关的时间段就可以相应延长完工(或交船)日期,根本不提及该事项有否对工程造成延误或延误程度。但进一步想,这种做法就算实际上能够做到,也只解决部分问题。因为近年来中国船厂败诉的案件不少是由于外国船东不合作甚至造成障碍的第二类延误,通常不会有条文针对而需要依赖"一般法律"(general law)向船东索赔损失,包括时间损失或延误。这样,中国船厂为了证明损失,还是需要一个合理、清晰、全面、详尽、客观与现实的计划作为基准。换言之,中国承建商(或船厂)还是要对关键路径方式有充分的了解并且尽快累积经验以保证能够作出尽量可以避免被对方攻击的分析,这也是对工程的良好管理所必需的。

§5 妨碍原则

"妨碍原则"(prevention principle)[6],就是任何一方不能做任何事情(不论是否有错)妨碍对方的履约,这与合约的延误是有密切关系。

5.1 妨碍原则适用在国际货物/商品买卖合约与程租合约

这个默示大原则早就在租约中的案例针对,如在 Ogmore Steamship Co Ltd v. H Borner & Co Ltd (1901) 6 CC 104 先例中,Gorell Barnes 大法官说的:"It is the ordinary and natural implication that neither party should prevent the other from performing that part of the contract which falls to be performed by that other; and if the charterers by themselves, or by their agents acting within the scope of their authority, have placed impediments in the way of the shipowner bringing their vessel into dock, the charterers ought to be responsible for the delay so caused, as if the vessel had in fact arrived in

---

〔6〕 这与本书第七章之10.2段介绍的双方必须给予协助/合作让对方顺利履行合约与10.3段介绍的合约一方不能通过自己的错误获利的默示责任有密切关系与相互呼应。

dock."(法律正常与自然的默示是任何一方不能妨碍对方履行他的合约承诺。如果一位承租人自己或通过其授权的代理人造成障碍,不让船东尽早靠泊船舶[靠泊后才能起算装卸时间与滞期费],承租人是要为船舶进不了港靠泊的延误作出赔偿。)

在该先例,案情涉及承租人作为卖方出售船上一批货物,买方也就是收货人在卸港有自己私人泊位。但由于收货人同时有其他三艘船舶抵达卸港,所以装运该批货物的 Deerhound 轮不被安排靠泊,事后船东向承租人索赔这延误造成的一笔滞期费。但法院不认为承租人要对收货人这个妨碍的行为负责,因为收货人,也就是买方,不严格是承租人的代理人。而承租人出售这批货给买方,在做法上完全合理、正常与有必要。Barnes 大法官说:"It is true that the consignees had, at the time of the vessel's arrival outside the dock, other vessels at berths in the dock and waiting to discharge, in consequence of which the plaintiffs' vessel was prevented from entering the dock, but the charterers are not, in my opinion, responsible for this. The engagements and actions of the consignees in relation to the other vessels were not entered into or taken by them as agents for the charterers. It was not contended that there was anything unreasonable in the charterers selling the cargo to the particular consignees. The charterers would not know what the engagements of the consignees would be at the time of the vessel's arrival. As between the shipowners and the charterers the delay is one of the risks taken by the shipowners when they agree to take their vessel a particular dock. They could guard against it by proper stipulations in the charterparty."

但如果案情有了改变,如不被安排靠泊的原因是承租人自己租的其他船舶造成妨碍,他就要对船东承担赔偿延误损失的责任了。这情况在 Aktieselskabet Inglewood v Millar's Karri Forests (1903) 8 Com Cas 196 先例出现,承租人在程租租约中有权指定在澳大利亚 Fremantle 港的装货泊位,但他迟迟不指定,因为该港的 4 个泊位中的 3 个被承租人所租用的船舶占用了。Kennedy 大法官是这样说:"If the ship is prevented from going to the loading place, which the charterer has a right to name, by obstacles caused by the charterer, or in consequence of the engagements of the charterer, the lay days commence to court as soon as the ship is ready to load, and would, but for such obstacles or engagements, begin to load at that place."

另也有先例针对延误是因为承租人没有备妥货物,导致船舶进不了港靠泊,而需要负责赔偿:Postlethwaite v Freeland (1880) 5 AC 599;Ardan SS. Co. v Weir (1905) AC 501; Gardiner v Macfarlane (2) (1893) 20 Sess. Cas. 4th Series, 414 等先例。也有同样的先例是由于承租人坚持自己方便的卸货方式,导致船舶不能马上靠泊(由于卸港的岸上堆场拥挤,港口当局只允许船舶靠泊卸到马上会离开港口范围的火车车皮。但承租人由于还没有出售货物,所以想把船上货物卸下岸上堆场,这种卸货在当时不允许,所以靠不了泊):The "Varing" (1931) 39 Ll. L. Rep. 205 先例。

5.2　妨碍原则适用在工程/建筑合约与造船合约

近期有许多针对妨碍原则的重要案例是出现在工程/建筑合约(包括造船合约)。针对这种合约,妨碍原则会在两方面有关:一是承建商(或船厂)在工程延误的情况下每天要向雇主赔付的议定赔偿;二是合约规定的完工时间(在造船合约就是交船时间)。

已经在本章较早的第1与第4段介绍过,这里简单重复或补充,在工程/建筑合约(包括造船合约),基本都会有一个双方约定的完工日期(在造船合约就是交船日期),这是双方经过谈判推测承建商所需要的合理时间在某天完成工程。但是如果在这段时间内发生一些承建商完全无法控制的外来因素造成工程的延误,这就不包括在原来推测合理时间内。所以合约中常常会有一条"不可抗力"(*force majeure*)条文针对,如果发生条文中所规定的事项造成延误,可以相应地延长完工日期。这些事项显然包括了各种天灾人祸,如台风、地震、海啸、瘟疫等天灾,或是战争、恐怖行为、骚乱、罢工等人祸。根据双方的谈判力量与水平,不可抗力条文所包括的事项会多会少,甚至包括一些承建商一定程度上可以控制的事项,如劳工短缺等。不可抗力条文也会规定一些先决条件,要求承建商必须遵守才能延长完工日期,最常见的是马上或尽早给雇主一个准确的通知,主要的目的是让雇主可以尽快作出调查是否发生所说的事项与有否真正造成工程的延误。

如果在完工日期之后工程还没有完成,显然承建商违反了承诺。在违约的情况下,不可抗力条文不再适用,而这种延误在大部分的情况下对雇主造成损失与不便。显然,雇主可以向承建商索赔损失,但这种损失往往很难计算与富争议性。例如,通往新机场的一条公路的工程无法在约定(加上不可抗力事项的延长)的完工日期前完成,导致新机场的交通拥挤与混乱,给很多人士造成不便,但把它们量化变成雇主的金钱损失就非常困难。所以,在工程/建筑合约(包括造船合约)也通常有条文规定一笔每天延误要支付的"议定赔偿"(liquidated damages),如每天10万美元。这种条文也可以有变化,如雇主对短暂的延误还可以接受,但延误一长,损失会更加严重,就可以把议定赔偿的金额相应提高。另外,合约会规定雇主在发生延误(或发生一段时间后)有权终止合约,这也是以明确的条文把时间上的延误提升为条件条文。但显然在一般的工程合约,雇主一般不会这样做,除非承建商的延误是重大原因所造成(如经济发生严重问题,甚至濒临破产倒闭),导致了他能否继续工程也有很大疑问,雇主才会被迫另找一家承建商继续没完成的工程。

显然,如果雇主(不论是否有错)对承建商进行的工程造成延误,而这种延误又不是在不可抗力条文下的事项,也没有合约其他条文针对,普通法下的妨碍原则就会适用。雇主的延误会发生在约定完工日期前,但也会发生在承建商违约后需要支付议定赔偿的期间内。这样,对承建商的公平合理的救济看来是延长完工日期或是可以不必支付相应的议定赔偿金额。但这方面的英国法以前是说如果妨碍原则适用,在解释有关的工程/建筑合约就会是约定的完工日期不再有效,而完工变为"无限期"(at large)。至于议定赔偿的支付,也变为不再有效。当然,无限期也不是说承建商之后可以随意延误,而是承建商不再有明确的合约完工日期约束,只需要在合理时间内完工。而什么是合理时间,也应该与妨碍原则到底造成了多长时间的延误有关,总不能妨碍原则只造成了 1 天的延误,就可以让合理时间变为合约规定的完工日期的 100 天后。这可节录较近期的 Multiplex v Honeywell (2007) EWHC 447 先例, Jackson 法官说:"The essence of the prevention principle is that the promisee cannot insist upon the performance of an obligation which he has prevented the promisor from performing. In the field of construction law, one consequence of the prevention principle is that the employer cannot hold the contractor to a specified completion date, if the employer has by act or omission prevented the contractor from completing by that date. Instead, time becomes at large and the obligation to complete by the specified date is replaced by an implied obligation to complete within a reasonable time."(妨碍原则的重点是被承诺方如果妨碍承诺方合约的履行,就不能坚持承诺方必须严格履行合约承诺。在建造行业的法律,后果之一就是在妨碍原则下,雇主再也不能坚持承建商要在双方约定的一天完工,只要是雇主曾经以他的行动或过错妨碍承建商在该天完工。双方约定的一天也变为无限期,换言之,承建商的责任变为只是在合理时间内完工的默示责任。)

针对议定赔偿,《The Law of Shipbuilding Contracts》(第 4 版,2012 年)之 65 页,说:"... a long line of English decisions commencing with Holme v Guppy holds that the buyer/employer is precluded from claiming any liquidated damages whatsoever where his conduct has in fact delayed the completion of the contract works."

但有说法是这样也不公平,也会有危险是雇主轻微的妨碍(如向承建商提一个小的规格更改要求),就已经造成了这个后果。这在 Adyard Abu Dhabi v SD Marine Services (2011) BLR 384 先例,Hamblen 大法官说:"This all the more so given the potentially extreme circumstances of the application of the prevention principle, as explained by Colman J in Balfour Beatty v Chestermount Properties (1993) 62 BLR 1, 27. A trivial variation may lead to the loss of the right to liquidated damages for a long period of culpable delay and, in this case, loss of the right to rescind as well."

没有在合约规定的一天完工,应该是承建商无法抵赖的事实。如果承建商想抗拒支付议定赔偿甚至被终止合约,就需要解释与证明什么造成了工程延误并可以为违反承诺开脱,而常见的原因之一就是妨碍原则,妨碍工程进度自然来自雇主或其代理人。这在今天暴跌的造船市场下,中国船厂面对大量外国船东以延误为由的弃船,往往也是以妨碍原则进行抗辩与反索赔。

5.3 承建商/船厂必须证明妨碍原则带来工程延误

船厂能否在违约后依赖这个妨碍原则,要船东/买方对妨碍所造成的延误负责,要看很多方面。首先是船厂能否提供证据证明船东/买方所造成的延误是什么,特别重要的是文件证据,不能依赖口头证据,因为口说无凭。可以很容易想到将来涉及诉讼,船东/买方肯定否认他们曾经做过任何妨碍船舶建造的事情。另外,即使证明有过妨碍的事情或行为,船厂还必须证明这妨碍或多或少确实造成了延误,这就要提供更大量的证据。买方对船厂(或承建商)会典型作出在这方面的抗辩可以节录笔者在近期一个仲裁案件中的抗辩请求,如下:

"1. It is denied that there was any loss of time, as alleged.

2. Alternatively, if there was any delay, which is denied, as is clear form the above, this wasequally caused and/or contributed to by 船厂. The prevention principle is not applicable to instances of concurrent delay – see Jerram Falkus Construction v Fenice Investments [2011] EWHC 1935 (TCC).

3. In any event, if there was any such delay, it did not affect the construction schedule. It certainly did not affect the preparation and provision of drawings as alleged, which were the cutting of steel and the construction of blocks. There was no 'net loss' of time.

4. It is submitted that the onus is squarely on 船厂 to prove:1. Delay;2. Caused By 船东;3. Which caused an actual 'net' loss of time to the construction schedule.

5. 船厂 have failed to prove or particularize any net loss of time."

船厂要提供大量的证据证明船东/买方在妨碍所造成的延误,主要就是"关键路径分析"(critical path analysis),这在本章之4.7段有详论。

5.4 妨碍原则使完工日期变为无限期

已经在较早提到如果妨碍原则适用,有关的工程/建筑合约约定的完工日期就不再有效,而完工变为"无限期"(at large),也就是承建商或船厂只需要在合理时间内完成建造。如果超过了合理时间依然没有完成,雇主或船东也只是有权索赔"一般损失"(general damages),而不能索赔议定赔偿。早在 Holme v Guppy (1838) 3 M&W 387 先例,法院判说只要雇主或船东的行为确实对承建商或船厂的完工造成了延误,就不能索赔任何议定赔偿,而不需要考虑多长时间的延误是由雇主或船东造成的。在 The "Cape Hatteras" (1982) 1 Lloyd's Rep 518 先例,案情涉及船舶维修合约中规定如果在某个特定的日子前不交船,每延迟一天就要支付给船东一笔议定赔偿。修理厂最后延迟交船,原因之一是船东不批准修理厂把曲轴交给承包商打磨抛光。Staughton 大法官认为船东的行为对修理厂的完工造成了妨碍,修理厂不需要支付延迟的议定赔偿,而无须调查与证明船东的行为造成了多长时间的延误,说:"The principle established by the authorities, that no liquidated damages for delay can be claimed if completion was in part delayed by conduct of the employer, is applicable in the present case. Had the parties wished to avoid that result, they could and should have inserted in the contract a term that the agreed date for completion should be extended in the event of delay caused by the [shipowners]."

如果是在雇主或船东完全没有妨碍的情况下，承建商或船厂没有在规定的时限内完工或交船，但在之后雇主或船东做出了妨碍行为，在这种情况下雇主或船东是否可以获得妨碍行为前的议定赔偿？在澳大利亚法院的 SMK Cabinets v Hili Modern Electrics Pty（1984）VR 391 先例，法院看来是持肯定意见，说："... the ordering of variations after the due date which must substantially delay completion will, unless the contract provides otherwise, and in the absence of an applicable extension of time clause, disable the proprietor from recovering or retaining liquidated damages which might otherwise have accrued after the giving of the order, the employer's right in respect of amounts that have already accrued by way of liquidated damages not being affected. In Anderson v Tuapeka County Council（1900）19 N. Z. L. R 1 Stout C. J.（with whose judgment Williams and Conolly JJ agreed）at p 11, and Martin J at p21 expressed the opinion that the ordering of extras in September after the due date for completion 'would set the penalties at large from September'; Martin J alone said in unequivocal terms that the right to recover sums that had already accrued would not be affected. These observations were applied by Williams J in Baskett v Bendigo Gold Dredging Co Ltd（1902）21 N. Z. L. R. 166 at p 174 – 175, where it was held that, assuming that there had been no previous act of prevention, liquidated damages need not be allowed by the contractor from the time when, about one month after the due date for completion, delay was occasioned by the ordering of extra work."

如果雇主或船东尽管由于自己的过错或行为造成了延误，但仍希望能获得由于承建商或船厂的过错或行为造成的延误的议定赔偿，就需要在合约中明示或"可推断"(by necessary inference)加入一个"延期条文"(extension of time clause)。如在造船合约，就通常会有明示条文针对船东/买方的过错/违约，如延误或不支付预付船价或拒绝接船，交船日期就会相应延长，并且在船东的违约延续超过 15 日或不等的时间后，船厂可终止合约。

有了这个延期条文，由雇主或船东的过错或行为造成的延误可以按照相应延长合约的时限。法院或仲裁庭唯一需要做的就是整个延误完工或交船分开哪些延误是由雇主或船东的过错或行为造成的，哪些是由承建商或船厂的过错或行为造成的，而后者需要支付议定赔偿。Phillimore 大法官在 Peak v McKinney（1970）1 BLR 111 CA 先例中总结说："The reason for that is that when the parties agree that if there is delay the contractor is to be liable, they envisage that the delay shall be the fault of the contractor and, of course, the agreement is designed to save the employer from having to prove actual damage which he has suffered... It follows, once the clause is understood in that way, that if part of the delay is due to the fault of the employer, then the clause becomes unworkable if only because there is no fixed date from which to calculate that for which the contractor is responsible and for which he must pay liquidated damages...

However, the problem can be cured if allowance can be made for that part of the delay caused by the actions of the employer; and it is for this purpose that recourse is had to the clause dealing with extension of time. If there is a clause which provides for the extension of the contractor's time in the circumstances which happen, and if the appropriate extension is [on the contract in that case] certified by the architect, then the delay due to the fault of the contractor is disentangled from that due to the fault of the employer and a date is fixed from which the liquidated damages can be calculated."

5.5 妨碍原则在合约有明示条文针对时不适用

如果妨碍原则的默示法律地位已经有明示条文针对,也就不适用默示了,而是要解释明示条文。例如,工程合约包括造船合约经常涉及船舶的规格需要“更改”(modification),这可能是因为雇主的原因,也可能是法律的改变(这种问题对船舶建造最多,因为在漫长的建造中经常会有国际公约或是船旗国的法律发生改动,导致非要更改船舶的规格不可)。但工程合约或造船合约经常会有特定的条文针对规格的更改,如要求在更改前双方必须达成价格与延长工程完工日期的约定。这样,双方就必须照这个明示规定的条文做,但如果在双方还没有达成约定的情况下,承建商(包括船厂)想做好人先动工更改,但双方后来谈不拢,承建商就不能以妨碍原则延长完工日期。因为完全存在可能是船东订了一个非常赚钱的长期租约,但销约期与合约规定的交船日期十分接近,在对船舶改动的要求会造成交船日期延期的情况下,船东会撤回这个更改的指令。

多举一个涉及有明示条文针对船东/买方过错或行为的例子是延误交付给船厂所订购与提供的设备/物料。这种安排经常会有,而且越是复杂的船舶(如游轮或钻油平台),买方提供的设备/物料越多。这样,经常发生买方提供的设备/物料迟延交付给船厂。而后果会根据不同的设备/物料而有所不同,如设备/物料是进行下一步工程所必需,买方延误交付会导致关键路径延误。但也会有设备/物料是对进行下一步工程无关紧要,如游轮上的一些装饰或名贵地毯。造船合约通常都会有明示条文针对这种复杂的情况,如一些相对简单的条文如下:“Should the BUYER fail to deliver any of the BUYER's supplies within the time designated, and if the delay affects the Delivery Date of the VESSEL, the Delivery Date shall automatically be postponed for the period of such delay. In such event, the BUYER shall be responsible and pay to the SELLER for all losses and damages incurred by the SELLER by reason of such delay in delivery of the BUYER's supplies and such payment shall be made upon delivery of VESSEL. ...(如果船东/买方没有在规定的时间交付提供的设备/物料,而带来的延误是影响交船日期,交船日期就会自动与相应延长。在这种情况下,买方还要负责与支付所有卖方/船厂由于延误带来的损失。)

If delay in delivery of any of the BUYER's supplies exceeds twenty (20) days, then the SELLER shall be entitled to proceed with construction of the VESSEL without installation thereof in or on the VESSEL, without prejudice to the SELLER's other rights as hereinabove provided, and the BUYER shall accept and take delivery of the VESSEL so constructed."(如果买方交付他提供的设备/物料的延误超出20天,卖方有权继续造船工程并不装配买方想提供的设备/物料。)

明显看来,有上述的明示条文,作为英国法律默示地位的妨碍原则就不会适用在买方延误或不交付他应该供应的设备/物料的特定过错/违约。

另一种稍有不同的情况是造船合约(或工程合约)会有明示条文针对如果买方(或雇主)怠慢与不合作,如不尽快与合理批准图纸、同意配件供应商或是买方总管不合作等,船厂就可以在一定时间后不必理会买方单方面推进工程。换言之,有一个合约机制避免买方的妨碍造成延误。例如,有合约条文明示规定如果对方不在7天内作出决定,船厂(或承建商)就可以按自己的决定继续进行工程或"视为"(deem to be)[7]买方(或雇主)同意他的决定。这样,如果船厂(或承建商)因为友好[8]或犹豫不决,甚至是不懂法律与合约条文,不在7天后果断推进工程,延误也不能依赖妨碍原则。在Turner Corp Ltd v Austotel Pty Ltd (1994) 13 BCL 378先例,Cole大法官说:"A party to a contract cannot rely upon preventing conduct of the other party where it failed to exercise a contractual right which would have negated the effect of that preventing conduct."

在Adyard Abu Dhabi v SD Marine Services (2011) BLR 384先例,案情涉及原告船厂为英国政府建造一批船舶。合约要求船舶必须满足英国海岸巡逻队与相关的特殊用途船舶安全条例的相关规定,并且如果在双方同意的日子有两艘船舶没有备妥进行试航,被告有权终止合约。之后船舶没有及时备妥,被告决定终止合约。法院要解决的争议是,被告是否有权终止合约。原告对船舶没有完工没有争议,但声称延误是由于根据英国海岸巡逻队的要求或被告的指示多加了各种新的设计,因此,被告妨碍了船舶备妥可以进行试航,被告无权终止合约。根据合约规定,如果在建造期间有任何改动,买方可以选择同意船厂根据改动提出的对合约价格、完成时间与合约其他条文的合理调整,也可以选择不进行改动。但是,合约中没有针对买方没有及时作出决定是否让船厂进行改动的情况。船厂声称因为买方没有及时作出选择造成了延

---

[7] 视为条文可看本书第十四章之第3段。

[8] 这个问题在中国企业/公司特别严重,常常只强调所谓的友好合作,罔顾合约条文的明示规定或/与法律地位。如在造船的仲裁案件,尽管合约有明示规定买方不在7天(或者合约规定的一段时间)内批准,船厂就可以自己推进工程,但船厂在3、4个月之后仍在催促买方尽快批准。这样,在发生争议进行仲裁时,船厂投诉买方的不合作导致延误(进而导致船厂需要支付议定赔偿甚至过了销约期),买方就攻击船厂不在7天后推进工程是自作自受,妨碍原则不适用。买方也会要求仲裁庭推断船厂另有隐情,因为买方不合作实际上没有对工程造成任何真正的延误。船厂唯一的抗辩就是为了跟买方友好合作,是善意,但这种抗辩没有法律基础。笔者虽然理解中国的文化背景,但作为仲裁员,还是要根据合约与法律作出判决。除非买方在言行或文书中对船厂造成了不公平的误导,让船厂以为这段时间的延误可以延长,这就涉及"禁止翻供"(estoppel)的问题。但现实中买方的不合作往往只是对船厂的催促保持沉默或要求更长时间才能回复,这并不足以构成禁止翻供。

误，并且合约没有针对这种情况的延期条文，因此妨碍原则适用。

英国高院接受了合约中实际存在延期条文，并且妨碍原则不适用的说法。但Hamblen大法官的判决根据的并不是合约中关于改动的条文，而是不可抗力条文。Hamblen大法官认为根据不可抗力条文，在船厂及时向买方递交了延误通知的情况下（在该案中船厂并没有递交延误通知），船厂理论上应该可以获得买方不作出决定的这段时间的延期。Hamblen大法官接着说，合约存在着一定程度的含糊，适用妨碍原则可能意味着一些琐碎的修改就可以导致雇主或船东丧失了索赔相当巨大的延误议定赔偿的权利。

但合约中有针对雇主或船东的过错的延期条文，不代表妨碍原则在任何情况都不再适用，毕竟妨碍行为有很多，过错只是其中之一。合约明示的延期条文没有针对的妨碍行为，妨碍原则依然适用。这也符合本书第七章之4.4.5段节录的Hoffmann勋爵在Johnson v Unisys Ltd（2001）UKHL 13先例中的说法："... any terms which the courts imply into a contract must be consistent with the express terms. Implied terms may supplement the express terms of the contract but cannot contradict them. Only Parliament may actually override what the parties have agreed."（默示条文必须与明示条文一致。默示条文可以补充合约的明示条文但不能与明示条文有冲突，只有议会通过立法才能超越双方当事人的约定。）

而如果延期条文有写得含糊不清楚的地方，应该选择对承建商或船厂有利的解释。在Multiplex v Honeywell（2007）EWHC 447先例，Jackson大法官总结说："From this review of authority I derive three propositions：（i）Actions by the employer which are perfectly legitimate under a construction contract may still be characterised as prevention, if those actions cause delay beyond the contractual completion date.（ii）Acts of prevention by an employer do not set time at large, if the contract provides for extension of time in respect of those events.（iii）In so far as the extension of time clause is ambiguous, it should be construed in favour of the contractor. The third proposition must be treated with care. It seems to me that, in so far as an extension of time clause is ambiguous, the court should lean in favour of a construction which permits the contractor to recover appropriate extensions of time in respect of events causing delay. This approach also accords with the principle of construction set out by Lewison in 'The Interpretation of Contracts'（3rd edition, 2004）. That principle reads as follows：'Where two constructions of an instrument are equally plausible, upon one of which the instrument is valid and upon the other of which it is invalid, the court should lean towards that construction which validates the instrument.'"

5.6 妨碍原则与同步延误

5.6.1 什么是同步延误

这里所指的问题就是雇主的确被证明妨碍了工程的进度，但在同一时间内也发生了承建商自己要承担责任的延误,如雇主通过文件披露[9]或调查发现与证明承建商在同一时间因为经济问题导致工人不足。John Marrin QC 在他的《Concurrent Delay》(2002) 18 Const LJ No 6 436 一文中对同步延误的定义如下:"a period of project overrun which is caused by two or more effective causes of delay which are of approximately equal causative potency."

这个定义也在 Adyard Abu Dhabi v SD Marine Services (2011) BLR 384 先例被认同。在现实中,真正是同步延误(两个原因同时造成,一个来自买方/雇主,另一个来自船厂/承建商)不多。。这样,同步延误能否延长完工日期,就变得很有争议性。而且买方/雇主能否索赔议定赔偿或/与承建商在工程合约下能否索赔"延长费用"(prolongation costs),就会变得更加有争议性。

5.6.2 船舶保险的"同时有多个近因"的说法

工程合约的同步延误让笔者想起一个类似的问题,即船舶保险的承保风险。船舶保险一直以来在英国只愿意接受"列名风险"(named perils)的承保,不像货物保险或少数其他国家的船舶保险(如挪威)肯接受"一切险"(all risks)。这导致作为受保人的船东遇上船舶的部分损坏或全损,都需要证明承保的列名风险中的一项是主因或近因,才可以获得赔付。但会有情况是船东证明不了,如一艘船舶在一个天气很坏并且属于战区的地方失踪,船东根本无法证明应该属于水险还是战争险,因为这两个风险是分开来投保的。另也会有情况是船东能够证明船舶损坏或全损的原因,但不只是一个而是多个,这就带来了所谓"同时有多个近因"(concurrent proximate causes)的说法。如果多过一个原因但都是属于承保的列名风险,显然保险公司必须要赔付。但如果一个原因是属于承保的列名风险,另一个原因是属于保单中没有提到的风险甚至是保单中明确排除/免责的风险,就会带来争议。尤其是后一种情况发生得更为频密,这是因为船舶保险承保的列名风险这些年来一直有所增加,因此保单中没有提到的风险已经很少。但保单明示或默示排除/免责的风险倒有不少,包括要求被保险人的船东必须"恪尽职责"(due diligence)。

有关同时有多个近因,可看 Carins 大法官在 Wayne Tank & Pump Co Ltd v Employer's Liability Assurance Corp Ltd (1974) QB 57 先例中说:"I do not consider that the court should strain to find a dominant cause if, as here, there are two causes both of which can properly be described as effective causes of the loss. Mr. Le Quesne(原告的代表大律师)recognised that if there are two causes which are approximately equal in effectiveness, then it is impossible to call one rather than the other the dominant cause. I should prefer to say that unless one cause is clearly more decisive than the other, it should be accepted that there are two causes of the loss and no attempt should be made to give one of them the quality of dominance."

---

[9] 这在本章之4.2段已经提到。

Potter 大法官在 The "Aliza Glacial" (2002) 2 Lloyd's Rep 421 先例中说:"It is only if the Court is driven to the conclusion that there was 'not one dominant cause, but two causes which were equal or nearly equal in their efficiency in bringing about the damage', one being a peril and the other an exception, that the exception prevails."

因此在"同时有多个近因"的说法下,可粗略地分为三种情况与保险公司是否需要作出赔付:(1)多个近因都属于承保的风险,保险人要承担赔付的责任,如船员疏忽造成海上灾难,而两个都是承保的列名风险,保险人显然要负责;(2)多个近因中有一个是承保的风险,但其他的既没有说承保也没有说排除,这种情况下保险人也需要负责,这方面的有关先例有 Grill v General Iron Screw Collier Co (1866) LR 1 CP 600; Dudgeon v Pembroke (1877) 2 App Cas 284; Reischer v Borwick (1894) 2 QB 548; The "Miss Jay Jay" (1987) 1 Lloyd's Rep 32 等;(3)多个近因中有一个是承保的列名风险,另有一个是被排除/免责的风险,这就涉及怎样全面解释有关的保险合约。这里涉及承保的列名风险与明示或默示排除/免责的风险之间的冲突,但又必须要让它们都有一定的解释。所以,会有情况是不允许排除/免责的风险完全否定承保的列名风险,也有情况是判特定排除/免责的风险超越了承保的列名风险。相关的先例有 The "Lydia Flag" (1998) 2 Lloyd's Rep 652; The "Aliza Glacial"; IF P&C Insurance Ltd (Publ) v Silversea Cruises Ltd (2004) Lloyd's Rep IR 696 等。

5.6.3 工程合约同步延误的对立面问题

工程合约的同步延误是比船舶保险中同时有多个近因导致损失的情况更加复杂/困难,发生的频率也相对更高。困难的情况是船舶保险只涉及保险公司是否需要赔付的单方面问题,但工程合约就会带来"对立面问题"(obverse problem)。这就是同步延误并不只是带来能否延长完工日期的问题,同时也带来承建商是否需要支付议定赔偿或/与承建商能否向雇主索赔工程"延长费用"(prolongation costs)的问题。如承建商向雇主索赔因为雇主的原因(如要求更改工程)而导致的延长费用,但同时雇主反索赔承建商的延误的议定赔偿。以常理来说,承建商的索赔与雇主的反索赔不能都成功。除非能够试图分摊,否则就非要支持其中一方的索赔。这个对立面问题在 John Marrin QC 的《Concurrent Delay Revisit》(2012 年)一文说:"The problem has significance which extends beyond monetary claims. Because the success of the employer's counterclaim for liquidated damages is inversely related to the success which the contractor achieves on his extension of time claim, it is necessary to have regard to the obverse problem when considering the proper approach to extension of time."

怎样在工程合约有同步延误的情况下处理延长完工日期、索赔延长费用与议定赔偿的问题目前十分不明朗。接下会分别探讨这方面有关的议题,很多都没有定论。

5.6.4 妨碍原则在同步延误是否适用

妨碍原则不是工程合约的明示条文,而是普通法的地位。所以大原则是承建商除了要证明雇主妨碍,还需要进一步证明妨碍的确造成了延误。这样,在同步延误就带来有关工程如果是由于承建商自己的原因造成延误,就谈不上雇主的妨碍造成了真正的延误。换言之,妨碍原则在同步延误的情况下不适用。既然不适用,就不能让承建商延长完工日期,更进一步让雇主对承建商造成的延误(虽然也有雇主的原因)可索赔议定赔偿。这显然看来有点说不通,并且在一些近期的先例与权威说法有不一致的观点。

可先介绍在 Jerram Falkus Construction v Fenice Investment (2011) EWHC 1935 先例,Coulson 大法官说:"Accordingly, I conclude that, for the prevention principle to apply, the contractor must be able to demonstrate that the employer's acts or omissions have prevented the contractor from achieving an earlier completion date and that, if that earlier completion date would not have been achieved anyway, **because of concurrent delays caused by the contractor's own default, the prevention principle will not apply.** "(加黑部分是笔者的强调)

在该先例 Coulson 大法官同意了 Hamblen 大法官在 Adyard Abu Dhabi v SD Marine Services (2011) BLR 384 先例的判法,说:"Hamblen J's analysis indicated that, if there were two concurrent causes of delay, one which was the contractor's responsibility, and one which was said to trigger the prevention principle, the principle would not in fact be triggered because the contractor could not show that the employer's conduct made it impossible for him to complete within the stipulated time. The existence of a delay for which the contractor is responsible, covering the same period of delay which was caused by an act of prevention, would mean that the employer had not prevented actual completion. Throughout his analysis, Hamblen J stressed the importance of the contractor proving delay to the actual progress of the work as a result of the alleged act of prevention..."

但澳大利亚法院在较早的 SMK Cabinets v Hili Modern Electrics Pty (1984) VR 391 先例,有不同的判法,并且说是法律上百年来一贯的判法,说:"The sole remaining matter is that of the soundness of the ground on which the arbitrator in fact rejected the defence of prevention. He evidently considered that where acts or omissions of a proprietor do in fact substantially delay completion, the proprietor nonetheless cannot be said to have prevented the contractor from completing by the relevant date unless the contractor would have been able to complete by that date had it not been for the supposed prevention. Mr. McCurdy(雇主代表大律师)asks us to uphold that view. **But it has been accepted for more than one hundred years that this is not the law. The cases are all one way.** "(加黑部分是笔者的强调)

在该先例法院是判雇主不能向承建商收取议定赔偿,因为延误也有雇主的原因。在 Jerram Falkus Construction v Fenice Investment 先例,Coulson 大法官也有针对这个澳大利亚先例,并认为该先例并不严格针对同步延误的情况。

如果按照 Coulson 大法官的说法,妨碍原则必须在雇主的妨碍是造成有关延误的唯一原因时才会适用,但这看来不是被普遍接受的说法。如在《Hudson on Building and Engineering Contracts》(第 12 版,2010 年)一书之 6 - 060 段说:"Thus, it is well established that an Employer is not entitled to liquidated damages if by their acts or omissions they have prevented the Contractor from completing their work by the completion date. **Whether concurrent with another Contractor delay or not, there is no reason why the principle should not be the same.** As Salmon L. J. observed: 'If the failure to complete on time is due to the fault of both the employer and the contractor, in my view the clause (giving the employer liquidated damages) does not bite. I cannot see how, in the ordinary course, the employer can insist on compliance with a condition if it is partly his own fault that it cannot be fulfilled ... I consider that unless the contract express a contrary intention, the employer, in the circumstances postulated, is left to his ordinary remedy; that is to say, to recover such damages as he can prove flow from the contractor's breach'."(加黑部分是笔者的强调)

工程合约如果有明示的延期条文(如不可抗力条文或雇主要求变更规格等),显然是妨碍原则不再会适用。毕竟,经常会有情况是延期条文中的事项与雇主的妨碍行为有重叠,但同步延误的困难与对立面问题还是同样存在。

5.6.5 分摊的说法

表面看来同步延误最公平的处理方式就是分摊雇主与承建商之间的时间与金钱损失。这也有一些近期的先例支持,特别是来自苏格兰。

在 Laing Management (Scotland) Ltd v John Doyle Construction Ltd (2004) BLR 295 先例,MacLean 勋爵说:"... we are of opinion that apportionment of loss between the different causes is possible in an appropriate case. Such a procedure may be appropriate in a case where the causes of the loss are truly concurrent, in the sense that both operate together at the same time to produce a single consequence. For example, work on a construction project might be held up for a period owing to the late provision of information by the architect(在工程合约建筑师是代表雇主), but during that period bad weather might have prevented work for part of the time. In such a case responsibility for the loss can be apportioned between the two causes, according to their relative significance."

接下来在 City Inn Ltd v. Shepherd Construction (2008) BLR 269 先例,一审法院的 Drummond Young 勋爵针对 JCT Standard Form of Building Contract, Private Edition with Quantities (1980)标准格式合约说:"Where there is true concurrency between a relevant event and a contractor default, in the sense that both existed simultaneously, regardless of which started first, it may be appropriate to apportion responsibility for the delay between the two causes; obviously, however, the basis for such apportionment must be fair and reasonable. Precisely what is fair and reasonable is likely to turn on the exact circumstances of the particular case."

该先例之后上诉到了 Inner House of the Court of Session:City Inn Ltd v. Shepherd Construction (2010) BLR 437,这个观点被多数意见所支持。

至于怎样分摊各自应该承担多少时间的延误,在做法上与侵权诉讼需要分摊原告与被告各自疏忽要承担的责任(contributory negligence)基本一样。根据过错的百分比与造成事故的重要性分摊,如车祸中驾驶员与行人各自的疏忽程度。而分摊雇主与承建商各自要承担的责任与延误,主要看两点:一是不同原因过错的比重;二是每个原因对工程所造成的延误的重要性。

Drummond Young 勋爵是这样说:"That leads on to the question of how the exercise of apportionment is carried out. That exercise is broadly similar to the apportionment of liability on account contributory negligence or contribution among joint wrongdoers. In my opinion two main elements are important: the degree of culpability involved in each of the causes of the delay and the significance of each of the factors in causing the delay. In practice culpability is likely to be the less important of these two factors. Nevertheless, I think that in appropriate cases it is important to recognise that the seriousness of the architect's failure to issue instructions or of the contractor's default may be relevant consideration. The causative significance of each of the factors is likely to be more important. In this respect, two matters appear to me to be potentially important. The first of these is the length of the delay caused by each of the causative events; that will usually be relatively straightforward factor. The second is the significance of each of the causative events for the Works as a whole. Thus an event that only affects a small part of the building may be of lesser importance than an event whose effects run throughout the building or which has a significant effect on other operations. Ultimately, however, the question is one of judgment ..."

上诉到了 Inner House of the Court of Session,Osborne 勋爵说:"... In such a situation, which could, as a matter of language, be described as one of concurrent causes, in a broad sense, it will be open to the decision - maker, whether the architect, or other tribunal, approaching the issue in a fair and reasonable way, **to apportion the delay in the completion of the works occasioned thereby as between the relevant event and the other event.** In that connection, it must be recognised that the background to the decision making, in particular, the possibility of a claim for liquidated damages, as opposed to one for extension of time, must be borne in mind and approached in a fair and reasonable manner."

看来分摊并不容易,所以也有说法是既然是同步延误,就干脆对半平摊。

苏格兰这个分摊的说法在英国法律并不支持,英国法律看来是不热衷分摊合约责任与损失,不论是合约双方各有不同比例的过错或是同步过错所造成的损失。这方面在笔者的《损失赔偿与救济》一书第八章之第 11 段有涉及,并介绍了上诉庭的 Vesta v Butcher (1986) 2 Lloyd's Rep 179 重要先例。而涉及工程合约的同步延误,有关的英国先例有 Tennant Radiant Heat Ltd v Warrington Development Corporation (1998) 1 EGLR 41, CA; W Lamb Ltd (t/a) The Premier Pump & Tank Co v Jarvis & Sons Plc (1998) 60 Con LR 1, QBD (OR); Hi – Lite Electrical Ltd v Wolseley UK Ltd (2010) BLR 225。

5.6.6　主因的说法

这说法出现在 H Fairweather & Company Ltd v London Borough of Wandsworth (1987) 39 BLR 106 先例,案情涉及罢工造成延误,但同时雇主的建筑师要求更改并延误作出指示。两个造成延误的原因都可以让承建商延长完工日期,但只有后一个原因才可以让承建商有权索赔延长费用/赔偿。在这个说法下,就会是在雇主与承建商共同造成的延误中找出"主因"(dominant cause)。《Keating on Construction Contracts》(第 5 版,1991 年)一书第 195 页总结说:"If there are two causes, one the contractual responsibility of the Defendant and the other the contractual responsibility of the Plaintiff, the Plaintiff succeeds if he establishes that the cause for which the Defendant is responsible is the effective, dominant cause. Which cause is dominant is a question of fact, which is not solved by the mere point of order in time, but is to be decided by applying common sense standards."

但显然这个说法下还是不能解决同步延误的问题,因为在一个真正的同步延误,两个原因都是主因。

5.6.7　Malmaison 方式

早在 Henry Boot Construction Ltd v. Central Lancashire New Town Development Corporation (1980) 15 BLR 8 先例中,Edgar Fay Q. C. 大法官针对 1963 年 JCT Standard Form of Building Contract 的标准格式合约有这样的说法:"The broad scheme of these provisions is plain. There are cases where the loss should be shared, and there are cases where it should be wholly borne by the employer. There are also cases which do not fall within either of these conditions and which are the fault of the contractor, where the loss of both parties is wholly borne by the contractor. But in cases where the fault is not that of the contractor the scheme clearly is that in certain cases the loss is to be shared: the loss lies where it falls. **But in other cases the employer has to compensate the contractor in respect of the delay**, and that category, where the employer has to compensate the contractor, should, one would think, **clearly be composed of cases where there is fault upon the employer or fault for which the employer can be said to bear some responsibility.**"(加黑部分是笔者的强调,这是说在一些雇主有过错或至少有部分过错的情况下,要赔偿承建商延误的损失。看来雇主有部分过错就会是同步延误的情况。)

Dyson大法官在 Henry Boot Construction Ltd v Malmaison Hotel（Manchester）Limited（1999）70 Con LR 32，QBD（TCC）先例中总结了这种处理同步延误的方式，所以被称为 Malmaison 方式。

这里的观点是只要是雇主造成了延误，那么会否因为承建商的原因导致工程无论如何都会延误是不重要，承建商都可以得到相应的延期。这种观点是认为，雇主一旦对工程的完工造成了妨碍，承建商就有权延长一段合理的时间完成合约。这 Malmaison 方式针对工程合约解释也说得通，正如《Keating on Construction Contracts》（第8版，2006年）一书之8－021段所说："Thus it now appears to be accepted that a contractor is entitled to an extension of time notwithstanding the matter relied upon by the contractor is not the dominant cause of delay, provided only that it has at least equal 'causative potency' with all other matters causing delay. The rationale for such an approach is that where the parties have expressly provided in their contract for an extension of time caused by certain events, the parties must be taken to have contemplated that there could be more than one effective cause of delay (one of which would not qualify for an extension of time) but nevertheless by their express words agreed that in such circumstances the contractor is entitled to an extension of time for an effective cause of delay falling within the relevant contractual provision."（第二句是针对说得通的理由，就是双方在工程合约明示规定了在一些事项下要延长完工日期，他们应该在订约时就会想到造成延误时会有其他同步的原因，但仍是作出这种规定。这就表示只要有发生明示规定的事项造成延误，承建商就有权根据合约条文延长完工日期。）

Malmaison 方式的说法也在其他的先例有涉及，如 Carloway 勋爵在苏格兰的 City Inn Ltd v. Shepherd Construction（2010）BLR 437 先例中的少数意见说："The proposition that delay caused by the contractor must also to be taken into account was rejected, and rightly so. It is irrelevant so far as the contractual exercise is concerned. **That exercise does not involve an analysis of competing causes.** It involves a prediction of a Completion Date, taking into account that originally stated in the contract and adding the extra time which a Relevant Event would have instructed, all other things being equal... the exercise remains one of looking at the Relevant Event and the effect it would have had on the original (or already altered) Completion Date. If a Relevant Event occurs (no matter when), the fact that the Works would have been delayed, in any event, **because of a contractor default remains irrelevant.**"（加黑部分是笔者的强调）

另在 De Beers UK Ltd v Atos Origin IT Services UK Ltd（2010）EWHC 3276（TCC）的英国先例，案情涉及 Atos 向 DB 提供一套软件系统。Edwards－Stuart 大法官认定 Atos 和 DB 同时对工程造成了延误，并且任何一方的延误都会造成 Atos 无法在合约规定的时限内完工。Edwards－Stuart 大法官判是 Atos 可以延期，说："The general rule in construction and engineering cases is that where there is concurrent delay to completion caused by matters for which both employer and contractor are responsible, **the contractor is entitled to an extension of time but he cannot recover in respect of the loss caused by the delay.** In the case of the former, this is because the rule where delay is caused by the employer is that not only must the contractor complete within a reasonable time but also the contractor must have a reasonable time within which to complete. It therefore does not matter if the contractor would have been unable to complete by the contractual completion date if there had been no breaches of contract by the employer (or other events which entitled the contractor to an extension of time), because he is entitled to have the time within which to complete which the contract allows or which the employer's conduct has made reasonably necessary."(加黑部分是笔者的强调,也就是判承建商可以延长完工日期但不能索赔延长费用/损失。有关后者,会在本章下一小段介绍。)

支持这种判法的还有 Royal Brompton Hospital NHS Trust v Hammond (2001) 76 Con LR 148; Walter Lilly & Company Limited v Giles Patrick Cyril Mackay, DMW Developments Limited (2012) EWHC 1773 (TCC)等先例。

5.6.8 同步延误下的延期费用/赔偿

以上 3 个小段的探讨都只是涉及完工日期的延长,没有详细针对双方各自向对方提出的金钱索赔。在上一小段提到的 De Beers UK Ltd v Atos Origin IT Services UK Ltd (2010) EWHC 3276 (TCC)先例,判承建商可以延长完工日期但不能索赔延长费用/损失。而针对后一点的判法,Edwards – Stuart 大法官说原因如下:"By contrast, the contractor cannot recover damages for delay in circumstances where he would have suffered exactly the same loss as a result of causes within his control or for which he is contractually responsible. This means, that as things stood out as at the date of termination, Atos would have been entitled to an extension of time until about mid December 2008 ..., but would not have been entitled to recover from DB the prolongation costs consequent upon the delay up to that date."

这是说承建商不可以索赔延长费用/赔偿,原因是在同步延误下,他根本没有因为对方或雇主的妨碍或过错蒙受更大的损失。众所周知,在一般的违约索赔也是同样道理,即使证明对方违约,也必须证明违约带来损失,才能成功索赔。但这个普通法的地位看来在工程合约的同步延误也很有争议,有说法是延长费用/赔偿应该在雇主与承建商之间分摊。这在 City Inn Ltd v. Shepherd Construction (2008) BLR 269 先例也有针对,一审法院的 Drummond Young 勋爵就认为应该根据责任的分摊分摊损失,说:"... in an appropriate case where loss is caused both by events for which the employer is responsible and events for which the contractor is responsible it is possible to apportion the loss between the two causes. In my opinion that should be done in the present case. This is a case **where delay has been caused by a number of different causes, most of which were the responsibility of the employer, through the architect, but two of which were the responsibility of the contractor. It is accordingly necessary to apportion the defenders' prolongation costs between these two categories of causes.** I consider that the same general considerations, the causative significance of each of the sources of delay and the degree of culpability in respect of each of those sources, must be balanced. On this basis, I am of opinion that the result of the exercise should be the same; I am unable to discover any reason for treating the two exercises under clause 25 and clause 26 on a different basis. I accordingly conclude that the defenders are entitled to their prolongation costs for nine weeks."(加黑部分是笔者的强调)

这也带来一种在近期被建议的处理同步延误的"混合方式"(hybrid approach),就是根据 Malmaison 方式延长完工日期,但针对承建商可以索赔的延长费用/赔偿就作出分摊,而不是按照普通法一贯的地位。至于雇主本来可以向承建商索赔的议定赔偿,则由于已经根据 Malmaison 方式延期,也就不存在工程延误的议定赔偿。

这个混合办法也有问题,这可节录 John Marrin QC 在《Concurrent Delay Revisit》(2012 年)一文中说:"**A hybrid approach has been suggested, the idea being that the decision - maker might apply the Malmaison approach to the extension of time claim and then apportion the monetary claims.** However, it is suggested that that would not necessarily achieve the intended result. It is convenient to return to the facts of the chosen example[10]. Applying the Malmaison approach to the contractor's extension of time claim, the decision - maker would grant an extension of time for the whole of the month of January 2012. If the decision - maker then went on to apply the apportionment approach to the monetary claims, he might award the contractor his prolongation costs for, say, the first three weeks of January. If the apportionment were to give rise to a true sharing of the costs during that month, one might expect the employer in those circumstances to recover a monetary remedy in respect of the fourth week of the month. Yet, where (as in the example) the contract provides for liquidated damages for delay, the employer's claim for compensation will be shut out. The contractor will already have recovered a full extension of time for the entire month of January, which necessarily precludes the recovery or deduction of any liquidated damages at all. For these reasons, it is suggested that the hybrid approach is unlikely to find favour."(John Marrin QC 认为在将 1 个月的延误损失分摊给雇主与承建商后,看起来雇主可以有金钱方式的部分救济,但是雇主实

---

〔10〕 在该文一开始,John Marrin QC 给了一个简单的例子:承建商承诺在 2011 年 1 月至 12 月完成一个工程,但一方面由于承建商要进行工程瑕疵的补救,另一方面由于雇主要求进行一些更改,工程延迟了 1 个月的时间才完工,并且这两方面都是主因。

际上陷入了两难的境地,并且不会有金钱上的好处。因为根据分摊损失后所得出的的雇主与承建商各自应该承担的份额,如分摊3个星期的损失给承建商,就表示承建商可以向雇主取回3个星期的延长费用/赔偿。但分摊还剩下的1个星期雇主的工程延误损失理论上是可以向承建商取回或对冲掉,但在合约中这笔损失已经被约定是一笔议定赔偿,而合约的机制也因为完工日期被延长而不适用。所以,雇主根本没有办法取回分摊到的1个星期的损失,而只有支付金钱给承建商。)

5.7 妨碍原则下不必是雇主的错误行为造成

雇主或船东的行为不必是违约,妨碍原则也同样适用在雇主或船东行使合约权利要求承建商或船厂做额外的工作或是上面提到过的对工程/船舶的规格做出更改,双方没有事前同意给承建商或船厂更长的时间来完成,而有关合约也没有条文针对的情况。这可见 Holme v Guppy (1838) 3 M&W 387; Thornhill v Neats (1860) 8 CB (NS) 831; Dodd v Churton (1897) 1 QB 562 CA; Wells v Army & Navy (1902) 86 LT 764; Trollope & Colls v North West (1973) 1 WLR 601 HL; Honeywell v. Multiplex (2007) EWHC 447 等先例。也可见《Chitty on Contracts》(第31版,2012年)之37-119段。

第十二章　惯用条文之一

从本章至第十四章,笔者介绍一些在任何类别合约都会出现的重要的"惯用条文"(boilerplate clauses)。有不少惯用条文已经在本书较早章节有涉及,如本书第八章的变数条件条文与第九章的善意谈判条文。笔者的其他书籍也有不少针对惯用条文的详尽介绍,如在《仲裁法》上下册充分介绍了"仲裁条文"(arbitration clause),在《损失赔偿与救济》一书介绍了"议定赔偿条文"(liquidated damages clause)等。另在《国际货物买卖》一书,杨大明律师介绍了"保留货权条文"(retention of title clause)。本章先介绍三条十分重要的惯用条文:免责条文、补偿条文与时效条文。

§1　免责条文(exception clause)

1.1　先例中对免责条文作出的定义与分类

普通法对免责条文没有给出完整与肯定的定义,一般的概念就是这种条文是抗辩合约索赔的盾牌。由于这种条文会有千变万化的写法,可先针对其类别。首先介绍一些重要先例中的说法,第一个是 Wilberforce 勋爵在 Suisse Atlantique Societe D'Armement Maritime SA v N. V. Rotterdamsche Kolen Centrale (1966) 1 Lloyd's Rep 529 先例中说:"I treat the words 'exceptions clause' as covering broadly such clauses as profess to exclude or limit, either quantitatively or as to the time within which action must be taken, the right of the injured party to bring an action for damages."(这句话针对时效条文属于免责条文。)

另是 Donaldson 大法官在 Kenyon, Son & Craven Ltd v Baxter Hoare & Co Ltd (1971) 1 WLR 519 先例中的说法:"Protective conditions are of three distinct types, namely, first, those which limit or reduce what would otherwise be the defendants' duty; second, those which exclude the defendants' liability for breach of specified aspects of that duty and third, those which limit the extent to which the defendant is bound to indemnify the plaintiff in respect of the consequences of breaches of that duty."(一是局限或减少被告的义务;二是在被告违约的时候免除他的责任;三是局限被告赔偿原告/无辜方的程度。)

最后要节录的是 Diplock 勋爵在 Photo Productions Ltd v. Securicor Transport Ltd

(1980) 1 Lloyd's Rep. 545 先例中的说法:"... an exclusion clause is one which excludes or modifies an obligation, whether primary, general secondary or anticipatory secondary, that would otherwise arise under the contract by implication of law. Parties are free to agree to whatever exclusion or modification of all types of obligations as they please within the limits that the agreement must retain the legal characteristics of a contract; and must not offend against the equitable rule against penalties; that is to say, it must not impose upon the breaker of a primary obligation a general secondary obligation to pay to the other party a sum of money that is manifestly intended to be in excess of the amount which would fully compensate the other party for the loss sustained by him in consequence of the breach of the primary obligation. Since the obligations implied by law in a commercial contract are those which, by judicial consensus over the years or by Parliament in passing a statute, have been regarded as obligations which a reasonable businessman would realize that he was accepting when he entered into a contract of a particular kind, the court's view of the reasonableness of departure from the implied obligations which would be involved in construing the express words of an exclusion clause in one sense that they are capable of bearing rather than another, is a relevant consideration in deciding what meaning the words were intended by the parties to bear. But this does not entitle the court to reject the exclusion clause, however unreasonable itself may think it is, if the words are clear and fairly susceptible of one meaning only." [免责条文是排除或更改法律默示的合约义务。订约方有自由约定怎样排除或更改这些法律默示的义务,只要不导致合约失去法律特征(如在本章之 1.7.4 段介绍的相悖理论,会导致合约变成只是一个意向书)或变为违反衡平法的惩罚条文。因为有一个假设是订约方的订约意图是接受这些法律默示的义务,所以会严格解释免责条文。这些法律默示代表法院多年的一致看法或由议会通过立法制定,而这些默示义务是合理的商业人士在订约时接受的公平合理的做法。所以免责条文要偏离,就必须要在文字上写得清楚。如果免责条文可以有多个解释,法院可以根据合理性决定到底双方的订约意图是什么。但只要该免责条文是写得清楚无误与客观地说只能有一个解释,法院即使认为免责条文完全不合理,也不允许否定它。]

1.2 立法与权威说法对免责条文作出的定义与分类

在立法中的 1977 年英国《不公平合约法》之第 13 条,有明确的定义说:"To the extent that this Part of this Act prevents the exclusion or restriction of any liability it also prevents - (a) making the liability or its enforcement subject to restrictive or onerous conditions; (b) excluding or restricting any right or remedy in respect of the liability, or subjecting a person to any prejudice in consequence or his pursuing any such right or remedy; (c) excluding or restricting rules of evidence or procedure; and (to that extent) section 2 and 5 to 7 also prevent excluding or restricting liability to reference to terms and notices which exclude or restrict the relevant obligation or duty."上述的立法，(c)包括了排除或局限证据或程序，这是较早前先例对免责条文的分类没有包括的类别。

笔者认为，Brian Coote 教授在他的《Exception Clauses》(1964 年)一书很清楚地说到什么合约条文属于免责条文：

"Type A：exception clauses whose effect, if any, is upon the accrual of particular primary rights.(A 类型的免责条文是针对合约的首要权利或义务。[1])

Thus where words relating to quality have been employed by a vendor of goods, an exclusion of conditions, warranties, or undertakings as to quality, helps determine the extent to which those words are contractually binding as, by the same token, would a stipulation by the vendor that he should not be required to make compensation for poor quality.(如条文/文字说明卖方对提供货物的质量不作出任何条件、保证或承诺。同样也包括条文/文字说是卖方对货物质量有缺陷，不需要作出任何赔偿。显然在货物买卖，卖方对货物的满意质量在 1979 年《货物销售法》下是默示责任，这也是卖方的首要义务。A 类型的免责条文就是排除卖方需要提供满意质量货物的首要责任。)

Type B：exception clauses which qualify primary or secondary rights without preventing the accrual of any particular primary right. Examples would be limitations on the time within which claims might be made, and limitations as to the amount which might be recovered on a claim. By contrast, a clause which purported to take away a buyer's right to reject goods would belong to Type A."(B 类型的免责条文不针对首要权利或义务，而是限制次要权利或义务。典型例子是一条时效条文限制受害方必须在一个比法律默示时效更短的时间内提出索赔，或是限制受害方即使胜诉能够索赔的最高金额等。而如果是一条条文规定买方即使货不对版也不能拒货，这种条文/文字属于 A 类型。)

看来在 1977 年《不公平合约法》第 13(c)条针对排除或局限证据或程序的免责条文也属于 Brian Coote 教授说的 B 类型。

在更近期的 Lewison 大法官所著的《The Interpretation of Contracts》(第 5 版，2011 年)一书之 12.01 段有大同小异的说法："The strands of the description reveal a division of exclusion clauses into six categories：(i) clauses which exclude primary obligations；(ii) clauses which modify primary obligations；(iii) clauses which exclude general secondary obligations；(iv) clauses which modify general secondary obligations；

---

〔1〕有关合约首要义务与次要义务的说法在笔者的《损失赔偿与救济》一书第十一章之 1.1 段有简单介绍，首要义务就是其中一方承诺做一些事情；而次要义务就是指作出承诺的合约方违反了作出的首要义务承诺，这会是拒绝履行或有缺陷履行首要义务，就会带来法律默示的次要合约义务，对这一违约产生的损失向受害方做出金钱上的赔偿，详见 Diplock 勋爵在 Photo Production v Securicor (1980) 1 Lloyd's Rep 545 先例的著名说法。

(v) clauses which exclude anticipatory secondary obligations; (vi) clauses which modify anticipatory secondary obligations. ”

以上6种免责条文的类别,前两种属于 Brian Coote 教授说的 A 类型,其余4种属于B类型。

1.3 区分免责条文与合约其他条文的原因

对免责条文作出定义与分类的原因之一是,法院在很长一段时间对解释免责条文充满了敌意。虽然这一直以来的敌意在近年来已经大幅度减少,令解释免责条文变得与解释合约其他条文的区别不大。这方面会在本章稍后进一步介绍。另一个原因是1977年英国《不公平合约法》对免责条文的管制,虽然这只是针对与消费者所签的合约。可节录 Lewison 大法官所著的《The Interpretation of Contracts》(第5版,2011年)一书之12.01段的说法:“The importance of defining or classifying what an exclusion clause is lies in part in the traditional hostility of the courts to exclusion clauses, and in the development of principles of construction which are applied to exclusion clauses; and in part because exemption clauses are subject to statutory controls. ”

总结而言,免责条文与合约其他条文有时不容易区分,所以也带来不少这方面的诉讼。

1.4 履行风险分摊条文与免责条文的区分

例如,在提单或程租租约经常出现的一条标准格式条文,名为“邻近条文”(near clause)或通常写为“or so near thereunto as the vessel may safely get”,就被视为属于 Lewison 大法官所说的(ii)类别的免责条文,更改船东的首要义务。船东在提单或程租租约承诺了某个特定卸港,就有了必须履行这一首要义务的绝对/严格的合约责任。但经常会遇上危险是该列名或指定卸港突然发生了事故(如航道发生事故而堵塞、冰封、政治原因而封港、罢工、天灾等)导致船舶进不去并带来严重延误。这样,有了邻近条文的保障,船东就可以根据合约的规定即他并非只承诺该特定卸港,也可以是船舶能够安全抵达的邻近港口,把船舶开该邻近港口将货物卸下也算是履行了首要义务。在 Renton (GH) & Co Ltd v Palmyra Trading Corporation of Panama (1957) AC 149 先例,Morton 勋爵接受邻近条文可以保障船东不去约定的卸港伦敦而去了汉堡把货物卸下,说:“The contract contained in the bill of lading must be read as a whole. So read, it provides, in effect, that the goods must be carried to London unless there occurs an event specified in one or other of the provisos already mentioned; but if such event happens, the goods may be discharged elsewhere, and such discharge is to be deemed to be due fulfilment of the contract. No conflict arises when an obligation in a contract, unqualified in its terms as it is first stated, is subsequently qualified by a proviso modifying or altering the obligation if certain events happen which are outside the control of either party. The original obligation and the qualification of it both form part of the intention of the parties and neither part is repugnant to the other. ”

这种区分是否是免责条文的诉讼近年来还是有不少，如在 Dorset County Council v Southern Felt Roofing Ltd (1989) 48 BLR 96, CA 先例，涉及的工程合约有条文要求雇主承担一些风险，说："2.1 BEAR THE RISK of loss or damage in respect of the Works and (where appropriate) the existing structure and contents thereof ... by fire, lightning, explosion, aircraft and other aerial devices or articles dropped therefrom."

这看来是双方约定分摊风险的条文，但上诉庭认为该条文有可能是豁免承建商对第三人的侵权责任（如火灾或爆炸都有可能涉及承建商的疏忽），所以应该属于免责条文。

这种区分免责条文与"规范"（regulate）或"局限"（limit）双方怎样履行合约的所谓"规范/局限合约履行条文"（limitation clause）的近期先例还有 JP Morgan Chase Bank v Springwell Navigation (2008) EWHC 1186 (Comm) 与 Lobster Group Ltd v Heidelberg Graphic Equipment Ltd (2009) EWHC 1919 (TCC) 等。作出区分的原因是法院对后者的规范/局限条文有较少的敌意，正如 Wilberforce 勋爵在 Ailsa Craig Fishing Co Ltd v Malvern Fishing Co Ltd (1983) 1 WLR 964 先例所说："Clauses of limitation are not regarded by the courts with the same hostility as clauses of exclusion: this is because they must be related to other contractual terms, in particular to the risks to which the defending party may be exposed, the remuneration which he receives, and possibly also the opportunity of the other party to insure." [法院在解释规范/局限合约履行条文时没有像对待免责条文一样的敌意，因为这些条文一定与合约其他条文有关联，特别是针对履约的风险、对价/收取费用的高低（如警卫合约要求警卫看管的通常是十分昂贵的商品/标的，但对价往往只是很低的警卫费用，这费用根本不足够警卫公司为该商品/标的投保盗窃险）、谁有机会或应该投保风险。]

对这两种条文不同对待的原因，Fraser 勋爵在 Ailsa Craig Fishing Co Ltd v Malvern Fishing Co Ltd 先例也说道："In my opinion these principles（指的是针对免责条文严格/敌意解释）are not applicable in their full rigour when considering the effect of clauses merely limiting liability. Such clauses will of course be read *contra proferentem* and must be clearly expressed, but there is no reason why they should be judged by the specially exacting standards which are applied to exclusion and indemnity clauses. The reason for imposing such standards on these clauses is the inherent improbability that the other party to a contract including such a clause intended to release the *proferens* from a liability that would otherwise fall upon him. But there is no such high degree of improbability that he would agree to a limitation of the liability of the *proferens*, especially when... the potential losses that might be caused by the negligence of the *proferens* or its servants are so great in proportion to the sums that can reasonably be charged for the services contracted for. It is enough in the present case that the clause must be clear and unambiguous."（后部分是解释为什么法院在解释规范/局限合约履行条文时没有同样

的敌意,因为订约方会愿意放弃与不追究对方应该承担的合约责任的可能性通常不大,但愿意局限合约履行的风险,特别是在其收费不高并且与潜在的损失不成比例的情况下订立条文保护其不因雇员疏忽造成损失而负责的话,就有这个可能性。)

事实上,免责条文与规范/局限合约履行条文的确不容易区分,如较早前提到航运与外贸中经常会遇到的"邻近条文"(near clause)被视为一条对船东列名或指定卸港的首要义务作出更改的规范/局限合约履行条文,令船东去邻近港口卸货也不是违约,根本不是一般认为的免责条文是面对索赔时抗辩的盾牌。另在 The "Angelia" (1972) 2 Lloyd's Rep 154 先例,针对的是因一些无可避免的障碍而无法提供货物与装货的情况下保护承租人的租约免责条文,Kerr 大法官指条文到底是免责或只是更改/局限首要义务只是文字游戏,说:"It is true that on the basis of its wording clause 2 is properly to be described as an exception clause. This has the consequence, for instance, that it must be strictly construed. But its effect in the context of the question whether or not it can be relied upon as an answer to an allegation of fundamental breach cannot depend on the semantic question whether the charterparty says: 'I promise to supply a cargo but shall not be liable if I do not do so due to unavoidable hindrances,' or 'I promise to supply a cargo unless prevented by unavoidable hindrances.' The conclusive answer to any allegation of fundamental breach is in my view that the relevant provision (whether it be properly described as an exception clause or as a qualification of the obligation) excuses non - performance due to circumstances which are not the fault of the charterers."

另一个例子是"时效条文"(time bar clause),这根据本章开始所介绍的 Wilberforce 勋爵在 Suisse Atlantique Societe D'Armement Maritime SA v N. V. Rotterdamsche Kolen Centrale (1966) 1 Lloyd's Rep 529 先例中所讲的话,看来是十分明确属于免责条文。但根据 Lewison 大法官所著的《The Interpretation of Contracts》(第 5 版,2011 年)一书之 12.17 段的说法,则不再明确到底时效条文是属于免责条文或是规范/局限合约履行条文,说:"However, the House of Lords has now pointed out an important distinction between exclusion clauses and limitation clauses. It is not yet clear whether a time bar clause will be construed by reference to the especially exacting standards applicable to exemption clauses or to the less rigorous standards applicable to limitation clauses. Since a time bar clause does not wholly remove the right of an injured party to claim against the other, it is submitted that it is more analogous to a limitation clause than to an exemption clause. In other words it limits a claim temporally rather than quantitatively."

1.5 对双方都会有好处的条文不是免责条文

在 BHP Petroleum Ltd v British Steel Plc (2000) 2 Lloyd's Rep 277 先例,该建筑合约的一条常见的条文(这种条文在造船合约中也常见,就是船厂交船给船东后 1 年或不等时间内的“担保修理”[guarantee repair]条文)如下:“17.5 The Supplier shall immediately remedy, at the contracted point of delivery, at his expense any defect in the Work due to faulty design, materials or workmanship which shall appear within eighteen (18) months of the date stated in the Purchase Order or such longer period as may be provided in the Purchaser Order, but not later than twenty - four months, the delivery of the Work to the Purchaser (whichever shall first occur), at which time all liability of the Supplier relating to the Work shall terminate. ... Provided — The obligations of the Supplier, in addition to the remedying of the Purchaser of repair or replacement at the contracted point of delivery shall also extend to include payment to the Purchaser of cost and expense directly and necessarily incurred by the Purchaser in the location, uplifting and replacement, of any Work proved not to comply with the requirements of the Contract. The Suppliers [sic] liability hereunder shall not exceed 15% (fifteen percent) of the Contract Price by Line Item — the payment of which shall fully discharge all liabilities of the Supplier howsoever arising out of the supply of work that does not comply with the requirements of the Contract.”

这条文被上诉庭判并非是免责条文,因为该十分广泛的条文在本质上对双方都有好处。对雇主的好处是承建商/供应商(在该先例是被告向原告的海上钻油台供应钢管,但供应后两年发觉钢管有不妥)要负责将缺陷修妥,而对承建商/供应商的好处是他有机会以更便宜的价格修妥或弥补缺陷。

这种对双方都可能有利的条文,虽然在个别的案情中看起来保护了一方并造成对另一方不利[这种情况很早就已经有先例,如在国际货物买卖与租船合约都有的“滞期费条文”(demurrage clause)或其他合约的“议定赔偿条文”(liquidated damages clause),会在不同案情的案件中对违约方有利,这主要是滞期费条文或议定赔偿的金额约定的太低],但已经有先例判这种条文对双方都潜在有利,所以不属于免责条文。在 Suisse Atlantique Societe D'Armement Maritime SA v N. V. Rotterdamsche Kolen Centrale (1966) 1 Lloyd's Rep 529 先例,Upjohn 勋爵说:“An agreed damage clause is for the benefit of both; the party establishing breach by the other need prove no damage in fact, the other must pay that, no less but no more. But where liability for damage is limited by a clause then the person seeking to claim damages must prove them at least up to the limit laid down by the clause; the other party, whatever may be the damage in fact, can refuse to pay more if he can rely on the clause.”

对双方有利也出现在“检验证书为终”(certificate final)条文,这种条文在国际货物买卖合约中也经常出现,文字上是“以装港对货物质量作出的检验证书为最终结果”,加入该条文的原因是卖方害怕货物运到卸港被买方检查后认为货不对版而拒货。进一步的介绍可看本书第十四章之第1段。在 Toepfer v Continental Grain Co (1974) 1 Lloyd's Rep 11 先例,案情涉及小麦的 CIF 买卖,相关条文可节录如下:

"Quality: No. 3 HARD AMBER DURAM WHEAT of U. S. Origin – **quality/condition final at loading as per Official Certificate.**"(加黑部分是笔者的强调)

Carins 大法官在此案说:"I see no grounds for saying that a provision of this kind should be construed with some special degree of strictness. It is not like an exceptional clause which is designed to operate to give protection to one party. Either buyer or seller benefit from this clause if some error of judgment on the part of the inspector led him to certify a quality in the goods different from their actual quality."

此外,针对一些合约经常出现的如"不可抗力条文"(*force majeure* clause)、"补偿条文"(indemnity clause)、"完整合约条文"(entire agreement clause)、"议定赔偿条文"(liquidated damages clause),"时效条文"(time – bar clause)等,都因与免责条文有关系而需要作出区分。部分条文会在本章或其他章节涉及,在此不重复。

1.6 解释免责条文的传统做法

1.6.1 订约自由下法院对免责条文的敌意解释

法院对免责条文的敌意解释有很长的历史,这是因为有订约自由的大原则,所以谈判力量强大与订约水平高的一方一直可以强加一些不公平/不合理的免责条文给弱小与水平低的对方订约方。随着资本主义的发展,出现了一些垄断企业,这在社会上造成了很大的不公平,因为大部分市民作为消费者几乎没有任何谈判力量。在这种情况与订约自由的大原则下,法院在其权利范围内能够作出的一些平衡就只能是怀有敌意的解释这些免责条文,尽量挑毛病与吹毛求疵,也就是所谓的"扭曲解释"(strained construction)。正如 Denning 勋爵在 Mitchell (George) (Chesterhall) Ltd v. Finney Lock Seed Ltd (1983) Q. B. 284 先例中说:

"None of you nowadays will remember the trouble we had—when I was called to the Bar—with exemption clauses. They were printed in small print on the back of tickets and order forms and invoices. They were contained in catalogues or timetable. They were held to be binding on any person who took them without objection. No one ever did object. He never read them or knew what was in them. No matter how unreasonable they were, he was bound. All this was done in the name of 'freedom of contract'. But the freedom was all on the side of the big concern which had the use of the printing press. No freedom for the little man who took the ticket or order form or invoice. The big concern said, 'Take it or leave it.' The little man had no option but to take it. The big concern could and did exempt itself from liability in its own interest without regard to the little man. It got away with it time after time. When the courts said to the big concern, 'You must put it in clear words', the big concern had no hesitation in doing so. It knew well that the little man would never read the exemption clauses or understand them ...

Faced with this abuse of power—by the strong against the weak—by the use of the small print of the conditions—the judges did what they could to put a curb upon it. They still had before them the idol, 'freedom of contract'. They still knelt down and worshipped it, but they concealed under their cloaks a secret weapon. They used it to stab the idol in the back. This weapon was called 'the true construction of the contract'. They used it with great skill and ingenuity. **They used it so as to depart from the natural meaning of the words of the exemption clause and to put upon them a strained and unnatural construction.** In case after case, they said that the words were not strong enough to give the big concern exemption from liability; or that in the circumstances the big concern was not entitled to rely on the exemption clause. If a ship deviated from the contractual voyage, the owner could not rely on the exemption clause. If a warehouseman stored the goods in the wrong warehouse, he could not pray in it the limitation clause. If the seller supplied the goods different in kind from those contracted for, he could not rely on any exemption from liability. If a shipowner delivered goods to a person without production of the bill of lading, he could not escape responsibility by reference to an exemption clause. In short, whenever the wide words—in their natural meaning—would give rise to an unreasonable result, the judges either rejected them as repugnant to the main purpose of the contract, or else cut them down to size in order to produce a reasonable result ... But when the clause was itself reasonable and gave rise to a reasonable result, the judges upheld it, at any rate, when the clause did not exclude liability entirely but only limited it to a reasonable amount. So where goods were deposited in a cloakroom or sent to a laundry for cleaning, it was quite reasonable for the company to limit their liability to a reasonable amount, having regard to the small charge made for the service."(加黑部分是笔者的强调)

1.6.2　对免责条文作出扭曲解释与近期的否定

像Denning勋爵所讲的法院把免责条文中文字的一般性意思作出扭曲解释、否定或事后说该免责条文可以写得更清楚无误的案例的确多不胜数,其中不少在提单方面。如Wade v Cockerline (1904) 10 Com. Cas. 47先例,判是由于瘟疫造成卸货工人短缺并不属于"事故对卸货造成妨碍或延误"(accident preventing or delaying the discharge)的免责事项。

至于其他的案例,可先举Wallis Son & Wells v. Pratt & Haynes (1911) A. C. 394, HL先例,该案判是免责条文中排除了的"保证"(warranty)不包括"条件"(condition)。这令很多免责条文把各种称谓的合约条文,不管实质上有没有区别,都明示加在一条免责条文内。如说"all terms, provisions, conditions, warranties, exceptions..." ,以防有所遗漏。

也被认为是存在扭曲解释的先例是White v Warwick (John) & Co Ltd (1953) 1 WLR 1285,相关的三轮车租用合约规定三轮车主对租用者的人身伤害免责说:"nothing in this agreement shall render the owners liable for any personal injuries to the riders of the tricycle hired."

法院判是三轮车主根据法律的默示地位要提供一辆"合理适合用途"(reasonably fit for the purpose)的三轮车,并要对他的疏忽负责。而该条文只能被解释为排除了默示责任,但还是要对疏忽负责。

另一种被视为扭曲解释的做法是把一条免责条文说成只是在订约时向对方作出的警告或通告而已。Olley v Marlborough Court Ltd (1949) 1 KB 532 与 Hollier v Rambler Motors (AMC) Ltd (1972) 2 QB 71 都属于这种案例,在后一个先例上诉庭的 Stamp 大法官是这样说:"I would hold that, where the words relied upon by the defendant are susceptible to a construction under which they become a statement of fact in the nature of a warning or to a construction which will exempt the defendant from liability for negligence, the former construction is to be preferred."

但这种扭曲解释的做法在比较近期的 Spriggs v Sotheby Parke Bernet & Co (1986) 1 Lloyd's Rep 487 先例被上诉庭否定,案情涉及原告交给被告 Sotheby 拍卖行进行拍卖的一颗钻石被盗,原告向被告提出索赔,但被告抗辩原告接受了拍卖条件内的一条广泛的免责条文。原告代表律师的一个争辩是该条文的第一句话只是警告或通告,该句话是"(原告)接受只要(拍卖行)采取所有合理小心处理客户的财产,就不必对任何的损失或损坏承担责任...(I accept that whilst you take all reasonable care in handling the property on behalf of clients, you are not responsible for loss or damage of any kind whether caused by negligence or otherwise, the property being accepted at the owner's risk...)"原告代表律师说:"...the opening words amounted to no more than an assertion of fact or a statement of general practice, then the whole clause was merely a notice or warning, or at any rate was capable of being so construed, and accordingly was not sufficient to exclude liability."

但这争辩被上诉庭拒绝,其中 Neill 大法官说:"It seems to me that the words '... whether caused by negligence or otherwise...' are quite clear and are adequate to exclude any liability for any act of negligence by Sothebys or by any person for whom Sothebys would be responsible. I cannot construe these words as a mere notice or warning..."

从上述的简单介绍中,可以看到 Denning 勋爵认为通过扭曲解释否定免责条文是厉害的"武器"的原因。其实,这在中长期没有任何作用,因为在订约自由下,谈判力量强大与订约水平高的一方可以在一个案例败诉后吸取教训,然后把合约(特别是标准格式合约或条件)订得更加缜密与有针对性。

以提单为例,历史上就有过无数不同写法的免责条文。在长达百年的时间(特别在"二战"之前)内,班轮公司与班轮公会(被公认为世界上最早出现的垄断组织)相对货方明显有"一面倒"的谈判力量。所以,在一些班轮公司的印本标准格式合约,特别是提单,在不少著名的权威书籍如《Scrutton on Charter - parties and Bills of Lading》就列举了足足有六七十项不同写法的免责条文。有说法是在这种提单免责条文下,船东只有无数的权利(如收取运费与其他费用),但无须对要托运的货物负任何责任。

这样,如果无法否定订约自由,明显是要想另外的办法对付这种强弱悬殊的订约自由,这在稍后介绍。

1.6.3　对免责条文作出分开解释与近期的否定

接下来有另一个解释免责条文的传统做法,先考虑免责条文以外的其他合约条文确立的是什么责任,然后才针对该免责条文看是否能够对该责任提供抗辩。这种分开来解释的做法先是 Scrutton 大法官在 Rutter v Palmer (1922) 2 KB 87 先例中所提出,说:"In construing an exemption clause certain general rules may be applied: First the defendant is not exempted from liability for the negligence of his servants unless adequate words are used; secondly, the liability of the defendant apart from the exempting words must be ascertained; then the particular clause in question must be considered; and if the only liability of the party pleading the exemption is a liability for negligence, the clause will more readily operate to exempt him."

后来的 Karsales (Harrow) Ltd v Wallis (1956) 1 WLR 936 先例,上诉庭的 Denning 大法官也有类似的说法,并显示了对分开解释免责条文的敌意,说:"It is necessary to look at the contract apart from the exemption clauses and see what are the terms, express or implied, which impose an obligation on the party. If he has been guilty of a breach of those obligations in a respect which goes to the very root of the contract, he cannot rely on the exemption clauses."

这种分开来解释对免责条文的不利之处也可以节录 Scrutton 大法官在 Calico Printers' Association v Barclays Bank Ltd (1931) 145 LT 51 先例所说:"First of all, in my view, you do not take part of the document and consider it by itself; you are to construe the whole document. The parties have used a set of words to express their legal relations to each other and it is no good saying: 'Here I find in sentence A clear words, so I need not trouble about sentence B, because sentence B, if it contradicts sentence A, I will reject a repugnant, and I will ... assume that these parties used these words not meaning anything by them, and therefore I need not trouble about them because they do use clear language in sentence A'."

这样解释免责条文的不利之处是只把它视为对责任的抗辩,但 Brian Coote 教授在《Exception Clauses》(1964 年)一书对免责条文的分类是包括了对合约首要义务的"更改"(modification)或作出局限,这就不仅是一个抗辩了。同样,如果免责条文与其他合约条文一并作出解释,就更有可能把所谓的免责条文解释为"规范"(regulate)或"局限"(limit)双方怎样履行合约的所谓"规范/局限合约履行条文"(limitation clause),这在本章之 1.4 段也提到过后者条文是不会受到法院的敌意解释。这也是在 Gardiner v. Agricultural and Rural Finance Pty Ltd. (2007) NSWCA 235 先例的说法，Basten 大法官说："If the contract is read as a whole, one is, perhaps, more likely to reach the conclusion that what might otherwise be seen as an exception which excuses liability for failure to perform, will rather be construed as a limitation on the scope of performance."

这种分开来解释免责条文的传统做法现在应完全被否定，已经有无数的权威先例与观点认为解释免责条文应该与其他合约条文一并与总体解释。只节录 Bingham 大法官在 Swiss Bank Corporation v Brink's Mat Ltd (1986) 2 Lloyd's 79 先例说："My task, therefore, is to construe cl. 13(免责条文) in the context of the contract as a whole and of the business relationship between these parties."

另是上诉庭的 Clarke 大法官在 National Westminster Bank v Utrecht – America Finance Co (2001) 3 All ER 733, CA 先例说："Like any clause, clause 8.2(免责条文) must be construed in its context and in the context of the contract as a whole having regard to its factual matrix or surrounding circumstances."

1.6.4 解决在订约方强弱悬殊的情况下订约自由被滥用的办法之一：立法禁止订约自由

中长期对付这种订约双方谈判力量强弱悬殊情况下(庞大与垄断企业面对消费者或班轮公司/公会面对货方)谈判力量强大一方滥用订约自由的问题，只能是通过立法而不能依赖法院对个别案件的审理。可以说，以立法禁止谈判力量强大与水平高的订约方利用订约自由大原则订立一面倒的免责条文排除应该合理承担的法律默示责任是一劳永逸的解决办法。这方面的立法最早出现在"提单"(bill of lading)，就是作为国际公约的 1924 年《海牙规则》与英国作为签约国相应的国内立法之 1924 年《海上货物运输法》。有关的条文禁止订约自由的是在《海牙规则》的 Article 3 (8)，如下："Article 3...8. Any clause, covenant, or agreement in a contract of carriage relieving the carrier or the ship from liability for loss or damage to, or in connection with, goods arising from negligence, fault, or failure in the duties and obligations provided in this article or lessening such liability otherwise than as provided in this convention, shall be null and void and of no effect..."

而针对岸上/本土的消费者，英国也是以立法解决这方面的严重问题。最重要与最具广泛性保护消费者的立法是 1977 年《不公平合约法》(《Unfair Contract Terms Act》)。但这个立法足足比《海上货物运输法》晚了半个世纪。这一立法给一些与消费者无关的商业合约，特别是国际性的商业合约内的免责条文带来了重要改变。法院对免责条文的敌意、"扭曲解释"(strained construction)与"基本违约"(fundamental breach)的说法，在该立法生效后的 Photo Productions Ltd v. Securicor Transport Ltd (1980) 1 Lloyd's Rep. 545 先例正式宣布告终。其中，可节录 Diplock 勋爵的说法："...the reports are full of cases in which what would appear to be very strained constructions have been placed upon exclusion clauses, mainly in what to – day would be called consumer contracts and contracts of adhesion. As Lord Wilberforce has pointed out, any need for this kind of judicial distortion of the English language has been banished by Parliament's having made these kinds of contracts subject to the Unfair Contract Terms Act 1977. In commercial contracts negotiated between business – men capable of looking after their own interests and of deciding how risks inherent in the performance of various kinds of contract can be most economically borne (generally by insurance), it is, in my view, wrong to place a strained construction upon words in an exclusion clause which are clear and fairly susceptible of one meaning only even after due allowance has been made for the presumption in favour of the implied primary and secondary obligations."(在1977年《不公平合约法》生效后,针对一般的商业合约,订约双方完全可以照顾自己利益的当事人,他们也可以决定将来合约履行的风险应该怎样最好与最经济地作出分摊[如谁对风险作出投保]。Diplock勋爵认为法院对这些非消费者的商业合约(特别是国际商业合约)不应该作出干预,而对免责条文作出一个扭曲的解释。)

Wilberforce勋爵在Ailsa Craig Fishing Co Ltd v Malvern Fishing Co Ltd (1983) 1 WLR 964先例也说:"法院不应该通过扭曲解释将免责条文硬说成是不明确(one must not strive to create ambiguities by strained construction)。"

1.6.5 解决在订约方强弱悬殊的情况下订约自由被滥用的办法之二:基本违约的说法

普通法曾经在20世纪50年代通过一连串的案例(如J. Spurling Ltd v. Bradshaw [1956] 1 W. L. R. 461; Sze Hai Tong Bank Ltd v. Rambler Cycle Co. Ltd [1959] 2 Lloyd's Rep. 114; Astley Industrial Trust v. Grimley [1963] 1 W. L. R. 1468等)带出了基本违约的理论。该理论是说,如果有一个基本违约(fundamental breach)或换一个说法是违反了合约中基本与重大的条文,违约方就不可以依赖合约中的免责条文,不论该免责条文写得如何清楚无误与只能有一个解释。这里可节录《Chitty on Contracts》(第31版,2012年)一书之14–020段:"It was at one time supposed that a party to a contract would be precluded from relying upon an exemption clause contained in it where he had been guilty of a fundamental breach of contract or the breach of a fundamental term. Statements in certain cases tended to encourage the view that there existed a rule of substantive law preventing a party from relying on an exemption clause in situations of fundamental breach or the breach of fundamental term, regardless of the wording of the clause. It was predicated that there were certain breaches of contract ('fundamental breaches') which was so totally destructive of the obligations of the party in default that liability for such a breach in no circumstances be excluded or restrictive by means of exemption clause. ..."

这可以Sze Hai Tong Bank Ltd v. Rambler Cycle Co. Ltd先例为例,该案是有关海上货物运输中的无单放货。显然,如果这样做,船东是违反了提单合约中的一条基本与重大条文,因为整个海上货物运输的根本目的是把货物运送至目的地然后准确地交给收货人,而不是随意侵占货物或者胡乱交给其他人。但在该案中,提单有一条十分广泛的免责条文,明确说明船东在船旁卸货后,不论是作为承运人或是托管人的所有责任都绝对终止。在文字的字义上,应该可针对无单放货的违约。但在上诉庭被判是属于基本违约而不让船东依赖免责条文。

笔者也无意多介绍,因为基本违约的说法已经过时。

1.7 近年解释免责条文的做法

在1977年《不公平合约法》生效后,普通法对免责条文的态度有重大改变。这改变也可以理解,因为针对谈判力量悬殊的情况已经有立法救济,不再需要法院扭曲解释合约内的免责条文以求主持公道。这重大的态度改变显示在两个贵族院先例:Photo Productions Ltd v. Securicor Transport Ltd (1980) 1 Lloyd's Rep. 545 与 Ailsa Craig Fishing Co Ltd v. Malvern Fishing Ltd (1983) 1 W. L. R. 964, HL。改变之一是 Photo Productions Ltd v. Securicor Transport Ltd 先例否定了基本违约的说法;改变之二是在两个先例中都说是要避免像以前一样扭曲解释免责条文,而要像对待其他合约条文一样作出一般性解释。

在接下来的段节会介绍部分这方面的重要先例,这里先节录近期重要案例对目前怎样解释免责条文的说法。首先是澳大利亚最高院在 Darlington Futures Ltd v Delco Australia Pty Ltd (1986) 61 ALJR 76 先例中说:"... the interpretation of an exclusion clause is to be determined by construing the clause according to its natural and ordinary meaning, read in the light of the contract as whole, thereby giving due weight to the context in which the clause appears including the nature and object of the contract and, where appropriate, construing the clause *contra proferentem* in case of ambiguity."(解释免责条文与解释其他条文一样,就是根据条文/文字的自然与一般性意思作出解释并配合整个合约以及语境与合约本质/目的。唯一不同之处是如果免责条文有含糊,就会作出不利于能从免责条文中获利一方的解释。)

另一个在 Whitecap Leisure Ltd v John H Rundle Ltd (2008) 2 Lloyd's Rep 216 先例,Moore - Bick 大法官讲:"One can find in the authorities many statements to the effect that exclusion clauses must be clear and unambiguous if they are to operate effectively, many of which date from a period when courts took a more literal approach to the construction of commercial documents in general than is now generally the case. **The modern approach to construction, which applies as much to exclusion and limitation clauses as to other contractual terms, is to ascertain the objective intention of the parties from the words used and the context in which they are found, including the document as a whole and the background to it**: see Mannai Investment Co Ltd v Eagle Star Life Assurance Co Ltd [1997] AC 749, and Investors Compensation Scheme v West Bromwich Building Society. However, in cases where there is uncertainty about the parties' intention, and therefore about the meaning of the clause, such uncertainty will be resolved against the person relying on the clause and the more significant the departure is said to be from what are accepted to be the obligations ordinarily assumed under a contract of the kind in question, the more difficult it will be to persuade the court that the parties intended that result."(加黑部分是笔者的强调)

1.7.1　先例之一:Photo Productions Ltd v. Securicor Transport Ltd

Photo Productions Ltd v. Securicor Transport Ltd (1980)1 Lloyd's Rep. 545 先例的案情是被告是一家提供警卫服务的公司,他与原告的合约中是包括每天晚上原告的工厂进行4次巡逻。收费是每周9英镑左右,相当于每一次巡逻只收费26便士。这个金额即使在1968年也是十分低廉。后来,被告的一位雇员在巡逻时放火烧毁了原告整个工厂。原告也没有指控被告本人雇佣这位肇事的雇员有疏忽,只是要求被告承担"代理人/替代责任"(vicarious liability)。而被告的抗辩就是合约中有一条非常广泛的免责条文说明被告对其雇员的疏忽与过错不必负责,除非被告能够恪尽职责的合理预见到这一事故并防止。合约还有另外一条免责条文,说明即使要赔偿原告,金额也是限制在25,000英镑,而不是原告索赔的615,000英镑。这两条免责条文可节录如下:

"1. Under no circumstances shall the Company be responsible for any injurious act ... by any employee of the Company unless such act ... could have been foreseen and avoided by the exercise of due diligence on the part of the Company as his employer, nor in any event shall the Company be held responsible for:(a) any loss suffered by the customer through ... fire ... except insofar as such loss is solely attributable to the negligence of the Company's employees acting within the course of their employment ...

2. If notwithstanding the foregoing provision any liability on the part of the Company shall arise ... for any injury to or loss or damage of whatsoever nature sustained by the customer, such liability shall ... be confined to claims of which written notification is received by the Secretary of the Company at its Head Office within one month of the happening of the default by the Company alleged to give rise to such liability; ... and shall be otherwise limited to a maximum of£ 25,000 for the consequences of each incident involving fire or explosion."

上诉庭判这是一个基本违约,所以不论免责条文订得怎样广泛与清楚无误,都不能保护被告。Denning 勋爵这样说:"... since the object of the contract was to safeguard the plaintiffs' premises from fire, and in setting fire to the premises the guard was doing the very thing he was employed to prevent, this was a fundamental breach of contract; and Securicor could not avail themselves of the exemption clause ... the exception clauses in the contract were not apt to cover the case of a deliberate destruction of the subject matter; ..."

但到了贵族院,上诉庭的判决被推翻。其中,Wilberforce 勋爵谈到在《不公平合约法》之后已经不再需要基本违约的普通法理论保护处于弱势的消费者。至于有平等谈判力量的订约方(特别是在商业合约),他们自己可以通过保险安排分摊合约责任与风险,不需要法院再插手作出平衡。Wilberforce 勋爵是这样说:"The doctrine of 'fundamental breach' in spite of its imperfections and doubtful parentage has served a useful purpose. There were a large number of problems, productive of injustice, in which it was worse than unsatisfactory to leave exception clauses to operate. ... But since then Parliament has taken a hand: it has passed the Unfair Contract Terms Act, 1977. This Act applies to consumer contracts and those based on standard terms and enables exception clauses to be applied with regard to what is just and reasonable. It is significant that Parliament refrained from legislating over the whole field of contract. After this Act, in commercial matters generally, when the parties are not of unequal bargaining power, and when risks are normally borne by insurance, not only is the case for judicial intervention undemonstrated, there is everything to be said, and this seems to have been Parliament's intention, for leaving the parties free to apportion the risks as they think fit and for respecting their decisions."

另外,也说是不像以前一样扭曲的解释免责条文,而要给予一般性但仍会是"严格"(strict)地解释。此外,免责条文也必须以清楚无误的文字表达。这在同一个先例,Diplock 勋爵说:"Since the presumption is that the parties by entering into the contract intended to accept the implied obligations exclusion clauses are to be construed strictly and the degree of strictness appropriate to be applied to their construction may properly depend upon the extent to which they involve departure from the implied obligations. Since the obligations implied by law in a commercial contract are those which, by judicial consensus over the years or by Parliament in passing a statute, have been regarded as obligations which a reasonable businessman would realize that he was accepting when he entered into a contract of a particular kind, the Court's view of the reasonableness of any departure from the implied obligations which would be involved in construing the express words of an exclusion clause in one sense that they are capable of bearing rather than another, is a relevant consideration in deciding what meaning the words were intended by the parties to bear. But this does not entitle the Court to reject the exclusion clause, however unreasonable the Court itself may think it is, **if the words are clear and fairly susceptible of one meaning only.**"(加黑部分是笔者的强调)

可以说,再引用 1980 年以前许多判例针对免责条文的解释时要极小心,因为现在不应该再采用扭曲的解释。

1.7.2 先例之二:Ailsa Craig Fishing Co Ltd v. Malvern Fishing Ltd

在 Ailsa Craig Fishing Co Ltd v. Malvern Fishing Ltd (1983) 1 W. L. R. 964, HL

这一先例,很巧合的是争议也是涉及警卫服务合约与同一个当事人 Securicor。它在一个提供港口警卫的服务合约中被认定履行合约有疏忽与要负责任,从而要赔偿原告的损失(一艘5.5万英镑的渔船)。但因为在合约中有明确条文规定每一次事故最多赔偿1000英镑(或如果在火灾与盗窃赔1万英镑),贵族院允许被告根据该条文限制责任。

1.7.3　针对免责条文的三种不同程度的严格性

虽然 Photo Productions Ltd v. Securicor Transport Ltd (1980) 1 Lloyd's Rep. 545 先例要求不再扭曲解释免责条文,但它仍是明确免责条文要适用"针对规则"(*contra proferentem*)。而免责条文有许多不同类别,解释起来的严格性也有三种不同程度的说法。

一是针对标准格式合约内的免责条文或是通过双方共同谈判拟定的免责条文,应是不适用针对规则。另一种更明显的例子是"相互免责条文"(mutually accepted clause),更是应该给一个"平衡的"(balanced)解释:Lloyds TSB General Insurance Holding v. Lloyds Bank Group Insurance Co Ltd (2003) UKHL 48 等先例。

二是针对一些限制责任的免责条文,如在较早前已经节录过的 Photo Productions Ltd v. Securicor Transport Ltd 先例的第2条文是限制赔偿责任在25,000英镑,针对这样的条文就应该以比较轻的严格性解释。这里的原因 Fraser 勋爵在 Ailsa Craig Fishing Co Ltd v. Malvern Fishing Ltd (1983) 1 W. L. R. 964, HL 先例有解释,说:"Later authorities which lay down very strict principles to be applied when considering the effect of clauses of exclusion or indemnity... In my opinion these principles are not applicable in their full rigor when considering the effect of the clauses merely limiting liability. Such clauses will of course be read *contra proferentem* and must be clearly expressed, but there is no reason why they should be judged by the specially exacting standards which are applied to exclusion and indemnity clauses. **The reason for imposing such standards on these clauses is the inherent improbability that the other party to a contract including such a clause intended to release the proferens from a liability that would otherwise fall upon him. But there is no such high degree of improbability that he would agree to a limitation of the liability of the preferens**, especially when, as explained in... the present contract, the potential losses that might be caused by the negligence of the proferens or its servants are so great in proportion to the sums that can reasonably be charged for the services contracted for. It is enough in the present case that the clause must be clear and unambiguous."(加黑部分是笔者的强调,Fraser 勋爵是说合约让获利方完全对其疏忽免责任有更大的潜在不可能性。但如果只是让获利方减轻责任,可减少赔偿,这一不可能性相对减低。)

三是要特别严格的解释,即免责条文是"排除责任条文与补偿条文"(exclusion and indemnity clauses)。要特别严格针对的原因在较早介绍的 Fraser 勋爵的判词中已经有解释,就是订约一方愿意让对方(获利方)免除其在合约或法律上应对自己负的责任的可能性几乎没有。所以双方如果真的想这样约定,合约的文字就要非常清楚无误、不含糊与只能有一种合理解释。

1.7.4 目前仍有的相悖理论(doctrine of repugnancy)

目前解释合约还有一种情况会否定或扭曲免责条文的适用,不管文字上写得怎样清楚无误。这主要是发生在免责条文违反了合约"目的"(purpose)的情况。这样解释免责条文的做法以前也一样,如在本书第四章之8.5段所介绍的Glynn v Margetson (1893) AC 351 先例。虽然1980年的Photo Productions Ltd v. Securicor Transport Ltd (1980) 1 Lloyd's Rep. 545 先例要求不要扭曲解释免责条文与否定了基本违约,但这个说法也仍存在。这是根据一个假设,即除非写得清清楚楚,否则不应该有订约意图把免责条文适用在一个违反"基本性条文"(fundamental term)的情况。正如Gerard McMeel 教授在《The Construction of Contracts—Interpretation, Implication and Rectification》(2007年)一书之21.12段中所说的,如下:"What remains is a rule of construction based on fundamental breach. This is linked to the generally strict approach to exemption clause. It is probably best characterized as a presumption that an exemption clause will not permit a party to commit a fundamental breach of contract unless it so provides by clear words. The principal manifestation is that a clause will be ignored or modified if it is inconsistent with the main object of the transaction."

也可以换一个说法是,订约方不会针对做某件事订一个合约但同时加入一条免责条文说,如果承诺方不做该事,也没有任何责任。这会导致该合约只是一份没有法律约束力的"意向书"(letter of intent),因为订约方承诺做又可以任意选择不做也不会有责任。

这可节录Brian Coote 先生的《Exception Clauses》(1964年)一书中的一个十分生动的例子:"Suppose, for example, that I sell a horse which I say is sound for jumping, but provide in the written agreement that I accept no responsibility whatever if the horse should prove unsound. What I am doing is to ensure that the purchaser has no primary contractual right to call for a horse which is sound for jumping. I am not contracting that the horse is sound and giving myself a shield in case of breach. I am simply refusing to contract on the point at all."

最后还可以另一个合约解释规则配合相悖理论来否定免责条文,这就是如果作出解释会导致合约的主要目的被否定,就会带来荒谬可笑的结果。正如Reid勋爵在Suisse Atlantique Societe D'Armement Maritime SA v. NV Rotterdamsche Kolen Centrale(1966) 1 Lloyd's Rep 529 先例中说:"... Or it may appear that the terms of the clause are so wide that they cannot be applied literally; that may be because this would lead to an absurdity or because it would defeat the main object of the contract . . . "[2]

根据相悖理论在 1980 年之后的判例,可作以下的介绍。

1.7.4.1　案例之一:Firestone Tyre Ltd. v. Vokins & Co. Ltd.

在 Firestone Tyre Ltd. v. Vokins & Co. Ltd. (1951) 1 Lloyd's Rep. 32 先例, Delvin 大法官说:"One may test the point by considering the construction of the contract if the phrase about pilferage of the goods were not there. The position would then be that the lightermen were saying: 'We will deliver your goods; we promise to deliver your goods at such and such a place, and in the condition in which we receive them, but we are not liable if they are lost or damaged from any cause whatsoever.' **That is not in a law a contract at all. It is illusory to say: 'We promise to do a thing but we are not liable if we do not do it'.** "(加黑部分是笔者的强调)

1.7.4.2　案例之二:Suisse Atlantique Societe D'Armement Maritime SA v. NV Rotterdamsche Kolen Centrale

在 Suisse Atlantique Societe D'Armement Maritime SA v. NV Rotterdamsche Kolen Centrale(1966) 1 Lloyd's Rep 529 先例,Wilberforce 勋爵说:"One may safely say that the parties cannot, in a contract, have contemplated that the clause should have **so wide an ambit as in effect to deprive one party's stipulations of all contractual force: to do so would be to reduce the contract to a mere declaration of intent.** To this extent it may be correct to say that there is a rule of law against the application of an exceptions clause to a particular type of breach. "(加黑部分是笔者的强调)

1.7.4.3　案例之三:Evans (J) & Son (Portsmouth) Ltd v. Merzario (Andrea) Ltd

在 Evans (J) & Son (Portsmouth) Ltd v. Merzario (Andrea) Ltd (1976) 1 WLR 1078 先例,Roskill 大法官说:"I ventured to ask . . . what the position would have been if when the defendants' first quotation had come along there had been stamped on the face of that quotation: 'No containers to be shipped on deck'; and the container had been shipped on deck. [Counsel] bravely said that the exemption clauses would still have applied. With great respect, that is an impossible argument. In the words which Devlin J. used . . . the defendants' promise that the container would be shipped on deck would be wholly illusory. "

1.7.4.4　案例之四:The "TFL Prosperity"

这个先例 The "TFL Prosperity" (1984) 1 Lloyd's Rep. 123 涉及一份期租合约,有关的船舶是一艘滚装船。承租人计划租用该船舶行走欧洲与中东之间的班轮航

[2]　如果会带来可笑的结果则可偏离字义上的解释的规则在本书多处有提及,包括第一章之第 5 段的"黄金规则"(golden rule)。

线,并在该船舶的主甲板放置堆装了40尺集装箱的托卡,这需要主甲板的高度必须是6.10米。这方面的船舶特征也在租约的第26条附加条文有明示。但在第一个航次从鹿特丹与其他欧洲港口装货后再去中东的Jeddah、迪拜、科威特与Damman港口卸货就出问题,在鹿特丹港发现船舶装不下这些托卡。事后量度主甲板的高度,只有6.05米。虽然只是相差一点,但关键就是装不下。该先例主要的争议是该期租租约(根据Baltime标准格式)的第13条免责条文可否保护船东。该免责条文是印本条文,而Baltime是著名的偏袒船东的标准格式,基本写法与金康租约一致。条文如下:"13. The Owners **only** to be responsible for delay in delivery of the Vessel or for delay during the currency of the Charter and for loss or damage to goods on board if such delay or loss has been caused by want of due diligence on the part of the Owners ... in making the vessel seaworthy and fitted for the voyage or any other personal act or omission or default of the Owners ... **The Owners not to be responsible in any other case nor for damage or delay whatsoever and howsoever caused ...** "

高院与贵族院的判决均认为该条文在文字上是针对在履行中的责任问题(如它针对晚了交船、租约期内的延误、船上货物的损坏与适航等方面),不像是有意图针对这种对船舶细节/特征的误述与合约承诺。高院的Bingham大法官是这样说:"the particular incidents mentioned in clause 13 suggested that that clause was concerned with claims arising from and during the operation of the vessel under the charter but the second sentence was drawn in very wide terms; since the parties had provided in clause 26, very precise details of a large number of structural mechanical and other features of the vessel, it was inconceivable that the parties intended the owners to be immune from liability in respect of breaches of clause 26, at least so far as the structural statistics of the vessel were concerned and a breach of these detailed provisions relating to matters outside the scope of clause 13 had to be regarded as falling outside the ambit of the protection afforded by that clause. ... "

但上诉庭将Bingham大法官的判决推翻,认为需要全面解释合约与尽量给每一条文/文字有一定的意思,所以判第26条文(长达两页纸的关于所有船舶细节/特征)不受第13条免责条文的影响是不可接受的做法。毕竟,第26条文中的一些船舶细节/特征如"船速"(speed)会影响第13条文中特别针对的一些履行中的责任问题,如迟延交船与租约期内的延误。第13条免责条文即使有效,也不会导致第26条文毫无意义(即船东对船舶细节/特征的陈述变为空话),因为承租人虽然不能索赔,但可以根据1967年的《误述法》终止合约。Donaldson大法官这样说:"Nevertheless this gives clause 26 some scope since misdescription can produce delay or damage to the goods and it would also leave a right of rejection. Furthermore, although this is not an aid to construction, the charterers would remain free, in appropriate cases, to avoid clause 13 under the Misrepresentation Act, 1967. If the argument which appealed to Mr.

Justice Bingham is to be accepted, it would I think follow that all the added clauses took effect free of clause 13 and this seems to me to be an impossible construction."

看来,这又是大家看法不一致与各有侧重地解释合约导致不同判决的好例子。但最后还是以贵族院的说法为准,而贵族院是支持Bingham大法官的相悖理论判法,认为从解释合约角度来说第13条免责条文并非有意图保护对第26条的违反。Roskill大法官这样说:"In truth **if clause 13 were to be construed so as to allow a breach of the warranties as to description in clause 26 to be committed or a failure to deliver the vessel at all to take place without financial redress to the charterers, the charter** virtually ceases to be a contract for the letting of the vessel and the performance of services by the owners, their master, officers and crew in consideration of the payment of time charter hire and **becomes no more than a statement of intent by the owners** in return for which the charterers are obliged to pay large sums by way of hire, though if the owners fail to carry out their promises as to description on delivery, are entitled to nothing in lieu. I find it difficult to believe that this can accord with the true common intention of the parties and I do not think that this conclusion can accord with the true construction of the charter in which the parties in the present case are supposed to have expressed that true common intention in writing."(加黑部分是笔者的强调)

1.7.4.5 案例之五:The "Chanda"

这个先例The "Chanda"(1989)2 Lloyd's Rep. 494涉及的是一份提单合约,包括有一条首要条文合并了1924年《海牙规则》。众所周知的是,《海牙规则》中有一个货物"件装的赔偿责任限制"(package limitation)。

在该案例中,案情是运送一座贵重机器(用来制造与弄干柏油)从德国去沙特阿拉伯。由于该机器的控制台有复杂的电子与电脑设备,价值高昂,占整座机器价值的90%。但可惜的是,船东在没有授权下把该控制台装在甲板上,结果在航次中途遇上10级风的坏天气,导致捆绑断裂与货物移动。最后船舶到了沙特阿拉伯的Jeddah港卸货,该控制台严重损坏,港口当局不允许其卸下。最后该控制台被抛弃,而要另付运一台新的控制台作为替代。之后,买方就向船东提出索赔。看来,责任应该非常明确,因为船东在没有授权下私自把控制台装在甲板。但船东的抗辩之一是即使要负责任,也可以根据《海牙规则》限制赔偿责任在1250德国马克。注意这是属于限制责任条文,理论上应该没有这么严格针对船东来解释(可见本章之1.7.3段)。但Hirst大法官判是相悖理论适用,说:

"... I am quite satisfied that that **neither ... case rested on the discredited fundamental breach rule, but rather on a principle of construction**, ... that clauses which are clearly intended to protect the shipowner provide he honours his contractual obligations to stow goods under deck do not apply if he is in breach of that obligation ... as Lord Wilberforce said, this rule is quite clearly based on contractual intention.

I am satisfied that the package limitation clause falls fairly and squarely within this category, since it can hardly have been intended to protect the shipowner who, as a result of the breach, exposed the cargo in question to such palpable risk of damage. Otherwise the main purpose of the shipowners' obligation to stow below deck would be seriously undermined....

As a result I hold that the package limitation clause, **being repugnant to and inconsistent with the obligation to stow below deck, was inapplicable.**"(加黑部分是笔者的强调)

从上述的判决可见,通过合约解释认为在这种基本违反合约的做法下(就是把控制台装在甲板),双方不会有订约意图让船东仍可享受责任限制。

1.7.4.6 案例之六:Motis v. Dampskibsselskabet

Motis v. Dampskibsselskabet (2000) 1 Lloyd's Rep. 211 先例是一个无单放货的案件,但船东是相当无辜,因为有人以假造的提单提走货物。船东的抗辩就是根据提单的一条广泛免责条文,说明货物一旦从船上卸下,船东就对货物的损失没有任何责任。条文是:"... the Carrier shall have **no liability whatsoever** for any loss or damage to the goods while in its actual or constructive possession before loading or **after discharge over ship's rail**, or if applicable, on the ship's ramp, **however caused.**"(加黑部分是笔者的强调)

由于无单放货是货物从船上卸下后发生的事情,所以船东就依赖上述的免责条文作出抗辩。其中一个船东给的比喻是货物从船上卸下后被"盗窃"(theft),上述免责条文应该适用。现在的情况是有人以假造提单提走货物,本质上与被盗窃没有不同。但 Rix 大法官在高院判无单放货与盗窃是两码事,而前者是非常严重的事。上诉庭同意,Stuart - Smith 大法官说:"In my judgment(该免责条文)is not apt on its natural meaning to cover delivery by the carrier or his agent, albeit the delivery was obtained by fraud. I also agree with the Judge that even if the language was apt to cover such a case, it is not a construction which should be adopted, involving as it does excuse from performance and obligation of such fundamental importance."

1.7.4.7 案例之七:The "Irbenskiy Proliv"

这一先例 The "Irbenskiy Proliv" (2005) 1 Lloyd's Rep. 383 涉及 19 份班轮提单下的货损索赔,而该 19 份提单合约中第 4 条免责条文非常广泛与细致,免责条文中的文字包括"however caused"、"or otherwise howsoever"、"arising or resulting from ... any other cause whatsoever"这种最广泛的用字。

在该先例中,有要求高院决定一个"预先争议"(preliminary issue),就是船东可否依赖提单的第 4 条免责条文而对该货损免责。

货方认为第 4 条文应该被排除,因为它与整个合约的目的有矛盾与相悖。否则,根据一般与自然的解释看第 4 条文,船东对不履行合约或怎样履行合约有完全的自由。

在高院,Ian Glick 大法官认为第 4 条文与提单合约的目的相悖。而且,它会令整个合约变成只是一份意向书,因为船东可以完全不顾合约的承诺,如单方面与没有任何理由地拒绝把货物运到卸港,但根据第 4 条文仍无须负责。Ian Glick 大法官这样说:

"The common law's approach to the construction of contracts, however, is not a literalist one. This is illustrated by *Glynn v. Margetson & Co.* itself, which was decided in 1893, and is even more clearly the case today: see, for example, the speech of Lord Steyn in *Sirus International Insurance Company (Publ) v. FAI General Insurance Ltd.*, (2004) *UKHL* 54, at par. 19.

If to give words in a contract, 'their full and complete meaning', would produce a result at odds with the main object of the contract then, as Lord Herschell, L. C. made clear in*Glynn v. Margetson & Co.* (at pp. 354 to 355), the Court will put upon those words a restricted meaning. In some cases, as Lord Halsbury pointed out (at p. 357), the Court may have to reject words, or even whole provisions, if they are inconsistent with the main purpose of the contract.

More commonly, however, and wherever possible, the Court will attribute to the words used a meaning consistent with that purpose.

In the present case it is in my judgement plain that the words, 'however caused', 'or otherwise howsoever' and 'arising or resulting from... any other cause whatsoever', when considered in their context as parts of contracts for the carriage of goods from one port to another, do not operate to relieve the carrier of liability for any and every breach of contract. These words bear a restricted meaning. They do not cover, for example, loss or damage **caused by dishonesty** on the part of the carrier. Whether this is because of a rule of law, or a principle of construction does not matter: the result is that the carrier would be liable for a breach of contract caused by its dishonesty. Moreover the words would not be strong enough to relieve the carrier from liability for loss of or damage to the goods caused by it arbitrarily refusing to ship them to the port of discharge at all. The clause shifts most risks which might result in loss of or damage to the goods shipped from the carrier to the holder of the bill of lading. But that is not inconsistent with the purpose of a commercial contract of carriage where the bearer of risk can insure against it.

In my judgement it is unnecessary, and indeed impossible, to imagine all circumstances in which it might be said by the carrier that clause 4 applies, and where a Court might have todecide whether it does or not. The fact that the application of the clause may have to be determined case by case does not make its meaning uncertain.

Moreover the principle that, in cases of doubt a contractual provision will be construed against the person who produced it, and for whose benefit it operates, **does not extend to construing a contractual provision as widely as possible so as to render it repugnant to the main object of the contract read as a whole** when it can be given a meaning consistent with that object.

For the reasons given above, in my view, clause 4 does not operate to relieve the carrier of all secondary obligations under the contracts. It follows that the question whether, if it did have the effect of reducing the contracts to mere declarations of intent, it should be rejected, falls away."(加黑部分是笔者的强调)

在上述判决第一处加黑的强调是说免责条文使用怎样广泛的用字都不能对不诚实或"欺诈"(fraud)免责,这是违反"公共政策"(public policy),不存在有订约自由,这可见本章之1.10段。这方面有关的先例有:HIH Casualty and General Insurance Ltd v Chase Manhattan Bank (2003) 2 Lloyd's Rep 61 与 Frans Maas (UK) Ltd v Samsung Electronics (UK) Ltd (2004) 2 Lloyd's Rep 251 等。

1.7.4.8 案例之八:Internet Broadcasting Corp v. MAR LLC (t/a MARHedge)

在 Internet Broadcasting Corp v. MAR LLC (t/a MARHedge) (2009) 2 Lloyd's Rep. 295 先例,Gabriel Moss QC 大法官说:"The principles I deduce from the authorities which are relevant to the present type of case of deliberate, repudiatory breach involving personal wrongdoing are as follows: (1) There is no rule of law applicable and the question is one of construction.... (5) Words which, in a literal sense, cover a deliberate repudiatory breach will not be construed so as to do so if that would defeat the 'main object' of the contract. (7) Words which in a literal sense cover a deliberate repudiatory breach cannot be relied upon if they are 'repugnant' ..."

1.8 什么是严格解释

在上述的小段已经提到现在解释免责条文,再也不会扭曲解释,但也提到法院还是会作出严格的解释。而且如果免责条文有含糊之处,就会针对获利方解释,也就是"针对规则"(*contra proforentem*)。这样,笔者想进一步探讨这个方面,特别是严格的解释会怎么样看待免责条文。

解释免责条文的文字在目前的先例中权威说法是有两种态度:一是要求文字清楚;二是只要求自然、平易的意思。但可以说在大部分的案件适用这两种态度最后的结果都不会有太大区别,所以不多提。只节录在 Stocznia Gdynia SA v Gearbulk Holdings Ltd (2009) 1 Lloyd's Rep 461 先例,上诉庭的 Moore - Bick 大法官说:"Mr Dunning(船厂代表大律师) submitted that since that decision the approach of the courts to the construction of exclusion clauses has developed in favour of a greater willingness to give them the meaning which the words used would naturally bear. I would accept that, but I would not accept his suggestion that as **the law stands today there are two competing approaches struggling for supremacy: one requiring clear express words, the**

other favouring the natural meaning of the words used. It is important to remember that any clause in a contract must be construed in the context in which one finds it, both the immediate context of the other terms and the wider context of the transaction as a whole. The court is unlikely to be satisfied that a party to a contract has abandoned valuable rights arising by operation of law unless the terms of the contract make it sufficiently clear that that was intended. The more valuable the right, **the clearer the language will need to be.**"(加黑是笔者的强调)

看来,法律还是要求免责条文的用字清楚无误,即使是严格解释的程度在不同类别与合理性的免责条文有差异。这样可看看怎样的用字才算是清楚无误。

1.8.1 什么是清楚无误之一:不可能有误解

这可以节录在 White v Warwick (John) & Co Ltd (1953) 1 WLR 1285 先例,Denning 大法官说:"In this type of case, two principles are well settled. The first is that, if a person desires to exempt himself from a liability which the common law imposes on him, he can do so by a contract freely and deliberately entered into by the injured party **in words that are clear beyond the possibility of misunderstanding.**"

1.8.2 什么是清楚无误之二:条文/文字只能有一个解释

这可节录在 Photo Productions Ltd v. Securicor Transport Ltd (1980) 1 Lloyd's Rep. 545 先例,Diplock 勋爵说:"But this does not entitle the Court to reject the exclusion clause, however unreasonable the Court itself may think it is, if **the words are clear and fairly susceptible of one meaning only.**"(加黑部分是笔者的强调)

1.8.3 什么是清楚无误之三:不要用新词或怪字

在 L. N W. R. v Neilson (1922) AC 263 先例,火车公司的标准合约中的免责条文是说明对货物运输不负责"loss, damage, **misconveyance**, delay or detention"。双方事后对加黑的一词有争议,在上诉庭,Scrutton 大法官这样说:"... he must use ordinary English and not inventive word of doubtful meaning."

这在贵族院也被认同,其中 Sumner 勋爵说:"... it is so wrapped up in deliberate obscurity as to be unavailable to the railway company, when read, as it should be, *contra proferentem.*"

1.8.4 什么是清楚无误之四:与合约其他条文一并看会带来含糊

在 Elderslie Steamship Co Ltd v Borthwick (1905) AC 93 先例,Macnaghten 勋爵说:"The clause which has been called the large print clause seems to me to be perfectly clear. The small print clause is equally clear. For my part I am unable to reconcile the two clauses. In such a case an ambiguous document is no protection."

1.8.5 什么是清楚无误之五:条文/文字有一个以上的解释

这种情况有不少,所以也带来不少先例。免责条文的文字如果可以有一个以上或通常是两个解释,根据针对规则就会作出不利获利方的解释。简单举个类似 Hollier v Rambler Motors (AMC) Ltd (1972) 2 QB 71 先例的例子,对"火灾"(fire)免责。火灾可以是与获利方无关的原因所引起,但也可以是与获利方有关的原因(如他或是他的雇员疏忽、维修保养不妥善等)所引起。这样对火灾的解释,对获利方不利的解释就会只局限在与获利方无关原因引起的火灾。

再举一个航运有关的例子,就是在国际上最普遍被使用的期租租约标准格式合约的 NYPE 46,在第 16 条文的一条相互免责条文是说:"... The act of God, enemies, fire, restrain of Princess, Rulers and People, and all dangers and accidents of the Seas, Rivers, Machinery, Boilers and Steam Navigation, and **errors of Navigation** throughout this Charter Party, always mutually excepted..."

上述加黑部分是有关的免责事项,文字上没有说是航行疏忽。但在航运,航行疏忽还是很大的风险。而历史上一直都允许船东免责,如在 1924 年的《海牙规则》或中国《海商法》,都允许船东免责。这里的问题是上述免责条文的"航行错误"(errors of navigation)是否包括了"航行疏忽"(negligence in navigation)。这方面的争议可参见杨大明律师的《期租合同》一书第三十七篇之 37.2.4 段。

以 The "Emmanuel C"先例的案情为例,该船舶涉及一个航次期租合约,但船舶装港时发生搁浅并导致全损。搁浅是由于航行疏忽所导致。由于船舶去不了装港装货导致承租人蒙受损失,他向船东提出 12 万美元的索赔。这被判是船东不能依赖航行错误的免责而需要赔偿这笔钱。

以下对这个严格解释的说法可节录一些权威先例:

1. 在 Price & Co v Union Lighterage Co (1904) 1 KB 412 先例,Alverstone 勋爵说:"... when a clause in such a contract as this is capable of two constructions, one of which will make it applicable where there is no negligence on the part of the carrier or his servants, and the other will make it applicable where there is such negligence, it requires special words to make the clause over non – liability in case of negligence."

2. 在 Lee (John) & Son (Grantham) Ltd v Railway Executive (1949) 2 All ER 581 先例,Evershed MR 大法官说:"We are presented with two alternative readings of this document and the reading which one should adopt is to be determined, among other things, by a consideration of the fact that the defendants put forward the document. ... I think the rule *contra proferentem* should applied ..."

3. 在 Hollins v Davy (J) Ltd (1963) 1 QB 844 先例,Sachs 大法官说:"I need, of course, hardly add that all exemption clauses are construed *contra proferentem* so that if there were here two reasonable constructions of a word or phrase, then the construction least favourable to the defendants will be adopted."

1.8.6 什么是清楚无误之六:条文/文字必须严格针对要求免责的事项

免责条文的用字必须针对要求免责的事项,这个严格解释一直存在,目前还是以这一原则作出解释。简单地说,如果对"火灾"(fire)免责,就不会对一些接近的事项免责,如爆炸或是发热。

这方面也带来了无数先例,可小部分节录如下:

1. 在 Wallis Son & Wells v Pratt & Haynes (1911) A. C. 394, HL 先例,法院判是免责条文中的"warranty"一词不包括"condition"。类似的先例还有 Baldry v Marshall (1925) 1 KB 260,在该先例,买方告诉卖方他想买一辆舒适与适合作为旅行用途的汽车。合约排除了"any other guarantee or warranty, statutory or otherwise"。之后证明该汽车并不舒适,也不适合作为旅行用途。法院判是"舒适与适合作为旅行用途"是"condition",不包括在免责条文的"any other guarantee or warranty"。

2. 在 Beck & Co v Szymanowski (K) & Co (1924) AC 43 先例,相关的时效条文是:"... **the goods delivered** shall be deemed to be in all respects in accordance with the contract and the buyers shall be bound to accept and pay for the same accordingly **unless the sellers shall within** 14 **days after the arrival of the goods at their destination receive from the buyers notice** of any matter or thing by reason whereof they may allege that the goods are not in accordance with the contract. (加黑部分是笔者的强调)" 法院判是时效条文只针对已经交付的货物,而短交货物的争议不受该时效条文的约束。

3. 在 Andrews Brothers (Bournemouth) Ltd v Singer and Co Ltd (1934) 1 KB 17 先例,合约明示规定是买卖一辆新车。相关的免责条文可节录如下:"all conditions, warranties and liabilities **implied** by statute common law or otherwise are excluded."但之后卖方交付的并不是一辆新车,法院判是免责条文只针对默示条文,而新车是合约的明示条文,卖方不能依赖该条文免责。

4. 在 Kendall (Henry) & Sons v Lillico (William) & Sons (1969) 2 AC 31 先例,相关的买卖合约有条文排除"潜在缺陷"(latent defect)带来的责任。法院判是该免责条文不能排除 1979 年英国《货物销售法》下"合理适合用途"(reasonably fit for purpose)的默示责任。

5. 在 Dorest County Council v Southern Felt Roofing (1989) 48 BLR 96 先例,建筑合约中规定雇主要承担由于"fire, lightning, explosion, aircraft and other aerial devices"所造成损失的风险与责任。判是部分风险如闪电不涉及人为的疏忽,所以条文也不够清楚让承建商在由于疏忽所导致的火灾并造成损失的情况下免责。

6. 在 Pegler Ltd v Wang (UK) Ltd (2000) BLR 218 先例,案情涉及供应电脑硬件与软件,合约中有条文限制运行与使用供应的电脑硬件与软件带来的责任。法院判是该条文只针对已经提供的电脑硬件与软件,不包括延误提供带来的责任。

7. 在 Insight Vacations Pty Ltd v Young (2011) HCA 11 先例,案情涉及旅行社的旅游合约,其中的免责条文是如下:"Where the passenger **occupies a motorcoach seat** fitted with a safety belt, neither the Operators nor their agents or co - operating organizations will be liable for any injury, illness or death or for any damages or claims whatsoever arising from any accident or incident, if the safety belt is not being worn at the time

of such accident or incident."旅行途中,一位游客从旅游大巴的座位上站起来拿放在行李架上的行李时,旅游大巴突然刹车,导致该游客摔倒并受伤。法院判是因为当时游客没有坐在座位上,该免责条文不适用。

1.9 疏忽免责条文的解释

以下针对不同类别的免责条文,其中针对疏忽的免责最经常见到。本质上,这种免责条文十分不合理与不大可能。因为根据普通法的默示地位,合约方要为自己以及雇员/代理人的疏忽所造成的损失负责,否则损失变为要无辜的对方负责显然很奇怪。正如 Fraser 勋爵在 Ailsa Craig Fishing Co Ltd v. Malvern Fishing Ltd (1983) 1 W. L. R. 964, HL 先例中说的,如下:"... the inherent improbability that the other party to a contract including such a clause intended to release the proferens from a liability that would otherwise fall upon him."

在订约自由下,如果双方的订约意图确是豁免疏忽方的责任,疏忽的后果反过来是要无辜方承担,就需要在条文/文字上清楚无误写明并且会理解到将来有了争议法院或仲裁庭会作出严格地解释。

1.9.1 对疏忽的免责条文必须严格解释的原因

这一方面在本章之第 1.8 段已经有了很多介绍,在本段只是更加针对疏忽的免责条文。但即使这样,还是有很多地方相同,笔者尽量不重复。

在 Hollier v. Ramble Motors (A. M. C.) Ltd (1972) 2 Q. B. 71 先例,该修理汽车的发票中有条文说"对火灾免责"(not responsible for damage caused by fire to customer's cars on the premises)。事后修车厂发生火灾,原因涉及修车厂疏忽没有检查与维修保养电线线路。上诉庭判是火灾可以由很多原因造成,排除因为修车厂的疏忽引起火灾也不表示这一免责条文失去了任何意思。而且,该条文因为对火灾可以有几种解释,所以是含糊而可适用针对规则。Salmon 大法官说是要对疏忽免责,必须文字的表面可以让一般非文盲与讲道理的人士一看就明了(its meaning plain on its face to any ordinary literate and sensible person)。另外,Latey 大法官也同意并说在文字上必须对一个没有受过法律训练的人士来说也可以有足够的理解,即修车厂不必对火灾负责,即使是由于他的过错而引起(the words used were not adequate to convey to a layperson that the garage would not be liable even if they were at fault)。

同样的解释也在 The "Super Servant Two" (1990) 1 Lloyd's Rep. 1 先例被适用在一条"不可抗力"(*force majeure*)条文,案件将在本书第十三章之第 1.5 段有介绍。

最后节录 Donaldson 大法官在 The "Raphael" (1982) 2 Lloyd's Rep. 42 先例中所说的:"When parties make an agreement governing their future relationship, human nature being on balance more inclined to optimism than pessimism, the parties are more likely to be thinking in terms of non – negligent rather than negligent performance of the contract. The law reflects this fact of life by assuming that if there are two potential grounds of liability, both of them real and foreseeable, but one involves negligence, *pri-*

ma facie any words of exemption will be directed at the non – negligent ground of liability."(当双方订约时,人性总是倾向乐观多于悲观。所以想到的通常是履约时万事顺境,不会涉及有疏忽的出现导致麻烦。法律为了反映这个人性的事实,就要假设如果文字上可以有两个不同的解释,但其中一个涉及疏忽而另一个并不涉及疏忽,免责条文就只是针对没有疏忽所导致的责任。)

对疏忽的免责条文严格解释也符合本书第四章之第10段与第七章之10.3段针对的一方不能通过他的错误获利,所以明示条文必须要写得清楚明确才能超越这个重要的法律默示地位。

1.9.2 除非相悖理论适用,否则必须给免责条文一定的意思

在本章1.7.1段已经提到Photo Productions Ltd v. Securicor Transport Ltd (1980) 1 Lloyd's Rep. 545先例判是不扭曲解释免责条文与否定了基本违约的说法,变为唯一可否定或扭曲解释免责条文的情况,就是在本章之1.7.4段介绍的"相悖理论"(doctrine of repugnancy)。但如果免责条文并没有违反合约目的,也就是相悖理论不适用,在解释时就必须让免责条文有一定的意思。这是本书第三章之第1段所讲的合约条文/文字都必须尽量给其一定的意思。

这就会带来一些困难与有趣的分析。如每个案件的"语境"(context)不同,对违约方会带来的法律默示责任不尽相同。虽然免责条文有同样的文字,但在一个案件中可免责,而在另一个案件中就不能免责。

以航运的"公共承运人"(common carrier)的责任为例,普通法认为他需要对货物的运输承担严格责任。但"火车承运人"(railway carrier)与一般的"受托人"(bailee)一样,只在托管期间有疏忽或过错,才需要承担责任。这样,如果有一条没有特别说明疏忽的免责条文,但用字广泛可以包括在疏忽或没有疏忽的事项,就会对火车承运人适用,因为他的责任只会是有疏忽才需要承担。在解释该免责条文必须要给其一定意思的原则下,就只能让它针对唯一需要承担责任的疏忽,否则免责条文没有意思。但同样文字的免责条文对航运的公共承运人(如班轮公司/集装箱公司)就不适用,因为在严格责任下不管疏忽与否,他仍要负责任,该免责条文大可以适用在没有疏忽下产生的责任。这说法可见Donaldson大法官在The "Raphael" (1982) 2 Lloyd's Rep. 42先例中所说的:"Thus in *Rutter v. Palmer*, (1922) 2 K. B. 87 Lord Justice Bankes contrasts the position of the common carrier and the railway carrier with that of the ordinary bailee. The former operate subject to liabilities independently of negligence; the latter do not. Similar words may therefore protect the bailee from liability for negligence, although they will not protect the carriers. A similar approach has been adopted by the law in relation to the implied warranty of initial seaworthiness. Here the parties are more likely to contemplate negligence than breach of the initial warranty, and accordingly an exception which in terms covers negligence does not protect the shipowner where the negligence has led to beach of the warranty: *Gilroy v. Price*, [1893] A. C. 56."

在 Donaldson 大法官的讲话中提到的 1922 年 Rutter v. Palmer 先例中,Scrutton 大法官所讲的也可以节录如下:"In construing an exemption clause certain general rules may be applied: First the defendant is not exempted from liability for the negligence of his servants unless adequate words are used; Secondly, the liability of the defendant apart from the exempting words must be ascertained; then the particular clause in question must be considered; and if the only liability of the party pleading the exemption is a liability for negligence, the clause will more readily operate to exempt him."

另也可节录 Greene 勋爵在 Alderlade v. Hendon Laundry Ltd (1945) 1 K. B. 189 先例中同样针对的说法,如下:"The effect of those authorities can I think be stated as follows: where the head of damage in respect of which limitation of liability is sought to be imposed by such a clause is one which rests on negligence and nothing else, the clause must be construed as extending to that head of damage because it would otherwise lack subject - matter. Where, on the other hand, the head of damage may be based on some ground other than that the clause must be confined in its application to loss occurring through that other cause, to the exclusion of loss arising through negligence."

在这个课题,最后多举一个案例名为 The "Kheti" (1949) 82 Ll. L. Rep. 525。案情是有关付运的洋葱发生损坏与短缺,该批洋葱是从埃及运去英国利物浦。根据提单合约,其印本第一条是合并了 1924 年的英国《海上货物运输法》,也就是 1924 年《海牙规则》。在《海牙规则》下,众所周知是它在 Article 3 要求船舶在航次前要"恪尽职责令船舶适航"(due diligence to make the ship seaworthy)。另也要求船东/承运人要"妥善与小心地装载、处理、堆装、付运、保管、照顾与卸下货物"(properly and carefully load, handle, stow, carry, keep, care for, and discharge the goods carried)。但在该提单的左边空白之处另有紫色的印章加上了一条"洋葱条文"(onion clause),内容是:

"It is specially agreed that no liability for loss or damage to and/or deterioration in onions shall attach to the master and/or owners of the steamer, even if such loss, damage and/or deterioration result from a cause for which but for this special agreement to the contrary, the steamer would have been liable.

The steamer shall not be responsible for obliteration of marks and numbers, delay in delivering or incorrect delivery involving loss whether in quality, condition, or other account, nor for protraction of voyage through any cause whatever."

有争议的第一段是说明船东/船长对货损货差免责,这包括如果没有这个约定,船东/船长本来可能需要承担的责任。

该案例的争议是船东是否对疏忽堆装货物要承担责任。显然,根据《海上货物运输法》的 Article 3,船东/船长要妥善与小心堆装货物。疏忽堆装显然是没有尽到责任,船东/船长需要负责。但多了一条"洋葱条文",是否说明了船东本来有责任,也在现在的约定下(就是可免责的洋葱条文)变为没有责任? 如果不是这样解释,怎能给这条洋葱条文一定的意思? 所以,最后的判决是"洋葱条文"所能针对的只是在船长因为疏忽而没有妥善与小心地装载、处理、堆装、付运、保管、照顾与卸下货物的情况。

1924 年的《海上货物运输法》不像 1971 年的《海上货物运输法》,后者是根据 1968 年《海牙—维斯比规则》,适用面有所扩大。在 1924 年的立法,它只适用从英国装货出口去其他外国港口的海上运输。换言之,它不强制适用在本案例利物浦卸货的航次。如果强制,就存在立法禁止船东以订约自由减轻责任,这就变为该"洋葱条文"其实无效。但由于不强制适用,本案例下的《海上货物运输法》只是凭合约法把立法合并在提单的第一条文。合并条文只是印本条文,所以分量上是比不上以紫色印章加上的"洋葱条文",所以非得把它们协调解释。而且,"洋葱条文"是为了装运洋葱而被双方特意加在提单的特定条文。所以作出解释,这洋葱条文的分量肯定要重得多。

1.9.3 疏忽免责条文解释的三个考验

加拿大上诉去了枢密院的著名先例 Canada Steamship Lines Ltd v. The King (1952) 1 Lloyd's Rep. 1(案情请看本书第五章之 6.6.3 段)中,Morton 勋爵对疏忽免责条文(该先例涉及一条"补偿条文"[indemnity clause],但解释的原则一致)解释的三种不同情况概括与分析如下:

"(1) If the clause contains language which expressly exempts the person in whose favour it is made (hereafter called 'the proferens') from the consequences of the negligence of his own servants, effect must be given to that provision. (补偿条文明确说明雇员的疏忽后果免责,这样作出解释就必须给它这个意思。)

(2) If there is no express reference to negligence, the court must consider whether the words are wide enough, in their ordinary meaning, to cover negligence on the part of the servants of the proferens. If a doubt arises at this point, it must be resolved against the proferens. (如果补偿条文没有明示针对疏忽,法院就需要考虑条文/文字是否作出一般解释是足够广泛包括雇员的疏忽。如果有怀疑,就必须作出对获利方不利的解释。)

(3) If the words used are wide enough for the above purpose, the court must then consider whether 'the head of damage may be based on some ground other than negligence'.... The 'other ground' must not be so fanciful or remote that the proferens cannot be supposed to have desired protection against it; but subject to this qualification ... the existence of a possible head of damage other than that of negligence is fatal to the proferens even if the words used are *prima facie* wide enough to cover negligence on the part of his servants."(这就是在本章之 1.8.5 段与 1.9.2 段所针对的情况。)

这在后来的一些相关案例中,经常会被说成是 Morton 勋爵的三个"考验"

(tests)。第一个考验其实最简单与明确，但现实中很少见，即依赖免责的订约方写明可对他或他的雇员疏忽的后果免责。这样明确写明疏忽免责的典型例子是在1924年的《海牙规则》，但这个航行疏忽的免责在最近几十年来不断受到批评，导致1980年的《汉堡规则》与在联合国通过但还没有生效的《鹿特丹规则》都排除了对船东/承运人航行疏忽的免责。

Morton勋爵的第二个考验是没有明示写明疏忽的免责，但有其他十分广泛的文字，根据一般性的解释，可与"疏忽"一词同义或可以包括获利方雇员的疏忽。这种情况在现实中很多，也比较容易在订约时被对方接受或被瞒骗过。这种文字在本章稍后1.9.4段会介绍，如"不为"(omission)，或是整条条文的如金康租约的免责条文[3]等。这种条文/文字，如果写法会带来一定的怀疑或含糊，就要适用针对规则针对获利方解释。

Morton勋爵第三个考验，也是针对足够广泛与可以包括疏忽的条文/文字。但法院还要进一步考虑受害方向获利方提出索赔是否必须依赖获利方的疏忽，或还会有其他的根据(如有其他的严格责任)。这根据当然要合情合理，但如果有其他根据，这足够广泛的免责条文就不足以保障获利方了。这可举上一小段介绍过的例子，就是航运的公共承运人，如果不把货物运到目的地，货方就可以提出索赔，而且不必理会公共承运人有疏忽与否，因为他是有必须完成航次的严格责任，只除了在普通法的绝少数的免责下(天意与公敌)可逃避责任。这样，海上运输合约的免责条文中只在一般解释下足够广泛(如说："整个海上运输是货方的风险，船东不负责")但没有明示疏忽就不足以对疏忽免责了。

在Canada Steamship Lines Ltd v. The King先例是有关Morton勋爵的第三种考验，可先节录起争议的第7条免责条文："That the lessee (船公司作为租用人) shall not have any claim or demand against the lessor (加拿大政府作为出租人) for detriment, damage or injury of any nature to the said land, the said shed, the said platform and the said canopy, or to any motor or other vehicles, materials, supplies, goods, articles, effects or things at any time brought, placed, made or being upon the said land, the said platform or in the said shed."

上述免责条文没有明示疏忽。双方争议是即使上述文字是足够广泛包括出租人雇员的疏忽(他们在维修码头货棚时，因疏忽而造成火灾)，租用人的大律师也举了三种情况会是与出租人疏忽与否无关但可以起到保护出租人的责任。换言之，这一条免责条文解释起来不会没有意思。第一种情况是根据《魁北克省民法典》第1614条，规定出租人所出租的东西如果有缺陷，即使出租人不知情，也要对后果负责。这表示码头货棚在出租期间因为缺陷而整个屋顶倒塌，但这事故完全不涉及出租人的疏忽与过错，在这种情况下，租用人向出租人索赔损失，后者就可以有效地依赖上述

[3] 条文可见本章之1.9.4.6段。

第7条免责条文。第二种是在民法典第1612(3)条,情况会是出租人(加拿大政府)把码头货棚旁边的一块地出租给其他人或授权第三方进行一些活动,但第三方/其他人对码头货棚造成了损坏。这样,也是与出租人的疏忽毫无关系,但面对租用人根据民法典的索赔,就可以依赖第7条免责条文了。第三种是民法典的第1617条与第1660条,情况会是有非法闯入的人士并造成破坏,如放火。这样租用人如果没有办法得到其他救济,就会根据民法典要求出租人减租,这也会是包括在第7条免责条文,而且与疏忽没有关系。

但出租人的代表大律师认为这种例子是想象力太丰富与遥远,不足以影响第7条免责条文足够广泛针对雇员的疏忽。枢密院不同意,认为订约双方在订约时不会没有想到民法典。Morton勋爵是这样说:"It was contended on behalf of the Crown(加拿大政府) that these instances of possible claims for damages were fanciful and remote, and would not have been within the contemplation of the parties when the terms of the lease were agreed. No doubt there may be cases in which it may be difficult to draw the line. In the present case, however, their Lordships are not prepared to assume that the obligations imposed upon lessors by the Civil Code were not in the minds of the parties. They think that the Crown may well have desired to protect itself from claims for damage arising out of any breach of these obligations, and yet may not have intended to go so far as to stipulate for protection from claims for damage resulting from negligence of its servants."

上述的Canada Steamship Lines Ltd v. The King先例中所谓的Morton勋爵的三个考验,在后来的不少有关先例有涉及。其中在Investors Compensation Scheme c. West Bromwich Building Society (1998) 1 W. L. R. 896先例有讲到这三个考验是否是"思维包袱"(intellectual baggage)的其中一种而要被丢掉。但在后来的贵族院先例H. I. H. Casualty and General Insurance Ltd v. Chase Manhattan Bank (2003) 2 Lloyd's Rep. 61,又再度明确Morton勋爵的三个考验还是十分有用的指引,但解释时还是要多考虑案件的背景,尤其是针对商业案件。Bingham勋爵是这样说:"There can be no doubting the general authority of these principles, which have been applied in many cases, and the approach in many cases, and the approach indicated is sound. The courts should not ordinarily infer that a contracting party has given up rights which the law confers on him to an extent greater than the contract terms indicate he has chosen to do; and if the contract terms can take legal and practical effect without denying him the rights he would ordinarily enjoy if the other party is negligent, they will be read as not denying him those rights unless they are so expressed as to make clear that they do. But ... Lord Morton was giving helpful guidance on the proper approach to interpretation and not laying down a code. The passage does not provide a litmus test which, applied to the terms of the contract, yields a certain and predictable result. The court's task of ascertaining what the particular parties intended, in their particular commercial context, remains."

1.9.4 其他试图对疏忽或过错免责的条文/文字

现实中有条文/文字清楚写明订约方不必对疏忽负责的情况不多,该条文可以是简单明确地说:"我们对于任何疏忽或过错不对你负责(We shall not be liable for any negligence or default on our part)。"原因在上一小段已经提到, Salmon 大法官在 Hollier v. Ramble Motors (A. M. C.) Ltd (1972) 2 Q. B. 71 先例也说,商业人士如果太直率地告诉对方他需要在疏忽的责任上受到保障会有点不好意思,并且会遭到对方抗拒。笔者也认为,水平较高的商业人士如果可以以较隐蔽的写法达到同样效果,就会更加喜欢。在订约自由下,不直率说明"疏忽"一词,就会有许多其他不同的写法,是否能成功对获利方的疏忽或过错免责就命运各异了,以下逐一介绍。

1.9.4.1 "liability at common law"

在 Ailsa Craig Fishing Co Ltd v. Malvern Fishing Ltd (1983) 1 W. L. R. 964 先例,一条限制责任条文中的这个措辞被判是倾向于包括疏忽责任。该条文的有关部分可节录如下:"If, pursuant to the provisions set out herein, any liability on the part of the company shall arise (**whether** under the express or implied terms of this contract, or **at common law**, or in any other way) to the customer for any loss or damage of whatever nature arising out of or connected with the provision of, or purported provision of, or failure in provision of, the services covered by this contract, such liability shall be limited to the payment by the company by way of damages of a sum ..."

Fraser 勋爵说:"... Liability at common law is undoubtedly wide enough to cover liability including the negligence of the proferens itself, so that even without relying on the final words 'any other way', I am clearly of opinion that the negligence of Securicor is covered."(普通法肯定是包括了疏忽的责任,所以条文应该包括被告 Securicor 的疏忽。)

1.9.4.2 "whatsoever"

这是一个广泛的文字,可翻译为"无论如何"。有时候还会加上同样的文字,如"不管怎样"(howsoever)。已经在本书第四章之 8.2 段说过,加上这一广泛文字可有效排除同类规则的适用。在这里进一步探讨可否包括疏忽。简单而言,可以包括疏忽,节录 Fraser 勋爵在 Smith v. South Wales Switchgear Co. Ltd (1978) 1 W. L. R. 165 先例所讲的:"The argument was that the words 'any liability, loss claim or proceedings whatsoever' amounted to an express reference to such negligence because they covered any liability however caused. The argument was supported by reference to the opinion of Lord Justice Buckley and Lord Justice Orr in *Gillespie Bros. & Co. Ltd. v. Roy. Bowles Transport Ltd.*, [1973] 1 Lloyd's Rep. 10, where great emphasis was placed on the word 'whatsoever' occurring in an indemnity clause as showing that the indemnity was intended to apply to all claims and demands however caused including claims for negligence. I agree with the decision in that case and with the statement by Lord Justice Buckley at page 421, that the clause was one 'which cannot sensibly be construed as subject to an implied qualification' ...."

有关"无论如何"一词还有很多其他案例,可介绍如下:

1. 在 Joseph Travers & Sons Ltd v Cooper (1915) 1 KB 73 先例,相关的免责条文是说"any damage to goods however caused which can be covered by insurance"。Phillimore 大法官说:"If you say 'any loss' you are directing attention to the kinds of losses and not to their cause or origin, and you have not sufficiently made it plain that you mean 'any and every loss' irrespective of the cause, and therefore you have not brought home to the person who is entrusting the goods to you that you are not going to be responsible for your servants on your behalf exercising due care for them, or possibly even for your own personal want of care. But if you direct attention to the causes of any loss, if you say '**any loss**', '**however caused**' or '**under any circumstances**', you give sufficient warning, and it is not necessary to say in express terms 'whether caused by my servants' negligence', or in the bill of lading phrase, 'neglect or default or otherwise'."

2. 在 White v Blackmore (1972) 2 QB 651 先例,Roskill 大法官说:"It will be observed that the exclusion is of 'all liabilities arising out of accidents causing damage or personal injury (whether fatal or otherwise) howsoever caused'. **Wider words of exemption are difficult to conceive. Indeed the words 'howsoever caused' have become in the last half century and more the classic phrase whereby to exclude liability for negligence.**"(加黑部分是笔者的强调)

3. 在 Gillespie Bros. &Co. Ltd. v. Roy. Bowles Transport Ltd. (1973) 1 Lloyd's Rep. 10 先例,相关合约中的免责条文没有"疏忽"一词,而是说:"all claims or demands whatsoever by whomsoever made ..."Buckley 大法官说,如果免责条文只是"all claims or demands"这几个字,确是不包括疏忽之责,虽然"所有"一词已经十分广泛。但多加了"whatsoever"这一更广泛的字,就不一样了,因为不能不给这一个字任何解释,说是加了也没有任何改变或意思,不能包括疏忽。他说:"... but if the word 'whatsoever' be added the proper interpretation may very well be different. 'Whatsoever' is a word which is *prima facie* inconsistent with any exception from the class of objects referred to. It is true that one might say colloquially 'any claim whatsoever except one due to negligence', but here the use of 'whatsoever' would be tautologous, for it adds nothing to the meaning of 'any claim except one due to negligence.' One must suppose that the word 'whatsoever' was inserted in clause 3(4) for some purpose and it should, if reasonably possible, be given some effect. ... all claims and demands of whatsoever kind must, in my opinion, extend to all claims and demands how-

ever caused, including claims for negligence."

4. 在 Hinks v Fleet (1986) 2 E. G. L. R. 243 先例,相关免责条文可节录如下:"Vehicles and caravans are admitted on condition that the Park Owner Shall Not be liable for loss or damage to (a) any vehicle or caravan (b) anything in, on or about any vehicle or caravan **however such loss or damage may be caused.** ..."上诉庭判是该条文可以包括疏忽。

5. 在 Brown v Drake International Ltd (2004) EWCA Civ 1629 先例,Pill 大法官说:"The expression '**however caused**' gives the clearest indication that negligence and breach of statutory duty are included. The expression should be given its plain meaning."

但要注意"无论如何"一词也有不同判法,这可以出现在以下两种情况:(1)解释合约是要整体解释,所以,如果从整体看会在一些特殊情况不让"无论如何"包括获利方的疏忽。这里先可举 Gerard McMeel 教授所著的《The Construction of Contracts—Interpretation, Implication and Rectification》(2007 年)一书第 21.47 段所说的:"The tendency has been to treat language which adopts a broad approach to potential heads of liability or causally effective events as being sufficient to cover negligence. However it is necessary to proceed with caution as the courts will construe the whole contract and are reluctant to decide cases purely on the basis of one word or phrase."这里可举的案例就是 The "Super Servant Two" (1990) 1 Lloyd's Rep. 1,该有关合约的不可抗力条文虽然也是有"无论如何"一词,但正如本书第十三章之 1.5 段所说,Bingham 大法官认为该条文所明示的不可抗力事项都是与船东疏忽无关,如天灾、战争、港口拥挤等。所以该条文在结构上不像是有意图包括船员疏忽。(2)在补偿条文,这也是免责条文的一种,目前也有不稳定的判法。在 Gillespie Bros. & Co. Ltd. v. Roy. Bowles Transport Ltd. 先例,合约合并了 Road Haulage Association 的标准条文,其中有一条补偿条文说是针对"all claims and demands whatsoever"。法院判是足够包括提出要求补偿方雇员的疏忽(雇员是卡车司机,运送一批金表去伦敦机场,但半途在无人看管下停留而导致车上金表被窃)。但在 Smith v. South Wales Switchgear Ltd 先例,有类似的措辞却被判不能包括因疏忽导致损失的补偿。贵族院适用了 Canada Steamship Lines Ltd v. The King (1952) 1 Lloyd's Rep. 1 一案的指引,判"any liability, loss, claim or proceedings whatsoever under statute or common law"包括了另一方雇员的疏忽,但要求补偿方自己雇员的疏忽就不能被包括在内了。Fraser 勋爵并对上一先例作出评论,认为"whatsoever"一词并非等同于必然排除了疏忽责任。所以还是要看整体合约的解释,不能生搬硬套,也不能只单独地针对"无论如何"一词解释。

1.9.4.3 "wilful neglect or default"/"wilful misconduct"

有时订约方会以另一种写法明示排除疏忽责任,就是把获利方所需要承担的合约责任约定在更高的层次，如获利方只是在"有意的疏忽/错误"(wilful neglect or default)或"有意的行为"的违约才需要负责。如 Circle Freight International Ltd v. Medeast Gulf Exports Ltd (1988) 2 Lloyd's Rep. 427, CA 先例的免责条文就是如下："18. The Company shall not be liable to the Customer or Owner (a) for loss or damage caused by any failure to carry out or negligence in carrying out the Customer's or Owner's instructions, or by any failure to perform or negligence in performing the Company's obligations (whether such obligations arise by contract or otherwise), **unless such loss or damage is due to the wilful neglect or default of the Company or its own servants.**"

有关"有意的疏忽/错误"的定义可节录 Romer 大法官在 In re City Equitable Fire Insurance Co Ltd (1925) 1 Ch. 407 先例中所说的："An act, or an omission to do an act, is wilful where the person of whom we are speaking knows that he is doing and intends to do what he is doing. But if that act or omission amounts to a breach of his duty, and therefore to negligence, is the person guilty of wilful negligence? In my opinion that question must be answered in the negative unless he knows that he is committing, and intends to commit, a breach of his duty, or is recklessly careless in the sense of not caring whether his act or omission is or is not a breach of duty."(加黑部分是笔者的强调)

至于"有意的行为"的定义可节录 Alverstone 勋爵在 Forder v Great Western Railway (1905) 2 KB 532 先例中说："**Wilful misconduct** in such a special condition means misconduct to which the will is party as contradistinguished from accident, and **is far beyond any negligence, even gross or culpable negligence**, and involves that a person wilfully misconducts himself who knows and appreciates that it is wrong conduct on his part in the existing circumstances to do, or to fail or omit to do (as the case may be), a particular thing, and yet intentionally does, or fails or omits to do it, or persists in the act, failure, or omission regardless of consequences.... or acts with reckless carelessness, not caring what the results of his carelessness may be."(加黑部分是笔者的强调)

在 National Semiconductors (UK) Ltd v UPS Ltd (1996) 2 Lloyd's Rep 212 先例，Longmore 大法官也对"有意的行为"定义说："If I summarize the principle in my own words, it would be to say that for wilful misconduct to be proved there must be either (1) an intention to do something which the actor knows to be wrong or (2) a reckless act in the sense that the actor is aware that loss may result from his act and yet does not care whether loss will result or not or, ... 'he took a risk which he knew he ought not to take'."

在这种免责条文下，就变成每次都要看不同的事实，然后适用此考验，看有没有有意的疏忽/过错。但有意的疏忽/或错与一般的疏忽/过错很不容易区分，特别是时间相隔很久的诉讼，变得很难证明在事发时到底是疏忽方有意或是一时的判断错误。

而当场的证据就会非常重要,如交通事故就是事发后警察的报告。

在 Circle Freight International Ltd v. Medeast Gulf Exports Ltd 先例,案情是有关原告的货代替被告的出口商把一批货物(成衣)运去希思罗机场出口。途中,原告的卡车停在伦敦的街道而且没有人看管,结果部分货物被窃。在此案例,货代作为原告的原因是想取回在账目被欠下的余款,而出口商就提出反索赔这批货物被窃的损失。其中重要的争议之一当然是货代或其雇员(卡车司机)是否有意疏忽。在事故的一刻,该司机是准备旁边的一条小马路交货(其他的货物)。他不知道交货的准确地点,包括要走上 5 层楼,所以他在离开卡车时根本不晓得要用多久完成这个交货。他只是希望能够尽快回来卡车,所以离开的时候也没有把车熄火,或担心卡车停在双黄线会有警察干预。在这些事实的认定下,高院与上诉庭都认为司机(Huggins 先生)是有意的疏忽/过错。Bingham 大法官是这样说:

"On the second issue concerning wilful neglect or default, I agree with the principle as stated by my Lord. Despite the long and detailed exegesis to which these words were subjected in *In re City Equitable Fire Insurance Co Ltd* (1925) 1 Ch. 407, I do not think the meaning of the words is obscure or illusive, although I have no doubt that its application to any given set of facts may be difficult.

Here the judge found—and these findings are not challenged—**first, that Mr. Huggins must have had in mind the risk of theft; second, that he took a deliberate choice to leave the van unattended, and, third, that in so doing he knew that he was disobeying instructions.** Those findings, in my judgment, amply justify the conclusion to which the learned Judge came on the second issue, and I would therefore dismiss the appeal on that point."(加黑部分是笔者的强调)

在针对公路运输的国际公约《Convention of Goods by Road》(或简称 C. M. R),其中有类似说法的免责,就是只要不是运输方的"有意的不良行为"(wilful misconduct)。这也带来了不少同样的案件,如卡车司机驾驶时打瞌睡是否是有意不良行为或只是一般的过错。在 Jones Ltd v. Bencher Ltd. (1986) 1 Lloyd's Rep. 54 先例中,卡车司机被指称在公路行驶时打瞌睡,导致卡车冲出公路与货物损坏。该案例判卡车司机明知道规定连续驾驶不能超出一定时限却还这样做是有意不良行为。但在一个较近期名为 TNT Global SpA v. Denfleet International Ltd. (2007) EWCA Civ 405 的上诉庭先例,推翻高院的判决,认为仅是卡车司机在驾驶时打瞌睡不足以构成有意不良行为。

1.9.4.4 "at sole risk"

航运经常针对甲板货会在租约与提单合约写明"at charterer's risks"或"at shipper's risks",这显然是因为甲板货在航次中会面对更大的海上风险。但一般的说法是这样的写法并不足够保护船东,如果是其雇员/船员疏忽造成甲板货的损坏。这方面可参见杨大明律师所著的《期租合同》一书第 25 篇之 25.2.5 段。

有关航运对甲板货风险的免责条文,还不断有一些近期的先例,如 Sunlight v Ever Lucky Shipping Company Ltd (2004) 2 Lloyd's Rep 174;Compania Sud Americana Vapores v ER Hamburg Schiff (2006) EWHC 483 (Comm);The "Socol 3" (2010) 2 Lloyd's Rep 221 等。这些先例有关的免责条文十分广泛,包括"howsoever caused"。但船东还是在部分先例中无法依赖免责条文。正如在《Voyage Charters》(第4版,2014年)一书之6.3.5段说:"Some deck cargo clauses, such as that in *The Danah* (1993) 1 Lloyd's Rep 351, use language of such width that it makes it clear that the owner is under no liability even if the loss results from the negligence of those for whom he would otherwise be responsible, and even if the improper stowage of the deck cargo renders the ship unseaworthy, but even such clauses have not always proved effective in all circumstances."

但甲板货的免责条文不是解释本小段"at sole risk"能否包括获利方的疏忽/过错的好例子,虽然在上述所讲也应该显示了不够清楚明确包括在内。原因是甲板货的风险十分独特,如果租约或提单合约适用1924年《海牙规则》,在开航前船东恪尽职责令船舶适航,是依赖免责事项的先决条件。虽然甲板货不受《海牙规则》的管制,理论上有订约自由,但普通法也有绝对适航的责任。所以,一旦涉及船舶不适航,不论怎样广泛写法的甲板货免责条文都不足以保障船东。除非是免责条文涉及不适航,如 Blackburn 勋爵在 Steel v State Line SS Co., (1877) 3 AC 72 先例的建议,说:"We(这是指船东)will take the goods on board, but we shall not be responsible at all, though our ship is ever so unseaworthy; look out for yourselves; if we put them on board a rotten ship, that is your look - out; you shall not have any remedy against us if we do."

但看来,如果合约把合约的风险转移到其中一方,并同时要求或约定他投保有关风险,这就会整体解释起来得出不一样的结果。换言之,把双方同意的风险转移不再被视为免责条文,而是在合约中大家愿意怎样分摊风险。在 Levison v. Patent Steam Carpet Cleaning Ltd (1978) Q.B. 69, CA 先例,争议涉及地毯清洁合约的第2条文与第5条文。根据第2条文,地毯的价值被视为不超过40英镑。而第5条文规定由"地毯所有人承担风险"(at owner's risk)并建议地毯所有人投保。但在所有人交出地毯后,地毯丢失。上诉庭判是合约的第5条文包括清洁地毯一方的疏忽。

另在有关建筑合约的先例,如 Archdale (James) & Co Ltd v Comservices Ltd (1954) 1 WLR 459 与 Scottish Special Housing Association v Wimpey Construction UK Ltd (1986) 1 WLR 995,也是有类似的案情与判决。在后一个先例,有关的免责条文可节录如下:"20 ... [C] The existing structures together with the contents thereof owned by him or for which he is responsible and the works and all unfixed materials and goods, delivered to, placed on or adjacent to the works and intended therefore ... **shall be at the sole risk of the employer as regards loss or damage by** fire, lightning, explosion, storm, tempest, flood, bursting or overflowing of water tanks, apparatus or pipes, earthquake, aircraft and other aerial devices or articles dropped therefrom, riot and civil commotion (excluding any loss or damage caused by ionising radiations or contamination by radioactivity from any nuclear fuel or from any nuclear waste from the combustion of nuclear fuel, radioactive toxic explosive or other hazardous properties of any explosive nuclear assembly or nuclear component thereof, pressure waves caused by aircraft or other aerial devices travelling at sonic or supersonic speeds), **and the employer shall maintain adequate insurance against those risks. .**"

在以上免责事项中,显然部分可以涉及承建商或他雇员的疏忽,如"火灾"、"爆炸"、"水箱、器具或水管的破裂或溢出"等。在本章之1.8.5段所讲,如果免责事项可以是与获利方无关的原因,但也可以是获利方有关的原因(如他或是他的雇员疏忽、维修保养不妥善等)所引起,解释时要针对获利方。但在这一条免责条文,有要求雇主投保这些风险(显然也包括了疏忽造成事故如火灾的风险),结果就不一样了。在贵族院,Keith 勋爵说:"Clause 20[C] provides that the existing structures and contents owned by the employer are to be at his sole risk as regards damage by *inter alia* fire. No differentiation is made between fire due to the negligence of the contractor and that due to other causes. The remainder of the catalogue of perils includes some which could not possibly be caused by the negligence of the contractor, such as storm, tempest and earthquake, but others which might be, such as explosion, flood and the bursting or overflowing of water pipes. There is imposed upon the employer an obligation to insure against loss or damage by all these perils, in quite general terms. **I have found it impossible to resist the conclusion that it is intended that the employer shall bear the whole risk of damage by fire, including fire caused by the negligence of the contractor or that of sub-contractors.** "(加黑部分是笔者的强调)

另在 Co-operative Retail Services Ltd v Taylor Young Partnership Ltd (2002) 1 WLR 1419 先例,也是涉及一个建筑的合约,合约要求其中一方以双方作为共同受保人投保一切险。这也被上诉庭判双方之间不能提出索赔,只要损失能够向保险人取回。

Wilberforce 勋爵在 Ailsa Craig Fishing Co Ltd v. Malvern Fishing Ltd (1983) 1 W.L.R. 964, HL 先例与上诉庭在 E.E. Caledonia Ltd v Orbit Valve Co Europe (1994) 1 WLR 1515 先例都有提到合约中有关保险的条文/文字,这可以显示双方是否对风险的分摊有所约定。

1.9.4.5 "act or omission"

这些文字会出现在一些免责条文,如在 The "Raphael" (1982) 2 Lloyd's Rep. 42 先例的有关合约第2条文就是说明"我们不负责任何你们的损失……如果它是由于任何我们的雇员或分包商的行为或不为所引起(we shall not be liable for any damage loss injury costs or expenses suffered by you or your servants or agents and which may arise from or be in any way connected with any act or omission of any person or corporation employed by us or by any sub – contractors or engaged in any capacity in connection herewith. . .)。"

在上述的两个文字,看来"行为"(act)一词就会有危险是不包括疏忽的行为而只包括不疏忽的行为。但"不为"(omission)一词就肯定是针对疏忽。也是这个原因,在 The "Raphael"先例中,想依赖有关免责条文的被告想避开行为而只针对不为,上诉庭的 May 大法官这样说:"Counsel(被告大律师)then pointed to the use of the phrase 'act or omission' and submitted that the word 'omission' must, again having regard to the opening words of clause 2, comprise something not within the *force majeure* clause 8. Thus, he argued, in its place in clause 2 the word 'omission' was certainly wide enough to cover negligence. Counsel was a little reluctant to accept an argument that the whole of the phrase 'any act or omission' was itself wider, and wide enough to cover negligence, because he thought he foresaw that if clause 2 could be held to cover other heads of liability and thus fail to pass Lord Morton's test three, this would be more likely through the use of the word 'act' than 'omission'. He felt that if he over – stressed the width of the relevant phrase in clause 2 in order successfully to pass test two, then he might be giving a hostage to fortune when he came to jump the third fence."

在 The "Raphael"先例,上诉庭判是这一句的"行为或不为"足够广泛包括疏忽,让被告可对他的雇员/工人在处理船舶堆载时因为疏忽而导致吊杆塌下来损坏船舶免责。其中 Donaldson 大法官这样说:"In the present case there is no express reference to negligence in clause 2, nor are there words which can be regarded as synonymous therewith. On the other hand, the words 'any act or omission' are certainly wide enough to comprehend negligence. Lord Atkins' classic definition in *Donoghue v. Stevenson*, [1932] A. C. 562 at p. 580, uses those very words:. . . You must take reasonable care to avoid acts and omissions which you can reasonably foresee would be likely to injure your neighbour."

1.9.4.6　金康租约的免责条文

金康租约的程租合约标准格式在中国大陆的航运与外贸经常被使用,但这一标准格式租约比较偏袒船东,其中最重要显露出来的就是第 2 条免责条文。其 1994 版本中的有关条文节录如下:

"2. Owners' Responsibility Clause

The Owners are to bc responsible for loss of or damage to the goods or for delay in deliveryof the goods only in case the loss, damage or delay has been caused by personal want of due diligence on the part of the Owners or their Manager to make the Vessel in all respects Seaworthy and to secure that she is properly manned, equipped and supplied, or by the personal act or default of the Owners or their Manager.

And the Owners are not responsible for loss, damage or delay arising from any other cause whatsoever, even from the neglect or default of the Master or crew or some other person employed by the Owners on board or ashore for whose acts they would, but for this clause, be responsible, or from unseaworthiness of the Vessel on loading or commencement of the voyage or at any time whatsoever."

笔者对上述的免责条文有以下观察:

1. 抬头是"船东责任条文",但其实其内容是千方百计说明船东不必负责。所以这一抬头有很大程度的误导,也难怪解释合约通常不给抬头任何或太大分量,这方面请看本书第二章之第 12 段。

2. 在文字上只针对船东作为获利方但没有针对承租人,标准格式也没有其他条文针对承租人的免责或"责任条文"。所以在金康租约下,承租人履行合约(如提供货物与装卸货物)是严格责任。即使遇上一些不可控制的事情如政府禁止出口,承租人还是不能对船东免责。

3. 第一部分只说明船东只有在两种情况下才需负责。第一种情况是船东或经理人没有尽到"本人应尽的恪尽职责"(personal want of due diligence)令船舶适航。第二种情况是"船东或船舶经理人本人的行为或过错"(by the personal act or default of the Owners or their Manager)。这样看来,该条文下需要负责只针对船东本人的过错,不包括船长/船员的疏忽/过错,除非船东参与。考虑到船舶在海上行走,绝大部分的工作涉及船员的疏忽/过错都不会有船东本人的参与,特别是在通讯不发达的年代。所以这一条免责条文对船东非常优待。这里可节录 McNair 大法官在 The "Brabant" (1965) 2 Lloyd's Rep. 546 先例中针对上述免责条文的类似文字,说:"... because the clause referred to 'personal' fault, the fault of employees did not, without more, render the owners liable."

4. 第二部分明确除了第一部分船东要负责的两种情况下,其他损失无论什么原因造成都一概不负责。注意是除了有十分广泛的"无论如何"(whatsoever)一词,也清楚说明船长、船员与船东其他在海上或岸上的雇员所犯的疏忽或过错,船东也不负责。明确有了"疏忽"(neglect)与"过错"(default)的文字,再否定就根本不是可以接受的解释合约做法了。

总结而言,这是清楚无误,毫无争议余地的一条包括疏忽的免责条文。看来,承租人/货方使用金康租约要特别小心,尽量加上附加条文如首要条文,令船东承担应该有的责任/义务。

1.10 针对欺诈的免责条文

如果对疏忽或过错的免责是要严格解释,至少还是有机会可以成功依赖。但针对欺诈想免责就可以说极不可能了,这是因为一个大原则,即"欺诈超越一切"(fraud unravels all)。这也是"公共政策"(public policy)的一部分,明示条文写得如何清楚显示订约意图对欺诈免责也不会被承认。所以在 Thomas Witter Ltd v. TBP Industries Ltd (1996) 2 All E. R. 573 先例,Jacob 大法官判一条排除误述的完整合约条文,是不包括欺诈性误述,说:"The clause does not distinguish between fraudulent, negligent or innocent misrepresentation. If it excludes liability for one kind of misrepresentation it does so for all. I cannot think it reasonable to exclude misrepresentation for fraudulent misrepresentation."

另在 Granville Oil and Chemicals Ltd v. Davies Turner and Co Ltd (2003) 2 Lloyd's Rep. 356 先例,上诉庭判一条 9 个月的时效条文只针对一般的合约索赔,不包括关于欺诈的索赔。

但对于代理人的欺诈而非订约方本人的欺诈,情况就有点不同了。唯一只是会严格解释这种类型的免责条文,正如 H. I. H. Casualty and General Insurance Ltd v. Chase Manhattan Bank (2003) 2 Lloyd's Rep. 61 先例所说的,合约要以可能相对疏忽免责更加清楚无误的条文写明(clear and unmistakable terms on the face of the contract)。

1.11 针对损失赔偿限制的条文

订约双方会对损失赔偿作出限制的约定经常出现在两种形式,一种是在需要负责赔偿的金额上作出限制,另一种是在可以提出索赔的损失种类作出局限。这些条文可被称为"规范/局限合约履行条文"(limitation clause)而不被视为"免责条文"(exception clause)。一直有看法是针对规范/局限合约履行条文,解释不像对免责条文的严格。针对这方面,Wilberforce 勋爵与 Fraser 勋爵在 Ailsa Craig Fishing Co Ltd v Malvern Fishing Co Ltd (1983) 1 WLR 964 先例有明确与权威的说法,这可看本章之 1.4 段。Fraser 的说法在后来的先例甚至被称为一个原则:Price Waterhouse v The University of Keele (2004) EWCA Civ 583 先例。但在 H. I. H. Casualty and General Insurance Ltd v. Chase Manhattan Bank (2003) 2 Lloyd's Rep. 61 先例,Hoffmann 勋爵对 Fraser 勋爵是否意图订立一个规则区分规范/局限合约履行条文与免责条文有疑问,说:"whether Lord Fraser intended to introduce one mechanistic rule (a distinction between limiting and excluding liability) to mitigate the rigour of another."

在 BHP Petroleum Ltd v British Steel Plc (2000) 2 Lloyd's Rep 277 先例,上诉庭的 Evans 大法官认为不需要原则性作出区分,反正是越极端的条文豁免责任(相比限制责任)就越严格作出解释,说:"I think it is unfortunate if the present authorities cannot be reconciled on the basis that no categorization is necessary and of a general rule that the more extreme the consequences are, in terms of excluding or modifying the liability which would otherwise arise, then the more stringent the Court's approach should be in requiring that the exclusion or limit should be clearly and unambiguously expressed."

在 Lewison 大法官所著的《The Interpretation of Contracts》(第 5 版,2011 年)一书第第 619 页,表示赞同 Evans 大法官的说法。

"议定赔偿条文"(liquidated damages clause),如国际货物买卖、程租合约与提单的"滞期费条文"(demurrage clause),被视为对双方都有好处,不会被视为免责条文或规范/局限合约履行条文(即使在个别案件议定赔偿的金额事实上偏低)严格或稍微严格针对获利方作出解释,这可看本章之1.5段。

1.11.1　金额上作出限制

Ailsa Craig Fishing Co Ltd v. Malvern Fishing Ltd (1983) 1 W. L. R. 964, HL先例是一个很好的例子,法院判是根据合约免责条文,被告Securicor对5.5万英镑的损失只需要赔偿1000英镑。为了让读者参考一条拟定得十分完善的免责条文,其中部分内容包括了对赔偿金额作出了限制,笔者把Securicor的合约中的免责条文节录如下:"1. Under no circumstances shall the company be responsible for any injurious act or default by any employee of the company unless such act or default could have been foreseen and avoided by the exercise of due diligence on the part of the company as his employer; nor, in any event, shall the company be held responsible for: (a) Any loss suffered by the customer through burglary, theft, fire or any other cause, except insofar as such loss is solely attributable to the negligence of the company's employees acting within the course of their employment ... (b) Any failure by the company to carry out the service by reason of strikes, lockouts, labour disputes, weather conditions, traffic congestion, mechanical breakdown, obstruction of any public or private road or highway or other cause beyond the company's control.... 2. If, notwithstanding the foregoing provision, any liability on the part of the company shall arise (whether under the express or implied terms hereof or at common law) for any injury to or loss or damage of whatsoever nature sustained by the customer, such liability shall under all circumstances be confined to claims of which written notification is received by the secretary of the company at its head office within one month of the happening of the default by the company alleged to give rise to such liability: and subject thereto, **shall be limited to the payment by the company by way of damages of a sum not exceeding £ 1,000 (inclusive of costs) in respect of any one claim arising from any duty assumed by the company** ...."(加黑部分是笔者的强调)

另可举Circle Freight v. Medeast (1988) 2 Lloyd's Rep. 427先例为例,它有一条限制赔偿金额条文如下:"19. In no case whatsoever shall any liability of the Company, however arising, and notwithstanding that the cause of loss or damage be unexplained, exceed (a) the value of the relevant goods, or (b) a sum at the rate of £ 800 per tonne of 1,000 kilos on the gross weight of the goods; or (c) £ 15,000 in respect of any one claim whichever shall be the least."

笔者见过不少中国公司/企业面对西方公司的损失索赔,金额比同类的违约/毁约案件高得多。主要的原因之一是中国公司/企业要价很低,如造船合约,中国造船厂的要价比订约时的市场价格低得多。这样,一旦中方成为被告,对方根据国际市场价格的“市场规则”(market rule)[4]所计算出来的“利润损失”(loss of profit)金额就会很高。例如,在其他外国船厂发生类似争议只能索赔5000万美元,但中国船厂面对基本相同的索赔但金额高达8000万美元。事实上,中国船厂以低廉的报价来承建船舶,在航运市场景气时吸引力很大,外国船东都争相来中国船厂造船。中国船厂拥有如此强大的市场谈判力量,完全可以像Photo Productions Ltd v. Securicor Transport Ltd (1980) 1 Lloyd's Rep. 545与Ailsa Craig Fishing Co Ltd v. Malvern Fishing Ltd先例的Securicor那样,将自己的责任或赔偿金额限制也相应约定在较低的水平。例如,加上条文说明由于船舶造价低(该原因其实也不必说明),任何违约/毁约“被证明的损失的赔偿金额要减半”(recovery of proven loss or damage howsoever/whatsoever caused shall be reduced by 50%)。此外还有很多其他的写法限制赔偿责任,这也不只是中国船厂,任何其他的中国企业都可以考虑这样做。

1.11.2　损失种类上作出局限

1.11.2.1　什么是间接或/与结果性损失?

这种规范/局限合约履行条文的写法通常会排除对“间接”(indirect)或/与“结果性”(consequential)的损失,换言之,只剩下要对“直接”(direct)损失负责赔偿。但问题是英国针对损失赔偿的法律从来没有这样分类,[5]所以这样的写法会带来不肯定。这种写法一定程度是受美国法律的影响,因为美国法院与法律书籍有尝试对这些种类作出区分。有关这方面的课题,在笔者的《损失赔偿与救济》一书第二章有详论。如果合约条文/文字有这样的写法对直接或间接损失作出区分,法院或仲裁庭也就必须作出解释并让它有一定的意思。这样,在Millar's Machinery Co Ltd v David Way and Son (1935) 40 Com. Cas. 204先例,针对一条免责条文说是不负责“consequential damages”被上诉庭判是不能对“自然或直接的损失”(damage occurring naturally or directly)免责。Maugham大法官是说:“The word 'consequential' had come to mean 'not direct'.”

在接下来的Saint Line v Richardsons Westgarth & Co Ltd (1940) 67 Ll. L. Rep. 62先例,Atkinson大法官说:“In my judgment, the words 'indirect or consequential' do not exclude liability for damages which are the direct and natural result of the breaches ... If one takes loss of profit, it is quite clear that such a claim may very well arise directly and naturally from the breach based on delay. The vessel was a trading vessel and

〔4〕 可见笔者《损失赔偿与救济》一书第十三、十四章。

〔5〕 英国法律对损失赔偿的分类,一直以来就是著名的Hadley v. Baxendale (1854) 9 Ex. 341先例把损失分为“一般性”(general)与“特别”(special)损失。主要的强调就是在订约时可否合理预见,前者是可以,但后者就不能。如果不能合理预见的损失,就有必要在订约前预先作出通知给对方,让对方可以考虑是否订约并接受面对这种可能庞大的不可预见的损失的风险才有机会成功索赔。当然,什么是订约前合理应该预见的损失,特别是订约方在某一些特殊行业中,会有争议。

the owners were deprived of the possession and use of the vessel for many months, and thereby of the obvious opportunity of making profit."(Atkinson大法官判是利润损失属于对船舶造成延误的一般性损失,完全可以预见。合约内的免责条文排除"间接"或"结果性"的损失类别没有保障违约方的作用。)

另在British Sugar Plc v NEI Power Projects Ltd (1997) 87 BLR 42先例,上诉庭的Waller大法官拒绝接受"consequential loss"包括利润损失。

1.11.2.2 需要局限利润损失赔偿的原因

以笔者熟悉的国际"商品"(commodity)买卖为例,如果发生违约要计算损失赔偿,在英国法律下是根据"市场规则"(market rule)与"违约一天计算损失规则"(breach date rule)计算无辜方的损失。原因是商品通常都会有可供买卖的市场,并且有明确或相对明确与客观的市场价格可供比较。例如,有关货物买卖涉及的违约是卖方交付了"次货"(defective goods),这样,买方就可以根据1979年《货物销售法》之section 14要求货物符合满意质量的默示条文的违约向卖方提出索赔。至于什么是Hadley v. Baxendale (1854) 9 Ex. 341先例的一般性损失,显然就是该立法的section 53 (3)的规定,即交货时也就是违约时,该批次货与正货之间的市场差价(In the case of breach of warranty of quality such loss is *prima facie* the difference between the value of the goods at the time of delivery to the buyer and the value they would have had if they had fulfilled the warranty)。

至于什么是Hadley v. Baxendale先例的特别损失(或可称为间接损失),这可能是买方对"分买方"(sub - buyer)在"分合约"(sub - contract)中的特殊赔偿责任或商品是买方自用但因为卖方违约而导致生产停顿所造成的损失。但这种索赔在商品买卖就会有很大的问题,原因之一是在市场规则下,前提就是有关货物(通常是商品)有可以进行买卖的市场。也就是假设无辜方的卖方或买方在对方违约下,不论是不付运货物、延误付运货物、交付了次货或拒绝接受货物,都可以马上去市场购买替代货物。这样,他的损失也就只会局限在市场价格的差价,不应该存在间接损失。换言之,买方可以购买市场的替代货物交付给分买方或分买方自己也可以从市场购买并向买方索赔差价。买方如果是自用,也可以购买市场的替代货物不让生产停顿。所以针对商品买卖的合约,很少会需要免责条文局限损失种类。

但如果买方实际上没有马上在市场购买替代货物,并导致分买方在分合约提出索赔。在该分合约下,买方能够赚取比市场差价高得多的利润,或分合约有一些特殊的条文针对延误付运货物或交付了次货需要面对惩罚。又或是,买方没有马上或尽快去市场购买替代货物导致生产停顿而蒙受庞大的利润损失,因为买方没有对这种商品/原料有储备。这种情况在Hadley v Baxendale先例下,显然是一种特别损失。[6] 换言之,索赔这种损失的无辜买方必须在订约前通知了违约的卖方有关这一

[6] Victoria Laundry v Newman Industries (1949) 2 KB 528先例。

分销合约或是自己紧急等这批商品用作生产,因为自己没有任何储存。否则违约的卖方不能被假设能够合理预见这种损失。

但上述的市场规则是不能适用在大量其他非商品或没有可供买卖市场的货物买卖。这样,直接损失或间接损失就很有关系。如在一个关于电脑软件安装工程合约的 Salvage Association v CAP Financial Services (1995) FSR 654 先例,有关合约内的免责或局限损失种类条文是:"CAP shall not be liable for any indirect or consequential losses, damage, injury, costs or expenses of any kind whatsoever including economic loss such as a loss of production, loss of profits or of contracts ..."

这种商业活动很需要这种条文,就是在不少的货物买卖合约或工程/服务合约,卖方/供应商或承建商由于对对方的业务不充分了解,但业务上又非得面对大量的不同买方,就会很担心如果自己的履约中发生延误或提供的货物/服务有缺陷会面对庞大的利润或生产损失的索赔。举例而言,工程合约包括像造船合约,如果事后发觉有缺陷,承建商/船厂很愿意修妥缺陷。修理费是可以预见到或是有限,但如果缺陷导致了利润损失就有危险是一个无底洞的赔偿。例如,船舶的缺陷导致交船后的船舶在一个租金高昂(2008 年金融海啸之前订立)的长期期租合约被承租人终止,因为该租约有条文约定停租超过 14 天承租人就有可以终止的选择权,而船舶的缺陷恰恰导致了 15 天的停租。这样,船东对船厂的损失索赔就可能是天文数字。即使船厂有机会对部分的损失成功根据 Victoria Laundry v Newman Industries 等先例作出抗辩,但诉讼的不肯定以及费用昂贵就已经要促使船厂以明示条文排除这一风险。

1.11.2.3　局限利润损失赔偿的类别必须明示规定

在本章之 1.11.2.1 段所介绍的先例,英国法院都把一些合理的利润损失当作"直接损失"(direct loss),并且强调在订约时可以预见,而不可以预见的只是一些不合理的利润损失。但即使是合理的利润,也经常是一大笔金额。而且,由于有不少商业活动对无辜方的业务不了解,需要履行的一方通常希望以明示条文排除利润损失。但在已经介绍过的先例,可以看到以一条经常见到的免责/局限条文,只针对"间接或/与结果性损失"是不足以作出保障。

这可介绍 Deepak Fertilisers Ltd v. I. C. I. Chemicals Polymers Ltd (1999) 1 Lloyd's Rep. 387 先例,案情涉及一个生产甲醇的工厂的建造,工厂设备是由被告的 ICI 通过技术转让所提供。但投入生产后半年发生严重问题,导致工厂停产与需要重建,损失高达 1 亿英镑。有关的技术转让合约中有一条免责条文明示排除利润损失责任与间接或结果性损失。上诉庭判工厂损毁的一般性损失,包括重建所需要的金钱和时间,加上期间的生产损失。这些损失都是违约方在订约时可以合理预见到。重建的费用与期间生产损失/利润损失本质上都一样,并非是特别损失,也不属于间接或/与结果性损失。但上诉庭最后判是利润损失不能索赔成功,因为有明示条文/文字同时排除了利润损失的赔偿。上诉庭的 Stuart - Smith 大法官这样说:"The direct and natural result of the destruction of the plant was that Deepak was left without a methanol plant, the reconstruction of which would cost money and take time, losing for Deepak any methanol production in the meantime. Wasted overheads incurred during the reconstruction of the plant, as well as profits lost during that period, are no more remote as losses than the cost of reconstruction. **Lost profits cannot be recovered because they are excluded in terms, not because they are too remote.**"(加黑部分是笔者的强调)

最后,作出的结论是要限制索赔损失的种类,最好是明确说明该种类如利润损失不能索赔,而避免使用一些与英国法律不一致的措辞,如"间接损失"。这里可节录Gerard McMeel 教授的《The Construction of Contracts—Interpretation, Implication and Rectification》(2007 年)一书第 21.69 段如下:"It is submitted that the best approach to drafting such clauses is to use terminology which has a settled meaning in English law. For example, in *Deepak* the clause excluding 'lost profits' was efficacious, whereas the boilerplate phrase of 'indirect and consequential losses' was ineffective. If such phrases are to be used, further definition or guidance as to what is intended should be included in the clause."

1.12 1977 年英国《不公平合约法》

普通法尊崇订约自由,所以不理会合约条文公平与否。这就带来了这一重要的立法,主要是保护缺乏谈判力量或/与水平的广大消费者。它也针对面对消费者一方所拟定的标准合约条文,这种标准合约条文经常会在日常生活中遇到。立法要求合理,而不再是放任订约自由的普通法做法。也是上述理由,这一立法不是本书所要针对。笔者只准备简单与选择性地略及。

该立法之 Section 2(1)规定由于疏忽造成人命伤亡的责任,是不能以任何合约条文或预先通知排除。另在 Section 2(2),针对其他因疏忽造成损失的责任,免责条文必须符合合理的要求:"In the case of any other loss or damage, a person cannot exclude or restrict his liability for negligence except in so far as the term or notice satisfies the requirement of reasonableness."

接下来 Section 3 规定如下:"(1) This section applies as between contracting parties where one of them deals as a consumer or on the other's written standard terms of business. (2) As against that party, the other cannot by reference to any contract term—(a) when himself in breach of contract, exclude or restrict any liability of his in respect of the breach; or(b) claim to be entitled: (i) to render a contractual performance substantially different from that which was reasonably expected of him; (ii) in respect of the whole or any part of his contractual obligation, to render no performance at all, except in so far as (in any of the cases mentioned above in this subsection) the contract term satisfies the requirement of reasonableness."

在上述立法所要求的合理,Potter 大法官在 Overseas Medical Supplies Ltd v. Orient Transport Services Ltd (1999) 2 Lloyd's Rep. 273 先例中作出了 8 个指引,如下:

"The treatment of various factors going to the question of reasonableness has been considered in a number of authorities from which the following observation of relevance emerge. (1) The way in which the relevant conditions came into being and are used generally is relevant. (2) Although not specifically applicable to cases falling within Section 3 of the 1977 Act, the five guidelines as to reasonableness set out in Schedule 2 are nonetheless relevant to the question of reasonableness, while bearing in mind that the Court is dealing with a commercial and not a consumer transaction. They ought therefore to be taken into account... Those which are relevant in this case are (a) the strength of the bargaining position of the parties relative to each other, taking into account (among other things) alternative means by which the customer's requirement could have been met; (b) whether the customer received an inducement to agree to the term or, in accepting it, had an opportunity of entering into a similar contract with other persons, but without having to accept similar terms; (c) whether the customer knew or ought to have known of the existence and extent of the term (having regard, among other things, to any custom of the trade and any previous course of dealing between the parties). (3) In relation to the question of equality of bargaining position, the Court will have regard not only to the question of whether the customer was obliged to use the services of the supplier but also to the question of how far it would have been practicable and convenient to go elsewhere... (4) The question of reasonableness must be assessed having regard to the relevant clause viewed as a whole: it must also be viewed against a breach of contract which is the subject matter of the present case... (5) The reality of the consent of the customer to the supplier's clause will be a significant consideration... (6) In cases of limitation rather than exclusion of liability, the size of the limit compared with other limits in widely used standard terms may also be relevant... (7) While the availability of insurance to the supplier is relevant, it is by no means a decisive factor... (8) The presence of a term allowing for an option to contract without the limitation clause but with a price increase in lieu is important ... However ... if the condition works in such a way as to leave little time to put such option into effect, this may effectively eliminate the option as a factor indicating reasonableness..."

上述有提到立法的 Section 3(1)有针对"标准合约条文"(written standard terms of business)。不少商业活动经常会面对这样的情况,甚至是国际性的,如班轮公司的提单。所以,最近有一些法院担忧这主要用来保护消费者的立法入侵商业活动,而这不是立法的本意。这里可举一些法院针对这方面的说法,首先是在 Salvage Association v. CAP Financial Service Ltd (1995) F. S. R. 654 先例中 Thayne Forbes 大法官说:"Generally speaking, where a party well able to look after itself enters into a commercial contract and, with full knowledge of all the relevant circumstances, willingly accepts the terms of the contract which provide for the apportionment of the financial risks of the transaction, I think that it is very likely that those terms will be held to be fair and reasonable."(一般而言,如果订约一方完全有能力订立一个商业合约,并全面知道所有的有关情况,自愿接受合约条文并承担有关经济上风险的分摊,在这种情况下有关的合约条文非常可能被判是公平与合理。)

另在 Watford Electronics Ltd v. Sanderson CFL Ltd (2001) E. W. C. A. Civ 317 先例,上诉庭认为免责条文在订约双方有平等谈判力量的商业合约将被法院确认与执行。Chadwick 大法官也说:"In circumstances in which parties of equal bargaining power negotiate price for the supply of a product under an agreement which provides for the person on whom the risk of loss will fall, it seems to me that the court should be very cautious before reaching the conclusion that the agreement which they have reached is not fair and reasonable."

最后介绍的是在 Granvile Oil and Chemicals Ltd v. Davis Turner and Co ltd (2003) 2 Lloyd's Rep. 356 先例,Tuckey 大法官也警告说:"The 1977 Act obviously plays a very important role in protecting vulnerable consumers from the effects of draconian contract terms. But I am less enthusiastic about its intrusion into contracts between commercial parties of equal bargaining strength, who should generally be considered capable of being able to make contracts of their own choosing and expect to be bound by their terms."(1977 立法明显对保护消费者非常重要,可免他们受到严酷的合约条文带来的影响。但对由有平等谈判力量的订约双方所订立的商业合约并不热衷于让此立法干预,因为他们完全可以根据自己的选择订立合约,并且可要求他们受这些合约条文的约束。)

§2 补偿条文(indemnity clause)

补偿条文[7]可以分两大类别,第一类就是一方承诺补偿另一方将来会面对的第三人责任。这种例子有很多,如在卸港船东被要求无单放货。笔者可节录 The "Houda" (1994) 2 Lloyd's Rep 541 先例,有关租约的条文是如下:"**Charterers hereby indemnify Owners against all consequences or liabilities that may arise from** the master, charterers or their agents signing bills of lading or other documents or from the master otherwise **complying with charterers' or their agent's orders**, (including **delivery of cargo without presentation of Bills of Lading**, or at port(s) different from the port(s) shown on the Bills of Lading) as well as from any irregularities in papers sup-

[7] 关于补偿条文,在本书第五章之 6.6 段也有详细针对。

plied by charterers or their agents. Letter of indemnity to owners' P & I club wording to be incorporated in this charterparty."(加黑部分是笔者的强调)

第一类别的补偿条文看来与免责条文没有太大关系,但接下来的第二类补偿条文就被称为"免责条文的相对面"(the obverse of an exempting clause)。这表示第二类的补偿条文作出解释与免责条文一样。这种条文可节录近期的一个有关北海钻油台供应船的一个期租合约先例,名为 The "Far Service" (2010) 2 Lloyd's Rep 387。有关争议的免责条文可节录如下:"33.5...[供应船船东的 Farstad] **shall** defend, **indemnify and hold harmless** [承租人的 ASCO] from and against any and all claims, demands, liabilities, proceedings and causes of action resulting from loss or damage in relation to the vessel (including total loss) or property of [Farstad], including personal property of [Farstad's] personnel or of anyone for whom [Farstad] may be responsible on the vessel, **irrespective of the cause of loss or damage**, **including** where such loss or damage is caused by [sic], or contributed to, **by the negligence of** [**ASCO**]..."(加黑部分是笔者的强调)

在该先例,承租人委任的一家清洁公司(名为 Enviroco)由于有雇员疏忽,导致该供应船被火灾严重损坏。船东向 Envioco 以侵权索赔损失,但在船东与承租人之间的租约也有争议,就是承租人或代理人的疏忽是否可以根据上述的补偿条文要求船东作出补偿?如果是,就像承租人免责一样不必承担疏忽的严重后果。在该先例,这方面的结果可以想得到,就是该免责/补偿条文(exception/indemnity)作为抬头的第33条文明示了承租人的疏忽,可以保障承租人。最高院的 Clarke 勋爵说:"Like any other term in a contract, clause 33.5 must be construed in its context as part of clause 33 as a whole, which must in turn be set in its context as part of the charterparty, which in its own turn must be considered against the relevant surrounding circumstances or factual matrix. The vessel was chartered for work in the oil rig supply industry and was a comparatively long-term contract. **Clause 33 contains a division of responsibility between the owner and charterer of a type which has become familiar.** However, that fact is no more than part of the factual matrix. Ultimately all depends upon the true construction of the language of the particular clause in its context.... The question is whether clause 33.5 excludes the charterer's liability to the owner in respect of damage to the vessel caused by the charterer's negligence. **In my opinion it plainly does.** As appears below, the word 'indemnify' is capable of having a wide meaning but, even assuming that by itself it might (depending upon the context) have a narrow meaning, it does not stand alone in the clause. The owner must 'defend... and hold harmless' the charterer, not only against liabilities and causes of action, but also against 'all claims, demands' and 'proceedings'. The natural meaning of that expression is that, since the owner must hold ASCO harmless from a claim by the owner in respect of damage to the vessel caused by

ASCO's negligence, **ASCO cannot be liable to the owner in respect of such damage.**"(加黑部分是笔者的强调)

但如果补偿条文没有明示写明"疏忽",就不会有这个结果,如在 Walters v Whessoe & Shell Refining Co Ltd (1960) 6 B. L. R 23 先例,死亡的建筑工人的遗孀向雇佣他的承建商与开发商的两位共同被告提出索赔。这显然涉及有疏忽的开发商能否在他与承建商的合约中取得补偿。该合约的相关补偿条文说:"...(the contractor to indemnify the employer against) **all claims** arising out of the operations being undertaken by the contractor under contract, **including personal injury and death.**"(加黑部分是笔者的强调)

上诉庭判是补偿条文虽然针对"所有的索赔"(all claims),但没有明示疏忽(或有同义的广泛文字),所以所有的索赔只针对不涉及疏忽的索赔。同样原则解释免责条文已经在本章之1.8.5段等段节有介绍。

最后介绍的是一个较近期的 Wilshire County Council v Crest Estates Ltd (2005) 4 PLR 86 先例,案情涉及筑路工程。政府当局与开发商之间的合约有一条补偿条文如下:"[开放商的 Crest] hereby indemnifies the Council(政府当局)in respect of all actions, claims, demands, expenses and proceedings **arising out of or in connection with or incidental to the carrying out of the works** other than those arising out of or in consequence of any act, neglect, default or liability of the council."(加黑部分是笔者的强调)

上述的补偿政府当局的条文用字是十分广泛针对有关的筑路工程。但由于双方的合约要求开发商在公路完毕后的1年继续负责维修保养,这就导致了有争议是上述补偿条文只适用在第三人在工程期间提出的索赔(如受到工程影响),或是可以延伸工程完毕后使用期间第三人提出的索赔。在上诉庭,判是补偿条文应该尽量狭窄地解释,所以只是在工程期间的索赔才有补偿。同样原则解释免责条文也在本章之1.8段有介绍。

§3 时效条文(time limit clause)

合约时效条文也是一种免责条文,正如在 Atlantic Shipping and Trading Co Ltd v Louis Dreyfus and Co (1922) 2 AC 250 先例,Sumner 勋爵所说:"There is no difference in principle between words which save them from having to pay at all and words which save them from paying as much as they would otherwise have had to pay."

另在 Suisse Atlantique Societe D'Armement Maritime SA v N. V. Rotterdamsche Kolen Centrale (1966) 1 Lloyd's Rep 529 先例,Wilberforce 勋爵说:"I treat the words 'exceptions clause' as covering broadly such clauses as profess to exclude or limit, either quantitatively or as to the time within which action must be taken, the right of the injured party to bring an action for damages."

但有一点还是不明确,就是在本章之1.4段提到的时效条文到底是属于"免责条文"(exception clause)还是"规范/局限合约履行条文"(limitation clause),而法院或仲裁庭在解释后者时不会同样严格。时效条文在本质上比较接近一条局限条文,因为条文并不是完全否定索赔的权利,只是在时间上作出局限。但在现实中问题不大,已经提到在BHP Petroleum Ltd v British Steel Plc (2000) 2 Lloyd's Rep 277先例,上诉庭的Evans大法官认为不需要作出原则性的区分,而是越极端的条文就越严格作出解释(如解释3个月或3年的时效)。并且在解释时,两种条文的严格程度的分水线事实上很不清晰。

3.1　合约时效条文要求索赔方必须开始诉讼

最为大家熟悉的合约时效条文是针对通过法院或仲裁提出索赔损失。在很多合约特别是国际性合约中都可以见到,理由不难理解,大致上如下:

1. 特别是国际性的合约,如果适用法不明确,就会带来争议与要根据冲突法原则确定,这会非常的不肯定。而时效的问题就是以合约的适用法为准,是属于实体法。这样,就会带来看是哪种类别的索赔而可能只有很短的时效与不同的计算办法(如法国在程租合约,索赔的时效是卸货后1年,而在期租合约就是还船后1年;日本则在债务欠下后的1年等)。而长的话,有一些索赔的类别在荷兰可以长达30年。至于中国大陆,时效也只有2年,而前来香港仲裁的案件经常会约定适用中国法。但也可能会有比较罕见的案件根据合约明示条文或默示的法律冲突,适用法是日本或是法国。针对这种不肯定的情况,如果加入一条明示条文说明是某个时效,是订约双方都可以接受,就会带来双方的肯定,因为很少国家的法律会否定合约中明示条文的规定。

2. 英国法的法定时效相对比较长,根据1980年《Limitation Act》,"简式合约"(simple contract)是诉因一天起算的6年,如果是"盖章合约"(contract under seal)更会是长达12年。这样长的时效在今天是不合时宜的。被告如果没有预先作出准备,可以说是出事的6年后才被原告起诉会措手不及,什么证据都没有,而且再也找不到。即使还有一些证据,如主要证人,也会因为时间的流逝而变得证据不再有帮助或可靠了。

所以,越来越多适用英国法的合约会加入一条明示条文针对更短的索赔时效,正如Rix大法官在Lazenby v. Mcnicholas (1995) 2 Lloyd's Rep. 30先例中所说的:"All that can be said is that if the parties to an arbitration agreement wish to emphasis the importance of speedy resolution of their disputes, then they must agree to curtail the statutory limitation period of six years for a contractual claim."其好处也很简单的在Ocean Chemical v. Exnor (2000) 1 Lloyd's Rep. 446先例中有提到,就是该合约中的6个月时效条文可带来肯定与终局,只要6个月一过,被告就可以把该合约的交易当作历

史。相关的部分可节录如下:"... able to advance and extol the benefits of certainty and finality. Upon expiry of six months the defendants would, if they wished, be able to treat any transaction as history."

针对开始诉讼的时效条文,在笔者的《损失赔偿与救济》一书第十七章有详论,内容包括时效的开始计算与如何保护时效、法律可以中断时效计算的例外情况、可以重新启动时效的情况等。

3.2 商业合约其他类别的时效条文

除了本章之3.1段介绍的规定在一个时限内要求索赔方必须开始诉讼的时效条文,另一大类的合约时效条文是规定一个时限内要求对方必须做一些事情(通常是要求作出通知),否则就会失去一些合约的权利或救济。如在国际货物买卖,就会有时效条文针对卖方如果在装港遇上"不可抗力"(*force majeure*)的事项导致无法及时付运货物,就必须在一个短时间内通知买方。又或是,买方如果在卸港发觉货损货差需要向卖方提出索赔,就必须在一个短时间内(如1个月内)通知卖方。在造船合约,就会有时效条文针对船厂如果以船东没有支付分期付款的船价而行使合约权利终止合约前,必须在一个短时间内(如7天内)先向船东作出通知。另也有时效条文针对船厂在造船的过程中如果遇上不可抗力事项延误工程,必须在一个短时间内向船东作出通知。另是交船后的1年担保期,本质上也是一条时效条文。在程租合约(也包括国际货物买卖合约),针对滞期费的索赔也通常有一条时效条文,要求船东(或派船的买卖方)在一个相对短时间内提出。

除了国际货物买卖与租约,在其他类别的合约也有同样的时效条文。如在本书多处提到的重要贵族院先例 Photo Productions Ltd v. Securicor Transport Ltd (1980) 1 Lloyd's Rep. 545 与 Ailsa Craig Fishing Co Ltd v. Malvern Fishing Ltd (1983) 1 W. L. R. 964,其合约的详尽免责条文中就有针对在一个时限内必须作出索赔通知,内容如下:"1. Under no circumstances shall the company be responsible for any injurious act or default by any employee of the company.... 2. If, notwithstanding the foregoing provision, any liability on the part of the company shall arise (whether under the express or implied terms hereof or at common law) for any injury to or loss or damage of whatsoever nature sustained by the customer, **such liability shall under all circumstances be confined to claims of which written notification is received by the secretary of the company at its head office within one month of the happening** of the default by the company alleged to give rise to such liability..."(加黑部分是笔者的强调)

3.3 其他类别时效条文的理由

主要支持这种时效条文(在一定程度上也包括必须开始诉讼的时效条文)的理由是,它让将来会面对索赔的一方可及时知道并马上调查取证以利双方和解或无法和解就将来有证据可抗辩。由于不是针对尽早提出起诉,所以这种时效条文在文字上并不是针对要求潜在的原告在某一个时限内提起诉讼。正如 Bingham 大法官在

The "Oltenia" (1982) 1 Lloyd's Rep. 448 先例所说:"The commercial intention underlying this clause seems to me plainly to have been to ensure that claims were made by the owners within a short period of final discharge **so that the claims could be investigated and if possible resolved while the facts were still fresh ....** This object could only be achieved if the charterers were put in possession of the factual material which they required in order to satisfy themselves whether the claims were well – founded or not..."(加黑部分是笔者的强调)

3.4 其他类别的合约时效条文的有效通知

至于被要求作出通知的一方,怎样通知才会是有效保护时效,主要是解释有关的时效条文看有什么明示要求:Forest v Glasser (2006) 2 Lloyd's Rep 277; ROK Plc v S Harrison Group Ltd (2011) EWHC 270 (Comm)等先例。如果合约时效条文只要求通知对方有一个索赔,就不需要提供索赔的细节:Forest v Glasser 先例。但如果合约时效条文要求包括"索赔的本质"(the nature of the claim),通知就必须有合理的细节针对有关的索赔:ROK Plc v S Harrison Group Ltd 先例。

即使是针对必须启动仲裁并开始诉讼的时效条文,如果有关的仲裁条文明示原告向被告作出仲裁通知的内容,也必须严格依照,否则就保护不了诉讼的时效。这方面最危险的例子就是在仲裁条文合并了 2010 年《联合国仲裁规则》(UNCITRAL Arbitration Rules)。它在 Article 3 对仲裁通知的要求如下:

"3. The notice of arbitration **shall** include the following: (a) A demand that the dispute be referred to arbitration; (b) The names and contact details of the parties; (c) Identification of the arbitration agreement that is invoked; (d) Identification of any contract or other legal instrument out of or in relation to which the dispute arises or, in the absence of such contract or instrument, a brief description of the relevant relationship; (e) A brief description of the claim and an indication of the amount involved, if any; (f) The relief or remedy sought; (g) A proposal as to the number of arbitrators, language and place of arbitration, if the parties have not previously agreed thereon.

4. The notice of arbitration **may** also include: (a) A proposal for the designation of an appointing authority referred to in article 6, paragraph 1; (b) A proposal for the appointment of a sole arbitrator referred to in article 8, paragraph 1; (c) Notification of the appointment of an arbitrator referred to in article 9 or 10."(加黑部分是笔者的强调)

3.5 严格解释时效条文的先例

时效条文由于本质上是免责条文,在较早的先例看来是有严格的解释针对获利方或是想依赖时效条文的一方。如针对滞期费的索赔,如果在文字上出现"含糊"(ambiguity)时就会适用"针对规则"(*contra proferentem*)。这可看 The "Pera" (1985) 2 Lloyd's Rep. 103 先例,该程租租约有一条文名为"Petroship Time Bar Clause"针对滞期费索赔的时效条文,内容如下:"... Demurrage, if any, shall be payable by charterers against owners' invoice supported by notice and statement of fact(s) from loading and discharging port(s) duly signed by shippers, respective receivers. **Any claim for demurrage to be accordingly presented within** 12 **months from completion of final discharge.**"

船舶是装了一船原油从利比亚去叙利亚的 Banias 港,在 1980 年 11 月 22 日卸货结束。到了 1981 年 7 月 7 日,船东向承租人提出了滞期费索赔,但可惜在支持文件中少了一份装港的"准备就绪通知书"(notice of readiness),而且装港的"事实记录"(statement of facts)也看不清。到了 1981 年 11 月 10 日(还差 11 天就届临 12 个月的时效),船东取得了上一次缺少与看不清的两份文件,并交给承租人。但可惜这些文件直到 1981 年 11 月 22 日才被承租人收到,时效只差 1 天,但承租人就是以时效已过为由作为抗辩。

注意是上述的条文写得并非清楚无误,首先是针对滞期费索赔时效条文,并没有说明不依照的严重后果。特别是在同一条文针对开始仲裁的诉讼时效有说明如果错过时效的后果是"the claim shall be deemed to be waived and absolutely barred"。另一个含糊之处是滞期费索赔条文中"accordingly"一字,这个字在高院被认为可以有两个解释,一是"因此"(therefore);二是"根据上述所要求的文件"(in the manner just described)。如果是"因此",这句话就变成"Any claim for demurrage to be therefore presented within 12 months from completion of final discharge"。这样解释船东就已经在 12 个月内通知了承租人有关滞期费的索赔,不存在时效已过。但如果是"根据上述所要求的文件",至少在这方面船东因为少了一份文件与另有一份文件看不清,就谈不上是有严格依照了时效条文中明示对文件的要求。Staughton 大法官判是"因此"的解释,毕竟是要针对获利方解释,所以承租人败诉。承租人了上诉庭,上诉庭也作出了与高院的一致判法,说:"It was impossible to say that the word 'accordingly' in the context of the clause clearly bore the meaning 'in accordance with the premises' rather than 'therefore'; the use of the word was ambiguous and ought to be construed *contra proferentem*; the second sentence of the demurrage clause was not sufficiently clear in its terms to require the documents to be presented within 12 months in order to prevent the claim becoming time barred, if the claim was otherwise presented in time."

另一个要介绍的案例是国际货物买卖合约,针对买卖双方之间的卸港滞期费索赔,名为 The "Yellow Star" (2000) 2 Lloyd's Rep. 637。案情有关一船 35,000 吨俄罗斯原油,买卖是"船旁交货"(Ex - ship),表示派船的一方是卖方。买卖合约中有一条滞期费索赔时效条文如下:"(1) Any demurrage is due provided owners actually claim it. (2) Pro rata quantity loaded if part cargo... (4) **Any claim barred** if not notified duly supported by relevant documents (whereof copy of charter - party and copy of owner's demurrage claim and invoice) **within 90 days from bill of lading date.**"

这条条文也是拟定得很差劲,像第一句应该是表示这个买卖合约的滞期费索赔属于“补偿性质”(indemnity),即船东真正向卖方提出,卖方才可向买方索赔要求补偿。另最有关时效的一句是在(4),说明在提单日期的90天内卖方必须交给买方有关的文件,内中包括一份租约与一份船东的滞期费索赔与发票。它针对的是船东的滞期费索赔与发票,而不是卖方。估计可能由于本条文是属于补偿性质,买方就希望知道船东真正索赔的滞期费是多少。

提单日期是1998年11月21日,所以90天的时效应在1999年2月19日届满。卖方是在1999年1月4日以信函向买方提出滞期费的索赔,并附上了通知书、事实记录、船长抗议书与租约。卖方也给了一份卸货时间/滞期费的计算,但该份文件的抬头是“Mabanaft Laytime/Demurrage Calculation”。这不是船东的计算,因为Mabanaft不是船东。另外还欠缺的是船东的一份发票,只有卖方自己的发票。就是这两份文件带来了买卖双方的争议。在法院,Hallgarten大法官判是因为没有在时效内递交船东的滞期费计算与发票给买方,而这两份文件是双方的买卖合约中明示要求的,这导致卖方索赔滞期费的时效已过。

针对船东的发票,卖方声称船东根本没有作出过发票,所以这份文件根本不存在而无法及时递交给买方,而法律是不应强求不可能做到的事情。但Hallgarten大法官不接受,认为卖方可以在时效没有届满之前主动向船东要求作出并取得一份发票,而事实上船东后来也的确提供了这一份发票。

这个先例不同的判法应是The“Pera”先例的条文有含糊之处,但该先例是明确要求这两份文件但卖方就是没有及时递交。在此也可以看到英国合约法的精神,就是合约条文/文字怎样写就怎样解释,不存在法院/仲裁庭有权代订约方重写合约。

在一些先例提到,如果不明确写明错过了时效的后果,就不能“排除”(barring)提起索赔的权利或假设对方接受责任。如在Bunge v Deutsche Conti (1980) 1 Lloyd's Rep 352先例,Donaldson大法官说:“Applying the general principle that claims are not to be barred, except by clear words.”

另在The“Pera”先例,Staughton大法官也有说:“A time bar clause must be clear and unambiguous if effect was to be given to it and since the clause was prepared and put forward by the charterers for inclusion in the charter - party any ambiguity must be construed against them.”

而上诉庭的Griffiths大法官是这样说:“... this clause is, at best, ambiguous, and that being so I return to the fundamental rule that a contractual clause intended to cut down the rights which a party to a contract would otherwise enjoy, must be expressed in clear and unambiguous language.”

但也有先例认为有没有明示的“排除”文字并不重要,原因是如果条文要求在一个期限内提起诉讼或仲裁,错过了时效,除非把有关的索赔视为过期外,不会有其他意思。所以,为了让条文有一定的意思,“排除”不明示也可以默示双方订约的意图是希望该条文达到令索赔过期并排除诉权的效果。

在 Metalimex Foreign Trade Corpn v Eugenie Maritime Ltd (1962) 1 Lloyd's Rep 378 先例,有关的程租合约有条文说是“在卸货后 6 个月内要提起伦敦仲裁”(Arbitration to be in London ... Any Claim arising under this Charter Party has to be made in writing within 6 months after final discharge. ...)。英国高院的 McNair 大法官判说:“Accordingly, approaching this case from the point of view of the words themselves, and from the point of view of reasonableness, it seems to me that the right construction is that contended for by the defendants here, namely, that unless the claim is made in writing within the time limited then the claim shall be barred or not admissible, or whatever words one cares to choose. **I am reinforced in that conclusion by the consideration that, as far as I have been able to understand, if that effect is not given to the clause, no effect is given to it at all.**”(加黑部分是笔者的强调)

另在 Metalfer Corporation v Pan Ocean Shipping Co Ltd (1998) 2 Lloyd's Rep 632 先例,有关租约的时效条文可节录如下:“Any dispute arising out of this charterparty to be referred to the London Arbitrators within 30 days of completion of the voyage and English law to apply. One Arbitrator to be appointed by each of the parties thereto and the third by the two so chosen.”

英国高院的 Longmore 大法官判在航次完结后的 30 天内必须提起伦敦仲裁,否则时效就会错过,说:“unless one reads this provision as a time bar it really has no meaning at all.”

已经在本章之 1.7 段提到现在不会再扭曲解释免责条文,而是像其他合约条文一样作出一般性解释,再加上在本书第三章之第 1 段介绍的要给每条有关条文甚至每个有关单词一定意思的解释合约规则,可以说今天的法院或仲裁庭解释一条免责条文的时效条文时不再要求有明确的“排除”文字。这不仅仅是局限在针对通过法院或仲裁提出索赔损失的时效条文,也包括规定一个时限内要求对方必须做一些事情(通常是要求作出通知),否则就会失去一些合约的权利或救济的时效条文,如“不可抗力”(*force majeure*)通知、货差货损通知等。因此,中国公司要特别小心不要答应做不到的时效条文,而一旦对时效达成协议,就要严格遵照履行合约。

第十三章　惯用条文之二

§1　不可抗力条文(*force majeure* clause)

1.1　合约受阻针对订约后情况有重大改变的不足之处

这个条文(即不可抗力条文)在很多尤其是较长期的合约中出现,主要针对履约期间的情况出现双方不可以完全合理预见与不想接受的"重大改变"(change of circumstance)。这是因为有了情况上的重大改变,根据英国法律,不影响合约中约定的义务,还是要严格/绝对履行,除非这个改变严重到可以令合约"受阻"(frustration)。但英国法律下,合约受阻通常不容易成立,因为门槛很高。通常多花金钱与时间可以解决的问题就都不会令合约受阻。有七八个案例关于在苏伊士运河因为埃及和以色列之间的战争而封闭时,船舶被迫要多花费大量时间与燃油绕道南非的好望角而产生争议,严重程度可以导致个别船东无法承担。但法院都拒绝判有关的租约或国际货物买卖合约受阻:The "Eugenia" (1963) 2 Lloyd's Rep. 381 等先例。更近期的例子是在金融海啸后,航运市场一度暴跌90%,许多高租金的长期期租租约被承租人拒绝履行而终止。部分承租人的抗辩之一是金融海啸造成了合约受阻,但这不被法院接受:Classic Maritime Inc v Lion Diversified Holding Berhad (2010) 1 Lloyd's Rep 59 先例。订约后的履行如果变得十分昂贵,或是市场的波动导致合约一方履行十分困难,都不是构成合约受阻的理由。

合约受阻在笔者所著的《国际商务游戏规则——英国合约法》一书第十二章有介绍,不重复,只在这里节录几个经典的说法。首先是在 Davis Contractors v Fareham UDC (1956) AC 696 先例,Radcliffe 勋爵说:"... frustration occurs whenever the law recognizes that without default of either party a contractual obligation has become incapable of being performed because the circumstances in which performance is called for would render it a thing radically different from that which was undertaken by the contract. *Non haec in foedera veni.* It was not this that I promised to do."

另是 Simon 勋爵在 National Carriers v. Panalpina (1981) A. C. 675 先例中所说:"Frustration of a contract takes place when there supervenes an event (without default of either party and for which the contract makes no sufficient provision) which so significantly changes the nature (not merely the expense or onerousness) of the outstanding contractual rights and/or obligations from what the parties could reasonably have contemplated at the time of its execution that it would be unjust to hold them to the literal sense of its stipulations in the new circumstances; in such case the law declares both parties to be discharged from further performance."

再是 Bingham 大法官在 The "Super Servant Two" (1990) 1 Lloyd's Rep. 1 先例中所说:"Since the effect of frustration is to kill the contract and discharge the parties from further liability under it, the doctrine is not to be lightly invoke, must be kept within very narrow limits and ought not to be extended ..."(因为合约受阻的后果是消灭一个有效的合约,所以这个理论并不轻易可适用,并且必须局限在非常狭窄的范围且不能扩展。)

英国普通法下的受阻说法还有一个问题是它没有说明如果情况有重大改变(如不知维持多久的罢工或禁止出口)可延长/延误履约的责任,但合约本身不必被"消灭"。正如 Gerard McMeel 教授所著的《The Construction of Contracts—Interpretation, Implication and Rectification》(2006 年)一书之 22.03 段所说如下:"The common law did not develop a doctrine permitting temporary suspension of performance for impediments to performance, such as strikes or export bans, whose duration is uncertain. Furthermore the common law insists that a frustrated contract is a dead contract ..."与 22.17 段:"The common law did not develop any doctrine or power of suspension for changes of circumstances which were likely to be temporary or of limited (but determinable) duration, this is a weakness of the common law compared to other legal systems and is one of the factors which makes necessary careful consideration of appropriate express terms, especially in long-term contracts"(普通法没有发展出可在暂时性的情况改变时允许暂停合约履行的理论或权利,这是普通法相比其他法律制度的弱点,并造成了一些特别是长期的合约需要加上明示条文针对。)

这样看来英国法律默示的受阻有很多令人不满意的地方,即有了情况上的重大改变,合约或者继续严格执行(否则就是违约/毁约),或者自动终止,没有中间选择。但偏偏商业人士更喜欢有中间选择,如可以有一段时间押后履行,可进一步观测情况会否变好。此外,情况有了重大改变会被合约双方视为不可抗力事项但不足以构成合约受阻也经常发生,如相对严重的延误,或是市场有重大波动等。在这种考虑下,就导致了许多商业合约会加上一条明示的不可抗力条文,希望超越法律默示的受阻。

这可举 Intertradex v. Lesieur (1978) 2 Lloyd's Rep. 509 先例,涉及一个 CIF 买卖,货物是 800 吨的非洲"马里的花生渣"(Mali groundnut expeller)。但由于 Koulikoro 榨油厂受到供电系统损坏的影响与火车运送花生工厂时受到干预,卖方只能交大约 500 吨货物。事发时,该商品市场价格猛涨,买方向卖方索赔损失。卖方抗辩的之一是依赖买卖合约中的第 22 条不可抗力条文,如下:"Sellers shall not be responsible for delay in shipment of the goods or any part thereof occasioned by any... breakdown of machinery... or any cause comprehended in the term '*force majeure*'."

英国法院判合约受阻不成立,但根据不可抗力条文就会成立,可见它们是有关联但实属两码事。Denning 勋爵是这样说:"First as to frustration: I do not think the board (GAFTA 的上诉仲裁庭) were right in finding that the contracts were frustrated. The events were not sufficient to warrant any finding of frustration. There was the breakdown of machinery at the factory. There was difficulty getting raw material down by rail. Such events are commonplace in the world of affairs. If a party desires to avoid such consequences, he must insert a stipulation to excuse him.... Second as to clause 22: it gives an exemption in case of *force majeure*... If the breakdown of machinery at Koulikoro had been proved to be by itself an effective cause of the non-delivery, the notices (*of force majeure*) would have been good...."

合约受阻与不可抗力条文不一致完全可以理解,毕竟后者是明示条文,在订约自由下任由双方约定哪些事项可包括在不可抗力条文内。如在 The "Super Servant Two"先例,该合约的不可抗力条文中的特定事项之一是"不正常的价格与工资上涨"(abnormal increases in prices and wages)。但根据普通法,这种以金钱可以解决的问题根本不会令合约受阻。

1.2 "不可抗力"一词的定义

"不可抗力"(*force majeure*)一词本身来自法国的《民法典》之 Article 1148,英文翻译是:"There is no occasion for damages where, in consequence of *force majeure* or accident the debtor has been prevented from conveying or doing that to which he was obliged or has done what he was debarred from doing."

在 Matsoukis v. Priestman & Co (1915) 1 K.B. 681 先例,Bailhache 大法官在听取了大陆法律师的专家意见后,说:"The words '*force majeure*' are not words which we generally find in an English contract. They are taken from the Code Napoleon and they were inserted by this Roumanian gentleman or his advisors, who were no doubt familiar with their use on the Continent. I have had the evidence of a Belgium lawyer as to their meaning, and he said that the words are understood on the Continent to mean 'causes you can not prevent and for which you are not responsible'."(不可抗力在英国法的合约下并不常见,这是来自拿破仑法典。Bailhache 大法官听取了作为专家证人的比利时律师的证言,就是不可抗力在欧洲大陆被解释为任何无法避免,也无需负责的事情。)

由于不可抗力条文有许多常用的不同版本,所以如果条文含糊,会被英国法院视为太不肯定而判是无效。在 British Electrical and Associate Industries (Cardiff) Ltd v. Patley Pressings Ltd (1953) 1 WLR 280 先例中,一个买卖钢材的合约中有一句说是"subject to *force majeure* conditions",这被法院判是不肯定哪个版本而无效。

Donaldson 大法官在 Thomas Borthwick (Glasgow) Ltd v. Faure Fairclough Ltd

(1968) 1 Lloyd's Rep. 16 先例中也针对“*force majeure*”一词的解释说：“the precise meaning of this term, if it has one, has eluded lawyer for years.”

但看来，今天英国法院更重视给双方的约定一定的解释，所以即使条文没有其他特定事项，也不会判“*force majeure*”一词无效。这可节录《Chitty on Contracts》(第 31 版，2012 年)一书之 14 – 150 段所说：“Sometimes the actual expression '*force majeure*' is employed. *Force majeure* is not a term of art in English law, although it is well known in continental legal systems, for example that of France. The meaning of *force majeure* may nevertheless be ascertained by reference....”

其中依据之一是可合并国际商会对不可抗力定义的一条标准条文。该条文名为 *Force Majeure* (Exemption) Clause of the International Chamber of Commerce，可节录如下：“(1) that the failure was due to an impediment beyond his control (无法履约是由于他无法控制的障碍); and (2) that he could not reasonably be expected to have taken the impediment and its effects upon his ability to perform the contract into account at the time of the conclusion of the contract; (他在订约时无法合理估计该障碍与其会影响履约能力的程度) and (3) that he could not reasonably have avoided or overcome it or at least its effects. (他无法合理避免或超越该障碍或它所造成的影响)”

1.3 不可抗力条文应该针对的方面

全面与拟定得好的不可抗力条文应该针对四个方面：(1)针对的事项是什么；(2)作出通知的责任；(3)发生不可抗力事项的后果；(4)有争议时谁裁定。以下逐一分析。

1.3.1 针对的事项是什么？

通常的不可抗力条文包括什么事项会有以下三种写法：一是只泛泛地说 *force majeure*，而没有其他特定事项；二是有一连串的特定不可抗力事项，然后在结尾加上兜底性语言，如 circumstances beyond the control of the parties，或干脆是 other *force majeure* events；三是说明一般的不可预见与不可控制的事项。

第一种写法在英国法律中已经解释，即使有效也不明确是包括什么，它也会带来双方不必要的争议，所以应该避免这种写法。至于第二种写法，有先例说在不可抗力条文结尾加兜底性语言并不会适用同类规则：Ambatielos v. Anton Jurgens Margarine Works (1923) A. C. 175 先例。现实中，多数的不可抗力条文会写出一连串的特定不可抗力事项，好处是至少可在 *force majeure* 的基础上包括或扩大某些特定事项并明确后，可减少争议。

1.3.1.1 不同版本不可抗力条文的介绍

笔者以下可节录一条不可抗力条文，显然是针对卖方如果受到特定不可抗力事项导致在买卖合约下无法供应货物给买方的情况：“the company shall not be liable to the customer for any loss or damage which may be suffered by the customer as a result, directly or however indirectly, of the supply of goods or services by the company being prevented, hindered, delayed or rendered uneconomic by reason of circumstances or events beyond the reasonable control of the company including but not limited to act of God, war, riot, strike, lock – out, trade dispute or labour disturbance, accident, break – down of plant or machinery, fire, flood, storm, difficulty or increased expense in obtaining workmen, materials or transport or other circumstances affecting the supply of the goods or of raw materials thereof by the company's normal source of supply or the manufacture of the goods by the company's normal means or the delivery of the goods by the company's normal route or means of delivery."

另是伦敦食糖商会拟定的标准格式合约 Refined Sugar Association Contract 之第17条的不可抗力条文如下：

"*Force Majeure*

Should EEC legislation, government intervention, ice, war, strikes, rebellion, political or labour – disturbance, civil commotion, fire, stress of weather, act of God or any cause of*force Majeure* (whether or not of like kind to these before mentioned) beyond the Seller's control prevent directly or indirectly within the delivery period stated in the contract:(a) the supply or delivery in whole or in part of the sugar allocated or to be allocated by the Seller against the contract, or (b) the means of transport declared or to be declared for loading the sugar and the Seller or his agent be unable to supply other means of transport of equal character to enable him to effect delivery within the contract period,

the Seller shall immediately advise the Buyer by cable or by teleprinter of such fact and the quantity so affected and the delivery period shall be extended by 45 days. If the Seller is prevented from advising immediately through the circumstances beyond his control he shall notify the Buyer as soon as possible. If the delivery is still prevented by the end of the extended period, the contract shall be void for such quantity without penalty payable or receivable."

另是在 The "Marine Star" (1996) 2 Lloyd's Rep. 383 先例一条非常详尽的针对买卖合约的不可抗力条文如下："*Force Majeure Clause* Neither party shall be liable for any breach, delay or non – performance hereunder which directly or indirectly results from or is caused, in whole or in part, by revolutions or other disorders, was, declared or undeclared, acts of public enemies, embargoes or other restrictions imposed by law, arrest or restraint of officials, rulers or people, perils of the sea or other acts of God, accidents or navigation, or by breakdown or injury to ships, pipelines, machinery or other facilities of the seller or those from whom the seller obtained products purchase hereunder, used for production transportation, receiving, manufacturing, handling, or delivery of the products purchased hereunder, or the raw materials from which such products are manufactured, or other impairment or interference with sellers means of supply, transportation or other facilities, or by fires, storms explosions, or other casualties, or by strikes, lockouts or restraint of labour, either partial or general from whatever cause, or if performance hereunder is hindered, delayed or prevented by, or would violate or controvert, any law, rule, order or request of government, federal, state or foreign, or any agency or representative thereof, or which directly or indirectly results from cause beyond sellers or buyers control, whether such other causes be of the classes herein specifically provided or not. In the event of the foregoing, seller shall not be obliged to pro - rate product/or deliveries hereunder nor shall seller be obligated to deliver from a terminal, use a berthing, loading or unloading facilities, type of carrier or manner of delivery other than those designated in the contracts and in the absence of any such designation(s) those customarily used in the performance hereunder, regardless of whether a commercially reasonable substitute is available."

1.3.1.2 应该包括在 *force majeure* 一词中的事项

在这方面也已经有过不少先例,首先是 Matsoukis v. Priestman & Co (1915) 1 K. B. 681 先例,案情涉及造船合约,工程受到 1912 年煤炭工人大罢工的影响而延误。该造船合约有条文针对延误交船要每天支付一笔议定赔偿,除非是包括在不可抗力条文的特定事项所导致的延误。Bailhache 大法官拒绝把"*force majeure*"一词视为等同于英国普通法中的"天意"(Act of God),判是煤炭工人大罢工可以被视为不可抗力事项。

在 Lebeaupin v. Richard Crispin & Co (1920) 2 K. B. 714 先例,案情涉及两个有关供应加拿大三文鱼罐头的合约下,卖方没有交货。McCardie 大法官判是三文鱼的供应数量并没有降低,不交货只是卖方或发货人/"罐头厂"(canners)自己可以控制的原因所造成。所以,McCardie 大法官不认为是合约受阻。但该合约中有一句"subject to *force majeure*",McCardie 大法官接受可包括战争、罢工、立法与行政干预(如禁令)、意外的设备故障,但不包括正常的坏天气(除了是非正常的风暴)与经济上的因素(如欠缺资源),说:"I take it that a '*force majeure*' clause should be construed in each case with a close attention to the words which precede or follow it, and a due regard to the nature and general terms of the contract. The effect of the clause may vary with each instrument."在该先例,由于不可抗力条文一开始就说明了"在罐头厂与发货人的控制以外",而事实的认定是事故在罐头厂的控制之内,所以判是卖方不能依赖不可抗力条文。这样看来,不可抗力条文的解释主要还是根据双方在订约自由下所选用的文字。

其他可被认定为 *force majeure* 的事项及先例可参见笔者的《国际商务游戏规则——英国合约法》一书。并可节录《Chitty on Contracts》(第 31 版,2012 年)一书之 14 - 151 段针对有哪些不可抗力事项,如下:"It has rightly been observed that the concept of *force majeure* in English law is wider than that of 'Act of God' or *vis major*, as these latter expressions appear to denote events due to natural causes, without any human intervention. In Lebeaupin v. Crispin & Co (1920) 2 K. B. 714 McCardie J. reviewed the previous authorities on *force majeure*, and it now seems that war, strikes, legislative or administrative interference, for example, an embargo, the refusal of a licence, or seizure, abnormal storm or tempest, flooding which inhabits shipment from river ports, interruption of the supply by rail of raw material, and even the accidental breakdown of machinery can amount to *force majeure*, but not 'bad weather, football matches or a funeral,' a failure of performance due to the provision of insufficient financial resources or to a miscalculation, a rise in cost or expense, the failure by a third party or by the other party to fulfil his contract[1], or any act, negligence, omission or default on the part of the party seeking to be excused. The words '*force majeure*' are, however, rarely unqualified. The type of circumstance envisaged by the parties will often be set out, so that those circumstances may apply to limit, extend or explain the meaning of '*force majeure*.' Further the clause may refer to performance being 'prevented,' 'hindered' or 'delayed' by *force majeure*. The expression must therefore be construed with regard to the words which precede and follow it and also with regard to the nature and general terms of the contract."(加黑部分是笔者的强调)

1.3.1.3　不可抗力事项怎样影响合约的履行

不可抗力事项会怎样影响合约的履行才适用不可抗力条文,通常在条文中规定。它会是以不同的动词说明,最常见的是“阻止”(prevented)、“妨碍”(hindered)或“延误”(delayed)。比较少见的甚至会出现不可抗力事项“导致不经济”(rendered uneconomic)履约等的规定,反正是订约自由。

“阻止”一词被解释为依赖的订约方无法履行他的合约义务,不论是“实质上”(physically)或“法律上”(legally)。但如果只是使履约更困难或要亏本,往往不足够。这可节录在 Tennants (Lancashire) Ltd v CS Wilson & Co (1917) AC 495 先例中,Finlay 勋爵说:“'prevention' in such a clause must refer to physical or legal prevention and not an economical unprofitableness.”

像受阻一样,不可抗力不会被解释为包括合约履行会变得十分昂贵或严重的市场波动的情况,除非明示规定。这在近期的先例也有提到,在 Thames Valley Power

---

〔1〕《Chitty on Contracts》一书在这里的写法应是指只约定“不可抗力”不包括第三人的行为导致合约一方无法履行。例如,在一连串的买卖下,最初的卖方拒绝供应货物并导致合约链中的其他卖方也无法向买方供应货物。对夹在当中的多位卖方即使是无奈/无助,也不能依赖“不可抗力”一词。但在 The “Marine Star” (1996) 2 Lloyd's Rep. 383 先例,相关的不可抗力条文中包括卖方的货源出了问题的特定事项,因此法院判是在上一手卖方拒绝交货的情况下,卖方可以依赖不可抗力条文。

Ltd v Total Gas & Power Ltd (2006) 1 Lloyd's Rep 441 先例,Christopher Clarke 大法官说:"the fact that a contract has become expensive to perform, even dramatically more expensive, is not a ground to relieve a party on the grounds of *force majeure* or frustration."

另在 Tandrin Aviation Holdings Ltd v Aero Toy Store LLC (2010) 2 Lloyd's Rep 668 先例,Hamblen 大法官说:"It is well established under English law that a change in economic/market circumstances, affecting the profitability of a contract or the ease with which the parties' obligations can be performed, is not regarded as being a *force majeure* event."

但受阻与不可抗力的区别是后者是来自订约自由的明示条文,合约双方喜欢怎样写都可以。所以可以像 Brauer v James Clark (1952) 2 All ER 497 先例把成本高涨与 The "Super Servant Two" (1990) 1 Lloyd's Rep. 1 先例把"不正常的价格与工资上涨"(abnormal increases in prices and wages),甚至在一个长期租约把运费的指标上涨或下跌 50% 作为不可抗力事项,解释起来就不一样了。

"妨碍"是比较广泛的文字,有更好的机会扩大不可抗力条文的适用。《Chitty on Contracts》(第 31 版,2012 年)一书之 14 - 146 段是这样解释:"A wider scope is, however, given to the word 'hindered' and Lord Loreburn said: '... to place a merchant in the position of being unable to deliver unless he dislocates his business and breaks his contracts in order to fulfil one surely hinders delivery.' Where, due to executive restrictions following a strike, charterers could not load unless they dislocated their business and broke other contracts, loading was 'hindered.' A contract of sale of goods which contemplates the carriage of goods by sea may be hindered by the shortage of ships due to enemy action and an increased risk with resultant rise in freight rates. Normally, however, a mere rise in price rendering the contract more expensive to perform will not constitute 'hinderance.' The words 'impede', 'impaired' and 'interfered with' may, in context, be construed as equivalent to 'hindered'."

在 Tennants (Lancashire) Ltd v CS Wilson & Co 先例,Atkinson 勋爵说:"'Preventing' delivery means, in my view, rendering delivery impossible; and 'hindering' delivery means something less than this, namely, rendering delivery more or less difficult, but not impossible."("阻止"交货是交货变得不可能做到。"妨碍"交货代表没有这么严重的情况,只是交货变得更困难,但不是不可能。)

至于"延误"一词,看来是与"妨碍"一词有差不多的意思。《Chitty on Contracts》(第 31 版,2012 年)一书之 14 - 147 段是这样解释这一词:"If provision is made for an extension of time for performance if 'performance' is delayed by circumstances beyond a party's control, the word 'delayed' is not necessarily to be treated as equivalent to 'prevented' and circumstances which merely hinder performance may fall within the provision."

至于在不可抗力条文中用的是哪个动词,甚至几个动词一起用上,就看需要针对什么或订约方的水平而定。如 BIMCO 标准格式造船合约 Standard Shipbuilding Contract 2007 第 24 条文,针对一些不可抗力事项可延长交船日期,所以条文中只是用"延误"一词就已足够。

1.3.2　作出通知的责任

1.3.2.1　作出通知的原因

不可抗力条文经常会规定想依赖的一方必须在特定的时限内作出通知,否则不可以依赖。这样规定有其原因,因为对方往往不知道有这种事项出现并且对合约的履行造成妨碍或延误,所以作出通知就可允许他马上进行调查,否则等到将来出争议时再调查就会导致什么证据都没有了。在针对通知的责任方面,条文最好也针对通知是给谁,如在一个建筑合约内会要求通知也给建筑师或工程师。

1.3.2.2　通知的时限

另一方面要针对的是作出通知的时限,理论上当然越短越好,但也要符合实际。在笔者有参与的 BIMCO 标准格式造船合约 Standard Shipbuilding Contract 2007 的拟定,大家还探讨过属于"公开消息"(public domain)的不可抗力事项,如地震或火山爆发,是否也要求依赖的船厂作出通知。毕竟,发生了这种巨大灾难,在现场的人士都忙着逃命,恐怕向船东作出不可抗力通知是船厂最后要关心的事情。但最后还是决定不区分哪些事项要作出通知,哪些不必作出通知。毕竟,会有地区性的地震影响造船进度是外国船东不一定能够从公开消息中知悉的。

1.3.2.3　通知的细节/内容

再一方面要针对的是,要求不可抗力通知有一定程度的细节/内容。例如,建筑合约经常会要求承建商提供不可抗力事项干预的程度与估计会带来的进度的影响。在 Intertradex v. Lesieur (1978) 2 Lloyd's Rep. 509 先例中,合约的不可抗力条文是要求"通知必须要说明延误的原因"(The notice shall state the reason[s] for the anticipated delay),但该通知由于只有说明一个原因(榨油厂供电系统损坏),但没有说明另一个同时发生的原因(火车运送花生工厂时受到干预)而被判是有缺陷。Denning 勋爵这样说:"That shows that if there are two reasons, the notice must give the reasons, stating the occurrences which caused non-performance. If they occur successively, two successive notices must be given. This is necessary so that buyers can check it up to see whether the reasons are valid. The eighth sentence said that 'the sellers shall provide, if required, satisfactory evidence' justifying the delay or non-fulfilment. Hence the necessity for notice of the occurrence. So it comes to this: if the break down of machinery would by itself have been sufficient to prevent delivery, the sellers would be protected by the *force majeure* clause, even though there may have also operated another cause, namely, the difficulty in getting raw materials. But, if the breakdown of machinery would not by itself have prevented delivery, and if the goods could have been delivered in time, but were prevented by the difficulty of getting raw materials, then the sellers could not rely on the *force majeure* clause: because they give no notice in regard to the difficulty in getting raw materials."

1.3.2.4　不及时/准确作出通知的后果

最后要在不可抗力条文针对的是说明上述的一些要求如果没有被严格遵守会带来的后果。很多条文会说明不依照就会导致不能依赖不可抗力事项,这样,及时与准确的通知就会是一个"先决条件"(pre-condition)。这种文字可以像 BIMCO Standard Shipbuilding Contract 2007 的相关条文,在列了一连串的不可抗力事项后,加上最后的一段是说:"The Builder shall notify the Buyer within [five (5)] running days of when the Builder becomes aware of the occurrence of any event of delay on account of which the Builder asserts that it may be entitled to claim an extension of the Delivery Date. **A failure to so notify shall bar the Builder from claiming any extension** to the Delivery Date."(加黑部分是笔者的强调)

如果条文没有规定,就会带来到底是"条件条文"(condition)或是想依赖不可抗力事项的先决条件,或只是"中间条文"(intermediate term)的争议。因为中间条文只会允许被通知方索赔收不到及时与准确通知所导致的损失,而在通知迟延半天/一天作出的情况下,损失可能是零。即使从来没有收到过通知,他也很难量化金钱损失,因为损失就是失去了及时调查与取证(包括对不可抗力事项与不履行或延误的因果关系)的机会。这方面在本书第十章之4.4段也有详细针对。

这种不肯定可举 Bremer v Vanden (1978) 2 Lloyd's Rep. 109 的重要先例为例,该买卖合约对通知的要求只是简单说"sellers shall advise buyers or reasons therefor",这被贵族院判是不足够明确可构成先决条件,不让卖方依赖该条文之不可抗力事项。该先例重要之处是 Wilberforce 勋爵给了三条指引,判断有关条文是否是先决条件或是中间条文。第一就是条文本身的用字,如在该先例就没有规定卖方必须作出通知的期限,如3天或5天不等,这就不像是先决条件。而第二条指引是合约整体考虑,包括其他条文的写法。如合约有其他针对通知的条文,说明是条件条文或是不作出的后果。但偏偏针对 *force majeure* 的通知只是泛泛一句,不针对不作出的后果,就很难被接受是先决条件。第三条指引是整体法律的考虑,重要之处之一是如果没有及时或从未作出任何通知,明显违反不可抗力条文要求作出通知的规定。如果这个违约可以让无辜方,即没有收到或迟延收到通知的一方量化与索赔金钱的损失,就很有可能被解释为中间条文。但已经提到无辜方通常很难证明迟延收到通知会有何金钱上的损失,变成如果不被解释为先决条件,就导致这个违约根本没有后果或带来任何救济。

在这里只介绍在本书第十章之4.4段已经提到过的 Mamidoil-Jetoil Greek Petroleum Co SA v. Okta Crude Oil Refinery AD (2003) 2 Lloyd's Rep. 635 先例,该合

约的通知条文是说:“shall give prompt notice to the other party”。这被上诉庭的 Aikens 大法官判是如果没有尽快作出通知,就不能依赖不可抗力事项。Aikens 大法官说:

“Okta submitted that Lord Wiberforce's speech establishes that there are three factors that determine whether the notice provision is a condition precedent:(i) the form or the clause itself;(ii) the relation of the clause to the contract as a whole; and (iii) general considerations of the law.

I would have been inclined to hold that notice provision in the 1993 contract is a condition precedent. The form of the notice provision is imperative; a party '*invoking force majeure shall give prompt notice to the other party*'. The implication behind that imperative is that if the party does not then it cannot rely on force majeure. The reason for requiring notice to be given must be that the '*other party*' can then investigate the alleged force majeure at the time. It can challenge whether it does prevent performance or delay in performance by the party invoking force majeure. Alternatively it can see if there are other means of enabling performance to be continued. Lastly, if the notice provision is only an innominate term, then I find it difficult to see when the innocent party could allege it had suffered additional damage as a result of not being told promptly of the force majeure event other than the very damages that it would wish to recover for the first party's failure to perform the contract at all. These factors would all lead me to conclude that the parties intended the notice provision to be a condition precedent.”

1.3.3　发生不可抗力事项的后果

不可抗力条文通常也写清楚一发生它所包括的特定事项会带来什么后果。它本可以写明一发生这种事项就会令合约终止,但很少有不可抗力条文会这样写,因为后果太极端,变成与普通法下的合约受阻一样。但这样写法的条文不是没有,如 The “Super Servant Two”(1990)1 Lloyd's Rep. 1 先例。通常约定的后果会有针对性,而其中允许一段更长时间履行最常见,如在买卖合约就允许延长付运期,在工程合约允许延长完工日期。它也会规定在延长一段时间后不可抗力事项仍然存在,这就会允许终止有关的合约,如在本章之 1.3.1.1 段介绍的 Refined Sugar Association Contract 就是这样针对的。

也会有不可抗力条文针对的后果是以另一种履约的方法作为替代(如只需要部分交货)或可以/不可以做些什么,如在上述节录 The “Marine Star”(1996)2 Lloyd's Rep. 383 的不可抗力条文。或是像 2003 年的 ICC Hardship Clause,要求双方谈判说:“... the continued performance of [a party's] contractual duties has become excessively onerous due to an event beyond its reasonable control, to negotiate alternative contractual terms which reasonably allow for the consequences of the event.”

反正是订约方要小心考虑不可抗力事项会带来怎样的后果,与怎样是恰当的在有关合约中作出针对,因为这完全只能依赖明示条文。例如,在冰天雪地的西伯利亚铺设油管的一个工程合约,其不可抗力条文不能只针对发生不可抗力事项就可以相应延期。因为在这种环境下的工作只能在每年的 4 月到 9 月进行,这导致在 9 月底发生了几天的不可抗力事项,就会需要延期至第二年的 4 月中旬了,只延期相应的几天是完全不够的。

1.3.4 有争议时谁裁定

如果双方对某些情况是否属于不可抗力事项或/与该事项是否带来合约规定的后果(因果关系的方面)有争议,这可以将来留待法院或仲裁庭作出判决/裁决,但这显然是一种不方便与昂贵的做法,所以有些不可抗力条文会规定由中立的第三人尽早作出裁决。在一些建筑合约内,通常的做法是让建筑师或者工程师裁定并决定后果(就是有关延长的时间)[2]:Hickman v. Roberts (1913) AC 229;Perini Corporation v. Commonwealth of Australia (1969) 12 BLR 82 等先例。

"因果关系"(causation),也就是即使发生了特定的不可抗力事项,也必须与后果(如延长履行时间或终止合约)有直接关系。如在买卖合约,如果卖方由于自己的问题根本没有货物可以作出付运,就不能碰巧遇上不可抗力事项作为"挡箭牌"。这在一些先例都有提到,如在 Bremer Handelsgesellschaft mbH v Westzucker GmbH (No. 2) (1981) 2 Lloyd's Rep 130 先例,Donaldson 大法官说:"If shippers or other sellers wish to take the benefit of the clause, they must still prove that the embargo would have prevented fulfillment of the contract on the assumption that they would otherwise have been in a position to fulfil it."

另在 The "Radauti" (1987) 2 Lloyd's Rep 276 先例,Staughton 大法官说:"I would suggest it is more a question of causation, whether the incidence of a particular peril which could have been foreseen can really be said to have caused one party's failure of performance."

在 Agrokor AG v Tradigrain SA (2000) 1 Lloyd's Rep 497 先例,Longmore 大法官说:"(a) that it is for the sellers to prove that they are entitled to rely on cl. 20 or equivalent; and (b) that, in order to do so, the sellers must show not merely that there was a ban which restricted the export of wheat, but also that the ban had the effect of restricting the performance of the actual contracts with Tradigrain."

1.4 不可抗力条文是否是免责条文

这个问题涉及两个方面,一是如果不可抗力条文属于免责条文中的一种,就会被"严格解释"(strict construction);二是不可抗力条文会受到 1977 年《不公平合约法》的管制。如果不可抗力条文属于免责条文,在 Photo Productions Ltd v. Securicor Transport Ltd (1980) 1 Lloyd's Rep. 545 先例前,还可能会被"扭曲解释"(strained

[2] 这种由第三人或专家决定,可看本书第十四章之第 1 与第 2 段。

construction)。但在该先例后,这一危险已经减低或不存在,这可看本书第十二章之1.6.2段。至于第二点只是针对英国的消费者。

看来这个问题是有些不同看法,毕竟区分合约条文说是“我承诺履行,但如果在某些特定的事项下,我不履行也不必承担责任”(I promise to perform, but will not be liable if I fail to do so for specific reasons)与另一个说法是“我承诺履行,除非受到某些特定事项下的阻止”(I promise to perform unless prevented by specific reasons)在本质上区分会是困难。Ewan Mckendrick 教授在其所著的《Force Majeure and Frustration of Contract》一书中认为,不可抗力条文只是针对订约方在一些无法合理控制的情况下有了重大改变作出怎样的替代履行,没有理由将其当作免责条文。在《Chitty on Contracts》(第31版,2012年)一书之14-140段也表达了同样的看法,但也说两种条文很难区分,因为它们都针对解除订约一方的严格履约义务/责任:“... *Force majeure* clauses have been said not to be exemption clauses, although it is difficult to draw any clear line of demarcation between the two types of clause, since the effect of each may be to relieve a contracting party of an obligation or liability to which he would otherwise be subject, and *force majeure* clauses may nevertheless be affected by the Unfair Contract Terms Act 1977.”

但看来也不绝对,因为有太多不同版本的不可抗力条文,有些版本属于或接近免责条文,但另一些版本就不应该是免责条文了。这里的区分可以先节录 Fairclough Dodd & Jones Ltd v. J H Vantol Ltd (1957) 1 WLR 136 先例中 Tucker 勋爵所说:“*Force majeure* clauses are of different kinds. In the case of an exception clause it is generally true to say that it only operates on the happening of an event which would otherwise result in a breach, but there is nothing to prevent the parties providing for an extension of the time for performance or for a substituted mode of performance on the occurrence of a *force majeure* event whether or not such event would have prevented performance.”

这样看来,如果不可抗力条文是对本来是违约的情况下免责,特别是针对的后果是极端,如让违约方终止合约,这就有较大的可能是本质上属于或接近免责条文(如 The “Super Servant Two” [1990] 1 Lloyd's Rep. 1 的不可抗力条文)。但在 Fairclough Dodd & Jones Ltd v. J H Vantol Ltd 先例中的不可抗力条文说明后果是延期两个月,然后让买方而不是依赖不可抗力事项的卖方有终止合约的选择权,所以贵族院判这不是免责条文。

在 Gerard McMeel 教授所著的《The Construction of Contracts—Interpretation, Implication and Rectification》(2006年)一书之22.36段对区分不同内容的不可抗力条文同样地说:“A *force majeure* clause is more likely to be treated as an exemption clause if its operation only benefits one party or is only likely in practice to benefit one party. In addition a power to suspend performance or render alternative and equivalent performance is less likely to lead to characterization as an exemption clause than a clause which brings the contract to an end."

但针对不可抗力条文会严格解释看来是明确,这与在本书第十二章之1.7段所讲的近年解释免责条文虽然不再需要扭曲解释但仍要严格解释一样。因此在笔者看来,不可抗力条文与免责条文的区分不再重要。

1.5 不可抗力条文是否适用针对规则

不可抗力条文如果属于免责条文,"针对规则"(*contra proferentem*)[3]就肯定要适用:Photo Productions Ltd v. Securicor Transport Ltd (1980) 1 Lloyd's Rep. 545, HL。但即使不属于免责条文,针对规则也会适用,只要该条文是偏袒订约一方或不公平,这可看本书第四章之5.1段。

这方面可介绍The "Super Servant Two" (1990) 1 Lloyd's Rep. 1先例,该先例是明确在合约内的不可抗力条文不是一条免责条文。但由于该条文是完全允许船东终止合约,在判决中还是以针对规则对待。该条文如下:"17.1 Wijsmuller(拖轮船东)has the right to cancel its performance under this Contract whether the loading has been completed or not, in the event of *force majeure*, Acts of God, perils or danger accidents of the sea, acts of war, warlike - operations, acts of public enemies, restraints of Princes, rulers or people or seizure under legal process, quarantine restrictions, civil commotions, blockade, strikes, lockout, closure of the Suez or Panama Canal, congestion of habours or any other circumstances whatsoever, causing extra - ordinary periods of delay and similar events and/or circumstances abnormal increases in prices and wages, scarcity of fuel and similar events, which reasonably may impede, prevent or delay the performance of this contract."(加黑部分是笔者的强调)

案情是该合约下,船东同意提供一艘拖轮把一个钻井平台(名为Dan King)从日本造船厂拖去鹿特丹附近海域。针对所用作履行的拖轮,该合约说明船东可以在两艘特定的拖轮中选择其中一艘:"Super Servant One or Super Servant Two in Wijsmuller's option"。船东本来计划以Super Servant Two拖带Dan King,但不幸在尚未开始拖时,前者在另一个拖带合约中因事故沉没。船东也无法以另一艘拖轮Super Servant One履行,因为已经有其他的任务,非要履行不可。

在上述的情况下,明显是英国普通法中的受阻无法成立。如果合约只规定Super Servant Two负责拖带,其沉没,特别是不涉及船东的过错/疏忽,就应该是合约受阻。但在本合约,因为涉及另外一艘拖轮的履行,而船东还没有行使选择权,就不能说是合约无法履行而受阻。

但针对不可抗力条文,由于Super Servant Two的沉没明确符合条文中最后一句针对后果的"会阻碍、防止或延误合约的履行"(reasonably may impede, prevent or de-

---

〔3〕 本书第四章之第5段有针对这一课题。

lay the performance of this contract.),而不可抗力事项也是该条文所包括的"海难"(perils or danger accidents of the sea)。所以判是 Super Servant Two 的沉没只要不涉及船东的过错/疏忽,就可以依赖不可抗力条文。但很有争议的是,如果 Super Servant Two 的沉没涉及船东要负责的船员疏忽(这点的事实还没有认定),船东能否依赖不可抗力条文。

船东的争议是"海难"可以包括船员有疏忽或没有疏忽,这在海上保险法律中最明显。保单只是说明这个承保风险,就已经包括了搁浅或碰撞等海上风险,不论船员有没有疏忽。保单并没有"船员航行的疏忽与过错"(error or negligence in navigation)的承保风险。这个事项只是在针对提单的 1924 年《海牙规则》中出现,这是由于它是免责事项,会适用针对规则。而且,《海牙规则》要求船东要在航次中小心与谨慎照顾货物,所以整体解释《海牙规则》,就有必要在免责事项中说明包括船员航行的疏忽与过错。而在本案件,不可抗力条文并不是免责条文,而且不存在《海牙规则》要整体解释的问题。而且,Super Servant Two 由于还没有被船东选择履行该拖带合约,船东不存在欠对方(Dan King 的所有人)小心与谨慎的责任。

但高院与上诉庭不同意,Bingham 大法官首先认为该不可抗力条文虽然不是免责条文,但还是适用针对规则,说:"The present clause is not, as the Judge accepted, an exceptions clause. It is not therefore directly covered by *Canada Steamship Lines Ltd v. The King* (1952) 1 *Lloyd's Rep*. 1. The clause is, however, one which confers on one party only a right exercisable in a very wide range of circumstances to nullify the contractual bargain made between the parties at no cost to itself and regardless of the loss which the other party may sustain. To such a clause the broad approach indicated by *Canada Steamship* is in my judgment appropriate."

Bingham 大法官接下来针对第 17.1 条的不可抗力条文从文字上看来是够广泛包括船员疏忽(主要是"无论任何"[whatsoever]一词),但从整个条文的结构看,特别是个别的不可抗力事项,都是与船东疏忽无关,如天灾、战争、港口拥挤等。他是这样说:"The language of clause 17 is, I think, wide enough to embrace events caused by Wijsmuller's(拖轮船东)negligence. But the general tenor of the clause, opening with a reference to *force majeure* and acts of God and including such events as acts of war, civil commotion, canal closure and harbour congestion, strongly points towards events beyond the direct or indirect control of Wijsmuller. Clause 17.1 is not deprived of a sensible application if read as excluding events brought about by the negligence of Wijsmuller their servants or agents. Almost all the events listed could only occur wholly independently of Wijsmuller and there is none which could only occur as the result of Wijsmuller's negligence."(第 17.1 条文完全可以给它一个合理的解释,因为所有明示的不可抗力事项都不涉及船东疏忽。)

所以,Bingham 大法官判是针对不可抗力的第 17.1 条文只针对船东没有疏忽的事项,而不包括船东有疏忽的事项。同样解释免责条文(或适用针对规则)在本书第十二章之1.9.1段有介绍。

再接下来Bingham大法官是针对合约整体的解释,即第16条免责条文说明拖带全部是Dan King所有人的风险,而船东完全免责,除非是船东本人故意的行为或错漏所造成(howsoever caused unless caused by the deliberate act or omission of Wijsmuller)。这种免责条文在拖带合约中经常见到,因为拖带的风险比较大,所以拖轮都不愿意承担。这一条文在文字上与第17.1条的不可抗力条文很不一样,导致Bingham大法官认为要局限不可抗力条文的解释说:"It could not be supposed that Wijsmuller could cancel under clause 17.1 where they had deliberately brought about the event relied on. But, in contrast with clause 16 there is no express exclusion of deliberate acts or omissions. So some restriction of the wide language of clause 17.1 is to be understood. In considering the breadth of the clause it is significant that the words 'howsoever caused' which appear in clause 16.1 do not appear here."(虽然17条文没有说明,大家不会认为由于船东本人故意行为所造成的事项他仍可以终止合约,不必像第16条文一样说明。所以,第17条文应该局限解释。)

最后,Bingham大法官也解释了这两条条文的不同针对是可以作商业背景上理解。针对免责条文,除了这是拖带合约一般的做法外,Dan King所有人很容易在保险市场为Dan King的拖带投保。但针对不可抗力条文,如果船东终止拖带合约,Dan King所有人的损失就很难在这种商业风险投保了。所以,该不可抗力条文应该严格解释,就是不包括由于船员过错/疏忽所引起的Super Servant Two的沉没。

另多举一个权威说法指出针对规则适用在不可抗力条文是British Shipping Law series的系列中之《C. I. F. and F. O. B. contracts》(第5版,2012年)一书在介绍了The "Marine Star" (1996) 2 Lloyd's Rep. 383先例后,在13-006段总结说:"Although the circumstances of this particular case were rather peculiar, the level of scrutiny given to the clause by the courts is clearly indicative of the *contra proferentem* approach judges have vis-à-vis generally-worded *force majeure* clauses."

1.6 不可抗力条文是否适用同类规则

同类规则在本书第四章之第8段有详述,在不可抗力条文的解释中适用的不多。这可节录Gerard McMeel教授所著的《The Construction of Contracts—Interpretation, Implication and Rectification》(2006年)一书之22.49段说:"The courts have generally not applied the restrictive rule of language - *ejusdem generis* - to the general phrases often found in *force majeure* clauses, whether at the head or the foot of the clause. On ordinary principles the sweeping words are more likely to be restrictively interpreted but in practice the courts do not appear to have done this."

原因之一可能是法院/仲裁庭会对不可抗力条文的敌意比较低,且这些条文通常本身就已经订得非常完整,对有可能出现的不可抗力事项包罗万有,并加上一些十分广泛的文字像"无论任何"(whatsoever),这会导致同类规则不适用:The "Mozart"(1985) 1 Lloyd's Rep. 239 先例。

1.7 不可抗力事项在依赖的订约方的控制以外

这是国际商会的 *Force Majeure* (Exemption) Clause of the International Chamber of Commerce(在本章之 1.2 段有介绍)中的第 1 条文,要求:"(1) that the failure was due to an impediment beyond his control"。这也是英国法律解释不可抗力条文的考虑,类似的文字更是经常在不同版本的不可抗力条文写明。这方面的案例也有不少,只介绍近期的 Mamidoil – Jetoil Greek Petroleum Co SA v. Okta Crude Oil Refinery AD (2003) 2 Lloyd's Rep. 635 先例。案情是有关一个前南斯拉夫的炼油厂声称无法履行合约供应与处理原油,原因是政府的要求。他依赖合约中的不可抗力条文说明是不必在"acts or compliance with requests of any governmental authority... beyond the control of the party affected"的事项下负责。但法院认定的事实是他自己挑起政府提出这一要求,所以事项并非在他的控制以外。上诉庭的 Longmore 大法官说:"... a *force majeure* event, if it is to be effective, still has to be beyond the control of the party affected."

可比较较早的另一个贵族院先例 Czarnikow v. Rolimpex (1978) 2 Lloyd's Rep. 305 中,涉及的是食糖的 FOB 买卖合约,装港是波兰,卖方是一家波兰的国有企业。1974 年秋天,大雨与水灾导致甜菜失收。波兰政府下令马上禁止食糖出口,这导致部分食糖无法交货。卖方依赖了不可抗力条文的有关部分:"Should the delivery in whole or in part within the delivery time specified be prevented or delayed directly or indirectly by government intervention... stress of weather... or any cause of *force majeure* (whether or not of like kind to those before mentioned), beyond the seller's control..."买方指称卖方是波兰国有企业,所以有关不可抗力事项并非在卖方的控制之外。但这不被法院接受,认为从证据上看来卖方不能视为波兰政府的机构,并且享有充分的自主权。

这种案件与中国还是非常有关系的,因为国有企业,甚至社会主义制度下的非国有企业如果要适用不可抗力事项,只要问题涉及政府(如无法取得出口证或进口证)都会有可能被外国公司指称这不是在中国公司的控制之外,也会容易让西方仲裁员有怀疑。这样,就要根据证据看中国公司是否享有充分的自主权。

不可抗力事项必须在依赖方的控制以外,也被进一步延伸依赖方必须采取合理步骤来避免或解决不可抗力事项所造成的后果。这方面会在本章稍后的 1.9 段详尽针对,在本质上这两个方面有密切关联。

1.8 不可抗力事项无法合理在订约时针对

这是国际商会的 *Force Majeure* (Exemption) Clause of the International Chamber of Commerce 中的第 2 条文,要求:"(2) that he could not reasonably be expected to have taken the impediment and its effects upon his ability to perform the contract into account at the time of the conclusion of the contract."

在合约受阻的理论下,造成受阻的事故需要双方在订约时无法合理预见(the parties could [not] reasonably have contemplated at the time of its execution):National Carriers v. Panalpina (1981) A. C. 675 先例。但合理预见并没有明确的定义,如果严格看待,所有会发生的不可抗力事项在一定程度上都可以预见,如战争、政治问题、自然灾难等。但事后分析与在商业谈判中准确预测并在合约内针对并不同,而且经常会有商业人士乐观地订约,并希望可能会发生的不可抗力事项将来不会出现。所以,"预见"(foreseeability)不到的事项是指不大可能会发生的情况而令合理的订约双方觉得没有必要在订约时明示针对与在将来发生时怎样分摊风险(an event so unlikely to occur that reasonable parties see no need explicitly to allocate the risk of it occurrence, although the impact it might have would be of such magnitude that the parties would have negotiated over it, had the event been more likely)。国际商会条文中的文字接近这个理念。

1.9 不可抗力事项是依赖的订约方无法合理避免或控制

这是国际商会的 *Force Majeure* (Exemption) Clause of the International Chamber of Commerce 中的第3条文,要求:"(3) that he could not reasonably have avoided or overcome it or at least its effects."

这个要求在英国普通法也有默示,就是依赖的订约方采取合理措施来避免或控制不可抗力事项带来的对合约履行的影响与后果。这与无辜方在对方违约后需要合理减少损失看来差不多,但不完全一样。合理减少损失是法律地位,也可以从另一个角度看,即无辜方可以减少损失,但不这样做就令有关的损失(或增加的损失)与违约的直接因果关系被中断。但不可抗力条文(或免责条文)需要依赖方合理避免影响是来自对有关条文的合理解释(或严格解释)。

第一个先例是 Bulman & Dickson v Fenwick & Co (1894) 1 QB 179,案情涉及航次租约,船上煤炭的货物因为罢工卸不下来。在上诉庭,Esher MR 勋爵说:"It is true that when the vessel arrived at the Regent's Canal there was a difficulty in taking delivery because of a strike of workmen; but a strike would in itself not be sufficient to exonerate the charterers from doing the best they could to accept delivery, and would not entitle them to fold their arms and do nothing. **If, notwithstanding the strike, they could by reasonable exertion have taken delivery of the cargo within the proper time, the strike would not have afforded them any defence.** But the jury have found that they could not, by any reasonable effort, have taken delivery. The delay, therefore, was caused entirely by the strike, and was within the exception in the charterparty."(加黑部分是笔者的强调)

这被视为要求依赖免责条文的订约方必须证明他采取了合理步骤避免后果的权威性先例,并带来以后的多个同样判法的先例。如在 B & S Contracts and Design Ltd v Victor Green Publications Ltd (1984) ICR 419 先例,上诉庭的 Griffiths 大法官说:**"Clauses of this kind have to be construed upon the basis that those relying on them will have taken all reasonable efforts to avoid the effect of the various matters set out in the clause which entitle them to vary or cancel the contract**: see Bulman & Dickson v. Fenwick & Co. [1894] 1 Q. B. 179, in the speech of Lord Esher M. R. at p. 185. Quite apart from that general principle this particular clause starts with the following wording: 'Every effort will be made to carry out any contract based on an estimate,' which is saying in express terms that which the law will imply when construing such a clause."(加黑部分是笔者的强调)

另是 Kerr 大法官也说了同样的话,并认为订约一方想依赖他自己工人的罢工作为不可抗力事项是有困难的,说:"it is clear that where an exception of strikes is invoked, then like all other exceptions it is subject to the principle that the party seeking to rely on it must show that the strike and its consequences could have been avoided by taking steps which were reasonable in the particular circumstances."

在 Hoecheong Products Co Ltd v Cargill Hong Kong Ltd (1995) 1 Lloyd's Rep 584 先例,Mustill 勋爵说:"The sellers would be required to show, first, that there had been an event of the kind stipulated by the clause operating at the relevant time; second, that this event had adversely affected the supply of the goods by the sellers; and third, that the sellers could not overcome this adverse effect by obtaining from a source other than the one which they had planned goods which matched the requirements of the contract."

另在 Mamidoil – Jetoil Greek Petroleum Co SA v. Okta Crude Oil Refinery AD (2003) 2 Lloyd's Rep. 635 先例,上诉庭的 Longmore 大法官说:"The question is not whether the request of the governmental authority is *within* the control of Okta but, rather, whether it is *beyond* the control of Okta. For Okta to be able to rely on the clause they have to show that the failure to perform is attributable to a request, which was beyond Okta's control."

最后可节录新加坡上诉庭的一个近期先例 Holcim (Singapore) Pte Ltd v Precise Development Pte Ltd (2011) SGCA 1 中,Andrew Phang Boon Leong 大法官说:"Whether the affected party must have taken all reasonable steps before he can rely on the force majeure clause depends, in the final analysis, on the precise language of the clause concerned. Nevertheless, it might well be the case that, at least where the clause in question relates to events that must be beyond the control of one or more of the parties, then the party or parties concerned ought to take reasonable steps to avoid the event or events stipulated in the clause. In such a situation (as is in fact the case in the present proceedings), there is, in our view, a persuasive case for requiring the affected party to take reasonable steps to avoid the effects of the event in question. The rationale for this approach is a simple and commonsensical one: to the extent that the party or parties concerned do not take reasonable steps to avoid the event or events in question, it cannot be said that the occurrence of the event or events was beyond the control of the party or parties concerned – in which case the clause would not apply."新加坡上诉庭的说法也十分正确,不可抗力条文下到底是否要求依赖方必须先采取所有合理步骤是根据有关条文文字的解释。但如果条文中的不可抗力事项是在合约方的控制以外,这就应该有这个要求。但不可抗力条文的事项是通过双方订约自由约定,会有可能双方约定的事项涉及其中一方的疏忽。这样,解释不可抗力条文原则性是要求依赖方/疏忽方必须先采取所有合理步骤避免这一后果就等于否定了这一不可抗力事项。

要强调的是,依赖不可抗力条文的订约方只需采取合理的步骤办事。如卖方在出现不可抗力事项时,手中只有足够在一个买卖合约中提供的货物,但他在当时订了好几个同样的买卖合约,他应该怎样做?看来,卖方应合理办事,如把货物提供给较早订的合约而再后来订的合约就依赖不可抗力条文。这种争议在 Intertradex v. Lesieur (1978) 2 Lloyd's Rep. 509 先例中出现,Denning 勋爵说:"Mr. Hallgarten(买方代表大律师)submitted that the defence of *force majeure* are not available: because(卖方)had some groundnuts available. They had, he said, sufficient to fulfil this contract, but instead of fulfilling it, they fulfilled two or three other contracts—which were earlier in point of date. I put to Mr. Hallgarten this instance: Suppose (卖方)had entered into 15 equal contracts and they had only enough groundnuts to fulfil one of these contracts. If they fulfilled one of them, would they be liable in damages on all the other 14? Mr. Hallgarten submitted that they would be. I cannot agree with that at all. This is a question which has often been discussed. It seems to me that, when a supplier had many contracts to fulfil, but only has enough of the goods to fulfil one of them, then, if he reasonably appropriated what he has to that one, he can rely on *force majeure* as to the others."

1.10 不可抗力事项是依赖的订约方订约时已知道的

这个问题与本章之 1.8 段的不可抗力事项是无法合理在订约时明示针对的区别是,本段针对订约时合理预知"一定会发生"(bound to operate),而不是合理预见"不大可能会发生"(unlikely to occur)而不针对的情况。如果想依赖免责条文或不可抗力条文的合约一方在订约前预知或可以合理预知某个特定的免责或不可抗力事项一定会发生,会造成不公平。例如,卖方知道或可以合理知道将会有禁令禁止有关货物出口,但仍与买方订合约承诺作出供应,不久后以免责或不可抗力的出口禁令作为理由终止合约。这看来不合理,特别是终止合约时市场上涨,等于剥夺了不知情买方在较早前更好的时间与其他可以供应有关货物的卖方订约的机会。在 The "Angelia" (1972) 2 Lloyd's Rep 154 先例,就发生了类似的情况。有关的磷矿货物的租约在订立时,承租人如果先作出调查,就可以知道以色列局势紧张,军方已经征用所有卡车。没有卡车是无法把磷矿从矿场运抵船旁并装上船舶。之后,承租人依赖租约中的免责或不可抗力条文,如下:"... shortage of cars, wagons ... or other unavoidable hindrances in mining, transporting, loading, discharging or receiving the phosphate ... are excepted and neither charterer nor shippers shall be liable for any loss or damage resulting from any such excepted causes..."

但这被 Kerr 大法官拒绝,判是承租人不能依赖该条文。类似的考虑也出现在很多较近期的先例,即使不涉及免责或不可抗力条文,如在 The "Product Star"(No 2)(1993) 1 Lloyd's Rep 397 与 The "Paiwan Wisdom"(2012) 2 Lloyd's Rep 416 先例。在 The "Product Star"先例,涉及期租合约中的战争条文,允许在履行中的港口/地区如果有战争的危险可以拒绝前往。在解释是否危险,法院认为战争风险没有比在订约时有所增加,所以船东不能拒绝前往。上诉庭的 Leggatt 大法官说:"For the purpose of construing 'dangerous' in cl. 40(战争条文) the common intention that the vessel should trade to UAE ports is relevant to the reasonableness of refusal by the owners to proceed there. ... Since cl. 40, even though strictly speaking not an exceptions clause, was a provision for the owners' benefit, it was ... for them to show that they were entitled to invoke it..... They were only entitled to object in the event that the risks had so far increased that in their discretion they considered such voyages to have become dangerous. ..."

但上述的说法或原则很有争议,这也可以理解,避免不了有例外的情况。例如,订约时双方(甚至是单方面)知道或可以合理知道免责或不可抗力的事项会影响合约履行,但乐观(而且没有不合理之处)认为有关的事项(不论是禁令或是罢工)会有很大机会迅速结束,所以冒险订立合约。但后来履行时事与愿违,有关的事项没有结束,难道不允许依赖双方同意的免责或不可抗力条文才是公平吗?

这方面可节录《Chitty on Contracts》(第 31 版,2012 年)一书之 14 - 143 段作为总结,如下:"...However, in Trade and Transport Inc v Lino Kaiun Kaisha Ltd (1973) 1 WLR 210 where the clause in question referred to 'unavoidable hindrances', Kerr J. stated that a party would be debarred from relying upon such a clause if the existence of facts which show that the clause was bound to operate should reasonably have been known to that party prior to the conclusion of the contract, and would have been expected by the other party to be so known. But subsequently in Channel Island Ferries Ltd v Sealink United Kingdom Ltd (1988) 1 Lloyd's Rep. 323, Parker L. J. expressed doubts whether, because of pre - contract improvidence, a party would be disable from relying on a *force majeure* clause, even if such clause would otherwise have applied; there was no principle of law that a party who entered into a contract could not rely on its terms because he was improvident in entering into it. It may, nevertheless, be argued that the parties to a contract cannot reasonably have intended that one party should be entitled to rely on a *force majeure* clause which, as the result of facts known to him at the time of entering into the contract, he could reasonably foresee would inevitably come into operation and so affect the performance expected of him by the other party. However, it has been held that there is no justification for limiting the ordinary meaning of words in a *force majeure* clause to events or states of facts not in existence at the date of the contract or to those which are unpredictable at the time it was made."

1.11 如果有替代履行办法通常不能依赖不可抗力条文

这方面可先举 Ross T Smyth & Co Ltd v W N Lindsay Ltd (1953) 1 WLR 1280 先例，案情涉及买卖合约，有关的货物是意大利西西里的蚕豆，付运期是 1951 年的 10 月与 11 月。合约有一条不可抗力条文是说："... should the fulfillment of this contract be rendered impossible by prohibition of export ... any unfulfilled part thereof to be cancelled."

订约时蚕豆是允许出口，但稍后意大利当局禁止出口，除了在 11 月份的出口可以通过申请批准被允许。卖方依赖上述的不可抗力条文，但这被法院拒绝，认为合约只是更困难履行，但不是不能履行。Devlin 大法官是说："It appears to me that if a party is going to rely on a prohibition of export or frustration, whichever it is, he has to show that it covers the whole contract period. If the prohibition covers only a part of the period which the contract gives for shipment then performance of the contract is not rendered impossible for the seller, it is merely rendered more difficult for him. Instead of having the full rights which the contract apparently gives him — two months in which to select a date — he has to select a date within a more limited period, but that is not rendering performance impossible. The position is exactly the same under a contract of this sort, where there is liberty to ship on any date during a given period, as it would be in a contract which offers to one party an option of doing a thing in two or more ways, let us say, to pay in gold in New York or in sterling in London. If after the contract it becomes illegal for him to pay in gold in New York he is not thereby relieved altogether from his obligation, he is merely deprived of his option. He has to pay in sterling in London. He cannot elect to tender gold in New York and then say: 'That is the way I chose to perform the contract, and as I cannot perform it in that way I am excused from performance altogether.'"

另在 Warinco AG v Fritz Mauthner (1978) 1 Lloyd's Rep 151 先例，Megaw 大法官说："It is, in general, no answer for the seller merely to say, and to prove, that he had intended, and had made arrangements, to perform the contract in a particular way or at a particular time, and that he could no longer, as a result of the event, carry it out in that way or at that time. In order to escape being in default, he has also, in general, to show, at least, that he could not have carried out the contract, in compliance with its terms, in some other way or at some other time within the contract period. The same applies where the contract gives him a number of ports from which the goods may be shipped, but he is obliged to supply goods shipped from one or the other of them."

这个说法或原则也带来了国际货物买卖的大问题,特别是涉及 CIF/CFR 买卖。众所周知,CIF 买卖本质上是付运文件的买卖,法律并不理会 CIF 卖方到底是否作出付运。他可以买进同样的一票货物(包括特定的货物、提单日期在付运期内等),但已经装在船舶上,是所谓的"浮动货物"(floating cargo)。正如 Evans 大法官在 The "Golden Rio" (1990) 2 Lloyd's Rep 273 先例,说:"'Sales afloat' contracts in practice are synonymous with c. i. f. and c. and f. contracts."所带来的问题是,买卖合约即使是有一条广泛的不可抗力条文保护(不论延长付运期或终止合约)卖方遇上不可抗力事项而无法在付运期内作出货物的付运,也不一定会成功。如在 1973 年美国对黄豆禁运(起因是密西西比河泛滥,影响黄豆收成并造成美国本土供应紧张,导致美国政府禁止出口)时带来无数著名案例,如:Toepfer v. Cremer (1975) 2 Lloyd's Rep. 118; Tradax Export SA v Andre & Cie SA (1976) 1 Lloyd's Rep 416; Finagrain SA v Kruse (1976) 2 Lloyd's Rep. 508; Bunge v. Kruse (1977) 1 Lloyd's Rep. 492; Bremer v. Vanden (1978) 2 Lloyd's Rep. 109 等。但即使因为美国政府禁运而无法作出付运,在 CIF/CFR 买卖的卖方还是可以买进一票浮动货物履行合约。这种浮动货物不多,而且市场价格会上涨至不可思议的高度。正如 McNair 大法官在 JH Vantol v Fairclough Dodd & Jones Ltd (1955) 2 All ER 516 先例中,说:"Generally, a seller cannot claim the protection of the clause(这是指不可抗力条文) which provides that the contract shall be cancelled if shipment is prevented by certain specific clauses unless he proves both (a) that he was himself so prevented from shipping and (b) that it was impossible for him to fulfil the contract by buying goods afloat which had been shipped during the contract period."

虽然有稍后的先例判是如果涉及"绕圈子"(circle 或 string transaction)的买卖,这些 CIF 卖方没有买进浮动货物的责任也可以依赖免责或不可抗力条文。原因是这种买卖涉及太多 CIF 卖方,随时有几十个甚至上百个。如果他们都不想违约/毁约,并市场买进浮动货物,就会给市场价格带来不可想象的影响。这是在 Tradax Export SA v Andre & Cie SA 先例,Denning 勋爵说:"If there were to be an obligation to buy afloat, who is to do the buying? Is each seller to do so in order to fulfil his obligation to the buyer? If that were so, there would be ... large numbers of buyers chasing very few goods and the price would reach unheard of levels."

看来,作为 CIF/CFR 卖方,如果有关的货物买进浮动货物不容易,也不想这样做,就需要买卖合约的不可抗力条文写得更好与有针对性。如在本章之 1.3.1.1 段所节录的 The "Marine Star" (1996) 2 Lloyd's Rep. 383 先例中的不可抗力条文,最后的一句是“... seller shall not be obliged to pro – rate product/or deliveries hereunder nor shall seller be obligated to deliver from a terminal, use a berthing, loading or unloading facilities, type of carrier or manner of delivery other than those designated in the contracts and in the absence of any such designation(s) those customarily used in the performance hereunder, **regardless of whether a commercially reasonable substitute is available.** (加黑部分是笔者的强调)”而如果在上述加黑的部分针对性写上浮动货物变为“regardless of whether a commercially reasonable substitute, such as floating cargo, is available”就会更加保险。

1.12 举证责任

这显然是要依赖不可抗力条文的订约方举证,通常是在三个方面。一是发生的事项是在条文内,不论是在个别事项或是在该条文的兜底性文字内;二是该不可抗力事项影响了合约的履行,这涉及因果关系;三是他已经采取了合理行动避免或减轻这一不可抗力事项的影响。针对举证责任,有很多先例有明确,包括 Bremer v Vanden (1978) 2 Lloyd's Rep. 109 等。这是一个很大的独立课题,此处不多说。

1.13 总结

本章只是粗略介绍了不可抗力条文,特别只针对原则上怎样解释,因为解释合约就是本书所要针对的内容,但不可抗力条文有太多内容,也有无数的重要先例。它也是一条非常重要与惯用的合约条文,特别是在国际性的合约内,如国际货物买卖与大型工程合约。这方面要留待有兴趣的读者看一些专门的书籍,如 Ewan Mckendrick 教授所著的《Force Majeure and Frustration of Contract》一书。本书第十一章也有大量内容针对造船/工程合约的不可抗力条文,请一并参阅。

§2 完整合约条文(entire agreement clause)

完整合约条文在英语中有几种叫法,除了 entire agreement clause 外,也被称为 merger clause 或 integration clause,该条文内部分内容也被称为 non – reliance clause。反正有许多不同版本,是近年来十分重要的一条惯用条文。

今天在一些比较复杂或有律师协助草拟的合约,都加上一条完整合约条文。这种条文会越来越多见到,如在合资、合并/收购、技术转让、保险、造船、提供服务、货物买卖、和解协议等合约中都可以见到。

这种条文在订约自由下可以有不同的写法,也会带来不同的后果。如在 Alman and Benson v. Associated Newspapers Group Ltd. Ch D (Unreported, 20 June 1980) 先例中一条比较简单的完整合约条文:“This agreement, when taken together with the agreed drafts or the executed engrossments of them, constitutes the entire agreement and understanding between the parties with respect to all matters therein referred to.”

又如 Deepak Fertilisers and Petrochemicals Corp v. ICI Chemicals & Polymers Ltd. (1999) 1 Lloyd's Rep. 387, CA 先例中的:"Entirety of agreement This CONTRACT comprises the entire agreement between the PARTIES, as detailed in the various Articles and Annexures and there are not any agreements, understandings, promises or conditions, oral or written, expressed or implied, concerning the subject matter which are not merged into this CONTRACT and superseded hereby. This CONTRACT may be amended in the future only in writing executed by the PARTIES."

另是 Inntrepreneur Pub Co v. East Crown Ltd (2000) 2 Lloyd's Rep. 611 先例中的:"Any variations of this Agreement which are agreed in correspondence shall be incorporated in this Agreement where the correspondence makes express reference to this Clause and the parties acknowledge that this Agreement (which the incorporation of any such variations) constitutes the entire Agreement between the parties."

再是在 Watford Electronics Ltd v Sanderson CFL Ltd (2001) EWCA Civ 317 先例中的:"(1) The parties agree that these terms and conditions ... represent the entire agreement between the parties ... and (2) that no statement or representations made by either party have been relied upon by the other in agreeing to enter into the Contract."(第一句是完整合约条文,第二句是"不依赖条文"[non - reliance clause]。)

笔者在最近的一个和解协议也见到了这样一条条文:"This agreement constitutes the entire agreement between the Parties relating to the subject matter of this Agreement. Each of the Parties acknowledges and confirms that in entering into this Agreement, it is not relying upon any statement or representation made by or on behalf of any other Party, whether or not in writing, at any time prior to execution of this Agreement which is not expressly set out herein. Each of the parties expressly agrees that it will not have any right of action in relation to any statement or representation, whether oral or written, made by or on behalf of any of the other Parties in the course of any negotiations which preceded the execution hereof. This agreement may be varied or modified only by the written agreement of the Parties."

简单而言,完整合约条文可分为三大类:一是上述 Deepak Fertilisers and Petrochemicals Corp v. ICI Chemicals & Polymers Ltd. 先例的条文,是一条典型的完整合约条文。二是确认双方订约并"没有依赖"(non - reliance),条文需要其中一方签一份宣告确认他没有依赖任何对方的陈述订这份合约。三是说明以前所有的承诺与约定全部作废,如 Fontana GB Ltd v. Fabio (unreported, 4 July 2002)先例中的条文说:"This Agreement shall be in substitution for any previous letters of appointment, agreements or arrangements, whether written, oral or implied."

这种条文的本意都是订约双方想局限或排除合约内明示条文/文字以外的争议,

如"附带保证/协议"(collateral warranty/contract)、"默示条文"(implied terms)[4]、"误述"(misrepresentation)、"引导"(inducement)、"商业习惯做法/惯例"(custom/usage)、"侵权的共同责任"(concurrent liability in tort)等。换言之,如果这种条文被法院/仲裁庭接受为有效,就表示解释合约只能看有关合约四个角之内的明示条文/文字。法院/仲裁庭不能或不该看的最主要的就是在谈判中与订约时的"口头证据"(parole evidence)或"外来证据"(extrinsic evidence),这在本书第六章之2.3.1段有介绍。因为上述的争议如误述,证明肯定需要这些口头/外来证据。

这种条文的重要是根据英国法律,如果双方签订了一个合约就是对双方同意的责任与权利有了终局,除非欺诈或误述所导致。这所谓的"签字规则"(signature rule)可节录Devlin勋爵在McGutcheon v David MacBrayne Ltd (1964) 1 WLR 125先例中的说法:"... the law is clear, without any recourse to estoppel, that a signature to a contract is conclusive."

另是在L'Estrange v F Graucob Ltd (1934) 2 KB 394 (DC)先例,Scrutton大法官说:"When a document containing contractual terms is signed, then, in the absence of fraud, or, I will add, **misrepresentation**, the party signing it is bound, and it is wholly immaterial whether he has read the document or not."(加黑部分是笔者的强调)

签字规则的重要性在近期的Peekay Intermark Ltd v Australia & New Zealand Banking Group Ltd (2006) 2 Lloyd's Rep 511先例,也被Moore - Bick大法官强调说:"It is an important principle of English law which underpins the whole of commercial life; any erosion of it would have serious repercussions far beyond business community."

所以如果一个合约变成对其中一方不利而想脱身,要证明欺诈不会容易(虽然明示欺诈的举证责任还是平衡的可能性,但这是严重的指控,需要更高的举证责任),变成剩下就是指称对方曾经在谈判时作出误述(不论是疏忽甚至是无辜),他有依赖(即使只是部分)这一误述才订立与签署该合约。这样,就表示该合约的产生有严重缺陷,在英国法下可终止,并可以在疏忽或欺诈性的误述下向对方索赔损失。这也解释了为什么需要一条不依赖条文,说明双方订约都没有依赖对方作出过的陈述,完全是依赖自己的订约意愿。在Alman and Benson v Associated Newspapers Group Ltd先例,Browne - Wilkinson大法官认为一般写法简单的完整合约条文只可以排除对附带协议/保证的"指称"(allegation),但不包括误述。这也解释了还要多加一条"不依赖条文"(non - reliance clause)的原因。他是这样说:"If it were designed to exclude liability for misrepresentation it would, I think, have to be couched in different terms, for example, a clause acknowledging that the parties had not relied on any representations in entering into the contract."

所以草拟一条好的完整合约条文(内容会包括不依赖条文)是需要一点技巧与

[4] 这方面可看本书第七章之第9段。

对法律的了解。

这种条文还可以带来另一个说法,就是一些不喜欢最近三四十年来英国法院在解释文书合约时从传统的“字义上解释”(literal 或 text)走向“广泛本质上解释”(expanded contextual)趋势的人士,希望通过完整合约条文扭转这一方向。在本书第六章提到对合约条文作出本质上的解释,往往要求接纳口头/外来证据,确定双方在订约时的“背景事实”(background facts)或者合约“目的”(purpose)。这样做显然会带来大量的证据与额外的争议,表示每个诉讼都会拖长与变得更昂贵。问题是有了这一完整合约条文,能否扭转方向?这个疑问也在本书第六章之2.3.1段有提到。但看来,通常这种条文的写法在措辞/文字中并没有针对这一点,也表示还是不能抗拒接纳口头/外来证据对合约条文(特别是写得含糊)进行解释。这可看 J J Spigelman 的《Contractual interpretation: A comparative perspective》(2011) 85 ALJ 412 一文。

另是在衡平救济的“合约变更”(rectification),也有说法是完整合约条文不能阻止法院接受口头证据并对双方已经签署的合约中的条文作出变更。有关的先例如 JJ Huber (Investment) Ltd v. The Private DIY Co. Ltd. (1995) NPC 102;Phillips Petroleum Co UK Ltd v. Snamprogetti Ltd (2001) EWCA Civ 889;澳大利亚的 Franklins Pty Ltd v Metcash Trading Ltd (2009) 76 NSWLR 603;Macdonald v. Shinki Australia Pty Ltd (1998) QCA 53,已经在本书第三章之13.1段有介绍。

2.1 完整合约条文的本质

看所用的文字,完整合约条文在本质上会被视为免责条文,所以解释起来会严格对待。而且,这种条文会带来严重后果(如太宽松解释可以阻止法院/仲裁庭考虑合约的本质/背景),所以在近年来很富有争议性。支持方会说这是订约自由的大原则,订约方没有理由不被允许在合约中说明这份文件就是双方完整的约定,而且以明示条文改变普通法地位是长久以来一直的做法。反对方会说在绝大部分情况下都不能在一份文件中包罗万有的制造一份完整合约,总会有一些变数是没有在文件中出现。所以必须对背景要有了解才会找到正确答案。

早在1959年 Wedderburn 勋爵在《Collateral Contracts》(1959) CLJ 58 一文中就提到这种附带保证/协议的必要,说:“In a society in which people are daily led to enter into written contracts which they do not understand on the basis of oral promises which they do understand, the value of this weapon of justice is likely to increase.”(每天都有人被引导订约,但他们其实对该文书合约的理解只是基于口头的承诺,只是对这种承诺有所理解,所以为了公正,保护他们的武器需要增加。)

这是现实情况,所以在订约方的合约知识强弱悬殊时,如果在文书合约多加入一条完整合约条文,就可以有效地排除附带保证/协议与误述,就表示假设弱方只理解这一条条文与它所带来的后果,但对合约其他所有的条文反而不理解。这显然不现实与对弱方不公平,毕竟不能排除弱方接受完整合约条文也是受到强方的误述引导。

难怪,特别是针对消费者的合约,这种条文很受到质疑与敌视。英国法律委员会在 1986 年名为《The Parol Evidence Rule》(Law Com 154) 的报告之2.15 段说到这种条文如果是排除或减免对误述的责任,是无效的。另针对附带保证/协议,该报告说:"Without legislative provision such a clause cannot, we think, have conclusive effect. It may have a very strong persuasive effect but if it were proved that, notwithstanding the clause, the parties actually intended some additional clause, the court would give effect to that term because such was the intention of the parties."

在判例中,也有不同的说法。如 McGrath v Shah (1987) 57 P&CR 452, Ch D. 先例中,John Chadwick 大法官就不认为这条文有违反 1967 年《误述法》与 1977 年《不公平合约法》。但 Jacob 大法官在 Thomas Witter Ltd v TBP Industries Ltd (1996) 2 All ER 573 先例中持相反看法。在这方面可节录 Gerard McMeel 教授的《The Construction of Contracts—Interpretation, Implication and Rectification》(2007 年)一书之24.08 段,如下:"Secondly, given their proximity to, and often close relationship with, exemption clauses, the question arises whether either the entire agreement clause or the non – reliance clause are within the scope of the restrictions on exemption clauses introduced by principally the Unfair Contract Terms Act 1977 and section 3 of the Misrepresentation Act 1967. Whilst there is authority both for and against statutory regulation, it is submitted that as a matter of principle and as a matter of statutory construction both clauses are vulnerable to the argument that they are regulated exemption clauses."

针对国际商贸,由于订约双方被视为有相同谈判力量,所以会宽松对待。上诉庭的 Chadwick 大法官在 EA Grinstead & Son Ltd v. McGarrigan (Unreported, 27 October 1999)先例中认为在业务收购的这种合约,由于大家都有平等的谈判水平,就应该尽量保护订约自由,说:"There are, as it seems to me, at least two good reasons why the courts should not refuse to give effect to an acknowledgement of non – reliance in a commercial contract between experienced parties of equal bargaining power—*a fortiori*, where those parties have the benefit of professional advice. First, it is reasonable to assume that the parties desire commercial certainty. They want to order their affairs on the basis that the bargain between them can be found within the document which they have signed. They want to avoid the uncertainty of litigation based on allegations as to the content of oral discussions at pre – contractual meetings. Second, it is reasonable to assume that the price to be paid reflects the commercial risk which each party—or, more usually, the purchaser—is willing to accept. The risk is determined, in part at least, by the warranties which the vendor is prepared to give. The tighter the warranties, the less the risk and (in principle, at least) the greater the price which the vendor will require and which the purchaser will be prepared to pay. It is legitimate, and commercially desirable, that both parties should be able to measure the risk, and agree the price, on the basis of the warranties which have been given and accepted."

在 North Eastern Properties v Coleman (2010) 3 All ER 528 先例,上诉庭的 Longmore 大法官说得更明确,就是双方同意文书合约完整,法院就不能干预,说:"If the parties agree that the written contract is to be the entire contract, it is no business of the courts to tell them that they do not mean what they have said."

完整合约条文与不依赖条文有逻辑不通之处,就是在较早时涉及的如果合约是依赖严重的误述而产生,而不依赖条文只是该合约的条文之一,会否整个合约包括该不依赖条文都一并无效?这个问题 Moore - Bick 大法官在 Peekay Intermark Ltd v. Australia & New Zealand Banking Group Ltd. (2006) 2 Lloyd's Rep 511 先例中是说:"The effectiveness of [a no reliance clause] may be challenged on the grounds that the contract as a whole, including the clause in question, can be avoided if in fact one or other party was induced to enter into it by misrepresentation."

这个复杂的问题在近期的一个上诉庭先例以及其他有关的一审先例中有解答,该上诉庭先例是 Springwell Navigation v JP Morgan Chase Bank (2010) EWCA Civ 1212,将会在本章稍后的 2.4.9 段介绍。

2.2　完整合约条文的好处

完整合约条文的好处主要是带来"商业上的肯定性"(commercial certainty)与减少争议,只要看文书合约的明示条文/文字,就可以知道订约双方的责任与义务。这不仅是对订约双方,也包括其他依赖有关合约的第三人,如银行。这尤其重要,现在的法律环境在放宽口头/外来证据,导致合约争议越来越多。这不但使诉讼费用昂贵,而且带来结果不肯定。依赖的第三人不能只看一份合约的四个角内的条文/文字,因为其解释再也不是法律问题,而是混合了法律与事实,而事实是要依赖第三人不知道的口头/外来证据。有关这方面本书有多章详论,如第一章与第六章。虽然有了完整合约条文,也不能完全避免对口头/外来证据的处理,但肯定可以大幅度减少:Proforce Recruit Ltd v Rugby Group Ltd (2006) EWCA Civ 69;Air New Zealand Ltd v Nipppon Credit Bank Ltd (1997) NZLR 218,224, BZCA 等先例。但显然法院/仲裁庭会有很大保留甚至是敌意,正如 Longmore 大法官在 Reeds Solicitors (a firm) v Norwich Union Insurance Ltd (2005) EWCA Civ 323 先例中所说的:"As always when an oral agreement is relied on... and there are subsequent written agreements with entire agreement clauses, any court would look at a claimant's case with a great deal of scepticism."

也有一些交易涉及多层面的谈判,如班轮公司通过代理人或职员揽货,谁也不知道他们为了揽货会对货方说什么。所以,把这些可能是真或是假的误述、引导或附带保证/协议排除在该运输合约外,就需要一条好的完整合约条文。这种情况在私人银行的业务也可以明显见到,就是经常会与他们提供投资服务的客户有大量谈话。为了小心与避免将来被客户指控错误的投资建议等,银行通常会把每次的谈话(特别是电话)都录音。但这样就难以避免有大量录音,有了争议就会涉及昂贵与复杂的文件披露[5]与争辩。所以最好的保障办法就是银行与客户之间的协议有一条好的完整合约条文与不依赖条文。

现实中,经常有订约方在出了争议后发觉合约条文/文字对他不利,就回想谈判的过程中对方是否曾经有误述、引导或作出附带保证/协议以扭转劣势。只要勉强能找到蛛丝马迹,就会毫不犹豫的争辩这些在文书合约外的争议。这经常导致诉讼变得十分昂贵与整个交易的最后结果不肯定。什么是误述或引导而导致合约的订立在笔者的《国际商务游戏规则——英国合约法》第五章有详论。至于附带保证/协议,是指双方在谈判时,其中一方曾经作出了一个"承诺"(promise),但该承诺并没有记录在文书合约内。有关附带保证/协议在本书第六章之2.3.2段有介绍。而有了完整合约条文就可以在这方面避免,并减少争议,这个好处的权威说法可看本章稍后的2.4.4段介绍的Inntrepreneur v. East Crown (2000) 2 Lloyd's Rep. 611先例。

2.3 完整合约条文的坏处

完整合约条文的坏处主要是令双方有此条文的文书合约变得至关重要,必须条文/文字订得好与对自己一方有利,因为将来决定争议的唯一依据就是这个合约内的明示条文。但这对中国的一方不利,因为中国人有一些无法配合国际做法的传统。如果合约中有一条完整合约条文(这种可能性越来越大)就会导致中国企业/公司在发生争议时更加无法为自己辩护。例如,笔者知道有一个合约被西方公司索赔将近一亿美元,中国企业坚持是在签署合约前,西方公司口头承诺肯定不会在中国企业拿不到担保/批准时向中国企业索赔。结果中国企业就在这个承诺下签署了合约并作出明示的严格保证会在一个月内拿到担保/批准。这严格保证其实就是西方公司所拟订的合约条文中规定中国企业要这样做。结果中国企业无法做到而被西方公司提出巨额索赔。如果中国企业相信他所坚持的事实(西方公司的口头承诺)就可以附带保证/协议作为抗辩,只要证据足够(中方有关于口头承诺的内部文书记录或双方电邮往来)与证人表现好,会有机会胜诉。但可惜在该书面合约中有一条完整合约条文,导致难以提出这一抗辩。可见是这种条文的危险之处。

2.4 完整合约条文的有关先例

在近二三十年来,开始有大量的先例针对完整合约条文的解释,内中也可以看到这条文普遍被采用,以下对部分先例作出介绍。

2.4.1 案例之一:Alman and Benson v. Associated Newspapers Group Ltd.

Alman and Benson v. Associated Newspapers Group Ltd. (Unreported, 20 June 1980)是近期大量有关完整合约条文案例中第一个解释该条文文字的先例,案情有关一家咨询公司的股份买卖,双方的争议涉及该合约的误述。该合约有一条相对简单

[5] 在Springwell Navigation v JP Morgan Chase Bank (2010) EWCA Civ 1212先例,原告作为客户对被告的摩根大通银行提出149个特定的误述,而摩根大通银行也需要披露1000个磁带与1500个电话交谈的录音。可以说这149个特定的指控,只要1个能够成立,就可以致摩根大通银行败诉。

的完整合约条文,如下:"11(1). This agreement, when taken together with the agreed drafts or the executed engrossments of them, constitutes the entire agreement and understanding between the parties with respect to all matters therein referred to."

Browne - Wilkinson 大法官判是该条文可以抗辩一个附带保证/协议的索赔,但不足以也没有明示可避免一个误述的索赔。换言之,该条文的文字/措辞不够广泛。他是这样说:"Clause 11 (1) provides that the written contract constitutes 'the entire agreement and understanding between the parties with respect to all matters therein referred to'. It is to be noted that it does not in terms refer to representations. The defendants, however, submit that the word 'understanding' covers the representation alleged in this case. I cannot accept this submission. Although it is true that, in one sense, the common assumption by all parties that the plaintiffs were to be in charge of the day - to - day running could be called 'an understanding' between them, the plaintiffs are not suing on that bilateral 'understanding' but on the representation of intention implicit in it. Clause 11 (1) plainly excludes any contractual claim based a bilateral understanding, but it does not go further. In my judgment the word 'understanding' is directed to excluding any claims arising from warranties collateral to the main agreement. If it were designed to exclude liability for misrepresentation it would, I think, have to be couched in different terms, for example, a clause acknowledging that the parties had not relied on any representation in entering into the contract. I therefore hold that the word 'understanding' in this contract is not apt to cover representation, and accordingly does not exclude the plaintiffs' claim."(Browne - Wilkinson 大法官说该条文只针对双方的"理解"[understanding]。有关原告负责该公司以后每天的业务可以是双方的理解,但这不代表一方向另一方作出的误述。要把误述也加在完整合约条文内,文字上就要有所不同,如说明双方都没有依赖对方的陈述订立本合约。由于"理解"一词并不能包括误述,原告可以根据误述向被告提出索赔。)

2.4.2　案例之二:Thomas Witter v. TBP Industries Ltd

Thomas Witter v. TBP Industries Ltd (1996) 2 All ER 573 先例的案情是有关收购一个地毯公司,收购价格是400万英镑,另加上利润分摊等的其他对价。之后卖方被指控在订约前曾经有过一连串的误述,包括口头与文书上对将来利润的预测,另有关一笔可收取的帐款,说是12万英镑,但其实夸大了7万英镑。该合约也有一条完整合约条文,如下:"This Agreement sets forth the entire agreement and understanding between the parties or any of them in connection with the Business and the sale and purchase described herein. In particular, but without prejudice to the generality of the foregoing, the Purchaser acknowledges that it has not been induced to enter into this Agreement by any representation or warranty other than the statements contained or referred to in Schedule 6."

但 Jacob 大法官判是该条文不足够包括有关的不真实误述,说:"The first thing to do is to construe the clause . . . in my judgment the first sentence does not operate to exclude remedies for pre – contractual misrepresentations. It simply does not say it does. If it said, for instance, 'The vendor [*scilicet* purchaser] agrees he will have no remedy in respect of any untrue statement made to him upon which he relied in entering this contract, and that his only remedies can be for breach of contract' the clause would probably have done the job. Then, if he is sold a pup, he will have no remedy, unless it is a contractually warranted pup . . . Unless it is manifestly made clear that the purchaser has agreed only to have a remedy for breach of warranty I am not disposed to think that a contractual term said to have this effect by a roundabout route does indeed do so. In other words, if a clause is to have the effect of excluding or reducing remedies for damaging untrue statements, then the party seeking that protection cannot be mealy – mouthed in his clause. He must bring it home that he is limiting his liability for falsehoods he may have told."

Jacob 大法官上述的解释与原因被后来的上诉庭先例 EA Grinstead & Son Ltd v. McGarrigan (Unreported, 27 October 1999)批评说:"The acknowledgement in the present case are not acknowledgements as to what representations were made to the purchaser; they are acknowledgements as to what acknowledgements the purchaser relied upon. I can see no difficulty in an acknowledgement by a purchaser that a representation which was made was not relied upon; but I cannot see how a purchaser who has acknowledged that a representation was not relied upon can afterwards say that that was nothing more than what he thought was the position at the time. Put another way, I reject the contention that it is open to a purchaser to assert both that he did not rely on a representation which was made to him and that he did rely upon that representation. He must be taken to know, at the time when he enters in to the agreement, what representations he is relying upon."

2.4.3 案例之三:Deepak Fertilisers and Petrochemicals Corp v. ICI Chemicals & Polymers Ltd.

Deepak Fertilisers and Petrochemicals Corp v. ICI Chemicals & Polymers Ltd. (1999) 1 Lloyd's Rep. 387, CA 先例是一个涉及技术转让的重要案例,案情有关在印度的 Deepak 计划建造一个生产甲醇的工厂。生产以一种名为 tube cooled methanol converters 的技术进行,ICI 公司称这是一种经过验证的新技术并可由它在伦敦的许可商 Davy 提供。之后,Deepak 与 Davy 直接签署了一份技术转让合约并在 Davy 的协助下建起了工厂。但工厂设备一直有温度超标的问题,并在投入生产后约半年,生产甲醇的转换器发生爆炸,导致工厂停产与需要重建,损失高达 1 亿英镑。Deepak 于是向 ICI 与 Davy 索赔损失,争议之一是 Deepak 指称 ICI 与 Davy 共做出过 8 项误述,而有关的合约是有一条完整合约条文如下:“Entirety of agreement This CONTRACT comprises the entire agreement between the PARTIES, as detailed in the various Articles and Annexures and there are not any agreements, understandings, promises or conditions, oral or written, expressed or implied, concerning the subject matter which are not merged into this CONTRACT and superseded hereby. This CONTRACT may be amended in the future only in writing executed by the PARTIES.”(加黑部分是笔者的强调)

这样,这一争议就是 Deepak 认为上述条文并不排除误述或附带保证/协议,但 Davy 说上述条文有排除,所以 Deepak 不能以误述为由提出索赔。这就涉及解释该条文所用的文字,Rix 大法官同意 Deepak 的说法,认为该条文的文字并没有针对陈述或误述。它所针对的四个字(agreements, understandings, promises, conditions)中,前两个已经在 Alman and Benson v. Associated Newspapers Group Ltd. Ch D (Unreported, 20 June 1980)先例有所针对并被 Browne – Wilkinson 大法官判是“理解”一词不包括误述。Rix 大法官同意这一判法,并指出在本案例的有关条文多的两个字 promises 与 conditions,对要把误述也包括在内起不了任何作用,只适合针对附带保证/协议。Rix 大法官的部分判决可节录如下:“I agree with Deepak's submission so far as concerns misrepresentation. Thus the clause's language – ‘agreements, understandings, promises or conditions’ – is not apt, expressly or impliedly, to include representations. This was the view of Mr. Justice Browne – Wilkinson in Alman and Benson v. Associated Newspapers Group Ltd. June 20, 1980, (unreported, Lexis transcript at p. 30)... – When it comes to excluding liability for collateral warranties, however, I agree with Davy that the clause effectively does so. That was the view, albeit *obiter*, of Mr. Justice Browne – Wilkinson in the passage cited above from the *Associated Newspapers Group* case, when he said that the word ‘understandings’ is directed to excluding any claims agreement. In the present case the clause goes further and refers to ‘promises or conditions ... which are not merged into this CONTRACT and superseded thereby’. It seems to me that the words ‘promises or conditions’ are particularly apt to deal with collateral warranties, and that the succeeding words make plain that all such collateral warranties have been merged into and superseded by the final contract. They have been either excluded or discharged...”

2.4.4 案例之四:Inntrepreneur v. East Crown

Inntrepreneur v. East Crown (2000) 2 Lloyd's Rep. 611 先例的案情已在本书第六章之 2.3.2 段有介绍,为了方便读者阅读,可部分重复。本案涉及一个伦敦酒吧的 30 年租赁,租赁合约中有一条文要求租客向一些房东指定的啤酒供应商购买啤酒。1996 年,租客购买了 280 桶啤酒。但之后急跌,到了 1998 年 4 月后,租客根本停止了向指定供应商购买啤酒,显示租客是通过其他渠道购买。房东法院申请禁令,试图禁止租客这样做。租客的抗辩是在签约前,房东曾经口头答应说到了 1998 年 3 月,就会放开对租客这些购买啤酒的约束,这构成了附带保证/协议。但该合约中有一条完整合约条文,如下:"14.1 Any variations of this Agreement which are agreed in correspondence shall be incorporated in this Agreement where that correspondence makes express reference to this Clause and the parties acknowledge that this Agreement (with the incorporation of any such variation) constitutes the entire Agreement between the parties."

双方的争议是上述条文是否包括了附带保证/协议与房东有否作出过被指控的附带保证/协议。Lightman 大法官判是证据不足以证明曾经作出过这种附带保证/协议,所以严格来说不必再针对上述的完整合约条文作出解释。但 Lightman 大法官还是有针对,并先解释该完整合约条文的目的与作用,说:"The purpose of an entire agreement clause is to preclude a party to a written agreement from threshing through the undergrowth and finding in the course of negotiations some (chance) remark or statement (often long forgotten or difficult to recall or explain) on which to found a claim such as the present to the existence of a collateral warranty. The entire agreement clause obviates the occasion for any such search and the peril to the contracting parties posed by the need which may arise in its absence to conduct such a search. For such a clause constitutes a binding agreement between the parties that the full contractual terms are to be found in the document containing the clause and not elsewhere, and that accordingly any promises or assurances made in the course of the negotiations (which in the absence of such a clause might have effect as a collateral warranty) shall have no contractual force, save insofar as they are reflected and given effect in that document. The operation of the clause is not to render evidence of the collateral warranty inadmissible in evidence as is suggested in Chitty on Contract, 28th ed. Vol. 1, par. 12-102: it is to denude what would otherwise constitute a collateral warranty of legal effect."

接下来,Lightman 大法官认为本合约条文中的文字足够包括附带保证/协议,说:"That is the question raised in this case, where the formula of words used in the clause is abbreviated to an acknowledgement by the parties that the agreement constitutes the entire agreement between them. In my judgement that formula is sufficient, for it constitutes an agreement that the full contractual terms to which the parties agree to bind themselves and that what might otherwise constitute a side legal effect. That can be the only purpose of the provision."

2.4.5　案例之五:Exxonmobil Sales and Supply Corp v. Texaco Ltd

Exxonmobil Sales and Supply Corp v. Texaco Ltd (2003) EWHC 1964 (Comm) 先例是有关 CIF 的买卖,货物是 15000 吨柴油,根据买卖合约,在装港时委任了一位独立专家取样以确定该票柴油符合合约规格,该专家也确认了是符合的。但到了卸港的卡迪夫,买方声称柴油不符合规格而拒货。在诉讼中,买方指控装港的专家犯了严重错误并要举证在装港的习惯做法,就是他应把样品保留一段合理的时间。针对习惯做法,卖方指出该买卖合约有一条完整合约条文,内容已经包括了排除习惯做法的争议。该条文如下:"... contains the entire agreement of the parties... and there is no other promise, representation, warranty, usage or course of dealing affecting it..."

Nigel Teare 大法官判上述条文有效排除习惯做法/惯例的默示条文的争议。但他也作出了有关不同种类的默示条文不是全都可包括在这种条文内的警告,说:"It seems to me arguable that where it is necessary to imply a term in order to make the express terms work such an implied term may not be excluded by the entire agreement clause because it could not be said that such a term is to be found in the document or documents forming part of the contract. The same cannot be said of an implied term based on custom or usage."

该警告是有道理的,有的默示条文必须加入合约而使合约有"商业效力"(business efficacy),否则合约无法操作。有关这方面的问题在本书第七章之第4段有详论。这样,任何广泛的完整合约条文都不足以排除这种默示条文。另外,一些立法的默示,如英国1979年的《货物销售法》里的各种默示条文,如卖方对货物的主权,也一般不能被排除,除非这个完整合约条文写得足够清楚。在 Gerard McMeel 教授的《The Construction of Contracts—Interpretation, Implication and Rectification》(2007年)一书中的24.32段对此有论述,如下:"It is submitted that this case correctly excluded the custom or usage, which were expressly referred to in the entire agreement clause. However other implied terms should be approached more cautiously. It is clear that an entire agreement clause would be insufficient to exclude the various statutory implied terms, as its language is insufficiently clear and express to meet the strict tests for *prima facie* exclusion of those general default rules. It also appears to be correct that the entire agreement clause is inapt to exclude those terms which are necessary to make the contract work. This may be for the reason suggested by the Deputy Judge, or it may be simply that the existence of the implied term contradicts the assertion in the entire agreement clause that it represents the totality of the agreement. In those circumstances the necessary implied term must trump."

2.4.6 案例之六:Infiniteland Ltd v. Artisan Contracting Ltd

Infiniteland Ltd v. Artisan Contracting Ltd(2006) 1 BCLC 632 先例的案情是有关一个房屋承建公司的买卖,在收购以前,买方曾经进行了一个全面的"经济上的尽职调查"(financial due diligence),包括可全面检查的"帐簿"(books)。另在一个长达7个星期的时间内,卖方也提供了一份十分详细的有关公司经济状况的资料。买方后来指控卖方误述,但这不被 Park 大法官接受。因为在上述详细调查的情况下,买方不可能会依赖在酒店喝咖啡时的短暂的交谈中涉及的公司业务状况的误述订约。所以误述在事实上不成立,但即使在法律上买方也是败诉,因为合约中有一条完整合约条文,内容包括陈述,所以可排除这个误述的指控。该条文是:“The purchaser has entered into this agreement on the basis of and in reliance on the Warranties and the Purchaser acknowledges that it has not been induced to enter into this agreement by any representation or warranty other than the Warranties.”

2.4.7 案例之七:Proforce Recruit Ltd v. Rugby Group Ltd

Proforce Recruit Ltd v. Rugby Group Ltd (2006) EWCA Civ 69 先例不是针对完整合约条文的解释,而是关于有了该条文是否可以避免针对口头/外来证据。在该先例,原告要提供事实证人(公司的主席与总经理)协助解释合约内的明示条文。该合约有一条完整合约条文,说道:“This agreement supersedes all prior representations, agreements, negotiations or understandings”

在高院,Field 大法官认为有这样的条文下,他不能考虑外来证据协助解释合约明示条文/文字,说:“The effect of the words... is that the things superseded are to have no bearing on the meaning of the agreement.”

但这在上诉庭被改变,认为该完整合约条文不应针对明示条文的解释,说道:

“Mr Sweeting(上诉申请人代表大律师)submitted clause 9.2 was an ‘entire agreement clause’ aimed at excluding attempts to use extrinsic evidence in order to incorporate further terms or representations into the contract, which the parties had not themselves included and thereby change the contents of the agreement. It was not apt to govern the construction of the written terms that the parties had included or to exclude evidence relevant to the ascertainment of their meaning. ProForce(上诉申请人)argued that it was not attempting to use what was agreed, understood or said before the making of the written contract in order to introduce a new term or a collateral contract, but to arrive at the proper meaning of the expression ‘preferred supplier status,’ which had no plain natural and ordinary meaning and which was not defined in the written agreement.(上诉申请人代表大律师指完整合约条文只是排除以外来证据企图加入其他条文或陈述,但该条文并非针对文书合约内的内容与通过外来证据作出解释。)

In my judgment, ProForce has a real prospect of succeeding at trial in its construction of clause 9.2. There is a reasonably arguable distinction between, on the one hand, ascertaining the contents of a written contract or setting up a collateral or side contract by reference to prior representations, agreements, negotiations and understandings and, on the other hand, ascertaining the meaning of a term contained in a written contract by reference to pre-contract materials. It is reasonably arguable that in clause 9.2 the parties intended to exclude the former, but not to inhibit the latter.”

2.4.8 案例之八:Peekay Intermark Ltd v. Australia & New Zealand Banking Group Ltd.

这个先例 Peekay Intermark Ltd v. Australia & New Zealand Banking Group Ltd.

(2006) 2 Lloyd's Rep 511 有关投资是 ANZ 银行推出的一种名为"Structured US Dollar hedged Russian Treasury bill deposit"的金融产品,它是与俄罗斯政府的债券挂钩。投资者是在 Isle of Man 注册的一家公司,而背后真正的投资者估计是阿拉伯国家的一些富商。投资者的代表在 ANZ 的合约表格中签了字,也另签了一份"风险披露声明"(Risk Disclosure Statement)。声明中有说明是投资者确认已经阅读与明白有关风险的披露,而在投资合约表格中也有各种风险警告,包括俄罗斯政府的"主权国违约"(sovereign default)与"新兴市场"(emerging markets)的风险。后来,该金融产品出了事,发生了主权国违约。投资者起诉 ANZ 并指控误述。高院的 Siberry 大法官不认为投资合约中的文件有排除订约前的误述,并认为投资者只是粗略看了有关的合约表格,并签了字。至于误述方面,Siberry 大法官认为有误述,认定 ANZ 曾经口头对投资者说这是一个在"俄罗斯债券的直接投资"(direct proprietary investment in Russian bonds),但事实上这一个金融产品是"对冲基金"(derivative)或 structure deposit contract。

但该案件被上诉庭推翻,上诉庭对有关投资合约的文件内容比高院重视得多,并不认为 ANZ 有任何错误的"引导"(inducement),判是投资者自己误解了该投资产品的性质。Moore - Bick 大法官是这样说:"It is common to include in certain kinds of contracts an express acknowledgment by each of the parties that they have not been induced to enter the contract by any representations other than those contained in the contract itself. The effectiveness of a clause of that kind may be challenged on the grounds that the contract as a whole, including the clause in question, can be avoided if in fact one or other party was induced to enter into it by misrepresentation. However, I can see no reason in principle why it should not be possible for parties to an agreement to give up any right to assert that they were induced to enter into it by misrepresentation, provided they make their intention clear, or why a clause of that kind, if properly drafted, should not give rise to a contractual estoppel of the kind recognised in *Colchester Borough Council v. Smith* (1991) *Ch* 448; *affd* (1992) *Ch* 421. However, that particular question does not arise in this case. A clause of that kind may (depending on its terms) also be capable of giving rise to an estoppel by representation if the necessary elements can be established."

2.4.9 案例之九:Springwell Navigation v. JP Morgan Chase Bank

Springwell Navigation v. JP Morgan Chase Bank (2010) EWCA Civ 1212 先例与 Peekay Intermark Ltd v. Australia & New Zealand Banking Group Ltd. (2006) 2 Lloyd's Rep 511 先例是同一类的争议,涉及在 1990 年年底,专业投资者在新兴市场(涉及发展中国家)债务危机而蒙受严重损失,试图向提供投资意见的私人银行提起诉讼并索赔损失。在该先例,原告是专业投资者,他的钱来自一个希腊船东(Polemis 家族),他们在航运赚了大钱(估计希腊船东不少是赚了中国贸易商与船厂的钱)并希望在航运以外找其他投资，在本先例就涉及投资7亿美元在新兴市场的债券，其中最重要的就是俄罗斯。由于俄罗斯在1998年发生经济危机（同时也是亚洲金融危机），在8月份对部分债券违约，这导致希腊船东蒙受严重损失，所以在英国法院向投资银行的摩根大通提出诉讼与索赔损失。这个昂贵的诉讼一审持续了68天，有390个开庭文件案卷，另有22个先例的案卷。其中关键的就是他们之间的协议有一条十分详尽的完整合约条文与不依赖条文，但问题是摩根大通银行能否依赖这条文的保障，这也是在上诉庭的法律争议。

这里也涉及较早时两个看来对摩根大通银行不利的先例。第一个是 Diplock 大法官在 Lowe v Lombank Ltd (1960) 1 WLR 196 先例中的判决，案情涉及一位65岁的老妇人通过租购合约向一家车行租了一辆车子。该合约中有条文说明老妇人已经检查过车辆并确认状况良好，但其实根本没有检查过。同样的条文也出现在交车的收据，但该老妇人依然没有检查过。事实上该车子不能安全使用，而且对一个像老妇人这样的外行人无法一下子看出来的。在后来的诉讼，老妇人在第一审败诉，因为她已经在有关的合约与文件中签字，根据本章之第2段介绍的签字规则，她无法不受到约束。而确认已经检查过与车辆状况良好也构成了“合约禁止翻供”（contractual estoppel），[6]不能推翻并声称这合约的规定并非事实的真相。

但上诉至上诉庭被推翻，认为老妇人的原告所确认的是过去的事实（也就是对车子作出了检验），是双方都知道不正确的事实（因为实际上没有检查过），这就不是一个合约的承诺。Diplock 大法官是这样说：“No doubt for the very good reason that there was no evidence (an it is difficult to see how there could be any truthful evidence) that the defendants believed in the truth of the representation. To call it an agreement as well as an acknowledgement by the plaintiff cannot convert a statement as to past facts, known by both party to be untrue, into a contractual obligation, which is essentially a promise by the promisor to the promise that acts will be done in the future or that facts exist at the time of the promise or will exist in the future.”

这显然对完整合约条文与不依赖条文有直接冲击，因为这种条文也会是说双方

---

[6] 合约禁止翻供的大原则在很多合约中会出现，包括所谓的“结论性证据条文”（conclusive evidence clause）。例如，国际货物买卖就经常有一条“装港检验证书为终”条文，以避免货物在卸港被买方以货物质量有问题而拒货所带来的严重损失与不便。这种做法包括一些著名的先例，如 Veba v Petrotrade (2002) 1 Lloyd's Rep 295 等先例，在杨大明律师的《国际货物买卖》一书第259页有详细介绍。根据合约禁止翻供，双方既然同意以装港的检验证书为终，只要该证书是证明货物质量符合买卖合约，买方就不能以卸港的检验证明不符合质量更准确或抨击装港检验不准确等理由推翻双方的约定。换言之，除了欺诈等极端的情况，买方禁止证明真相，这也是禁止翻供的精神。这种结论性证据条文也出现在其他类型的合约，如银行担保：Bache v Banque Vernes (1973) 2 Lloyd's Rep 437；IIG Capital LLC v Van der Merwe (2008) 2 Lloyd's Rep 187 与 AXA Sun Life Services plc v Campbell Martin Ltd and others (2011) 2 Lloyd's Rep 1 等先例。这方面在本书第十四章之第1段有详论。

没有依赖对方的陈述(或误述)甚至否定曾经作出过任何陈述,如在 Trident Turboprop (Dublin) Ltd v First Flight Couriers Ltd (2008) 2 Lloyd's Rep 581 先例,案情涉及飞机买卖合约中有一条条文说:"... the supplier has not and shall not be deemed to have made any warranties or representations, express or implied, about the Aircraft."

但通常是双方的确在谈判中有作出过陈述,甚至被依赖,双方也知道这个事实。所以,如果在一条完整合约条文或不依赖条文的情况下作出双方都知道是不正确的事实陈述,能否有效存有疑问。

根据 Lowe v Lombank Ltd 先例,在 EA Grinstead & Son Ltd v. McGarrigan (Unreported, 27 October 1999)与 Watford Electronics Ltd v Sanderson CFL Ltd (2001) EWCA Civ 317 这两个先例,Chadwick 大法官认为一条不依赖条文的有效性必须满足三方面的考验。一是该条文必须清楚与不含糊(the statement of non-reliance must be clear and unambiguous)。二是作出没有依赖的陈述一方必须是想到对方会接受或依赖(the maker of the statement of non-reliance must have intended that the other should act on or rely on it)。三是对方必须相信与依赖了这个没有依赖的陈述(the other party must in fact have believed and relied on the statement of non-reliance)。换言之,把"没有依赖"也当作独立的陈述,陈述方想到对方会依赖与对方也的确依赖了这个"没有依赖"的陈述。Chadwick 大法官自己也知道这些考验很难或不可能做得到,说:"that may present insuperable difficulties; not least it may be impossible for a party who has made representations which he intended should be relied upon to satisfy the court that he entered into the contract in the belief that a statement by the other party that he had not relied upon those representations was true."

所以有说法是在这两个判例后,完整合约条文与不依赖条文的有效性被判了死刑。但在 Peekay Intermark Ltd v. Australia & New Zealand Banking Group Ltd 先例,特别是 Springwell Navigation v JP Morgan Chase Bank 先例后,完整合约条文与不依赖条文的有效性"死而复生"。首先,在 Springwell 先例的上诉庭不认为 Lowe v Lombank Ltd 先例对他们有约束,该先例只是针对消费者,与适用保护消费者的《Hire Purchase Act 1938》,Aikens 大法官说:"... are not binding authority for the far-reaching proposition that there can never be an agreement in a contract that parties are conducting their dealings on the basis that a past event had not occurred or that a particular fact was the case, even if it was not the case and both the parties knew it was not."

Aikens 大法官也不认为双方为什么不可以在合约中约定双方都知道不是正确的事实,说:

"Before I examine Lowe v Lombank and subsequent cases on this issue, I will try and analyse the matter from principle. If A and B enter into a contract, then, unless there is some principle of law or statute to the contrary, they are entitled to agree what they like. Unless Lowe v Lombank is authority to the contrary, **there is no legal principle**

that states that parties cannot agree to assume that a certain state of affairs is the case at the time the contract is concluded or has been so in the past, even if that is not the case, so that the contract is made upon the basis that the present or past facts are as stated and agreed by the parties...(加黑是笔者的强调)

So, in principle and always depending on the precise construction of the contractual wording, I would say that A and B can agree that A has made no pre – contract representations to B about the quality or nature of a financial instrument that A is selling to B. Should it make any difference that both A and B know at and before making the contract, that A did, in fact, make representations, so thatthe statement that A had not is contrary to what each side knows is the case? Apart from the remarks of Diplock J in Lowe v Lombank, Mr Brindle [这是原告 Springwell 的代表大律师] did not show us any case that might support the proposition that parties cannot agree that X is the case even if both know that is not so. I am unaware of any legal principle to that effect. The only possible exception might be if the particular agreement between A and B on the certain state of affairs concerned contradicts some other specific or more general rule of English public policy. Like Moore – Brick LJ in Peekay, I see commercial utility in such clauses being enforceable, so that parties know precisely the basis on which they are entering into their contractual relationship."

2.4.10 案例之十:AXA Sun Life Services Plc v. Campbell Martin Ltd

AXA Sun Life Services Plc v. Campbell Martin Ltd(2011) 2 Lloyd's Rep 1 先例,案情涉及 AXA 的保险公司授权 Campbell Martin 作为其代表销售保险产品,他们之间的合约有一条完整合约条文说:"This Agreement and the Schedules and documents referred to herein constitute the entire agreement and understanding between you and us in relation to the subject matter thereof. Without prejudice to any variation as provided in clause 1.1, **this Agreement shall supersede any prior** promises, agreements, **representations**, undertakings or implications **whether made orally or in writing** between you and us relating to the subject matter of this Agreement but this will not affect any obligations in any such prior agreement which are expressed to continue after termination."(加黑部分是显示这一条完整合约条文所用的文字是说本文书合约超越了以前不论是口头或文书所作出的陈述。)

在该先例,Campbell Martin 指 AXA 曾经作出误述,但 AXA 以上述完整合约条文作为抗辩之一。上诉庭在这一点是判 AXA 败诉,其中 Rix 大法官是说:"In context the language of 'representations' and 'supersede' is the language of defining contractual obligations rather than the language of excluding liability in misrepresentation. There was there, as here, no language to the effect that the parties were agreed that no representations had been made or relied upon."

他也说："No doubt all such cases are only authority for each clause's particular wording：nevertheless it seems to me that there are certain themes which deserve recognition. Among them is that the exclusion of liability for misrepresentation has to be clearly stated. It can be done by clauses which state the parties' agreement that there have been no representations made；or that there has been no reliance on any representations；or by an express exclusion of liability for misrepresentation. However, save in such contexts, and particularly where the word 'representations' takes its place alongside other words expressive of contractual obligation, talk of the parties' contract superseding such prior agreement will not by itself absolve a party of misrepresentation where its ingredients can be proved."（虽然每个先例只是有关完整合约条文特定文字的权威先例，但还是可以看到解释这种条文的共同认知。其中之一就是排除误述的责任需要明确写明。写法上可以是说明双方同意在谈判中没有作出过任何陈述，或是对这些陈述没有任何依赖，或明示排除误述的责任。但在本先例，只把以前的陈述与其他合约的承诺［以前的承诺、协议、承担与默示］一并说是被文书合约超越是不足够。）

第十四章　惯用条文之三

§1　最终与有约束力条文(final and binding clause)

任何商业合约的履行往往都会涉及双方会面对的技术性问题,如果双方不想带来昂贵与不会有结论的争议,甚至最终要以诉讼解决,就会想到尽早由双方委任/约定一位在技术方面可以信赖的第三人及时或尽早作出决定。但第三人作出的决定如果对其中一方不利,就会经常出现不利一方挑战、质疑并试图推翻该第三人的决定。如果不利一方作出挑战并成功推翻,并由另一个第三人作出不同决定,难否定后一个决定会比原来的决定更加准确。特别是,原来的决定作出后,不利一方针对性提供更多的证据与争议,会有可能是后来的决定会更加全面与正确。但允许这样做就会没完没了,所以不少商业合约,都经常会以明示条文规定一旦有双方同意的第三人作出了决定,就不能推翻。这种条文可被称为造成"合约禁止翻供"(contractual estoppel)。

例如,双方如果同意以香港国际仲裁中心的管理规则进行仲裁,根据2013年仲裁规则之Art 3.2,香港国际仲裁中心的任何决定(如否合并仲裁)都是终局,不能上诉。这里唯一的例外是对仲裁员的挑战,因为根据香港法律(英国法律也是一样)这会涉及"自然公正"(natural justice),必须由法院来监督,不存在可以通过合约条文制造禁止翻供。同样的道理也在仲裁条文,即使双方约定了仲裁是终局,在英国法律下也一直存在这样约定是违反公共政策,所以是无效的说法:Czarnikow v Roth Schmidt & Co (1922) 12 Lloyd's Rep 195先例。原因之一是法律问题最后的决定权是在法院,而不是仲裁庭。另一个重要的原因是英国商法,而商业争议绝大部分都是以仲裁解决,所以只能通过让仲裁裁决上诉至法院才能持续英国商法的发展与完善。这种情况直到1979年英国《仲裁法》才有了一定程度对双方约定仲裁裁决是最终与有约束力的承认。

当然,即使法律承认最终与有约束力条文或合约禁止翻供,也不表示是绝对。以仲裁裁决为例,通常被视为对有关的争议造成了禁止翻供,不论这说法是"一审终局"(*res judicata*)或"一事不再理"(issue estoppel)。败诉方事后拿出新的与强有力的证据显示原来的裁决有错误,甚至是根据已经提供的证据显示了原来的裁决有错误,也会因为禁止翻供被拒绝"找出真相"。例外的情况是原来的裁决是通过欺诈获得，如有证据显示仲裁庭受贿，这显然会导致裁决书被撤销或不能执行。另一种例外情况是原来的裁决是通过非双方所约定的程序进行，如仲裁员人数或是仲裁员资格。这样，就涉及了仲裁管辖权的问题。

1.1　商业合约与证书/证明

商业合约如货物买卖合约与建筑合约（包括造船合约）常常会有条文规定某些技术性问题由证书决定，并会说明是最终与有约束力。如国际货物买卖合约，就经常会有条文规定装港/卸港对货物质量或来源地由某机构签发的证书为准，或是在卸港由双方共同委任的机构对货损货差作出检查与签发的报告/证书为准。如果发生不可抗力事件导致无法或延误履行，需由当地的商会作出证明。这方面可节录《Benjamin's Sale of Goods》（第18版，2010年）一书之13-041段说："Provision is often made for certification and testing by various methods. Such clauses may be treated as exemption clauses, and where appropriate subjected to strict interpretation. Sometimes, however, the contractual duty is itself simply to supply goods that satisfy the certifier, or fulfil certain contractual standards and also satisfy the certifier. Unless the contract so provides expressly or by necessary implication, however, approval of the certifier is not conclusive that the contractual terms have been duly performed. But the contract may so provide: provisions for conclusive certifications as to quality are common. Sometimes much more complex terms are laid down which require specific analysis. Thus in 'Agroexport' v NV Goorden Import Cy SA (1956) 1 Lloyd's Rep 319 there was what Sellers J. called: '... a comprehensive code for rejection or acceptance or allowance based on the evidence derived from the certificate of control and the certificates of the analysts as prescribed.'..."

造船合约也同样涉及大量证书/证明。双方约定的船级社在检查后会签发大量针对性的证书，如针对船舶的主机与设备、吨位、吃水、船舶结构、安全与适航等。这些证书通常要求"不能有要求、限制或批注"（free of recommendations, restrictions or qualifications），也就是无条件显示有关船舶的建造是依照船级社或有关当局（如船旗国[1]）的要求。这些都是船厂在交船时需要按照造船合约交出给船东让其在将来营运所必需的文件。另在建造的过程中，如果船厂与船东发生技术性争议，条文通常约定由船级社检验师的决定为准。[2]

这种情况在岸上的工程合约也是同样道理，正如在London and Regional (St George's Court) Ltd v Ministry of Defence (2008) 121 Con. L. R. 56先例，一审法院的Coulson大法官说："Under most standard forms of construction and engineering con-

---

〔1〕船旗国所签署的国际公约或对船舶的各种要求是授权船级社作出检查，如果符合要求签发证书。

〔2〕在这种情况，看来是把船级社验船师的决定视为"专家决定"（expert determination），这方面会在本章之第2段详论。

tracts, certification regimes are commonplace. The contract will spell out the particular issue that the certifier is required to decide; what information is to be provided to the certifier to allow him to reach that decision, and when it must be provided; and the circumstances in which the certifier will then decide, on the basis of the information provided by both sides, the answer to the issue before him. The certificate is the final step in a process designed to ensure fairness, with the mechanism spelled out carefully in the contract itself. **Moreover, where the certificate is anything other than an interim or provisional statement of the position — if it is intended to be final, and oust the jurisdiction of the courts or an arbitrator to review it — then that must be made plain in the clearest possible terms.**"(加黑部分是说签发的证书如果想作为最终,并排除法院或仲裁庭重新考虑有关事实真相的管辖权,就需要明确规定。)

这解释了商业合约有大量最终与有约束力条文规定某个或某些技术性问题由证书决定,这可以大量减少昂贵与耗时的事后争议。可以说,证书对相关事实的认定经常会被判是结论性,也就是说即使证书有错误,不满意的一方也不能提出异议。这导致在某些先例,法院认为是"证书最终条文"(certificate final clause)是一条"免责条文"(exemption clause),应该严格解释。如在 Kollerich & Cie SA v State Trading Corporation of India (1979) 2 Lloyd's Rep 442 先例,Parker 大法官说:"The clause is one which is, as to the certificate, an exemption clause and must therefore be narrowly construed."

但在 Toepfer v Continental Grain Co (1974) 1 Lloyd's Rep 11 先例,Carins 大法官指出两者(这种条文与免责条文)之间存在不同,因为这种条文是对合约双方都有利,说:"I see no grounds for saying that a provision of this kind should be construed with some special degree of strictness. It is not like an exceptional clause which is designed to operate to give protection to one party. Either buyer or seller benefit from this clause if some error of judgment on the part of the inspector led him to certify a quality in the goods different from their actual quality."

1.2 对人证书与对物证书

很多商业合约中都有条文规定由证书证明履行的质量是否有达标,如国际货物买卖合约是以货物描述进行买卖,或是工程合约必须符合某些特定的规格。这就产生了一个疑问,取得合约规定的证书是否表示合约一方已经是结论性完成了合约的承诺/责任,或只是给他多一重保障?如果是后果,就表示双方事后对事实有争议,有关的证书也只是其中一份文件证据,即使这份证据会在法院或仲裁庭有较重的分量。

在 Minster Trust Ltd v Traps Tractors Ltd (1954) 1 WLR 963 先例,Devlin 大法官把证书分为两类,说:"If work under a contract has to be completed to the satisfaction of a certifier, it may mean that his duty is merely to see that the requirements of the contract are met, or it may mean that he is entitled to impose a standard of his own. It may be that his standard is that to which the parties submit and that it constitutes the only provision in the contract about quality; or it may be that his standard is an added protection, so that performance under the contract must satisfy both the contract requirements and the certifier. . . there is a distinction between a certificate that is given only for the purposes of a particular contract and one that, although it may be called for by a particular contract, is not particularly related to that contract. The certifier may not then be an agent of either party. That is so in the case of a Lloyd's certificate or of a certificate by a public analyst, or others that may be obtainable on a fee. It has now become quite common to include among documents which have to be tendered against payment a certificate of inspection or of quality. Certificates of this sort are addressed to all the world or to all who may be concerned. If the phrase is not used as more than a label, they might be called certificates *in rem*, as compared with certificates *in personam*, which concern only particular contracts and are addressed only to particular parties. The former carry the same meaning to all who read them. The latter may have to be interpreted in the light of particular contractual requirements or of information known only to the addressees. **A certificate in rem certifies a standard of quality extraneous to the contract. It may be the certifier's own standard or it may be taken from some public or independent source. A certificate *in personam* may be based on the certifier's own standards or on standards prescribed by the contract. It may be a certificate of quality or a certificate that a contract has been carried out.**"(上述所讲,特别是加黑的部分,是把证书区分为两类,第一类是"对物"[in rem],第二类是"对人"[in personam]。大致上第一类证书是针对所有人士,包括合约双方与其他的第三人所作出。而签发有关证书的机构也不属于合约双方的代理人,即使合约方需要支付一定的费用才能取得。而第二类是针对有关的合约,证书也是给合约双方而不针对第三人,而签发这类证书的机构往往是合约一方或双方的代理人。)

所以在本章之1.1段提到的例子中,国际货物买卖合约由双方共同委任的机构对货物质量作出的报告/证书,应该是属于对人证书,而从有关当局取得的出口证则应该属于对物证书。造船合约所涉及的大量证书/证明,有很多船级社在检查后为自己或为授权的船旗国所签发的"船级社与营运证书"(classification and trading certificates),应属于对物证书。但同样是船级社检验师针对在建造的过程中船厂与船东发生的技术性争议所作出的证明/证书,则属于对人证书。

有说法是法院"有更大的可能"(more likely)判对物证书是结论性,也就是合约一方是结论性符合了合约的承诺/责任,这可看Lewison大法官所著的《The Interpretation of Contracts》(第5版,2011年)一书第655页。这表示对人证书有更大机会被法院或仲裁庭认为是给合约一方加多一重保障,或对有关技术性争议多了一份证据。现实中,这两种类型证书的分水线很难判断,到底是表示合约一方卸下了合约责任还是只是让另一方增加一重保障,还要根据特定合约的条文/文字进行解释。

因此,如果合约方希望该证书(不论是对物或是对人)是结论性,安全的做法还是以明示条文规定,造成合约禁止翻供。在 Lindsay (W. N.) & Co Ltd v European Grain & Shipping Co Ltd (1963) 1 Lloyd's Rep. 437 先例,Diplock 大法官说:"There may be good business reasons for modifying the ordinary common - law remedies for breach of contract, or for prescribing one method to the exclusion of all others for proof of a particular breach, but if this is to be done, it is better done clearly and expressly rather than by relying upon an implied term to that effect, for this is a field in which the Courts are always slow to find an implication of that kind."

1.3 证书/证明只是多了一重保障或多了一份文件证据

一般情况下,有了一份证书/证明只是多了一重保障。首先介绍一些工程合约,这可以看 Newton Abbott Development Co Ltd v Stockman Bros (1931) 47 T. L. R 616 先例,承建商同意根据一定的规划和规格建造房屋,并且工程要获得测量师与政府当局卫生检查员的满意。测量师和政府当局卫生检查员签发了批准证书,但法院判是这不代表承建商卸下了工程质量的合约责任,而只是让雇主增加了一重保障。

另是在 National Coal Board v Neil (William) & Son (St Helens) Ltd (1985) QB 300 先例,也有类似判法。建筑合约要求工厂的建造符合一定的规格并要工程师合理满意。之后工程师没有注意到一些隐藏的缺陷,签发了证书。法院判是工程师满意的事实不能让承建商卸下必须承担符合一定规格的合约责任。

同样的判法也出现在其他的商业合约,如在 Sleigh v Tyser (1900) 2 QB 333 先例,案情涉及航次保险合约。有条文要求船舶在开航前需要劳合社验船师检查与批准船上的设施,这也事后被通过并获取证书/证明。但到了航次履行,有关设施并不足够而导致出了事故。这被法院判在 1906 年英国《海上保险法》针对航次保险是有默示的适航保证,这个保证并非是劳合社验船师作出了检查与批准就可以被忽视。

另在 The "Gianna M" (1937) 57 Lloyd's Rep 247 先例,案情涉及租约条文允许承租人先检查满意后才开装汽油的货物。条文如下:"(1) That the steamer being tight staunch and strong and every way fitted for the voyage, and to be maintained in such condition during the voyage, perils of the sea excepted ... (16) The captain is bound to keep the tanks, pipes and pumps of the steamer always clean... (27) Steamer to clean for the cargo in question to the satisfaction of charterers' inspector."

事实上也的确进行了检查并获得满意,但最后装船的汽油仍受到污染。上诉庭判船舶适航与适货的责任是基本与重大,不是让承租人先检查满意就可以超越。承租人多了这个检查的权利只是希望预防事故与多一重保障,并非要替代船东适航的责任。类似的条文普遍在油轮租约存在,如在 ASBATANKVOY 标准格式的第 18 条文说:"Cleaning: The Owner shall clean the tanks, pipes and pumps of the vessel to the satisfaction of the charterer's Inspector."

涉及散粮的运载在美国、加拿大、澳大利亚等主要装货港都有十分严格的装货前验(货)舱程序,散粮受污染的事故现在已经很少见。例如,在美国港口对散粮装船前的严格检查,由美国农业部(USDA)或 N. C. B. (National Cargo Bureau)负责,确认货舱清洁及货物不受污染后才准许开始装货,从而就会大幅度减少这种事故。但这种事故一旦发生,船东还是不能以装货前的检验替代保证适航/适货的责任,最多只是多了一份可能是强而有力的文件证据。

1.4 合约规定证书/证明是最终与有约束力造成合约禁止翻供

而如果合约有约定一些证书/证明是最终与有约束力(或类似明确的语言),就会造成合约禁止翻供。即双方同意了该证书是不能事后否定。

1.4.1 文字上造成合约禁止翻供

如在"Agroexport" v NV Goorden Import Cy SA (1956) 1 Lloyd's Rep 319 先例,合约第 9 条文规定:"... The control certificate and the samples drawn and sealed at shipment will be definitive."

在该先例,有关的检验机构在装港已经作出了一份检验报告,也就是上述条文所针对的证书。卸货后买方要求进一步检验,同一检验机构对同一份样品作出了第二份不同结果的检验报告。于是,买方开始仲裁,要求以第二份检验报告为准。仲裁庭判是买方胜诉,卖方上诉至法院,要求撤销裁决书,理由是第二份检验报告不能被接受。Sellers 大法官同意卖方的说法,如下:"The contract expressly provided that the certificate of superintendence [or control certificate] and the samples drawn and sealed at shipment were to be final and conclusive (definitive). The rights of the parties, it was said, were dealt with contractually and exclusively in respect of description and quality by Clauses 8, 9 and 10 of Form 15."

当然这也会有例外,如在 Studebaker Distributors v Charlton Steam Shipping Co (1938) 1 KB 459 先例,案情涉及从美国运输汽车英国,提单有条文说是纽约保险人指定的验船师对船舶的堆货满意就被视为"结论性证据"(conclusive evidence)。事实上,该验船师也作出了一份证书/证明。但这在法院被判是证书并非结论性,而且这个条文因为 1893 年美国《哈特法》(也就是等同 1924 年《海牙规则》)禁止以订约自由减轻承运人的责任而变为无效。Goddard 大法官是说:"... the clause does offend against the Act because it enables the shipowner to escape the liability from which the Act intends he should not escape, if he can produce a surveyor's certificate saying that he has done that which in fact he may not have done..."

1.4.2 证书/证明必须有针对性与清楚明确才能造成合约禁止翻供

固然,除了订约双方的合约条文,要造成合约禁止翻供也需要作出的有关证书是一份有针对性与清楚明确的文件。在 Minster Trust Ltd v Traps Tractors Ltd (1954) 1 WLR 963 先例,Devlin 大法官说:"I think that a certificate of this sort must, to satisfy the contract, be unambiguous and readily understandable. When a document is tendered under a contract, the recipient has often to make up his mind whether he is going to pay out money upon it or to accept or reject goods; he has no right and may not have time to cross – examine the certifier or to ask him to clear up doubts."(这是说依赖有关证书作出重大决定的人士不会有机会或有权查问或盘问作出/签发证书的人士。)

这点也在 Token Construction Co Ltd v Charlton Estates Ltd (1973) 1 BLR 48, CA 先例被上诉庭确认,Roskill 大法官说:"Though neither condition 2(e) nor condition 16 . . . prescribes any form in which the architect is to grant any extension or to certify his opinion, it is, in my judgment, essential that, **while the architect is left free to adopt what form of expression he likes for the grant or certificate**, **as the case may require**, **he must do so clearly so that the intent and substance of what he does is clear.** The court should not be astute to criticize documents issued by an architect merely because he may not use the precise language which a lawyer might have selected in order to express a like determination, but while this amount of latitude is permissible, it cannot extend to the court's treating as due compliance with contractual requirements documents which, however liberally interpreted, **do not plainly show that they were intended to comply with, and, fairly understood, do comply with those contractual requirements.**"(加黑部分是笔者的强调)

上述两个先例针对的是证书内包括的信息,看来法院在解释时会采取与解释单方面合约同样的解释规则。在一些合约会明示规定有效的证书/证明要符合某些条件,在这种情况,法院会相对严格地解释有关的证书/证明是否符合了合约的要求。因此,如果合约中有列名证明人或有对证明人的描述,必须严格遵从,否则证书/证明就会无效,也构成不了合约禁止翻供。

1.5 国际货物买卖约定以装港检查为终的条文

这种装港"证书最终条文"(certificate final clause)是笔者熟悉而且已经有大量先例。问题是在国际货物/商品买卖,货物都是 1979 年英国《货物销售法》视为的"将来货物"(future goods)或"不确定货物"(unascertained goods)。该立法针对这种货物是允许买方在首次有合理机会时对卖方交出的货物作出检查,如果发觉货不对版,就有终止合约也就是拒货的权利。这个对货物作出检查的合理机会通常是在卸港。但卖方如果在卸港被买方拒货,会面对一个十分艰巨与困难的情况。而且,会有卖方对买方在卸港作出的检验不放心。所以在过去三四十年,已经有不少卖方坚持一条在装港付运前对货物作出检验的条文。如果检验的结果符合买卖合约的货物描述与质量等,就视为最终与结论性。这种证书最终条文的效力在较早期的上诉庭 Toepfer v Continental Grain Co. (1974) 1 Lloyd's Rep 11 先例被总结(并在 Berger & Co Inc v Gill & Duffus SA [1984] 1 Lloyd's Rep 7 先例获得了贵族院同意)如下:"Where a certificate is to be conclusive as to the quality of goods, the buyer will be precluded from recovering damages from the seller, if, contrary to the statement contained in the certificate, they are not of the contract quality, even if, in fact, the person giving the certificate has been negligent in making it."

这一方面在杨大明律师的《国际货物买卖》一书有更详尽的解释,可参阅。

1.5.1 近期有关重要先例之一:The "Mercini Lady"

The "Mercini Lady"先例涉及一个"气油"(gasoil)的FOB买卖,在装港的岸上油柜测试显示了有关的货物是符合买卖合约的描述。而有关的买卖合约的第12条文说:"12. QUANTITY/QUALITY Quality and quantity, basis shoretank, to be determined by a mutually agreed independent inspector at the loading installation, in the manner customary at such installation. **Such determination shall be final and binding for both parties**, except in case of fraud or manifest error..."(加黑部分是笔者的强调)

但该批气油到了西班牙卸港后的测试是货物并不符合买卖合约的描述,这导致了双方的争议与买方提出300万美元以上的索赔。由于有上述节录的第12条文,买方接受是受到约束,也就是该批气油在装船的一刻是符合买卖合约的描述。这样,在普通法下以及该买卖合约的第15条文明确规定了货物在装船后所有的风险转移给买方,卖方的争议就是即使该批气油事后在航次中有了变化,这也是买方的风险。但在Mash v Murrell Ltd v Joseph I Emmanuel Ltd (1961) 2 Lloyd's Rep 326先例,Diplock勋爵判有关货物必须能够承受一个卸港的正常航次并维持其可以作为商售质量(在1979年《货物销售法》把这个条件变为是满意质量)直到卸港:"... to be capable of standing a normal voyage to Liverpool and to be of merchantable quality at the time of arrival."

这个普通法的要求也完全可以理解,因为有很多货物如易腐的货物或鱼粉等,都必须在装船前有过恰当的处理或包装才可以保证他们能够承受正常的运输并能够完整无缺抵达卸港。所以,有说法是涉及付运的买卖,对货物商售质量的保证是一个"持续性保证"(continuous warranty),正如Diplock勋爵所说的:"... these goods being bought c&f Liverpool, the warranty as to merchantability was a warranty that they should remain merchantable for a reasonable time, the time reasonable in the circumstances, which means a time for the normal transit to the destination, and for disposal after..."

也有说法是装船后卖方对货物的风险通常转移给买方,但上述的持续性保证是其中一个例外(其他的例外之一是CIF/CFR卖方把货物付运在一艘根本不适合的船舶,如货物需要冷藏但船舶没有这种设备)。

这表示如果在卸港的测试发觉货物的质量有问题,是可以推算装货时的质量也会有问题。反正在The "Mercini Lady"先例,第一审的结果是卖方不能依赖装港证明为终条文逃避这个默示责任。但在上诉庭被改变过来,Rix大法官说:"... the contract makes it clear that the specification has to be met at the time of delivery, that the intention is that the gasoil should be inspected by an independent inspector prior to loading, 'basis shoretank' (ie not even on the basis of the gasoil in the ship's tanks), and that the inspector's determination should be conclusive (ie final and binding in the absence of fraud or manifest error). It is accepted that, even though the gasoil's sediment was measured by the wrong test, nevertheless the sediment was within specification limits at the time of loading and delivery. Therefore gasoil of the correct specification was delivered. The buyer's acceptance of that fact supplants the want of a valid inspector's certificate. Moreover, the intention of the contract remains, that specification should be determined conclusively at loading. Therefore it matters not that things may change thereafter, or even, if a conclusive determination has once been made, that things may not change but that a new test may show a different result which is outside specification limits. After delivery the buyer 'assumes all risks pertaining thereto' (clause 15). **All risks are all risks.** They include the risk of transport, and **they include the risk of cargo instability** — unless that risk has already been taken by the seller under a term of the contract which relates to the condition of the cargo pre – delivery. But a clause for conclusive inspection and determination on loading replaces or redefines the implied terms as to quality *pro tanto*. A fortiori it prevents any further implication that it is legitimate to take account of changes in the cargo's specification after delivery."(加黑部分是笔者的强调)

Rix 大法官接着说,如果在卸港发现货物有一些潜在的内在缺陷无法在装港检查时发现,或是不包括在检查的货物描述,就不会受到这种最终与有约束力条文的保障。这也表示还是有不少情况(大部分在杨大明律师的《国际货物买卖》一书提及),最终与有约束力条文也不是绝对能够对卖方起到保障。但在订约自由下,这种条文如果拟定的更好与有更广泛的针对性(但许多在国际货物买卖合约中的条文并非如此),还是可以起到更加肯定的保护作用。

1.5.2 近期有关重要先例之二:RG Grain Trade LLP v. Feed Factors International Ltd

最后简单介绍另一个先例 RG Grain Trade LLP v. Feed Factors International Ltd (2011) 2 Lloyd's Rep 432,有关的货物是向日葵渣,该 FOB 买卖合约有如下条文:"Quality and condition to be **final** at time and place of loading as per certificate of first class superintendent **approved by GAFTA at seller's choice and expense. The buyers have the right to appoint their own GAFTA approved supervisor at their expense.** In this case the sampling to be done conjointly, as per GAFTA terms and conditions. **2**nd analysis, if any, as per Salamon and Seaber, London..."(加黑部分是笔者的强调)

卖方在装港作出了检查,并且是符合买卖合约的描述与质量。但根据上述条文,买方行使了他对货物样品作出第二次测试的权利。在 Salamon and Seaber 所作出的第二次测试,发觉货物的蛋白质与纤维不达标,这导致了买方拒绝货物。虽然双方最后达成了另一个协议以更低的价格买卖该批货物,但双方事后向对方提出索赔与反索赔,卖方是索赔差价,买方是索赔货不对版的损失。卖方的立场是在装港作出检查与签发的第一份证书就是最终与有约束力，但这争议不被法院接受。这里主要的原因是 Hamblen 大法官认为如果第一份证书是最终，就会令上述条文的允许买方行使权利进行第二次测试没有任何意思。这是违反本书第三章之第 1 段介绍的解释合约的大原则之一，也就是要给每一条文/文字一定解释。

看来这又是另一个例子显示了装港检验证书为最终条文如果拟定的不好，就达不到最终与有约束力的效果。

§2　专家决定(expert determination)

商业合约中经常会规定技术性的问题由第三人(通常是专家)来决定，专家作出决定后也往往会作出一份报告，这可被视为一份证书/证明。这样看来，与上述所讲的有关"最终与有约束力条文"(final and binding clause)情况也差不多，毕竟这种条文经常还是以第三人(通常会是专家)的决定所作出的证书/证明为准。如果笔者一定要挑些区别，会是专家决定通常被视为解决双方争议的一种办法。这样，本小段所针对的专家决定是双方有了争议，并约定以一位专家作出的决定为准，也就是他的决定被视为最终与有约束力。这样又会与另一种解决争议办法的仲裁分不开，毕竟还是有不少仲裁也是委任专家作为仲裁员，因为不少争议有很强的技术性。而且，现在的仲裁很大一部分是"不正式的程序"(informal procedure)，如不需要开庭。这也在 1996 年的《仲裁法》或香港的《仲裁条例》所允许。这表示，以前有一个看法是专家决定不正式，而仲裁程序就正式的说法也不能作准。

2.1　专家决定与仲裁的区别

有关专家决定与仲裁的区别(或难以区分)可先节录《Russell on Arbitration》(第 23 版，2007 年)一书之 2－028 段与 2－031 段如下：

"**Expert determination (or valuation).** Like arbitration, expert determination provides for the final resolution of disputes by a private individual or individuals to whom issues are referred for a binding decision. Traditionally a distinction has been drawn between the two on the basis that a tribunal must act judicially by applying the law whereas an expert, unless the parties agree some other basis for his decision, decides according to his own expert opinion. This has become a less clear distinction now that, if agreed by the parties, a tribunal is entitled to base its decision on 'other consideration', although if the requirement to act judicially can be established it will resolve the issue. Experts are often appointed more to get the benefit of their professional (non－legal) expertise in deciding technical issues, but arbitrators appointed for their technical expertise have long been a feature of English arbitration. Experts have traditionally been involved in determinations prior to the existence of a dispute, whereas an arbitration tribunal deals with disputes after they have arisen. A more recent development is the use of experts, notably lawyers, to decide all aspects of a dispute, rather than particular technical issues. As a result of these factors the distinction between experts an arbitrators has in some cases become somewhat blurred although there are significant practical differences since expert determination is not governed by the Arbitration Act 1996. . . .

Expert determination treated differently from arbitration. The following features demonstrate how expert determination is treated differently from arbitration in a number of important respects.

- An expert determination is constrained by the terms of the clausereferring the matter to expert determination, whereas much is incorporated into an arbitration agreement by statute and by judicial precedent. For example, the court generally has no power to appoint an expert, whereas statute provides the court with the power to appoint an arbitrator. Similarly there is no obligation of confidentiality in relation to expert determination unless one has been contractually agreed.
- An arbitration award can be challenged on grounds of 'serious irregularity' in the conduct of the arbitration, but this is a statutory remedy for which there is no common law analogue in expert determination.〔3〕
- An expert's decision can only be enforced as a matter of contract and not pursuant to the statutory machinery available in respect of an arbitration award.
- An expert can be sued for negligence〔4〕, while an arbitrator has immunity.
- There can be no appeal on a point of law from an expert determination, unless the wrong law has been applied to the issue for determination, in which case there is not, strictly speaking, an appeal, but rather the decision can be challenged〔5〕. The parties to an arbitration can appeal against a tribunal's award on a point of law in certain limited circumstances. "

2.2 专家决定针对技术性争议有合约的约束力

专家决定对合约双方的约束力不像仲裁裁决(或法院判决)有法律规定,只能通过合约关系。所以,合约条文针对专家决定也是最好写上这个决定"最终与有约束

〔3〕 仲裁员是司法的角色,所以如果在程序上有"严重不正常"(serious irregularity),就会导致裁决书被挑战并有可能被法院撤销。严重不正常经常会涉及"自然公正"(natural justice),这在英国与香港都是立法规定的。即使主要针对建造行业的"审裁"(adjudication),英国在1996年的立法《Housing Grants, Construction and Regeneration Act》之section 24有规定审裁员必须遵循自然公正。但针对专家决定,不止是没有立法,连普通法也没有类似要求。这是一个复杂的课题,会在本章之2.6.2段针对。

〔4〕 Arenson v Casson Beckman Rutley & Co (1975) 3 WLR 815的贵族院先例。

〔5〕 Nikko Hotels (UK) Ltd v MEPC Plc (1991) 2 EGLR 103先例。

力”。但也有说法是即使没有这种文字/措辞,现在法院也会这样看待或默示。在 Homepace Ltd v Sita South East Ltd (2008) 1 P & CR 24 先例,Lloyd 大法官说:“The structure of these provisions seems to me to be such that, despite the absence of any words such as ‘final and binding’, the surveyor is given exclusive power to determine the questions to which his certificate is directed, whether it be as to the exhaustion of all Minerals, or as to their not being economically recoverable, and with no prospect of being so within 10 years. If his certificate does no more (and no less) than determine one or other of those matters, it seems to me that it is not open to either party (it would in practice be the landlord) to contend that this is not the correct view of the facts. There would be no point to the certificate if the question to which it relates were to remain in contention between the parties after a valid certificate has been issued.”

2.3 专家决定针对技术性争议的好处

以专家决定解决技术上的争议有很大好处,一是专家是作出决定的合适人选,二是相对便宜与快捷,三是这种争议通常不需要太正式,甚至不需要一个文书的决定。如在造船合约,它在造船中经常会遇到各种各样的技术上的争议,因为通常船东会有总管住在船厂监督工程并参加各种测试。这样,如果通过仲裁解决这种争议(即使委任的仲裁员是专家),也会是一个复杂与耗时的程序。虽然早期笔者曾经听过有个别仲裁员(如已故的 Cedric Barclay 先生)飞船厂停留几天实地检查后对大量与不同的技术性争议作出个别口头(后来再追加简单的文书)决定,并号称在 1 天作出上百个裁决书。但这种例子在今天的仲裁中只是典故或是非常罕见的例外。而且,经常有个别的争议除非是即时有了决定,整个造船工程需要停顿。

所以造船合约的标准格式通常会把技术性的争议约定是通过专家决定为准,而其他非技术性的争议就通过仲裁解决。例如,中国造船厂经常会依照的“日本造船格式”(SAJ Form)的 Article XIII,就有非常详尽的仲裁条文,但在后部分有一段针对专家的决定解决技术性的争议,说:“Notwithstanding the preceding provisions of this Paragraph, it is recognized that in the event of any dispute or difference of opinion arising in regard to the construction of the VESSEL, her machinery or equipment, or concerning the quality of materials or workmanship thereof or thereon, such dispute may be referred to the Classification Society upon mutual agreement of the parties hereto as far as the Classification Society agrees to determine such dispute. The decision of the Classification Society shall be final and binding upon the parties hereto.”

2.4 专家决定会被法院否定的理由

针对专家决定(包括针对争议或本章之第 1 段的最终与结论性证书/证明),不论有否明示是最终与有约束力,法律地位应该是明确,即使有错误(甚至有明显错误),约定的双方还是受到约束,除非涉及专家欺诈、同谋、真正偏私与偏离双方委任的指示。

在 Campbell v Edwards (1976) 1 Lloyd's Rep 522 先例,Denning 勋爵说:"It is simply the law of contract. If two persons agree that the price of property should be fixed by a valuer on whom they agree, and he gives that valuation honestly and in good faith, they are bound by it. Even if he has made a mistake they are still bound by it. The reason is because they have agreed to be bound by it. If there were fraud or collusion, of course, it would be very different. **Fraud or collusion unravels everything.**"(专家决定纯是合约法。如果双方同意房子的价格是由一位他们约定的估价师作出决定,该估价师也诚实与善意作出估价,双方就受到约束,即使他会是犯了错误。原因是双方同意受到约束。但如果涉及欺诈或同谋就很不一样,欺诈与同谋超越所有。)

另是 Cooke 大法官在 Bernhard Schulte v Nile Holdings (2004) 2 Lloyd's Rep. 352 先例所说:"The determination **will be binding** between them unless it can be challenged on the basis of **fraud, collusion, bias or material departure from instructions**, but if there has been negligence on the part of the expert, the damaged party may sue the expert in respect of any loss suffered."(加黑部分是笔者的强调)

针对这四个可否定专家决定的理由,欺诈或同谋应该不必多解释。专家决定不利的一方想以这两个理由推翻专家决定也不容易,因为即使是事实也很难会有证据或/与满足沉重的举证责任。接下来的段节可探讨其他两个理由,先是专家偏离了双方委任的指示,再是专家偏见的问题,这也涉及了自然公正的大原则与善意。

2.5 专家决定不能偏离双方的委任与指示的错误/疏忽

第一个理由可以说是涉及专家的管辖权问题,因为像仲裁员一样,专家的关系权是来自双方当事人的协议。如在 Veba v Petrotrade (2002) 1 Lloyd's Rep 295 先例,双方约定以 D1298 测试气油,但专家决定是根据一种名为 ASTM D4052 的更新与更准确的测试。这一专家决定被高院与上诉庭否定,因为偏离了双方委任所约定的测试办法。正如第一审的 Morison 大法官说:"it was not the business of the Court to weigh the importance of a stipulation in a contract; if the requirement to use the method specified in cl. 4 was contractual that was an end of the matter, whether or not the Court thought it was important or would have made a difference; the assumption that the Court made was that the parties had chosen to define their rights and obligations according to their own needs whatever they might have been; it was no business of the Court to inquire why the claimants asked for this particular test; this was what was agreed and had Caleb Brett(专家)been aware of this contractual requirement they would have used it."

看来,如果偏离了双方委任时作出的指示,即使作出的专家决定(不论双方是否有争议)更加正确,也不能作准,因为这不是双方所同意的。这样看来,偏离委任与指示等同于专家超出了管辖权。显然,这种问题往往来自专家的错误或疏忽,如没有留心看他的委任,甚至是合约有关条文,而冒然根据自己的习惯做法作出决定。这就带来另一个困难的分水线,也就是有了很多先例明确了的说法,专家决定即使错误也是对合约双方最终与有约束力:Toepfer v Continental Grain (1974) 1 Lloyd's Rep 11 (CA); Campbell v Edwards (1976) 1 Lloyd's Rep 522; Nikko Hotels v MEPC (1991) 2 EGLR 103; Jones v Sherwood (1992) 1 WLR 277 (CA); The "Glacier Bay" (1996) 1 Lloyd's Rep 370; Morgan Sindall v Sawston Farms (1998) EGCS 177; Bernhard Schulte v Nile Holdings (2004) 2 Lloyd's Rep. 352 等先例。这样,专家决定的错误到底分水线是在哪里?

这方面会带来以下进一步探讨的问题。

2.5.1　专家决定可管辖的范围来自双方的约定

这种专家决定的错误应该简单与明显,如双方委任一位专家对某栋房屋作出估价或检查,如果这位专家错误把另一栋房屋作出估价或检查,显然他作出的决定不会是最终与有约束力,因为他从基本性偏离了双方的委任。

针对专家决定的委任与他能够管辖的范围,显然是来自双方的约定,这也表示这种争议往往需要解释有关的合约条文/文字。在 Homepace Ltd v Sita South East Ltd (2008) 1 P & CR 24 先例,Lloyd 大法官说:"Each case depends on the terms of the contract under which the determination is made, both as to what it is that the expert has to decide, and as to how far his decision is binding on the parties. In each case it is necessary to examine the determination, in order to see whether it lies within the scope of the expert's authority. If it does not, then it has no effect as between the parties. If on the other hand it does, then the contract also governs the question whether the determination is binding or whether, and if so to what extent or on what grounds, the determination can be questioned."(专家决定管辖的范围必须是看双方的约定。如果双方有约定,合约会决定哪些问题的决定有约束力,约束力到什么程度,或在哪些情况下专家决定可以受到质疑。)

在较早的 Jones v Sherwood Computer Services Plc (1992) 1 WLR 277 先例,Dillion 大法官说:"On principle, the first step must be to see what the parties have agreed to remit to the expert, this being,... The next step must be to see what the nature of the mistake was, if there is evidence to show that. If the mistake made was that the expert departed from his instructions in a material respect - e.g. he valued the wrong number of shares, or valued shares on the wrong basis or if, as in Jones (M.) v. Jones (R.R) [1971] 1 W.L.R. 840, the expert had valued machinery himself whereas his instructions were to employ an expert valuer of his choice to do that - either party would be able to say that the certificate was not binding because the expert had not done what he was appointed to do."(大原则是第一步看双方同意把什么问题交给专家作出决定,第二步是看专家决定的错误本质,如果这个错误是在一个重要的层面偏离了双方的委任或指示,如把错误的股票数目估值,或估值是根据错误的办法,双方就可以说专家的证书/证明对他们没有约束,因为专家没有做他所被委任的事情。)

对专家的委任可以是简单,如在本章之1.5段提到的装港检验证书为最终条文,会有情况是只需要把合约描述交给专家,然后专家作出决定该货物是否符合描述,具体的检验方式由专家自己决定。在这种情况下,很难说该专家决定会偏离他的委托/指示。但还是会有争议,如在 Toepfer v Continental Grain Co (1974) 1 Lloyd's Rep 11 先例,相关的买卖合约所针对的"No. 3 Hard Amber Durum Wheat"的货物有一条装港检验为终条文,如下:"**Quality final** as per official Lakes Loading Inspection certificate or any other official inspection certificate."(加黑部分是笔者的强调)

货物实际上是另一种稍有不同的 Amber Durum Wheat,但之后作出的装港检验证书仍是写作 Hard Amber Durum Wheat。换言之,证书/证明对货物的描述有错误/疏忽。作为原告的买方的其中一个争辩是该检验证书只对货物质量为终,而不对货物描述为终,而这份证书真正是货物描述的错误。但这不被上诉庭接受,Denning 勋爵说:"The 'description' of goods often includes a statement of their quality. Thus 'new-laid eggs' contains both quality and description all in one. 'Quality' is often part of the description. In this very case the word 'hard' is a word both of quality and of description. If a certificate is final as to the quality 'hard', it is final as to that description also. The quality and description cannot be separated. Finality as to one means finality as to the other."

如果双方对专家决定的约定与委任十分详尽与复杂,特别是表达有含糊之处,解释起来就会带来更多与更复杂的争议:Conoco (UK) Ltd v Phillips Petroleum Co (UK) Ltd, 19 August 1996, unreported;British Shipbuilders v ESEL Consortium Plc (1997) 1 Lloyd's Rep 106;Shell UK Ltd v Enterprise Oil Plc (1999) 2 Lloyd's Rep 456 等先例。

笔者也估计针对这方面专家决定条文的解释比仲裁条文严格,所以对它的拟定也要小心。毕竟仲裁条文在 Fiona Trust & Holding Corporation & Ors v Yuri Privalov & Ors (2008) 1 Lloyd's Rep 254 先例下,解释的起点就是假设双方的订约意图是通过仲裁"一站式"解决所有争议。所以,如果再争议仲裁庭的管辖只能针对合约内的争议而不包括合约外或本质上是侵权的争议,因为仲裁条文用字不够广泛等,已经很难会成功。但这种宽松解释显然不会适用在专家决定条文。例如,笔者在不久前的一个香港仲裁就面对一个技术性争议(船舶的油漆是否有缺陷)的管辖权质疑,船厂认为这是应该属于船级社专家决定管辖范围内,因为属于技术性的争议。但这被否定,包括笔者在内的仲裁庭解释有关的专家决定条文,认为只是适用在造船工程的期间。而有关油漆的争议,是发生在交船后并在船舶已经营运了一两个航次后才出现的。

2.5.2 如何区分是否在重要层面偏离了委任/指示的错误/疏忽

另是更常见不利一方会提出的争议是专家决定是否"在重要层面偏离了他的委任/指示"(departed from his instruction in the material respect)。这种错误/疏忽往往来自专家错误解读了合约的专家决定条文或双方提出的问题:Mercury Communications Ltd v Director – General of Telecommunication (1996) 1 WLR 48 先例。这里也涉及回答了错误的问题,与回答了正确的问题(但答案错误)的区分:Nikko Hotels (UK) Ltd v MEPC Plc (1991) 2 EGLR 103 先例。在本章之2.5段已经提到过,这个区分十分重要,因为前者的疏忽会导致专家决定被否定,但后者仍会约束双方。

这方面的先例有很多,只少数介绍。在 Doughy Hanson & Co Ltd v Roe (2008) 1 BCLC 404 先例,涉及股权转让合约与对有关股票的合理价格通过投资银行或会计师所作出估价的决定,但被其中一方指称专家决定是基于一个错误的假设。法院是这样作出区分说:"If he adopts a hypothesis that would not be adopted by other valuers, then he may have made an error in his valuation, but it does not mean that he has valued something different. It means he has made a mistake."

上诉庭的 Simon Brown 大法官也曾经在 Veba v Petrotrade (2002) 1 Lloyd's Rep 295 先例说到怎样作出区分:"A mistake is one thing; a departure from instructions quite another. A mistake is made when an expert goes wrong in the course of carrying out his instructions. The difference between that and an expert not carrying out his instructions is obvious..."

另是在 Bernhard Schulte v Nile Holdings (2004) 2 Lloyd's Rep. 352 先例,案情涉及船舶买卖,卖方指称专家决定所针对的时间并不符合有关合约的条文(专家针对是交船一天的船舶状况与船价,但卖方认为应该是买方检查的一天)。Cooke 大法官同意这个错误是偏离了他的委任/指示,但由于这是"初步争议"(preliminary issue)的审理,所以没有作出最终的决定。但 Cooke 大法官说到怎样区分两个阶段对专家的错误/疏忽到底属于哪一类:

"The Purchasers contended that in circumstances where **the contract did not expressly instruct the expert** as to the date to which his valuation and assessment were to refer, the point was left to him to determine as part of the expert reference so that any mistake which he might have made in that respect, whether or not it was a question of law, **was a mistake in the reference, rather than a failure to follow instructions.**

The authorities show there are **two steps** in the reasoning process to be applied by the Court in assessing where the line is to be drawn for the purposes of this distinction. The **first** is to ascertain what the parties have agreed to remit to the expert, whilst the **second** is to ascertain the nature of the mistake made – what has the expert done and why did he do it? Did the expert do what he was appointed to do, albeit in a mistaken manner, or did he carry out a different task as a result of his mistake?"(加黑部分是笔者的强调,第一段是说如果合约没有明示指示专家以哪天作出估价与核算,就是让专家自己作出决定。如果专家的决定有错误,这只是在他的程序上犯错,不是偏离了委任/指示。而第二段所谈到的两个阶段作出区分,一是看双方同意了的委任专家的职权范围;二是看专家错误/疏忽的本质。)

Cooke 大法官也提到 Simon 勋爵在 Arenson v Casson Beckman Rutley & Co (1975) 3 WLR 815 的贵族院先例曾经说:“... the expert, **subject to the express provisions of his remit**, is entitled to carry out his own investigations, form his own opinion and come to his own conclusion regardless of any submissions or evidence adduced by the parties themselves.”(专家可以凭自己的调查与专业知识作出决定,不必理会双方当事人的陈述或证据,但先决条件就是专家必须依照明示规定的职权范围。)

这也可以配合上述所讲的 Veba v Petrotrade 先例,合约约定以 D1298 测试气油,专家就不能根据另一种测试作出决定,即使该测试会是更新与更准确。但如果合约只是泛泛地要求专家作出决定,该专家就可以有完全的自主权决定怎样测试,即使测试的结果不理想或错误。

上述介绍只是原则或理论,适用到实际案件还是困难重重。如一个专家决定需要对有关标的作出 50 个不同的测试,这是全球普遍与习惯性的做法,也只有这一种做法。如果专家少做了 1 个测试,或其中 1 个测试是给了一个不被正式承认的实验室进行,这样到底属于哪一类别的错误?如果有关的专家条文没有明示测试的做法,或是条文多余地加上一句测试以习惯性做法为准,后者条文会否带来区别?

在过去五年,中国有大量的造船合约争议去伦敦仲裁。[6] 其中有一方面的争议就是外国船东/买方攻击有关的船级社验船师,指称他们作出的证书/证明或决定有错误,所以船厂不能按照合约交船或外国船东可以拒船。如 Non Destructive Test (NDT)[7] 不符合船级社的规定,但还是被验船师批准而不是要求再做多一次 NDT (因为时间上不允许),所以船级社作出的“船舶安全结构证书”(safety construction certificate)应被否定,因为造船合约是约定以该船级社规定建造,这种错误属于偏离他的委任/指示。

但笔者很难接受来自外国船东的这种争议(但也不容易说服部分伦敦仲裁员),原因在于:(1)大前提是船级社规定十分详尽,一旦有偏离,就算是偏离他的委任/指示,就会导致船级社所作出的证书/证明或检验师的“即场决定”(contemporaneous decision)都不能作准,这会带来非常严重的后果。(2)船级社规定通常也为自己保留了一定弹性,就是有条文说明对有关的规定的解释权利属于船级社。这也表示即场的检验师也应该有一定弹性的裁量权。(3)船级社规定除了详尽,通常还是在技术上十分先进与正确。这样,如果一旦偏离就属于偏离他的委任/指示,不会有空间留给另一类的错误了。也就是说,如果验船师完全按照船级社规定,就根本不会有错误

〔6〕 可看本书第四章之第 8 段,第六章之第 14 段,第十章之 4.4 段与第十一章。

〔7〕 NDT 测试是针对船壳钢板接驳的焊接是否符合要求,因为这种焊接是船壳钢板持续性力度的弱点。测试是通过超声波与 X 光,这是十分繁重的工作。针对 NDT 的 X 光片的密度,不同船级社有不同的规定。船东与船厂在这方面经常会有争议,船东的总管会认为焊接工作做得并不好,但 NDT 的通过率却很高,怀疑(或说服仲裁庭怀疑)船厂作假。

了。(4)造船合约针对某船级社的规定只是泛泛一提(即使有明示条文要求船厂作出 NDT,但实际上明示没有必要因为船级社规定包括了 NDT),这是否算是明示的约定?(5)船级社规定对 NDT 有许多细节,会长达两三页。这样即使任何偏离都属于偏离了船级社的委任/指示,也有问题是哪些偏离属于重要,哪些偏离属于轻微,正如在 Bernhard Schulte v Nile Holdings 先例所说:"It was common ground between the parties, after examination of the authorities, that the test as to whether or not a departure from instructions was material is that which is set out in Veba Oil v Petrotrade [2002] 1 LLR 295 (CA) where the majority decided that 'any departure is material unless it can be characterised as trivial or de minimis '..."(6)这可以从另一个角度看到底船级社有否错误/疏忽(不论属于哪个类别),这就是不利的一方可否成功以合约/侵权向船级社索赔,指他们错误并违反了自己的规则。笔者认为答案是显然不会成功。

2.5.3 总结专家决定职权范围的说法

在 British Shipbuilders v. VSEL Consortium plc (1997) 1 Lloyd's Rep 106 先例中, Lightman 大法官将这方面的原则总结如下:

"(1) Questions as to the role of the expert, the ambit of his remit (or jurisdiction) and the character of his remit (whether exclusive or concurrent with a like jurisdiction vested in the Court) are to be determined as a matter of construction of the agreement. (专家的角色或是他的管辖权范围是根据对合约的解释。)

(2) If the agreement confers upon the expert the exclusive remit to determine a question, (subject to[3] and [4] below) the jurisdiction of the Court to determine that question is excluded because (as a matter of substantive law) for the purposes of ascertaining the rights and duties of the parties under the agreement the determination of the expert alone is relevant and any determination by the Court is irrelevant. It is irrelevant whether the Court would have reached a different conclusion or whether the Court considers that the expert's decision is wrong, for the parties have in either event agreed to abide by the decision of the expert. (如果合约约定让专家决定一个问题,法院[或仲裁庭]针对该问题的管辖权就被排除。法院[或仲裁庭]会有一个不同的决定或认为专家决定错误是完全无关,因为双方约定了受到专家决定的约束。)

(3) If the expert in making his determination goes outside his remit e. g. by determining a different question from that remitted to him or in his determination fails to comply with any conditions which the agreement requires him to comply with in making his determination, the Court may intervene and set his decision aside. Such a determination by the expert as a matterof construction of the agreement is not a determination which the parties agreed should affect the rights and duties of the parties, and the Court will say so. (如果专家决定是超越了他的管辖范围或没有按照双方约定的一些条件[如取样本的做法、测试所根据的资料、测试的程式与办法、测试的次数与时间、测试的设备等]

作出决定,法院就可以作出干预并撤销这一决定。)

(4) Likewise the Court may set aside a decision of the expert where (as in this case)[8] the agreement so provides if his determination discloses a manifest error.(法院也会撤销一个有重大错误的专家决定,如果相关的专家决定条文有这个明示约定。)

(5) The Court has jurisdiction ahead of a determination by the expert to determine a question as to the limits of his remit or the conditions which the expert must comply with in making his determination, but (as a rule of procedural convenience) will (save in exceptional circumstances) decline to do so. This is because the question is ordinarily merely hypothetical, only proving live if, after seeing the decision of the expert, one party considers that the expert got it wrong. To apply to the Court in anticipation of his decision (and before it is clear thathe has got it wrong) is likely to prove wasteful of time and costs – the saving of which may be presumed to have been the, or at least one of the, objectives of the parties in agreeing to the determination by the expert."(法院有权在专家决定之前作出有关他的管辖权与必须符合的条件的判决,但通常会等到专家作出决定后,其中一方觉得错误才针对这个问题。注意是针对仲裁员的管辖权,有关的仲裁法如 1996 年英国《仲裁法》或香港《仲裁条例》,这是由仲裁庭决定,虽然这个决定可以自动上诉到法院,但已经可以看到是与专家的管辖权很不一样的做法。)

2.6 专家决定不能偏私[9]

这是在 2.4 段所介绍的另一个专家决定会被法院否定的理由。在笔者看来,这也是另一个在英国法下困难而且分水线不明确的地方。这个问题可以分两个方面探讨,一是专家是否需要合理与善意,二是专家是否要遵循自然公正的天条。

2.6.1 决定的专家是否需要合理与善意?

针对这点的法律地位是如果一个决定(不论是否涉及争议)是由第三人(这当然是双方约定,也往往是专家)作出,针对这方面是与合约其中一方作出决定很不一

---

[8] 该先例的专家决定条文可节录如下:"5.3 If any disagreement arises between the Accountants in connection with the certification referred to in Clause 5.2 above, the subject matter of such disagreement shall, if the disagreement has not been resolved within a period of 14 days of such disagreement arising, be referred for settlement to such firm of Chartered Accountants... The firm of Chartered Accountants (or person) selected as aforesaid (the "Expert") shall act as an expert and not as an arbitrator and its (or his) decision shall, in the absence of manifest error, be final and binding on the parties hereto."

[9] 本段并非针对另一种专家,就是并非对双方的争议作出决定而只是向法院或仲裁庭提供他的专业意见的专家,也就是"专家证人"(expert witness)。涉及这方面专家证人偏私而导致专家意见被拒绝提供或不给与任何分量的也有不少重要的近期先例,如 SPE International Ltd v Professional Preparation Contractors (UK) Ltd (2002) EWHC 881; R (Factortame Limited & Ors) v Secretary of State for Transport, Local Government and the Regions (No. 8) (2003) QB 381; Hussein v William Hill Group (2004) EWHC 208 QB; Meat Corporation of Namibia Limited v Dawn Meats (UK) Limited (2011) EWHC 474 等,但本段不准备详论。

样。在后者的情况,可以说就是在本书第九章之第 3 段介绍的让合约一方作出决定或裁量权,法律是默示有裁量权的一方必须善意与公平合理。这里的区别可以节录 Lewison 大法官所著的《The Interpretation of Contracts》(第 5 版,2011 年)一书之 14.05 段的标题,说:"Where a contract is to be performed to the satisfaction of a third party, the third party is not usually required to act reasonably in deciding whether or not to express satisfaction or to issue a certificate. But where the contract is to be performed to the satisfaction of one of the parties to it, it will usually be implied that he should act reasonably."

在 Caney v Leith (1937) 2 All ER 532 先例,一个土地买卖合约规定以买方律师批准卖方所有权为准。看来,买方律师被视为第三人,法院判是在没有恶意或不合理行为的情况下,律师是否批准所有权的决定是结论性。Farwell 大法官解释这里的"不合理"并非一般性的不合理,说:"What do the judges mean when they talk about unreasonableness? In my judgment, when they are using the word 'unreasonable', they are dealing with a position where the solicitors are not acting in good faith - that is to say, where, to assist their client, and get him out of the contract, or for some other reason, the solicitors refuse to approve the lease, without giving the matter any consideration at all, or where their reasons for disapproval **are so patent and absurd that court can say in a moment: 'This is ridiculous and the solicitors cannot possibly make such an objection at that.'**"(加黑部分是笔者的强调)

也就是说 Farwell 大法官认为"不合理"并非是一般的说法,而必须达致荒谬或可笑的地步,这个"高度"不合理的考验也被广泛接受。在香港终审法院的 Regal Success Venture Ltd v Jonlin Ltd (2000) 2 HKFCAR 364 先例,Ribeiro 大法官也有提到上述先例说:"While it may not be necessary to go so far as to require the opinion to be so objectionable that it suggests bad faith on the part of the solicitor, Farwell J's approach of permitting a challenge only where the objection can quickly be seen to be absurd or ridiculous, is a test that has been widely adopted and is plainly the appropriate approach to 'unreasonableness' in this context."

在 Bernhard Schulte v Nile Holdings (2004) 2 Lloyd's Rep. 352 先例,Cooke 大法官也同意说英国法律没有善意的大原则,[10] 即使合约双方有一条"最大努力条文"(best endeavours clause)也不代表要善意。

2.6.2　专家决定是否必须遵循自然公正的天条?

这个重要的问题是关系到一个专家决定会否在法院被挑战,而这种情况现在也越来越多地发生。专家决定是否涉及偏私经常会是不利一方的怀疑,如在本章之 1.5 段提到会有卖方对买方在卸港作出的检验不放心,但买方对卖方在装港作出的检

〔10〕 可看本书第九章。

验并被视为最终与有约束性也同样不放心。但这种问题会是在双方有了争议以专家决定解决时最为尖锐，因为这涉及了互动与整个程序，会导致不利一方觉得曾经受到不公平的对待。不论对否，专家决定不利的一方就像仲裁败诉方的心态，总会是觉得决定对他不公平。而如果在程序上能够挑得出毛病，这个专家决定就避免不了会受到质疑。

法律上专家决定与仲裁的区别还是明确，后者是“诉讼”（litigation）的一种，另一种就是法院审理。所以，“自然公正”（natural justice）是通过法律（普通法与《仲裁法》）强加在仲裁。但没有立法强加同样的要求在专家决定。毕竟两个角色不一样。仲裁员是有司法的角色，但专家只是以他的专业知识对技术性问题或争议作出决定。所以在《Russell on Arbitration》（第23版，2007年）一书之2－029段有说：“A tribunal arrives at its decision on the evidence and submissions of the parties and must apply the law or, if the parties agree, other considerations. An expert, unless it is agreed otherwise, makes his own inquiries, applies his own expertise and decides on the basis of his own expert opinion.[11]”

从上述就已经看到重要区别之一，就是仲裁员必须避免依赖“秘密证据”（secret evidence）作出决定，这会是严重不正常行为。但专家决定就可以自己进行调查，以自己的专业知识作出决定。这样看来，专家决定不像是要求遵循自然公正的天条。事实上，这方面也在很多的先例中有明确，如在 Bernhard Schulte v Nile Holdings (2004) 2 Lloyd's Rep. 352 先例，Cooke 大法官说：“There is no requirement for the rules of natural justice or due process to be followed in an expert determination in order for that determination to be valid and binding between the parties.”

另在更近期的 Owen Pell Limited v Bindi (London) Ltd (2008) EWHC 1420 先例，Kirkham 大法官也说：“I see no reason to depart here from the guidance given by Cooke J in Bernhard Schulte namely that there is no requirement for the rules of natural justice or due process to be followed in an expert determination in order for that determination to be valid and binding between the parties.”

在现实中，合约双方约定专家决定的第三人（如造船合约的船级社），会考虑专家的公信力与独立性。这会导致双方在谈判中不容易约定谁是专家。他们也会采用委任独任仲裁员的办法，如通过双方递交一份有几位他们认为可以接受的专家名单然后看看有否同样的名字。其他的做法会是在合约中规定委任的专家必须“独立”（independent）：Bernhard Schulte v Nile Holdings 先例。或是在委任时明示要求专家必须公正持平，在程序上要求让双方提交各自的立场与有关的文件后才作出决定等。另在做法上的约定也会减少或避免这个危险，如双方一起作出委任、各自支付一半的费用等。换言之，在保障公正持平的做法上是通过合约而不是法律的要求。

---

〔11〕 Palacath v Flanagan (1985) 2 All ER 161 先例。

但也有一些先例看来有不同的说法,如在 Worrall v Topp (2007) EWHC 1809 先例,就判作出决定的专家有一个默示责任公平对待双方当事人。另在近期的 Macro v Thompson (No. 3) (2002) BCLC 36 先例,Robert Walker 大法官说:"On the authorities as a whole I accept the submission... that when the court is considering a decision reached by an expert valuer who is not an arbitrator performing a quasi - judicial function, **it is actual partiality, rather than the appearance of partiality, that is the crucial test.** Otherwise auditors (like architects and actuaries) who have a long - standing professional relationship with one party (or persons associated with one party) to a contract might be unduly inhibited, in continuing to discharge their professional duty to their client, by too high an insistence on avoiding even an impression of partiality."(加黑部分是笔者的强调)

另在 Bernhard Schulte v Nile Holdings 先例,Cooke 大法官说:"If an expert is guilty of actual bias, then his determination could be set aside."

这不同说法的先例要找出一条分水线,这分水线也会是专家决定与仲裁庭对自然公正方面的区分。首先分析的是"表面偏私"(apparent bias)与"真正偏私"(actual bias)。

表面偏私的考验是在著名的贵族院先例 Porter v Magill (2002) 2 AC 357 所说:"whether the fair - minded and informed observer, having considered the facts, would conclude that there was a real possibility that the tribunal was biased."

而真正偏私的考验是 Re Medicaments and Related Classes of Goods (2001) 1 WLR 700 先例所说:"The cases draw a distinction between thc cases draw a distinction between 'actual bias' and 'apparent bias'. The phrase actual bias has not been used with great precision but has been applied to the situation (1) where a judge has been influenced by partiality or prejudice in reaching his decision, and (2) where it has been demonstrated that a judge is actually prejudiced in favour of or against a party..."

针对仲裁员对自然公正的要求,Porter v Magill 先例的考验,也就是表面偏私适用。如果过不了这一关,就不应该被委任为仲裁员或委任了也会被法院赶走。而他作出的裁决书也会是严重不正常而被撤销。但针对专家决定,对自然公正的要求看来还是有,但程度上是真正偏私才会过不了关。看来,法院也应该把好这一关,不要轻易让专家决定被不利的一方否定。

Worrall v Topp 先例的默示责任公平对待双方当事人,这也是对自然公正的要求。在该先例,案情涉及法院的诉讼,但双方同意把争议交出给一位专家作出决定。而在法院文件中的附件二,有列出专家决定的程序,并在第 7 条文说明这个决定是约束双方。第 4 条文是针对双方有机会提交他们的争议与证据给专家说:"The parties shall be at liberty to set out their factual evidence in support of their contentions as to the position of the boundary by a date to be agreed or determined by the surveyor but will not be permitted to rely on any other expert evidence."

但在后来的程序中，被告的律师提交的一封电邮与4份附件（都是一些图纸）并没有抄本给原告，原告也不知道。这样，在最后作出对原告不利的专家决定后，原告试图在法院否定这个专家决定。虽然最后的判决是被告的这些文件对专家决定没有重大影响，但 Kitchin 大法官是说专家有一个默示的公平责任："Nevertheless, I am satisfied there was an implied obligation upon Mr Caruth（专家）to act fairly. Clearly it is highly desirable that any communications between one party and an expert in the position of Mr Caruth are copied to all other parties. Fairness must generally demand that each party should have an opportunity to respond to contentions made by any other party. If this course is not followed then a court may hold that any decision reached by the expert cannot stand. Whether it does so or not must depend upon all the circumstances and, in particular, the nature of the communication, the extent to which it concerned matters of which the other party or parties were already aware and the effect it had on the expert in reaching his decision."

笔者可以试图总结说，英国法律应该是没有法律默示〔12〕或政策上要求专家决定必须遵循自然公正，这可看 Bernhard Schulte v Nile Holdings 与 Owen Pell Limited v Bindi（London）Ltd 先例。但会在个别案件作出事实默示，〔13〕如在 Worrall v Topp 先例。而不论有否默示责任，专家决定如果有明显的真正偏私，就会被法院否定。这可节录 Cooke 大法官在 Bernhard Schulte v Nile Holdings 先例所说："The determination will be binding between them **unless** it can be challenged on the basis of fraud, collusion, **bias** or material departure from instructions, but if there has been negligence on the part of the expert, the damaged party may sue the expert in respect of any loss suffered."（加黑部分是笔者的强调）

在不同的案情，可作出事实默示也可以理解。但正如在本书第七章之第4段所介绍，事实的默示必须满足五个条件，即一定要合理，必须是合约有商业效力所必须，要满足好事第三人的考验，必须能够清楚地表达出来与不能与明示条文起冲突。这就带来另一个在本章之2.5.2段提到的有关中国船厂的造船合约争议去伦敦仲裁的另一个会面对的争议就是外国船东/买方攻击有关的船级社（即使是外国船级社，并且是由外国船东指定）的验船师偏私，并作出对船东不利的决定。这也无可避免带来了船级社是否有公正持平的默示责任。如上述所讲，这个默示是事实的默示，而且有像 Worrall v Topp 的先例。但事实的默示要看每个不同案件的事实，并要看是否满足这五个条件。对笔者而言，也是觉得不应该要这个默示（虽然也是不容易说服部分伦敦仲裁员），原因在于：（1）重要与必须的条件之一是合约有商业效力所"必

〔12〕 可看本书第七章之第3段。

〔13〕 可看本书第七章之第4段。

须”(necessary),笔者觉得是不能满足。船级社的委任与费用的支付来自船厂,但在造船合约的谈判中往往是由外国船东所指定。通常指定的外国船级社也就是几家国际著名的如劳合社、美国船级社、挪威船级社(DNV)、德国船级社(GL)、日本船级社(NKK)、法国船级社(BV)等。会指定这些船级社,就是因为其信誉与可依赖性的高程度,也可以假设他们在作出每份证书/证明或作出决定都会谨慎与持平,因为这是与自己长久以来的信誉有莫大关系。在这种情况下,没有必要再作出事实的默示要求船级社必须公正持平,否则造船合约会失去效力。(2)在同样的道理下,笔者也觉得另一个重要的条件,即满足好事第三人的考验也无法满足。外国船东在整个造船过程中都有他的“总管”(superintendent),甚至是多过一位作出监督。(3)如果默示船级社有公正持平或自然公正的责任,就会与现实的做法完全不配套。如船级社经常会与船厂或船东私下接触,而如果船级社有危险作出对船东不利的决定,船东经常会私下向船级社的总部施加压力,希望把压力转给在船厂的验船师。这样的程序会否是符合公正持平或自然公正?而且船级社面对这些压力不论是否顶住,也不会像仲裁员向另一方(船厂)作出披露并让船厂有答辩的机会。(4)至于说会否有十分例外的情况,如船级社验船师涉及欺诈、受贿或所作出的决定荒谬或可笑,是明显有真正偏私,这些极端的情况在普通法都有救济,就是决定会被否定,没有必要默示公正持平。

§3　视为条文(deeming clause)

3.1　如何解释视为条文

视为条文是拟定合约条文经常被使用的技巧,并会带来各种不同的后果。其中有不少后果与“合约禁止翻供”(contractual estoppel)〔14〕有关,也有可能本质上被视为属于一条免责条文:Demco Investments & Commercial SA v SE banken Forsakring Holding AB (2005) 2 Lloyd's Rep 650 先例。所以与所有其他合约条文,特别是会被针对作出解释的条文一样,视为条文用字必须清楚与不含糊:Tai Hing Cotton Mill Ltd v Liu Chong Hing Bank Ltd (1986) AC 80 与 Financial Institutions Services Ltd v Negril Negril Holdings Ltd (2004) UKPC 40 等先例。如果文字不明确,法院会以针对原则作出解释:WJB Chiltern Plc v Olympia Securities Commercial Plc (2003) EWHC 3464 (Ch)先例。

就算是一条明确的视为条文,也会有困难决定到底被视为什么:Barhados Trust Co v Bank of Zambia (2007) 1 Lloyd's Rep 495 先例。在该先例,案情涉及一笔1亿美元的贷款安排给赞比亚银行以进口原油。这种“主权国债务”(sovereign debt)在

---

〔14〕 可看本书第十三章之脚注。

市场上也有通过“转让”(assign)进行买卖,但有关贷款安排的合约有“限制转让条文”(non - assignment clause),因为欠下债务的主权国国家银行会担心债务转让给一些不愿意打交道的人士。该条文有一个例外,就是债权人在转让前取得赞比亚银行“事前”(prior)的文书同意。另有一条视为条文,是赞比亚银行没有在提出要求的15天内回复,就视为同意,文字上如下:“... provided that any such assignment may only be effected if (save in the case where the Assignee is a member of the same group as the assignor, no such consent then being required) the **prior written consent** thereto of the Borrower shall have been obtained (**such consent** not to be unreasonably withheld and to **be deemed to have been given** if no reply is received from the Borrower within fifteen days after the giving of a request for consent by a Bank).”(加黑部分是笔者的强调)

显然赞比亚银行没有在15天的限期内回复,上诉庭的3位大法官在解释该视为条文是视为什么都得出了不同结论。其中作为少数意见的Waller大法官认为视为条文中的“such consent”指的是“事前文书同意”,即如果赞比亚银行没有及时回复,就视为给了事前文书同意,不论没有及时回复发生在转让前或转让后。但多数意见的Rix大法官认为在15天后就视为给了事前文书同意,但事实上这谈不上在转让的“事前”(prior),因为转让发生在1999年12月10日,但被视为有文书同意的一天是12月17日,所以无法令该转让视为有效。与Rix大法官作为多数判决的Hooper大法官认为“such consent”只是简单的同意,笔者看来Hopper大法官与Rix大法官的意见差不多,可是他们在判决中说明是有不同看法。

总体而言,解释视为条文与解释其他条文一样,很重要的是根据个别案件的“背景/语境”(context)与有关合约的其他条文整体解释。在Re Cosslett (Contractors) Ltd (1998) Ch 495先例,上诉庭的Millett大法官说:“Where, however, as in the present case the contract provides only that the plant and materials ‘shall be deemed’ or ‘shall be considered’ to be the property of the employer, **the words are regarded as ambiguous. In such a case other provisions of the contract may be taken into account** in order to decide whether the contract has the effect of passing the legal property in the plant and materials to the employer or **whether, as the prima facie meaning of the words suggests,** it does not have this effect but merely entitles the employer to act as if the property in the plant and materials had passed to him.”(加黑部分是笔者的强调)

3.2 “视为”一词的两个不同解释

只是看“视为”(deeming)一词可以有两个不同解释。一是把它视为假设的事实或后果,但可以推翻;二是被视为的事实或后果是结论性,[15]不能推翻。关于这说法,Giles大法官在澳大利亚先例Abigroup Contractors Pty Ltd. v. ABB Services Pty Ltd. (2004) NSWCA 181,说:“The word ‘deemed’ may create a fictitious situation, or

---

〔15〕 或是definitive或universal application等的同义称呼。

it may simply state an indisputable conclusion."

另在英国的 Starmark Enterprises Ltd. v. CPL Distribution Ltd. (2002) Ch. 306 先例,上诉庭的 Arden 大法官说:"Proviso (2) is a deeming provision and the natural meaning of the word 'deem' in my judgment is to introduce a conclusive state of affairs. There has to be some indication that the deemed state of affairs is not to survive on particular circumstances to exclude that normal meaning."(视为条文在 Arden 大法官的判决带来了一个结论性的事实,除非有些情况显示了视为的事实在一些特别的情况下不应该存在,并排除视为一词的一般性解释。)

在 Lafarge (Aggregates) Ltd. v. Newham London Borough Council (2005) 2 Lloyd's Rep. 577 先例,Cooke 大法官说:"The word 'deemed' can mean 'presumed until the contrary is proved', but it an also be used as a word of definition, stating how matters are to be regarded definitively for the purposes of the contract or document in question."

这在稍后介绍的先例可以进一步了解它们不同的判法。看来,除了个别案件的背景/语境外,视为条文所选用的文字也有很大影响。如说明"视为最终"(deem to be final)或"视为是结论性"(deem to be conclusive)等措辞显然加强了双方的订约意图。

在立法的视为条文,会有比较明确的规定,如在 1889 年《Interpretation Act》之 section 26 是说:"... this Act authorises or requires any document to be served by post ... then, unless the contrary intention appears, the service **shall be deemed to be** effected by properly addressing, prepaying, and posting a letter containing the document, and **unless the contrary is proved** to have been effected at the time at which the letter would be delivered in the ordinary course of post."(加黑部分是笔者的强调)

例如在法院告票的送达,如果以上述办法邮寄就会被视为送达。这样,如果被告没有及时向法院告知已经收到与稍后提出抗辩,就会有危险很快原告会向法院取得"缺席判决"(default judgment)。但这个视为并非结论性,缺席的被告可以向法院事后证明他并没有收到告票与有关文件,并成功撤销缺席判决。

3.3 单方面的视为条文没有法律效力

经常会见到单方面加上一条视为条文向另一方作出警告或要求,如说"如果你不在 3 天内同意,将被视为违约/毁约"或"如果你不在 5 天内回复,将被视为同意"。这种单方面而不是双方同意的视为条文没有法律效力,不能作准。如果是向另一方作出警告,这充其量只是单方面的"最后通牒"(ultimatum)。这可节录 The "Hermosa" (1982) 1 Lloyd's Rep 570 先例,上诉庭的 Donaldson 大法官说:"But the ultimatum had no formal legal status. It was not directed to making time of the essence[16].

---

〔16〕 这个课题可看本书第十章之第 5 段。

... The letter was no more than a very strongly worded demand for reassurance. The fact that it did not provoke a helpful response was calculated to increase Nitrates'(作出最后通牒的一方)anxiety, but was not, in my judgment, enough to transform anxiety into conviction."

3.4 视为条文的作用之一:扩大特定条文/文字的一般性解释

视为条文第一个作用是扩大一个特定条文/文字的一般性解释。在 Dairy Containers Ltd v Tasman Orient Line CV (2005) 1 WLR 215 先例,相关提单有一条视为条文可节录如下:"... for the purpose of this sub - paragraph the limitation of liability under the Hague Rules shall be deemed to be £ 100 sterling, lawful money of the United Kingdom per package or unit and references in the Hague Rules, to carriage by sea, **shall be deemed to include** references to carriage by inland waterways and the Hague Rules shall be construed accordingly ..."(加黑部分就是视为条文)

在枢密院,Bingham 勋爵是这样说:"In each instance, the need for the deeming provision arises because without it the term in question does not have the meaning it is to be deemed to have. The limitation of liability under the Rules is not '£ 100 sterling, lawful money of the United Kingdom per package or unit': it is the limitation provided by article IV, rule 5 as qualified by article IX. The references to carriage by sea in the Rules do not include carriage by inland waterways. Thus the purpose of the deeming provision is to give the Rules a meaning different from that which they would have in the absence of a deeming provision."

上述提单的条文合并了 1924 年的《海牙规则》,注意是许多国家承认《海牙规则》并立法成为它们的《海上运输法》并在涉及有关国家的海上货物运输强制适用。但会有情况是没有强制适用的立法,这样提单合并 1924 年的《海牙规则》就通过订约自由的大原则适用。但《海牙规则》针对货物件装或单位的责任限制是以 1924 年 100 英镑的黄金价格为准:The "Rosa S" (1988) 2 Lloyd's Rep 574 先例。这些年来黄金价格飙升,在 2006 年,1924 年 100 英镑可以买的黄金已经变为 14000 美元。这表示上述提单的视为条文是把《海牙规则》的 100 英镑视为纸币,与 1924 年的黄金价格无关。显然如果有个别国家(包括英国)的《海上运输法》强制适用,并且是高出 100 英镑的责任限制,就表示上述的提单条文违反了《海上运输法》,变为无效。但如果不是此情况,订约自由完全有效,变成怎样写就怎样解释。上述提单条文也把《海牙规则》视为适用在内河运输,这也是在《海牙规则》以外。《海牙规则》是国际公约,只适用在国与国之间的海上运输,不适用在内河运输。但双方通过订约自由的视为条文扩大《海牙规则》的适用,也不会有人反对。

有类似作用的例子很多,如在 Hotgroup Plc v Royal Bank of Scotland Plc (2010) EWHC 1241 (Ch)先例,有视为条文扩大租客对房东作出通知的要求,说:"... no notice will be deemed to be validly served on the Landlord unless a copy of the notice is also served on Schroder Property Investment Management Limited. . . ”(不视为是有效送达,除非通知的副本同时送达给房东的管理代理人。)

3.5 视为条文的作用之二:假设/约定一个事实

在 Howells v IGI Insurance Co Ltd (2003) Lloyd's Rep I. R. 803 先例,涉及一个英超足球运动员的保险合约。该保单有条文说明在该运动员受伤后的 12 个月,如果他参赛多过 5 次,“受保人/运动员就会被结论性地视为完全康复与不能再提出索赔”(the Insured shall be deemed conclusively to have been fully rehabilitated and no claim shall be payable hereunder. . .)。该运动员的膝盖受伤后,一直没有恢复到原来的状况参加英超比赛,但曾经在 12 个月内参加了较低层次的 8 次比赛。他向保险公司索赔,被判是败诉,其中上诉庭的 Potter 大法官是说:“It is plain that clause 11 is a deeming clause, designed to define and put beyond doubt the test or definition of permanent total disablement from employment as a professional footballer. ”

在一定的角度看来,这里的视为条文有点像“定义条文”(definition clause),就是把什么视为“康复”作出了一个定义。这在 Lafarge (Aggregates) Ltd. v. Newham London Borough Council (2005) 2 Lloyd's Rep. 577 先例对视为一词的解释,就是结论性。

只要定义是双方能够接受,也可以看到它的好处,就是双方可以避免要法院认定一个复杂的事实,也就是运动员受伤程度的昂贵与不肯定。

3.6 视为条文的作用之三:说明合约双方之间的后果

3.6.1 通知/文件视为收到或送达

第一种经常发生的情况涉及合约双方之间的通知,这通常会有条文针对通知怎样作出(如谁是收件人与以什么方法如传真/电邮加上快递/挂号信等),并会有视为条文说明在多久后视为收到并会有什么后果。这种条文也往往是双方同意分摊通知到底是否有收到的风险,因为任何的传达办法都会有危险不成功(虽然这个风险在今天的社会越来越小)或被“忽视”(overlook)。此外,条文也给了双方肯定性,不论有关的通知或文件是早收到、迟收到或没有收到。毕竟,很多合约会同时说明视为收到通知后但没有作出回复或行动的一些严重后果。对作出通知的一方还有一个重要的好处就是他可以避免证明收件人已经完整无缺地收到文件的困难。

这种视为条文到底是一个假设(如没有办法明确通知有否收到与什么时候收到)或是结论性有不同判法的案例,这显然是根据个别案件的背景/语境但也有一定程度的不肯定。

首先介绍的是 Carne v Debono (1988) 1 WLR 1107 先例,涉及土地的买卖。双方的合约中涉及双方作出的通知有一条视为条文,如下:“12(h) Any notice given by either party to the other under the provisions of this agreement shall be in writing and **shall be deemed to have been served at the expiration of 48 hours after it has been posted . . .** ”

简单的案情是根据双方的通知,成交日期是在2月5日。但双方对完成交易所要支付的金额,特别是利息有一点疑议。这导致买方代表律师在2月4日通过电话要求卖方代表律师给一份“完成交易文件”(completion statement),内中有卖方认为正确的金额。这份文件在2月5日早上由卖方作出,显然要在当天中午完成交易来不及,而且买方也认为文件中的金额不正确。如果是根据视为条文,买方应在48小时后,也就是2月7日早上才算收到。结果在没有完成交易的情况下,卖方终止合约并没收10%的定金。这导致双方的诉讼,但买方在上诉庭败诉,原因包括完成交易文件并非一份必须作出的文件,另是买方即使对完成交易的金额有异议,也应该在成交日期交出他所认为正确的金额才能避免违约/毁约。而针对视为条文,看来上诉庭认为不是结论性,其中Browne - Wilkinson大法官说:“Clause 12(h) is a deeming provision which does not exclude the possibility of proving an earlier receipt. It is not a statement that for all purposes the document shall only be treated as having been received at a particular time.”

接下来介绍的另一个先例也有同样判法,即视为条文并不是结论性。但该案情有十分独特的事实,导致这样的判法看来十分公平合理。这是Re Thundercrest Ltd (1995) 1 BCLC 117先例,案情涉及一家私人公司决定发行3万股新股以增加公司资本。公司有3位持有同样数量股份的股东,这表示发行的新股也应该每人分配1万股。如果其中有一位股东拒绝供股,其余的两位股东就可以作出分配。这可节录公司章程的一条视为条文针对如果在21天的时间内不接受新股将被视为拒绝供股,如下:“Subject to any direction to the contrary that may be given by the company in general meeting, any original shares for the time being unissued and **any new shares** from time to time to be created shall, **before they are issued, be offered to the members in proportion as nearly as possible** to the nominal value of the existing shares held by them and **such offer shall be made by notice** specifying the number of shares to which the member is entitled and limiting a time within which the offer, **if not accepted, shall be deemed to be declined**; and after the expiration of such time or on receipt of an intimation from the member to whom the notice is given that he declines to accept the shares, the directors may dispose of the same in such manner as they think most beneficial to the company. The provisions of s. 17 of the Companies Act 1980 shall have effect only in so far as they are not inconsistent with this article.”(加黑部分是笔者的强调)

该先例独特的事实是向其中一位股东作出的通知被邮局退回,表示另外两位股东完全知道该股东没有与不可能收到通知。另是该两位股东也知道另一位股东想接受新股。但结果到了21天后,该两位股东就把另一位股东的1万股平均分摊。这被法院判是不可以接受,也就是视为条文不被接受是结论性。Paul Baker QC大法官说:“The purpose of deeming provisions in the case of management of companies is clear. In the case of uncertainty as to whether a document has been delivered, with large numbers of shareholders and so forth, there has to be some rule under which those in charge of the management can carry on the business without having to investigate every case where some shareholder comes along and says he has not got the document. The directors have to proceed and transact the company's business on the basis of the deeming provisions. **But, in my judgment, all that falls away when you find it is established without any possibility of challenge that the document has not been delivered.**"(加黑部分是笔者的强调)

最后在这方面想介绍的是 Lafarge (Aggregates) Ltd v Newham London Borough Council (2005) 2 Lloyd's Rep 577 先例。而在这个先例,英国高院是判视为条文是结论性,但它涉及的案情很不一样,所以背景/语境也不一样。案件涉及一个工程合约,其中也有一条通知条文,并说明送达后的两天视为送达/收到,说:"(3) Any notice shall be deemed to be served two working days following service in accordance with this clause."

双方的争议有关一条"争议解决条文"(dispute resolution clause),这种在英国的工程/建筑合约,是先由"审裁员"(adjudicator)很快作出决定。而如果败诉方不服气,他必须在一个特定时间内(工程合约是 3 个月内)作出通知,把争议提交给"仲裁"(arbitration)。在该先例,涉及败诉方有否在 3 个月内作出通知。法院判是审裁员作出的决定是在 8 月 13 日(虽然这是一份电邮并没有签字,而书面的决定是在 8 月 17 日才寄出),而败诉方是在 11 月 11 日以信函作出通知要提交给仲裁。但这个信函直到 11 月 11 日后的两个工作日才能被视为收到,其中涉及周末。所以法院认为在视为条文下,败诉方的信函是在 11 月 15 日才视为收到。这超出了审裁员决定后的 3 个月,所以仲裁无效。针对视为条文的解释,Cooke 大法官说:"I therefore agree with the arbitrator that the deeming provision in clause G44 is of universal application and applies to all notices served under the contract. The allowance of two working days is to give some scope for the matter to come to the actual attention of those dealing with it on behalf of the recipient but the provision is of benefit to the person serving the notice inasmuch as there is clarity as to the point at which service is effective."

3.6.2 日后不得对事实或情况提出异议

第二种经常发生的情况是视为条文被用在一些富争议性的事实或情况,并说明对方如果不提出异议的后果就是一方提出的事实变为最终或结论性。这通常会被视为结论性,特别是视为条文写明"最终"(final)或"结论性"(conclusive)。如在国际外贸或程租合约,涉及装卸港的"事实记录"(statement of facts)与相关文件,通常也包括根据这些文件所计算出来的滞期费,经常会有条文说是给了对方(CIF/CFR 买方、FOB 卖方或租约的承租人)后多少天,对方如果不提出异议,该事实记录与相关文件就被"视为是最终"(deem to be final)。这种条文也有道理,因为在外国的装卸港,要对事实作出调查并不容易,如果对方对某些记录的事实有异议就尽快提出,可让派船的卖方或买方或船东尽早作出调查。而这种在外国装卸港通过代理人的调查,更加是越早越有机会成功。所以不论在用字上或作出解释的背景/语境,都更加倾向是结论性。

这方面的先例可先介绍 Burrough's Adding Machines Ltd v Aspinall (1925) 41 TLR 276,案情涉及计算器生产商与销售员之间的佣金合约,其中有条文规定生产商作出的账目如果销售员在收到后 30 天不提出异议,该账目"将被视为接受为正确"(shall be deemed to be accepted by the salesman as correct)。这被判是销售员没有在 30 天内提出异议,就受到生产商账目的约束,即使内中有错误。

在另一个较近期的先例 Starmark Enterprises Ltd v CPL Distribution Ltd (2002) Ch 306,涉及房屋租赁合约的"租金调整条文"(rent review clause)。该条文规定房东可以作出通知告知他希望的新的租金价格,如果租客不在一定时间内向房东作出反通知,就会被"视为接受房东提出的新租金"(deem to have agreed to pay the increased rent specified in the rent notice)。尽管在租金调整条文内规定的时间一般不视为重要,[17]但在该先例是说如果规定的时间加上了一条视为条文,就应该被视为重要,上诉庭的 Arden 大法官说:"... the normal presumption in rent review cases that time was not of the essence could be displaced if the contracting parties had shown clear contra - indications in their wording of the rent review clauses in the lease; that where by way of a deeming provision the contract expressed a clear intention as to the consequence of a party's failure to comply with the stipulated timetable the court would not read such a deeming provision as mere administrative direction or conclude that time was not of essence, since such a construction would amount to a rewriting of the contract by which the parties had agreed to be bound."

Arden 大法官也针对视为条文说:"That proviso may loosely be referred to as a 'deeming' provision. The word 'deem' as used in legal drafting denotes a device for introducing a fiction. The word 'deem' in this type of context signals that the draftsman is about to introduce a fiction as if proviso (2) had read 'if the lessees shall fail to serve a counter - notice within the period aforesaid they shall be deemed to have agreed that black is white'. The concept of agreement in this situation is an artificial one."

这方面也有稍微不同的判法,就是视为条文到底不允许日后提出什么争议。这是在 WJB Chiltern Plc v Olympia Securities Commercial Plc (2003) EWHC 3464 (Ch) 先例。案情是雇主(一家国际企业)与税务顾问之间的合约,合约规定了后者的收费主要根据省下税金的百分比作为报酬,另加上工作时间。合约另有一条视为条文说如果不在一个时间段内对税务顾问作出的发票提出争议,就视为接受发票内的条件。该第 3 条文可节录如下:"Our Fees will be invoiced from time to time and will be sub-

---

[17] 这在本书第十章之 4.2.2.3 段有详述。

ject to VAT where applicable. Invoices will take the form of a final account for all work carried out during the period covered by the relevant invoice and will be due for payment (in full, in sterling, without any deduction, set – off or counterclaim) within 30 days of the invoice date. If an invoice is not paid within that time we reserve the right to charge interest on any outstanding balance at 2% above the prevailing daily base lending rate of Barclays Bank plc, from the 30 th day after the invoice date until the date of settlement ... If you disagree with an invoice you must notify us in writing within twenty one days of the invoice date, **failing which you will be deemed to have agreed to its terms.** You agree that you will in any event pay all undisputed amounts in accordance with this Contract."(加黑部分是笔者的强调)

这被判是雇主不能对发票内的工作时间日后提出异议,但可以对有否成功减税提出争议。Langan QC 大法官说:"The success fee is a sum payable from the happening of an event. In my judgment the terms of clause 3 are not so plain that they should be construed as creating liability for that payment irrespective of whether the event has occurred. Mr Pearson(税务顾问的代表大律师)was unable to point to any case in which a deeming provision like clause 3 had been given so extensive an effect. In my judgment, applying the modern principles of construction of commercial documents for clause 3, it can be no more than a nuts and bolts provision. It might, for example, prevent a client from disputing the number of hours shown on the bill delivered on a time charge basis after the lapse of the specified period. Clause 3 cannot go to a fundamental question of the kind with which this litigation is concerned. In so far as it is of doubtful meaning, it must be construed *contra proferentem* and therefore in favour of Olympia(雇主)."

3.6.3 外来事件/不可抗力事项的后果

有关不可抗力条文,在本书第十三章已经有提到。要依赖不可抗力条文需要满足不少条件,看来也不容易。如在 1.7 段要在依赖方的控制以外,在 1.9 段要是依赖方无法合理避免或控制与 1.11 段如果有替代履行办法(如卖方可以买进浮动货物)通常不能依赖等。但在不可抗力条文加上一条视为条文,会有机会避免这些条件的满足。如在 Pancommerce SA v Veechema BV (1982) 1 Lloyd's Rep 645 先例,买卖合约的不可抗力条文是说:"In case of prohibition of export ... or in case of any executive or legislative act done by or on behalf of the government of the country of origin ... restricting export, whether partially or otherwise, any such restriction **shall be deemed** by both parties to apply to this contract and to the extent of such total or partial restriction to prevent fulfilment ... and to that extent this contract or any unfulfilled portion thereof shall be cancelled ..."(如果货物来源地的当局禁止或限制出口,不论是部分或全部,这个限制将被双方视为适用在本合约并阻止合约的履行,本合约或还没有提供的部分货物将被取消。)

第一审的 Bingham 大法官是说:"It also follows by virtue of the clause that the restriction is deemed to the extent of the restriction to prevent fulfilment. **I accept without reservation that the purpose of this deeming provision is to outlaw any factual enquiry into whether, but for the restriction, the seller could have performed the contract and whether his position was short or long and whether he could or should have obtained goods of the contractual description elsewhere...**"(加黑部分是笔者的强调)

但在该案例,卖方在高院与后来的上诉庭(1983) 2 Lloyd's Rep 304,都败诉。原因是卖方手中有出口批文(这是在当局作出禁令之前取得),可以满足与履行有关的买卖合约,可以说根本没有受到出口禁令的阻止。在上诉庭,Donaldson 大法官这样说:

"Mr. Longmore(卖方代表大律师)submits that the new clause(这是指以 GAFTA 标准格式为准的买卖合约内的被修改过的不可抗力条文)is designed to restrict the inquiry much further, by excluding 'loophole goods'(这是指出口禁令前已经装在驳船的货物,本质上与浮动货物一样不受到禁令的影响), such as, in this case, goods to which an existing licence could be applied. Properly construed the clause applied the restriction to the contract and so produced a deemed total prohibition of fulfilment ...

It is an interesting argument, but one which I find wholly unconvincing. As Mr. Justice Bingham pointed out, **the commercial consequences would be startling in the extreme. Prohibitions of export are a sellers' nightmare, but the clause, so construed, would convert them into a sellers' dream. Possessed of goods which they had contracted to sell and a licence for a sufficient quantity to export them all, sellers would be able to re-negotiate the price to reflect the effect of the prohibition of export, notwithstanding that they could honour their contracts without let or hindrance.** (加黑部分是说明如果接受卖方对不可抗力条文的解释会带来严重后果,就是卖方即使持有出口批文与货物,完全没有任何障碍履行合约,卖方也可以敲买方竹杠。)

No doubt the draftsman of the clause overlooked the possibility that restrictions on export might be applied to goods generally rather than to goods under particular contracts, ... The clause falls to be construed according to its terms. **The restriction which is deemed to apply to the contract with the buyers is, in effect, a restriction upon the export of sugar beet pellets(有关货物)not covered by a licence granted before July 1, 1976. It can be notionally written into the contract in these terms.** If and insofar as this prevents shipment, the contract is cancelled. But on the facts it did not prevent shipment. Accordingly the sellers are in breach, ..."(加黑部分是说本合约的不可抗力条文所针对的禁止或限制只适用在 7 月 1 日取得的出口批文不包括的货物,这个条件

可以默示在该合约内。)

3.7　视为条文的作用之四:造成合约禁止翻供

在 Trident Turboprop (Dublin) Ltd v First Flight Couriers Ltd (2008) 2 Lloyd's Rep 581 先例,涉及一架飞机的租赁合约中的"没有依赖条文"(non – reliance clause)。合约中针对有关的飞机有一条视为条文,说:"The Lessee also agrees and acknowledges that save as expressly stated in this Agreement and the other Transaction Documents to which the Lessor is a party, **the Lessor has not and shall not be deemed to have made any warranties or representations**, express or implied, about the Aircraft, including but not limited to the matters referred to above."(加黑部分是笔者的强调)

这被视为合约规定了即使对有关的飞机作出过陈述,也被视为没有发生过。Aikens 大法官说:"The parties who agree such a clause are thus agreeing that no representations were made by Trident (as lessor), or, if any representations were made, then it is 'deemed' that they were not. The legal effect of provisions such as this has been analysed by the courts in terms of an estoppel created by contract ... As Moore – Bick LJ points out at para 56 in the *Peekay* case, it is commercially convenient and desirable for parties to a contract to agree that a certain state of affairs (ie that no pre – contractual representations were made) is the case, so as to provide a clear basis for the contract itself. If the parties do agree a certain factual basis on which the contract is made, the contractual agreement is that neither party can subsequently deny that basis. **Hence the phrase 'estoppel by contract'.**"(加黑部分是笔者的强调)

3.8　视为条文的作用之五:对合约承诺/责任作出局限

在 William Sindall Plc v Cambridgeshire County Council (1994) 1 WLR 1016 先例,涉及一大片土地(可以建几十栋房子)的买卖。买卖合约有以下的条文,包括视为条文:

"14. Without prejudice to the duty of the vendor to disclose all latent easements and latent liabilities known to the vendor to affect the property, the property is sold subject to any rights of way and water, rights of common and other rights, easements, quasi – easements, liabilities and public rights affecting the same. ...(土地的卖方需要把他所知道会影响该土地的潜在的地役权或潜在的责任在订约前作出披露。)

17. The purchaser **shall be deemed to purchase with full notice** of and subject to:... (e) all easements quasi – easements rights and privileges (whether of a public or private nature) now affecting the property but without any obligation on the part of the vendor to define the same."(土地的买方视为有了完整的通知买下该土地……)

但在交易完成后,买方进行工程时发觉地下有污水渠,严重影响该土地的价值。这导致买方以卖方的误述或双方有基本性的"共同错误"(common mistake)终止合约或令合约无效。[18] 但法院判买方不能终止合约,因为即使有一个双方的共同错误,也并非是基本性可以令该合约变为无效。至于是误述,虽然卖方不知道地下有污水渠令他没有在订约前作出披露,但通过立法 1967 年《误述法》之 Section 2(2),即使是"无辜误述"(innocent misrepresentation),也可以通过金钱赔偿替代终止合约。而针对上述的视为条文,上诉庭的 Hoffmann 大法官说:"They **qualify the obligations** to convey as beneficial owner and give vacant possession and therefore **qualify any representation** which could be implied from having undertaken these obligations."(加黑部分是笔者的强调)

§4 法院管辖条文(court jurisdiction clause)

在近年来,法院管辖条文的惯用远远比不上仲裁条文,但还是会有。如在一份著名的油轮租船标准格式合约的 Shelltime,其第 41 条文名为"law and litigation clause"就规定是英国法院的管辖,但在双方同意下有权选择伦敦仲裁。这一条文带来的争议可看 The"YM Saturn"(2012) EWHC 2652 先例。

在商业合约,法院管辖条文的受欢迎程度比不上仲裁条文,有很多原因。其中普遍被接受是在 1958 年《纽约公约》下,仲裁条文的效力与裁决书的执行已经有了 150 个国家承认,这在最近三四十年的全球化经济十分重要。但涉及法院管辖条文,还没有世界性的国际公约针对。在 2005 年《海牙选择法院协议公约》(2005 Hague Convention on Choice of Court Agreements)[19] 承认选择法院管辖权的有效性,但该公约至今没有生效。[20]

显然在国际性的商业合约,最多被选择的管辖法院就是英国法院。在很多调查中,可举一个比较近期的在 2008 年由 Oxford Institute of European and Comparative Law and the Oxford Centre for Socio - Legal - Studies 作出的调查,[21] 针对了 100 家欧盟的大企业(包括在法国、德国、意大利、荷兰、波兰、西班牙、比利时与英国),在它们的国际商业合约中最喜欢选择适用英国法与英国法院的管辖。而主要的考虑是法官与法院的质量、判决的可预测性、英国合约法、程序与判决的公平性、不存在贪污受贿与作出决定的速度。

这样,在商业合约中作出选择,就必须拟定一条好的英国法院管辖条文。例如,是一条"专属管辖权条文"(exclusive jurisdiction clause)而不是一条"非专属管辖权

---

〔18〕 可见本书第三章之 13.3 段。

〔19〕 公约内容可见 http://www.hcch.net/index_en.php? act = conventions.text&cid = 98 。

〔20〕 墨西哥在 2007 年加入该公约,美国与欧共体在 2009 年签署该公约。

〔21〕 可见 the Institute of European and Comparative Law 的网页 www.iecl.ox.ac.uk/。

条文”(non – exclusive jurisdiction clause)。它们的区别是根据对有关条文的解释,如果条文是可被解释为有“积极或作为义务”(positive obligation)要求双方把争议交出给选择的法院,这就有更大的可能被视为一条专属管辖权条文。但如果是受制于一个选择的法院管辖权,就会有危险被视为一条非专属管辖权条文。正如 Hobhouse 大法官在 Pathe Screen Entertainment Ltd v Handmade Films (Distributors) Ltd, 11 July 1989, (2005) Lloyd' s Rep IR 32 先例的判决说,如果“submit”是用作“及物动词”(transitive verb),如“the parties submit their disputes to the jurisdiction of the English courts”(合约方将他们的争议递交英国法院),那么该条文就是专属管辖权条文。但如果“submit”是用作“不及物动词”(intransitive verb),如“the parties submit to the jurisdiction of the English courts”(合约方受制于英国法院的管辖权),该条文就有可能属于非专属管辖权条文。

从解释合约的角度看,如果双方约定受制于某个法院的管辖权,只能解释为任何一方不能抗拒该法院的管辖,如申请中止审理,因为有其他更适合的法院。但这不能被解释为双方同意把所有会发生的争议只递交给该法院。换言之,如果一条条文是说明把双方所有的争议递交给某个法院,或同样的文字,更不用说明示说明“专属”(exclusive)一词,就应该被视为一条专属管辖权条文。

在 Pathe Screen Entertainment Ltd v Handmade Films (Distributors) Ltd 先例,Hobhouse 大法官也提到法院管辖条文会有三类,到底是哪类完全根据有关条文/文字解释,说:“Broadly, jurisdiction clauses which are mutual may be of three types. First there can be a clause which specifically provides that a certain court is to have exclusive jurisdiction. Second there can be a clause, like an arbitration clause, by which the parties agree to refer to a particular court the determination of certain disputes. Thirdly, the parties can simply agree that a certain court will have jurisdiction over them or to submit to the jurisdiction of that court. In the first two categories to attempt to litigate a relevant dispute before some other forum is a breach of the clause although under English law, the remedies for such breach may be limited and discretionary; this is because under English law no agreement, apart from some statutory provision can oust the jurisdiction of the court. The function of the third category is to confer jurisdiction and avoid disputes about jurisdiction; it can accordingly confer useful and valuable rights.”

4.1 专属管辖权条文与非专属管辖权条文的区分

Austrian Lloyd Steamship Co v Gresham Life Assurance Society Ltd (1903) 1 KB 249 应该是最早被报道有关这个问题的先例,相关法院管辖条文被判是一条专属管辖权条文:“For all disputes which may arise out of the contract of insurance, all the parties interested expressly agree **to submit to the jurisdiction of the Courts of Budapest** having jurisdiction in such matters.”(双方明示同意受制于布达佩斯法院的管辖权)

Romer 大法官有以下的解释说:“The question is this: Does the condition merely mean that, if one of the parties to the contract is sued by the other in the Court of Budapest, he will not take any objection to its jurisdiction; or, does it mean that the parties mutually agree that, if any dispute arises under the contract, it shall be determined by the Court in Budapest? Having regard to the nature of the contract and its language, I am of opinion that the latter construction is the correct one. It is not as if the insurance company only had agreed that they would submit to the jurisdiction of the Court at Budapest: both parties mutually agree to submit to that jurisdiction in respect of any dispute which may arise under the contract. If there had been an agreement by the parties in similar terms to submit to the decision of a particular individual, I think there could have been no doubt that it would have amounted to an agreement to submit any dispute under the contract to the arbitration of that person. In this case, instead of nominating a particular individual as arbitrator, the parties agree to submit any dispute arising under the contract to the Courts at Budapest."

之后,在 Pathe Screen Entertainment Ltd v Handmade Films (Distributors) Ltd, 11 July 1989, (2005) Lloyd's Rep IR 32 先例,Hobhouse 大法官不认同 Austrian Lloyd Steamship Co v Gresham Life Assurance Society Ltd 先例的判决,说:"The phrase in the *Austrian Lloyd* case was 'agree to submit' but in that case it was construed in a transitive sense as an agreement to submit disputes to a particular court in the same way as one can agree to submit disputes to the decision of an arbitrator. The clauses which I have to construe do not lend themselves to a transitive construction; the sense is that the parties submit themselves to the jurisdiction of the court not that the parties submit disputes. In the *Austrian Lloyd* case it was open to the court to construe the words as if they read 'agree to submit all such disputes'. I do not consider that it would be appropriate to make such an inferential insertion in these clauses. Words are an accurate tool and relatively small differences in wording will produce different contractual effects. In these clauses the parties have used neither the word exclusive nor a sentence construction which is transitive."(Hobhouse 大法官认为该先例的法院管辖条文中的"submit"一词用作不及物动词,有关的条文规定是合约方受制于布达佩斯法院的管辖权,而不是将争议递交给该法院,因此不认同该先例的判法。)

在该先例,有关的法院管辖条文是:"The parties hereby [consent and] submit to the jurisdiction of the Court of England in connection with any dispute arising hereunder."

在 Pathe Screen Entertainment Ltd v Handmade Films (Distributors) Ltd 先例之后,有关及物动词与不及物动词的说法,几乎在所有有关这个问题的先例都有针对与分析。如在 Sinochem International Oil (London) Co Ltd v Mobil Sales and Supply Corporation (2000) 1 Lloyd's Rep 670 先例,Rix 大法官说:"The test which has been developed for distinguishing an exclusive from a non – exclusive jurisdiction clause is whether on its proper construction the clause obliges the parties to resort to the relevant jurisdiction, irrespective of whether the word ‘exclusive’ is used: Dicey and Morris, 13th ed. 2000 at par. 12 – 078. Or to put the issue in another way: is the obligation contained in the clause the intransitive one to submit to a jurisdiction if it is chosen by the other contracting party, or is it the transitive one to submit all disputes to the chosen jurisdiction?"(发展出来的到底是专属或是非专属管辖权条文[不论有没有写明]的考验,是看在文字上到底是作为不及物动词受制于某个由对方选择的法院的管辖权,或是作为及物动词要求把所有的争议交出给一个双方约定的法院。)

Waller 大法官在 Sabah Shipyard (Pakistan) Ltd v Pakistan (2003) 2 Lloyd's Rep 571 先例也有类似的说法:"In my view cl. 1.9.1 does not lend itself to a transitive construction, and when taken with cl. 2.6, it seems to me that it is not an exclusive clause in the sense of making it a breach of contract for either party to commence proceedings in a jurisdiction other than England."(大致说是解释第 1.9.1 条文并加上第 2.6 条文,这应该属于一条非专属管辖权条文。)

在该先例,第 1.9.1 条文是说:"Each Party consents to the jurisdiction of the Courts of England for any action filed by the other Party under this agreement to resolve any dispute between the Parties and may be enforced in England . . ."

另第 2.6 条文是说:

"2.6 Sovereign Immunity

The Guarantor hereby irrevocably and unconditionally agrees that the execution, delivery, and performance by it of this Guarantee constitute private and commercial acts.

The Guarantor hereby irrevocably and unconditionally agrees that: (i) should any proceedings be brought against the Guarantor or its assets, other than its military aircraft, naval vessels and other defense related assets or assets protected by the diplomatic and consular privileges under the 1978 Immunity Act of the United Kingdom or the 1976 Sovereign Immunities Act of the United States orany analogous legislation (the ‘Protected Assets’) in any jurisdiction in connection with this Guarantee or any of the transactions contemplated by this Guarantee, no claim of immunity from such proceedings will be claimed by or on behalf of the Guarantor on behalf of itself or any of its assets (other than the Protected Assets); (ii) it waives any right of immunity which it or any of its assets (other than the Protected Assets) now has or may in the future have in any jurisdiction in connection with any such proceedings; and (iii) consents generally in respect of the enforcement of any judgment against it in any such proceedings in any jurisdiction to the giving of any relief or the issue of any process in connection with such proceedings (including without limitation, the making, enforcement or execution against or in respect of any of its assets whatsoever (other than the Protected Assets) regardless of its use or intended use)."(这条文是针对主权国的豁免权,因为其中一方的当事人[也是该先例的被告]是巴基斯坦的主权国。条文约定巴基斯坦不会以主权国的豁免权作为被原告 Sabah Shipyard 提出索赔时的抗辩,而它作出的担保是一份私人与商业合约。)

另在 AXA Re v Ace Global Markets Limited (2006) Lloyd's Rep I. R. 683 先例,Gloster 大法官说:"... my judgment, the jurisdiction clause, even taken on its own, is not necessarily an exclusive jurisdiction agreement, because it does not transitively require all disputes to be submitted to an English court."

但"submit"用作不及物动词并不代表该条文就一定是非专属管辖权条文,还是要根据合约条文(甚至是合约其他有关条文)的整体解释。在 Continental Bank NA v Aeakos Compania Naviera SA (1994) 1 WLR 588 先例,相关银行借贷合约的法院管辖条文可节录如下:"21.02 Each of the borrowers ... hereby irrevocably submits to the jurisdiction of the English courts ... but the bank reserves the right to proceed under this agreement in the courts of any other country claiming or having jurisdiction in respect thereof."(每个借款人无条件受制于英国法院的管辖……但银行保留在任何其他有管辖权的法院提出起诉的权利。)

看来,银行这样规定是给自己更大的弹性,因为它们向"借款人"(borrowers)采取的行动,往往是追债。这在许多法院可以获得"简易判决"(summary judgment),会快捷与便宜得多。但如果在英国法院取得简易判决,还需要外国向借款人执行。解释这样的条文,如果只是看第一句的文字是属于非专属管辖权条文,而第二句的文字就更加是属于非专属管辖权条文。这样岂非两条写法完全不同的条文是同一个解释?所以,上诉庭判这条文对借款人是专属管辖权条文,但对银行是非专属管辖权条文也可以理解。Steyn 大法官说:"We regard the concluding words as significant: 'but the bank reserves the right to proceed under this agreement in the courts of any other country claiming or having jurisdiction in respect thereof.' The juxtaposition of a submission by the defendants to the jurisdiction of the English courts and the option reserved in favour of the bank to sue elsewhere brings into play the *expressio unius exclusio alterius* canon of construction. It suggests that a similar option in favour of the defendants was deliberately omitted. In our judgment the language of clause 21.02 evinces a clear intention that the defendants, but not the bank, would be obliged to submit disputes in connection with the loan facility to the English courts."

在 Middle Eastern Oil v National Bank of Abu Dhabi (2009) 1 Lloyd's Rep 251 先例也有类似的判法,相关的条文说:"The Bank and the Customer submit to the jurisdiction of the Civil Courts of the United Arab Emirates but without prejudice to the Bank's general right to take proceedings, where necessary, in any court wheresoever."

Teare 大法官说:"The words used in the phrase 'The Bank and the Customer submit to the jurisdiction of the Civil Courts of the United Arab Emirates' are capable of meaning that the bank and the customer agree that they will submit disputes concerning their banking relationship to the jurisdiction of the civil courts of the UAE. But they are also capable of meaning that the bank and the customer agree that if one commences proceedings against the other concerning their banking relationship in the civil courts of the UAE the other will submit to the jurisdiction of those courts, leaving untouched the parties' right to commence proceedings elsewhere if they are able to do so. However, the clause must be construed as a whole. The clause ends by saying: 'but without prejudice to the Bank's general right to take proceedings, where necessary, in any court whereso-ever'. This indicates that the draftsman has addressed the question of proceedings concerning the banking relationship being brought in other jurisdictions and has expressly provided that the bank may do so. No mention is made of the customer being able to do so. In my judgment the obvious inference to be drawn from that omission is that, properly construed, the jurisdiction clause was intended to oblige the customer to commence proceedings concerning its banking relationship in the courts of the UAE but not to oblige the bank to do so. The customer's general right to do so was prejudiced. The bank's general right to do so was not prejudiced. That is the meaning which, in my judgment, the clause would convey to a reasonable person in the situation of the parties at the time they entered into their banking relationship."

4.2 合约同时明示适用英国法对英国法院有专属管辖权的影响

如果合约条文中在规定了英国法院的管辖权的同时选择适用英国法,那么该条文很可能属于专属管辖权条文,尤其是在合约双方都不是英国公司的情况下。在Sohio Supply Co v Gatoil (USA) Inc (1989) 1 Lloyd's Rep 588 的上诉庭先例,相关合约涉及两个美国特拉华州的公司之间的石油买卖,其中的法院管辖条文可节录如下:"This agreement shall be governed by the Laws of England under the jurisdiction of the English courts without recourse to arbitration."

该条文被判是专属管辖权条文,Staughton 大法官说:"To my mind, it is manifest that these business men intended that clause to apply to all disputes that should arise between them. I can think of no reason at all why they should choose to go to the trouble of saying that the English Courts should have non-exclusive jurisdiction. I can think of every reason why they should choose that some Court, in this case the English Court, should have exclusive jurisdiction. Then, both sides would know where all cases were to be tried."

在 Svendborg v Wansa (1997) 2 Lloyd's Rep 183 先例,法院也有同样的判法,Staughton 大法官说:"I conclude that the clause does confer exclusive jurisdiction on the English Courts. My reasons are in substance, first those which I stated in Sohio Supply

Co. v. Gatoil (U. S. A.) Inc., [1989] 1 Lloyd's Rep. 588 at pp. 591 – 592, and in particular that I could think of no reason why businessmen should choose to go to the trouble of saying that the English Courts should have non – exclusive jurisdiction. My second reason is that the parties in the second part of the clause were plainly saying that English law was to be mandatory if the American Carriage of Goods by Sea Act did not apply; it seems to me that they must have intended English jurisdiction likewise to be mandatory in that event."

Waller大法官在 British Aerospace Plc v Dee Howard Co (1993) 1 Lloyd's Rep 368 先例中也说:"... there is no real purpose as I see it in submitting disputes to the jurisdiction of the English Court as well as choosing English law unless the intention is to make England exclusive."(双方没理由将争议递交给英国法院并选择适用英国法,除非双方的订约意图是想约定英国法院有专属管辖权。毕竟,适用法是用在解决双方实体的争议。)

Waller大法官的判决也在后来的 Sinochem v. Mobil Sales (2000) 1 Lloyd's Rep. 670 先例被认同,这包括两方面的原因,一是一条香港法院管辖条文同时约定适用法是香港法,二是商业人士通常不会同意一条非专属管辖权条文,判该先例的管辖权条文应是专属。Rix 大法官说:"In the present case the clause in the Hong Kong contract **not only provides for Hong Kong law**, but states that the Hong Kong Courts 'are to have jurisdiction to settle any disputes' between the parties and that the parties 'submit to the jurisdiction of those courts'. In my judgment, this is a clause which contains a transitive obligation to submit disputes to the Courts of Hong Kong. It has all the indicia of such a clause. It is mutual, it refers to 'any disputes' i. e. all disputes, and the language 'are to have jurisdiction', pace Mr. Hollander(被告代表大律师) who contrasts the word 'shall' in the opening line of the clause, is the language of obligation and not option. Moreover, although a choice of law clause may well exist without any jurisdiction clause to accompany it, nevertheless, as Mr. Justice Waller remarked in British Aerospace v. Dee Howard at p. 375, **there is not much point in choosing a specific law to accompany a jurisdiction clause unless the intention is to make the Courts where such law operates exclusive.** Mr. Berry did not stress the unusual presence of the word 'irrevocably', and so I do not do so either, but it strikes me that if anything this word underlines the transitive commitment. Therefore, the starting point is that the Hong Kong contract, like the London contract, where indeed the word 'exclusive' is expressly found, is an exclusive jurisdiction clause."(加黑部分是笔者的强调)

但即使是明示约定适用英国法,也不保证法院管辖条文会被解释为专属管辖权:AXA Re v Ace Global Markets Limited (2006) Lloyd's Rep I. R. 683 先例与 The "Athena" (No. 2) (2007) 1 Lloyd's Rep 280 先例。在后一个先例,案情涉及船东与他

的互保协会之间有了争议，在互保协会的规则中有关法院管辖条文是说："44.1 The Association and each Owner hereby submits to the jurisdiction of the High Court of Justice of England in respect of any dispute or difference between the Owner and the Association arising out of or in connection with these Rules or out of or in connection with any contract between the Owner and the Association."

Langley 大法官对 Svendborg v Wansa, British Aerospace Plc v Dee Howard Co 与 Sinochem v. Mobil Sales 先例的一个判决理由，就是说商业人士没有理由同时同意一条非专属管辖权条文与法律适用条文，有不同的看法。Langley 大法官说："... even a non-exclusive jurisdiction clause does have a purpose. It makes it difficult, if not impossible, to argue that the chosen forum is not an appropriate one for the resolution of the dispute."

虽然笔者认为 Langley 大法官的说法也不太有说服力，但可以说是管辖权条文到底是专属或非专属解释起来也不容易与不稳定。这方面笔者认同 Langley 大法官所说："I have also been referred to a number of authorities on this issue. **They are not all easy to reconcile. The language of 'transitive' and 'intransitive' does not leap to every mind.** But one of the, if not the, most often cited cases and judgments is the decision of Hobhouse J given in July 1989 in Pathé Screen Entertainment v Handmade Films (Distributors) Ltd, 11 July 1989, which has recently been fully reported as an attachment to the judgment of Morison J in Tonicstar Ltd v American Home Insurance Co [2005] Lloyd's Rep IR 32."（加黑部分是笔者的强调）

看来把一条好的专属法院管辖权条文拟定得清楚无误，会比一条仲裁条文[22]困难得多。另是，加上"专属"(exclusive)一词对有关条文的解释肯定有帮助。但已经在本书第二章之第 12 段有介绍，条文的抬头（或定义）并不重要。即使相关条文的抬头是"exclusive jurisdiction clause"，如果更详尽的内容有冲突，如说是让一方甚至双方有选择权将争议递交到其他法院，显然也不能根据抬头的"exclusive"一词认定相关的法院有专属管辖权。

4.3　法院管辖条文的范围

4.3.1　法院管辖条文本质上与仲裁条文一样有宽松解释

这方面法院管辖条文与仲裁条文是同样的道理，如合约中有一条管辖权条文，那么不论该条文是专属管辖权条文[23]或是非专属管辖权条文，[24]都应该假设双方的

---

〔22〕 关于仲裁条文的宽松解释在 Fiona Trust & Holdings Corporation v Privalov (2008) 1 Lloyd's Rep 254 先例有了定论。

〔23〕 Skype Technologies SA v Joltid Ltd (2009) EWHC 2783 (Ch)先例。

〔24〕 Cinnamon European Structured Credit Master Fund v Banco Commercial Portugues SA (2009) EWHC 3381 (Ch)先例。

定约意图是由合约规定的法院决定他们之间所有的争议。在 Fiona Trust & Holdings Corporation v Privalov (2007) 2 Lloyd's Rep 267 先例,相关的争议涉及一条仲裁条文,但上诉庭的 Longmore 大法官的判决也顺便包括了法院管辖条文,说:"Ordinary businessmen would be surprised at the nice distinctions drawn in the cases and the time taken up by argument in debating whether a particular case falls within one set of words or another very similar set of words. If businessmen go to the trouble of agreeing that their disputes be heard in the courts of a particular country or by a tribunal of their choice they do not expect (at any rate when they are making the contract in the first place) that time and expense will be taken in lengthy argument about the nature of particular causes of action and whether any particular cause of action comes within the meaning of the particular phrase they have chosen in their arbitration clause. If any businessman did want to exclude disputes about the validity of a contract, it would be comparatively simple to say so. As it seems to us **any jurisdiction or arbitration clause in an international commercial contract should be liberally construed....**"(加黑部分是笔者的强调)

贵族院也同意了 Longmore 大法官的判决,因此这种对仲裁条文的宽松解释的道理也应该适用在法院管辖条文:(2008) 1 Lloyd's Rep 254。笔者也认同这一看法,商业人士在谈判中同意一条仲裁条文或法院管辖条文,通常想到的就是把有关合约将来会发生的争议交出给这个双方同意的仲裁庭或法院解决。他们不会是想把争议的一部分,如双方是否有合约关系递交给法院审理,而把另一部分如否有违约/毁约递交给仲裁庭审理。毕竟把一个争议切割出来递交给不同的人审理,会带来很严重的不良后果,如有矛盾的判决/裁决与高昂的费用等。所以,正如在 Fiona Trust & Holdings Corporation v Privalov 先例,贵族院的 Hoffmann 勋爵说:"In my opinion the construction of an arbitration clause should start from the assumption that the parties, as rational businessmen, are likely to have intended any dispute arising out of the relationship into which they have entered or purported to enter to be decided by the same tribunal. The clause should be construed in accordance with this presumption unless the language makes it clear that certain questions were intended to be excluded from the arbitrator's jurisdiction."

4.3.2 双方有多个合约,各有不同的法院管辖条文

表面看来,这种情况不应该经常发生,但这方面也有不少被报道的先例,显示情况的确存在。这种情况会出现在一些大型的工程项目、公司并购计划、衍生品的买卖等。即使在航运,也见过由双方先订立一个长期的"主运输合约"(master agreement)并约定了一个框架,让以后每个不同的航次订立个别的合约。这样,如果双方在这前后两份有效合约同意不同的法院管辖条文或仲裁条文,就会带来问题是谁有权管辖。

在 Sebastian Holdings Inc v Deutsche Bank AG (2011) 1 Lloyd's Rep 106 先例,案情涉及衍生品的买卖,双方在 2006 年 5 月订立了一个主合约(根据 1992 年 International Swap Dealers Association 的标准格式合约，称为 Equities ISDA Master Agreement），并给将来订立的衍生品合约提供了框架。这个主合约有一条英国法院的专属管辖权条文。之后，双方订立了多个衍生品合约，其中有英国法院管辖条文、伦敦仲裁与美国法院管辖条文。但之后双方发生争议，原告在美国法院起诉被告的银行，而被告在英国法院向原告索赔债务。这里的案情可节录上诉庭 Thomas 大法官的介绍，如下：

"The principal issue in this appeal is the construction of jurisdiction clauses in a series of agreements between a bank and its customer; most provided for the jurisdiction of the English courts; one provided for the jurisdiction of the courts of New York. The agreements related to trading in the financial markets made over a two – year period. The trading ended in October 2008 when losses in the region of US $ 750 million were made by the appellant (Sebastian) in trading through the respondent (the bank); the bank claims unpaid debts due under two of the agreements and Sebastian claims damages in respect of the losses it has funded.

Sebastian wishes to pursue its claims inNew York; accordingly in November 2008 it brought proceedings against the bank in the Supreme Court of New York to recover approximately US $ 750 million as damages for breach of one of the agreements. The bank wishes to pursue its claim in England; accordingly in January 2009, the bank brought proceedings in the Commercial Court in London to recover approximately US $ 250 million which it contends Sebastian should have paid under two agreements, each of which contained English jurisdiction clauses. Sebastian contends that the English court does not have jurisdiction under the jurisdiction clauses in the agreements on the true construction of the series of agreements looked at together or that if it has, the claim should be stayed in favour of New York.

In the Commercial Court Walker J held on 14 August 2008 that the bank was entitled to bring the claim under the jurisdiction clauses in the two agreements under which the outstanding sums were claimed by the bank..."

在这种情况，涉及争议之一就是有关的仲裁条文或法院管辖条文的范围，这就需要解释有关的条文，并要考虑整体的交易，如争议是出自哪个合约与应该由谁来管辖最适合，因为可以假设商业人士不会愿意同一个争议夹在一个"同步诉讼"（parallel litigation）。在 UBS AG v HSH Nordbank AG（2009）2 Lloyd's Rep 106 先例，Lawrence Collins 大法官说："Whether a jurisdiction clause applies to a dispute is a question of construction. Where there are numerous jurisdiction agreements which may overlap, the parties must be presumed to be acting commercially, and not to intend that similar claims should be the subject of inconsistent jurisdiction clauses."

在 Sebastian Holdings Inc v Deutsche Bank AG 先例，上诉庭的 Thomas 大法官也

说:"It is generally to be assumed on these principles that just as parties to a single agreement do not intend as rational businessmen that disputes under the same agreement be determined by different tribunals, parties to an arrangement between them set out in multiple related agreements do not generally intend a dispute to be litigated in two different tribunals. **However, where there are multiple related agreements, the task of the court in determining whether a dispute falls within the jurisdiction clauses of one or more related agreements, depends upon the intention of the parties as revealed by the agreements against these general principles.**"(加黑部分是说决定争议应该落在哪条管辖条文要看所有有关合约显示出来的双方订约意愿。)

在 PT Thiess Contractors Indonesia v PT Kaltim Prima Coal (2011) EWHC 1842 (Comm)先例,Blare 大法官同意新加坡高院在 Transocean Offshore International Ventures Ltd v Burgundy Global Exploration Corp (2010) 2 SLR 821 先例的说法,说:"... in Transocean Offshore International Ventures Ltd v Burgundy Global Exploration Corp [2010] 2 SLR 821, Andrew Ang J. In that case, the plaintiff sought to stay proceedings on an escrow agreement, on the basis that the parties had agreed to refer disputes under the principal agreement between them (an offshore drilling contract) to arbitration. Refusing a stay, the High Court of Singapore held at [21] that the parties had carved out disputes under the escrow agreement. At [26], applying recent English authorities, the judge said that, 'In addition, I was of the view that where different but related agreements contained overlapping and inconsistent dispute resolution clauses, **the nature of the claim and the particular agreement out of which the claim arose ought to be considered. Where a claim arose out of or was more closely connected with one agreement than the other, the claim ought to be subject to the dispute resolution regime contained in the former agreement, even if the latter was, on a literal reading, wide enough to cover the claim'.** I agree with this approach."(加黑的部分是说必须要考虑双方争议的本质与发生争议的特定合约。如果有关的争议出自某个特定合约或有密切关系,就应该属于该合约的管辖条文,即使其他有关合约的管辖条文也足够广泛包括该争议。)

在 Sebastian Holdings Inc v Deutsche Bank AG 先例,判是英国法院有管辖权也不会中止,美国法院有管辖权不影响这个决定。上诉庭的判决理由是:"The parties plainly intended the bank to be able to bring a claim under an agreement under which a debt was due in the jurisdiction provided for in that agreement. It was impossible to see how it could be said that the bank and Sebastian(原告) were to be taken to have agreed that the bank would analyse its claim and ascertain under which agreement the cause or origins of the debts arose before issuing its proceedings. Rational businessmen entering into agreements relating to different aspects of trading in the financial markets would understand that the bank would wish to be entitled to bring proceedings to enforce payment of debts under each agreement which gave rise to the specific debt. Businessmen agreeing to different jurisdiction clauses in a series of related contracts could not have been taken to have intended that the entitlement to bring that claim in the chosen forum in respect of one contract should depend on whether a defence had been raised prior to the bringing of the claim and that the defence to that claim might place the centre of gravity of the dispute as being related to a different contract with a different jurisdiction clause. Not only would it give rise to a complete lack of certainty, but could seriously prejudice an institution such as a bank bringing a claim if there was a limitation period about to expire or there was otherwise a need to bring a claim urgently."

说到底这是双方的协议,并可能带来无可避免的"多重诉讼"(multiplicity of proceedings was inevitable)。这种情况别说会发生在多个合约,就算只有一个合约,也会有这种莫名其妙的约定。在笔者涉及的一个香港仲裁,双方的合约中就有一条以下的条文:"... disputes and conflicts shall be governed by the court of the place at which the main assets of all aforementioned assets are located and/or arbitrated by the Hong Kong arbitration department."

在该案件,合约一方开始香港仲裁,而另一方在中国法院提出诉讼(因为有关的资产都在中国境内)。在中国法院提出诉讼的一方(被告)在香港仲裁应诉,但要求中止程序。这被笔者作为首席的仲裁庭拒绝,因为根据双方的仲裁条文,仲裁庭明显有管辖权。裁决书中针对同步或多重诉讼的部分原因是如下:

"... as regards the parallel proceedings in Mainland China commenced by the Claimant, it is something which is within the contemplation of the parties, as is evidenced by the Arbitration Clause. Indeed, this Tribunal is constrained by the terms of the Arbitration Clause. The parties have agreed that a proper construction of the Arbitration Clause admits the possibility of concurrent litigation and arbitration. That being the case unless the Respondents can show that somehow, the actions of the Claimant estop them from availing itself of this possibility, we do not have the power or discretion to deny the exercise of our jurisdiction, when we have been validly appointed. In this regard, we do not see any evidence, nor has it been argued, that the Claimant is estopped from availing themselves of the possibility of concurrent litigation and arbitration.

In this regard, it is pertinent to note that even in cases of anti – suit injunction, the courts do not necessarily find the existence of parallel proceedings objectionable. Unless and until the foreign proceedings can be said to be vexatious or oppressive or is commenced in bad faith, no anti – suit injunction would be granted..."

4.3.3 独立原则

仲裁条文的"独立原则"(separation principle)已经众所周知,在英国的 1996 年

《仲裁法》之 section 7,已经有了明确规定,说:“unless otherwise agreed by the parties, an arbitration agreement which forms or was intended to form part of another agreement (whether or not in writing) shall not be regarded as invalid, non - existence or has become ineffective, and it shall for that purpose be treated as a distinct agreement.”

同样的独立原则也适用在法院管辖条文,不论是在英国的法律[25]或是欧共体法律。[26] 独立原则的好处是双方约定的法院可以管辖主合约是否有效或存在的争议,也就是最后的判决是主合约无效或不存在,也不影响表面看来是双方约定的专属或非专属法院管辖权条文,因为后者是独立的合约关系。这种争议在现实中很多,如合约涉及非法、胁迫、欺诈、误述、共同错误、[27]没有满足先决条件、[28]双方谈判还没有结束而没有合约关系、[29]欠缺约因、双方没有订约意图、起诉的对象有错误、没有授权订立合约、合约受阻等等。这可节录在 Vee Networks Ltd v Econet Wireless International Ltd (2005) 1 Lloyd's Rep 192 先例,Coleman 大法官说:“If, in accordance with s. 7, an arbitrator determines that the matrix contract is, for example, void *ab initio* by reason of illegality and it is not in issue whether the arbitration agreement is also illegal and void, the tribunal can continue to exercise such jurisdiction under the arbitration agreement as its scope permits. For example, if there were an alternative claim in tort or for restitution which was within the scope of the clause, the tribunal would continue to have jurisdiction conclusively to determine that claim.”

§5 适用法条文(choice of law clause)

合约的另一个惯用条文是适用法条文,它可能与仲裁条文或法院管辖条文写在一起,也可能分开,因为两条条文针对的是两码事,虽然它们之间是有密切关系。这里的原因是在订约自由下,双方完全有权选择在某个地方/国家仲裁或接受该地法院的管辖,但适用另一个国家的法律。在香港,就经常会见到商业合约同意在香港仲裁,但适用中国大陆(也见过是其他国家,如英国最常见或间中有德国或日本)的法律。在香港,像英国一样,不论是仲裁或是法院审理商业合约的争议,完全按照双方约定的适用法,即使是外国/外地的法律。显然这并不是好的安排,因为在香港或在英国作出审理与判决/裁决的人士,他们通常不会熟悉其他法律,包括中国大陆的法

---

〔25〕 Mackender v Feldia (1967) 2 QB 590 先例。

〔26〕 Benincasa v Dentalkit Srl (1997) E. C. R. I-3767 先例。

〔27〕 可看本书第三章之 13.3 段。

〔28〕 可看本书第八章之第 2 段。

〔29〕 可看本书第二章之第 2 段。

律。他们会需要依赖中国法律的专家证人协助理解并作出决定,这样显然会增加诉讼的费用与带来更大的错判危险,但做法上完全可以。这方面的问题在法院的审理会更严重,因为英国的法官只会熟悉英国法,即使是听了外国法律专家证人的证言,仍会以英国法律的思维作出最后的决定。但在一个国际仲裁,就经常见到当事人或有关的仲裁机构委任一个熟悉双方约定的适用法的人士作为独任仲裁员或首席。这样,即使避免不了昂贵的专家证人,错判的机会也会相应降低。所以,在没有明示的适用法而要默示的情况下,如果双方同意伦敦仲裁就可以假设双方的订约意图是适用英国法,因为这是一种合理的安排而默示就必须是合理:Compagnie D' Armement Maritime S. A. v. Compagnie Tunisienne de Navigation S. A. (1970) 2 Lloyd's Rep 99 先例。但这个判决在变化多端的国际仲裁是否有很大的说服力也很难说,如 ICC 仲裁还是有一定数量的案件双方是没有同意仲裁地点,而是由 ICC 仲裁庭作出决定。这就很难接受如果 ICC 仲裁庭决定新加坡仲裁就导致合约的适用法也是新加坡法,而决定瑞士仲裁就导致适用法变为瑞士法。另一个例子是会有"浮动仲裁条文"(floating arbitration clause),说明是由被告选择伦敦或北京仲裁,这在 The "Star Texas" (1993) 2 Lloyd's Rep 445 先例被判是有效。这就很难接受被告选了伦敦就适用英国法,选了北京就适用中国法。

5.1 默示适用法条文

如果双方没有在合约中规定一条明示的适用法条文,就会需要仲裁庭或管辖法院根据当地的"冲突法"(conflict of law)[30] 找出与有关合约最密切与最直接关系的法律。[31] 针对仲裁庭,在 1996 年英国《仲裁法》之 section 46(3)给予仲裁庭更大的裁量权决定,说:"If or to the extent that there is no such choice or agreement, the tribunal shall apply the law determined by the conflict of laws rules **which it considers applicable.**"(加黑部分是笔者的强调)

同样的裁量权也出现在一些仲裁机构的规则,如 2012 年 ICC 仲裁规则的第 21(1)条说:"The parties shall be free to agree upon the rules of law to be applied by the arbitral tribunal to the merits of the dispute. In the absence of any such agreement, the arbitral tribunal shall apply the rules of law which it determines to be appropriate."

但在一个国际性的合约,如果没有一条明示的适用法条文而要依赖默示条文或地位,并非是一件好事。一是有争议时会增加诉讼的费用,因为先要决定到底什么是适用法。二是什么是最密切关系的法律会涉及很多方面,如当事人所在地与营业地

---

〔30〕 Amin Rasheed v Kuwait Insurance (1984) AC 50; CGU International Insurance Plc v Astrazeneca Insurance Co Ltd (2006) 1 CLC 162 等先例。

〔31〕 《Contracts (Applicable Law) Act 1990》之 Schedule 1 Article 4。

点、合约的本质与标的、签约地点、合约格式、[32]主要的履行地点、支付金钱地点、仲裁或管辖法院地点等。所以经常会带来不肯定,并带来了第三个问题,就是双方还没有争议时履行合约,他们假设的合法或正确履行的做法有机会在后来决定的一套不同的适用法下是不正确的做法。[33] 所以,国际性合约特别是与多个国家有千丝万缕的关系的合约,应该在订约时约定一条明示的适用法条文。而在本章之第 4 段已经提到,最多人选择适用的是英国法。

5.2 明示适用法条文的解释

双方是否有在合约中规定适用法是解释有关条文/文字的问题,适用本书介绍的合约解释规则。在 Compagnie D' Armement Maritime S. A. v. Compagnie Tunisienne de Navigation S. A. (1970) 2 Lloyd's Rep 99 先例,Diplock 勋爵说:"... when any question arises between parties to a contract as to the proper law applicable to it, is to determine whether the parties intended by their contract to exercise any choice at all and, if they did, to determine what was the system of law which they selected. In determining this the English court applies the ordinary rules of English law relating to the construction of contracts."

通常解释一条适用法条文相对简单(这是相比一条仲裁条文或一条法院管辖条文是专属或非专属的争议),条文也不会太长。但这里也会有例外,如在 Compagnie D' Armement Maritime S. A. v. Compagnie Tunisienne de Navigation S. A. 先例,有关的租约适用法条文是船旗国的法律,另一条条文是伦敦仲裁。这显然不是一条好的适用法条文,特别是订立租约时是不会知道船东会指定的船舶。这可以是船东自己的船舶(悬挂的是法国旗),但也可以以二船东的身份指定他所租用的船舶。再说,今天的船舶已经是多数悬挂方便旗,这可以是巴拿马、利比里亚、塞浦路斯等。订约的双方不大可能真的想适用这些国家的法律。

这也带来了另一个问题,就是"浮动适用法条文"(floating governing law clause)。在较早前已经提到一个浮动的仲裁条文或法院管辖条文可以有效,但这种条文在适用法方面就有一点不明朗。这可介绍 The "Iran Vojdan" (1984) 2 Lloyd's Rep 380 先例,在提单上的一条适用法条文如下:"2 (a) The contract of carriage, the bill of lading and all disputes arising hereunder or in connection therewith ... shall ... **in the option of the carrier to be declared by him on the merchant's request be gov-**

---

〔32〕 如在 The "Al Wahab" (1983) 1 Lloyd's Rep 235 先例,有关保险合约与英国毫无关系,但双方订约使用了英国的标准格式合约,也就是劳合社的保单,这就是足够重要的因素假设双方订约意图是适用英国法。

〔33〕 不同的法律体系会有很大区别,如在英美法下,大原则是不能改写双方的合约条文/文字,而只能推敲双方的订约意图作出解释。但在中国法(《合同法》第 54 条),看来就可以以法院或仲裁庭自己认为的公道与否,在善意的原则下改写双方的合约。另一个例子可以是中国法有不可抗力导致合约无法或困难履行的说法,但英国法律的受阻比不可抗力窄得多(本书第十三章之 1.1 段)。

erned (i) either **by Iranian law**, in particular by the Hague Rules ... as enacted in the Iranian Maritime Code ... with exclusive jurisdiction of the Courts in Teheran Iran; (ii) **or by German law**, in particular by the Hague Rules as enacted in German Commercial Code ... with exclusive jurisdiction of the Courts in Hamburg ... ; (iii) **or by English law**, in particular by the Hague Rules as enacted in the Carriage of Goods by Sea Act, 1924 ... with exclusive jurisdiction of the Courts in London ... (b) In case the law of the country in which a suit is filed does not recognize this agreement on the exclusive jurisdiction of the Courts of Teheran, Hamburg or London ... and/or this agreement on the exclusive application of Iranian, German or English law ... then the Hague Rules as enacted in that country shall apply."(加黑部分是笔者的强调)

上述条文是选择适用三个国家的法律,伊朗、德国或英国,并由承运人(被告的伊朗国家船公司)在对方提出要求时选定。但该条文被判是无效,Bingham 大法官是这样说:"I must, however, proceed to review the matter on the alternative assumption that Iranian and not German law is the proper law. I have no evidence whatever of Iranian law and I therefore proceed on the assumption that it is the same as English law. As a matter of English law, it is, I think, clear and not disputed that this clause in the bill of lading is bad insofar as it envisages what may be called a 'floating proper law.' So much appears from the Court of Appeal decision in The Armar, [1980] 2 Lloyd's Rep. 450; [1981] 1 W. L. R. 207. That appears to me, with respect to the Court of Appeal, to be an obviously correct decision. **The proper law is something so fundamental to questions relating to the formation, validity, interpretation and performance of a contract that it must in my judgment, be built into the fabric of the contract from the start and cannot float in an indeterminate way until finally determined at the option of one party.** As I say, it is, as I understand, common ground that as a matter of English law effect cannot be given to that part of this clause. That is, however, the limit of the common ground."(加黑部分是笔者的强调)

这样看来在英国法律下一条浮动适用法条文是不被承认。但在后来的 Heath Lamber v Sociedad De Corretaje De Seguros (2004) 1 Lloyd's Rep 495 先例,案情涉及委内瑞拉与英国当事人的海事再保险合约。其中适用法条文是:"Subject to Venezuelan Law and/or Venezuelan Jurisdiction **if required**."(加黑部分是笔者的强调)这被英国高院认定是一条浮动适用法条文,但法院并没有判该条文无效,而只是指条文的措辞是给委内瑞拉被告一个选择权。但被告从来没有作出选择适用委内瑞拉的法律。所以,还是适用英国法。但在该先例的报道中,双方代表大律师不像有向法院提出与依赖 The "Iran Vojdan"先例。

5.3 明示适用超国家体的法律

在一个英国法院管辖的合约,是不承认一些"超国家体"(supra – national body)

的"法律规则"(rule of law)。如"习惯商法"(*lex mercatoria*)、[34]"伊斯兰教法"(Sharia'a)、[35]"犹太教律法"(halacha)[36]的适用。这可介绍 Shamil Bank of Bahrain EC v Beximco Pharmaceuticals Ltd (2004) 2 Lloyd's Rep 1 先例,有关的适用法条文是:"Subject to the principles of the Glorious Sharia'a, this agreement shall be governed by and construed in accordance with the laws of England."

上诉庭的 Potter 大法官说:"The general reference to principles of Sharia in this case affords no reference to, or identification of, those aspects of Sharia law which are intended to be incorporated into the contract, let alone the terms in which they are framed. It is plainly insufficient for the defendants to contend that the basic rules of the Sharia applicable in this case are not controversial. Such 'basic rules' are neither referred to nor identified. Thus the reference to the 'principles of... Sharia' stands unqualified as a reference to the body of Sharia law generally. As such, they are inevitably repugnant to the choice of English law as the law of the contract and render the clause self-contradictory and therefore meaningless."

但看来超国家体的法律适用在仲裁没有问题,在 Halpern v Halpern (2007) 2 Lloyd's Rep. 56 先例,Waller 大法官说:"Section 46 of the Arbitration Act 1996 expressly recognises that arbitral tribunals can and indeed should decide disputes in accordance with the law chosen by the parties 'or if the parties so agree, in accordance with such other considerations as are agreed by them or determined by the tribunal'. Thus an English court would stay proceedings brought in breach of the arbitration clause even though some set of principles not law or a law other than the law of a particular country had been chosen as the applicable law to govern their disputes. It would furthermore enforce an award made by arbitrators applying any 'considerations' agreed between the parties. Thus, if parties wish some form of rules or law not of a country to apply to their contract, then it is open to them to so agree, provided that there is an arbitration clause. The court will give effect to the parties' agreement in that way."

这也是《联合国示范法》(UNCITRAL Model Law)所允许,在 Article 28(1)说:"The arbitral tribunal shall decide the dispute in accordance with **such rules of law** as are chosen by the parties as applicable to the substance of the dispute. Any designation of **the law or legal system of a given State** shall be construed, unless otherwise expressed, as directly referring to the substantive law of that State and not to its conflict of laws rules."(加黑部分是笔者的强调)

---

〔34〕 Halpern v Halpern (2007) 2 Lloyd's Rep. 56 先例。

〔35〕 Shamil Bank of Bahrain EC v Beximco Pharmaceuticals Ltd (2004) 2 Lloyd's Rep 1 先例。

〔36〕 Halpern v Halpern (2007) 2 Lloyd's Rep. 56 先例。

更进一步的是允许仲裁庭在双方当事人没有作出选择时适用超国家体的法律规则。这在印度的1996年《仲裁法》之Section（28）（b）（iii）说："the arbitral tribunal shall apply **the rules of law** it considers to be appropriate given all the circumstances."（加黑部分是笔者的强调）

在香港国际仲裁中心2013年的《机构仲裁规则》之Article 35(1)，也有说："... Failing such designation by the parties, the arbitral tribunal shall apply **the rules of law** which it determines to be appropriate."（加黑部分是笔者的强调）

5.4　针对仲裁条文的明示适用法条文

已经在本章之4.3.3段提到仲裁条文是一个独立的合约，虽然在现实中仲裁条文经常是主合约的条文之一。但有了"独立原则"(separation principle)，就带来了一个疑问，就是主合约的明示或默示适用法条文是否也同样适用在仲裁协议。这个问题会带来严重的后果，包括仲裁条文的有效性、管辖权、有关争议"可否仲裁"(arbitrability)、仲裁员与当事人之间的关系等。这个问题在独立原则的说法还没有发展前，[37]仲裁条文作为主合约的一条条文显然是适用主合约的适用法。但有了独立原则，就带来一个说法是仲裁协议既然独立于主合约，就完全可以有自己的适用法，而如果没有明示，就可以是默示。而如果是默示(这也会是绝大部分的情况)，就是找出与仲裁协议有最密切与直接关系的法律。这样，仲裁协议最密切关系的法律很大可能不会与主合约一样。有最密切关系的显然是仲裁地点的法律，而仲裁地点往往也决定了仲裁的程序法(有时候被称为lex fori或lex arbitri)，这也包括了监督的法院。虽然在大部分的情况下，lex fori与仲裁协议的适用法会一致，但还是在少数的情况下有偏离，正如Mustill大法官在Black Clawson International Ltd v Papierworke Waldhof – Aschaffenburg AG（1981）2 Lloyd's Rep 446先例中说："In the great majority of cases, [the lex causae, the law applicable to the arbitration agreement, and the lex fori] will be the same. But this will not always be so. It is by no means uncommon for the proper law of the substantive contract to be different from the lex fori; and it does happen, although much more rarely, that the law governing the arbitration agreement is also different from the lex fori."

这种少见的例子会是如ABB v. Keppel（1999）2 Lloyd's Rep 24先例，涉及新加坡船厂Keppel建造一个海上储油船舶的合约，它的适用法条文与仲裁条文如下："37.1 This contract shall be governed by and interpreted in accordance with English Law. 37.2 Disputes arising in connection with or as a result of the contract, and which are not resolved by mutual agreement, shall be referred to the London Court of International Arbitration. Disputes shall be settled in accordance with Singapore Law."

---

〔37〕 Harbour Assurance Co（UK）Ltd v Kansa General International Insurance Co Ltd（1993）1 Lloyd's Rep 455等先例。

这不同的法律在 Arsanovia Ltd v Cruz City 1 Mauritius Holdings（2013）1 Lloyd's Rep 235 先例,Andrew Smith 大法官有提到说:"Neither the law of the reference nor the law of the arbitration agreement needs be the same as the law (or any of the laws) applicable to any matrix contract containing the arbitration agreement or to the substantive dispute that is the subject of the reference (sometimes called the lex causae). Equally, they need not be the same as the curial law which governs the conduct of the reference (sometimes called the lex fori or lex arbitri), which is often determined by the choice of the seat of the arbitration and therefore often involves acceptance that that law governs the supervision of the arbitration by the courts."

而其中有最多争议的就是仲裁协议的适用法到底是否与主合约,也就是针对实体争议的适用法一致。这方面在英国的判例也有不同结果,正如上诉庭的 Neuberger 勋爵在 Sul America Cia Nacional de Seguros SA v Enesa Engenharia SA（2012）1 Lloyd's Rep 671 先例所说:

"Accordingly:(i) there are a number of cases which support the contention that it is rare for the law of the arbitration to be that of the seat of the arbitration rather than that of the chosen contractual law, as the arbitration clause is part of the contract; but (ii) the most recent authority is a decision of this court which contains clear dicta (albeit obiter) to the opposite effect, on the basis that the arbitration clause is severable from the rest of the contract and plainly has a very close connection with the law of the seat of the arbitration.

Faced with this rather unsatisfactory tension between the approach in the earlier cases and the approach in C v D[38], it seems to me that, at any rate in this court, we could take one of two courses. The first would be to follow the approach in the most recent case, given that it was a decision of this court, namely C v D. The alternative course would be to accept that there are sound reasons to support either conclusion as a matter of principle. Whichever course is adopted, it is necessary to consider whether there is anything in the other provisions of the contract or the surrounding circumstances which assist in resolving the conundrum."(早期的部分先例认为仲裁条文是主合约的条文之一,所以主合约的适用法也适用在仲裁协议。但近期的先例认为在独立原则下,仲裁协议与仲裁地点的法律有十分密切的关系。接下来的一段 Neuberger 勋爵是说在该先例他可以采纳任何一种判法。)

---

〔38〕（2008）1 Lloyd's Rep 239,在该先例有关的保险合约明示适用纽约法,但仲裁是在伦敦。在伦敦仲裁败诉的保险公司试图根据美国联邦仲裁法在美国联邦法院质疑该裁决书,但受保人向英国法院取得了止诉禁令。这就带来了保险公司的上诉,指称当事人选择伦敦仲裁但仲裁协议是适用纽约法,但这被上诉庭否定。

而 Longmore 大法官在 C v D (2008) 1 Lloyd's Rep 239 先例是这样说:"... if there is no express law of the arbitration agreement, the law with which that agreement has its closest and most real connection is the law of the underlying contract or the law of the seat of arbitration. It seems to me that if (contrary to what I have said above) this is a relevant question, the answer is more likely to be the law of the seat of arbitration than the law of the underlying contract."

另在一个更近期的 Habas Sindi Ve Tibbi Gazlar Istihsal Endustrisi AS v VSC Steel Co Ltd (2014) 1 Lloyd's Rep 479 先例,Hamblen 大法官把这方面的英国法律地位总结如下:

"(1) Even if an arbitration agreement forms part of a matrix contract (as is commonly the case), its proper law may not be the same as that of the matrix contract.

(2) The proper law is to be determined by undertaking a three - stage enquiry into: (i) express choice; (ii) implied choice; and (iii) the system of law with which the arbitration agreement has the closest and most real connection.

(3) Where the matrix contract does not contain an express governing law clause, the significance of the choice of seat of the arbitration is likely to be 'overwhelming'. That is because the system of law of the country seat will usually be that with which the arbitration agreement has its closest and most real connection.

(4) Where the matrix contract contains an express choice of law, this is a strong indication or pointer in relation to the parties' intention as to the governing law of the agreement to arbitrate, in the absence of any indication to the contrary.

(5) The choice of a different country for the seat of the arbitration is a factor pointing the other way. However, it may not in itself be sufficient to displace the indication of choice implicit in the express choice of law to govern the matrix contract.

(6) Where there are sufficient factors pointing the other way to negate the implied choice derived from the express choice of law in the matrix contract the arbitration agreement will be governed by the law with which it has the closest and most real connection. That is likely to be the law of the country of seat, being the place where the arbitration is to be held and which will exercise the supporting and supervisory jurisdiction necessary to ensure that the procedure is effective."

这方面的问题或疑点也不止是英国法律,因为国际仲裁会涉及许多其他国家/地方的法律。如在 Gary Born 教授的《International Commercial Arbitration》(2009 年)一书,就在多处提到了这一问题,以及针对了日本、德国、瑞士与瑞典的法律地位,并提到在做法上并不一致。其他国家如比利时与意大利的说法是倾向适用主合约的适用法。其他还会涉及这方面的先例有印度的 Shin - Etsu Chemical Co Ltd v Aksh Optifibre Ltd (2005) 7 SCC 234,新加坡的 Philippines v Philippine International Air Terminals Co Inc (2007) 1 SLR 278 与更近期的 FirstLink Investments Corporation Ltd v GT Payment Pte Ltd (2014) SGHCR 12 等。

这个问题的实质重要性可举例说明,就是中国大陆的企业/公司前来香港仲裁的仲裁条文经常是简单的一句“arbitration in HK,PRC Law to govern”,这可翻译为“香港仲裁,中国大陆法适用”。这是一条典型的“临时仲裁”(ad hoc arbitration)条文,在香港以及英国或世界上大部分的国家/地区,都是有效的仲裁条文。但根据中国的《仲裁法》就不一样,中国大陆不承认临时仲裁,而需要法律认可的仲裁机构管理。这样上述所讲的简单一句根本不可能是机构仲裁,它也没有提到任何仲裁机构的名字,更说不上是中国法律认可的仲裁机构。所以如果仲裁协议的适用法是香港法,就不会有问题。但如果适用法是与主合约一致,适用中国大陆法,这条经常见到的仲裁条文/协议就变为无效。

为了肯定,香港国际仲裁中心在 2013 年推出的《机构仲裁规则》与建议使用的标准仲裁条文,已经加上了一句“The law of this arbitration agreement shall be (Hong Kong law)”。也就是加上一条明示的适用法条文,而这适用法条文往往与主合约的适用法不一致,不论是适用中国大陆法律或更加普遍会见到是适用英国法。

§6 保密条文(confidentiality clause)

这种条文需要针对如下方面:首先是定义什么是机密资料;其次针对保护机密的责任/义务是什么,如什么可以做与什么不可以做;最后是机密责任/义务的例外情况、违约的救济与最后退还/销毁机密资料。

条文的文字/措辞是根据不同的合约与情况而定。首先是对机密资料的定义,可以是简单的如“某产品的相关技术性资料”或“某公司业务的商业资料”,但也可以是比较详尽的如通过附件把机密资料逐份列出并加上在履行时双方向对方提供的所有资料等。如果机密资料只是由一方提供,在谈判中需要得到保护的一方会尽力把机密资料的定义制定的广泛,而另一方应该就相反,最后可能是双方各退一步。即使双方都会提供机密资料,但仍有提供多少之分,双方在谈判时也会有同样的心态。以下节录 Richard Christou 律师的《Boilerplate: Practical Clauses》(第 5 版,2010 年)一书提到的惯用条文的一些例子(同类的书籍也有不少,如 Deborah Fosbrook 与 Adrian C Laing 律师的《The A – Z of Contract Clauses》[第 3 版,2010 年],但特定合约的条文还是要更有针对性的拟定),如下:“‘Confidential Information’ shall mean all that technical information relating to(有关产品) which is disclosed to the Receiving Party by the Disclosing Party, or is otherwise obtained by the Receiving Party from the Disclosing Party [including without limitation the information contained in the document listed in the Schedule hereto]."

或另一条更广泛的条文:"'Confidential Information' shall mean all information (including all oral and visual information, and all information recorded in writing or electronically, or in any other medium or by any other method) disclosed to, or obtained by one party from, the other party or a third party acting on that other party's behalf, and without prejudice to the generality of the foregoing definition shall include but not be limited to (i) any information ascertainable by the inspection or analysis of samples, (ii) the information detailed in the Schedule hereto, and (iii) any information relating to a party's operation, processes, plans, intentions, product information, knowhow, designs, trade secrets, software, market opportunities, customers and business affairs [PROVIDED THAT information disclosed orally shall not fall within this definition if it is not identified as confidential at the time of its disclosure and confirmed as such in writing by the disclosing party within thirty days of such disclosure]."

接下来是针对机密的责任/义务是什么,内容除了稍早提到规定什么是可以做与什么是不可以做外,还会约定保密的期限等。可能是3年或5年不等,但也可以是没有期限。这样,法律会默示一个合理期限:Compere Associates Ltd v Keith Halsey and Ors (2004) EWHC 1317 (Ch)先例。这种条文的例子可以是:"Each party will take all proper steps to keep confidential all Confidential Information of the other which is disclosed to or obtained by it pursuant to or as a result of this Agreement, and will not divulge the same to any third party and will allow access to the same to its own staff only on a 'need to know' basis, except to the extent that any such Confidential Information becomes public through no fault of that party. Upon termination of this Agreement, each party will return to the other any equipment and written data (without retaining copies thereof) provided for the purposes of this Agreement. Notwithstanding the termination or expiry of this Agreement for whatever reason the obligation and restrictions in this clause shall be valid for a period of(3年或5年不等)from the date of signature hereof."

或者是更详细地写作:

"In consideration of the mutual exchange and disclosure of Confidential Information, each party undertakes in relation to the other party's Confidential Information:

(a) To maintain the same in confidence and to use it only for the purposes of this Agreement and for no other purpose and in particular, but without prejudice to the generality of the foregoing, not to make any commercial use thereof or use the same for the benefit of itself or of any third party other than pursuant to this Agreement or a further agreement with the other party;

(b) Not to copy reproduce or reduce to writing any part thereof except as may be reasonably necessary for the aforesaid purposes and that any copies reproductions or reductions to writing so made shall be the property of the disclosing party;

(c) Not to disclose the same whether to its employees or to third parties except in confidence to such of its employees or directors who need to know the same for the aforesaid purposes and provided that (i) such employees and directors are obliged by their contracts of employment or service not to disclose the same, and (ii) the receiving party shall enforce such obligations at its expense and at the request of the disclosing party in so far as breach thereof relates to the disclosing party's Confidential Information;

(d) To be responsible for the performance of sub – clause (a), (b) and (c) above on the part of its employees or directors to whom the same is disclosed pursuant to sub – clause (c) above;

(e) To apply thereto no lesser security measures and degree of care than those which the receiving party applies to its own confidential or proprietary information [and which the receiving party warrants as providing adequate protection of such information from unauthorised disclosure, copying or use]; and

(f) To treat the Confidential Information at all times in accordance with the Data Protection Act 1998."

再接下来是针对机密资料的例外,这方面普通法也有针对,如最重要的是"公开资料"(public domain 或是 public knowledge)就不会被接受是机密资料。这方面也有不少先例:Saltman Engineering Co Ltd v Campbell Engineering Co Ltd (1948) 65 R. P. C 203; Coco v AN Clark (Engineers) Ltd (1969) R. P. C 41; A – G v Guardian Newspapers (No. 2) (1990) 1 AC 109, HL; Lancashire Fires Ltd v S. A. Lyons & Co. Ltd (1996) F. S. R. 629; Bunn v BBC (1998) 2 All ER 552; Poeton Industries Ltd v Horton (2000) I. C. R. 1208, CA; A – G v Times Newspapers Ltd (2001) EWCA Civ 97, CA; A – G v Greater Manchester Newspapers Ltd (2002) 99(6) L. S. G. 30, QBD; EPI Environmental Technologies Inc v Symphony Plastic Technologies Plc (2006) EWCA Civ 3; Aegis Defence Services v Stoner Ltd (2006) EWHC 1515 (Ch); Mosley v News Group Newspapers (2008) EWHC 687, Q. B 等。什么是公开资料涉及事实与法律的争议,每个案件都会不一样。为了避免昂贵的诉讼与不肯定,更好还是以明示条文针对,把双方同意的或广或窄的不属于机密的资料,也就是不受机密条文约束的资料列明。当然这也必须与较早的机密资料的定义配合,不要产生矛盾。这种条文可举以下的例子:"The obligations of confidentiality under this Clause shall not apply to any information or material which the recipient party can prove: (1) Was already known to it prior to its receipt thereof from the disclosing party; (2) Was subsequently disclosed to it lawfully by a third party who did not obtain the same (whether directly or indirectly) from the disclosing party; or (3) Was in the public domain at the time of receipt by the recipient party or has subsequently entered into the public domain other than by reason of the breach of the provisions of this Clause or of any obligation of confidence owed by the recipient party or by any of its Sub – Contractors or Sub – Licensees to the disclosing party."

另一个例子是："Nothing in this definition of Confidential Information shall be construed to limit each party's use or dissemination of information that: (1) Was in the lawful possession of the receiving party at the time of disclosure by the disclosing party without an obligation to keep it confidential; (2) Was in the public domain at the time of receipt or disclosure or subsequently becomes so; (3) Is not identified in writing as being proprietary or confidential; (4) Was originally considered proprietary under this Clause but which subsequently becomes part of the public knowledge or literature through no fault of the receiving party; (5) Is developed by or for the receiving party at any time independently of the information disclosed to it by the disclosing party [by persons who have had no access to or knowledge of the said information]; (6) Has been or hereafter may be rightfully acquired from third parties without obligation to keep confidential; or (7) Consists solely of generalized ideas, concepts, knowhow or techniques relating to [data processing]."

或是简单写作："Notwithstanding the foregoing, the receiving party shall be entitled to make any disclosure required by law, by a court or tribunal of competent jurisdiction or by any governmental or other regulatory authority (including without limitation the [香港证券交易所]) of the other party's Confidential Information provided that it gives the other party not less than two business days' notice of such disclosure [and prior to making such disclosure it shall consult with the disclosing party as to the contents of such disclosure and the possible steps to avoid or limit disclosure and take those steps where they would not result in significant adverse consequences to the receiving party.]"

再接下来是救济，通常针对破坏机密条文的救济是以称职法院的禁令阻止对方，因为金钱损失往往很难证明与不足够。合约有以下的文书条文，估计会对称职法院在考虑作出禁令时有更大说服力，也增加了违约方抗拒禁令的困难。条文可以如下："The Purchaser agrees that the Vendor could be harmed by a breach of this agreement by the Purchaser and that damages alone may not be an adequate remedy and that the Vendor shall in addition to all other remedies available at law or in equity be entitled without proof of special damage to the remedies of injunction, specific performance and other equitable relief for any actual or threatened breach of the provisions of this agreement and the Purchaser agrees that it will not oppose the granting of such relief."

最后是归还/销毁机密文件，条文可以如下："The Purchaser will, forthwith upon request at any time return, and procure the return by any director, employee, adviser or third party to whom disclosure has been made of all Confidential Information to the Seller or as the Seller may direct, and the Purchaser will destroy, and procure that any such director, employee, adviser or third party will destroy, all Confidential Information (including all Secondary Material prepared by or for the Purchaser) and, to the extent possible, expunge and destroy any Confidential Information from any computer or other device in the Purchaser's possession or under its control, or the possession or control of any such director, employee, adviser or third party, and pending such expunging or destruction, the provisions of this agreement shall continue to apply to such Confidential Information. The requirement for destruction or delivery up of Confidential Information does not apply to any Confidential Information store electronically pursuant to an existing routine back – up exercise provided no attempt is made to recover such Confidential Information. The Purchaser will, forthwith upon the Seller's request (within [天数] of the request) to expunge and destroy the Confidential Information, provide written confirmation in such form as the Seller may reasonably request, that the Confidential Information has been expunged and destroyed. [Nothing in this paragraph shall require the Purchaser to return or destroy Confidential Information or any copies that the Purchaser, or the persons to whom the Confidential Information or copies have been disclosed, are required to retain by applicable law or to satisfy the rules or regulations of a regulatory body or stock exchange to which such person is subject.]"

除了上述比较有针对性的机密条文之外,一般的商业合约也经常会见到比较简单但本质上属于机密条文的条文,主要是希望有关的合约(包括是价格与条文等)不被其他业内人士(如竞争对手)知道。这条文可以是简单的:"The parties agree to keep confidential the terms of this Agreement, and neither shall make any announcement in relation to or otherwise publicise [its existence or] its contents."或是要求对方披露前要获得自己的同意,说:"Terms, conditions and general provisions of this Agreement, and any agreements or arrangements entered into pursuant to it, shall be held in confidence by both parties, and only disclosed as may be agreed to by both parties or as may be required to meet stock exchange disclosure or export permit requirements or any other legal or regulatory requirement. Neither party shall make public statements or issue publicity or media releases with regard to this Agreement or the relationship between the parties thereunder without the prior written approval of the other party."

以下的保密条文写法是要求双方在披露前进行咨询,条文与上一条文的不同在于没有要求双方同意才能披露。这表示一旦向对方提出合理咨询就可以披露,即使并没有获得对方的同意:"The Vendor and the Purchaser shall consult together as to the terms of, the timetable for the manner of publication of, any announcement (unless specified by law or The Stock Exchange) to shareholders, employees, customers and suppliers or to The Stock Exchange or other authorities or to the media or otherwise which either may desire or be obliged to make regarding this Agreement."

最后一提的是,在笔者《仲裁法——从 1996 年英国仲裁法到国际商务仲裁》一书第十三章所讲的仲裁机密性。该章之第 1 段就提到,英国法律默示[39]了仲裁的机密性。但世界上还是有许多国家不明确或不承认仲裁机密的法律地位,如澳大利亚、[40]美国、[41]瑞典[42]等。这在经济全球化的今天,不一定让商业企业/公司满意,因为对有些企业/公司来说,它们所签订个别的合约中所涉及的技术保密或商业上的机密会十分重要,这也是令仲裁比国家法院优胜的重要原因之一。这样,为了避免对方在一些不承认仲裁机密性的国家泄露有关仲裁的资料与结果,就需要一条明示的机密条文。另是一些仲裁机构的仲裁规则中也会对仲裁的机密性进行规定,如香港国际仲裁中心 2013 年的《机构仲裁规则》Article 47 针对的就是这一方面。

§7　知识产权条文(intellectual property rights clause)

知识产权条文也是根据合约不同的本质(涉及高科技的买卖合约、合作研发或生产合约、"许可合约"[Licence Agreement]与任何涉及知识产权的合约)与各种写法。知识产权条文与保密条文在结构上与需要针对的方面有很多类似之处,如也需要先定义知识产权。但知识产权条文也有一些独特的方面要针对,如在合约中会需要提供知识产权一方保证他拥有有关知识产权的所有权。

另是需要明确订约前、在合约履行期间或合约履行完毕后知识产权分别属于谁以及被许可方(在一个许可合约)在合约履行期间或合约履行完毕后所研发的新的知识产权又是属于谁。笔者作为仲裁员的一个早期仲裁就涉及了这种争议。案情涉及一家美国公司与中国公司签订了一个为期 3 年的许可合约,授权中方使用美方拥有知识产权的技术为中国市场生产某种设备。合约履行完毕后,中方继续生产同类设备并且生意越做越大,因为价廉物美,在美国也接到很多订单。于是,美国公司在美国多个不同州的法院取得禁令,禁止中国公司的销售与交货。这马上带来"雪球

〔39〕这可看本书第七章之第 3 段。

〔40〕Esso Australia Resources Ltd. and Others v. Plowman (Minister for Energy and Minerals) and Others (1995) 128 ALR 391 等先例。

〔41〕Milone V Gen Motors Corp., 446 N. Y. S. 2d 650 (N. Y. App. Div. 1981); Industrotech Constructors, Inc v Duke Univ., 314 S. E. 2d 272 (N. C. App. 1984); Giacobazzi Grandi Vini Spa v. Renfield Corp. (1987) US Dist Lexis 1783; USA v. Panhandle Eastern Corp. (1988) 118 FRD 346; A. T. v State Farm Mut. Auto Ins. CO., 989 P. 2d 219 (Colo. App. 1999); Caringal v Karteria Shipping, Ltd, 2001 WL 874705 (E. D. La 2001); Contship Container Lines, Ltd v PPG Indus., Inc., 2003 WL 1948807 (S. D. N. Y. 2003)等先例。

〔42〕AI Trade Finance Inc. v the Bulgarian Foreign Trade Bank Limited, XXVI Y. B. Comm. Arb. 291 (Swedish Supreme Court)等先例。

效应"(snowball effect),因为这令中国公司在大量的销售合约中违约,并带来无可抗辩的巨额金钱索赔。该仲裁中,双方最主要的争议就是中国公司声称它在国际上销售的设备是用所研发的新技术制造,而并非是使用美国公司订约前拥有与合约规定要退还的知识产权。但由于中国公司没有足够的证据,最后在仲裁中败诉。看来,这种条文除了要订得好与明确外,对证据保存也要十分小心。例如,双方订立合约前委任一个信托人保存有关知识产权的资料、样品、蓝图等。

知识产权条文再接下来要针对的是根据合约的性质与双方的谈判力量,一方(如许可方)会向另一方保证对知识产权拥有合法的所有权,并加上一条补偿条文,补偿因为第三人(声称他才是拥有有关知识产权的人士)申请禁令并提出诉讼给另一方所造成的损失。最后是针对如果在合约履行期间,有第三人侵犯了知识产权,是应该由许可方(在一个许可合约)还是被许可方采取法律行动并索赔相关损失?

以下节录 Richard Christou 律师的《Boilerplate: Practical Clauses》(第 5 版,2010 年)一书的两条比较详尽的相关条文,如下:

1."(1) The Licensor represents and warrants to the Licensee that:

1.1 The Licensor has registered the Trade Mark in each of the countries listed on Schedule A;

1.2 The Trade Mark may be used by the Licensee in any country listed on Schedule A; and

1.3 The Software, as used in the Licensor's business as of the date of this Agreement, does not include any software which is not owned or controlled by the Licensor.

(2) The Licensor agrees to indemnify and hold harmless the Licensee against any and all loss, costs, expenses and damages of whatsoever nature (collectively 'Losses') arising out of or related to (i) any breach of the Licensor's warranty in Clause1.3, or (ii) any claim that the Licensee's use of any of the Software infringes or violated the Intellectual Property Rights of any third party, or that the Licensor is not the owner thereof, or that the Licensee is not authorised to utilize the same, and the Licensor shall defend and settle at its sole cost, expense and control all suits or proceedings arising out of the foregoing. The foregoing indemnity is the Licensee's sole remedy for any such infringement or violation.

(3) The Licensor agrees to indemnify and hold harmless the Licensee against any and all Losses arising out of or related to any breach of the Licensor's warranty in Clauses 1.1 and 1.2, and the Licensor shall defend and settle at its sole cost, expense and control all suits or proceedings arising out of any such breach, PROVIDED HOWEVER THAT the Licensor's obligations under this Clause 3 shall (i) only apply with respect to any claim for breach of such warranty for which notice thereof has been provided to the Licensor on or prior to(某天), and (ii) be limited to £ ... in the aggregate (including

the Licensor' s costs incurred in conducting such litigation, if any, arising out of such breach). The foregoing indemnity is the Licensee' s sole remedy for any such breach.

(4) The Licensor shall have no obligations under Clauses 2 or 3 to the extent that such Losses arise as a direct result of the Licensee' s negligence or willful misconduct or its material breach of the terms of this Agreement. The Licensee shall, with respect to any claim which is indemnifiable under Clause 2 or 3 provide the Licensor with: (i) prompt notice of any such claim of which it learns; (ii) assistance in the defence of the action as the Licensor reasonably requires (as the Licensor' s sole cost and expense); and (iii) control over the defence of such action.

[The failure to give any such notice referred to in this Clause 4 shall not affect the Licensor' s obligations hereunder except to the extent the Licensor is actually prejudiced therefrom, and then only to the extent of such prejudice.]

(5) In any infringement actionprovide for in Clauses 2 or 3, the non - prosecuting party, at its own expense, shall be entitled to non - controlling participation in such action through counsel of its own selection.

(6) Except as provided in Clause 1, the Software is offered by the Licensor and accepted by the Licensee 'as is' and the Licensor makes no other representation or warranty, express or implied, regarding the Software, including but not limited to any implied warranty of suitability quality merchantability or fitness for a particular purpose.

(7) Under no circumstances (including, for theavoidance of doubt, under Clauses 2 and 3) shall a party hereto be liable for any loss of business, profits, contracts or revenues, or for any special, incidental or consequential damages suffered by the other party hereto (other than any such damages suffered by any third party for which the Licensor may be liable under Clauses 2 or 3 as the case may be), even if it has been or is hereafter advised of the possibility of such damages.

(8) Except (i) in the case of the Licensor' s obligations under Clause 2 and (ii) in the case of the Licensee' s failure to make any royalty payments due hereunder, the entire liability of each party and the exclusive remedy of the other party against it for damages from any cause whatsoever arising under this Agreement other than as a result of a willful breach of, or willful failure to perform, this Agreement, and regardless of the form of action, shall be limited £ ... PROVIDED HOWEVER THAT the Licensee shall also be entitled to a credit in an amount equal to the Annual Royalty (or a *pro rata* portion thereof) for any period during which the Licensee does not receive fundamentally all of the benefits of this Agreement."

2. "(1) In the event that the Licensee becomes aware of any actual or suspected unauthorised use or infringement of any Software (including any Intellectual Property

Rights or Confidential Information relating thereto) or any infringement of the Trade Mark by any third party in the Licensed Area, the Licensee shall promptly notify the Licensor. The Licensee shall, at its sole cost and expense, have first option to take such action (including without limitation bringing a suit against such third party) as may be reasonable required in order to protect fully the Software (including any related Intellectual Property Rights) and/or the Trade Mark. In such event, the Licensor (at the Licensee's sole cost and expense) shall provide any assistance in the prosecution of such action reasonably requested by the Licensee, including (if necessary) joining as a claimant in any suit brought by the Licensee against such third party or assigning to the Licensee the Licensor's right to prevent and protect against the unauthorised use or infringement referred to in this Clause 1.

(2) In the event that the Licensee determines not to act pursuant to the provisions of Clause 1 above, it shall promptly so notify the Licensor. Upon receipt of such notice, the Licensor shall have the right, but shall not be obliged, to take such action, at the Licensor's sole cost and expense, to protect fully the Software (including any Intellectual Property Rights or Confidential Information relating thereto) or the Trade Mark. In such event the Licensee shall provide, at the Licensor's sole cost and expense, any assistance reasonably requested by the Licensor in the prosecution of such action, including joining as a claimant in any suit brought against such third party.

(3) Any recoveries, damages or settlement amounts received by the prosecuting party as a result of any action taken hereunder shall, unless otherwise agreed by the parties hereto, be retained by the prosecuting party [PROVIDED THAT, if such amounts represent in part any loss, damage, cost or expense (collectively 'Losses') that the non-prosecuting party suffered as a result of the matter which is the subject of the action, such non-prosecuting party shall receive its proportional share of such recoveries, damages or settlement amounts (by reference to the relevant Losses suffered by the Licensor, on the one hand, and the Licensee, on the other hand), after deducting the prosecuting party's reasonable legal fees and other costs incurred in conducting such litigation]."

第十五章　有关解释合约的香港仲裁案件

正如本书序言所说,Denning 勋爵在其自传《The Discipline of the Law》中写道:"In the daily practice of the law, the most important subject is the construction of documents."(在每天的法律实务,最重要的工作是解释文件。)

这也是笔者作为仲裁员的深刻体会,笔者的仲裁案件几乎每个都会涉及有关合约或有关文件的解释。为了让读者更好地了解合约解释规则并能活学活用,笔者在本章节录4个自己曾经作出的仲裁裁决书。读者可以从中看到本书所介绍的部分解释合约的规则,如背景/语境,如何整体协调合约的条文/文字,私人字典,合约合并其他标准格式,默示条文等。也希望读者能够从这些实例中看到,只要掌握了解释合约的全面知识,就可以从草拟合约的第一步直到作为仲裁员或是法官都可以游刃有余。

§1　香港仲裁案件之一

以下是一个笔者的香港"宣告裁决书"(declaratory award),是在裁决书宣告法律的认定,这通常是对双方有争议的合约条文/文字作出权威与有约束力的解释。笔者被双方委任为独任仲裁员,争议是有关期租合约的纠纷,涉及租期的计算。期租像房屋租赁一样,船东与承租人会约定1年或3年不等的出租期限。这等于是船东把有关船舶交给承租人,之后在承租人营运了1年或3年不等的期限后,就必须在双方约定的还船地点交还船舶。但期租合约经常涉及全球的营运,加上每个航次的快慢也不是承租人可以控制,所以经常导致无法准时在约定地点交还船舶给船东。这导致承租人经常违约并需要赔偿船东损失。而承租人为了避免或减少这种麻烦,也在订立期租合约时加入一些明示条文作出保障。如比默示更广泛的"明示伸缩性"(express tolerance),如1年的期租"加减30天"(30 days more or less),可允许承租人合法在11个月或13个月内交船。另一种明示的写法是把这1年的期限在期租合约写为"最少11个月,最多13个月"(minimum 11 months, maximum 13 months)。另一种常见的写法是加上一条"最后航次条文"(final voyage clause):The "World Symphony" (1992) 2 Lloyd's Rep 115; The "Kriti Akti" (2004) 1 Lloyd's Rep 712 等先例。至于比较短的期限如"航次期租"(TCT),会对约定的期限加上"不担保"(without guarantee):The "Lendoudis Evangelos II" LMLN 408 24.06.95 等先例。

以上各种写法能够在一定程度对承租人起到保障,特别是承租人真诚与努力准时还船,只是不幸地在最后一个航次遇上了他不可以控制但也不严重的天灾人祸(坏天气、海难、卸货时遇上罢工、装卸港拥挤等)而导致最后的航次比预算的更慢(或在极少的情况下更快,如原定卸港突然变得十分拥挤或进不去而导致改港,令预算航次缩短)。但在接近还船时间市场如果上涨,承租人就会尽量用尽租期以及其伸缩性,这往往会导致"超期还船"(overlap)的违约。而如果接近还船时间市场下跌,承租人就会尽量提早交船,这往往会导致"提早还船"(underlap)的违约。而众所周知,航运会在很短时间暴涨暴跌,导致这些争议经常出现,并有无数的先例,包括贵族院/最高院的先例。近年来,在损失计算方面几个最著名的贵族院先例,如 The "Golden Victory" (2007) 2 Lloyd's Rep 164 与 The "Achilleas" (2008) 2 Lloyd's Rep 275 就是涉及这种争议。这方面的问题可参阅杨大明律师的《期租合同》一书,很多争议本质上就是解释合约(期租合约只是比较复杂与国际性的一种合约)。

这个仲裁也是针对这方面的问题,但涉及另一方面的复杂性。双方对一个本来打算 5 年的期租合约不简单地说是 5 年,至多加上明示伸缩,如 3 个月不等,而约定一个十分复杂的期限,如下:"36 *months* + 12 *months* (*first optional period*) + 11 *to* 13 *months* (*Second optional period*) + *at Charterers' option any off-hire time as per Clause* 83 +/-15 *days for 'about' in Charterers' option.*"

这期限与期租合约的其他有关条文导致了双方的争议,而船东与承租人各自按照自己的办法计算有关的两个期租合约的租期,长短相差几个月。在接近的还船的时间,航运市场高涨,也表示期租合约所订立的租金偏低。如果承租人的计算被接受,就可以多跑一两个航次才合法还船给船东,这会涉及可多赚取 200 万美元以上的差价。至于情况紧急是由于双方委任笔者作为独任仲裁员时,已经十分接近船东计算应该还船的时间。所以,如果笔者能够尽快作出裁决并判船东胜诉,就表示船东可以马上去市场寻找下一票货物。

这个裁决书涉及本书好几个部分的内容,会在以下节录的裁决书中以脚注的形式说明相关的章节或段节,方便大家深入了解。

IN THE MATTER OF THE ARBITRATION ORDINANCE (CAP. 341)

AND

IN THE MATTER, OF AN ARBITRATION

BETWEEN

承租人	(The Charterers)
AND	
甲轮船东	(The Owners of "甲轮")
乙轮船东	(The Owners of "乙轮")

DECLARATORY AWARD

WHEREAS:

I) By two identical time charterparties dated 28th July 2000 for the "甲轮" and 1st August 2000 for the "乙轮", the Owners agreed to charter the two vessels to the Charterers upon the terms and conditions set out therein.

2) The two charterparties provided for, in Clause 17, for any disputes to submit to Hong Kong arbitration with English law to govern.

3) A dispute having arisen between the Charterers and the Owners and on21st September 2005, the parties entered into an agreement to appoint me, the undersigned Philip Yang of 18A, Casey Building, 38, Lok Ku Road, Sheung Wan, Hong Kong, as the sole arbitrator.

4) The dispute referred to me concerned the precise durations of the two charterparties.

5) The parties provided me with extensive written submissions and submissions in response, together with the relevant documentary evidence they rely on.

6) Neither party requested an oral hearing.

7) Under the Hong Kong Arbitration Ordinance, I am obliged to issue a Reasoned Award and my reasons are accordingly attached hereto and form part of this my **DECLARATORY AWARD.**

NOW I, the said Philip Yang, having taken upon myself the burden of this my reference and having carefully and conscientiously read and considered the submissions made by the Owners and the Charterers, and the documentary evidence they put before me, **DO HEREBY MAKE, ISSUE AND PUBUSH** this my **DECLARATORY AWARD** as follows:

A) **I AWARD, ADJUDGE AND DECLARE** that the two charterparties' precise durations should be 36 *months* + 12 *months* (*first optional period*) + 11 *to* 13 *months* (*second optional period*) + *at Charterers' option any off-hire time as per Clause* 83 +/- 15 *days for "about" in Charterers' option.*

B) I tax and settle the costs of this my **DECLARATORY AWARD** at the sum of HK $...

C) **I RESERVE** for later determination all questions as to liability on costs (both the parties' costs and the costs of this my Award).

GIVEN under my hand this 3rd November, 2005.

Philip Yang

Sole Arbitrator Witness

“甲轮”/“乙轮”

REASONS

For and forming part of DECLARATORY AWARD

1) In this reference, the parties have agreed to jointly appoint me as the sole arbitrator with a view to come to a “quick” decision on the precise redelivery dates of the two (2) vessels, “甲轮” and “乙轮” under their governing Time Charter – parties (T – C/Ps). It has to be quick or instant because the Owners' position is that the redelivery dates ought to be as early as 21/11/2005 for “乙轮” and 1/12/2005 for “甲轮”. If the Owners prevail in this arbitration, they need to start looking for next employments for the vessels. Likewise, if the Charterers prevail, they also need time to look for next employments. In that sense, 21/11/2005 is not far off.

2) The precise redelivery dates must necessarily depend on the durations of the two T – C/Ps. Briefly put, the Owners position is: the durations in both T – C/Ps should be “36 *months* + 12 *months* (*first optional period*) + 11 *to* 13 *months* (*Second optional period*) + *at Charterers' option any off – hire time as per Clause* 83 +/ – 15 *days for* ‘*about*’ *in Charterers' option*”. But the Charterers' position is that they are entitled to use the vessel for a maximum period of: “*maximum* 38 *months* +13 *months* 15 *days* + 13 *months* 15 *days* + (*off – hire time as per Clause* 83”. This kind of dispute is common when the freight market rises substantially and the Charterers logically wish to use the vessel having chartered – in at lower rate for as long as possible. Whether the Charterers are entitled to do so must depend on the construction of the governing T – C/P.

3) I must therefore first set out the material provisions in the two governing T – C/Ps

(which are the same) as follows:

“Lines 13 – 15 – ”*That the said Owners agree to let, and the said Charterers agree to hire the said vessel, from the time of delivery, for about minimum* 34 *and maximum* 38 *months Time Charter exact period in Charterers option. Charterers option further about* 11 / *about* 13 *months Time Charter: Charterers option additional further about* 11/*about* 13 *months time Charters. About means*15 *days more or less in Charterers option. Optional period to be declared latest* 3 *months prior to the expiry of the previous period* (*I.*

E. latest the last date of the 33rd *month and last date of* 45th *month respectively). Hire for optional period to count from expiry of the* 36th *month and the* 48th *month respectively....*

Clause 4 – "*That the Charterers shall pay for the use and hire of the said Vessel at the rate of USD*10,600. – *daily including overtime payable*15 *days in advance for the first* 3 *years period and USD*11,400. – *daily including overtime for the optional period (s)* ·

Clause 83 – "*Charterers' option to add any off hire time to Charter Party*"

Addendum No. 6 – "*Notwithstanding the terms and conditions of above Charter Party ... Charterers hereby exercise their first option for further about* 11 *months/*13 *months time charter for M/V* "甲轮" *as per subject Charter Party dated* 28th *July* 2000. *Hire for the optional period start to count from* 37th *month* (1st *November*; 2003) *and the hire rate to be USD*11,400. – *daily including overtime.*"

Addendum No. 10 – "*Notwithstanding the terms and conditions of above Charter Party ... Charterers hereby exercise their second option for further about* 11 *months/*13 *months time charter for M/V*'"甲轮" *as per subject Charter Party dated* 28th *July* 2000. *Hire for the optional period start to count from* 49th *month* (1st*November*, 2004) *and hire rate to be USD*11,400. – *daily including overtime.*"

For the "乙轮", the Charterers had also exercised their two options in similar wording, recorded in Addendums Nos. 6 &9, which I shall not repeat.

4) Both parties exchanged initial written submissions concurrently (no doubt with a view to expedite the process) and had a second round of exchanging submissions in response. The submissions are very lengthy or wordy which make it very difficult for me to decide quickly or instantly. As an illustration, the submissions in response have 9 pages and 14 pages from the Charterers and the Owners respectively.

5) Essentially, the dispute boils down to the following issues:

(i) Factual Matrix[1]/private dictionary[2] or mutual understanding during negotiation.[3]

(ii) Construction of the material provisions as set out in Paragraph 3.

I will deal with these issues and the main arguments of the parties in paragraphs to follow.

---

〔1〕 请看本书之第六章。

〔2〕 请看本书第三章之第 14 段。

〔3〕 请看本书第三章之 13.1 段。

Factual Matrix

6) I shall first deal with this issue. The Owners' solicitors had initially applied for the specific disclosure of two other fixtures relating to a vessel called "ABC 轮" and an unnamed vessel in what is called "XYZ 轮". They were mentioned by the Charterers during negotiations and there was suggestion of private dictionary[4] in that the parties reached mutual understanding with regard to the charter duration. The Charterers strongly resisted.

7) I sent a fax to the parties on 6/10/2005, stating, *inter alia*:

"*...I am happy to express my initial impression to the arguments with regard to specific disclosure and factual matrix...*

c) If 1*am to consider factual matrix in my construction (if the executed C/Ps, I must consider what transpired between the parties during the earlier negotiations. No doubt I will receive the fixture files in due course, ...*

d) But my rough understanding of factual matrix or "relevant circumstances" which then exist ought to be limited to those within the common knowledge of the parties[5] *at the time when they made their C/Ps. Thus, I am not altogether persuaded that further disclosure should be ordered, which are the documents the Owners did not see during negotiations...* "

8) The Owners pursued no further on specific disclosure. But in subsequent written submissions and submissions in response, *factual matrix*[6] remains a main issue in dispute. The parties argued extensively which had taken up a lot of time.

9) I have looked at the fixtures negotiations submitted by the Owners[7]. It started with the Owners' offering the "甲轮" (then a Panamax newbuilding under construction) for a period of "*minimum* 58/ *maximum* 62 *months time charter*; *exact period in Charterers' option*". It was back on 26/4/2000.

10) But the Charterers countered on 3/5/2000 with "*minimum* 331*maximum* 39 *months time charter exact period in Charterers' option, Charterers ' further* 10/14 *months time charter and Charterers ' further*10/14 *months time charter.* "

---

〔4〕 请看本书第三章之第14段。

〔5〕 请看本书第六章之第7段。订约时的语境既然必须是订约双方都知道或应该知道,就表示针对语境的证据不能向仲裁庭申请披露,因为要求披露就显示对方才有这方面的文件证据,但自己就没有,也等于订约时不会知道。

〔6〕 请看本书第六章。

〔7〕 根据本书第六章之2.5.1段的谈判除外规则,笔者不应该看双方谈判的证据。但在本案件,双方都邀请笔者看这方面的证据,理由是双方谈判时有私人字典,在本书第三章之14.3段已经介绍,私人字典应该属于谈判除外规则的例外。

11) On 10/5/2000, the Owners had also used the words of "minimum" and "maximum" to describe the initial or basic period by counter – offering:

"*minimum* 47 *maximum* 49 *months time charter exact period in Charterers' option. Charterers' option further minimum* 11/*maximum* 13 *months time charter*; *such option to be declared latest on the* 1st *day of the* 44th *month after delivery*, *if option period be declared by Charterers*, *optional period and rate of hire for optional period to count from the starting of the* 49th *month after delivery.*"

12) The Owners further conceded on 12/6/2000 at 11 :58H to a shorter initial or basic period and granted to the Charterers two (2) further optional periods. It reads as follows:

"*minimum* 35/*maximum* 37 *months time charter exact period in Charterers' option. Charterers' option further minimum* 11/*maximum* 13 *months time charter. Charterers' option further minimum* 11/*maximum* 13 *months time charter. Optional period to be declared latest* 3 *months prior to the expiry of the previous period* (*I. E. latest the last date of the* 3. 3*th* (*sic*) *month and the last date of the* 45th *month respectively*). *Hire for optional period to count from the expiry of the* 36th *month and the* 48*th month respectively.*
"

13) On 13/6/2000, the Charterers attempted to further increase the span or spread between "minimum/maximum" charter duration to "*minimum* 34/*maximum* 38 *months time charter exact period in Charterers' option*" At the same time, the Charterers accepted the declaration and hire commencement.

14) In the morning of 14/6/2000, the Owners maintained position in the time charter period to be "*minimum* 35/*maximum* 37 *months time charter exact period in Charterers' option.* ".

15) The parties' respective positions kept changing and by 14/6/2000, in late afternoon, the Owners conceded to and settled at "*about* 35/*about* 37 *months time charter exact period in Charterers' option*, *Charterers' option further about* 11/*about* 13 *months time charter*, *Charterers' option further about* 11/*about* 13 *months time charter.* "*A bout*" *means* 10 *days more or less Charterers' option* (*MOLCO*) ".

16) By 15/612000, the Owners' further conceded to "*about*" being "15 days MOLCO" instead of "10 days MOLCO".

17) It was finally agreed and recorded in the fixture recap and in the executed T – C/Ps that the durations should be "*minimum* 34 *maximum* 38 *months time charter exact period in Charterers' option*, *Charterers' option further about* 11/*about* 13 *months time charter*, *Charterers' option further about* 11/*about* 13 *months time charter*, '*about*' *means* 15 *days MOLCO*".

18) In my view and my general experience in chartering, I find it to be a perfectly normal negotiations process, with some signs of the Owners yielding to the Charterers' demand insofar as the duration is concerned and a continuous change of position. Clearly, it must be to the Charterers' advantage in having two (2) periods of options than a flat period initially proposed by the Owners, even with a tolerance of "min/max".

19) The parties referred me to several authorities and the leading text in Chitty on Contracts. I shall only repeat one citation here of what Lord Wilberforce said in Prenn v. Simmonds (1971) 1WLR 1381, of:

"*In my opinion, then, evidence of negotiations, or of the parties' intentions, and a fortiori of[the plaintiff's] intentions, ought* **not** to be received, and evidence should be restricted to evidence of the factual background **known to the parties** at or before the date of the contract, including evidence of the 'genesis' and objectively the 'aim' of the transaction. (*bold words are my emphasis*)

20) *I see it as a warning not to be influenced by what is in truth a finding of the subjective intention of the parties*[8] *at the relevant time (which was, in this, more than* 5 *years ago), instead of carrying out what I believe should be the correct exercise of determining objectively the mutual/shared intention*[9] *of the parties all the way through to the conclusion of the C/P*[10] *from the words of the documents in the fixture file in the light of the circumstances surrounding the transaction.*

21) *With the above in mind, I must conclude that I have difficulty accepting the Owners' arguments of* factual matrix. *To start off, the relevant words used by the parties such as* "minimum/maximum" *are exceedingly clear and unambiguous*[11] *to people in the chartering business. There is no imperfection of language which I need to enquire further. Furthermore, there were many rounds of offers and counters, part of which is being cited by me from Paragraphs* 9 *to* 17 *above. I cannot find any factual background "known to the parties"*[12] *or "special circumstances"*[13] *that could lead to the con-*

---

〔8〕 请看本书第三章之14.3段与第六章之2.5.1段，这也是这两段所讲的不接受谈判证据的原因，就是担心仲裁庭会受到谈判双方的主观意图的影响。仲裁庭即使看了，也应该避免受到影响。

〔9〕 请看本书第三章之13.1.4段与13.1.5段。

〔10〕 请看本书第三章之13.1.6段。

〔11〕 这是针对"最短/最长"一词的解释，笔者认为清楚无误，不会有第二种解释，所以根据本书很多内容，包括第一章之第5段介绍的解释合约的"黄金规则"(golden rule)与本书第四章之4.2段所讲，就必须给它这个解释。

〔12〕 在这个案件笔者看不到任何语境证据可以帮助解释这个清楚无误的词，这也可参阅本书第一章之8.6段介绍的Rainy Sky SA and others v Kookmin Bank (2012) 1 Lloyd's Rep 34先例。

〔13〕 特殊情况可以是私人字典。

struction or "*manipulation*" *of* "minimum 34/maximum 38 months time charter" *as meaning the same as* "3 *years*" *or* "36 *months*". *Indeed with several counters back – and – forth in narrowing or expanding the* "minimum/maximum" *period* (*such as*, *in Paragraph* 14, *the Owners countered with* "minimum 35/maximum 37 months" *against Charterers' last of* "minimum 34/maximum 38 months"), *I have difficulty in accepting all the different descriptions of the precise time charter periods used by the parties can all be taken to mean* "3 *years*". *In any event*, *I find the Owners* (*and indeed the Charterers*) *are very experienced and knowledgeable in that they know precisely*[14] *what was meant by the use of the description of* "minimum/maximum" *for the time charter period at the time of negotiations.*

22) *Therefore*, *I reject the Owners' argument of* factual matrix *or mutual understanding during the negotiation. As mentioned*, *it has taken up a lot of time in this reference. In today' s environment of awarding costs based on success and failure of different issues*, *I have a feeling that if I am asked to deal with costs later by the parties*, *I will take this matter into account. If any authority is needed to support my intended cause of action with regard to costs*, *I can cite* NLA Group Ltd v. Bowers (1999) 1 *Lloyd' s Rep.* 109.

Construction of the Time Charter – parties

23) I now turn to the construction of the various material provisions in the two (2) T – C/Ps, of which I have cited in Paragraph 3 above. In the written submissions, both parties cited many important rules of construction, such as, the famous canon of construction by Lord Reid:

"*The fact that a particular construction leads to avery unreasonable result must be a relevant consideration. The more unreasonable the result*, *the more unlikely it* is *that the parties can have intended it*, *and if they do intend it*, *the more necessary it is that they should make that intention abundantly clear*".

24) I was also referred by the Owners' solicitors to Chitty, 29th Ed. Paragraph 12 – 078 of:

"*an effort should be made to give effect to every clause in the agreement and not to reject a clause unless it is manifestly inconsistent with or repugnant to the rest of the agreement.*"

25) The Charterers referred me to Glynn v Margetson & Co. (1893) A. C. 351 of:

---

〔14〕 这表示笔者解释合约也必须考虑合约的本质与谈判时可以推断的语境，就是谈判双方都是很有经验与水平的人士，不会不知道"最短/最长"一词的意思。加上这个词在很多标准格式合约有出现，并有过不少有关的先例，不能轻易偏离，这可参阅本书第四章之第 2 段。

"*Looking at the whole of the document, and seeing what one must regard ... as its main purpose, one must reject words, indeed whole provisions, if they are inconsistent with what one assumes to be the main purpose of the contract.*"

The Charterers also referred me to a Canadian case ofSawley Agency v Ginter (1964) regarding the same principle when it comes to inconsistency.

26) I remember other rules of construction such as: "*One should be reluctant to hold that parts of a contract are inconsistent with each other, and will give effect to any reasonable construction which harmonises such clauses.*" (see The Interpretation of Contracts, 3rd Ed.). Lord Goff said in Vien Yieh Commercial Bank Ltd. v. Kwai Chung Storage Co. Ltd. (1989) 2 HKLR 639, PC:

"*Their Lordships wish to stress that to reject one clause in a contract as inconsistent with another involves a rewriting of the contract which can only be justified in circumstances where the two clauses are in truth inconsistent...*"

27) The parties also referred me to many cases on time charter durations, such as: The "Peonia" (1991) 1 Lloyd's Rep. 100; The "Gregos" (1995) I Lloyd's Rep. 1 (H. L.), etc. But the parties argued before me mostly on the case of The "Aspa Maria" (1976) 2 Lloyd's Rep. 643. In that case, the initial time charter period was agreed for "*six months* 30 *days more or less at charterers' option*". Then a further clause 13 said:

"*the charterers shall have the option of continuing this charter for a further period of further six months* 30 *days ... at charterers' option ...*"

The charterers in that case said to have a total duration of "12 *months pins* 60 *days*". But it was rejected by the High Court and the Court of Appeal and held that the margin of tolerance of 30 days either way applies only once and not twice.

It seems to me that the cases being cited to me have little application to this dispute, except in The "Aspa Maria", I have a feeling of construing in that case the charter period option against the charterers. In another word, the rule of *contra proferentem* [15] may apply because the option is in favour of the charterers.

28) Having said the above, I understand fully that the rules of construction are not the law. With every contract differs in the words used by the contractual parties, I know my duty as the arbitrator of having to consider the contract (in this case, the *T - C/P*) as a whole [16], in support of all the provisions and harmonise any inconsistent terms (if at all possible), not to rewrite the parties' contract, etc., and come up with a hopefully reasonable and objective result. Last but not the least, I say that in the construction of

---

〔15〕 请看本书第四章之第5段。

〔16〕 请看本书第三章之第1段。

contract, it is in many cases a matter of an overall impression[17].

29) I must also mention that the Owners had presented to me the reasons for a Declaratory Award dated 17/9/2004, which on the face appears to be strikingly similar to the dispute in this reference. The material clause/provision in that time charter can be cited as follows:

"Lines 13 - 15 - - *That the said Owners agree to let, and the said Charterers agree to hire the said vessel, from the time of delivery, for about Minimum* 11*months/maximum* 13 *months timecharter, Charterers' option further minimum* 11*months/maximum* 13 *months timecharter. Optional period to be declared latest within*8 *months after vessel's delivery*".

Briefly put, it was decided by a London sole arbitrator (name of which is not disclosed due to confidentiality) that the charterers prevailed on a true construction of the charterparty that they were entitled to the use of vessel for an initial or basic period of 13 months (maximum period) plus a further 13 months (maximum period).

This is notwithstanding a rider clause entitled "Rate of Hire" stated a hire rate of USD17,500 daily for the optional year and the option year is to be commenced on the first day of the thirteenth month period. That means the 13th month in the initial or basic period the charterers must pay an increase of daily hire from the original rate of USD15,500 to USD17,500. This apparent anomaly was criticized by the disponent owners in that case as "absurd".

The arbitrator said that there was no doubt that the draughtsmanship of clause 75 in this respect was somewhat unfortunate. He concluded that because clause 75 was entitled "Rate of Hire" it was dealing simply with the rates of hire and not with the duration of the basic or extended hire periods.

The above, I hope, is a very brief summary of what my understanding of the reasoning in the London arbitration award to be.

30) I appreciate that the London arbitration award is only of persuasive value at its best, especially with no knowledge to other documents of the case. But I have considered it very carefully and humbly because it will be most unfortunate in differ with the London arbitrator for no good reason in the construction of identical contractual wording/provisions and cause the Charterers to be caught in between, whom I understand to be the disponent owners in that case. Especially, the amount in dispute, as I was told, is substantial in this case.

---

〔17〕 请看本书第四章之4.2段与本书第五章之第2段介绍的 The "Mariasmi" (1970) 1 Lloyd's Rep. 247 先例。

31) To facilitate reading, I repeat the most important provisions in the two disputed T - C/Ps in this reference, which I have already cited earlier in Paragraph 3. I will also highlight the different wording which I can detect in comparison with the charterparty wording faced with in the London arbitration award cited in Para. 29. It is as follows:

"Lines 13 - 15 - "*That the said Owners agree to let, and the said Charterers agree to hire the said vessel, from the time (if delivery, for about minimum* 34 *and maximum* 38 *months Time Charter exact period in Charterers option. Charterers option further* **about 11/about 13** months Time Charter. Charterers option additional further **about 11 / about 13** months 'time Charters. **About means 15 days more or less in Charterers option.** Optional period to be declared **latest 3 months prior to the expiry of the previous period (I. E. latest the last date of the 33rd month and last date of 45th month respectively). Hire for optional period to count from expiry of the 36th month and the 48th month respectively ....** "

It should be a lot clearer now that the words used are not the same. Much more has been said and agreed in the two T - C/Ps of the "甲轮" *and the* "乙轮". *The words used and added are a lot more precise and definite.*

32) *I have carefully considered the arguments of both parties. They proposed various constructions or interpretations to the highlighted words or provisions. Briefly put, the Charterers argued*, inter alia, *that*:

(*i*) *The initial or basic period of* "maximum" 38 *months is exceedingly clear and unambiguous. There is no* "*expiry*" *of this period until it reaches the last day of the* 38*th* *month.*

(*ii*) *Having to pay increased or higher hire rate for the optional period per* <u>*Addendum No. 6*</u> "from 37th month (1st November, 2003)" *does not necessarily mean the commencement of the optional period must start to run on that date. In another word, the Charterers argued that in the remaining* 2 *months of the initial period of* 37*th* & 38*th* *month, the higher optional period hire rate should be paid. No doubt the Charterers are relying on the reasoning of the London arbitration award referred to in my Paragraph* 29.

(*iii*) *Nowhere in the Addenda says that by agreeing to pay different hires for different specified periods, the optional periods should commence at the same time when different hires are to be paid.*

(*iv*) *Nowhere in the T - C/Ps says when optional periods are to be commenced once the options are exercised.*

(*v*) *The expiry of the initial or basic period and the first optional period should be the end of the* 38*th* *month and the* 51. 5*th* *month respectively instead of the end of the* 36*th* *month and the* 48th *month, as alleged by the Owners.*

(*vi*) *The words used in* <u>*Lines* 13 – 15</u> *of* "**latest three months prior to the expiry of the previous period**" *should be rejected due to inconsistency. It is in contradiction with the clear description of the* "maximum" *initial or basic period.*

33) *The Owners argued, predominantly and forcefully, on the words used in* <u>*Line* 13 – 15</u> (*the duration clause*) *of* "**the expiry of the previous period**" *and said the whole clause makes perfect sense as an agreed mechanism whereby, on exercise of the Charterers' option for an additional* 11 – 13 *months, the previous time charter period*(*s*) *shall expire on the last dates of the preceding calendar years, i. e. as expressly defined to be* "**the last date of the** $\mathbf{33^{rd}}$ **month and last date of the** $\mathbf{45^{th}}$ **month respectively.**"

<u>My deliberation and decision</u>

34) On a fine balance, I have some difficulty in accepting the Charterers' arguments. Whilst I agree that the term of "minimum/maximum" is exceedingly clear to people in the chartering business (and I am sure to the Owners' knowledge during the negotiations), it is not the only term or words in the "duration clause" of <u>L 13 – 15</u>. As pointed out and highlighted in Paragraph 31, there are a lot more specific words or provisions in the same clause, which I must try to give them meaning and read them as a whole.〔18〕

35) The Charterers urged me to reject some words in the duration clause of "**latest three months prior to the expiry of previous period'** *due to inconsistency, presumably in contradiction with* "maximum 38 months" *earlier in the same clause. But based on the rules of construction that I have mentioned earlier, in particular, the guidance of Lord Goff in Paragraph* 26, *I should not reject words in an executed contract lightly or else it amounts to a rewriting of the contract or T – C/Ps.*〔19〕

36) *It will also involve the change or manipulation of the clear words used by the parties, defining in brackets the last dates of* "33rd *month and* 45th *month*" *to* "38th*month and* 51.5^{th} *month*". *This, in my view, is going too far into rewriting the T – C/Ps. Obviously if the Charterers are to exercise the option to extend a charter, the market then must be buoyant. It is logical that the Charterers would like to enjoy the maximum initial*

---

〔18〕请看本书第三章之第1段。注意在本案件,笔者虽然支持承租人对"最短/最长"一词的解释,但这不是本租约中唯一有关租期长短的文字。而如果把租约其他的条文/文字一并解释,并给每个条文/文字一定的意思,就非要把"最短/最长"一词的解释作出局限。这等于整体解释合约是承租人败诉。

〔19〕承租人要求笔者漠视/删除一些其他看来与"最短/最长"一词有矛盾的条文/文字,但笔者拒绝,认为这样是改写双方的合约。换言之,能够整体作出解释,笔者要尽量避免漠视/删除合约中的任何的条文/文字。这可看本书第三章之第2段。

or basic charter period. But in this case, the duration clause in Line13 – 15 *specifically says, I repeat*: **"latest 3 months prior to the expiry of the previous period (I. E. latest the last date of the 33rd month ant/last date of 45th month respectively)"**.

37) I am also mindful that the first optional period (as against the initial or basic period) of "about 11/about 13 months" does not use the strong words of "minimum/maximum".

38) With regards to the Charterers' arguments in Paragraph 32(ii) and (iii), it is true that it was the same conclusion in the London arbitration award that was brought to my attention. Although this conclusion is not "unreasonable", it is at least in my view "unusual". If the Charterers wish to pay higher hire rate to the Owners by reason of having exercised the option, they can agree on an even higher rate for the optional period or periods. There is no need to disturb the original rate agreed upon for the initial or basic period in the last 2 months. If this "unusual" contractual arrangement is intended, I expect much clearer words should be used by the parties – as stated in the famous canon of construction by Lord Reid in Paragraph 23. Afterall, adequate and punctual hire payment is crucial in a time charter, especially when the market is buoyant, failing which the Owners can use as an excuse to withdraw the vessel.

39) Incidentally, in this case, the parties had also made reference to hire payment in the duration clause (Line 13 – 15) of "*Hire for optional period to count from expiry of the 36th month and the 48th month respectively*". Therefore, the reasoning in the London arbitration award of "Rate of Hire" clause was dealing simply with the rate of hire and not with the duration of charter is inapplicable in this case before me.

40) With all the considerations I have mentioned in Paragraph 28 in the construction, in particular with an intention to support all the provisions/words and to give meanings to them, notwithstanding the apparent inconsistency, I accept the proposed construction put forward by the Owners. That is, to harmonise the whole duration clause as:

(i) If the Charterers do not exercise the option, they can use the vessel for a period within the span or spread of "*minimum* 34 *months and maximum* 38 *months*".

(ii) If the Charterers exercise the option or options, then the "*expiry of the previous period*" (i. e. initial or basic period) will be 36 months and the first option must be declared latest 3 months prior on the last date of the 33rd month. The first optional period hire rate must then start from 37th month as stated in Addendum No. 6.

By this way of construction, I can give meanings to all the words or provisions used by the parties in Lines 13 – 15, the duration clause.

41) The Charterers may think that in Paragraph 40 (i) above, what I have decided is artificial because if the Charterers do not exercise the option to extend, the freight mar-

ket is more likely to be depressed. There is accordingly no way that the "maximum 38 months" will be utilized. Thus, I am still not giving meaning or weight to this clear and common description to the charter period or duration. But I believe even if the freight market is marginally better than the time of fixture, there can still be scenarios of the Charterers not to exercise the option. Such as, the vessel in hand is a problematic vessel. Another scenario could be: the Charterers do not exercise the option on the last date of the 33rd month and is thus considered as waived. But thereafter, the freight market sharply increases and the Charterers are only left with the initial or basic period, which they will try to use for as long as possible, up to or close to the "maximum 38 months".〔20〕

42) I feel unhappy that I must decide against one party, the Charterers in this instance. I appreciate it has major financial consequence. But regrettably this is not a mediation or conciliation. I must come to a decision, sometimes on a fine balance of probability, against one party who has put trust and confidence in me by accepting me as the sole arbitrator. I can only hope that my speedy service to the parties in avoiding uncertainty and further escalation of losses or damages can makeup this unfortunate result to the Charterers.

43) I must also mention that I did not extensively cover every arguments &/or cases referred to me. But I can assure the parties that I have read and/or considered all of them. If have to be comprehensive, the reasons of this Declaratory Award will go on much longer This is a quick or an instant arbitration and I do not intend to hold back from the parties my decision.

§2 香港仲裁案件之二

以下的仲裁裁决书是有关国际货物(丙烷与丁烷)的中国某港口船旁交货(*Delivery Ex-Ship*,或简称 *DES*)的买卖合约,卖方是一家欧洲公司,而买方是一家中国企业/公司。在该仲裁,双方有好几个争议,笔者只介绍其中有关解释合约的争议(*Issue* 4),该争议涉及金额最大,也是双方争议的重点。这笔金额实际上是一笔庞大的滞期费,船舶在中国的卸港受到严重延误,因为不能靠泊卸货。外国卖方想把这笔支付给了船东的滞期费转嫁给中国买方,认为在买卖合约的条文/文字是买方要承

〔20〕 将合约作为整体协调解释后,"最短/最长"一词的意思虽然有所局限,但仍有一定的意思,也就是说笔者没有漠视/删除该词,否则就变成改写租约。在这里笔者举了两个"最短/最长"一词可以适用的情况。

担。换言之,笔者作为独任仲裁员又需要解释买卖合约的条文/文字,看中国买方是否要承担。

为了让读者更好地理解这份裁决书,笔者首先简单介绍 *DES* 买卖。根据一般商业上的理解,包括国际商会的 *Incoterms* 与英国普通法,*DES* 买卖与 *CIF* 买卖十分接近,是要求卖方租船与作出海上运输,并在双方约定的卸货地点让买方从船上提货。而在整个过程中,直到买方可以从船上提货,卖方需要承担所有的风险,包括对货物与时间损失等的风险。这样看来,卖方所租用的船舶如果在中国卸港受到不能靠泊的延误,这个风险明确应该属于卖方而不是中国买方。另一个不合理之处是该买卖合约中的货物(丙烷与丁烷),只是船上的一部分货,让中国买方负责整条船的滞期费说不过去。但在订约自由下,双方可以清楚无误的条文/文字约定不合理或偏离正常的做法。[21] 举例而言,双方约定一条条文说明买方需要承担所有装港与船舶通过巴拿马运河的费用,买方也就不能说在 *DES* 买卖下原来是卖方要负责这些费用。[22] 笔者觉得在这个争议,需要看 *DES* 卖方有否在买卖合约的条文/文字做到这一点。

卖方所依赖的是双方订立的买卖合约,其中有第 15 条文简单说:"本买卖合约的商业条文是合并 *Incoterms* 2000。"另第 16 条文简单说:"本买卖合约的'海运条文'(*maritime terms*)是合并一份名为'*Asbatankvoy*'的油轮租约标准格式。"*Asbatankvoy* 标准格式租约中的第 9 条文是承租人作出承诺在船舶抵达时有一个马上可以挂靠的泊位(*the charterers to provide a berth reachable on vessel's arrival*)。这个承诺的解释已经有贵族院先例,而且是标准格式合约,所以它的意思是肯定。这样,如果该条文可以成功合并在这份 *DES* 买卖合约,承租人就可以把他篡改为买方(作为非派船方),就表示买方因为没有提供一个马上可以挂靠的泊位,导致船舶在卸港受到延误而不能进港是构成违约,并需要承担这笔滞期费的损失。

简单总结,笔者作为独任仲裁员要解释这个 *DES* 买卖合约与有关争议,是要考虑几个方面,包括有关合并其他合约的问题、[23] 标准格式合约条文/文字已经有了先例的解释、[24] 什么是"海运条文"这个不常见的用语与有否涉及私人字典、[25] 整体解释合约并给每一个条文/文字一定的意思[26] 等。笔者最后是判中国买方不必为这笔庞大的滞期费的损失承担合约责任。

---

〔21〕 请看本书第四章之第 4 段。

〔22〕 这可见本书第三章之 5.3 段,即面窄与特别针对一件事的条文超越广泛与一般性的条文。

〔23〕 请看本书第二章之第 8 段。

〔24〕 请看本书第四章之第 2 段。

〔25〕 请看本书第三章之第 14 段。

〔26〕 请看本书第三章之第 1 段。

IN THE MATTER OF THE ARBITRATION ORDINANCE (CAP. 341)
AND
IN THE MATTER OF AN ARBITRATION
B E T W E E N

(卖方) Claimants/Sellers

AND

(买方) Respondents/Buyers

“(运载货物的船舶)” Sales Contract dated 8 September 2002

FINAL ARBITRATION AWARD

1) By a Sales Contract dated 8 September 2002, (卖方) (“the Sellers”) agreed to sell and deliver Delivery Ex Ship/DES (中国某卸港的某泊位), and (买方) (“the Buyers”) agreed to purchase, receive and pay for a cargo of 30,000 MT +/- 5% Propane and Butane.

2) The said Sales Contract provides for:

“17. *Law and Arbitration*

This contract shall be governed by and construed in accordance with the English law and the arbitration shall be held in Hong Kong in English.”

3) Disputes (hereinafter more particularly defined) did arise between the parties. The Sellers applied to the Hong Kong International Arbitration Centre (“HKIAC”) for the appointment of arbitrator pursuant to the Arbitration Ordinance.

4) On 31 January 2003, the HKIAC approached me, the undersigned Philip Yang of 18th Floor, Casey Building, 38 Lok Ku Road, Sheung Wan, Hong Kong and asked if I was available to be the sole arbitrator in this reference. I confirmed my availability and the ability to act independently and impartially between the parties. The parties were formally informed on 19 March 2003 by the HKIAC of my appointment.

5) The dispute referred to me as the sole arbitrator is the Sellers' claim for demurrage of a total sum of US $ 400,000.00.

6) The parties subsequently exchanged written submissions (including but not limiting to Claim Submissions, Defence & Counterclaim Submissions, Reply & Defence to Counterclaim Submissions, Rejoinder Submissions), attached with documentary evi-

dence they relied on.

7) The parties called for an oral hearing and a hearing was held at the HKIAC on 15 – 16 June 2006. The Sellers were represented by Counsel and have adduced expert evidence by (X 先生) who was subject to cross – examination. The Buyers were represented by a law firm in Shanghai and they did not adduce expert evidence. Both parties did not adduce factual witness.

8) After the oral hearing, the parties exchanged written closing submissions before I was invited to proceed to my Award.

9) Under the Hong Kong Arbitration Ordinance, I am obliged to issue a Reasoned Award and my reasons are accordingly attached hereto and form part of this my **FINAL AWARD.**

NOW I, the said Philip Yang, having taken upon myself the burden of this reference and having carefully and conscientiously read, heard and considered the submissions and evidence put before me by the Sellers and the Buyers, and having given due weight thereto, **DO HEREBY MAKE, ISSUE AND PUBLISH** this my **FINAL AWARD**, as follows:

A) **I HEREBY FIND AND HOLD** that the Sellers' claim for US $ 400,000.00 succeeds only to the extent of US $ 85,000.00 and no more.

B) **I THEREFORE AWARD AND ADJUDGE** that the Buyers shall forthwith pay to the Sellers the sum of US $ 85,000.00 **TOGETHER** with interest at the rate of 4.5% p. a. or *pro rata* calculated from 24 October 2002 until the date of actual payment.

C) **I FURTHER AWARD AND ADJUDGE** that the Buyers shall bear and pay their own legal costs and in addition, the Buyers shall pay 25% of the Sellers' legal costs in the reference (to be assessed/determined by me, if they cannot agree) **AND** in respect of the costs of this my **FINAL AWARD** which I hereby assess/determine and settle at the sum of HK $ ___, the Sellers shall pay 40% of such costs while the Buyers shall pay 60% of such costs **PROVIDED ALWAYS** that if, in the first instance, the party who has paid in excess of its share of the costs of this my **FINAL AWARD**, it shall be entitled to an immediate refund from the other party of the sum so paid.

GIVEN UNDER MY HAND in Hong Kong this 1st November, 2006.

Philip Yang Sole Arbitrator	Witness

<u>"(运载货物的船舶)" - Sales Contract dated 8 September 2002</u>

<u>REASONS, for and forming part of FINAL AWARD</u>

<u>THE FACTS</u>:

1) By a Sales Contract ("Sales Contract") dated 8 September 2002, (卖方) ("the Sellers") agreed to sell and deliver "DES (中国某卸港的某泊位)", and, (买方) ("the Buyers") agreed to purchase, receive and pay for a cargo of 30,000 MT +/- 5% Propane and Butane.

2) The cargo was carried and delivered by two (2) vessels, a cargo of 20,000 MT of Propane onboard the "(运载货物的船舶)" (sometimes referred to as "the Vessel") and 10,000 MT of Butane onboard the "另一艘船舶". The movements of "另一艘船舶" were described in the Sellers' opening submissions in Paragraph 4 as follows:

"*The Vessel carrying the Cargo arrived at* (中国卸港) *on* 29. 9. 02 *at* 1800 *and tendered NOR at the same date and time. At about the same time, the* "另一艘船舶" *also arrived at* (中国卸港) *and was given priority to berth. The* "另一艘船舶" *completed discharge at* 1. 10. 02 *at* 12 10 *hours. She cleared the berth at* 1418 *on the same day*"

Whereas the movements of "(运载货物的船舶)" were, according to the Sellers' "Time Sheet", as follows:

"*Arrival (end of Sea Passage)*	1800	29. 09. 2002
Pilot onboard	0840	12. 10. 2002
Completed mooring	1100	12. 10. 2002
Pratique granted	1315	12. 10. 2002
Notice of Readiness (tendered)	1800	29. 09. 2002
Notice of Readiness (accepted)	1500	12. 10. 2002
Commenced discharging	1620	12. 10. 2002
Completed discharging	2235	17. 10. 2002"

3) In the Sales Contract, the following terms and conditions are relevant and/or material to the dispute:

03. *<u>Product</u>*

Propane and Butane (Segregated) with C3/C4 50/50 +/- 5% at Seller's option.

05. *<u>Quantity</u>*

As per original supplier's specification (Cargo Origin: Algeria and/or Arabian Gulf and/or Malaysia).

06. *<u>Vessel</u>*

“(运载货物的船舶)” *or sub.*

08. *Delivery*

DES(中国某卸港的某泊位)

0.9. *Price*

USD 265.00/*MT Fixed Price DES one safe berth* (中国卸港)

10. *Laytime for discharge*

60 hours SHINC + 6 hours NOR basis 18,000 *MTS, extra laytime shall be given on pro rata basis for quantity over* 18,000 *MTS.*

For demurrage calculation purpose only, Seller shall guarantee vessel is capable to discharge min. 200 *MT/hr for propane and min.* 500 *MT/hr for butane.*

If Seller's vessel fails to meet the high tide in daytime (0600 – 1800) *on the day of arrival at* (中国卸港) *Pilot Station, then waiting time till next available high tide in daytime or till vessel is fully alongside, whichever is earliest, shall not be counted as laytime.*

11. *Demurrage*

*USD*29,000 *per day or pro rata*

Claims, if any, shall be communicated in written with in 90 *days after NOR.*

15. *Commercial Terms*

Incoterms 2000 *plus amendments for Ex – Ship sales shall be applied.*

16. *Maritime Terms*〔27〕

As per Asbatankvoy C/P.

19. *Title and Risks*

Title, beneficial ownership and risks of loss shall pass from Seller to Buyer as the product passes vessel's flange at disport.

THE CLAIM AND THE ISSUES:

4) The Sellers claimed the permissible fixed laytime for discharge in the Sales Contract was 60 hours but the total time used by the “(运载货物的船舶)” was 392 hours. Therefore, the Vessel was on demurrage for 330 hours and at the demurrage rate of US $29,000 per day, the total demurrage due from the Buyers is accordingly US $400,000.00. The Buyers denied any demurrage is due to the Sellers.

5) The issues in dispute can be broken down as follows:

(A) Whether “(运载货物的船舶)” was an arrived ship on 29 September 2002 at 1800 hours when the Notice of Readiness (“NOR”) was tendered?

(B) Whether the 1st NOR tendered on 29 September 2002 at 1800 hours was to the

〔27〕 这就是起争议的“海运条文”。

correct and/or proper party/parties?

(C) Whether the 1st NOR was a valid NOR in light of the free pratique and expiry of Deratting Exemption Certificate?

(D) The construction of the Sales Contract and to what extent the Asbatankvoy C/P was incorporated?

(E) Whether the Sellers were in breach by delivering the cargo by two vessels of "另一艘船舶" and "(运载货物的船舶)"?

(F) The Buyers' duty, if any, in ensuring early berthing of "(运载货物的船舶)"

(G) Whether the Vessel was in breach of the discharging capacity and possible problem of back pressure?

There are many other sub – issues being raised by the parties, especially by the Buyers, which I will attempt to cover all of them in the discussionsor deliberations that follow.

Issue No. 1 – Whether "(运载货物的船舶)" was an arrived ship on 29 September 2002 at 1800 hours when the Notice of Readiness ("NOR") was tendered?

...

Issue No. 2 – Whether the 1st NOR tendered on 29 September 2002 at 1800 hours was to the correct and/or proper party/parties?

...

Issue No. 3 – Whether the 1st NOR was a valid NOR in light of the free pratique and expiry of Deratting Exemption Certificate?

...

Issue No. 4 – The construction of the Sales Contract and to what extent the Asbatankvoy C/P was incorporated?

24) This is the primary case for the Sellers and a most difficult issue for me. So much so, I have invited the parties' lawyers at the end of the oral hearing for further and better explanation/clarification in their written closing submissions, particularly with regard to the extent of incorporation by the qualification of "Maritime Terms".

A) Sellers' arguments

25) Briefly put, the arguments or submissions of the Sellers are, inter alia: Clause 16 of the Sales Contract provided that: "*Maritime Terms As per Asbatankvoy C/P*". Laytime and demurrage are matters which properly fall within the definition of "maritime terms" and Clauses 10 and 11 of the Sales Contract are to be supplemented with the appropriate provisions of the Asbatankvoy form of C/P. Accordingly, Clause 6 of Asbatankvoy as cited in Paragraph 6 was incorporated which was to "advance" the time for the tendering of a valid NOR (*at customary anchorage*) when the Vessel arrived at (中

国卸港) on 29 September 2002. It has also triggered the commencement of laytime at 1418 hours on 1 October 2002.

26) In the written closing submissions, the Sellers further referred me, belatedly, to the House of Lords' decision in The "Laura Prima" (1982) 1 Lloyd's Rep. 1 which has to do with an absolute warranty of the charterers to provide "a berth reachable on vessel's arrival" in Clause 9 of the Asbatankvoy C/P.[28]

27) The Sellers also argued that all those terms that are "maritime" in nature, which could supplement the laytime and demurrage clauses in Clauses 10 &11 and should be incorporated. That includes Clause 6 of the Asbatankvoy C/P, which effectively "advanced" the tendering of NOR and triggered the commencement of laytime. In support of similar situations in practice, the Sellers cited the case in The "Adolf Leonhardt" (1986) 2 Lloyd's Rep. 395 which has a clause on laytime and demurrage in the sales contract, reading as follows:

"*special conditions ... Time to count as per Centrocon charter party, WIBON, WIPON, WIFPON. Demurrage/Despatch as per C/P ... Other Conditions as per Centro Exportadores term* ... (my emphasis).

28) As to the case of The "Handy Mariner" (1991) 1 Lloyd's Repl. 378 heavily relied on by the Buyers (see Paragraph 30), the Sellers pointed out that the material clause in that case only read as follows:

"*Discharge* 400 *metric tones per hold/weather working day Sundays and Holidays excepted unless used with maximum* 2000 *metric tones per day. Demurrage U. S.* $3,500 *per day pro rata with half despatch.* ".

Although the sales contract in that case has also incorporated GAFTA 100, the Sellers submitted that it did not incorporate any standard C/P and had no provision (express or by incorporation) for the tendering of NOR and "notice time". This is different with the present case in which Asbatankvoy C/P was specifically incorporated.

B) Buyers' arguments

29) The first main argument advanced by the Buyers was that the sale is on the basis of "*DES* (中国某卸港的某泊位)" and therefore the Sellers were obligated to deliver the cargo to the exact spot as agreed. The Buyers also referred me to the Incoterms 2000 which explain the term "DES (Delivery Ex Ship)" as follows:

"'*Delivered Ex Ship' means that the seller delivers when the goods are placed at*

---

〔28〕 这就是 Asbatankvoy 标准格式租约中要求承租人必须在船舶抵达时提供一个马上可以挂靠的泊位的第 9 条文。因为这是标准格式,为了肯定性/可循性,笔者必须依从先例曾经作出过的解释,这可以参阅本书第四章之第 2 段。

the disposal of the buyer on board the ship not cleared for import at the named port of destination. The seller has to bear all the costs and risks involved in bringing the goods to the named port of destination before discharging. If the parties wish the seller to bear the costs and risks of discharging the goods, then the DEQ term should be used.

This term can be used only when the goods are to be delivered by sea or inland waterway or multimodal transport on a vessel in the port of destination."

Then the Incoterms 2000 provide for in "A. THE SELLER'S OBLIGATIONS" as follows[29]:

"*A3 Contracts of carriage and insurance*

a) Contract of carriage

The seller must contract at his own expense for the carriage of the goods to the named point, if any, at the named port of destination. If a point is not agreed or is not determined by practice, the seller may select the point at the named port of destination which best suits his purpose. (Emphasis added)

b) Contract of insurance

No obligation.

A4 Delivery

The seller must place the goods at the disposal of the buyer on board the vessel at the unloading point referred to in A3 a), in the named port of destination on the date or within the agreed period, in such a way as to enable them to be removed from the vessel by unloading equipment appropriate to the nature of the goods. (Emphasis added)

A5 Transfer of risks

The seller must, subject to the provisions of B5, bear all risks of loss of or damage to the goods until time as they have been delivered in accordance with A4."

30) The second main argument advanced by the Buyers was the reference to the case in The "Handy Mariner" (1991) 1 Lloyd's Rep. 382. It was about a "CIF sale, Free Out, Lorient". In the sales contract, the material clause with regard to discharge laytime and demurrage has been cited in Paragraph 28 earlier, which I shall not repeat. But in the clause, there was nothing concerning when the vessel could be deemed to be an "arrived ship" at Lorient and could commence laytime counting against the buyers. It so happened that there was delay to the berthing of the vessel after she arrived the port of Lorient. So, the dispute between the sellers and the buyers was: Were the buyers liable to pay demurrage to the sellers in respect of the period between the arrival of the vessel in port of Lorient and the time when the vessel was berthed?

---

〔29〕 以下是节录 Incoterms 2000 对 DES 买卖下卖方所要承担的责任与风险的规定。

31) The High Court and the Court of Appeal reversed the arbitration award. In the High Court, Hobhouse J. held:

"*that on the proper construction of the contract the buyers' obligation to discharge did not begin until the goods were ready for discharge at the discharge berth; the clause did not impose on the buyers any risk with regard to waiting time ...*"

32) In the Court of Appeal, Staughton LJ, said, *inter alia*, as follows:

"*To undertake a liability for demurrage while the vessel is in port but waiting for a berth would be an open-ended commitment in a contract for the purchase of what must probably be a part cargo. It would also be open-ended for a full cargo, since the receiver cannot normally control congestion in the port. In the case of a part cargo the problem is worse and the result may be capricious; the buyer does not know when he makes the contract how much other cargo will be carried on the vessel and so share his liability pro rata - unless some or all of it has been discharged at a previous port. I would require rather clearer words before holding that the buyers had assumed such a liability in this case.*"

33) The Buyers had also referred me in the written closing submissions to the judgment of Hobhouse J regarding the difference between a charter-party and a CIF sales contract, unless the latter has put in clear words that would radically transform the scheme of the CIF contract. His Lordship said as follows:

"*... There is no provision in this contract for the tendering of any notice of readiness, or for any lapse of time between the time when the vessel was an 'arrived vessel' and the time at which an obligation to discharge, or the running of laytime, starts. It is an indication in my judgment of this confusion, that the appeal board has treated this contract as if it included some laytime provision which provided for the serving of a notice of readiness, and for the commencement of laytime at some interval after the notice of readiness had been served. I accept that before me that was no an essential part of the sellers' submissions. But it does indicate and illustrate that it is mistaken to incorporated into a c. i. f contract ... considerations which are not in that contract and would be considerations that would have to be derived from some express provision of some charter-party or similar contract. If this contract, or this demurrage provision, was drafted on some basis of indemnity, then there would be either an implied or express cross-reference to a charter-party which would justify the introduction of such concepts because there would be need to refer to the charter-party and therefore to consider what were the terms of the charter-party. But that is not the case here. It is common ground that there is no cross-reference to a charter party and the provisions of this contract stand on their own as between seller and buyer. ... It would have been easy to include such a* *provision, and the most obvious way in which it could have been done is to include some reference to a charter – party which would radically transform the scheme of this contract. There are other ways in which it could be to done, which would be to expand the discharge provision so as to include some words like 'whether in berth or not' or 'time waiting for berth to be treated as discharging time', or indeed to expand it into a full – blooded laytime provision together with notice of readiness and so on. None of these things have been done. ... In those circumstances, in my judgments, the buyer's contentions are right and ought to have been accepted."*

34) The third argument by the Buyers raises matters or issues such as the meaning in < Black Law Dictionary > on words such as: "terms", "as per" and "incorporated" in the context of whether the disputed clauses in the Asbatankvoy C/P could have been incorporated. Furthermore, the Buyers argued that there are several versions of Asbatankvoy C/P, etc. The Buyers also argued that the control of berthing was in the hands of the (中国卸港) Port Authority and they have no control whatsoever. Finally, the Buyers argued that the main cause of the delay in berthing had to do with bad weather/gale wind.

C) My Deliberations & Decisions on this issue

35) This is the most difficult issue in this reference as far as I am concerned. I found it difficult at the hearing on 15 – 16 June 2006. In fact I have specifically asked the parties to fully address me in written closing submissions on this issue of "Maritime Terms" in Asbatankvoy C/P to be incorporated in Clause 16. One of my doubts was: being a C/P pro – forma, I would regard all terms therein should be classified as "maritime terms". Accordingly, would all the terms and every word in Asbatankvoy C/P be incorporated, subject only to necessary or reasonable "verbal manipulations"? Would there be any limitation as the title of Clause 16 of "Maritime Terms" seems to suggest or infer[30], or I shall give little or no weight to the title of a clause[31]?

36) In essence, it boils down to one important question, as the Sellers putting it in Paragraph 28, of whether the incorporation of Asbatankvoy C/P in this Sales Contract, which is lacking in The "Handy Mariner" (1991) 1 Lloyd's Rep. 382, would have made the difference or distinction that leads to a completely opposite result to the trading terms used by the parties (CIF or DES)? It is very much an exercise of the construction

---

〔30〕 这里是笔者对"海运条文"这个不常见的词的疑惑，因为 Asbatankvoy 标准格式租约既然是一份租约，它所有的条文都可以说是海运条文。但总不会可以把每条租约条文都合并进一份买卖合约，毕竟合并的条文不能超越买卖合约的明示条文。

〔31〕 本书第二章之第 12 段已经介绍过条文的抬头不重要，但在本案件，笔者觉得这个解释规则不适用，原因是"海运条文"的抬头后不是一句完整的条文，而只是简单说合并 Asbatankvoy 标准格式租约。另注意是在本案件，双方最后都同意海运条文不涉及私人字典。

of the Sales Contract. The fundamental rule is to ascertain, by objective means, the meaning which the Sales Contract should convey, as a whole, to a reasonable person.

37) As I understand it, to incorporate another contract (actual or standard pro – forma) is to bring in all its terms, conditions and exceptions that are relevant and/or germane to the main contract. It is a very common practice in charter – party bills of lading and there have been a lot of well – known principles of construction dealing with the extent or limitation of a general incorporation clause. [32] Such as:

– an incorporation clause does not incorporate a clause that would otherwise render a party in breach of his basic duty;

– inconsistent and repugnant clauses ought not be incorporated generally;

– unreasonable and unusual terms in the trade ought notto be incorporated generally;

– overall rationality, business sense or commercial commonsense ought to be considered when it comes construction of incorporation clause;

– ancillary clause (such as arbitration clause or time bar clause) ought not to be incorporated generally;

– oral agreement ought not to be incorporated generally;

– etc.

38) Therefore, it is general knowledge in shipping that a general incorporation clause in bills of lading is insufficient to incorporate an arbitration clause in the charter – party. [33] More so, the demurrage clause and the discharge laytime clause, even though they are clearly germane to the voyage, may not be incorporated especially if it involves a part cargo and/or verbal manipulation, because it would be unreasonable and umcommercial to expose the bills of lading holder to potential liability of such demurrage. It would not make business sense to say he has intentionally entered into a contract with such potential liability in his mind. As far as part cargo is concerned, there is the added difficulty of how to operate between different consignees of different parts of the cargo.

39) Turning to this case, I observe that firstly, the Sales Contract provides for "DES" (Delivery Ex – Ship) and a named point of "中国卸港某泊位" at the named port of destination of "(中国卸港)" has been agreed upon. As I understand it and in the

---

〔32〕 这是合并其他合约/文件的一些大原则,可参阅本书第二章之第8段。

〔33〕 有关提单一般性合并租约条文,请参阅本书第二章之8.4.2段。在本案件,虽然不涉及提单,但笔者认为DES买卖合约合并Asbatankvoy标准格式租约,并且在订立买卖合约时卖方还没有租船作出付运,表示租约还不存在,中国买方也不可能知道有关的条文/文字,在本案件解释什么是有效或无效的合并也应该有同样考虑。这等于是在本书第二章之8.4.3段节录的Lewison大法官总结的四种情况的第一种(A and B make a contract incorporating terms agreed between A [or B] and C),是否能够成功合并需要严格解释。

Incoterms 2000 that was also expressly incorporated, the term "DES" itself bears the clear meaning of the Sellers having to deliver, at their own expense, for the carriage of cargo to the named point at the named port of destination (see my added emphasis in Paragraph 29). Therefore, the starting point must clearly be, it should be the Sellers who must bear the consequence of delay in berthing (or arriving at the agreed point of destination), unless it is the fault of the Buyers. With freedom of contract, the Sellers can pass the risk of delay in berthing to the Buyers, thus changing the basic framework or structure of "DES". But it has to be achieved by very clear and unambiguous terms or provisions in the Sales Contract. Such as, in The "Adolf Leonhardt" (1986) 2 Lloyd's Rep. 395, it has specifically stated in the laytime clause the well - known and unmistakable acronyms of "WIBON, WIPON".

40) Secondly, I take note of the case in The "Handy Mariner" (1991) 1 Lloyd's Rep. 382, heavily relied on by the Buyers, was a "CIF sale, Free Out, Lorient". But still, it was decided that the sellers could not pass on to the buyers the risk of delay from the time of vessel's arrival at the port of Lorient until the time of berthing to the buyers. Yet, in this case, it is a "DES sale, (中国某卸港的某泊位)" which gives a stronger impression that the Sellers must deliver the cargo closer to the "home" of the Buyers. Accordingly, if the Sellers wished to pass the risk of delay (in particular, navigational risks such as bad weather/gale wind) from the time of vessel's arrival at the "customary anchorage" of (中国卸港) (which can be inside or outside of port limit) until the time of berthing at the agreed named point, I expect even clearer, totally unambiguous and unmistakable words[34] have to be used by the Sellers (and agreed by the Buyers).

41) Thirdly, I shall now examine whether or not the Sellers have achieved this duty in order to change the basic framework of "DES". In the written closing submissions, the Sellers essentially argued that:

(1) Demurrage is plainly a maritime term as opposed to commercial terms within the framework of the distinction between Clauses 15 & 16 in the Sales Contract.

(2) Questions of laytime and demurrage are matters which properly fall within the definition of "maritime terms" in Clause 16 of the Sales Contract and Clauses 10 & 11 are to be "supplemented" with the appropriate provisions of the Asbatankvoy C/P.

(3) The Sales Contract and the Asbatankvoy C/P must be read together.

(4) This case is rather like The "Adolf Leonhardt" (1986) 2 Lloyd's Rep. 395 which incorporated the standard form of Centrocon C/P.

---

〔34〕 请看本书第四章之第4段。

42) I accept some of the arguments/submissions of the Sellers, such as the Asbatankvoy C/P must be read together with the Sales Contract, which has been expressly incorporated. So would be the Incoterms 2000, expressly incorporated in Clause 15. The question is to what extent the Asbatankvoy C/P should be incorporated. Would it incorporate Clauses 6 &9 of the Asbatankvoy C/P, which as the effect of substantially advancing the commencement of laytime and passing the risk of delay in berthing (even if it was caused by navigational hazards) to the Buyers, thus upsets the basic framework of a "DES" sale set out in Incoterms 2000?

43) My problem is - if Clauses 6 &9 of the Asbatankvoy C/P were intended to be incorporated and to "supplement" Clause 10 entitled "Laytime for discharge", why was the incorporation not expressly stated in Clause 10. The Sellers relied on The "Adolf Leonhardt". But the important distinction is that the incorporation of Centrocon C/P in that very case was in or together with the laytime and demurrage provisions (which was entitled "Special Conditions" and please see my Paragraph 27). In this case, the Asbatankvoy C/P was incorporated in a completely separate and different clause (Clause 16) to the "Laytime for discharge" clause of Clause 10. The two clauses were far removed from each other. Furthermore, Clause 16 has no express (certainly no implied) link to Clause 10.

44) I also bear in mind that in The "Adolf Leonhardt", the relevant clause has also expressly stated "WIBON, WIPON" to make it beyond doubt that the intention was to pass on the berthing delay to the Buyers. But in this case, there is no such clear, unambiguous and unmistakable agreement in Clause 10. Yet, I expect even clearer words/clauses must be used in order to change the basic framework of a "DES" sale, more so than a CIF sale in The "Adolf Leonhardt".

45) I am not suggesting in earlier paragraphs that the incorporation of Asbatankvoy C/P has no meaning. There are still a lot of "Maritime Terms" in the Asbatankvoy C/P that could be incorporated in Clause 16. Such as, the General Exceptions Clause, the Paramount Clause, the General Average Clause, the Limitation of Liability Clause, the War Risks Clause, the Agents Clause, etc. It is just the irrelevant clauses such as the nomination of loading port or tendering of notice of readiness for loading that should not

be included in incorporation.[35] Also not included are the inconsistent clauses to a "DES" sale unless the incorporation itself is clearly meant to override the "DES" framework, such as, *at the very least*, the incorporation clause is expressly stated in Clause 10 or Clause 16 is linked to Clause 10.

46) Even better and clearer, the Sellers could have inserted (with the Buyers' agreement) in Clause 10 of the Sales Contract clauses or provisions like:

"Berth Reachable on arrival", or

"The Master is entitled to give notice of readiness upon arrival at the customary anchorage of (中国卸港)", or

"WIBON, WIPON",

Etc.

But there is nothing of this sort in this Sales Contract.[36]

47) In support of my construction of this DES Sales Contract which is apparently against the Sellers, I repeat the words of Hobhouse J in the first instance judgment of The "Handy Mariner", which I fully accept and humbly follow, as below:

"*It would have been easy to include such a provision, and the most obvious way in which it could have been done is to include some reference to a charter – party which would radically transform the scheme of this contract. There are other ways in which it could be to done, which would be to expand the discharge provision so as to include some words like 'whether in berth or not' or 'time waiting for berth to be treated as discharging time', or indeed to expand it into a full – blooded laytime provision together with notice of readiness and so on. None of these things have been done. ... In those circumstances, in my judgments, the buyer's contentions are right and ought to have been accepted.*"

48) Finally, I must also say that I have reservation as to whether or not laytime and demurrage clauses are strictly "Maritime Terms". It is because they can be found in both

---

〔35〕 海运条文合并 Asbatankvoy 标准格式租约必须有一定的意思与解释。所以笔者列举了一些有效合并进买卖合约的海运条文，如免责条文、首要条文、共同海损条文、限制责任条文、战争条文、代理条文等。但还有一些条文明显与买卖合约没有关系甚至会起冲突，如有关装港的指定、船舶准备就绪通知书的递交与装货条文包括装货时间计算与滞期费等，就不可能成功合并了。

〔36〕 笔者在这里是举了两个以清楚无误的写法成功以明示条文把卸港等待泊位的延误转嫁给 DES 买卖的买方的例子，至于什么才能够满足清楚无误的要求，可参阅本书第十二章之 1.8 段。

charter - parties and sales contracts.〔37〕 Thus, they should be "maritime" as well as "commercial" terms in nature. Indeed, it is becoming one of the main terms in the negotiation of international sales contracts. But I need not deal with this matter in light of my earlier construction of the Sales Contract. Likewise, I need not deal with other arguments raised by the Buyers such as the meaning of "as per" or "incorporated", and what version of Asbatankvoy C/P should be incorporated, if at all. Save to say, I am not persuaded by the Buyers over these arguments or issues. But this would not affect the result in my construction.

Issue No. 5 - Whether the Sellers were in breach by delivering the cargo by two vessels of"另一艘船舶"*and*"(运载货物的船舶)"?

...

Issue No. 6 - The Buyers' duty, if any, in ensuring early berthing

...

Issue No. 7 - Whether the Vessel was in breach of the discharging capacity and possible problem of back pressure?

§3 香港仲裁案件之三

以下是另一个笔者在香港仲裁的裁决书,有关程租合约的争议,涉及承租人是否要支付运费,因为船舶在装货后起航不久沉没,造成了租约的"受阻"(frustration)。

〔37〕 这里是笔者对"海运条文"这个不常见的词的疑问,就是Asbatankvoy标准格式租约的第9条文与装卸时间与滞期费有密切关系。但国际货物买卖也涉及装卸时间与滞期费的问题,合约中都会有条文针对不派船一方承诺在固定时间完成装货或卸货,否则向派船一方赔偿滞期费。这样,有争议的装卸时间与滞期费条文可以归类于买卖合约第16条的"海运条文",但也可以归类于第15条的"商业条文"(commercial terms)。在本合约,商业条文是合并Incoterms 2000而并没有像海运条文一并合并Asbatankvoy标准格式租约。而Incoterms 2000是明确规定DES卖方必须承担所有时间损失的风险,直到买方可以到船旁提货的一刻。这表示DES卖方的争辩在合约的第15条与第16条有直接的冲突或矛盾,整体解释就必须协调或在无法作出协调时根据条文的不同分量漠视/删除其中的一条,这可看本书第三章之第4段与第5段。由于第15条文与第16条文都是合并其他的文件,分量不重,所以,难以说是第15条文超越第16条文。但第15条文针对的DES买卖下卖方必须承担所有时间风险,在有关的买卖合约下也并非只有第15条文的合并才有提到。买卖合约很多其他地方包括第8条文要求卖方在中国某卸港的某泊位交货都是清楚无误的明示条文,虽然没有进一步明示DES卖方必须承担所有时间损失的风险直到这一刻,但也没有明示DES卖方不需要承担某些风险。这表示解释第8条文卖方所作出的严格承诺,就必须承担所有的风险,而且这也是英国法下对DES买卖的默示地位。此外,已经多次提到由于卖方争辩的法律地位不合理,必须以清楚无误的文字表明,而显然只靠合并另一份文件并与买卖合约其他条文(包括第15条文)起冲突就肯定不是清楚无误,必须严格针对DES卖方解释,所以笔者最后判DES卖方败诉。

如果租约约定与欠下的运费支付日期是在受阻前，承租人就必须支付给船东。但如果支付的日期是在受阻后，承租人就无须支付。有关受阻的课题在本书第十三章之1.1段有介绍，但只局限在怎样的严格条件下才会导致合约的受阻。而在本案件涉及合约受阻的另一个课题，虽然最后双方都达成共识，因此，在本裁决书只需要简单在裁决书原因的第33段一提，也就是1943年《Frustrated Contracts Act》的立法。

在Taylor v Caldwell (1863) 122 ER 309先例[38]与Chandler v Webster (1904) 1 KB 493先例及其他一连串"英皇加冕典礼先例"(Coronation Cases)承认合约可以受阻的理论后，很快就带来一个问题。这个问题可以Fibrosa Spolka Akcyjina v. Fairbain Lawson Combe Barbour Ltd. (1942) 73 Lloyd's Rep. 45先例为例，该先例的被告以1600镑的对价为原告制造一台机器然后交付波兰。在签约时，原告按照合约的约定先支付了1000镑。在制造半途，德国占领波兰，令整个合约变为非法而受阻。原告成功向被告索回已付的1000镑，原因是"完全得不到对价好处"(total failure of consideration)。但Fibrosa先例也带出了受阻理论的一些重要缺点：(1) 看来，如果只是"部分得不到对价好处"(partial failure of consideration)，Fibrosa先例的说法不适用，不公平情况仍在。这会是制造的机器(或其他货物或服务)已交付或提供了一部份。(2) 被告退回已支付的1000镑，是依据完全得不到对价好处，与公平合理无关，普通法(不是衡平法)也不会理会个别案件的公平合理。本案例对原告公平合理，因为他没有获得这台机器就不应该付钱。但考虑被告的地位就不一样，是没有一个法律的依据让被告可以在1000镑中保留制造机器半途已花费了的成本(金钱)，有剩余才退给原告。

这带来了1943年《Frustrated Contracts Act》的立法，立法的目的是避免在合约受阻后，其中一方会因此而"不当得利"(unjust enrichment)。立法提供了灵活的机制把合约受阻所带来的损失作出公平分摊。立法的Section 1 (1) 说："Where a contract governed by English law has become impossible of performance or been otherwise frustrated, and the parties thereto have for that reason been discharged from the further performance of the contract, the following provisions of this section shall, subject to the provisions of section two of this Act, have effect in relation thereto."

该立法条文要注意两点：(1) 合约一定要适用英国实体法，所以去伦敦仲裁但合约明示或默示适用外国法律，1943年立法仍不适用。(2) 1943年立法说明适用情况是合约"变为"(become)不能履行或受阻，所以合约不是"变为"而是"自始无效"

---

〔38〕 在该先例之前，英国法律对履行合约承诺的责任是相当严格，甚至可以说是绝对责任，这可看本书第八章之脚注1。该先例涉及英国的Surrey Music Hall音乐厅，该音乐厅可以容纳1万人，但一场不涉及当事人疏忽的火灾把该音乐厅烧毁。原告Taylor向被告索赔损失，因为他们订立的合约中被告承诺提供该音乐厅作为1861年夏天的4个晚上音乐表演的场地。当时的英国法律承认"天意"(Act of God)，换言之，除非火灾是闪电直接击中而导致，被告不能免责。该先例首次带来合约可以受阻的说法。

(void *ab initio*),即合约"错误"(mistake)[39]的情况,本立法也不适用。其他不适用情况是合约下订明的情况,如本书第十三章之第1段介绍的"不可抗力条文"(*force majeure* clause)所带来的不能履行与合约终止。

立法的 Section 1(2) 是公平分摊金钱的大原则所在,说:"All sums paid or payable to any party in pursuance of the contract before the time when the parties were so discharged (in this Act referred to as 'the time of discharge') shall, in the ease of sums so paid, be recoverable from him as money received by him for the use of party by whom the sums were paid, and, in the case of sums so payable, cease to be payable: Provided that, if the party to whom the sums were so paid or payable incurred expenses before the time of discharge in, or for the purpose of, the performance of contract, the court may if it considers it just to do so having regard to all the circumstances of the case, allow him to retain or, as the case may be, recover the whole or any part of the sums so paid or payable, not being an amount in excess of the expenses so incurred."

该立法条文要注意以下几点:

1. 容许合约一方向对方取回在受阻前"已支付的钱"(sums so paid)。

"在受阻后"(after the time of discharge),双方仍会有瓜葛,但这不是1943年立法所要管的。例如,受阻后一方在不知情下仍付了一笔钱,如期租合约下的承租人不知船舶已沉没仍付出一笔租金,这可以错误,即"事实搞错"(mistake of fact)为由取回。这是"复原"(restitution)的精神。

如在受阻后,一方仍在替另一方服务,如法律改变或战争令租约或提单受阻后承租人或收货人仍要求船东把船上的货物卸去某处,这也不是1943年立法所要管的。这会是双方另订一份新合约,或是船东根据他们的要求提供服务(与花了使费)后,可取回"合理报酬"(*quantum meruit* sum),在 The "Zuiho Maru" (1977) 2 Lloyd's Rep. 552 先例,承租人所依赖的抗辩就涉及这一方面。

2. 容许合约受阻前已到期应支付的一方,若该款项"尚未付出"(sums so payable),则"不必再支付"(cease to be payable)。

3. 该立法没有再要求"完全得不到对价好处"才适用。

4. 该立法也改变了 Fibrosa 先例,容许退还受阻前已支付的钱的一方,保留他"已花的使费"(incurred expenses),只要这使费是"为了履行这合约而花费掉的"(for the purpose of the performance of contract)。但合约订立以前已经花费的钱就不包括。此外,立法的 Section 1(4) 也允许包括合理的"固定成本"(overhead)。

5. 法院在合理情况下,会允许花费一方"保留"(retain)或"取回"(recover)使费,后者是针对第二种情况。但不明朗之处是全部或一半的使费?因为大前提是要法院"认为是公平合理"(considers it just to do so)。如花费一方在合约受阻前收了5万美

[39] 请看本书第三章之13.7段。

元,但同时他花了2万美元的使费,他能在5万美元中保留多少?一个说法是花费一方只能保留一半,即1万美元,因为双方应共同承担受阻后果。有说法是这立法既然是针对“受阻是双方均没有责任”(one or two parties has to suffer loss for which neither is responsible)的情况,公平合理的做法应是让花费一方保留或取回一半使费(the normal cases the just course would be to order the retention or repayment of half the loss incurred)。也有说法是花费一方能保留全部的2万美元使费,因为1943年的立法带来了“位置的改变”(change of position),这是Goff大法官在B. P. v. Hunt (1979) 1 WLR 783先例与英国法律改革委员会Seventh Interim Report (Rule in “Chandler v Webster”) Cmnd. 6009所讲。1943年的立法,因为年代长久,有不少的批评,这方面可看Ewan MeKendrick教授所著的《*Force majeure* and Frustration of Contract》(第2版,1995年)一书,本书不在此详论。

该立法之Section 2(5)(a)是说明不适用在程租合约或提单,而只适用在期租合约(与光租合约)。另在Section 2(5)(b)与(c)也说明部分其他类别的合约不适用。在程租合约(与提单),主要的支付就是“运费”(freight),而普通法下船东能够赚取运费与承租人需要支付运费是在船舶把货物运抵卸港并可以交出货物的一天:Dakin v Oxley (1864) 15 C. B. (N. S.) 646与Appleby v Myers (1867) L. R 2 CP 651先例。而如果在运输中途(即使已经十分接近卸港),发生了受阻的情况如船舶或货物本身因意外全损,导致没有货物可在卸港交出,就根本不能赚取任何运费。这是因为程租合约因受阻而自动终止后,赚取与支付运费的一天永远不会再来临。这也是船东需要为运费投保的原因,因为航次能否赚取运费的风险由其承担。但由于CIF/CFR买卖频多,越来越多的做法就是承租人需要一份“运费预付”(freight pre-paid)的提单,这导致租约条文也经常配合约定全数的运费或很高百分比(如90%)的运费在装完货后就预付。但即使约定预付也不代表可以改变普通法下运费是在卸港交货时才赚取的法律地位:[40] The “Lorna 1” (1983) 1 Lloyd's Rep 431先例。所以运费即使是预付,但如果稍后在运输途中遇上受阻,预付的这笔运费也有危险被承租人(与货方)根据Fibrosa先例的“完全得不到对价好处”(total failure of consideration)的说法向船东取回。至于船东已经花费了的使费,如装港的费用、燃油等,也由于1943年立法的不适用无法让船东作出保留。这导致程租合约会加上其他的明示条文希望对船东作出保障,如规定“船货全损运费概不退还”(freight non-returnable cargo and/or vessel lost or not lost...)。另一个常见的写法就是索性以清楚无误的条文/文字改变普通法的地位,约定运费在装港作出付运时就已经赚取,正如Donaldson大法官在The “Lorna 1”先例中作出的建议,说:“Forms of words appropriate to alter this position are well known, e. g. ‘Freight to be considered earned on shipment.”

这样,在货物付运后的航次发生了任何受阻,都不影响承租人需要支付运费,因

---

〔40〕 请看本书第四章之第11段。

为已经成为一笔欠下的债务。

在上述的介绍后,估计读者会更容易理解以下的裁决书(只节录部分)。该仲裁的事实是,船舶于2005年4月19日23时装完货,并在4月20日1时30分开航。但船舶开航不久后于4月25日在印度洋沉没,有关的程租合约与提单也就受阻。程租合约下有第9条文约定所有的运费在“装完货”(completion of loading)的3个“银行工作日”(banking day)内支付,而期间的4月24日与4月25日是周六周日,在香港不是银行工作日。而双方在仲裁前与委任笔者作为独任仲裁员时,就已经同意约定与接受法律的地位是如果受阻是在装完货的3个银行工作日内,承租人就不必支付高昂的运费。但如果受阻是在装完货的3个银行工作日后,承租人就必须支付。而船东认为4月19日23时后有足足4个银行工作日:4月20日(周二)、21日(周三)、22日(周四)、23日(周五),船舶之后才沉没与程租合约受阻。

承租人的抗辩看来希望不大,他的争辩是希望把开始起算3个银行工作日的时间往后推,说是第9条文的“装完货”一词应是在装港的“水尺检验”(draft survey)或/与签署提单后。这个检查是在装完大宗货后根据船舶的吃水计算船舶所装货物的数量,用来作为提单的货物数量或确认岸上提供的装货数量。而在该案件,船舶是在4月20日的凌晨在开航前才作出这一水尺检验,而提单也随即签署。这样,根据承租人的争辩,装完货的日子就不是4月19日而是4月20日。而承租人的争辩理由之一是如果水尺检验发觉货物装船的数量不足以满足买卖合约与信用证的最低装货量要求,会需要继续加装。这种情况也有发生,虽然在本案件没有。但即使是4月20日才起算3个银行工作日,还是勉强足够。所以,承租人也同时争辩是第9条文的约定应被解释为3个银行工作日届满“之后”(after),而不是在3个银行工作日“内”(within)。

承租人另一个争辩是租约的第9条文虽然只是针对装完货,但应该有一个默示条文是只有在签署与交出提单后才需要支付运费,这发生在4月21日,而3个银行工作日是从这一时间开始起算。

但这些理由都被笔者拒绝,认为第9条文所使用的文字清楚无误,作出一般性的解释无法支持承租人的抗辩,原因请看以下部分节录的裁决书。

IN THE MATTER OF THE ARBITRATION ORDINANCE (CAP. 341)
AND
IN THE MATTER OF AN ARBITRATION
BETWEEN

原告船东　　　　Claimants/Owners

AND

被告承租人　　　　Respondents/Charterers

M. V. "船舶": C/P dd. 05.04.2005

FINAL ARBITRATION AWARD

1) By a fixture note or charter - party dated 05th April 2005 (the "F/N") the Claimant, 原告船东, entered into a voyage charter in respect of M. V. "船舶" ("the Vessel") with the Respondent, 被告承租人 for a voyage from 印度装港 to 中国甲卸港 or 中国乙卸港, upon the terms and conditions set out therein.

2) The said F/N provided for:

"18. *ARBITRATION IN HK WITH ENGLISH LAW TO APPLY.*"

3) Disputes (hereinafter more particularly defined) did arise between the parties. The Arbitration Clause did not provide for the appointment of a sole arbitrator. A three - man tribunal was required in this arbitration.

4) The Owners and the Charterers subsequently agreed to appoint the undersigned Philip Yang of Unit A, 18th Floor, Casey Building, 38 Lok Ku Road, Sheung Wan, Hong Kong as the sole arbitrator to deal with all disputes arising out of or in connection with the above F/N.

5) The Owners' claims (hereinafter more particularly defined) related to the freight of US $ 750,000.00 which has failed to be paid by the Charterers. The Owners also claimed interest and costs.

6) The parties through their respective lawyers delivered written submissions attaching the documents and evidence upon which they relied.

7) Under the Hong Kong Arbitration Ordinance, I was obliged to issue a Reasoned Award and my Reasons are accordingly attached hereto and form part of this FINAL AWARD.

NOW I, the said Philip Yang having taken upon myself the burden of this reference and having carefully and conscientiously read and considered the submissions and the documentary evidence put before me by the Owners and the Charterers, and having given due weight thereto and being in agreement, **DO HEREBY MAKE, ISSUE AND PUBLISH** this my **FINAL AWARD**, as follows:

A) **I HEREBY FIND AND HOLD** that the Owners' claim succeeds in full in the total sum of US $ 750,000.00.

B）**I AWARD AND ADJUDGE** that the Charterers shall pay forthwith to the Owners the sum of US $750,000.00 **TOGETHER** with interest at 6.5% p.a. from 24th April 2005 until the actual date of payment.

C）**I FURTHER ORDER AND ADJUDGE** that the Charterers shall bear their own costs and the Owners' costs of this arbitration on party and party basis (to be assessed and determined by me, if not agreed) **AND** the Charterers shall also bear and pay the full amount of the costs of this my **FINAL AWARD** which I hereby assess, determine and settle at the sum of HK $ ______, **PROVIDED ALWAYS** that if, in the first instance, the Owners having paid any part of the costs of this my **FINAL AWARD**, they shall be entitled to an immediate refund from the Charterers of the sum so paid.

GIVEN UNDER MY HANDS in Hong Kong this 10 March, 2007.

______________________	______________________
Philip Yang	Witness

"船舶" C/P dd. 05. 04. 2005

(Reasons, for and forming part of Final Arbitration Award)

THE FACTS：

1）By a fixture note ("F/N") or charter－party dated 05th April 2005 (the "F/N") the Claimant, 原告船东, as the Owners, entered into a voyage charter in respect of M. V. "船舶" ("the Vessel") with the Respondent, 被告承租人, as the Charterers for a voyage from 印度装港 to 中国甲卸港 or 中国乙卸港, with a cargo of minimum 20,000 Metric Ton 有关货物 in Bulk.

2）The Vessel completed loading cargo at 印度装港 on 19th April 2005 and a draft survey made by 检验公司 on 20th April 2005 showed that a quantity of 20,100 mt 货物 has been loaded on board. Bill of lading No. 01 ("the Bill of Lading") was issued with the date 19th April 2005 and marked "Freight payable as per charter－party dated 05/04/2005". On 20th April 2005 the Vessel left 印度装港 to sail for 中国乙卸港. On 25th April 2005, the Vessel sank in the Indian Ocean.

3）The movements of the Vessel in the Statement of Facts ("the SOF") and Time Sheet were, inter alia：

"*Arrival at Pilot Station*:	1600 *Hours* 15/04/05
...	
Notice of Readiness Tendered:	1600 *Hours* 15/04/05
Notice of Readiness Accepted:	2150 *Hours* 15/04/05
Commenced Loading:	2150 *Hours* 15/04/05
Completed Loading Hatch 1:	0530 *Hours* 18/04/05
...	
Completed Loading Hatch 2:	2150 *Hours* 19/04/05
Completed Loading Hatch 3:	2300 *Hours* 19/04/05
Time Sailed:	0130 *Hours* 19/04/05"

4) The material or relevant provisions in the F/N can be cited as follows:

"(2) *CARGO AND CARGO QUANTITY*: *MINIMUM* 20,000 *MT TO VESSEL' S FULL CAPACITY AT CHARTER' S OPTION* 有关货物 *IN BULK*, *CARGO QUANTITY TO DETERMINED BY DRAFT SURVEY AT BOTH ENDS.*

(6) *FREIGHT*: *USD*40.00 *PER MT ON FREE IN AND OUT STOW AND TRIM*, ... *FOR* 中国甲卸港 *DISCHARGE USD*44.50 *PER MT* ... *FOR* 中国乙卸港[41] *DISCHARGE*

(9) *FULL FREIGHT LESS ADDRESS COMMISSION TO BE PAID IN USD TO OWNER' S NOMINATED ACCOUNT WITHIN* 3 *BANKING DAYS AFTER COMPLETION OF LOADING AND SIGNED B/L....*

(22) *OTHER TERMS AND CONDITIONS AS PER GENCON* 76."

***<u>THE CLAIM AND THE ISSUES</u>*:**

5) The Owners' case is that the freight, <u>US $ 750,000.00</u>, became due and payable by the Charterers to the Owners "*within* 3 *banking days after completion of loading*", namely 3 banking days after 19th or 20th April 2005. It is alleged by the Owners that 19th, 20th April, 21st, 22nd and 23rd April 2005 were all banking days in Hong Kong and thus the freight, <u>US $ 750,000.00</u>, was due and payable by the Charterers by 22nd or 23rd April 2005. This was prior to the date of Vessel's sinking on 25th April 2005, hence its timely payment was not affected or frustrated by the sinking of the Vessel.

...

7) The Charterers denied that any amount was due to the Owners.

8) The issues in dispute can be broken down as follows:

(A) Whether the loading was completed on 19th April 2005 or after the Draft Survey on 20th April 2005?

---

〔41〕 乙卸港比甲卸港远,所以运费较高。

...

(D) Whether there was an implied term that the 3 banking days should start to count after releasing of B/L?

(E) When was the end of the three banking day period?

(F) Whether the freight accrued due and payable by the Charterers before the vessel sank?

A) The Owners' Arguments

...

B) The Charterers' Arguments

...

DISCUSSIONS & DELIBERATIONS

33) Both the Owners and the Charterers accepted that if the date of advance freight payment under Clause 9 of the F/N was prior to the date of the Vessel's sinking on 25th April 2005, it remained payable despite the Vessel's loss which should frustrated the C/P.[42] Likewise, if the date of advance freight payment happened to be later than the date of Vessel's sinking, no payment would be due by reason of the frustration of the C/P. It is not disputed that the Frustrated Contracts Act 1943 (the F/N is governed by English law) does not apply to freight payment under F/N or C/P. Therefore, there is no subsequent adjustment of loss or return of freight payment, in full or in part, short of a proven breach of contract by the Owners having caused the Vessel's sinking. For the reasons mentioned above, it is understandable why the parties have gone into such extensive arguments regarding the commencement and the counting of "3 banking days" (within which period advance freight has to be paid) under Clause 9, in order to arrive at the payment date of advance freight.

34) The Owners and the Charterers also accepted that the physical loading was completed at 2300 hours on 19th April 2005 and the Bill of Lading ("B/L") was released to the Charterers (who were also the Shippers) on 21st April 2005. Furthermore, both parties did not dispute that 21st, 22nd & 23rd April (Wednesday - Friday) 2005 were banking days in Hong Kong and that 24th & 25th April 2005 were not banking days.

---

〔42〕 这个案件笔者作为仲裁员的疑虑之一是租约第9条文并没有类似 The "Lorna 1" (1983) 1 Lloyd's Rep 431 先例中 Donaldson 大法官所建议的条文改变普通法地位,只是说运费要在装完货与签署提单后的3个银行工作日作出支付,但没有针对提前赚取运费的类似文字。这样,就算是承租人在计算第9条文的装货后在3个银行工作日内要支付运费的争议败诉,也可以根据 Fibrosa Spolka Akcyjina v. Fairbain Lawson Combe Barbour Ltd. (1942) 73 Lloyd's Rep. 45 先例的"完全得不到对价好处"(total failure of consideration)说法,向船东取回这笔即使是预付了的运费。但由于双方已经同意,笔者的委任只是裁决第9条文的解释与计算支付运费的日期,所以只能私下有疑虑。

35) Accordingly, if the commencement date for the purpose of counting 3 banking days was on 19th March 2005, the advance freight would become payable at the latest on 22nd April 2005 and if the commencement date was on 20th April 2005, the advance freight would become payable at the latest on 23rd April 2005, both of which dates were before the sinking of the Vessel. This, understandably, is the Owners' position. The Charterers' main position is that the commencement date should be on 21st April when the B/L was released. Therefore the 3 banking days were 22nd, 23rd & 26th April 2005 which would mean that the last payment date of advance freight was subsequent to the sinking of the Vessel. The Charterers also raised other issues in support of their position that advance freight was not due or payable. To facilitate reading, the various issues in dispute are dealt with in sequence, as follows:

A) Effect of draft survey

36) The first argument related to the time to carry out the draft survey. It was raised by the Charterers in Paragraph 7(a) & (b) of the Re – Amended Points of Defence, served with the Respondent's Final Submissions. It has to do with the completion of the draft survey which was recorded to be on 20th April 2005 in the Provisional Draft Survey Report. The Charterers argued:

"*Until and unless draft survey at the load port had been carried out loading operation of the Vessel had not been completed. Since draft survey at the load port was conducted by* 检验公司 *only on* 20*th April* 2005 *the loading of the Vessel could not be said to have completed on* 19*h April* 2005. *Unless such loading operation had been completed no shipped bill of lading could have been issued by the Claimants, the Master of the Vessel and/or their agents* (船东代理)."

37) Briefly put, the Tribunal finds difficulty in accepting that the draft survey is to be treated as part of the loading operation. It is accepted that the purpose of the draft survey is to ascertain (or sometimes to countercheck) the quantity of cargo being loaded onboard the vessel. In addition to a draft survey to ascertain the cargo quantity, there may be other surveys to ascertain the condition of the cargo loaded (as one example) the purpose of which is to determine whether "clean" or "clause/unclean" bills of lading be issued. It would not make sense to say that until all surveys are completed, the loading operation would not be considered as completed. Furthermore, what if the result of the initial survey or surveys are disputed by the parties, calling for a further survey(s) to be held? Would it mean that the completion of the loading operation has to be put back continuously or indefinitely? Last but not the least, if cargo was loaded on the last few days of the shipment period permissible under the sales contract and/or the letters of credit, can the charterers by disputing the draft survey or condition survey findings, turns a

"timely" shipment to an "untimely" shipment, giving rise to a fresh but lawful excuse under the sales contract to reject the cargo by the buyer?

38) To conclude, I consider that the phrase "completion of loading" in Clause 9 should be given its ordinary and natural meaning[43], limited to the physical operation of cargo loading. The phrase does not include other ancillary matters relating to loading such as the draft survey or signing of bills of lading. I go further to say that the time taken for the draft survey should not even be counted, unless otherwise agreed, as loading laytime or demurrage. A London arbitration award is reported in LMLN No. 488 (1998) which appears to take the same view as mine.

...

D) Construction of Clause 9 and Implied term

50) This issue was raised by the Charterers in the Re - Amended Points of Defence in

Paragraph 7(h) and can be cited as follows:

"*Further or alternatively, the Respondents will say that in construing Clause* 9 *of the Fixture Note it is necessary, so as to give business efficacy to the provision, to imply a term to the effect that in any event the* 3 *banking day period for payment of freight will not start to run until the Bill of lading is actually released. It is admitted and averred that the Bill of Lading was released on* 21*st April* 2005. *In the premises, if which is denied, freight ever became due and payable, it did not do so until* 26*th April* 2005 *by which date the Vessel had sunk.*"

51) I also find difficulty with this argument of the Charterers. The reasons are:

Firstly, there is a complete and express clause (i. e. Clause 9) dealing with the freight payment. Namely, it has to be paid within 3 banking days "after completion of loading" (which was on 19th April 2005) ... These provisions should override any implied position with regard to freight payment.

Secondly, I am not aware of any implied term that freight is payable upon the release of the bills of lading. The Charterers did not show me any authority or persuasive material in support of the term sought to be implied by them.

Thirdly, if the parties intended to pay freight only after the release of bills of lading, they should have expressed this clearly in Clause 9 of the F/N. It is not uncommon for parties to state that freight should be paid*before or after* the release of bills of lading, as explained in the report by the Owners' expert, 专家证人. This is also my general experience as a shipping man. For instance, it is not uncommon for owners to insist that

〔43〕 请看本书第一章之第5段介绍的"黄金规则"。

freight must be paid prior to the release of bills of lading marked "freight prepaid". This is motivated by a concern that if such bills of lading fall into the hands of innocent holders, the owners would be bound. Therefore, if in this F/N nothing was said about the release of B/L, I consider it wrong to imply such a term which would contradict parties' expressed stated contractual intention[44] as shown in Clause 9 of the F/N.

52) The Owners referred me to what Lord Simon has said in BP v. Hastings (1977),[45] setting out the five stringent requirements which needed to be satisfied in order to imply any term into a contract. Namely, it must be reasonable and equitable; it must be necessary to give business efficacy to the contract; it must be so obvious that it goes without saying; it must be capable of clear expression and it must not contradict any express term of the contract. I have to say that in this case, none of the five requirements have been satisfied for implying the term sought by the Charterers to be implied in Clause 9 of the F/N.

E) The period of 3 banking days

...

55) I accept the argument of the Owners. The word used in Clause 9 of the F/N is "*within*" the 3 banking days of say, 21st, 22nd & 23rd April 2005 so the freight payment must have become due by midnight on 23rd April 2005. If Clause 9 had used another common word "*after*" the 3 banking days, then the Charterers' argument that freight became due only on 26th April 2005 may well be correct. But it is not the case here.

F) Conclusion about the payment of advance freight

56) To summarize the above, I find that the advance freight became due for payment prior to the sinking of the Vessel on 25th April 2005. Accordingly, the Charterers must pay to the Owners the sum of US $750,000.00 together with interest at 6.5% p.a., from 24th April 2005 until the date of actual payment.

...

§4 香港仲裁案件之四

以下是另一个笔者在香港仲裁的裁决书,涉及的金额并不高,争议是在国际货物买卖合约与程租合约经常发生的"滞期费"(demurrage)。这两种合约经常有条文/文字要求负责装卸货物的一方作出承诺在固定的装卸时间内完成作业,否则就是违约

〔44〕 请看本书第七章之4.4.5段。

〔45〕 请看本书第七章之4.4段。

并需要支付“议定赔偿”(liquidated damages)的滞期费。合约中针对多少天的固定装卸时间,通常会加以限制,“周日与假期不算在内”(Sundays and Holidays Excluded,简称 SHEX)。本案件涉及一份程租合约,双方的争议是“周六”(Saturday)是否算在固定装货时间内。显然,周六并没有明示加在对固定装货时间限制的 SHEX 一词内。但希望有更多固定装货时间的承租人以中国的《劳动法》作为支持,因为立法规定了周六也算是假期,争辩说是即使周六没有明示,也在中国的装港不算在固定装货时间内。

笔者判是这一说法不成立,理由在于:(1)中国《劳动法》与国际外贸/航运的“本质”(context)是两码事,这在本书第一章之 5.2.2 段与本书其他部分都有讲到。(2)合约条文已经特别针对一件事情,但不提其他同类事情,这在本书第四章之第 7 段有详论。如果周末在双方的订约意图下算是假期,何必把周日独立出来针对并加在 SHEX 一词内?周日应该比周六更接近属于周末的假期。所以只加上周日,双方的订约意图有更大可能是不考虑周六,而不大可能是将周六视为包括在假期内。(3)笔者在航运租船业务有多年的经验,知道市场上有专门针对不包括周六或只包括部分周六的时间的标准条文,如 Baltimore Form C Saturday Clause。所以在本租约,如果什么都没有明示就支持周六可以被包括在假期的限制内,不包括在固定装卸时间内,笔者认为这样的解释并不合理与违反商业常识,等于否定了市场上历史悠久与大量被使用的明示不包括周六或周六部分时间的著名标准条文。这可看本书第四章之第 3 与第 4 段,正如 Diplock 勋爵在 The “Antaios” (No. 2) (1984) 2 Lloyd's Rep. 235 先例所说的:“... if detailed semantic and syntactical analysis of words in a commercial contract is going to lead to a conclusion that flouts business common sense, it must be made to yield to business common sense.”

IN THE MATTER OF THE ARBITRATION ORDINANCE (CAP. 341)

AND

IN THE MATTER OF AN ARBITRATION

BETWEEN

A 公司 Claimants (Owners)

AND

B 公司 Respondents (Charterers)

"X 轮" C/P dated 28 APRIL 2007

FINAL ARBITRATION AWARD

1) By a Charter – Party (the "C/P") evidenced by a Fixture Note (the "F/N") dated 28 April 2007, it was mutually agreed between A 公司 as the Owners (the "Owners") and B 公司 as the Charterers (the "Charterers") to charter the MV "X 轮" (the "Vessel") for a voyage from one safe port/one safe berth Shanghai, China to one safe port/one safe berth Calcutta, India.

2) The said C/P (evidenced by a F/N of 28 April 2007) provides for:

"17. *Dispute, differences, controversies, if any, TB settled by arbitration in Hong Kong and English law to apply with LMAA rule including LMAA small claim procedure up to USD*25,000."

3) Disputes (hereinafter more particularly defined) did arise between the parties. By agreement of the parties, I, the undersigned Philip Yang of 18A, Casey Building, 38, Lok Ku Road, Sheung Wan, Hong Kong, was appointed as the sole arbitrator in respect of all disputes arising out of or in connection with the C/P on 8 June 2007. I accepted the appointment on the same day.

4) The dispute referred to me as the sole arbitrator was the Owners' claim against the Charterers for demurrage accrued in the loading port of a total sum of US $ * * * * *.

5) The parties subsequently exchanged written submissions (including but not limiting to Claim Submissions, Defence Submissions, Reply Submissions), attached with documentary evidence they relied on.

6) Neither party asked for an oral hearing and they invited me to proceed to my Award based on the submissions and documents presented.

7) Under the Hong Kong Arbitration Ordinance, I am obliged to issue a Reasoned Award and my reasons are accordingly attached hereto and form part of this my FINAL AWARD.

NOW I, the said Philip Yang, having taken upon myself the burden of this reference and having carefully and conscientiously read and considered the submissions made by the Claimants, and the documentary evidence they put before me, **DO HEREBY MAKE, ISSUE AND PUBLISH** this my **FINAL AWARD**, namely: –

A) I FIND AND HOLD that the Owners' claim for US $ * * * * * * * succeeds in full.

*B) I THEREFORE AWARD AND ADJUDGE that the Charterers shall pay to the Owners the sum of US $ * * * * * * * within seven days after completion of discharging at Calcutta which is estimated to be on* 15 *June* 2007.

C) I FURTHER AWARD AND ADJUDGE that the Charterers shall pay the costs of my FINAL AWARD which I tax and settle at HK $ * * * * * * * PROVIDED ALWAYS that if, in the first instance, the Owners has paid any part of the costs of this my FINAL AWARD, they shall be entitled to an immediate refund from the Charterers of the sum so paid.

GIVEN UNDER MY HAND in Hong Kong this day of June, 2007

____________________ ____________________

Philip Yang Witness
Sole Arbitrator

"X 轮" C/P dated 28 APRIL 2007

REASONS

For and forming part of FINAL AWARD

THE FACTS:

1) By a Charter - Party (the "C/P") evidenced by a Fixture Note (the "F/N") dated 29 April 2007, it was mutually agreed between A 公司 as the Owners (the "Owners") and B 公司 as the Charterers (the "Charterers") to charter the MV "X 轮" (the "Vessel") for a voyage from one safe port/one safe berth Shanghai, China to one safe port/one safe berth Calcutta, India.

2) According to the Statement of Facts (the "SOF"), the Vessel arrived at the loading port of Shanghai and tendered Notice of Readiness (the "NOR") at 0640 hours on 15 May 2007.

3) The relevant and/or material terms and conditions in the C/P (evidenced by a F/N of 28 April 2007) are as follows:

2. *QUANTITY*: *MIN* 10,500*MT FERTILIZER IN BAG STOWAGE FACTOR ABT* 1.15

5. *LOADING/DISCHARGING RATE*: 2,500*MT*/1,500*MT PER WEATHER WORK-*

ING DAY SUNDAY & HOLIDAY EXCLUDED UNLESS USED

21. *HOLIDAYS IN THIS FIXTURE NOTE SHALL DENOTE NATIONAL HOLIDAY AND HOLIDAYS AS DECLARED BY GOVERNMENT.*

4) Whereas the movements of the Vessel were, according to the Owners' SOF, as follows:

Date		Time From	To	Description
15 – May	TUE		0640	ARRIVED AT FANGCHENG P/S N TENDERED NOR
		0640	2400	AWAITED FOR BERTHG DUE TO PORT CONGESTION
16 – May	WED	0000	2400	AWAITED FOR BERTHG DUE TO PORT CONGESTION
17 – May	THU	0000	2400	AWAITED FOR BERTHG DUE TO PORT CONGESTION
18 – May	FRI	0000	2400	AWAITED FOR BERTHG DUE TO PORT CONGESTION
19 – May	SAT	0000	2400	DITTO(0400 – 0800 RAIN)
20 – May	SUN	0000	2400	AWAITED FOR BERTHG DUE TO PORT CONGESTION
21 – May	MON	0000	2400	AWAITED FOR BERTHG DUE TO PORT CONGESTION
22 – May	TUE	0000	2400	AWAITED FOR BERTHG DUE TO PORT CONGESTION
23 – May	WED	0000	2400	AWAITED FOR BERTHG DUE TO PORT CONGESTION
24 – May	THU	0000	2048	AWAITED FOR BERTHG DUE TO PORT CONGESTION
24 – May		2048	2345	PILOT ON BOARD AND ALL LINES FAST
24 – May		2345	2400	JOINT INSPECTION N INWARD FORMALITIES
25 – May		0000	0100	JOINT INSPECTION N INWARD FORMALITIES
25 – May	FRI	0100	0800	AWAITEDCARGO HOLD INSPECTION DUE TO RAIN
25 – May		0800	1050	CARGO HOLD INSPECTION AND PREPARATION FOR LOADING
25 – May		1050	2400	LOADING COMMENCE AND CONTINUE
26 – May	SAT	0000	2400	LOADING CONTINUE
27 – May	SUN	0000	2400	LOADING CONTINUE
28 – May	MON	0000	1600	LOADING SUSPENDED DUE TO RAIN
28 – May		1600	2400	LOADING RESUMED AND CONTINUE
29 – May	TUE	0000	0900	LOADING CONTINUE
29 – May		0900	1300	LOADING SUSPENDED DUE TO RAIN
29 – May		1300	2400	LOADING RESUMED AND CONTINUE
30 – May	WED	1300	2400	LOADING CONTINUE AND COMPLETED

THE CLAIM AND THE ISSUES:

5) The Owners' claim against the Charterers for demurrage accrued in the loading port of * * * * * * days amounts to a total sum of US $ * * * * * * *. The Charterers denied such demurrage was due.

6) The issues of the disputes can be broken down as follows:

i) Whether aSaturday is a holiday in Fangcheng?

ii)...

<u>OWNERS' ARGUMENTS</u>

...

8) In the Claim Submission, the Owners argued that, pursuant to Clause 21 of the F/N and the government declared that the holidays include the New Year's Day (one day), the Labour Day (three days), the National Day (three days), the Lunar New Year's Day (three days), Saturdays were not holidays. The Owners submitted that the "S" in "SHEX" in Clause 5 of the F/N should stand for "Sundays" or "Saturdays". Then, if Sundays could be excluded, then Saturdays could not. Similarly, if Saturdays could be excluded, then Sundays could not. As a result, the Owners alleged that, in order to exclude both Sundays and Saturdays, SSHEX should be expressly stated in the F/N. Finally, the Owners argued that if Saturdays were holidays, there was no need to state SHEX in the F/N and merely HEX would exclude both Sundays and Saturdays. This cannot be right in Owners' submissions.

9) In the Reply Submissions, the Owners further agued that the "Weekly Holidays" (周休息日) provided in the "Provisions of the State Council on Working Hours of Workers and Staff" were not the same thing as "Holidays".

...

<u>CHARTERERS' ARGUMENTS</u>

11) In the Defense Submissions, the Charterers argued that, pursuant to Article 7 of the "Provisions of the State Council on Working Hours of Workers and Staff" and the Decision of the State Council on Revising the "Provisions of the State Council on Working Hours of Workers and Staff" promulgated on 25 March 2007, both Sundays and Saturdays were "Holidays".

The saidArticle 7 are, *inter alia*:

"*All state organs and institutional organizations shall institute a unified working hour system under which Saturday and Sunday shall be arranged as weekly holidays.*

Enterprises and institutional organizations that cannot institute the unified working hours prescribed in the preceding paragraph may make flexible arrangements for weekly holidays in the light of their actual conditions."

(《国务院关于职工工作时间的规定》

第七条　国家机关、事业单位实行统一的工作时间,星期六和星期日为周休息日。

企业和不能实行前款规定的统一工作时间的事业单位，可以根据实际情况灵活安排周休息日。)

12) Further, the Charterers argued that no matter what the "S" stood for, whether it was Sunday or Saturday, it would not matter because both days or either one of the two would be holidays within the meaning of the official document referred to in Para. 11.

...

MY DECISIONS

A) Whether a Saturday is a Holiday in Fangcheng?

15) I shall first deal with the question of whether a "Saturday" should be a "Holiday" in this F/N. In chartering, "Holidays" can be described in many ways such as: "general or local holidays", "legal holidays", "official and local holidays", "charterparty holidays", "legal and local holidays", "non – working holidays", etc. These terms have precedent cases with slightly varying meanings. But I need not be bothered because the term used in this F/N to denote "Holidays" is in Clause 21 of: "*HOLIDAYS IN THIS FIXTURE NOTE SHALL DENOTE NATIONAL HOLIDAY AND HOLIDAYS AS DECLARED BY GOVERNMENT.*"

16) Without this Clause 21, I have little or no hesitation that in normal chartering practice, week – ends or weekly breaks (i. e. Saturdays and/or Sundays) are not "Holidays". This can be supported at least by two reasons. One is the well – known definition of "Holidays" in all of commonly used chartering rules or codes, namely, *The Charterparty Laytime Definitions* 1980, *Voyrules* 1993 and *Baltic Code* 2003 as:

"*HOLIDAY – a day other than the normal weekly day(s) of rest or part thereof, when by local law or practice the relevant work during what would otherwise by ordinary working hours is not normally carried out.*"

Although the above rules or codes were not incorporated in this F/N, they nevertheless illustrate the common understanding in chartering.

17) Another reason in supporting of my belief is the common chartering practice of using the acronyms SHEX (which stands for "Sundays & Holidays Excluded") and/or SHINC (which stands for "Sundays and Holidays Included"). Indeed it is the case in this F/N. If Sundays (and/or Saturdays) can be considered as "Holidays", then as the Owners argued in Para. 8, people in chartering needs only the acronym of HEX, which is all – inclusive, rather than to negotiate for SHEX/SHINC or even further for SatSHEX, which are all suplusages. I agree and further add it is common in chartering to use clear words or provisions to exclude Saturdays by a so – called "Weekend Clause" which typically reads: "*Time shall not count between noon on Saturday and* 8 *am on Monday*" or an even more elaborated "Baltimore Form C Saturday Clause".

18) *But in this case, there is the very difficult problem created by Clause* 21, *which I have never seem before in my many years of chartering experience. The said clause has*

stated that as long as holidays declared by the Government (and in this case the PRC Government), they should be holidays within the meaning of this F/N for the calculation of laytime. Then in Para. 11, the Charterers produced the "Provisions of the State Council on Working Hours of Workers and Staff" issued by the PRC Government which defines "Saturdays" as "Weekly Holidays" in the English text.

19) *It is appreciated that due to the small amount in dispute, parties did not adduce experts (legal experts) in the relevant PRC law to better explain to me what is the meaning of by "Weekly Holidays" in that piece of official document and the difference, if any, with other public holidays. The Owners' argument was essentially that it would be ridiculous and wholly unrealistic to claim so many holidays (over 100 in a year) in the PRC.*

20) I have to say that I cannot tell the difference, if any, by reading the official document in English, between the terms "Weekly Holidays" and "Holidays". Thus, if it has only the English text, I might be persuaded that Saturdays are intended to be "Holidays" within the meaning of this F/N because the parties have chosen to incorporate Clause 21. However, if I go on to read the Chinese text of the official document, the corresponding term of "Weekly Holidays" is "周休息日", it literally means "Weekly Resting Days". In the Chinese text, I do not find a reference to "Holidays" which in my view should more commonly read as "假期". Of importance, I am confident that the Chinese text should prevail over the English text in a Chinese government document.

21) I should also point out that in the Chinese text (人事部贯彻《国务院关于职工工作时间的规定》的实施办法) presented to me by the Charterers, in page 3, Article 3, there is another term of "节假日" following the term of "周休息日". The literal translation of the former term appears to be "Festival Holidays". I understand that there is other official document issued by the PRC Government defining what those days are, such as the National Day, the Lunar New Year's day, etc. I am therefore persuaded that the word "Holidays" in this F/N is more appropriate to equate to "Festival Holidays" declared by PRC Government.

22) To therefore conclude on this issue, I have decided in favour of the Owners in that Saturdays at Fangcheng are not "Holidays" within the meaning of the F/N and/or within the meaning of the "Provisions of the State Council on Working Hours of Workers and Staff" issued by the PRC Government.

...

C) Conclusion

36) To conclude, I decide that the Owners' claim of US $ * * * * * * must prevail. ...

案 例 目 录

图书在版编目(CIP)数据

合约的解释:规则与应用 / 杨良宜著. -- 北京:
法律出版社, 2015.3(2025.6 重印)
ISBN 978 -7 -5118 -7593 -8

Ⅰ. ①合… Ⅱ. ①杨… Ⅲ. ①国际贸易-贸易法-研
究 Ⅳ. ①D996.1

中国版本图书馆 CIP 数据核字(2015)第 041376 号

合约的解释:规则与应用
HEYUE DE JIESHI:GUIZE YU YINGYONG

杨良宜 著

责任编辑 吴 昉
装帧设计 凌点工作室

出版发行 法律出版社
编辑统筹 法律教育出版分社
责任校对 陈 慧
责任印制 刘晓伟
经　　销 新华书店

开本 720 毫米×960 毫米 1/16
印张 63.25 **字数** 1273 千
版本 2015 年 3 月第 1 版
印次 2025 年 6 月第 7 次印刷
印刷 永清县金鑫印刷有限公司

地址:北京市丰台区莲花池西里 7 号(100073)
网址:www.lawpress.com.cn
投稿邮箱:info@lawpress.com.cn
举报盗版邮箱:jbwq@lawpress.com.cn
销售电话:010-83938349
客服电话:010-83938350
咨询电话:010-63939796

书号:ISBN 978-7-5118-7593-8
定价:128.00 元

凡购买本社图书,如有印装错误,我社负责退换。电话:010-83938349

